Encyclopedia of the
New York School Poets

TERENCE DIGGORY

Facts On File
An imprint of Infobase Publishing

To People of the Future

don't worry about your lineage
—Frank O'Hara, "A True Account of Talking to the Sun at Fire Island"

ENCYCLOPEDIA OF THE NEW YORK SCHOOL POETS

Copyright © 2009 by Terence Diggory

Facts On File, Inc.
An imprint of Infobase Publishing
132 West 31st Street
New York NY 10001

Library of Congress Cataloging-in-Publication Data

Encyclopedia of the New York School Poets / Terence Diggory.
p. cm.
Includes bibliographical references and index.
ISBN 978-0-8160-5743-6 (acid-free paper)
1. Poets, American—New York (State)—Encyclopedias. 2. Poets,
American—Biography—Encyclopedias. 3. American poetry—Encyclopedias.
4. New York school of art—Encyclopedias. I. Diggory, Terence, 1951–
PS255.N5E53 2008
811'.540903—dc22
2008036842

Facts On File books are available at special discounts when purchased in
bulk quantities for businesses, associations, institutions, or sales promotions.
Please call our Special Sales Department in New York at
(212) 967-8800 or (800) 322-8755.

You can find Facts On File on the World Wide Web at
http://www.factsonfile.com

Text design by Erik Lindstrom
Cover design by Semadar Megged/Takeshi Takahashi
Illustrations by Jeremy Eagle

Printed in the United States of America

VB KT 10 9 8 7 6 5 4 3 2 1

This book is printed on acid-free paper and
contains 30 percent postconsumer recycled content.

CONTENTS

ACKNOWLEDGMENTS

Many of the poets represented in this volume responded to a questionnaire, supplied copies of publications, reviewed drafts, or otherwise contributed in the New York School spirit of creative collaboration. It is impossible to name them all here without doubling the size of the encyclopedia, but they have all earned my gratitude. I am especially indebted to the generous hospitality of Bill Berkson, Larry Fagin, the late Barbara Guest, Grace Hartigan, Brenda Iijima, Charles North, Paul Violi, Marjorie Welish, and Trevor Winkfield. Sandy Berrigan and William Corbett deserve special thanks for going out of their way to supply out-of-the-way materials.

The New York Public Library is the essential repository for materials relating to the New York School. In particular, I want to acknowledge the assistance of Isaac Gewirtz and the staff of the Henry W. and Albert A. Berg Collection of English and American Literature and Margaret Glover and the staff of the Print and Spencer Collections, Miriam and Ira D. Wallach Division of Art, Prints and Photographs. Access to other valuable collections was graciously provided by Nicolette A. Schneider of the Special Collections Research Center, Syracuse University Library, and Melissa Watterworth of the Thomas J. Dodd Research Center, University of Connecticut Libraries. At New York School headquarters, the Poetry Project at St. Mark's Church, Corrine Fitzpatrick dug into the archives and responded cheerfully to numerous queries.

The staff of the Lucy Scribner Library at Skidmore College provided invaluable support, as always. Special thanks go to Ruth Copans, College Librarian and Special Collections Librarian; John Cosgrove, Humanities Librarian; Amy Syrell, Interlibrary Loan Supervisor; and Wendy Anthony, Special Collections Associate. Also at Skidmore, Charles M. Joseph, then dean of the faculty and vice president for academic affairs, provided both moral and financial support from the Andrew W. Mellon Foundation's Upstate New York Four-College Consortium Grant to Support Faculty Career Enhancement. My successor as English department chair, Linda Simon, protected my time during a sabbatical leave and set an inspiring example of productive scholarship that encouraged me after I returned to teaching. The faculty and the students of the Skidmore English department together maintain a community in which scholarship thrives. I consider myself lucky to work with them all.

At home I have the best possible colleague in my wife, Anne Diggory. Together we have enjoyed many of the adventures that research on this book has led to, and she has lovingly tolerated my moments of absence, even when it looks like I am present. Her engagement in her own art of painting has continually stimulated me in thinking about poetry that is closely associated with the visual arts.

My former student David Schaffer contributed diligently to the formatting of files and compiling of the bibliography. My friend and colleague Jay Rogoff lent his keen editorial eye at a crucial stage of the project's development. Jim McMahon expertly prepared the maps. Henry Rasof initially proposed this project to Facts On File, and Jeff Soloway has proven to be an exemplary editor, showing much understanding and patience throughout what must have seemed a very slow process.

The list of contributors in the appendix names those who in some way participated in the actual writing of various entries in the encyclopedia. The forms of participation have been so varied, and the stages of revision have been so complex, that it would be inaccurate to attach individual names to particular entries. Moreover, I need to take full responsibility for errors that have surely persisted and that I hope will be brought to my attention. Those on the list of contributors, as well as all of those referred to above, simply deserve, once again, my sincere thanks.

INTRODUCTION

The NEW YORK SCHOOL poets embody the avant-garde spirit informing all the arts in the United States in the period following World War II (1939–45). The avant-garde—"vanguard," in English—is by definition supposed to lead, but prior to World War II American writers and artists who identified with the avant-garde were usually viewed, and viewed themselves, as following developments that originated in Europe (hence the retention of the French term *avant-garde*). World War II placed the United States in a new position of power on the world stage, not only politically, but also artistically. Reflecting a new spirit of independence, a group of painters became known as the School of New York, no longer taking their cues from the previously dominant School of Paris (Pablo Picasso, Henri Matisse, and followers). Poets with close ties to the painters came to be known, in turn, as the New York School. These poets were one of several groups that challenged the literary establishment during the 1950s. The BEATS first gained the attention of the general public, as much by their scandalous lifestyle as by their literary innovation. But a strong case can be made that the New York School has had a more profound and pervasive influence on the actual practice of writing. Certain aspects of New York School style—the casual movement through the events of a day or the fluid alternation between concrete, even surreal, imagery and abstract, philosophical reflection—have become so pervasive as to call into question whether it still makes sense to assign particular poets to the "School." Nevertheless, this book attempts that

assignment, not so much in the hope of providing a definitive answer as out of a conviction that the question itself remains relevant and illuminating. One advantage of the encyclopedia format is that it offers as many ways to answer the question as there are users of the book.

There is a fair amount of agreement about membership of the "first generation" of New York School poets. Five poets are named most frequently: JOHN ASHBERY, BARBARA GUEST, KENNETH KOCH, FRANK O'HARA, and JAMES SCHUYLER. Schuyler was the first to settle in NEW YORK CITY, following his discharge from the navy in 1944. Guest arrived in New York with her husband, John Dudley, in 1946. Then came Koch (1948), Ashbery (1949) and O'Hara (1951), all of them recent graduates of Harvard. Ashbery introduced Koch to O'Hara, but the gregarious O'Hara was most responsible for galvanizing the sense of a group identity in a spirit of fun that kept the group distinct from anything institutional. In a prose poem titled "Day and Night in 1952," O'Hara describes himself and his friends "grinning and carrying on as if it were a picnic given by somebody else's church" (94).

In the aftermath of World War II, the New York literary scene was dominated by a group of critics, centered on the journal *Partisan Review* (edited by Philip Rahv and William Phillips), who identified an agenda for intellectuals; the group came to be know as the New York Intellectuals. Big questions posed by the war—for example, the meaning of existence, the nature of evil, the ethics of social order—demanded seriousness in both thought and tone. That tone was the quality shared by the New York Intellectuals and the New Critics (such as John Crowe Ransom and Cleanth Brooks), whose doctrine of poetic form is sometimes misleadingly posed as the chief constraint against which the New York School poets rebelled. In fact, the poets embraced a range of forms, some of them quite traditional, and they objected to current poetic practice partly for its failure to pay sufficient attention to the medium of language, a basic tenet of formalism. As Ashbery later observed, "the new poets who began publishing after the war, like ROBERT LOWELL, were very serious and depressing, and not, to me anyway, verbally engaging" (Ashbery, *Mark Ford* 32).

Seeking an alternative, Ashbery and his fellow poets found inspiration in the painters of the "School of New York," as Robert Motherwell dubbed them in 1951. Their mode was primarily abstract, or abstract expressionist (see ABSTRACT EXPRESSIONISM), another label frequently applied. But, again, it was not their mode as much as their mood that attracted the poets. In his poem "Radio" (1955), O'Hara describes how a painting by WILLEM DE KOONING, the leader of the New York School painters during the 1950s, dispelled a mood of depression by presenting "more than the ear can hold" (234). It was "almost more than the imagination can hold, but not quite," Koch commented. "One's feeling of being overwhelmed gives way to a happy awareness of expanded powers of perceiving and holding in mind" (27). "Happy awareness" as the condition of art for the New York School poets set them in direct opposition to the seriousness of the New York Intellectuals, as DAVID LEHMAN has documented in the case of one member of that group, Lionel Trilling (192). No wonder O'Hara and LeRoi Jones (AMIRI BARAKA) decide "we don't like Lionel Trilling" (O'Hara 336) during a lunchtime conversation recorded in the former's "Personal Poem" (1959). O'Hara exits the poem "happy at the thought" that the person he loves may be thinking of him.

It is impossible to separate the imaginative excitement that the painters stimulated in the poets from the sexual excitement that pulsed through their social interaction. A shared commitment to freedom and experimentation inspired both artistic and sexual expression. The TIBOR DE NAGY GALLERY (1950–   ), a focus of interaction between the poets and painters during the 1950s, was also a center for New York's gay community, thanks to the connections of JOHN BERNARD MYERS, the gallery's director. Three of the five poets who formed the core of the first-generation New York School—Ashbery, O'Hara, and Schuyler—were gay. This fact further helps account for the separation between the New York School and the New York Intellectuals, whose "Jewish moral seriousness," according to Susan Sontag, contrasts with "homosexual aestheticism and irony" in an opposition that defines "the two pioneering forces of modern sensibility" (290). The poetry of the New York School unquestionably exhibits the latter, yet the community that the poets formed has implications beyond aestheticism. In the work of PAUL GOODMAN, an acquaintance of New York School poets from the start of the 1950s, and in the work of the Beat writers published in the second half of the decade, erotic energy informed a vision of society more explicit than the hints contained in the work of the New York School, nevertheless marking obvious affinity. During the 1960s that affinity led a second generation of New York School poets to engage in the emerging counterculture as well as to extend the first generation's counter-aesthetic.

While the Beats had already made news with their challenge to conventional lifestyles, the 1960s opened with a major challenge to conventional poetry in the anthology The NEW AMERICAN POETRY, 1945–1960 (Grove Press, 1960), edited by Donald Allen. Collectively, its contents opposed the "academic" conformity represented in *The New Poets of England and America* (Meridian, 1957), edited by Donald Hall, Robert Pack, and Louis Simpson. Parallel to the Beats, Allen identified other anti-academic groups, including the "New York Poets." Myers first designated this group as a "school" two years later, in an article published in a special issue of the magazine *Nomad*. Little magazines like *Nomad* (small circulation, low production costs) proliferated during this decade, as part of a countercultural trend toward democracy of expression. However, the magazines started by the first-generation poets, *LOCUS SOLUS* (1961–62) and *ART AND LITERATURE* (1964–67), maintained the image of the avant-garde as an elite, both in the high quality of their production and in their orientation toward Europe, where they were published. In contrast, the cheap mimeograph magazines started by second-generation poets, such as ED SANDERS's FUCK YOU (1962–65) and TED BERRIGAN's "C" (1963–66), expressed the rawness of New York's Lower East Side, where the younger poets acted out their creative and communal experiments.

Second-generation poets continued to find inspiration in the other arts, but they particularly embraced POP ART, whose comic book images and soup cans scandalized abstract expressionist purists. Meanwhile, rock MUSIC gained ascendancy over the visual arts as the voice of the counterculture. Live performances gathered the tribe, so by 1966 New York School poets had established their own performance center at the POETRY PROJECT AT ST. MARK'S CHURCH IN-THE-BOWERY, the site of protests against the Vietnam War as well as poetry readings. In the same year O'Hara's "bizarre accidental death" prompted a memorial essay by Ashbery, "Writers and Issues," reflecting on the awkward position that O'Hara—and by implication, Ashbery, as well—occupied with regard to cultural trends: "too hip for the squares and too square for the hips" (80–81). Ted Berrigan proved his hipness by composing a "found poem"—"Frank O'Hara's Question"—out of Ashbery's essay. To Berrigan, a poet's language belonged to the people as much as the image of a Campbell's soup can.

Increasing diversity among the poets of the second generation complements the populism of their poetry. Especially notable was the expanded role of women. ANNE WALDMAN directed the Poetry Project for most of its formative years (1968–78). BERNADETTE MAYER conducted an influential series of Poetry Project workshops (1971–75) and later served a term as director (1980–84). MAUREEN OWEN used the mimeograph equipment at the Poetry Project to launch TELEPHONE, one of the longest running New York School magazines (1969–82). If the one woman of the first generation, Guest, thus found herself in the company of women, the one Jew, Koch, found himself among "Our Crowd," as LARRY FAGIN titled his list poem that named 52 Jewish writers, including MICHAEL BROWNSTEIN, DAVID SHAPIRO, and LEWIS WARSH among the second generation. Another second-generation writer,

RON PADGETT, Poetry Project director from 1978 to 1980, not only came from Tulsa, Oklahoma, but from a working-class background, like his friend Berrigan. Both poets drew on this background to reenvision the elite aura surrounding the avant-garde. Padgett attended Columbia University, where he studied with Koch and developed an enthusiasm for the French modernist poets, but for his own reasons: Blaise Cendrars, for example, was "a seaman and a real tough guy" (Padgett 90). Of Koch and company, Berrigan commented: "[T]hey were all sophisticated sons-of-bitches, all these Harvard-educated poets who knew very well very talented painters and we were a little bit more barbarian and yet we had the advantage of having seen things that their sophistication had produced" (Berrigan, *Tranquility* 114).

The civil rights struggles of the 1960s redrew racial divisions that an earlier bohemian spirit pretended to erase. Jones, O'Hara's lunch partner in 1959, moved Uptown to Harlem in 1965, taking the name Amiri Baraka and founding the Black Arts Repertory Theatre. Nevertheless, other black writers, such as ISHMAEL REED and LORENZO THOMAS, associated with the Downtown UMBRA group in the early 1960s, participated in the workshops and publications of the Poetry Project later in the decade. In the early 1970s the Natural Process Workshop, founded in East Harlem by TOM WEATHERLY, merged with the Poetry Project. FRANK LIMA brought the experience of Spanish Harlem to classes at the New School and, eventually, collaboration with O'Hara. Meanwhile, an ethnic Puerto Rican community was establishing residence on the Lower East Side, with consequences for poetry performance. The NUYORICAN POETS CAFÉ, founded in 1974, would become a center for SLAM POETRY and a proving ground for such poets as EDWIN TORRES, who went on to join the board of directors of the Poetry Project. Despite the recent announcement of a "NuyorAsian" poetry by Bino Realyuo, Asian-American writers working in the New York School context have relied less on group identity than on individual voice, as implied in the title of YUKI HARTMAN's first collection, *A One of Me* (Genesis: Grasp, 1968). JOHN YAU's first collection, meanwhile, was entitled *Crossing Canal Street* (Bellevue Press, 1976), referring to the boundary between the Lower East Side and New York's Chinatown.

Along with increased diversity, the New York School experienced considerable divergence during the 1970s. Colonies of poets formerly based in New York sprang up in distant locations. For example, TOM CLARK, BILL BERKSON, and ARAM SAROYAN, among others, found refuge in BOLINAS, CALIFORNIA, from urban blight and the nationwide political stalemate under President Richard Nixon. In Boulder, Colorado, Waldman cofounded the Jack Kerouac School of Disembodied Poetics at the NAROPA INSTITUTE in 1975. Berrigan, who spent some time in both Bolinas and Boulder, traveled to a series of temporary teaching appointments, beginning at the University of Iowa in 1968 and ranging from the University of Michigan and Northeastern Illinois University in CHICAGO to the University of Essex in England. Not all of the divergence during this period was geographical, however. When the critic Harold Bloom began writing Ashbery into the main line of American poetry dating back to Ralph Waldo Emerson, and major awards were heaped on Ashbery's SELF-PORTRAIT IN A CONVEX MIRROR (1975), it appeared that a leading voice of the New York School had been co-opted into the academy that "new American poets" were supposed to oppose. About the same time, a group of Downtown poets, many of them participants in Mayer's Poetry Project workshops, began producing and judging poetry according to a theoretical program based on linguistics and Marxist politics. With these "Language poets," as they came to be known, the academy had invaded the avant-garde, or at least so it seemed to New York School poets who recalled Ashbery's lesson that "Frank O'Hara's poetry has no program" (Ashbery, "Writers and Issues" 81). It may have come as some relief that the first book-length studies of O'Hara and Ashbery, by Majorie Perloff (1977) and David Shapiro (1979), respectively, attended to each poet in the particularity of his work rather than the generality of a theoretical program.

For the third generation of New York School poets emerging in the late 1970s, it would have been easy to form an identity in opposition to LANGUAGE POETRY, but to do so would mean, ironically, turning an antiprogrammatic attitude into a program of its own. Some polemical statements were published, and a few protest walkouts occurred at poetry readings, but for the most part the New York School community maintained the eclectic, even anarchic spirit that had characterized it from the beginning. Language poetry offered a new perspective on the attention to language that had always been one component of New York School practice, while subjective experience—regarded with skepticism by Language writers—found new FORMs of expression in the New York School poets' continuing fascination with autobiography and the content of daily life. For his work in these areas Schuyler (*A Few Days,* Random House, 1985) achieved greater recognition as a link between the first generation and younger poets. Schuyler's former assistant, EILEEN MYLES, served as director of the Poetry Project from 1984 to 1986. Sadly, the passing of the generations was brought home when both Berrigan and EDWIN DENBY, a kind of grandfather figure to the New York School, died the same month in 1983.

Communal as well as individual survival was in question during much of the 1980s. The AIDS epidemic cast a pall over sexual freedom. Real estate speculation was driving up rent and driving out poets on the Lower East Side. Under President Ronald Reagan, federal funding for the arts was drastically reduced and redistributed; funds awarded to the Poetry Project by the National Endowment for the Arts shrank from $50,000 to $20,000 in 1985 and to $5,000 by 1989. The community rallied with benefit fund-raising events and considerable political savvy. In 1986 the leadership of the Poetry Project was stabilized with the appointment of ED FRIEDMAN as director, a position he held until 2003.

Not surprisingly, the theme of survival looms large in assessments of the situation of poetry at the start of the 1990s (Ginsberg xxx, Jarnot 2, Evans 651–652), but this, too, was a theme already present in the postwar poetry of the first-generation New York School. "Outside the gods survive," Guest had concluded in a poem published in 1960 in her first collection, *The Location of Things* (Tibor de Nagy, 1960, 10). Guest herself ensured survival by shifting location in 1994 to California, where she was rediscovered by West Coast Language poets. The mythical resonance in her allusion to the survival of "the gods" echoes throughout the various forms of "feminine" epic explored during the 1990s, as in Waldman's IOVIS I and II (Coffee House Press, 1993, 1997) and in The DESCENT OF ALETTE (in The SCARLET CABINET, 1992) and *Désamère* (1995) by ALICE NOTLEY, widow of Ted Berrigan. Notley and Berrigan's sons, EDMUND and ANSELM BERRIGAN, debuted as poets during this decade; Anselm later succeeded Friedman as director of the Poetry Project (2003–07). In a New York School lineage that grounded the notion of "generations" in biological reality, the Berrigan brothers joined the older poet sons of painters, for example, VINCENT KATZ (son of ALEX KATZ) and Paul and Elio Schneeman (sons of GEORGE SCHNEEMAN). For herself, however, Notley determined a mythical lineage (in *Doctor Williams' Heiresses*) as one of the daughters of a race of "male-females," including O'Hara and PHILIP WHALEN, who descended from the "marriage" of William Carlos Williams and Gertrude Stein, the two modernist poets most important to the New York School.

In contrast to these gestures of survival, various statements implying the end of the New York School have issued from poets otherwise associated with it. A notable instance is Lehman's *The Last Avant-Garde* (Doubleday, 1998), one of the first book-length attempts to view the New York School as a group, but placing that view at some historical distance, as signaled by the word *last* in the title. More recently, Daniel Kane's anthology of critical essays about second-generation poets, *Don't Ever Get Famous* (2006), places those poets in its subtitle "after the New York School." Even Notley was described as "formerly associated with the New York School" on the dustjacket of her volume of selected poems *Grave of Light* (2006). In the case of Kane and Notley the motive is clearly to invite attention to the poets' individual qualities, apart from any group identity, but something more is at stake in the case of Lehman. His thesis is that any form of art—indeed, any claim that something is art—is so readily accepted today that the notion of an avant-garde, which defines itself in opposition to an establishment, has lost its force. However, this view has the unfortunate consequence of confining the definition of the New York School to the category "art." While it is art, it is art that defines itself in relation to life, even to the point of erasing the distinction—a characteristic of postmodernism as well as the avant-garde, according to some accounts (for example, Andreas Huyssen). Shortly after Lehman published *The Last Avant-Garde*, a grim challenge to contemporary life arrived on the doorstep, so to speak, of the New York School poets, when the twin towers of the World Trade Center in Downtown New York were destroyed by terrorist attacks on SEPTEMBER 11, 2001. In their writing, New York School poets, including Lehman, responded individually yet with enough of a common sensibility to permit comparison with the first generation's response to the horrors of World War II. TONY TOWLE, former student of both O'Hara and Koch, summarized the situation in his post–9/11 poem "Diptych": "wit, laughter / and ambiguity are made to carry gloom, / lamentation and humorlessness on their shoulders" (47). As it continues to evolve, New York School poetry does not deny the burdens of life, but it lightens the weight by its art.

HOW TO USE THIS BOOK

Users interested in a particular author or work may first search for him, her, or it in the alphabetical sequence of main entries. If the item of interest does not appear as an entry, it can be found elsewhere by consulting the index at the back of the book. The index is also useful for tracking the number of times a particular name or topic is referred to throughout the encyclopedia. Within each main entry, SMALL CAPITAL LETTERS indicate cross-references to other entries.

Users interested in acquiring an overview of New York School poetry may find it most helpful to begin with the List of Entries by Subject. This includes a grouping of New York School poets into three "generational" categories, according to the period in which a particular poet began to publish or first connected with the network of associations that make up the New York School. Such categories are necessarily arbitrary and incomplete. Some poets might be surprised to find themselves included; others, unfortunately, might be disappointed to find themselves excluded. Especially for the third category of "Later Generations (published or connected after 1975)," there are too many possible candidates to be covered adequately by any list. The aim in this case has been to represent the variety of directions in which New York School poetry continues to evolve.

The bulk of this encyclopedia consists of bio-bibliographical entries on individual writers and descriptive-interpretive entries on individual works. In addition to the New York School poets themselves, other writers related in some way to the New York School or especially important to the time period are also covered. Writers more distantly related but important for context are treated in group entries, for instance, on modernist poetry, French literature, or Russian poetry. Entries on individual works include fiction and drama as well as poetry, because the writers of the New York School, although known primarily as poets, were interested in working in all genres.

The importance of the other arts to New York School poetry is represented in numerous entries, but these are not confined to painting, which is sometimes mistakenly represented as the New York School poets' exclusive concern. Music has been of equal importance, and the entries included here cover music of all sorts, from the art music of John Cage to the punk rock of PATTI SMITH. Similarly, within the visual arts not only abstract expressionism but also pop art, minimalism, conceptual art, and performance art are treated in separate entries in order to trace the continuing engagement of New York School poets in the development of visual art since World War II.

Despite its name, the New York School is not confined to New York City. The category of "scenes" includes a variety of sites where significant interaction with New York School poetry has occurred (such as the cities of Boston, Chicago, and Providence) or that could even be said to have been colonized by New York School poets (such as Bolinas, California, or the Naropa Institute in Boulder, Colorado). The category of "topics" includes attention to the reception of the New York School among poets in Canada, Great Britain, Ireland, Australia, and New Zealand. The maps in the front matter, meanwhile, approach geography in a different way, confined more narrowly to New York but not to a single time period. They show points of interest relevant to the history of the New York School at some time but not necessarily at the same time.

Dates provided for individual poems represent one of following, in order of preference, depending on information available: 1) date of composition, 2) date of first periodical publication, or 3) date of first publication in a collection of the author's work. The time line in the appendix shows the chronological relationship among events of special significance to the New York School, including major publications and awards, arrivals and departures, and deaths of some of the leading poets. A narrative chronology and overview are offered in this introduction.

Bibliographical information appears in several forms. References to a poet's work are embedded in the narrative entry about the poet. In most cases these references have not been repeated in the supplementary bibliography at the end of the entry unless a specific edition has been cited for quotation. The bibliography that appears at the end of the volume, rather, lists secondary sources of most value to the general reader and principal publications of the major poets in the movement. Periodicals run by the poets themselves have played an especially important role in transmitting the work of the New York School. Many of these periodicals are covered by title in separate entries in the body of the encyclopedia; more periodicals are covered for the early, formative period of the New York School than for more recent years.

The best way to use this book is to identify poets who sound particularly interesting, find their poems through the bibliographic information supplied, and then read the poem.

In some author-date citations in the text, publishers' names have been included. This information is of particular interest to students of the New York School. The network of alternative publishers established by these poets was initially essential to the distribution of their work, and the poets' subsequent publication by mainstream publishers marked a significant moment in the movement's development.

Bibliography

Ashbery, John. *John Ashbery in Conversation with Mark Ford*. London: Between the Lines, 2003.

———. "Writers and Issues: Frank O'Hara's Question" (1966). In *Selected Prose*, edited by Eugene Richie, 80–83. Ann Arbor: University of Michigan Press, 2004.

Berrigan, Ted. "Frank O'Hara's Question from 'Writers and Issues' by John Ashbery" (1969). In *The Collected Poems of Ted Berrigan*. Edited by Alice Notley, Anselm Berrigan, and Edmund Berrigan. Berkeley: University of California Press, 2005, 159–160.

———. Interview by Charles Ingham (1978). In *Talking in Tranquility: Interviews with Ted Berrigan*, edited by Stephen Ratcliffe and Leslie Scalapino, 106–125. Bolinas, Calif.: Avenue B; Oakland, Calif.: O Books, 1991.

Bloom, Harold, ed. *John Ashbery: Modern Critical Views*. New York: Chelsea House, 1985.

Evans, Steve. "The American Avant-Garde after 1989: Notes toward a History." In *The World in Time and Space: Towards a History of Innovative American Poetry in Our Time*, edited by Edward Foster and Joseph Donahue, 646–671. Jersey City, N.J.: Talisman House, 2002.

Fagin, Larry. "Our Crowd." In *Rhymes of a Jerk*. New York: Kulchur Foundation, 1974. 22–23.

Ginsberg, Allen. Foreword to *Out of This World: An Anthology of the St. Mark's Poetry Project, 1966–1991*, edited by Anne Waldman, xxiv–xxx. New York: Crown, 1991.

Guest, Barbara. "The Hero Leaves His Ship." In *The Location of Things*. New York: Tibor de Nagy Editions, 1960, 17–18.

Huyssen, Andreas. "The Search for Tradition: Avantgarde and Postmodernism in the 1970s." In *After the Great Divide: Modernism, Mass Culture, Postmodernism*, Bloomington: Indiana University Press, 1986. 160–177.

Jarnot, Lisa. Preface to In *An Anthology of New (American) Poets,* edited by Lisa Jarnot, Leonard Schwartz, and Chris Stroffolino, 1–2. Jersey City, N.J.: Talisman House, 1998.

Kane, Daniel, ed. *Don't Ever Get Famous: Essays on New York Writing after the New York School*. Champaign, Ill.: Dalkey Archive Press, 2006.

Koch, Kenneth. "All the Imagination Can Hold" (1972). In *The Art of Poetry: Poems, Parodies, Interviews, Essays, and Other Work*. Ann Arbor: University of Michigan Press, 1996, 23–29.

Lehman, David. *The Last Avant-Garde: The Making of the New York School of Poets*. New York: Doubleday, 1998.

Motherwell, Robert. Preface ["The School of New York"] to *Seventeen Modern American Painters* (1951). In *The Collected Writings of Robert Motherwell*. Edited by Stephanie Terenzio. New York: Oxford University Press, 1992, 82–84.

Myers, John Bernard. "In Regards to This Selection of Verse, or Every Painter Should Have His Poet." *Nomad New York* nos. 10, 11 (Autumn 1962): 30.

Notley, Alice. *Doctor Williams' Heiresses*. Berkeley, Calif.: Tuumba Press, 1980.

O'Hara, Frank. *The Collected Poems*. Rev. ed. Edited by Donald Allen. Berkeley: University of California Press, 1995.

Padgett, Ron. "Poets and Painters in Paris, 1919–39." *Art News Annual* 34 (1968): 88–95.

Perloff, Marjorie. *Frank O'Hara: Poet among Painters*. New York: Braziller, 1977.

Realyuo, Bino A., ed. *The NuyorAsian Anthology: Asian American Writings about New York City*. New York: Asian American Writers' Workshop, 1999.

Shapiro, David. *John Ashbery: An Introduction to the Poetry*. New York: Columbia University Press, 1979.

Sontag, Susan. "Notes on 'Camp'" (1964). In *Against Interpretation and Other Essays*. New York: Dell-Delta, 1966, 275–292.

Towle, Tony. "Diptych." In *Poetry after 9/11: An Anthology of New York Poets,* edited by Dennis Loy Johnson and Valerie Merians, 47. Hoboken, N.J.: Melville House, 2002.

New York School Poets in Manhattan

CENTRAL PARK

Columbus
Circle

W. 57th St.   E. 57th St.

W. 55th St.   E. 55th St.

W. 50th St.   E. 50th St.

Rockefeller
Center

W. 45th St.   E. 45th St.

TIMES
SQUARE   MIDTOWN

Bryant
Park

W. 40th St.   E. 40th St.

East
River

W. 35th St.   E. 35th St.

Tenth Ave. Ninth Ave. Eighth Ave. Seventh Ave. Sixth Ave. Fifth Ave. Madison Ave. Park Ave. Lexington Ave. Third Ave. Second Ave. First Ave.

W. 30th St.

Roosevelt
Island

W. 25th St.

CHELSEA

W. 20th St.   E. 20th St.

Broadway

FDR Dr.

Long Island Sound
CT
NY
NJ
Long Island
Area of
main map
New
York
City
ATLANTIC
OCEAN

W. 15th St.   E. 15th St.
W. 14th St.   Union   E. 14th St.
W. 13th St.   Square

Hudson River

Westside Highway

Greenwich Ave.

WEST
VILLAGE

Horatio St.
W. 12th St.
Bank St.
W. 11th St.
Perry St.
Charles St.
W. 10th St.
Christopher St.

Bleecker St.
W. 4th St.

E. 13th St.
E. 12th St.
E. 11th St.
E. 10th St.
E. 9th St.
E. 8th St.
E. 7th St.
E. 6th St.
E. 5th St.
E. 4th St.
E. 3rd St.
E. 2nd St.
E. 1st St.

4th Ave.
Ave. A
Ave. B
Ave. C

St. Mark's Pl.

Tompkins
Square
Park

EAST
VILLAGE

Washington
Square
University Pl.
Broadway

GREENWICH
VILLAGE

Bleecker St.

Bedford St.
West St.
Washington St.
Greenwich St.
Hudson St.
Varick St.
Macdougal St.
Sullivan St.
Thompson St.
West Broadway
Wooster St.
Greene St.
Mercer St.
Lafayette St.
The Bowery

Houston St.

SOHO

N

0   .5 mile
0   .5 km

© Infobase Publishing

New York School Poets in Manhattan

Midtown

1. 57th St. commercial galleries
Art of This Century (Peggy Guggenheim) **30 W. 57th St.**
Green Gallery (Richard Bellamy) **15 W. 57th St.**
various galleries (Samuel Kootz, Julien Levy, Betty Parsons, Sidney Janis) **15 E. 57th St.;** (Charles Egan) **63 E. 57th St.**
2. Birdland, 1678 Broadway (SE corner W. 53rd St.): Miles Davis clubbed by police on August 26, 1959
3. Museum of Modern Art, 11 W. 53rd St. (between Fifth and Sixth Aves.)
4. View, 1 E. 53rd St.
5. Seagram Building, 375 Park Ave. (between 52nd and 53rd Sts.)
6. Tibor de Nagy Gallery, 219 E. 53rd St. (near Third Ave.): opens 1951
7. Frank O'Hara, 326 E. 49th St. ("Squalid Manor"), 1952–57; shared with Schuyler, and from 1955, with Joe LeSueur; Schuyler shared with John Ashbery, 1957–58
8. Gotham Book Mart, 41 W. 47th St., 1946–2004
9. UN Headquarters, E. 45th St. (at East River)

Chelsea

10. Jack Kerouac, 454 W. 20th St.: writes *On the Road*, 1951
11. Chelsea Hotel, 222 W. 23rd St.
12. Edwin Denby, 145 W. 21st St.
13. Paul Blackburn, 322 W. 15th St.

Union Square Area

14. Living Theater, 530 Sixth Ave. (NE corner W. 14th St.), from 1958
15. John Cage, 12 E. 17th St.
16. Union Square
Teachers and Writers Collaborative, 5 Union Square W.
Andy Warhol, The Factory, 33 Union Square W.
Partisan Review, 41 Union Square W.
Max's Kansas City, Park Ave. S. (off Union Square)
17. Kenneth Koch, Jane Freilicher, Third Ave. (at E. 16th St.): Koch shares his apartment briefly with John Ashbery in 1949

Greenwich Village

18. André Breton, 265 W. 11th St.
19. The Old Place, 139 W. 10th St.
20. *The Village Voice*, **22 Greenwich Ave.** (now relocated)
21. David Amram, 461 Sixth Ave. (SW corner W. 11th St.)
22. The New School, 66 W. 12th St.
23. W. 8th St.
Eighth Street Bookshop, 32 W. 8th St.
Hans Hofmann School, 52 W. 8th St. (between Sixth Ave. and Macdougal St.)
24. Marcel Duchamp, E. 10th St. (just off Fifth Ave.)
25. University Pl.
Frank O'Hara, 90 University Pl., 1957–59
Cedar Tavern, 24 University Pl. (now at no. 82)
26. Washington Square
Judson Church, 55 Washington Square S.
New York University
27. Frank O'Hara, 791 Broadway (near 10th St.), from spring 1963; Joe LeSueur leaves January 1965
28. E. 8th St.
Artists Club, 39 E. 8th St.
Atelier 17 (Stanley William Hayter Print Studio), 43 E. 8th St.
Jackson Pollock and Lee Krasner, 46 E. 8th St.
29. Theatre de Lys, 121 Christopher St.; first season of Artists Theater, 1953

30. Grove Press, 18 Grove St. (now relocated)
31. Sheridan Square
Stonewall Bar, 51 Christopher St. (now at no. 53 Sheridan Square)
Circle in the Square Theater, 5 Sheridan Square
32. Cornelia St.
Phoenix Bookshop, 18 Cornelia St.
Kenward Elmslie, 28½ Cornelia St.
Caffe Cino, 31 Cornelia St.
33. Cherry Lane Theater, 38–42 Commerce St.
34. LeRoi and Hettie Jones, 7 Morton St.: launch *Yūgen*, 1958
35. Gregory Corso birthplace, 190 Bleecker St. (SW corner Macdougal St.)
36. San Remo, 93 Macdougal St. (NW corner of Macdougal and Bleecker Sts.)

East Village

37. Alfred Leslie loft, 108 4th Ave. (location of *Pull My Daisy*)
38. Artist Co-Op Galleries, E. 10th St. (between Third and Fourth Aves.): south side: Camino, 92 E. 10th St.; Tanager, 90 E. 10th St.; Area, 80 E. 10th St.; north side: Brata, 89 E. 10th St.;
Also on E. 10th St.: Willem de Kooning studio, 88 E. 10th St.; Tenth Street Coffee House, 80 E. 10th St.
   In the neighborhood: Hansa Gallery (Richard Bellamy and Ivan Karp, Directors), 70 E. 12th St.; Reuben Gallery, 61 Fourth Ave. (between 9th and 10th Sts.)
39. Harold and May Rosenberg, 117 E. 10th St.
40. St Mark's-in-the-Bouwerie (Poetry Project), 131 E. 10th St. (NW corner Second Ave.)
41. Allen Ginsberg and Peter Orlovsky, 437 E. 12th St.
42. Stanley's Bar, 551 E. 12th St. (corner Ave. B)
43. Peace Eye Bookstore, 383 E. 10th St.
44. Café Le Metro, 149 Second Ave.
45. Frank O'Hara and Joe LeSueur, 441 E. 9th St., 1959–63: taken over by Tony Towle and, briefly, Frank Lima; Joe Brainard replaces Lima 1963–64
46. Tompkins Square: The East Village Other, 147 Ave. A
47. St. Mark's Pl.
Bridge Theatre, 4 St. Mark's Pl.
The Dom, 23 St. Mark's Pl. (later The Electric Circus)
George and Katie Schneeman, 29 St. Mark's Pl.
Anne Waldman and Lewis Warsh, 33 St. Mark's Pl.
Joan Mitchell, 60 St. Mark's Pl.; W. H. Auden, 77 St. Mark's Pl.; Larry Rivers, 77 St. Mark's Pl.; Ted Berrigan and Alice Notley, 101 St. Mark's Pl.
48. Fillmore East, 105 Second Ave.
49. Les Deux Mégots, 64 E. 7th St.
50. Five Spot, 5 Cooper Square (at 5th St. and Third Ave.)
51. Off-Off Broadway Theater Row, E. 4th St. (between The Bowery and Second Ave.): East End Theater, 85 E. 4th St. (present site of KGB Bar); Atelier East, 83 E. 4th St.; Café La Mama ETC, 74A E. 4th St.
52. Artist's Studio (George Nelson Preston's club), 48 E. 3rd St. (south side near Second Ave.)
53. Nuyorican Poets Café, 236 E. 3rd St. (between Aves. B and C)
54. Bowery Poetry Club, 308 The Bowery at Bleecker (across from the former CBGB) **315 The Bowery** (SE corner E. 2nd St.)
55. Anthology Film Archives, 32 Second Ave. (at 2nd St.): formerly first home of Poetry Project workshops and Millennium Film Workshop
56. Diane Di Prima, 309 E. Houston St. (south side, near Clinton St.): launches *The Floating Bear*, 1961

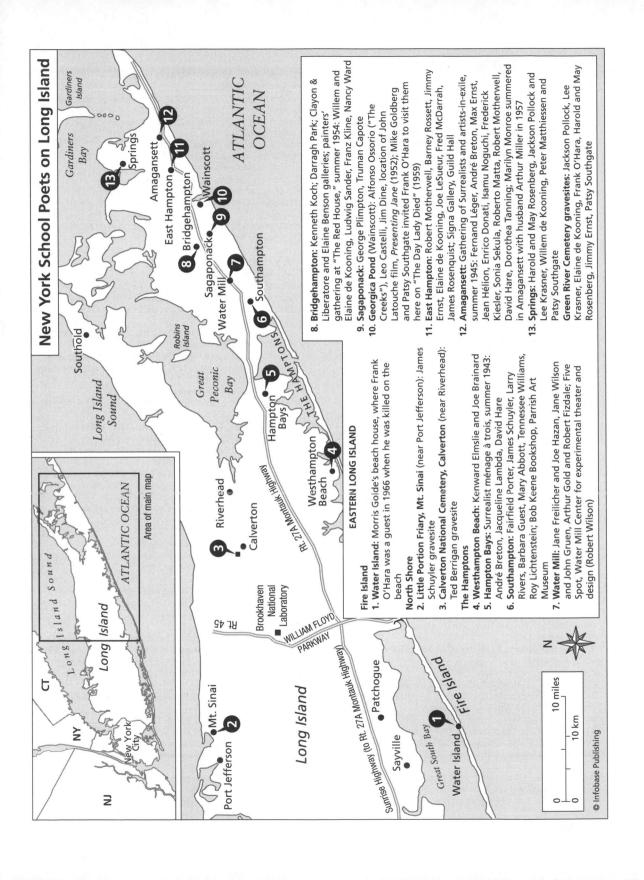

New York School Poets on Long Island

ATLANTIC OCEAN

Gardiners Island

Gardiners Bay

Springs

Amagansett

East Hampton

Bridgehampton

Wainscott

Sagaponack

Water Mill

Southampton

Long Island Sound

Southold

Robins Island

Great Peconic Bay

Hampton Bays

THE HAMPTONS

Riverhead

Calverton

Brookhaven National Laboratory

WILLIAM FLOYD PARKWAY

Rt. 27A Montauk Highway

Westhampton Beach

Sunrise Highway (to Rt. 27A Montauk Highway)

Rt. 45

Patchogue

Mt. Sinai

Port Jefferson

Sayville

Great South Bay

Fire Island

Water Island

Long Island

N

10 miles

10 km

© Infobase Publishing

Inset map:

NJ

NY

CT

Long Island Sound

Long Island

New York City

ATLANTIC OCEAN

Area of main map

8. Bridgehampton: Kenneth Koch; Darragh Park; Clayon & Liberatore and Elaine Benson galleries; painters' gathering at "The Red House," summer 1954: Willem and Elaine de Kooning, Ludwig Sander, Franz Kline, Nancy Ward

9. Sagaponack: George Plimpton; Truman Capote

10. Georgica Pond (Wainscott): Alfonso Ossorio ("The Creeks"), Leo Castelli, Jim Dine, location of John Latouche film, *Presenting Jane* (1952); Mike Goldberg and Patsy Southgate invited Frank O'Hara to visit them here on "The Day Lady Died" (1959)

11. East Hampton: Robert Motherwell, Barney Rossett, Jimmy Ernst, Elaine de Kooning, Joe LeSueur, Fred McDarrah, James Rosenquist; Signa Gallery, Guild Hall

12. Amagansett: Gathering of Surrealists and artists-in-exile, summer 1945: Fernand Léger, André Breton, Max Ernst, Jean Hélion, Enrico Donati, Isamu Noguchi, Frederick Kiesler, Sonia Sekula, Roberto Matta, Robert Motherwell, David Hare, Dorothea Tanning; Marilyn Monroe summered in Amagansett with husband Arthur Miller in 1957

13. Springs: Harold and May Rosenberg, Jackson Pollock and Lee Krasner, Willem de Kooning, Peter Matthiessen and Patsy Southgate

Green River Cemetery gravesites: Jackson Pollock, Lee Krasner, Elaine de Kooning, Frank O'Hara, Harold and May Rosenberg, Jimmy Ernst, Patsy Southgate

Fire Island
1. Water Island: Morris Golde's beach house, where Frank O'Hara was a guest in 1966 when he was killed on the beach

North Shore
2. Little Portion Friary, Mt. Sinai (near Port Jefferson): James Schuyler gravesite

3. Calverton National Cemetery, Calverton (near Riverhead): Ted Berrigan gravesite

The Hamptons
4. Westhampton Beach: Kenward Elmslie and Joe Brainard

5. Hampton Bays: Surrealist ménage à trois, summer 1943: André Breton, Jacqueline Lambda, David Hare

6. Southampton: Fairfield Porter, James Schuyler, Larry Rivers, Barbara Guest, Mary Abbott, Tennessee Williams, Roy Lichtenstein; Bob Keene Bookshop, Parrish Art Museum

7. Water Mill: Jane Freilicher and Joe Hazan, Jane Wilson and John Gruen, Arthur Gold and Robert Fizdale; Five Spot, Water Mill Center for experimental theater and design (Robert Wilson)

EASTERN LONG ISLAND

Abel, David (1956–)

Born in Salt Lake City, Utah, David Abel came east to complete his studies at Bard College in Annandale-on-Hudson, New York, where he received an M.F.A. Like his teachers, for example, Charles Stein (1944–), Abel explores the conjunction of literature and MUSIC directly, as a student of Indian classical vocal music, and indirectly, as many of his works involve time and the musical aspects of language. In NEW YORK CITY throughout the 1980s he participated in the sound poetry and new music performances of JACKSON MAC LOW and Franz Kamin (1941–). MITCH HIGHFILL credits Abel with introducing him to the new music scene while they were rooming together in 1980.

In addition to writing and performance, Abel contributed to expanding the range of poetry available in print as a publisher and bookseller. From 1987 through 1989 he ran the Bridge Bookshop in New York's East Village. He collaborated in the editing of *Red Weather* magazine (1988–90), with Highfill, KIMBERLY LYONS, and Jim Hydock, and the publishing of diwan books, most notably *Opening the Eyelid* (1990) by David Rattray (1936–92). Increasingly interested in the art of the book, Abel participated in early projects of the Soho-based Granary Books, culminating in the exhibit "Library: Book Artists' Invitational" (1992), curated by Abel, Katherine Kuehn (1956–), and Steve Clay (1951–), Granary Books's publisher.

Soon afterward, Abel issued his own first volumes in collaboration with Kuehn, under her Salient Seedling imprint, from Albuquerque, New Mexico, where they had both relocated. *Near the Mimbres* (1992) was followed by *Selected Durations* (1994) and *Rose* (1997). In Albuquerque, Abel founded Passages Bookshop and Gallery, which he continues to run from his present location in Portland, Oregon. Recent volumes include *Cut* (Situations, 1999) and *Black Valentine* (Chax, 2006). *Threnos* (2001) is a recent collaboration with Kuehn, who sewed Abel's text onto a 37-foot ribbon.

Abel's writing includes journal entries focusing on the everyday, the local, and its variants—a practice closely identified with the NEW YORK SCHOOL. With constant attention given to the music of human experience, Abel creates poems that negotiate the silences between speech and intellection. The shorter poems tend to expand in the mind's eye after reading them once, seemingly delivering crucial observations in the spaces between the lines. His poetic works also include larger experimental pieces that often illuminate our perception of time and experience of duration. When taken in combination with his intermedia works, his range is inclusive of many different schools or coteries.

Bibliography

Highfill, Mitch. Interview by Gary Sullivan. *Readme* 3 (Summer 2000). Available online. URL: http://home. jps.net/~nada/highfill.htm. Accessed December 16, 2008.

abstract expressionism

The style of NEW YORK SCHOOL painting is most commonly designated *abstract expressionism,* a term that originated with *New Yorker* art critic Robert Coates in 1946. Although the style or look of a painting was less important to the New York School poets than the process of creation—better captured in HAROLD ROSENBERG's term ACTION PAINTING—both abstraction and expression, as concepts, identify key problems in the poets' inheritance from modernism. That inheritance was fully elaborated in *Abstract Painting* by THOMAS B. HESS (1952), the work that made the concept of abstract expressionism a topic of debate among the artists themselves (Pavia).

From its origins in the first decades of the 20th century, modernist abstraction asserted, in varying degrees, the independence of art from the world, in contrast to the dependent relation of representing the world as it appears to ordinary experience. Certain modes of abstraction, such as the cubist painting of Pablo Picasso, presented aspects of the world as if it had been sampled, taken apart, and measured for purposes of analysis—hence the term *analytic cubism.* Alternatively, expressionist painters, such as Henri Matisse or the German painters called expressionists (Emil Nolde, Ernst Kirchner, Franz Marc), distorted natural FORMS as a means of highlighting the artist's feeling of being in the world. While both of these alternatives abstracted from the visible world, a third mode, pioneered by Wassily Kandinsky, assumed total independence. In this mode, which has been called "expressive abstraction" (Osborne 111–115), the feeling expressed by the artist is not so much that of being in the world but of being *"in* the painting," as JACKSON POLLOCK famously asserted (546). Color, shape, and composition become not only the means of expression but also, to a large extent, the painting's subject. The feelings expressed are specifically art feelings, "The Subjects of the Artist," as a group of New York School artists (including Robert Motherwell, Barnett Newman, and Mark Rothko) called a school they ran briefly in 1948–49.

Newman and Rothko, especially, became identified with one branch of abstract expressionism that explored the abstract world of "color fields." Another branch, identified especially with Pollock

and WILLEM DE KOONING, emphasized the expressive gesture by which the artist applied paint to canvas. During the 1950s, the formative period for the New York School poets in their relation to painting, gestural painting was dominant. In the course of the decade its tone modulated from raw violence to lyric pastoralism, terms employed by critics at the time that could be taken to imply an increasing approximation between painting and poetry (Sandler, *New York School* 51–55). In fact, however, literary parallels pervade the discourse of abstract expressionism from the beginning, for instance, in Newman's appeal to the aesthetic of the sublime or in Motherwell's choice of the GENRE of elegy for his series of paintings, *Elegy to the Spanish Republic,* begun in 1949. Even the violent gestures of de Kooning, as Robert Goldwater observed (135), could find a literary analogue in the genre of epic as opposed to lyric poetry.

For their part, the first generation of New York School poets drew vital inspiration from "the cresting of the 'heroic' period of Abstract Expressionism," as JOHN ASHBERY called it, which coincided with their arrival in NEW YORK CITY (241). Typically, the poets responded to an individual painter or even a particular painting without measuring the achievement in terms of some abstract expressionist program. "Variety is what, of course, abstract expressionism insisted on all along," stated FRANK O'HARA ("Grand Manner" 177). Nevertheless, the full implications of abstract expressionist theory apply to poetry in O'Hara's definition of *"PERSONISM"* (1959). Like Pollock's immersion in his painting, the kind of abstraction that O'Hara advocates places the poet in the poem, and "the poet's feelings towards the poem" become the feelings that the poem expresses (O'Hara, *Collected Poems* 499). Other features of abstract expressionist practice that were particularly important to the poets are expansive scale—"works as big as cities," as O'Hara explained the connection between his poem *Second Avenue* (1953) and the work of de Kooning—and an emphasis on "surface" ("Notes" 38). In painting, the latter quality was associated with the assertion of the two-dimensional surface of the canvas and the elimination of the traditional illusion of three-dimensional depth. The elimination of symbolic depth, "hidden" meaning, bore some analogy in poetry, but a more important analogue was the assignment of equal value to all elements in a composition, what the critic CLEMENT GREENBERG referred to as "all-over" composition. All areas of the compositional field became evenly active, rather than gathering around a "figure" (in painting) or a climax (in poetry).

Bibliography

Ashbery, John. "Jane Freilicher" (1986). In *Reported Sightings: Art Chronicles, 1957–1987*, edited by David Bergman, 239–245. Cambridge, Mass.: Harvard University Press, 1991.

Coates, Robert M. "The Art Galleries: Abroad and at Home." *New Yorker*, 30 March 1946, 83–84.

Cook, Albert. "Expressionism Not Wholly Abstract: Ashbery and O'Hara." In *Figural Choice in Poetry and Art*. Hanover, N.H.: University Press of New England, 1985, 167–202.

Goldwater, Robert. "Reflections on the New York School" (1960). In *Abstract Expressionism: A Critical Record*, edited by David Shapiro and Cecile Shapiro, 126–138. Cambridge: Cambridge University Press, 1990.

Greenberg, Clement. "The Crisis of the Easel Picture" (1948). In *Art and Culture: Critical Essays*. Boston: Beacon, 1965, 154–157.

Hess, Thomas. *Abstract Painting: Background and American Phase*. New York: Viking, 1951.

Libby, Anthony. "O'Hara on the Silver Range." In *Frank O'Hara: To Be True to a City*. Edited by Jim Elledge. Ann Arbor: University of Michigan Press, 1990 131–155.

Moramarco, Fred. "John Ashbery and Frank O'Hara: The Painterly Poets." *Journal of Modern Literature* 5, no. 3 (September 1976): 436–462.

Newman, Barnett. "The Sublime Is Now" (1948). In *Theories of Modern Art: A Source Book by Artists and Critics*, edited by Herschel B. Chipp, 552–553. Berkeley: University of California Press, 1971.

O'Hara, Frank. "The Grand Manner of Motherwell" (1965). In *Standing Still and Walking in New York*. Edited by Donald Allen. San Francisco: Grey Fox, 1983, 174–179.

———. "Notes on *Second Avenue*." In *Standing Still and Walking in New York*. Edited by Donald Allen. San Francisco: Grey Fox, 1983, 38–40.

———. "Personism: A Manifesto" (1959). In *The Collected Poems of Frank O'Hara*. Rev. ed. Edited by Donald Allen. Berkeley: University of California Press, 1995, 498–499.

Osborne, Harold. *Abstraction and Artifice in Twentieth-Century Art*. Oxford: Oxford University Press, 1979.

Pavia, P. G. "The Unwanted Title: Abstract Expressionism." *It Is* 5 (Spring 1960): 8–11.

Pollock, Jackson. Excerpt from "My Painting" (1947). In *Theories of Modern Art: A Source Book by Artists and Critics*, edited by Herschel B. Chipp, 546–548. Berkeley: University of California Press, 1971.

Sandler, Irving. *The New York School: The Painters and Sculptors of the Fifties*. New York: Harper & Row, 1978.

———. *The Triumph of American Painting: A History of Abstract Expressionism*. New York: Praeger, 1970.

Wolf, Leslie. "The Brushstroke's Integrity: The Poetry of John Ashbery and the Art of Painting." In *Beyond Amazement: New Essays on John Ashbery*, edited by David Lehman, 224–254. Ithaca, N.Y.: Cornell University Press, 1980.

action painting

The term *action painting*, coined by HAROLD ROSENBERG in an essay in *Art News* in 1952, designates what was most important to the first generation of NEW YORK SCHOOL poets in contemporary avant-garde painting. Rosenberg's term implies, first of all, art that focuses attention on the process of its creation, a priority that carries over to "Frank O'Hara's concept of the poem as the chronicle of the creative act that produces it," as JOHN ASHBERY explained (viii–ix). On a more philosophical level, inspired by the current vogue of French existentialism, action painting asserted the absolute freedom of the artist to create without any prior determining influences, which Rosenberg symbolically erased in the formula "It's not that, it's not that, it's not that" ("American Action Painters" 29). JAMES SCHUYLER invoked this formula when he asserted that "Harold Rosenberg's Action Painting article is as much a statement for what is best about a lot of New York poetry as it is for New York painting" (418).

Rosenberg, who was himself a poet, conceived of action painting in poetic terms. A phrase from the French poet Apollinaire about "gestures among the solitudes" offered the most specific clue to what Rosenberg expected the viewer to look for in action painting ("American Action Painters" 23); it became synonymous with gestural painting, particularly the slashing brushwork of WILLEM DE KOONING, who "provided the model" for action painting, Rosenberg later revealed ("De Kooning" 117). (Rosenberg's "American Action Painters" article had avoided naming any contemporary painters.) At the same time, the criticism of Wallace Stevens and the example of Walt Whitman framed Rosenberg's critique of American culture as too ready to furnish comfortable substitutes for "painting in the medium of difficulties" ("American Action Painters" 33). Stevens also supplied the key conception of poetry as "a process of the personality of the poet" ("American Action Painters" 29), which, translated back from the language of action painting, became the basis for FRANK O'HARA's "PERSONISM." For O'Hara, as for Rosenberg, the "person" projected through the creative act was a result of the creation, not a prior existence being "expressed." As O'Hara wrote in his characterization of JACKSON POLLOCK's action painting, there is "no reference to exterior image or environment"; the painter as actor is one with his painting, "in a oneness which has no need for the mediation of metaphor or symbol" ("Jackson Pollock" 35). Such a statement exemplifies, on the one hand, how action painting encouraged the New York School poets to reject traditional features of poetry and, on the other hand, how action painting itself relied on the "poetic" style of criticism that O'Hara and his associates perfected.

While the poetry of the New York School can be read as "action poetry," such a reading needs to be attuned to the spontaneous energy of the poem rather than any superficial resemblance to painting, which could only restrain the energy. Even if painters showed poets the way, Schuyler insisted, "'writing like painting' has nothing to do with it" (Schuyler 418). In fact, action poetry as a concept is likely to appear as an object of parody in New York School poetry. In "Far from the Porte de Lilas and the Rue Pergolèse" (1958), O'Hara reports with self-conscious melodrama: "a dream of immense sadness peers through me / as if I were an action poem that couldn't write" (*Collected Poems* 311). In KENNETH KOCH's

mock epic *Ko, or a Season on Earth* (1959), the action poet Joseph Dah has the power to make imaginary actions come to life in reality, with the accompanying sadness that his "poems do not lie in any book / And so are dead to his posterity" (40). Action painting has suffered a similar fate in art history, which has favored the alternative categories "New York School" or "ABSTRACT EXPRESSIONISM" to designate the art once identified with action. In its isolation of spontaneous action as unique and individual, the concept of action painting set itself at odds with historical explanation (Rosenberg, "Action Painting" 45–46). Nevertheless, poems inspired by the concept remain alive to posterity in the books of the New York School poets.

Bibliography

Ashbery, John. Introduction to *The Collected Poems of Frank O'Hara*. Rev. ed. Edited by Donald Allen. Berkeley: University of California Press, 1995, vii–xi.

Horvath, Brooke. "James Schuyler's Early Art Criticism and the Poetics of Action Poetry." *Denver Quarterly* 24, no. 4 (Spring 1990): 53–68.

Koch, Kenneth. *Seasons on Earth*. New York: Penguin, 1987.

O'Hara, Frank. *The Collected Poems of Frank O'Hara*. Rev. ed. Edited by Donald Allen. Berkeley: University of California Press, 1995.

———. "Jackson Pollock" (1959). In *Art Chronicles, 1954–1966*. New York: Braziller, 1990, 12–39.

Rosenberg, Harold. "Action Painting: Crisis and Distortion" (1962). In *The Anxious Object*. 1966. Reprint, Chicago: University of Chicago Press, 1982. 38–47.

———. "The American Action Painters" (1952). In *The Tradition of the New*. 1960. Reprint, New York: Da Capo, 1994, 23–39.

———. "De Kooning 1: 'Painting Is a Way'" (1963). In *The Anxious Object*. 1966. Reprint, Chicago: University of Chicago Press, 1982, 108–120.

Schuyler, James. "Poet and Painter Overture." In *The New American Poetry, 1945–1960*, edited by Donald Allen, 418–419. 1960. Reprint, Berkeley: University of California Press, 1999. 418–419.

actualism   *See* IOWA WRITERS' WORKSHOP.

Adventures in Poetry (1968–1975, 2001–)
LARRY FAGIN published his mimeograph magazine *Adventures in Poetry* during a crucial transitional stage in the evolution of the NEW YORK SCHOOL. *Adventures* picked up where magazines of the 1960s left off: *FUCK YOU* (1962–65), *C* (1963–66), *LINES* (1964–65), *MOTHER* (1964–69), *ANGEL HAIR* (1966–69), and *0 TO 9* (1967–69). *Adventures* also complemented another new publication, *The WORLD,* begun in 1967 as an official journal of the POETRY PROJECT OF ST. MARK'S CHURCH IN-THE-BOWERY. Fagin often drew contributions from readings he heard at the Project, and by the seventh issue (summer 1971), the masthead of *Adventures in Poetry* announced that it was "published at the Poetry Project" as a token of thanks for the use of the Project's mimeograph equipment. But *Adventures* was always published by Fagin. Whereas *The World* reflected the community in its spontaneity—like a pickup basketball game, in Fagin's analogy (Kane 8)—*Adventures in Poetry* shaped a community in which the sensibility of the editor was reflected. As Fagin explains: "You build up a mailing list, a very particular readership, people who'll actually be *reading* what you've put together and who'll maybe notice how you've done it . . . the combinations, your style" (Waldman and Fagin 511).

Adventures in Poetry strikes a unique balance between individuality and community. Fagin preferred to publish substantial selections of work by a few authors rather than a scattering of many authors represented only by one or two poems each. For the most part, collaborative exercises that merge the voices of several authors are conspicuously absent from *Adventures in Poetry,* despite their popularity among New York School writers and despite the fact that Fagin himself engaged in the practice. On the other hand, an entire issue (number 10, undated) is anonymous, omitting even the name of the magazine. This experiment implies allegiance with other contemporary attacks on the traditional idea of the author, but Fagin's comments on the experiment suggest that he is equally concerned with thwarting the tendency to associate an author's identity with membership on a particular "team" (Fagin 9). Instead, the reader is forced to confront the individual style of the work, freed from preconceptions about the author's status. Avoidance of a team mentality is further evident in the range of authors published in *Adventures* overall. While the magazine brings together the first (JOHN ASHBERY, EDWIN DENBY, FRANK O'HARA, JAMES SCHUYLER) and second (ANSELM BERRIGAN, JOSEPH CERAVOLO, TOM CLARK, RON PADGETT, ANNE WALDMAN, LEWIS WARSH) generations of the New York School, it also features the work of writers associated with other "teams": Michael McClure, PHILIP WHALEN, Ebbe Borregard, David Meltzer, Jack Spicer, ALLEN GINSBERG, and GREGORY CORSO, to list some of the names Fagin himself offers as examples (Fagin 9).

In addition to the magazine, the Adventures in Poetry label attached to a series of chapbooks, most notably Ashbery's *The New Spirit* (1970), later collected as one of *Three Poems* (1972). In 2001 Fagin started a new Adventures in Poetry chapbook series with the publication of Ashbery's *100 Multiple Choice Questions,* which originally appeared in issue number 5 of the magazine (January 1970). However, Fagin has shown less concern for what a name like Ashbery can bring to his press than for what his press can do for less famous poets who deserve more recognition. "Helping a poet like STEVE MALMUDE get going is really gratifying," Fagin explains, adding MARY FERRARI and JOHN GODFREY to the list of writers whom he has published. "The small press is there to start them," says Fagin. "That's the reward if you have a small press: you're the intermediary" (Waldman and Fagin 512–513).

Bibliography

Adventures in Poetry Web site. Available online. URL: http://www.adventuresinpoetry.com/home.html.

Clay, Steven, and Rodney Phillips. *A Secret Location on the Lower East Side: Adventures in Writing, 1960–1980.* New York: New York Public Library/Granary Books, 1998, 195–196.

Fagin, Larry. Interview by Daniel Kane. "Adventures in Poetry." *Poetry Project Newsletter* 185 (Summer 2001): 6–11.

Waldman, Anne, ed. *Out of This World: The Poetry Project at St. Mark's Church-in-the-Bowery, an Anthology 1966–1991.* New York: Crown, 1991, 637–638.

Waldman, Anne, and Larry Fagin. "Discussion of Little Magazines and Related Topics." In *The Little*

Magazine in America: A Modern Documentary History, edited by Elliott Anderson and Mary Kinzie, 496–513. Yonkers, N.Y.: Pushcart Press, 1978.

Adventures of Mr. and Mrs. Jim and Ron, The **Jim Dine and Ron Padgett** (1970)

The joyful spirit of early modernism returns in the COLLABORATION between JIM DINE and RON PADGETT on *The Adventures of Mr. and Mrs. Jim and Ron* (London: Cape Goliard; New York: Grossman, 1970). Previously, Dine had supplied illustrations for Padgett's TRANSLATION of Apollinaire's early modernist prose work *The Poet Assassinated* (London: Rupert Hart-Davis; New York: Holt, Rinehart and Winston, 1968). The lives of the collaborators had also been captured by the spirit of adventure. The emergence of the second generation of NEW YORK SCHOOL poets in the POETRY PROJECT AT ST. MARK'S CHURCH IN-THE-BOWERY and such journals as LARRY FAGIN's *ADVENTURES IN POETRY* was confirmed by Padgett and DAVID SHAPIRO's *ANTHOLOGY OF NEW YORK POETS* (1970), in which an excerpt ("The Farmer's Head") from *The Adventures of Mr. and Mrs. Jim and Ron* appears. Also in 1970, Dine's status as a major contemporary artist was confirmed by a retrospective exhibit at the Whitney Museum, accompanied by a catalog to which Padgett contributed. Meanwhile, Dine and his family had gone off to London, like the fictional family of Henry Mayhew's novel *1851*, published that same year, with illustrations by George Cruikshank and the explanatory subtitle *The Adventures of Mr. and Mrs. Sandboys and Family, Who Came up to London to "Enjoy Themselves," and to See the Great Exhibition.*

Neither Jim nor Ron nor their families appear as characters in the fragmentary narratives and images in *The Adventures of Mr. and Mrs. Jim and Ron,* laid out by Dine on 8-by-11-inch pages. In Padgett's prose, sudden swerves in perspective destabilize any sense of fixed identity. For example, in "The Farmer's Head" episode (not titled in this context), someone named Ernest sees that the farmer's head is on fire. But the exclamation "Fire! Fire!" is attributed to a "she," as if the event that has transformed the farmer has also transformed Ernest's gender. The collage photo that appears on the facing page (in black and white, like all of the images in the book) similarly transforms identity by replacing the head of a woman in bridal costume with a bouquet of flowers. While grotesque in a way, the image seems to emphasize the beauty of the transformation rather than its danger. In the form of photography—the medium Dine employs in this book in about equal proportion to drawings—the image also invites acceptance of this surreal transformation as simple matter-of-factness, paralleling the farmer's response to the news that his head has been struck by lightning: "By gum! So it has!"

Bibliography

Balken, Debra Bricker, ed. "Interactions Between Artists and Writers." *Art Journal* 52, no. 4 (Winter 1993): 72.

Gordon, John. *Jim Dine.* New York: Whitney Museum of American Art/Praeger, 1970.

"Letter and Spirit." *Times Literary Supplement,* 2 October 1970, 1,139–1,140.

Agnes and Sally **Lewis Warsh** (1984)

Set in a small New England town, LEWIS WARSH's novella *Agnes and Sally* looks at the adult lives of the two title characters, friends since high school. Agnes, a failed actress-turned-housewife, lives in NEW YORK CITY with her affable but unfaithful husband, Jacob, an aspiring writer. Meanwhile, Sally, a former valedictorian, is now the unlikely wife of the high school basketball hero. The book explores how past mistakes can undercut present goals. This theme is reflected in the plot, which begins with Sally's stated intention of visiting Agnes but ends just before that trip takes place; instead of moving decisively forward, the characters maintain a kind of holding pattern around their tangled memories and fantasies.

Although Agnes and Sally never appear together in the present, we come to understand the dynamics of their relationship through Warsh's perpetual digressions into each woman's daydreams and recollections. In this manner the author establishes quiet emotional complexity and familiar, subdued tensions (for example, low self-esteem, marital disaffection, feelings of unfulfilled potential) in lieu of specific, rising conflict.

Certain sections of *Agnes and Sally* are divided into two distinct scenes, one occupying the top half of the page and the other, printed in a different typeface, in the space below. While most chapters start with only one narrative focus, the author repeatedly introduces a second "tangential" scene, which is then brought to a close shortly before the upper "main" chapter ends. In more than one case, the secondary scene follows an extramarital affair that occurs behind the back of the main story's protagonist.

Another salient feature of *Agnes and Sally* is the diverse chorus of narrative voices that Warsh brings to bear on the action. An example is the following passage, which begins with Sally's husband lying in bed after his wife leaves for New York City:

Going away for three days was a small intermission in the imaginary drama which he didn't know was happening since the only time he'd gone to a play (other than the highschool play Sally had directed) he'd fallen asleep with the program open on his knees. These days, the performers no longer wear clothing. The house lights went on. "Wake up son, it's time to leave." He was in bed but she wasn't with him anymore (104).

Agnes and Sally was published in 1984 by the Fiction Collective, with help from the TEACHERS & WRITERS COLLABORATIVE. The book received a number of favorable reviews and earned praise from writers ROBERT CREELEY, BARBARA GUEST, and Russell Banks.

AIDS

NEW YORK CITY was one of the first population centers in the United States to experience the epidemic potential of the disease known, since 1982, as AIDS (acquired immunodeficiency syndrome). Although the nation was kept complacent by the early and gravely mistaken identification of AIDS exclusively with HOMOSEXUALITY, the arts community in New York quickly recognized the threat to sexual liberation as a threat to the broader cultural emancipation that the city stood for. JIM CARROLL wrote around 1990 that since the advent of AIDS,

"To be modern / In the city is to be a victim in time" (266). On those who had previously enjoyed the city's freedoms, AIDS imposed the chill of waiting. "[T]he incubation period may be up to four years," JAMES SCHUYLER wrote in his diary in 1984, "so even if you 'reform' you still don't know if you're safe for a long, long time" (136). Indeed, it was nearly a decade after the emergence of AIDS that its most direct impact on the community of NEW YORK SCHOOL poets began to be felt in a tragic series of deaths: TIM DLUGOS in 1990, JIM BRODEY in 1993, JOE BRAINARD in 1994.

Understandably, the impact of AIDS on the poetry itself can be seen most clearly in individual elegies by, for instance, EILEEN MYLES for Dlugos ("PV"), JOHN GODFREY for Brodey, and ANNE WALDMAN and KENWARD ELMSLIE for Brainard. DAVID TRINIDAD's "Driving Back from New Haven" is a kind of anticipatory elegy for Dlugos, in which the inadequacy of conventions, both poetic and social, is chillingly summarized in the last line, quoting Dlugos: "I resent that we do not know how to die" (Klein 221). The detail of Dlugos's response to his AZT pill—"Poison"—echoes the clinical details of the poems that Dlugos himself wrote about his journey toward death, most notably the long poem G-9, named for the AIDS ward at Roosevelt Hospital. Myles has placed this poem in the tradition of FRANK O'HARA, observing that "Tim used that New York School immediacy to allow his own demise to be translucent" ("Chewing the Fat"). Schuyler's "Payne Whitney Poems," based on hospitalization for mental illness rather than AIDS, also stand somewhere in the background.

The details of lived experience that characterize Dlugos's last poems point in the direction of a GENRE distinct from the elegy and distinctive of the emerging literature of AIDS. The genre might be called "living with AIDS." How to approach sex is one of its central questions, with answers ranging from EDWARD FIELD's "put sex away" in "The Veteran" (Klein 76) to the hypersexual abandon indulged in such poems as JOHN GIORNO's "Hi Risque" and Brodey's "In the Sky Church." Such poems, as Giorno explained in a 1990 interview, are "very erotic for a particular reason. I mean, sexuality, and everything that became liberated in the last twenty-five years, came to an end eight years ago. So when I perform, I'm talking about things that people used to do, and don't do anymore, and want to do, and long for it" (interview by Zurbrugg 166). The aim is to transmute sexual energy into poetic energy, an "AIDS chant piece" as WALDMAN describes the goal of her "Paean: May I Speak Thus?" ("Grasping" 282).

Brodey, Waldman, and Giorno exemplify the various practical ways in which poets have responded to the AIDS crisis. During his last years, Brodey served as a volunteer counselor to hospitalized AIDS patients in the San Francisco Bay area. Waldman has worked with an ethics committee in the state of Colorado to explore the issue of assisted suicide for terminal AIDS and cancer patients. Giorno continues to administer the AIDS Treatment Project, which he founded in New York in 1984 to provide financial assistance to persons afflicted with AIDS.

Bibliography

Brodey, Jim. "In the Sky Church." In *Heart of the Breath: Poems, 1979–1992*. Edited by Clark Coolidge. West Stockbridge, Mass.: Hard Press, 1996, 317–321.

Carroll, Jim. "In Time, AIDS." In *Fear of Dreaming: Selected Poems*. New York: Penguin, 1993, 266.

Dlugos, Tim. *G-9*. In *Things Shaped in Passing: More "Poets for Life" Writing from the AIDS Pandemic*, edited by Michael Klein and Richard McCann, 45–60. New York: Persea, 1997.

Elmslie, Kenward. "Letter to Joe." In *Agenda Melt*. New York: Adventures in Poetry, 2004, 38–39.

Giorno, John. "AIDS Monologue." In *You Got to Burn to Shine: New and Selected Writings*. London and New York: High Risk Books/Serpent's Tale, 1994, 32–35.

———. "Hi Risque." In *You Got to Burn to Shine: New and Selected Writings*. London and New York: High Risk Books/Serpent's Tale, 1994, 28–31.

———. Interview by Nicholas Zurbrugg. In *Art, Performance, Media: 31 Interviews*, edited by Nicholas Zurbrugg, 156–171. Minneapolis: University of Minnesota Press, 2004.

Godfrey, John. "The James Brother." In *Push the Mule*. Great Barrington, Mass.: The Figures, 2001, 39–41.

Klein, Michael, ed. *Poets for Life: Seventy-six Poets Respond to AIDS*. New York: Crown, 1989. [Includes poems by Tim Dlugos, Edward Field, Eileen Myles, David Trinidad, and others.]

Myles, Eileen. "Chewing the Fat about AIDS—Arts Today with Eileen Myles." Artery: The AIDS-Arts Forum. Available online. URL: http://www.artistswithaids.org/artery/symposium/symposium_myles.html.

———. "PV." In *Maxfield Parris: Early and New Poems*. Santa Rosa, Calif.: Black Sparrow, 1995, 63–65.

Schuyler, James. *The Diary*. Edited by Nathan Kernan. Santa Rosa, Calif.: Black Sparrow, 1997.

———. "The Payne Whitney Poems." In *The Collected Poems*. New York: Noonday/Farrar, Straus & Giroux, 1993, 252–258.

Waldman, Anne. "Grasping the Broom More Tightly Now." Interview by Eric Lorberer. In *Vow to Poetry: Essays, Interviews, and Manifestos*. Minneapolis, Minn.: Coffee House Press, 2001, 281–296.

———. "Paean: May I Speak Thus?" In *In the Room of Never Grieve: New and Selected Poems, 1985–2003*. Minneapolis, Minn.: Coffee House Press, 2003, 234–236.

———. "There was a time an eclipse." In *Iovis: Book II*. Minneapolis, Minn.: Coffee House Press, 1997, 217–226.

Aldan, Daisy (1923–2001)

In accounts of the NEW YORK SCHOOL, Daisy Aldan is usually cited as the editor of *FOLDER* magazine, but she played a more integral role, closer to that of theatrical producer, in the activities of artists and writers who were just beginning to come together as a group in the early 1950s. The production of the first issue of *Folder* in 1953 was itself an event, as the contributors—including FRANK O'HARA, JOHN ASHBERY, and GRACE HARTIGAN— "walked around a table putting the pages together like a smorgasbord" (Aldan, "Interview" 274). In 1954 the same cast of characters gathered at Hartigan's studio to pose for her painting *Masquerade* (Mattison 35–37); Aldan stares out at the viewer from the center of the group. In 1955 Aldan produced a film, *Once Upon an El*, in which 18 poets and painters respond in more or less fanciful ways to the closing of the Third Avenue elevated railway and O'Hara "pretends to throw himself in front of an oncoming train" (Aldan, "Interview" 277). When *A New Folder* was published in 1959, Aldan staged a celebratory reading at the LIVING THEATRE, with slides of artwork from the anthology projected behind the poets while they read (Berkson and LeSueur 71).

Aldan was born in NEW YORK CITY and was one of the child actors in the CBS radio series *Let's Pretend*. She edited a literary magazine as a student at Hunter College and went on to New York University to pursue a Ph.D., her dissertation, never completed, on "The Influence of French Surrealism on American Literature." Her husband, Richard Miller (1920–71), and his friend Floriano Vecchi (1920–2005) helped her establish TIBER PRESS in order to publish *Folder*, which she financed with her salary from teaching at New York's High School of Art and Design. During the 1950s Aldan's most notable publication, apart from her editorial work, was her TRANSLATION of Stephane Mallarmé's *Un coup de dés* (A *Throw of the Dice*, Tiber Press, 1956), the first English rendering of that poem to reproduce the unusual spacing. Inclusion of such work in *Folder* attracted the attention of members of the transatlantic avant-garde. At the invitation of Anaïs Nin (1903–77), Aldan served briefly (1961–62) as the U.S. editor of the journal *Two Cities*, based in New York and Paris.

Aldan's first major collection of verse, *The Destruction of Cathedrals*, was published by Two Cities Press in 1963. It contains poems in the spirit of BARBARA GUEST—"The shadow of a street-lamp may be an upside-down / Parachute" (4)—or Frank O'Hara—"How sprightly New York is at the end of April" (63)—but in the *New York Times Book Review*, M. L. Rosenthal compared Aldan to e. e. cummings for "combining daring technique with sentimental conception" (4). The latter quality evolved into a spiritualism informed by Aldan's study of Rudolf Steiner, with the consequence that her later work failed to engage the avant-garde audience that she had originally attracted.

Bibliography

Aldan, Daisy. "Books and the Living Hand." In *Celebration with Anaïs Nin*, edited by Valerie Harms, 66–72. Riverside, Conn.: Magic Circle Press, 1973.

———. *Collected Poems*. Troy, Mich.: Sky Blue Press, 2002.

———. *The Destruction of Cathedrals and Other Poems*. Paris and New York: Two Cities Press, 1963.

———. "An Interview on *Folder*." By Dennis Barone. In *The Little Magazine in America: A Modern Documentary History*, edited by Elliott Anderson and Mary Kinzie, 263–279. Yonkers, N.Y.: Pushcart Press, 1978).

———. "Poetry and a One-Woman Press." In *The Publish-It-Yourself Handbook: Literary Tradition and How-To*, edited by Bill Henderson, 95–107. Yonkers, N.Y.: Pushcart Book Press, 1973.

Berkson, Bill, and Joe LeSueur, eds. *Homage to Frank O'Hara*. Bolinas, Calif.: Big Sky, 1988.

Malanga, Gerard. "Three Women Poets." *Wagner College Literary Magazine* (1960–61): 67–70.

Mattison, Robert Saltonstall. *Grace Hartigan: A Painter's World*. New York: Hudson Hills, 1990.

Nin, Anaïs. *The Diary*. Vol. 6 (1955–66) and Vol. 7 (1966–74). Edited by Gunther Stuhlmann. New York: Harcourt Brace Jovanovich, 1976, 1980.

Rosenthal, M. L. "Sharp Glimpses of Reality." *New York Times Book Review*, 8 March 1964, 4.

Alfred and Guinevere James Schuyler (1958)

JAMES SCHUYLER's first novel, *Alfred and Guinevere*, appeared before the author had gained prominence as one of the original NEW YORK SCHOOL poets. Relying exclusively on dialogue, letters, and journal entries, this short book chronicles the emotional life of the title characters—a precocious brother and sister at two different stages of preadolescence—sent to spend a summer at the country home of their aloof uncle and grandmother. The reader becomes acquainted with Alfred and Guinevere—along with their respective playmates, Stanley and Betty—through a series of revealing vignettes, set in places ranging from a hospital sickbed to a train compartment to the deck of an ocean liner. Throughout, Schuyler uses the children's perceptions of their social microcosm as a window into the complex adult world that surrounds them.

At the time of its release, the novel was singled out for its inventiveness, "pitch-perfect" dialogue, and reverence for the absurd. Nevertheless, several critics identified it (either implicitly or explicitly) as children's literature, a label that was reinforced by the Paul Sagsoorian drawings that illustrated the first edition. The author's friend and fellow poet, KENNETH KOCH, rebuked such categorization and praised the text as a mature work of adult fiction, pointing to its consonance with Schuyler's poetry. "Prose as poetry really should be," Koch wrote, "among other things fresh, surprising, artful, and clear" (221).

The book's favorable reviews, however, belie the author's difficulties in getting it into print. Harcourt Brace had agreed to publish *Alfred and Guinevere* as early as 1954 on the condition that the manuscript be heavily revised. But that process proved more tedious than Schuyler had anticipated, and it placed him under a great deal of stress, as he related in an interview.

> Getting *Alfred and Guinevere* published was a kind of a nightmare, with niggling criticisms about, like, whether I should call a skillet a spider, and would the vitamin C in orange juice oxidize, and this went on and on (162).

The novel has received renewed attention in recent years thanks to a 2002 edition from the *New York Review of Books*, which includes a new introduction by JOHN ASHBERY.

Bibliography

Davison, Dorothy P., ed. *Book Review Digest.* Vol. 54. New York: H. W. Wilson, 1959.

Koch, Kenneth. Review of *Alfred and Guinevere. Poetry* (Fall 1959): 221.

Robertson, Peter. Review of *Alfred and Guinevere. Booklist* 15 April 1958, 477.

Schuyler, James. Interview by Carl Little. *Agni* 37 (January 1993): 152–182.

Allen, Donald M. (1912–2004) *editor*

Working quietly behind the scenes, Donald Allen redrew the map of contemporary poetry as the editor of several key publications, most notably his anthology *The NEW AMERICAN POETRY, 1945–1960.* Allen came to the avant-garde from a conservative Midwestern background. He was born in Muscatine, Iowa, and attended the University of Iowa through to a master's degree in English, which he obtained in 1935. A period of extensive travels followed, culminating in wartime service in the Pacific as a U.S. Navy translator. His knowledge of Japanese language and culture extended into the practice of Zen Buddhism throughout his later life. After completing his military service in Europe in 1947, Allen pursued graduate studies at the University of California, Berkeley, where he met the poets of the SAN FRANCISCO RENAISSANCE, Robert Duncan, Jack Spicer, and Robin Blaser. They remained his principal reference point as he went on to explore the full range of experimentation in poetry during the postwar decades.

Having decided against a career in teaching, Allen left Berkeley in 1949 without taking a degree and headed for NEW YORK CITY to try his hand in publishing. At a publishing seminar at Columbia University he met Barney Rossett, who invited Allen to join Grove Press, which Rossett had recently purchased. Together they launched *The Evergreen Review* in 1957, with Allen drawing on his West Coast connections to produce the sellout issue number 2, "The San Francisco Scene." In the same year Grove published FRANK O'HARA's *Meditations in an Emergency,* and O'Hara became Allen's chief guide to the New York scene. In turn, Allen became a trusted editorial adviser to O'Hara, helping to shape the latter's *Lunch Poems* (1964) and acquiring experience that Allen drew upon to produce a series of posthumous editions of O'Hara's work: *Collected Poems* (Knopf, 1972), *Selected Poems* (Knopf, 1974), *Early Writings* (Grey Fox, 1977), *Poems Retrieved* (Grey Fox, 1977), and a volume of selected essays, *Standing Still and Walking in New York* (Grey Fox, 1983).

In 1960 Allen moved back to California, residing in San Francisco and then BOLINAS during its peak decade as a literary community (1968–78). He followed up on the success of *The New American Poetry* with other anthologies: *New American Story* (with ROBERT CREELEY, 1965), *New Writing in the U.S.A.* (with Creeley, 1971), *The Poetics of the New American Poetry* (with Warren Tallman, 1973), and *The Postmoderns* (with George F. Butterick, 1982). In 1965 he helped organize the BERKELEY POETRY CONFERENCE. While continuing to serve as West Coast editor for Grove Press until 1970, Allen began to issue books under two of his own imprints. His Four Seasons Foundation and Grey Fox Press published several volumes by O'Hara as well as CHARLES OLSON, Duncan, Spicer, Creeley, Ed

Dorn, JOANNE KYGER, Lew Welch, JACK KEROUAC, and ALLEN GINSBERG. The "hippie" cult author Richard Brautigan, one of Allen's discoveries, sold well for Four Seasons after being dropped by Grove. Grey Fox issued a number of titles of special interest to gay and lesbian readers, establishing a context for the reception of O'Hara's explicitly gay poems.

Bibliography

Allen, Donald. "Don Allen: Grove's First Editor." Interview by S. E. Gontarski. *Review of Contemporary Fiction* 10, no. 3 (September 1990): 132–136.

———. Interview by David Chadwick. *Crooked Cucumber.* Available online. URL: http://www.cuke.com/Cucumber%20Project/interviews/allen.html. Accessed December 16, 2008.

"Donald Allen Feature." *Jacket* 25 (February 2004). Available online by subscription. URL: http://jacket magazine.com/25/index.html. Accessed December 16. 2008.

LaBonte, Richard. "What They Forgot to Say about Donald M. Allen." *Lambda Book Report* 13, no. 4–5 (November–Decenber 2004): 66.

Saxton, Wolfgang. "Donald Allen, 92, Book Editor of Bold New Voices in Poetry," *New York Times,* 9 September 2004, 31.

Altos, The
Barbara Guest and Richard Tuttle (1991)

BARBARA GUEST collaborated on *The Altos* with the artist Richard Tuttle and the master printer Hank Hine, who produced this artist's book in 1991 at his Limestone Press, then based in San Francisco.

The format of the book is outsized, with a cover measuring 17¼-by-14¼ inches and composed of pigskin, into which the title has been embossed. Inside, the handset type is correspondingly large (30 points): For instance, the left vertical of the letter *h* measures ⅜ inches. While the sans serif font adds to the effect of boldness, the soft gray ink of the lettering appears to fade into, or gradually to emerge from, the cream-colored Somerset paper. Correspondingly, Tuttle's hand-colored soft-ground etchings employ color sparingly; the drawing is attenuated and often suggests erasure. In proportion to the size of each sheet, the number of words in the text or of marks

in each print is relatively sparse. Image and text are presented separately, rather than on facing sheets. Eleven prints and 10 units of text alternate in sequence. The reader-viewer may experience the text visually or, alternatively, may attempt to "read" the marks in the prints, as a FORM of glyph. The unfolding drama evokes evanescence, apparition, suspension, isolation—keynotes of Guest's late aesthetic and of the MINIMALISM that has characterized Tuttle's art throughout his career.

Poet and artist also share a commitment to abstraction. Tuttle deploys geometrical shapes—circle, square, triangle—and a repeated kidney-shaped form reminiscent of some of the whimsical figures in the art of Joan Miró. However, Tuttle's forms are frequently left incomplete, or their boundaries are somehow opened up by overlapping or faintness of line. Even the identity of a single line is challenged by the modulation of color over its trajectory, for instance, aqua, green, blue, orange in varied sequence in the final print. This instability or permeability of borders is inscribed thematically in Guest's text, where *border* is the last word, but it completes the phrase "cross the border." A symmetrical structure is formed in conjunction with the reference to crossing a river in the opening unit. More generally, fragmented syntax keeps the language of the poem open throughout. There are few complete sentences, and there is much uncertainty as to whether successive phrases are to be read continuously or in isolation, so they cannot make sense in a conventional way. This problem of succession is present from the very beginning of the text, which opens with ellipsis points (. . .) and then the words *the warbler* placed at the far right of the sheet, rather than the far left, where our eyes are accustomed to begin reading. Guest has credited Tuttle with this placement, and she describes "spacing" as a consideration of design that was of special importance to both of them (Guest 27).

If *The Altos* does not tell a coherent story or even describe a recognizable world, it does compose a space that can be characterized as otherwordly. *Altos* is the Spanish word for "heights," as in Los Altos, the town just south of San Francisco that may have helped to suggest the name to Guest. But to Guest, high places designate the world of the imagination rather than any specific locale (in the original text of *The Altos*, the word *altos* is not capitalized). Moreover, the world of the imagination has the peculiar quality of being characterized by mobility rather than stasis; it is not fixed in place. The ability to move fluidly between text and image is one of the features of this world, as is the ability to move between present and past texts and ultimately between the living and the dead. The final phrase of unit 9 of *The Altos*, "with full hands," echoes a famous passage from Virgil's *Aeneid* (6.883), in which Anchises, the dead father of Aeneas, foresees the death of the young Marcellus, and mourns, "with full hands, give me lilies" (Mandelbaum's translation). "The lily" is named a few lines above in Guest's text and is figured in references to "the stalk image" and "a gestural branch." Tuttle's print accompanying this text, with a long, thin line extending from the bottom left and curving into a slightly hooked shape at top center, comes closer to representing Guest's imagery than at any other point in this collaboration (Diggory 91). But the word *gestural* is a more significant point of contact than the image of the branch. In the spirit of ACTION PAINTING, a line in drawing or a line of poetry is most meaningful as a trace of the activity of the artist, the agent of the imagination.

As reprinted in *Defensive Rapture* (Sun & Moon, 1993), the text of *The Altos* varies from the original printing, to some extent in wording and to a considerable degree in spacing and sequence. The opening and closing units are the same, but the sequence of the intervening units has been rearranged and an additional unit, beginning "the embonpoint" (96), has been inserted.

Bibliography

Diggory, Terence. "Barbara Guest and the Mother of Beauty." *Women's Studies* 30 (2001): 75–94.

Guest, Barbara. Interview by Mark Hillringhouse. *American Poetry Review* (July–August 1992): 23–30.

Richard Tuttle: Books and Prints. Exhibit brochure. Hartford, Conn.: Widener Gallery, Trinity College, 1996, New York: New York Public Library, 1997.

Amelia Earhart   Maureen Owen   (1984)

Just as the pioneer aviator Amelia Earhart (1897–1937) claimed a space for women in the sky, MAUREEN OWEN revised the legend of Earhart to claim a space for women writers in the "open field" of experimental poetry. Kathleen Fraser, who published drafts of Owen's *Amelia Earhart* in the second issue of her journal of women's writing, *HOW(ever)* (1983), remarks on the influence of CHARLES OLSON's theory of "PROJECTIVE VERSE" in the "Working Notes" that Owen supplied to accompany the drafts: "[T]he spaces between the words breathe because there is no finished poem" (Fraser 158). Fraser adds, "we also recognize the New York School's valuing of process," for instance, in Owen's claim that "the process of the poem being written becomes the actual poem" (Fraser 158). Thematically, as well, Owen's Earhart belongs to a NEW YORK SCHOOL lineage somewhere between the juvenile adventure hero—the "Beryl of the By-plane" who features in JOHN ASHBERY's "Europe" (1962) or the aviators of KENNETH KOCH's *The Red Robins* (1975)—and the mythic protagonist of ALICE NOTLEY's *The Descent of Alette* (1992), who flies like an owl.

In the development of Owen's own work, *Amelia Earhart* is prefigured in several aviation poems in her collection *Hearts in Space* (Kulchur Foundation, 1980), as well as in the title of that collection. "It's about space," declares the protagonist of *Amelia Earhart*, "& claustrophobia" (section 10; sections are unnumbered and unpaginated, thus references to sections are by order of sequence). These two phrases are separated on the page by white space, a device that breathes the air of poetry into Owen's lines, whose margins otherwise suggest the shape of prose. Open space has special autobiographical significance for Owen, who identifies with Earhart as a fellow Midwesterner. In one of their imagined dialogues, Owen connects Earhart's "love of flying" with Midwestern geography: "I myself get claustrophobic if I can't see / for five or six miles in all 4 directions" (sect. 7). The freedom of open spaces connects with the freedom of childhood: "I feel / like a girl again" (sect. 10). On the other hand, the experience of claustrophobia connects with a mother's role of caring for children, the role that Owen was trying to balance with her writing during the composition of *Amelia Earhart*. As Fraser deduces from Owen's "Working Notes," the desire to fly that animates Owen's poem connects with her desire "to free herself from the confines of literal interruptions by her children's everpresent claims" (158).

While experience such as Owen's provided a new feminist rationale for the modernist aesthetic of fragmentation (Rich 173–175), Owen seeks in *Amelia Earhart* to transcend fragmentation with a new vision of the whole work, a spatialized version of the SERIAL POEM that defines much New York School experimentation. Owen's spatialization derives from her identification with the point of view of the aviator, looking down on a landscape that appears flat yet readable, like a map. "O geography My Great Flat Home," she writes at the end of *Amelia Earhart* (sect. 25), returning to her home on the flat Midwestern plains. Her "Working Notes" make the relevance to poetic composition explicit: "Flat geographies can be invented w/ intersecting plains & meandering waters that are little stories merging from different sources." Though the sources are "different," the process of "intersecting" and "merging" prevents them from appearing fragmented. Owen finds a visual equivalent to such composition in the art of her friend Yvonne Jacquette, whose signature vision of New York streets seen from high above is represented in the frontispiece to *Amelia Earhart*.

Despite the theoretical clarity of her poem, Owen asserts in her "Working Notes" that it is "the mystery" that excites her. Certainly, the achievements of Earhart as an aviator might be forgotten were it not for the persistent mystery of her disappearance somewhere over the Pacific Ocean during an attempt to fly around the world. Owen concludes *Amelia Earhart* on that note of mystery, following her assertion of "My Great Flat Home" with an uncanny image of depth:

> *the corpse floated a strange shaped emerald under the sea* (sect. 25).

Bibliography

Fraser, Kathleen. "Line. On the Line. Lining up. Lined with. Between the lines. Bottom line" (1988). In *Translating the Unspeakable: Poetry and the Innovative Necessity.* Tuscaloosa: University of Alabama Press, 2000, 141–160.

Friedman, Ed. Review of *Amelia Earhart, Poetry Project Newsletter* 110 (December 1984), n.p.

Owen, Maureen. *Amelia Earhart.* San Francisco: Vortex Editions, 1984.

———. "Working Notes." *HOW(ever)* 1, no. 2 (October 1983). Available online. URL: http://www.asu.edu/pipercwcenter/how2journal/archive/print_archive/monotes.html.

Rich, Adrienne. "When We Dead Awaken: Writing as Re-vision" (1971). In *Adrienne Rich's Poetry and Prose.* Edited by Barbara Charlesworth Gelpi and Albert Gelpi. New York: Norton, 1993, 166–177.

America: A History in Verse
Ed Sanders (2000–)

Based on his theory that "poetry should again assume responsibility for the description of history" (INVESTIGATIVE POETRY, 3), ED SANDERS projects a nine-volume chronicle for *America: A History in Verse,* covering the 15th century up to the present time. He has completed the five volumes relating to the 20th century and published three of them: *Volume 1, 1900–1939* (Black Sparrow, 2000), *Volume 2, 1940–1961* (Black Sparrow, 2000), and *Volume 3, 1962–1970* (Godine, 2004). While several other books by Sanders constitute what he calls "investigative poetry," his *America* chronicle is by far his most ambitious attempt to set in verse a comprehensive archive of information. In *America,* Sanders juxtaposes textbook American history with a revisionist version that emphasizes cultural innovations, dissident organizations, and injustices perpetrated through the abuse of power.

The form of *America* develops the free-verse patterns championed in Sanders's *Investigative Poetry* (City Lights, 1976). The underlying theory is that of CHARLES OLSON's "PROJECTIVE VERSE," namely, that "the poem itself must, at all points, be a high energy construct and . . . an energy discharge" (Olson 387), which Sanders extends to the discharge of data. *America* reads as a passionate, chronological encyclopedia of 20th-century American policies, headlines, and histories. While the events of each decade dictate the content, Sanders creates a poetic voice full of inflections, pauses, commentary, and questions. He manipulates the pace of his language relative to his subject, changing tones and shifting moods to produce poetic effects far beyond those of conventional nonfiction history. At times, however, Sanders's apparent desire for *America* to compete with other almanacs swamps the poetry with "gargantuan lists" (MacAdams 7).

Most of *America* sounds like a silenced witness finally allowed to speak. Sanders focuses on the people and groups behind policy decisions and speculates on the various motives that shaped the events. Introducing the Spanish-American War, he quotes Teddy Roosevelt confiding in a friend, "I should welcome almost any war / for I think this country needs one" (1:13). With all his topics, especially war, Sanders invokes opposition views, with a particular emphasis on communist, socialist, and pacifist movements, such as the Anti-Imperialist League. He also illuminates the hypocrisies and conflicts of victory, as when describing Roosevelt's triumphant parade up Fifth Avenue: "To his credit he publicly thanked the black troops for their bravery / yet the heroes he praised / could not get served / in the restaurants of the south / upon their return" (1:25).

Sanders directs his harshest condemnation at Americans who lobbied on behalf of greed; his harrowing retelling of the Ludlow Massacre of April 20, 1914, castigates a nation that has shamefully forgotten not only the anniversary but the event itself: "Goony war whoops gooned the smoke / 13 were shot dead / . . . Only by keeping the images alive / in text & song / does a massacre teach tomorrow / as Euripides keeps alive the women of Troy" (1:127).

In addition to major events and conflicts, Sanders dutifully records cultural progress with landmarks big and small: for example, the first traffic lights (August 5, 1914), the strange death of Isadora Duncan (September 14, 1927), and the five months ROBERT LOWELL spent in prison for protesting "indiscriminate bombing of civilians" during World War II (1944).

In his review of *America*'s third volume, LEWIS MACADAMS aligns Sanders with the public poetry of the BEATS in contrast to "the so-called personal poem" (7), implicitly a reference to a mode identified with FRANK O'HARA and the NEW YORK SCHOOL. However, the documentary method held considerable fascination for the second generation of the New York School, who also inclined toward the Beat sensibility much more than their elders did. Both in method and in sensibility, *America: A History in Verse* affirms the place assigned to Sanders by RON PADGETT and DAVID SHAPIRO in their ANTHOLOGY OF NEW YORK POETS (Random House, 1970).

Bibliography

MacAdams, Lewis. "A Poet's Song of the '60s," *Los Angeles Times Book Review,* 4 July 2004, 6–7.

Olson, Charles. "Projective Verse" (1950). In *The New American Poetry, 1945–1960,* edited by Donald Allen, 386–397. 1960. Reprint, Berkeley: University of California Press, 1999.

Sanders, Ed. *Investigative Poetry.* San Francisco: City Lights, 1976.

American Book of the Dead, The
John Giorno (1964)

Although the title dates to a collection privately circulated in 1964, *The American Book of the Dead* represents an ongoing experiment in "found poetry" that JOHN GIORNO pursued throughout the 1960s. Selections appear in his first published volume, *Poems by John Giorno* (1967), and in An ANTHOLOGY OF NEW YORK POETS, edited by RON PADGETT and DAVID SHAPIRO (1970).

Unlike the "found" texts incorporated into major modernist poems such as Ezra Pound's *Cantos* or William Carlos Williams's *Paterson*, the poems in *The American Book of the Dead* are nothing but quotations given poetic shape simply by Giorno's choice of line breaks and stanza divisions. This condition led TOM CLARK, reviewing Giorno's *Poems* in the *New York Times Book Review,* to argue that "there is no invention in Giorno's poems, only composition" (32). On the other hand, JOHN PERREAULT, in a review in the *Village Voice* (36), claimed that Giorno had introduced "a major innovation, long overdue" by applying to poetry "the use of found materials" that had become established practice in the visual arts, as the Museum of Modern Art had recently confirmed (1961) in its major survey *The Art of Assemblage.*

POP ART is the contemporary art movement most relevant to Giorno's found poems. During the early 1960s Giorno was a close associate of ANDY WARHOL; he was the subject of Warhol's first film, *Sleep* (1963), which simply documents for eight hours the image of Giorno asleep. Like his films, Warhol's paintings have a strong documentary impulse, though it may be less apparent in paintings of objects, such as the famous soup cans, than in paintings of events, such as the Death and Disaster series from the same period. Just as Warhol reproduces newspaper photographs of auto accidents, race riots, and suicides, Giorno's poems reproduce newspaper stories in which death or the threat of death is a recurrent theme. The impersonal language of newspaper reporting confers on the poem a *deadpan* tone, a term frequently applied by critics to pop art and by Perreault to the work of Giorno (42). However, Giorno achieves subtle inversions in our expectations of the personal or impersonal dimensions of subject matter. In a poem about the assassination of President John F. Kennedy, an event of great public significance, Giorno chooses to focus on a first-person account by the president's wife. In contrast, the suicide of the dancer Fred Herko, another member of Warhol's circle whom Giorno knew well, is distanced through a quotation about the memorial service to be held at the Judson Church.

Cumulatively, *The American Book of the Dead* offers a record of a particular historical moment in American culture. Giorno has explained elsewhere his response to the Kennedy assassination in 1963: "There was so much unexpressed optimism, the moment of JFK's death seemed the absolute indication of the complete failure of everyone's aspirations, portending what was to come" (124). The poet's minimal interference with the material leaves any emotion "unexpressed," whether optimistic or otherwise, while also extending aspirations, and their failure, to an anonymous, collective "everyone." Underlying this cultural critique is a religious perspective specific to Giorno, who, as an undergraduate at Columbia University, had begun the study of Buddhism under one of its leading American interpreters, Alan Watts. The title of *The American Book of the Dead* alludes to the Buddhist text known as the Tibetan Book of the Dead, which is used to guide the initiate toward a good death by encouraging detachment from the life of sensory existence, regarded by Buddhists as illusion. Thus, disillusionment, experienced as a negative moment for the culture, takes on positive value for the individual soul seeking enlightenment.

The combination of cultural critique and religious quest that informs *The American Book of the Dead* is usually regarded as more characteristic of the BEATS than of the NEW YORK SCHOOL poets, and, indeed, Giorno is today often classified as a Beat writer, partly due to his later association with WILLIAM S. BURROUGHS. Historically, it is more accurate to recognize in *The American Book of the Dead* the intertwining of strands whose separation into "schools" can be misleading. The derivation of Giorno's method from contemporary visual art is typical of New York School practice. During the same period JOHN ASHBERY and TED BERRIGAN were also exploring the possibilities of "found texts." The experience of such texts as objective material—*objets trouvés* in French, or "found objects"—invited the kind of multisensory manipulation that made Giorno into one of the star performers at the POETRY PROJECT AT ST. MARK'S CHURCH IN-THE-BOWERY.

Bibliography

Clark, Tom. "Two and Three," *New York Times Book Review*, 31 March 1968, 32.

Giorno, John. *You Got to Burn to Shine: New and Selected Writings*. London and New York: High Risk Books/ Serpent's Tail, 1994.

Perreault, John. "Pop Poetry." Review of Giorno, *Poems*. *Village Voice*, 7 September 1967, 6 ff.

American Literary Anthology, The
(1968–1970)

If the sad history of *The American Literary Anthology* is any indication, the gathering of NEW YORK SCHOOL poets into their "own" anthologies during the same period (*The POETS OF THE NEW YORK SCHOOL,* 1969; *An ANTHOLOGY OF NEW YORK POETS,* 1970) was equivalent to placing an infected population under quarantine. The inclusion of New York School poets among the "mainstream" writers in *The American Literary Anthology* not only led to the demise of the project but also spread like a virus into debates about the legitimacy of a federal government agency.

The *American Literary Anthology* was the brain-child of George Plimpton, editor of the PARIS REVIEW, who secured funding from the National Endowment for the Arts (NEA), just founded in 1965, for a series of annual anthologies that would "bring before a wider public the best work from little magazines" (Anderson and Kinzie 525). *Little* did not necessarily imply "underground," and the work culled from the original survey of 1966 publications included already distinguished names, such as W. H. AUDEN, and current trendsetters, such as Joyce Carol Oates and Susan Sontag. Sontag was also one of the panel of judges for the interview category, who awarded the top prize to TED BERRIGAN's "interview" with JOHN CAGE, originally published in MOTHER. In reality, this piece was an experiment in the FORM of the interview (Berrigan 99), with content lifted entirely from published interviews with other people, not Cage. When the announcement of prize money forced Berrigan to explain these circumstances, Plimpton decided he ought at least to consult Cage. Having already been assured by JOHN ASHBERY that Berrigan was on his side, Cage raised no objection to publication, and the "interview" appeared, above an explanatory note, in the first installment of the anthology, published after some delay in 1968 by Farrar, Straus & Giroux. The Berrigan incident proved to be merely a warning of more trouble to come.

For the second annual *American Literary Anthology,* published by Random House in 1969, Robert Duncan awarded prize money to ARAM SAROYAN for one of his minimalist poems, consisting of the single "misspelled" word *lighght,* originally published in the *Chicago Review.* In this case controversy arose as an issue not of authenticity but of expense: $107 per letter, as calculated by the Republican member of Congress William Scherle of Iowa (Saroyan, *Friends* 83). Congressmen like Scherle, who already disliked the idea of funding the NEA, jumped on this example in an effort to portray the entire enterprise as irresponsible. They succeeded in cutting funding for the anthology series, which managed to publish with Viking Press only one more volume (1970) before the ax fell. The NEA survived but remains subject to attacks, in which Saroyan's poem is still used as ammunition (Doolittle letter). Setting the incident in the context of the Vietnam War and the assassinations of Martin Luther King Jr. and Robert Kennedy, Saroyan recalls: "[W]hat troubled me most at the time was a recognition that my work comprised a sensibility that was being fiercely challenged, not to say effectively obliterated by the surge of world events" ("Flower Power" 5).

Bibliography

Anderson, Elliott, and Mary Kinzie. Introduction to "Enterprise in the Service of Art: George Plimpton." In *The Little Magazine in America: A Modern Documentary History.* Yonkers, N.Y.: Pushcart Press, 1978, 525–526.

Balakian, Nona. "Angel Hair, *Partisan Review* Et Al.," *New York Times,* 26 June 1968, 45.

Berrigan, Ted. "Interview with CITY" (1977). In *Talking in Tranquility: Interviews.* Edited by Stephen Ratcliffe and Leslie Scalapino. Bolinas, Calif.: Avenue B; Oakland, Calif.: O Books, 1991, 90–105.

Doolittle, John T. Letter addressed "Dear Colleague," 9 April 1997. U.S. House of Representatives Web site. Available online. URL: http://www.house.gov/doolittle/dearcolleague/dc04097.htm.

Saroyan, Aram. "Flower Power." In *Starting Out in the Sixties: Selected Essays.* Jersey City, N.J.: Talisman House, 2001, 3–6.

———. *Friends in the World: The Education of a Writer.* Minneapolis, Minn.: Coffee House Press, 1992.

American poetry

The recruitment of the NEW YORK SCHOOL poets under the banner of the NEW AMERICAN POETRY inevitably raises the question of what makes them American as well as "new"—that is, modern. The fact that the leading examples of MODERNIST POETRY IN ENGLISH were also American complicates the question, though it is notable that the modernists who had the greatest influence on the New York School, Wallace Stevens and William Carlos Williams, were the two who stayed home, in contrast to the European exile of T. S. Eliot and Ezra Pound. As much as the New York School poets looked to France for models, there is a strong case behind Harold Bloom's claim that "[John] Ashbery goes back through Stevens to [Walt] Whitman" ("John Ashbery" 110), just as FRANK O'HARA, in

"PERSONISM" (1969), traces his own lineage back to Whitman by way of Williams and Hart Crane (*Collected Poems* 498). Following Bloom, though arriving at different conclusions, recent critics such as Michael Magee and Andrew Epstein have emphasized the tradition's philosophical as well as aesthetic dimensions, placing New York School writers in the context of American pragmatism derived from Ralph Waldo Emerson. Henry David Thoreau, as a philosopher of nature, has seemed less relevant, though he has been invoked as precursor for the realism shared by JAMES SCHUYLER and FAIRFIELD PORTER (Spring 324).

The persona that the BEATS found so attractive in Whitman seems to have been of most interest to KENNETH KOCH among the New York School poets. "It's as if some wild Marlovian hero had wandered into nineteenth century America," observed Koch (interview 189), who heard "a sort of Whitmanian I" functioning as "the chief persona" in O'Hara's *Second Avenue* ("Poetry Chronicles" 130). Certainly the urban scene that underlies that poem links O'Hara to Whitman as the poet of "Manahatta," although O'Hara's evocation of the scene in *Second Avenue* is more abstract than Whitman's catalogs. It is no accident that Whitman ("City of Ships") and O'Hara ("Meditations in an Emergency") are the two poets whose lines in celebration of the city are inscribed on a harborside railing in Lower Manhattan, in the plaza designed (1989) by Siah Armajani and Scott Burton for the World Financial Center (Johnson). But O'Hara and Whitman share a vision that extends beyond the city into a realm that is equally abstract for both poets, frequently expressed by Whitman as a sense of overwhelming vastness, encapsulated in O'Hara's phrase "the enormous bliss of American death" (*Collected Poems* 326). This is the American sublime that descends from Whitman to JOHN ASHBERY in Bloom's analysis, for instance, in his "misreading" of Whitman's "As I Ebb'd with the Ocean of Life" and Ashbery's "As You Came from the Holy Land" (*A Map of Misreading* 178–184, 203–206).

Emily Dickinson, Whitman's great counterpart in 19th-century American poetry, paradoxically condensed "the enormous bliss of American death" into tightly compressed lines, sentences, and stanzas. In general, New York School poetry seems to

owe more to Whitman's long line, explicitly praised by Ashbery, who avoided comment on Dickinson by claiming, "I think I should read her more" (Ashbery, *Mark Ford* 33–34). Koch, however, has observed how "Dickinson's poems are like high explosives hidden in small, neat boxes" (*Making* 210), making them sound rather like the constructions of JOSEPH CORNELL, a confessed admirer of Dickinson (Porter). O'Hara compared Dickinson to the minimalist MUSIC of MORTON FELDMAN: "Its form reveals itself after its meaning is revealed, as Dickinson's passion ignores her dazzling technique" ("New Directions" 118). O'Hara's poem "Off the Kerb & after Emily Dickinson" (1961) is the first of a line of New York School poems "after" Dickinson, especially by women writers (MAUREEN OWEN, ANNE WALDMAN). Women also appear more likely to make Dickinson the subject of critical reflection (ANN LAUTERBACH, ALICE NOTLEY). BARBARA GUEST, the only woman of the first-generation New York School, was prompted by the work of younger writers, specifically Susan Howe's *My Emily Dickinson*, to offer her own reflection on the "very Byzantine turn" in Dickinson's work, "a preference for abrupt connections with the remote in order to establish a concrete interior" ("Mysteriously" 13). Interestingly, in the much revised version of these remarks that Guest later collected, Dickinson disappears and Edgar Allan Poe makes one of his very rare appearances in a New York School context (Guest, *Forces* 84).

The intangible quality that Williams called the "American idiom" registers in the vernacular diction and rhythm of New York School poetry, though here, again, a distinction of generations is useful. The painter ALEX KATZ, who felt especially attuned to "the use of the vernacular, and of vernacular images" in the poets of the second generation, shrewdly observes: "With Ron Padgett, there's no English poetry in his work. The words are more American than English. With Frank [O'Hara], there's a lot of French Surrealism, but basically it always seems like the roots are in Elizabethan English" (15). It is symptomatic that Koch would characterize Whitman as "a wild Marlovian hero"—that is, a character from an Elizabethan play by Christopher Marlowe—and the comparison may say as much about Whitman as it does about Koch. Williams praised Whitman not as an oracle whose words American poets needed to obey but as a prophet who pointed to a promised land that he himself never entered. There was hope, in other words, that American poetry would grow closer to the American idiom than it had been in the 19th century. New York School poetry fulfills that hope in small details, such as the roughening of the smooth iambic flow in "a certain slant of light," from Emily Dickinson's poem (number 258), by the extra syllable in A CERTAIN SLANT OF SUNLIGHT, the title of TED BERRIGAN's final volume (O Books, 1988). The cumulative effect is the persuasive force of "the 'civil meter' of American English," as identified by DOUGLAS CRASE, the second-generation poet who has devoted most explicit attention to the question of what it means to call poetry "American." He concedes: "If you write in this civil meter, it's true you have to give up the Newtonian certainties of the iamb. But you gain a stronger metaphor for conviction by deploying the recognizable, if variable patterns of the language of American power" (38).

Bibliography

Ashbery, John. "As You Came from the Holy Land." In *Self-Portrait in a Convex Mirror.* Harmondsworth, U.K.: Penguin, 1976, 6–7.

———. *John Ashbery in Conversation with Mark Ford.* London: Between the Lines, 2003.

Bloom, Harold. "John Ashbery: The Charity of the Hard Moments." In *Contemporary Poetry in America: Essays and Interviews,* edited by Robert Boyers, 110–138. New York: Schocken, 1974.

———. *A Map of Misreading.* Oxford: Oxford University Press, 1975.

Crase, Douglas. Commentary on "Once the Sole Province." In *Ecstatic Occasions, Expedient Forms: 85 Leading Contemporary Poets Select and Comment on Their Poems,* edited by David Lehman, 36–39. 2d ed. Ann Arbor: University of Michigan Press, 1996.

Dickinson, Emily. *The Complete Poems.* Edited by Thomas H. Johnson. Boston: Little, Brown, 1960.

Epstein, Andrew. *Beautiful Enemies: Friendship and Postwar American Poetry.* Oxford: Oxford University Press, 2006.

Guest, Barbara. *Forces of Imagination: Writing on Writing.* Berkeley, Calif.: Kelsey St. Press, 2003.

———. "Mysteriously Defining the Mysterious: Byzantine Proposals of Poetry." *HOW(ever)* 3 (October 1986): 12–13.

Johnson, Ken. "Poetry and Public Service." *Art in America* 78, no. 3 (March 1990): 160–163ff.

Katz, Alex. Interview by Vincent Katz. *Poetry Project Newsletter* 184 (April–May 2001): 11–15ff.

Koch, Kenneth. Interview by Jordan Davis (1995). *The Art of Poetry: Poems, Parodies, Interviews, Essays, and Other Work.* Ann Arbor: University of Michigan Press, 1996, 187–214.

———. *Making Your Own Days: The Pleasures of Reading and Writing Poetry.* New York: Scribner, 1998.

———. "Poetry Chronicles." *Partisan Review* 28 (January–February 1961): 130–136.

Lauterbach, Ann. "The Night Sky III" (1996). In *The Night Sky: Writings on the Poetics of Experience.* New York: Viking, 2005, 80–94.

Magee, Michael. "Tribes of New York: Frank O'Hara, Amiri Baraka, and the Poetics of the Five Spot." *Contemporary Literature* 42, no. 4 (2001): 694–726.

Notley, Alice. "Voice" (2000). In *Coming After: Essays on Poetry.* Ann Arbor: University of Michigan Press, 2005, 147–157.

O'Hara, Frank. *The Collected Poems.* Rev. ed. Edited by Donald Allen. Berkeley: University of California Press, 1995.

———. "New Directions in Music: Morton Feldman" (1959). In *Standing Still and Walking in New York.* Edited by Donald Allen. San Francisco: Grey Fox, 1983, 115–120.

———. "Off the Kerb & after Emily Dickinson." In *Poems Retrieved.* Rev. ed. Edited by Donald Allen. San Francisco: Grey Fox, 1996, 216.

Owen, Maureen. "For Emily (Dickinson)." In *Hearts in Space.* New York: Kulchur Foundation, 1980, 45.

Porter, David. "Assembling a Poet and Her Poems: Convergent Limit—Works of Joseph Cornell and Emily Dickinson." *Word & Image* 10, no. 3 (July–September 1994): 199–221.

Spring, Justin. *Fairfield Porter: A Life in Art.* New Haven, Conn.: Yale University Press, 2000.

Waldman, Anne. "Complaynt." In *First Baby Poems.* Rev. ed. New York: Hyacinth Girls, 1983, 22.

Whitman, Walt. *Leaves of Grass: Comprehensive Reader's Edition.* Edited by Harold W. Blodgett and Sculley Bradley. New York: Norton, 1965.

Williams, William Carlos. "The American Idiom." *New Directions* 17 (1961): 250–251.

Angel Hair (1966–1978)

For coeditors ANNE WALDMAN and LEWIS WARSH, *Angel Hair* magazine was a more personal enterprise than *The WORLD*, the magazine that Waldman edited, frequently in collaboration with Warsh, for the POETRY PROJECT AT ST. MARK'S CHURCH IN-THE-BOWERY. *Angel Hair* came first, soon after Waldman and Warsh met at the BERKELEY POETRY CONFERENCE in 1965. They named their magazine after a poem by Jonathan Cott, who had introduced them. *Angel Hair* was produced elegantly by letterpress, by the same printer whom Waldman had worked with as editor of the Bennington College literary magazine. By contrast, *The World* aimed for speed and quantity of production, facilitated by the quick and inexpensive mimeograph process. The entire run of *Angel Hair* consisted of only six issues, published between spring 1966 and spring 1969, a period that saw the first 18 issues of *The World*. Stricter editorial discrimination also shaped *Angel Hair*. Warsh tells the story of rejecting TED BERRIGAN's first submissions, as they represented *The SONNETS*, which "everyone knew" ("Publishing Ted" 25). To keep his magazine "special" and "to expand people's notions of Ted's work," Warsh accepted a chapter from the novel CLEAR THE RANGE for Berrigan's first appearance in *Angel Hair* (number 2, fall 1966), and work by Berrigan appeared in every subsequent issue.

Although "by the fifth issue, the magazine became associated almost exclusively with the New York School," as Warsh concedes, both he and Waldman emphasized "variousness" as their editorial goal (Warsh, Introduction xxvi). Warsh points proudly to the number of West Coast writers included: Ebbe Borregard, PHILIP WHALEN, Robert Duncan, JOANNE KYGER, John Thorpe, and Jim Koller. Waldman, meanwhile, focuses on the empowerment of a younger generation to depart from their elders in a variety of ways (Waldman, Introduction xxvi). Nevertheless, the core of the first-generation NEW YORK SCHOOL poets (JOHN ASHBERY, BARBARA GUEST, KENNETH KOCH, FRANK O'HARA, and JAMES SCHUYLER) were published in *Angel Hair* along with nearly all of the second-generation poets (except for DAVID SHAPIRO and ED SANDERS) represented in RON PADGETT and Shapiro's ANTHOLOGY OF NEW YORK POETS (1970).

By "a natural progression" (Warsh, Introduction xxiv), *Angel Hair* expanded into a publishing enterprise that outlasted the magazine as well as Warsh and Waldman's marriage. Each continued to issue chapbooks and broadsides under the Angel Hair imprint until 1978, eventually compiling a list of more than 60 publications. Especially notable titles include JIM BRODEY's *IDENTIKIT* (1967), CLARK COOLIDGE's *Ing* (1968), O'Hara's, *Oranges* (1969), BILL BERKSON's *Shining Leaves* (1969), JOE BRAINARD's *I REMEMBER* installments (1970, 1972, 1973), ALICE NOTLEY's *Incidentals in the Day World* (1973), EDWIN DENBY's *Snoring in New York* (in conjunction with ADVENTURES IN POETRY, 1974), Berrigan's *Nothing for You* (1977), and BERNADETTE MAYER's *The GOLDEN BOOK OF WORDS* (1978). Printing methods ranged from mimeograph to high-quality letterpress by the Grabhorn-Hoyem Press in San Francisco. Covers were produced by a distinguished list of artists including JIM DINE, PHILIP GUSTON, ALEX KATZ, James Rosenquist, and Raphael Soyer as well as the poets' "house artists," Brainard and GEORGE SCHNEEMAN.

Bibliography

Waldman, Anne. Introduction to *The Angel Hair Anthology*. Edited by Anne Waldman and Lewis Warsh. New York: Granary Books, 2001, xix–xxvii.

———. Statement on *Angel Hair*. In *A Secret Location on the Lower East Side: Adventures in Writing, 1960–1980*, by Steven Clay and Rodney Phillips, 177. New York: New York Public Library/Granary Books, 1998.

Warsh, Lewis. Introduction to *The Angel Hair Anthology*. Edited by Anne Waldman and Lewis Warsh. New York: Granary Books, 2001, xix–xxvii.

———. "Publishing Ted." In *Ted Berrigan: An Annotated Checklist*, edited by Aaron Fischer, 15–20. New York: Granary Books, 1998.

———. Statement on *Angel Hair*. In *A Secret Location on the Lower East Side: Adventures in Writing, 1960–1980*, by Steven Clay and Rodney Phillips, 179. New York: New York Public Library/Granary Books, 1998.

anthologies, canonical

The entry of NEW YORK SCHOOL poets into the canon is dramatically illustrated in the three editions of the *Oxford Book of American Verse* (the third edition substitutes *Poetry* for the musty term *Verse*). The first edition appeared in 1950, just as the core group of New York School poets was beginning to form. As students at Harvard, they had had contact with the editor, Professor F. O. Matthiessen, but he would not have noticed them as anthology prospects; the youngest poet represented in his anthology is ROBERT LOWELL. The second edition (1976), edited by Richard Ellmann, includes JOHN ASHBERY and FRANK O'HARA but devotes more space to poets in the Black Mountain line (CHARLES OLSON, ROBERT DUNCAN, ROBERT CREELEY, DENISE LEVERTOV, ED DORN, AMIRI BARAKA). The third edition, edited by New York School poet DAVID LEHMAN, not surprisingly shifts the emphasis toward the New York School. Lehman drops Dorn and Baraka and reduces Olson to one poem, but in a volume that expands the total number of poets from Ellmann's 78 to 212, Lehman supplements Ashbery and O'Hara with the full roster of first-generation New York School writers: EDWIN DENBY, BARBARA GUEST, KENNETH KOCH, HARRY MATHEWS, and JAMES SCHUYLER. Later generations are represented by TED BERRIGAN, JOSEPH CERAVOLO, TOM DISCH, TOM CLARK, ANN LAUTERBACH, RON PADGETT, DOUGLAS CRASE, PAUL VIOLI, JOHN KOETHE, BERNADETTE MAYER, ALICE NOTLEY, DAVID SHAPIRO, and JOHN YAU. Moreover, Lehman fills out the tradition with other poets important to the New York School. Each of the formerly noncanonical American poets (John Wheelwright, Laura Riding, David Schubert) whom Ashbery treated in his Harvard lectures on *Other Traditions* receives space in Lehman's anthology. Among other past favorites and contemporary associates of the New York School, Lehman includes Gertrude Stein, Joan Murray, W. H. AUDEN (excluded by Ellmann as essentially English), Lincoln Kirstein (director of the NEW YORK CITY BALLET), PAUL GOODMAN, Anne Porter (wife of FAIRFIELD PORTER), and PATTI SMITH.

In another arena of canon formation—the textbook market—the flagship Norton anthologies have been slow to recognize the New York School. Koch was the sole New York School poet included in the first edition of the *Norton Anthology of Poetry* (1970), compiled by an editorial team under Arthur M. Eastman. In each

subsequent edition Koch was joined by one more colleague, Ashbery in 1975, Schuyler in 1983, and, finally, O'Hara in 1996, under a new editorial team (Margaret Ferguson, Mary Jo Salter, and Jon Stallworthy). The quartet of Ashbery, Koch, O'Hara, and Schuyler remains in the fifth edition (2004). The *Norton Anthology of American Literature* has consistently represented the New York School with selections from Ashbery and O'Hara since its first edition in 1979, under David Kalstone's editorial leadership. The *Norton Anthology of Modern Poetry* has presented the triad of Ashbery, Koch, and O'Hara since its first edition, compiled by Ellmann in 1973. Berrigan also appeared in that edition but not in later revisions (1988, edited by Ellmann and Robert O'Clair; 2003, edited by Jahan Ramazani, with the title expanded to *Modern and Contemporary Poetry*). For later New York School poets the big breakthrough in Norton's list came in 1994 with PAUL HOOVER's *Postmodern American Poetry: A Norton Anthology.* As in the case of Lehman's *Oxford Book*, appointing an editor with strong New York School affiliations guaranteed substantial representation, with Guest and Mathews added to the first generation and some 30 younger poets bringing the tradition up to date. However, the separate status assigned to these poets under the rubric "postmodern," as opposed to inclusion under Ramazani's heading, "contemporary," implies a position on the threshold of the canon but not yet inside.

Bibliography

Ashbery, John. *Other Traditions.* Cambridge, Mass.: Harvard University Press, 2000.

Golding, Alan. *From Outlaw to Classic: Canons in American Poetry.* Madison: University of Wisconsin Press, 1995.

Norton Anthologies Web site. Available online. URL: http://www.wwnorton.com/college/english/anthologies_home.htm.

The Oxford Book of American Poetry Web site. Available online. URL: http://www.oup.com/us/companion.websites/9780195162516/.

Perloff, Marjorie. "Whose New American Poetry? Anthologizing in the Nineties." *Diacritics* 26, nos. 3–4 (Fall–Winter 1996): 104–123. Marjorie Perloff home page. Available online. URL: http://epc.buffalo.edu/

authors/perloff/anth.html. Accessed December 16, 2008.

anthologies, polemical

NEW YORK SCHOOL poetry has played an important role in anthologies that can be called polemical in relation to making a case for a particular kind of poetry—or at least celebrating its existence—as opposed to offering a supposedly impartial historical survey. The *new* in the title of DONALD M. ALLEN's *The NEW AMERICAN POETRY, 1945–1960* (Grove, 1960) promised an advance beyond earlier poetry—as in "advance guard." It was interpreted as a challenge to *The New Poets of England and America* (Meridian, 1957), the title of a recent anthology edited by Donald Hall, Robert Pack, and Louis Simpson, which was new in terms of the poets' ages but traditional in mode; the leading figures were ROBERT LOWELL and Richard Wilbur (1921–). Although publication of *The New American Poetry* seemed to open a "war of the anthologies" (Carroll 226–228), the traditionalist camp had already begun to suffer defections, presaged in Lowell's *Life Studies* (Farrar, Straus and Cudahy, 1959). The most significant defection with regard to the production of future anthologies was that of Donald Hall (1928–). A Harvard classmate of JOHN ASHBERY's, Hall proved himself to be open to younger poets he encountered while teaching at the University of Michigan, including TOM CLARK (1960–63) and TED BERRIGAN (1969). As early as 1962, in his anthology *Contemporary American Poetry*, published by Penguin, Hall recognized "a kind of imagination new to American poetry," "expressionist" rather than "exhibitionist" (32–33), as Lowell's confessional mode had already become in the work of imitators. Although Hall identified the new imagination by quoting Robert Bly (1926–) and Louis Simpson (1923–), he included Ashbery in his anthology, and in the second edition (1972), he expanded the representation of the New York School with selections from FRANK O'HARA, Clark, and RON PADGETT. The worldwide distribution network available to Penguin publishers expanded the influence of Hall's anthology. Poets in Australia and New Zealand remember Hall rather than Allen for introducing

them to Ashbery in a meaningful context (Tranter n.p.; Manhire n.p.).

Nevertheless, *The New American Poetry* became synonymous with experimental poetry in the United States during the second half of the 20th century. Its title is echoed in many subsequent anthologies, from *New American Writers* (edited by Richard Kostelanetz, Funk and Wagnalls, 1967) to *An Anthology of New (American) Poets* (edited by LISA JARNOT, Leonard Schwartz, and CHRIS STROFFOLINO, Talisman House 1998). Poets associated with the New York School appear under each of these titles, evidently with less discomfort than they feel under the "New York School" label itself, which has not been repeated in an anthology title since JOHN BERNARD MYERS's *The POETS OF THE NEW YORK SCHOOL* (University of Pennsylvania, 1969). During the 1960s it was more acceptable to be part of a "scene" than part of a school, which may explain how Padgett and DAVID SHAPIRO intended *New York* to function in the title of *An ANTHOLOGY OF NEW YORK POETS* (Random House, 1970). Interestingly, in the same year as *The New American Poetry*'s publication, many New York School poets showed up in *The Beat Scene* edited by Elias Wilentz (Corinth, 1960), an effort to attach the suddenly trendy BEAT label to all of downtown "Bohemia" (Wilentz 9). Allen DeLoach chose the title *The East Side Scene* (State University of New York Press, 1968) on the basis of location alone, and a few poets with New York School connections (Berrigan, ED SANDERS) appear in this eclectic company. By this time New York School poets had a scene of their own at the POETRY PROJECT AT ST. MARK'S CHURCH IN-THE-BOWERY, from which two *World* anthologies issued in rapid succession (Bobbs-Merrill, 1969, 1971). However, the anthology of this period that did the most to circulate the work of the second-generation New York School was PAUL CARROLL's *The Young American Poets* (Follett, 1968), a work that substitutes "generation" for "scene" as the organizing principle and that seems to substitute youth for the quality of newness that Allen was after. In fact, Carroll would later be criticized for being too "conciliatory" in the range of qualities he was willing to include (Codrescu xxxiii), but roughly one-third of his 54 poets have New York School affiliations.

The 1970s opened with the demise of a short-lived project, *The AMERICAN LITERARY ANTHOLOGY*, brought about by a conflict between official sponsorship and the subversive imagination of at least one New York School poet, ARAM SAROYAN. Later anthologies associated with the New York School either played with or flatly rejected established categories, even those established by the avant-garde. Clark threw a curveball in the canon game, applying a title from baseball, *All Stars* (Grossman/Goliard, 1972), to his gathering of personal preferences. In *None of the Above* (The Crossing Press, 1976), MICHAEL LALLY acknowledged the antecedents of his poets in "The New York School, Black Mountain, the Beats, conceptual art, feminism, the new left, etc." (Lally 7), but denied that the work could be explained by these categories—hence his title. Having found a warmer reception outside New York after Allen placed him, anomalously, among the New York poets, EDWARD FIELD mapped out *A Geography of Poets* (Bantam, 1979), recognizing the many scenes in which poetry flourished between as well as on America's two coasts.

Anthologizing in the 1980s started out on a hopeful note with Dennis Cooper's *Coming Attractions* (LITTLE CAESAR, 1980), which EILEEN MYLES, one of the poets included, has characterized as "really important to my generation . . . a photo of a moment" (Myles e-mail). The anthologies that followed, however, tended to look to the past. Allen, now with coeditor George F. Butterick, issued a revised edition of *The New American Poetry* under the title *The Postmoderns* (Grove, 1982). Several of the original poets were dropped (including Field); a total of nine were added, only one of whom (ANNE WALDMAN) was born after 1940—a fact highlighted by the arrangement of poets simply in order of birth rather than the previous groupings that had identified "New York poets." In general, *The Postmoderns* leaves the impression of an avant-garde now canonized, open only to minor revision. The problem posed by this circumstance to the contemporary avant-garde was directly addressed in ANDREI CODRESCU's *American Poetry Since 1970: Up Late* (Four Walls Eight Windows, 1987), the decade's most comprehensive anthology

of "outsiders" (Codrescu xxxv). Although his title manifested, unintentionally, the anxiety of "being a latecomer," as Harold Bloom diagnosed it in Ashbery (12), Codrescu's introduction attempted to counter that anxiety by recalling O'Hara's advice in "PERSONISM": "just go on your nerve" (Codrescu xxxii). Codrescu's reassurance that "contemporaneity is a given" was put to the test in the series of *Best American Poetry* annuals launched by DAVID LEHMAN in 1988. Ashbery, the editor of the first volume, "enjoyed juxtaposing poets as unlike each other as Kenward Elmslie and Richard Wilbur, Joseph Brodsky and Kenneth Koch" (Ashbery 206), based on the simple premise that these poets had published work in the same year.

The 1990s brought quasi-canonical status to New York School poets of the second and later generations through their inclusion in PAUL HOOVER's Norton anthology, *Postmodern American Poetry* (1994). The effort to modify the historical framework of *The New American Poetry* continued in Eliot Weinberger's *American Poetry since 1950: Innovators & Outsiders* (Marsilio, 1993) and Douglas Messerli's *From the Other Side of the Century: A New American Poetry, 1960–1990* (Sun & Moon, 1994). In two significant ways these two very different anthologies agreed in their revision of Allen's work: They restored the OBJECTIVIST poets to consideration, and they reduced attention to the Beats (in each case represented only by ALLEN GINSBERG). They also agreed on assigning an important role to New York School poetry, though in Weinberger's much smaller book that role was correspondingly limited (to Ashbery, O'Hara, and CLARK COOLIDGE). Paradoxically, the breadth of the New York School has been conveyed more adequately in anthologies that focus narrowly on specific projects, such as the third *World* anthology (*Out of This World*, Crown, 1991), edited by Waldman, or *The Angel Hair Anthology* (Granary Books, 2001), edited by Waldman and LEWIS WARSH. MARK FORD's two anthologies of *The New York Poets* (Carcanet, 2004, 2006, the latter coedited with TREVOR WINKFIELD) offer less that was not already accessible to American readers, but the books' publication in England further extends the poets' influence as a group, if not as a "school."

Bibliography

Ashbery, John. "Introduction to *The Best American Poetry*" (1988). In Ashbery, *Selected Prose.* Edited by Eugene Richie. Ann Arbor: University of Michigan Press, 2004, 202–207.

Best American Poetry Web site. Available online. URL: http://bestamericanpoetry.com/index.php.

Bloom, Harold. *The Anxiety of Influence.* 1973. Reprint, New York: Oxford University Press, 1997.

Carroll, Paul. *The Poem in Its Skin.* Chicago: Follett, 1968.

Codrescu, Andrei. "Up Late: An Introduction." In *American Poetry since 1970: Up Late.* New York: Four Walls Eight Windows, 1987, xxxi–xxxvii.

Golding, Alan. *From Outlaw to Classic: Canons in American Poetry.* Madison: University of Wisconsin Press, 1995.

Hall, Donald. Introduction to *Contemporary American Poetry.* 2d ed. London: Penguin, 1972, 25–34.

Lally, Michael. Introduction to *None of the Above: New Poets of the USA.* Trumansburg, N.Y.: Crossing Press, 1976, 7–8.

Manhire, Bill. "Breaking the Line: A View of American and New Zealand Poetry" (1987). New Zealand Electronic Poetry Centre. Available online. URL: http://www.nzepc.auckland.ac.nz/authors/manhire/breaking.asp.

Moramarco, Fred. "Restoring Whitman's Vision: The Anthologies of the Eighties." In *Containing Multitudes: Poetry in the United States since 1950,* edited by Fred Moramarco and William Sullivan, 314–328. New York: Twayne, 1998.

Myles, Eileen. E-mail to Terence Diggory, 24 November 2006.

Perloff, Marjorie. "Whose New American Poetry? Anthologizing in the Nineties." *Diacritics* 26, nos. 3–4 (Fall–Winter 1996): 104–123. Marjorie Perloff home page. Available online. URL: http://epc.buffalo.edu/authors/perloff/anth.html. Accessed December 16, 2008.

Rasula, Jed. *The American Poetry Wax Museum: Reality Effects, 1940–1990.* Urbana, Ill.: National Council of Teachers of English, 1996.

Tranter, John. Interview by Leonard Schwartz (2003). Audio file. *Cross-Cultural Poetics,* show no. 30. KAOS-FM. Evergreen State College, Olympia, Washington. Formerly available online. URL: http://kaos.evergreen.edu/programs/cc_poetics.html.

Wilentz, Elias. Introduction to *The Beat Scene.* Illustrated by Fred McDarrah. New York: Corinth Books, 1960, 8–15.

Anthology of New York Poets, An (1970)

In retrospect, *An Anthology of New York Poets* signals the emergence of the "second generation" of the NEW YORK SCHOOL out of the literary underground and into public view. The editors, RON PADGETT and DAVID SHAPIRO, had each recently published individual volumes with mainstream publishers, and they used the resulting connections to place their anthology with Random House (Kane 266, note 93). At the time the idea of the New York School was itself still new enough that reviewers tended to concentrate on general characteristics rather than drawing distinctions between generations (Lask 29; Vendler 16). The editors encouraged this tendency by presenting their 27 poets in random order to avoid an impression of "lineage or historical arrangement," as stated in the preface. "This is, after all," they quip, "a Random House book" (xxxvi).

The editors also protest against "the gruesome possibility of the 'New York School of Poets' label" (xxx), but they lay claim to an unlabeled "sense of solidarity" based on "acquaintances and friendships, . . . sharings of tastes and affections" (xxix). Similar ambivalence is evident in the observation that "most of the poets in this book would probably decline, with a smile, the invitation to write anything as eternal as a manifesto," followed immediately by quotation, in full, of FRANK O'HARA's "PERSONISM" manifesto since "it in many ways speaks for us all" (xxxi). That sense of "us all" made it inevitable that Padgett and Shapiro's anthology would be taken to represent a "school" of some sort, and the inclusion in the anthology of all but one of the poets included in JOHN BERNARD MYERS's *The POETS OF THE NEW YORK SCHOOL* (1969) made it inevitable that Myers's label would stick to Padgett and Shapiro.

The one poet from Myers's list who was cut by Padgett and Shapiro is BARBARA GUEST, an exclusion that upset her first-generation colleagues (Schuyler 190, 341) and drew fire from later feminist critics (DuPlessis 190; Keller 225, note 1; Kinnahan 231), even after David Shapiro apologized for the "misjudgment" (Shapiro, "Salon" 39). On the other hand, Padgett and Shapiro expand the first generation beyond either Myers's or Donald M. Allen's lists by including Edwin Denby and Harry Mathews along with John Ashbery, Kenneth Koch, O'Hara, and James Schuyler. Among the second-generation writers, the omission of women is still notable; Bernadette Mayer is the only woman included in the entire anthology. Her work fits the editors' preference for radical experimentation in form or theme, reflected also in the inclusion of Clark Coolidge, John Giorno, Aram Saroyan, Ed Sanders, and Tom Veitch. Giorno extends his experimentation with the "found poem" into his biographical note, which appropriates Elvis Presley's biography as his own.

An Anthology of New York Poets makes less of the connection to the visual arts than Myers's anthology does. Nevertheless, that connection can be traced throughout Padgett and Shapiro's selection, from O'Hara's "Why I Am Not a Painter" through Peter Schjeldahl's "The Page of Illustrations" and John Perreault's "The Metaphysical Paintings" to Padgett's "Joe Brainard's Painting 'Bingo.'" Joe Brainard designed the cover for the anthology and vignettes that punctuate the text throughout.

Bibliography

DuPlessis, Rachel Blau. "The Gendered Marvelous: Barbara Guest, Surrealism and Feminist Reception." In *The Scene of My Selves: New Work on New York School Poets*, edited by Terence Diggory and Stephen Paul Miller, 189–213. Orono, Me.: National Poetry Foundation/University of Maine, 2001.

Kane, Daniel. *All Poets Welcome: The Lower East Side Poetry Scene in the 1960s*. Berkeley: University of California Press, 2003.

Keller, Lynn. "Becoming 'a Compleat Travel Agency': Barbara Guest's Negotiations with the Fifties Feminine Mystique." In *The Scene of My Selves: New Work on New York School Poets*, edited by Terence Diggory and Stephen Paul Miller, 215–227. Orono, Me.: National Poetry Foundation/University of Maine, 2001.

Kinnahan, Linda A. "Reading Barbara Guest: The View from the Nineties." In *The Scene of My Selves: New Work on New York School Poets*, edited by Terence Diggory and Stephen Paul Miller, 229–243. Orono, Me.: National Poetry Foundation/University of Maine, 2001.

Lask, Thomas. "Lines from Gotham," *New York Times*, 6 June 1970, p. 29.

Padgett, Ron, and David Shapiro. Preface to *An Anthology of New York Poets*. New York: Random House–Vintage, 1970, xxix–xxxvii.

Schuyler, James. *Just the Thing: Selected Letters, 1951–1991*. Edited by William Corbett. New York: Turtle Point Press, 2004.

Shapiro, David. "A Salon of 1990: Maximalist Manifesto." *American Poetry Review* (January–February 1991), 37–47.

Vendler, Helen. "27 poets, 363 poems—9 poets, 95 poems." *New York Times Book Review*, 15 November 1970, 16.

Antlers in the Treetops
Ron Padgett and Tom Veitch (1973)

A collaboration by "second-generation" New York School poets Ron Padgett and Tom Veitch, *Antlers in the Treetops* (Coach House Press) is a 131-page prose poem that traverses a vast cartoon landscape. It is "grounded" in no reality other than text, "which is made up," Padgett explained, "entirely of found paragraphs lightly altered to fit together" (Padgett 52). In the way it fits together, *Antlers in the Treetops* owes a substantial debt to founding New York School poets John Ashbery and Kenneth Koch (with whom Padgett studied at Columbia University). Like these poets, Padgett and Veitch revel in flights of absurdist fancy and privilege word sound and line rhythm over narrative continuity or intelligibility. In pursuit of these interests the authors employ a fragmented style that capriciously veers every description into something else, producing a collage of non-sequitur juxtapositions and single-line changes of context, often based on chance association and pun.

Instead of allowing such shifts to disrupt the poetic flow, however, the authors seamlessly blend the divergent textual layers so that they assume a kind of harmonic unity. The resulting work occupies the space between coherent meaning and nonsense—a space invoked in the suggestive motto on the back cover: "Imagine an almost complete trace of meaning." This phrase, which also appears in the body of the text, offers a useful conception of the book as a whole: a series of narrative glimmers whose meaning is almost, but not quite, clear, inducing a state of perpetual readiness for a semantic closure that never arrives.

Notwithstanding its manic, comic-book sensibility, the book is suffused with brief passages of "domestic" observation like the one below, more akin to FRANK O'HARA than to Ashbery or Koch:

> Then, rising, he shook out the long roll of his robe in a regal, virile line, knocking his cigar from the table as with love and eagerness, strode like a conqueror down the hall, the cigar riding, for awhile, in the folds of his robe (99).

Antlers in the Treetops speaks in both a serious and a comic register, but, on the whole, it exudes the same impish mirth and excitement that seems to characterize all of the collaborations within the New York School circle. Published in 1973, this book is rarely read, owing to its limited print run of 1,000 copies. It features cover art, drawn in the style of early pulp novels, by longtime New York School associate GEORGE SCHNEEMAN.

Bibliography

Eshleman, Clayton. "Padgett the Collaborator." *Chicago Review* (Spring 1997): 8.

Hoover, Paul. "Fables of Representation: Poetry of the New York School." *American Poetry Review,* (1 July 2002): 20–30.

Padgett, Ron. "Collaborating with George: A Conversation with George Schneeman." In *Painter Among Poets: The Collaborative Art of George Schneeman.* New York: Granary Books, 2004, 35–62.

Padgett, Ron, and Tom Veitch. *Antlers in the Treetops.* Toronto, Canada: Coach House Press, 1973.

Sorrentino, Gilbert. "The New York School, Continued." *New York Times Book Review,* 19 September 1976, 8.

architecture   See ART, VISUAL.

Arshile (1993–1999)

Poet Mark Salerno began the magazine *Arshile* in Los Angeles in 1993 with the intention of providing a national and international editorial view, in contrast to the "local" orientation historically adopted by many of that city's literary magazines. As it turned out, *Arshile* became one of several publications, including *Ribot,* launched by veteran Angelino Paul Vangelisti in the same year, moving to open up the Los Angeles scene at this time. However, *Arshile* was distinguished by the extent to which its cosmopolitanism, represented partly by work in TRANSLATION, took on a New York accent.

Salerno was born in New York, in 1956, but more important, his taste was formed there. The press release for his first book, *Hate,* published in 1995 under the same imprint (96 Tears Press) that issued *Arshile,* aligns Salerno with PAUL BLACKBURN, JOEL OPPENHEIMER, and GILBERT SORRENTINO, the latter an especially frequent contributor to *Arshile.* Equally prominent among *Arshile*'s contributors are poets specifically of the NEW YORK SCHOOL. It is as if the literary POLITICS that had separated the Black Mountain group from the St. Mark's group in New York dwindled to insignificance from the distance of Los Angeles, freeing *Arshile* to reassert the more profound aesthetic affinities between these groups.

Arshile's orientation toward the New York School is signaled in its title, which honors Arshile Gorky, a seminal figure in the New York School of painting. Work by WILLEM DE KOONING, JASPER JOHNS, and Michael Goldberg is featured on covers of the magazine. New York School historian Dore Ashton contributes essays from the first issue and extending to "Some Thoughts on Poetry and Painting" in the fifth (1996). An excerpt from William Corbett's memoir of PHILIP GUSTON appears in the second issue (1993). Like Corbett, ALICE NOTLEY is represented in *Arshile* by both poetry and essays. The first three essays in Notley's collection *Coming After* (2005)—on FRANK O'HARA, JOANNE KYGER, and RON PADGETT—all first appeared in *Arshile,* as did Notley's introduction to TED BERRIGAN's *Selected Poems* (1994). A "Special Selection" of Berrigan's last poems is featured in the sixth issue (1996). The entire run of *Arshile* presents an unusually full procession of New York School writers, from first generation (JOHN ASHBERY, KENWARD

ELMSLIE, BARBARA GUEST, KENNETH KOCH) to second generation (BILL BERKSON, JIM BRODEY, TOM CLARK, CLARK COOLIDGE, LEWIS MACADAMS, RON PADGETT, ARAM SAROYAN, TONY TOWLE) and beyond (EDMUND BERRIGAN, PETER GIZZI, AMY GERSTLER, GILLIAN MCCAIN, EILEEN MYLES, ELENI SIKELIANOS). The climax of the procession comes in the final issue of the magazine (number 11, 1999) with a "Special Project" on O'Hara, featuring art by Don Bachardy and Alfred Leslie and essays by Jacques Debrot and Joe LeSueur.

Bibliography

Arshile Web site. Available online. URL: http://home. earthlink.net/~arshile/.

Schaefer, Standard. "Impossible City: A History of Literary Publishing in L.A." In *The World in Time and Space: Towards a History of Innovative American Poetry in Our Time,* edited by Ed Foster and Joseph Donahue, 289–297. Jersey City, N.J.: Talisman House, 2002.

art, visual

NEW YORK SCHOOL poets vary considerably in the extent to which they display a specifically visual sensibility in their work, but they share an attachment to visual art as the leading medium of the avant-garde in the 20th century. In 1950 it appeared that "poetry was declining" while "painting was advancing," as FRANK O'HARA wrote in his 1957 COLLABORATION with the painter LARRY RIVERS, *Stones* (Ferguson 53). "Artists in any genre are of course drawn to the dominant art movement in the place where they live," explained JAMES SCHUYLER in "Poet and Painter Overture" (Schuyler, *Selected* 1–2), his statement for *The NEW AMERICAN POETRY, 1945–1960* (1960).

Of all of the visual arts, painting had achieved dominance because it best suited the combination of qualities represented by the term ABSTRACT EXPRESSIONISM, a combination that spoke to the moment in both art history and cultural history. The poets found their own ways to cultivate these qualities in their medium, but their attention to painting was not limited to the contemporary moment. References range from the Renaissance artists Pinturrichio (BARBARA GUEST, "Piazzas" [1960]) and Parmigianino (JOHN ASHBERY, "SELF-PORTRAIT

IN A CONVEX MIRROR" [1974]) to such modernist pioneers as Pablo Picasso (O'Hara, "Memorial Day 1950"), Wassily Kandinsky (Guest, "The View from Kandinsky's Window" [1986]), and Piet Mondrian (O'Hara, "Early Mondrian" [1952]). Among contemporaries, the first-generation New York School poets championed realist painters such as FAIRFIELD PORTER and JANE FREILICHER without disavowing the advances of JACKSON POLLOCK and WILLEM DE KOONING in the development of abstraction. Such openness to a range of styles, based on response to individual work rather than a preference for a predefined type, extended to second-generation poets who embraced POP ART during the 1960s and developed especially close ties to pop-related artists such as JOE BRAINARD and GEORGE SCHNEEMAN. Although critics attempted to package pop art as an attack on abstract expressionism, the imagery of popular culture from which pop derived its name had already entered New York School poetry in the work of the first generation during the 1950s.

Printmaking rose in the hierarchy of the visual arts during the reign of pop, since mechanical process implied at least the potential for mass production appropriate to pop's imagery. However, artists devoted to the individual and immediate painter's gesture of abstract expressionism required special inducements to explore printmaking, one of which was the opportunity to collaborate with poets. During the 1950s FOLDER magazine not only published early work by New York School poets but also introduced a number of their artist friends to the silk screen process, through the encouragement of printer Floriano Vecchi, later of TIBER PRESS. Tatyana Grosman of Universal Limited Art Editions (ULAE) set up collaborations between poets and artists as occasions for printmaking, including *Stones* by Rivers and O'Hara. JASPER JOHNS's *Skin with O'Hara Poem* (1963–65), another ULAE production, dramatizes the tension between mechanical reproduction and immediate expression that formed a central dynamic in the art of the 1960s (Ferguson 136). The text of O'Hara's poem "The clouds go soft" (1963) appears to be typewritten, while the images of Johns's own face and hands were created directly by the artist pressing himself against the lithographic stone.

Another important tension in the art of the period, between painting and sculpture, is exhibited in Johns's *In Memory of My Feelings—Frank O'Hara* (Ferguson 129). Primarily a painted canvas, the work, created in 1961, is also treated as an object, assembled at a hinged joint and attached to an actual fork and spoon that dangle from a wire. Such "art of assemblage," as a 1961 exhibition at the Museum of Modern Art designated the GENRE, was as much an extension of modernist collage as it was a projection into three-dimensional space, the space occupied by sculpture. The assemblage artist lifts "found objects" into the space of the imagination, where they are transformed, according to Schuyler's account of ROBERT RAUSCHENBERG (*Selected* 83) or O'Hara's of Claes Oldenburg (*Standing Still* 131). O'Hara saw a similar process even in sculpture that fits more traditional definitions of the medium, such as the work of David Smith, whose development parallels the development of abstract expressionist painting. "Using the inspiration of the material's quality as a start," O'Hara wrote, "Smith does not hesitate to urge change, advancement or conceal-ment, as the image of the particular work takes form" (*Standing Still* 123). The work is an image, not merely an object, because it lives in the imagi-nation. In turn, the viewer comes under the spell of the work's "enchantment," as Guest describes the effect of a sculpture by her close friend Tony Smith. Although Tony Smith is often designated as a minimalist (see MINIMALISM) for his concentration on simple geometric forms, Guest's account of his *Amaryllis* at the Walker Art Center in Minneapolis, Minnesota, picks up on the sculpture's title and credits it with an organic life capable of transform-ing the entire city (*Countess* 42).

Architecture is the art that transforms cities in a more literal sense. In the years following World War II, NEW YORK CITY was transformed by the erection of new monuments in the International style, the modernist architecture that had long been championed in concept by the Museum of Modern Art. The apartment on East 49th Street that O'Hara and Schuyler shared during the mid-1950s was within view of the new United Nations headquarters, with its glass tower designed by Le Corbusier (1951). Schuyler offers a glimpse of "the UN building on big evenings / green and wet" in his poem "February" (1955). Toward the end of the decade Mies van der Rohe's Seagram Building (1958) rose on Park Avenue, just a few blocks away from the Museum of Modern Art where O'Hara worked. His writing responds to the challenge of the Seagram Building repeatedly, once as the mea-sure for the "overpowering effect" of a de Kooning painting (*Standing Still* 95), once as the scene for accidentally dropping his hotdog in a fountain in the building's outdoor plaza in the 1964 poem "Walking" (see also "Personal Poem" [1959] and "Steps" [1960]). As this comic gesture implies, the monumentality of International-style architecture was essentially at odds with the New York School preference for "distinct, individual meaningfulness," as O'Hara found it in the painters (*Standing Still* 95). On these grounds, later poets particularly objected to the graceless dilution of the International style in the twin towers of the World Trade Center, designed by Minoru Yamasaki in 1972 (Lehman xv; Lauterbach 229). While the symbolic boastfulness of the twin towers made them the target of terrorist attack, a more modest and more urbane example of civic design by Siah Armajani survives nearby in the waterfront plaza of the World Financial Center (1989), which features a railing inscribed with quotations from Walt Whitman ("City of Ships" [1865]) and O'Hara ("Meditations in an Emergency" [1954]). As in the bridge Armajani had installed the previous year at the Walker Art Center in Minneapolis, bearing a quotation from ASHBERY ("[Untitled]"), the architect seems to have recog-nized in the New York School poets an affinity for what might be called the art of the passage.

Photography provides an essential complement to that art by capturing the images a viewer experi-ences in passing through the city, much like the New York School "walk poem." That correspon-dence, along with the adaptability of photography to book publication, led naturally to such collabo-rations as EDWIN DENBY and RUDY BURCKHARDT's *IN PUBLIC, IN PRIVATE* (James A. Decker, 1948) and *MEDITERRANEAN CITIES* (Wittenborn, 1956). The genre extends to VINCENT KATZ's *BOULEVARD TRANSPORTATION* (TIBOR DE NAGY EDITIONS, 1997), with photos by Burckhardt; JOHN YAU's collabora-tions with Bill Barrette, *BIG CITY PRIMER* (Timken, 1991) and *Berlin Diptychon* (Timken, 1995); and the unusually complex *Lowell Connector* (Hard Press, 1993), with poems by Yau, CLARK COOLIDGE, and MICHAEL GIZZI and photographs by Barrette and Celia Coolidge (Clark Coolidge's daughter). The moving image underscores the passage of time implicit in passage through city streets or natural landscape in Burckhardt's documentary films, such as *The Climate of New York* (1948), with text by Denby; *City Pasture* (1974), with text by Denby, KENNETH KOCH, RON PADGETT, and TREVOR WINKFIELD; and *Tree Streets* (1995), with text by Katz. Still images provide documentation of a quasi-scientific nature in BERNADETTE MAYER's MEMORY (exhibited 1972; North Atlantic Books, 1975), which abstracts the idea of the passage of time from the visual realm into a dimension that came to be identified with CONCEPTUAL ART.

Bibliography

Ashbery, John. "Self-Portrait in a Convex Mirror." In *Self-Portrait in a Convex Mirror*. New York: Penguin, 1976, 68–83.

———. "Siah Armajani" (1983). In *Reported Sightings: Art Chronicles 1957–1987*. Edited by David Bergman. Cambridge, Mass.: Harvard University Press, 1991, 346–348.

———. "[Untitled] And now I cannot remember . . ." In *Hotel Lautréamont*. New York: Knopf, 1992, 127.

Diggory, Terence. "Picturesque Urban Pastoral in Post-War New York City." In *The Built Surface 2: Architecture and the Pictorial Arts from Romanticism to the Twenty-first Century*, edited by Karen Koehler, 283–303. Aldershot, Hants: Ashgate, 2002.

Ferguson, Russell. *In Memory of My Feelings: Frank O'Hara and American Art*. Exhibit catalog. Los Angeles: Museum of Contemporary Art. Berkeley: University of California Press, 1999, 53.

Guest, Barbara. *The Countess from Minneapolis*. Providence, R.I.: Burning Deck, 1976.

———. "Piazzas." In *Poems: The Location of Things/ Archaics/The Open Skies*. Garden City, N.Y.: Doubleday, 1962, 13–14.

———. "The View from Kandinsky's Window." In *Fair Realism*. Los Angeles: Sun & Moon, 1989, 13–14.

Lauterbach, Ann. "9/11." In *The Night Sky: Writings on the Poetry of Experience*. New York: Viking Penguin, 2005, 225–234.

Lehman, David. "The World Trade Center" (1996). *Poetry after 9/11: An Anthology of New York Poets*, In edited by Dennis Loy Johnson and Valerie Merians, xv. Hoboken, N.J.: Melville House, 2002.

O'Hara, Frank. *The Collected Poems*. Rev. ed. Edited by Donald Allen. Berkeley: University of California Press, 1995.

———. *Standing Still and Walking in New York*. Edited by Donald Allen. San Francisco: Grey Fox, 1983.

Rudy Burckhardt. Exhibit catalog. Valencia, Spain: IVAM Centre Julio González, 1998.

Schuyler, James. "February." In *Collected Poems*. New York: Noonday/Farrar, Straus & Giroux, 1993, 4–5.

———. "Is There an American Print Revival? New York." *Art News* 60, no. 9 (January 1962): 36–37.

———. *Selected Art Writings*. Edited by Simon Pettet. Santa Rosa, Calif.: Black Sparrow, 1998.

Whitman, Walt. "City of Ships." In *Leaves of Grass*. Edited by Harold W. Blodgett and Sculley Bradley. New York: Norton, 1968, 294.

Art and Literature (1964–1967)

Art and Literature was so broadly international and interdisciplinary in scope that it can hardly be identified as a journal of NEW YORK SCHOOL poetry, yet it provides an outstanding example of the New York School presence on the international scene. It was modeled on *LOCUS SOLUS*, with JOHN ASHBERY once again playing a leading editorial role, this time in partnership with two painters, Anne Dunn (1929–　) and her husband, Rodrigo Moynihan (1910–90), who provided financial backing. France remained the base of operations, as it had been for *Locus Solus*, but Ashbery relocated to the United States just as the magazine was launched. Dunn and Moynihan brought with them an extensive set of connections with the British art world, including the influential group associated with Cyril Connolly (1903–74) at the magazine *Horizon*. Connolly's essay on "Fifty Years of Little Magazines" appeared in the first issue of *Art and Literature* (March 1964). Sonia Orwell (1918–80), widow of the writer George Orwell (1903–50) and a former editor at *Horizon*, played a role in editing *Art and Literature* for the first six of its 12 issues. Her "much more conservative taste," according to Ashbery, gave rise to "a number of disputes" (Ashbery quoted in Kermani 99).

A directory of the European-American avant-garde could be extracted from the table of contents of *Art and Literature*, but, short of reading the work itself, the excitement of the magazine is best conveyed by the sequence of names as they are encountered in a particular issue. For instance, the first issue opens with a prose work by the British modernist poet David Jones (1895–1974), moves to FICTION by the Italian novelist Carlo Emilio Gadda (1893–1973), and then presents poems by DAVID SHAPIRO, 17 years old at the time and the first of many New York School poets who would eventually appear in the magazine. Poems by KENWARD ELMSLIE and TONY TOWLE appear later in the first issue. KENNETH KOCH is represented by a prose work, "The Postcard Collection," followed by "Figure," written by the French painter Jean Hélion (1904–87). Some pages after that, "The Wide Sargasso Sea" by Jean Rhys (1894–1979), a close friend of Sonia Orwell, is followed by a "Dialogue" between ALEX KATZ and JANE FREILICHER, two painters who were especially close to the New York School poets. In representing the visual arts, *Art and Literature* often included photographic reproductions in black and white, an advance beyond *Locus Solus*, which was otherwise similar in format.

In the context of New York School poetry, Ashbery's "The SKATERS" (number 3, autumn–winter 1964) and a group of TED BERRIGAN's SONNETS (number 4, spring 1965) are the most important publications in *Art and Literature* in terms of their influence on subsequent developments. For eccentricity, nothing beats two poems published under the name of "Koichi K. O'Hara" (number 8, spring 1966), evidently a collaborative invention of Koch and FRANK O'HARA, though the "Contributor's Note" provides a straight-faced identification of the author as "a Japanese poet and critic in the field of literature and Russian problems." The final issue of *Art and Literature* (number 12, spring 1967) includes a memorial tribute to O'Hara, who had died the previous spring. It includes seven poems by O'Hara; a poem by George Montgomery, O'Hara's former college roommate; BILL BERKSON's essay "Frank O'Hara and His Poems"; examples of

O'Hara's collaborations with LARRY RIVERS (*Stones*, 1957–60) and Norman Bluhm (*Poem-Paintings*, 1960); and portraits of O'Hara painted by Elaine de Kooning, Freilicher, and Katz.

Bibliography

Ashbery, John. "The Skaters." In *Rivers and Mountains*. 1966. Reprint, New York: Ecco, 1977, 34–63.

Berkson, Bill. "Frank O'Hara and His Poems." In *Homage to Frank O'Hara*, edited by Bill Berkson and Joe LeSueur, 161–165. Bolinas, Calif.: Big Sky, 1988.

Berrigan, Ted. Review of *Art and Literature*, no. 1. *Kulchur* 15 (Autumn 1964): 93–95.

———. Sonnets 43, 46, 47, and 49. In *The Collected Poems of Ted Berringan*. Edited by Alice Notley, Anselm Berrigan, and Edmund Berrigan. Berkeley: University of California Press, 2005, 52–56.

Clay, Steven, and Rodney Phillips. "*Art and Literature*." In *A Secret Location on the Lower East Side: Adventures in Writing, 1960–1980*. New York: New York Public Library/Granary Books, 1998, 170–171.

Connolly, Cyril. "Little Magazines." In *The Evening Colonnade*. New York: Harcourt Brace Jovanovich, 1975, 375–386.

Kermani, David. *John Ashbery: A Comprehensive Bibliography*. New York: Garland, 1976.

Koch, Kenneth. "The Postcard Collection." In *The Collected Fiction*. Edited by Jordan Davis, Karen Koch, and Ron Padgett. Minneapolis, Minn.: Coffee House Press, 2005, 13–39.

Spurling, Hilary. *The Girl from the Fiction Department: A Portrait of Sonia Orwell*. New York: Counterpoint, 2002, 132–133.

"Artist, The" Kenneth Koch (1962)

Whether it is read as a serious meditation or a comic send-up, or both, the poem "The Artist" reflects the emphasis on process over product that is characteristic of the NEW YORK SCHOOL aesthetic. In a series of diary entries the artist in question, a fictional character, charts his rapid progression from one work to another. The excitement of conceiving the new work seduces him into "abandoning" whatever he has just completed.

"The Artist" was first collected in KENNETH KOCH's volume *Thank You and Other Poems* (1962).

In the later collection *On the Great Atlantic Rainway* (1994), a note connects the Artist with the surrealist painter and sculptor Max Ernst (1891–1976) and the diary FORM with the *Journal Intime* (*Private Diaries*) of the French novelist Stendhal (1783–1842), but the nature of the Artist's work reflects, and even anticipates, more recent trends. The celebration of process and the projection of immense scale (nothing "less than what I think should girdle the earth") are both in keeping with the spirit of New York School painting, but in his choice of materials Koch's Artist has moved "beyond painting," a direction that had been signaled in the title of a collection of writings by Ernst (1948). Abandoning earlier works that anticipate the pop sculptures exhibited by Claes Oldenburg in the early 1960s—"cherrywood smokestack," "steel cigarettes"—the Artist turns to reshaping the Earth itself, as in the "earthworks" of the early 1970s by such artists as Christo and Robert Smithson. The final project of Koch's Artist, re-creating (or perhaps displacing) the Pacific Ocean with "sixteen million tons of blue paint," calls into question whether the aim is to return art to nature or to absorb nature in art or the artist. The underlying connection to New York School painting may be JACKSON POLLOCK's claim "I am nature."

Unlike Pollock but very much like Koch, the Artist tries to remember not to take himself too seriously. Accurately gauging the mixture of comedy and seriousness is perhaps the greatest challenge to reading Koch's poem. As in satire, the subject is deliberately blown up to excessive proportions, but rather than leading to deflation, the process feels exhilirating. Appropriately, "The Artist" was adapted in the FORM of an opera, produced at the Whitney Museum in 1972, with MUSIC by Paul Reif and set by LARRY RIVERS.

Bibliography

Chinitz, David. "'Arm the Paper Arm': Kenneth Koch's Postmodern Comedy." In *The Scene of My Selves: New Work on New York School Poets*, edited by Terence Diggory and Stephen Paul Miller, 311–326. Orono, Me.: National Poetry Foundation, 2001.

Howard, Richard. "Kenneth Koch." In *Alone with America*. Enlarged ed. New York: Atheneum, 1980, 331–341. [340–341 for "The Artist"].

Koch, Kenneth. *On the Great Atlantic Rainway: Selected Poems, 1950–1988*. New York: Knopf, 1994, 62–69, 321.

Artists' Theatre (1953–1956)

JOHN BERNARD MYERS's vision of a community of artists joined in COLLABORATION was realized partly through the Artists' Theatre, which Myers cofounded with his partner Herbert Machiz. Machiz's THEATER experience included work in Paris, where he had been struck by the visual impact created by "the best modern painters" rather than "professional scene designers" ("Challenge" 73). As director of the TIBOR DE NAGY GALLERY, Myers was able to supply not only painters but also poets associated with them, the group whom Myers would eventually dub the "poets of the NEW YORK SCHOOL."

Contrary to Myers's unreliable memoir, the plays the poets supplied were not, in most cases, "written for us" (166). Of the inaugural program, produced in February 1953 at the Theatre de Lys in Greenwich Village, FRANK O'HARA's TRY! TRY! had already been staged by the POETS' THEATRE in Cambridge, Massachusetts, JAMES SCHUYLER's *Presenting Jane* had been written for a film directed by JOHN LATOUCHE the previous summer, and KENNETH KOCH's *Red Riding Hood* had been written while the poet was still at Harvard, under the influence of "Yeatsean symbolic drama" (Koch 202). What was new in the Artists' Theatre production was, first of all, the visual dimension provided by the collaborating artists: LARRY RIVERS with O'Hara; Elaine de Kooning (plus clips from LaTouche's film) with Schuyler; and GRACE HARTIGAN with Koch. Second, Machiz insisted on engaging professional actors. JOHN ASHBERY and VIOLET R. (Bunny) LANG had performed in the original production of *Try! Try!* and the cast for the film version of *Presenting Jane* included Ashbery, O'Hara, and JANE FREILICHER (the "Jane" of the title). The cast assembled by Machiz, however, included actors such as Anne Meacham, who later starred under Machiz's direction in the premier of Tennessee Williams's *Suddenly Last Summer* (1958). O'Hara found himself so inspired by these circumstances that he "rewrote the play for Anne Meacham, J. D. Cannon, Louis Edmonds [the complete cast] and Larry's set" ("Larry Rivers" 172).

As reproductions illustrate (O'Hara, *Amorous Nightmares* 219), what Rivers provided was really a painting rather than a set, calling into question whether the independent strength of the art pulled it away from collaboration. Ashbery, who participated in a later Artists' Theatre program in May 1953 with his play *The HEROES,* was pleased with the evocation of the city of Troy in flames that Nell Blaine created for his play (Perl 200–201). He also recalled "a very beautiful set done by Jane Freilicher for another of the plays on the program . . . called *The Lady's Choice* by Barbara Guest" (Ashbery 19). On the other hand, JAMES MERRILL, the author of the third play, *The Bait,* complained that "the set [by Al Kresch]—a café table in Venice juxtaposed with the stern of a fishing boat in the Gulf Stream—looked messy and abstract expressionist rather than spare and ambivalent" (254).

Machiz's direction was another source of dissatisfaction. In 1954, when the Artists' Theatre produced Lang's *Fire Exit,* another revival from the Cambridge Poets' Theatre, Lang reported, "Herbert Machiz is about the worst director in NY or anywhere" (Gooch 230). John Gruen, who provided the MUSIC for *Fire Exit,* recalled: "Machiz once confessed to me that these intellectual plays were not his cup of tea, that he was cut out to direct Noel Coward" (90).

At various locations in New York, the Artists' Theatre produced work by other playwrights, including Tennessee Williams, Federico García Lorca, Parker Tyler, Robert Hivnor, and Lionel Abel. In spring 1956 the Tibor de Nagy Gallery mounted an exhibition of stage designs for the Artists' Theatre in conjunction with the final production, Abel's *Absalom.* Myers and Machiz briefly revived the company name for an Artists' Theatre Festival they conducted in Southampton, Long Island, during the summers of 1968 and 1969.

Bibliography

Ashbery, John. "Poet in the Theater." Interview by Roger Oliver. *Performing Arts Journal* 3, no. 3 (Winter 1979): 15–37.

Gooch, Brad. *City Poet: The Life and Times of Frank O'Hara.* New York: Knopf, 1993.

Gruen, John. *The Party's Over Now: Reminiscences of the Fifties—New York's Artists, Writers, Musicians, and Their Friends.* Wainscott, N.Y.: Pushcart, 1989.

Koch, Kenneth. Interview by Jordan Davis (1995). In *The Art of Poetry: Poems, Parodies, Interviews, Essays, and Other Work.* Ann Arbor: University of Michigan Press, 1996, 187–214.

Machiz, Herbert. "The Challenge of a Poetic Theatre." *Theatre Arts* 40, no. 2 (February 1956): 72–74ff.

———, ed. *Artists' Theatre: Four Plays.* New York: Grove, 1960. [Includes Frank O'Hara, *Try! Try!;* John Ashbery, *The Heroes;* James Merrill, *The Bait;* Lionel Abel, *Absalom.*]

Merrill, James. *A Different Person: A Memoir.* New York: Knopf, 1993.

Myers, John Bernard. *Tracking the Marvelous: A Life in the New York Art World.* New York: Random House, 1983.

O'Hara, Frank. *Amorous Nightmares of Delay: Selected Plays.* Baltimore, Md.: Johns Hopkins University Press, 1997, 218–225.

———. "Larry Rivers: A Memoir" (1965). In *Standing Still and Walking in New York.* Edited by Donald Allen. San Francisco: Grey Fox, 1983, 169–173.

Perl, Jed. *New Art City: Manhattan at Mid-Century.* New York: Knopf, 2005.

Playbook: Five Plays for a New Theatre. Norfolk, Conn.: New Directions, 1956. [Includes three Artists' Theatre texts: Lionel Abel, *The Death of Odysseus;* Robert Hivnor, *The Ticklish Acrobat;* James Merrill, *The Immortal Husband.*]

"Stage-sets at De Nagy by Members of the Gallery." *Art News* 55 (May 1956): 48.

"Theatre Sets at Tibor de Nagy Gallery." *Arts Magazine* 30 (May 1956): 56.

Ash, John (1948–) *British poet*

Born in Manchester, England, poet John Ash helped galvanize the NEW YORK SCHOOL from the mid-1980s to mid-1990s. He now stays in touch from Istanbul, Turkey. Ash's apartment on 15th Street in Manhattan became the location of "Ash Wednesdays," a weekly salon-workshop for works in progress. Elegantly tall, a charming host, he offered a working community to writers and poets, including HARRY MATHEWS, the late GERRIT HENRY, Jaime Manrique, Maggie Paley, Marc Cohen, Susan

Baran, Ted Castle, Jane DeLynn, Roberta Allen, EUGENE RICHIE, and ROSANNE WASSERMAN. He also assisted KENNETH KOCH in organizing manuscripts. According to Ash, the milieu suited him: "Americans in general are much more open than the English. English politeness can be unbearable. In New York you can say exactly what you feel and people won't think you're weird. They're all doing it too" ("Writer's Almanac" n.p.).

Ash graduated from the University of Birmingham and taught briefly in Manchester and Cyprus. He had four published books already when he arrived in New York: *The Casino* (Oasis, 1978), *The Bed* (Oasis, 1981), *The Goodbyes* (Carcanet, 1982), and *The Branching Stairs* (Carcanet, 1984). The title poem of his first New York collection, *Disbelief* (Carcanet, 1987), set to MUSIC by Aaron Jay Kernis, was written while stuck in traffic on the Triboro Bridge. *The Burnt Pages* followed in 1991 (Random House). He taught poetry seminars at the University of Iowa and the University of California, Berkeley, and reviewed gallery shows for *Art Forum* and *Art in America*. His honors include a Guggenheim Fellowship, Ingram Merrill Grant, and Whiting Foundation Writers Award. In the early 1990s, however, he left New York to travel in Anatolia and produced *A Byzantine Journey* (Random House, 1995). Another move, this time to Istanbul, was followed, by *Selected Poems* (Carcanet, 1996). More recently, in *Two Books: The Anatolikon/ To the City* (Carcanet, 2002) he still considers urban themes, ancient and contemporary. An expert on Byzantine antiquities as well as Manhattan postmodernism, Ash sharpens his avant-garde poetry against his classical learning. Knowledge of the destruction of one great empire underlines celebrations of NEW YORK CITY with a dark, delighted appreciation. The past inspires as much disbelief as today does: "In Byzantium," too, "fans of the rival chariot teams / wore their hair long / 'in the Hunnish fashion' / and wore the colours of their teams" ("Language Poem: 2000 BC–2000 AD," in *The Anatolikon*).

Although a few British critics would have preferred Ash to stay British, his New York School and Turkish allegiances charm many others. New Yorkers found his poems witty, surreal, and nostalgic, with influences from Constantine Cavafy to Ronald Firbank. Like FRANK O'HARA, Ash could hold his own in a conversation on obscure musicians with JOHN ASHBERY, whose work some find most influential on Ash's. But Ash's vision seems founded in a Mediterranean landscape; for example, in "Advanced Choreography for Beginners" (*The Branching Stairs*), his poetics calls for the establishment of "a new lyricism in which all these things will find their place / equally like buildings on the loop of a promenade / doors and windows open."

Bibliography

Ash, John. *A Byzantine Journey.* New York: Random House, 1995.

———. *Selected Poems.* Manchester, U.K.: Carcanet, 1996.

———. *Two Books: The Anatolikon/To the City.* Manchester, U.K.: Carcanet, 2002.

The Writer's Almanac, with Garrison Keillor. "Sonnet 18: Shall I Compare Thee to a Summer's Day?" 29 June 1999. Available online. URL: http://writersalmanac. publicradio.org/index.php'date/1999/06/29.

Ashbery, John (1927–)

Ashbery defines the NEW YORK SCHOOL by its "absence of any program," its way of "not planning the poem in advance but letting it take its own way." Its poetry is not surreal but embraces surrealism's "big permission" (*Selected Prose* 115–116). Ashbery's poetry is as comfortable with lines from a Val Lewton or Guy Maddin movie as with images from Parmigianino or the *Kalevala*. Critical response to his work ranges from outrage to adulation, though even detractors recognize his excellence. All-embracing, multifaceted, and unassuming, Ashbery is, according to the influential critic Helen Vendler, "an undeniably original poet" (33).

Born in Rochester, New York, Ashbery lived there with his grandparents during elementary school, spending summers with his parents, Chester and Helen, on their farm near Sodus. Fascinated with language, he won a "Quiz Kid" contest at 14. He attended Deerfield Academy and Harvard University (1945–49), where he started lifelong friendships with KENNETH KOCH and FRANK O'HARA. When they relocated to NEW YORK CITY, their circle included JAMES SCHUYLER and BARBARA GUEST, as well as painters such as JANE FREILICHER, FAIRFIELD PORTER, and LARRY RIVERS.

At Columbia University (1951), Ashbery wrote his master's thesis on British novelist HENRY GREEN. After four years as a copywriter in New York, he spent a decade in Paris, first on a Fulbright, then as a *New York Herald Tribune* and *Art International* art critic. Living with Pierre Martory, he discovered lost work by RAYMOND ROUSSEL and cofounded the journals *LOCUS SOLUS* in 1960, with Koch, Schuyler, and HARRY MATHEWS, the American member of OULIPO; and *ART AND LITERATURE* in 1963, with Anne Dunn, Rodrigo Moynihan, and Sonia Orwell. In 1965, returning to New York, he became executive editor of *ARTNews*. Soon after, he met David Kermani, with whom he founded Flow Chart Foundation in 1998. He has taught at Brooklyn College, City University of New York (1974–90), Harvard (1989–90), and Bard College since 1990.

In 1953 TIBOR DE NAGY GALLERY published Ashbery's *Turandot and Other Poems* with Freilicher's drawings, along with books by O'Hara, Koch, and Schuyler. Alfred Corn included it on a 1970 list of the most important events "in the history of twentieth-century avant-garde art" (4). For the 1956 Yale Series of Younger Poets Prize, W. H. AUDEN chose Ashbery's *Some Trees*. The poems mystified Auden, but he approved of Ashbery's concern with how "in dreams and daydreams entirely, the imaginative life of the human individual stubbornly continues to live by the old magical notions" (13), foreshadowing the "hymn to possibility" and the poet's "*real* reality" (Ashbery, *Selected Prose* 12–13) that Ashbery found in Gertrude Stein, ELIZABETH BISHOP, and O'Hara. O'Hara generously declared it "the most beautiful first book to appear in America since *Harmonium*," praising its "faultless music" and "originality of perception" (312).

The controversial *Tennis Court Oath* (1962) prompted Marianne Moore to call Ashbery "prepossessing" but provoked "outrage and disbelief" in Harold Bloom, who thought it "a fearful disaster" of "calculated incoherence" (51–53). Opposing Auden's placing Ashbery in the Rimbaud tradition, Bloom preferred Ashbery's American roots: Ralph Waldo Emerson, Walt Whitman, and Wallace Stevens. Five books followed, and then *SELF-PORTRAIT IN A CONVEX MIRROR* (1975) won the Pulitzer Prize, the National Book Award, and the

National Book Critics Circle Award: a trifecta catapulting Ashbery into the spotlight. New collections have followed every few years, from *Houseboat Days* (1977) to *A Worldly Country* (2007).

Ashbery has written plays, notably, *The HEROES* (1952); produced Off-Broadway in the ARTISTS' THEATRE (*Three Plays*, 1978); and cowritten with Schuyler the novel *NEST OF NINNIES* (1969). He has collaborated with artists and composers including JOE BRAINARD, Siah Armajani, TREVOR WINKFIELD, Rivers, and Elliot Carter. His art writings appear in *Reported Sightings* (1989); his Harvard Charles Eliot Norton Lectures, in *Other Traditions* (2000); and his essays, reviews, and introductions about writers, artists, and filmmakers, in *Selected Prose* (2004). A forthcoming volume of French TRANSLATIONs includes Pierre Martory, Max Jacob, Raymond Roussel, Giorgio de Chirico, Pierre Reverdy, René Char, Franck André Jamme, Pascalle Monnier, and others.

Ashbery's poetry, championed by major arbiters Bloom, Vendler, and Marjorie Perloff, provokes intense responses. Early complaints about its difficulty seem obsolete beside LANGUAGE POETRY, which claims as inspiration Ashbery's "Europe" and "America" (in *Tennis Court Oath*). His detractors often sound like baffled critics of Igor Stravinsky's *Rite of Spring* or Pablo Picasso's *Les demoiselles d'Avignon*. Ashbery uses figuration and surface, like WILLEM DE KOONING and Freilicher; writes listening to postmodern composers such as JOHN CAGE, Arvo Pärt, or Robin Holloway; and, in Stevens's meditative vein, considers language and its limits in reflecting perceptions and feelings. His allusions range from global and erudite to pop culture and corny vulgarities, as in "Daffy Duck in Hollywood" (*Houseboat Days*)—"a mint-condition can / Of Rumford's Baking Powder"—or "Farm Implements and Rutabagas in a Landscape" (*Double Dream of Spring*, 1970)—"Popeye chuckled and scratched / His balls: it sure was pleasant to spend a day in the country." As "A Mood of Quiet Beauty" (*April Galleons*) puts it: "Museums then became generous, they live in our breath." In New York School style, his work elevates irony above romanticism, celebrating speech, humor, and cultural bric-a-brac, yet creates poems resonant and deep as the meditation on love and death in "At North Farm" (*A Wave*,

1984): "Somewhere someone is traveling furiously toward you, / At incredible speed."

Ashbery's work engages the polyphonic "instant mix," "one of the real achievements of the New York School" (Ashbery, *Selected Prose* 118–119). Pioneering new approaches, he used the Malaysian pantoum in *Some Trees* and adapted the *Kalevala* FORM in "Finnish Rhapsody" (*April Galleons*). Long poems include *The* SKATERS (*Rivers and Mountains*, 1966); *Three Poems* (1972); *Self-Portrait in a Convex Mirror*; the tour-de-force *Litany* (*As We Know* [1979]), two parallel columns meant to be read simultaneously; and FLOW CHART (1991), created when Winkfield suggested he write a 100-page poem. Conversely, *As We Know* also includes one-line poems; "The Cathedral Is" reads: "Slated for demolition." "How much of anyone of us survives?" he asks in *The Skaters*, catching "whispers out of time" (*Self-Portrait*), echoing the mind's perceptions. Embracing and resisting metaphor, "What Is Poetry" (*Houseboat Days*) begins with metapoetic humor: "The medieval town, with frieze / Of boy scouts from Nagoya?" Such play continues in such lines as "Cut the mustard, curvaceous" from "Coma Berenices" (*Where Shall I Wander*, 2005), an imitation of a family New Year's letter alluding to Egyptian queen Berenice's hair and a constellation near Leo, Ashbery's birth sign.

Ashbery's honors include the Bollingen Prize, Horst Bienek Prize for Poetry, Ruth Lilly Poetry Prize, Feltrinelli Prize, and Guggenheim and MacArthur Foundation fellowships. He was named an *officier* in the French Légion d'Honneur and is recipient of the Robert Frost Medal (Poetry Society of America), Wallace Stevens Award (Academy of American Poets), and Gold Medal for Poetry (American Academy of Arts and Letters). Studies of his work range from DAVID SHAPIRO's (1979) to David Herd's (2001); collections edited by DAVID LEHMAN, Susan Schultz, and Bloom; and histories of the New York School such as Lehman's and Geoffrey Ward's. Ashbery is a quintessential New York School poet, but as he told MARK FORD, "We began, when we first knew each other, by copying each other's poetry; and then I think it became more a question of example" (34), which is to say that the New York School was born in an enduring magnetic community, one of its most provocative and lasting human qualities.

Bibliography

Ashbery, John. *Collected Poems, 1956–1987.* Edited by Mark Ford. New York: Library of America, 2008.

———. *Notes from the Air: Selected Later Poems.* New York: Ecco, 2007.

———. *Selected Poems.* New York: Viking, 1987.

———. *Selected Prose.* Edited by Eugene Richie. Ann Arbor: University of Michigan Press; Manchester, U.K.: Carcanet, 2004.

Ashbery Resource Center: A Project of the Flow Chart Foundation for Bard College. Available online. URL: http://www.flowchartfoundation.org/arc/.

Auden, W. H. Foreword to *Some Trees,* by John Ashbery, New Haven, Conn.: Yale University Press, 1956.

Bloom, Harold. "John Ashbery: The Charity of the Hard Moments" (1973). In *Modern Critical Views: John Ashbery.* New York: Chelsea House Publishers, 1985, 49–79.

Corn, Alfred. "The Notion of the Avant-Garde." *University Review* (December 1970): 4ff.

Ford, Mark. *John Ashbery in Conversation with Mark Ford.* London: Between the Lines, 2003.

Herd, David. *John Ashbery and American Poetry.* New York: Palgrave-Macmillan, 2001.

Lehman, David. *The Last Avant-Garde: The Making of the New York School of Poets.* New York: Doubleday, 1998.

O'Hara, Frank. Review of *Some Trees. Poetry* (February 1957): 312.

Shapiro, David. *John Ashbery: An Introduction to the Poetry.* New York: Columbia University Press, 1979.

Vendler, Helen. "Attention, Shoppers." *New Republic,* 7 March 2005, 30–33.

Ward, Geoffrey. *Statues of Liberty: The New York School of Poets (Language, Discourse, Society).* 2d ed. New York: Palgrave-Macmillan, 2001.

Auden, W(ystan) H(ugh) (1907–1973)
British poet

W. H. Auden was the most important contemporary English poet to influence the NEW YORK SCHOOL, both in his poetry and in person. In his native England during the 1930s he became well known as the leading figure in a group of young writers—including Christopher Isherwood (1904–86), C. Day Lewis (1904–72), Louis MacNeice (1907–63), and Stephen Spender (1909–95)—whose work hinted at political revolution but saved more revolutionary energy for art than much of the left-wing verse being produced in the United States at the time. In 1939 Auden moved to the United States to escape the burdens of his own reputation as well as the oncoming war in Europe; he became a U.S. citizen in 1947. Soon after his arrival, with a new American lover, Chester Kallman (1921–75), Auden joined an exotic communal housing experiment in Brooklyn along with other writers such as Carson McCullers and Paul and Jane Bowles, the composer Benjamin Britten, and the stripper Gypsy Rose Lee. Although Auden soon changed his residence, he continued to move among New York's bohemian and especially gay networks, where he became acquainted with EDWIN DENBY and JOHN BERNARD MYERS. In 1947, on the occasion of a reading at Harvard, Auden met FRANK O'HARA and JOHN ASHBERY through George Montgomery, another New York acquaintance. However, the closest personal connection between Auden and the New York School came through JAMES SCHUYLER, a friend of Kallman's since 1943. Between 1948 and 1949 Schuyler spent various periods of time with Kallman and Auden on the Italian island of Ischia, a scene Schuyler recalled in his memorial poem "Wystan Auden" (1973). Auden's long-term residence on St. Mark's Place in NEW YORK CITY, from 1953 until he left the United States in 1972, placed him on the scene of the second-generation New York School, to whom the mere sight of Auden on his "early morning 'constitutional'" affirmed their dedication to the life of poetry (Waldman xxii).

In his poetry Auden opened a door that led from modernism to a future of new creative possibilities. His work had been praised by T. S. Eliot, but unlike Eliot's work, Auden's had not yet been sealed away in the canon where it could only be admired rather than used. In his senior honors thesis at Harvard on "The Poetic Medium of W. H. Auden" (1949), Ashbery emphasized Auden's role in bringing poetry closer to "the everyday world," with an "immediacy and concreteness" lost in Eliot's symbolism (quoted in Epstein 21). In his poem "Memorial Day 1950," O'Hara associated Auden and Arthur Rimbaud, an association based on the surrealist quality of Auden's early work,

which New York School writers continued to prefer. By the 1950s Auden had turned against that style and disapproved when it showed up in his followers. Although he gave Ashbery's career a significant boost by selecting *Some Trees* for the Yale Younger Poets prize in 1956, Auden's placement of the book in the "school" of Rimbaud implied reservations, which he made explicit in a letter to O'Hara, whose submission for the Yale prize had been rejected. "I think you (and John, too, for that matter)," Auden wrote to O'Hara, "must watch what is always the great danger with any 'surrealistic' style, namely of confusing the authentic non-logical relations which arouse wonder with accidental ones which arouse mere surprise and in the end fatigue" (quoted in Epstein 24–25).

Just at this time KENNETH KOCH expressed a sense of fatigue in Auden's work, in a review of *The Old Man's Road* (1956), a small gathering of poems later collected in *Homage to Clio* (1960). Auden was replacing real persons with abstractions, Koch complained. In a letter to Koch before the review was completed, Schuyler expressed similar misgivings about Auden's notorious revisions of his early work (*Just the Thing* 73–75). One example Schuyler cited was a poem ("January 1, 1931") reprinted from *The Orators* (1932), in which a line addressing "Wystan, Stephen, Christopher" (*English Auden* 94)—the sort of personal naming that was to become a trademark of the New York School—was redirected toward generalities: "Subjects, Objects, all of you" (*Collected Poems* 153). Schuyler's objection was based not only on the shift in language but on the poem's removal from its original dramatic context, where such language might have resonated ironically in the speech of a character. This effect made Auden's plays exciting to the New York School poets, who applied Auden's example in their own work for the THEATER and in other ways of "staging" prose to produce a kind of poetry. Auden himself praised the stylized dialogue of Ashbery and Schuyler's novel A NEST OF NINNIES, recognizing its ancestry in the FICTION of Ronald Firbank, a personal favorite of Auden's. The hypersophisticated speech of Caliban in *The Sea and the Mirror* (1944), Auden's reexamination of William Shakespeare's *The Tempest*, served as a model for Ashbery's *Three Poems* (Viking, 1972), written in prose (Kostelanetz 103). But the prose work most deeply influenced by Auden is Koch's *The RED ROBINS*, both as a novel (Random House–Vintage, 1975) and a play (*Performing Arts Journal*, 1977). It is the story of a band of youthful adventurers such as Auden depicts in *The Orators* and his first play, *Paid on Both Sides* (1930), which Koch excerpted in his anthology *Making Your Own Days* (Scribner, 1998). The ability of the New York School poets to envision themselves as such a band was aided by their acceptance of Auden as a leader, made all the more acceptable by being grumpy, slightly disheveled, and a little tired (Shaw 59–62).

The energy of Auden's art is transmitted most powerfully in the play of FORMS and language that characterizes much of New York School poetry. His bravura in handling traditional forms was, paradoxically, one of the ways that he pointed beyond modernism, which had become identified with free verse, especially in AMERICAN POETRY. To Koch, Auden's work seemed to offer "a great poetic amusement park, a park of poetic forms to try out" (interview 193). ALLAN KAPLAN employed a circus metaphor to capture the fun of Auden's rhyming "curtain rod" and "God" in "Victor" (1937) (*English Auden* 221). The conjunction was "pretty for being a bit grotesque," according to Kaplan, "like the thighs of the female aerialist clutching the trapeze bar, / And flying!" (Kaplan 48). This is the sort of verbal "happening" that especially interested TED BERRIGAN: "Hits between words, things like that, things that Auden talks about in his poems" (93). When Ashbery reviewed the 1967 edition of Berrigan's SONNETS, he explained the operative principle, that "poetry is made of words rather than ideas," by quoting Auden: "even a presumably 'idea' poet like W. H. Auden once said that poems are written not by intellectuals but by 'the man who likes to hang around words, trying to figure out what they mean'" (Ashbery 117).

Bibliography

Ashbery, John. Unpublished review of Ted Berrigan's *The Sonnets*." In *Selected Prose*. Edited by Eugene Richie. Ann Arbor: University of Michigan Press, 2004, 117–119.

Auden, W. H. *The Collected Poetry*. New York: Random House, 1945.

———. *The English Auden: Poems, Essays, and Dramatic Writings, 1927–1939*. Edited by Edward Mendelson. New York: Random House, 1977.

———. Foreword to *Some Trees*, by John Ashbery. New Haven, Conn.: Yale University Press, 1956.

———. "A Piece of Pure Fiction in the Firbank Mode." *New York Times Book Review*, 4 May 1969, 5, 20.

———. *The Sea and the Mirror: A Commentary on Shakespeare's The Tempest*. Edited by Arthur Kirsch. Princeton, N.J.: Princeton University Press, 2003.

Berrigan, Ted. "Interview with CITY" (1977). In *Talking in Tranquility: Interviews*. Edited by Stephen Ratcliffe and Leslie Scalapino. Bolinas, Calif.: Avenue B; Oakland, Calif.: O Books, 1991, 90–105.

Carpenter, Humphrey. *W. H. Auden: A Biography*. Boston: Houghton Mifflin, 1981.

Epstein, Andrew. "Auden and the New York School Poets." *W. H. Auden Society Newsletter* 22 (November 2001): 19–28. Andrew Epstein home page. Available online. URL: http://www.english.fsu.edu/faculty/aepstein.htm. Accessed December 16, 2008.

Kaplan, Allan. "Mind and Body." In *Paper Airplane*. New York: Harper & Row, 1971, 48–49.

Koch, Kenneth. Interview by Jordan Davis (1995). In *The Art of Poetry: Poems, Parodies, Interviews, Essays, and Other Work*. Ann Arbor: University of Michigan Press, 1996, 187–214.

———. "New Books by Marianne Moore and W. Auden." *Poetry* 90, no. 1 (April 1957): 47–52.

Kostelanetz, Richard. "John Ashbery" (1976). In *The Old Poetries and the New*. Ann Arbor: University of Michigan Press, 1981, 87–110.

Schuyler, James. *Collected Poems*. New York: Noonday/Farrar, Straus & Giroux, 1995.

———. *Just the Thing: Selected Letters of James Schuyler, 1951–1991*. Edited by William Corbett. New York: Turtle Point Press, 2004.

Shaw, Lytle. *Frank O'Hara: The Poetics of Coterie*. Iowa City: University of Iowa Press, 2006.

Waldman, Anne. Introduction to *The Angel Hair Anthology*. New York: Granary Books, 2001, xix–xxvii.

Australian and New Zealand poetry

To the young poets of Australia and New Zealand during the 1960s, responding to the New American poetry was not "Americanizing" but "globalizing" a culture that felt provincial. New Zealand poet Ian

Wedde (1946–) recalls: "[T]here was a surge of feeling connected to a global culture—not of being 'influenced' by, but of being part of, an international culture" (Wedde, "Antipodean Hipster" n.p.). There was also a sense of connecting at last with modernism (Stead), overcoming the traditional bias of BRITISH POETRY that had supplied the chief models in Australia and New Zealand up to this time. The French poet Arthur Rimbaud was the initial inspiration for the Australian John Tranter (1943–), who subsequently discovered the Franco-American connection, "from Desnos, Reverdy and Raymond Roussel back to Ashbery and O'Hara in New York" (Tranter, interview by Kinsella n.p.). Finally, in the spirit of the 1960s, the Australian poets especially, who came to be known as "the generation of '68," connected their reading of such poets as JOHN ASHBERY, FRANK O'HARA, and the younger TED BERRIGAN with the upsurge of the young and the new. In New Zealand, Arthur Baysting's anthology *The Young New Zealand Poets* (Heinemann, 1973), including work by Wedde, Bill Manhire (1946–), and Alan Loney (1940–), echoed the title of PAUL CARROLL's *The Young American Poets* (1968). Meanwhile, echoing the title of DONALD M. ALLEN's *The NEW AMERICAN POETRY* (1960), Tranter published *The New Australian Poetry* (Makar, 1979), including John Forbes (1950–98), Laurie (Laurence) Duggan (1949–), and Robert Adamson (1943–). Tranter recalls that Forbes "helped to give my romanticism a more adult perspective, by insisting on the importance of poets like Frank O'Hara (John did a thesis on O'Hara [at the University of Sydney]) and Ted Berrigan" (Tranter, interview by Tower n.p.). Interestingly, Tranter presents the NEW YORK SCHOOL influence as a check on the youthful enthusiasm inspired by Rimbaud.

During the post–World War II period both Australia and New Zealand experienced rapid growth in urban centers, which made the association of New York School poetry with city life especially relevant. Ken Bolton (1949–), another close friend of Forbes, describes a split in Australian poetry along an urban/rural divide: "The binary proposed in the 1970s was that of a new, more with-it, urban, American-derived poetic opposed to a more traditional range of forms and diction much attuned to a 'rural' Australia and Anglo-Australian

values: Les Murray [1938–], A. D. Hope [1907–2000], Robert Gray [1945–], say" (n.p.). In the "more with-it" poetry, the city will sometimes play a central role as content, as in Tranter's *The Floor of Heaven* (1992) or many of the poems collected by Pam Brown (1948–) in *Dear Deliria* (Salt, 2002), which takes its epigraph from JAMES SCHUYLER. More pervasively, urban experience inflects rhythm, or as Forbes called it, "timing":

> I think our sense of timing's
> the most important thing
> O'Hara taught us
> don't you Ken?

Forbes poses this question at the conclusion of his poem "Thin Ice" (1989), addressed to Ken Bolton. This passage is quoted in an experimental novel, *Genre* (136), by a younger friend of Forbes, John Kinsella (1963–), who imports the city poet's jagged sense of incident back into the experience of rural western Australia, where he grew up. The resulting "anti-pastoral" (Kinsella, "Landscape Poetry?" n.p.) complements the urban pastoral of the New York School poets. However, American readers are in danger of missing this connection because their introduction to Kinsella has been provided by Harold Bloom (Henry), who attempts to sublimate Kinsella into "deep subjectivity" (Bloom, Introduction xxiii), the realm to which Bloom had previously assigned "his precursor," Ashbery (Bloom, jacket blurb).

Admitting that he does not understand Kinsella's "curious attachments to Dennis Hopper and to Warhol" (Introduction xv), Bloom points to another dichotomy in Australian and New Zealand poetry in which the New York School has become involved: "high" culture versus "low," or popular, culture. Kinsella has praised Tranter as "a poet who really understands the discourse between popular art and perceived notions of high art" (Kinsella, interview n.p.). In his poem "nature morte: Oh, Rhetoric!" which is dedicated to Tranter, Kinsella explores this topic partly in relation to Ashbery. The "high" versus "low" debate has been formulated with special application to New Zealand by Wystan Curnow (1939–), son of Allen Curnow (1911–2001), a leading poet in New Zealand's equivalent of the Auden generation. After a period of residence in the United States, Wystan Curnow returned to New Zealand in 1970 eager to engage his compatriots in three developments that would unfold over the next decade in American "high," or avant-garde, culture: "conceptual art, post-structuralist theory and L=A=N=G=U=A=G=E poetry" (Curnow, "High Culture Now!" n.p.). On the other side of the debate, Wedde has warned against a "hieratic" imposition of a "will-to-language" and celebrated the liberating effect on New Zealand poetry of a more "demotic" relation, "language with a spoken base, adaptable and exploratory codes, and a 'lower' and more inclusive social threshold emphasising cultural mobility and immediacy" (Wedde, Introduction n.p.). Dating this liberation to the late 1960s, Wedde implicitly counters Curnow with a different set of Franco-American influences: "Black American rhythms, the liberated subject (Frank O'Hara's 'I was walking along the street . . .'), and the suicidal, sophisticated ennui of French existentialism" (Wedde, "Antipodean Hipster" n.p.). Mark Young (1941–   ), the poet whom Wedde describes as the "guru" of this moment in New Zealand, has recently resurfaced with a poem containing an invitation from O'Hara ("Lunch with Frank O'Hara"), which Young read at a publication party for *Big Smoke* (Auckland University Press, 2000), an anthology documenting the period 1960–75.

At the intersection of poetry and performance, as practiced in Australia and New Zealand, New York School and LANGUAGE POETRY meet and diverge in a bewildering variety of ways. The three editors of the *Big Smoke* anthology, Alan Brunton (1946–2002), Murray Edmond (1949–   ), and Michele Leggott (1956–   ), provide an illustration. Brunton played a pioneering role in the Auckland arts scene as a magazine editor (*Freed*, 1969–70, and *Spleen*, 1975–77, with Wedde) and founder of Red Mole (1974–   ), an experimental THEATER company that spent a period of residence (1978–84) on New York's Lower East Side. From the standpoint of performance, Brunton objected to Ashbery's reading style as typical of the "anti-voice" stance of Language poetry (n.p.). On the other hand, Edmond, Brunton's successor as editor of *Freed* (1970–71), traced a continuous development from the Poets' Theater of the New York School to the West Coast Poets' Theater of the Language poets (Edmond, n.p.). Brunton's collaboration with Leggott on a poetry video, *Heaven's Cloudy Smile* (Red Mole and GG Films, 1998), exemplifies the extension of performance into new media that has especially excited poets Down Under, where the need to transmit the immediacy of performance across long distances is acutely felt. Australian poet Hazel Smith (1950–   ) has described O'Hara's construction of "hyperscapes" in his poetry as an anticipation of the possibilities of "hypertext" on the World Wide Web. The outstanding example of the use of the Internet to make Australian and New Zealand poetry "part of an international culture" ("Antipodean Hipster"), as Wedde envisioned, is Tranter's online magazine, *Jacket*, launched in 1997. Throughout the magazine, as in his poetry, Tranter has included the voices of the New York School in a global conversation.

Bibliography

Bloom, Harold. Introduction to *Peripheral Light: Selected and New Poems*, by John Kinsella. New York: Norton, 2004.

———. Jacket blurb for *The New Arcadia*, by John Kinsella. New York: Norton, 2005.

Bolton, Ken. "Modern Australian Poetry: An Introduction for *Poetry Ireland*" (2004). Australian Literature Resources. Available online. URL: http://www.austlit.com/a/bolton-k/mod-aust-po.html. Accessed December 16, 2008.

Brunton, Alan. "Alan Brunton Gets Jaamed" (2001). Interview by Mark Pirie. New Zealand Electronic Poetry Centre. Available online. URL: http://www.nzepc.auckland.ac.nz/authors/brunton/jaamed.asp. Accessed December 16, 2008.

Curnow, Wystan. "A Brief Description of Poetry in New Zealand." *Boundary 2* 26, no. 1 (Spring 1999): 75–78.

———. "High Culture in a Small Province." In *Essays in New Zealand Literature*. Auckland, New Zealand: Heinemann Educational Books, 1973, 155–170.

———. "High Culture Now! A Manifesto" (1998). New Zealand Electronic Poetry Centre. Available online. URL: http://www.nzepc.auckland.ac.nz/misc/wystan.asp. Accessed December 16, 2008.

Edmond, Murray. "No Paragraphs: Meditations on Noh, Poetry, Theatre and the Avant-Garde." *Jacket* 16

(March 2002). Available online. URL: http://jacketmagazine.com/16/ov-edmo.html. Accessed December 16, 2008.

Forbes, John. "Frank O'Hara's 'In Memory of My Feelings.'" *Scripsi* 2, nos. 2&3 (1983): 199–219.

———. "Thin Ice." In *New and Selected Poems*. Pymble, Australia: Angus & Robertson, 1992, 104–105.

Henry, Brian. "Bloom's Kinsella: The Politics of Selection in *Peripheral Light*." *Jacket* 27 (April 2005). Available online. URL: http://jacketmagazine.com/27/henr-bloom-kins.html. Accessed December 16, 2008.

Kinsella, John. *Genre*. South Fremantle, Australia: Fremantle Arts Centre Press, 1997.

———. Interview by Ted Slade (1998). The Poetry Kit Interviews. Available online. URL: http://www.poetrykit.org/iv98/kinsella.htm. Accessed December 16, 2008.

———. "Landscape Poetry?" (2004). John Kinsella home page. Available online. URL: http://www.johnkinsella.org/essays/landscapepoetry.html. Accessed December 16, 2008.

———. "nature morte: Oh, Rhetoric!" *Tinfish* 4 (1997). Available online. URL: http://wings.buffalo.edu/epc/ezines/tinfish/tinfish04/tf4.html#kinsella. Accessed December 16, 2008.

Loney, Alan. "The Influence of American Poetry on Contemporary Poetic Practice in New Zealand." *Journal of New Zealand Literature* 10 (1992): 92–98.

Manhire, Bill. "Breaking the Line: A View of American and New Zealand Poetry" (1987). New Zealand Electronic Poetry Centre. Available online. URL: http://www.nzepc.auckland.ac.nz/authors/manhire/breaking.asp. Accessed December 16, 2008.

Mead, Philip. "The American Model II." In *Assembling Alternatives: Reading Postmodern Poetries Transnationally*, edited by Romana Huk, 169–193. Middletown, Conn.: Wesleyan University Press, 2003.

Smith, Hazel. *Hyperscapes in the Poetry of Frank O'Hara: Difference/Homosexuality/Topography*. Liverpool, U.K.: Liverpool University Press, 2000.

Stead, C. K. "From Wystan to Carlos—Modern and Modernism in Recent New Zealand Poetry" (1979). In *In the Glass Case: Essays on New Zealand Literature*. Auckland, New Zealand: Auckland University Press, 1981, 139–159.

Tranter, John. "Anaesthetics: Some Notes on the New Australian Poetry." In *The American Model: Influence and Independence in Australian Poetry*, edited by Joan Kirkby, 99–116. Sydney, Australia: Hale & Iremonger, 1982.

———. Interview by John Kinsella (1991, 1995). John Tranter home page. Available online. URL: http://johntranter.com/interviewed/1995-jk-jt.shtml. Accessed December 16, 2008.

———. Interview by C. K. Tower. *Riding the Meridian* 1, no. 1 (1999). Available online. URL: http://www.heelstone.com/meridian/word1.html. Accessed December 16, 2008.

———. *Urban Myths: 210 Poems (New and Selected)*. St. Lucia, Australia: University of Queensland Press, 2006.

———, ed. *Jacket* Web site. Available online. URL: http://jacketmagazine.com/00/home.shtml.

Wedde, Ian. "Antipodean Hipster" (2001). New Zealand Electronic Poetry Centre. Available online. URL: http://www.nzepc.auckland.ac.nz/authors/young/hipster.asp. Accessed December 16, 2008.

———. Introduction to *The Penguin Book of New Zealand Verse*. Auckland, New Zealand: Penguin, 1985, 23–52. New Zealand Electronic Poetry Centre. Available online. URL: http://www.nzepc.auckland.ac.nz/authors/wedde/penguin.asp. Accessed December 16, 2008.

Young, Mark. "Lunch with Frank O'Hara." *Big Smoke*. New Zealand Electronic Poetry Centre. Available online. URL: http://www.nzepc.auckland.ac.nz/features/bigsmoke/bs_o-y.asp. Accessed December 16, 2008.

Autobiography Tony Towle (1970–1973)

The long poem *Autobiography* may be TONY TOWLE's finest work, as PAUL VIOLI suggests (88). It is also certainly a major example of the NEW YORK SCHOOL's challenge to the "confessional" poetry identified with ROBERT LOWELL. Towle has stated that in writing *Autobiography* he felt he had finally realized the implications of FRANK O'HARA's "PERSONISM" (Pataphysics n.p.). "On His Name" (1973), in Towle's volume *"Autobiography" and Other Poems* (Sun/Coach House South, 1977), humorously describes an imaginary encounter with Lowell, who published three volumes of autobiographical verse in 1973. Towle's response to the publication of O'Hara's *Collected Poems* in 1971 was far more serious, as recorded in "Nearing Christmas" (1971–72), which also appeared in *"Autobiography" and Other Poems*. The weight of O'Hara's example posed such a burden to Towle that he felt "the impulse to close up shop" (*History of the Invitation* 103), but, instead, he decided to write against that impulse. *Autobiography*, written over this same period, needs to be understood primarily as writing, literally "life writing," as contemporary theorists of autobiography sometimes refer to it. Towle is writing for his life, composing "the polemics of survival, / in the enigmas posed by the use of the words themselves," as he states in the poem. In doing so, "he provided an inspiring alternative," Violi claims, "to the dry, lifeless linguistic exercises into which some experimental poetry [i.e., LANGUAGE POETRY] was beginning to sink" (85).

Autobiography does not present a linear narrative, but it is punctuated by references to some key dates, neatly aligned with decades. "I start off the Seventies, publish a book [*North*, 1970], and fall back exhausted," Towle writes midway through the poem (HI 121). Presumably, he is writing *Autobiography* partly as a means to recover creative energy. Looking back, Towle identifies 1960 as the year when he began writing poems, as well as the year when he "returned in anonymous triumph" from Washington, D.C., to Manhattan, "the island of my birth," after the breakup of a marriage not described in the poem but recorded in Towle's prose *Memoir*. The year 1950 marks a moment of epiphany for Towle at age 10 on a school playground in Queens. He sees "that no matter when I looked back from the future / all the previous years would have flown in a second." This vision poses the central problem that the entire poem struggles with, since it not only destroys the possibility of coherent narrative, but also calls into question the "location" of the self who exists only in "time without place." Towle seeks to create an alternative mode of existence in language by employing words in alternative ways, not as conventional vehicles for information, but rather "in phrases built up like brushstrokes, / but apprehended in a sequential structure, like music."

Bibliography

Bolton, Ken. Review of *The History of the Invitation*. *Jacket* 16 (March 2002). Available online. URL: http://www.jacketmagazine.com/16/ov-bolt-r-towl.html. Accessed December 16, 2008.

Lally, Michael. "Economou and Company," *Washington Post Book World*, 1 January 1978, p. E7.

Seidman, Hugh. "Overstated, Understated," *New York Times Book Review*, 14 May 1978, 7.

Towle, Tony. *The History of the Invitation: New & Selected Poems, 1963–2000*. Brooklyn, N.Y.: Hanging Loose Press, 2001.

———. Interview. *Pataphysics* 9 (2003). Formerly available online. URL: http://www.pataphysicsmagazine.com/towle_interview.html.

———. *Memoir, 1960–1963*. Cambridge, Mass.: Faux Press, 2001.

Violi, Paul. "Tony Towle in the '70s." In *The History of the Invitation*, by Tony Towle, 85–88. Brooklyn, N.Y.: Hanging Loose Press, 2008.

B

Baraka, Amiri (LeRoi Jones) (1934–)

One of the most significant and controversial African-American writers since World War II, Amiri Baraka played an important, if undersung, role around the edges of the developing NEW YORK SCHOOL of poetry in the 1950s and 1960s. In fact, Baraka was one of the only African-American writers to be closely affiliated with the original members of the New York School. Most discussions of Baraka's career highlight his association with BEAT writers such as ALLEN GINSBERG and JACK KEROUAC and his debt to BLACK MOUNTAIN/projectivist poets CHARLES OLSON and ROBERT CREELEY before moving on to describe his role in the founding of THE BLACK ARTS MOVEMENT in the late 1960s, yet it has been less well recognized that he was closely intertwined with the New York School poets during these formative years. In fact, between 1958 and 1965, Baraka shared a particularly close and productive friendship with FRANK O'HARA, regularly published work by New York School poets in the journals he coedited, included numerous references to O'Hara in his own works, and wrote poems dedicated to New York School poets (for example, "The Rare Birds," which is dedicated to TED BERRIGAN) (Waldman 174). Although his career has notoriously featured dramatic shifts and renunciations of former positions, his early and substantial connection to the poets of the New York School should not be overlooked.

Baraka was born Everett Leroy Jones in 1934, in Newark, New Jersey. After changing his name to LeRoi in high school, Jones attended Howard University, where he studied with E. Franklin Frazier and Sterling Brown. When he flunked out of Howard, Jones joined the air force, serving three years before being dishonorably discharged in 1957. He immediately moved to New York, where he suddenly found himself happily immersed in the bohemian, relatively integrated literary world of Greenwich Village. He married a white woman and fellow writer, Hettie Cohen, had two daughters, and quickly became a central, galvanizing figure in the white avant-garde literary scene. As coeditor of the influential small journals YŪGEN (with Cohen) and the FLOATING BEAR (with DIANE DI PRIMA), Jones even served as a kind of bridge between different factions of the New American poetry: the Black Mountain, Beat, and New York School camps. A tireless promoter, editor, critic, and writer of the new poetry, Jones was also the only African-American writer among the 44 poets gathered together in the landmark anthology The NEW AMERICAN POETRY, 1945–1960, edited by DONALD M. ALLEN in 1960.

When Jones's first book of poems, Preface to a Twenty-Volume Suicide Note (Corinth), appeared in 1961, it clearly showed the influence of the various strains of the new avant-garde poetries and announced the arrival of a major new talent. The poems in Jones's first two books are elliptical, pained, and introspective, employing visceral images and fragmented syntax to convey the agonized self-consciousness of a soul tormented by self, society, and racial strife. In their use of open FORM and collage, their slangy, demotic voice and ironic humor, their embrace of comic-book heroes and other pop culture materials, and their attention to the daily ("wives, gardens, jobs, cement yards where cats pee"), they also show the impact of O'Hara and New York School poetics (*Baraka Reader* 16). (Baraka would later recall the importance of O'Hara's "openness" to the development of his own poetic voice.) During these highly frenetic, creative years, Jones and O'Hara were deeply involved in each other's lives and works, publicly supporting each other's writing, performing together frequently, working as editors together on the journal KULCHUR, and so on. When Jones needed help on a new play he was writing, he met with O'Hara for advice; when his play *The Toilet* was staged in 1963, Jones collaborated with New York School artist LARRY RIVERS, who created the set. When JOHN ASHBERY edited an issue of the New York School journal LOCUS SOLUS in 1962, he included four poems by Jones alongside a roster of the usual New York School suspects. For his part, O'Hara frequently sang the praises of Jones's works, seemed inspired by his friend's passionate involvement in the civil rights struggle, and included the figure of Jones himself in several crucial works, including his famous mock manifesto "PERSONISM" and its companion piece, "Personal Poem."

Despite, or perhaps because of his close involvement with poets like O'Hara, by the early 1960s Jones was growing increasingly disillusioned with the white bohemian literary world. After a life-changing visit to revolutionary Cuba in 1960, Jones became more and more impatient with what he saw as the apolitical stance of the white avant-garde and its separation of art from POLITICS, and ever more angered by racial prejudice and injustice. The painful confusion and strain of this period, and the friction they caused between the poet and his allies, erupted in the poems of Jones's powerful second volume of poetry, *The Dead Lecturer* (Grove Press, 1964), as well as in his plays and the experimental novel *The System of Dante's Hell* (Grove Press, 1965). With the success of his incendiary, controversial 1964 play *Dutchman*, which uncomfortably probed issues of racial misunderstanding and hatred by staging a violent encounter between a white woman and a black man in a subway car, Jones's national reputation was established.

Pressured by the increasingly urgent racial politics of the time to rediscover his connection to African-American culture, Jones left his white wife and their children immediately after the assassination of Malcolm X in 1965, cut ties with his former companions in Greenwich Village, and moved uptown to Harlem, eventually returning to Newark. He changed his name from LeRoi Jones to Amiri Baraka, became a founder and central creative force within the Black Arts Movement, a public spokesman for black cultural nationalism, and a militant political organizer and leader. In the books *Black Magic* (Bobbs-Merrill, 1968) and *It's Nation Time* (1970), he began writing fierce, polemical (and frequently anti-white and anti-Semitic) poems that attacked white racism and advocated violence and black separatism in much more straightforward language, in part inspired by African-American MUSIC and oral tradition.

By 1974 Baraka's political stance and poetry had undergone another radical shift. He now rejected his earlier black nationalism and began to espouse what he called "Third World Marxism," and his poems became even more concerned with direct political statement and activism, now dedicated to challenging not only racism but also the inequities of Western capitalism and imperialism. Over the course of the past 30 years, the innovative use of black vernacular and emphasis on the musical, performative dimension of poetry in Baraka's later work have been extremely influential. In 2002 Baraka once again found himself in the national spotlight. After he was named poet laureate of New Jersey, a furious controversy erupted when Baraka read a polemical poem about SEPTEMBER 11TH and American imperialism that critics considered anti-Semitic. (Because Baraka adamantly refused to resign, the state of New Jersey abolished the position of poet laureate altogether.)

Baraka's sharp break with his white companions in the mid-1960s and the course of his later career have taken him quite far from his original connection to the New York School of poetry. Furthermore, his critique of the hypocrisy and passivity of the white avant-garde and his vision of poetics as a form of political action raise complex questions about the status of the political within New York School poetics. But there is little question that the exciting conversation and collaboration across racial lines that occurred between Baraka and the poets of New York in the 1950s and 1960s stands as an important chapter not only in his own career but in the development of the New York School and of postwar AMERICAN POETRY in general.

Bibliography

Baraka, Amiri. *The Autobiography of LeRoi Jones.* Chicago: Lawrence Hill Books, 1984.

———. *Black Magic: Collected Poetry, 1961–1967.* Indianapolis, Ind.: Bobbs-Merrill, 1969.

———. *The Dead Lecturer.* New York: Grove, 1964.

———. *The LeRoi Jones/Amiri Baraka Reader.* 2d ed. Edited by William J. Harris. New York: Thunder's Mouth Press, 2000.

———. *Preface to a Twenty-Volume Suicide Note.* New York: Totem Press/Corinth Books, 1961.

———. *The System of Dante's Hell.* New York: Grove, 1965.

———. *Transbluesency: The Selected Poems of Amiri Baraka/LeRoi Jones (1961–1995).* Edited by Paul Vangelisti. New York: Marsilio, 1995.

Benston, Kimberly W. *Baraka: The Renegade and the Mask.* New Haven, Conn.: Yale University Press, 1976.

———, ed. *Imamu Amiri Baraka (LeRoi Jones): A Collection of Critical Essays.* Englewood Cliffs, N.J.: Prentice-Hall, 1978.

Epstein, Andrew. *Beautiful Enemies: Friendship and Postwar American Poetry.* New York: Oxford University Press, 2006.

Gooch, Brad. *City Poet: The Life and Times of Frank O'Hara.* New York: Knopf, 1993.

Gwiazda, Piotr. "The Aesthetics of Politics/The Politics of Aesthetics: Amiri Baraka's 'Somebody Blew Up America.'" *Contemporary Literature* 45, no. 3 (2004): 460–485.

Harris, William J. *The Poetry and Poetics of Amiri Baraka: The Jazz Aesthetic.* Columbia: University of Missouri Press, 1985.

Jones, Hettie. *How I Became Hettie Jones.* New York: Dutton, 1990.

Lehman, David. *The Last Avant-Garde: The Making of the New York School of Poets.* New York: Doubleday, 1998.

LeSueur, Joe. *Digressions on Some Poems by Frank O'Hara.* New York: Farrar, Straus & Giroux, 2003.

Magee, Michael. "Tribes of New York: Frank O'Hara, Amiri Baraka, and the Poetics of the Five Spot." *Contemporary Literature* 42, no. 4 (2001): 694–726.

Nielsen, Aldon Lynn. *Writing between the Lines: Race and Intertextuality.* Athens: University of Georgia Press, 1994.

Posnock, Ross. *Color and Culture: Black Writers and the Making of the Modern Intellectual.* Cambridge, Mass.: Harvard University Press, 1998.

Sollors, Werner. *Amiri Baraka/LeRoi Jones: The Quest for a "Populist Modernism."* New York: Columbia University Press, 1978.

Waldman, Anne, ed. *Nice to See You: Homage to Ted Berrigan.* Minneapolis, Minn.: Coffee House Press, 1991.

Watts, Jerry Gafio. *Amiri Baraka: The Politics and Art of a Black Intellectual.* New York: New York University Press, 2001.

Barg, Barbara (1947–)

Barbara Barg was born in Memphis and raised in a small Arkansas town, where hers was the only Jewish family. After studying with TED BERRIGAN at Northeastern Illinois University, she moved to NEW YORK CITY and became involved in a number of individual and collaborative projects, including the rock group Homer Erotic, which came to life spontaneously during a lull in a poetry reading in 1991. The group is composed of seven women interested in MUSIC as a performative art FORM. Barg's poetry is attuned to notions of feminism, Buddhism, and what she calls "voluntary evolution," a realization and incarnation of sublimity in contemporary existence.

Barg is the author of two books, *The Origin of THE Species* (Semiotext(e), 1994) and *Obeying the Chemicals* (1984). She has also appeared in a number of anthologies, including *Poems for the Nation: A Collection of Contemporary Political Poems* (Seven Stories Press, 1999); *American Poets Say Goodbye to the 20th Century,* edited by ANDREI CODRESCU and Laura Rosenthal (1996); *Am Lit: Neue Literatur aus den USA* (Edition Druckhaus/ Germany, 1992); *Out of This World: The Poetry Project at St. Mark's Church-in-the-Bowery: 1966– 1991,* edited by ANNE WALDMAN (1991); and *The L=A=N=G=U=A=G=E BOOK* (Southern

Illinois University Press, 1984). She wrote the exhibition catalog for Barbara Ess's photography exhibit *I Am Not This Body* at the Curtis Marcus Gallery. As a singer-songwriter-drummer, Barg has released two CDs with Homer Erotic (*Homerica the Beautiful* and *Yield*) and has contributed to three of Elliot Sharp's multi-artist compilations—*Hey George, Phone Noir,* and *Late 20th Century Sexual Practices*—as well as to *One World Poetry,* a multi-artist compilation recorded at Amsterdam's One World Poetry Festival, and *Sugar, Alcohol & Meat,* produced by JOHN GIORNO Poetry Systems. Barg features in two multi-artist compilation tapes: *Noise Fest,* with the band Avant Squares (produced by Thurston Moore and Kim Gordon of Sonic Youth), and *Tellus #5* with Ess (produced by Harvest Works in New York).

Barg has performed poems and vocals for a number of videos, including *Duties of My Heart; Poetry Spots,* produced for the Public Broadcasting Service by BOB HOLMAN; and *Uh-Oh Plutonium,* Waldman's music video produced by ROSE LESNIAK and Out There Productions. She has written and narrated for such films as *If You Meet the Buddha on the Road, Kill Him/Her/It,* and *Pop Quiz.* In the THEATER, the play *Fibs,* produced in CHICAGO, was based on a short story by Barg, and *Rhythm of Torn Stars,* produced in Los Angeles, incorporated text by Barg as well as JIM CARROLL, FRANK O'HARA, Berrigan, and other poets. Barg has hosted and edited *Poetry International,* a radio magazine. She has curated the EAR INN reading series in New York and the Out There reading series in Chicago. She has taught at the St. Mark's Poetry Project, as an adjunct professor at Brooklyn College, and at various New York City high schools.

Bibliography

Barbara Barg Web site. Available online. URL: http://www.barbarabarg.com/.

Barg, Barbara. Statement in *Out of This World: An Anthology of the St. Mark's Poetry Project, 1966–1991,* edited by Anne Waldman, 618–619. New York: Crown, 1991.

Basketball Diaries, The   Jim Carroll   (1978)

JIM CARROLL's *The Basketball Diaries* enacts the scenario envisioned in the founding of the POETRY PROJECT AT ST. MARK'S CHURCH IN-THE-BOWERY: A street kid from the Lower East Side, hooked on drugs, explores the act of writing as an alternative source of power, escape, and revenge. Carroll's conflicting motives are deliberately left unresolved. Within the scope of the diaries themselves, which cover the period 1963–66, it is not at all clear that writing offers redemption from drugs and delinquency, though that was the premise on which the Poetry Project received inaugural funding in 1966 and the premise on which the Hollywood film version of *The Basketball Diaries* was based in 1995. The film concludes with the main character (Jim Carroll), played by Leonardo DiCaprio (1974–   ), rejecting an offer of dope and proceeding to read from his diaries before an appreciative audience. Carroll, in fact, found such an audience at the Poetry Project, though his initial involvement in that community did not free him from drugs, as he documents in *Forced Entries,* the "sequel" to *The Basketball Diaries.* In reality, withdrawal from drugs required withdrawal from New York, to a methadone clinic in California and a period of seclusion in BOLINAS. *The Basketball Diaries* was first published there in book form (Tombouctou Press, 1978), with an introduction by TOM CLARK, who had been instrumental in the publication of an excerpt from the diaries in the *PARIS REVIEW* (Number 50, fall 1970).

The two keywords in the title of *The Basketball Diaries* symbolize two opposite directions in Carroll's fortunes. A promising career as a high school basketball player disintegrates as drugs take over his life. On the other hand, the act of writing the diaries provides a means of control over the chaos he is experiencing. "I think of poetry," he writes, "and how I see it as just a raw block of stone ready to be shaped, that way words are never a horrible limit to me, just tools to shape" (159). The diary itself is written in prose that to some extent fictionalizes content and frequently approaches prose poetry in style. In one entry Carroll quotes a poem in verse that "I wrote on L.S.D. a while ago" (140). Its final line is repeated as the last sentence in the book: "I just want to be pure" (210). The same poem is repeated in the film version, which is remarkably faithful both to the book's words, which are often quoted, and to its incidents until the point where the film takes the Carroll character through incarceration and sudden rehabilitation. The atmosphere of poetry is heightened in the film by quotations from additional poems by Carroll—"Blood Bridge" and "Little Ode on St. Anne's Day"—and by musical selections, including Carroll's songs "Catholic Boy" (sung by Carroll with Pearl Jam) and "People Who Died" (sung by Carroll with the JIM CARROLL BAND). That this is NEW YORK SCHOOL poetry is underscored by the fact that much of the film was shot on location in NEW YORK CITY, adding a documentary dimension that is also very much in the spirit of the diaries. In fact, contrary to the usual associations of the diary form with private subjectivity, Carroll explicitly presents his work as public documentary, or even epic: "Now I got these diaries that have the greatest hero a writer needs, this crazy fucking New York" (*The Basketball Diaries* 159).

Bibliography

Carroll, Jim. *The Basketball Diaries*. New York: Penguin, 1995.

———. *Fear of Dreaming: The Selected Poems*. New York: Penguin, 1993.

———. *Forced Entries: The Downtown Diaries, 1971–1973*. New York: Penguin, 1987.

Carter, Cassie. *Shit into Gold: Jim Carroll's* The Basketball Diaries *and* Forced Entries. Catholicboy.com. Available online. URL: http://www.catholicboy.com/chapter1.php. Accessed December 16, 2008.

Kalvert, Scott, dir. *The Basketball Diaries*. DVD. New York: Palm Pictures, 1998.

Lehmann-Haupt, Christopher. Review of *The Basketball Diaries* and *Forced Entries*. *New York Times*, 9 July 1987, p. C23.

Maslin, Janet. "Looking for Poetry in All the Wrong Places," *New York Times*, 21 April 1995, p. C12.

Bean Spasms **Ted Berrigan and Ron Padgett** (1967)

Bean Spasms includes poems; interviews; short stories about dogs, policemen, and milkmen; parodies; plays; cartoons; an epistolary travel narrative; and other hard-to-characterize FORMs. Beyond this astonishing variety of GENREs, what is perhaps most original about *Bean Spasms* is its approach to authorship.

As stated by TED BERRIGAN in the text, *Bean Spasms* was partly inspired by "Kenneth Koch's marvelous magazine anthology of collaborations, LOCUS SOLUS II" (201). In a section of *Bean Spasms* entitled "Collaborations," there is no indication as to which poet wrote which line in the various texts. Additionally, authorship is mostly undesignated for the other sections in *Bean Spasms*; readers literally do not know who wrote what. Such a practice suggests that Berrigan and RON PADGETT reject the privilege of stable authorship in favor of a far more communal and chaotic approach. For example, though the cover of the book lists Berrigan and Padgett as sole authors, we find out in the "Notes" section of the book that "[s]ometimes friends who came by would write a few lines" (199).

Producing a collaborative work means that an individual writer cannot treat a given text as his or her property. Indeed, to a letter from LITA HORNICK (editor of *KULCHUR*) in which she wrote, "I forgot to ask you which pieces in *Bean Spasms* are yours, which are Ron's and which are collaborations," Berrigan responded, "Don't Know—we each did one like this—don't know if this is R's or Mine." Texts written by an individual author lose all traces of origin thanks to their place within the democratic context of the collaborative book.

In his review of *Bean Spasms* JOHN PERREAULT predicted the book would "infuriate most poets and writers because of its uncompromising insistence upon 'abstraction.' It will also infuriate many because of the collaboration devices employed and because of the apparent lack of 'self-expression' and/or psychological and sociological 'content'" (10). Repudiating the idea of the poem as self-expression, the texts in *Bean Spasms* are language centered; that is, they are free to explore the very materiality of words independent of conventional signification. "To," the first poem in the book, is made up entirely of variations on the name *Linda*. The first word of the text is *Linda*, the second is *Ilnda*, the third is *Nilda*, and so on (7). The choice to begin the book with such a poem points to the overall ethos of *Bean Spasms*: Words do not represent transparently but are arbitrary signs that can be happily disassembled and imaginatively recombined; play in community is the true source of pleasure and meaning.

Such themes are evoked repeatedly throughout *Bean Spasms*. JOE BRAINARD's illustration *Policeman Dan* (15) is an image of a dog's shaggy head, the words *POLICEMAN DAN* inscribed directly underneath the picture. In a hilarious interview with the composer JOHN CAGE in the book, we learn at the end that "John Cage served neither as collaborator nor as interviewee" (67). The poem "In Four Parts" ends with a description of William Carlos Williams as

> a
> strong
> and
> vigorous
> poet
> who
> spoke
> in
> the
> American
> idiom (57).

Like the "Linda" poem mentioned above, the tendency in these images and texts is to radically reassign meaning, to challenge our assumptions of naturalness and authorial presence in favor of what could be called textual anarchy. Even Williams's belief that a "natural" speech-based "American idiom" be replicated in poetry is implicitly critiqued by the wildly stilted lineation of "In Four Parts."

With its deep humor, its delight in surface wordplay, its references to names specific of a given social scene, and its use of complicated and often bizarre forms, *Bean Spasms* fits within what might loosely be called the overall NEW YORK SCHOOL scene. More important, however, is the way in which *Bean Spasms* so radically foregrounds writing itself as its subject. As Berrigan writes in the "Notes" section: "There are no tricks. It was New York City and friends, and most of our friends were writers or painters, and when we got together (the writers not being able to afford 'Cedar Bar') we wrote" (200). (See CEDAR STREET TAVERN.)

Bibliography

Berrigan, Ted, and Ron Padgett. *Bean Spasms*. New York: Kulchur Press, 1967.
Berrigan, Ted. Letter to Lita Hornick, 8 February 1967. Ted Berrigan Papers. Rare Book and Manuscript Library, Columbia University, New York.
Clark, Tom. "Two and Three," *New York Times Book Review*, 31 March 1968, 32–34.
Perreault, John. "Bean Spasms: A Book by Ron Padgett and Ted Berrigan," *Village Voice*, 7 December 1967, 10–11.

Beats

Although the Beat writers emerged at the same time as the first-generation NEW YORK SCHOOL poets, the two groups are often placed at opposite poles aesthetically and sometimes identified with opposite coasts geographically. San Francisco provided the stage for the public performances in the mid-1950s that first drew attention to ALLEN GINSBERG, GREGORY CORSO, and JACK KEROUAC, three leading Beat writers. But each of these writers had roots on the East Coast and particularly in NEW YORK CITY, where Corso was born and both Ginsberg and Kerouac attended Columbia University. The clubs, bars, and lofts of DOWNTOWN MANHATTAN offered a hospitable scene in which Beat writers and New York School poets frequently intermingled, though the Beats were generally more receptive to the language of the street. In Times Square, Kerouac met the "hipsters" who described themselves as "beat" (Kerouac 568). He later applied that term to the attitude of an entire generation of young people who were eager to appear defeated, beaten, by the standards of the dominant culture if it meant holding on to the "wild selfbelieving individuality" that America once had promised (Kerouac 568)

As a means of ensuring individuality, both the Beat writers and the New York School poets were devoted to spontaneity. In artistic practice the Beats found their model especially in JAZZ improvisation, while the New York School poets looked to the immediate gestures of the action painter. In lifestyle the Beats especially valued certain "peak" experiences for the sensation of spontaneous release: sexual orgasm, the drug-induced high, driving a car at high speed. To the New York School sensibility each moment is to be valued as much as the next or preceding moment; spontaneity is experienced less as a visionary breakthrough than as a random sequence of actions: FRANK O'HARA's "I do this I do that." If there is a privileged moment for the New York School, it is the moment of art. In contrast to the Beats, therefore, the New York School poets can seem to be aesthetes. In their foregrounding of art, they are more resolutely modernist than the romantic Beats.

The Beats initially received more attention than the New York School poets because the Beats were both more accessible and more sensational. Kerouac and WILLIAM BURROUGHS—a father figure to the younger Beats in many ways—both wrote in the popular medium of prose. Beat defiance of conventions extended beyond aesthetic norms to challenge social structures. If it was scandalous, and therefore attention grabbing, that the Beats described the pursuit of sexual release in explicit terms, it was doubly scandalous that they were actually living the life they described. The idea of a "Beat generation," proclaimed as early as 1952 in a *New York Times Magazine* article by John Clellon Holmes, played into contemporary anxieties about a rise in juvenile delinquency. The term *beatnik*, coined in 1958 by *San Francisco Chronicle* columnist Herb Caen, darkly implied the menace of communism posed by the Soviet Union, whose *Sputnik* satellite had beaten America in the race into space the previous year. While a New York School poet might fear, at worst, having his publications ignored by the general public, a Beat writer could expect either attempts at legal suppression, such as greeted the publication of Ginsberg's *Howl* (1956) and excerpts of Burroughs's *Naked Lunch* (1958–59), or harsh critical condemnation, such as Norman Podhoretz's attack "The Know-Nothing Bohemians," provoked by the publication of Kerouac's *On the Road* (1957).

The Beats' ability to attract public attention inevitably made it tempting to market the broader avant-garde movement, including the New York School poets, through association with the Beats. From this perspective the inclusion of the Beats was crucial to the success of DONALD ALLEN's anthology *The NEW AMERICAN POETRY* (1960), although Allen assigned separate sections to the Beats and the New York School poets. In the same year Elias Wilentz of the EIGHTH STREET BOOKSTORE lumped together the entire "young literary world of New York's Greenwich Village" under the title *The Beat Scene.* Along with Ginsberg, Corso, and Kerouac, Wilentz included O'Hara, KENNETH KOCH, Joseph LeSueur, KENWARD ELMSLIE, and many other writers across a wide range of styles.

In addition to publication, another outlet for writers to which the Beats attracted a spotlight was the public poetry reading. JOHN ASHBERY and O'Hara reluctantly went along with this trend but maintained a dry manner of delivery that seemed to insist on the surface of the written page, rather than the depths of the poet's soul, as the source of what the audience was hearing. Only Koch, among the first-generation New York poets, occasionally experimented with reading his work to jazz accompaniment, after the Beat fashion. For poets of the second generation, performance became a standard mode of operation. Greater public engagement characterized not only their relation to their audience but also their stance of open opposition to the dominant culture. Such engagement was implicit in such predecessors as O'Hara but might not have become so explicit without the influence of the Beats.

Bibliography

Charters, Ann. *Beat Down to Your Soul: What Was the Beat Generation?* New York: Penguin, 2001.

Kerouac, Jack. "*Beatific*: The Origins of the Beat Generation" (1959). In *The Portable Jack Kerouac.* Edited by Ann Charters. New York: Penguin, 1995, 565–573.

Tytell, John. *Naked Angels: Kerouac, Ginsberg, Burroughs.* New York: Grove, 1976.

Watson, Steven. *The Birth of the Beat Generation: Visionaries, Rebels, and Hipsters, 1944–1960.* New York: Pantheon, 1998.

Wilentz, Elias, ed. *The Beat Scene.* New York: Corinth Books, 1960.

Berkeley Poetry Conference (1965)

"One of the major convergences of the poets in the Don Allen anthology [*The NEW AMERICAN POETRY*]," according to LEWIS WARSH (xx), the Berkeley Poetry Conference was held from July 12 to 24, 1965, under the auspices of the Extension program of the University of California, Berkeley.

DONALD M. ALLEN was one of the conference organizers, together with Richard Baker of the Extension program, who had been a former colleague of Allen's at Grove Press in New York and was now a fellow member of the San Francisco Zen Center. To serve as cohosts of the conference, Allen and Baker enlisted Robert Duncan and Berkeley professor Thomas Parkinson, an early advocate of the BEAT writers inside academia. BEATS and SAN FRANCISCO RENAISSANCE and BLACK MOUNTAIN POETS received top billing on the program, with dual lecture-reading assignments going to Duncan, Jack Spicer, Gary Snyder, Ed Dorn, ALLEN GINSBERG, ROBERT CREELEY, and CHARLES OLSON. The audience at one of these main events could number more than 1,000 (Faas 304).

The Berkeley Poetry Conference is significant in the development of the NEW YORK SCHOOL in several ways, though not necessarily in ways one might expect. None of the first-generation New York School poets attended. Although JOHN ASHBERY and FRANK O'HARA had been invited, TED BERRIGAN reports (106), their attention was turned toward Europe, where, on O'Hara's recommendation, Ashbery had just appeared with Olson at the SPOLETO FESTIVAL OF TWO WORLDS. Berrigan made sure that he got invited to Berkeley, and his reading there, from his recently published SONNETS (1964), received favorable notice from Duncan (501), Creeley ("Colloquy" 88), and Dorn (Clark 15). Berrigan himself reports that his meeting with PHILIP WHALEN, with whom he had been in correspondence, was a highlight of the conference (106). For ANNE WALDMAN, the highlight was Olson's performance in his controversial marathon reading at the end of the conference, the event from which Waldman dates her "confirmation of a life in poetry" (145). Thus, in various ways the conference provided second-generation New York School writers with a form of initiation into a larger tradition. But they also forged ties with one another. Waldman and Warsh first met at Duncan's reading. Others who attended the conference and who were to contribute further to the evolution of the New York School included JIM BRODEY, CLARK COOLIDGE, Jonathan Cott, LARRY FAGIN, ED SANDERS, and Hannah Weiner.

In the radical atmosphere of the Berkeley campus, a proving ground for the New Left during the 1960s, the poetry conference inevitably took on a political burden, explicitly in remarks by many of the poets, implicitly in their commitment to free expression in their poems. In *The Nation*, a traditional voice of the Old Left, Donald Wesling took Sanders's FUCK YOU magazine as evidence of the irresponsible extreme to which the free speech movement, a recent cause at Berkeley, might lead. But Duncan found it possible to respond even to Sanders's performance at the conference as genuine poetry. Writing to DENISE LEVERTOV, then poetry editor of *The Nation*, he singled out the program in which Sanders read with Berrigan as "a delight" (501).

Bibliography

Berrigan, Ted. "To Propitiate the Gods" (1978). In *Nice to See You: Homage to Ted Berrigan*, edited by Anne Waldman, 104–115. Minneapolis, Minn.: Coffee House Press, 1991.

Clark, Tom. *Late Returns: A Memoir of Ted Berrigan.* Bolinas, Calif.: Tombouctou, 1985.

Creeley, Robert. "A Colloquy" (1965). In *Contexts of Poetry: Interviews, 1961–1971.* Bolinas, Calif.: Four Seasons, 1973, 71–124.

———. "Sense of Measure" (1964). In *Collected Essays.* Berkeley: University of California Press, 1989, 486–488.

Dorn, Ed. *The Poet, the People, the Spirit.* Vancouver, Canada: Talonbooks, 1976.

Duncan, Robert. "At the Poetry Conference, Berkeley, after the New York Style" (1965). In *Nice To See You: Homage to Ted Berrigan*, edited by Anne Waldman, 12–14. Minneapolis, Minn.: Coffee House Press, 1991.

Duncan, Robert, and Denise Levertov. *The Letters of Robert Duncan and Denise Levertov.* Edited by Robert J. Bertholf and Albert Gelpi. Stanford, Calif.: Stanford University Press, 2004.

Faas, Ekbert. *Robert Creeley: A Biography.* Hanover, N.H.: University Press of New England, 2001.

Olson, Charles. *Muthologos: The Collected Lectures and Interviews.* Vol. 1. Edited by George F. Butterick. Bolinas, Calif.: Four Seasons, 1978. [Includes transcripts of Olson's Berkeley lecture and reading.]

Snyder, Gary. "Poetry and the Primitive." In *Earth House Hold.* New York: New Directions, 1969, 117–130. [A version of Snyder's Berkeley lecture.]

Spicer, Jack. "Poetry and Politics." In *The House That Jack Built: The Collected Lectures of Jack Spicer.* Edited by Peter Gizzi. Hanover, N.H.: University Press of New England/Wesleyan University Press, 1998, 149–172. [Transcript of Spicer's Berkeley lecture.]

Waldman, Anne. "'I Is Another': Dissipative Structures." In *Fast Speaking Woman.* New ed. San Francisco: City Lights, 1996, 127–159.

Warsh, Lewis. Introduction to *The Angel Hair Anthology.* New York: Granary Books, 2001, xix–xxvii.

Wesling, Donald. "Berkeley: Free Speech and Free Verse." *The Nation* 201, no. 15 (8 November 1965), 338–340.

Berkshires, the

This region in westernmost Massachusetts, named for the Berkshire Hills, has served over the years as an idyllic outpost for a number of poets affiliated with the NEW YORK SCHOOL. During the late 1970s and early 1980s, TED BERRIGAN and ALICE NOTLEY spent several summers in Cummington. For 27 years CLARK COOLIDGE resided atop a mountain in Hancock. The UNITED ARTISTS editors BERNADETTE MAYER and LEWIS WARSH took up residence in Worthington in the mid-1970s and soon relocated to the center of Lenox, where Mayer composed *Midwinter Day* (Tutle Island, 1982).

In the mid-1980s, MICHAEL and PETER GIZZI invigorated the poetry scene in Berkshire County. Peter edited the influential journal *O-BLEK* in Stockbridge, while his brother Michael coordinated two important reading series, first at Simon's Rock of Bard College and then at Arrowhead, home of Herman Melville and the Berkshire Historical Society. Many New York School poets participated in these readings, among them JOHN ASHBERY and Pierre Martory, JAMES SCHUYLER, DAVID SHAPIRO, BARBARA GUEST, LARRY FAGIN, HARRY MATHEWS, Coolidge, JOHN GODFREY, Mayer, and WILLIAM CORBETT. Ashbery, from nearby Hudson, New York, participated in both venues.

In the early 1990s Michael Gizzi began editing at Hard Press and on its arts journal *Lingo.* In addi-tion to features on FRANK O'HARA and Shapiro, *Lingo 2*, dedicated to the New York School, featured an interview with Ashbery and artwork by TREVOR WINKFIELD. Most significantly, Hard Press published the Profile series whose titles included *The Desire of Mothers to Please Others in Letters* by Mayer, *The Heart of the Breath* by JIM BRODEY (edited by Coolidge), and *New and Selected Poems of Frank Lima* (edited by Shapiro).

Geoffrey Young in Great Barrington ran and was editor of, until 2003, The Figures, the longest lived literary press in the Berkshires. Begun in Berkeley, California, as a publisher of LANGUAGE POETRY, The Figures relocated in 1982 to Berkshire County. The Figures has published half a dozen important books by RON PADGETT and Coolidge, including their COLLABORATION *Radiant Silhouette.* Under Young it also published TOM CLARK, JOHN GODFREY, and Michael Gizzi.

Berkson, Bill (1939–)

A pioneer of the second-generation NEW YORK SCHOOL poets, Bill Berkson is now recognized as "a serene master of the syntactical sleight and transformer of the mundane into the marvelous" (review 82). He was born in NEW YORK CITY, where his father, Seymour Berkson, was the publisher of the *New York Journal–American* and his mother, Eleanor Lambert, was a "high-fashion" publicist, credited with being "the Empress of Seventh Avenue" (Nemy). When his father died in 1959, Berkson left his studies at Brown University and returned to New York, where he signed up for KENNETH KOCH's poetry workshop at the New School. The workshop offered him an invigorating introduction to FRENCH POETRY by Max Jacob, Pierre Reverdy, Blaise Cendrars and RAYMOND ROUSSEL as well as the work of Koch and his friends, FRANK O'HARA and JOHN ASHBERY. Koch soon introduced Berkson to O'Hara in person, teasing him that O'Hara would function as a "germ" in his life (Gooch 350).

Despite the differences in ages (Berkson 19 when they met, O'Hara 32), the two quickly developed a close friendship. O'Hara wrote several poems to and about the younger poet, including "For the Chinese New Year & For Bill Berkson"

(1961) and "BIOTHERM" (1962). The two men also collaborated on several projects, recently collected as the *Hymns of St. Bridget & Other Writings* (Owl Press, 2001). The cover of this edition includes ALEX KATZ's painting of both men, entitled *Marine and Sailor* (1961). After O'Hara's death, Berkson edited the memorial volume *In Memory of My Feelings* (Museum of Modern Art, 1967); *Homage to Frank O'Hara* (with Joe LeSueur; BIG SKY, 1978); and *What's Wth Modern Art?* (Mike & Dale's Press, 1999), a collection of O'Hara's art criticism.

Berkson's first collection of poems, *Saturday Night* (TIBOR DE NAGY, 1961), was among the volumes that JOHN BERNARD MYERS first advertised as representing the "New York School" (advertisement, *Wagner Literary Magazine*). Having a prior claim on "school" membership, Berkson initially kept aloof from the new influx of younger poets, particularly TED BERRIGAN and his circle, who struck Berkson as rather "bumptious" (interview by Diggory). He learned to better appreciate the new work from students in his own classes at the New School (1964–70), including MICHAEL BROWNSTEIN, BERNADETTE MAYER, and PETER SCHJELDAHL. An electrifying reading by Berrigan at the POETRY PROJECT AT ST. MARK'S CHURCH IN-THE-BOWERY in 1967 further helped convert Berkson. Eventually, after he moved to 10th Street in late 1968, Berkson's apartment became a regular DOWNTOWN MANHATTAN gathering place for the younger poets, many of whom appeared in Berkson's "one shot" magazine *Best and Company* in 1969. When Berkson moved to BOLINAS, CALIFORNIA, in 1970, he maintained New York ties through personal contact with other poets who had moved west and through his new publishing venture, BIG SKY (1971–78).

Following the example of O'Hara, Ashbery, and JAMES SCHUYLER, Berkson educated himself in the world of contemporary visual arts by writing for *Art News* and other publications. As associate producer for the *Art New York* series for WNDT-TV in 1964, he arranged two shows in which O'Hara separately interviewed Barnett Newman and David Smith (Gooch 448), and he worked with O'Hara as a guest editor of the Museum of Modern Art. As a poet, Berkson COLLABORATED with PHILIP GUSTON (ENIGMA VARIATIONS, 1975) and Alex Katz (*Gloria*, 2005), as well as with the "in-house" artists of the second-generation poets, JOE BRAINARD and GEORGE SCHNEEMAN. In 1984 Berkson began teaching at the San Francisco Art Institute, and his art criticism once again began to appear on a regular basis. He has been a corresponding editor for *Art in America* and a regular contributor to *Artforum, Modern Painters,* and *American Craft.*

As of 2008, Berkson had published 15 books and pamphlets of poetry. His principal collections are *Blue Is the Hero: Poems, 1960–75* (L Publications, 1976) and *Serenade: Poetry and Prose, 1975–1989* (Zoland Books, 2000). *Portrait and Dream: New & Selected Poems* is scheduled for publication by Coffee House Press in 2009. *Publishers Weekly* described the work in *Serenade* as "evidence of the aesthetic cross-fertilization between 'late' New York School writing and the Language-centered avant-garde of the '70s and '80s," but added, "beyond such documentary value, the volume retains a jubilant contemporaneity and a dazzling verbal wit" (Review 82).

Bibliography

Advertisement for the New York School of Poets, Tibor de Nagy Editions. *Wagner Literary Magazine* 3 (1962): n.p., back section.

Berkson, Bill. "George's House of Mozart." In *Painter among Poets: The Collaborative Art of George Schneeman,* edited by Ron Padgett, 90–98. New York: Granary Books, 2004.

———. Interview by Robert Glück (2005). *Jacket* 29 (April 2006). Available online. URL: http://jacketmagazine.com/29/berk-gluc-iv.html. Accessed December 16, 2008.

———. Interview by Terence Diggory (2005).

———. *Sudden Address: Selected Lectures, 1981–2006.* Berkeley, Calif.: Cuneiform Press, 2007.

———. *The Sweet Singer of Modernism and Other Art Writings, 1985–2003.* Jamestown, R.I.: Qua Books, 2003.

———. "Working with Joe." *Modern Painters* 14, no. 3 (Autumn 2001): 62–65.

Berkson, Bill, and Bernadette Mayer. *What's Your Idea of a Good Time? Letter and Interviews, 1977–1985.* Berkeley, Calif.: Tuumba Press, 2006.

Berkson, Bill, and Frank O'Hara. *Hymns of St. Bridget and Other Writings.* Woodacre, Calif.: Owl Press, 2001.

Gooch, Brad. *City Poet: The Life and Times of Frank O'Hara.* New York: Knopf, 1993.

Gruen, John. *The Party's Over Now: Reminiscences of the Fifties.* Wainscott, N.Y.: Pushcart, 1989.

LeSueur, Joe. "The Bill Berkson Period." In *Digressions on Some Poems by Frank O'Hara: A Memoir.* New York: Farrar, Straus & Giroux, 2003, 233–239.

O'Hara, Frank. *The Collected Poems.* Rev. ed. Edited by Donald Allen. Berkeley: University of California Press, 1995.

Review of *Serenade. Publishers Weekly,* 24 April 2000, 82.

Berrigan, Anselm (1972–)

Anselm Berrigan is one of the most distinct voices to emerge from the NEW YORK SCHOOL in the late 1990s. Born in CHICAGO, he is the son of TED BERRIGAN and ALICE NOTLEY and the older brother of EDMUND BERRIGAN. He currently lives in NEW YORK CITY's East Village with the poet Karen Weiser. From 2003 to 2007 he served as artistic director of the POETRY PROJECT AT ST. MARK'S CHURCH IN-THE-BOWERY, after serving as program assistant and Monday Night Reading Series coordinator.

Although he cites his brother, Edmund, and his late stepfather, DOUGLAS OLIVER, as his biggest poetic influences (e-mail), his first full-length collection, *Integrity & Dramatic Life* (Edge, 1999), suggests a wider influence. In "WE WIN!" he writes: "I was on the phone / the other day & realized I could just as easily be writing a poem / so I hung up" (*Integrity* 63), mirroring FRANK O'HARA's "PERSONISM." The telephone becomes a constant image as Berrigan searches for pure correspondence in a world severely lacking integrity. The poem "Looking through a slant of light" is a recasting of the title poem in Ted Berrigan's *A CERTAIN SLANT OF SUNLIGHT,* itself a recasting of Emily Dickinson's "There's a Certain Slant of Light." In "Ghost town," he writes, "So much depends upon / three planes and a landing lane," echoing William Carlos Williams's "The Red Wheelbarrow," though he concludes, "What worked the other day fails this one" (*Integrity* 55). In his search for integrity, looking through the work of an older poet is ultimately not enough.

Berrigan claims that he has never willingly taken on the "New York School" moniker (e-mail),

and in his impressive second collection, *Zero Star Hotel* (Edge, 2002), he truly comes into his own. About the section "Zeros and Ones," he says, it "was written directly out of a process of copying the pages of Elastic Latitudes, a typewriter-written poem made entirely of the numbers 0 and 1, into duplicate lines with the numbers spelled out. By the end of each page I would be in a trance-like empty state and write what turned out to be all the poems in that middle section" (*Zero* iv). The book's centerpiece, *Zero Star Hotel,* a 35-page elegy for Oliver, is deeply moving. Composed of 10-line fragments arranged to resemble the windows of a French hotel, the poem syntactically approximates the mental process of memory and grief and feeling "bad at first / then a little better" (*Zero* 97). His other books include *On the Premises* (Gas, 1995); *They Beat Me Over the Head with a Sack* (Edge, 1998); *In the Dream Hole* (MAN, 2000), with Edmund Berrigan; and *Strangers in the Nest* (Dolphin Press/New Lights Press, 2002).

Bibliography

Berrigan, Anselm. E-mail correspondence with Nick Moudry. 23 and 26 October 2003.

———. *Integrity & Dramatic Life.* Washington, D.C.: Edge Books, 1999.

———. *Zero Star Hotel.* Washington, D.C.: Edge Books, 2002.

Dickinson, Emily. No. 258 ["There's a Certain Slant of light"]. In *The Complete Poems.* Edited by Thomas H. Johnson. Boston: Little, Brown & Company, 1960, 118–119.

Williams, William Carlos. "The Red Wheelbarrow" (1923). In *The Collected Poems,* vol. 1: *1909–1939.* Edited by A. Walton Litz and Christopher MacGowan. New York: New Directions, 1986, 224.

Berrigan, Edmund (1974–)

The younger of ALICE NOTLEY and TED BERRIGAN's two sons, Edmund Berrigan was born in Colchester, England, where his father had accepted a year-long teaching appointment at the University of Essex. Shortly thereafter, the family returned to the United States, where Berrigan was raised in NEW YORK CITY, in and around the POETRY PROJECT AT ST. MARK'S CHURCH IN-THE-BOWERY. His childhood was interrupted by the death of his father in 1983, and again by the death of his half-sister, Kate, five years later. Berrigan began attending poetry readings when he was an infant and started writing poems as soon as he was able to read and write. He gave his first public reading before he had turned 10 and gave several other readings before the age of 15. During his childhood Berrigan took writing workshops with NEW YORK SCHOOL luminaries, and, with his parents, traveled frequently to Boulder, Colorado, for NAROPA INSTITUTE's Summer Writing Program. His parents, however, were his first and most important writing instructors. Through them Berrigan had contact with not only all of the major New York School writers but also such figures as ROBERT CREELEY, PHILIP WHALEN, Leslie Scalapino, and ALLEN GINSBERG. Berrigan attended the State University of New York–Purchase from 1991 to 1995, receiving his B.A. in literature. For the three years that followed, Berrigan lived in San Francisco and then returned to New York City in 1999. In addition to writing poems, Berrigan is also a musician, playing guitar in the loosely formed group I Feel Tractor.

Berrigan's work, while informed by and situated within New York School traditions, in many ways operates outside those traditions. While he maintains the lyricism and humor of his predecessors—as well as their "charm" and "moral force," the potent combination that Notley finds in FRANK O'HARA (8)—Berrigan has also absorbed the attention to the materiality of language characteristic of the Language poets (LANGUAGE POETRY), among others. Among his own brief list of influences are JACK KEROUAC, Kathy Acker, Dylan Thomas, JAMES SCHUYLER, Laura (Riding) Jackson, Will Alexander, ELENI SIKELIANOS, and, more recently, the later work of Paul Celan. Berrigan is the author of several chapbooks and one full-length collection, *Disarming Matter* (Owl Press, 1999). With Notley and his brother, the poet ANSELM BERRIGAN, Berrigan coedited *The Collected Poems of Ted Berrigan* (University of California Press, 2005) and is currently editing a collection of poems by Steve Carey.

Bibliography

Berrigan, Edmund. *Disarming Matter.* Woodacre, Calif.: Owl Press, 1999.

Berrigan, Ted. *The Collected Poems of Ted Berrigan.* Edited by Alice Notley, Anselm Berrigan, and Edmund Berrigan. Berkeley, Calif.: University of California Press, 2005.

Notley, Alice. "O'Hara in the Nineties" (1996). In *Coming After: Essays on Poetry.* Ann Arbor: University of Michigan Press, 2005, 3–14.

Berrigan, Sandy (Sandra Alper) (1942–)

In 1962, at the age of 19, Sandra Alper was swept up into the world of poetry in the most romantic fashion, by eloping with TED BERRIGAN after spending a weekend with him at Tulane University in New Orleans, Louisiana, where she was a student and Ted was visiting another student, his friend DICK GALLUP. Alper was born in Detroit, Michigan, but moved with her parents in 1956 to Miami, Florida, which she hated, so she was eager for escape when she met Ted. The bohemian existence the couple led in NEW YORK CITY was strained by poverty (Clark 27–29) but enlivened by family ties that extended from their two children, David (1963–) and Kate (1965–87), to the young poets whom Ted delighted in taking under his wing (Saroyan 136–137). The life that Sandy and Ted built together led to the creation of poems that are "domestic in a certain way," as Ted elaborated with respect to his own work: "[T]hey're involved with love and friendship, the rituals of daily life" (Ted Berrigan, interview 84). Sandy's first book of poems is entitled *Daily Rites* (Telephone, 1974), with cover and illustrations by Paula North. It was published, however, six years after her marriage with Ted had ended and two years after she had moved to the northern California coast, where she still resides, in the small town of Albion, some 140 miles north of the "poets' commune" in BOLINAS.

Sandy "began writing at the urging of Ted" (questionnaire n.p.), but her poems are very different from his. Rather than the "harum scarum haze on the [Jackson] Pollock streets" (Ted Berrigan, Sonnet XIX 39), Sandy's reflect the meditative calm of "Blue sky and quilt cover," a line from an untitled poem in her second collection *Summer Sleeper* (Telephone, 1981; cover by Sophia Sutherland). Quilting and gardening—an occasion for getting under the "blue sky"—are two of her favorite activities, and both inform the patterns of her poetry, as does her passion for DANCE, appropriately represented in GEORGE SCHEENMAN's cover illustration for the privately printed *Public Display of Affection* (1987). However, as she states explicitly in the poem "Sunday" from that volume, Berrigan also responds directly to "word order." Her sense of "my own linguistics," as she calls it, has evidently been heightened by contact with West Coast Language poets such as Carla Harryman (1952–) and Lyn Hejinian (1941–), both of whom are invoked by name in this collection. The support of MAUREEN OWEN, Berrigan's publisher (in TELEPHONE magazine and books) as well as collaborator ("Hey Ted"), is frequently acknowledged throughout Berrigan's work. She has also collaborated recently with Pat Nolan (1943–) in the composition of renku, the Japanese linked-verse FORM.

In a recent collection as yet unpublished, entitled *Love in a Mist*, the English poet LEE HARWOOD emerges as a kind of muse figure for Berrigan. They had first met during Harwood's residence in New York during the 1960s, and a love affair began when Berrigan visited England in 1971 (she figures in Harwood's poem of that year entitled "Qasida") A resumption of the affair during the 1980s led to series of poems by each of them: for instance, Harwood's "György Kurtág Meets Sandy Berrigan," "Gilded White," and "The Wind Rises: Istvan Martha Meets Sandy Berrigan"; Berrigan's "A Word" and "Fancy That," both dedicated "for Lee" (*Public Display of Affection*). In *Love in a Mist*, however, the figure of Harwood merges so completely with the English landscape that he becomes a quasi-mythological figure, "the green man." *Love in a Mist* subtitled *English Journey/A Summer Pastoral*, becomes Berrigan's means of revisiting not only a former love but the English pastoral tradition, perhaps her clearest point of departure from the "urban pastoral" of the NEW YORK SCHOOL.

Bibliography

Berrigan, Sandy. Questionnaire response for *Encyclopedia of the New York School Poets*. 19 January 2006.
———. "Sandy's Believe It or Not: A Few Aspects of My Friendship with Joe [Brainard]." *Pressed Wafer 2* (March 2001): 159–162.
Berrigan, Ted. Interview by Ralph Hawkins (1974). In *Talking in Tranquility: Interviews*. Edited by Stephen Ratcliffe and Leslie Scalapino. Bolinas, Calif.: Avenue B; Oakland, Calif.: O Books, 1991, 73–89.
———. "Letter to Sandra Alper Berrigan" (1962). In *Nice to See You: Homage to Ted Berrigan*, edited by Anne Waldman, 3–6. Minneapolis, Minn.: Coffee House Press, 1991.
———. "Sonnet XIX" (1964). In *The Collected Poems of Ted Berrigan*. Edited by Alice Notley, Anselm Berrigan, and Edmund Berrigan. Berkeley: University of California Press, 2005, 39.
———. "Words for Love" (ca. 1963). In *The Collected Poems of Ted Berrigan*. Edited by Alice Notley, Anselm Berrigan, and Edmund Berrigan. Berkeley: University of California Press, 2005, 15–16.
Clark, Tom. *Late Returns: A Memoir of Ted Berrigan*. Bolinas, Calif.: Tombouctou, 1985.
Harwood, Lee. *Collected Poems, 1964–2004*. Exeter, U.K.: Shearsman, 2004.
Owen, Maureen, and Sandy Berrigan. "Hey Ted" (1983). In *Nice to See You: Homage to Ted Berrigan*, edited by Anne Waldman, 172–173. Minneapolis, Minn.: Coffee House Press, 1991.
Saroyan, Aram. "A Personal Memoir" (1983). In *Nice to See You: Homage to Ted Berrigan*, edited by Anne Waldman, 135–138. Minneapolis, Minn.: Coffee House Press, 1991.

Berrigan, Ted (1934–1983)

Edmund Joseph (Ted) Berrigan was born in PROVIDENCE, RHODE ISLAND, in 1934 and died in NEW YORK CITY on July 4, 1983. He was among the most celebrated of the second-generation NEW YORK SCHOOL poets, and largely through his works and instruction, the poetics associated with the New York School passed to a third and fourth generation. His first wife was SANDY BERRIGAN, with whom he had two children, David and Kate. His second wife was the poet ALICE NOTLEY. Their children are the poets ANSELM and EDMUND BERRIGAN.

Ted attended Providence College, served in the U.S. Army in Korea, and completed his B.A. and M.A. at the University of Tulsa, in Oklahoma. In Tulsa he met the poets RON PADGETT and DICK GALLUP and the artist and poet JOE BRAINARD. All four moved to New York and joined DAVID

SHAPIRO, ANNE WALDMAN, TONY TOWLE, and BILL BERKSON, among others, in constituting the second generation of the New York School.

In 1963 Berrigan founded "C" magazine and "C" Press, both of which became important venues for avant-garde writing in the 1960s. His first book was *The SONNETS* (1964), republished in 1966, 1982, and 2000; it remains his best-known book. Among his numerous other publications (all poetry except where noted) are *Living with Chris* (1965), *Many Happy Returns* (1969), *Peace* (1969), *Train Ride* (1971), *The Drunken Boat* (1974), *A Feeling for Leaving* (1975), *Red Wagon* (1976), CLEAR THE RANGE (novel, 1977), *Nothing for You* (1977), *Carrying a Torch* (1980), *In a Blue River* (1981), *A CERTAIN SLANT OF SUNLIGHT* (1988), *Talking in Tranquility* (interviews, 1991), and *On the Level Everyday* (talks and interview, 1997). He also collaborated on several works, including *Seventeen* (1964), *Some Things* (1966), BEAN SPASMS (1967), and *NOH* (1969), all with Padgett; *Doubletalk* (1969) with ANSELM HOLLO; MEMORIAL DAY (1971) with Waldman; *Back in Boston Again* (1972) with TOM CLARK and Padgett; and *Yo-Yo's with Money* (1979) with HARRIS SCHIFF. His poems were collected in *So Going around Cities: New & Selected Poems, 1958–1979* (1980) and *The Collected Poems of Ted Berrigan* (2005). His *Selected Poems*, edited by ARAM SAROYAN, was published in 1994.

Wherever Berrigan lived—England, CHICAGO, New York's Lower East Side—his home soon became a gathering place for young writers interested in New York School poetics. From 1968 until his death he taught writing workshops at the POETRY PROJECT AT ST. MARK'S CHURCH IN-THE-BOWERY as well as at colleges and universities, including the IOWA WRITERS' WORKSHOP, the University of Michigan at Ann Arbor, Yale, the NAROPA INSTITUTE, the University of Essex in England, the Stevens Institute of Technology, the City University of New York, and others; some of his lectures were transcribed and published in *On the Level Everyday* (1997). That book, in turn, helped pass New York School poetics to a new generation.

Berrigan began writing in the 1960s, a time of crisis for the romantic notion of the author as a creator rather than merely as a craftsman. In a much discussed essay, "The Death of the Author"

(1968), Roland Barthes argued that a text should be seen not as "the 'message' of the Author-God" but as "a fabric of quotations, resulting from a thousand sources of culture" (1968). Writers who accepted Barthes's position were among those who believed that the tradition of lyric poetry had ended. Language was a communal rather than a personal instrument, they insisted, and it was language itself, not the writer, that spoke in the poem. Intimations of the poet's subjective presence in the work were denied or treated ironically. As Ron Silliman wrote in the introduction to his anthology, *In the American Tree* (1986), poets would now "look . . . at what a poem is actually made of—not images, not voice, not characters or plot, all of which appear on paper, or in one's mouth, only through the invocation of a specific medium, language itself" (xvi). "Language writers" such as Bruce Andrews and Barrett Watten adopted this position in their own works and defended it in their critical writings, and it soon dominated much of the more adventurous and innovative poetry written and published in the United States in the 1970s and 1980s.

A collage of materials drawn from his own poems and his readings of works such as by JOHN ASHBERY and FRANK O'HARA, Berrigan's *Sonnets* might at first seem a harbinger of this movement. In fact, however, the author's subjectivity is always present, selecting and arranging the phrases to include, and the bits and scraps of language and quotations from various sources merge in works that are anything but a random or impersonal juxtaposition of words. In his "Sonnet Workshop" at the Poetry Project, Berrigan told his students that he had begun the book by selecting six of his earlier works that he thought "were not bad poems, but . . . [not] really successful enough," although they contained things he liked. He would look at one of these poems until he found a line that would "resonate" (Berrigan, *On the Level* 95). He would type that into the new poem and turn to another of the older works for the next line, and so forth, until he had borrowed from all six. Then he reversed the process, going backward through the pile of poems until he had 12 lines. "And by the time I had done that," he said, "I already knew what the final two [lines] would be, and that's how I made the first sonnet. I made some others like that too, and then again there are many I wrote straight through, all the way" (Berrigan, *On the Level* 95).

The words and lines that went into the sonnets contained the stamp of his personality. Even when the lines were drawn from other texts, they were integrated into the new poems not in some impersonal or ironic way but rather as instances of what the poet, for whatever personal reason, found amusing or engaging. Thus, he concluded his "Sonnet Workshop" by insisting that "my poems are about what happens to me in my life as I see it or imagine it or fantasize it or do whatever. The 'I' that I'm about, the 'me,' is just a person in this world. I . . . write my poems . . . about 'me' Ted Berrigan" (Berrigan, *On the Level* 96).

By saying this, Berrigan placed himself in opposition to the Language writers. He reasserted that poetry, or at least his own poetry, was essentially lyrical. Language was the medium for poetry, but it was not its subject. Berrigan was not advocating the lyricism of confessional poetry with its roots in psychological notions of personality but rather Frank O'Hara's "PERSONISM," in which abstraction and theory are jettisoned and the work becomes a matter "between two persons instead of two pages" (499). Berrigan's later poems, including such often reprinted and anthologized works as "Things to Do in Providence," "Red Shift," and "A Certain Slant of Sunlight," are unmistakably lyrical and personal. He could insist, as he did in a workshop transcribed for *On the Level Everyday,* that "poems are just the words" (25), but he viewed words as inextricable from the poet who spoke them. As he wrote in "Red Shift," "I'm only pronouns, & I am all of them. . . ."

Bibliography
Barthes, Roland. "The Death of the Author" (1968). Translated by Stephen Heath. *The Norton Anthology of Theory and Criticism.* Edited by Vincent B. Leach. New York: Norton, 2001, 1,466–1,470.
Berrigan, Ted. *The Collected Poems of Ted Berrigan.* Edited by Alice Notley with Anselm Berrigan and Edmund Berrigan. Berkeley: University of California Press, 2005.
———. *On the Level Everyday: Selected Talks on Poetry and the Art of Living.* Edited by Joel Lewis. Jersey City, N.J.: Talisman House, 1997.
Clark, Tom. *Late Returns: A Memoir of Ted Berrigan.* Bolinas, Calif.: Tombouctou, 1985.
Fischer, Aaron. *Ted Berrigan: An Annotated Checklist.* New York: Granary Books, 1998.
Foster, Edward. *Code of the West: A Memoir of Ted Berrigan.* Boulder, Colo.: Rodent Press, 1994.
Hornick, Lita. *The Green Fuse.* New York: Giorno Poetry Systems, 1989.
Lehman, David. *The Last Avant-Garde: The Making of the New York School of Poets.* New York: Doubleday, 1998.
Myles, Eileen. *The Chelsea Girls.* Black Sparrow Press, Los Angeles, Calif. 1994.
Notley, Alice. Introduction to *Selected Poems,* by Ted Berrigan. New York: Viking/Penguin, 1994.
O'Hara, Frank. "Personism" (1959). In *The Collected Poems of Frank O'Hara.* Rev. ed. Edited by Donald Allen. Berkeley: University of California Press, 1995, 498–499.
Padgett, Ron. *Ted: A Personal Memoir of Ted Berrigan.* Great Barrington, Mass.: The Figures, 1993.
Rifkin, Libbie. *Career Moves: Olson, Creeley, Zukofsky, Berrigan, and the American Avant-Garde.* Madison: University of Wisconsin Press, 2000.
Saroyan, Aram. *Friends in the World: The Education of a Writer.* Minneapolis, Minn.: Coffee House Press, 1992.
Silliman, Ron. "Language, Realism, Poetry." *In the American Tree,* edited by Ron Silliman, xv–xxiii. Orono: National Poetry Foundation/University of Maine at Orono, 1986.
Waldman, Anne, ed. *Nice To See You: Homage to Ted Berrigan.* Minneapolis, Minn.: Coffee House Press, 1991.

Beyond Baroque (1968–　)
Founded in 1968 in Venice, California, as an avant-garde literary magazine, Beyond Baroque developed into an arts center that has become best known for its poetry readings and workshops. George Drury Smith, its founder, was a high school English teacher who used a small inheritance to buy a large, run-down storefront on West Washington Boulevard. He converted a portion of it into a print shop that he used to produce the magazine, and opened the rest to the public. Two poets, Joseph Hansen and John Harris, started a free workshop

on Wednesday nights that is still running. Directors of the workshop have included Jim Krusoe, Jack Grapes, Michelle T. Clinton, and Bob Flanagan.

By the early 1970s a reading series on Friday night began attracting overflow audiences, and *Beyond Baroque* magazine split into two entities, *NewLetters* and *New*. The former concentrated on experimental prose and poetry, while the latter featured a blend of old and young poets on the West Coast. Along with the POETRY PROJECT AT ST. MARK'S CHURCH IN-THE-BOWERY, Beyond Baroque has endured as an example of a poetry community directly evolving out of the idealism of the counterculture of the 1960s. It should be noted, though, that in contrast to the Poetry Project, Beyond Baroque received no grant support whatsoever until 1974, and only very modest support during the last six years that its founder led the organization. Subsequent directors, including Manazar Gamboa, Jocelyn Fisher, Dennis Phillips, and D. B. Finnegan, struggled with constantly fluctuating budgets, and the organization nearly folded in both the mid-1980s and mid-1990s.

Both the NEW YORK SCHOOL of poets and poets affiliated with Beyond Baroque were vigorous participants in the small press movement that flourished in the 1970s in the United States. (Contrary to widespread misconception, M.F.A. programs were not the centrifuge of AMERICAN POETRY during the 1970s.) One distinguishing trait of Beyond Baroque as an alternative literary center, however, is that it incorporated a typesetting center, NewComp Graphics, into the services it provided to the literary community, which by the late 1970s had become larger than the original building could accommodate. A nearby two-story building on Venice Boulevard, the Venice City Hall, became available at that time, and by October 1979 Beyond Baroque had moved its rapidly expanding small press library, typesetting equipment, and magazine operations into its new home, where it has remained. DENNIS COOPER took over the reading series from James Krusoe shortly after the move to the new building and, with the help of the first substantial grants Beyond Baroque had ever received, significantly expanded the scope of the reading series. In particular, he emphasized poets from the New York School as well

as Language writers. Subsequent directors of the reading series include Benjamin Weissman, Tosh Berman, and Fred Dewey, who has served as artistic director of Beyond Baroque since 1995. Dewey has also revived the book publishing projects of Beyond Baroque, which began in the mid-1970s with collections by poets such as MAXINE CHERNOFF, K. Curds Lyie, and Eloise Klein Healy.

Big City Primer John Yau and Bill Barrette (1991)

New York is the "Big City" presented by poet JOHN YAU and photographer Bill Barrette (1947–) in *Big City Primer* (Timken Publishers, 1991), but the climate of NEW YORK CITY has chilled considerably since EDWIN DENBY and RUDOLPH BURCKHARDT's 1948 COLLABORATION, establishing a NEW YORK SCHOOL GENRE, *IN PUBLIC, IN PRIVATE*. The city that Denby and Burckhardt celebrate is a setting for human interaction and its verbal medium is human speech. Yau and Barrette present a city that has swallowed up its inhabitants, "like a vast jaw," an image from Yau's final poem, echoed in the accompanying photograph by a long, heavy cloud that seems about to clamp down on the city's skyline. Typically, Barrette's photographs, all in black and white, do not show people. Yau's language achieves a comparable dehumanization by calling attention to itself through writing, removed from the human presence of living speech, brought down from poetic heights to the street level of prose. The condition described is typically postmodern, including the tendency to view the general decay represented in the book as the product of representation itself rather than of socioeconomic or natural forces. With self-conscious irony a poem entitled "Camera" is accompanied by a photograph of the Camera family tomb in a Queens cemetery.

The close correspondence between text and photograph in specific details suggests that Yau composed the poems in response to the photographs. This impression is reinforced by the format, which pairs each poem with a photograph on a facing page, each 10 inches square (the sole exception is the text of "Permanent and Temporary," which runs across two pages). In all, there are 33 poems but 90 photographs, as intervening pages present series of photographs without text, grouped thematically: cars and trucks (typically derelict), bridges, office buildings and factories, religious buildings, entertainment buildings, government buildings, libraries and schools, houses and apartment buildings, hospitals and clinics, memorials, and gravesites. The subjects are deliberately ordinary; except for the frontispiece showing the Brooklyn Bridge, none of the photographs presents a major New York landmark, at least not in an iconic view. Although the sequence of themes suggests a narrative progression, in general the book's orderliness seems arbitrary, like the order of the alphabet implied in the notion of a "primer" and signaled in the titles of some of the poems (presented out of order): "F Is for Forecast," "A Is for Automobile," "L Is for Lodge," "D Is for Diagnosis." Within the poems, arbitrary sequence lends a surreal air to the imagery. In a parody of Walt Whitman, Yau addresses a "City of prose, fantasy, and / automatic fire" ("First and Last Views" [1]).

Bibliography

Friedman, B. H. "Always Street-Smart." *American Book Review* 14, no. 4 (October–November 1992): 20,

Hales, Peter B. "Photography," *New York Times Book Review,* 1 December 1991, 22.

Big Sky (1971–1978)

The most important publishing venture linking the NEW YORK SCHOOL poets to the arts community in BOLINAS, CALIFORNIA, Big Sky was launched by BILL BERKSON in 1971, the year after he moved to Bolinas. Just as the mimeograph machine at the POETRY PROJECT AT ST. MARK'S CHURCH IN-THE-BOWERY, in NEW YORK CITY, served multiple purposes, an old multilith printer in a redwood shed in Bolinas was understood to be at the disposal of the community and produced many publications, including the first copies of *Big Sky* magazine and Big Sky books. Initially, Berkson approached the magazine in the spirit of inclusiveness with which he had edited *Best and Company* (1969), an anthology published in New York. However, a magazine proved to require a firmer editorial hand to preserve its identity over several issues. After two "chaotic" issues, Berkson focused the third issue

(1972) on the work of CLARK COOLIDGE, producing "the best introduction to Coolidge's excellence," according to Richard Kostelanetz (135). The fourth issue (1972) returned to a multi-author format, but Berkson felt he "hit [his] stride" as an editor with a selection anchored in "especially powerful contributions by [Robert] Creeley, Ron Padgett and Bernadette Mayer" (183). Publication of *Big Sky* concluded with a double issue (nos. 11–12, 1978) devoted to FRANK O'HARA, reissued in revised form as the Big Sky book *Homage to Frank O'Hara* (1988), now established as an indispensable document for O'Hara scholarship.

The main run of Big Sky books, including more than 20 titles, extends from JOE BRAINARD's *Bolinas Journal* (1971) to TOM VEITCH's *Death College and Other Poems* (1976). Two especially notable volumes of 1975, Coolidge's *Polaroid* and BERNADETTE MAYER's *Studying Hunger,* were published in collaboration with LARRY FAGIN's ADVENTURES IN POETRY; Big Sky also issued collaborative poems by Berkson and Fagin, *Two Serious Poems and One Other* (1971), and Fagin's solo pamphlet, *Seven Poems* (1976). Berkson's ENIGMA VARIATIONS (1975) includes a cover and a series of drawings by PHILIP GUSTON, part of an extended exchange with the artist that is also represented in issues 4 and 5 of *Big Sky* magazine and in the cover of a Big Sky book by David Anderson, *The Spade in the Sensorium* (1974). The cartoon quality of Guston's work during this period was well matched to the sensibility that Berkson sought to evoke at Big Sky. "My original concept was a comic-book format, which was impractical for small print runs," Berkson explains, "so I held to something like comic-book size" (183). "Underground" cartoonist Greg Irons (1947–84) provided the cover for the first issue of *Big Sky* magazine and for the Big Sky books *Tales of Virtue and Transformation,* by Jim Gustafson (1974), and *Blues of the Egyptian Kings,* by JIM BRODEY (1975). Irons's frequent collaborator in comics, Veitch, suggested the title for *Big Sky,* based on the 1968 song of the same title by the British rock group The Kinks.

Bibliography

Berkson, Bill. Statement in *A Secret Location on the Lower East Side: Adventures in Writing, 1960–1980,* edited by Steven Clay and Rodney Phillips, 183. New York: New York Public Library/Granary Books, 1998.

Kostelanetz, Richard. "The New Poetries" (1973). In *The Old Poetries and the New*. Ann Arbor: University of Michigan Press, 1981, 121–149.

Opstedal, Kevin. "A Literary History of the San Andreas Fault: Bolinas Section." *Jack Magazine* 1, no. 3 (2001). Available online. URL: http://www.jackmagazine.com/issue3/renhist.html. Accessed December 16, 2008.

Biography Barbara Guest (1980)

In her nine-part sequence of poems, *Biography*, BARBARA GUEST reflects on the experience of writing her biography HERSELF DEFINED: THE POET H.D. AND HER WORLD (1984). The poems do not refer to H.D. directly, though her presence can be detected in a keyword, "a word like Egypt" (Number 3), or a set of images, "whorlshell Shade" (Number 9). Guest seems to be interested in involving the reader in the activity of detection, one of the principal activities of the biographer. A complementary activity, as Guest practices the art, is what she calls "introspection" (Number 1). As the biographer comes to identify with her subject, she can conduct research, so to speak, through self-examination. However, the self in this case is a fictional construction, a composite figure rather than a "natural" identity. What is "natural" comes under critical scrutiny in Guest's poems, along with the relationship to nature that we call "knowledge." Guest recognizes "an urge / really to 'know'" (Number 3), yet the quotation marks she places around the verb leave in doubt the possibility of fulfilling the urge. "Biography," she writes, "is a dubious route" (Number 8), meaning it is alive with doubt.

In contrast to the urge to know scientifically, Guest posits a mode of intuition leading to experience that might be called "supernatural." As in H.D.'s work, "the Angel descends" in *Biography* (Number 5). However, Guest performs a distinctive twist on H.D.'s mysticism, a difference that makes Guest a key link in the chain that connects NEW YORK SCHOOL poetry to LANGUAGE POETRY. In Guest, supernatural experience does not enter the text from beyond but rather arises from the activity of language itself: "When we foundered in the labyrinth of word / puns set like traps, and when the

first Angel . . ." (Number 2). Any word is haunted by other words, the essential condition of the pun. Studying the words of her subject, the biographer feels haunted by the subject's voice. *Biography* is both an invocation and an exorcism of that haunting. As much as she enjoys the act of identification, Guest also feels "a need to escape so we breathed separately" (Number 4).

Biography was first published in 1980 by BERNADETTE MAYER and LEWIS WARSH in their magazine *United Artists* (Number 10) and issued later the same year as a separate chapbook by Burning Deck Press. It was reprinted in *H.D.: Woman and Poet* (1986), excerpted in *Signets: Reading H.D.* (1990), and was finally collected in *The Collected Poems of Barbara Guest* (Wesleyan University Press, 2008).

Bibliography

Friedman, Susan Stanford. "H.D." *Contemporary Literature* 26, no. 1 (Spring 1985): 107–113.

Guest, Barbara. "The Intimacy of Biography." *Iowa Review* 16, no. 3 (Fall 1986): 58–71.

"Biotherm" Frank O'Hara (1962)

The method of fragmentation identified with modernist art and literature reaches an end and a new, postmodernist beginning in FRANK O'HARA's "Biotherm," "his last great poem and one of the important poems of the sixties," according to the critic Marjorie Perloff (178). While T. S. Eliot declared in *The Waste Land* (1922), "These fragments I have shored against my ruins" (50), the fragments in "Biotherm" are simply "shored," that is, washed up like so much driftwood on the shore of the "ego-ridden sea" (*Collected Poems* 448). O'Hara bids good riddance to ego; he has no desire to "shore it up." However, as "Biotherm" conveys through its highly charged verbal energy, O'Hara has plenty of sexual desire, in contrast to the failure of desire that renders the waste land sterile for Eliot. "Biotherm" is a love poem addressed to BILL BERKSON, whose heterosexuality prevented the two men from sharing their love physically. But as poets who lived partly in language, they formed an intimate relationship through the "stylish alacrity" of camp speech (Berkson, "Air" 11)—spoken through a mask, simultaneously denying what it appears to affirm, refusing to be pinned down to any "true" meaning. The line "I am a woman in love," which appears toward the end of "Biotherm" (*Collected Poems* 447), was Berkson's response ("delivered in Garboesque accent") when JOHN ASHBERY, having drinks with Berkson and O'Hara in Paris, asked what was going on between them (Berkson, "Air" 11). For over a year prior to this encounter (in October 1961), Berkson and O'Hara had been exchanging poems with titles based on some variant of the office memo heading "F.Y.I" (For Your Information). One of the working titles that O'Hara assigned to "Biotherm" was "M.L.F.Y" (My Love for You).

The title finally assigned to "Biotherm" is the name of an expensive "after sun" skin lotion, "which Bill's mother fortunately left around," O'Hara explained in a letter to DONALD M. ALLEN (*Collected Poems* 554). It belongs to a set of beach references running throughout the poem (Perloff 174), but to ground the poem's mobility in a particular setting is no more appropriate than to harmonize its many tones in the voice of a single "ego." None of the imagery in "Biotherm" is symbolic in the traditional sense; each word is a verbal gesture, as in ACTION PAINTING, and its function is to keep the action moving—a key principle that O'Hara shares with the "PROJECTIVE VERSE" of CHARLES OLSON, who admired "Biotherm" (Olson 178). O'Hara was delighted to report that the poem, begun as a celebration of Berkson's birthday in August 1961, was "still going" when he wrote to Allen in September (*Collected Poems* 554). He did not stop writing the poem until January 1962. The title of "Biotherm" signals the process of writing rather than its meaning. Just as the skin of the body absorbs the ingredients of the skin lotion—including "plankton" (*Collected Poems* 448), an ingredient that seems to have struck O'Hara as delightfully incongruous—so the many disparate references in the poem have been *absorbed*—the poem's concluding word—in its "skin," which is thus continually revitalized. The implication of a poem having a skin is part of its sexual charge as well as its aesthetic context. The visual art with which O'Hara was most closely aligned emphasized surface rather than depth, as in JASPER JOHNS's "Skin with O'Hara Poem" (1963–65).

Because "Biotherm" seems simply to have discarded "all referential frameworks of meaning" (Molesworth 88) or to admit "only gradually" the reader into the framework (Perloff 178), the poem has received relatively little critical attention. The most extended reading, by Mutlu Konuk Blasing, draws on psycholinguistic theory to supply a depth that runs counter to the poem's insistence on surface, not to mention the poet's lack of interest in probing the unconscious (Berkson, "O'Hara" 230). On the other hand, "Biotherm" is "still going," as O'Hara experienced it, in a succession of later poems and art works that take O'Hara's poem as a starting point and move off in a variety of directions. According to ALICE NOTLEY, TED BERRIGAN took off from "Biotherm" to produce the "open form" of TAMBOURINE LIFE (677), a touchstone of the second-generation NEW YORK SCHOOL. For the Language poets (see LANGUAGE POETRY), too, "Biotherm" has supplied a standard of measurement, as when Barrett Watten praises Lisa Samuels's *The Seven Voices* (O Books, 1998) on the book's cover for "some of the most evocative spatial allegories for meaning since Frank O'Hara's 'Biotherm.'" In 1990 Arion Press published an edition of "Biotherm" with 42 lithographs by JIM DINE and an essay by Berkson. Dine's account of his process echoes O'Hara's account of producing the poem, though Dine worked even more quickly: "I pinned mylar on the walls of my studio that summer and simply responded to Frank's text in a free associative way as it came up in the poem. It was done in less than a week and poured out of me the way images flash for one when the engine is stoked" (interview n.p.).

Bibliography

Berkson, Bill. "Air and Such: An Essay on *Biotherm*." In *Biotherm*, by Frank O'Hara, 8–13. Lithographs by Jim Dine. San Francisco: Arion Press, 1990.

———. "Frank O'Hara and His Poems" (1967, 1969). In *Frank O'Hara: To Be True to a City*, edited by Jim Elledge, 226–233. Ann Arbor: University of Michigan Press, 1990.

Blasing, Mutlu Konuk. "Frank O'Hara: The Speech of Poetry" (1987). In *Frank O'Hara: To Be True to a City*, edited by Jim Elledge, 301–320. Ann Arbor: University of Michigan Press, 1990.

Dine, Jim. "Interview with Artist Jim Dine," by Jed Birmingham. 14 November 2007. RealityStudio. org. Available online. URL: http://realitystudio.org/ bibliographic-bunker/bunker-interviews/interview-with-artist-jim-dine/. Accessed December 16, 2008.

Eliot, T. S. *The Waste Land*. In *The Complete Poems and Plays, 1909–1950*. New York: Harcourt, Brace & World, 1971, 37–55.

Molesworth, Charles. *The Fierce Embrace: A Study of Contemporary American Poetry*. Columbia: University of Missouri Press, 1979.

Notley, Alice. Note on Ted Berrigan, *Tambourine Life*. In *The Collected Poems of Ted Berrigan*. Edited by Alice Notley, Anselm Berrigan, and Edmund Berrigan. Berkeley: University of California Press, 2005, 676–677.

O'Hara, Frank. *The Collected Poems*. Rev. ed. Edited by Donald Allen. Berkeley: University of California Press, 1995.

Olson, Charles. "Note" (1969). In *Homage to Frank O'Hara*, edited by Bill Berkson and Joe LeSueur, 178. Bolinas, Calif.: Big Sky, 1988.

Perloff, Marjorie. *Frank O'Hara: Poet Among Painters*. 1977. Reprint, Chicago: University of Chicago Press, 1998.

Bishop, Elizabeth (1911–1979)

To a certain extent the NEW YORK SCHOOL poets formed themselves in opposition to the young writers who dominated the poetic mainstream in the years just after World War II, those "trembling" academics of the "Poem Society" whom KENNETH KOCH satirizes in "FRESH AIR." Elizabeth Bishop was a close friend and colleague of such key members of the society as Randall Jarrell and ROBERT LOWELL and, thus, "an establishment poet," as JOHN ASHBERY notes, and yet, he adds, one for whom "the establishment ought to give thanks; she is proof that it can't be all bad" ("Throughout" 120). Ashbery has recalled how he "read, reread, studied and absorbed Miss Bishop's first book" ("Throughout" 122), *North and South*, when it came out in 1946, and his admiration for her work deepened over time. In 1997 Ashbery gave a public reading of his favorite Bishop poem, "Over 2000 Illustrations and a Complete Concordance." "When he reached the last stanza," DAVID LEHMAN reports, "he cried" (134).

What might Ashbery's attachment to this establishment poet tell us about his own complex attitude toward the literary establishment? Both poets cite as early influences Wallace Stevens, W. H. AUDEN, and Marianne Moore (who became Bishop's lifelong friend and mentor), both have a surrealist streak, and both spent extended periods of their lives in self-imposed exile (Ashbery in Paris and Bishop in Brazil) that reinforced their sense of themselves as cultural outsiders. Still, Bishop's plain, pure diction and deceptively straightforward descriptions of scenes imagined and observed would seem to have little in common with Ashbery's mongrel rhetorics and rapidly shifting ground. Yet both are stringently impersonal and anti-expressive (in ways that set them apart from peers like Lowell and FRANK O'HARA) while remaining poets of the inner life. As Ashbery puts it, he and Bishop are in the same "quandary": For them, "it is not a dualistic conflict between inner and outer reality; it is rather a question of deciding how much the outer reality is our reality, how far we can advance into it and still keep a toe-hold on the inner, private one" ("Throughout" 121). Their ambivalent relationship to "outer reality" is the source both of their poems' somewhat specialized appeal—Ashbery famously called Bishop "a writer's writer's writer"—and of their personal reticence, a reticence always in tension with a powerful ambition to establish themselves as major poets.

Bishop's ambition was perhaps better hidden than Ashbery's, and certain traits—her penchant for self-corrections and parenthetical asides, her reliance on "mere" description—have led critics such as Howard Moss, JOHN KOETHE, and Michael Hoffman to compare her to the similarly "modest" JAMES SCHUYLER. Bishop herself felt an affinity with Schuyler, liked O'Hara's work, and responded to Ashbery's admiration in kind (*One Art*, 371, 572; Lehman, 255, 355). Her influence on the group can be felt more generally in that "the horrid appearance of sestinas in our midst," as Schuyler termed it, "can be traced directly, by way of John Ashbery's passion for it, to one by Elizabeth Bishop" (110), as in "A Miracle for Breakfast," which inspired Ashbery to write "The PAINTER" (1948).

Bibliography

Ashbery, John. "Second Presentation of Elizabeth Bishop." In *Selected Prose*. Edited by Eugene Richie. Ann Arbor: University of Michigan Press, 2004, 164–171.

———. "Throughout Is This Quality of Thingness: Elizabeth Bishop." In *Selected Prose*. Edited by Eugene Richie. Ann Arbor: University of Michigan Press, 2004, 120–124.

Bishop, Elizabeth. *The Complete Poems, 1927–1979*. New York: Farrar, Straus & Giroux, 1983.

———. *One Art: Elizabeth Bishop, Letters*. Edited by Robert Giroux. New York: Farrar, Straus & Giroux, 1994.

Ford, Mark. "Mont D'Espoir or Mount Despair: Early Bishop, Early Ashbery, and the French." In *Poetry and the Sense of Panic: Critical Essays on Elizabeth Bishop and John Ashbery*, edited by Lionel Kelly, 9–27. Amsterdam, Netherlands: Rodopi, 2000.

Lehman, David. *The Last Avant-Garde: The Making of the New York School of Poets*. New York: Anchor Books, 1999.

North, Charles. "Abstraction and Elizabeth Bishop." In *No Other Way: Selected Prose*. Brooklyn, N.Y.: Hanging Loose Press, 1998, 35–45.

Schuyler, James. *Just the Thing: Selected Letters of James Schuyler*. Edited by William Corbett. New York: Turtle Point Press, 2004.

Black, Star (1946–)

Star Black skillfully constructs complex NEW YORK SCHOOL FORMS and wields its ironic tone, while her humor and emotional accessibility quickly win readers, as in the double sestina "Hi Yo:" "We / like Tonto. He is our buddy. I myself am the Lone Ranger's / busted-up bride" (*Double Time* 43). DAVID SHAPIRO, on the back cover of her *October for Idas*, calls Black "a late symbolist . . . faithful to a child's perspective," which "adds up to an adult masque and a self-focusing lens."

Born in Coronado, California, to a journalist mother and a career-army father, Black was raised in Hawaii, Paris, and Washington, D.C. After receiving her B.A. in 1968 from Wellesley in English and art history, she wrote travel guides in Southeast Asia. In NEW YORK CITY by 1977, she studied with JOHN ASHBERY, William Matthews, and C. K. Williams at Brooklyn College, obtaining an M.F.A. in 1984. She joined workshops with Galway Kinnell, Bill Knott, Joseph Brodsky, Derek Walcott, and Alfred Corn and taught poetry writing at Eugene Lang College of the New School (2000–04) and elsewhere. Her five books are *Ghostwood* (2003); the sonnet sequences *Balefire*, its cover bearing one of her collages (1999), and *Waterworn* (l995); *October for Idas* (1997); and *Double Time* (1995), which consists of eight double sestinas inspired by Ashbery's FLOW CHART. She has won grants from the Fund for Poetry and the New York Foundation for the Arts, and she has often been a fellow at Yaddo, MacDowell, and elsewhere. With DAVID LEHMAN she cofounded Manhattan's KGB Bar poetry reading series in 1997.

Black is unique among New York School poets for her simultaneous, notable career in photography and her gently surreal collages; although there are many artists among its poets, and vice versa, photographers are rare. In addition to her poetry, she has created photo portraits of many New York School and other poets, including BARBARA GUEST and Louise Glück. She joined United Press International as a staff news photographer in 1977 and went freelance in l980, publishing photographs in the *Philadelphia Inquirer*, the *New York Times*, *Women's Wear Daily*, and *Avenue* magazine, and covering art openings at the Museum of Modern Art and the Whitney. She has also photographed for the Metropolitan Museum of Art, the Guggenheim, the Frick, and the Dia Center for the Arts. The Library of Congress and the New York Public Library have collected her photographs. The Poet's House held an exhibition of her collages, *A Poet's Eye for Collage*, in spring 2005.

Bibliography

Black, Star. *Balefire*. New York: Painted Leaf Press, 1999.

———. *Double Time*. Hudson, N.Y.: Groundwater Press, 1995.

———. *Ghostwood*. Hoboken, N.J.: Melville House, 2003.

———. *October for Idas*. New York: Painted Leaf Press, 1997.

———. *Waterworn*. A Gathering of the Tribes series. New York: Fly by Night Press, l995.

Black Arts Movement

The Black Arts Movement established NEW YORK CITY as a capital for writers and artists of the African diaspora during the 1960s and 1970s. Many of its important leaders, activists, authors, and artists lived on the Lower East Side and in Harlem, and by the mid-1970s had spread the movement's enthusiasm and optimism to other cities and countries. Some had belonged to the UMBRA workshop, a group of black writers on the Lower East Side associated with the NEW YORK SCHOOL. Umbra writers Askia Mohammed Touré (Rolland Snellings) and Al Haynes founded the Uptown Writers Movement in Harlem in late 1964, shortly after the neighborhood had erupted in violence following the fatal shooting of a black youth by a white police officer in July. Urban rebellion sparked by racial tension became a pattern in U.S. cities over several successive summers.

After Malcolm X's assassination in Harlem in February 1965, many African-American artists abandoned a politics of integration in a society perceived as violently uncertain about its social commitments to its citizens. The Black Arts Movement began symbolically when LeRoi Jones, who named the new movement "Black Arts" and renamed himself AMIRI BARAKA, left the Lower East Side for Harlem in March 1965. Baraka's ubiquitous presence at workshops and events had given him an iconic status on the Lower East Side, where he edited and published YŪGEN, FLOATING BEAR, and the anthology *The Moderns* (Corinth, 1963). His exit ended the optimistic vision of Downtown bohemia as a utopia for young artists. In Harlem, Baraka opened the Black Arts Repertory Theatre/School (BARTS), along with Touré, the brothers Charles and William Patterson, and Steve Young. That particular project foundered after Baraka relocated to Newark, New Jersey, in December 1965, but by that time, "there were similar efforts rising all over the country," as Baraka observed (*Baraka Reader* 503).

The Black Arts Movement's main media were THEATER, poetry performances, and publications, though prominent visual artists belonged, too (Touré was both a writer and an artist). The 1968 "Black Theatre" issue of *Drama Review* (volume 12, number 4), edited by Ed Bullins,

featured several movement authors: Bullins, Larry Neal, Baraka, Ben Caldwell, Jimmy Garrett, John O'Neal, Sonia Sanchez, Marvin X, Ron Milner, Woodie King Jr., Bill Gunn, and Adam David Miller. Other important movement figures included Hoyt Fuller, Addison Gayle Jr., Harold Cruse, Julian Mayfield, Ron Karenga, and Nikki Giovanni. Important theaters in New York included the New Lafayette Theatre, directed by Bob MacBeth, and the National Black Theatre, under Barbara Ann Teer. Two New York movement magazines, *Freedomways* and Dan Watts's *Liberator*, achieved national readership. The sheer number of authors and theorists and the volume of their publications characterize Black Arts as an intensely creative and heterogeneous movement.

Many Black Arts advocates believed the movement should subscribe to the political objectives of the Black Power movement. Black Arts writers addressed empowerment through poetry that echoed political speech. As Neal wrote in his 1968 essay "The Black Arts Movement," Black Arts and Black Power both desired "self-determination and nationhood. Both concepts are nationalistic. One is concerned with the relationship between art and politics; the other with the art of politics" (272).

The relationship between art and politics is a key point of disagreement between New York School poets and proponents of the Black Arts movement. For the former, art was primary; for the latter, politics. TED BERRIGAN's ironically titled poem "Black Power" (1970) seems to dismiss the need for politics: thanks to (black) coffee, "'the living is easy' / Tho the art is hard" (*Collected Poems* 211). Both the tone of Berrigan's poem and its conception of art stand in stark contrast to Baraka's notorious poem "Black Art" (1965), which submits art to the service of the most violent politics: "We want 'poems that kill'" (*Baraka Reader* 219). Nevertheless, enduring personal ties among the writers of the two movements and their "shared . . . sense of a cultural crisis" (Thomas 120) fostered a degree of mutual understanding. In his memoir of Berrigan, RON PADGETT recalls: "[A]t the height of the black power movement, when black political leaders were making their most extreme statements, Ted patiently explained to me why this was necessary, and how some good would come of it" (87). And in a memorial poem dedicated to Berrigan, Baraka says of Berrigan and his fellow artists, "I heard these guys," and their "message" was "from like a very rare bird" ("Rare Birds" 174).

Bibliography

Baraka, Amiri. *The LeRoi Jones/Amiri Baraka Reader.* 2d ed. Edited by William J. Harris. New York: Thunder's Mouth Press, 2000.

———. "The Rare Birds." In *Nice to See You: Homage to Ted Berrigan,* edited by Anne Waldman, 174. Minneapolis, Minn.: Coffee House Press, 1991.

Baraka, Amiri, and Larry Neal, eds. *Black Fire: An Anthology of Afro-American Writing.* New York: Morrow, 1968.

Berrigan, Ted. *The Collected Poems.* Edited by Alice Notley, Anselm Berrigan, and Edmund Berrigan. Berkeley: University of California Press, 2005.

Neal, Larry. "The Black Arts Movement." In *The Black Aesthetic,* edited by Addison Gayle Jr., 272–290. Garden City, N.Y.: Doubleday, 1971.

Padgett, Ron. *Ted: A Personal Memoir of Ted Berrigan.* Great Barrington, Mass.: The Figures, 1993.

Smethurst, James. *The Black Arts Movement: Literary Nationalism in the 1960s and 1970s.* Chapel Hill: University of North Carolina Press, 2005.

Thomas, Lorenzo. "Roots of the Black Arts Movement: New York in the 1960s." In *Extraordinary Measures: Afrocentric Modernism and Twentieth-Century American Poetry.* Tuscaloosa: University of Alabama Press, 2000, 118–144.

Blackburn, Paul (1926–1971)

In NEW YORK CITY, Paul Blackburn held readings at CAFÉ LE METRO, where the BEATS, NEW YORK SCHOOL poets, BLACK MOUNTAIN POETS, and others communed and collaborated. "The different groups coexisted because Paul knew how to do it" (Holman n.p.). Furthermore, Blackburn disliked "the division of poets into schools and . . . the role of Black Mountain poet into which he was cast" (Jarolim in Blackburn, xxii–xxiii). Blackburn got his notion of open FORM from the troubadours he translated in *Proensa* (1953). William Carlos Williams and Ezra Pound, whom Blackburn visited, were also major influences. However, Blackburn found value in all forms of poetry. He towed a heavy Wollensack reel-to-reel recorder to coffeehouse readings, capturing a culture in the process of defining itself. Ultimately, he helped institute the POETRY PROJECT AT ST. MARK'S CHURCH-IN-THE-BOWERY.

Not only did New York School poets and Blackburn share a carefree attitude and sense of wit; their techniques in common include image displacement and fragmentation, and process, that is, that the poem's construction can be monitored in present tense. The distinguishing characteristic of Blackburn's poems lies in the oral poetry that makes much of raw experience, breaking it into odd but evocative juxtapositions on the page. "Blackburn was adept at this technique, adjusting line breaks, margins, and spacing to reflect his desired reading pace and breathing patterns" (West 870). Words scatter over the page like paint in an abstract expressionist ACTION PAINTING, but delivered in sync with Blackburn's hospitable voice, his natural rhythms and unique sensibility put the reader at the scene.

Raised by his maternal grandparents, Blackburn rejoined his mother, Frances Frost, in New York's Greenwich Village in 1963. She gave him a copy of W. H. AUDEN's *Collected Poems* and encouraged him to write. He entered New York University in 1946, joined the army the following year, and later in 1947 reentered NYU where he read Pound. Blackburn visited Pound at St. Elizabeth's Hospital before taking a B.A. from University of Wisconsin in 1950. Blackburn's first books appeared in print, thanks to ROBERT CREELEY, who published *Proensa* (1953) and *The Dissolving Fabric* (1955). In the preface to Blackburn's *Against the Silences* (1980), Creeley admits that Blackburn was "a far more accomplished craftsman" (11), and critics agree that Blackburn was a master poet, a poet's poet. His major works include *The Cities* (1967), *In, on or about the Premises* (1968), and *The Journals* (1975), a document of the last four years before his death in Cortland, New York, on September 13, 1971.

Bibliography

Blackburn, Paul. *The Collected Poems of Paul Blackburn.* Edited by Edith Jarolim. New York: Persea Books, 1985.

Creeley, Robert. Preface to *Against the Silences,* by Paul Blackburn. New York: Permanent Press, 1981, 11–13.

Gilmore, Lyman. *Don't Touch the Poet: The Life and Times of Joel Oppenheimer.* Jersey City, N.J.: Talisman House, 1998.

Holman, Bob. "Just a Moment: Paul Blackburn and the Fragmentation of the New American Poetry." 4 August 1998. About.com:Poetry. Available online. URL: http://poetry.about.com/library/weekly/aa080498. html. Accessed October 9, 2008.

Lehman, David. *The Last Avant-Garde: The Making of the New York School of Poets.* New York: Doubleday, 1998.

West, Robert. "Paul Blackburn." In *American National Biography,* edited by John A Garraty and Mark C. Carnes, 870–871. New York: Oxford University Press, 1999.

Black Mountain College (1933–1956)

Located in North Carolina, Black Mountain College was an experimental institution that provided students an alternative liberal arts education gained through communal experience and interdisciplinary study. Students and faculty both studied and lived closely together. Its concentration on cross-GENRE arts education inspired the programs of many major American institutions while promoting future artistic innovation.

From its inception in 1933 until its closure in 1956, the college was one of the only schools in America earnestly committed to educational and artistic experimentation. Faculty members included Josef and Annie Albers, former teachers at Germany's famed Bauhaus School of Design; composer JOHN CAGE; dancer Merce Cunningham; and architect Buckminster Fuller. Many of these artists were members of the avant-garde. Encouraged by the liberal intellectual atmosphere, their work at Black Mountain advanced influential movements in their respective disciplines.

One such movement concerned poetry. The BLACK MOUNTAIN POETS, headed by CHARLES OLSON, one-time rector of the college, included writers ROBERT CREELEY, Ed Dorn, Robert Duncan, and DENISE LEVERTOV. These writers were devoted to a new, improvised FORM of poetics that sought to reflect exactly the content of the poem. Their unique approach to poetry focused on the use of breath to determine the poetic line. The employment of this "essential" poetics endorsed direct connection between art and life. The college also was a breeding ground for ABSTRACT EXPRESSIONISM. Visual artists Elaine and WILLEM DE KOONING, Robert Motherwell, and ROBERT RAUSCHENBERG all taught at Black Mountain, sharing their interest in exploring the deeper sense of reality beyond the recognizable image. They sought to create essential images that revealed emotional truth and authenticity of feeling. Their use of abstraction peeled away the inessential and presented the necessary.

The poets of the NEW YORK SCHOOL engaged these movements' search for the essential. They also continued Black Mountain's experimental and collaborative ways. The New York poets lived and worked directly with abstract expressionists to create a conjoined art as they ultimately modified and advanced the work of the Black Mountain poets. Black Mountain College cultivated what became the continuing effort of the New York poets to assume a communal approach in the expansion of consciousness through experimental rendering of contemporary life by way of artistic and intellectual effort.

Bibliography

Duberman, Martin. *Black Mountain: An Exploration in Community.* New York: Norton, 1993.

Harris, Mary Emma. *The Arts at Black Mountain College.* Cambridge, Mass.: MIT Press, 1987.

Katz, Vincent, ed. *Black Mountain College: Experiment in Art.* Cambridge, Mass.: MIT Press, 2003.

Black Mountain poets

The Black Mountain poets included writers CHARLES OLSON, ROBERT CREELEY, Ed Dorn, Robert Duncan, Larry Eigner, PAUL BLACKBURN, Hilda Morley, JOHN WIENERS, Jonathan Williams, Fielding Dawson, JOEL OPPENHEIMER, and DENISE LEVERTOV.

The group derived its name from BLACK MOUNTAIN COLLEGE, an experimental institution located in North Carolina that fostered communal experience by emphasizing the connection between living and learning. Most, but not all, of the Black Mountain poets were associated with the college in some form, either as students or instructors. Some are included in the group by virtue of their having published work in the BLACK MOUNTAIN REVIEW.

While at Black Mountain as an instructor, Olson published his seminal essay, "PROJECTIVE VERSE" (1950). This essay contained what was to become the central poetic guidelines for the Black Mountain poets. Olson called for an essential poetry of "open field" composition to replace traditional closed poetic FORMs. The use of open form facilitates the direct transference of "energy" from object to reader in order to remove the "mind" from the observer. Erasing thought from the creative process eliminates any preconceived meaning gathered from observation. The poem then extols the meaning of the direct relationship between perceiver and object, self and world.

The way to reveal this relationship is through a poetics that "projects" the self-object situation. The result is a poem containing an improvised form based on the poet's position that should reflect exactly the content of the poem, as each poetic line contains a single human "breath."

Poets Blackburn and Oppenheimer helped establish a direct link between Black Mountain and NEW YORK SCHOOL poetry. The POETRY PROJECT AT ST. MARK'S CHURCH IN-THE-BOWERY, in NEW YORK CITY, long considered the "epicenter of a new poetic genre, the postmodern urban poem," and the breeding ground of many of the New York School poets, began when Blackburn initiated a popular reading series there, one "made up of a great many Black Mountain folk who were the Project's principal readers" (Kimmelman n.p.).

Though the New York poets were more unprogrammatic than the Black Mountain poets—FRANK O'HARA, for example, wrote an essay "PERSONISM," in opposition to Olson's "Projective Verse," finding Olson "too grandiose, too bent on making 'the important utterance'" (Perloff xxi)—they were joined in the effort to expand consciousness by forging a vernacular language that gave expression to contemporary life.

Bibliography

Kimmelman, Burt. "From Black Mountain College to St. Mark's Church: The Cityscape Poetics of Blackburn, di Prima, and Oppenheimer." *Rain Taxi* (Spring 2002). Available online. URL: http://www. raintaxi.com/online/2002spring/poetryproject.shtml. Accessed December 16, 2008.

Perloff, Marjorie. *Frank O'Hara: Poet among Painters.* Chicago: University of Chicago Press, 1997.

Black Mountain Review (1954–1957)

The *Black Mountain Review* was an influential magazine of the arts published by BLACK MOUNTAIN COLLEGE, an experimental liberal arts institution located in North Carolina whose avant-garde faculty promoted artistic innovation. Launched as a result of correspondence between poets CHARLES OLSON and ROBERT CREELEY, two of the leading BLACK MOUNTAIN POETS, the review sought to be an "'active, ranging' section for critical writing that would be 'prospective' . . . would break down habits of 'subject' and gain a new experience of context generally" (Duberman 410). Olson, as rector of the college, asked Creeley to edit the magazine in 1953. Creeley edited all seven issues of the magazine, which was published from 1954 to 1957.

The *Review* indeed became a platform for the "projective" theories of writing the two men had formulated in their exchange of ideas as well as a showcase for the Black Mountain poets, whose work was guided by these theories. It was also one of the few outlets in publication for cutting-edge ideas that was not backed by the traditional publishing and academic establishment at that time. The *Black Mountain Review* was the rebellious cousin to the popular *Hudson, Kenyon, Partisan,* and *Sewanee* reviews, containing the antidote to what Creeley called—in defense of an essay written by Martin Seymour-Smith and published in the *Review* that attacked the academic verse of Theodore Roethke—the "diffusion, generality, and completely adolescent address to the world" found in a "large portion of what passes for critical writing in America" (Duberman 413).

Established and guided by Creeley's keen eye for emerging alternative talent, the *Black Mountain Review* published not only poems but also FICTION and essays, letters and reviews, artistic reproductions, and photographs. Contributions included such important works as Jorge Luis Borges's "Three Versions of Judas," Carl Jung's "The Mass & the Individual Process," ALLEN GINSBERG's "America," a section from WILLIAM BURROUGHS's then-unpublished *Naked Lunch,* and photographs and art by the abstract expressionists (see ABSTRACT EXPRESSIONISM) Franz Kline, PHILIP GUSTON, and Aaron Siskind.

The *Black Mountain Review* helped expose and promote the many areas of unconventional art and thought being produced in mid-century America, groundbreaking work that led to further experimentation by artists of the 1960s and 1970s.

Bibliography

Clay, Steven, and Rodney Phillips. *"The Black Mountain Review." A Secret Location on the Lower East Side: Adventures in Writing, 1960–1980.* New York: New York Public Library–Granary Books, 1998, 106–108.

Duberman, Martin. *Black Mountain: An Exploration in Community.* New York: Norton, 1993.

Bolinas, California

From the late 1960s through the 1970s, the small rural hamlet of Bolinas, California, on the Pacific coast 30 miles north of San Francisco, attracted a community of writers that rivaled and, through continuous exchange, revitalized the community struggling through transition on the Lower East Side of NEW YORK CITY. So many New York poets settled in or passed through Bolinas that it could be taken for "New York School West" (Berkson n.p.), but in fact the community included a variety of affiliations: SAN FRANCISCO RENAISSANCE (JOANNE KYGER), BEAT (PHILIP WHALEN), and BLACK MOUNTAIN (ROBERT CREELEY). TOM CLARK, who moved to Bolinas in 1968, led the exodus of the NEW YORK SCHOOL, followed by BILL BERKSON, JIM BRODEY, JIM CARROLL, LEWIS MACADAMS, ARAM SAROYAN, TOM VEITCH, and LEWIS WARSH, to name only those who stayed for longer periods.

A combination of time and place accounts for the attraction of Bolinas. The Vietnam War and racial conflict seemed to be tearing the country apart, and Bolinas offered, alternatively, a retreat from the pressures of history or a place to start POLITICS afresh. "In effect I was called upon to make myself a citizen," recalls Saroyan, "whereas in the city I could float for days at a time on the high seas of my own mood, free of the responsibility implicit in any real sense of community" (82).

For some Bolinas residents, notably, among the poets, Kyger and MacAdams, responsibility to the community took the form of specific local action to keep the human population in balance with nature. The pastoral sensibility that had been a strong undercurrent in New York School writing from the beginning merged with the practical concerns of environmentalism. At the same time, the desire to "float for days at a time" that Saroyan expresses was hardly abandoned. Rather, it too went communal in a (relatively) uninhibited sharing of drugs and sexual partners. This sparked the pastoral air with a certain electricity. Warsh, in the midst of a developing relationship with Kyger, observed: "[B]ig dramas are taking place in the air around us constantly."

Like the community based at DOWNTOWN MANHATTAN's POETRY PROJECT AT ST. MARK'S CHURCH IN-THE-BOWERY, Bolinas became the base for a number of publishing enterprises. Jim Koller and Bill Brown arrived in the mid-1960s with *Coyote's Journal* and Coyote Press. DONALD ALLEN issued Grey Fox and Four Seasons books from Bolinas during the decade of his residence there (1968–78). Warsh continued the series of Angel Hair books from Bolinas between 1969 and 1971, the year Berkson launched BIG SKY. Other imprints issued at various times from Bolinas include Avenue B (Stephen Ratcliffe), Blue Millennium (Duncan McNaughton), Tombouctou (Michael Wolfe), Smithereens (Charley Ross), Tree (David Meltzer), and Yanagi (Louis Patler). Bolinas has its own anthology, *On the Mesa,* edited by Joel Weishaus (City Lights, 1971), including work by Clark, Berkson, and Warsh, among others. A few individual volumes announce their origin in their titles: JOE BRAINARD's *Bolinas Journal* (1971), MacAdams's *A Bolinas Report* (Zone, 1971), Saroyan's *The Bolinas Book* (Other Publications, 1974). *Bolinas Eyewash,* a COLLABORATION between TED BERRIGAN and Clark, composed during Berrigan's visit in 1971, has never been published in full, perhaps because Berrigan proved to be too much of a city dweller to find sufficient creative stimulus in a pastoral retreat.

Bibliography

Berkson, Bill. Interview by Robert Glück. *Jacket* 29 (April 2006). Available online. URL: http://www.

jacketmagazine.com/29/berk-gluc-iv.html. Accessed December 16, 2008.

Berrigan, Ted, and Tom Clark. "Bolinas Eyewash" (excerpts). *GAS: High Octane Poetry* 3 (Summer 1991): n.p.

Kane, Daniel. *All Poets Welcome: The Lower East Side Poetry Scene in the 1960s.* Berkeley: University of California Press, 2003, 176–179.

Opstedal, Kevin. *Dreaming as One: Poetry, Poets and Community in Bolinas, California, 1967–1980.* Big Bridge. Available online. URL: http://www.bigbridge. org/bol-cont.htm. Accessed December 16, 2008.

———. "A Literary History of the San Andreas Fault: Bolinas Section." *Jack Magazine* 1, no. 3 (2001). Available online. URL: http://www.jackmagazine. com/issue3/renhist.html. Accessed December 16, 2008.

Saroyan, Aram. "The Town after the City." In *Starting Out in the Sixties: Selected Essays.* Jersey City, N.J.: Talisman, 2001, 81–86.

Schell, Orville. *The Town That Fought to Save Itself.* New York: Pantheon, 1976.

Warsh, Lewis. "California Diary" (1969). In *Part of My History.* Toronto, Canada: Coach House Press, 1972, n.p.

Weishuas, Joel. *On the Mesa: An Anthology of Bolinas Writing.* San Francisco: City Lights, 1971.

Boston, Massachusetts

Although JOHN ASHBERY, KENNETH KOCH, and FRANK O'HARA graduated from Harvard University shortly after World War II, their work had little influence in Boston and Cambridge, Massachusetts, through the 1950s. To the extent that the region had avant-garde affiliations, they involved the group that became identified as the BLACK MOUNTAIN POETS: CHARLES OLSON, who conferred mythic dimensions on nearby Gloucester, Massachusetts, in his *Maximus Poems* (1960); ROBERT CREELEY, a Harvard drop-out; and Cid Corman (1924–2004), whom Olson and Creeley encouraged to launch the magazine *Origin* (1951–84) from the Boston suburb of Dorchester. Corman's outrage at VIOLET R. (BUNNY) LANG's less than reverential staging of his play *The Circle* for the Cambridge POETS' THEATRE in 1952 (Lurie 19–23) is symptomatic of the distance between his sensibility and that of the

"Harvard wits" (Schuyler 161) at the core of the NEW YORK SCHOOL. A more productive exchange arose from O'Hara's meeting with JOHN WIENERS in 1956, also at the Poets' Theatre.

Upon appearance in 1960 of *The NEW AMERICAN POETRY, 1945–1960,* not a single contributor to DONALD M. ALLEN's landmark anthology lived in the Boston area. There were no Boston equivalents of little magazines such as JOHN BERNARD MYERS's *Semi-Colon* and LeRoi Jones's (AMIRI BARAKA) *YŪGEN,* presses such as Totem-Corinth and Grove, or galleries active in the poetry scene, such as TIBOR DE NAGY. Boston native ROBERT LOWELL dominated the poetry scene even after he moved to New York in 1960. Poets connected to the avant-garde such as New York native Michael Palmer (1943–   ), who attended Harvard (B.A., 1965; M.A., 1968), were a rarity. What influence the New York School had came through magazines and books available at Gordon Cairnie's Grolier Bookshop.

The wanderings of the second-generation New York School poets that began in the late 1960s brought some of them to the Boston area. The TELEGRAPH BOOKS publishing venture "began in Harvard Square" when ARAM SAROYAN reconnected there with Andrew Wylie in 1971 (Clay and Phillips 213). In 1973 LEWIS WARSH took up residence in Cambridge for a few years. He collaborated with English poet LEE HARWOOD, then living in Boston, and Boston poet WILLIAM CORBETT to publish one of the few Boston mimeograph magazines, *The Boston Eagle,* which published its third and last issue in 1974. That year EILEEN MYLES left Boston for New York, where her "New England working class speech" (Myles 63) enriched the vernacular mix in New York School poetry. Inspired by the presence of Wieners, JACK KIMBALL remained in Boston a while longer, but he forged a connection with New York through his magazine, *Shell* (1976–79).

Starting in the 1980s at Harvard's Woodberry Poetry Room, curator Stratis Haviaras opened his reading series to a wide range of poets. Gail Mazur did the same at her Blacksmith House reading series. Ashbery, BARBARA GUEST, RON PADGETT, JOE BRAINARD, and BERNADETTE MAYER appeared at these venues. In the early 1990s poet Michael

Franco began Word of Mouth in the basement of a Cambridge restaurant. His events drew poet Gerrit Lansing, Harvard classmate of Ashbery and O'Hara; Ed Barrett, who had studied with Ashbery at Brooklyn College; and the just-getting-started ANGE MLINKO. In 1993 Barrett and Corbett organized a memorial reading for JAMES SCHUYLER at the Massachusetts Institute of Technology (MIT), in which many first- and second-generation New York School poets participated. The POETRY PROJECT AT ST. MARK'S CHURCH IN-THE-BOWERY began to invite Boston poets to give readings in New York, and a lively culture of readings developed in the Boston area under the auspices of Joseph and Molly Torra's *lift* magazine (1990–96); Corbett, Torra, and Dan Bouchard's PRESSED WAFER Press (1999–   ); Bouchard's magazine *Poker* (2003–   ); and poet-impresario Jim Behrle's numerous reading series. While no definitive list of Boston poets exists, the "Boston 1999" issue of Kimball's online magazine the *East Village,* coedited with Bouchard, offers a relevant and representative sample and, appropriately, an introduction by Creeley.

Bibliography

Clay, Steven, and Rodney Phillips, eds. *A Secret Location on the Lower East Side: Adventures in Writing, 1960–1980.* New York: New York Public Library/Granary Books, 1998.

Kimball, Jack, and Daniel Bouchard, eds. "Boston 1999" issue. *East Village.* Available online. URL: http://www.theeastvillage.com/vb.htm. Accessed December 16, 2008.

Lurie, Alison. "V. R. Lang: A Memoir." In *Poems and Plays,* by V. R. Lang. New York: Random House, 1975, 1–71.

Myles, Eileen. "The End of New England." In *On My Way.* Cambridge, Mass.: Faux Press, 2001, 61–69.

Schuyler, James. *Just the Thing: Selected Letters, 1951–1991.* Edited by William Corbett. New York: Turtle Point, 2004.

Boulevard Transportation
Rudolph Burckhardt and Vincent Katz (1997)

Published by a revived press at the TIBOR DE NAGY GALLERY, *Boulevard Transportation* is only one of many collaborative enterprises between Rudolph Burckhardt and Vincent Katz. An earlier volume of Katz's poems, *New York Hello!* (Ommation, 1990), also contains Burkhardt photos; Burckhardt's short film *Tree Streets* (1995) features a poem by Katz; and Katz himself (with his wife, Vivien Bittencourt) has made a documentary film about Burckhardt entitled *Man in the Woods* (2003). Katz has also curated (and written catalog texts for) a number of exhibits of Burckhardt's photography and painting, including *Street Dance: The New York Photographs of Rudy Burckhardt* (Museum of the City of New York, 2008), *Rudy Burckhardt's Maine* (Colby College Museum of Art, 2002), *Rudy Buckhardt & Friends: New York Artists of the 1950s and '60s* (Grey Art Gallery, New York University, 2000), and the artist's first retrospective, *Rudy Burckhardt* (IVAM Centre Julio González, Valencia, 1998).

Modeled on the two EDWIN DENBY–Burckhardt COLLABORATIONS, *Boulevard Transportation*'s four sections have the same subjects as Denby's sonnets (New York, Europe, and Maine); many of the Burckhardt photos themselves can also be found in either IN PUBLIC, IN PRIVATE or MEDITERRANEAN CITIES. All three books tread the same literal and figurative thoroughfares, a relation acknowledged by Katz: "Again, influence / of [Willem] de Kooning dictum," he writes (*Boulevard* 23), proceeding to quote Denby on "the designs on the sidewalk Bill pointed out" (Denby 10). Yet *Boulevard Transportation* differs from its predecessors. In the way the book is printed, the Katz poems alternate with and often face the photos (in the Denby-Burckhardt collaborations, the photographic images are collected at the center or end of the volumes). Katz's poems therefore have a quality of spontaneous description, an effect consistent with Burckhardt's visual aesthetics: "He gives you / something you see, / not something you / 'should' see" (*Boulevard* 66). Yet this relation of word and image is quite different from Denby and Burckhardt's stereoscopy; Katz's poems do not lend the same kind of depth to Burckhardt's images as did Denby's work. This is perhaps in part a result of the temporal distance between Katz's Manhattan and the world Burckhardt's photographs have captured (after all, the book's first images of New York date from 1939–40). Describing a "sensitive-lipped / big nosed / guy," Katz quips, "He's probably still / around" (*Boulevard* 32). While Katz's poems are a far cry from Denby's deliberate lyrics, *Boulevard Transportation* is an interesting project, nevertheless, one whose energizing tension is provided by the interplay of change and continuity between generations.

Bibliography

Burckhardt, Rudy, dir. *Tree Streets* (1995). With poem by Vincent Katz. In *Films by Rudy Burckhardt*. Videorecording. New York: Poetry Project, 2003.

Burckhardt, Rudy, and Simon Pettet. *Talking Pictures: The Photography of Rudy Burckhardt*. Cambridge, Mass.: Zoland, 1994.

Denby, Edwin. "The Silence at Night" (1948). In *The Complete Poems*. Edited by Ron Padgett. New York: Random House, 1986, 10.

Katz, Vincent. *Boulevard Transportation*. With photographs by Rudolph Burckhardt. New York: Tibor de Nagy Editions, 1997.

———, curator. *Rudy Burckhadt's Maine*. 2003. New York Studio School. Available online. URL: http://www.nyss.org/rudy/welcome.html. Accessed December 17, 2008.

Katz, Vincent, and Vivien Bittencourt, dirs. *Man in the Woods: The Art of Rudy Burckhardt*. Videorecording. New York: Checkerboard Foundation, 2003.

Lopate, Phillip. *Rudy Burckhardt*. With an essay by Vincent Katz. New York: Abrams, 2004.

Bowery Poetry Club (2002–)

Opened in 2002, the Bowery Poetry Club symbolizes the ongoing evolution of the poets' community on NEW YORK CITY's Lower East Side in the face of increasing pressures toward gentrification. According to the *Village Voice*, the club's founder, BOB HOLMAN, "suggests that instead of watching a neighborhood turn into a theme park of itself, artists must begin to think about business" (Carr n.p.). Holman found a group of investors to buy the building (number 308) on the Bowery, where the club is located, across the street from where the legendary PUNK ROCK venue CBGB's reigned until 2005, five blocks west of the NUYORICAN POETS CAFÉ, and eight blocks south of the POETRY PROJECT AT ST. MARK'S CHURCH IN-THE-BOWERY. The club makes some money through sales of food and drinks, as well as CDs and publications sold on consignment, but major financial support, including federal and state grants, is channeled through a nonprofit foundation, Bowery Arts and Science. Holman continues to apply the lessons in "poetic economy" that he learned while working for the Poetry Project (1977–80) under CETA (the Comprehensive Employment and Training Act), "the largest federally-funded arts project since the WPA" during the Great Depression (Holman n.p.).

Rather than running its own readings series, the Bowery Poetry Club serves as host to series under a variety of independent sponsors, ranging from JORDAN DAVIS's "The Million Poems Show" to the Segue series, long identified with the Language poets (see LANGUAGE POETRY). One-time events have included a benefit for victims of Hurricane Katrina, coordinated with the Poetry Project (September 30–October 1, 2005), and a "Poets for Peace Speak Out" against the war in Iraq (March 19, 2007).

Amid all the variety, Holman's influence has encouraged the emergence of a house style, emphasizing "spoken word" performance, or what Holman calls "the reemergence of the oral tradition in the digital age" (Holman n.p.). Those of the NEW YORK SCHOOL poets who have been most closely involved with performance have naturally been among the first to appear at the Bowery. ANNE WALDMAN and JIM CARROLL performed in a joint appearance (October 25–26, 2002) just a month after the club opened. Poet-actor TAYLOR MEAD and Tuli Kupferberg of The FUGS have each featured in their own solo reading series. However, Holman's understanding of the oral tradition includes a dynamic relation with writing, realized at the Bowery Poetry Club through innovative approaches to the writing of the New York School. For instance, the club's first "podcast" (posted on the Bowery Poetry Club Web site in summer 2007) leads off with Holman reading an excerpt from TED BERRIGAN's "The Art of the Sonnet" to saxophone accompaniment. During the John Ashbery Festival organized by the New School in April 2006, the Bowery Poetry Club was the site of a performance of JOHN ASHBERY's "Litany" (1979), with participation by Ashbery, ANN LAUTERBACH, James Tate, and Dara Wier. The Bowery Poetry Club Web site continues a line extending from Ashbery ("Last

Month") through Berrigan (Sonnet LXXIV) and Jim Carroll ("'The Academy . . .'") with an allusion embodying Holman's vision of the club as "the Academy of the Future."

Bibliography

Ashbery, John. "Last Month" (1963). In *Rivers and Mountains.* 1966. Reprint, New York: Ecco, 1977, 13.

Berrigan, Ted. "Sonnet LXXIV" (1964). In *The Collected Poems of Ted Berrigan.* Edited by Alice Notley, Anselm Berrigan, and Edmund Berrigan. Berkeley: University of California Press, 2005, 68.

Bowery Poetry Club Web site. Available online. URL: http://www.bowerypoetry.com/.

Carr, C. "Po Show: Bringing Poetry Alive on the Bowery." *Village Voice.* 25 September–1 October 2002. Available online. URL: http://www.village voice.com/news/0239,carr,38604,1.html. Accessed December 17, 2008.

Carroll, Jim. "'The Academy of the Future Is Opening Its Doors . . .'" (1986). In *Fear of Dreaming: Selected Poems.* New York: Penguin, 1993, 127.

Davis, Jordan. "The Million Poems Show" Web page. Available online. URL: http://www.jordandavis. com/Talkshow.html. Accessed December 17, 2008.

Holman, Bob. Interview by Monica de la Torre. *Brooklyn Rail* (May 2006). Available online. URL: http:// brooklynrail.org/2006/05/poetry/bob-holman-with-monica-de-la-torre. Accessed December 17, 2008.

Richardson, Lynda. "A Poet (and Proprietor) Is a Beacon on the Bowery," *New York Times,* 12 November 2002, p. B2.

"Segue at the Bowery Poetry Club." Audio archives. PENNsound. Available online. URL: http://writing. upenn.edu/pennsound/x/Segue-BPC.html. Accessed December 17, 2008.

Brainard, Joe (1942–1994)

Born in Salem, Arkansas, Joe Brainard was raised in Tulsa, Oklahoma, where he met his lifelong friends DICK GALLUP, RON PADGETT—who invited Brainard to be co–art editor of the *WHITE DOVE REVIEW*—and TED BERRIGAN—who was attending Tulsa University on the G.I. Bill. After high school, Brainard received a scholarship to the Dayton Art Academy. Dissatisfied with school, he quit and moved to NEW YORK CITY.

In an interview about his artwork, Padgett asked Brainard:

> RP: Do you think the work you're doing now is new, I mean historically new? I mean are you doing something that's never been done before?
>
> JB: Not terribly. The only way I'm doing anything new is more in attitude. . . . The objects I select make my work new because the selection is personal, but it's not revolutionary (Lewallen 92).

Brainard speaks directly to the viewer in a modest, gentle way that, in itself, is revolutionary. His work is void of the cynicism, hype, and ego of other artists of the 1960s, '70s, and '80s. Where Brainard succeeds magnificently is in an instant sense of camaraderie; one feels at home and not at all intimidated.

Brainard is often associated with the POP ART movement, and his work was exhibited in pop shows, but he is not a pop artist. Though he painted 7UP logos and cartoons and used Tide boxes, Prell bottles, and cigarette butts and packaging in his works, he used these objects more for their aesthetic interest than their ability to comment on consumer culture. Brainard refreshed the art scene with his ability to broach topics in less disconcerting ways. For example, he questions the authenticity of genius by humorously placing the cartoon *Nancy* in a Leonardo da Vinci sketch or a WILLIAM DE KOONING painting; his mimicry is playful and kind. JOHN ASHBERY describes Brainard's work as having "confrontation without provocation"; Brainard confronts issues, Ashbery concedes, "but there's no apparent effort on the artist's part to cause stress or wonderment in the viewer" (Lewallen 1).

Brainard's friendships with second-generation NEW YORK SCHOOL poets brought about many COLLABORATIONs. In such collaborative books as *The Champ* (Black Sparrow, 1968), with KENWARD ELMSLIE, Brainard's images act as autonomous yet essential parts of the text. The simple, graphic drawing style likely stems from Brainard's early interest and job as a draftsman. As Brainard wrote in *Ten Imaginary Still Lifes* (1981), "[O]ne gets the impression that something is going on that cannot be seen" (Lewallen 82). This implied narrative is found throughout Brainard's drawings and lends them an openness wherein the viewer feels a sense of place.

Brainard also worked on collaborative COM-ICS for "C" Comics and designed covers for countless journals and books. About The GOLDEN BOOK OF WORDS (ANGEL HAIR, 1978), BERNADETTE MAYER says:

> The most interesting thing about it to me was having Joe Brainard do the cover for which Joe asked me what I'd want it to be. Joe wasn't doing many covers at the time either and I loved getting his wonderful printed correspondences so I'd write him as often as possible (Mayer 591).

Other collaborators include Ashbery, BILL BERKSON, Berrigan, ROBERT CREELEY, BARBARA GUEST, KENNETH KOCH, FRANK O'HARA, Padgett, JAMES SCHUYLER, and ANNE WALDMAN. The interplay of text and writing is key to Brainard's work and collaborations and can be found in nearly everything he touched.

Brainard's artwork alone is enough to secure his reputation, but remarkably, he is equally well known for his writing. This eclectic output defies classification. As Brainard himself said:

> I don't have a definite commodity, and that's the only way to make money. I change every year, and it's very slow. . . . I've had oil-painting shows that were very realistic, then I've done jack-off collages, cut-outs one year and drawings . . . it's all been different. And the writing too confuses people (Lewallen 99).

In I REMEMBER, published in its first installment by Angel Hair Press (1970), Brainard takes anaphora, a FORM far from new, and creates a 167-page memoir of concise recollections. In addition, his countless poetic and journal-like writings about museum exhibitions, artists, and daily occasion resound with a voice of generosity, kindness, and honesty second to none.

Bibliography

Berkson, Bill. "Working with Joe." Modern Painters 14, no. 3 (Autumn 2001): 62–65.

Brainard, Joe. Bolinas Journal. Bolinas, Calif.: Big Sky, 1971.

———. I Remember. New York: Granary Books, 2001.

———. Selected Writings, 1962–1971. New York: Kulchur Foundation, 1971.

Corbett, William, Elaine Equi, and David Trinidad, eds. "Hello Joe: A Tribute to Joe Brainard." Pressed Wafer 2 (March 2001): 85–237.

Lewallen, Constance M. Joe Brainard: A Retrospective. Exhibit catalog. Berkeley: Art Museum, University of California, Berkeley; New York: Granary Books, 2001.

Mayer, Bernadette. "The Writing of Moving, Eruditio Ex Memoria and The Golden Book of Words." In The Angel Hair Anthology, edited by Anne Waldman and Lewis Warsh, 590–591. New York: Granary Books, 2001.

Padgett, Ron. Joe: A Memoir of Joe Brainard. Minneapolis, Minn.: Coffee House Press, 2004.

British poetry

To NEW YORK SCHOOL poets the entire history of English literature became simultaneously available, a reflection of the postmodern spirit that encouraged eclectic mixtures of different periods as well as "high" and "low" GENRES. As they read Edmund Spenser together at Harvard University, JOHN ASHBERY told KENNETH KOCH that reading The Faerie Queene was as much fun as reading a comic book (interview 194). Since then, Ashbery has applied John Milton's Paradise Lost to his own reading of his 1975 poem "Daffy Duck in Hollywood" (Ashbery, Mark Ford 59). FRANK O'HARA's allusions to Thomas Wyatt range from the obscene ("After Wyatt" [1951]) to the elegiac (BIOTHERM [1962]). Koch drew on James Thomson for "The Seasons" (1998) and on Lord Byron for SEASONS ON EARTH (1987). Poets of later generations followed suit. TED BERRIGAN insisted that his SONNETS (1964) were "very narrowly within the confines of the form of the Shakespearean sonnet" (73), and ALICE NOTLEY adopted a "quasi-Spenserian stanza" (Notley 591) for the title poem of Incidentals in the Day World (1973). From the more obscure recesses of the tradition, CHARLES NORTH referred to William Cowper ("For a Cowper Paperweight" [1989]), and PAUL VIOLI turned to Samuel Daniel ("The Curious Builder" [1993]). Perhaps most surprising is the appearance of Alexander Pope in the work of JIM CARROLL ("Next Door" [1973]; *The BASKETBALL DIARIES* [1979]) and JOHN YAU ("For Alexander Pope's Garden" [1983]).

The New York School poets were attracted to British poets who offered an alternative version of modernism, including D. H. Lawrence, a favorite of O'Hara's (Gooch 365–366), and, from the next generation, Dylan Thomas and W. H. AUDEN (Ashbery, *Selected Prose* 246–247). Auden is a crucial figure in the early formation of Ashbery, O'Hara, and JAMES SCHUYLER as poets. Ironically, Auden's move from England to the United States in 1939 became identified, by influential critics on both sides of the Atlantic, with either a betrayal of England or a betrayal of modernism. To the New York School poets betrayal was more evident in "the Movement" that gained ascendancy in Britain following World War II (for example, Philip Larkin, Kingsley Amis), which O'Hara dismissed as an expression of "the new bourgeoisie sensibility" (O'Hara, interview 26)—1950s conformism extended to the realm of art. A favorable climate for the reception of New York School poetry in the United Kingdom did not begin to emerge until the youth rebellion of the 1960s. Meanwhile, two significant events in Anglo–New York School relations occurred in 1956: the publication of Ashbery's *Some Trees* as Auden's selection in the Yale Younger Poets series and Ashbery's first trip to Great Britain, during which he met F. T. Prince. Ashbery's enthusiasm for Prince's work, which never gained a wide readership, was passed on to the second-generation New York School as one of the signs of membership (Ashbery, *Selected Prose* 178–180, 304–306; Padgett 85–87; North, "Words").

In 1960 the publication of *The NEW AMERICAN POETRY, 1945–1960* helped spark a parallel movement that became known as the *British Poetry Revival*. This term connotes primarily a new burst of energy, fueled especially by the example of the BEATS. To the extent that the "revival" was a return to a moment in the past, it was the modernist moment of Ezra Pound, represented in *The New American Poetry*, especially by the BLACK MOUNTAIN POETS. Ironically, while both Pound and CHARLES OLSON took part in a gathering that included a significant number of New York School poets at the SPOLETO FESTIVAL OF TWO WORLDS in summer 1965, the breakthrough event for the British Poetry Revival occurred that same summer at the International Poetry Incarnation in London's Royal Albert Hall, where the Beats (ALLEN GINSBERG, GREGORY CORSO, Lawrence Ferlinghetti, and WILLIAM BURROUGHS) starred but the New York School was scarcely in evidence. Two poets who were to become involved in the New York School, TOM CLARK and ANSELM HOLLO, read at the Albert Hall, and Hollo was adopted as one of the "Children of Albion" in the anthology of the same name edited by Michael Horovitz (Penguin, 1969) that grew out of the Albert Hall event. Less nationalistic publishing ventures exposed poets in the United Kingdom to the work of the second-generation New York School. For instance, in 1966 Tom Raworth published Clark, Hollo, RON PADGETT, and ARAM SAROYAN through the Goliard Press. Between 1968 and 1970 Opal L. Nations invited Padgett, ANNE WALDMAN, and LARRY FAGIN to edit special issues of the magazine *Strange Faeces*. TREVOR WINKFIELD's *JUILLARD* (1968–72) included these names and more. In general, second-generation writers were preparing the ground for the reception of the first generation. In 1971 ANN LAUTERBACH, then a resident in London, brought Ashbery to read at an international "Poetry Information" festival that she had organized under the auspices of the Institute of Contemporary Art. In the same year Ashbery shared volume 19 of the Penguin Modern Poets series with Tom Raworth and LEE HARWOOD.

The cultural shift of the 1960s, in which the new poetry played a role, affected traditional institutions in the United Kingdom in various ways during the 1970s. As editor from 1971 to 1977, Eric Mottram opened the pages of *Poetry Review*, the journal of the Poetry Society, to many representatives of the British Poetry Revival and U.S. associates such as Ashbery. For a brief period the governing body of the Poetry Society itself came to be dominated by the new poets, including Harwood and Tom Pickard, both of whom had first-hand experience of the New York School from trips to the United States in the late 1960s. At Cambridge University close study of Ashbery and O'Hara contributed to the emergence of the so-called Cambridge School, both in poetry (J. H. Prynne, John James) and in criticism (VERONICA FORREST-THOMSON). However, the spirit of the DOWNTOWN MANHATTAN'S POETRY PROJECT AT ST. MARK'S CHURCH IN-THE-BOWERY was exported more readily to less traditional institutions and to unofficial "little magazines." Berrigan taught for the 1973–74 academic year at the new University of Essex, where poet and Pound scholar Donald Davie had established a strong orientation toward the new (and American) poetry as soon as the doors opened in 1964. Davie recruited Black Mountain poet Ed Dorn as the first poet in residence and Clark, his former student at Cambridge, as an instructor. While Berrigan was poet-in-residence at Essex, he met a number of poets who would later find their way to New York, including DOUGLAS OLIVER and SIMON PETTET. Not far from the University of Essex, in the neighboring county of Suffolk, Martin Stannard launched his little magazine, *Joe Soap's Canoe*, in 1978. Stannard's advocacy of the New York School poets, particularly his friends North, TONY TOWLE, and Violi, persisted through the final issue of his magazine (in 1993) and continues to be reflected in his poetry and reviews.

While Ashbery's international reputation still sets him apart, British poets and critics (often combined in the same person) have recently devoted considerable attention to the New York School poets in various groupings. The first book-length study of the New York School, Geoff Ward's *Statutes of Liberty* (Macmillan, 1993; 2nd ed., Palgrave, 2000), concentrated on Ashbery, O'Hara, and Schuyler. William Watkin's *In the Process of Poetry* (Associated University Presses, 2001) added Koch to the group, as did MARK FORD's anthology, *The New York Poets* (Carcanet, 2004). Its sequel, *The New York Poets II*, edited by Ford with Winkfield (Carcanet, 2006), offered an expanded view of the first generation (EDWIN DENBY, KENWARD ELMSLIE, BARBARA GUEST, and HARRY MATHEWS) while introducing second-generation poets (Berkson, Berrigan, JOSEPH CERAVOLO, CLARK COOLIDGE, BERNADETTE MAYER, North,

and Padgett). Although his own poetry is closest to Ashbery's, Ford helped to make the work of O'Hara more widely available in his selection entitled *Why I Am Not a Painter* (Carcanet, 2003). Similarly, although Ashbery is the focus of David Herd's *John Ashbery and American Poetry* (Manchester University Press, 2000), that book takes great care in setting Ashbery in the context of the New York School, in particular, as well as AMERICAN POETRY more generally.

Bibliography

Ashbery, John. "Daffy Duck in Hollywood." In *Houseboat Days*. New York: Penguin, 1977, 31–34.

———. *John Ashbery in Conversation with Mark Ford*. London: Between the Lines, 2003.

———. *Selected Prose*. Edited by Eugene Richie. Ann Arbor: University of Michigan Press, 2004.

Berrigan, Ted. Interview by Ralph Hawkins (1974). In *Talking in Tranquility: Interviews with Ted Berrigan*. Edited by Stephen Ratcliffe and Leslie Scalapino. Bolinas, Calif.: Avenue B; Oakland, Calif.: O Books, 1991, 73–89.

Carroll, Jim. *The Basketball Diaries*. New York: Penguin, 1995.

———. "Next Door." In *Fear of Dreaming: Selected Poems*. New York: Penguin, 1993, 12.

Clark, Tom. "Confessions." In *Contemporary Authors, Autobiography Series 22*, edited by Joyce Nakamura, 1–26. Detroit, Mich.: Gale, 1996.

Gooch, Brad. *City Poet: The Life and Times of Frank O'Hara*. New York: Knopf, 1993.

Koch, Kenneth. *The Collected Poems*. New York: Knopf, 2005.

———. Interview by Jordan Davis (1995). In *The Art of Poetry: Poems, Parodies, Interviews, Essays, and Other Work*. Ann Arbor: University of Michigan Press, 1996, 187–214.

———. *Seasons on Earth*. New York: Penguin, 1987.

Lauterbach, Ann. "John Ashbery—Mapping the Real: The Given and the Chosen" (2005). Ashbery Resource Center. Available online. URL: http://www.flowchart foundation.org/arc/home/special_features/lauterbach. htm. Accessed December 17, 2008.

North, Charles. Commentary for *Joe Soap's Canoe* (on "For a Cowper Paperweight") (1991). In *No Other Way: Selected Prose*. Brooklyn, N.Y.: Hanging Loose Press, 1998, 118–119.

————. "For a Cowper Paperweight." In *New and Selected Poems*. Los Angeles: Sun & Moon Press, 1999, 126–127.

————. "Words from F. T. Prince" (1980). In *No Other Way: Selected Prose*. Brooklyn, N.Y.: Hanging Loose Press, 1998, 38–41.

Notley, Alice. "Incidentals in the Day World" and contributor's statement. In *The Angel Hair Anthology*, edited by Anne Waldman and Lewis Warsh, 418–424, 591. New York: Granary Books, 2001.

O'Hara, Frank. *The Collected Poems*. Rev. ed. Edited by Donald Allen. Berkeley: University of California Press, 1995.

————. Interview by Edward Lucie-Smith (1965). In *Standing Still and Walking in New York*. Edited by Donald Allen. San Francisco: Grey Fox, 1983, 3–26.

Oliver, Douglas. "The Year in Essex." In *Nice to See You: Homage to Ted Berrigan*, edited by Anne Waldman, 204–206. Minneapolis, Minn.: Coffee House Press, 1991.

Padgett, Ron. *Ted: A Personal Memoir of Ted Berrigan*. Great Barrington, Mass.: The Figures, 1993.

Sheppard, Robert. *The Poetry of Saying: British Poetry and Its Discontents, 1950–2000*. Liverpool, U.K.: Liverpool University Press, 2005.

Stannard, Martin. "*Joe Soap's Canoe* and New York School Poetry." *Joe Soap's Canoe* 10 (1986): 3–8.

Violi, Paul. "The Curious Builder." In *Breakers: Selected Poems*. Minneapolis, Minn.: Coffee House Press, 2000, 137–150.

Yau, John. "For Alexander Pope's Garden." In *Corpse and Mirror*. New York: Holt, Rinehart & Winston, 1983, 6.

Broadway: A Poets and Painters Anthology
(1979, 1989)

JAMES SCHUYLER and CHARLES NORTH published two installments of *Broadway: A Poets and Painters Anthology* a decade apart (SWOLLEN MAGPIE PRESS, 1979; HANGING LOOSE PRESS, 1989). They thus form a sequence with the two initial NEW YORK SCHOOL anthologies published by JOHN BERNARD MYERS (1969) and by RON PADGETT and DAVID SHAPIRO (1970), each sampling the state of the art at a distinct phase of development. Of the nine poets chosen by Myers, *Broadway* includes all but FRANK O'HARA (Schuyler and North chose only living poets); of the 27 poets chosen by Padgett and Shapiro, *Broadway* includes 17. Through Schuyler's connections, *Broadway* was able to attract significant work by first-generation poets, for instance, KENNETH KOCH's "The Burning Mystery of Anna in 1951" and a portion of BARBARA GUEST's "The Türler Losses" (both in the original *Broadway*). In addition, by limiting each poet to only one poem, *Broadway* made room for a much larger number of poets than appeared in the earlier anthologies. The first *Broadway* offers 51 poets, including such newcomers as Douglas Crase, VINCENT KATZ, EILEEN MYLES, and ALICE NOTLEY. *Broadway 2*, published by HANGING LOOSE PRESS and consisting of 61 poets, traces the widening geographical range of New York School influence, drawing in new poets such as MAXINE CHERNOFF, ELAINE EQUI, PAUL HOOVER, JEROME SALA, and DAVID TRINIDAD. A letter that Schuyler wrote to Trinidad in California in 1985 provides interesting detail of Schuyler's interest in as well as resistance to some of the poets the younger man recommended for the new anthology in progress (Schuyler, *Just the Thing* 418). "Boy, could he be tough," North recalls of Schuyler. "I remember him absolutely putting his foot down about certain potential contributors" (11).

North proposed the *Broadway* project to Schuyler on the model of a "one-shot" magazine called *49 South* that Schuyler had edited in 1972. In both cases the title denoted the editor's address, since Schuyler had moved from FAIRFIELD PORTER's home at 49 South Street in Southampton, Long Island, to Broadway on New York's Upper West Side. The cover of the first *Broadway* shows a view of the avenue from North's apartment nearby, drawn by North's wife, Paula. Overall, the artwork in both *Broadway*s is representational rather than abstract, by artists with close ties to Schuyler, including Mary Abbott, Nell Blaine, JOE BRAINARD, RUDOLPH BURCKHARDT, JANE FREILICHER, Yvonne Jacquette, ALEX KATZ, Porter, and GEORGE SCHNEEMAN. TREVOR WINKFIELD provided the cover for *Broadway 2*. A reviewer for the British magazine *Beat Scene* found the "highly traditional" artwork "an odd, yet successful companion to the post modern intellectual tendencies of the poets" (Dougherty).

Bibliography

Dougherty, Sean Thomas. Review of *Broadway 2* in *Beat Scene*. Undated clipping in the collection of Charles North.

North, Charles. Interview by Ange Mlinko. *Poetry Project Newsletter* 183 (February–March 2001): 10–14, 27.

Schuyler, James. *Just the Thing: Selected Letters, 1951–1991*. Edited by William Corbett. New York: Turtle Point Press, 2004.

Brodey, Jim (1942–1993)

Among the poets of the second-generation NEW YORK SCHOOL, Jim Brodey was one of the closest to FRANK O'HARA, even sharing O'Hara's bed occasionally (Brodey, *Heart* 217, 260; LeSueur 292–293). However, Brodey's poetry is a unique combination of a wide range of influences. After studying with Louise Bogan at New York University (Towle 59), he took workshops at the New School with KENNETH KOCH and LeRoi Jones (AMIRI BARAKA), as well as O'Hara (from 1963 to 1965). At the BERKELEY POETRY CONFERENCE (1965), Brodey acquired first-hand experience of the breath-based poetics of CHARLES OLSON, but the "heart of the breath" in Brodey's poems resounds to the beat of JACK KEROUAC's prose and the MUSIC of JAZZ, blues, and rock, which Brodey reviewed professionally in such magazines as KULCHUR, the *East Village Other*, and *Creem*. As TED BERRIGAN wrote in his preface to Brodey's first book, *Fleeing Madly South* (1967), "The discipline inherent in Kerouac's locomotive meditations (which look so easy when read), is fed-back to him, but in mad overdubbing stanzas." At the time, Berrigan could not have predicted the extent to which the discipline of stanzas would unleash Brodey's creativity. In 1981 he hit upon a FORM, 10 stanzas of three lines each, that inspired him to produce a torrent of poems over the next four years, sometimes as many as 30 poems a day (Brodey, *Heart* 15, 109–203). Each of these poems bears the name of a writer, artist, or musician important to him, but, in a twist on O'Hara's "personal poem," the name does not lead back to a social occasion in the poet's life but rather forward to new, transcendent possibilities that cannot be named. For instance, "Ted Berrigan 9" ends:

The mind reeling the page spinning
The poem taking shape the meaning's
So clear we cannot stop to read it.

In addition to publishing two issues of his own magazine, *Clothesline* (1965, 1970), Brodey contributed to the full run of magazines affiliated with the New York School during the 1960s, from WAGNER LITERARY MAGAZINE (number 4, 1963–64) to ADVENTURES IN POETRY (number 5, January 1970). A similarly representative list of publishers issued Brodey's books and pamphlets, starting with *Fleeing Madly South* (Clothesline, 1967) and IDENTIKIT (ANGEL HAIR, 1967) and extending through the next decade: *Breathlahem* (Sun, 1972), *Last Licks* (Telephone Books, 1973), *Blues of the Egyptian Kings* (BIG SKY, 1975), *Unless* (Jawbone, 1977), *Piranha Yoga* (Jim Brodey Books, 1977), and *Judyism* (UNITED ARTISTS, 1980). During this period Brodey shifted residence back and forth between his native New York and California. As it did for many New Yorkers who colonized BOLINAS, northern California encouraged a pastoral mood in Brodey (for example, "Stone Free"), but by the late 1970s he had decided that "new yawk is all joy" (Brodey, *Heart* 22), and he seemed determined to settle there. His workshops at the POETRY PROJECT AT ST. MARK'S CHURCH IN-THE-BOWERY stimulated the development of a third generation of New York School poets, including ELINOR NAUEN, STEVE LEVINE, EILEEN MYLES, SUSIE TIMMONS, GREG MASTERS, MICHAEL SCHOLNICK, and BARBARA BARG. Jim Brodey Editions published Myles's first pamphlets (*The Irony of the Leash*, 1978) and TOM SAVAGE's work (*Personalities*, 1978).

Most of Brodey's abundant production of poetry during the 1980s awaited publication in the posthumous edition *Heart of the Breath* (Hard Press, 1996), edited by his close friend CLARK COOLIDGE. The last decade of Brodey's life was a difficult one, marred by the death of friends (for instance, EDWIN DENBY and Berrigan, both in 1983) and the ravages of cocaine addiction. Eventually homeless, Brodey squatted in Tompkins Square Park in the East Village before leaving again for California, where he died of AIDS in 1993. His late work is uneven, a persistent problem that his staunchest supporters have acknowledged (JOHN GODFREY, CHARLES

NORTH), but at its best it contributes powerfully to the transformation of elegy that is one of the lasting achievements of the New York School. For example, Brodey writes in memory of Berrigan:

> Ted, we sing thee
> As once we knew you
> And here we learn how not to survive, . . .

With his own work in mind as well as that of his friends, he adds, "The poems and the songs remain."

Bibliography

Berrigan, Ted. "Note on Jim Brodey's Poems and Him." In *Fleeing Madly South: Poems, 1962–1966.* New York: Clothesline Books, 1967, n.p.

Brodey, Jim. *Heart of the Breath: Poems, 1979–1992.* Edited by Clark Coolidge. West Stockbridge, Mass.: Hard Press, 1996.

———. "Homeward Bound." Sound recording (1977). Ubuweb. Available online. URL: http://www.ubu.com/sound/big_ego.html. Accessed December 17, 2008.

———. "Stone Free" (1968). In *The Angel Hair Anthology,* edited by Anne Waldman and Lewis Warsh, 138. New York: Granary Books, 2001.

———. "2-Egg Cake." In *Homage to Frank O'Hara,* edited by Bill Berkson and Joe LeSueur, 154–155. Bolinas, Calif.: Big Sky, 1988.

Coolidge, Clark. "Brodey Notes." In *Blues for the Egyptian Kings,* by Jim Brodey, n.p. Bolinas, Calif.: Big Sky, 1975.

Godfrey, John. "Preface" (1993). In *Heart of the Breath: Poems, 1979–1992,* by Jim Brodey, 17–18. Edited by Clark Coolidge. West Stockbridge, Mass.: Hard Press, 1996.

LeSueur, Joe. *Digressions on Some Poems by Frank O'Hara: A Memoir.* New York: Farrar, Straus & Giroux, 2003.

North, Charles. "On & for Jim Brodey" (1993). In *No Other Way: Selected Prose.* Brooklyn, N.Y.: Hanging Loose, 1998, 148–151.

Towle, Tony. *Memoir, 1960–1963.* Cambridge, Mass.: Faux Press, 2001.

Brown, Lee Ann (1963–)

Born in Saitama-ken, Japan, and raised in Charlotte, North Carolina, poet Lee Ann Brown enjoys ties to the NEW YORK SCHOOL that are both literary and personal. Her poetry takes FRANK O'HARA's tongue-in-cheek manifesto "PERSONISM"—which advises to put the poem "squarely between the poet and the person"—literally. Brown's frequent use of the poem as a personal address to poets, family, friends, and lovers gives her take on ephemeral experience an unexpected depth and sweetness. In addition, Brown's friendships with BERNADETTE MAYER and JOE BRAINARD, and her deep identification with and long residency in the city itself, place her firmly in the New York School lineage.

Brown received her B.A. from Brown University in 1987. During this period she also spent several summers at the NAROPA INSTITUTE in Boulder, Colorado, first as a student (1980s) and then as a visiting faculty member (1990s). Brown's association with BEAT poets such as ALLEN GINSBERG and ANNE WALDMAN stimulated her love of performance. Her poetry readings often include songs and audience participation. The dominant Beat-inspired poetic devices of anaphora, JAZZ cadence, and political rant, however, are rare in Brown's poetry. The unique style of her writing owes more to two apparently incongruous influences: the American South and the New York School.

Brown's work is strongly self-identified with southern history and culture, as seen in poems such as "Gossip North Carolina," "South of the Mind," and "Cafeteria" (in *Polyverse*) and "The Ballad of Vertical Integration" (in *The Sleep That Changed Everything*). Much of Brown's work is also inspired by folk culture, church life, the Appalachian ballad, and her grandmother, Agnes Lee Wiley Dunlop (called Obaa, from *obaa-san,* or "grandmother," in Japanese). The poetic FORMs and mode of address in which she integrates her southern experience, however, owe much to the New York School. "Obaa I Remember" (*Sleep*) inhabits the form Brainard pioneered in his 1975 book *I REMEMBER.* Brainard's awkward gay adolescence and pop-culture registers are replaced in Brown's poem by a space of female intimacy and suburban interiors: "I remember your den's knotty pine paneling / faces grinning out through the grain."

After college Brown moved to NEW YORK CITY. She became involved in the Lower East Side poetry scene centered on the POETRY PROJECT AT ST. MARK'S CHURCH IN-THE-BOWERY. There she met Mayer, who became Brown's most important mentor and strongest link to the New York School. In 1989 Brown founded Tender Buttons Press, for which Brainard designed a logo. The first Tender Buttons book was Mayer's *Sonnets.*

In 1991 Brown returned to PROVIDENCE, RHODE ISLAND, to earn her M.F.A. at Brown University. She lived in Providence until 1996 before moving back to New York City permanently. During this period Brown finished *Polyverse,* which won the New American Poetry Series in 1996 and was published in 1999 by Sun & Moon.

The influence of Brown's New York School mentor Mayer is everywhere apparent in *Polyverse.* The book is dedicated to Mayer, includes a poem written "during a phone conversation with . . . Mayer," several collaborations with the older poet, and an imitation ("Thang"). The multipart "Crush," which concludes *Polyverse,* owes its tone and address (and lines such as "The desire of mothers to please others in letters") to Mayer, as well as to Gertrude Stein. Mayer's use of the personal address, her affirmation of the complexity of female desire, as well as her insouciant intertextuality, are everywhere present in Brown's *Polyverse.* Even the book's endnotes, where Brown writes, "There's a lot more to say about these poems so ask me" owes something to Mayer's *Utopia* (UNITED ARTISTS, 1984), the acknowledgments of which include Mayer's address and phone number so that readers may "call or write me if there's any problem."

FRANK O'HARA is also an important predecessor of *Polyverse.* In "Demi-Queer Notion," Brown writes: "I'm sorry Frank O'Hara isn't as cute / as you expected." And in "To Jennifer M." she concludes: "But Frank O'Hara / has faith in you & me even / though or because we're girls." Brown's personal addresses to Sappho ("After Sappho") and references to Vladimir Mayakovsky ("Mayakovsky," and "The Thousand-and-One Nights of the Inside-Out Gown") also recall O'Hara's casual transcultural/historical literary dialogues. About *Polyverse* Robert Hass writes: "Among younger American poets, Lee Ann Brown is one of the wittiest and most inven-

tive. . . . inspired doodling, something in the spirit of the late New York poet Frank O'Hara" (X12). *Polyverse* is "the most entertaining book of poetry I've read in years," writes Patrick Pritchett (n.p.)

In 1996 Brown was hired to teach literature at St. John's University, and in 2000 she was made assistant professor. Her second full-length collection, *The Sleep That Changed Everything,* was published by Wesleyan University Press in 2003. Dedicated to Brainard, Brown's grandmother, and several others, this collection is a departure from *Polyverse* insofar as Brown's style is more individuated. The poems are longer and complicate both their formal devices and emotional register. A negativity enters, reminiscent of O'Hara's "Ode to Joy." "You are gorgeous and I am not getting to know you any better / I feel Broken into I feel drench dreamed," opens a poem wittily titled after O'Hara, "You Are Not Gorgeous and I Am Coming Anyway." Variations on traditional form replace the COLLABORATIONs and experiments of *Polyverse.* *Sleep* includes ballads, sonnets, villanelles, odes, and an epithalamium. The "Ballad of Amiri B. (60's)" evinces a touching homage to the history of the Lower East Side, relating a story in which the BLACK ARTS MOVEMENT poet AMIRI BARAKA, distanced from his white friends, still gives them a wink on the subway. *Sleep* is Brown's wink to the New York School; though it is still part of her history, she has moved into new territory. The immediacy of experience becomes complicated by memory, the outward address interiorized. Heidi Lynn Staples writes about *Sleep,* "Brown lights this unsettling plight of ours that we call being; she goes by the grace of humor, assuring us that 'Cruel behavior's handiwork—undone— / All phenomenon O Lord—can laugh'" (n.p.).

Bibliography

Hass, Robert. Review of *Polyverse, Washington Post,* 18 July 1999, p. X12.

Pritchett, Patrick. Review of *Polyverse. Jacket* 8. Available online. URL: http://jacketmagazine.com/08/prit-r-brown.html. Accessed December 17, 2008.

Staples, Heidi Lynn. Review of *The Sleep That Changed Everything, Verse* (October 14, 2004). Available online. URL: http://versemag.blogspot.com/2004/10/new-review-of-lee-ann-brown.html.

Brownstein, Michael (1943–)

Michael Brownstein conveys BEAT vision with NEW YORK SCHOOL speed. Like many other New York School poets, he has been attracted to the prose poem as a "one page novel," as pioneered by the French modernist Max Jacob: "[H]e was the first writer to realize the sheer speed with which people see each other today" (Brownstein, introduction iv). Yet, there is an expansiveness to Brownstein's vision that has led him to write full-length novels, three of them to date: *Country Cousins* (Braziller, 1974), *The Touch* (Autonomedia, 1993), and *Self-Reliance* (Coffee House Press, 1994). And in *World on Fire* (Open City Books, 2002), Brownstein has composed a "treatise/poem" that culture critic Eric Schlosser has called "a howl for the twenty-first century" (n.p.), with a deliberate nod to ALLEN GINSBERG's epic *Howl*.

The poles of Brownstein's vision are love and power, identified with west and east, respectively, in his poem "Geography," one of the "big masterpieces" that RON PADGETT singled out for particular praise in a review of Brownstein's collection *Strange Days Ahead* (Z PRESS, 1975). A repeated image of power, resonating with JACK KEROUAC's *On the Road,* is the position of being "behind the wheel," the title of Brownstein's first collection (1967). Behind the wheel is the place of the ego: "I got in my car and someone was already behind the wheel—/ it was me," writes Brownstein in "Personnel Poem" (1977), a paranoid version of the "personal poem" descended from FRANK O'HARA. In *World on Fire* the image is grounded explicitly in autobiography: "The first time I got behind the wheel, what joy! / Sixteen years old, a Jewboy trapped in Bible-Belt fifties Tennessee. / What better way to seek release!"

Making his way to NEW YORK CITY in 1965 was another means of seeking release for Brownstein, who quickly plugged into the circuits of power, such as they were, extending from the POETRY PROJECT AT ST. MARK'S CHURCH IN-THE-BOWERY. *Behind the Wheel* was published by TED BERRIGAN's "C" Press, and a second selection, *Highway to the Sky* (Columbia University Press), was published by Columbia University Press as the 1969 recipient of the Frank O'Hara Poetry Award. In 1970 Brownstein appeared in Padgett and DAVID SHAPIRO's ANTHOLOGY OF NEW YORK POETS, and Angel Hair published his first set of prose poems, *Three American Tantrums.*

As an expression of rage associated with the American will to power, the tantrum is opposed in Brownstein's personal mythology to tantra ("Memoir" 577), a body of esoteric knowledge and practice specifically Hindu and Buddhist but more generally non-Western, as Brownstein's eclectic research defined it. The role that love occupies in opposition to power in Brownstein's writing must be understood in this context, a context alien to the Eurocentric focus of the first-generation New York School but of increasing importance to the second generation. Brownstein's interaction with ANNE WALDMAN in this regard was especially fruitful. Brownstein introduced Waldman to the recordings of the Mazatec shaman María Sabina, an inspiration for Waldman's chant poems (Waldman 44), and when the Tibetan Buddhist teacher Chögyam Trungpa invited Ginsberg and Waldman to organize a poetics program at the NAROPA INSTITUTE, she recruited Brownstein to teach there, which he did from 1976 to 1983. *Oracle Night: A Love Poem* (Sun & Moon, 1982) is a product of this period. As in tantric practice, its engagement with the beloved is explicitly erotic, but the figure of the beloved is more cosmic than individual. She prefigures the "unnamed other who could be the gaea [Mother Earth] itself" (n.p.), as Brian Kim Stefans characterizes the recipient of "an erotic love letter" interspersed throughout the pages of *World on Fire*. In any case she is a being in whose embrace the lover can abandon his ego without fear, a "better way to seek release," Brownstein concludes, than being "behind the wheel."

Bibliography

Brownstein, Michael. Introduction to *The Dice Cup: Selected Prose Poems,* by Max Jacob. Edited by Michael Brownstein. New York: SUN, 1979, i–v.

———. "Memoir." In *The Angel Hair Anthology,* edited by Anne Waldman and Lewis Warsh, 576–577. New York: Granary Books, 2001.

———. "Personnel Poem." *Poetry Project Newsletter* 47 (July 1, 1977): 8.

Padgett, Ron. "Strange Indeed." *Poetry Project Newsletter* 48 (October 1, 1977): 3.

Schlosser, Eric. Quoted in publisher's press release for *World on Fire*, by Michael Brownstein. New York: Open City Books, 2002.

Stefans, Brian Kim. Review of *World on Fire. Arras: New Media Poetry and Poetics*. Available online. URL: http://www.arras.net/the_franks/brownstein_world. htm.

Waldman, Anne. "My Life a List" (1976). In *Vow to Poetry: Essays, Interviews, and Manifestos*. Minneapolis, Minn.: Coffee House Press, 2001, 25–50.

Buffalo, University of; Poetics Program

Albert Cook (1925–1998) was hired as chairman of the English department at the University of Buffalo (State University of New York at Buffalo) in 1963. Cook believed that poets and novelists should teach literature classes, so in the following years he hired CHARLES OLSON, ROBERT CREELEY, Leslie Fiedler, John Barth, John Logan, Mac Hammond, and Carl Dennis. However successful these writers were as scholars, their value to the department was as writers. The Poetry Collection at Buffalo was started in 1937 by Charles D. Abbott, so by the mid-1960s the library had already achieved an international reputation as a research library. The English department and the Poetry Collection sponsored poetry readings alone and together and brought a great range of poets to the campus for readings. There was a constant insertion of new ideas about poetry. MORTON FELDMAN, Lukas Foss, and NED ROREM all taught in the music department and were all on the cutting edge of contemporary MUSIC and composition. The students were also editors, so Ralph Maud began *Audit*, Douglas Calhoun began *Athanor*, and Al Glover began the *Magazine of Further Studies*. The energy and accomplishments of the 1960s, including Cook's innovations for the English department, became the foundation for the Poetics Program.

Creeley was appointed to Samuel P. Capen Chair of Poetry and Letters in spring 1989, and that following fall he had meetings with Raymond Federman, Dennis Tedlock, and Robert Bertholf to formulate a program in poetics. Charles Bernstein began his tenure in the Grey Chair of Poetry and Letters in fall 1990; the Poetics Program became an administrative unit of the English department in May 1991. Creeley served as its director until 1995, when Bernstein took over. In the Poetics Program poets and writers would teach courses in literature and subjects that informed poetry, what went under, as Olson understood it, the process of making a poem. The faculty did not conduct classes or workshops in writing poetry. The English department and the comparative literature department had taken strong positions about literary theory, and there was an institute for psychoanalytic studies, so both theory and psychoanalysis came into the program. From the beginning the Poetics Program was not proscriptive and resisted rigid guidelines for teaching. It welcomed multiple approaches then and interdisciplinary approaches to literary, cultural, and textual studies now. Again there were many poetry readings by many different poets; and there were new magazines, *The Apex of the M*, *Chloroform*, and *Chain*, *Deluxe Rubber Chicken*, to name only a few; again students formed groups to read poems to one another. Steve McCaffery succeeded Bernstein as the Grey Chair of Poetry and Letters. Susan Howe and Myung Mi Kim also currently teach in the Poetics Program. The students are trained to define an area of scholarship at the same time that they honor the multiphasic process of making poetry.

Burckhardt, Rudy (Rudolph Burckhardt)
(1914–1999) *filmmaker, painter*

The films of Rudolph (Rudy) Burckhardt frequently provide a medium for NEW YORK SCHOOL poetry and always treat the medium of film poetically. "My films are more like painting or poetry, they're not like big films," Burckhardt has stated (interview by Sawin n.p.). Indeed, rather than reaching the wide audiences of "big films," the exposure of Burkhardt's films could be limited to the "inner cell" that JAMES SCHUYLER reported to be on hand for a showing at Burckhardt's studio one night in 1959 (Schuyler, *Just the Thing* 95). While Burckhardt feared the hint of tragedy in Schuyler's poetry would weigh down his films, he found JOHN ASHBERY's work to be especially well suited for inclusion, either in written titles (*The Nude Pond* [1985]) or spoken voiceover (*Ostensibly* [1989]). As Burckhardt explained, Ashbery's "lines are like dreams, and when you put them over a film image it helps the viewer to see the image in a dreamlike way" (Lopate 42). Burckhardt's collaborator of longest standing, EDWIN DENBY, felt that he learned to see city life through Burckhardt's eyes (Denby 259), as two of Denby's collections—IN PUBLIC, IN PRIVATE (Decker, 1949) and MEDITERRANEAN CITIES (Wittenborn, 1956)—demonstrate by their incorporation of his friend's still photography. In elaborating on what he saw, specifically with reference to Burckhardt's images of city streets, Denby implicitly acknowledged the urban pastoral vision—"the bluish haze on the city as if you were in a forest" (Denby 259)—that distinguishes the New York School attitude toward the urban environment.

A native of Switzerland, Burckhardt met Denby in Basel in 1934 and followed him to NEW YORK CITY the next year. In 1936 Burckhardt made his first film, *145 West 21*—the address of the loft he shared with Denby in New York's Chelsea neighborhood. The cast included Denby, Paul Bowles (1910–99), Aaron Copland (1900–90), JOHN LATOUCHE (1917–56), and Virgil Thomson (1896–1989), a reflection of Burckhardt's place in the world of the arts, especially MUSIC, which would remain important in the structure of Burckhardt's film as well as the carefully chosen soundtracks. Appropriately, the last of four films that Burckhardt made during the mid-1950s with Joseph Cornell is entitled *What Mozart Saw on Mulberry Street* (1956). FRANK O'HARA plays piano music by Claude Debussy, Francis Poulenc, and Aleksandr Scriabin in *The Automotive Story* (1954), based on a text by KENNETH KOCH. O'Hara selected the music for *Lurk* (1964), a version of the Frankenstein story, with Denby as the doctor and the painter Red Grooms (1937–) as the monster.

Burckhardt was involved with painting from the very beginning of the New York School. WILLEM DE KOONING, a neighbor in Chelsea during the 1930s, painted a series of portraits using Denby and Burckhardt as models (Perl 110–115). In 1947 Burckhardt married a painter, Edith Schloss (1919–), an émigré from Germany, and he soon began formal art studies under French émigré Amédée Ozenfant (1886–1966), who encouraged Burckhardt's temperamental preference for structure over expressionism. Although Burckhardt

expressed dissatisfaction with the "primitive" quality of his painting (Burckhardt and Denby n.p.), he exhibited his work (at the Green Mountain Gallery co-op and, during the 1990s, at TIBOR DE NAGY GALLERY) and always counted painters among his close friends. His second wife, whom he married in 1964, was the painter Yvonne Jacquette (1934–). Their son, Tom (1964–), is also a painter; Jacob (1949–), Burckhardt's son by his first wife, is a filmmaker. Starting in 1965, Rudy, Yvonne, and Denby—who remained essentially a member of the family—regularly spent summers in an area of central Maine where friendships with other painters flourished, notably Rackstraw Downes (1939–), ALEX KATZ, and Neil Welliver (1929–2005). Katz's son VINCENT KATZ, who shuttled between New York and Maine throughout his childhood, concludes his book *BOULEVARD TRANSPORTATION* (Tibor de Nagy Editions, 1997) with a group of poems responding to Burckhardt's photographs of Maine.

Like the poets, Burckhardt learned from the painters an aesthetic of process. Still photography was "too quick," whereas "painting takes time" (Burckhardt and Denby n.p.). As a professional photographer, Burckhardt was assigned to take pictures of paintings in progress for the X Paints a Picture series featured in *Art News*. (When Burckhardt and Schuyler were assigned to do the feature on Alex Katz, both the photographer and the writer ended up in the painting.) Making films provided an ideal opportunity for Burckhardt to combine his experience as a photographer with the painter's concern for process, a concern that became the film's content in the same way that the painter's gestures became the subject of ACTION PAINTING. Burckhardt's "story" films are essentially HAPPENINGS, often involving poets as actors, for example, in MOUNTING TENSION (1950), with Ashbery, or *Inside Dope* (1971), with Denby, JIM CARROLL, LARRY FAGIN, PETER SCHJELDAHL, and ANNE WALDMAN. *Tarzam* (1969), with TAYLOR MEAD, is the closet Burckhardt came to working with a film "star." Closer to the work of the poets are Burckhardt's "diary films," as they have been called (Lopate 40–42), which function like the diary or journal poems of the New York School to foster an acceptance of each passing moment as of equal value.

In Burckhardt's photographs, paintings and films, "the transience of the images was also what made them so enduring," observed LEWIS WARSH (Waldman 12), one of the principal practitioners of this mode in poetry. The occasion for Warsh's comment was Burckhardt's death by means he chose, drowning himself in a lake near his home in Maine. Like his friend Denby, who also committed a gentle suicide, Burckhardt accepted his own passing as part of life's process.

Film Distribution:

Film-Makers' Cooperative in New York City. Online catalog of Rudolph Burkhardt's films. Available online. URL: http://www.film-makerscoop.com/search/search.php?author=Rudolph+Burckhardt. Accessed December 17, 2008.

Poetry Project. *Films by Rudy Burckhardt.* 2003. VHS. Poetry Project Web site. Available online. URL: http://www.poetryproject.com/artwork.php. Accessed October 11, 2008.

Bibliography

Ashbery, John. "The Enabler." *New York Times Magazine,* 2 January 2000, 20.

———. "Long Ago with Willem de Kooning." *Art Journal* 48, no. 3 (Fall 1989): 222–227.

———. "New York? Mais Oui!: Rudy Burckhardt" (2003). In *Selected Prose.* Edited by Eugene Richie. Ann Arbor: University of Michigan Press, 2004, 290–291.

Burckhardt, Rudy. "But Here's a Funny Story." Interview by William Corbett. *Modern Painters* 12, no. 4 (Winter 1999): 48–51.

———. Interview by Martica Sawin (1993). Archives of American Art, Smithsonian Institution. Available online. URL: http://www.aaa.si.edu/collections/oralhistories/transcripts/burckh93.htm, Accessed December 17, 2008.

———. *Mobile Homes.* Calais, Vt.: Z Press, 1979.

———. "Photographing Pollock: Rudy Burckhardt Remembers." Interview by William Corbett. *Modern Painters* 12, no. 1 (Spring 1999): 27ff.

Burckhardt, Rudy, and Edwin Denby. "The Cinema of Looking" (ca. 1976). Interview by Joe Giordano. *Jacket* 21 (February 2003). Available online. URL: http://jacketmagazine.com/21/denb-giord.html. Accessed December 17, 2008.

Burckhardt, Rudy, and Simon Pettet. *Talking Pictures: The Photography of Rudy Burckhardt.* Cambridge, Mass.: Zoland, 1994.

Denby, Edwin. "Dancers, Buildings, and People in the Streets" (1954). In *Dance Writings and Poetry.* Edited by Robert Cornfield. New Haven, Conn.: Yale University Press, 1998, 252–260.

Katz, Alex. "Rudolph Burckhardt: Multiple Fugitive." *Art News* 62, no. 8 (December 1963): 38–41.

Katz, Vincent, ed. *Rudy Burckhardt.* Exhibit catalog. Valencia, Spain: IVAM Centre Julio González, 1998.

Lippard, Lucy. "Rudy Burckhardt: Moviemaker, Photographer, Painter." *Art in America* 63, no. 2 (March–April 1975): 75–81.

Lopate, Phillip, with Vincent Katz. *Rudy Burckhardt.* New York: Abrams, 2004.

MacDonald, Scott. "The City as the Country: The New York City Symphony from Rudy Burckhardt to Spike Lee." *Film Quarterly* 51, no. 2 (Winter 1997–98): 2–20.

Perl, Jed. *New Art City: Manhattan at Mid-Century.* New York: Knopf, 2005.

Schuyler, James. "Alex Katz Paints a Picture" (1962). In *Selected Art Writings.* Edited by Simon Pettet. Santa Rosa, Calif.: Black Sparrow, 1998, 36–44.

———. *Just the Thing: Selected Letters of James Schuyler, 1951–1991.* Edited by William Corbett. New York: Turtle Point Press, 2004.

Waldman, Anne, et al., "Tribute to Rudy Burckhardt." *Poetry Project Newsletter* 177 (December 1999–January 2000): 11–13.

Burroughs, William (William S. Burroughs) (1914–1997)

William Burroughs's novel *Naked Lunch* (Paris: Olympia, 1959) is one of the three main classics of BEAT writing, along with ALLEN GINSBERG's *Howl* (1956) and JACK KEROUAC's *On the Road* (1957). Ginsberg and Kerouac met Burroughs in NEW YORK CITY in 1944, and the older man developed a complex relation as both mentor and student to his young friends as the three of them evolved the themes and styles that became identified as Beat by the late 1950s. As Burroughs lived outside the United States for much of this period, his reputation reached the NEW YORK SCHOOL poets largely secondhand, through Ginsberg, Kerouac, and GREGORY CORSO. Burroughs's publications achieved extra notoriety through censorship battles, starting with the suppression of the spring 1958 issue of the *Chicago Review,* which included the first chapter of *Naked Lunch,* and continuing with federal prosecution of the FLOATING BEAR (number 9, June 1961) for publishing the satirical "routine," "Roosevelt after Inauguration." Although LITA HORNICK had refused to print that work in KULCHUR, correctly recognizing the risk of prosecution, the pre-Hornick *Kulchur* opened with Burroughs's "The Conspiracy" in the inaugural issue (spring 1960). Soon afterward, publications even more closely identified with the New York School featured Burroughs's work. His "cut-ups" of Arthur Rimbaud, composed with Corso, appeared in the "COLLABORATION" issue of LOCUS SOLUS (number 2, 1961). A three-column composition, "Who Is the Third That Walks Beside You?" led off the summer 1964 issue of ART AND LITERATURE.

As these publications indicate, Burroughs was initially of more interest to New York School writers for his avant-garde techniques than for his Beat content. The practice of "cutting up" preexisting text to produce new compositions, to which Burroughs was introduced in 1959 by the painter Brion Gysin (1916–86), had antecedents in DADA that the New York School poets were already familiar with. JOHN ASHBERY, who was exploring the technique at the same time as Burroughs, has disavowed the motive of destruction that came to be associated with Burroughs's theory of language itself as an alien power that needed to be attacked as the body's immune system attacks a virus (Ashbery 43–44). For writers of the second-generation New York School, the cut-up technique acquired additional weight through Burroughs's example, and his science fiction imagery fit the poets' growing interest in the creative potential of prose FORMs derived from popular culture. TED BERRIGAN's "review" in *Kulchur* (number 18, summer 1965) of Burroughs's *Nova Express* (Grove, 1964) employs the cut-up technique that Berrigan explored at the same time in the prose paragraphs of "Great Stories of the Chair." Though published later, TOM VEITCH's *The LUIS ARMED STORY* (Full Court, 1978) dates from the same period. Its satirical treatment of Lyndon Johnson's inauguration in 1965 recalls Burroughs's

satire of Roosevelt, and Burroughs's appropriation of popular prose GENREs, from science fiction to crime fiction, echoes throughout Veitch's novel, which cuts up passages from *Naked Lunch,* among other sources.

From Burroughs's perspective his most significant contact with New York School poetry came through JOHN GIORNO, whom he first met during a brief period of residence in New York in 1964–65. When Burroughs returned to New York in 1974, Giorno involved him in performance, starting with a joint reading at the POETRY PROJECT AT ST. MARK'S CHURCH IN-THE-BOWERY that Burroughs recalled as "the gateway to a new dimension in my life as a writer" (Burroughs, Contributor's Note 626). Burroughs soon moved into a windowless apartment he called "The Bunker" in Giorno's building at 222 Bowery. The Phoenix Theater nearby on Second Avenue was the scene of the Nova Convention in 1978, a three-day festival organized by Giorno, celebrating Burroughs's performance in the company of JOHN CAGE, Merce Cunningham, PATTI SMITH, Laurie Anderson, and others. Publication of Burroughs's *Cities of the Red Night* (Holt, Rinehart and Winston, 1981) became the occasion for a national tour by Burroughs and Giorno, on which the two men performed with a synergy that Burroughs appreciated: "John's rock-and-roll delivery never failed to electrify our crowds, and then I would go on stage with my carefully-chosen reading pieces, like a Grandpa from hell" (Burroughs, "Voices" 6). One such performance in Toronto, Canada, became the inspiration for Ron Mann's documentary film *POETRY IN MOTION.*

In 1981 Burroughs followed his companion James Grauerholz (1953–   ) to Lawrence, Kansas, where he lived for the rest of his life. ANNE WALDMAN, who worked with Burroughs during the foundation of the NAROPA INSTITUTE, provides a moving account of visiting Burroughs in Lawrence in a section of IOVIS II (1997). Anticipating Burroughs's imminent death, Waldman draws on the Tibetan Book of the Dead—a source of common interest to Burroughs, Giorno, and Waldman—to depict Burroughs as a monster-deity and herself as his "consort" (*Iovis* II:209). Against death, she is recalling a moment of psychic rebirth recorded in her earlier poem "Eyes in All Heads to Be Looked Out Of," in which the ability to form "a new beast" was inspired in part by Burroughs's shamanistic instruction: "to take on the powers of the animals that transcend his/her own, to adorn, to proclaim oneself with the skin and hair, the magical implements that both stand in and activate power, to inhabit the persona" (Waldman, "'I Is Another'" 209).

Bibliography

Ashbery, John. *John Ashbery in Conversation with Mark Ford.* London: Between the Lines, 2003.

Berrigan, Ted. "Great Stories of the Chair" (1965–68). In *The Collected Poems of Ted Berrigan.* Edited by Alice Notley, Anselm Berrigan, and Edmund Berrigan. Berkeley: University of California Press, 1965, 88–97.

Burroughs, William. Contributor's Note. In *Out of This World: An Anthology of the St. Mark's Poetry Project, 1966–1991,* edited by Anne Waldman, 626. New York: Crown, 1991.

———. "Voices in Your Head." Introduction to *You Got to Burn to Shine: New and Selected Writings,* by John Giorno, 1–6. New York: High Risk Books/Serpent's Tail, 1994.

Morgan, Ted. *Literary Outlaw: The Life and Times of William S. Burroughs.* New York: Holt, 1988.

Waldman, Anne. "'I Is Another': Dissipative Structures" (1975). In *Vow to Poetry: Essays, Interviews, and Manifestos.* Minneapolis, Minn.: Coffee House Press, 2001, 193–213.

———. *Iovis* II. Minneapolis, Minn.: Coffee House Press, 1997.

But Not for Love May Natalie Tabak (1960)

Beginning in the mid-1940s, increasing numbers of Greenwich Village bohemians—including several NEW YORK SCHOOL painters and poets—were taking up part-time residence in the HAMPTONS, an area of Long Island famous for its scenic beaches. The artistic community that took shape in this region provided the source material for May Natalie Tabak's satiric novel *But Not for Love* (1960). Tabak, along with her husband, famed art critic HAROLD ROSENBERG, was among the many creative New Yorkers who migrated to the Hamptons after World War II. At that time the area's landed, WASP families were facing displacement by the influx of freewheeling, devil-may-care bohemians. Tabak explores the latter group's social milieu through the eyes of some dozen painters and writers as they maneuver and compete for sex, social prestige, and artistic greatness—all of which blur together in the neurotic minds of the protagonists. The author shrewdly dissects each character's singular foibles and then accentuates those qualities through the cast's interactions with one another.

Although Tabak's novel is not a genuine roman à clef, it does include some transparent fictionalizations of real-life figures. Most notable is her celebrated abstract painter, Brian Cooper (referred to by many—including his wife—as simply "Cooper"); prone to self-aggrandizing hyperbole and sporadic drunkenness, Cooper is a thinly veiled surrogate for JACKSON POLLOCK. *But Not for Love* portrays Cooper (one of the "older Young Artists") as a ridiculous hack, whose reputation is built on the financial connections and publicity stunts of his rich wife, Amy. For her part, Amy is probably based on Pollock's devoted patron, Peggy Guggenheim, rather than on his wife, fellow painter Lee Krasner, with whom he lived in East Hampton. Other real-life figures who have fictional doubles in the book are WILLEM and Elaine DE KOONING and Ruth Kligman (Pollock's mistress at the time of his death).

But Not for Love was very well received by critics, many of whom praised the sense of humanity that Tabak brings to her characters, in spite of her sharp-edged satirical acuity. In the words of Hope Hale, "Ms. Tabak brings to her report a special mingling of mischief and sympathy" (20).

Bibliography

Cahill, Holger. Review of *But Not for Love, New York Herald Tribune,* 12 June 1960, p. BR10.

Gruen, John. *The Party's Over Now: Reminiscences of the Fifties—New York's Artists, Writers, Musicians, and Their Friends.* New York: Pushcart Press, 1989.

Hale, Hope. Review of *But Not for Love. Saturday Review,* 23 July 1960, 20.

Harrison, Helen A., et al. *Hamptons Bohemia: Two Centuries of Artists and Writers on the Beach.* New York: Chronicle Books, 2002.

Nyren, Karl. Review of *But Not for Love. Library Journal*, 1 June 1960, 2,197.

Tabak, May Natalie. *But Not for Love.* New York: Horizon Press, 1960.

Bye, Reed (1948–)

Bye was born in Plainfield, New Jersey, on October 20, 1948. His parents met outside London in 1945 on an air force base at which his American father was stationed and where his British mother worked with the Red Cross. After the war Bye's father continued to work for the U.S. Air Force in Washington, D.C., and later for a civil engineering firm in New Jersey. Bye spent his youth not far from New York, in the New Jersey suburbs. After high school he briefly attended Cornell University, dropping out after a year. Shortly thereafter he moved to Boulder and there attended the University of Colorado, but did not complete his degree.

It was in Boulder, strangely enough, that Bye's connections with the NEW YORK SCHOOL really began. There he met, along with other first- and second-generation New York School luminaries (in town for the NAROPA INSTITUTE's Summer Writing Program), ANNE WALDMAN, to whom he was later married and with whom he had a son, Ambrose. Waldman and Bye lived with their son in NEW YORK CITY in the early 1980s, during which time Bye's connections with the New York School were solidified. In the middle of the '80s, Bye and Waldman returned to Boulder, where they began teaching full time at Naropa. In the 10-year period between 1985 and 1995, Bye completed his B.A., M.A., and Ph.D. in English literature at the University of Colorado, writing his doctoral dissertation on modernist prosody in the work of Gertrude Stein, Ezra Pound, and William Carlos Williams—the influence of whom can be seen in Bye's work. Waldman and Bye were divorced in the early '90s.

Although it is appropriate to group Bye with his second-generation New York School counterparts, his work perhaps owes less to their company (or to first-generation figures such as FRANK O'HARA and JOHN ASHBERY) than to ROBERT CREELEY, whom Bye classifies as "an enormous poetic beacon since I began reading poetry at around 20 years old" (interview). His poems are also marked by his longtime friendship with the poet JACK COLLOM, whose work is notable for, among other things, its "everyday" quality. Bye's poems, which are frequently humorous, are interesting not only for their immediacy of perception but for their deeply probing, contemplative nature. Often personal in content, his poems are by turns inventive, big-hearted, musical, and surreal. A core faculty member at Naropa since the 1980s, Bye teaches year-round and lives with his wife, Jill, in Boulder. His book of selected poems, *Join the Planets*, was released in 2005.

Bibliography

Bye, Reed. *Border Theme.* Calais, Vt.: Z Press, 1981.

———. *Erstwhile Charms.* Boulder, Colo.: Rocky Ledge Cottage Editions, 1980.

———. *Gaspar Still in His Cage.* Boulder, Colo.: Erudite Fangs/Smokeproof Editions, 2002.

———. *Heart's Bestiary.* Boulder, Colo.: Rocky Ledge Cottage Editions, 1987.

———. Interviewed by Erik Anderson, 2005, unpub.

———. *Join the Planets.* New York: United Artists Books, 2005.

———. *Passing Freaks and Graces.* Boulder, Colo.: Rodent Press & Erudite Fangs, 1996.

———. *Some Magic at the Dump.* New York: Angel Hair Books/Songbird Editions, 1978.

C

"C" (1963–1967)

TED BERRIGAN's "C": A *Journal of Poetry* established the first link in the chain connecting the periodical publications of the first-generation NEW YORK SCHOOL poets with those of the second generation. Although the mimeograph revolution, continued by "C" and later magazines, began in 1962 with ED SANDERS's *FUCK YOU*, "C" focused more exclusively on literature and art, like *LOCUS SOLUS*, Berrigan's acknowledged model ("Some Notes" 2). The first issue of "C" contained Berrigan's "Poem in the Traditional Manner," which had previously appeared in the final issue of *Locus Solus* (number 5, 1962). However, the four contributors to the first issue of "C"—Berrigan, RON PADGETT, DICK GALLUP, and JOE BRAINARD—shared a connection with another magazine, the *WHITE DOVE REVIEW*, published in Tulsa, Oklahoma, where they had all met.

How the "TULSA SCHOOL," as JOHN ASHBERY jokingly referred to them (Padgett and Shapiro xxx), moved to the center of the New York School using "C" as their vehicle has been the subject of much recent criticism (Wolf, Rifkin, Kane, Thorne). Publicity attended "C" at every stage of its existence, and even before. The idea for the magazine arose amid a controversy surrounding censorship of a student publication at Columbia University, which got Padgett, then a student at Columbia, a spot on TV news. A *Censored Review*, produced in cheap mimeograph format, bypassed university officials and gave Berrigan the idea—and perhaps the title (Kane 104)—for "C." Lorenz

Gude (1942–), another Columbia student, took on the role of publisher.

What seems to have fixed attention on "C" within the New York School was Berrigan's decision to devote the fourth issue (September 1963) to EDWIN DENBY. Through GERARD MALANGA, whose work had appeared in "C," number 3 (July–August 1963), Berrigan was able to arrange for ANDY WARHOL to design both the front and back covers of the issue, featuring photographs of Denby and Malanga in sexually suggestive poses (on the back cover, Malanga is kissing Denby). Reva Wolf has argued that Warhol may have been using these images to get through to FRANK O'HARA, who had so far shunned him. There is no doubt that the Denby issue helped Berrigan get through to O'Hara, who contributed both a previously published review of Denby (excerpted from "Rare Modern") and a new poem, "Edwin's Hand." With a bridge between "C" and the first generation now firmly in place, other poets soon followed. Ashbery, BARBARA GUEST, and JAMES SCHUYLER contributed to issue number 5 (October–November 1963), and later issues published so many recognized names, including BEATS such as WILLIAM S. BURROUGHS and ALLEN GINSBERG, that Berrigan felt the need to reassert his interest in promoting unknown writers ("Some Notes" 10). But by this time the image of "C" was in the public domain, beyond Berrigan's control. A trade paperback anthology, *The New American Arts* (Collier Books, 1965), edited by Richard Kostelanetz (1940–), advertised coverage of the full range of contemporary poetry, "from

ROBERT LOWELL's *Life Studies* to the 'C' magazine nihilists" (back cover blurb).

While the contents of "C" grew increasingly diverse (Thorne), the original Tulsa School remained central to other aspects of the enterprise. For instance, Brainard designed covers for eight of the magazine's 13 issues and produced most of the artwork for two separate issues of "C" *Comics* (number 1, 1964; number 2, 1965), in collaboration with New York School poets of both the first (Ashbery, Denby, KENWARD ELMSLIE, Guest, KENNETH KOCH, O'Hara, Schuyler) and second generations (BILL BERKSON, Berrigan, Gallup, FRANK LIMA, Padgett, PETER SCHJELDAHL, TONY TOWLE, TOM VEITCH). "C" Press issued the debut collections of Berrigan (*The Sonnets*, 1964), Padgett (*In Advance of the Broken Arm*, 1964), and Gallup (*Hinges*, 1965), which Berrigan and Padgett followed up by reviewing each other's books in the same issue of KULCHUR (number 17, spring 1965). The 13th and final issue of "C" appeared in May 1966 (issues are numbered consecutively but divided into two volume numbers, the second volume starting with issue number 11, summer 1965). "C" Press essentially ceased operation in 1967 with the publication of pamphlets by MICHAEL BROWNSTEIN (*Behind the Wheel*) and Elmslie (*The Power Plant Poems*). Berrigan, however, revived the imprint to sponsor a few later titles, including *165 Meeting House Lane* (1971) by ALICE NOTLEY and *In February I Think* (1978) by Elio Schneeman (1961–97), the son of the artist GEORGE SCHNEEMAN.

Bibliography

Berrigan, Ted. Letter to James Schuyler, January 30, 1964. In *Nice to See You: Homage to Ted Berrigan*, edited by Anne Waldman, 7–8. Minneapolis, Minn.: Coffee House Press, 1991.

———. "Poem in the Traditional Manner" (1962). In *The Collected Poems of Ted Berrigan*. Edited by Alice Notley, Anselm Berrigan, and Edmund Berrigan. Berkeley: University of California Press, 2005, 32.

———. "Some Notes about C." (1964). Ted Berrigan Papers. Syracuse University Library, Special Collections Research Center, Syracuse, N.Y.

Clay, Steven, and Rodney Phillips. *A Secret Location on the Lower East Side: Adventures in Writing, 1960–1980*. New York: Granary Books, 1998, 160–165.

Kane, Daniel. *All Poets Welcome: The Lower East Side Poetry Scene in the 1960s*. Berkeley: University of California Press, 2003, 100–122.

O'Hara, Frank. "Edwin's Hand" (1963). In *The Collected Poems*. Rev. ed. Edited by Donald Allen. Berkeley: University of California Press, 1995, 238–239.

———. "Rare Modern" (1957). In *Standing Still and Walking in New York*. Edited by Donald Allen. San Francisco: Grey Fox, 1983, 73–81.

Padgett, Ron, and David Shapiro. Preface to *An Anthology of New York Poets*. New York: Vintage–Random House, 1970, xxix–xxxvii.

Rifkin, Libbie. "'Worrying about Making It': Ted Berrigan's Social Poetics." In *Career Moves: Olson, Creeley, Zukofsky, Berrigan, and the American Avant-Garde*. Madison: University of Wisconsin Press, 2000, 108–135.

Thorne, Harry. "'The New York School is a Joke': The Disruptive Poetics of C: A Journal of Poetry." In *Don't Ever Get Famous: Essays on New York Writing after the New York School*, edited by Daniel Kane, 74–89. Champaign, Ill.: Dalkey Archive Press, 2006.

Wolf, Reva. *Andy Warhol, Poetry, and Gossip in the 1960s*. Chicago: University of Chicago Press, 1997.

Café Le Metro (Metro Café)

Café Le Metro was originally owned by Moe and Cindy Margulies and stood at 149 Second Avenue in the East Village. The Metro was a dimly lit and sparsely decorated antique furniture store that doubled as a coffeehouse. It began hosting regular literary gatherings after LES DEUX MÉGOTS Coffeehouse (a previous reading venue) closed down in February 1963. The following year the Metro became the center of a landmark First Amendment battle; after attending a reading by poet JACKSON MAC LOW, a city license inspector issued a summons citing the New York Coffee House Law of 1962—a law prohibiting the presentation of "entertainment" without a costly cabaret license. If the city had won, it would have effectively shut down the small (and unlicensed) neighborhood coffeehouses that gave voice to many of the era's most important poets. The case gained the attention of poets such as ALLEN GINSBERG of the BEATS, PAUL BLACKBURN of the *BLACK MOUNTAIN REVIEW*, and the second-generation

NEW YORK SCHOOL poet TED BERRIGAN, all of whom fought for, and eventually won, the right to read poetry without a cabaret permit.

Blackburn served as the primary coordinator of events at the Metro, which featured, in addition to the poets already mentioned, readings by WILLIAM S. BURROUGHS, GREGORY CORSO, DIANE DI PRIMA, DICK GALLUP, LeRoi Jones (AMIRI BARAKA), GERARD MALANGA, RON PADGETT, and JOHN WIENERS. More than merely a place to share their work, the Metro gave artists a sense of community, born out of their shared creative energy. Significantly, the Metro was much less formal than many subsequent poetry reading venues. At the Metro audience members did not necessarily give the poet their full attention but, rather, allowed the poetry to meld into the ambient noise and conversation.

In 1965 friction between café management and the African-American writers associated with the UMBRA workshop caused the readings to move from the Metro to St. Mark's Church (also on Second Avenue).

Cage, John (1912–1992) *musician, artist*

"John Cage is a quintessential artist of this century," writes ANNE WALDMAN in *IOVIS* I (309). It is significant that Waldman identifies Cage simply as an "artist," without specifying a medium. Although Cage first established a reputation as a musician, he extended his theories of composition to writing, graphic arts, and unclassifiable performance events in ways that broke down boundaries between the arts, as between art and life. He would probably object to Waldman's term *artist* as implying such a boundary.

Cage was born and raised in Los Angeles and spent some time there studying with the great modernist composer Arnold Schoenberg. After moving to NEW YORK CITY in 1942 he met Marcel Duchamp, whose ideas would be transmitted through Cage to younger artists in a FORM that critics came to call "neo-dada." Most requests for Cage's compositions came at this time from dancers, particularly Merce Cunningham, with whom Cage formed a lifetime partnership, both personal and professional. Painters made up the core of the audience. By the late 1940s Cage was participating in the artists' CLUB and contributing to artists' journals such as *Possibilities* and the *Tiger's Eye*. Likeminded musicians, including MORTON FELDMAN, David Tudor, Earle Brown, and Christian Wolff, soon gathered around Cage to form an "'abstractionist' pressure group," bringing MUSIC up to speed with painting (Thomson 76).

Cage acknowledged an affinity between his music and NEW YORK SCHOOL painting with regard to the principle of "all-over" composition, "a surface which in no sense has a center of interest" (Sandler 255). The work is not defined internally, by a visual "figure" or a harmonic "key" but rather externally by the frame in painting or a unit of time in music. The arbitrariness of this organization is meant to be felt in the sense that "it looks as if it could have continued beyond the frame," in the case of painting, or as if it has "no beginning, middle, or ending," in the case of music (Sandler 255). All of these elements register in JOHN ASHBERY's account of Tudor's performance of Cage's the *Music of Changes*, which Ashbery attended with FRANK O'HARA on New Year's Day 1952: "It was a series of dissonant chords, mostly loud, with irregular rhythm. It went on for over an hour and seemed infinitely extendable. The feeling was an open determinism—that what happens was meant to happen, no matter how random or rough or patchy it seemed to be" (Kostelanetz 93). This openness to "what happens" displaces the artist from his traditional role in Western art as the center of intention. It "profoundly refreshed" Ashbery, who felt freed from a writer's block he had been suffering for nearly two years. Cage had absorbed the attitude from his study of Eastern philosophy, including Zen Buddhism and the *I-Ching,* or *Book of Changes.* He employed the latter system of decision making by random procedure, the tossing of coins, in composing the *Music of Changes.*

To the extent that painting incorporated accident—the way paint happened to flow from a stick or splash onto a canvas—it was aligned with this aspect of Cage's aesthetic also. However, the expressionist intention of so-called ABSTRACT EXPRESSIONISM was diametrically opposed to the decentering of the ego that Cage saw as a chief benefit of submitting to the discipline of randomness (Jones). In this regard he found allies in the next generation of painters, especially ROBERT RAUSCHENBERG and JASPER JOHNS, and in poets who, like these painters, explored the use of found materials as a challenge to the originality associated with authorship. Again Duchamp stands in the background, and Ashbery, who made significant use of found material in *The Tennis Court Oath* (1962), provides the connection to NEW YORK SCHOOL poetry. Cage's "26 Statements re Duchamp," celebrating "the things he found," first appeared in Ashbery's journal ART AND LITERATURE (number 3, autumn–winter 1964). The following year TED BERRIGAN made up an "interview" with Cage, appropriating text by other authors ranging from the Spanish playwright Fernando Arrabal to Berrigan's friend DICK GALLUP (Clark 36–39). When PETER SCHJELDAHL published the interview in MOTHER magazine (number 7, 1966), Cage was reportedly upset by a slight to his mother (Lehman 362–364), but presumably he did not object to the method. His "mesostic" poems, a variation of acrostic that he began to write about this time, "read through" preexisting texts by following a pattern of letters that spell out a predetermined key word or name, which is then highlighted as the "spine" running down the middle of a text sample. Cage contributed two such mesostics in the name of FRANK O'HARA to *Big Sky* magazine's memorial issue, "Homage to Frank O'Hara" (1978).

As a musician, Cage was especially interested in mining text for its sound properties, an interest that encouraged poets in the exploration of both live and recorded performance. In his Dial-a-Poem series, JOHN GIORNO included Cage on several albums, for instance *Disconnected* (1974), which also features work by Giorno, Ashbery, CLARK COOLIDGE, BERNADETTE MAYER, Anne Waldman, and others. Waldman's "Pieces of an Hour," which is introduced in *Iovis* by the statement about Cage quoted above, was written to accompany a performance of Cage's music. The title refers to his method of composing music by units of duration. In performance, Waldman plays on one of Cage's most famous technical innovations, the "prepared piano," in which everyday objects like nuts and bolts and pieces of wood are placed between the piano's strings to produce a new range of percussive sounds. Using her body like one of these objects,

Waldman at various moments lies under the piano (Waldman, *In the Room* 126), "accompanying the 'text' or 'score' with knocks on the underbelly of the instrument, animal noises, and the like" (Waldman, "Go-Between" 273). Like Ashbery, Waldman finds Cage's repositioning of the author "extraordinarily liberating" ("Go-Between" 273).

Bibliography

Cage, John. *Music of Changes* (1951). In *The Complete John Cage Edition*, Vol. 29: *Piano Works 6*. CD. Martine Joste, piano. Mode 147, 2005.

———. *Silence: Lectures and Writings*. 1961. Reprint, Middletown, Conn.: Wesleyan University Press, 1973.

———. "26 Statements re Duchamp" (1964). In *A Year from Monday*. Middletown, Conn.: Wesleyan University Press, 1967, 70–72.

———. "2 Mesostics." In *Homage to Frank O'Hara*, edited by Bill Berkson and Joe LeSueur, 182. Bolinas, Calif.: Big Sky, 1988.

Clark, Tom. *Late Returns: A Memoir of Ted Berrigan*. Bolinas, Calif.: Tombouctou, 1985.

Giorno, John, et al. *Disconnected*. Sound recording. Giorno Poetry Systems, 1974. UbuWeb. Available online. URL: http://www.ubu.com/sound/disconnected.html. Accessed December 17, 2008.

Jones, Caroline A. "Finishing School: John Cage and the Abstract Expressionist Ego." *Critical Inquiry* 19, no. 4 (Summer 1993): 628–665.

Kostelanetz, Richard. "John Ashbery" (1976). In *The Old Poetries and the New*. Ann Arbor: University of Michigan Press, 1981, 87–110.

Lehman, David. *The Last Avant-Garde: The Making of the New York School of Poets*. New York: Doubleday, 1998.

Sandler, Irving. *A Sweeper-up after Artists: A Memoir*. New York: Thames & Hudson, 2003.

Thomson, Virgil. "The Abstract Composers" (1952). In *Writings about John Cage*, edited by Richard Kostelanetz, 73–76. Ann Arbor: University of Michigan Press, 1996.

Tomkins, Calvin. "John Cage." In *The Bride and the Bachelors: Five Masters of the Avant-Garde*. New York: Penguin, 1976, 69–144.

Waldman, Anne. "Go-Between Between." In *Vow to Poetry: Essays, Interviews, and Manifestos*. Minneapolis, Minn.: Coffee House Press, 2001, 269–279.

———. *In the Room of Never Grieve: New and Selected Poems, 1985–2003*. Minneapolis, Minn.: Coffee House Press, 2003.

———. *Iovis* I. Minneapolis, Minn.: Coffee House Press, 1993.

———. "Pieces of an Hour." Recorded excerpt in *Alchemical Elegy—Selected Songs and Writings*. PENNsound Web site. Available online. URL: http://www.writing.upenn.edu/pennsound/x/Waldman.html. Accessed December 17, 2008.

Carroll, Jim (1950–)

More famous than most NEW YORK SCHOOL poets, Jim Carroll is less famous as a poet than as the leader of The JIM CARROLL BAND and the author of the sensational memoir of NEW YORK CITY street life, *The BASKETBALL DIARIES* (1978). Yet poetry has been Carroll's one constant occupation and the means by which he has come closest to realizing his desire "to sleep / inside a strange language" (*Fear* 260).

Born in New York and raised on the Lower East Side, Carroll attended Catholic schools and won a scholarship to the elite Trinity School in 1964, where he starred at basketball. While at Trinity, Carroll also began to write and shoot heroin; both would define his life over the next eight years. His experiences on the streets of New York, where he resorted to hustling and muggings to support his addiction, forced an early reckoning with heartache and isolation. He stoked his writing ambition while attending readings at the POETRY PROJECT AT ST. MARK'S CHURCH IN-THE-BOWERY, where he saw poets like JOHN ASHBERY and ALLEN GINSBERG. In 1967 he published his first poems in *The WORLD* and in a mimeograph pamphlet, *Organic Trains* (Penny Press), with an epigraph from FRANK O'HARA's "To the Harbormaster" (1954). He presented the pamphlet to TED BERRIGAN, and the two became fast friends. In 1969 Berrigan praised the young Carroll in *Culture Hero*, a tabloid published by the artist Les Levine (1935–).

Forced Entries (1987), reconstructed diary entries of 1971–73, document Carroll's many connections in the art world during this period. He worked for ANDY WARHOL at the Factory, assisted ANNE WALDMAN at the Poetry Project, and alternated between LARRY RIVERS's studio and Clarice Rivers's apartment, looking after the kids. (The section of *Forced Entries* entitled "Christmas with D. M. Z." [81–98] describes Rivers under a pseudonym.) Carroll's poems of this period, collected in *4 Ups & 1 Down* (ANGEL HAIR, 1970) and *LIVING AT THE MOVIES* (1973), explore personal relationships at a more intimate level. As is so often the case in New York School poetry, names that might not be identifiable to the general reader enhance the air of intimacy: "I hope that George [Schneeman] enjoys the gifts / that Ron [Padgett] will give him tonight" ("Birthday Poem"). More conventionally, Carroll also employs the traditional lyric address to an unnamed "you": "depth is approaching everywhere in the sky and in your touch" ("Poem"). Carroll longs for depth in his poems as much as he condemns the shallowness of contemporary life in his diaries. For instance, he writes of Warhol's Factory: "The poles are greased so thoroughly with bullshit and artifice that depth hasn't a chance" (*Forced Entries* 34–35).

In 1973 Carroll left New York for BOLINAS, CALIFORNIA, where he lived a solitary existence and concentrated on overcoming his addiction to heroin. With encouragement from TOM CLARK, he shaped his basketball diaries into a book, which was first published in Bolinas (Tombouctou Press, 1978). The attention that book ultimately received, in its second edition (1980), owed much to Carroll's simultaneous emergence as a rock star, with the release of the album *Catholic Boy* (1980) by The Jim Carroll Band. This development, too, stems from Carroll's West Coast sojourn. A Bolinas neighbor, Rosemary Klemfuss, whom Carroll married in 1978, took him to hear PUNK ROCK/new wave bands in the San Francisco area. A former girlfriend from New York, PATTI SMITH ("Jenny Ann" in *Forced Entries*), had Carroll perform with her band when she needed an opening act in San Diego, and he felt himself hooked on a new kind of high.

By 1980 Carroll was back in New York with his wife and a new career that channeled much of his writing energy into song lyrics. He did not publish another book of poems until after his band broke up. *The Book of Nods* (Penguin, 1986) includes work dating as far back as 1970, when *The World* (number 20) published one of the first "nods," prose poems evoking drug-induced fantasies. However, the style of the section entitled "California Variations" is no less surrealistic. Rather than varying with his experience, Carroll's inspiration stems continuously from writing and writers such as the French poet Arthur Rimbaud, a hero of *The Book of Nods*, or Frank O'Hara, the dedicatee of "Poem" ("My footsteps in the shallow"). Carroll's memorial poem for Berrigan, "Calm under Fire," appears in the "New Work" section of his collection *Fear of Dreaming* (Penguin, 1993). *Void of Course* (Penguin, 1998) opens with a memorial poem for grunge rocker Kurt Cobain (1967–94), drawing on the terms of O'Hara's advice to JOHN WIENERS in "A Young Poet" (1957). Carroll confesses that he might have preceded Cobain in suicide except that the urge to keep writing "kept me alive, above any wounds" ("8 Fragments for Kurt Cobain").

Bibliography

Berrigan, Ted. "Jim Carroll." *Culture Hero* 1, no. 5 (1969): 9–10.

Carroll, Jim. "The Catholic Boy Confesses: Jim Carroll." Interview by Clarice Rivers. *Interview* (January 1980): 54–55.

———. "8 Fragments for Kurt Cobain." In *Void of Course: Poems, 1994–1997.* New York: Penguin, 1998.

———. *Fear of Dreaming: Selected Poems.* New York: Penguin, 1993.

———. *Forced Entries: The Downtown Diaries, 1971–1973.* New York: Penguin, 1987.

Carter, Cassie. "The Sickness That Takes Years to Perfect: Jim Carroll's Alchemical Vision." *Dionysos: The Literature and Addiction TriQuarterly* 6, no. 1 (Winter 1996): 6–19.

Gray, Timothy. "'A World without Gravity': The Urban Pastoral Spirituality of Jim Carroll and Kathleen Norris." *Texas Studies in Literature and Language* 47, no. 3 (Fall 2005): 213–252.

Kuennen, Cassie Carter. "Jim Carroll: An Annotated, Selective, Primary and Secondary Bibliography, 1967–1988." *Bulletin of Bibliography* 47, no. 2 (1990): 81–112. CatholicBoy.com. Available online. URL: http://www.catholicboy.com/bulletin_of_bibliography_7-2.html. Accessed December 17, 2008.

O'Hara, Frank. *The Collected Poems.* Rev. ed. Edited by Donald Allen. Berkeley: University of California Press, 1995.

Carroll, Paul (1927–1995)

Born and raised in CHICAGO, ILLINOIS, where he conducted most of his career, poet and editor Paul Carroll contributed greatly to the history and development of the post–World War II avant-garde through his editing of the literary magazine *Big Table* (1959–60) and the anthology *The Young American Poets* (1968), as well as serving as a conduit for BEAT, NEW YORK SCHOOL, and BLACK MOUNTAIN poetics in the nation's major noncoastal city.

Carroll's father, an Irish immigrant, had achieved social prominence in Chicago by amassing a fortune in banking and real estate, much of it lost in the Great Depression. The ambiguous psychological legacy he left his son is recorded in Carroll's "Father," the one poem of his included in *The NEW AMERICAN POETRY, 1945–1960* (1960). Carroll is placed in that anthology among the Black Mountain poets because he had published in the magazines *Origin* and BLACK MOUNTAIN REVIEW, but he was best known as a champion of the Beats. In 1958 works by WILLIAM S. BURROUGHS and JACK KEROUAC had been main targets of censorship of the *Chicago Review* by University of Chicago officials, leading Carroll and fellow editor Irving Rosenthal to start *Big Table* in order to publish the suppressed works. Subsequent issues of *Big Table*, edited by Carroll, included a number of New York School poets (JOHN ASHBERY, KENNETH KOCH, FRANK O'HARA, and BILL BERKSON).

What was important about Carroll's attention to the New York School poets was precisely that it did not isolate them as a "school" but instead presented them as part of a much larger generational shift in AMERICAN POETRY, eventually identified by Carroll as "the generation of 1962" (*Poem in Its Skin* 203). For Carroll this shift required a turn away from the formalist principles of literary criticism in which he had been trained at the University of Chicago and toward something that sounded much like O'Hara's "PERSONISM." At the outset of his critical study *The Poem in Its Skin* (1968), Carroll declares: "Every good poem is like a person: it has its own skin." This does not mean that the critic is to look for the poet inside the poem but rather to observe the poem's individual behavior, not just its FORM. Carroll is particularly delighted when the poem defies any rules that might be formalized. This sort of behavior makes him choose Ashbery's "Leaving the Atocha Station"—"an anti-poem" (23)—and O'Hara's "The DAY LADY DIED"—an "impure poem" (161)—as two of the 10 poems that each supply the focus of a chapter in Carroll's book. For his anthology of poets under 35, *The Young American Poets*, Carroll chose TED BERRIGAN's *TAMBOURINE LIFE* despite the fact that its "skin" fleshed out to 26 pages. "'Tambourine Life' is my most famous poem because of that anthology," Berrigan later acknowledged (37). In Carroll's judgment, that poem established Berrigan as "a leader of the young American poets" (Note on Berrigan 119), not just of the second-generation New York School, who make up roughly one-third of the 55 poets represented in the anthology overall.

Carroll continued to publish his own poetry, including two selected editions, *New and Selected Poems* (Yellow Press 1978) and *Poems, 1950–1990* (Another Chicago Press, 1991), but his work failed to develop beyond its promising beginning, and it attracted little critical attention. His later influence came chiefly through his teaching at the University of Illinois–Chicago. The careers of former students such as PAUL HOOVER and BOB ROSENTHAL testify to Carroll's role in spreading the news of the New York School. Carroll's last two books, *The Beaver Dam Road Poems* (1994) and *Straight Poets I Have Known and Loved* (1995), were self-published under the Big Table imprint from Vilas, North Carolina, where he moved with his wife, Maryrose Carroll, a sculptor, upon his retirement from teaching.

Bibliography

Berrigan, Ted. Interviewed by Barry Alpert (1972). In *Talking in Tranquility: Interviews*. Edited by Stephen Ratcliffe and Leslie Scalapino. Bolinas, Calif.: Avenue B; Oakland, California: O Books, 1991, 31–54.

Carroll, Paul. "Father" (1959). In *The New American Poetry, 1945–1960*. Edited by Donald Allen, 1960, 88–89. Reprint, Berkeley: University of California Press, 1999.

———. Note on Ted Berrigan. In *The Young American Poets*. Chicago: Follett/Big Table, 1968, 119.

———. *The Poem in Its Skin*. Chicago: Follett/Big Table, 1968.

Carroll Band   *See* JIM CARROLL BAND, THE.

Cedar Street Tavern

Described by painter LARRY RIVERS as "the G-spot of the whole art scene" (Lehman 68), the original Cedar Street Tavern at 24 University Place (1945–63) was a social nexus of avant-garde artists in the 1950s and 1960s. In contrast to the genteel trendiness of its later incarnation at 82 University Place (1963–2006), the old bar was a seedy, smoke-filled dive where drinking to excess was the rule and violent brawls were not uncommon. Both JACKSON POLLOCK and JACK KEROUAC were kicked out of the tavern for misconduct, and WILLEM DE KOONING once punched art critic CLEMENT GREENBERG in the jaw there.

Sexual tensions inherent in the diversity of bohemian lifestyles were forced into the open in such an environment. The painter Mike Goldberg (1924–2007) recalled: "[T]he Cedar Bar *was* a macho place. A lot of us had been in the service. Even the few women in there were tough cookies" (Ferguson 98). FRANK O'HARA's longtime roommate, Joe LeSueur (1924–2001), described the painter Joan Mitchell (1925–1992) as one of the "tough cookies," though he also remembers a different type of woman, "the camp-follower types, who hung out at the Cedar, abject, sycophantic females dubbed 'art tarts' by one of us, possibly by me" (162).

The macho style of the Cedar was much less hospitable to gay men than some of the other downtown bars like the SAN REMO. Cedar patrons have recorded many antigay outbursts, from Pollock especially. Nevertheless, though many of the NEW YORK SCHOOL poets were gay, "even the people who didn't read respected poets," Goldberg explained (Ferguson 98). O'Hara was especially fond of the Cedar and lived just up the street from 1957 to 1959. In numerous poems the bar features as a meeting spot for O'Hara and various friends (Gooch 202). It is the setting for the unfinished play *Kenneth Koch: A Tragedy* that O'Hara co-authored with Rivers, as well as for a play by Alfred Leslie (1927–   ), simply called *The Cedar Bar* (1952, 1986), recently reincarnated by Leslie as a film (2001).

Memoirs of the Cedar give the impression that bar patrons witnessed the mayhem as if they were watching a play. In O'Hara's judgment, "[I]f Jackson Pollock tore the door off the men's room in the Cedar it was something he just did and was interesting, not an annoyance. You couldn't see into it [the men's room] anyway, and besides there was then a sense of genius" (169).

Bibliography

Ferguson, Russell. *In Memory of My Feelings: Frank O'Hara and American Art.* Exhibit catalog. Los Angeles: Museum of Contemporary Art; Berkeley: University of California Press, 1999.

Gooch, Brad. *City Poet: The Life and Times of Frank O'Hara.* New York: Knopf, 1993.

Lehman, David. *The Last Avant-Garde: The Making of the New York School of Poets.* New York: Doubleday, 1998.

LeSueur, Joe. *Digressions on Some Poems by Frank O'Hara: A Memoir.* New York: Farrar, Straus & Giroux, 2003.

O'Hara, Frank. "Larry Rivers: A Memoir" (1965). In *Standing Still and Walking in New York,* edited by Donald Allen, 169–173. San Francisco: Grey Fox, 1983.

O'Hara, Frank, and Larry Rivers. "Kenneth Koch: A Tragedy" (1954). In *Amorous Nightmares of Delay: Selected Plays,* by Frank O'Hara. Baltimore, Md.: Johns Hopkins University Press, 1997, 121–132.

Ceravolo, Joseph (1934–1988)

The poetry of Joseph Ceravolo (pronounced cheh/RAV/o/lo) abounds with the lyric intensity of first things. His short poem "Drunken Winter" opens, "Oak oak! like like / it then," because there is no likeness other than the thing itself ("it"), nothing prior to the word other than the word itself: *oak* precedes *oak.* Ceravolo's work is characterized by a seemingly alien syntax. As KENNETH KOCH says, "What these lines say, in a prose way, doesn't make sense. . . . But what the lines suggest . . . makes sense of a kind that is only found in poetry" (9–10). Ceravolo told DAVID SHAPIRO that "he didn't so much express emotions as observe the linguistic constellations that grouped themselves during or around an emotion. [He wanted] to create only one

school, The School of Everyday Life, with courses in the seasons" (Hoover 291).

Ceravolo was born in the NEW YORK CITY borough of Queens, the first son of Italian immigrants. He graduated from City College of New York with a degree in civil engineering and, in 1959, attended Koch's poetry workshop at the New School. Ceravolo spent most of his adult life in Bloomfield, New Jersey, where he worked as a hydraulics engineer. His books include *Fits of Dawn* (C Press, 1965); *Wild Flowers Out of Gas* (Tibor de Nagy Editions, 1967); *Spring in This World of Poor Mutts* (Columbia University Press, 1968), winner of the first-ever Frank O'Hara Award; *Transmigration Solo* (Toothpaste Press, 1979); *Millennium Dust* (KULCHUR, 1982); and the posthumous *The Green Lake Is Awake: Selected Poems* (Coffee House Press, 1994).

Although Ceravolo is commonly associated with the second-generation NEW YORK SCHOOL, his singular work bears little aesthetic resemblance to that of other poets of that group beyond a shared affinity for William Carlos Williams and the French cubist poets. Despite the efforts of his close friends Shapiro and Koch, Ceravolo's work has, unfortunately, received little critical attention. Perhaps this is due to the fact that most critical studies of the second-generation New York School have focused on sociological aspects, and Ceravolo was not a major player in the group's social network. Ceravolo died of cancer in 1988, leaving behind two unpublished manuscripts: *Mad Angels* and the book-length poem *The Hellgate.*

Bibliography

Ceravolo, Joseph. *The Green Lake Is Awake: Selected Poems.* Minneapolis, Minn.: Coffee House Press, 1994.

Koch, Kenneth. "On the Poetry of Joseph Ceravolo." In *The Green Lake Is Awake: Selected Poems.* Minneapolis, Minn.: Coffee House Press, 1994, 9–13.

Hoover, Paul. Headnote to Ceravolo selection. In *Postmodern American Poetry.* New York: Norton, 1994, 291.

Certain Slant of Sunlight, A Ted Berrigan (1988)

In early 1982 Ken and Ann Mikolowski of Alternative Press sent TED BERRIGAN 500 blank postcards to do whatever he wanted with. The postcards were eventually to be packaged with other Alternative Press materials and sent to their subscribers. In her introductory note to *A Certain Slant of Sunlight* (O Books, 1988), ALICE NOTLEY writes:

> Early on in the project Ted discovered he was writing a book of poems . . . & sometimes characterized the projected book as a book of postcard-like messages, sometimes as a book of short, or shorter, poems. Neither of these characterizations is particularly apt for what happened: a realm of shorter poems, written in a newly freed voice, that drifts among day-book, epigram & lyric, in all literary awareness, describing the feel of a difficult year.

The book was written over the course of 1982, the year of Berrigan's mother's death and the year before his own, but Berrigan faces this subject with typical bravado; in the opening, "Poem," he writes:

> *Yea, though I walk*
> *through the Valley of*
> *the Shadow of Death, I*
> *Shall fear no evil—*
> *for I am a lot more*
> *insane than*
> *This Valley.*

The idiosyncratic capitalization and use of the dash as an end stop are only a couple of the book's nods to Emily Dickinson. The title poem, "A Certain Slant of Sunlight," is also a reworking of the theme in Dickinson's "There's a certain Slant of light" (number 258). Like most of Berrigan's appropriations, the source material is seamlessly woven into a wholly original work. Interestingly enough, "A Certain Slant of Sunlight" itself gets a makeover in ANSELM BERRIGAN's "Looking through a slant of light."

The other way in which these poems relate to Dickinson is in their dual function as lyric poems and acts of correspondence. At times Berrigan takes this notion at its most literal; the whole of "Christmas Card" reads as follows:

> *O little town of Bethlehem,*
> *Merry Christmas*
> *to Jim*
> *& Rosemary.*

In doing so, Berrigan suggests that the act of correspondence is an act of poetry. The fact that the book is not paginated enhances the lyric day-book quality of the text, as though the book really were a stack of postcards inviting the reader to flip through them at random.

The final product was collected and edited by Notley, after Berrigan died, in 1983. Despite the confined space of the postcard—which is reminiscent of the formal organization of Berrigan's first book, *The SONNETS* (1964)—he is able to create works in the open-field style that characterized his later work. Berrigan is always aware of the space at his disposal: "Oops! Wait a minute. Will this fit on a / Postcard? Joseph Conrad, here I come." Then he writes in "Eureka!" In "Interstices," Berrigan revisits the compositional technique of *The Sonnets*, arranging lines from that book and from other works in a sonnet-like FORM. By repackaging the familiar, "Interstices" achieves the same sort of detached commentary on stardom and commodity as Marcel Duchamp's *Green Box* (1934).

Notley claims that Berrigan often began these poems by giving the postcards to an artist or another poet to draw or write something on before finishing them himself. As in BEAN SPASMS, Berrigan's 1967 COLLABORATIVE book with RON PADGETT, the collaborators in *A Certain Slant of Sunlight*—who include ALLEN GINSBERG, EILEEN MYLES, Notley, ANNE WALDMAN, and GEORGE SCHNEEMAN—are not credited on the individual works. At times the poems feel static in their rather conventional presentation. The poem "Windshield," for example, simply reads, "There is no windshield." As the original postcard is reproduced in the cover, however, we see the word *windshield* written at the top in Schneeman's handwriting and a drawing of a windshield with a wiper moving across it. Under the drawing, in Berrigan's handwriting, is the sentence, "There is no windshield." As such, the postcard has the same complex, symbolic properties as surrealist painter Renè Magritte's *The Treachery of Images* (1928–29). The true impact of these works is best experienced in the few reproductions printed on the covers and at the end of the book, where both the verbal and visual elements are allowed to exist simultaneously.

Bibliography

Berrigan, Anselm. *Integrity & Dramatic Life*. Washington, D.C.: Edge Books, 1999.

Dickinson, Emily. *The Complete Poems of Emily Dickinson*. Edited by Thomas H. Johnson. Boston: Little, Brown & Company, 1960.

Notley, Alice. *"A Certain Slant of Sunlight"* (1999). *Coming After: Essays on Poetry*. Ann Arbor: University of Michigan Press, 2005, 67–82.

Chelsea Girls Eileen Myles (1994)

Chelsea Girls is a series of personal memoirs by third-generation NEW YORK SCHOOL poet EILEEN MYLES. This collection of 28 stories canvases some 30 years of the author's life, from her Catholic upbringing in BOSTON, MASSACHUSETTS during the late 1950s and 1960s, to her emergence as a lesbian poet in NEW YORK CITY in the 1970s. The chapters vary in length and are organized according to a combination of theme and chronology. The author has a scattershot writing style that often approaches stream of consciousness, though she never wanders too far from the primary focus of a given chapter. She does, however, frequently allude to people and events without providing the context necessary to comprehend fully her meaning. (This is not unlike the name-dropping and in-joking found in some of FRANK O'HARA's poems). Still, the various threads that Myles picks up—sometimes out of nowhere—eventually find coherence within the larger framework of the collection.

One of the defining aspects of *Chelsea Girls* is the visceral shock that many of its passages—particularly the graphic sex sequences and pervasive "background noise" of drugs and alcohol—induce. Myles describes countless scenes of emotional and psychological turmoil—the death of her alcoholic father, the gang-rape of her high school friend, her addiction to diet pills—yet her tone is always one of casual detachment, bordering on callous indifference. This intentional disparity between grim content and deadpan expression effectively heightens the reader's emotional response.

Myles devotes much of the title chapter, "Chelsea Girls," to her 1979 stint as a caretaker for JAMES SCHUYLER at the CHELSEA HOTEL. Schuyler, a founding member of the New York School poets, was living at the legendary hotel while recovering from poor health and financial problems. Myles was charged with preparing his food, bringing him his pills and newspaper, and doing his laundry. In the course of these activities, the two gay poets became friends and exchanged both poetry and personal sexual anecdotes. While never stated explicitly, they seem to recognize part of themselves in the other. Near the end of the book, the line separating creative influence and erotic intimacy is blurred somewhat when Myles rhetorically links Schuyler with Mary, one of her lesbian lovers. Because many critics were put off by the book's explicit content and pretense of stony self-absorption, *Chelsea Girls* received very few positive reviews.

Bibliography

Furtsch, Stephanie. Review of *Chelsea Girls*. *Library Journal* (July 1994): 131.

Latiolais, Michelle. Review of *Chelsea Girls*. *Review of Contemporary Fiction* (Spring 1995): 173.

Myles, Eileen. *Chelsea Girls*. Santa Rosa, Calif.: Black Sparrow Press, 1994.

Pepper, Rachel. "Stealing Tampax." *Lambda Book Report* (September 1994): 16.

Richard, Frances. "Never Real, Always True: An Interview with Eileen Myles." *Provincetown Arts* (2000). Eileen Myles.com. Available online. URL: http://www.eileenmyles.com/proart.html.

Simson, Maria. Review of *Chelsea Girls*. *Publishers Weekly*, 27 June 1994, 71.

Chelsea Hotel (Hotel Chelsea)

The Chelsea Hotel building at West 23rd Street between Seventh and Eighth Avenues was constructed in 1884 as the city's first cooperative apartment building; it did not become a hotel until 1905. The red brick, 12-story building is famous for its many artistic residents, some of whom are memorialized by plaques near the front entrance. These include authors Mark Twain,

Brendan Behan, and Thomas Wolfe, along with NEW YORK SCHOOL poet JAMES SCHUYLER, who lived at the Chelsea from 1979 until his death in 1991. Other famous occupants include BEAT poets such as WILLIAM S. BURROUGHS (who wrote *Nova Express* and *Naked Lunch* there), GREGORY CORSO, Lawrence Ferlinghetti, Herbert Huncke, and JACK KEROUAC (who wrote the first draft of *On the Road* there). The Chelsea has also been home to New York School painters such as WILLEM DE KOONING, JACKSON POLLOCK, and LARRY RIVERS. These painters are just a few of those who have donated paintings to the hotel in lieu of rent, adding to the collection that decorates the lobby and corridors. Many of these guests developed lasting friendships at the hotel; for instance, composer Arnold Weinstein, who has lived at the Chelsea off and on since the 1960s, recalls gleeful evenings spent drinking with Kerouac, Rivers, and ALLEN GINSBERG.

Although the Chelsea today is relatively subdued, it has retained the reputation for all-night parties and drug abuse that it acquired in the late 1950s and '60s. This notoriety was surely amplified by the release of ANDY WARHOL's delirious *Chelsea Girls*, which was filmed on location in 1966. The film's cast includes poet GERARD MALANGA, who stayed at the Chelsea with JOHN WIENERS during the 1960s.

Aside from its iconic status, the hotel's continued popularity among artists and performers is due to the efforts of Stanley Bard, who has managed the building since 1957, when he took over from his father. For more than 45 years, Bard has welcomed creative individuals with open arms, often providing them with special accommodations and payment arrangements.

Recently, the second-generation New York School poet DAVID LEHMAN wrote *The Last Avant-Garde: The Making of the New York School of Poets* while renting a studio there, thus marking a continued link between the New York School and the Chelsea Hotel.

Bibliography

Cale, John. "Chelsea Mourning." *Observer* (U.K.), 3 September 2000, Life section.
Miller, Cathleen. "Chelsea Moaning: In NYC, Bunk with the Ghosts of America's Greatest Drunks, Dreamers and Other Artists," *Washington Post*, 24 January 1999, section E.
Morgan, Bill. *The Beat Generation in New York: A Walking Tour of Jack Kerouac's City.* San Francisco: City Lights Books, 1997.
Waldman, Anne. "A Literary Guide to Beat Places." In *The Beat Book: Poems and Fiction of the Beat Generation.* Boston: Shambhala, 1996.

Chernoff, Maxine (1952–)

Born in CHICAGO, ILLINOIS, poet, novelist, and short-story writer Maxine Chernoff edits NEW AMERICAN WRITING, one of the most hospitable venues for the various generations of NEW YORK SCHOOL poets, with her husband PAUL HOOVER. She is the chair of the Creative Writing Program at San Francisco State University. Chernoff began her writing career as a poet, but as she said in an interview in *Bold Type*, "in my twenties I was getting poems published in nice places like the PARIS REVIEW. I think the turning point for me was realizing that I valued what people say to each other and how people solve problems and articulate their issues in life more than I was finally interested in how to line up language on the page, as I was doing through poetry. I moved to FICTION. . . . My turning point was simply knowing that I could write fiction and that my interest in social relations and how people get along could be explored there instead of in poetry, which I was first drawn" ("Transformation" n.p.).

This proclivity toward prose has been manifest since Chernoff's first book of poems. *A Vegetable Emergency* (BEYOND BAROQUE Foundation, 1976) consists, tellingly, of prose poems, a FORM that she continues to return to in her poetry. Some of her other books of poems include *Utopia TV Store* (The Yellow Press, 1979), *New Faces of 1952* (Ithaca House, 1985), *Japan* (Avenue B Press, 1988), *Leap Year Day: New & Selected Poems* (Another Chicago Press, 1990; Jensen Daniels, 1999), *World: Poems, 1991–2001* (Salt Publications, 2001), and another collection of prose poems, *Evolution of the Bridge* (Salt Publications, 2004). Chernoff's prose—including the critically acclaimed collections of short stories *Bop* (Coffee House Press, 1986; Vintage Contemporaries, 1987) and *Signs of Devotion* (Simon

& Schuster, 1993), a *New York Times* Notable Book of 1993, and the novels *A Boy in Winter* (Crown Publishing, 1999; Harper Flamingo Australia, 2002) and *American Heaven* (Coffee House Press, 1996)—has garnered serious attention.

Chernoff uses a sinuous poetic line that at times is reminiscent of a prose paragraph and at other times fluctuates down the page with ample caesuras, excisions, and lacunae. Her poetic model often seems to be drawn from JAZZ and the improvisational nature of the medium, and she intersperses dialogue, quotation, and witty observation with portentous silences that only the most skilled musicians can make. As Ethan Paquin has written in *Jacket* about *World: Poems, 1991–2001,* "The book's eponymous, central poem (a long poem, it comprises one of the book's four sections) is a rambling jazz suite of sorts, and typifies the sonic and syntactical quirkiness for which Chernoff is known and celebrated. . . . Chernoff's poetry is not about the science of prosody, it is about nothing but music" (n.p.).

Occasionally, that MUSIC is closer to an absurdist play than to a lyricism found with any frequency in contemporary poetry. For instance, "Heavenly Bodies," from *Evolution of the Bridge,* channels both Samuel Beckett and Eugene Ionesco.

Chernoff's other role, as coeditor of *New American Writing,* is equally important. Founded in 1986, the annual journal is dedicated to experimental writing and includes cover art by leading artists, including ALEX KATZ, Robert Mapplethorpe, and FAIRFIELD PORTER, and poems, essays, and reviews by such writers as JOHN ASHBERY, ROBERT CREELEY, DENISE LEVERTOV, BARBARA GUEST, Lyn Hejinian, and Charles Bernstein. In the "Gender and Editing" edition of *Chain* magazine, Chernoff has written, "the magazine does receive a high number of serious submissions by women, perhaps because it is a 'general' magazine co-edited by a woman and has historically published a large number of women. Do women respond to my name on the masthead? Perhaps. Though I would like to think, as Paul Hoover has observed in his workshop at Columbia College, Chicago, that many of the best poets today simply are women. Their numbers may be disproportionately high in the general population" ("Home in the Mind" n.p.). Indeed, a look at some of the past contributors of the journal shows new work by MARJORIE WELISH, ANN LAUTERBACH, Lydia Davis, Rosmarie Waldrop, Susan Wheeler, ALICE NOTLEY, ANNE WALDMAN, CONNIE DEANOVICH, and Wanda Coleman, among many other contemporary women poets.

Bibliography

Chernoff, Maxine. "Heavenly Bodies." In *Evolution of the Bridge.* Cambridge: Salt Publishing, 2004.

———. "A Home in the Mind." *Chain 1: Gender and Editing.* (October 1, 1994). Available online. URL: http://people.mills.edu/jspahr/chain/1_chernoff.htm. Accessed October 12, 2008.

———. "Transformation." *Bold Type* 3, no. 6 (October 1999). Available online. URL: http://www.randomhouse.com/boldtype/1099/chernoff/. Accessed December 18, 2008.

Paquin, Ethan. "Ethan Paquin reviews *World: Poems 1991–2001* by Maxine Chernoff." *Jacket* 19 (October 2002): Available online. URL: http://jacketmagazine.com/19/paq-rev2.html. Accessed December 18, 2008.

Chicago, Illinois

During the 1970s NEW YORK SCHOOL poetry tapped into a new stream of energy flowing out of Chicago, originating in early American modernism and descending through the NEW AMERICAN POETRY of the late 1950s. Chicago had been the home of *Poetry* magazine since its founding in 1912; despite the load of history it had accumulated by the 1950s, the magazine, under the eclectic editorship of Henry Rago (1955–69), proved to be remarkably receptive to new developments such as the New York School. However, the big breakthrough for the New American Poetry in Chicago came, ironically, through an attempt to prevent the publication of Beat writers in the *Chicago Review,* a journal published under the auspices of the graduate division at the University of Chicago. Editors Irving Rosenthal and PAUL CARROLL transferred the suppressed material to the first issue of *Big Table,* which quickly attracted international attention as a result of the censorship controversy. As contributors to later issues of *Big Table,* New York School poets JOHN ASHBERY, KENNETH KOCH,

FRANK O'HARA, and BILL BERKSON reached new readers, but the BEATS stole the media spotlight, with ALLEN GINSBERG giving a benefit reading of *Howl* to an audience of 1,000 at Chicago's Palmer House in 1959.

A decade later another controversy hit Chicago with consequences of broader scope but still including poetry. Protests at the Democratic Party Convention in Chicago in August 1968 led to violent clashes with police, reminiscent of scenes at Columbia University in New York during the student strike the previous spring. Poets were on the scene in Chicago, with Ginsberg, once again, leading the crowd, and ED SANDERS storing up impressions that he transposed into his satirical novel *SHARDS OF GOD*. The collaborative sequence of poems *Chicago* (ANGEL HAIR, 1969), by LEWIS WARSH and TOM CLARK (included in Warsh's *PART OF MY HISTORY*), typifies the New York School position in relation to such events: distant psychologically, geographically, and chronologically (it was written in BOLINAS, CALIFORNIA, during the trial of the "Chicago Seven," part of the aftermath of the convention). But for many young writers in Chicago, disillusioned with what they had seen of POLITICS firsthand, it was poetry that they wanted to get closer to (Jacobus).

By coincidence, 1968 was also the year in which Carroll revived the Big Table imprint for a series of books, including his critical study *The Poem in Its Skin*, with extensive essays on Ashbery and O'Hara, and his anthology *The Young American Poets*, presenting within a wide range of styles such New York School writers as RON PADGETT, ANNE WALDMAN, and TED BERRIGAN. These were the poets whom PAUL HOOVER remembers discovering in the anthology, which encouraged him to start "taking more chances" (Hoover, interview n.p.). Hoover and BOB ROSENTHAL, another young writer excited by the New York School, were among the first students to enroll in the Program for Writers that Carroll founded at the University of Illinois–Chicago in 1971. In that same year Ed Dorn left a newly established position in poetry at Northeastern Illinois University, to be replaced by Berrigan. The circuit between NEW YORK CITY and Chicago was now complete, and the energy could start to flow in both directions.

If Chicago supplied the setting for poems by Berrigan ("Chicago Morning") and ALICE NOTLEY ("Getting to Sleep, Chicago"), who were married shortly after their arrival in the city, they returned full value in the sense of "making the scene" for poetry. According to Hoover, "Ted was the Pope of the scene, and he made everything around him seem important" ("Last Chicago Days" 200). At the Body Politic, a venue for poetry readings as well as the experimental comedy of Paul Sills, cofounder of Second City, Berrigan regularly occupied a seat in "the middle of the second row, commenting on the reader's work with laughs and asides" (Hoover, "Last Chicago Days" 200). BOB HOLMAN, another recent arrival from New York, recalls reading at the Body Politic as his first experience of being "engaged in a poetry scene" (Holman and Snyder n.p.). At Berrigan's suggestion, Notley started the magazine *Chicago* (1972–74) as "a way to make contacts" (Russo 260). Another magazine, *Out There* (1973–79), was started by ROSE LESNIAK and BARBARA BARG, students in Berrigan's workshop at Northeastern Illinois. In 1977 they followed Berrigan and Notley to New York, where a number of other participants in the Chicago scene (Rosenthal, ROCHELLE KRAUT, Holman, SIMON SCHUCHAT, STEVE LEVINE) had already relocated. During the 1980s a second wave of transplants from Chicago to New York included KIMBERLY LYONS, ELAINE EQUI, and SHARON MESMER, all students of Hoover at Columbia College–Chicago. When Hoover left that position in 2002, the New York School connection was maintained through the appointment of DAVID TRINIDAD.

Since the 1980s Chicago has been especially identified with SLAM POETRY, which originated there. Slam, however, is only a recent manifestation of a style deriving, according to Lyons, "from Chicago's particular working class politics, African American culture (think of the avant-garde African American jazz performers coming out of Chicago), comedy, and Chicago's longtime involvement with surrealism" (Piombino n.p.). The terms that describe this style—"funny, talky, kind of surreal," according to Sharon Mesmer (Piombino n.p.)—transfer so readily to the style of the New York School that the transference of so many Chicago poets to New York can be easily understood.

Bibliography

Berrigan, Ted. "Chicago Morning" (1972). In *The Collected Poems of Ted Berrigan*. Edited by Alice Notley, Anselm Berrigan, and Edmund Berrigan. Berkeley: University of California Press, 2005, 391.

Holman, Bob, and Margery Snyder. "Three Generations in the 70s: Memoirs of a Chicago Po-Renaissance." About.com:Poetry. Available online. URL: http://poetry.about.com/od/poetryhistory/a/chicago70s.htm. Accessed December 18, 2008.

Hoover, Paul. Interview by Vittorio Carli (1995). Vittorio Carli's Art Interviews. Formerly available online. URL: http://www.artinterviews.com/PoetPaulHoover.html.

———. "Last Chicago Days." In *Nice to See You: Homage to Ted Berrigan*, edited by Anne Waldman, 200–201. Minneapolis, Minn.: Coffee House Press, 1991.

Jacobus, Terry. "The Air of June Sings." *Cento*. Formerly available online. URL: http://centomag.org/dorn/jacobus.

Notley, Alice. "Getting to Sleep, Chicago." *Chicago* 5, no. 1 (November 1, 1972): n.p.

Piombino, Nick. Blog entry, 2 April 2005. Fait Accompli. Available online. URL: http://nickpiombino.blogspot.com/2005_03_27_archive.html. Accessed December 18, 2008.

Russo, Linda. "'F' Word in the Age of Mechanical Reproduction: An Account of Women-Edited Small Presses and Journals." In *The World in Time and Space: Towards a History of Innovative American Poetry in Our Time*, edited by Edward Foster and Joseph Donahue, 243–284. Jersey City, N.J.: Talisman House, 2002.

Warsh, Lewis, and Tom Clark. *Chicago*. In *The Angel Hair Anthology*, edited by Anne Waldman and Lewis Warsh, 275–279. New York: Granary Books, 2001.

child, the

The legacy of romanticism in the poetry of the NEW YORK SCHOOL is strikingly evident in the presence of children both as image and as inspiration for the creative process. William Blake (*Songs of Innocence*) and William Wordsworth ("The child is father of the man") are the ultimate though usually unacknowledged sources. As in so many other respects, contemporary visual art provided the New York School with validation for a poetic practice that conservative critics condemned as childishness. FRANK O'HARA defended KENNETH KOCH against this charge by citing the art of Jean Dubuffet, which aspired to the look of children's drawings in celebration of "spontaneity and freedom from formalistic constraints" (O'Hara 63). The painter FAIRFIELD PORTER also had much to say about the quality of "original childishness" (222) in Koch and his colleagues that was brought out in a series of COLLABORATIONs with painters, published by TIBER PRESS (1961).

Among first-generation poets, the child is often viewed nostalgically as an image of lost or unrealized selfhood, as in JOHN ASHBERY's "The Picture of Little J. A. in a Prospect of Flowers" (*Some Trees*, 1956) or O'Hara's "Poem (There I could never be a boy)" (*Meditations in an Emergency*, 1957). The associated mood is elegiac, though the child can function to counter that mood, as so often occurs in Wordsworth. In O'Hara's "Ode on Causality" (*Odes*, 1960), an encounter with a child at the grave of JACKSON POLLOCK inspires the poet, in defiance of mortality, to pray, "like that child at your grave make me be distant and imaginative." Koch is the "first generation" poet who seems least distanced from the pure imaginative exuberance of childhood, but even in his work there is mediation. "Aus Einer Kindheit" (*Thank You and Other Poems*, 1962) has been refracted through the German poet Rainer Rilke, the source of Koch's title, which means "from a childhood." The imitation of children's adventure stories in Koch's *The RED ROBINS* (1977) shares in the camp sensibility that produced the cut-ups of *Beryl of the Biplane* in Ashbery's "Europe" (*The Tennis Court Oath*, 1962). The simplicity—and the brevity—of Koch's ONE THOUSAND AVANT-GARDE PLAYS (1988) may owe something to the example of Koch's student, RUTH KRAUSS, a professional children's author.

Koch is well known for teaching children to write poetry, a practice that has helped many second-generation writers support themselves as "poets in the schools." In fact, this sort of direct engagement with a real rather than an imaginary child may be an instance of the "second generation"—the poetic children, so to speak—influencing the first. DAVID SHAPIRO recalls that it took some arguing to convince Koch to take seriously

Shapiro's experiment in collaborating with his four-year old sister in "Five Poems," published in Shapiro's first book, *January* (1965), when Shapiro himself was only 18. Other instances of such collaboration include a series of poems written by Shapiro and his son (in *A Burning Interior*, 2002); TONY TOWLE's narrative composed with his daughter, "An Interesting Story" (*Some Musical Episodes*, 1992); and STEPHEN PAUL MILLER's volume *Skinny Eighth Avenue* (2005), which includes texts produced in collaboration with his son as well as his son's artwork. In other cases a child may provide a model of language applied to new purposes. ANNE WALDMAN reports that the repetition of the word *closed* in the final section of MEMORIAL DAY (1970), her collaboration with TED BERRIGAN, is based on Berrigan's hearing DICK GALLUP's daughter, during a car trip, rapidly naming various places "closed" as they passed by the car window (Fischer 42, 45).

With the increase in the number of women associated with the New York School, the treatment of the child in poetry has expanded to include special associations between women and children, both biologically and culturally. The mother's view of her child is reflected variously in ALICE NOTLEY's *Songs for the Unborn Second Baby* (1979), Waldman's FIRST BABY POEMS (1983), and BERNADETTE MAYER's *The Desires of Mothers to Please Others in Letters* (1994). Direct quotation from the child, as in Notley's "January" (*How Spring Comes*, 1981), keeps the focus on language as the ultimate subject of experimental poetry, while opening poetry to the experiments in living that the poets were conducting at the same time. The parallel inevitably raises such questions as "Who is speaking that way?" and "Why?" when "baby talk" appears in a poem, questions that BRENDA IIJIMA has applied to Carla Harryman's *Baby* (2005) and work by other contemporary poets.

Bibliography

Fischer, Aaron. *Ted Berrigan: An Annotated Checklist.* New York: Granary Books, 1998.

Flynn, Richard. "'Infant Sight': Romanticism, Childhood and Postmodern Poetry." In *Literature and the Child: Romantic Continuations, Postmodern Contestations*, edited by James Holt McGavran, 105–129. Iowa City: University of Iowa Press, 1999.

Iijima, Brenda. "Time and Crisis: The Phenomenon of Baby Talk in Female Poets' Work." CUNY Conference on Contemporary Poetry. The Graduate Center, City University of New York, 5 November 2005.

Martiny, Erik. "'There I Could Never Be a Boy': Frank O'Hara and the Cult of the Child." *Cambridge Quarterly* 34, no. 1 (2005): 23–32.

O'Hara, Frank. "On and On about Kenneth Koch: A Counter-Rebuttal" (1955). In *Standing Still and Walking in New York*. Edited by Donald Allen. San Francisco: Grey Fox, 1983, 62–63.

Plotz, Judith. *Romanticism and the Vocation of Childhood.* New York: Palgrave, 2001.

Porter, Fairfield. "Poets and Painters in Collaboration" (1961). In *Art on Its Own Terms: Selected Criticism, 1935–1975.* Edited by Rackstraw Downes. 1979. Reprint, Cambridge, Mass.: Zoland, 1979, 220–225.

Wordsworth, William. "My Heart Leaps Up." In *Selected Poems and Prefaces*. Edited by Jack Stillinger. Boston: Houghton Mifflin/Riverside, 1965, 160.

"Circus, The" Kenneth Koch (1961, 1974)

Two poems by KENNETH KOCH bear the title "The Circus," the second (here designated II) reflecting on the circumstances in which the first (I) was composed, almost 20 years earlier (1955–56, according to DAVID LEHMAN's estimate [240]). At that time Koch and his wife, Janice, were living in Paris, caught up in the romance of Europe and the rapture of young love. This is the spirit Koch attempted to capture in "The Circus" I, a simple narrative of incidents involving various characters associated with a circus, especially the "circus girls." A subplot involving "Minnie the Rabbit" poses the contrast of death—"What is death in the circus?"—without seriously darkening the mood, as Minnie lives (and dies) the one-dimensional life of a cartoon character. In "The Circus" II, Koch himself steps forward as a real person, and the distance of time from which he looks back at his youthful composition complicates without repudiating the emphasis on "surface" that marks both poems as products of the NEW YORK SCHOOL. As LEWIS WARSH put the distinction, "The first poem was all about an attempt to stay on the surface, while the second poem gives itself up to the struggle to stay above ground" (158).

Both poems reflect the crucial influence of FRANK O'HARA on Koch's work. If "The Circus" I is like O'Hara's "Second Avenue" (1953) in its attempt "to keep the surface of the poem high and dry, not wet, reflective and self-conscious" (O'Hara, "Notes" 40), "The Circus" II is like O'Hara's "personal poems," self-conscious both in its naming of the poet's intimate friendships and in the sense of loss that darkens the tone of intimacy, marking what some readers view as a turning point in Koch's career (North 67). "Frank was alive" still, Koch recalls of the time when he wrote "The Circus" I, but what Koch seeks to recapture in "The Circus" II is not so much the presence of his friends as his former feeling for them, as well as his feeling for Janice, from whom he was now separated. The feeling of separation, or "aloneness," as Koch calls it in "The Circus" II, poses the strongest contrast between that poem and the feeling of being a member of a company that "The Circus" I, even in its title, celebrates. Yet, as he looks back on his former self, Koch recognizes the impulse toward separation even then: "I treasured secretly the part of me that was individually changing." Even at that earlier time Koch's friends recognized this impulse as a quality that, paradoxically, strengthened their connection to him. Referring to Koch's travels in Europe, where he wrote "The Circus" I, O'Hara observed: "Kenneth continually goes away and by this device is able to remain intensely friendly if not actually intimate" ("Day and Night" 94).

The circus community narrated in "The Circus" I and the network of friendships recalled in "The Circus" II together compose a complex picture of the New York School as it was experienced by one of its leading members. Like JOHN ASHBERY's "The Lithuanian Dance Band" (1973), another poem that has been read as an image of this band of poets (Epstein 163–165), "The Circus" II ends with an acknowledgment that "you are meant to be alone . . . in order to work" (Ashbery 53). Koch recalls the night that he did not take Janice out to the Cirque Medrano, one of the sources for "The Circus" I, but instead stayed home to write about it. "And [I] am writing about that now," he observes in "The Circus" II, "and now I'm alone."

Bibliography

Ashbery, John. "Lithuanian Dance Band." In *Self-Portrait in a Convex Mirror.* 1975. Reprint, New York: Penguin, 1976, 52–53.

Epstein, Andrew. *Beautiful Enemies: Friendship and Postwar American Poetry.* Oxford: Oxford University Press, 2006.

Koch, Kenneth. *The Collected Poems.* New York: Knopf, 2005.

Lehman, David. *The Last Avant-Garde: The Making of the New York School of Poets.* New York: Doubleday, 1998.

North, Charles. "Kenneth Koch in Public" (1982). In *No Other Way: Selected Prose.* Brooklyn, N.Y.: Hanging Loose, 1998, 50–71.

O'Hara, Frank. "Day and Night in 1952" (1952). In *The Collected Poems.* Rev. ed. Edited by Donald Allen. Berkeley: University of California Press, 1995, 93–95.

———. "Notes on *Second Avenue.*" In *Standing Still and Walking in New York.* Edited by Donald Allen. San Francisco: Grey Fox, 1983, 37–40.

Warsh, Lewis. Interview by Edward Foster (1991). In *Poetry and Poetics in a New Millennium,* edited by Edward Foster, 147–159. Jersey City, N.J.: Talisman House, 2000.

Clark, Tom (1941–   )

Most of Tom Clark's extensive interaction with the NEW YORK SCHOOL has taken place outside New York. His is not one of the "urban voices" that he admired in TED BERRIGAN (Clark, "Ted" 130), but by entering into dialogue and frequently collaborating with those voices, Clark tuned his own poetry to the full range of contemporary experience. In addition, by concentrating on New York School poetry during his tenure as poetry editor of the influential PARIS REVIEW (1964–73), Clark helped expand the range of recognition accorded to the movement.

Clark's upbringing in CHICAGO, ILLINOIS, made him a fan of baseball, the subject of several of his nonfiction books and some of his poems. What made him a poet, however, was the experience of reading Rainer Maria Rilke, Boris Pasternak, Wallace Stevens, and Theodore Roethke during undergraduate study at the University of Michigan

(1960–63), where Clark won a Hopwood Prize for poetry, as FRANK O'HARA had done before him. One of Clark's professors at Michigan, Donald Hall, was the first poetry editor of the *Paris Review* and recommended Clark for that position in 1963. By this time Clark was in England, immersing himself in the work of Ezra Pound under the tutelage of Donald Davie, first at Cambridge University (1963–65) and later at the newly formed University of Essex (1965–67). The arrival of Ed Dorn to teach at Essex in 1965 not only provided Clark with a direct link to the Pound tradition by way of BLACK MOUNTAIN but also his first "live" exposure to the New York School. Dorn had tapes of Berrigan and ED SANDERS reading at the BERKELEY POETRY CONFERENCE, and listening to them was a revelation for Clark. "The speech I *knew*," in contrast to the speech of "English academic institutions" that surrounded him, "was very much present in Ted's reading, moving and jumping to the tune of a new kind of comic surrealism that sounded, I thought, like a message from the immediate literary future" (*Late Returns* 16).

From England Clark reached out to the New York School poets first through correspondence, soliciting contributions for the *Paris Review* and his series of mimeograph magazines (*Once, Twice, Thrice,* and so on). He met LARRY FAGIN and ARAM SAROYAN when they visited England, and RON PADGETT, when Clark visited France. Clark published Padgett's *Tone Arm* (1967) under the imprint of Once Books, a venture limited to only two other titles: Clark's *Airplanes* (1966), with an introduction by Saroyan, and TOM VEITCH's *Toad Poems* (1966). In 1967 Clark returned to the United States and spent a year based in NEW YORK CITY's Lower East Side. His brief but intense involvement in the local poetry scene was capped in March 1968 by his marriage at St. Mark's Church to Angelica Heinegg, the muse who inspired the title of ANGEL HAIR magazine. Padgett served as best man; Berrigan gave the bride away; Fagin, DICK GALLUP, DAVID SHAPIRO, and painter Mike Goldberg provided MUSIC; ANNE WALDMAN and LEWIS WARSH hosted the reception at their apartment. The next month Clark and his wife left for BOLINAS, CALIFORNIA, where they became a magnet for the involvement of New York School

poets in the writers' community that developed there over the next decade.

Residence in Bolinas (1968–78), Santa Barbara (1980–84, after a brief sojourn in Colorado), and Berkeley (since 1984) has nurtured Clark's development not only as "a quintessentially California poet" but also as a "nature poet" (Equi n.p.), sensitive to the play of light and shade that is staged so dramatically on the California coast. *Light & Shade* is the title of Clark's most recent "new and selected" volume (Coffee House Press, 2006), but the fact that the title quotes a letter of John Keats affirms literary tradition as an influence of equal importance to that of the natural environment. Clark undertook an extended meditation on Keats's life, in both prose and verse, in *Junkets on a Sad Planet: Scenes from the Life of John Keats,* published by Black Sparrow (1994), the California firm that has issued several of Clark's volumes since the 1970s. Since the publication of his first major collection, *Stones* (Harper and Row, 1969), Clark's voice has been recognized as essentially "lyrical" (Warsh 441; Lehman 231). This is the voice that is emphasized in the selections that compose *Light & Shade.* A more representative selection of the FORMS of experiment in which Clark engaged through his association with the New York School is contained in *The Angel Hair Anthology,* including two products of a visit to KENWARD ELMSLIE's property in Calais, Vermont, in 1967 ("The Lake" and *Bun,* the latter a COLLABORATION with Padgett); a response to Berrigan's SONNETS mediated through Wordsworth ("Sonnet [Five a.m. on East Fourteenth Street]," 1968); a collaboration with Warsh composed in Bolinas in 1969 ("Chicago"); and an extensive excerpt from *Neil Young* (1970), Clark's arrangement of lines from his favorite singer at the time.

Since 1987 Clark has taught part time at New College of California in San Francisco, but for the most part he has made a living as a writer in many GENREs. His first novel, *Who Is Sylvia?* (Blue Wind, 1979), fictionalizes Clark's experience of the psychedelic revolution in England during the 1960s. Of his many works of nonfiction, his biographical accounts of JACK KEROUAC, CHARLES OLSON, ROBERT CREELEY, Dorn, and Berrigan are especially relevant to Clark's interests as a poet, as is his collection of critical essays, *Poetry Beat* (University of Michigan Press,

1990). This collection includes "Stalin as Linguist" (1985, 1987), Clark's controversial itemization of charges against the Language poets (see LANGUAGE POETRY), not least of which is the charge of distorting literary history to create "an Olson without soul and a Berrigan without heart" (Clark, *Poetry Beat* 75). As AMY GERSTLER argues in her introduction to *Light & Shade*, "the word 'heart' and the concept of *heart* in poetry" provide keys to Clark's lyricism (iii).

Bibliography

Clark, Tom. *Charles Olson: The Allegory of a Poet's Life.* New York: Norton, 1991.

———. "Confessions." In *Contemporary Authors, Autobiography Series* 22, edited by Joyce Nakamura, 1–26. Detroit: Gale, 1996.

———. *Edward Dorn: A World of Difference.* Berkeley, Calif.: North Atlantic Books, 2002.

———. Interview by Kevin Ring. *Jacket* 21 (February 2003). Available online. URL: http://jacketmaga-zine.com/21/clark-iv1.html. Accessed December 18, 2008.

———. *Jack Kerouac: A Biography.* San Diego, Calif.: Harcourt Brace Jovanovich, 1984.

———. *Late Returns: A Memoir of Ted Berrigan.* Bolinas, Calif.: Tombouctou, 1985.

———. *Light & Shade: New and Selected Poems.* Minneapolis, Minn.: Coffee House Press, 2006.

———. *The Poetry Beat: Reviewing the Eighties.* Ann Arbor: University of Michigan Press, 1990.

———. *Robert Creeley and the Genius of the American Common Place: Together with the Poet's Own Autobiography.* New York: New Directions, 1993.

———. "Ted" (1983). In *Nice to See You: Homage to Ted Berrigan,* edited by Anne Waldman, 129–130. Minneapolis, Minn.: Coffee House Press, 1991.

Equi, Elaine. "The Natural." *Jacket* 29 (April 2006). Available online. URL: http://jacketmagazine.com/29/equi-clark.html. Accessed December 18, 2008.

Gerstler, Amy. Introduction to *New and Selected Poems, Light & Shade,* by Tom Clark. Minneapolis, Minn.: Coffee House Press, 2006, iii–vi.

Lehman, David. "The Whole School." *Poetry* 199, no. 4 (1972): 224–233.

Waldman, Anne, and Lewis Warsh, eds. *The Angel Hair Anthology.* New York: Granary Books, 2001.

Warsh, Lewis. "Out of Sight." *Poetry* 115, no. 6 (March 1970): 440–446.

Clear the Range Ted Berrigan (1977)

TED BERRIGAN's collage novel *Clear the Range* chronicles the disjointed adventures of a tramp, aptly named "The Sleeper"—one of several overt references to the story's dreamlike quality. Most of the action involves a one-dimensional rancher named Cole Younger and a series of nondescript, southwestern backdrops, the ambiguity of which renders much of the text opaque. Our uncertainty regarding the story's setting is exacerbated by the author's reliance on lyrical vagaries in place of explicit, communicative prose. This obscure writing style is consistent with Berrigan's poetry. Here, however, he uses it to explode the roughneck imagery and vocabulary of traditional western novels, one of which supplied an immediate source. The manuscript in the collection of Aaron Fischer (53) shows that Berrigan used different color inks to mark passages in a paperback reissue of *Twenty Notches* (originally published in 1932) by Max Brand (1892–1944). "Writing through" Brand's text—a technique developed by JOHN CAGE—yielded the language that Berrigan reassembled into slightly off-kilter scenes such as the following from chapter 13:

> He cut off as he heard the first stealthy braying of women weeping in the distance.
>
> The Sleeper started forward again, and ran straight to the table. He was about to rush it when he heard voices inside.
>
> "Give me three," said the voice of Drengk.
>
> "Gonna hold those aces, eh," said the voice of Bonney.
>
> Two of them ensconced within, and such a two!
>
> He saw them in the merciless sunshine of his memory, every feature and every line.
>
> Drengk and Bonney! He would rather have had two basilisks in his way. And then he froze, cold with wonder (36).

Berrigan had completed substantial portions of *Clear the Range* by the middle of 1968, at which time he read from the work at the POETRY PROJECT AT ST. MARK'S CHURCH IN-THE-BOWERY. Part of the text also appeared in a 1968 issue of the literary magazine *ANGEL HAIR*, edited by LEWIS WARSH and ANNE WALDMAN. The finished novel was released in 1977 by Adventures in Poetry and Coach House South in a limited edition of 750 copies. The drawing featured on the front cover is a collaborative effort by Berrigan and painter GEORGE SCHNEEMAN.

In 1979 Berrigan adapted *Clear the Range* into a stage play (a copy of which now resides at Indiana University). Although the play was never published, it was produced at St. Clement's under the direction of BOB HOLMAN.

Bibliography

Berrigan, Ted. *Clear the Range*. New York: Adventures in Poetry/Coach House South, 1977.

Fischer, Aaron. *Ted Berrigan: An Annotated Checklist.* New York: Granary Books, 1998.

Foster, Edward. *Code of the West: A Memoir of Ted Berrigan*. Boulder, Colo.: Rodent Press, 1994.

Club, the (1949–1962)

The artists who launched the Club at 39 East 8th Street in 1949 did not want to assign it a name any more than they wanted to name themselves as a group. Nevertheless, they became known as abstract expressionists, and the Club came to be seen as their headquarters. According to art historian Dore Ashton, "[W]hile the artists used the headquarters to relax and stay in intimate contact with one another, they also used it to confirm their widening audience among the educated strata of the society and to establish the visual artist as a member of the intelligentsia on an equal footing with writers and composers" (198). The first organized discussion that HAROLD ROSENBERG recalled at the Club was on "the relationship between art and poetry." His friend WILLEM DE KOONING, a primary instigator of the Club's formation, was especially fascinated by "the relation between Cézanne and Mallarmé," Rosenberg reported (Gruen 178).

From its origins the Club thus provided fertile ground for the introduction of the NEW YORK SCHOOL poets along with their friends among the rising "second generation" of painters. Many of the younger painters were included in the Ninth Street Show in 1951, an extension of Club activ-

ity. At the Club itself their debut moment can be pinpointed to a panel discussion on March 7, 1952, moderated by JOHN BERNARD MYERS of the new TIBOR DE NAGY GALLERY and featuring four of that gallery's artists (GRACE HARTIGAN, Alfred Leslie, Joan Mitchell, LARRY RIVERS) and one poet, FRANK O'HARA. This was the third in a series of eight evenings at the Club prompted by the publication of *Abstract Painting* by THOMAS B. HESS (1951), who traced the convergence of two strains of modernist painting, abstraction and expressionism, in its current "American phase." By 1955 the second-generation challenge to the purity of abstraction had found a spokesman in O'Hara, whose essay "Nature and New Painting" (*Folder 3*, 1954) provided the basis for another series of Club panels.

O'Hara and his poet colleagues brought to the Club a challenge to the tone of high seriousness that may have been precisely what the older artists hoped to acquire through their association with writers. The younger poets, however, identified that tone with the dead hand of the past from which they sought to liberate themselves. In a 1952 panel on "The Image in Poetry," in which O'Hara was joined by EDWIN DENBY and British poets David Gascoyne and Ruthven Todd, O'Hara protested against the "deadening and obscuring and precious effect" of T. S. Eliot (Gooch 216). Only one month later, on May 14, 1952, several alternatives to Eliot were presented in a joint reading by O'Hara, JOHN ASHBERY, BARBARA GUEST, and JAMES SCHUYLER. The only poet missing from this roster of the original New York School is KENNETH KOCH, but O'Hara was able to introduce Koch's "FRESH AIR" (1955)—his satirical antidote to the "baleful influence" of Eliot and company (Koch 123)—in an otherwise properly "serious" talk at the Club on "Design etc" (date uncertain). In their uncompleted play "Kenneth Koch, a Tragedy" (1954), O'Hara and Rivers have Ad Reinhardt, known for his advocacy of "pure" painting, suggest to Philip Pavia, the sculptor who ran the Club program, that Koch be invited to speak at the Club (132). Koch's reply, "Greatness in art isn't heavy, it's light," presumably serves as fair warning of the challenge such an invitation would entail.

By 1955 the spirit of the younger generation was taking over the Club. "Older members, Pavia's 'boys,' began to attend less often, and younger artists replaced them," explains Irving Sandler (*Sweeper-Up* 32). Pavia himself stepped down from his organizing role, which he eventually transferred to the magazine *It Is,* an extension of the Club in print. Sandler headed the program committee from 1956 to the end of the Club in 1962. The titles of panels during this period, such as "Has the Situation Changed?" (winter 1958–59) and "What Is the New Academy?" (spring 1959), reflect increasing anxiety over the congealing of avant-garde art into an academic style.

Poets offered alternative responses to the problem of anxiety. ALLEN GINSBERG, whom Sandler had recruited for a panel in order to bring the Club up to date with the recent BEAT phenomenon, ended the evening by literally throttling art historian Peter Selz (Sandler, *Sweeper-Up* 37). A less violent, but still deadly serious performance by Ginsberg appeared in the pages of *It Is* (number 3, winter–spring 1959) under the title "Abstraction in Poetry," the taking-off point for O'Hara's manifesto "PERSONISM" (*Yūgen* 7, 1961). Meanwhile, in what appears to have been O'Hara's last appearance on a Club program, April 25, 1958, he joined in the performance of a "Hearsay Panel," later published in the same issue of *It Is* as Ginsberg's essay. This panel spoofed current anxieties by drawing a parallel between imitating style in painting and repeating conversation at second and third hand: "style as hearsay" (O'Hara et al. 149)—the kind of thing that occurred all the time in conversation at the Club. In the script of the "Hearsay Panel," the painter Norman Bluhm cites O'Hara in a witty remark that anticipates both the style and the substance of "Personism": "Frank says: Style at its lowest ebb is method. Style at its highest ebb is personality" (O'Hara et al. 149).

Bibliography

Ashton, Dore. *The New York School: A Cultural Reckoning.* 1973. Reprint, Berkeley: University of California Press, 1992.

Gibson, Ann Eden. "*It Is*: A Magazine for Abstract Art." In *New York School: Another View.* Exhibit catalog. Albany, N.Y.: Opalka Gallery/Sage Colleges, 2005, 28–36.

Ginsberg, Allen. "Abstraction in Poetry." In *Deliberate Prose: Selected Essays, 1956–1995.* Edited by Bill Morgan. New York: HarperCollins, 2000, 243–245.

Gooch, Brad. *City Poet: The Life and Times of Frank O'Hara.* New York: Knopf, 1993.

Gruen, John. *The Party's Over Now: Reminiscences of the Fifties.* Wainscott, N.Y.: Pushcart Press, 1989.

Hess, Thomas. *Abstract Painting: Background and American Phase.* New York: Viking, 1951.

Koch, Kenneth. "Fresh Air." In *The Collected Poems.* New York: Knopf, 2005, 122–128.

O'Hara, Frank. "Design, etc." In *Standing Still and Walking in New York.* Edited by Donald Allen. San Francisco: Grey Fox, 1983, 33–36.

———. "Nature and New Painting." In *Standing Still and Walking in New York.* Edited by Donald Allen. San Francisco: Grey Fox, 1983, 41–51.

———. "Personism." In *The Collected Poems.* Rev. ed. Edited by Donald Allen. Berkeley: University of California Press, 1995, 498–499.

O'Hara, Frank, and Larry Rivers. "Kenneth Koch, a Tragedy." In *Amorous Nightmares of Delay: Selected Plays,* by Frank O'Hara. Baltimore, Md.: PAJ Books/ Johns Hopkins University Press, 1997, 121–132.

O'Hara, Frank, et al. "Five Participants in a Hearsay Panel" (1959). In *Art Chronicles, 1954–1966.* New York: Braziller, 1990, 149–156.

Pavia, Philip. *Club without Walls: Selections from the Journals.* Edited by Natalie Edgar. New York: Midmarch Arts Press, 2007.

———. "The Unwanted Title: Abstract Expressionism." *It Is* 5 (Spring 1960): 8–11.

Sandler, Irving. "The Club." In *Abstract Expressionism: A Critical Record,* edited by David Shapiro and Cecile Shapiro, 48–58. Cambridge: Cambridge University Press, 1990.

———. *A Sweeper-Up after Artists: A Memoir.* New York: Thames & Hudson, 2003.

———. "Sweeping Up after Frank." In *Homage to Frank O'Hara,* edited by Bill Berkson and Joe LeSueur, 78–80. Bolinas, Calif.: Big Sky, 1988.

Codrescu, Andrei (1946–)

Andrei Codrescu was born in Romania and immigrated to the United States in 1966 to escape the oppression of the Communist regime there. "I applied for visas in several countries," Codrescu has written, "and was accepted by three: Australia, Canada, and the United States. All were English-speaking countries, which would now be my new language. There was no question as to which I would choose: the drumbeats I had heard on the smuggled tapes of Western music came directly from the United States. That's where the Pied Piper lived" (42). He soon met ANNE WALDMAN and become involved with the POETRY PROJECT AT ST. MARK'S CHURCH IN-THE-BOWERY, which he called, "the literary heart of the lower east side, which was the number one Bohemia in the world in 1968" (Monroe). In New York, Codrescu began writing poems marked by witticism and social inquiry, infused with a sense of metaphoric and literal exile. He has since experimented with many GENREs, including novels, essays, travelogues, screenplays, TRANSLATIONs, book reviews, manifestoes, and audio recordings. His books of poems include *It Was Today—New Poems by Andrei Codrescu* (Coffee House Press, 2003); *Poezii Alese/Selected Poetry*, a bilingual English-Romanian edition (Editura Paralela 45, 2000); *Alien Candor: Selected Poems, 1970–1995* (Black Sparrow Press, 1996); *Belligerence* (Coffee House Press, 1993); and *Comrade Past and Mister Present* (Coffee House Press, 1991). He has won National Endowment for the Arts Fellowships for poetry, editing, and radio; an ACLU Freedom of Speech Award; and the Literature Prize of the Romanian Cultural Foundation, Bucharest, and currently is a distinguished professor of English at Louisiana State University in Baton Rouge. He is also the founding editor of *Exquisite Corpse* (1983), a literary journal that is decidedly subversive, sarcastic, and occasionally bizarre. It has featured the work of such poets as TED BERRIGAN, ANSELM HOLLO, and ALICE NOTLEY. Codrescu has become a kind of media maven, regularly appearing on National Public Radio as a commentator, starring in a documentary that was shown on the Public Broadcasting Service, and even appearing on *Charlie Rose, The Today Show,* and the *David Letterman Show.*

Bibliography

Codrescu, Andrei. *The Disappearance of the Outside: A Manifesto for Escape.* Reading, Mass.: Addison-Wesley, 1990.

Exquisite Corpse. Available online. URL: http://www.corpse.org.

Monroe, Wanda. "Post-Beat Poet Anne Waldman Draws Rave Reviews." *University Record*, University of Michigan, March 18, 2002. Available online. URL: http://www.vcurnich.edu/0102/Mar18-02/11.htm. Accessed December 18, 2008.

collaboration

Not all NEW YORK SCHOOL poets engage in collaborative work, but the practice of collaboration typifies several key aspects of the New York School aesthetic. In collaboration the process matters at least as much as the final product. It is a social process but usually on an intimate scale, "between two persons instead of two pages," as FRANK O'HARA envisioned for "PERSONISM" (499). The separateness of the collaborators ensures an element of surprise in the creative process, while the intimacy of the collaborative relationship can create the sense that one has been surprised by an encounter with oneself, facing the challenge posed by French poet Arthur Rimbaud: *"je est un autre"* (I am an other) (6). Multiple selves find expression in multiple media, and collaboration with artists in other media as well as with each other has enabled New York School poets to respond as directly as possible to the stimulus of other arts, especially painting and printmaking.

During the modernist period, collaboration featured most prominently in DADA AND SURREALISM, two movements that profoundly influenced the development of the New York School during World War II and the years immediately following. To derail conscious control of the artistic process and promote the spontaneous emergence of images, the surrealists played the game of "exquisite corpse," in which a succession of writers (or artists) each wrote (or drew) on a piece of paper, which was then folded over before it was handed to the next participant, who then added his contribution to work that he could not read (or see). The dadaist Tristan Tzara made similar use of accident by cutting up a newspaper article and then producing a new text by drawing the cut-up words at random out of a hat. Each of these techniques is represented in an issue of LOCUS SOLUS (number 2, 1961), edited by KENNETH KOCH and devoted to the process of collaboration. In this issue the example of cut-up technique qualifies doubly as collaboration, as it is performed by two participants, WILLIAM S. BURROUGHS and GREGORY CORSO, on a preexisting text by Rimbaud. In the New York School context the process of working together with other people is as important to collaboration as the process of liberating words from conscious control. Significantly, the examples in *Locus Solus* begin with the Eastern tradition of "linked verse" (Japanese *renga*) that resembles the "exquisite corpse" but places greater emphasis on the social occasion, "an atmosphere of mutual esteem and emulation," as Koch expresses it ("Note on This Issue" 193–194).

The earliest collaborations that may be identified with New York School poetry date to 1948, when EDWIN DENBY published *IN PUBLIC, IN PRIVATE*, incorporating photographs by RUDY BURCKHARDT, and Burckhardt produced the film *The Climate of New York*, incorporating poems by Denby. In Burckhardt's film *MOUNTING TENSION* (1950), JOHN ASHBERY collaborated as actor rather than poet, as Denby had done in earlier films. The FORMS of collaboration multiplied throughout the ensuing decade. O'Hara provided texts in 1952 for GRACE HARTIGAN's *Oranges*, a series of "POEM-PAINTINGS"; the same year Koch wrote his first collaborative poem (with O'Hara), an unpublished sestina for the daughter of art dealer Leo Castelli (Koch, "Note on Frank O'Hara" 26), and Ashbery and JAMES SCHUYLER began their collaborative novel, *A NEST OF NINNIES* (Lehman 80). In February 1953 the ARTISTS' THEATRE was launched with three productions pairing poets and painters: Koch with Hartigan, O'Hara with LARRY RIVERS, and Schuyler with Elaine de Kooning. In 1954 the duo piano team of ARTHUR GOLD and Robert Fizdale commissioned musical compositions based on texts by O'Hara (*FOUR DIALOGUES*) and Schuyler (*Picnic Cantata*). From 1957 to 1960 Rivers and O'Hara produced the series of lithographs entitled *Stones*. Since text and images were produced in spontaneous interaction while both poet and artist worked on each print together, O'Hara recalled this as "the only time that I think that I've really collaborated" with a visual artist (interview 4), though the same criteria would

seem to apply to the poem-paintings he produced with Norman Bluhm in 1960.

In the 1960s the second generation of New York School poets emphasized collaboration to such a degree that one commentator, Daniel Kane, has taken it as the sign of "a shift in aesthetics" ("ANGEL HAIR" 351). If the second generation "picked up" collaboration "from a more primitive place," as TED BERRIGAN claimed (114), it was still within the bounds of the tradition, closer to the madness of dada than to the "marvelous" of surrealism. Moreover, the younger poets carried their elders with them, as the example of "C" *Comics* (number 2, 1964) demonstrates with its texts by Ashbery, Koch, O'Hara, Schuyler, and BARBARA GUEST, all set in comic strips drawn by JOE BRAINARD. As visual artists, Brainard and GEORGE SCHNEEMAN played a role in collaborations of the second-generation equivalent to that played by Hartigan and Rivers in the first. Meanwhile, the poets explored the full range of intertextual collaboration, as represented in *BEAN SPASMS* (Berrigan and RON PADGETT, 1967), *MEMORIAL DAY* (Berrigan and ANNE WALDMAN, 1971), *PART OF MY HISTORY* (LEWIS WARSH, with Berrigan, Waldman, and TOM CLARK, 1972), and *ANTLERS IN THE TREETOPS* (Padgett and TOM VEITCH, 1973). Collaboration also featured prominently in such journals as "C" (1963–66), which sponsored "C" *Comics*; *The World*, which issued a special number devoted to collaboration (number 12, June 1968); and *Unnatural Acts* (1972–73), which published work produced collectively and anonymously in BERNADETTE MAYER's workshop at the POETRY PROJECT AT ST. MARK'S CHURCH IN-THE-BOWERY (Kane, *All Poets* 199–201).

As many key players on the poetry scene moved away from NEW YORK CITY during the 1970s, the frequency of collaboration diminished; however, the practice extended to long-distance exchanges such as that between BILL BERKSON and PHILIP GUSTON, leading to the publication of *ENIGMA VARIATIONS* (1975). New forms of collaboration emerged in DOWNTOWN MANHATTAN with the growth of PUNK ROCK and PERFORMANCE ART and, by the early 1990s, the importation of the poetry SLAM. Staged "contests" between poets produced collaborative works, such as "Popeye and William Blake Fight to the Death" by Koch and ALLEN GINSBERG (1979), and expressed the competitive spirit that has always lain just beneath the surface, and sometimes erupted, in New York School collaboration.

The theory of postmodernism that dominated the art world in the 1980s tended to give an opposite spin to collaboration as a critique of *individualization,* the term used by Michel Foucault in his much-cited essay "What Is an Author?" (Shapiro 53). New York School collaboration stands as a critique of this critique. Even in his theoretical statement on "Art as Collaboration" (1984), poet DAVID SHAPIRO warned that "the disappearance of the producer has perhaps been too fashionably unsettled, and tactless misreadings have replaced the 'collaborative' act of critique" (54). In contrast to Foucault's theoretical position, which locks him into "a static embrace" with traditional defenders of the author function, CARTER RATCLIFF has celebrated the dynamic freedom enjoyed by the poets who collaborated with Schneeman: "[F]eeling no need to score theoretical points, they simply left such obstacles behind as they moved out into the open spaces where the new is possible. That is where they still are" (25).

Bibliography

Berrigan, Ted. Interview by Charles Ingham (1978). In *Talking in Tranquility: Interviews.* Edited by Stephen Ratcliffe and Leslie Scalapino. Bolinas, Calif.: Avenue B; Oakland, Calif.: O Books, 1991, 106–125.

Duhamel, Denise, Maureen Seaton, and David Trinidad, eds. *Saints of Hysteria: A Half-Century of Collaborative American Poetry.* Brooklyn, N.Y.: Soft Skull Press, 2007.

Herd, David. "The Art of Life: Collaboration and the New York School." In *John Ashbery and American Poetry.* New York: Palgrave, 2000, 52–68.

Kane, Daniel. *All Poets Welcome: The Lower East Side Poetry Scene in the 1960s.* Berkeley: University of California Press, 2003.

———. "*Angel Hair* Magazine, the Second-Generation New York School, and the Poetics of Sociability." *Contemporary Literature* 45, no. 2 (2004): 331–367.

Koch, Kenneth. "Collaborating with Painters" (1993). In *The Art of Poetry: Poems, Parodies, Interviews, Essays,* *and Other Work.* Ann Arbor: University of Michigan Press, 1996, 168–175.

———. "A Note on Frank O'Hara in the Early Fifties" (1964). In *Homage to Frank O'Hara,* edited by Bill Berkson and Joe LeSueur, 26–27. Bolinas, Calif.: Big Sky, 1988.

———. "A Note on This Issue." *Locus Solus* 2 (1961): 193–197.

Koch, Kenneth, and Allen Ginsberg. "Popeye and William Blake Fight to the Death." *Jacket* 15 (December 2001). Available online. URL: http://www.jacketmagazine.com/15/koch-popeye.html. Accessed December 18, 2008.

Lehman, David. *The Last Avant-Garde: The Making of the New York School of Poets.* New York: Doubleday, 1998.

O'Hara, Frank. Interview by Edward Lucie-Smith (1965). In *Standing Still and Walking in New York.* San Francisco: Grey Fox, 1983, 3–26.

———. "Personism" (1959). In O'Hara, *The Collected Poems.* Edited by Donald Allen. Rev. ed. Berkeley: University of California Press, 1995, 498–499.

Ratcliff, Carter. "Schneeman and Company: How to Do Things with Words and Pictures." In *Painter Among Poets: The Collaborative Art of George Schneeman,* edited by Ron Padgett, 11–28. New York: Granary Books, 2004.

Rimbaud, Arthur. Letter to Georges Izambard, May 1871. In *Collected Poems.* Edited by Oliver Bernard. London: Penguin, 1986, 5–7.

Shapiro, David. "Art as Collaboration: Toward a Theory of Pluralist Aesthetics, 1950–1980." In *Aesthetic Collaboration in the Twentieth Century,* by Cynthia Jaffe McCabe. Exhibit catalog. Washington, D.C.: Smithsonian Institution Press, 1984, 45–62.

Waldman, Anne. "'Surprise Each Other': The Art of Collaboration" (1998–99). In *Vow to Poetry: Essays, Interviews, and Manifestos.* Minneapolis, Minn.: Coffee House Press, 2001, 319–326.

Collom, Jack (1931–)

Colorado poet, teacher, and birdwatcher, Jack Collom was instrumental in expanding the boundaries of the NEW YORK SCHOOL past its urban origins. Born in CHICAGO, ILLINOIS, on November 8, 1931, Collom grew up in Western Springs, Illinois, and moved to Colorado at age 15. At age 11, he discovered bird-watching, which was to become a lifelong passion and poetic inspiration. He received a degree in forestry and then joined the U.S. Air Force, writing his first poems in Libya. After working at factories for 20 years, he now teaches as a poet-in-the-schools and at NAROPA University. A primary fomenter of the still-emerging field of ecological poetry, he has written essays and poems and taught courses on how poetry can incorporate ecological concepts in a deeply structural and experimental way. While he was a close friend and COLLABORATOR with many second-generation New York School poets, such as TED BERRIGAN, ALICE NOTLEY, REED BYE, and ANNE WALDMAN, he also has spoken of his equally close relationship to the BLACK MOUNTAIN and LANGUAGE poets, particularly Lyn Hejinian, with whom he wrote the collaborations, *Sunflower* (The Figures, 2000) and *Situations, Sings* (ADVENTURES IN POETRY, 2008).

In 2001 *Red Car Goes By* (Tuumba Press), a compendium of Collom's work from 1955 to 2000 (selected by poets including Bye, CLARK COOLIDGE, LARRY FAGIN, Merril Gilfillan, and Hejinian) was published. Ron Silliman has written of it, "Part of what is so very interesting reading these earliest poems by Jack Collom is that he seems to have already figured out what it seems to have taken so many other poets another 20 years to get straight—it's not a zero sum competition. Liking the New York School need not preclude an interest in the Beats, the Projectivists nor anything else for that matter" (n.p.). Mark DuCharme, in a review of *Extremes & Balances* (Farfalla, 2004), concurs: "Collom can swerve from an almost latter-day Projectivist all-over-the-page plainspeak; to rhyme & other formal devices . . . to the humorously didactic, & the didactically humorous; toward a kind of folk-song poetics; to the use of found text and collaboration; toward an ongoing engagement with visual poetry . . . toward a kind of 'indeterminacy' which seems to anticipate/coexist with/follow from/ignore similar approaches by some of his contemporaries; toward the rigorously descriptive, the prosaic, the expansive, the concrete, & the minute" (n.p.).

Collom, the recipient of two National Endowment of the Arts grants, is married to the writer Jennifer Heath. His most recent collection is *Exchanges of Earth & Sky* (Fish Drum, 2006).

Bibliography
DuCharme, Mark. "Extremes of Startle." *Jacket* 26 (October 2004). Available online. URL: http://jacketmagazine.com/26/duch-coll.html. Accessed December 18, 2008.
Silliman, Ron. "Thursday, June 05, 2003." Silliman's Blog. Available online. URL: http://www.ronsilliman.blogspot.com/2003_06_01_archive.html.

conceptual art

The elusive movement known as conceptual art is the missing link in the evolutionary chain connecting NEW YORK SCHOOL poetry to LANGUAGE POETRY. The two movements of poetry, which have been sharply distinguished in subsequent polemics, prove to have much in common when viewed within the context of the art world that they shared during the 1970s.

The fundamental assumption of conceptual art is that the artist is primarily an inventor of ideas rather than a maker of things. During the 1910s, Marcel Duchamp demonstrated this assumption when he declared "ready-made" objects—a bottle rack, a shovel, a urinal—to be art solely because he conceived of them as such. The influence of Duchamp, and more broadly of DADA, can be traced in more immediate antecedents of 1960s conceptual art—in lettrism and situationism in Europe and in fluxus and neo-dada (particularly the work of ROBERT RAUSCHENBERG) in NEW YORK CITY. From HAPPENINGS, in which Rauschenberg crossed paths with the New York School poets, to minimalist art, the 1960s seemed headed toward "the dematerialization of the art object" (Lippard 1973). In a 1965 article focused on MINIMALISM, the critic Barbara Rose looked ahead to conceptualism by quoting JOHN ASHBERY: "[W]hat matters is the artist's will to discover, rather than the manual skills he may share with hundreds of other artists" (278). In 1967 the artist Sol LeWitt echoed this distinction in "Paragraphs on Conceptual Art," the document from which conceptualism as a movement is often dated. "When an artist uses a conceptual form of art," LeWitt declared, "it means that all of the planning and decisions are made beforehand and the execution is a perfunctory affair" (214).

To convey their ideas, conceptual artists placed a new emphasis on forms of language: declaration, documentation, instructions—practices that readily suggested parallels in the work of poets. Given the simultaneous emergence of conceptual art and the second generation of New York School poets, a case can be made for viewing the idea of the New York School as a work of conceptual art. TED BERRIGAN's offer to enroll poets in the New York School for a fee of $5 (Berrigan 91), based on his say-so, has a direct precedent in Rauschenberg's telegram to the Parisian gallery owner Iris Clert: "This is a portrait of Iris Clert if I say so" (1961). Berrigan's "Things to Do" poems parallel the conceptual artist's list of instructions for acts that might or might not actually be performed. As DAVID SHAPIRO has noted, the "conceptual bareness" of Berrigan's lists contrasts with the "PERSONISM" of FRANK O'HARA's "I do this I do that" poems (226). Indeed, the persistence of subjectivity in New York School writing is the principal feature that distinguishes it from conceptual art and later Language writing. Ashbery's *Three Poems* (1972) would otherwise be a central document of conceptual art. Written in prose, Ashbery's texts seem to point to the idea of a poem rather than its embodiment, a possibility that O'Hara had already suggested in connection with his "Oranges": "It is even in / prose, I am a real poet" (O'Hara 361). Like the conceptual artist, Ashbery introduces his texts as "examples" of a predetermined procedure: "these are examples of leaving out" (3). Unlike conceptual art, however, the barest statement by Ashbery has a way of evoking "our private song" (Ashbery 109), suggesting his closer affinity to abstract expressionist painting or modernist MUSIC.

The closest affinity with conceptual art in New York School poetry is evident in the work of BERNADETTE MAYER and CLARK COOLIDGE. In Mayer's journal *0 TO 9*, coedited with Vito Acconci, texts by Mayer and Coolidge appeared alongside statements by conceptual artists such as LeWitt and Robert Smithson. Smithson's interest in language as material—a tendency of conceptual art that seemed to arise as a corollary to the "dematerialization of the object"—directly inspired Coolidge's *Smithsonian Depositions* (1980). Mayer's interest in treating the materials of auto-biography with the methods of documentary, as in her project MEMORY (1972, 1975), parallels the autobiographical experiments of the artist Jennifer Bartlett, who published in *The WORLD* and in the *ADVENTURES IN POETRY* pamphlet series (*Cleopatra*, 1971). In a series of influential workshops at the POETRY PROJECT AT ST. MARK'S CHURCH IN-THE-BOWERY (1971–75), Mayer developed writing exercises—"systematically eliminate the use of certain kinds of words" (557)—that correspond as much to the procedures of conceptual art as they do to KENNETH KOCH's strategies as a teacher or to HARRY MATHEW's experiments as a member of OULIPO. Many poets who became identified with the Language movement, including Bruce Andrews, Charles Bernstein, Nick Piombino, and Hannah Weiner, participated in Mayer's workshops. However, neither Mayer nor Coolidge has pursued the conceptual purity that congealed Language poetry as a movement. Coolidge recalls the response among the West Coast Language writers to a marathon reading he gave in San Francisco: "I remember somebody saying to me, 'Well, it's really a conceptual work isn't it?'—this was in the late seventies—'It's kind of like a conceptual-athletic thing, the number of words you're reading. It doesn't really matter what so-called content it has.' And my God, no! It *does* depend on what the content is" (n.p.).

Bibliography

Ashbery, John. *Three Poems.* 1972. Reprint, New York: Penguin, 1978.

Bartlett, Jennifer. Excerpt from *Autobiography.* In *Out of This World: An Anthology of the St. Mark's Poetry Project, 1966–1991,* edited by Anne Waldman, 172–173. New York: Crown, 1991.

Berrigan, Ted. "Interview with CITY" (1977). In *Talking in Tranquility: Interviews.* Edited by Stephen Ratcliffe and Leslie Scalapino. Bolinas, Calif.: Avenue B; Oakland, Calif.: O Books, 1991, 90–105.

Coolidge, Clark. Interview by Tyler Doherty. *Jacket* 22 (May 2003). Available online. URL: http://jacketmagazine.com/22/doher-cooli.html. Accessed December 18, 2008.

LeWitt, Sol. "Paragraphs on Conceptual Art" (1967). In *Conceptual Art,* edited by Peter Osborne, 213–215. London: Phaidon, 2002.

Lippard, Lucy, ed. *Six Years: The Dematerialization of the Art Object from 1966–1972.* New York: Praeger, 1973.

Mayer, Bernadette, and members of the St. Mark's Church Poetry Project Writing Workshop (1971–75). "Experiments." In *In the American Tree,* edited by Ron Silliman, 557–560. Orono: National Poetry Foundation/University of Maine at Orono, 1986.

O'Hara, Frank. "Why I Am Not a Painter" (1956). In *The Collected Poems.* Rev. ed. Edited by Donald Allen. Berkeley: University of California Press, 1995, 260–261.

Rose, Barbara. "A B C Art" (1965). In *Minimal Art: A Critical Anthology,* edited by Gregory Battcock, 274–297. New York: Dutton, 1968.

Shapiro, David. "On a Poet." In *Nice to See You: Homage to Ted Berrigan,* edited by Anne Waldman, 223–227. Minneapolis, Minn.: Coffee House Press, 1991.

Construction of Boston, The   Kenneth Koch
(1962)

KENNETH KOCH wrote the text of *The Construction of Boston* for a performance by artists ROBERT RAUSCHENBERG, Jean Tinguely, and Niki de Saint Phalle on May 4, 1962, at the Maidman Theater on 42nd Street in NEW YORK CITY, where Koch's GEORGE WASHINGTON CROSSING THE DELAWARE had been produced two months earlier. As representatives of the new "art of assemblage," "new realism," or more broadly, POP ART, each of the artists involved was big news at the time. Word had spread of their COLLABORATION the previous year in a performance at the U.S. Embassy in Paris, and all tickets for the New York performance quickly sold out. Whereas the Paris performance played against an event, a piano recital by David Tudor, the New York performance acted out a story, the construction of a city, a theme that Koch pursued in other dramatic work (*Angelica* [1962], *The Building of Florence* [1964]). For *The Construction of Boston* each artist chose what he or she wanted to contribute: Rauschenberg supplied "weather" by means of a rain machine and "people" simply by ushering in a cast of extras; Tinguely supplied "architecture" by building a brick wall at the edge of the stage, eventually blocking out the view of the audience; and de Saint Phalle supplied "art" by a device that had made her notorious—shooting at a target embedded with balloons of colored paint, in this case a white plaster copy of the Venus de Milo.

Koch's difficult task was to supply a text that would somehow frame the artists' actions and speak for them, through doubles, in the case of Tinguely and Saint Phalle, or through words projected on a screen, in the case of Rauschenberg. Recognizing that the action constituted a procession rather than a dramatic plot—and no doubt recognizing also the nature of the egos involved—Koch chose the FORM of a Renaissance masque, with the text, mostly in suitably archaic rhyming couplets, describing the artists' actions as an allegory of quasi-divine creativity. A certain amount of dramatic tension is provided through the conflict between the sublime of nature and the sublime of art, resolved in the mood of urban pastoral that animates much NEW YORK SCHOOL poetry. The courtly form adopted by Koch removed the performance from the rawness and, according to Allan Kaprow, even the freshness of HAPPENINGS, the artist's THEATER that Kaprow and others had lately pioneered (n.p.). FRANK O'HARA, however, viewed *The Construction of Boston* as a happening because the collaborators performed independently (18–19), submitting neither to the script nor to the direction, nominally provided by Merce Cunningham.

In 1989 the composer Scott Wheeler (1952–   ) adapted the text for *The Construction of Boston* as the libretto for a one-act opera that has been performed several times in BOSTON, MASSACHUSETTS, generally to more favorable reviews than the original New York version received. Poet and MUSIC critic Lloyd Schwartz has praised the opera for its "charm" and "sophisticated delicacies," among which is the "urban pastoral" quality reinforced by Wheeler's music (n.p.).

Bibliography

Diggory, Terence. "Picturesque Urban Pastoral in Post-War New York City." In *The Built Surface,* Vol. 2: *Architecture and the Pictorial Arts from Romanticism to the Twenty-first Century,* edited by Karen Koehler and Christy Anderson, 283–303. Aldershot, U.K.: Ashgate, 2002.

Kaprow, Allan. Review of *The Construction of Boston. Floating Bear* 30 (1964): n.p.

Koch, Kenneth. *A Change of Hearts: Plays, Films, and Other Dramatic Works, 1951–1971.* New York: Random House, 1973.

———. "Collaborating with Painters" (1993). In *The Art of Poetry: Poems, Parodies, Interviews, Essays, and Other Work.* Ann Arbor: University of Michigan Press, 1996, 168–175.

O'Hara, Frank. Interview by Edward Lucie-Smith (1965). In *Standing Still and Walking in New York.* Edited by Donald Allen. San Francisco: Grey Fox, 1983, 3–26.

Schwartz, Lloyd. "Constructive Criticism: Ralph Shapey at NEC, Scott Wheeler at Boston Conservatory." *Boston Phoenix* (February 14–21, 2002). Available online. URL: http://www.bostonphoenix.com/boston/music/other_stories/documents/02156380.htm. Accessed December 18, 2008.

Tomkins, Calvin. *The Bride and the Bachelors: Five Masters of the Avant-Garde.* New York: Penguin, 1976, 228–229.

Conversions, The Harry Mathews (1962)

HARRY MATHEWS's first novel, *The Conversions*, is the tale of an antiquarian's quest for information about a decorated adze (a hatchet-like tool), belonging to a deceased millionaire. The story's anonymous protagonist and narrator is undistinguished save for the absurdly arcane knowledge he calls forth to reconstruct the artifact's mysterious origins; nevertheless, he serves as an excellent mechanism for retrieving testimony from more richly imagined characters. Hence, nearly every chapter is framed around a story that the narrator either hears or reads. In many cases, these embedded narratives occupy multiple layers, as when the protagonist interviews a writer, who, in the course of relating events from his own life, recounts the plot of his most recent novel. Each "guest narrative" introduces new puzzles and expectations, leading both reader and narrator into a web of mysteries that the author leaves deliberately unresolved.

Aided by its perpetual sidetracking, *The Conversions* canvases everything from the 15th-century origins of a Scottish religious sect to a recent plague in a remote Indian village. Unlike Mathews's later FICTION, however, the myriad detours that account for the novel's bulk are strung together with only the most slender thread of continuity. If there is an underlying theme that unites the plot's endless diversions, it is the sense of ritual significance that each conveys. This effect stems from the author's meticulously—even pathologically—thorough treatment of his material, which confers upon it a kind of religious aura. Examples are his comprehensive genealogy of a prize-winning racehorse named Gypsum, his pseudoscientific log of a chemist's experiments with unstable metal, and his account of the process required to decode secret messages in the MUSIC of a renowned composer. These carefully wrought sequences range from the playfully improbable to the surrealistically grotesque, but all are depicted in the mechanically sober tone and style of a scholarly journal, complete with footnotes and appendices.

Initial responses to the book's 1962 release were a mix of lukewarm and favorable. Yet, even the most positive critics had difficulty categorizing the novel. In an article for the *Library Journal*, L. W. Griffin described it as "a surrealistic kind of book composed of a blend of Kafka, Branch Cabell, Dali, Stith Thompson, and a dash of Thomas Edison" (2, 158). American critics might have come up with a more coherent set of comparisons if they had been more familiar with the new French fiction, but the most important French model for Mathews was his new discovery, RAYMOND ROUSSEL (Sawyer-Lauçanno 250–252). Appropriately, *The Conversions* first appeared in serial installments (1961–62) in the journal named after a novel by Roussel, *LOCUS SOLUS*, edited by JOHN ASHBERY, KENNETH KOCH, and JAMES SCHUYLER. Koch's enthusiasm for Mathews's work persuaded Jason Epstein (1928–) to publish *The Conversions* at Random House (Sawyer-Lauçanno 258–259).

Bibliography

Ash, John. "A Conversation with Harry Mathews." *Review of Contemporary Fiction* (Fall 198): 21–32.

Griffin, L. W. Review of *The Conversions. Library Journal* (June 1, 1962): 2,158.

Mathews, Harry. *The Conversions.* New York: Random House, 1962.

Sawyer-Lauçanno, Christopher. *The Continual Pilgrimage: American Writers in Paris, 1944–1960.* San Francisco: City Lights, 1992.

Southern, Terry. Review of *The Conversions. Nation*, 29 September 1962, 184.

Coolidge, Clark (1939–   )

Throughout his long and varied career, Clark Coolidge has been affiliated with a number of literary movements but has produced a body of work that does not readily lend itself to critical categorization. He has drawn much inspiration from the example of JACK KEROUAC, and he is considered an important forerunner of LANGUAGE POETRY. However, like BERNADETTE MAYER, he prefers a mode of experimentation that is improvisatory rather than programmatic, a preference that is much in the spirit of the NEW YORK SCHOOL.

Coolidge was born in PROVIDENCE, RHODE ISLAND, and attended Brown University, where his father was chair of the MUSIC department. Coolidge lived intermittently in NEW YORK CITY throughout the 1960s and became acquainted with a number of New York School poets, including TED BERRIGAN, LARRY FAGIN, ARAM SAROYAN, and Mayer. His first two collections, *Flag Flutter & U.S. Electric* (1966) and *Clark Coolidge* (1967), were published by Saroyan under the Lines imprint. *Ing* (1969) was published by Angel Hair. He coedited three issues of his own magazine, *Joglars*, with the poet Michael Palmer (1943–   ) from 1964 to 1966. His appearance in *An ANTHOLOGY OF NEW YORK POETS* (Random House, 1970), coupled with the publication of *SPACE* (Harper & Row, 1970), firmly situated him within the New York School. *Space* remains Coolidge's only book published by a major commercial house; he has become closely identified with a nationwide network of small presses that have issued more than 40 volumes of his work.

Much of Coolidge's early work focuses on creating "constellations" of language that amplify the materiality of each component part. Words are treated as objects, and their arrangement on the page suggests the hanging of paintings in a gallery, with each image serving as both a self-contained work and part of the larger exhibition. Lines such as "erything/eral/stantly" provide pieces of words—affixes, stems, roots—and force one to consider them as one might a painting. When confronted by such literature, the reader is compelled to wonder about the phonemic structure of language. In other words, what is the smallest unit of language that can be used to convey meaning? By reducing language to its most basic level, Coolidge obliges the reader to proceed carefully and concentrate on the act of reading itself.

The late 1970s saw a palpable shift in Coolidge's work, with volumes such as *Mine: The One That Enters the Stories* (The Figures, 1982), *Solution Passage: Poems, 1978–81* (Sun & Moon, 1985), and *The Crystal Text* (The Figures, 1986) tracing a progression that favored the line and phrase over the compressed potency of the individual word. Unlike such contemporaries as Ron Silliman (1946–   ), whose work uses the sentence as its basic unit, Coolidge's line is more of a musical phrasing than a linguistic entity, as is evident in these lines from *The Rova Improvisations* (Sun & Moon, 1994): "it was pacific, deck of a carrier / bluing puffs and / no trains were run, I see, do not do, they have / all their sayings trundled, scared the bat, apt to fire" (45). Such extended meditations are evocative of the extended line of JAZZ music, where a "sentence" may run on for pages at a time, rough and unpunctuated.

Bob Perelman (1947–   ) observes that one of the characteristics of modern poetry is that it reflects the actions of the thinking mind (16). Jerome McGann extends this by saying that Coolidge's work treats "words not as the dress but as the physique of thought" (266). Within Coolidge's work the reader sees the thought process mapped directly to the page, using language as music uses notes—as a means of "creating a time phase within which things can get articulated" (Coolidge, interview 15).

In a prefatory note to *The Rova Improvisations*, Coolidge explains that the poems comprising the book originated from liner notes solicited by the Rova Saxophone Quartet for their album *The Crowd*. Each poem in the book has two versions: one written while listening to the music of Rova, the second written after having read through the first series of poems. Thus, the separate "takes" of each poem "exist as two parallel surges of improvisation. One written in the hollows of the music. The other in the silence of the words" (n.p.).

Rather than restricting his forays to the musical, Coolidge mines imaginative material from a variety of sources, most notably from the fields of geology and photography. Where many writers are content to borrow terminology or images from other disciplines, Coolidge also borrows their procedures. If movement, like musical notes, creates time within which things are articulated, then Coolidge's appropriation of the procedures of other disciplines introduces what Michael Golston calls a "shared grammar" (298). In some instances this sharing has extended to actual COLLABORATION, notably in Coolidge's "POEM-PAINTINGS" with PHILIP GUSTON.

When two vocabularies are introduced into a single work, the result is often a chorus of overlapping and competing voices. *On the Nameways* (The Figures, 2000) was composed while watching old second-run movies, whose hackneyed dialogue provided fodder for Coolidge's poetry. The lines shift awkwardly and break oddly, tearing themselves from statements they have not yet made: "we'd just been to the doll store / where they had/as is heard/ the party plods onward" (77). There is an off-kilter transition from scene to scene, where what one expects to find is not what one encounters.

The "silence of the words" is induced by a number of different vocabularies being spoken simultaneously, as if poetry were little more than white noise, a series of discrete sounds raised to an overarching intonation. Coolidge appropriates the material of the world, filters it through musical staves, makes it transitive, and produces a poetry that shows us the limits of language, while suggesting how those boundaries might be breached. This task is never complete, for as Coolidge states near the close of *The Crystal Text*, "I have made up a procedure here to which / there never can be an end" (138).

Bibliography

Berrigan, Ted. "A Conversation with Clark Coolidge" (1970). In *Talking in Tranquility: Interviews*. Edited by Stephen Ratcliffe and Leslie Scalapino. Bolinas, Calif.: Avenue B; Oakland, Calif.: O Books, 1991, 171–202.

Coolidge, Clark. "Clark Coolidge: 'A constant retrogression, and this is not memory.'" In *Talking Poetry: Conversations in the Workshop with Contemporary Poets*, edited by Lee Bartlett, 2–15. Albuquerque: University of New Mexico Press, 1987.

———. Interview by Edward Foster (1989). In *Poetry and Poetics in a New Millennium. Postmodern Poetry: The Talisman Interviews*, edited by Edward Foster, 1–20. Jersey City, N.J.: Talisman Housec, 2000.

Dworkin, Craig, ed. Eclipse Web site. Available online. URL: http://english.utah.edu/eclipse/projects/. [Includes facsimile editions of 15 Coolidge collections.]

Golston, Michael. "At Clark Coolidge: Allegory and the Early Works." *American Literary History* 13, no. 2 (2001): 295–316.

McGann, Jerome. "Truth in the Body of Falsehood." *Parnassus* 15, no. 1 (1989): 257–280.

Perelman, Bob. *The Trouble with Genius*. Berkeley: University of California Press, 1994.

Shaw, Lytle. "Faulting Description: Clark Coolidge, Bernadette Mayer and the Site of Scientific Authority." In *Don't Ever Get Famous: Essays on New York Writing after the New York School*, edited by Daniel Kane, 151–172. Champaign, Ill.: Dalkey Archive Press, 2006.

Cooper, Dennis (1954–)

Although Dennis Cooper is now primarily known as a FICTION writer and art critic, his literary career began as a poet and the editor and publisher of a small-press venture that was significantly influenced by the NEW YORK SCHOOL of poets. Born in Los Angeles, Cooper briefly attended Pitzer, a private college near Pomona, California, where he studied with Bert Meyers before dropping out to travel in Europe for several months. Returning to Los Angeles, he studied poetry with Ron Koertge at Pasadena City College and by 1977 had started a magazine, LITTLE CAESAR, which soon expanded into a small press that published full-length collections of poetry.

Cooper's attraction to the New York School of poets can be traced back to his adolescence, when he bought a copy of RON PADGETT's and DAVID SHAPIRO's ANTHOLOGY OF NEW YORK POETS in 1971. "I liked the entire book," he told DAVID TRINIDAD in an interview in *Bachy* magazine, and "my interest has fallen there ever since. . . . [S]how me any New York school poet and I'll get some delight out of him or her. I just love that kind of language use and that kind of sensibility" (256). In a handwritten introduction to issue number two of *Little Caesar* (1976), Cooper noted that *The WORLD* magazine, produced by the POETRY PROJECT AT ST. MARK'S CHURCH IN-THE-BOWERY, was one of his major influences. Espousing a poetics he defined as "casual but sharp" (Mohr), heavily influenced by the New York School, Cooper gathered around him a cluster of young poets living in Los Angeles, including AMY GERSTLER, Trinidad, Bob Banagan, and Jack Skelley, and secured the support of older poets in Los Angeles such as James Krusoe. Cooper ran the reading series at BEYOND BAROQUE for four years and was the pivotal figure in making this literary arts center a nationally recognized alternative poetry site. In addition to poets such as TIM DLUGOS, EILEEN MYLES, PETER SCHJELDAHL, and MICHAEL LALLY, Cooper brought in poets whose work could be aligned with earlier experimental underground scenes of the Lower East Side in NEW YORK CITY as well as Language writers (see LANGUAGE POETRY) such as Ron Silliman, Barrett Watten, Kit Robinson, and Steve Benson.

Sea Horse Press published Cooper's *Idols* in 1979. His second collection of poems, *The Tenderness of the Wolves,* was published by Crossing Press in 1982, and this became the second book by a gay Los Angeles poet in a three-year span to be nominated for the *Los Angeles Times* book award for poetry. Cooper's poetry continued to appear in anthologies, such as *Poetry Loves Poetry* (1989) and *The Norton Anthology of Postmodern American Poetry* (1994) but he increasingly concentrated on fiction, which was published by Grove Press. After living in New York and Amsterdam for a number of years, Cooper returned to Los Angeles and presently works as a writer, teacher, and critic.

Bibliography

Cooper, Dennis. "Of Idols and Innocence." Interviewed by David Trinidad. *Bachy* 18 (1981): 254–263.

Mohr, Bill. Email to Terence Diggory. 26 November 2008.

Corbett, William (1942–)

Since 1966 William Corbett's poems and presence have nourished the BOSTON-Cambridge area with a wide-ranging curiosity extending to the NEW YORK SCHOOL and beyond. His poetry is steeped in the local. Boston's history, geography, POLITICS, and people (some well known, others not) distinguish his *New & Selected Poems* (Zoland, 1995) and *Boston Vermont* (Zoland, 1999). Moreover, Corbett's connections with the New York School have been integral in bringing to Boston poets who otherwise might not have been accessible in the city. No other Boston poet has been so influential in this regard.

The poetry scene in Boston-Cambridge has long been dominated by the universities and under the influence of poets such as ROBERT LOWELL, Sylvia Plath, and Anne Sexton. Their dominion left little room for poets connected with DONALD M. ALLEN's *The NEW AMERICAN POETRY, 1945–1960* anthology. Almost single-handedly, Corbett has maintained a lifeline to his city that brings in alternative poetry from the outside. He has done this through his editing of magazines such as *Fire Exit* (1968–74); *The Boston Eagle* (1973–74), coedited with LEWIS WARSH and LEE HARWOOD; and *PRESSED WAFER* (1999–). In addition, Corbett has held editorial roles on such journals as *Ploughshares, Agni,* and *Grand Street.* Corbett has also been active in bringing poets associated with the New York School to Boston-Cambridge for readings. An incomplete list includes BARBARA GUEST, Warsh, BERNADETTE MAYER, JOHN ASHBERY, CHARLES NORTH, ALICE NOTLEY, KENWARD ELMSLIE, ANNE WALDMAN, PAUL VIOLI, RON PADGETT, and HARRY MATHEWS.

New York School poet JAMES SCHUYLER cited the young Corbett as a poet to watch. The poetry of the two writers shares a directness and clarity. Their content is culled from the daily experience of lives being lived. They write of friendships, their localities, and the man-made and natural worlds that thrive simultaneously around them. Each has a passion for visual art, MUSIC, and the literary. In 1999 Corbett, along with the poet Ed Barrett, organized a James Schuyler Memorial Reading at the Massachusetts Institute of Technology (MIT). To mark that event, Corbett and Geoffrey Young edited *That Various Field* (The Figures, 1991) in honor of Schuyler. Later Corbett edited *Just the Thing:*

Selected Letters of James Schuyler (Turtle Point, 2004) and *The Letters of James Schuyler to Frank O'Hara* (Turtle Point, 2006). Corbett also included a profile of Schuyler in his historical compendium, *New York Literary Lights* (Graywolf, 1998).

Corbett's association with NEW YORK CITY is based not only on poetry. His passion for visual art has held his eyes on that city as well. He has written extensively, both in his poetry and as an art critic, about New York artists, from abstract expressionists to contemporaries. His friendship with PHILIP GUSTON developed while Guston was teaching at Boston University (1973–77). Guston designed the cover for Corbett's Angel Hair book, *Columbus Square Journal* (1976), and collaborated with Corbett on a number of "POEM-PAINTINGS" (Balken). Corbett's book *Philip Guston's Late Work* (Zoland, 1994) takes the FORM of a memoir. Corbett continues to write essays for catalogs and reviews of exhibits, many of which are collected in *All Prose* (Zoland, 2001).

Corbett and his wife, Beverly, are famous for their hospitality. Their summer home in Greensboro, Vermont, is near Kenward Elsmlie's home in Calais, and dinners with the Corbetts, Elmslie, JOE BRAINARD, and Ron and Pat Padgett became "a summer ritual," according to Padgett (210). In Boston the Corbett home at 9 Columbus Square has provided a nexus for poets, artists, and musicians. Countless poets from New York, San Francisco, Europe, and Asia have graced the Corbett's dinner table in the company of local artists and writers. Over the years the Corbett's hospitality has done more to expand the horizons of the local community than many of the official institutions of the area. Corbett has inspired numerous readers with his poetry and innumerable friends with his company.

Bibliography

Balken, Debra Bricker. *Philip Guston's Poem-Pictures.* Andover, Mass.: Addison Gallery of American Art, Phillips Academy; Seattle: University of Washington Press, 1994.

Padgett, Ron. *Joe: A Memoir of Joe Brainard.* Minneapolis, Minn.: Coffee House Press, 2004.

Selinger, Eric Murphy. "This Personal Maze Is Not the Prize." *Parnassus* 24, no. 2 (2000): 77–116.

Cornell, Joseph (1903–1972)
assemblage artist

At the age of 10, JOHN ASHBERY discovered Joseph Cornell, an artist best known for his glass-fronted shadowboxes that enclose lyrical assemblages of images and objects, via an article on surrealism in *Life* magazine. The future poet felt strongly drawn to the artist, and a decade later, Ashbery recalled: "[T]he same force, which is so delicate and so powerful that one hesitates to talk much about it, hit me when I had my first chance to see a show of Cornell's boxes at the Egan Gallery" (Foreword 9–10). Ashbery has since written essays and a poem ("Pantoum" [1953]) dedicated to Cornell and placed one of his collages on the cover of *Hotel Lautréamont* (1992). FRANK O'HARA, too, paid tribute to the artist in a poem ("Joseph Cornell" [1955]) and an admiring review. Ashbery's and O'Hara's efforts were early entries in what has turned out to be a burgeoning GENRE. Since the early 1970s, NEW YORK SCHOOL poets who have written "Cornell poems" include KENWARD ELMSLIE, ANN LAUTERBACH, MAUREEN OWEN, and JOHN YAU.

Why Cornell? For one, he is the most "literary" of artists, whose collages often include pages from old books and newspapers, fragments of print, scrolls in bottles, and bits of narrative and are rife with allusions to Cornell's favorite writers, many of them the same French poets (see FRENCH POETRY), from Lautréamont to André Breton, who inspired the New York School. More specifically, Cornell's work unfolds at the juncture between word and image; it "exists," as Ashbery says, "beyond questions of 'literature' and 'art' in a crystal world of its own making" (*Reported Sightings* 17). This illusion of a world elsewhere attracts the sort of writers for whom the space between literature and art signifies the possibility of working in the margins of existing institutions.

The self-taught artist, who lived in his mother's house on Utopia Parkway in Queens, was always himself a marginal figure, an outsider adopted by art-world insiders, from Julien Levy and the surrealists who frequented Levy's gallery in the 1930s to later artists, such as JASPER JOHNS and ROBERT RAUSCHENBERG. What the latter learned from Cornell, O'Hara wrote, was "that there is no aspect (or for that matter artifact) of modern life which can *not* become art" (*Standing Still* 149). Cornell collected many of the artifacts that fill his boxes in his wanderings around NEW YORK CITY; Charles Simic associates Cornell and O'Hara as walkers in the city in his book of Cornell poems, *Dime-Store Alchemy* (15). And Johns's *Memory Piece (Frank O'Hara)* (1961, 1970), a wooden box filled with sand that is repeatedly imprinted with a cast of the poet's foot attached to its lid (Ferguson 133), at once recalls the artist's friend and the box-maker who influenced them both.

Bibliography

Ashbery, John. Foreword to *Joseph Cornell's Theater of the Mind: Selected Diaries, Letters and Files.* Edited by Mary Ann Caws. New York: Thames & Hudson, 1993, 9–12.

———. *Hotel Lautréamont.* New York: Farrar Straus & Giroux, 1992.

———. "Pantoum: Homage to Saint-Simon, Ravel and Joseph Cornell." In *A Joseph Cornell Album,* edited by Dore Ashton, 119–120. New York: Viking, 1974.

———. *Reported Sightings: Art Chronicles, 1957–1987.* Edited by David Bergman. Cambridge, Mass.: Harvard University Press, 1991.

Elmslie, Kenward. "Joseph Cornell Box." In *Album,* illustrated by Joe Brainard. New York: Kulchur Press, 1969.

Ferguson, Russell. *In Memory of My Feelings: Frank O'Hara and American Art.* Los Angeles: Museum of Contemporary Art; Berkeley: University of California Press, 1999.

Foer, Jonathan Safran, ed. *A Convergence of Birds: Original Fiction and Poetry Inspired by the Work of Joseph Cornell.* New York: Distributed Art Publishers, 2001. [Includes Lauterbach and Yau.]

O'Hara, Frank. "Joseph Cornell." In *The Collected Poems of Frank O'Hara.* Edited by Donald Allen. Berkeley: University of California Press, 1995, 237.

———. "Joseph Cornell and Landes Lewitin." *Art News* 54, no. 5 (September 1955): 150.

———. *Standing Still and Walking in New York.* Edited by Donald Allen. San Francisco: Grey Fox, 1985.

Owen, Maureen. "6 from the Joe Cornell Series." In *Erosion's Pull.* Minneapolis, Minn.: Coffee House Press, 2006, 47–57.

Simic, Charles. *Dime-Store Alchemy: The Art of Joseph Cornell.* New York: Ecco, 1992.

Solomon, Deborah. *Utopia Parkway: The Life and Work of Joseph Cornell.* New York: Noonday, 1997.

Corso, Gregory (Gregory Nunzio Corso) (1930–2001)

Hailed by ALLEN GINSBERG as "probably the greatest poet in America" (Introduction 16), Gregory Corso did not live up to his early promise, but for a brief period in the 1950s he played a key role in the interaction between BEAT and NEW YORK SCHOOL poetry. FRANK O'HARA's admiration for Corso's work persuaded Ginsberg that O'Hara was "hip" (Gooch 280). Ironically, O'Hara seems to have met Corso in the genteel setting of Cambridge, Massachusetts, rather than the hipsters' hangout of NEW YORK CITY's Greenwich Village, where he was born as Nunzio Corso. O'Hara's friend VIOLET R. (BUNNY) LANG had planted Corso in Cambridge like a human bomb that would shake up the establishment with his street kid's language and his tales of petty crimes and prisons (Sayre 102–103). What both O'Hara and Ginsberg admired in Corso, however, was "the strangest phrasing picked off the streets of his mind" (Ginsberg, Introduction 13), a way of handling language that seemed abstract rather than realistic. Corso is Ginsberg's leading example in his essay on "Abstraction in Poetry," first published in the journal of the abstract expressionist painters, *It Is* (number 3, winter 1959).

In O'Hara's poem "To Hell with It" (1957), he offers a glimpse of himself, Corso, and Lang as actors in JOHN ASHBERY's *The Compromise* at the POETS' THEATRE in Cambridge in 1956. O'Hara drafted but never published reviews of Corso's first two collections: *The Vestal Lady on Brattle* (1955), published in Cambridge by subscription among Lang's circle of friends (Corso, *Accidental* 55); and *Gasoline* (1958), published in San Francisco at Lawrence Ferlinghetti's City Lights bookstore. While the first review notices Corso's sound—"rhythms and figures of speech of the jazz musician's world" (O'Hara, "Gregory Corso" 83)—the second review ("Gregory Corso: *Gasoline*"), poetic enough to be included in O'Hara's *Collected Poems* (315–317), concentrates on key aspects of Corso's vision, particularly memories of childhood and forebodings of death, which are taken up again in O'Hara's elegy for Lang,

"The 'Unfinished'" (1959). As Corso explained to the students of the WAGNER LITERARY MAGAZINE (*Accidental* 192–193), the Beats' response to contemporary anxiety about death, exacerbated by the fear of nuclear war, was a return to CHILD-like innocence, evoked in the phrase that became the title of Corso's third collection, *The Happy Birthday of Death* (New Directions, 1960).

While he could appreciate the commitment to happiness in O'Hara and his fellow New York School poets, Corso had his doubts about whether they shared the profundity of the Beats' vision (interview 157). He nearly caused a rift between the two groups when he wrote dismissively of O'Hara, Ashbery, and KENNETH KOCH as "three ex-chichi academics" in an article on "The Literary Revolution in America" for *Litterair Paspoort* (November 1957), but O'Hara, at least, was able to laugh off what "Gregory says in that Dutch magazine" (*Poems Retrieved* 183 and note, 241). Corso sent letters of apology (Corso, *Accidental* 81–82) and soon made better use of his temporary residence in Europe by working with Walter Höllerer (1922–2003), a leading advocate of experimental poetry in Germany, to prepare *Junge Amerikanische Lyrik* (young American lyric) published in 1961 as a German counterpart to *The* NEW AMERICAN POETRY, *1945–1960* (1960). The Höllerer-Corso anthology included translations of poems by O'Hara, Ashbery, Koch, and BARBARA GUEST. Meanwhile, back in the States, Corso blundered into another confrontation when he read with O'Hara at the LIVING THEATRE in March 1959. Corso read his poem "Marriage," which soon appeared in *The New American Poetry* under a dedication to the recently married Goldbergs, the Mike and Patsy of O'Hara's "The DAY LADY DIED" (1959). But at the Living Theatre, Corso spun the poem against O'Hara, remarking, "You see, you have it so easy because you're a faggot. Why don't you get married?" (Gooch 322).

If the gay poets of the first-generation New York School remained suspiciously "chichi" in Corso's eyes, the married poets of the second generation would look too "domestic" (Lenhart 102). Though Corso himself was married three times and fathered several children, these circumstances entered his poetry only toward the end of his life. Unlike Ginsberg, who embraced all of the Downtown

poets as extended family, Corso seemed intent on maintaining the quasi-orphaned status that he had known as a child. After the publication of *Long Live Man* (New Directions, 1962), he began to withdraw from the public eye, spending more time abroad, publishing less frequently, and descending deeper into drug addiction. His elegy for JACK KEROUAC, the title poem of *Elegiac Feelings American* (New Directions, 1970), is as much an elegy for himself, though it explicitly rejects that possibility. As one of the original Beats, Corso remained a legendary figure among the poets of the Lower East Side, though the legend acquired an ironically "domestic" coloration. The third of three Corso issues published by the DOWNTOWN MANHATTAN magazine *Unmuzzled Ox* (number 22, winter 1981), opens with a photograph by GERARD MALANGA of Corso and his father and closes with a photograph of Corso with his youngest child, Max (born in 1976). Corso returned to Greenwich Village during the last decade of his life, and he died in 2001, "the last of the 'Daddies'" (Morgan xiii).

Bibliography

Corso, Gregory. *An Accidental Autobiography. The Selected Letters.* Edited by Bill Morgan. New York: New Directions, 2003.

———. Interview by Michael Andre (1973). *Unmuzzled Ox* 22 (Winter 1981): 123–158.

———. "Marriage." In *The New American Poetry, 1945–1960*, edited by Donald Allen, 209–212. 1960. Reprint, Berkeley: University of California Press, 1999.

———. *Mindfield: New and Selected Poems.* New York: Thunder's Mouth, 1989.

Ginsberg, Allen. "Abstraction in Poetry" (1959). In *Deliberate Prose: Selected Essays, 1952–1995.* Edited by Bill Morgan. New York: HarperCollins, 2000, 243–245.

———. Introduction to *Gasoline*, by Gregory Corso. San Francisco: City Lights, 1958, 13–16.

Gooch, Brad. *City Poet: The Life and Times of Frank O'Hara.* New York: Knopf, 1993.

Lenhart, Gary. *The Stamp of Class: Reflections on Poetry and Social Class.* Ann Arbor: University of Michigan Press, 2006.

Morgan, Bill. Editor's Introduction. In *An Accidental Autobiography. The Selected Letters*, by Gregory Corso. New York: New Directions, 2003, xiii–xvi.

O'Hara, Frank. *The Collected Poems*. Rev. ed. Edited by Donald Allen. Berkeley: University of California Press, 1995.

———. "Gregory Corso." In *Standing Still and Walking in New York*. Edited by Donald Allen. San Francisco: Grey Fox, 1983, 82–85.

———. *Poems Retrieved*. Rev. ed. Edited by Donald Allen. San Francisco: Grey Fox, 1996.

Olson, Kirby. *Gregory Corso: Doubting Thomist*. Carbondale: Southern Illinois University Press, 2002.

Sayre, Nora. "The Poets' Theatre: A Memoir of the Fifties." *Grand Street* 3, no. 3 (Spring 1984): 92–105.

Skau, Michael. *"A Clown in a Grave": Complexities and Tensions in the Works of Gregory Corso*. Carbondale: Southern Illinois University Press, 1999.

Coultas, Brenda (1958–   )

Coultas was born on the Ohio River Bridge, between Kentucky and Indiana. She grew up in the small Indiana town of Bloomfield, the population of which (at the time around 50) was mostly composed of her mother's family, the Yearbys. Her father was a rural mail carrier and a part-time farmer; her mother was a housewife. As a child, Coultas traveled during the summers, when her family worked at the carnival, making and selling taffy. After receiving her B.A. from the University of Southern Indiana in 1991, Coultas attended the NAROPA INSTITUTE in Boulder, Colorado, graduating with an M.F.A. in 1994. Soon after graduation she moved to NEW YORK CITY where she began work as a program assistant at the POETRY PROJECT AT ST. MARK'S CHURCH IN-THE-BOWERY, then under the direction of ED FRIEDMAN. Coultas joined with such figures as MARCELLA DURAND, JO ANN WASSERMAN, ANSELM BERRIGAN, ELENI SIKELIANOS, and others to form the loose constellation informally dubbed the "third generation" of the NEW YORK SCHOOL.

Her first book, *Early Films* (Rodent Press, 1996), was followed by *A Handmade Museum* (Coffee House Press, 2003) and *The Marvelous Bones of Time* (Coffee House Press, 2007). She is also the author of three chapbooks. An assistant professor of English and the Introduction to College Writing coordinator at Touro College in New York since 1998, Coultas has also taught at Naropa University, Long Island University, the

Poetry Project, and elsewhere. She has received awards from the Fund for Poetry, Academy of American Poets, Poetry Society of America, and New York Foundation for the Arts.

Coultas's work—while sharing with the other poets of the New York School what ALICE NOTLEY has identified as its hallmark, "extraordinary in both its charm and what you might call moral force" (8)—enlivens its New York School roots by embracing the local (also a hallmark of the New York School) through documentary techniques that owe more to ED SANDERS's INVESTIGATIVE POETRY than to FRANK O'HARA. Notable for its personal immediacy and public engagement, Coultas's work remains both highly lyrical and humorous. The disarming, sometimes deceptive simplicity of JOE BRAINARD's I REMEMBER marks a definite strain in Coultas's work, but her most marked influences (other than her direct contemporaries) are the second-generation New York School figures ANNE WALDMAN and BERNADETTE MAYER, whose highly personal work of the 1970s and 1980s nevertheless maintains the playful interrogation of language characteristic of much post–World War II AMERICAN POETRY.

Bibliography

Coultas, Brenda. "Dumpster Surveillance: A Conversation with Brenda Coultas." Interview by Douglas Manson, Isabelle Pelissier, and Jonathon Skinner. *Ecopoetics* 1 (2001): 25–32.

———. "Brenda Coultas Tells the Truth." Interview by Marcella Durand. *Poetry Project Newsletter* 200 (October/November 2004): 13–19.

Notley, Alice. *Coming After: Essays on Poetry*. Ann Arbor: University of Michigan Press, 2005.

Wallace, Mark. Review of *Early Films*. *Poetry Previews*. Available online. URL: http://www.poetrypreviews.com/poets/poet-mccain.html.

Countess from Minneapolis, The
Barbara Guest (1976)

BARBARA GUEST's *The Countess from Minneapolis* (PROVIDENCE: Burning Deck, 1976, reprint 1991) is a sequence of 42 brief texts, some in verse and some in the FORM of prose poems, evoking the experience of her fictional Countess in Minneapolis.

The preposition *from* in the title may be taken to suggest that the texts are somehow dispatches from the Countess to a sympathetic audience in a more sophisticated world, although the point of view in most of the texts is that of a narrator who describes the Countess in the third person. It is more fitting to understand the Countess as being from Minneapolis in the sense that she has learned to draw from her environment even as she remains opposed to it. This is the position of art and the artist in Guest's aesthetic. Above all, the Countess is an aristocrat of art.

To a degree that is unusual in Guest's work, *The Countess from Minneapolis* registers the details of the ordinary world before it has been translated into art. The Minnesota winter is long and cold. The prairie is flat. Grain elevators are the most distinctive feature of local architecture, and the air seems to be permeated with the dust of grain or the flour milled from it. The street gutters are muddy, and so is the Mississippi River, which makes the Countess wonder at the "river worship" evident among the locals (perhaps a swipe at T. S. Eliot's hymn to the Mississippi in *Four Quartets*). As for the people themselves, they belong in the "beer joint" where a visiting lecturer on the fall of Rome has a vision of their barbarian ancestors: "The athletes still of medium height, in their Atilla hiatus, i.e., the hefty maidens and the food as junky as that served in a mead hall" (#14). It is noteworthy that the lecturer "liked what he saw." There are strength and vitality in "the crowd" that the Countess likens to the "rich traces" of minerals carried along in the Mississippi mud (#7). If art is to draw on these riches, the artist's task is not to purify the stream of life but to channel it. The difference between the Seine in Paris, as the Countess dreams of it, and the Mississippi in Minneapolis, as the Countess experiences it, is a question of "limits" (#8).

The role of art in imposing limits is repeatedly and variously enacted in *The Countess from Minneapolis*. If the locals worship the undisciplined river, with its tendency to overflow its banks, "the Countess worshipped that confinement, the enclosure of the scoured space" that she finds in paintings of Dutch interiors (#23). An equally sacred precinct is the artist's studio, which the reader visits in a section of the poem, based on the studio of Guest's friend,

the painter Mary Abbott, who was teaching at the University of Minnesota in the early 1970s. Guest's trips to Minneapolis to visit her friend provide the immediate background for *The Countess*, though it is not clear whether the "I" who speaks in the "River Road Studio" section (#5) is to be understood as the Countess or Guest herself. In any case the focus is on painting, how "black organizes the ochre," and how "everyone gropes toward black," the limit of color. The aesthetic principle that Guest cites to justify such reduction, "less is more," was formulated by the architect Mies van der Rohe, but Guest correctly attributes the related term MINIMALISM to John Graham, an influential theorist of modernism in the early days of the NEW YORK SCHOOL, whom she imagines driving by coach through Minneapolis on his way to visit the Countess (#20).

As a movement that came into its own during the 1960s, long after Graham introduced the term, minimalism literally sets a limit to Guest's poem. She concludes with a celebration of a sculpture, *Amaryllis* (1965, 1968), by her friend Tony Smith, which entered the collection of the Walker Art Center in Minneapolis in 1968. As Guest treats it, *Amaryllis* epitomizes the dual relation of art to the world, both drawing from it and opposing it. Like the golden bird in W. B. Yeats's "Sailing to Byzantium," Smith's sculpture derives its abstract, minimalist form from a natural thing, the plant for which it is named, but its material is metal, lifting it out of the natural cycle of growth and decay. Having "come to dwell in Minneapolis," however, the sculpture does not merely remain "aloof"; it adopts "a regal stance." Like the jar that "took dominion" over Tennessee in Wallace Stevens's "Anecdote of the Jar," *Amaryllis* casts an "enchantment" over Minneapolis that gives the city artistic form. That is the only Minneapolis in which the Countess can ever hope to feel at home.

Bibliography

Diggory, Terence. "Barbara Guest and the Mother of Beauty." *Women's Studies* 30 (2001): 75–94.

Lundquist, Sarah. "The Midwestern New York Poet: Barbara Guest's *The Countess from Minneapolis*." *Jacket* 10 (October 1999). Available online. URL: http://www.jacketmagazine.com/10/gues-by-lund.html. Accessed December 18, 2008.

Crase, Douglas (1944–)

Ever-expanding possibility is an article of faith for Douglas Crase, so it is fitting that his work opens up possibilities for NEW YORK SCHOOL poetry that, so far, he alone has explored. He finds his point of departure in JOHN ASHBERY, but in Ashbery's rhetoric, in his mode of address to the reader, rather than in surrealist imagery or fragmented FORM. Particularly in Ashbery's work of the 1970s, *Three Poems* (1972) and *Houseboat Days* (1977) more than *SELF-PORTRAIT IN A CONVEX MIRROR* (1975), Crase found the promise of "a new American measure," the "civil meter" that Crase went on to explore in his own work, where America itself becomes "the meter-making argument" that Ralph Waldo Emerson identified as the essence of poetry (Commentary 38; "Justified Times" 148). However, rather than turning his portrait of America into a self-portrait, in the tradition that runs continuously from Emerson to Ashbery, Crase renders the obdurate facts of landscape, particularly that of his native Michigan and New York State, both rural and urban. His respect for "things as they are" was nurtured through his acquaintance with the great realist of the New York School poets, JAMES SCHUYLER (Schuyler, "Dec. 28, 1974").

Crase met Ashbery in 1972 in Rochester, New York, where Crase worked as a speech writer for executives of the Eastman Kodak Company, an occupation that informs his interest in rhetoric. In 1973 Crase met Schuyler in Sagaponack, Long Island, at the home of Robert Dash, a realist painter who has provided a common point of reference in poems by both Crase ("Sagaponack" and "Sagg Beach" in *The Revisionist*) and Schuyler. Schuyler's "Dec. 28, 1974" is based on a house party hosted by Dash that included Schuyler, TREVOR WINKFIELD, the painter Darragh Park, Crase, and his partner, Frank Polach. Earlier in 1974 Crase and Polach had moved to the Chelsea neighborhood of NEW YORK CITY, where Schuyler eventually became their neighbor. In "Dining Out with Doug and Frank," Schuyler employs their friendship as the loom on which to weave a complex tapestry of city life. The first installment of *BROADWAY: A POETS AND PAINTERS ANTHOLOGY* (1979), edited by Schuyler and CHARLES NORTH, includes poems by both Crase and Polach.

Crase's poetry has been collected to date in only one volume, *The Revisionist* (Little, Brown, 1981), which won such wide acclaim that it immediately established him as a poet of significance beyond the narrow confines of a "school." Commenting on Crase's achievement in *A History of Modern Poetry*, David Perkins proposed "that America and its history are only formally his subject matter, that the deeper meaning of his poetry lies in his vision of process, of unresting, somehow orderly change in natural things and also in buildings, cities, or 'history'" (Perkins 633). Crase takes an unusual approach to cultural history in *AMERIFIL.TXT* (University of Michigan Press, 1996), a "commonplace book" in which quotations from American writers are arranged to compose a kind of "map of home," as the preface explains. Crase's home in the New York School is confirmed by the frequent quotations from Ashbery, Schuyler, and FAIRFIELD PORTER and other, more expected authors such as Emerson, David Thoreau, Walt Whitman, and Emily Dickinson. A third book by Crase, *Both: A Portrait in Two Parts* (Pantheon, 1994), makes a special contribution to the history of the New York School. It is a double biography of Dwight Ripley, founding sponsor of the TIBOR DE NAGY GALLERY, and his partner, Rupert Barneby. In his later years Barneby had come to know Polach through their shared expertise in botany, and recognizing that Polach and Crase belonged to the community that had grown up around the de Nagy Gallery, Barneby willed to Polach his collection of papers and artwork relating to the gallery. Drawing on this material, Crase has composed both a history of the times in which Ripley and Barneby lived and a meditation on what it means to live in a long-term relationship such as his own with Polach. Similarly, the title poem of *The Revisionist* is both a sketch of America's character and a love poem, one "vision of process" serving to illuminate both national and personal history.

Bibliography

Crase, Douglas. Commentary on "Once the Sole Province." In *Ecstatic Occasions, Expedient Forms: 85 Leading Contemporary Poets Select and Comment on Their Poems*, 2d ed., edited by David Lehman, 36–39. Ann Arbor: University of Michigan Press, 1996.

———. "Justified Times," *The Nation,* 1 September 1984, 146–149.

———. "Plainsongs," *The Nation,* 16 November 1985, 506–508, 510.

———. "The Prophetic Ashbery." In *Beyond Amazement: New Essays on John Ashbery,* edited by David Lehman, 30–65. Ithaca, N.Y.: Cornell University Press, 1980.

———. "A Schuyler Ballade." *Denver Quarterly* 24, no. 4 (Spring 1990): 25–32.

———. "A Voice Like the Day." *Poetry* 163, no. 4 (January 1994): 225–238.

Molesworth, Charles. "Three American Poets," *New York Times Book Review,* 23 August 1981, 3, 29.

Perkins, David. *A History of Modern Poetry* Vol. 2: *Modernism and After.* Cambridge, Mass.: Harvard University Press, 1987.

Schuyler, James. *Collected Poems.* New York: Noonday/ Farrar, Straus & Giroux, 1995.

Shetley, Vernon. "Ask the Fact," *New York Review of Books,* 29 April 1982, 43.

Creeley, Robert (1926–2005)

Of the several poetic heirs to CHARLES OLSON, Robert Creeley did the most to construct the institutions that Olson's poetic revolution required if it was to have lasting impact. Adept at critical formulation, Creeley supplied the famous expression "Form is never more than an extension of content" that Olson incorporated in his manifesto "PROJECTIVE VERSE" (1950). Together, Creeley and Olson sought to fashion magazines that would be friendly to their cause: first the BOSTON-based *Origin* (1951–57), edited by Cid Corman, then *The BLACK MOUNTAIN REVIEW* (1954–57), edited by Creeley as an organ of the experimental college where both he and Olson taught. Creeley was one of seven featured speakers, including Olson, at the BERKELEY POETRY CONFERENCE in 1965. The following year Creeley succeeded Olson as the anchor of the Poetics Program at the University of BUFFALO, where Creeley taught until 1995. Meanwhile, after appearing in DONALD M. ALLEN's *The NEW AMERICAN POETRY, 1945–1960,* Creeley joined Allen in coediting *New American Story* (Grove, 1965) and *The New Writing in the U.S.A.* (Penguin, 1971).

The institution that might have first connected Creeley with the NEW YORK SCHOOL was Harvard University, which he attended in the late 1940s at the same time as JOHN ASHBERY, KENNETH KOCH, and FRANK O'HARA. But Creeley was not interested in acquiring cultural credentials and left Harvard in 1947 without taking a degree. A more rugged New England mattered more to him and provided a bond not only with Olson but with later writers associated with the New York School, such as TED BERRIGAN and WILLIAM CORBETT (*Collected Essays* 323–329). As for the institution that launched the New York School, Creeley was well aware of the process-oriented aesthetic developed by the abstract expressionist painters, several of whom taught at BLACK MOUNTAIN COLLEGE (*Collected Essays* 367–376). Nevertheless, the taut, stripped-down poetic style of Creeley and DENISE LEVERTOV looked to O'Hara not like spontaneous action but rather obsessive control (O'Hara 23). Ashbery has been more generous, suggesting that Creeley's "succinctness is like the unfettered flashing of a diamond," but he has still placed this very American trait, in his judgment, at the opposite pole from his own "European and maximalist" predilections (242–243). Despite these differences, influential critics have compared Creeley with O'Hara, for writing that refuses to turn in on itself as a self-contained artifact (Altieri 35), and with Ashbery, for writing "about the orders that silently prevail over hardly noticed details of daily life, and about where those orders begin to dissolve" (von Hallberg 54).

Creeley himself had more to say about KENNETH KOCH than about any other member of the first-generation New York School (*Collected Essays* 249–250, 342–343), perhaps because a writer so obviously different could be considered without interference from competitive instincts. On the whole second-generation poets developed closer relations with Creeley, both in their writing and in their personal interaction. At the Berkeley Poetry Conference, Creeley heard TED BERRIGAN read from *The SONNETS* and recognized their derivation from O'Hara and Ashbery but also recognized that Berrigan was using new "feedback" techniques, creating the voice of a poem through echoing phrases rather than imitating a person speaking (*Contexts*

88). In BOLINAS, CALIFORNIA, where Creeley lived from 1970 to 1973, he came in contact with other New York School writers. ARAM SAROYAN had reviewed Creeley's novel *The Island* (Scribners, 1963) in spring 1964 and sought him out that summer in New Mexico. Catching up with Saroyan in Bolinas, Creeley found that he had obtained "brilliant" effects with his concrete poetry. TOM CLARK's excavation of "found poetry" from the songs of Neil Young seemed, like Berrigan's *Sonnets*, to liberate language from attachment to an "original" speaker (*Contexts* 196–197).

Creeley's contribution to this movement of liberation was a type of SERIAL POEM in which brief daily notations, each followed by a line of a few dots, accumulate as a series determined merely by chronology rather than narrative or thematic design. As if responding to O'Hara's criticism of his earlier work, Creeley explained, "I wanted to trust writing, I was so damned tired of trusting my own opinion as to whether or not this was a good piece of poetry or a bad piece of poetry" (*Contexts* 193). *Pieces* (Black Sparrow, 1968) was the simple title assigned to his first publication in this mode. LEWIS WARSH, another Bolinas transplant, published a successor, *In London* (ANGEL HAIR, 1970), eventually included in Creeley's *A Day Book* (Scribners, 1972). Creeley's example in this regard can be traced in the work of JOANNE KYGER (*Joanne*, 1970), LARRY FAGIN (*Twelve Poems*, 1972), and Berrigan ("London Air," 1977).

Bibliography

Altieri, Charles. *Postmodernisms Now: Essays on Contemporaneity in the Arts.* University Park: Pennsylvania State University Press, 1998.

Ashbery, John. "Introduction to a Reading by Robert Creeley and Charles Tomlinson" (1995). In *Selected Prose.* Edited by Eugene Richie. Ann Arbor: University of Michigan Press, 2004, 241–243.

Clark, Tom. *Robert Creeley and the Genius of the American Common Place.* New York: New Directions, 1993.

Creeley, Robert. *Collected Essays.* Berkeley: University of California Press, 1989.

———. *Collected Poems, 1945–75.* Berkeley: University of California Press, 1982.

———. *Contexts of Poetry: Interviews, 1961–1971.* Edited by Donald Allen. Bolinas, Calif.: Four Seasons, 1973.

———. "Stories: Being an Information: An Interview." *Sagetrieb* 1, no. 3 (Winter 1982): 35–56.

Faas, Ekbert, with Maria Trombacco. *Robert Creeley: A Biography.* Hanover, N.H.: University Press of New England/McGill Queen's University Press, 2001.

O'Hara, Frank. Interview by Edward Lucie-Smith (1965). In *Standing Still and Walking in New York.* Edited by Donald Allen. San Francisco: Grey Fox, 1983, 3–26.

Saroyan, Aram. "'An Extension of Content.'" *Poetry* 104 (April 1964): 45–47.

von Hallberg, Robert. *American Poetry and Culture, 1945–1980.* Cambridge, Mass.: Harvard University Press, 1985.

Waldman, Anne, and Lewis Warsh, eds. *The Angel Hair Anthology.* New York: Granary Books, 2001.

Cyberspace Kenward Elmslie and Trevor Winkfield (2000)

Since the groundbreaking "Special Issue of Collaborations" of *LOCUS SOLUS*, edited by KENNETH KOCH in summer 1961, the writers, artists, and some publishers associated with the NEW YORK SCHOOL have been known for their inspired COLLABORATIONs. Poet KENWARD ELMSLIE and painter TREVOR WINKFIELD's *Cyberspace*, published by Granery Books in 2000, takes its place among the most enjoyable and successful collaborations, including Elmslie's collaborations with JOE BRAINARD collected in *Pay Dirt* (Bamberger Book, 1992) and Winkfield's numerous artist books made with many of the principal poets of both the first and second generations of the New York School.

Cyberspace is a strange contemporary masterpiece, both resistant to and the artful product of its historical moment. Drawing on modernism, surrealism, and other vanguard traditions, the book builds upon three-and-a-half decades of back-and-forth poet-painter collaborations between Elmslie and Winkfield. *Cyberspace*'s distinction is this: It not only joins the two fantastic imaginations of Elmslie and Winkfield, but it also theatrically plays along the fault lines of two epochs as well—one of the material world and culture and the other of the age of cyberspace itself. Both epochs are fully coded and masterfully embodied in the book. Elmslie writes:

Hoofed it. Why reinvent the wheel online via an all-pixel dream? Grrr! Drunk, we smashed the *NextPreviousHome* server that'd so relentlessly harassed us.

Both Elmslie and Winkfield employ collage techniques and are steeped in highly stylized aesthetic sensibilities. However, it is their respective rhythmical virtuosity that shines above all other characteristics of their mysteriously affecting work. Elmslie's uninhibited rhythmical sense is an extension of his musical plays, opera librettos, song lyrics, and what he calls his "poem songs." The extreme rhythmical play of Elmslie's poems propels the reader through his topsy-turvy world of buzzwords, cyber jargon, and breathtaking juxtapositions. Elmslie's poems are unique in that they have a wildly perfect pitch. In the second section, "Solo Imbroglio," he writes:

Funny money decal coins gummed up tax haven jackpots. Offshore, bubble-wrapped, Auntie T wound up in bruise-free Isle of Man nut-house. "Keep me safe from downtime, Help Desk! Over to you, help Desk! Help Desk? Get me Help Desk!" Double strapped, jaw jutting, nose hole cones unswabbed, she'd shriek (from *On The Town*).

The genius of Winkfield's artwork may be his ability to create exquisite (sometimes orderly, sometimes tangled) rhythmical patterns. Winkfield's images provide visual echoes, which open up and suggest the most subtle and pleasurable contours of the mind. The collages feature objects where one thing often becomes another. The perfect apple rhythmically transforms itself into a face with a single yellow eye and two rosy cheeks; or with the greatest of ease, a bird becomes an Asian fan; or goat hooves twirl into asparagus spears, and three-dimensional triangles keep one's eyes in motion in Winkfield's exacting sense of play. JOHN ASHBERY has described the rhythmical aspects of Winkfield's paintings in this way: "It's as though seeing and hearing merged into a single act, and the 'meaning' of the picture were lodged at the intersection of two

of the senses, where one is pleasurably enmeshed, deliciously hindered" (260).

It is apt to mention Granary Books and small-press publisher Steven Clay as a key force along with Elmslie and Winkfield. Clay's decade-long commitment to publishing artist books, both in limited editions and high-quality trade paperbacks, is fully realized in the exquisite printing and production of *Cyberspace*.

The art of *Cyberspace* is that the poems and paintings here continually dazzle in a field of new relationships. The play of these relationships can be as unsettling as they are alluring. As Winkfield has discussed, "Something comes so close to whimsy but veers off at the last moment to become tragedy" (Winkfield interviewed by Shapiro, 37). Neither Winkfield nor Elmslie avoids the wicked ways of the world or the coded mysteries of cyberspace. As Elmslie writes, in "Diddly Squot," the third and final section of *Cyberspace*, "Deep trouble? You bet!"

Oddly, the paradox of this book is that each painting and each poem seems to be able to stand alone as much as it stands in relation to, and complements, its companion. The paintings do not illustrate the poems any more than the poems supply elaborate captions for the paintings. To the credit of both Elmslie and Winkfield, each page faces inward, the one calling the other by its secret name: poet, painter, and friend.

Bibliography

Ashbery, John. Introduction to *Trevor Winkfield's Pageant: Selected Prose*. Edited by Eugene Richie. Ann Arbor: University of Michigan Press, 2004, 259–261.

Corbett, William. "A Mysterious Clarity." *Modern Painters* 16 (Summer 2002): 92–95.

Esplund, Lance. "Winkfield's Vocations." *Art in American* (January 2003): 92–95.

Winkfield, Trevor. "How They Wrote Certain of My Drawings." In *Trevor Winkfield's Drawings*. Whitmore Lake, Mich.: Bamberger Books, 2004, 7–12.

———. *In the Scissors' Courtyard: Selected Writings, 1967–75*. Flint, Mich.: Bamberger Books, 1994.

———. "A Resurrected Childhood." Interview by David Shapiro. *Arts Magazine* 60 (May 1986): 36–40.

D

dada and surrealism

Within the international movement of modernism, dada and surrealism were the French contribution to the avant-garde, rivaling in significance German expressionism and Italian-Russian futurism. NEW YORK SCHOOL poets paid special attention to the French avant-garde, but, in addition, there were two specifically New York moments in the history of dada and surrealism when European artists sought refuge in the city during the two world wars of the 20th century. Before the term *dada* had been invented, a New York dada group gathered (1915–19) around the presence of Marcel Duchamp (1887–1968), whose 1912 painting *Nude Descending a Staircase, No. 2* (Rubin 12) had aroused scandal at the "Armory Show" in NEW YORK CITY in 1913. Both William Carlos Williams and Wallace Stevens met Duchamp during his first New York sojourn. Later, as favorites of the New York School poets, Williams and Stevens helped transmit the influence of both dada and surrealism. The New York–based magazine *View* (1940–47) published Williams and Stevens in a context dominated by the surrealist writers and artists who had immigrated to New York during World War II. Their leader, the poet André Breton (1896–1966), gave his first American interview for a special surrealist issue of *View* (numbers 7–8, October–November 1941). Even before they arrived in New York, the poets who were to form the New York School were reading *View* for the latest word on surrealism (Ashbery, *Selected Prose* 246; Koch, interview n.p.). Meanwhile, in his role as managing editor of *View*, JOHN BERNARD MYERS absorbed the aesthetic principles that he later applied to New York School poetry as an instance of the surrealist "marvelous" (Myers 12–13).

In between these two New York moments dada and surrealism evolved on the European continent, and not only in France. Among a circle of artists centered on Tristan Tzara (1896–1963) in Zurich, the term *dada* emerged in 1916 as a nonsense word aimed at exposing the irrationality underlying social institutions, now revealed in the horror of total war. Although art as a social institution was a specific target of dada, its "anti-art" thrust has been resisted by New York School poets (Ashbery, *Mark Ford* 44) except insofar as the goal was to erase the boundary between art and life. The "ready-mades" that Duchamp exhibited in New York, such as his famous *Fountain* (1917)—a urinal purchased from a plumbing supply store—perform this erasure while also transforming everyday objects by displacing them into an art context. Through a similar procedure Tzara produced dadaist poems by cutting up newspaper articles and rearranging the words (Motherwell 92). New York School poets from JAMES SCHUYLER ("A New Yorker," "Walter Scott") to TED BERRIGAN (*The SONNETS*) later employed some version of this "cut-up" technique, for which the German dadaist Kurt Schwitters (1887–1948) receives Schuyler's thanks (Schuyler interview 179). Poems in Ashbery's *The Tennis Court Oath* (Wesleyan University Press, 1962), such as "Europe" and "America," are the most significant examples of the technique in terms of their influence on later New York School writing.

Surrealism arose in Paris, first as a term employed by Apollinaire (*The Breasts of Tiresias: A Surrealist Drama* [1917]) and eventually as a movement led by Breton ("Manifesto of Surrealism" [1924]), who organized the energy released by dada as dada itself dispersed in anarchy. The term *surrealism* means "super-realism" and points to a "superior reality" that Breton and his followers identified especially with the state of dreaming (Breton 26). New York School poets have shown little interest in the psychoanalytic implications of dream, which Breton derived from Freud (Breton 10), but the evocation of dream as an aesthetic objective links New York School poetry directly to surrealism. Ashbery's *The Double Dream of Spring* (Dutton, 1970) takes its title from a 1915 painting (Rubin 79) by Giorgio de Chirico (1888–1978), one of many works whose "dreamlike spaces" (Ashbery, "de Chirico" 402) earned de Chirico a place in the pantheon of surrealist forerunners, as determined by Breton (Rubin 82). But Breton defined surrealism proper less by mood than by method, the operation of "psychic automatism" (26) by which a writer or artist suspended all conscious control and gave free rein to the unconscious "depths of the mind" (10). In Ashbery's view the psychic transformation prescribed in the surrealist program too often failed to yield a corresponding transformation in language. Compared to most supposedly "automatic writing," he preferred the syntactical experiments of Pierre Reverdy (1889–1960), another surrealist forerunner (Ashbery, *Selected Prose* 20–21). As a writer himself, de Chirico produced *Hebdomeros* (1929), which Ashbery praised as "the finest" surrealist novel, again on the basis of the language: "long run-on sentences, stitched together with semicolons," permitting "a cinematic freedom of narration" similar to what many experience in reading Ashbery's poems (Ashbery, *Selected Prose* 90).

The bridge that surrealism formed between writing and painting proved to be of enormous consequence to the New York School. "In that creative atmosphere of magical rites," as BARBARA GUEST referred to the surrealist ambience, "there was no recognized separation between the arts" (51). The "POEM-PAINTING," combining word and image, thrived as a surrealist GENRE (Rubin 94), descended both from cubist collage and from dadaist COLLABORATION (Motherwell). However, with the ascent of Salvador Dalí (1904–89) during the 1930s, the style of depicting images in surrealism grew increasingly conservative. The automatism that the surrealists imported into New York in the 1940s was more a theory than a practice, but it became powerfully joined to practice in the art of Arshile Gorky (1904–48), his friend WILLEM DE KOONING, and their younger associate JACKSON POLLOCK. The techniques they developed for transferring the artist's physical action immediately onto the painting's surface, without premeditated, conscious intention, became the basis for ACTION PAINTING and for the action writing that the painters inspired in the New York School poets. In describing the immediacy of Pollock's work, FRANK O'HARA laid bare an ethical foundation that writing and painting shared, both under obligation to surrealism: "Surrealism enjoined the duty, along with the liberation, of saying what you mean and meaning what you say" (18).

The personality of Breton, who "excluded any tone of frivolity" (Myers 10), can still be felt in O'Hara's statement of surrealist obligation, though it was written in 1959, more than a decade after Breton had left New York. Duchamp, who remained in New York, exerted a counter-influence, in which every statement implied a meaning different from what was said, every appearance concealed a different reality. The frivolity that such conditions could inspire is evident in O'Hara's early (1949) poem "Homage to Rrose Sélavy," addressed to the camp female persona that Duchamp sometimes assumed (Rubin 17). The tone persists as a dadaist strain in the work of both O'Hara and KENNETH KOCH throughout the 1950s, notably in their long poems "Second Avenue" (1953) and "When the Sun Tries to Go On" (1953), respectively. What came to be called "neo-dada" entered the art world at the end of the 1950s with the cooler ironies of JASPER JOHNS, but the term was extended to the more blatantly frivolous examples of POP ART as it emerged in the early 1960s.

In this context the second generation of New York School poets inclined more toward dadaism than surrealism. RON PADGETT recalls that for him and TED BERRIGAN, Duchamp was "like a god" (Padgett 10). The ironic title of Duchamp's snow shovel "ready-made," *In Advance of the Broken Arm* (1915), echoes in Berrigan's *Sonnets* (1964) and as the title of Padgett's first collection of poems ("C" Press, 1964). JOHN PERREAULT interviewed Duchamp in 1965, at a time when Perreault was making a transition from poetry to CONCEPTUAL ART, Duchamp's main mode of production since his renunciation of painting in 1918. His last painting of that year, *Tu m'* (Rubin 20), supplies the title of a section of ANNE WALDMAN's *IOVIS*, Book II. The title has been interpreted as Duchamp's comment on the act of painting: *"tu m'emmerdes"* (meaning "you piss me off," though excrement is the French image) (Rubin 21). But in the spirit of dada, Waldman accepts the "cut-up" phrase as a whole sound, on which she rings changes from "tomb" to "dictum" (saying). She thus enacts the principle that Duchamp's saying always differs from what it means.

Bibliography

Apollinaire, Guillaume. *The Breasts of Tiresias: A Surrealist Drama.* Translated by Louis Simpson. In *Modern French Theatre: The Avant-Garde, Dada and Surrealism,* edited by Michael Benedikt and George E. Wellwarth, 55–91. New York: Dutton, 1966.

Ashbery, John. "A de Chirico Retrospective" (1982). In *Reported Sightings: Art Chronicles, 1957–1987.* Edited by David Bergman. Cambridge, Mass.: Harvard University Press, 1991, 401–404.

———. *John Ashbery in Conversation with Mark Ford.* London: Between the Lines, 2003.

———. *Selected Prose.* Edited by Eugene Richie. Ann Arbor: University of Michigan Press, 2004.

Berrigan, Ted. *The Collected Poems of Ted Berrigan.* Edited by Alice Notley, Anselm Berrigan, and Edmund Berrigan. Berkeley: University of California Press, 2005.

Breton, André. "Manifesto of Surrealism" (1924). In *Manifestoes of Surrealism.* Translated by Richard Seaver and Helen R. Lane. Ann Arbor: University of Michigan Press, 1972, 1–47.

Chirico, Giorgio de. *Hebdomeros.* Cambridge, Mass.: Exact Change, 1992.

Dijkstra, Bram. *Cubism, Stieglitz, and the Early Poetry of William Carlos Williams: The Hieroglyphics of a New Speech.* Princeton, N.J.: Princeton University Press, 1969.

Ford, Charles Henri. *View: Parade of the Avant-Garde 1940–1947.* New York: Thunder's Mouth Press, 1991.

Guest, Barbara. "The Shadow of Surrealism" (1986). In *Forces of Imagination: Writing on Writing.* Berkeley, Calif.: Kelsey St. Press, 2003, 51–54.

Koch, Kenneth. Interview by David Kennedy (1993). Al Filreis Web site, University of Pennsylvania. Available online. URL: http://writing.upenn.edu/~afilreis/88/koch.html. Accessed December 18, 2008.

———. "When the Sun Tries to Go On." In *Sun Out: Selected Poems, 1952–54.* New York: Knopf, 2002, 71–140.

MacLeod, Glen. *Wallace Stevens and Modern Art: From the Armory Show to Abstract Expressionism.* New Haven, Conn.: Yale University Press, 1993.

Motherwell, Robert, ed. *The Dada Painters and Poets: An Anthology.* 2d ed. Cambridge, Mass.: Harvard University Press, 1988.

Myers, John Bernard. "The Poets of the New York School." In *The Poets of the New York School.* Philadelphia: Department of Fine Arts, University of Pennsylvania, 1969, 7–29.

O'Hara, Frank. "Jackson Pollock" (1959). In *Art Chronicles, 1954–1966.* Rev. ed. New York: Braziller, 1990, 12–39.

Padgett, Ron. "On *The Sonnets*" (1978). In *Nice to See You: Homage to Ted Berrigan,* edited by Anne Waldman, 9–11. Minneapolis, Minn.: Coffee House Press, 1991.

Perreault, John. "Dada perfume: A Duchamp interview. Making mischief: Dada invades New York at the Whitney through February 23." December 1996. Available online. URL: http://plexus.org/review/perreault/dada.html. Accessed December 18, 2008.

Rubin, William S. *Dada, Surrealism, and Their Heritage.* Exhibit catalog. New York: Museum of Modern Art, 1968.

Schuyler, James. *Collected Poems.* New York: Farrar, Straus & Giroux, 1993.

———. Interview by Carl Little. *Agni* 37 (January 1993): 152–182.

Tashjian, Dickran. *A Boatload of Madmen: Surrealism and the American Avant-Garde, 1920–1950.* New York: Thames & Hudson, 1995.

———. *Skyscraper Primitives: Dada and the American Avant-Garde, 1910–1925.* Middletown, Conn.: Wesleyan University Press, 1975.

Waldman, Anne. "Tu m'." In *Iovis: Book II*. Minneapolis, Minn.: Coffee House Press, 1997, 252–257.

Zweig, Paul. "The New Surrealism." In *Contemporary Poetry in America: Essays and Interviews,* edited by Robert Boyers, 314–329. New York: Schocken, 1974.

dance

"Ballet is the most modern of the arts," wrote FRANK O'HARA and BILL BERKSON in 1961. "It is made up exclusively of qualities which other arts only aspire to in order to be truly modern: daring, risk, chance, personality, individual and unique beauty" (O'Hara and Berkson 39). If it is surprising to read such a statement from poets who are supposed to have taken their lead from painting, it is important to recognize that the concept of ACTION PAINTING posited dance as an ideal condition (Rosenberg 27). Hans Namuth's film of JACKSON POLLOCK painting (1951), accompanied by the MUSIC of MORTON FELDMAN, stages Pollock's action as a dance (Naifeh and Smith 663). If it is surprising that the poets refer to ballet as modern, rather than so-called modern dance, it is worth remembering that for the poets ballet meant the NEW YORK CITY BALLET under the direction of George Balanchine (1904–83), a direct link to the fusion of ballet and modernism under Serge Diaghilev (1872–1929) earlier in the century. A more profound fusion occurred in NEW YORK CITY during the 1950s as the ballet of Balanchine and the new modern dance emerging under the leadership of Merce Cunningham (1919–   ) converged in mutual allegiance to abstraction (Garafola 176–177, 181).

In dance as in painting, abstraction meant a rejection of "literary" reference—story-telling—and a concentration on the essential qualities of the medium: Painting is about paint; dance is about movement. "Risk," as O'Hara and Berkson imply, is fundamental to dance in this sense. EDWIN DENBY, who was better known as a dance critic than as a poet for much of his career, explained: "In dancing one keeps taking a step and recovering one's balance. The risk is a part of the rhythm" (288). But the poet in Denby, and in the other poets who learned how to see dance through his eyes, also saw abstraction in a quality that Denby called "momentum," a quality akin to poetry because it

had to do not with physical movement but with the imaginative shapes projected in the viewer's mind by the dancer's gesture (Denby 287, 302). In an "Ode" (1960) addressed to Tanaquil LeClercq (1929–2000), Balanchine's wife and prima ballerina until she was stricken by polio in 1956, O'Hara wrote: "when you disappeared in the wings nothing was there / but the motion of some extraordinary happening" (*Collected Poems* 364).

Though O'Hara may not have intended the allusion in this instance, his poetic view of ballet is related to performances called HAPPENINGS that grew out of the cross-fertilization among the arts—dance, THEATER, painting, and poetry—at this time. Cunningham served as nominal director for a kind of happening called *The CONSTRUCTION OF BOSTON* (1962), with text by KENNETH KOCH. As the name implies, however, happenings were supposed to embrace "whatever happens," subject as much to chance as to direction. Cunningham's main collaborator, JOHN CAGE, supplied the theoretical foundation, and Cunningham, like Cage, introduced chance into his method of composition, but he applied the method in the service of a minimalist style that remained closer to the cool classicism of ballet than the highly charged expressionism toward which happenings naturally tended. A choreographer more in tune with the latter spirit was James Waring (1922–75). In addition to his work in dance, Waring directed plays by O'Hara and others at the LIVING THEATRE and, with the poet DIANE DI PRIMA, one of his dance students, founded the NEW YORK POETS THEATRE. Other students of his, including Yvonne Rainer (1934–   ) and Fred Herko (ca. 1935–64), became founding members of the Judson Dance Theater, the leading laboratory for modern dance experiment during its brief existence from 1962 to 1967. O'Hara's poem "Dances Before the Wall" takes its title from a dance staged by Waring in 1958, but it crams in references to several different performances in a chaotic sequence that anticipates the mood of later happenings at JUDSON MEMORIAL CHURCH.

The spirit of performance that radiated from Judson Church informed "the dynamic ritual enactment atmosphere of countless poetry events" at nearby St. Mark's Church (Waldman 201), where the POETRY PROJECT AT ST. MARK'S CHURCH IN-

THE-BOWERY was founded in 1966. In 1974 the Poetry Project acquired a dance counterpart in Danspace, cofounded by poet LARRY FAGIN and dancer Barbara Dilley (1938–   ), who founded the dance program at the NAROPA INSTITUTE the following year. Dilley had performed with the Judson Dance Theater, the Cunningham company, and the Grand Union, a dance collective that flourished as a kind of successor to Judson from 1970 to 1976. Another Cunningham alumnus and member of the Grand Union, Douglas Dunn (1942–   ), is especially notable for COLLABORATIONs with NEW YORK SCHOOL poets. In 1983 he presented *The Secret of the Waterfall,* in which six dancers performed to verbal music recited by ANNE WALDMAN and REED BYE. "Language (an act of mind) actually shapes the acts of the body," according to Jena Osman's description (n.p.). Charles Atlas directed a film version of *The Secret of the Waterfall.* Dunn also performs dance segments in several films by RUDY BURCKHARDT, including *The Nude Pond* (1985), with poems by JOHN ASHBERY, and *Tree Streets* (1995), with poems by VINCENT KATZ.

Bibliography

Denby, Edwin. *Dance Writings and Poetry.* Edited by Robert Cornfield. New Haven, Conn.: Yale University Press, 1998.

Garafola, Lynn. "Toward an American Dance: Dance in the City." In *New York: Culture Capital of the World, 1940–1965,* edited by Leonard Wallock, 156–187. New York: Rizzoli, 1988.

Naifeh, Steven, and Gregory White Smith. *Jackson Pollock: An American Saga.* New York: Clarkson N. Potter, 1989.

O'Hara, Frank. *The Collected Poems.* Rev. ed. Edited by Donald Allen. Berkeley: University of California Press, 1995.

———. "Cunningham, Here and Now" (1957). In *Merce Cunningham: Dancing in Time and Space: Essays, 1944–1992,* edited by Richard Kostelanetz, 31–32. Chicago: A Capella Books, 1992.

O'Hara, Frank, and Bill Berkson. "Notes from Row L." In *Hymns of St. Bridget and Other Writings.* Woodacre, Calif.: Owl Press, 2001, 39–40.

Osman, Jena. "Tracking a Poem in Time: The Shifting States of Anne Waldman's 'Makeup on Empty Space.'" *Jacket* 27 (April 2005). Available online. URL: http://jacketmagazine.com/27/w-osma.html. Accessed December 18, 2008.

Rosenberg, Harold. "The American Action Painters." In *The Tradition of the New.* 1960. Reprint, New York: Da Capo, 1994, 23–39.

Satin, Leslie. "James Waring and the Judson Dance Theater." In *Reinventing Dance in the 1960s: Everything Was Possible,* edited by Sally Banes, 51–80. Madison: University of Wisconsin Press, 2003.

Waldman, Anne. "'I Is Another': Dissipative Structures." In *Vow to Poetry: Essays, Interviews, and Manifestos.* Minneapolis, Minn.: Coffee House Press, 2001, 193–213.

Davis, Jordan (1970–   )

Jordan Davis was born in New York and educated at Columbia College (B.A., 1992), where he studied with KENNETH KOCH, edited the arts section of the *Columbia Spectator,* won the Academy of American Poets Prize, and hosted a poetry radio show, *Composed on the Tongue,* on WKCR. Along with CHRISTOPHER EDGAR, he founded in 1998 the literary journal *The Hat,* which has brought the NEW YORK SCHOOL poets up to date in its six extant issues. As an editor he has worked for the *Poetry Project Newsletter* (1992–94) and *Teachers & Writers* (1999–2000). Recently he began hosting *The Million Poems Show* at the BOWERY POETRY CLUB, "a new format," as he describes it, "mixing talk, reading, collaboration, and audience participation. No podium, no self-flattering exegesis" (jordandavis.com). Featured guests have included Terrance Hayes, Susan Wheeler, ANSELM BERRIGAN, and JENI OLIN. Prior to that, Davis was the host and curator of the Poetry City reading series at TEACHERS & WRITERS (1995–2000).

One of Davis's main projects has been the "Million Poems Journal," the inception of which was a dream in which Davis was told to write a million poems. He immediately embarked on the seemingly absurd endeavor, creating an eponymous blog entrusted to releasing his latest creations. To date, he has written nearly 2,000 poems and the project by dint of its sheer magnitude is impetus enough to keep him writing for the rest of his life. As poet Susan Wheeler has written about his work, "there is a whiff of the downtown/Tulsa/beats/New York School tradition . . . but there are also strains of Marcel Janco, Paul Reverdy, and Matsuo Basho; of W. H. Auden and Louis MacNeice as well as Tom Raworth and Jeremy Prynne; props to the American transcendentalists; and an assimilation of the L=A=N=G=U=A=G=E inheritance. The mix is a rich one, and wholly his own" (n.p.).

Davis has published two full-length collections, *Million Poems Journal* (Faux, 2003) and *The Moon Is Moving: MPJ 2* (Faux, 2005), and four chapbooks, *A Little Gold Book* (Golden Books, 1995), *Upstairs* (Barque Press, 1997), *Poem on a Train* (Barque Press, 1998), and *Yeah, No* (Detour, 2000). His work has also been anthologized in *Anthology of New (American) Poets*, edited by LISA JARNOT, Leonard Schwartz, and CHRIS STROFFOLINO (Talisman House, 1998), and *Heights of the Marvelous*, edited by Todd Colby (St. Martin's Griffin, 2000). Along with Sarah Manguso, Davis coedited *Free Radicals: American Poets before Their First Books* (Subpress, 2004). He is also a permanent columnist for the acclaimed online literary review *The Constant Critic*, produced by *Fence* magazine, and his reviews and poems have appeared in such places as the *Village Voice, Paper,* and *Boston Review.* He currently authors a second blog entitled *Equanimity.*

One of Davis's primary influences has been Koch, with whom he developed programs for teaching writing in public schools and for whom he is now the literary executor. He was the coeditor of both *The Collected Poems of Kenneth Koch* (Knopf, 2005) and *The Collected Fiction of Kenneth Koch* (Coffee House Press, 2005).

Davis married Anna Malmude in 1997, with whom he had a son, James Malmude Davis, in 2000. He separated from his wife in 2002 and is currently married to the poet Ali Davis (formerly Alison Stine). In the past he has lectured at the POETRY PROJECT AT ST. MARK'S CHURCH IN-THE-BOWERY, the New School, the University of Massachusetts at Amherst, the University of Kansas, and within the NEW YORK CITY public school system. He has read his poetry around the world, from Copenhagen, Denmark, to San Diego, California, giving several readings a year in New York City, where he currently makes his residence.

Bibliography

Davis, Jordan. "Equanimity" blog. Available online. URL: http://equanimity.blogspot.com/. Accessed December 18, 2008.

———. "Million Poems" blog. Available online. URL: http://millionpoems.blogspot.com/. Accessed December 18, 2008.

———. Web site. Available online. URL: http://www.jordandavis.com/about.html. Accessed December 18, 2008.

Wheeler, Susan. "Emerging Poet: On Jordan Davis" (2001). Academy of American Poets Web site. Available online. URL: http://www.poets.org/viewmedia.php/prmMID/7887. Accessed December 18, 2008.

"Day Lady Died, The" Frank O'Hara (1959)

FRANK O'HARA's position at the turning point between modernism and postmodernism comes into brilliant focus in his most famous poem, "The Day Lady Died," first published in the groundbreaking anthology *The NEW AMERICAN POETRY, 1945–1960* (1960). O'Hara's poem belongs to the traditional GENRE of the elegy, finding its occasion in the death of the JAZZ singer, Billie Holiday (1915–59), whose nickname, "Lady Day," is playfully echoed in O'Hara's title. In a typically modernist gesture, the poem's conclusion equates the stillness of death with the transcendence of art, as O'Hara recalls a performance by Holiday about a year before her death at the East Village jazz club the FIVE SPOT: "and everyone and I stopped breathing." What makes the poem most memorable, however, is the way O'Hara keeps moving through the details of daily existence up until the moment when he sees a newspaper announcing Holiday's death. Attention to the simple succession of moments, each of equal significance or insignificance, was to become a characteristic of postmodernist art. O'Hara's followers in the NEW YORK SCHOOL, such as TED BERRIGAN and RON PADGETT, pursued the cataloging of particular facts but dropped the culmination into a "meaningful" whole (Perloff 183).

Critics have shown more reluctance than poets to accept the preponderance of fact over FORM or meaning in "The Day Lady Died." Marjorie Perloff performs a structuralist reading by classifying

O'Hara's observations into two categories: "foreign or exotic" (the books O'Hara considers purchasing, the Italian liqueur, the French cigarettes) and "native American" (the shoeshine, the hamburger, the john door) (181–182). These two categories combine, Perloff suggests, in Holiday, an African-American woman who was exotic in her artistry. Andrew Ross proposes a different kind of dialectic, structured around the poles of the personal and the political that combined in the liberation movements of the late 1960s, such as feminism and gay rights. Ross understands O'Hara, as a gay man, to be staging a "camp" performance of a "lady's day," seemingly devoted to shopping but in fact committed to the "survivalist" strategy of taking things into one's own hands (390). Though without the gender-bending connotations of "camp," Charles Altieri's reading of "The Day Lady Died" as "domestic lyric" gets closer to accepting the radical contingency of the poem's details (203). Nevertheless, Altieri insists on something "organic" in the poem, if not in its form, then in its "lyric emotion" (203).

At this point Altieri is arguing with PAUL CARROLL, the critic who, very early in the unfolding debate, predicted most accurately the use that poets would make of O'Hara's example. Carroll calls "The Day Lady Died" an "impure poem," by which he means that O'Hara "refuses to step away . . . from immediate but fragmentary and 'unpoetic' experiences" in order to enter the "pure" realm of "the organic and well-made work" ("Impure" 376–377). Avoiding even the dialectic of modernism and postmodernism, Carroll aligns O'Hara's work with the unplaceable movement of DADA. In an appendix to the original version of his essay he cites a striking precedent for "The Day Lady Died" in a poem of 1917 by the French dadaist Pierre Albert-Birot (*Poem in Its Skin* 164–168). And Carroll compares O'Hara's implicit claim that "The Day Lady Died" is a poem to the audacity of the contemporary "neo-dadaist" ROBERT RAUSCHENBERG, who produced a portrait by the sheer act of claiming to do so: "This is a portrait of Iris Clert because I say it is." "In short," Carroll writes of "The Day Lady Died," "here is an original 'act' in creating a poem." He concludes: "Such audacity is exciting" ("Impure" 378).

Bibliography

Altieri, Charles. "From 'Varieties of Immanentist Expression'" (1979). In *Frank O'Hara: To Be True to a City*, edited by Jim Elledge, 189–208. Ann Arbor: University of Michigan Press, 1990.

Carroll, Paul. "An Impure Poem about July 17, 1959" (1968). In *Frank O'Hara: To Be True to a City*, edited by Jim Elledge, 373–379. Ann Arbor: University of Michigan Press, 1990.

———. *The Poem in Its Skin*. Chicago: Follett, 1968.

Elledge, Jim, ed. *Frank O'Hara: To Be True to a City*. Ann Arbor: University of Michigan Press, 1990.

LeSueur, Joe. "The Day Lady Died." In *Digressions on Some Poems by Frank O'Hara: A Memoir*. New York: Farrar, Straus & Giroux, 2003, 191–196.

O'Hara, Frank. "The Day Lady Died." In *The Collected Poems*. Rev. ed. Edited by Donald Allen. Berkeley: University of California Press, 1995, 325.

Perloff, Marjorie. *Frank O'Hara: Poet among Painters*. 1977. Reprint, Chicago: University of Chicago Press, 1998.

Ross, Andrew. "The Death of Lady Day" (1989). In *Frank O'Hara: To Be True to a City*, edited by Jim Elledge, 380–391. Ann Arbor: University of Michigan Press, 1990.

Deanovich, Connie (1960–)

Born in East Chicago, Indiana, an industrial suburb of CHICAGO, ILLINOIS, where her father was a steelworker, Connie Deanovich is a widely respected poet of the NEW YORK SCHOOL's younger generation and a frequent contributor to its leading journals, including NEW AMERICAN WRITING. She has lived primarily in Chicago, where she founded the literary magazine *B City*, and in the Madison, Wisconsin, area.

With ELAINE EQUI, JEROME SALA, PAUL HOOVER, MAXINE CHERNOFF, and SHARON MESMER, Deanovich was one of the Chicago poets of the late 1970s to early 1990s associated with New York School poetics of humor, casualness, popular culture, and surrealist disjuncture. Her wryness and use of the American idiom is also consistent with New York School poetics. In its twisted imagism, set against a metaphysical urban ground, such work is also consistent with the work of Chicago imagist painters Ed Paschke, Jim Nutt, and Roger Brown.

Responding to the question "How would you explain what a poem is to my seven year old?" posed by the Here Comes Everybody blog, Deanovich replied:

> I would say words have secrets and special powers. I would smile and wait for the child to smile back or to smirk. Then I'd say it is a poet's job to discover these secrets and powers. I'd say a poet is like a honeybee except instead of going from flower to flower the poet goes from word to word to get what she needs. The bee makes honey and the poet makes poems. Both are workers, explorers, and participants in the world of beauty. A poet puts words together so the secrets and powers can be revealed to anyone who reads the poems ("Tuesday, July 19, 2005" n.p.).

In her poem entitled "Ted Berrigan" (1988), the reader can follow the poet moving "from word to word"—"Phoney baloney San Antoni"—rather than from thing to word. Rather than grounding the poem in a world of reference, the poet unfolds a list of "what she needs": "pray for me"; "isolate me"; "lurch at me." It may be that these appeals are addressed to the title figure, TED BERRIGAN, but it seems more likely that the movement of the words themselves is intended to compose an abstract portrait of Berrigan as representative poet, after the manner of Gertrude Stein's verbal portraits.

Deanovich has been honored with the General Electric Award for Younger Poets in 1990 and the Whiting Writer's Award in 1997. Of her first collection, *Watusi Titanic* (Timken Publishers, 1996), one reviewer notes: "[C]asual reflections on daily life . . . are the hallmark of the New York School, but here those reflections have been displaced to a Midwestern city obsessed with the White Sox and Cubs, family restaurants, and questions like whether it can have real punk rockers" (Wallace n.p.). A second collection, *Zombie Jet,* appeared in 1999 (Zoland). *The Spotted Moon,* a long poem that has been widely published in excerpt, awaits publication.

Bibliography

Deanovich, Connie. Excerpt from *The Spotted Moon.* *Chicago Review* 44, nos. 3–4 (1998): 167–170.

———. "Ted Berrigan." In *Under 35: The New Generation of American Poets,* edited by Nicholas Christopher, 46–47. New York: Doubleday, 1989.

———. "Tuesday, July 19, 2005." Here Comes Everybody blog. Available online. URL: http://herecomesevery body.blogspot.com/2005/07/connie-deanovich-is-recipient-of.html.

Wallace, Mark. Review of *Watusi Titanic. Poetry Previews.* Available online. URL: http://www.poetrypreviews. com/poets/poet-mccain.html. Accessed December 18, 2008.

Deep Image

The poets of the Deep Image share the location as well as much of the history of the second-generation NEW YORK SCHOOL. Advocacy by Robert Bly from his isolated position in rural Minnesota has tended to associate the theory of the Deep Image with the ideal of solitude, but simultaneous with Bly's pronouncements, from 1959 into the later 1960s, a practice of the Deep Image evolved in NEW YORK CITY through a network of coffeehouses, bookstores, and little magazines. The same network, though not necessarily the same nodes, fostered a sense of the New York School as a communal activity. On the scene, Jerome Rothenberg and Robert Kelly issued statements about and offered examples of the Deep Image in their magazines, *Poems from the Floating World* (1959–63, edited by Rothenberg) and *Trobar* (edited by Kelly, his wife, Joan, and George Economou). They were joined in publication and performance by a core of fellow poets including David Antin, Clayton Eshelman, JACKSON MAC LOW, Rochelle Owens, Armand Schwerner, and Diane Wakoski.

In the practice of Deep Image, the emphasis is on the depth of feeling from which the poem is presumed to well up naturally, rather than on the structure of the image as a crafted artifact—a distinction from the earlier imagism of Ezra Pound and his descendants in the Black Mountain School. At the same time, the proponents of Deep Image distinguished themselves from surrealism in the matter of depth, "automatic writing" being a technique "which too often just hits the surface of things," according to Rothenberg (Ossman 31). This distinction extends to the New York School poets, who not only embraced the surrealists but also acquired from the abstract expressionist painters "a love for surfaces and surface effects," as Rothenberg and his coeditor, Pierre Joris, have noted in describing the work of FRANK O'HARA in their anthology *Poems for the Millennium* (192). The editors also note, however, the "nearly elegiac sensibility" that will often bring O'Hara and other New York School writers momentarily close to the tone of Deep Image work (192).

A second key difference between New York School and Deep Image poets is reflected in *Poems for the Millennium*'s inclusion of TED BERRIGAN to represent "a deflationary / self-deflationary view of poet & of poet's stance" (530). In contrast to such a stance, tapping into the Deep Image presumed a visionary power that conferred on the poet the status of the shaman in traditional cultures. From the New York School perspective, claims to such power were overinflated, as TONY TOWLE conveys satirically in *AUTOBIOGRAPHY*, when he presents the atomic bomb as "the scientific equivalent of the Deep Image." Nevertheless, as the New York School writer who comes closest to the Deep Image aesthetic in her practice of oral performance, ANNE WALDMAN has compared her experience to that of traditional shamans, and she has participated in the study of "ethnopoetics" pursued by Rothenberg's magazine *Alcheringa* (1970–73, 1975–80). *Poems for the Millennium* presents excerpts from Waldman's *IOVIS* as well as from ALICE NOTLEY's *Désamère*, both poems of epic proportions and universal rhythms that represent to the editors a departure "from early New York School verbal wit & speed" (746). Movement toward the Deep Image is implied in a quotation from Notley about the source of her poetry "in the same depths where dreams originate, where worlds & new worlds are born" (Rothenberg and Joris 744).

Bibliography

Kane, Daniel. *All Poets Welcome: The Lower East Side Poetry Scene in the 1960s.* Berkeley: University of California Press, 2003.

Ossman, David. *The Sullen Art: Interviews.* New York: Corinth Books, 1963. [See especially interviews with Rothenberg, Kelly, Bly, and Creeley.]

Rothenberg, Jerome, and Pierre Joris, eds. *Poems for the Millennium*, Vol. 2. Berkeley: University of California Press, 1998.

de Kooning, Willem (1904–1997)

The reputation of Willem de Kooning rose to such prominence during the 1950s that by the end of the decade NEW YORK SCHOOL painting meant "the school of de Kooning," as his friend FAIRFIELD PORTER observed (36). To de Kooning's admirers, who included the first generation of New York School poets, this meant "there is de Kooning, then the others" (Schuyler 21); de Kooning was leading the pack on the basis of his individual achievement. To skeptics, such as the critic CLEMENT GREENBERG, the "school of de Kooning" consisted of imitators who sacrificed individual achievement in favor of a common style: the "gestural" brushwork that Greenberg called "the Tenth Street touch" (194). Whether or not de Kooning's influence was "beneficent" (Schuyler 219), to acknowledge that influence was a point of pride among the younger painters with whom the New York School poets were most closely associated (Schuyler 9). However, de Kooning was important to the poets not only indirectly, because his art was important to their friends, but also directly, through his personal presence, both forceful and congenial. Unlike the unsociable JACKSON POLLOCK, the other principal claimant to the position of leadership in the New York School, de Kooning was gregarious. The sense of beauty that the poets came to associate with him was not only aesthetic but moral, "the beauty that instinctive behavior in a complex situation can have," according to EDWIN DENBY (4).

Denby met de Kooning as early as 1935, some 10 years after the painter had emigrated (illegally) from his native Holland. As neighbors in NEW YORK CITY's Chelsea district, they participated in one of the several arts communities from which de Kooning derived vital stimulation throughout his career. These included BLACK MOUNTAIN COLLEGE, where de Kooning taught during summer 1948; the area of 10th Street, where he maintained studios after 1946 and helped to found the artists' CLUB (on 8th Street) in 1949; and the HAMPTONS, on Long Island, where he embarked on the construction of a studio of mythic proportions during the 1960s. The East Hampton home of art dealer Leo Castelli, where de Kooning stayed during summer 1952, was the scene of his introduction to JOHN ASHBERY, KENNETH KOCH, and FRANK O'HARA, dramatically staged by JOHN BERNARD MYERS with the connivance of de Kooning's wife (Myers 136). Elaine de Kooning (1918–89), a distinguished painter in her own right, matched her husband in the ability to enliven any gathering. Dubbing her "the White Goddess," O'Hara confessed, "we all adored (and adore) her" (Standing Still 170), even after she separated from de Kooning in 1956.

De Kooning's "breakthrough" into ABSTRACT EXPRESSIONISM dates from 1948, the year that he and Pollock exhibited their alternative approaches to the new mode in shows scheduled only one month apart. However, the show that brought de Kooning into the public eye and established his leadership in the art world was the exhibition Paintings on the Theme of the Woman at the Sidney Janis Gallery in 1953. Woman I had already caused a stir as the subject of the Art News feature "De Kooning Paints a Picture," written by THOMAS B. HESS, a powerful champion of de Kooning, and illustrated with photographs by RUDY BURKHARDT, a friend of de Kooning from his Chelsea days. The painting was purchased from the Janis show by the Museum of Modern Art. In composition it shows the same crowding of FORMS in shallow space that had produced the distinctive surface tension in works such as Excavation (1950), but the forms are no longer abstractly biomorphic—they actually compose the body of a woman. Younger painters took de Kooning's example as "permission" to combine abstract style with figurative content of various sorts, generally categorized as "nature," that is, the recognizable world. In "Nature and New Painting" (1954), a defense of this trend, O'Hara acknowledged the example of the "moral image," as Denby would call it (4), both in de Kooning's abstract work and in the newer figurative work: "In a manner of speaking, this artist's great Excavation shows us what we do to the earth just as his Woman shows us what we do to women" (Standing Still 42).

The influence of de Kooning on New York School poetry shows up most clearly in O'Hara's work because, once again, the debt is explicitly acknowledged. In a passage of "Second Avenue" (1953) that O'Hara called "a little description of a de Kooning WOMAN that I'd seen recently in his studio" (Standing Still 39), "red lips of Hollywood" appear "soft as a Titian and as tender"—the sort of marriage of popular culture and "high" art that de Kooning found especially inspiring (studies retain clippings from magazine advertisements that provided some of the original models for the Women paintings). As a whole, "Second Avenue" aspires to produce the effect of "works as big as cities" (O'Hara, Standing Still 40) such as de Kooning's Ashville (1949) or Gansevoort Street (1950–51), an effect that has as much to do with the density of forms crowded into the composition as with the size of the canvas. For de Kooning abstraction depended on the presence of "many things" (de Kooning 557), rather than their removal. In "Radio" (1955), O'Hara celebrates the presence of "many things," "more than the ear can hold," such as de Kooning's early abstraction Summer Couch (1943), which Porter had lent to O'Hara for his apartment (LeSueur 78–81). Here, ambiguity of form permits the viewer to see the couch of the painting's title also as a reclining female figure, a "visual metaphor" that is characteristic of de Kooning's method (Rosenberg 115) and, of course, a connection to the metaphorical function of poetry.

Sometimes, like the metaphysical poets, de Kooning yokes together such disparate objects that the resulting metaphor feels violent, a feeling that some viewers have misconstrued as de Kooning's attitude toward his subject. When one critic speculated that slashes of red paint in the Women paintings were like blood dripping from wounds, de Kooning responded that red belonged as much to rubies as to blood (Hartigan 158). O'Hara incorporated this observation into the conclusion of his "Ode to Willem de Kooning" (1957), adding one further image to the complex metaphor: "'maybe they're wounds, but maybe they are rubies' / each painful as a sun."

During the 1960s de Kooning raised the temperature of his expressionism, as if in defiance of the newly emerging varieties of "cool" art, from POP ART to MINIMALISM. Although many poets of the second-generation New York School were in sympathy with the newer trends, de Kooning's importance to the first generation ensured that he would remain a point of reference, from the brief mention, "up the de Kooning," in RON PADGETT's "Tone Arm" (1967), to the book manuscript that TED BERRIGAN assembled (1973–83) under the title *Easter Monday*, the title of one of de Kooning's city paintings (1956). The poets took note as de Kooning explored new media during the 1970s, including lithography (Ashbery) and sculpture (PETER SCHJELDAHL). When a show of paintings from the 1980s toured major museums across the country in 1996–97, BILL BERKSON published an eloquent defense against charges that senility was diminishing the quality of de Kooning's work. Quoting de Kooning's own words, Berkson reminded his readers of the poetic function that had always unsettled de Kooning's work: "The surface of it is a metaphor" (145).

Bibliography

Ashbery, John. "Willem de Kooning" (1971). In *Reported Sightings: Art Chronicles, 1957–1987*. Edited by David Bergman. Cambridge, Mass.: Harvard University Press, 1991, 181–187.

Berkson, Bill. "As Ever, de Kooning" (1997). In *The Sweet Singer of Modernism and Other Art Writings, 1985–2003*. Jamestown, R.I.: Qua Books, 2003, 142–149.

Berrigan, Ted. *Easter Monday*. In *The Collected Poems of Ted Berrigan*. Edited by Alice Notley, Anselm Berrigan, and Edmund Berrigan. Berkeley: University of California Press, 2005, 389–425.

de Kooning, Willem. "What Abstract Art Means to Me" (1951). In *Theories of Modern Art: A Source Book by Artists and Critics*, edited by Herschel B. Chipp, 556–561. Berkeley: University of California Press, 1971.

Denby, Edwin. "The Thirties: An Essay" (1957). In *Dance Writings and Poetry*. Edited by Robert Cornfield. New Haven, Conn.: Yale University Press, 1998, 1–5.

Gaugh, Harry F. *Willem de Kooning*. New York: Abbeville, 1983.

Greenberg, Clement. "Post Painterly Abstraction." (1964). In *The Collected Essays and Criticism*. Vol. 4: *Modernism with a Vengeance, 1957–1969*. Edited by John O'Brian. Chicago: University of Chicago Press, 1993, 192–197.

Hartigan, Grace. Interview by Cindy Nemser. In *Art Talk: Conversations with 12 Women Artists*, edited by Cindy Nemser, 148–172. New York: Scribner's, 1975.

Hess, Thomas B. "De Kooning Paints a Picture." *Art News* 52, no. 1 (March 1953): 30–33ff.

LeSueur, Joe. *Digressions on Some Poems by Frank O'Hara: A Memoir*. New York: Farrar, Straus & Giroux, 2003.

Myers, John Bernard. *Tracking the Marvelous: A Life in the New York Art World*. New York: Random House, 1983.

O'Hara, Frank. *The Collected Poems*. Rev. ed. Edited by Donald Allen. Berkeley: University of California Press, 1995.

———. *Standing Still and Walking in New York*. Edited by Donald Allen. San Francisco: Grey Fox, 1983.

Padgett, Ron. "Tone Arm." In *Great Balls of Fire*. 1969. Reprint, Minneapolis, Minn.: Coffee House Press, 1990, 63–78.

Porter, Fairfield. "Willem de Kooning" (1959). In *Art in Its Own Terms: Selected Criticism, 1935–1975*. Edited by Rackstraw Downes. Cambridge, Mass.: Zoland, 1979, 36–38.

Rosenberg, Harold. "De Kooning 1: 'Painting Is a Way'" (1963). In *The Anxious Object*. 1966. Reprint, Chicago: University of Chicago Press, 1982, 108–120.

Schjeldahl, Peter. "De Kooning's Sculpture." In *De Kooning: Drawings/Sculptures*, edited by Philip Larson and Peter Schjeldahl. Exhibit catalog. New York: Dutton, 1974.

Schuyler, James. *Selected Art Writings*. Edited by Simon Pettet. Santa Rose, Calif.: Black Sparrow, 1998.

de Nagy Gallery See TIBOR DE NAGY GALLERY.

Denby, Edwin (1903–1983)

Born in Tianjin, China, Denby was the son of Martha Orr and Charles Denby II, a U.S. diplomat. Denby attended Harvard University but left without earning a degree. Instead, in 1925 he went on to study modern DANCE at the Hellerau-Laxenburg School in Germany. From 1929 until 1934 he worked in the State Theater of Darmstadt, Germany, as a dancer and choreographer. He later gained fame in the United States as a dance critic for *Modern Music* (1936–43) and the *New York Herald Tribune* (1942–45); he also contributed articles to *Dance Magazine, Ballet,* and the *Evergreen Review.* Denby's dance criticism has been noted for its clarity and poetic detail. In his introduction to *Dancers, Buildings, and People in the Street* (Horizon, 1965), FRANK O'HARA wrote of Denby: "He sees and hears more clearly than anyone I have ever known" (182). Denby wrote about such famed dancers as Martha Graham, Merce Cunningham, and Jerome Robbins. His first book, *Looking at the Dance* (Pelligrini and Cudahy, 1949), has been described as "one of the most influential critical works of the century" (Beukel n.p.). Other notable books by Denby include the aforementioned *Dancers, Buildings, and People in the Street,* which one critic suggests "could be read as a pleasurable handbook to New York School poetics" (Beukel n.p.), and *Dance Writings* (Knopf, 1986), which won the National Book Critics Circle Award for criticism.

Although Denby is well recognized for his dance criticism, he also worked with his lifelong friend RUDY BURCKHARDT on a number of film projects, including *145 West 21st* (1936), *Lurk* (1964), and *Money* (1967). He also gained acclaim as a poet, most notably for his use of the sonnet in an era when William Carlos Williams had pronounced the FORM dead. Many of Denby's sonnets are compressed and use dissonance to break up the form's rhythmical expectations. RON PADGETT admitted: "[I]nitially I found Edwin's sometimes herky-jerky rhythms to be distracting. I think I suspected at first that maybe he was simply inept! (Like thinking that Jackson Pollock was messy.)" (Smith and Padgett n.p.). The poems often draw upon the quick, spasmodic pace and vibrant imagery of city life.

Denby has been quoted often for his explanation regarding the origins of the name *New York School poets.* He explained: "[T]he poets adopted the expression 'New York School' out of homage to the people who had de-provincialized American painting. It's a complicated double-joke" (Waldman 32). He was influential to several of the younger members of the New York School, particularly TED BERRIGAN, Padgett, ALICE NOTLEY, and ANNE WALDMAN. A special issue of Berrigan's

"C" magazine (number 4, September 1963) was devoted to Denby's work.

In 1948 Denby published his first book of poems, *IN PUBLIC, IN PRIVATE* (Decker). In his essay "Rare Modern" (1957), O'Hara credits Denby's book "for the risks it takes in successfully establishing a specifically American spoken diction which has a classical firmness and clarity under his hand" (O'Hara 78). In particular, O'Hara highlights for attention the poem "Elegy: The Streets." Denby's next book of poems, *MEDITERRANEAN CITIES* (Wittenborn, 1956), includes Burckhardt's photographs. O'Hara describes these poems as Proustian, particularly in regard to "a progression which proceeds from the signal absorption in locale ('place names') and its accidental characteristics to the emergence of the poet's being from his feelings in 'the place'" (O'Hara 78). O'Hara places Denby's sonnets in the tradition of the English romantics, specifically in the line of Percy Bysshe Shelley. The title poem of Denby's next collection of poetry (Angel Hair / Adventures in Poetry, 1974) is the long elegy *Snoring in New York.* His *Collected Poems* appeared in 1975 as the first book from Full Court Press, a project of Padgett, Waldman, and Joan Simon. Padgett edited *The Complete Poems* (Random House, 1986), which appeared after Denby's death. After struggling with physical ailments, Denby committed suicide on July 12, 1983, in Maine.

Bibliography

Beukel, Karlien van den. "Dance." *Poetry Review* 93, no. 4 (2003–04). Available online. URL: http://www. poetrysociety.org.uk/review/pr93-4/beukel.htm. Accessed December 18, 2008.

O'Hara, Frank. *Standing Still and Walking in New York.* Edited by Donald Allen. San Francisco: Grey Fox, 1983.

Smith, Simon, and Ron Padgett. "A Conversation about Edwin Denby." *Jacket* 21 (February 2003). Available online. URL: http://jacketmagazine.com/21/denb-smith-padg.html. Accessed December 18, 2008.

Waldman, Anne. "Paraphrase of Edwin Denby Speaking on the 'New York School'" (1974). In *Homage to Frank O'Hara,* edited by Bill Berkson and Joe LeSueur, 32–33. Bolinas, Calif.: Big Sky, 1988.

Dent, Tom (1932–1998)

Born in New Orleans, Louisiana, Tom Dent was a founding member of the UMBRA poets workshop on DOWNTOWN MANHATTAN's Lower East Side in the early 1960s. Inspired by Umbra's dynamism and the activism of NEW YORK CITY, Dent used his experiences there to help transform the New Orleans arts community as a leading cultural worker in THEATER, publishing, and African-American historical preservation.

Dent received his bachelor's degree from Morehouse College in 1952 and studied in the doctoral program at Syracuse University's School of International Studies (1952–56). He left Syracuse for the U.S. Army before completing his doctorate, and in 1959 arrived in New York City, where he worked for the Harlem newspaper the *New York Age* and later for the NAACP Legal Defense Fund.

Always active in community politics, by 1960, Dent was a member of On Guard for Freedom, a black literary group that included LeRoi Jones (AMIRI BARAKA) and future Umbra workshop members. Meetings of Umbra held in Dent's apartment on East 2nd Street led to friendships with LORENZO THOMAS, ISHMAEL REED, CALVIN HERNTON, DAVID HENDERSON, and others. The workshop provided an experimental and intellectual exchange of ideas. Beyond his poetry, Dent proved himself an effective organizer, mediator, and leader, qualities he developed further as his career progressed in New Orleans.

Discouraged by deteriorating conditions on the Lower East Side but encouraged by Umbra and the Civil Rights movement, Dent returned to New Orleans in 1965. He became an integral figure in the Free Southern Theater (1966–70); its workshop publication, *Nkombo* (1968–73); and the succeeding project BLKARTSOUTH, with Kalamu ya Salaam (1947–   ). In 1976 Dent, Charles Rowell (1940–   ), and Jerry Ward (1943–   ) founded the journal *Callaloo*, which has become a distinguished showcase for scholarship in African-American literature, though it has drifted from Dent's original intention of providing an incubator for new writers (Dent, interview 339). Dent's preface to the first issue of *Callaloo* shows him still "tired and disgusted with the New York scene" and hoping to prove the viability of "advanced, progressive" literature in the South (5–6).

The poems published in Dent's two collections, *Magnolia Street* (privately printed, 1976) and *Blue Lights and River Songs* (Lotus Press, 1982), are set primarily in New Orleans, though Dent's New York experience persists as an undertone and occasionally comes to the surface. For instance, in "Third Avenue, Near Fourteenth Street," from *Blue Lights*, "Dent playfully parodies Allen Ginsberg, Bob Kaufman, and Frank O'Hara as the city's streets become magically animated," as Thomas has observed (181). In Thomas's account the qualities that link Dent most closely to the NEW YORK SCHOOL aesthetic are the "faithful rendering . . . of everyday speech" and an attunement to "the contradictions of what passes for everyday life" (176, 178). The documentary impulse in Dent's work extends to his collecting of African-American oral histories and culminates in *Southern Journey* (University of Georgia Press, 2001), a personal, lyrical, and learned collection of travel essays retracing signature locations and events from the Civil Rights movement.

Bibliography

Dent, Tom. "Enriching the Paper Trail: An Interview with Tom Dent." *African-American Review* 27, no. 2 (Summer 1993): 327–344.

———. Preface to *Callaloo*, no. 1 (December 1976): 5–6.

———. "Umbra Days." *Black American Literature Forum* 14, no. 3 (1980): 105–108.

Thomas, Lorenzo. *Extraordinary Measures: Afrocentric Modernism and Twentieth-Century American Poetry.* Tuscaloosa: University of Alabama Press, 2000.

Descent of Alette, The Alice Notley (1992)

ALICE NOTLEY's *The Descent of Alette* is a book-length poem—148 pages in the Penguin Books edition (1996)—modeled on classical epic but simultaneously mounting a critique of the model from a feminist perspective. In its pattern of action it rejects war, the traditional subject of the epic, in favor of initiation, focusing on the journey to the underworld that is conventionally the central event of epic narrative. For that focus Notley acknowledges an ancient model in the Sumerian poem *The Descent of Inanna* ("'Feminine' Epic" 174–176), where the protagonist, like Notley's Alette, is female. Notley departs even from that model in having her protagonist recount her adventures in first-person voice, displacing the traditional third-person narrator. She recalls her name, Alette, only at the end of the story, as one of the last insights gained through her initiation. But she has acquired power as well as knowledge. Also at the end of the story she kills a male figure called "the tyrant" who is responsible for her amnesia, for war, and for the literal suppression underground of all authentic life. In another inversion of epic convention, the underworld into which Alette descends is the realm of life rather than death. Even her killing of the tyrant is life-giving since his existence is essentially a "lie" (22) that is dispelled by his death.

The fact that the story and some of its lessons can be so neatly summarized points up Notley's challenge to postmodern aesthetics as well as epic tradition. "*Alette* reacts against the prohibition against the use of continuous narrative in poetry," Notley flatly stated (interview n.p.). In this respect *Alette* is unlike other long or SERIAL POEMs produced by the NEW YORK SCHOOL, in which fragmentation predominates over a sense of the whole. Nevertheless, Notley's defiance of orthodoxy, including the orthodoxy of the avant-garde, is very much in the New York School spirit, recalling LARRY RIVERS's decision to paint GEORGE WASHINGTON CROSSING THE DELAWARE because it would outrage the purists of abstract art. Another link to the New York School is Notley's adaptation of popular narrative FORMs such as movies and comic books. Alette is closer to Spiderman than to Achilles or Odysseus in the power she eventually acquires to transform herself into an owl (a transformation suggested by her name). This power is the key to Alette's victory over the tyrant, and thus, in terms of the story it needs to be taken seriously. Yet in order to take it seriously, the reader has to be able to enter into the spirit of play that produces the invention. As a talking snake advises Alette,

"Humor" "is closer" "to the
divine than" "you might think" (76).

The idiosyncratic use of quotation marks in this manner throughout the poem may look like fragmentation from a postmodern perspective (McCabe 41), but Notley's prefatory note to the Penguin edition explains the practice as part of her interest in reclaiming the narrative function: "each phrase is a thing said by a voice: this is not a thought, or a record of thought-process, this is a story, told."

The new measure signaled by the use of quotation marks to frame phrases began to emerge for Notley in two elegies of the late 1980s: "Beginning with a Stain," prompted by the death of her stepdaughter Kate Berrigan in a traffic accident in 1987, and "White Phosphorus," a memorial for Notley's brother, who died in 1988 of an accidental drug overdose following a long period of stress caused by service in the Vietnam War. Both poems were collected, along with *The Descent of Alette*, in *The* SCARLET CABINET (1992), an anthology of work by Notley and DOUGLAS OLIVER. Together the two elegies contain the seeds of female and male principles embodied in characters whom Alette encounters at the end of her descent: in the female, "the breath that we all breathe" ("Beginning with a Stain"), the source of life, ultimately a mother figure; in the male, an embodied wisdom, ultimately a father figure, but identified in *Alette* with the owl, as Notley's brother (named Al) is identified in "White Phosphorous." To this combination of the personal and the archetypal, *Alette* adds a third, public dimension, corresponding to the social criticism in Oliver's PENNILESS POLITICS, also collected in *The Scarlet Cabinet*. The first level of the underworld in *Alette* is a city subway system populated by homeless people, who seemed to be "everywhere" during the years of Ronald Reagan's presidency, Notley recalls ("'Feminine' Epic" 177; autobiography 234). The third level of the underworld includes a city of tents in a parklike setting, a recollection of the squatters' settlement that sprang up in Tompkins Square Park, just a few blocks from Notley's home on the Lower East Side, and that was brutally dispersed by police in 1988. As a story of NEW YORK CITY, *The Descent of Alette* reveals further affinity with the New York School, all the more so by telling the story in surreal terms.

Bibliography

DuBois, Page. "'An Especially Peculiar Undertaking': Alice Notley's Epic." *Differences: A Journal of Feminist Cultural Studies* 12, no. 2 (Summer 2001): 86–97.

Glenum, Lara. "The Performance of Crisis in Alice Notley's *The Descent of Alette*." *Jacket* 25 (February 2004). Available online. URL: http://www.jacketmagazine. com/25/glen-notl.html. Accessed December 18, 2008.

McCabe, Susan. "Alice Notley's Experimental Epic: 'An Ecstasy of Finding Another Way of Being.'" In *We Who Love to Be Astonished: Experimental Women's Writing and Performance Poetics*, edited by Laura Hinton and Cynthia Hogue, 41–53. Tuscaloosa: University of Alabama Press, 2002.

Notley, Alice. Autobiography in *Contemporary Authors Autobiography Series* 27. Edited by Joyce Nakamura. Detroit, Mich.: Gale, 1997, 221–240.

———. *The Descent of Alette*. New York: Penguin, 1996.

———. "The 'Feminine' Epic" (1995). In *Coming After: Essays on Poetry*. Ann Arbor: University of Michigan Press, 2005, 171–180.

———. Interview by Brian Kim Stefans. *Jacket* 15 (December 2001). Available online. URL: http://www.jacketmagazine.com/15/stef-iv-not.html. Accessed December 18, 2008.

———. *Selected Poems*. Hoboken, N.J.: Talisman House, 1993. [Includes "Homer's Art" (essay), "White Phosphorous," and excerpts from *The Descent of Alette*.]

Notley, Alice, and Douglas Oliver. *The Scarlet Cabinet: A Compendium of Books*. New York: Scarlet Editions, 1992.

Dine, Jim (1935–) *Pop artist*

Jim Dine entered the New York art world by way of HAPPENINGS at the Judson and Reuben galleries in 1960 and the landmark *New Realists* show at the Sidney Janis Gallery in 1962. His participation in the latter event, along with ANDY WARHOL, Roy Lichtenstein, James Rosenquist, and others, identified him as a pop artist, but Dine has always insisted that his art is more subjective than POP ART is. He depicted bathrobes as self-portraits and treated conventional "heart" shapes as vehicles for genuine feeling. This subjective quality helped win him the favor of the NEW YORK SCHOOL poets, who expected art to produce "experiences which transcend the objects," as JOHN ASHBERY wrote in the *New Realists* catalog ("New Realists" 82). Ashbery names no artists in his essay, but FRANK O'HARA, reviewing the show for *KULCHUR* magazine, listed Dine among the better artists, in whom it was possible to trace a continuous lineage from ABSTRACT EXPRESSIONISM (in Dine's case: "Barnett Newman through Jasper Johns and Bob Rauschenberg") (147). Among the first generation of the New York School poets, Dine became closest to KENNETH KOCH, who shared Dine's background as a Jew from Cincinnati, Ohio. In 1966 they collaborated on a lithograph produced at Universal Limited Art Editions in West Islip, Long Island, and on a unique text published in *Art News*: a "Test in Art" prepared by Koch and completed by Dine, whose answers, both handwritten and drawn, are reproduced photographically in the journal.

From 1967 to 1970 Dine deliberately withdrew from the intensifying political and financial pressures of the New York gallery scene by moving with his wife and three sons to London, suspending the production of paintings, and deepening his engagement with poetry. Dine provided visual accompaniment to the work of several second-generation New York School writers during this period: RON PADGETT's TRANSLATION of Apollinaire's *The Poet Assassinated* (Holt, Rinehart and Winston, 1968); *Bun*, by Padgett and TOM CLARK (ANGEL HAIR, 1968); and *Fragment*, by TED BERRIGAN (Cape Goliard, 1969). In 1970 Dine and Padgett produced two genuine COLLABORATIONs with presses based in London: *The ADVENTURES OF MR. AND MRS. JIM AND RON*, an "artist's book" (Cape Goliard); and *Oo La La*, a portfolio of 15 lithographs. (Petersburg Press). Meanwhile, Dine illustrated and published an edition of his own poems (*Welcome Home Lovebirds*, Trigram Press, 1969), which have been linked to the New York School for "their obvious surreality" but also for their personality: "[L]aughing poems secure in their wisdom that they can, in the end, only reach as far as their own hearts" (Coleman n.p.).

Following a major retrospective exhibition at New York's Whitney Museum in 1970, Dine resumed work in every visual medium at a prolific rate. New York School poets (GERRIT HENRY,

CARTER RATCLIFF, PETER SCHJELDAHL, DAVID SHAPIRO) have kept in touch with his career primarily through their critical writing. In 1990 Arion Press in San Francisco issued a suite of 42 lithographs by Dine to accompany an edition of O'Hara's *BIOTHERM*, with an essay by BILL BERKSON.

Bibliography

Ashbery, John. "New Dine in Old Bottles." *New York*, 22 May 1978, 107–109.

———. "The New Realists." In *Reported Sightings: Art Chronicles, 1957–1987*. Edited by David Bergman. Cambridge, Mass.: Harvard University Press, 1991, 81–83.

Coleman, Victor. "Look at My Product: Notes, More or Less Specific, on Jim Dine." *Artscanada* (December 1970). Available online. URL: http://www.ccca.ca/c/writing/c/coleman/col010t.html. Accessed December 18, 2008.

Dine, Jim, and Ron Padgett. Statement in "Interactions between Artists and Writers." *Art Journal* 52, no. 4 (Winter 1993): 72.

Gordon, John. *Jim Dine*. New York: Whitney Museum of American Art/Praeger, 1970.

Koch, Kenneth. "Jim Dine." In *Poets and Painters*, edited by Dianne Perry Vanderlip and David Shapiro, 38. Denver, Colo.: Denver Art Museum, 1979.

Koch, Kenneth, and Jim Dine. "Test in Art." *Art News* 65, no. 6 (October 1966): 54–57.

"Letter and Spirit." *Times Literary Supplement*, 2 October 1970, 1,139–1,140.

Livingstone, Marco. *Jim Dine: The Alchemy of Images*. New York: Monacelli, 1998.

O'Hara, Frank. "Art Chronicle III." In *Standing Still and Walking in New York*. Edited by Donald Allen. San Francisco: Grey Fox, 1983, 140–151.

Padgett, Ron. "Making OO LA LA." *Modern Painters* 12 (Spring 1999): 62–65.

Shapiro, David. *Jim Dine: Painting What One Is*. New York: Abrams, 1981.

di Prima, Diane (1934–)

Diane di Prima was born in Brooklyn, New York, the eldest of three children of middle-class Italian-American parents. Her close relationship with her anarchist grandfather has influenced her political views throughout her life. She determined at a very early age to be a writer and dropped out of Swarthmore College when she was 19 in order to pursue a bohemian writing life in NEW YORK CITY's Greenwich Village. During her time in the Village, she cofounded the NEW YORK POETS THEATRE, where plays by Robert Duncan, FRANK O'HARA, and JAMES SCHUYLER were produced, and coedited the *FLOATING BEAR* literary newsletter with LeRoi Jones (AMIRI BARAKA). She also established and edited Poets Press (1964–69) and published the work of writers such as Audre Lorde, Herbert Huncke, and GREGORY CORSO.

Di Prima published her own first book of poems, *This Kind of Bird Flies Backward*, in 1958 and since then has published almost 40 books of poetry, memoir, and drama. Although the 1950s and '60s were a difficult time for women writers to establish themselves in the forefront of new American writing, di Prima nevertheless stands as the one woman whose work was known and respected at the time by the more prominent male writers around them. She has received a number of distinctions, including a National Poetry Association Lifetime Service Award in 1993 and an honorary doctorate from St. Lawrence University in 1999. She has lived in San Francisco for the last three decades, raising her five children, and has most recently published *Recollections of My Life as a Woman* (Viking, 2000) and an expanded edition of her ambitious book-long poem *Loba* (Penguin, 1998), a pan-female mythology, with a planned third book pending. Di Prima continues to write, teach writing workshops, and present readings from work that spans over half a century of life in American letters.

Bibliography

Libby, Anthony. "Diane di Prima: Nothing Is Lost; It Shines in Our Eyes." *Girls Who Wore Black: Women Writing the Beat Generation*. Edited by Ronna C. Johnson and Nancy M. Grace. New Brunswick, N.J.: Rutgers University Press, 2002, 45–68.

Disch, Tom (1940–2008)

An eclectic poet and FICTION writer, Tom Disch worked throughout his literary life at blurring GENRES and producing a prolific corpus of varied works, including lyric and dramatic poetry; science, historical, computer-interactive, collaborative, and children's fiction; criticism; cultural reviews; autobiography; and even opera libretti. Disch also wrote under a number of pseudonyms, including Thomas M. Disch, Leonie Hargrave, and the collaborative joint-pseudonyms, Cassandra Knye and Thom Demijohn. His protean output notwithstanding, Disch always considered poetry his entrance into the literary world, and the timing of his entrance coincided with the rise of the second generation of the NEW YORK SCHOOL.

Born in Des Moines, Iowa, Disch worked as a trainee steel draftsman after graduating high school, saving enough money to move to Manhattan, where he worked as a supernumerary for the Metropolitan Opera (carrying a spear in *Swan Lake*), at a bookstore, and at a newspaper, then enlisted in the army and was discharged to a mental hospital, returning to NEW YORK CITY to work at a THEATER cloakroom, take night school classes at New York University on architecture, serve as a full-time claims adjuster at an insurance company, copyedit, and serve as a mortuary attendant, all the while writing at night and in his spare hours. In May 1962 Disch wrote the short story, "The Double Timer," which he sold to *Fantastic Stories* for $112.50, and soon after he began publishing his poems in such places as the *Minnesota Review.*

In time he would review New York School poets JOHN ASHBERY and KENNETH KOCH, but aesthetically he felt closer to new formalists Dana Gioia, Richard Howard, and Marilyn Hucker than to the first-generation New York School. With the second-generation poets, many of whom were Disch's friends, he shared the dystopian outlook reflected in his anthology *Bad Moon Rising* (Harper & Row, 1973), which includes contributions by PETER SCHJELDAHL, RON PADGETT, and DICK GALLUP. During this period Disch's novels in the same dystopian vein, *Camp Concentration* (Doubleday, 1968) and *334* (MacGibbon & Kee, 1972), firmly established his reputation as a master of the new science fiction.

Disch went on to publish more than a dozen novels and 10 collections of poetry. His two collections of criticism, *The Castle of Indolence* (Picador, 1995) and *The Castle of Perseverance* (University of Michigan Press, 2002), turn his willingness to acknowledge the dark side of the creative effort into a critical strength. In one of his sermonettes, broadcast 1999–2000 in a weekly series on WNYC radio in New York City, he observed: "[T]here is no better way to learn to write well than to study the work of geniuses, of course, but also those who write execrably. Not just a quick giggle at some prize blooper but earnest analysis of the worst examples."

Bibliography

Disch, Thomas M. *Dark Verses and Light.* Baltimore: Johns Hopkins University Press, 1991.
———. *Haikus of an Ampart.* Minneapolis: Coffee House Press, 1991.
———. "Sermonettes." *Strange Horizons* (July 30, 2001). Available online. URL: http://www.strangehorizons.com/2001.20010730/sermonettes.shtml. Accessed December 18, 2008.
———. *Yes, Let's: New and Selected Poems.* Baltimore: Johns Hopkins University Press, 1989.

Dlugos, Tim (1950–1990)

Tim Dlugos was a prolific poet, tireless fund-raiser and activist, and longtime contributing editor to *Christopher Street* magazine. His poems combine an appreciation for pop culture and clever silliness with a moral seriousness rooted in his Christian faith and exuberant gay identity. DENNIS COOPER described him as "like Frank O'Hara or Oscar Wilde must have been to earlier generations. . . . One was always trailing after Tim as he flew between cocktail parties, poetry readings, art openings, the baths, services at his local church, and elsewhere, often over the course of a single evening" (xi).

Dlugos published his first chapbook, *High There* (Some of Us Press, 1973), only four years after leaving the order of the Christian Brothers in Philadelphia. In 1976 his poems appeared in MICHAEL LALLY's anthology, *None of the Above* (The Crossing Press), and he soon after relocated from Washington, D.C. to NEW YORK CITY. After meeting Cooper, he used his gift for friendship to link poets from Los Angeles's BEYOND BAROQUE with those in New York and Washington. Cooper's Little Caesar Press published Dlugos's first books, *Je Suis Ein Americano* (1979) and *Entre Nous* (1982). DAVID TRINIDAD published a chapbook edition of his long poem *A Fast Life* (Sherwood Press) in 1982.

Dlugos was an energetic and magnetic presence on the New York poetry scene throughout the 1980s, reading and publishing widely poems that would not be collected until after his death. In 1986 Dlugos returned to school and studied to become an Episcopal priest. In 1987 he discovered he was HIV positive, and in 1988 he entered Yale Divinity School. He died of AIDS in 1990, and his last books were published posthumously: *Strong Place* (Amethyst, 1992), *G-9* (Hanuman, 1992), and *Powerless: Selected Poems, 1973–1990*, edited by Trinidad and published by High Risk (1996).

Whether writing about Gilligan's Island, the Nicaraguan Revolution, the fast life of gay cruising, the tragedy of AIDS, or the B-actor Edmond O'Brien, Dlugos's poems are characterized by his candid, sophisticated voice and mercurial, embracing imagination. He wrote: "Grace, in a very orthodox sense, is my major preoccupation" (187). His work reflects, in Cooper's words, "his ravenous fascination with the innumerable ways in which grace could be represented through artfulness" (xi).

Bibliography

Cooper, Dennis. Introduction to *Powerless: Selected Poems 1973–1990*, by Tim Dlugos. Edited by David Trinidad. New York and London: Serpent's Tail / High Risk, 1996, xi–xiii.

Dlugos, Tim. "Statement." In *None of the Above: New Poets of the USA*. Edited by Michael Lally. Trumansburg, N.Y.: The Crossing Press, 1976, 187.

Downtown Manhattan

As NEW YORK CITY centers on the island of Manhattan, New York's artistic avant-garde has traditionally centered on Lower Manhattan. Greenwich Village had established itself as the bohemian capital during the 1910s and 1920s, and in the years following World War II it still supported that function in its THEATERS, cafés, bars, and other institutions. A productive laboratory for NEW YORK SCHOOL painting operated at Hans Hofmann's school on West 8th Street, not far from the EIGHTH STREET BOOKSTORE. Classes at the New School on West 12th Street offered

new ideas in MUSIC (from Henry Cowell to JOHN CAGE), theater (Erwin Piscator) and, by the early 1960s, poetry (KENNETH KOCH, FRANK O'HARA, LeRoi Jones [AMIRI BARAKA], BILL BERKSON). Also in the 1960s, JUDSON MEMORIAL CHURCH on Washington Square, the center of Greenwich Village, became a magnet for innovation in DANCE. In 1955 the *Village Voice* newspaper was launched by Norman Mailer, Edwin Fancher, and Dan Wolf especially to serve a liberal political agenda (in opposition to repressive government of the sort promoted by Senator Joseph McCarthy) but also to keep its readers informed about the cultural avant-garde. To the extent that early New York School poetry received attention, it was likely to receive it in the *Voice*, but the paper was more important as a channel for critical writing by poets, such as the art reviews of PETER SCHJELDAHL and JOHN PERREAULT.

Some New York School poets, including EDWARD FIELD, KENWARD ELMSLIE, and, for brief periods, O'Hara, have resided in Greenwich Village, but its fashionable cachet promoted higher rents than surrounding areas, and these areas accordingly played a larger role in the daily lives of most of the poets. As early as 1935, EDWIN DENBY and RUDY BURCKHARDT had taken up residence in Chelsea, north of Greenwich Village, where former warehouse space could be cheaply converted into residential lofts. JOHN ASHBERY moved to Chelsea shortly after his return to the United States from France in 1965. From 1976 JAMES SCHUYLER lived at several Chelsea addresses, concluding with the CHELSEA HOTEL, associated with many famous names in the arts. During the 1990s the entire Chelsea area became identified with the arts, but this followed earlier developments to the east of Greenwich Village, in an area of the Lower East Side that became known as the East Village, and to the south, in SoHo, a shortening of the designation "south of Houston" Street.

Visual artists led the way in both the East Village and SoHo. By 1946 WILLEM DE KOONING had moved his studio from Chelsea to Fourth Avenue, often regarded as the eastern boundary of Greenwich Village. Again, the attraction was cheap loft space ($35 a month [Stevens and Swan 227]). While the abstract expressionist breakthrough of the late 1940s brought de Kooning and his peers connections with Uptown commercial galleries, the presence of these artists Downtown encouraged as many as eight cooperative galleries to spring up during the 1950s, most of them concentrated in a single block on East 10th Street, where de Kooning eventually moved. On the same block, between 1960 and 1962, Mickey Ruskin ran poetry readings at the Tenth Street Coffeehouse, forerunner of LES DEUX MÉGOTS, which opened in 1962 on East 7th Street, closer to the heart of the East Village at Tompkins Square. Such institutions played a role in the conversion of the East Village from a workplace, which it was for the painters, into a lifestyle, where "hippies" sought to live the freedom that the poets wrote about. It seemed, at least for a time, a natural alliance, even an identity, for some individuals. During the 1960s, when the East Village reigned as the East Coast capital of the "counterculture," counterpart to San Francisco's Haight-Ashbury district, resident poets included ALLEN GINSBERG, O'Hara, Berkson, TONY TOWLE, FRANK LIMA, TED BERRIGAN, ANNE WALDMAN, LEWIS WARSH, ED SANDERS, RON PADGETT, LARRY FAGIN, and Schjeldahl. For the *East Village Other* (1965–72), poets were part of the news, much more so than for the *Village Voice*. The paper owes its name to Berrigan or ISHMAEL REED, depending on whose account one reads (Padgett 85; Reed 1,135). Allen Katzman, one of the founders of the *East Village Other*, was himself a poet and an organizer of poetry readings both at Les Deux Mégots and CAFÉ LE METRO. It seemed a natural outgrowth of the spirit of the East Village when, in 1966, the POETRY PROJECT AT ST. MARK'S CHURCH-IN-THE-BOWERY opened on East 10th Street, just one block east of the former Block of the Artists (Rosenberg 103; Schjeldahl).

The availability of loft space played roughly the same role in attracting artists to SoHo as to the East Village (both of these names arose after the artists arrived). However, commercial galleries, in contrast to cooperatives, played a much larger role in the second wave of development of SoHo, starting in the late 1960s. The resulting rise in real estate values became a barrier to poets who might otherwise have followed the artists in taking up residence in SoHo. Poetry readings were sponsored by some of the first SoHo galleries, notably those of Paula Cooper and Holly Solomon. BERNADETTE MAYER's MEMORY was exhibited at Solomon's gallery in 1972 and later, in book FORM (1975), reviewed by Simon Schuchat in the *SoHo Weekly News* (1973–82). Eventually, independent reading series arose, such as that at the EAR INN (1978–   ), though it is significant that this venue soon became identified with the Language poets. The New York School still had St. Mark's in the East Village, where their poetry intersected with new identities defined partly in opposition to the hippie lifestyle of the 1960s. Youth culture turned to PUNK ROCK, centered on clubs such as CBGB on the Bowery, and the Puerto Rican immigrant community to the east of Tompkins Square Park symbolized its dissension from "East Village" chic by adopting the name *Loisaida*, a Hispanic pronunciation of "Lower East Side." The NUYORICAN POETS CAFÉ was founded there in 1974.

The viability of the East Village area as an affordable living space was clearly threatened by the late 1970s, as real estate pressures similar to those in SoHo began to increase. Evidence of the parallel, though it was promoted as a contrast, was a cluster of new art galleries that flourished briefly in the East Village during the early 1980s, based on a visual expression of punk in the work of such artists as Keith Haring and Jean-Michel Basquiat. Real estate speculation proved to be a more enduring trend. While in the early 1960s a tenement apartment (bathtub in kitchen) in the East Village rented for as little as $25 a month (Jones 172), by 2006 one-bedroom apartments in the "new" Lower East Side started at $1,700 a month to rent or $4,500 a month to purchase in a co-op building (Vandam). Poets such as DOUGLAS OLIVER and ALICE NOTLEY, whose work (*PENNILESS POLITICS* [1991], *THE DESCENT OF ALETTE* [1992]) responds to the displacement of low-income tenants by East Village landlords, indirectly chronicles the end of a way of life for poets. While New York School poetry persists, it has lost its identification with a specific area of New York City.

Bibliography

Dunlap, David. "The New Chelsea's Many Faces," *New York Times*, 13 November 1994, p. R1.

Gruen, John. *The New Bohemia.* Chicago: A Cappella Books, 1966.

Jones, Hettie. *How I Became Hettie Jones.* New York: Dutton, 1990.

Kane, Daniel. *All Poets Welcome: The Lower East Side Poetry Scene in the 1960s.* Berkeley: University of California Press, 2003.

Mele, Christopher. *Selling the Lower East Side: Culture, Real Estate, and Resistance in New York City.* Minneapolis: University of Minnesota Press, 2000.

Padgett, Ron. *Joe: A Memoir.* Minneapolis, Minn.: Coffee House Press, 2004.

Reed, Ishmael. Interview by Shamoon Zamir. *Callaloo* 17, no. 4 (Fall 1994): 1,131–1,157.

Rosenberg, Harold. "Tenth Street: A Geography of Modern Art." In *Discovering the Present: Three Decades in Art, Culture, and Politics.* Chicago: University of Chicago Press, 1973, 100–109.

Schjeldahl, Peter. "Survival on 10th Street," *New York Times,* 19 November 1967, p. 155.

Simpson, Charles R. *SoHo: The Artist in the City.* Chicago: University of Chicago Press, 1981.

Stevens, Mark, and Annalyn Swan. *De Kooning: An American Master.* New York: Knopf, 2004.

Stosuy, Brandon, ed. *Up Is Up, but So Is Down: New York's Downtown Literary Scene, 1974–1992.* New York: New York University Press, 2006.

Sukenick, Ronald. *Down and In: Life in the Underground.* New York: William Morrow/Beech Tree, 1987.

Taylor, Marvin J. *The Downtown Book: The New York Art Scene, 1974–84.* Princeton, N.J.: Princeton University Press, 2006.

Vandam, Jeff. "Living on The Lower East Side: A New Page in an Unpredictable Tale," *New York Times,* 26 February 2006, sec. 11, p. 9.

Wetzsteon, Ross. *Republic of Dreams: Greenwich Village, the American Bohemia, 1910–1960.* New York: Simon & Schuster, 2002.

drama   *See* THEATER.

Dubris, Maggie   (date of birth withheld)

Although she did not publish her first book until 1998, Maggie Dubris has been active in poetry and performance on NEW YORK CITY's Lower East Side since the 1970s, when the allure of the avant-garde and a love of rock and roll drew her from her home in Michigan. Through workshops with BILL ZAVATSKY and PAUL VIOLI at the POETRY PROJECT AT ST. MARK'S CHURCH IN-THE-BOWERY, she connected with the rising third generation of the NEW YORK SCHOOL, a generation impatient with conventional ideas of succession or inheritance, or with convention, period. PUNK ROCK style and feminist POLITICS helped to fuel the impatience. The magazine *Koff* (1976–77), which Dubris coedited with ELINOR NAUEN and Rachel Barker, featured photos of male poets in the nude. *Caveman,* another new mimeograph magazine, published in 1979 Dubris's nose-thumbing dismissal of first-generation icons entitled "Good Riddance to Bad Rubbish": "Who would want Frank O'Hara around now   one more withered old queen trying to get laid   one more prune for young poets to appease." In her later work Dubris has shown more sympathy for the ways in which the poets of the past survive.

In the early 1980s Dubris began working as an ambulance paramedic in the city's Hell's Kitchen neighborhood, experience that became the basis for her prose poem sequence *WillieWorld* (CUZ Editions, 1998), her novel *Skels* (Soft Skull Press, 2004), and *In the Dust Zone,* a text-and-image collaboration with artist Scott Gillis (yet to be published in hard copy). Reviewing *WillieWorld* for the *Poetry Project Newsletter,* Ammiel Alcalay noted that the book's grounding in the rawest urban reality lends to its "exhilarating flights of lyric . . . the redemptive noise of great rock songs"—an apt comparison, since during the time she was at work on *WillieWorld* Dubris was composing rock songs. In 1991 she teamed up with poet BARBARA BARG to form the all-woman band Homer Erotic, which released two CDs during a decade of performance.

The most extensive collection of Dubris's writing is *Weep Not, My Wanton* (Black Sparrow, 2002), consisting of eight short stories, a reprint of *WillieWorld,* and a lyric sequence entitled *Toilers of the Sea.* Dubris's titles signal her interweaving of texts. "Weep not" alludes to a poem by the Elizabethan writer Robert Greene, and "toilers" comes from a Victor Hugo novel. The title of Dubris's novel, *Skels,* is archaic English slang for beggars or con men, which Dubris was surprised to discover in current use among the police and medics who dealt with New York's homeless people ("Maggie Dubris" n.p.). But the whole novel is about the resurfacing of words and wordsmiths, as the protagonist Orlie Breton (whose name recalls a French poet) encounters writers of the past—Jack London, Walt Whitman, Arthur Rimbaud, Mark Twain—in the consciousness of the street people she attends to. Repetition of the past similarly patterns "The Ruin," a poem modeled on an Old English elegy, which Dubris wrote in response to the destruction of the World Trade Center on SEPTEMBER 11, 2001. She was involved in the event as a paramedic, but as a poet she was simultaneously removed from the event into another realm of meaning. As she writes in *In the Dust Zone*, also based on her 9/11 experience, "I never wanted to live through something like this. I wanted to be born in Europe a hundred years ago and hang out in cafes, a poet in the fire-age of poetry" (excerpt n.p.).

Bibliography

Alcalay, Ammiel. Review of *WillieWorld*. *Poetry Project Newsletter* 175 (June 1999): 19–20.

Dubris, Maggie. Excerpt from part 5 of *In the Dust Zone*. Maggie Dubris Web site. Available online. URL: http://www.maggiedubris.com/events.htm. Accessed December 18, 2008.

———. "Good Riddance to Bad Rubbish." *Caveman* January 30, 1979: n.p.

———. "Maggie Dubris: Saving Lives and Blowing Minds." Interview by Tricia Warden. *DigitalHammer*. Formerly available online. URL: http://www.digital-hammer.com/interviews/md/

———. "The Ruin." In *110 Stories: New York Writes after September 11*, edited by Ulrich Baer, 78–79. New York: New York University Press, 2002.

Hudspith, Vicki. Review of *Weep Not, My Wanton*. Available online. URL: Poetz.com. http://www.poetz.com/reviews/rev-dubris.htm.

Sicha, Choire. "Deadlier Than the Male," *New York Times*, 22 August 2004, p. A23.

Durand, Marcella (1967–   )

Durand refreshes the NEW YORK SCHOOL's French, visual arts, and LANGUAGE POETRY connections. As JOHN ASHBERY's assistant since 2002 and working as program coordinator (1997–2000) and newsletter editor (2003–05) at the POETRY PROJECT AT ST. MARK'S CHURCH-IN-THE BOWERY she became, as Durand says, "involved with just about everything to do with second and third generation New York School poetry" (questionnaire response).

She was born near her grandparents' Pennsylvania farm to French-American artists Suzan Frecon and Michel Durand. Raised in BOSTON and NEW YORK CITY, she has studied in Paris and New Orleans. After a 1985 English B.A. from Tulane University, she earned a Sorbonne certificate (1991) and Brooklyn College M.F.A. in poetry (1995). She married artist Richard O'Russa. *The Anatomy of Oil* (2005) and the full-length *Western Capital Rhapsodies* (2001) followed four earlier chapbooks.

She says she "first saw Ashbery read in 1988, after my college writing teacher forbade me from attending. His fears were justified—my poetry was completely altered" (questionnaire response). Studies with JOHN YAU and ALLEN GINSBERG followed. Her interviews and articles feature New York School and other writers, including Will Alexander, ANSELM BERRIGAN, JACK COLLOM, CLARK COOLIDGE, BRENDA COULTAS, Kevin Davies, KIMBERLY LYONS, HARRY MATHEWS, BERNADETTE MAYER, MAUREEN OWEN, EDWIN TORRES, and ANNE WALDMAN, and she has collaborated with poet Tina Darragh. Other influences include Francis Ponge, ancient Chinese poetry, Susan Howe, Nicole Brossard, and PAUL BLACKBURN. Her artist COLLABORATIONs, with O'Russa and Karoline Schleh, include etchings, books, and sculpture; she curated a Center for Book Arts reading series (2002–04). Her art reviews appear in *New York Perspectives* and *Publishers Weekly*.

Her elegantly handled words present "spheres spinning according to their music," according to Joe Elliot (Faux Press Web site). Interests in ecology, astronomy, and geology enrich her work, creating inspired juxtapositions of sound, scale and image: "If / you handed me a glass of champagne / and saw in the bubbles a whole / new way of building traintracks / through the ruffled sides of geological / monuments" ("Ode to Planetarium," *Western Capital Rhapsodies* 11–12). In *City of Ports* 22, she invokes "somatosensology," spatial awareness of body and surroundings, offering a startlingly precise one-word summary of the New York School project.

Bibliography

Durand, Marcella. *The Anatomy of Oil.* Brooklyn, N.Y.: Belladonna Books, 2005.

———. *The Body, Light and Solar Poems.* 2002. Durationpress.com (e-chapbook). Available online. URL: http://www.durationpress.com/bookstore/ebooks/durand/durand.pdf.

———. *City of Ports: Numbers 1–25.* New York: Situations, 1999.

———. *Floored.* 2000. Fauxpress.com (e-chapbook). Available online. URL: http://www.fauxpress.com/e/floored/index.html.

———. "An Interview with Marcella Durand," by Christopher McCreary, *Poppycock* (Summer 2002): 5–7. Available online. URL: http://www.durationpress.com/ixngy/poppycockonepdfipdf.

———. Questionnaire response for *Encyclopedia of the New York School Poets.* December 3, 2005.

———. *Western Capital Rhapsodies.* Cambridge, Mass.: Faux Press, 2001.

Faux Press Web site. Available online. URL: http://www.fauxpress.com/b/d.htm.

E

Earhart, Amelia   *See* AMELIA EARHART.

Ear Inn

The Ear Inn is located in SoHo (DOWNTOWN MANHATTAN) at 326 Spring Street in the James Brown House, a National Historic Building built in 1817. The bar takes its unusual name from the MUSIC magazine *The Ear*, which was published in a room upstairs beginning in 1975. In that same year, part of the letter *B* in the neon "Bar" sign was painted over, making it read *Ear*. While the magazine stopped running in 1992, the Ear Inn has kept the title.

The Ear is a relatively low-key bar, filled with old etchings, maritime artifacts, and ear sculptures. Its old-fashioned charm has made it the subject of many urban myths (a sailor named Mickey, who was killed by a car out front, is rumored to haunt the bar and upstairs apartment). Before the expansion of Manhattan, the building stood at the very edge of the Hudson River. This made it a natural hotspot for smugglers, prostitutes, and sailors. In the last half century, however, the Ear has catered to a more culturally savvy crowd, who are drawn to the bar's musical and literary offerings. Some of the Ear Inn's most famous artistic patrons are John Lennon, Salvador Dalí, Tom Waits, Philip Glass, and JOHN CAGE.

In 1978 the poet STEPHEN PAUL MILLER launched the Ear Inn reading series, which was soon taken over by Charles Bernstein and TED GREENWALD and developed under the sponsorship of the Segue Foundation. Although identified with Language writing(see LANGUAGE POETRY), the series has presented many NEW YORK SCHOOL poets, from JOHN ASHBERY to LEE ANN BROWN. In the mid-1990s Segue readings moved to a bar in Chinatown, Double Happiness, and eventually to the BOWERY POETRY CLUB. An independent series has continued sporadically at the Ear Inn.

Bibliography

"Readings at the Ear Inn." (1977–92). Audio recordings. PennSound, University of Pennsylvania. Available online. URL: http://writing.upenn.edu/pennsound/x/Ear-Inn.html. Accessed December 17, 2008.

Edgar, Christopher (1961–   )

Christopher Edgar's debut volume, *At Port Royal* (2003), was published in the revived ADVENTURES IN POETRY series with an enthusiastic blurb by JOHN ASHBERY on the back cover: "Edgar's poems are unlike any I've ever read: deep, beautiful, and laugh-out-loud funny." While the originality of the work is indisputable, at the same time it offers evidence of the creative possibilities in a mode that Ashbery himself helped establish. The underlying experience is that of wandering and its psychological counterpart, daydreaming. "Pint-sized Lilliput" offers a tour of a miniature village with a dreamlike atmosphere similar to that of Guadalajara, as Ashbery imagines it in "The Instruction Manual." However, Edgar characteristically attributes visionary effects to optical processes, looking through "the wrong end of the binoculars" (*At Port Royal* 14). The implication is that "the illusion of reality" in which we all participate is produced by the lens of rationality, a particular way of looking at the world that Michel Foucault traced, among other sources, to the philosophers of the 17th-century French school of Port Royal—hence the title of Edgar's volume. Like Giorgio di Chirico in painting or RAYMOND ROUSSEL in literature—two of the favorite predecessors of the NEW YORK SCHOOL—Edgar exposes the surrealism inherent in realistic means of representation, such as logic and geometrical perspective. The impossible objective is somehow to step outside of representation into unique presence, "a point zero or a locus solus" ("Them Blue Lakes," *At Port Royal* 36), as Edgar describes it in the terms of Roussel.

After graduating from Oberlin College in Ohio with a B.A. degree in history and Russian (1983), Edgar took up editorial work in NEW YORK CITY, first for the art book dealer Ex Libris (1983–88) and then for the TEACHERS & WRITERS COLLABORATIVE (1987–2006). His knowledge of Russian literature shows up both in his editing (*Tolstoy as Teacher*) and in his poetry. "Norderney," (for example, *At Port Royal* 24) is "after" Viktor Shklovsky's novel *Zoo* (1923). Edgar's poems have appeared in many journals associated with the New York School, including GARY LENHART's *Transfer*, MICHAEL FRIEDMAN's *Shiny*, and LARRY FAGIN's *Sal Mimeo*. Since 1998 Edgar has coedited *The Hat* with JORDAN DAVIS. In 2002 Cube Press issued "Cheap Day Return" (the concluding poem in *At Port Royal*) as a chapbook, with illustrations by TREVOR WINKFIELD, who has also published Edgar in his new magazine, *The Sienese Shredder*. In 2006 Edgar moved to Geneva, Switzerland, to work as an editor for the United Nations.

Bibliography

Ashbery, John. "The Instruction Manual" (1955). In *Some Trees*. 1956. Reprint, New York: Ecco Press, 1978, 14–18.

Edgar, Christopher. *At Port Royal*. New York: Adventures in Poetry, 2003.

———. Segue reading at Bowery Poetry Club, 14 February 2004. Audio file. PennSound, University of Pennsylvania. Available online. URL: http://writing.upenn.edu/pennsound/x/Segue-BPC.html. Accessed December 17, 2008.

Foucault, Michel. *The Order of Things: An Archeology of the Human Sciences*. New York: Vintage/Random House, 1973.

Mlinko, Ange. Review of *At Port Royal*. *Poetry Project Newsletter* 202 (February–March 2005): 22.

Tolstoy, Leo. *Tolstoy as Teacher: Leo Tolstoy's Writings on Education*. Edited and translated by Christopher Edgar. New York: Teachers & Writers Collaborative, 2001.

Eighth Street Bookstore

The venerable Eighth Street Bookstore, at 32 West 8th Street, was the center of the literary universe for Beat writers and poets throughout the 1950s, '60s, and '70s. The old, three-story shop was opened by Ted and Eli Wilentz in 1947 after they returned from World War II. In the proceeding years the store came to embody the maxim made famous by Ted Wilentz, that a successful bookseller stays "behind the writers and ahead of the readers." Indeed, the store's progressive philosophy and practices gave it a privileged position among New York's literary avant-garde. ANDREI CODRESCU, Hettie Jones, and JOHN WIENERS all held jobs in the bookstore, and ALLEN GINSBERG stayed in a room upstairs for a brief time after returning from India in 1964. That same year Al Aronowitz, one of the first journalists to cover the BEATS, came to the store to introduce then-unknown folk singer Bob Dylan to Allen Ginsberg. The Wilentz brothers themselves were very friendly with many of the poets and held parties for DONALD M. ALLEN, Ray Bremser, Ginsberg, Lawrence Ferlinghetti, LeRoi Jones (AMIRI BARAKA), and others.

In 1959, a little over a decade after opening the store, the brothers decided to branch out into book publishing. The realization of this ambition was Corinth Books, an independent press featuring poetry and prose that reflected the wide-ranging tastes of its two founders.

During the 1960s and early '70s Corinth released important works by a number of young writers. These included DIANE DI PRIMA's *Dinner and Nightmares* (1961), CHARLES OLSON's *The*

Maximus Poems (1960), ANNE WALDMAN's *Giant Night* (1970), Kerouac's *The Scripture of the Golden Eternity* (1960), and Ginsberg's *Empty Mirror* (1961). Some of these titles were put out jointly with Totem Books, an offshoot of Leroi Jones's magazine, *YŪGEN*. Indeed, Corinth's collaboration with Totem spawned many of the era's defining poetry collections, including volumes from each of the major Beat writers. In February 1965, the bookstore moved across the street to 17 West 8th Street, where it remained until 1979 when the Wilentzes closed shop to pursue other areas of publishing.

Bibliography

Howell, Kevin. "Consummate Bookseller Ted Wilentz Dies at 86." *Publishers Weekly,* 14 May 2001, 33.

Morgan, Bill. *The Beat Generation in New York: A Walking Tour of Jack Kerouac's City.* San Francisco: City Lights Books, 1997.

Wilentz, Elias. *The Beat Scene.* New York: Corinth Books, 1960.

electronic poetry

The World Wide Web circulates text with elusive properties pertaining less to physical turf and communities than is the case in most other publishing categories. In this sense the Web challenges the social and historical basis implicit in the term *New York School.* This is not to say that New Yorkers are underrepresented on the Web or that NEW YORK SCHOOL practices have no electronic counterpart. But the idea of a solidified electronic or Internet tradition for voices, attitudes, and stylistics unique to New York is at best decentralized and further atomized by a plethora of alternative Web offerings and competing media for delivering them.

First- and second-generation New York School Web material appears as mostly html print-media conversions of poems, photos, bios, interviews, and critical summaries, along with occasional e-media files (mostly audio). The New York–based Academy of American Poets site (www.poets.org) typifies the conversion model, a primary but bare-bones approach to Web publishing by current standards. Its four-paragraph entry "A Brief Guide to the New York School" cites principal participants, such as BARBARA GUEST,

JOHN ASHBERY, BERNADETTE MAYER, and TED BERRIGAN, and incorporates hyperlinks to the academy's author pages, similarly modeled, and links elsewhere on the Internet. More comprehensive surveys of key New York School poets are available at the Electronic Poetry Center (EPC) Author Homepage Library at the University at Buffalo (www.epc.buffalo.edu). Not many first- or second-generation poets maintain their own Web pages, although a few have posthumous sites maintained for them, such as JOE BRAINARD and FRANK O'HARA. KENWARD ELMSLIE's pages (www. kenwardelmslie.com) break from the conversion model, serving up written, spoken, and sung texts engineered for Web consumption, images by Red Grooms, multiple audio and video files, nonlinear menu navigation, and so forth. Criticism has begun to perform a type of conversion in readings of conventional printed texts by New York School poets that highlight processes comparable to electronic hypertext (Smith; Tabbi).

Among pioneer New York Internet experimentalists are poet Aya Karpinska, whose "arrival of the beeBox" creates graphical interfaces that extend text three dimensionally; poet and musician Alan Sondheim, programmer of multiple e-platforms for ill-tempered personae-avatars and other trickster techno phenomena; sculptor Janet Zweig, who digitally permutes text to engender mechanical and kinetic art pieces; poet and theorist Stephanie Strickland, whose early adaptations of maps, "tiles," "zooms," and other narrative iconography demonstrate methods for redistributing alphabetic text; and poet and teacher Chris Funkhouser, developer of college syllabi that integrate e-poetics and information design. With regard to e-theory building, essays by New York Language poets (see LANGUAGE POETRY) are influential, in particular, Bruce Andrews's "Electronic Poetics" and Charles Bernstein's "Electronic Pies in the Poetry Skies" and "State of the Art."

Like counterparts around the globe, younger generations of New York School poets are adapting to the Internet's various and swiftly evolving opportunities for Web authorship, publishing, and communications. Gary Sullivan, Nada Gordon, JORDAN DAVIS, and others have produced "flarf"—self-consciously bad text composed of fragments lifted from a variety of Web postings—in the tradition of, but not necessarily in the spirit of, the long-standing New York School practice of "found poetry." As sites for "original" authorship, personal home pages, e-mail lists, and blogs are departure points for integrating texts within distinctively defined Internet spaces that deploy interactive and data-rich technologies. Brian Kim Stefans's Arras (www.arras.net), subtitled "New Media and Poetics," is exemplary as a personal domain in its extensive holdings of cyber poems, often composed with Flash, Shockwave, and other Web-oriented software, as well as archives and hyperlinks for diverse editorial initiatives. Stefans's "/ubu Editions" offers e-books by a range of writers, including New Yorkers Michael Scharf, LYTLE SHAW, and Hannah Wiener. In turn, UbuWeb (www.ubu.com), curated by Kenneth Goldsmith, functions as a massive repository for historical and contemporary conceptual and performance pieces, poems, poetic texts, hyperart, audio, video, and film. The repurposing for the Internet of work by such performance-oriented poets and artists as JOHN CAGE, Vitto Acconci, JACKSON MAC LOW, John Baldesarri, TAYLOR MEAD, Carolee Schneeman, Richard Kostelanetz, and Robert Ashley renders their earlier audio and visual constructs as Web compatible as the freshly minted new-media pieces by younger New York poets. Other large archives of multiple media works, Web poems, and poetics by New York School members include institutional sites—PennSound and Kelly Writers House (www.writing.upenn.edu), Slought (www.slought.org), Eclipse (www.english.utah.edu/eclipse/), Poets & Poems (www.poetryproject.com), Poets on Poetry (www.twc.org), and *Brooklyn Review* Online (www.depthome.brooklyn.cuny.edu/english/bkrvw)—and independent e-zines and e-presses sponsored by poets—*Jacket* (www.jacketmagazine.com), *Readme* (www.home.jps.net/~nada), *The East Village* (www.theeastvillage.com), Pompom (www.pompompress.com), Faux/e (www.fauxpress.com/e), Coach House (chbooks.com), and *$lavery* (www.cyberpoems.com). Finally, among many poets from New York and beyond there is rapid proliferation of the blog, a diary-like Web site where one updates texts, images, comment boxes, and hyperlinks in reverse chronological order. New York School examples include Lally's Alley, by MICHAEL LALLY (www.lallysalley.blogspot.com), and Equanimity, by Jordan Davis (www.equanimity.blogspot.com). The blog illustrates how the Internet can hybridize GENREs into a new, medium-specific entity that crosses personal and public e-spaces, a vehicle that encourages new FORMS of experimentation to circulate, allowing for timely publication, redrafting, self-promotion, and debate.

Bibliography

Andrews, Bruce. "Electronic Poetics" (2002). Ubuweb. Available online. URL: http://www.ubu.com/papers/andrews_electronic.html. Accessed December 17, 2008.

Bernstein, Charles. "Electronic Pies in the Poetry Skies." Electronic Book Review. Available online. URL: http://www.electronicbookreview.com/thread/technocapitalism/poetic. Accessed December 17, 2008.

———. "State of the Art." In *A Poetics.* Cambridge, Mass.: Harvard University Press, 1992, 1–8.

Magee, Michael. "The Flarf Files." Electronic Poetry Center, University at Buffalo. Available online. URL: http://epc.buffalo.edu/authors/bernstein/syllabi/readings/flarf.html. Accessed December 17, 2008.

Smith, Hazel. *Hyperscapes in the Poetry of Frank O'Hara: Difference/Homosexuality/Topography.* Liverpool, U.K.: Liverpool University Press, 2000.

Tabbi, Joseph. "Hypertext Hotel Lautréamont." *SubStance* 26, no. 1 (1997): 34–55.

elegy   *See* GENRE.

Elliot, Joe (1960–   )

Joe Elliot was raised in Albany, New York, and New Haven, Connecticut, within a large family of eight children. Elliot graduated from Yale University in 1982 with a B.A. in American studies. He studied acting at HB studios and the Williamstown Theater Festival in the 1980s. He received an M.A. in creative writing from the City University of New York, where he was a student of ANN LAUTERBACH. Elliot had studied the works of T. S. Eliot, Robert Frost, and W. B. Yeats at Yale; Lauterbach exposed him to the work of later modernists.

Elliot's poetry, literary activities, and encouragement have been important to a subset of writers who coalesced around the POETRY PROJECT AT ST. MARK'S CHURCH IN-THE-BOWERY and other DOWNTOWN MANHATTAN venues in the 1990s. With his wife, the book artist Anne Noonan, he started Soho Letter Press. Alongside their commercial venture of fine printing, Elliot and Noonan have experimented with innovative chapbook and broadside formats, publishing (under the two imprints of A Musty Bone and Situations) the works of Bill Luoma, LISA JARNOT, MARCELLA DURAND, CHRIS STROFFOLINO, Rich O'Russa, Brendan Lorber, Rob Fitterman, and others. Elliot has always been an advocate of friendly independent outposts of literary activity. He cofounded lively reading series at Biblio's Bookstore and later at the Zinc Bar in SoHo.

Elliot's poems are often colloquial in style, imparting an ongoing, elliptical conversation that can suddenly swerve into a rigorous and succinct philosophical proposition or a scathing critique. A notational MINIMALISM in his early chapbooks, *Reduced, 15 Clanking Radiators, 14 Knots*, and *Poems to Be Centered on Much Larger Sheets of Paper*, has expanded in the myriad FORMS and confident sweep of recent works, such as *Opposable Thumb* (Subpress, 2006) and *101 Designs for the World Trade Center* (faux press e-books, 2004). Throughout all of his works, perspective wobbles, unhinging the reader's expectations. Digressions lead to revelations; ontological clarity shifts the subject onto entirely new ground. In this way his work is reminiscent of PHILLIP WHALEN. Later works are more discursive and luxuriant, offering social commentary often with a surprising voltage. Elliot has also collaborated on books with artists, for example, with Julie Harrison (*If It Rained Here*, Granary Books, 2000) and Rich O'Russa (*Object Lessons*, Situations, 2001).

Elliot's presence on the NEW YORK SCHOOL poetry scene coincides with that of many peers, such as Kevin Davies, Durand, KIMBERLY LYONS, Brendan Lorber, JO ANN WASSERMAN, Diedre Kovac, Douglas Rothschild, and Shannon Ketch. Elliot's work is particularly effective in a live reading format, and his various readings at the Segue series, the Zinc Bar, the Poetry Project, and elsewhere around town are legendary.

He has written essays and reviews that have appeared in the *Journal of Artist's Books* and *Poetry Project Newsletter*. His poems have been published in many magazines, including *The WORLD, Arras, Object, Torque, Lungfull, Synaesthetic*, the *Poker*, and the *Poetry Project Newsletter*.

Elliot lives with his wife and three children in the Windsor Terrace area of Brooklyn.

Elmslie, Kenward (1929–)

Kenward Elmslie was born on April 27, 1929, in NEW YORK CITY. His father, William Gray Elmslie, was a British subject, and his mother was Constance Helen Pulitzer, daughter of publisher Joseph Pulitzer. Until age nine he lived in Colorado Springs, Colorado. After his mother's death in 1938, his father moved with Elmslie and his two older sisters to Washington, D.C., where he worked for the British embassy. As a teenager, Elmslie discovered and became enamored of musical THEATER, and in his senior year of prep school he wrote the lyrics for the school's spring musical. In 1946, on a vacation to Nassau, he gave up his British passport and became a U.S. citizen. He attended Harvard University, graduating in 1950, all the while continuing his apprenticeship in writing musicals. While working at a theater in Cleveland, Ohio, he contacted noted librettist JOHN LATOUCHE (*The Ballad of Baby Doe, Cabin in the Sky*), who came to Cleveland to see some of his and Elmslie's work performed. Elmslie soon moved to New York City to live with him. The pair also bought a farmhouse in Calais, Vermont, where Elmslie still spends his summers.

Living in New York City, Elmslie met playwrights, composers, actors, and young poets such as JOHN ASHBERY, KENNETH KOCH, and FRANK O'HARA. While he continued to write lyrics for revues and musicals, he also decided to try his hand at writing poetry. His first published poem, "Letter from Eldorado," appeared in *FOLDER* in 1956. (LaTouche died of a heart attack this same year.) In 1957 *The Sweet Bye and Bye*, Elmslie's first opera with composer Jack Beeson, was produced. In 1959 Nat King Cole had a minor hit with Elmslie's song "Love-wise," and in 1961 Elmslie's first poetry collection, *Pavilions*, was published by the TIBOR DE NAGY GALLERY. *Motor Disturbance* was published by

Columbia University Press in 1971 as the winner of that year's Frank O'Hara Award.

In 1964 Elmslie met artist JOE BRAINARD, who had only recently arrived from Tulsa, Oklahoma. Elmslie and Brainard began a personal and artistic relationship that would last until Brainard's death in 1994.

Over the years Elmslie's career has followed much this same pattern: poetry collections alternating with musical productions, alternating with a novel (*The Orchid Stories*, Doubleday, 1973) or COLLABORATION with artists such as Brainard, Donna Dennis, and TREVOR WINKFIELD, alternating with operas. This wide range of interests—and talents—seems to have worked against him to some extent. Critics seem unsure about including him with more easily categorized "poets." For example, his poet friends and contemporaries—such as Ashbery, JAMES SCHUYLER, Koch, and O'Hara, among others—are credited as being NEW YORK SCHOOL poets, his name is almost always conspicuously absent.

Elmslie's simultaneous loves for theater and poetry have resulted in a style of language no other poet or librettist even approaches, one at once dense and self-conscious of a variety of inner personae jousting with each other in lingos effervescent with slang, emotionally compelling, and linguistically obsessed. Highlights among his more than 40 separate publications include *26 Bars* (Z PRESS, 1987), an alphabetical tour of imaginary drinking establishments (with drawings by Dennis); *Sung Sex* (Kulchur Foundation, 1989), poems in a range of styles from the almost impossibly dense to haiku simplicity (with drawings by Brainard); and CYBERSPACE (Granary Books, 2000), with collages by Winkfield. *Routine Disruption: Selected Poems & Lyrics* was published in 1998 by Coffee House Press.

As time has passed, Elmslie has moved more into performing his own works. In addition to reading his poems, he has set a number of them to MUSIC, and his readings/performances also frequently include renditions of some of the songs he has written for both Off-Broadway and Broadway musicals. He has recorded several albums and CDs of his songs and poems, including *Kenward Elmslie in Palais Bimbo Lounge Show* (1985) and *26 Bars* (1987).

Bibliography

Ashbery, John. "The Figure in the Carport: Kenward Elmslie." In *Selected Prose*. Edited by Eugene Richie. Ann Arbor: University of Michigan Press, 2004, 159–163.

Bamberger, William C. *Kenward Elmslie: A Bibliographical Profile*. Flint, Mich.: Bamberger Books, 1993.

Elmslie Kenward. Web site. Available online. URL: http://www.kenwardelmslie.com/interactive/index02.html.

Notley, Alice. "Elmslie's *Routine Disruptions*." In *Coming After: Essays on Poetry*. Ann Arbor: University of Michigan Press, 2005, 52–56.

Enigma Variations Bill Berkson and Philip Guston (1975)

Facing each other across the pages of *Enigma Variations* (BIG SKY), BILL BERKSON's poems and PHILIP GUSTON's drawings tacitly acknowledge a common enigma by varied means. Poem and drawing do not represent each other but stand in an abstract relation to something inexpressible, enigmatic. Guston had recently abandoned abstract art, in the formal sense of nonfigurative, but his inclusion of both earlier abstract drawings and more recent figurative ones in *Enigma Variations* suggests a continuity in his underlying concerns, just as the pairing of drawing and poem suggests continuity between the two media. Guston's notes on the COLLABORATION suggest that poetry's dependence on "everyday" language corresponds to Guston's schematic representation of simple objects in a room—chair, rug, curtain, lamp—in the drawing that he pairs with the title poem of the volume. The mood of abstraction remains in this variation, which Guston refers to as "clear enigma." Fittingly, Berkson's title poem appropriates the text of an earlier "POEM-PAINTING" collaboration between FRANK O'HARA and Norman Bluhm (1960), in which O'Hara names both objects and enigmas:

> There's an apple
> on the table
> it's dawn
> I die.

The collaboration between Berkson and Guston came about at Berkson's request several years into their friendship, which continued largely through correspondence after Berkson moved to BOLINAS, CALIFORNIA, in 1970. In 1974 Berkson "finally got up the gumption" to ask Guston for drawings to accompany a group of his poems in a book ("Ideal Reader" 43). Guston was excited by the discoveries he made by using drawing as a means of reading the poems, a process he pursued further in a series of "poem-pictures" incorporating texts by Berkson and others in the same space as the drawing, unlike the facing-page format of *Enigma Variations*. That format was, however, Guston's suggestion, as recorded in notes he sent to Berkson along with the drawings. In most cases, the notes further specify which drawing is to accompany which poem.

In all, Guston supplied drawings to go with 16 of the 23 poems in *Enigma Variations*. Interestingly, he did not supply drawings for poems that were already collaborations, "Waves of Particles" (with MICHAEL BROWNSTEIN and RON PADGETT) and "Variations on a Theme by William Carlos Williams" (with LARRY FAGIN and Padgett). Although the choice of pairing was itself a creative act, some of the drawings had been done before Guston received the poems, just as the poems themselves had been written over a number of years. Only one of the poems, "Belgian Reflexes," was written specifically for Guston; according to his notes, he read it as confirmation that "poetry can be made of anything . . . just like painting."

The title poem arose from an occasion involving other artists and other arts: JIM CARROLL, who shared Berkson's apartment for a time before the latter left New York, was going with EDWIN DENBY to a performance of Frederick Ashton's ballet *Enigma Variations* (1968), choreographed to MUSIC by Edward Elgar (1899). Nevertheless, the association between Guston and "enigma" had been on Berkson's mind for some time. When Guston had exhibited his new figurative work at the Marlborough Gallery in New York in 1970, Berkson wrote a review that connected the work with that of the protosurrealist painter Giorgio di Chirico, whose titles repeatedly refer to some type of "enigma." Berkson concluded: "Guston's questions are lumbersome enigmas not so much to be answered as to paint on, which he does, with care

and enthusiasm and strange magic" ("The New Gustons" 85).

Bibliography

Berkson, Bill. E-mail to Terence Diggory, 11 November 2005.
———. "The Ideal Reader." In *Philip Guston's Poem-Pictures*, by Debra Bricker Balken, 43–45. Andover, Mass.: Addison Gallery of American Art, Phillips Academy; Seattle: University of Washington Press, 1994.
———. "The New Gustons." *Art News* 69, no. 6 (October 1970): 44–47, 85.
Guston, Philip. Notes on *Enigma Variations*. Bill Berkson Papers. Archives and Special Collections, Thomas J. Dodd Research Center, University of Connecticut Libraries.

epic   *See* GENRE.

Equi, Elaine (1953–)

Born and raised in CHICAGO, ILLINOIS, where with JEROME SALA she was a vital part of the PUNK ROCK poetry scene of the 1980s, Elaine Equi is a minimalist and ironist whose work reflects DEEP IMAGE and surrealist influences within the overall frame of NEW YORK SCHOOL casualness, lightness of tone, and pop reference. In the 1980s she was identified with Los Angeles poets DENNIS COOPER, AMY GERSTLER, and DAVID TRINIDAD as part of a post–NEW AMERICAN POETRY vanguard.

In a review of her work the poet TOM CLARK refers to her "Dorothy Parkerish kit of weapons: arched eyebrow barbs, nervy, catchy hooks of pop-conscious metaphor, and double meanings stitched in light-handedly" (194). A reviewer for *Publishers Weekly* writes of *The Cloud of Knowable Things* (Coffee House Press, 2003): "Equi's most frequent attitude is a gently appalled feminism, a stance one step back from everything; her best work combines lyric depth with restrained and epigrammatic wit, respecting not just 'the so-called power of words' but a quiet resistance to them" (71).

Equi's attention to objects derives not only from a surrealist fetishizing of them but also from imagist-OBJECTIVIST attention to the "thing itself," as seen especially in William Carlos Williams and Lorine Niedecker. Hers is a close seeing, with depth and mystery that also relates to the protosurrealist art of Giorgio de Chirico. Seen closely enough, objects take on both strangeness and serenity. In "Desire in Winter," included in *Voice-Over* (Coffee House Press, 1999), she addresses "a drifter / with edges that are not distinct," yet imbues this indistinctness with a pleasing sensory concreteness in a catalogue of colors: "your white / that is almost blue"; "your blue / that is almost gray"; and so on.

For a "pop" poet, Equi's work is surprising in its philosophical gravity and perceptual accuracy. This combination of depth and surface is characteristic of the New York School as a whole, especially in the work of JAMES SCHUYLER. Equi differs, however, in the ceremonial stillness and silence she can bring to language. In *Voice-Over* her deep wit overturns Williams's famous statement, "A poem is a small (or large) machine made of words" (Williams 54). In "Thesis Sentence" Equi declares: "The poem is a small machine made of God."

Coffee House Press published *Ripple Effect: New and Selected Poems* in 2007. Equi's other collections include *Surface Tension* (1989) and *Decoy* (1994), both from Coffee House Press, and the earlier publications *Federal Woman* (Dainaides Press, 1978), *Shrewcrazy* (Little Caesar Press, 1981), *The Corners of the Mouth* (Iridescence Press, 1986), and *Accessories* (The Figures, 1988). Since 1988, she has resided in NEW YORK CITY, where she teaches at City College and New York University. From 1998 to 2002 she was senior editor of the literary magazine *Conjunctions,* which published her provocatively titled essay, "Frank O'Hara: Nothing Personal."

Bibliography

Clark, Tom. "Pop Hooks." In *The Poetry Beat: Reviewing the Eighties.* Ann Arbor: University of Michigan Press, 1990, 194–195.

Equi, Elaine. "Frank O'Hara: Nothing Personal." *Conjunctions* 29 (Fall 1997). Available online. URL: http://www.conjunctions.com/archives/C29-ee/htm.

Review of *The Cloud of Knowable Things. Publishers Weekly,* 17 February 2003, 71.

Skbot, Floyd. "The Air Is Full of Secrets." *New York Times Book Review,* 1 April 2007, 11.

Williams, William Carlos. Introduction to *The Wedge* (1944). In *The Collected Poems.* Vol. 2, *1939–1962.* Edited by Christopher MacGowan. New York: New Directions, 1988, 53–55.

F

Fagin, Larry (1937–)

Larry Fagin combines broad experience in the international avant-garde with intensive involvement in the NEW YORK SCHOOL scene. Although he was born in NEW YORK CITY, Fagin moved with his family to many different locations during his youth, following his father's assignments as a civilian employee of the U.S. Army Corps of Engineers. Fagin became acquainted with the BEAT writers in Europe, visiting the "Beat Hotel" in Paris in 1958 and reading with GREGORY CORSO and Günter Grass in Berlin. After completing a bachelor's degree in English at the University of Maryland in 1960, he made his way to San Francisco and joined the circle surrounding the poet Jack Spicer. When Spicer died in 1965, Fagin rejoined his family in England, where, through contact with TOM CLARK, he began to read a full range of contemporary New York School writing. A visit by LEWIS WARSH and ANNE WALDMAN convinced him that New York had the creative energy he was seeking. In 1967 he left England with Joan Inglis, whom he married in 1969, the same year he began working with Waldman in helping to run the activities of the POETRY PROJECT AT ST. MARK'S CHURCH IN-THE-BOWERY. From 1971 to 1976 he served as assistant director, thereafter shifting his attention to Danspace, the Poetry Project's counterpart for DANCE, which he and Barbara Dilley launched in 1974.

Fagin has described "Occasional Poem," written in 1966, as "a breakthrough (?) of sorts" (interview by Brockris-Wylie 9), a judgment that seems to be confirmed by the number of times the poem has been reprinted. It certainly marks a breakthrough into the New York School mode of "I do this I do that," in this case reporting an excursion to Greenwich, outside London, in the company of Clark. Inflected with a pop sensibility, "Occasional Poem" goes beyond FRANK O'HARA and even TED BERRIGAN in striking a deadpan attitude toward ordinary experience, perhaps closest to the diary entries of LEWIS WARSH. But the reader is brought up short by Fagin's closing statement: "Then I / turned out the light and had this terrible dream." Even at its most flippant a certain poignancy, an existential moodiness hovers over much of Fagin's work, recalling his mentors in the Spicer circle, particularly George Stanley. Fagin writes in many voices, however. As PETER SCHJELDAHL noted in an early review, Fagin seems less interested in claiming a "voice" of his own than in exploring "the possibilities of poetry as an activity" (268–269). In frequent COLLABORATIONs with CLARK COOLIDGE he has pursued that exploration to the level of the most fundamental properties of language. Fagin's range is most fully represented in two collections: *Rhymes of a Jerk* (Kulchur Foundation, 1974), with cover design by Ed Ruscha), and *I'll Be Seeing You: Poems, 1962–1976* (Full Court Press, 1978). *Rhymes of a Jerk* contains a substantial section of TRANSLATIONs from work by Saint-Pol-Roux, Pierre Albert-Birot, Paul Scheerbarth, and Philippe Soupault.

In the New York School tradition of involvement with the visual arts, Fagin has produced collaborations with GEORGE SCHNEEMAN (*Landscape*,

ANGEL HAIR, 1972), Richard Tuttle (*Poems/ Drawings*, 1977), and TREVOR WINKFIELD (*Dig & Delve*, Granary Books, 1999). He has also made an art of editing, publishing, and teaching. He began editing magazines in 1962 in San Francisco with *Horus* and *Bacedifogu*. In New York, his ADVENTURES IN POETRY (1968–75) shared honors with *The WORLD* at the head of the list of New York School magazines, backed up by a series of 37 pamphlets published under the Adventures in Poetry label. Fagin edited a new magazine, *Un Poco Loco* (1977–79), as a new "generation" of writers came into the scene and a number of veterans left. Fagin himself spent increasing periods of time outside New York, teaching at the newly founded NAROPA INSTITUTE in Boulder, Colorado, where he directed the poetics program from 1982 to 1984. More recently, New York has once again become the base for his teaching as he has renewed outreach to public schools, partly through the Teachers & Writers Collaborative, and offered workshops at the New School. In 1999 he started yet another magazine, *Sal Mimeo*. In 2001 he revived Adventures in Poetry as a publishing label. For other publishers, Fagin has coedited collections of poems by JOSEPH CERAVOLO (1994) and George Stanley (2003).

Bibliography

Fagin, Larry. Interview by Victor Bockris and Andrew Wylie. *Contact* 4 (January 1973): 3–12.

———. Interview by Daniel Kane. "Adventures in Poetry." *Poetry Project Newsletter* 185 (Summer 2001): 6–11.

———. "Occasional Poem." In *I'll Be Seeing You: Poems 1962–1976*. New York: Full Court Press, 1978, 5–6.

Schjeldahl, Peter. "Around the Corner." *Poetry* 117, no. 4 (January 1971): 261–275.

Fame and Love in New York Ed Sanders (1980)

ED SANDERS's comic novel *Fame and Love in New York* (Turtle Island Foundation) is a four-part satire mixing materials, themes, and GENRES in a postmodern pastiche that chides the economics of both elite and popular culture. *Fame and Love* irreverently tells how an artist, a detective, a poet leading a secret literary society, and a world-famous rock band defend the integrity of American poet Hart Crane, the Brooklyn Bridge, and a revolutionary socialist movement.

Borrowing from science FICTION and the detective genre, Sanders sets *Fame and Love* "in New York City in the near future, with technology slightly more advanced than it actually is," as an introductory note explains. Part 1 tracks the embattled multimedia artist Milton Rosé's desperate attempts to sell his latest work, *Circles of Paradise,* with the help of international cocaine dealer Count Volpe.

In part 2, the narrator, Fitz McIver, comes to NEW YORK CITY in pursuit of papers of French novelist and playwright Honoré de Balzac stolen from the Count. During his investigation McIver stumbles upon a conspiracy involving Hart Crane's lost trunk of personal possessions and manuscripts. He then pursues bounty-seekers competing for the priceless collection, precious in an "Age of Archives." It turns out that artist Milton Rosé has stolen them and moved to Mars, site of a projected Hart Crane Museum.

In part 3, a group of poets, led by Ione Appleton, America's most popular creator of apothegms, revives their flagging careers by publishing novels with plots stolen from Balzac, updating them to reflect current events. Their enormous success has led them to steal Count Volpe's collection of Balzac manuscripts to provide them with fresh material. McIver discovers the Balzac Study Group is behind the theft when he overhears Ione and Milton Rosé trading declarations of love and revealing their secrets, and he ends up protecting Ione from the Count's vengeful henchmen.

Part 4 breaks from the narrative to interject the history of J'Accuse, the popular rock band of the 2000 Society, a secret socialist organization connecting almost all the book's characters, including McIver. In the final chapter the characters all convene for a J'Accuse concert. Overseeing security for the show, McIver finds that Hunk Forbes of the American Security Command is plotting against J'Accuse, but in his attack Forbes inadvertently shoots Milton Rosé. J'Accuse survives to close the book by leading a song of optimism on Eighth Avenue.

In *Fame and Love* Sanders mocks nearly every aspect of the art and literary world. The numerous inside jokes, often related in footnotes, provide two concurrent visions of the future of New York. In one, New York continues to offer a sanctuary to a generation of poverty-stricken poets, and the media demonstrate a passionate interest in great American artists like Hart Crane and Claes Oldenburg. In the other vision, New York becomes the cynical landscape of artists and writers selling useless trends to a society infatuated with scandal, gossip, and media celebrities.

Bibliography

Olsen, Lance. "Divining the Avant-Pop Afterburn: *Fame & Love in New York*." *Review of Contemporary Fiction* 19, no. 1 (Spring 1999): 91–100.

Feldman, Morton (1926–1987)
musician, composer

In his memorial essay for his friend FRANK O'HARA, composer Morton Feldman distinguishes "those who typified an era from those who thrust themselves above it" (*Give My Regards* 108). His desire to place himself, along with O'Hara, in the former category, says a great deal about the approach both to life and to art that these two men shared. Feldman, a physically large man who loved the give-and-take of ideas at the artists' CLUB or the CEDAR STREET TAVERN, was also a man of practical affairs who supported himself for much of his life by working in his family's clothing business. His MUSIC can seem austere, as if it were Feldman's means of withdrawing from the world, but once the listener's ear is attuned to it, it becomes evident that Feldman has found a way of entering into his music as he engaged in the world, sensually and emotionally as well as intellectually, just as JACKSON POLLOCK claimed to be in his painting (Namuth and Falkenburg).

Early in his career, on the recommendation of his mentor, JOHN CAGE, Feldman received the commission to write the score for the film about Pollock by Hans Namuth and Paul Falkenburg (1951). In the scenes of Pollock painting, the correspondence between notes plucked from the strings of a cello and paint flung from the stick in Pollock's hand implies that Feldman entered his music by means of gesture, yet that analogy can be misleading. More important to Feldman was the notion of the unit of composition as an open field in which the placement of notes was not determined by any preexisting system, whether the traditional octave scale or the 12-tone row that had become the preferred structure for avant-garde composers. Especially during the 1950s—though not in the score for the Pollock film—Feldman applied the example of painting to experiments in "graphic" notation: "Pollock placed his canvas on the ground and painted as he walked around it. I put sheets of graph paper on the wall; each sheet framed the same time duration and was, in effect, a visual rhythmic structure" (*Give My Regards* 147). Later, CLARK COOLIDGE would describe Feldman's method in terms of "open field" poetry, advocated by CHARLES OLSON in his essay on "PROJECTIVE VERSE" (1950). In fact, Feldman's first experiments in this mode were entitled *Projections* (1950–51).

How sounds were projected into time, as Feldman conceived of his "canvas" (*Give My Regards* 147), made all the difference. The gesture of ACTION PAINTING, a term Feldman disliked (*Give My Regards* 99), is highly theatrical, and it connotes, of course, movement. Feldman's music, when it is not trying to keep up with Pollock, moves very slowly, and even when its open field seems vast, as Coolidge notes, "it is all intimate detail" (n.p.), often no louder than a whisper. As Feldman himself puts it: "There is still movement—but it has become nothing more than the breathing of the sound itself" (*Give My Regards* 13). O'Hara called this "a personal and profound revelation of the inner quality of sound" (120), and it testifies to the composer's ability to enter into his work. What we hear is "human breathing," Feldman assures us (*Give My Regards* 61). To convey the intimacy of this presence, O'Hara traces the composer's "touch" rather than his "gesture" (117). O'Hara experienced first-hand the "lightness of touch" that Feldman's work demanded when he joined the composer in a four-hand piano duet at a benefit for the *FLOATING BEAR* at the LIVING THEATRE in 1961 (Berkson n.p.). Feldman acknowledged the demand explicitly when he described his *Piano Piece (to Philip Guston)* (1963) as "involved very much with touch" (Bernard 199). Among the abstract expressionist painters, PHILIP GUSTON was personally closest to Feldman, who placed him with the painter Piet Mondrian and the composer Edgar Varèse in a short list of "artists who are *in* the work" (*Give My Regards* 66).

Feldman named compositions in honor of several painters (Franz Kline, WILLEM DE KOONING, Mark Rothko, Guston) but only one NEW YORK SCHOOL poet, O'Hara, who was twice so honored, with *The O'HARA SONGS* (1962) and *For Frank O'Hara* (1973), an instrumental piece. The second-generation poets whom BILL BERKSON gathered for a reading at the New York Studio School, where Feldman served as dean from 1969 to 1971, did not impress Feldman (Berkson n.p.). He was more deeply disappointed when Guston turned to figurative work in 1970 (LeSueur 144). In 1972 he took up a professorship at the State University of New York at Buffalo and deliberately kept at some distance from NEW YORK CITY. The minimalist composers who came to prominence there during the 1970s (Philip Glass, Steve Reich, Terry Riley, LaMonte Young) were sometimes compared with Feldman, but the "touch" that O'Hara had identified preserved Feldman's uniqueness (Johnson 218, 245). As Feldman explained, "[I]t is not freedom of choice that is the meaning of the fifties, but the freedom of people to be themselves" (*Give My Regards* 99).

Bibliography

Berkson, Bill. Interview by Chris Villars (2001). Morton Feldman Page. Available online. URL: http://www.cnvill.demon.co.uk/mfbbint.htm.

Bernard, Jonathan W. "Feldman's Painters." In *The New York Schools of Music and Visual Arts*, edited by Steven Johnson, 173–215. New York: Routledge, 2002.

Coolidge, Clark. "Regarding Morton Feldman's Music and Wherever It All Now Goes" (1988). Morton Feldman Page. Available online. URL: http://www.cnvill.demon.co.uk/mfcooldg.htm. Accessed December 18, 2008.

Feldman, Morton. *Chamber Music*. WER 6273-2. Sound recording. Mainz, Germany: Wergo, 1996. [Includes *For Franz Kline, The O'Hara Songs, De Kooning, Piano Piece (to Philip Guston), For Frank O'Hara.*]

———. *Give My Regards to Eighth Street*. Edited by B. H. Friedman. Cambridge, Mass.: Exact Change, 2000.

Johnson, Steven. "Jasper Johns and Morton Feldman: What Patterns?" In *The New York Schools of Music and Visual Arts*. New York: Routledge, 2002, 217–247.

LeSueur, Joe. *Digressions on Some Poems by Frank O'Hara: A Memoir*. New York: Farrar, Straus & Giroux, 2003. 141–145.

Namuth, Hans, and Paul Falkenburg. *Jackson Pollock*. 16mm film. New York: Film Images, 1951.

O'Hara, Frank. "New Directions in Music: Morton Feldman" (1959). In *Standing Still and Walking in New York*. Edited by Donald Allen. San Francisco: Grey Fox, 1983, 115–120.

Ross, Alex. "American Sublime: Morton Feldman's Mysterious Musical Landscapes." *New Yorker* 19 June 2006, 84–88.

Ferrari, Mary (1928–   )

Mary Ferrari was a prominent member of a group of women poets, many of whom studied with KENNETH KOCH, that flourished in the late 1970s. Among other NEW YORK SCHOOL poets, Ferrari was close to LARRY FAGIN, ANNE WALDMAN, CHARLES NORTH, MAUREEN OWEN, and BILL ZAVATSKY. In 1968 Ferrari formed part of Adrienne Rich's poetry workshop at the 92nd Street Y, and Rich was responsible for Ferrari's first poem being published, in John Logan's anthology *Choice* (1971). Ferrrari also was part of a writing group of women poets, such as Catherine Murray, Annette Hays, Miriam Finkelstein, and Frances Waldman, who helped nurture and critically appraise one anothers' work for many years. Ferrari taught a poetry writing workshop at the POETRY PROJECT AT ST. MARK'S CHURCH IN-THE-BOWERY in spring 1978, and she read her poems at many venues, including Poet's House and the Poetry Project.

Ferrari counts Koch's seminal poetry workshop at the New School as chief among her influences. In 1965 she won the New School's Dylan Thomas Memorial Award for Poetry. "Eternity," a poem published in *ANGEL HAIR* 5 (spring 1968), and dedicated to Koch, reflects his spirit in mood and imagery:

*at the end of every cigarette that burns there is of
   course
a soft little bright light which means hope!*

As Nadine Gordimer observed on the jacket of
Ferrari's *Why the Sun Cannot Set,* "Mary Ferrari's
poetry has the unexpectedness of life." Among
her books are *The Flying Glove,* edited by Fagin
(Chapbook, 1973); *The Mocking Bird and Other
Poems,* edited by CHARLES NORTH (SWOLLEN MAGPIE
PRESS, 1980); *The Isle of the Little God* (KULCHUR,
1981); *The Poet Exposed: Portraits by Christopher
Felver* (Alfred van der Marck, 1986); and *Why the
Sun Cannot Set: New and Selected Poems* (HANGING
LOOSE PRESS, 1994).

Ferrari was born to Earle and Eloise Selby
in New Orleans, Louisiana, and educated at
the College of New Rochelle (B.A., 1950), New
York University (M.A., English), and Columbia
University (M. Phil., English). She currently lives in
Larchmont, New York, where she has lived for the
last 40-odd years, save three years in Johannesburg,
South Africa (1992–94). She is married to Frank
Ferrari, a political consultant on Africa, and has
four children.

Bibliography

Ferrari, Mary. "Eternity." In *The Angel Hair Anthology,*
   edited by Anne Waldman and Lewis Warsh, 130.
   New York: Granary Books, 2001.

fiction

The NEW YORK SCHOOL poem is "always threatening to become a novel," as JOHN ASHBERY described
Gertrude Stein's "Stanzas in Meditation" (*Selected
Prose* 12–13). In offering this description, Ashbery
has in mind a new conception of the way things
happen—the basis of fictional narrative—that
modern poets and novelists shared. As inheritors
of modernism, the New York School poets easily
crossed the boundary between poetry and fiction,
not only incorporating into their poems devices
they learned from fiction but also producing short
stories and novels themselves. Ashbery further
complicated the relationship by assigning the title
of novel to a verse poem ("A Long Novel" [1956])
and a prose poem (*Novel* [1954]).

An interview that Ashbery conducted with
HARRY MATHEWS, the New York School writer who
is best known as a novelist, contrasts their shared
sense of "the way things really happen" with the
appearance of reality in "the traditional short story
or novel" (Mathews 42). Paradoxically, the more
that events appear probable—the touchstone of
traditional realism—the less real they feel, according to Ashbery's definition of realism as "a sort
of casual, unbuttoned quality"—the quality of
freshness and surprise (41–42). Mathews goes on
to explain how this quality is instilled in writing
by the observance of arbitrary constraints such as
those employed by RAYMOND ROUSSEL, to whom
Ashbery introduced Mathews, or by the writers of
the OULIPO group with whom Mathews became
affiliated. Fundamentally, writing captures "the
way things really happen" by making words do
surprising things rather than using words to translate unexpected events in the "real" world. In the
novel *Hebdomeros* (1929), by the painter Giorgio
de Chirico, "the setting and the cast of characters
frequently change in mid-clause," noted Ashbery,
who praised the result as "a cinematic freedom of
narration" (*Selected Prose* 90).

While Roussel and de Chirico align roughly with the French surrealist movement, which
Ashbery designated "the most powerful single influence on the twentieth-century novel" (Ashbery,
Selected Prose 88), the New York School poets also
responded strongly to a native strain of eccentricity in British fiction such as in the work of
HENRY GREEN, the subject of Ashbery's master's
thesis. JAMES SCHUYLER's novels, including his
collaboration with Ashbery, *A NEST OF NINNIES*
(Dutton, 1969), and KENWARD ELMSLIE's linked
sequence *The Orchid Stories* (Doubleday, 1973) owe
a great deal to Ronald Firbank's comedy of manners. BARBARA GUEST's novel *SEEKING AIR* (Black
Sparrow, 1978) explicitly acknowledges a debt to
Dorothy Richardson for what might be called the
comedy of consciousness. Less self-conscious but
no less artful, certain examples of GENRE fiction
delighted the poets for the fresh effects that were
stimulated by their constraints, as in Roussel.
Schuyler had "a special fondness" for the Nancy
Drew mystery series (Ashbery, *Selected Prose* 282),
and Ashbery directly appropriated language for his

poem "Europe" (1962) from *Beryl of the Biplane,* an example of the children's adventure genre that KENNETH KOCH imitated in his novel *The RED ROBINS* (Vintage, 1975). At least two writers with ties to the second-generation poets have made a mark in genre fiction professionally: TOM DISCH in science fiction and Charlotte Carter (1947–) in detective fiction.

For most of the poets of the second generation, the news in fiction was the arrival of the BEAT writers WILLIAM S. BURROUGHS and JACK KEROUAC. Burroughs's "cut-up" technique provided up-to-date encouragement for a series of experiments in dadaist prose by TOM VEITCH (*The LUIS ARMED STORY* [Full Court, 1978]); TED BERRIGAN (*CLEAR THE RANGE* [ADVENTURES IN POETRY/Coach House South, 1977]); RON PADGETT, with Veitch (*ANTLERS IN THE TREETOPS* [Coach House, 1973]); and Johnny Stanton (*Slip of the Tongue* [ANGEL HAIR, 1969]). Although he writes exclusively in prose, Stanton (1943–) has been an integral part of the poets' social network. Kerouac's "spontaneous prose" made an immediate impact on poetry, for instance, in the work of CLARK COOLIDGE. In content, though not always in style, *On the Road* and *The Subterraneans* helped to define the "subterranean" novel as a genre. In *The System of Dante's Hell* (Grove, 1965), LeRoi Jones (AMIRI BARAKA) claimed a more ancient literary precedent while at the same time reconnecting the genre to its roots in the black experience, further explored in fiction by ISHMAEL REED (*Mumbo Jumbo* [Doubleday, 1972]) and CALVIN HERNTON (*Scarecrow* [Doubleday, 1974]). ARAM SAROYAN (*The Street,* [Bookstore Press, 1974]), ED SANDERS (*SHARDS OF GOD* [Grove, 1970]), MICHAEL BROWNSTEIN (*Self-Reliance* [Coffee House, 1994]), TOM CLARK (*Who Is Sylvia?* [Blue Wind, 1979]), and PAUL HOOVER (*Saigon, Illinois* [Vintage, 1988]) drew on their "subterranean" or countercultural experience from varying degrees of retrospective distance. Hoover provided an extra twist to retrospection by reflecting on the composition of his novel *Saigon, Illinois* in his long poem *The Novel* (New Directions, 1990).

The two tendencies of expressionism and abstraction that underlie the New York School aesthetic produce unexpected combinations in

"punk" prose, a variant of the subterranean novel, as the novels of PUNK ROCK musician RICHARD HELL most clearly demonstrate: *Go Now* (Scribner, 1996) and *Godlike* (Little House on the Bowery–Akashic, 2005). The punk genre includes such works as JIM CARROLL's *The BASKETBALL DIARIES* (Tombouctou Press, 1978) and EILEEN MYLES's *Cool for You* (Soft Skull, 2000), which are barely fictionalized autobiography. Heightened attention to the body and sexuality gives the work an expressionistic cast even when the author projects that attention through a persona, as in the fiction of DENNIS COOPER or through "found text," as in the work of Kathy Acker (1947–). Acker's association with the POETRY PROJECT AT ST. MARK'S CHURCH IN-THE-BOWERY, which she describes as a relation of "interior antagonism" (616), encouraged her experimentation with techniques that abstract the function of authorship while suffusing the work with personality, a fulfillment of FRANK O'HARA's vision of "PERSONISM" that O'Hara himself probably would not have anticipated.

Where the narrative function and the narrator become abstract, fiction verges on the prose poem, a distinct FORM that has its own history in the evolution of the New York School. The prose poem and shorter forms of fiction have developed through co-evolution in the work of certain poets, for example JOHN YAU and SHARON MESMER. MAXINE CHERNOFF, another practitioner of the prose poem, has translated the focused attention that characterizes that form into the extended scope of her novel *PLAIN GRIEF* (Summit, 1991). Further experiment is likely to produce new hybrids such as LEWIS WARSH has bred from his extended cultivation of prose fiction. Recalling Ashbery on the "cinematic freedom" of *Hebdomeros,* Warsh has said of his recent work *The Origin of the World* (Creative Arts, 2001): "What I wanted is a form where I wasn't confined to either/or, where I could break down the boundaries between poetry and fiction, where I could include all my impulses toward writing with as few restrictions as possible" (158).

Bibliography

Acker, Kathy. Statement in *Out of This World: An Anthology of the St. Mark's Poetry Project, 1966–1991,* edited by Anne Waldman, 616. New York: Crown, 1991.

Ashbery, John. "A Long Novel." In *Some Trees*. 1956. Reprint, New York: Ecco, 1978, 64–65.

———. *Novel*. Drawings by Trevor Winkfield. New York: Grenfell Press, 1998.

———. *Selected Prose*. Edited by Eugene Richie. Ann Arbor: University of Michigan Press, 2004.

Mathews, Harry. Interview by John Ashbery. *Review of Contemporary Fiction* 7, no. 3 (Fall 1987): 36–48.

Warsh, Lewis. Interview by Daniel Kane. In *What Is Poetry: Conversations with the American Avant-Garde*, edited by Daniel Kane, 157–162. New York: Teachers & Writers, 2003.

Field, Edward (1924–)

Protesting that he "never belonged" to the fast set of poets and painters grouped around FRANK O'HARA, Edward Field explains his inclusion among the "New York Poets" in *The NEW AMERICAN POETRY, 1945–1960* anthology (1960) as a consequence of a brief affair he had with O'Hara in 1955 and of O'Hara's intervention on Field's behalf with DONALD M. ALLEN, the anthology's editor (*The Man* 84–85). In a letter to KENNETH KOCH, JAMES SCHUYLER wrote approvingly of Field as O'Hara's "new friend": "He seems sweet and good, qualities I never found it in my heart to attribute to Larry Rivers" (Schuyler 26). Sweetness is a dominant quality in Field's poems, invoked by name in key passages and described in reviews as "innocence" (Dickey) or "sentimentality" (Howard; Mazzocco). Balanced with this quality is a direct engagement in the immediate situation and an often humorous recognition of its distance from the desired condition of innocence. The resulting combination creates a FORM of urban pastoral that qualifies Field's poetry for the "NEW YORK SCHOOL" designation, however alien that designation might seem to the poet himself.

After an unhappy childhood in Lynbrook, on Long Island, New York, and service as an air force navigator in Europe during World War II, Field explored the bohemian circles of Paris and NEW YORK CITY because they promised sexual freedom and expressed the alienation from the social "norm" that he felt personally. O'Hara represented to Field a "new breed" of bohemian who simply accepted society as it was (*The Man* 77). While Field found it difficult to adopt this view of life, a corollary

attitude of self-acceptance freed him from a writing block he had suffered throughout the early 1950s. "You didn't have to put on an act," Field discovered in O'Hara's example. Echoing O'Hara's "PERSONISM," Field elaborates, "a poem could even be what you might say to a friend over the phone" (*The Man* 79). Starting from where he happened to find himself, Field wrote a series of poems reflecting on the view across the Hudson River to New Jersey from an office where he worked every day. Some of these poems are included in *The New American Poetry*, where they connect generically with JOHN ASHBERY's "The Instruction Manual," a similarly wistful response to dreary circumstances. Eventually, the full sequence appeared as the second section, "A View of Jersey," in Field's first collection, *Stand Up, Friend, with Me* (Grove, 1963), published auspiciously as the Lamont Poetry Selection of the Academy of American Poets.

Field's second collection, *Variety Photoplays* (Grove, 1967), contains a group of poems about the movies, a use of popular culture "prefigured" in the New York School, as Field has acknowledged (*The Man* 76) and reviewers have noted (Mazzocco). However, Field's work has developed in a direction that is not only "pop" but "populist" ("Poetry File" 212–218); that is, it is more or less explicitly political in its identification with "the slobs, the misfits, the victims, for whom poetry is an act of rebellion, the secret voice speaking out, however crudely" ("Poetry File" 180). While such identification resembles the stance of the Beat poets, Field has steered clear of the BEATS' style of "preaching" in favor of the quality of "talk" he heard in O'Hara ("Poetry File" 211, 215), a quality that Field strips to such a degree of plainness that M. L. Rosenthal, reviewing *A Full Heart* (Sheep Meadow Press, 1977) for the *New York Times*, refused to regard the work as poetry. In contrast, a group of southern California writers (Gerald Locklin, Charles Stetler, Ron Koertge) found in Field a model of people's poetry to set beside the example of Los Angeles poet Charles Bukowski (1920–94). This reception outside New York gave Field the idea of editing an anthology, *A Geography of Poets* (Bantam, 1979), representing the variety of poetry across the country. Ironically, the *New York Times* reclaimed the anthology for New York in describing its populist premise: "Since the time of the Beats and the New York School of the 1950's, American verse has been dominated by a grass-roots movement" ("Paperbacks" 10).

The West Coast firm Black Sparrow (Bukowski's publisher) has issued Field's most recent collections of poetry: *Counting Myself Lucky: Selected Poems, 1963–1992* (1992) and *A Frieze for a Temple of Love* (1998). With his partner, Neil Derrick, Field has also coauthored several novels, of which *Village* (Avon, 1982; revised edition, *The Villagers,* Painted Leaf Press, 2000) is of particular interest for its portrayal of New York's bohemian headquarters, where Field still resides.

Bibliography

Dickey, James. "Tactics of Shock, Discoveries of Innocence." *New York Times Book Review,* 1 September 1963, 3.

Field, Edward. *After the Fall: Poems Old and New.* Pittsburgh, Pa.: University of Pittsburgh Press, 2007.

———. Interview by David Bergman. *American Poetry Review* (November–December 1991): 30–34.

———. *The Man Who Would Marry Susan Sontag and Other Intimate Portraits of the Bohemian Era.* Madison: University of Wisconsin Press, 2005.

———. "The Poetry File." In *Frieze for a Temple of Love.* Santa Rosa, Calif.: Black Sparrow, 1998, 145–228.

Howard, Richard. "Edward Field." In *Alone with America: Essays on the Art of Poetry in the United States Since 1950.* Enlarged ed. New York: Atheneum, 1980, 143–157.

Locklin, Gerald, and Charles Stetler. "Edward Field, Stand-Up Poet." *Minnesota Review* 9, no. 1 (1969): 63.

Mazzocco, Robert. "Counter-Songs." *New York Review of Books,* 23 November 1967. Available online. URL: http://www.mybooks.com/articles/11898. Accessed December 5, 2008.

"Paperbacks: New and Noteworthy." *New York Times Book Review,* 21 January 1979, 10.

Rosenthal, M. L. "Lyric and Prosaic." *New York Times Book Review,* 14 May 1978, 6.

Schuyler, James. *Just the Thing: Selected Letters, 1951–1991.* Edited by William Corbett. New York: Turtle Point Press, 2004.

film See ART, VISUAL.

First Baby Poems Anne Waldman (1982–1983)

Published in two small-press editions (Rocky Ledge Cottage, 1982; Hyacinth Girls, 1983), the first of ANNE WALDMAN's *First Baby Poems* were composed in 1980, the year of Waldman's marriage to REED BYE and of the birth of their son, Ambrose. In terms of literary history Waldman implies a much earlier conception for her poems by acknowledging or alluding to a range of sources as far back as Ovid. The title of "Song: Time Drawes Neere" quotes Hercules' mother, Alcmena, recalling the difficult birth of her son in the words of George Sandys's TRANSLATION (1632) of Ovid's *Metamorphoses* (ca. 8 C.E.). Waldman interprets motherhood from the mythological perspective that she later elaborated in *IOVIS* (1993, 1997), in which her son serves as her guide on an epic journey.

The role of shape-shifter that Waldman's son also plays in *Iovis* is foreshadowed in the theme of metamorphosis that runs throughout *First Baby Poems.* The theme is grounded in the biological fact that the embryo developing in the womb "recapitulates" earlier forms of life in evolutionary history. The poem "Animals" connects this process with the poet's creation of metaphor, spinning out a series of animal images to depict sensations arising from pregnancy, for instance, "I have a whale's appetite." The same connection confers symbolic significance on the great variety of FORMs exhibited in this collection. Waldman has explained that "Baby's Pantoum," the poem most often noted by reviewers of the volume, "was the first successful formal poem I had ever written" (*Vow* 59). Writing from the infant's point of view, Waldman employs the pantoum's repetitive structure to approximate a consciousness groping its way toward perceptual focus, self-consciousness, and language. The exercise proved to be a learning process for the poet herself. As she later described the experience, "A baby entered a writing world to interpret (translate) form: mind-form, poem-form. And until then the elder 'I' didn't know any of these words or things yet" (*Vow* 106).

While *First Baby Poems* are very much "songs of innocence"—William Blake's songs are another obvious model—they also celebrate the achievement of maturity on the part of the 35-year-old Waldman, who in her earlier work had deliberately suppressed her knowledge of literary history in deference to immediate sensation and who in her life had avoided motherhood in deference to her work as a poet. The ambivalence toward motherhood in the "new" women's movement of the 1970s had been anticipated by Waldman's own mother, who told Waldman at the time of her first marriage in 1966, "I swear if I see you pushing a baby carriage a few months from now, I'll come and shoot you" (*Vow* 210). The riff on the word *baby* in Waldman's early poem "Baby Breakdown" (1970) responds to all of these pressures with an irony that has continued to surface even after the period of *First Baby Poems*. In 1990 Waldman collaborated with the artist Red Grooms on *Triptych: Madonnas and Sons*, in which the "sons" are the writers JACK KEROUAC, William Carlos Williams, and Marianne Moore (*Vow* 325). But by directly confronting her own experience of motherhood in *First Baby Poems*, Waldman developed the ability to treat a potentially "sentimental" subject without ironic defensiveness. As she writes in "December Song,"

> the deficient sentimental
> tongue cries I am emotional / yes.

Bibliography

Waldman, Anne. *Vow to Poetry: Essays, Interviews, Manifestos.* Minneapolis, Minn.: Coffee House Press, 2001.

Five Spot

Originally located at 5 Cooper Square in DOWNTOWN MANHATTAN's East Village, the Five Spot was one of the premiere JAZZ venues of the 1950s and 1960s. The club's proprietors were Iggy and Joe Termini, who took over from their father in the mid-1940s when the club was just another neighborhood dive. It was not until the mid-1950s, when increasing numbers of artists began to frequent the establishment (thanks, in part, to its cheap drinks and free jukebox), that the Five Spot really gained distinction. Painters such as GRACE HARTIGAN, Alfred Leslie, David Smith, WILLEM DE KOONING, and LARRY RIVERS moved into the East Village, followed by such writers as JACK KEROUAC, ALLEN GINSBERG, FRANK O'HARA, and KENNETH KOCH. With the influx of this creative community the bar was able to attract legendary jazz musicians. Thelonious Monk, John Coltrane, Billie Holiday, Charlie Mingus, David Amram, Cecil Taylor, Sonny Rollins, and Ornette Coleman all performed at the original Five Spot in the late '50s and early '60s.

Because the bar could accommodate fewer than 100 people, there were usually long lines to get in. As one of the first art FORMS born in the United States, jazz thrived on much the same excitement that spurred the NEW YORK SCHOOL movements in the visual arts and poetry. It is not surprising, then, that for many of the painters and poets, the MUSIC they heard at the Five Spot had a profound influence on the style and substance of their work. One example is O'Hara's poem "The DAY LADY DIED," written in honor of Holiday and set at the Five Spot.

In some cases, Five Spot musicians entered the social (and collaborative) circles of the painters and poets who came to see them perform. Amram, for instance, would often hang out with the Beat poets. Rivers, a musician as well as a painter, organized some jazz and poetry performances at the Five Spot in the spirit of the BEATS but with a twist of New York School irony. One night Rivers played his saxophone while Koch read from the telephone book.

In 1962 the Five Spot moved around the corner to a larger, more expensive location at 2 St. Mark's Place. It remained there until its closing in the 1970s.

Bibliography

Magee, Michael. "Tribes of New York: Frank O'Hara, Amiri Baraka, and the Poetics of the Five Spot." *Contemporary Literature* 42, no. 4 (Winter 2001): 694–726.

Fizdale, Robert   *See* GOLD, ARTHUR, AND ROBERT FIZDALE.

Floating Bear (1961–1969)

LeRoi Jones (AMIRI BARAKA) and DIANE DI PRIMA began the mimeograph newsletter the *Floating Bear* in 1961 as a quicker, more informal alternative to YŪGEN, which di Prima had helped Jones and his wife, Hettie, produce. Simultaneously, Jones pursued an alternative to his marriage in a love affair with di Prima. In terms of literary affairs, FRANK O'HARA, a "big brother" figure to di Prima (di Prima, "For Frank" 156) and a would-be lover to Jones (di Prima, *Recollections* 220–221), occupied the third point of a triangle. Compared to other NEW YORK SCHOOL poets, O'Hara's "political sense" induced Jones to take him seriously (Gooch 425), while the whimsical spontaneity of the New York School that O'Hara epitomized appealed to di Prima, who named the *Floating Bear* after Winnie-the-Pooh's boat: "Sometimes it's a Boat, and sometimes it's more of an Accident" (di Prima, "Introduction" vii). O'Hara was also attuned to the camp spirit of the DANCE and THEATER worlds that James Waring, Freddie Herko, and Alan Marlowe brought to the *Floating Bear* through their friendship with di Prima, who was married to Marlowe from 1962 to 1969. This spirit, which became more prominent in the newsletter after Jones resigned as coeditor in 1963, even spawned a camp parody, the *Sinking Bear,* based in the arts projects at JUDSON MEMORIAL CHURCH (di Prima, "Introduction" xvi).

The most notorious works published in the *Floating Bear* are a short scenario by Jones depicting a homosexual rape, drafted for his novel-in-progress, *The System of Dante's Hell,* and a satire of Franklin D. Roosevelt by WILLIAM S. BURROUGHS, which later became one of his most popular routines in public readings. Jones and di Prima were charged with violation of federal obscenity laws for mailing the issue in which these pieces appeared together (number 9, June 1961), but the charges were eventually dropped by the grand jury. The most famous, though hardly as scandalous, work by a New York School poet published in the *Floating Bear* is O'Hara's "For the Chinese New Year & for Bill Berkson" (number 15, November 1961). A group of six poems by BILL BERKSON had already appeared in issue number 7 (May 1961), and he later served as guest editor of issue number 36 (January–July 1969), which included a full roster of New York School writers, both first-generation (JOHN ASHBERY, KENNETH KOCH) and second generation (Berkson, MICHAEL BROWNSTEIN, TOM CLARK, CLARK COOLIDGE, LARRY FAGIN, RON PADGETT, DAVID SHAPIRO, ANNE WALDMAN, LEWIS

WARSH). Di Prima, who had moved temporarily to the West Coast, worried that "most of that East Coast poetry didn't seem very relevant," and she assembled issue number 37 (March–July 1969) in a deliberate effort to evoke "a West Coast feeling," primarily BEAT ("Introduction" xviii). The two issues were mailed out together, but their failure to achieve "cross-pollination" (di Prima, *Recollections* 283–284), in the words of one of the West Coast writers represented, Kirby Doyle (1932–2003), was one factor in di Prima's decision to cease publication of the *Floating Bear.* She drew on the backlog of manuscripts for an issue of the Buffalo, New York, magazine *Intrepid* (number 20) that she guest-edited in 1971.

Bibliography

Clay, Steven, and Rodney Phillips. *A Secret Location on the Lower East Side: Adventures in Writing, 1960–1980.* New York: New York Public Library/Granary Books, 1998, 74–75.

di Prima, Diane. "For Frank O'Hara: An Elegy." In *Homage to Frank O'Hara,* edited by Bill Berkson and Joe LeSueur, 156–157. Bolinas, Calif.: Big Sky, 1988.

———. "Introduction." *The Floating Bear.* Reprint, La Jolla, Calif.: Laurence McGilvery, 1973, vii–xviii.

———. *Recollections of My Life As a Woman: The New York Years.* New York: Viking, 2001.

Gooch, Brad. *City Poet: The Life and Times of Frank O'Hara.* New York: Knopf, 1993.

Flow Chart **John Ashbery** (1991)

Even for a poet who has made a specialty of writing long poems, JOHN ASHBERY's *Flow Chart* stands out as especially long: 213 pages in a book all its own. It continues the tradition of the MODERNIST long poem in both theme and FORM—"nothing to check the flow," as W. B. Yeats noted of Ezra Pound's *Cantos* (Yeats xxiv). However, as in earlier long poems of the NEW YORK SCHOOL, such as FRANK O'HARA's *Second Avenue* (1953) or KENNETH KOCH's *When the Sun Tries to Go On* (1953), the experience that propels the length of *Flow Chart* is primarily the experience of writing itself. At the prompting of his friend the artist TREVOR WINKFIELD (who eventually designed the book's cover), Ashbery determined that he would write a page a day for 100 days. A personal symbolic significance was added to this arbitrary procedure by the fact that the 100 days began at the end of the year (1987) that had opened with the death of Ashbery's mother; the end of the 100 days was fixed at Ashbery's 61st birthday, July 28, 1988. These links between mother and son further connect *Flow Chart* to another long poem of the New York School, JAMES SCHUYLER's *A Few Days* (1985), which ends with the death of Schuyler's mother.

Between the dailiness of Schuyler and the dadaism of Koch, Ashbery moves back and forth within a "field of action," as William Carlos Williams defined the poem. The following sentence, for instance, ends in a very different place from where it began: "There is nothing beside the familiar / doormat to get excited about, yet when one goes out in loose weather / the change is akin to choirs singing in a distance nebulous with fear / and love" (7). The subject of *Flow Chart* is neither doormats nor choirs, but rather the mental process of moving through those positions as well as many others. *Flow Chart* is an instance of "The poem of the act of the mind" that Wallace Stevens identified with modern poetry (240). The "flow" is the "stream of consciousness." However, while that technique in modernist FICTION is often discussed as a form of naturalism—getting as close as possible to the way the mind "really" works—Ashbery accepts the artificiality of trying to represent in words a process that is essentially nonverbal. Words segment the continuous stream of consciousness into grammatical units, making of every sentence a "flow chart." As John Shoptaw has observed, the sentence is the measure of *Flow Chart* as much as the line, and both, like the poem as a whole, are very long (303). Ashbery seems to be exposing the artifice of grammar by stretching it out almost to the breaking point. The impression is not merely of flow but of overflow.

Flow Chart is divided into six numbered sections, though this aspect of structure, too, is largely "artificial," Ashbery has said (interview n.p.)— merely a means of reassuring the reader that it is OK to stop reading for a while. Where one resumes reading is equally arbitrary. Skipping 20 pages in the middle is "not going to matter very much," according to Ashbery (interview n.p.); indeed, Shoptaw

discovered that an entire page of the original typescript (reproduced in Shoptaw 373–374) was accidentally omitted when the text was transferred to a computer. Although hints of stories appear and disappear as the text unfolds, there is no continuous narrative nor any clearly discernible climax, whether narrative or thematic. The nearest approximation to a climax is purely formal: Out of the nearly shapeless ebb and flow of the long lines, a double sestina suddenly emerges (186–193), repeating the end words of a poem by Algernon Charles Swinburne (1837–1909). The range of allusion in *Flow Chart*, from literary models to all kinds of the "subliterary," as Helen Vendler defines it (133), creates a linguistic mixture that is Ashbery's trademark. For instance, toward the end of the poem he crosses the famous "To be or not to be" soliloquy from William Shakespeare's *Hamlet* with the name of a children's board game, producing "the snakes and ladders / of outrageous fortune" (211).

The extent to which Ashbery pushes linguistic experimentation in *Flow Chart* has led Fred Moramarco to claim that "*Flow Chart* is surely Ashbery's least accessible book since *The Tennis Court Oath* [1962], although it is also one of his most important" (43). Without denying the importance, John Bayley challenges the claim of difficulty. Whereas Ashbery's early work "still had the exoticism of new device and a new speech," *Flow Chart* seems to employ the accepted common idiom of contemporary poetry (Bayley n.p.). What has changed is not Ashbery's style but the habits of readers, shaped by the persuasive force of Ashbery's example. "To have sounded, in poetry, the standard tones of the age," Bayley concedes, "is no small feat" (n.p.).

Bibliography

Ashbery, John. *Flow Chart*. New York: Knopf, 1991.

———. Interview by Sarah Rothenberg. *Annandale* 131, no. 3 (Spring 1992). Ashbery Resource Center. Available online. URL: http://www.flowchartfoundation.org/arc/home/special_features/annandale. htm. Accessed December 5, 2008.

Bayley, John. "Richly Flows Contingency." *New York Review of Books*, 15 August 1991. Available online. URL: http://www.nybooks.com/articles/3172. Accessed December 5, 2008.

Koch, Kenneth. "When the Sun Tries to Go On." In *Sun Out: Selected Poems, 1952–54*. New York: Knopf, 2002, 71–140.

Moramarco, Fred. "Coming Full Circle: John Ashbery's Later Poetry." In *The Tribe of John: Ashbery and Contemporary Poetry*, edited by Susan M. Schultz, 38–59. Tuscaloosa: University of Alabama Press, 1995.

O'Hara, Frank. "Second Avenue." In *Collected Poems*. Rev. ed. Edited by Donald Allen. Berkeley: University of California Press, 1995, 139–150.

Schuyler, James. "A Few Days." In *Collected Poems*. New York: Noonday/Farrar, Straus & Giroux, 1995, 354–379.

Shoptaw, John. "Anybody's Autobiography: *Flow Chart*." In *On the Outside Looking Out: John Ashbery's Poetry*. Cambridge, Mass.: Harvard University Press, 1994, 301–341.

Smith, Dinitia. "Poem Alone." *New York* 24, no. 20 (May 20, 1991), 46–52.

Stevens, Wallace. "Of Modern Poetry" (1940). In *Collected Poems*. New York: Vintage/Random House, 1990, 239–240.

Vendler, Helen. "A Steely Glitter Chasing Shadows: John Ashbery's *Flow Chart*" (1992). In *Soul Says: On Recent Poetry*. Cambridge, Mass.: Harvard University Press, 1995, 130–140.

Williams, William Carlos. "The Poem as a Field of Action" (1948). In *Selected Essays*. New York: New Directions, 1969, 280–291.

Yeats, William Butler. Introduction to *The Oxford Book of Modern Verse, 1892–1935*. 1936. Reprint, Oxford: Oxford University Press, 1972, v–xlii.

Folder (1953–1956) **and** *A New Folder* (1959)

The first periodical to become identified with the NEW YORK SCHOOL poets, *Folder* was founded by DAISY ALDAN, a poet, actress, and teacher at the School of Art and Design in NEW YORK CITY. Through her connections in the art world she made the acquaintance of both the artists and poets associated with the TIBOR DE NAGY GALLERY, who in turn provided a nucleus of contributors to *Folder*. The first issue (winter 1953) included writing by JOHN ASHBERY, KENNETH KOCH, FRANK O'HARA, and JAMES SCHUYLER, as well as three original silkscreen prints by GRACE HARTIGAN. Under the supervision of Aldan's associate, Floriano Vecchi (1921–2005), printmaking became a vital component of the production of the magazine, complementing Aldan's attention to the visual presentation of text. She chose fine-laid paper and handset the first issue (later issues were set in Linotype) in sans serif Vogue, a style that looked particularly avant-garde to her eye ("Poetry" 100). Pages in 8½-by-11-inch format were left loose (as in the case of prints) or gathered in fascicles (for instance, a group of poems by one author) and then placed together in a folder, hence the magazine's name. Aldan's model for this presentation was Caresse Crosby's *Portfolio* (Aldan, "Daisy Aldan" 272), issued from Paris during the 1940s. *Hanging Loose* magazine adopted the practice during the 1960s, though in that case the implied message was "throw away what you don't want" rather than "suitable for framing." In general, the aesthetic emphasis of *Folder* was markedly different from the pragmatism that drove the small-press movement of the 1960s.

KENWARD ELMSLIE joined the roster of poets in the second issue of *Folder* (1954) and BARBARA GUEST in the third issue (1954–55). O'Hara appeared in all four issues because, Aldan explained, "In those days he was my favorite" ("Daisy Aldan" 276). In addition to poetry, O'Hara's important essay "Nature and New Painting" was published in the third issue of *Folder*. His "Ode to Willem de Kooning" was included in *A New Folder* (1959), a conventionally bound anthology that anticipates DONALD M. ALLEN's presentation of the full range of the avant-garde in *The NEW AMERICAN POETRY, 1945–1960*, though Allen's range does not extend to the visual arts as does Aldan's.

Along with Ashbery, Elmslie, EDWARD FIELD, Guest, Koch and O'Hara, *A New Folder* includes poets whom Allen would classify as BLACK MOUNTAIN POETS (CHARLES OLSON, DENISE LEVERTOV, PAUL BLACKBURN, ROBERT CREELEY, Larry Eigner), SAN FRANCISCO RENAISSANCE (James Broughton, Madeline Gleason), BEAT (JACK KEROUAC, ALLEN GINSBERG, GREGORY [NUNZIO] CORSO), and "other" (LeRoi Jones [AMIRI BARAKA]). As a result of this effort to be representative, there is discord in *A New Folder* that is not sensed in the earlier issues of *Folder*, which for all their variety remain in harmony with the editor's sensibility. Aldan has admitted that she felt the Beats exercised a destructive influence on literature ("Daisy Aldan" 277). One of the contributors to *A New Folder*, Levertov, lumped the Beats together with the New York School in expressing her reservations about the anthology to Robert Duncan: "In all that school—or say, the interlocking schools, New York and Beat—there is a sense of the poets keeping their weather eye on the potential reader—not, as you say 'living within the medium'" (179).

Bibliography

Aldan, Daisy. "Daisy Aldan: An Interview on *Folder.*" In *The Little Magazine in America: A Modern Documentary History,* edited by Elliott Anderson and Mary Kinzie, 262–279. Yonkers, N.Y.: Pushcart Press, 1978.

———. "Poetry and a One-Woman Press." In *The Publish-It-Yourself Handbook: Literary Tradition and How-to,* edited by Bill Henderson, 95–107. Yonkers, N.Y.: Pushcart Book Press, 1973.

Levertov, Denise, and Robert Duncan. *The Letters of Robert Duncan and Denise Levertov.* Edited by Robert J. Bertholf and Albert Gelpi. Stanford, Calif.: Stanford University Press, 2004.

O'Hara, Frank. "Nature and New Painting." In *Standing Still and Walking in New York.* Edited by Donald Allen. San Francisco: Grey Fox, 1983, 41–51.

Ford, Mark (1962–   ) *British poet*

Currently Mark Ford appears to be the United Kingdom's greatest champion of the NEW YORK SCHOOL and particularly of his friend JOHN ASHBERY. Ford wrote his doctoral dissertation on Ashbery's poetry at Oxford University and served as a visiting lecturer at Kyoto University in Japan from 1991 to 1992. He now teaches at University College London as a senior lecturer in the department of English and writes regularly for the *Times Literary Supplement* and *London Review of Books.*

Ford's first collection of poetry, *Landlocked* (Chatto & Windus, 1992), most clearly manifests the influence of FRANK O'HARA and Ashbery, despite the latter's claim that he only detects "echoes" of other poets in the work (Ashbery,

Selected Prose 232). For one, the title poem shows an exuberance comparable to O'Hara's, as the opening lines indicate: "See, no hands! she cried / Sailing down the turnpike." After describing the nature of O'Hara's influence on *Landlocked,* Ian Gregson notes, "But while Ford employs many of O'Hara's tricks to make the poem breathe and bustle, he keeps calling into question its ability to speak authentically or immediately" (22). This differentiation of Ford from O'Hara in fact points out an important connection between Ford's and Ashbery's poetry.

Ford has shown a critical interest not only in Ashbery's poetry but in his prose with his study *Raymond Roussel and the Republic of Dreams* (Faber, 2000), for which Ashbery supplied a foreword (Ashbery, *Selected Prose* 272–276). In the introduction Ford writes that his interest in RAYMOND ROUSSEL was originally incited by Ashbery's essays "Re-establishing Raymond Roussel" (1962; rpt. Ashbery, *Selected Prose* 33–45) and "In Darkest Language" (1967), and thus this book might be said to take up the dissertation Ashbery never finished. As Ford reports, Ashbery's passion for Roussel inspired others associated with the New York School, "such as Harry Mathews, Ron Padgett and Trevor Winkfield, to explore and translate Roussel's work" (introducton xxv). (See MATHEWS, HARRY; PADGETT, RON; and WINKFIELD, TREVOR.)

Ford's second collection of poems, *Soft Sift,* appeared shortly thereafter (Faber, 2001), again with a foreword by Ashbery (Ashbery, *Selected Prose* 291–294). As Helen Vendler remarks in her review, he "has absorbed technical possibilities from Roussel's stylistic obsessions, Ashbery's montages . . . and the insouciance of Frank O'Hara. But nobody could now mistake Ford for any of the writers who have influenced him" ("Fronds" 25). In both of his books of poetry, while Ford has evidently learned from the New York School, he has developed an independent style, especially with his second volume.

Ford has published *John Ashbery in Conversation with Mark Ford* (London: Between the Lines, 2003), a 20,000-word interview. He has also edited two selected editions of O'Hara, *"Why I Am Not a Painter" and Other Poems* (Carcanet, 2003) and *Selected Poems* (Knopf, 2008), and two New York

School anthologies, *The New York Poets* (Carcanet, 2004) and *The New York Poets* II (Carcanet, 2006), the latter coedited by Trevor Winkfield. Both as a poet and an editor, Ford has gained wider acceptance for the New York School in the world of BRITISH POETRY.

Bibliography

Ashbery, John. "In Darkest Language." *New York Times Book Review,* 29 October 1967, 58ff.

———. *Selected Prose.* Edited by Eugene Richie. Ann Arbor: University of Michigan Press, 2004.

Ford, Mark. Introduction to *Raymond Roussel and the Republic of Dreams.* Ithaca, N.Y.: Cornell University Press, 2001, xxi–xxviii.

Gregson, Ian. "Eternal Feminine." *London Review of Books* 15, no. 1 (January 7, 1993), 22.

Vendler, Helen. "'The Circulation of Small Largenesses': Mark Ford and John Ashbery." In *Something We Have That They Don't: British and American Poetic Relations Since 1925,* edited by Steve Clark and Mark Ford, 182–195. Iowa City: University of Iowa Press, 2004.

———. "Fronds and Tendrils." *London Review of Books* 23, no. 23 (November 29, 2001), 25.

form

The statement "Form is never more than an extension of content" became the mantra of the New American Poetry, first published in the 1959 manifesto on "PROJECTIVE VERSE" by CHARLES OLSON (148), who was quoting a letter from ROBERT CREELEY dated June 5, 1950. The underlying concept descends via the modernist precept that "form follows function" and derives ultimately from the romantic concept of "organic form" (Levertov 315); that is, form should grow simultaneously along with content in one inseparable record of experience, for instance, a poem. Form is not to be conceived as something prior to content or as a separate container into which content is forced to fit. The unity of form and content was so important to this doctrine that the Creeley-Olson formulation was itself attacked for implying too much separation in the word *extension.* DENISE LEVERTOV substituted the term *revelation* (Levertov 317). TED BERRIGAN objected: "Form is not an extension of anything.

Form and content are the same thing. Inseparable and interwoven" ("Business" 80).

The NEW YORK SCHOOL solution to the problem of unifying form and content was to reject another set of oppositions, between surface and depth (Koch, *Art* 214). As long as experience was located at some level of depth, whether of subjective consciousness or objective history, a poem that brought that experience to the surface was necessarily removed from the experience itself. For New York School poets, the present fact of the poem, or its "surface," was itself the scene of experience, where the self that mattered was the one coming into being through the act of writing, and history was the succession of immediate moments in which the poem was written or read. (That *or* conceals another opposition that becomes troubling for the New York School.) Although the poets' notion of "surface" was influenced by the mode of painting known as ABSTRACT EXPRESSIONISM (O'Hara, *Collected Poems* 497), their approach to form was not expressionist, as in the romantic tradition, but rather performative, as in ACTION PAINTING, or rhetorical, as in the classical literary tradition. FRANK O'HARA would simply call it "sexy," following the approach to form that he sets forth in "PERSONISM" (1959): "As for measure and other technical apparatus, that's just common sense: if you're going to buy a pair of pants you want them to be tight enough so everyone will want to go to bed with you" (O'Hara, *Collected Poems* 498). Although the tight fight aims at an "organic" effect, O'Hara's view of form is at the same time highly arbitrary. If the desired effect is not achieved, you can always try another pair of pants.

This attitude opened the New York School to a much wider range of forms than the "free verse" that had become the hallmark of modernist innovation. In terms of the war between "closed" and "open" form that raged in AMERICAN POETRY during the 1950s and 1960s (Breslin 62), the New York School was neutral territory that derived much (poetic) profit from trafficking in the weapons of both sides. The early work reviews the history of free verse, from the long run-on lines of Walt Whitman—as in JOHN ASHBERY's "The Instruction Manual" of 1955 (Ashbery, *Mark Ford* 33–34)—to the short, tightly enjambed lines of William Carlos

Williams—as in KENNETH KOCH's, "Sun Out" of 1952 (Koch, *Art* 163). At the same time, W. H. AUDEN's virtuosity in traditional forms was a major inspiration. As Koch recalled, "Auden's *Selected Poems* [1938] was for me a great amusement park, a park of poetic forms to try out" (*Art* 193).

New York School poets have shown special interest in forms that impose strict rules on composition. Some derive from Western tradition: canzone (Ashbery), rondeau (ANNE WALDMAN), sestina (James Cummins and DAVID LEHMAN), sonnet (EDWIN DENBY, Ted Berrigan, ALICE NOTLEY, BERNADETTE MAYER), triolet (O'Hara), and villanelle (MARJORIE WELISH). Some derive from Eastern tradition: haiku (RON PADGETT), pantoum (Ashbery), renga or renku (SANDY BERRIGAN and Pat Nolan), and tanka (PAUL VIOLI). Each of these forms is defined from a New York School perspective in *The Teachers & Writers Handbook of Poetic Forms,* edited by Padgett. Despite their traditional origins, these forms were directed by New York School poets toward avant-garde aims, closely allied to the *procédé* (procedure) of RAYMOND ROUSSEL, the "constraints" of OULIPO, and the "procedural" composition of JOHN CAGE. In all of these cases the application of rules substituted for choices that might have been made by the author (though, of course, the author chose to apply the rules in the first place). Although this sounds like a limitation on freedom—the opposite of "free verse"—the attraction of such methods lay in their potential for expanding the freedom of language. Mental habit tends to direct language into well-worn paths, "The Songs We Know Best," in Ashbery's formulation. Imposing rules that force new combinations of words also forces the mind out of its rut and creates new meanings.

Other forms have permitted New York School poets to arrive at new discoveries more intuitively. The "found poem" is similar to procedural verse insofar as the poet starts with given materials: text "found" in a newspaper, a legal document, another poem, etc. But in the "found poem" no predefined rules determine how (or whether) the material is "cut up" and recombined or "collaged." Ted Berrigan's SONNETS (1964) and JOHN GIORNO's *The AMERICAN BOOK OF THE DEAD* (1964) represent the continuum of possibilities from radical to minimal

rearrangement. A variant of the found poem is the found form, for instance, Ashbery's "100 Multiple Choice Questions," CHARLES NORTH's "Lineups," or Violi's "Index." In found form the poet's intuition is applied in the choice of content used to fill in the form. Still another variant is signaled in the many New York School poems titled "variations," an adaptation of the musical structure of "theme and variations." Such variation may use neither the language nor the form of the original text that supplies the "theme," and the nature of the relationship may be left to the reader to intuit. However, some form of parody is often involved, as in Koch's "Variations on a Theme by William Carlos Williams" (1962) or Ashbery's "Variations, Calypso and Fugue on a Theme of Ella Wheeler Wilcox" (1969).

No dimension of poetic form is left unexplored in New York School poetry. JAMES SCHUYLER has pursued both extremes of line length, very short ("Blue," 1972) and very long ("HYMN TO LIFE," 1974), the former producing the "skinny" poem that has become an important form in the work of Schuyler's successors, such as EILEEN MYLES (Myles 52). Whether long or short, Schuyler's lines break to produce "little jolts of pleasure, . . . surprises," as analyzed by North ("Schuyler's Mighty Line" 116). The traditional pleasure of rhyme at the end of lines has been exploited to great comic effect by Koch, especially as he uses the OTTAVA RIMA stanza in the long narrative poems collected in *SEASONS ON EARTH* (1987). Other stanza forms have helped generate long works, for instance, the 10-line stanza in Ashbery's *Fragment* of 1966 (Ashbery, "Craft Interview" 125) and the four-line stanza (in groups of four) in *Shadow Train* of 1981 (Ashbery, "Imminence" 75–76). To sustain a long series of related works, JIM BRODEY used a three-line stanza (in groups of 10) in his "name" poems (1981–85).

Alternatively, long works such as O'Hara's "Second Avenue" (1953) or Koch's "When the Sun Tries to Go On" (1953) employ stichic form, that is, a continuous succession of lines without stanza divisions, though sometimes with the paragraph or "chapter" divisions familiar in prose. The next step in this direction is the prose poem, a form very popular in the New York School from O'Hara ("Oranges," 1949) to MAXINE CHERNOFF ("Phantom Pain," 1979), but exploited at greatest length in Ashbery's *Three Poems* (1972). Formally, the prose poem offers the sentence rather than the line as the basic unit of composition. Waldman's *Marriage: A Sentence* (2000) builds on this basis both formally and thematically, drawing on the traditional prose-poetry mixture of Japanese *haibun*. An important avant-garde model is Gertrude Stein, whose sentence-based poetics can be traced through the New York School (Mayer, LEWIS WARSH) to LANGUAGE POETRY.

Given the close ties between New York School poetry and visual art, one might have expected more experiment than there has been with visual forms such as those of "shaped" or "concrete" poetry. There are rare attempts to imitate Guillaume Apollinaire's "calligrammes" (O'Hara, "Poem [WHE EWHEE]," 1950) or to explore the emerging visual possibilities of ELECTRONIC POETRY (JACK KIMBALL), but for the most part New York School poets have left visual art to their collaborators in the POEM-PAINTING. On the other hand, the visual dimension of the printed page has been recognized and exploited as an inherent property of the poet's art. As in the case of line length, page layout has been explored at both minimalist (ARAM SAROYAN, CLARK COOLIDGE, LARRY FAGIN) and maximalist (double columns in Ashbery's "Litany") extremes. Olson's "open field" format, in which words are spread over the page at intervals corresponding to patterns of breathing, was adopted with sufficient frequency by New York School poets after 1960 as to constitute a GENRE of its own, evident in O'Hara's "BIOTHERM" (1962), Ted Berrigan's "TAMBOURINE LIFE" (1966), and Notley's *Songs for the Unborn Second Baby* (1979). A similar format distinguishes the late work of BARBARA GUEST, though in this case a more likely model is Stéphane Mallarmé's "*Un Coup de dés*" (A throw of the dice, 1897).

Bibliography

Apollinaire, Guillaume. *Calligrammes: Poems of Peace and War (1913–1916)*. Translated by Ann Hyde Greet. Berkeley: University of California Press, 1980.

Ashbery, John. "Canzone" (1956). In *Some Trees*. 1956. Reprint, New York: Ecco, 1978, 44–46.

———. "Craft Interview with John Ashbery." In *The Craft of Poetry: Interviews from* The New York Quarterly, edited by William Packard, 111–132. Garden City, N.Y.: Doubleday, 1974.

———. *The Double Dream of Spring*. 1970. Reprint, New York: Ecco, 1976.

———. "The Imminence of a Revelation" (1981). In *Acts of Mind: Conversation with Contemporary Poets*, edited by Richard Jackson, 69–76. Tuscaloosa: University of Alabama Press, 1983.

———. "The Instruction Manual" (1955). In *Some Trees*. 1956. Reprint, New York: Ecco, 1978, 14–18.

———. *John Ashbery in Conversation with Mark Ford*. London: Between the Lines, 2003.

———. *Litany* (1978). In *As We Know*. New York: Penguin, 1979, 1–68.

———. *100 Multiple Choice Questions*. 1970. Reprint, New York: Adventures in Poetry, 2001.

———. *Shadow Train*. New York: Penguin, 1981.

———. "The Songs We Know Best." In *A Wave*. New York: Penguin, 1985, 3–5.

———. *Three Poems*. 1972. Reprint, New York: Penguin, 1978.

———. "Variation on a Noel" (1979). In *Ecstatic Occasions, Expedient Forms*, edited by David Lehman, 3–4. 2d. ed. Ann Arbor: University of Michigan Press, 1996.

Berrigan, Sandy, and Pat Nolan. *Red-Haired Woman*. Privately printed, 2003.

Berrigan, Ted. "The Business of Writing Poetry" (1976). In *On the Level Everyday: Selected Talks on Poetry and the Art of Living*. Edited by Joel Lewis. Jersey City, N.J.: Talisman House, 1997, 64–81.

———. *The Sonnets*. New York: Penguin, 2000.

———. *Tambourine Life* (1966). In *The Collected Poems of Ted Berrigan*. Edited by Alice Notley, Anselm Berrigan, and Edmund Berrigan. Berkeley: University of California Press, 2005, 121–150.

Breslin, James E. B. *From Modern to Contemporary: American Poetry, 1945–1965*. Chicago: University of Chicago Press, 1985.

Brodey, Jim. *Heart of the Breath: Poems, 1979–1992*. Edited by Clark Coolidge. West Stockbridge, Mass.: Hard Press, 1996.

Chernoff, Maxine. "Phantom Pain" (1979). In *Ecstatic Occasions, Expedient Forms*, edited by David Lehman, 26. 2d ed. Ann Arbor: University of Michigan Press, 1996.

Cummins, James, and David Lehman. *Jim and Dave Defeat the Masked Man*. Illustrated by Archie Rand.

Brooklyn, N.Y.: Soft Skull, 2006. [A collaborative sequence of sestinas.]

Denby, Edwin. *Mediterranean Cities: Sonnets.* Photographs by Rudolph Burckhardt. New York: Wittenborn, 1956.

Kimball, Jack. "Webpraxis." Available online. URL: http://www.jackkimball.com/.

Koch, Kenneth. *The Art of Poetry: Poems, Parodies, Interviews, Essays, and Other Work.* Ann Arbor: University of Michigan Press, 1996.

———. *The Collected Poems.* New York: Knopf, 2005.

———. *When the Sun Tries to Go On.* In *Sun Out: Selected Poems, 1952–54.* New York: Knopf, 2002, 71–140.

Lehman, David, ed. *Ecstatic Occasions, Expedient Forms: 85 Leading Contemporary Poets Select and Comment on Their Poems.* 2d ed. Ann Arbor: University of Michigan Press, 1996.

Levertov, Denise. "Some Notes on Organic Form" (1965). In *The Poetics of the New American Poetry,* edited by Donald Allen and Warren Tallman, 312–317. New York: Grove, 1973.

Mallarmé, Stéphane. *A Throw of the Dice Will Never Abolish Chance.* Translated by Daisy Aldan. New York: Tiber, 1956.

Mayer, Bernadette. *Sonnets.* New York: Tender Buttons, 1989.

Myles, Eileen. Interview by Edward Foster (1997). In *Poetry and Poetics in a New Millennium,* edited by Edward Foster, 50–63. Jersey City, N.J.: Talisman House, 2000.

North, Charles. "Lineups." In *Ecstatic Occasions, Expedient Forms,* edited by Lehman, 168–170. 2d ed. Ann Arbor: University of Michigan Press, 1996.

———. "Schuyler's Mighty Line (with an Essay Question)" (1990). In *No Other Way: Selected Prose.* Brooklyn, N.Y.: Hanging Loose, 1998, 110–117.

Notley, Alice. *165 Meeting House Lane.* New York: "C" Press, 1971.

———. *Songs for the Unborn Second Baby.* Lenox, Mass.: United Artists, 1979.

O'Hara, Frank. *The Collected Poems.* Rev. ed. Edited by Donald Allen. Berkeley: University of California Press, 1995.

———. "Triolet" (1947). In *Early Writing.* Edited by Donald Allen. Bolinas, Calif.: Grey Fox, 1977, 22.

Olson, Charles. "Projective Verse" (1959). In *The Poetics of the New American Poetry,* edited by Donald Allen

and Warren Tallman, 147–158. New York: Grove, 1973.

Olson, Charles, and Robert Creeley. *The Complete Correspondence.* Vol. 1. Edited by George F. Butterick. Santa Barbara, Calif.: Black Sparrow, 1980.

Padgett, Ron. "Haiku." In *Tulsa Kid.* Calais, Vt.: Z Press, 1979, 66.

———, ed. *The Teachers & Writers Handbook of Poetic Forms.* 2d ed. New York: Teachers & Writers, 2000.

Schuyler, James. *Collected Poems.* New York: Noonday/ Farrar, Straus & Giroux, 1995.

Violi, Paul. "Index" (1982). In *Ecstatic Occasions, Expedient Forms,* edited by David Lehman, 217–218. 2d ed. Ann Arbor: University of Michigan, 1996.

———. "Tanka." In *The Curious Builder.* Brooklyn, N.Y.: Hanging Loose, 1993, 20.

Waldman, Anne. "Rondeau." In *Marriage: A Sentence.* New York: Penguin, 2000.

———. *First Baby Poems.* 2d ed. New York: Hyacinth Girls, 1983, 17.

Welish, Marjorie. "Street Cries" (1991). In *Ecstatic Occasions, Expedient Forms,* edited by David Lehman, 223. 2d ed. Ann Arbor: University of Michigan, 1996.

Forrest-Thomson, Veronica (1947–1975)

Veronica Forrest-Thomson brought early attention to the NEW YORK SCHOOL in Great Britain through her discussion of JOHN ASHBERY and FRANK O'HARA in her essay "Dada, Unrealism, and Contemporary Poetry" (1974) and of Ashbery's *The Tennis Court Oath* (1962) in her book *Poetic Artifice* (1978), published posthumously. In what is probably the first extended critical treatment of Ashbery in Britain, she counts him among "thinking poets" who recognize that the poet must perform "a new and shocking revaluation of all that poetic language has been" and cites as an exemplary "masterpiece," his poem "They Dream Only of America" (*Poetic Artifice* 154). Similarly, in her essay she analyzes his and O'Hara's use, as she sees it, of a dadaist aesthetic, such that the poetry acknowledges its own artifice and thereby undermines a simplistic realism, a quality she would like to see in more contemporary poetry.

Born in Malaya in 1947, Forrest-Thomson was raised in Scotland. She published a chapbook of poems, *Identi-kit* (London: Outposts), in 1967, the same year as JIM BRODEY's pamphlet of the same title. The following year she obtained her B.A. from the University of Liverpool. She went on to Girton College, Cambridge, where she worked with J. H. Prynne (1936–) and Graham Hough (1908–90). In 1970 she privately published *twelve academic questions,* and the next year, poet-judges Edwin Morgan (1920–) and Peter Porter (1929–) selected her first complete collection, *Language Games,* as the second New Poets Award winner (School of English Press, University of Leeds, 1971). That same year she married Jonathan Culler (1944–), the now renowned theorist, and submitted her Ph.D. thesis, "Poetry as Knowledge: The Use of Science by Twentieth-Century Poets." From 1972 to 1974 she worked as a research fellow in English at the University of Leicester. In 1974, now divorced from Culler, she published a pamphlet, *Cordelia or 'A poem should not mean but be'* (Omens Press) and was appointed a lecturer in English at the University of Birmingham. She died on April 26, 1975.

Two collections of her poetry and a volume of criticism have been posthumously published: *On the Periphery* (Street Editions, 1976) and *Collected Poems and Translations* (Allardyce, Barnett, 1990), as well as the aforementioned *Poetic Artifice.* Her own poetry has come to be associated with Language poetics (see LANGUAGE POETRY), which complements her interest in and praise of Ashbery's *The Tennis Court Oath* in particular.

Bibliography

Ashbery, John. "They Dream Only of America." In *The Tennis Court Oath.* Middletown, Conn.: Wesleyan University Press, 1962, 13.

Forrest-Thomson, Veronica. "Dada, Unrealism, and Contemporary Poetry." *Twentieth-Century Studies* 12 (December 1974): 77–93.

———. *Poetic Artifice: A Theory of Twentieth-Century Poetry.* Manchester, U.K.: Manchester University Press, 1978.

Mark, Alison. *Veronica Forrest-Thomson and Language Poetry.* Tavistock, U.K.: Northcote House, 2001.

Tranter, John. ed. "Veronica Forrest-Thomson Feature." *Jacket* 20 (December 2002). Available online. URL: http://jacketmagazine.com/20/index.shtml. Accessed December 18, 2008.

found poem   *See* FORM.

Four Dialogues for Two Voices and Two Pianos Ned Rorem and Frank O'Hara (1954)

Songs for male and female soloists with two-piano accompaniment, *Four Dialogues* was composed in 1954 by NED ROREM (1923–) to lyrics written expressly for that purpose by FRANK O'HARA. Rorem, who rejects the atonality of the postwar musical avant-garde in favor of a neoromantic tonal idiom, conceives of this 20-minute work as "somewhere between concert cantata and staged opera," specifying in the score that it be presented dramatically, with the vocalists, in street clothes, enacting "the old comedy of boy meets girl." The first song, entitled "The Subway," depicts the two principals meeting on a ride from Manhattan to Brooklyn, with the MUSIC alternating, sometimes abruptly, between passages of frenetic, percussive keyboard ostinatos depicting the train's motion, and calmer, more lyrical episodes where the text expresses the characters' growing feelings toward each other. Each section is based on a static tonal field with triadic harmony that lacks traditional diatonic syntax. Rorem takes a more harmonically conservative approach to the second song, "The Airport," employing an overtly theatrical style whose recitative-like opening, as the characters arrive at the airport parking lot, precedes a passionate love duet in slow waltz tempo that highlights the repeated words *fire* and *desire* with flamboyant melismas. A short instrumental interlude featuring florid keyboard figures introduces the third song, "The Apartment." As the voices enter, the continuing figuration provides a flowing accompaniment, but when the couple begin quarrelling, percussive, syncopated dissonances heighten the scene's emotional intensity. At the argument's crucial moment, when the woman declaims "You hateful man!" and her partner responds "I'm going to leave you," Rorem reconfigures O'Hara's linear text to create a series of unaccompanied rapid exchanges that crescendo to a dramatic climax. The poignant final song, "In New York and Spain," finds the former lovers' thoughts turning to each other from afar, with O'Hara's text, originally written in side-by-side columns, rendered as intricately intertwined phrases. Rorem considers the work a "strict sonata" in which the pianists "may consider themselves of equal importance to the singers: the music was created as a Quartet of Dialogues."

Bibliography

Rorem, Ned. *Four Dialogues for Two Voices and Two Pianos*, New York: Boosey & Hawkes, 1969.
———. *War Scenes, Five Songs, Four Dialogues*. Sound recording. PHCD 116. Donald Gramm, bass-baritone; Eugene Istomin, piano. Phoenix, 1991.

Free Man, A Lewis Warsh (1991)

LEWIS WARSH's second novel, *A Free Man*, chronicles the tumultuous love lives of seven working-class New Yorkers: Frank, a depressed cop; his adulterous wife, Gina; Rosemary, a beleaguered lesbian; Irene, the abused wife of Frank's partner; Bienvenido, a troubled young Latina; her drug-addicted boyfriend, Mickey; and Max, an attractive young writer. This ensemble converges around the murder of an elderly woman, an event to which they are all, in some way, connected.

While the text is consistently sidetracked by the personal histories of its protagonists, the primary narrative takes place during the week following the murder. The chapters shift among each character's unique experiences of that time period, and each account sheds light on the interpersonal bonds that reside at the heart of the book. The reader's interest is sustained, not by a desire to identify the killer, but by the depth of Warsh's characters and the ambivalence of their relationships. In fact, the eventual revelation of the murderer is deliberately anticlimactic—even irrelevant—since it fails to satisfy the novel's tacit search for an ultimate explanation of human behavior. Central to this search are the connected themes of marriage, sex, and individual freedom. Instead of using authorial commentary to expound upon these three topics, the author simply highlights their frequent incompatibility within the story, leaving their reconciliation up to the reader.

Like the author's first book, AGNES AND SALLY, *A Free Man* employs a wide variety of intermingled narrative voices, including frequent, parenthetical interjections by unidentified speakers. This selection from chapter 9 demonstrates the polyphonic effect of Warsh's style:

> One became a teacher not because one had any particular attribute that made one a good teacher (or a better teacher than the next person) but because one thought, in a rational way, that it was something one could do. It was a position that commanded—at least in the past—a modicum of respect within the so-called community. "What do you do for a living?" "I'm a teacher." (I'm just doing it for the money.) The teachers drove up each morning (201).

Despite the positive response to Warsh's previous work, *A Free Man* seems to have escaped critical attention. It was published by Sun & Moon, an imprint of the Contemporary Arts Educational Project, a small nonprofit corporation.

Bibliography

Warsh, Lewis. *A Free Man*. Los Angeles: Sun & Moon Press, 1991.

Freilicher, Jane (1924–) *painter*

The paintings of Jane Freilicher, principally landscapes and still lifes, appear calm and unassuming; therefore, it seems paradoxical that Freilicher herself should have inspired highly theatrical responses from the painters and poets who gathered around her during the formative years of the NEW YORK SCHOOL. In RUDY BURCKHARDT's film MOUNTING TENSION (1950), LARRY RIVERS and JOHN ASHBERY have a fistfight in Freilicher's presence (Ashbery ends up with Freilicher). The following year Rivers slit his wrists in despair over losing Freilicher to a real rival (he immediately phoned FRANK O'HARA for help) (Rivers 258–266). O'Hara fantasized about paddling down a jungle river with Freilicher "towards / orange mountains, black taboos, dada!" ("A Terrestrial Cuckoo" [1951]). JAMES SCHUYLER wrote the scenario for another movie, *Presenting Jane* (1952), in which Freilicher walked on water (Myers 136). Inspiring, yet, at the same time restraining such extravagance, "tone and style were set by Jane," according to O'Hara's roommate, Joe LeSueur. "Her subdued, astringent personality kept the others from getting out of hand—no mean accomplishment" (LeSueur 126–127).

Born Jane Niederhoffer in Brooklyn, she acquired the name *Freilicher* from her first husband, who played JAZZ in the same band as Rivers in 1945. Freilicher persuaded Rivers to enter Hans Hofmann's school, where she was already studying painting. Later, Rivers would return the favor by urging Freilicher's inclusion in the roster of artists JOHN BERNARD MYERS was assembling for the TIBOR DE NAGY GALLERY. Before her first exhibit at de Nagy in 1952, Freilicher had been meeting the poets who were also to become identified with the gallery. She lived in the same building on Third Avenue at 16th Street where KENNETH KOCH took up residence after graduating from Harvard University in 1948. Koch let Ashbery stay in his apartment the following summer. When Ashbery and Freilicher met, Koch recalled, "it's as if they'd both been thrown into a swimming pool / Afloat with ironies jokes sensitivities perceptions and sweet swift sophistications" (Koch 24). Ashbery has given an unusually direct account of the correspondence between his poetry and Freilicher's painting as exemplified by a work he purchased in 1954 and reproduced much later on the cover of his collection of art criticism, *Reported Sightings:* "Perhaps I chose the painting-table still life because of my own fondness for a polyphony of clashing styles, from highbred to demotic—in a given poem, musical composition . . . or picture" (Ashbery 22). Freilicher felt that realism offered greater opportunity for such polyphony than the reigning abstraction of the time (Porter 47), because rather than imposing unity through "composition," the realist painter seeks "to leave things as they are" (Schuyler 32) in their individuality.

Critical appreciation of Freilicher became a subgenre of New York School poetry. She was "a poet's painter who may yet become the public's painter," Schuyler remarked hopefully in 1958 (25), but the public's recognition of Freilicher has remained about as limited as its enthusiasm for poetry. TED BERRIGAN's discussion of Freilicher as "Painter to the New York Poets" in 1965 employed the latest poetic techniques, creating a pastiche of unattributed "found" phrases from past reviews, including Schuyler's 1958 statement quoted above. PETER SCHJELDAHL emphasized something new in Freilicher's work in 1971. After a decade of immersion in the natural environment of the HAMPTONS, where she had moved after her marriage to Joseph Hazan in 1957, Freilicher was painting scenes of DOWNTOWN MANHATTAN in the mood of "urban pastoral." VINCENT KATZ has identified the latest development of this mood in "Urban Meditations": "The new paintings are open in a different way than are her 1950s paintings; they are not expressing but meditating, and it seems that what they are meditating on is natural rhythms (including those one finds in urban contexts)" (156).

Bibliography

Ashbery, John. "Jane Freilicher" (1986). In *Reported Sightings: Art Chronicles, 1957–1987*. Cambridge, Mass.: Harvard University Press, 1991, 239–245.

Berrigan, Ted. "Painter to the New York Poets." *Art News* 64, no. 7 (November 1965): 44ff.

Freilicher, Jane, and Alex Katz. "A Dialogue." *Art and Literature* 1 (March 1964): 205–216.

Katz, Vincent. "Urban Meditations." *Art in America* (November 2004): 156–157, 191.

Koch, Kenneth. "A Time Zone." In *One Train*. New York: Knopf, 1994, 22–30.

Lehman, David. *The Last Avant-Garde: The Making of the New York School of Poets*. New York: Doubleday, 1998.

LeSueur, Joe. *Digressions on Some Poems by Frank O'Hara: A Memoir*. New York: Farrar, Straus & Giroux, 2003.

Myers, John Bernard. *Tracking the Marvelous: A Life in the New York Art World*. New York: Random House, 1983.

O'Hara, Frank. *The Collected Poems*. Rev. ed. Edited by Donald Allen. Berkeley: University of California Press, 1995.

Porter, Fairfield. "Jane Freilicher Paints a Picture." *Art News* 55, no. 5 (September 1956): 46ff.

Rivers, Larry, with Arnold Weinstein. *What Did I Do? The Unauthorized Biography*. New York: HarperCollins, 1992.

Schjeldahl, Peter. "Urban Pastorals." *Art News* 69, no. 10 (February 1971): 33ff.

Schuyler, James. *Selected Art Writings.* Edited by Simon Pettet. Santa Rosa, Calif.: Black Sparrow, 1998.

Waldman, Anne. "Edwin Denby Speaking after Seeing a Show by the Artist Jane Freilicher, Spring 1983" (1989). In *In the Room of Never Grieve: New and Selected Poems, 1985–2003.* Minneapolis, Minn.: Coffee House Press, 2003, 61.

French poetry

When they arrived in NEW YORK CITY in the late 1940s, KENNETH KOCH, JOHN ASHBERY, and FRANK O'HARA came to a city that had harbored artists and writers of the French avant-garde during World War II. The notion of the NEW YORK SCHOOL itself arose in relation to a formerly dominant French movement, the "School of Paris." The interaction between poets and painters in the tradition of French modernism became a model for the New York School community, symbolized in PHILIP GUSTON's remark about O'Hara: "He was our Apollinaire" (Gooch 11). Despite the historical fact that Guillaume Apollinaire (1880–1918) and his colleagues had flourished in the early decades of the 20th century, they seemed more contemporary to the New York School poets than the dominant English-language writers of their own day: "Mallarmé, Valéry, Apollinaire, Eluard, Reverdy, French poets are still of our time," declared Koch in "FRESH AIR" (1955) (123).

The contemporary relevance of French modernism was reinforced by publications such as Marcel Raymond's *From Baudelaire to Surrealism* (Wittenborn, Schultz, 1950) and Robert Motherwell's *The Dada Painters and Poets* (Wittenborn, Schultz, 1951). In 1955 Wallace Fowlie published his *Mid-Century French Poets,* which made available poetry by Max Jacob (1876–1944), Saint-John Perse (1887–1975), Robert Desnos (1900–45), and others. Fowlie also evaluated the "legacy of Symbolism" (11), insisting on "the complete freedom of poet," which the New York School poets would put into practice (18).

Their interest in French literature was also fueled by trips to France. Koch, Ashbery, and RON PADGETT all went to France on Fulbright fellow-ships. Koch brought back RAYMOND ROUSSEL's *Nouvelles impressions d'Afrique* (New impressions of Africa; 1932), which he and his friends enthusiastically explored as a model of linguistic experimentation based on arbitrary literary methods. Ashbery lived in France for most of the decade between 1955 and 1965 and developed close friendships with French writers, including his partner, Pierre Martory (1920–98), and two poets associated with the influential journal *Tel Quel* (1960–82), Marcelin Pleynet (1933–) and Denis Roche (1937–). From 1961 to 1962 Ashbery, Koch, HARRY MATHEWS, and JAMES SCHUYLER published the magazine *LOCUS SOLUS,* named after a book by Roussel, out of Lans-en-Vercors, the site of Mathews's country home in France. In 1973 Mathews became the only American member of the French experimental group OULIPO. He still maintains a residence in France and is married to the novelist Marie Chaix (1942–).

French literature provided "other traditions," as Ashbery calls them, and allowed the New York School poets to steer away from the tired conventions of the late 1940s in BRITISH POETRY and AMERICAN POETRY. Charles Baudelaire (1821–67) and Arthur Rimbaud (1854–91) paved the way for experiments with the prose poem in English. Baudelaire's *Les Fleurs du mal* (Flowers of evil; 1857) and *Le Spleen de Paris* (Paris spleen; 1864) placed the city at the heart of poetry, calling for a new type of beauty. Rimbaud's radical redefinition of the self allowed one to stay clear of the "confessional" self-indulgence that became identified with ROBERT LOWELL. Baudelaire, Rimbaud, and, later, Apollinaire showed that nothing was unworthy of becoming the subject of a poem. Apollinaire, who sang 20th-century modernity, provided a model of experimental and lyrical poetry to O'Hara, TED BERRIGAN, Padgett, and others. The moving poetic self and *reportage universel* of Blaise Cendrars (1887–1961), spoken in a strong discursive voice, are echoed in the works of O'Hara, Koch, BILL BERKSON, and Padgett, who masterfully translated his *Complete Poems* (University of California Press, 1992). *The Magnetic Fields* (1920), by André Breton (1896–1966) and Philippe Soupault (1897–1990), and Breton's *Nadja* (1928) became New York School classics. Louis Aragon (1897–1982), Paul

Eluard (1895–1952), Desnos, even Francis Picabia (1879–1953; known principally as a painter) were read, quoted, translated, and saluted, as were the "French Negro Poets" in O'Hara's ode of 1958 (*Collected Poems* 305).

The French writers whom New York School poets seem to be most interested in are writers on the edges of surrealism (see DADA AND SUR-REALISM), whether great predecessors such as Lautréamont (Isidore Ducasse, 1846–70) and Roussel, or contemporaries of the surrealists such as Jacob and Pierre Reverdy (1889–1960). Reverdy's influence is considerable, as O'Hara makes clear in the concluding lines of "A Step Away from Them" (1956): "My heart is in my / pocket. It is Poems by Pierre Reverdy" (*Collected Poems* 258). After Reverdy died in 1960, Ashbery invited Berkson and O'Hara to write a poem for a special memorial issue of the *Mercure de France* (number 1,181, January 1962). The simultane-ous obscurity and simplicity of Reverdy's poetry, the "severity of light" (Padgett, "The Rue de Rennes" 27) in his world and the poetic enigmas his poems offer made a lasting impression on the New York School. In this sense Reverdy is close to Jacob's "enigmaism" (Ashbery, interview 18–19); Jacob's prose poems are akin to dream narra-tives presented in a certain light so as to unveil the elements of the poetic enigma. His humor and irony is also echoed in the work of Koch and Padgett. Jacob's influence grew as TRANSLA-TIONs by Ashbery, MICHAEL BROWNSTEIN, ANDREI CODRESCU, Padgett, and others became available. In 1979 BILL ZAVATSKY's SUN press published Jacob's *The Dice Cup*.

The relationship between French literature and the New York School of poets may be best seen in their compulsive work as translators. Translation even became a collaborative effort when *The Poems of A. O. Barnabooth* by Valéry Larbaud (1881–1957) was translated by Padgett and Zavatsky (Grossman, 1975). *The Random House Book of Twentieth Century French Poetry* (1982), edited by Paul Auster, gives an idea of the range and of the excellence of trans-lations by New York School poets, with examples by Ashbery, Brownstein, Mathews, Padgett, and Zavatsky. The only woman in the anthology, Anne-Marie Albiach (1937–), has been of particular interest to BARBARA GUEST, and Albiach has her-self translated O'Hara.

Michel Deguy (1930–) omitted O'Hara from his anthology *Vingt poètes américains* (Twenty American poets, Gallimard 1980) on the grounds that O'Hara was already well known in France, but Ashbery, Koch, Mathews, and Schuyler were included. The following year a special issue of the magazine *Change* (number 41, March 1981) entitled "L'Espace américain" (The American space) led off a section on the New York School with a long poem by Jacques Darras (1939–), *Notes abruptes sur la poésie de Frank O'Hara* (Quick notes on the poetry of Frank O'Hara), incorporating many excerpts from O'Hara's texts. Translations of Ashbery, PAUL BLACKBURN, CLARK COOLIDGE, Padgett, and Berrigan filled out the rest of the section. The appearance of a complementary section on LANGUAGE POETRY signaled rising interest in that movement among French writers, which increased over the following decade as theory became the principal currency of literary exchange between France and the United States. Particular interest in the New York School has remained in evidence, however, in such maga-zines as *Banana Split* and *L'Oeil de Boeuf* and the online publication *Double Change*.

Bibliography

Ashbery, John. Interview by Olivier Brossard. *L'Oeil de Boeuf* 22 (December 2001): 7–29. Available online. URL: http://www.doublechange.com/issue3/ashbery-odb.pdf. Accessed December 18, 2008.

———. *Other Traditions*. Cambridge, Mass.: Harvard University Press, 2000.

———. *Selected Prose*. Edited by Eugene Richie. Ann Arbor: University of Michigan Press, 2004. [Includes essays on Martory, Reverdy, and Roussel.]

Bennett, Guy, and Béatrice Mousli. *Charting the Here of There: French & American Poetry in Translation in Literary Magazines, 1850–2002*. New York: New York Public Library/Granary Books, 2002.

Fowlie, Wallace. Introduction. *Mid-Century French Poets*. New York: Twayne, 1955, 11–27.

Koch, Kenneth. *The Collected Poems*. New York: Knopf, 2005.

O'Hara, Frank. *The Collected Poems*. Rev. ed. Edited by Donald Allen. Berkeley: University of California Press, 1995.

O'Hara, Frank, and Bill Berkson. "Reverdy" (1961). In *Hymns of St. Bridget and Other Writings.* Woodacre, Calif.: Owl Press, 2001, 41–42.

Padgett, Ron. "Poets and Painters in Paris, 1919–39." *Art News Annual* 34 (1968): 88–95.

———. "The Rue de Rennes." In *The Big Something.* Great Barrington, Mass.: The Figures, 1990, 27.

Perloff, Marjorie. "Traduit de l'américin: French Representations of the New American Poetry." In *Poetic License: Essays on Modernist and Postmodernist Lyric.* Evanston, Ill.: Northwestern University Press, 1990, 53–69.

Sawyer-Lauçanno, Christopher. "*Locus Solus et Socii:* Harry Mathews and John Ashbery." In *The Continual Pilgrimage: American Writers in Paris, 1944–1960.* San Francisco: City Lights, 1992, 233–259.

"Fresh Air" Kenneth Koch (1955)

Written in the same year as ALLEN GINSBERG's *Howl,* KENNETH KOCH's "Fresh Air" exhibits "the same explosion of fearless humor, poetic energy, expansive and unchecked," as Ginsberg himself acknowledged (Koch, "Writing" 182–183). Lacking the obscenity of *Howl* and the exhibitionism of its author, "Fresh Air" made a relatively quiet debut in the little magazine *i.e., the Cambridge Review* (1955). However, after it was reprinted in *The NEW AMERICAN POETRY, 1945–1960* (1960), "Fresh Air" came to symbolize the revolutionary thrust of that anthology. "The great 'Fresh Air,'" LeRoi Jones (AMIRI BARAKA) recalled, "single-handedly demolished the academic poets (even if they couldn't dig it)" (233). At the same time Koch helped establish the distinctive allegiance of the NEW YORK SCHOOL with the avant-garde in the visual arts. He personifies "Fresh Air" as a sexy art student who dispels the "poisonous fumes and clouds" hovering over the poetic establishment. Her influence is more benign than that of Koch's other protagonist, the Strangler, who goes around strangling bad poets, "the students of myth," "the maker of comparisons / between football and life."

An immediate provocation for Koch's satire was an essay by Donald Hall (1928–) that appeared in the 1955 volume of the paperback annual *New World Writing.* "Fresh Air" records Koch's encounter with this article as a "misfor-

tune" that spoils the pleasure of "a fresh spring day." Hall's title, "The New Poetry: Notes on the Past Fifteen Years in America," eventually became mixed up in Koch's memory with the title of a later essay by Stanley Kunitz, "American Poetry's Silver Age" (Koch, interview by Shapiro n.p.). But in "Fresh Air," Koch accurately reflects the charges that were commonly brought against the "academic" poetry that Hall attempts to defend in his essay and would soon canonize as coeditor of the anthology *The New Poets of England and America* (1957).

First was the charge that poets had cashed in their artistic independence for the security of university teaching jobs, the root cause for the "academic" label. "They are trembling in universities, they are bathing the library steps with their spit," writes Koch in "Fresh Air" (he would shortly begin a university teaching career himself). The second charge was the sacrifice of individual voice to the common style of "magazine verse." The anonymous speaker in "Fresh Air" hates the dominant magazines with such a passion that he contemplates criminal action against them, but he hesitates at the thought of ending up in prison "with trial subscriptions / To the *Partisan, Sewanee,* and *Kenyon Review!*" The most serious charge, finally, was the separation of poetry from common speech, a betrayal of the movement that Hall identifies with William Carlos Williams (Hall 246). Williams is among a long list of predecessors that Koch acknowledges in "Fresh Air," but Koch's twist on common speech looks ahead to POP ART. The speech of "Fresh Air" is common but self-consciously mediated through reference to the mass media of comic books. The exclamations "Agh! Biff!" accompany an attack by the Strangler, and "stale pale skunky pentameters" receive comic praise: "the only honest English meter, gloop gloop!" Ginsberg drew a parallel between this line and "the subconscious bloops of the hand grenades" in a draft version of *Howl* (19, 132).

Criticism of "academic" verse was not unique to Koch, nor did it specially mark an avant-garde position. The charges that Hall was attempting to answer could be found in *Time* magazine (Hall 231). The "freshness" of "Fresh Air" lies rather in its transformation of criticism into creativity. By the end of the poem Koch has turned his back on "the hideous fumes" to face the sea, which presents, as it often does in his work, the excitement of limitless possibility: "Hello, sea! good morning, sea! hello, clarity and excitement, you great expanse of green."

Bibliography

Baraka, Amiri. *The Autobiography of LeRoi Jones.* Chicago: Lawrence Hill, 1997.

Ginsberg, Allen. *Howl.* Annotated ed. Edited by Barry Miles. New York: HarperPerennial, 1995.

Hall, Donald. "The New Poetry: Notes on the Past Fifteen Years in America." *New World Writing* 7. New York: New American Library, 1955, 231–247.

Koch, Kenneth. "Fresh Air." In *The Collected Poems.* New York: Knopf, 2005, 122–128.

———. Interview by David Shapiro (1972). *Jacket* 15 (December 2001). Available online. URL: http://jacketmagazine.com/15/koch-shapiro.html. Accessed December 18, 2008.

———. "Writing for the Stage." Interview by Allen Ginsberg (1978). In *The Art of Poetry: Poems, Parodies, Interviews, Essays, and Other Work.* Ann Arbor: University of Michigan Press, 1996, 176–185.

Kunitz, Stanley. "American Poetry's Silver Age." *Harper's* (October 1959), 173–179.

Vernon, John. "Fresh Air: Humor in Contemporary American Poetry." In *Comic Relief: Humor in Contemporary American Poetry,* edited by Sarah Blacher Cohen, 304–323. Urbana: University of Illinois Press, 1978.

Friedman, Ed (1950–)
playwright, performance artist

Ed Friedman holds the record for the longest term (1986–2003) anyone has served as director of the POETRY PROJECT AT ST. MARK'S CHURCH IN-THE-BOWERY, but his contributions to the Project began even earlier, shortly after his arrival in NEW YORK CITY in 1971. The workshop with BERNADETTE MAYER that Friedman enrolled in at the Project was about as far from the academic study of literature, which he had pursued at the University of California, San Diego (UCSD), as New York was from California, Friedman's native state. Out of the workshop Mayer and Friedman assembled

the magazine *Unnatural Acts* (1972–73), in which all work was presented anonymously, as a "collaborative writing experiment" (Kane 200). Soon Friedman was overseeing other FORMs of experimentation in the Poetry Project's Monday night readings series. "Ed Friedman's Monday nights invent performance poetry," notes BOB HOLMAN under the dates 1974–76 in a chronology of the Project (Holman, Contributor's note 648).

Through the concept of performance Friedman takes writing off the page in a variety of ways. His play *Chinoiserie,* performed at The Kitchen in 1978, presents what might be called "background writing," "conceived of as verbal ambience or Muzak" (Friedman, "Total Poetry?" 14). His texts for *The New York Hat Line* (Bozeaux of London, 1979) "were written to be read while a series of hats made by Robert Kushner were being presented by models descending a spiral staircase" (Friedman, "Total Poetry?" 14). Kushner (1949–   ), a college classmate of Friedman's, also designed a production of Friedman's play *The White Snake* (1982) and provided images for their collaborative artist's book, *Away* (Granary Books, 2001). Another UCSD artist, Kim MacConnel (1946–   ), collaborated with Friedman on several projects based on the experience of learning a foreign language, including a set of placemats, *Lingomats* (1980), and an illustrated phrasebook, *La Frontera,* presented both in performance (at the Poetry Project, 1979, and The Kitchen, 1980) and in book format (Helpful Books, 1983).

In two projects originating in 1979, Friedman reconceives the book itself as a performance space. *The Telephone Book* (Telephone / Power Mad Press, 1979) presents direct transcriptions of Friedman's telephone conversations recorded over a period of several weeks. "Is this the end of Personism?" Holman asked in a review, recalling FRANK O'HARA's account of the birth of "PERSONISM" in his realization "that if I wanted to I could use the telephone instead of writing the poem" (499). A second project, *Space Stations,* derives from the example of WILLIAM S. BURROUGHS, who divided the pages of a journal into three columns in order to record shifts of attention that occur during the act of writing. Although Friedman has not published *Space Stations* in its entirety, he credits that journal as the source of most of his published writing since 1979 (Friedman, "Total Poetry?" 15), collected in *Humans Work: Poems 1982–86* (Helpful Books, 1988), *Mao and Matisse* (Hanging Loose, 1995), and *Space Stations: The Funeral Journal* (Jensen/Daniek, 2001).

Bibliography

Friedman, Ed. "How Space Stations Gets Written." *Poetics Journal* 5 (May 1985): 22.

———. "Pure Stealing." *L=A=N=G=U=A=G=E* 1, no. 2 (April 1978): 6–8.

———. Statement on *Away* (2000). Granary Books Web site. Available online. URL: http://www.granarybooks.com/pages.php?which_page=product_view&which_product=61&search=Away&category. Accessed December 18, 2008.

———. "Total Poetry?" *Poetry Project Newsletter* 191 (October–November 2002): 14–15.

Friedman, Ed, and Kim MacConnel. "The Frontiers of Language." *Teachers and Writers* (May–June 1984): 9–10.

Holman, Bob. Contributor's note. In *Out of This World: An Anthology of the St. Mark's Poetry Project, 1966–1991*, edited by Anne Waldman, 647–648. New York: Crown, 1991.

———. Review of *The Telephone Book. L=A=N=G=U=A=G=E* 3, no. 11 (January 1980): 21.

Kane, Daniel. *All Poets Welcome: The Lower East Side Poetry Scene in the 1960s*. Berkeley: University of California Press, 2003.

Nemet-Nejat, Murat. Review of *Mao and Matisse. Big Bridge* 1, no. 5 (n.d.). Available online. URL: http://www.bigbridge.org/issue5/fi_nejat.htm. Accessed December 18, 2008.

O'Hara, Frank. "Personism" (1959). In *The Collected Poems*, Rev. ed. Edited by Donald Allen. Berkeley: University of California Press, 1995, 498–499.

Friedman, Michael (1960–)

Poet, editor, critic, and FICTION writer Michael Friedman was born in New Rochelle, New York. He studied at Columbia University and received his M.A. in English literature from Yale University in 1983 and his J.D. from Duke University in 1986. He is married to Dianne Perry, has two children, and currently resides in Denver, Colorado, where he is a practicing attorney.

Friedman's involvement with the NEW YORK SCHOOL includes studying with KENNETH KOCH at Columbia and interviewing RON PADGETT for the campus arts journal, *Upstart*, which Friedman coedited. He includes TIM DLUGOS and LARRY FAGIN as two important early mentors and counts the work of Padgett, Fagin, Dlugos, JOE BRAINARD, DAVID SHAPIRO, JOHN ASHBERY, Bob Perelman, Stephen Rodefer, CLARK COOLIDGE, Kit Robinson, and TED BERRIGAN as particularly influential. Friedman also credits Geoff Young, editor-publisher of the small press The Figures, which published two chapbooks of his prose poems, a broadside, and his full-length collection *Species*. In 1986 Friedman cofounded *Shiny* with Padgett, Fagin, and EILEEN MYLES, a literary journal that he continues to edit.

Shiny, in Friedman's own words, tracks an influential group of poetry innovators, especially those who have emerged out of the NEW YORK SCHOOL of poets and, in particular, its second generation. Friedman writes that, "the focus of the magazine has been both on New York School poets and certain Language poets (see LANGUAGE POETRY), as well as the cross-fertilization between the two groups evident in the work of subsequent generations. Some of the poets featured in the magazine qualify as both New York School poets and Language poets; and certain others featured in the magazine are both associated with the New York School and regarded as precursors of Language poetry" (Questionnaire Response). *Shiny* has received grants from the New York State Council on the Arts and the Fund for Poetry, as well as a Merit Award from the Society of Publication Designers.

Friedman has published a number of collections of his poetry, including *Celluloid City* (with drawings by Jim Ringley; Potato Clock Editions, 2003), *Species* (The Figures, 2000), *Arts & Letters* (with drawings by Duncan Hannah; The Figures, 1996), *Cameo* (The Figures 1994), *Special Capacity* (Intermezzo Press, 1992), and *Distinctive Belt* (Mary House, 1985). His work has been anthologized in *Great American Prose Poems: From Poe to the Present* (Scribner, 2003), *The Blind See Only This World: Poems for John Wieners* (Granary Books/PRESSED

WAFER, 2000), and *Writing from the New Coast* (O-BLEK, 1993). His first book of fiction, the comic novella *Martian Dawn,* was published in 2006 by Turtle Point Press.

Friedman was a member of the board of directors of the POETRY PROJECT AT ST. MARK'S CHURCH IN-THE-BOWERY in Manhattan from 1990 to 1995 and the board president from 1993 to 1995. He has taught a writing workshop at NAROPA University and given a talk in 1998 on Coolidge, Rodefer, JACKSON MAC LOW, and HARRY MATHEWS as part of the Museum of American Poetics' American Poet Greats lecture series in Boulder, Colorado.

Bibliography

Friedman, Michael. American Poet Greats lecture. 20 January 1998. Museum of American Poetics. Video recording. Available online. URL: http://www.poetspath.com/apg/apgls97_98.html. Accessed December 5, 2008.

———. Questionnaire response for *Encyclopedia of the New York School Poets.* 21 February 2006.

Fuck You: A Magazine of the Arts
(1962–1965)

Deliberately shocking and subversively satirical, *Fuck You: A Magazine of the Arts* was published in mimeograph by ED SANDERS from various locations on Manhattan's Lower East Side. In it, Sanders published many poets, including FRANK O'HARA, LeRoi Jones (AMIRI BARAKA), DENISE LEVERTOV, and ALLEN GINSBERG. Beyond serving as an outlet for poetry, however, *Fuck You* challenged the limits of free speech in NEW YORK CITY at a time of conservative cultural norms regarding language, sexuality, political philosophy, and morality.

Starting in the basement office of Dorothy Day's *Catholic Worker,* Sanders, a Greek studies student at New York University, published a combination of stenciled artwork and typewritten poems in the magazine. Alongside the featured work of his friends, Sanders added editorial commentary about the political issues he celebrated: pacifism, unilateral disarmament, civil disobedience, and sexual liberation, for example. Sanders reported on events such as protests and arrests, some of them related to the distribution of the magazine itself.

He also promoted venues like CAFÉ LE METRO, where many poets performed. In 1965, when *Fuck You* announced the formation of Sanders's folk-rock band, The FUGS, the magazine marked the promotion of both poetry and MUSIC as collective experiences, anticipating the early performances at the POETRY PROJECT AT ST. MARK'S CHURCH IN-THE-BOWERY, as well as the 1970s and 1980s rock bands formed by poets JIM CARROLL, PATTI SMITH, JOHN GIORNO, and others.

When Sanders opened his PEACE EYE BOOKSTORE in 1965 he distributed *Fuck You* there alongside other alternative press books, magazines, and pamphlets. In January 1965, he was arrested at the bookstore on obscenity charges. The arrest was part of a broader neighborhood crackdown by the police. The New York Civil Liberties Union represented Sanders but advised him not to release any more issues of *Fuck You.* KENNETH KOCH and JOHN ASHBERY testified on Sanders's behalf at the trial.

Sanders won the case in summer 1967, but largely because he was busy with the Fugs, he never published another issue. *Fuck You,* however, had served its purpose: It recorded a catalog of the community's members and activities and created a mystique and mythology for the poets it published and the neighborhood it described.

Bibliography

Kane, Daniel. *All Poets Welcome: The Lower East Side Poetry Scene in the 1960s.* Berkeley: University of California Press, 2003, 64–79.

Sanders, Ed. Statement in *A Secret Location on the Lower East Side: Adventures in Writing, 1960–1980,* by Steven Clay and Rodney Phillips, 167. New York: New York Public Library/Granary Books, 1998.

Fugs, The (1964–   )

Along with his friend Tuli Kupferberg, ED SANDERS started the folk-rock band the Fugs in 1964. Growing out of the "HAPPENINGS" common then in NEW YORK CITY's Lower East Side community, The Fugs began with Sanders and Kupferberg writing songs by the dozens, inspired by influences ranging from Alfred Jarry's early absurdist play *Ubu Roi* (1896) to the songs of the Civil Rights movement.

The band's name derived from Norman Mailer's 1948 war novel, *The Naked and the Dead,* in which "fug" and "fugging" substituted for then-unprintable profanities in the soldiers' dialogue.

The Fugs performed at the opening of the PEACE EYE BOOKSTORE in February 1965 and began recording their first album that April. In addition to Sanders (percussion, vocals, guitar) and Kupferberg (percussion, vocals), John Anderson played bass, and Vinny Leary, guitar.

In fall 1965 The Fugs traveled as part of an antiwar protest tour, with a lineup now consisting of Sanders, Kupferberg, Steve Weber on guitar, and Ken Weaver on drums. They shared the bill with ALLEN GINSBERG, Country Joe and the Fish, and Frank Zappa and the Mothers of Invention. Late in 1965 Verve/Folkways released the group's first album, *The Village Fugs—Ballads and Songs of Contemporary Protest, Points of View and General Dissatisfaction.*

Through 1966 The Fugs performed frequently at such venues as the Cafe au Go-Go on Greenwich Village's Bleecker Street and the Astor Street Playhouse and even appeared on several television shows. Controversy followed them: Coca-Cola threatened suit over their song "Coca Cola Douche," and fire and building inspectors' worries over rumors of flag burnings forced them to leave their Astor Place Playhouse engagement after four months. One of their shows did involve setting a "Lower East Side" scenery flat on fire, an event distorted in press reports. Personnel changes continued, with the band hiring new guitarist Pete Kearney and keyboardist Lee Crabtree.

The Fugs' second album appeared in March 1966, with liner notes by Ginsberg, and reached number 89 on the album charts. That summer The Fugs began a long-term relationship with the Players Theatre on MacDougal Street, where they would play several hundred times. They befriended Jimi Hendrix and Zappa and attracted such admirers as Richard Burton, Tennessee Williams, and Leonard Bernstein.

In winter 1966–67 The Fugs—now Sanders, Weaver, Kupferberg, Crabtree, and Jake Jacobs (guitar, vocals)—recorded tracks for Atlantic Records (not released) but then moved to Reprise, which issued *Tenderness Junction* and *It Crawled into My Hand, Honest* in 1968 with a new line-up includ-ing, variously, Kenny Pine (guitar, vocals), James Jarvis (bass), Charles Larkey (bass), and Danny Kortchmar (guitar). In October 1967 Sanders and The Fugs led an infamous "exorcism" of the Pentagon, creating images that would come to represent the 1960s protest movement.

Over the years since the 1960s Fugs members have occasionally reconvened for special projects and reunions, including performances at the Bottom Line, the 1985 album *No More Slavery,* and the 1987 opera *Star Peace,* produced at Syracuse Stage in Syracuse, New York, and at the Oslo International Poetry Festival and recorded for Denmark's Olufsen Records and France's New Rose label. They headlined the Real Woodstock Festival in August 1994 before touring Europe and played at the memorial tribute to Ginsberg in 1998. The Fugs continue to convene annually to play.

Bibliography

The Fugs Web site. Available online. URL: http://www. thefugs.com.

Fyman, Cliff (1954–   )

After studying at NAROPA INSTITUTE in 1977, Cliff Fyman returned to DOWNTOWN MANHATTAN, where he was born, and became a vital presence in the reading and publishing community that centered on the POETRY PROJECT AT ST. MARK'S CHURCH IN-THE-BOWERY. His poems, performances, and visual art reveal the inspiration of BEAT, BLACK MOUNTAIN, and NEW YORK SCHOOL models but are also rooted in Hebrew texts, Japanese pen and brush work, and his committed social conscience.

Raised in Queens, he received elementary and secondary education in orthodox yeshivas. While he was studying at Hebrew University in Jerusalem, the Yom Kippur War broke out (October 1973), and he spent three wartime months as a civilian volunteer. After returning to NEW YORK CITY and eventually dropping out of college, he gravitated with a friend to Berkeley, California. At the first San Francisco Poetry Festival, in fall 1976, he heard ANNE WALDMAN read and describe the start of the Jack Kerouac School of Disembodied Poetics. The following March he took a Greyhound bus to Boulder, Colorado, where he studied at Naropa Institute with ALLEN GINSBERG, DICK GALLUP, and Waldman. Strongly drawn to the work of Gary Snyder (1930–), he also traveled in Japan. He was inspired by the model of Lew Welch (1926–71) to write poems about his own experience driving a taxi in New York City and has continued to inspect and dramatize his own working life in his later work as busboy and bartender at the Algonquin Hotel and as a waiter at Sardi's Restaurant.

At the Poetry Project in the late 1970s he attended workshops led by HARRIS SCHIFF, MICHAEL BROWNSTEIN, and, later, BERNADETTE MAYER, and met MICHAEL SCHOLNICK, who published Fyman's first book, *Stormy Heaven*, in 1981 under the Misty Terrace imprint (reviewed by EILEEN MYLES as "Mimeo Opus" in the *Poetry Project Newsletter*, no. 89, March 1982). While continuing to write poetry,

in the late '70s and '80s he studied full time for three years at the Art Students League.

Fyman is an excellent performer of his own work, and his appearances are always highlights of the Poetry Project's New Year's benefits, where he has recited his poems while juggling flaming torches. One of his poems was also included on the recording *Sugar, Alcohol and Meat* (Giorno Poetry Systems, 1981). The thoughtful and outspoken political content of his poems can be seen in his contributions to *Poems for the Nation* (Seven Stories Press, 2000) and in his moving antiwar poems. He continues to paint, draw in pencil, conte crayon, and pen and ink, and his "23 Ink Brush Sketches" are included in the Berg Collection of the New York Public Library. Recent collections of his poems are *Nylon Sunlight* (Nylon Sunlight Press, 2004) and *FEVER* (Nylon Sunlight Press, 2006).

G

Gallup, Dick (1942–)

Part of the group jokingly referred to as the TULSA SCHOOL, Dick Gallup was born in Greenfield, Massachusetts. In 1952 he moved to Tulsa, Oklahoma, and in the late 1950s became close friends with RON PADGETT and JOE BRAINARD, with whom he helped produce The WHITE DOVE REVIEW, an art and literary magazine. In its five issues the magazine published ALLEN GINSBERG, JACK KEROUAC, ROBERT CREELEY, LeRoi Jones (AMIRI BARAKA), and others. Through his friendship with Padgett and Brainard, Gallup met the poet TED BERRIGAN who was then a graduate student at the University of Tulsa. All four of them moved to NEW YORK CITY in the early 1960s and became part of the second generation of the NEW YORK SCHOOL of poets, befriending ANNE WALDMAN, LEWIS WARSH, TOM CLARK, MICHAEL BROWNSTEIN, BERNADETTE MAYER, and ALICE NOTLEY.

Gallup's publisher, Coffee House Press, describes his poetry as "simultaneously elegant and goofy." He navigates the terrain between the personal and the political, seamlessly moving from evocations of everyday objects and situations to larger historical and literary ideas. During the late 1960s and early 1970s, Gallup published widely and collaborated with Brainard on the covers of his books and on other multimedia artifacts. Then, for a period of nearly 20 years Gallup stopped publishing and, for all intents and purposes, disappeared from the poetry scene, though he still appeared as a presence in the work of poets

such as JOHN ASHBERY and CLARK COOLIDGE. He reemerged when Coffee House Press brought out his new and selected poetry in 2001.

In addition to being the author of Shiny Pencils at the Edge of Things: New and Selected Poems (Coffee House Press, 2001), Gallup also has written and published a number of books, including Above the Tree Line (BIG SKY, 1976), The Wacking of the Fruit Trees: A Poem in 13 Parts (Toothpaste Press, 1975), Where I Hang My Hat (Harper & Row, 1970), The Bingo (1966), and Hinges (C Press, 1965). He has taught at the POETRY PROJECT AT ST. MARK'S CHURCH IN-THE-BOWERY, the Boulder Public Library, and at the NAROPA INSTITUTE. His work has been anthologized in American Poetry Since 1970: Up Late, edited by ANDREI CODRESCU; Out of This World: An Anthology of the St. Mark's Poetry Project, 1966–1991, edited by Waldman; and The Best American Poetry 1997, edited by James Tate. Gallup currently resides in San Francisco.

Bibliography

Coffee House Press Web site. Available online. URL: http://www.coffeehousepress.org/shinypencils.asp.

General Returns from One Place to Another, The Frank O'Hara (1964)

Poetry forms the absent center of FRANK O'HARA's The General Returns from One Place to Another, a play written in prose, about the length of one act but divided into 21 scenes. The unnamed title character, based on General Douglas MacArthur

(1880–1964), detests poetry because it is useless, as he explains in a central scene where he has wandered unaccountably into a field of useless but beautiful flowers (O'Hara 202). Yet, the General's wandering throughout the play, among various Far Eastern locales that recall the region of MacArthur's wartime triumphs, is a sign of his own uselessness at a time when "there isn't even a war on" (188). The condition of poetry seems to pursue the General as relentlessly as does the wealthy traveler, Mrs. Forbes, who falls in love with him. At the end of the play, he dies at her feet in another field of flowers, an ironic fulfillment of his perpetual desire to "return."

The historical General MacArthur famously declared "I shall return" after fleeing from the Philippine Islands in the face of Japanese invasion at the beginning of World War II. He had the satisfaction not only of returning to the Philippines but of presiding over the Japanese surrender in Tokyo Bay in 1945, a ceremony that O'Hara witnessed as a crewman on a navy destroyer. O'Hara's biographer Brad Gooch speculates that MacArthur's imperial airs on this occasion marked him as an object for O'Hara's satire (88–89); other critics have generalized O'Hara's concern to include an indictment of American imperialism in the Far East (Perloff 169; Bottoms 81), a timely topic in 1964 on the eve of the Vietnam War. However, the play lacks the satiric edge that would be required to fulfill either of these tasks. Joe LeSueur, O'Hara's former roommate and a shrewd drama critic, observes that *The General Returns* is "too good-natured, too low-keyed" to have "the bite of real satire," nor does it try for laughs "in the manner of a farce" (LeSueur xvi). Although O'Hara claimed Bertolt Brecht as his model (Perloff 216 note 2), the mood he creates is closer to that of Strindberg. When the General wonders, "If it is true that the lily springs from the dung heap" (O'Hara 202), he is returning to a central image of August Strindberg's *A Dream Play* (1902).

Before its initial publication in *Art and Literature* (number 10, 1965), *The General Returns* was produced in March 1964 "at a makeshift East Village venue called the Writers' Stage Theatre" (Bottoms 81). Jerry Benjamin directed, JOE BRAINARD designed the sets and costumes, and TAYLOR MEAD played the role of the General. The production of *The Baptism* by LeRoi Jones (AMIRI BARAKA) on the same bill diverted the attention of reviewers, since Jones had just made headlines with the racially charged *Dutchman*, which began an extended run at the Cherry Lane Theatre at the same time. However, Mead's performance in both plays at the Writers' Stage drew special notice, and he received an Obie (the Off-Broadway theater award sponsored by the *Village Voice*) for his role in *The General Returns*. Susan Sontag, writing in the *New York Review of Books*, judged him to be "more varied, and even more captivating" in O'Hara's play (157–158). Mead's gift for improvisation, and for what Sontag called "somnambulistic concentration," seemed perfectly suited to O'Hara's deconstruction of the hero (157–158). "Rather than a role, this part is more like a set of charades," Sontag observed (157–158). Mead has criticized Jones, and racial politics, for the collapse of plans to move *The General Returns* and *The Baptism* "to a really good off-Broadway theater" (Mead quoted in Gooch 417). However, in 2002, once again at an East Village venue (The Modern Arts), under the direction of Amy Wallin, Mead revived the role of the General on a double bill with Michael McClure's *Spider Rabbit* (1971).

Bibliography

Bottoms, Stephen J. *Playing Underground: A Critical History of the 1960s Off-Off-Broadway Movement.* Ann Arbor: University of Michigan Press, 2004.

Gooch, Brad. *City Poet: The Life and Times of Frank O'Hara.* New York: Knopf, 1993.

LeSueur, Joe. Introduction to *Amorous Nightmares of Delay: Selected Plays*, by Frank O'Hara. Baltimore, Md.: Johns Hopkins University Press, 1997, xv–xxv.

O'Hara, Frank. *The General Returns from One Place to Another.* In *Amorous Nightmares of Delay: Selected Plays.* Baltimore, Md.: Johns Hopkins University Press, 1997, 187–217.

Perloff, Marjorie. *Frank O'Hara: Poet Among Painters.* 1977. Reprint, Chicago: University of Chicago Press, 1998.

Sontag, Susan. "Going to the Theater, etc." (1964). In *Against Interpretation and Other Essays.* New York: Dell/Delta, 1966, 140–162.

Genghis Chan: Private Eye John Yau (1987–)

In the sequence of poems entitled *Genghis Chan: Private Eye*, JOHN YAU investigates the instability of personal identity. The identity of the sequence itself is not fixed by time or location. It has evolved through installments published in various collections since the first poem appeared in an issue of *Sulfur* magazine (number 19, 1987) and later in JOHN ASHBERY's selection of *The Best American Poetry 1988*. There is no single edition of the entire series, which now numbers 30 poems. Stylistically the series has evolved from surrealistic narrative—"I was floating through a cross section / with my dusty wine glass, when she entered" ("Genghis Chan" I)—to minimalist word play—"shoo war / torn talk" ("Genghis Chan" XXX). At each pole, however, identity is unstable: the "I" is "floating," the "talk" is "torn."

Since the title conflates two stereotypes of Asian identity, the warrior Genghis (Chinggis) Khan and the Hollywood movie detective Charlie Chan, critics tend to read the sequence for evidence of Yau's construction of his own identity as a Chinese American. In a controversial review of Yau's *Forbidden Entries*, Marjorie Perloff, citing the "Genghis Chan" poems in particular, judged such construction to be inauthentic, an attempt on Yau's part to position himself as a leader of the new Asian-American literature rather than a follower of the NEW YORK SCHOOL, specifically, "Yau's mentor John Ashbery" (39). Responding to such critique, Juliana Chang argues that "the schema of in/authenticity is irrelevant to Yau's thinking on racial and cultural difference" because "Yau presents the U.S.-Asian as always already reproduced in the media and mass culture, and the psyche of the Asian American subject as to some extent part of this reproduction" (Chang 227). This is why, Chang reasons, the "Genghis Chan" poems appear in *Forbidden Entries* in a section entitled "Hollywood Asians," along with another group of poems based on Peter Lorre's role as Mr. Moto.

Reading the "Genghis Chan" sequence as an instance of media critique rather than identity POLITICS reinforces the continuity between this sequence and Yau's New York School origins. Popular culture, and the movies in particular, have always played an important role in the imagery of the New York School, although for Yau such imagery no longer conveys the air of innocence that it did, for instance, for FRANK O'HARA. Yau and O'Hara are much closer in their mutual engagement with the imagery of visual art, which has mounted its own critique of popular culture with increasing acerbity during the years that Yau has chronicled as an art critic following O'Hara's death.

Of special relevance is the art of Ed Paschke (1939–2004), who produced 18 etchings for a limited edition of the first 20 "Genghis Chan" poems published by the Art Institute of Chicago in 1997. In a 1983 review of Paschke's work, Yau had proposed that "what Paschke seems to be saying is that our egos, so attuned to being persuaded, if not instructed, by mass media, can no longer see for themselves" ("How We Live" 66). Indeed, one's self becomes the most difficult object to see, as Paschke suggested in an image multiplied throughout his work, the completely bandaged masklike face of the "Invisible Man," from the Hollywood movie of that title (1933). A version of that face appears on the head of a serpent in the etching that accompanies "Genghis Chan" VIII, which echoes the theme of invisibility:

> Had I been as visible as a chameleon
> I would have crossed my eyes
> so as to look more like you
> than your silver reflection—

Presumably this is a reflection on the "silver screen" of the movie THEATER (Zhou 86). The confrontational stance of this passage, a stance Yau admires in Paschke ("Ed Paschke" 144; "The Self" 113), counters the desire for passive reflection with a demand for active engagement on the part of the reader/viewer. In the cultural condition in which Yau has implicated us, every identity, not just that of the Asian American, is at risk. Against the imagery of mass media, Yau enlists the "private eye" to restore the self to visibility.

Bibliography

Chang, Juliana. Review of *Forbidden Entries*. MELUS 23, no. 3 (Fall 1998): 226–228.

Perloff, Marjorie. Review of *Forbidden Entries*. *Boston Review* 22, no. 3 (Summer 1997): 39–41.

Yau, John. "Ed Paschke." *Artforum* 25, no. 9 (May 1987): 144.

———. *Genghis Chan: Private Eye.* Etchings by Ed Paschke. Chicago: Art Institute of Chicago/Landfall Press, 1997.

———. "Genghis Chan: Private Eye" I–VII. In *Radiant Silhouette: New and Selected Work, 1974–1988.* Santa Rosa, Calif.: Black Sparrow, 1989, 189–195.

———. "Genghis Chan: Private Eye" VIII–XX. In *Edificio Sayonara.* Santa Rosa, Calif.: Black Sparrow, 1992, 73–87.

———. "Genghis Chan: Private Eye" XXI–XXVIII. In *Forbidden Entries.* Santa Rosa, Calif.: Black Sparrow, 1996, 92–106.

———. "Genghis Chan: Private Eye" XXIX–XXX. In *Borrowed Love Poems.* New York: Penguin, 2002, 37–38.

———. "How We Live: The Paintings of Robert Birmelin, Eric Fischl, and Ed Paschke." *Artforum* 26, no. 8 (April 1983): 60–67.

———. "The Self as Subject, the Subjected Self: The Paintings of Ed Paschke." In *Ed Paschke*, by Neal Benezra. New York: Hudson Hills Press; Chicago: Art Institute of Chicago, 1990, 107–113.

Zhou, Xiaojing. "Postmodernism and Subversive Parody: John Yau's 'Genghis Chan: Private Eye.'" *College Literature* 31, no. 1 (Winter 2004): 73–102.

genre

NEW YORK SCHOOL poets have opposed the shrinking of the poetic field to the genre of the short lyric, which became the paradigm of "academic" verse, as opponents described it, in the years following World War II. On the other hand, New York School poets have not subscribed to the programmatic rejection of lyric voice that came to define LANGUAGE POETRY in the 1980s. The personal "I" may be as provisional as the relationship described in love poetry, a traditional subgenre of lyric that FRANK O'HARA and KENNETH KOCH notably brought up to date (Berkson 149). O'Hara's *Love Poems (Tentative Title)* (1965) signals provisionality in its title. Koch's love poems of the 1970s, in *The Art of Love* (1975) and *The Burning Mystery of Anna in 1951* (1979), establish an elegiac mood, though no one mood can represent the variety of this genre in the New York School (as

evidenced in the works of BARBARA GUEST, TED BERRIGAN, JAMES SCHUYLER, CHARLES NORTH, MAUREEN OWEN, LORENZO THOMAS, EILEEN MYLES, LEE ANN BROWN). As a separate subgenre of lyric, elegy performs its traditional function of responding to death, with O'Hara again leading the way in modernizing his "Four Little Elegies" (1955) for the movie actor James Dean (*Collected Poems* 248–252). Elegies for O'Hara, after his tragic death in 1966, became a distinct subset of this subgenre (Perloff 183–190). Later elegies continued to mark specific deaths, for instance, Berrigan's in 1983 (ALICE NOTLEY, "At Night the States," 1985; *Grave* 153–162) and his daughter Kate's in 1987 (Notley, "Beginning with a Stain," 1987; *Grave* 174–183), or mourned the passing of an entire generation (ANNE WALDMAN, "In the Room of Never Grieve," 2003).

Elegy is important to the New York School lyric for what Barbara Guest calls its "musicality," a matter of tone or, literally, sound. And, "'How you sound??' is what we recent fellows are up to," wrote LeRoi Jones (AMIRI BARAKA) in *The NEW AMERICAN POETRY, 1945–1960* (1960; 424), including O'Hara among the "young wizards" whose influence was already spreading. At the enthusiastic urging of Jones and others, African-American blues helped to "bend," like a blue note, O'Hara's sound ("THE DAY LADY DIED," 1959; *Collected Poems* 325) and the lyric poetry that followed (Waldman, Thomas). Still, New York School writers acknowledged the musical foundation of lyric by preserving classical genre designations such as "ode" (O'Hara, RON PADGETT), which means "song," or "eclogue" (JOHN ASHBERY, O'Hara), the dramatic framework for songs attributed to shepherds in pastoral. Pastoral may seem the most unlikely of the lyric modes for New York School poets to adopt, given their status as city poets; however, the poet's removal from the actual conditions of country life has always provided pastoral with an artificial frame, through which New York School poets have viewed the rural settings important to them, such as eastern Long Island (Schuyler), New England (WILLIAM CORBETT), or California (TOM CLARK). Moreover, acknowledging the artificiality of pastoral has made it possible to transfer some of the attitudes typical of the genre onto the urban scene, as in O'Hara's

"Poem (It was snowing)" (1960; *Collected Poems* 382–383), originally titled "A Little Elegy (A Little Pastoral Too)." The resulting "urban pastoral" has received much attention in critical studies of the New York School (Clark, Joseph Conte, Terence Diggory, Timothy Gray, Helen Vendler, Ann Vickery). It has distinctly American antecedents, most immediately in the poetry of William Carlos Williams.

In the work of Williams and his fellow modernists Ezra Pound and T. S. Eliot, the genre of epic poetry, traditionally deemed the superior alternative to lyric, had devolved into the "modernist long poem" (Altieri), essentially a sequence of lyrics strung together on very thin narrative thread. This development continued in the SERIAL POEM, a term imported to the New York School from the SAN FRANCISCO RENAISSANCE. A characteristic New York School twist on the serial poem produced the diary or journal poem (LEWIS WARSH, Corbett, BERNADETTE MAYER), in which the only link among the accumulated fragments is the fact that they were observed in chronological sequence by the recording poet. An influential model was provided by O'Hara's "I do this I do that" poems, as he calls them in "Getting Up Ahead of Someone (Sun)" (1959; *Collected Poems* 341). Especially in the journal poems of the second-generation New York School, the function assumed by the "I," that of documenting impressions rather than expressing feelings, provides a measure of the difference between this genre and traditional lyric as well as contemporary "confessional" poetry, identified with ROBERT LOWELL. At the same time, the "flatness" of the journal sequence, the implication that no one incident is more important than any other, distinguishes it from traditional narrative. However, New York School poets have also experimented with epic narrative both in its mock or comic FORM (Koch, SEASONS ON EARTH, 1987) and in the pattern of myth (Notley, THE DESCENT OF ALETTE, 1992). Mockery assumes the pattern of satire in such poems as Koch's "FRESH AIR" (1955).

Generally wary of theory, New York School poets have never developed a theory of genre, but the practice of genres held a special fascination for Berrigan and contributed to his role in promoting the notion that a New York School might actually exist. For instance, while O'Hara applied the title "Personal Poem" only once (1959; *Collected Poems* 335–336), as a description rather than a genre designation, Berrigan elevated that type of poem to the status of a genre by applying the title as many as nine times (if his system of numbering can be trusted). O'Hara's "I do this I do that" poem was further generalized by Berrigan into the "Things to Do" poem, another phrase that Berrigan repeated in titles, though in this case the specific title originated with Gary Snyder rather than O'Hara (Fagin, "Things to Do" 85–86). On the concrete level, literally, the "walk poem" is a variant of the "things to do" poem much favored by New York School writers as a medium for urban experience (Padgett, Philip Lopate, Roger Gilbert). More abstractly, the "things to do" poem can be subsumed under the broader category of the "list poem," another New York School favorite (LARRY FAGIN, Waldman). Fagin wrote a "things to do" poem under the title "Occasional Poem," a traditional genre commemorating an important occasion in the life of a community. In an essay much valued by O'Hara (Gooch 187), PAUL GOODMAN had proposed occasional poetry as the genre of the contemporary avant-garde in its task of restoring community to alienated society (376).

The occasional poem occupies a special position as a genre because it bridges art and life. New York School poets expanded the range of literature by adopting genres that belonged to ordinary life or to the realm of popular culture, somewhere between ordinary life and "high art." In Corbett's *Columbus Square Journal* (1975), the entry for November 27, 1974, is a simple list of subjects represented in postcards, copied from a magazine that Corbett had picked up that day at a postcard exhibition (Corbett, "Journal Poetics" 281). Postcards appealed to New York School poets both as a genre of ordinary life and as a formal constraint, imposing a tight frame on both word and image. Ashbery composed visual collages on postcards in the early 1970s. Berrigan wrote a series of poems on postcards (A CERTAIN SLANT OF SUNLIGHT, 1988), forming a journal of the last months of his life. With Wallace Stevens's "A Postcard from the Volcano" (1936) somewhere in the "high art" background, postcards feature in

O'Hara's poem "A Postcard from John Ashbery" (1951; *Collected Poems* 56–57), Koch's short story "The Postcard Collection" (1964), and KENWARD ELMSLIE's play *Postcards on Parade* (1993). One of Elmslie's characters has a crush on Roy Rogers, the subject of his favorite postcard and, of course, a hero of another popular genre, the Hollywood western. Through a process that involves both gender- and genre-bending, New York School writers transform the western into another version of pastoral, from O'Hara's "Red Rydler" comics with JOE BRAINARD (ca. 1964) through Berrigan's collage novel CLEAR THE RANGE (1977) to Coolidge's sequence of poems *Far Out West* (2001).

Bibliography

Altieri, Charles. "Ashbery as Love Poet." In *The Tribe of John: Ashbery and Contemporary Poetry,* edited by Susan M. Schultz, 26–37. Tuscaloosa: University of Alabama Press, 1995.

———. "Motives in Metaphor: John Ashbery and the Modernist Long Poem." *Genre* 11 (1978): 653–687.

Ashbery, John. "Eclogue" (1953). In *Some Trees.* 1956. Reprint, New York: Ecco, 1978, 12–13.

———. "Postcard Collages." *The Sienese Shredder* 1 (Winter 2006–07): 137–146.

Berkson, Bill. Interview by John Gruen. In *The Party's Over Now: Reminiscences of the Fifties,* by John Gruen. Wainscott, N.Y.: Pushcart Press, 1989, 148–152.

Berrigan, Ted. *A Certain Slant of Sunlight* (1988). In *The Collected Poems of Ted Berrigan.* Edited by Alice Notley, Anselm Berrigan, and Edmund Berrigan. Berkeley: University of California Press, 2005, 565–616.

———. *Clear the Range.* New York: Adventures in Poetry/ Coach House South, 1977.

———. *The Collected Poems of Ted Berrigan.* Edited by Alice Notley, Anselm Berrigan, and Edmund Berrigan. Berkeley: University of California Press, 2005.

Brown, Lee Ann. "Love." In *Polyverse.* Los Angeles: Sun & Moon, 1999, 38–39.

Clark, Tom. *Cold Spring: A Diary.* Austin, Tex.: Skanky Possum, 2000.

———. "The Lyric" (1991). In *Light and Shade: New and Selected Poems.* Minneapolis, Minn.: Coffee House Press, 2006, 209.

———. "Schuyler's Idylls: Notes and Reflections on the *Collected Poems.*" *American Poetry Review* (May–June 1994): 7–13.

Conte, Joseph. "Predetermined Form: John Ashbery, the Pastoral and the Urbane." In *Unending Design: The Forms of Postmodern Poetry.* Ithaca, N.Y.: Cornell University Press, 1991, 169–185.

Coolidge, Clark. *Far Out West.* New York: Adventures in Poetry, 2001.

Corbett, William. *Columbus Square Journal* (1975). In *New and Selected Poems.* Cambridge, Mass.: Zoland, 1995, 59–117.

———. "Journal Poetics." In *All Prose: Selected Essays and Reviews.* Cambridge, Mass.: Zoland, 2001, 279–285.

———. *Runaway Pond* (1981). In *New and Selected Poems.* Cambridge, Mass.: Zoland, 1995, 121–152.

Diggory, Terence. "'Picturesque' Urban Pastoral in Post-War New York City." In *The Built Surface 2: Architecture and Pictures from Romanticism to the Millennium,* edited by Christy Anderson and Karen Koehler, 283–303. Aldershot, U.K.: Ashgate, 2002.

Fagin, Larry. "Occasional Poem" (1967), including reproduction of broadside designed by George Schneeman. In *Painter Among Poets: The Collaborative Art of George Schneeman,* edited by Ron Padgett, 109. New York: Granary Books, 2004.

———. "Things to Do." In *The List Poem: A Guide to Teaching and Writing Catalog Verse.* 1991. Reprint, New York: Teachers & Writers, 2000, 85–90.

———. "Thirty Girls I'd Like to Fuck" (1968). In *The World Anthology: Poems from the St. Mark's Poetry Project,* edited by Anne Waldman, 29–30. Indianapolis: Bobbs-Merrill, 1969.

Gilbert, Roger. *Walks in the World: Representation and Experience in Modern American Poetry.* Princeton, N.J.: Princeton University Press, 1991.

Gooch, Brad. *City Poet: The Life and Times of Frank O'Hara.* New York: Knopf, 1993.

Goodman, Paul. "Advance Guard Writing in America, 1900–1950." *Kenyon Review* 13, no. 3 (Summer 1951): 357–380.

Gray, Timothy. "New Windows on New York: The Urban Pastoral Vision of James Schuyler and Jane Freilicher." *Genre* 33, no. 2 (Summer 2000): 171–198.

Guest, Barbara. *Musicality.* Illustrated by June Felter. Berkeley, Calif.: Kelsey St. Press, 1988.

———. "Parachutes, My Love, Would Carry Us Higher" (1960). In *Poems: The Locations of Thing/Archaics/ The Open Skies.* New York: Doubleday, 1962, 27.

Jones, LeRoi. "'How You Sound??'" In *The New American Poetry, 1945–1960,* edited by Donald Allen, 424–425.

1960. Reprint, Berkeley: University of California Press, 1999.

Koch, Kenneth. "Fresh Air." In *The Collected Poems*. New York: Knopf, 2005, 122–128.

———. "The Postcard Collection" (1964). In *The Collected Fiction*. Edited by Jordan Davis, Karen Koch, and Ron Padgett. Minneapolis, Minn.: Coffee House Press, 2005, 13–39.

———. *Seasons on Earth*. New York: Penguin, 1987.

Lopate, Phillip. "The Pen on Foot: The Literature of Walking Around." *Parnassus: Poetry in Review* 18, no. 2/19, no. 1 (1993): 176–212.

Magee, Michael. "Tribes of New York: Frank O'Hara, Amiri Baraka, and the Poetics of the Five Spot." *Contemporary Literature* 42, no. 4 (2001): 694–726.

Mayer, Bernadette. *Midwinter Day*. 1982. Reprint, New York: New Directions, 1999.

Myles, Eileen. "Warrior." In *Maxfield Parrish: Early and New Poems*. Santa Rosa, Calif.: Black Sparrow, 1995, 117.

North, Charles. "From the French" (1977). In *New and Selected Poems*. Los Angeles: Sun & Moon Press, 1999, 42.

Notley, Alice. *The Descent of Alette*. 1992. Reprint, New York: Penguin, 1996.

———. *Grave of Light: New and Selected Poems, 1970–2005*. Middletown, Conn.: Wesleyan University Press, 2006.

O'Hara, Frank. *The Collected Poems*. Rev. ed. Edited by Donald Allen. Berkeley: University of California Press, 1995.

———. Five "Eclogues." In *Amorous Nightmares of Delay: Selected Plays*. Baltimore, Md.: Johns Hopkins University Press, 1997, 75–94, 155–161.

———. *Odes*. New York: Tiber Press, 1960.

O'Hara, Frank, and Joe Brainard. "Red Rydler and Dog" (ca. 1964). In *In Memory of My Feelings: Frank O'Hara and American Art*, by Russell Ferguson. Exhibit catalog. Los Angeles: Museum of Contemporary Art; Berkeley: University of California Press, 1999, 107.

Owen, Maureen. "'Wanting You'" (1977). In *American Rush: Selected Poems*. Jersey City, N.J.: Talisman House, 1998, 61.

Padgett, Ron. Five "Odes." In *Great Balls of Fire*. 1969. Reprint, Minneapolis, Minn.: Coffee House Press, 1990, 50–54.

———. "Walk Poem." In *The Teachers & Writers Handbook of Poetic Forms*. 2d ed. New York: Teachers & Writers, 2000, 200–206.

Perloff, Marjorie. *Frank O'Hara: Poet Among Painters*. 1977. Reprint, Chicago: University of Chicago Press, 1998.

Schuyler, James. "June 30, 1974"–"December 28, 1974." In *Collected Poems*. New York: Noonday/Farrar, Straus & Giroux, 1995, 228–234.

———. "Loving You." In *Collected Poems*. New York: Noonday/Farrar, Straus & Giroux, 1995, 120–136.

Stevens, Wallace. "A Postcard from the Volcano" (1936). In *Collected Poems*. New York: Vintage/Random House, 1990, 158–159.

Thomas, Lorenzo. "Guilt" (1979). In *American Poetry Since 1979: Up Late*, edited by Andrei Codrescu, 152–153. New York: Four Walls Eight Windows, 1987.

———. "South St. Blues" (1963). In *Dancing on Main Street*. Minneapolis, Minn.: Coffee House Press, 2004, 12–13.

Vendler, Helen, "New York Pastoral: James Schuyler." In *Soul Says: On Recent Poetry*. Cambridge, Mass.: Harvard University Press, 1995, 62–70.

Vickery, Ann. "'A Mobile Fiction': Barbara Guest and Modern Pastoral." *TriQuarterly* 116 (Fall 2003): 245–260.

Waldman, Anne. "Blues Cadet." In *Journals and Dreams*. New York: Stonehill, 1976, 75–76.

———. "In the Room of Never Grieve" (2003). In *In the Room of Never Grieve: New and Selected Poems, 1985–2003*. Minneapolis, Minn.: Coffee House Press, 2003, 323–389.

———. "Thirty Guys I'm Glad I Didn't Fuck" (1978). *Caveman* (January 30, 1979): n.p.

Warsh, Lewis. "New York Diary 1967." In *Nice to See You: Homage to Ted Berrigan*, edited by Anne Waldman, 63–67. Minneapolis, Minn.: Coffee House Press, 1991.

Welish, Marjorie. "The Lyric Lately." *Jacket* 10 (October 1999). Available online. URL: http://jacketmagazine.com/10/welish-on-guest.html. Accessed December 5, 2008.

George Washington Crossing the Delaware

The motif of George Washington Crossing the Delaware plays a complicated role in the relation of NEW YORK SCHOOL poets and painters to avant-garde art and American culture. Based on a historical event in December 1776 during the New Jersey campaign of the Revolutionary War, the motif received its iconic treatment in visual art in a large canvas by Emanuel Leutze (1851; De Salvo and Schimmel 23), presently housed in the collection of the Metropolitan Museum of Art in NEW YORK CITY. By the mid-20th century this image had acquired a currency in popular culture that made it a natural subject for POP ART, a development already evident in early paintings by Roy Lichtenstein, for instance, *George Washington Crossing the Delaware II* (ca. 1951; De Salvo and Schimmel 83). However, pop was not yet recognized as a movement during the 1950s, and when LARRY RIVERS painted his version of *Washington Crossing the Delaware* in 1953 (De Salvo and Schimmel 18), it was viewed as a deliberate challenge to the movement then dominant, ABSTRACT EXPRESSIONISM (Rivers, "Larry Rivers" 111–113). Although Rivers employed the gestural brushwork of abstract expressionism, he challenged abstraction by depicting recognizable figures, and he challenged expressionism by presenting his figures in conventional "heroic" poses that could not meet the contemporary standard of "authenticity." The purchase of Rivers's painting by the Museum of Modern Art, also in New York, seemed, however, to recognize an underlying allegiance to modernism, and when Rivers painted a second version in 1960—fearful that the museum might not be able to restore the original version from damage sustained in a fire—he went even further in the direction of abstraction (Harrison 70).

The relevance of the George Washington theme to the contemporary avant-garde is clearly evident in the responses of Rivers's poet friends, FRANK O'HARA and KENNETH KOCH. O'Hara's poem "On Seeing Larry Rivers' *Washington Crossing the Delaware* at the Museum of Modern Art" (1953) celebrates the painting as a revival of "revolutionary" desire capable of burning up "theoretical considerations and / the jealous spiritualities of the abstract," including, presumably, the "theoretical considerations" that dictated abstraction as the only acceptable mode of avant-garde painting. In contrast, O'Hara ascribes to Rivers a kind of realism that is true to the complexity and the fluidity of feelings rather than a fixed position or identity. "Dear father of our country," as O'Hara invokes George Washington, "so alive / you must have lied incessantly to be / immediate." While turning on its head the legend of Washington's inability to tell a

lie, this view takes seriously Washington's formative role in American national identity. "See how free we are! as a nation of persons," O'Hara exclaims. In the abstract terms that the poem permits itself, the goal of Washington's crossing the river of "history" appears to be "freedom," "a shore / other than that the bridge reaches for," as O'Hara concludes in a wry allusion to Upper Manhattan's George Washington Bridge.

Freedom is also a core value in KENNETH KOCH's play *George Washington Crossing the Delaware* (1962), though Koch's mockery of abstract language makes the word *freedom* appear to be just that, a word. Dispelling any pretense of "natural" speech, Koch has one of Washington's soldiers expound: "The method of our struggle exemplifies its end—freedom for every man from the English" (Koch 24). The flatness of such language was nicely complemented by the flat "cut-out" figures that ALEX KATZ designed for the professional production of the play in 1962 (Sandler 35). However, Koch originally wrote the play to be performed at the school of Rivers's son Steven (Rivers, *What Did I Do?* 313), which provides a clue to the level at which freedom operates genuinely for Koch. It is the freedom of the imagination, often identified in Koch's work with the unspoiled imagination of the CHILD. The central episode in the play is a dream sequence in which Washington recalls the childhood incident of the cherry tree, leading, by Koch's playful logic, to the idea of tricking the British by crossing the Delaware. Rivers claimed that the main inspiration for his painting was "the patriotic grade school plays I sat through or participated in," which he "never took . . . seriously" but nevertheless "enjoyed" (Rivers, *What Did I Do?* 312). This is the spirit of enjoyment to which the critic Bonnie Marranca was responding when she called Koch's *George Washington* "a first-rate play in the American theatrical cartoon style" (Marranca 6).

Bibliography

Davidson, Michael. "Ekphrasis and the Postmodern Painter Poem." *Journal of Aesthetics and Art Criticism* 42 (1983): 69–79.

De Salvo, Donna, and Paul Schimmel. *Hand-Painted Pop: American Art in Transition 1955–62*. Exhibit catalog. Los Angeles: Museum of Contemporary Art; New York: Rizzoli, 1992.

Harrison, Helen A. *Larry Rivers*. New York: Harper & Row, 1984.

Koch, Kenneth. *George Washington Crossing the Delaware.* In *The Gold Standard: A Book of Plays*. New York: Knopf, 1998, 19–38.

Marranca, Bonnie. "Kenneth Koch." In *American Playwrights: A Critical Survey*. Vol. 1. New York: Drama Book Specialists, 1981, 3–14.

O'Hara, Frank. "On Seeing Larry Rivers' *Washington Crossing the Delaware* at the Museum of Modern Art." In *The Collected Poems*. Rev. ed. Edited by Donald Allen. Berkeley: University of California Press, 1995, 233–234.

Rivers, Larry. "Larry Rivers: 'Why I Paint as I Do'" (1959). In *Art Chronicles, 1954–1966*, by Frank O'Hara, 106–120. Rev. ed. New York: Braziller, 1990.

Rivers, Larry, with Arnold Weinstein. *What Did I Do? The Unauthorized Biography*. New York: HarperCollins, 1992.

Sandler, Irving. *Alex Katz*. New York: Abrams, 1979.

Gerstler, Amy (1956–)

A West Coast inheritor of the NEW YORK SCHOOL of poets, Amy Gerstler transports their postmodernist spirit of experimentation, irreverence, sensuality, and subversion to a new locale and to her own unique sensibility. Gerstler was born in San Diego and studied psychology at Pitzer College near Los Angeles. She now lives with her husband in the Los Angeles neighborhood of Eagle Rock and teaches at the Art Center, College of Design, in Pasadena. One of the central Los Angeles postmodernists, Gerstler works at the intersection of poetry, art, and film, just as members of the New York School did before her.

Gerstler has commented that she is particularly drawn to American films because their titles "seem to present the funny, irrepressible melodramatics of American English in a nutshell—our language with its distinctive mixture of slang and preachiness, the elevated and the silly" ("What Is American" n.p.). She has also spoken of being influenced by comic books, the thesaurus, recipes, and old science textbooks "where people try to explain the world, but they explain it wrong" (interview n.p.). Gerstler's poems subversively plumb the bottomless gulfs just below the seemingly placid surface of our culture: the haunting presences of separation, loss, grief, bitterness, greed, lust, illness, and death, things that "are dark, in the head" (interview n.p.). As Amy Robbins was first to note, Gerstler also provides vivid "portrayals of women" and of homophobia, childhood sexuality, and gendered power relations (Robbins 140). Although Gerstler's work evokes the rhythms of Los Angeles domestic life and cultural productions and has been influenced by the avant-garde BEYOND BAROQUE movement centered in the Venice section of Los Angeles, Gerstler downplays the impact that location makes. She does not see "much difference between one place or the other" except that NEW YORK CITY has more of a concentrated poetry "scene," whereas in Los Angeles the scenes are more spread out, providing a sense of "privacy" in which to do one's work (interview n.p.).

In Gerstler's first major volume, *The TRUE BRIDE* (Lapis Press, 1986), the poems and prose poems echo fairy tales, radio shows, Hollywood cinema, popular songs, and such diverse cultural figures as Henry Wadsworth Longfellow, Patsy Cline, and Boy George. But when a Gerstler text looks "under the spreading chestnut tree," it finds a "dismembered maiden" rather than a village smithy (*True Bride* 55). When a Gerstler heroine announces, "I fall to pieces" (*True Bride* 17), she does not mean it in a good way. Echoing the title of *The True Bride,* the poem "Marriage," included by JOHN ASHBERY among *The Best American Poetry of 1988,* is one of several poems collected in Gerstler's second volume, *Bitter Angel* (North Point Press, 1990), that focus on the failures and pains of sexuality. "A Love Poem," for example, ends: "Me zilch, you nada" (*Bitter Angel* 75). This volume also includes unsettling revisions of classic popular texts such as the Nancy Drew and Perry Mason mysteries. Noting Gerstler's penchant for transforming pop imagery, Laurence Goldstein observes that her poems "do not imitate the New York poetry of Frank O'Hara or James Schuyler, surveying Manhattan and describing its minute particulars like latter-day Whitmans. Rather, she internalizes the abundance and converts it to autonomous images fit for enumeration as an imaginary city of words" (728). *Bitter Angel* received the National Book Critics Circle Award for poetry in 1990 and was reissued in 1997 by Carnegie Mellon Press.

Nerve Storm (Penguin, 1993) and *Crown of Weeds* (Penguin, 1997) continue Gerstler's project of spinning popular culture, folklore, factitious science, and bent autobiography into a textual world that is by turns witty, enjoyable, and disturbing. *Medicine* (Penguin, 2000) is even more extravagant, bringing to the fore a multitude of odd voices and subject positions and an elusive play of language. "Scorched Cinderella," for example, is spoken by the heroine's stepsisters in tones that oscillate between sadistic resentment—"It's getting harder / to slap her awake every day"—and a guidebook's solicitude—"but she's still worth a detour, / if you happen to be passing through" (*Medicine* 180). In *Ghost Girl* (Penguin, 2004), Gerstler again deploys a variety of popular idioms and verbal obsessions to riff on our contemporary "Circus of Perversity" (*Ghost Girl* 38).

Bibliography

Ashbery, John, ed. *The Best American Poetry of 1988.* New York: Collier, 1988.

Axelrod, Rise B., and Steven Gould Axelrod. "Amy Gerstler's Rhetoric of Marriage." *Twentieth Century Literature* 50, no. 1 (Spring 2004): 88–105.

Birkerts, Sven. "Prose sic." *Parnassus* 15 (1989): 163–184.

Gerstler, Amy. "Contributor's Note." In *Out of this World: An Anthology of the St. Mark's Poetry Project, 1966–1991,* edited by Anne Waldman, 642. New York: Crown, 1991.

———. Interview. *Ignition* 1. Formerly available online. URL: http://www.ignitionmag.net/issue1/agi.html.

———. "What Is American about American Poetry?" Poetry Society of America website. Available online. URL: http://www.poetrysociety.org/gerstler.html.

Goldstein, Laurence. "Looking for Authenticity in Los Angeles." *Michigan Quarterly Review* 30 (1991): 717–731.

Robbins, Amy Moorman. "Amy Gerstler." In *Contemporary American Women Poets: An A-to-Z Guide,* edited by Catherine Cucinella, 138–141. Westport, Conn.: Greenwood Press, 2002.

Ginsberg, Allen (1926–1997)

Allen Ginsberg grew up in William Carlos Williams's Paterson, New Jersey, and spent much of his life in FRANK O'HARA's NEW YORK CITY. In a letter of 1950 that appears in Williams's *Paterson,* book 4 (1951), Ginsberg informs the older poet that he has "inherited" his experience of the city (Williams 173), just as he was to write to O'Hara, in the memorial poem "City Midnight Junk Strains" (1966), "I see New York thru your eyes" (Ginsberg, *Collected Poems* 467). Both Ginsberg and O'Hara are, in this sense, New York poets, but Ginsberg is properly identified with the BEATS rather than the NEW YORK SCHOOL as a group. His beatness is manifested in the sympathetic imagination that informed his reading of both Williams and O'Hara and found expression in a tremendous generosity toward everyone he met. That generosity made it possible for the New York School poets to benefit from the fame that Ginsberg acquired early as the author of *Howl* (1955). In January 1957, shortly after Ginsberg gave him a copy of the book that contains that poem, O'Hara wrote to KENNETH KOCH that Ginsberg was "even moved to mention Ashbery-Koch-O'Hara in his promotion as being part of the 'new' poetry" (Gooch 318). For later poets of the New York School, Ginsberg's dynamic performance style and his genial presence as a resident of the Lower East Side in DOWNTOWN MANHATTAN brought assurance that "the tradition of the new" was still alive.

While studying at Columbia University (B.A., 1948), Ginsberg formed friendships, particularly with WILLIAM S. BURROUGHS and JACK KEROUAC, that became the nucleus of the New York Beats. In 1950 he met GREGORY CORSO, whose work inspired an enthusiasm that Ginsberg eventually shared with O'Hara (Gooch 280). O'Hara's biographer, Brad Gooch, says that Ginsberg and O'Hara met in Boston in 1956 while O'Hara was working with the POETS' THEATRE (318). However, Ginsberg himself has implied an earlier meeting. He credited O'Hara with introducing him to the work of Russian poet Vladimir Mayakovsky, whose "At the Top of My Voice" was one of the texts that inspired Ginsberg to write "Howl" in August 1955 (*Howl* 175). By that time Ginsberg was living in San Francisco, where the first public reading of sections of *Howl* took place at the Six Gallery in September 1955 (*Howl* 165–168). This occasion connected Ginsberg with West Coast Beats such as Michael McClure, Gary Snyder, and PHILIP WHALEN. The attention they attracted as a group established the popular image of the Beat movement as a West Coast phenomenon (Eberhart), especially after a much publicized trial in San Francisco in 1957 attempted—ultimately unsuccessfully—to prevent City Lights Books from distributing *Howl and Other Poems* on the grounds that it would expose children to obscenity (*Howl* 169–174).

Howl has received so much attention as a sociological document that it takes some effort to recover "the beauty of abstract poetry of mind" that Ginsberg emphasized in his 1960 statement published in *The New American Poetry, 1945–1960* (Ginsberg, "Notes" 415). His essay on "Abstraction in Poetry," first published in the journal of the abstract expressionist painters, *It Is* (number 3, winter 1959), cites O'Hara's "Second Avenue" (1953) and Koch's *When the Sun Tries to Go On* (1953) as examples. In turn, Ginsberg's essay provides one of the starting points for O'Hara's discussion of "Personism" (1959). More than either abstraction or Personism, however, the quality most crucial to the dialogue between Ginsberg and the New York School is the "fearless humor" that Ginsberg felt *Howl* shared with "Fresh Air" by Koch (Koch, "Writing for the Stage" 182–183), the poet most noted for his comedy among the first generation of the New York School. In a remarkable journal entry for 1961, Ginsberg recorded a dream in which he and Koch engaged in a "Poetry Tournament." Koch's tactic is to parody Ginsberg "in eloquent funny Dada style." Ginsberg despairs of coming up with "anything that will out-serious his fancy rhetorical gaiety & style & wit & wisdom. Because," Ginsberg explains, "by comparison I seem just hung-up on myself & he seems a vast whitmanic canary" (*Journals* 240).

Ginsberg's obsession with "My Sad Self," as he called it in a 1958 poem dedicated to O'Hara, carried a potential for paranoia that he confronted in extreme form in his mother's mental illness, portrayed in the title poem of *Kaddish* (1961). Fearing that Ginsberg's attraction to Eastern religion might push him further in that direction, O'Hara joked about "Associated Paranoia" as an American institution but warned that the cure was not to be sought in India, where "Allen and Peter" Orlovsky (1933–), Ginsberg's companion, was headed

(O'Hara, *Collected Poems* 399–400). Rather, in accordance with the title of his poem "Vincent and I Inaugurate a Movie Theater" (1961), O'Hara escapes paranoia at the movies, the proper realm of "Fantasy" (1964), the title of another movie-based poem in which O'Hara prescribes a cure for Ginsberg, quite literally: "two aspirins a vitamin C tablet and some baking soda" (*Collected Poems* 488). As it turned out, Ginsberg's travels through the Far East culminated in an acceptance of himself, within the limitations of mortality, rather than a desire to "be cosmic consciousness, immortality" (Ginsberg, interview by Clark 48–49). As expressed in the pivotal poem "The Change: Kyoto-Tokyo Express" (1963), Ginsberg overcomes paranoia by renouncing "the hate I have spent / in denying my image" (*Collected Poems* 328). He accepts the world of images, including "old movies" (*Collected Poems* 327).

This is the point at which the second generation of the New York School started to engage meaningfully with Ginsberg. Before it appeared in Ginsberg's collection *Planet News* (1968), "The Change" was published in Ted Berrigan's "C" magazine, in the same issue (number 9, summer 1964) as O'Hara's "For the Chinese New Year & for Bill Berkson." Ginsberg explained the message of "The Change" to Tom Clark in an interview conducted in England in 1965 and eventually published in *The Paris Review* (number 37, spring 1966). Always a teacher as well as a poet, Ginsberg devoted both his life and his art to delivering a fundamental message against the harmfulness of abstract authority and in favor of "the return of all authority back to person," in the terms he identified with O'Hara (Schjeldahl 143). While the world witnessed Ginsberg's more sensational confrontations with public authority, for instance, during the demonstrations at the Democratic National Convention in Chicago, Illinois, in 1968, the poets were touched by "ordinary Allen . . . the guy flossing his teeth and cooking chicken soup," as Anne Waldman remembered him at Naropa Institute, where they taught together for 22 years (Waldman 260). In the spirit of the New York School, Ginsberg embodied a kind of "dailiness" for the poets who worked with him (for instance, Bob Rosenthal, his secretary for 20 years) or who lived in the same building that Ginsberg and Orlovsky occupied on East 12th Street (the long list of fellow residents includes JIM BRODEY, LARRY FAGIN, JOHN GODFREY, RICHARD HELL, JACK KIMBALL, GARY LENHART, GREG MASTERS, SIMON PETTET, and MICHAEL SCHOLNICK). To Ginsberg's Beat sensibility, however, the Lower East Side was not just a scene of dailiness but a stimulus for meditation on the transience of life, "Charnel Ground" (1992).

Bibliography

Eberhart, Richard. "West Coast Rhythms" (1956). In *Howl, Original Draft Facsimile, Fully Annotated*, edited by Barry Miles, 154–155. New York: HarperPerennial, 1995.

Ginsberg, Allen. "Abstraction in Poetry" (1959). In *Deliberate Prose: Selected Essays, 1952–1995*. Edited by Bill Morgan. New York: HarperCollins, 2000, 243–245.

———. "Allen Ginsberg Talks about Poetry," *New York Times Book Review*, 23 October 1977, pp. 9ff.

———. *Collected Poems, 1947–1997*. New York: HarperCollins, 2006.

———. *Howl, Original Draft Facsimile, Fully Annotated*. Edited by Barry Miles. New York: HarperPerennial, 1995.

———. Interview by Thomas Clark (1965). In *Spontaneous Mind: Selected Interviews, 1958–1996*. Edited by David Carter. New York: HarperCollins, 2001, 17–53.

———. *Journals: Early Fifties, Early Sixties*. Edited by Gordon Ball. New York: Grove, 1977.

———. "Notes for *Howl and Other Poems*" (1959). In *The New American Poetry, 1945–1960*, edited by Donald Allen, 415–418. 1960. Reprint, Berkeley: University of California Press, 1999.

Gooch, Brad. *City Poet: The Life and Times of Frank O'Hara*. New York: Knopf, 1993.

Hartman, Anne. "Confessional Counterpublics in Frank O'Hara and Allen Ginsberg." *Journal of Modern Literature* 28, no. 4 (Summer 2005): 40–56.

Hyde, Lewis, ed. *On the Poetry of Allen Ginsberg*. Ann Arbor: University of Michigan Press, 1984.

Koch, Kenneth. *When the Sun Tries to Go On*. In *Sun Out: Selected Poems, 1952–54*. New York: Knopf, 2002, 71–140.

———. "Writing for the Stage" (1978). Interview by Allen Ginsberg. In *The Art of Poetry: Poems, Parodies, Interviews, Essays, and Other Work*. Ann Arbor: University of Michigan Press, 1996, 176–185.

Morgan, Bill. *I Celebrate Myself: The Somewhat Private Life of Allen Ginsberg*. New York: Viking, 2006.

O'Hara, Frank. *The Collected Poems*. Rev. ed. Edited by Donald Allen. Berkeley: University of California Press, 1995.

Schjeldahl, Peter. "Frank O'Hara: 'He Made Things and People Sacred'" (1966). In *Homage to Frank O'Hara*, edited by Bill Berkson and Joe LeSueur, 139–143. Bolinas, Calif.: Big Sky, 1988.

Shinder, Jason, ed. *The Poem That Changed America: "Howl" Fifty Years Later*. New York: Farrar, Straus & Giroux, 2006.

Waldman, Anne. "Last Days, Hours." In *Vow to Poetry: Essays, Interviews and Manifestos*. Minneapolis, Minn.: Coffee House Press, 2001, 259–264.

Williams, William Carlos. *Paterson*. Edited by Christopher MacGowan. New York: New Directions, 1992.

Giorno, John (1936–)

Drawing on artists' fascination with new media during the 1960s, John Giorno brought to NEW YORK SCHOOL poetry an innovative style, emphasizing sound, repetition, and live performance. A native New Yorker, he worked for a while as a stockbroker after graduating from Columbia University (B.A., 1958). As a young gay man, he connected with a number of the rising stars in the NEW YORK CITY art world, starting with ANDY WARHOL, who made Giorno the subject of his first movie, *Sleep* (1963). A later lover, ROBERT RAUSCHENBERG, introduced Giorno to Robert Moog (1934–2005), creator of the "Moog synthesizer" of electronic sounds that Giorno used in his poetry performances. Rauschenberg's art of "assemblage" was also a model for the "found poems" that Giorno began to circulate in 1964 under the title *The AMERICAN BOOK OF THE DEAD*. Another important model was the "cut-up" technique of WILLIAM S. BURROUGHS, who became a close friend of Giorno's and eventually took up residence in the same building that Giorno still occupies on the Bowery on DOWNTOWN MANHATTAN's Lower East Side.

Through "found poetry" Giorno's work began to incorporate voices from ordinary life, such as newspapers and advertisements, borrowing from

American culture in much the same manner as Warhol for his soup cans. When Giorno mixed his "found" language into a collage, or juxtaposed it with his own refrains, it produced both an echo and a critique of his sources and thus of contemporary life. Meanwhile, Giorno began to expand the medium of poetry itself through "sound poetry." In collaboration with Burroughs's associate Brion Gysin (1916–86), he produced "Subway Poem," a recording of sounds on the New York subway, which was presented in the 1965 Biennale at the Museum of Modern Art in Paris. At the POETRY PROJECT AT ST. MARK'S CHURCH IN-THE-BOWERY in New York, Giorno created "electronic sensory poetry environments." For instance, a performance in April 1969 played Giorno's poems "Johnny Guitar" and "Cunt" on a stereo Moog tape while a "light organ" translated the sounds in variations of color and brightness and "Time-Mist aerosol dispensing units" spread odors throughout the sanctuary of St. Mark's Church.

Also in 1969 Giorno arranged for the Architectural League of New York to rent six telephones that he hooked up to a tape recorder to provide a "Dial-a-Poem" service, playing poems recorded by BILL BERKSON, Burroughs, ALLEN GINSBERG, Giorno, DAVID HENDERSON, TAYLOR MEAD, RON PADGETT, JOHN PERREAULT, ED SANDERS, PETER SCHJELDAHL, ANNE WALDMAN, LEWIS WARSH, and Emmett Williams. The experiment ended when the telephone company warned that too many callers were tying up the lines. Going wireless, Giorno launched local area "Radio Free Poetry" from St. Mark's Church as part of the Poetry Project's New Year's Day marathon in January 1970, but federal regulators brought broadcasts to a halt. The most enduring result of these experiments was the series of recordings that Giorno issued under the label of Giorno Poetry Systems, starting with *The Dial-A-Poem Poets* album in 1972.

Giorno's poetry spans a dozen books, several record albums, and countless public performances. He invented a poetic style notable for its incantatory use of repetition and its consequent dependence on PERFORMANCE ART. During his readings Giorno engages his audience with gestures and with changes in tone and volume. Music played an especially prominent role when Giorno per-

formed with the JOHN GIORNO BAND during the 1980s. The content of his poems varies, but Giorno predominantly writes about his intimate and erotic relationships, Buddhism, social unrest and military combat, the human body, and life in New York City.

Giorno's print publications include *Poems by John Giorno* (Mother, 1967), *Johnny Guitar* (Poetry Project, 1969), *Balling Buddha* (Kulchur, 1970), *Cum* (Adventures in Poetry, 1971), *Birds* (Angel Hair, 1971), *Cancer in My Left Ball* (Something Else, 1973), *Grasping at Emptiness* (Kulchur, 1985), *You've Got to Burn to Shine* (High Risk–Serpent's Tail, 1994), and *Subduing Demons in America: Selected Poems, 1962–2007* (Soft Skull, 2008).

Beyond his art, Giorno has worked tirelessly throughout his career as a community leader and social activist, most notably by founding the AIDS Treatment Project in 1984, providing cash grants to AIDS patients in emergency situations.

Bibliography

Giorno Poetry Systems. Recordings. Ubuweb: Sound. Available online. URL: http://www.ubu.com/sound/gps.html.

Kane, Daniel. *All Poets Welcome: The Lower East Side Poetry Scene in the 1960s.* Berkeley: University of California Press, 2003, 5–6, 183–185.

Shepard, Richard F. "Dial-A-Poem, or Even a Hindu Chant," *New York Times,* 14 January 1969, p. 34.

Smith, Howard. "Scenes." *Village Voice,* 1 January 1970, pp. 26–27.

Giorno Band   *See* JOHN GIORNO BAND.

"Girl Machine" Kenward Elmslie (1971)

For poet KENWARD ELMSLIE, "Girl Machine" has become a signature performance piece. More broadly the poem is emblematic of the diverse meanings that attach to PERFORMANCE ART in the NEW YORK SCHOOL, particularly as a reflection of popular culture and of the reflection of that culture in POP ART. ANDY WARHOL's associate GERARD MALANGA planted the seed for "Girl Machine" by asking Elmslie, who wrote for musical THEATER, to provide "a think-piece about Busby

Berkeley's films" for *Interview* magazine, which Warhol and Malanga had just launched (Elmslie, "Girl Machine" and Author's note 584). Instead of a "think-piece," a poem evolved. In *Interview* the poem is called "Time Step Ode," recalling a series of dance-step paintings produced by Warhol in the early 1960s, but the magazine provides visual accompaniment in the FORM of photographs from some of Busby Berkeley's song-and-DANCE productions, which make it clear that the lines of Elmslie's text are arranged visually to reflect the patterns formed by Berkeley's dancers. Subsequent versions under the title "Girl Machine," published as a separate pamphlet by Angel Hair (1971) and collected in Elmslie's volume *Motor Disturbance* (1971), retained such visual patterning, leading ALICE NOTLEY to describe the text as "concrete poetry" (Notley 54).

If "Girl Machine" resembles concrete poetry visually, it is also, as BILL BERKSON describes it, "one of Elmslie's most self-sonorous poems" (n.p.), thereby resembling concrete MUSIC (*musique concrète*). As in that avant-garde method of composition, Elmslie brings out patterns of sound as he finds them in preexisting material. For instance, in the first stanza, the repeated phrase "Ma Marine" is the actual name of a character in the 1937 movie *The Singing Marine*, referred to throughout "Girl Machine" and, of course, rhyming with that title. To bring the musical qualities of his text fully to life, Elmslie began to perform it as a song, starting in 1981 at the inaugural event in a series of readings organized by LITA HORNICK at the Museum of Modern Art in New York. "Kenward's high camp singing brought down the house," Hornick recalled (125). Shortly afterward, musician Steven Taylor (1955–), who had worked with ALLEN GINSBERG for over a decade, set "Girl Machine" to a reggae beat, well suited to the insistent repetition in the further-evolving text. This setting has been incorporated in a cabaret program of Elmslie's works, *Palais Bimbo Lounge Show*, and performed by Elmslie, usually in drag, at such venues as the POETRY PROJECT AT ST. MARK'S CHURCH IN-THE-BOWERY in New York and BEYOND BAROQUE in Los Angeles.

As Elmslie's performance in drag suggests, within gay subculture the notion of a "Girl Machine" fits the potentially liberating view of gender as performance or as the product of an artificial process—a machine that makes girls. However, within the dominant heterosexual culture of the time, there was a tendency in the opposite, repressive direction to make girls into machines, "dolls," as in a 1961 pop song called "Girl Machine," sung by Johnny Walsh (Stratton). Reflecting Berkeley's choreography, Elmslie captures the fate of one such "doll" as her man "carries her shot dead / down a shadowy endless Dream Corridor!"

Bibliography

Berkson, Bill. "Millennium Plainsongs." *New York Native* (April 14, 1986). Kenward Elmslie Web site. Available online. URL: http://www.kenwardelmslie. com/interactive/index02.html. Accessed December 18, 2008.

Elmslie, Kenward. "Girl Machine." Kenward Elmslie Web site. Available online. URL: http://www. kenwardelmslie.com/interactive/index02.html. Accessed December 18, 2008.

———. "Girl Machine" and Author's note. In *The Angel Hair Anthology*, edited by Anne Waldman and Lewis Warsh, 353–358, 584–585. New York: Granary Books, 2001.

Hornick, Lita. *The Green Fuse: A Memoir.* New York: Giorno Poetry Systems, 1989.

Notley, Alice. "Elmslie's *Routine Disruptions.*" In *Coming After: Essays on Poetry.* Ann Arbor: University of Michigan Press, 2005, 52–56.

Stratton, Jon. "Man-Made Women." *Australian Humanities Review* (September 1996). Available online. URL: http://www.lib.latrobe.edu.au/AHR/ archive/Issue-Sept-1996/stratton.html. Accessed December 18, 2008.

Wolf, Reva. *Andy Warhol, Poetry, and Gossip in the 1960s.* Chicago: University of Chicago Press, 1997.

Gizzi, Michael (1949–)

Michael Gizzi's ties to the NEW YORK SCHOOL of poetry date back to the early 1970s and the avant-garde poetry group spearheaded by Keith and Rosmarie Waldrop at Brown University in PROVIDENCE, RHODE ISLAND, where Gizzi earned both a B.A. and an M.F.A. His friendships with JOHN ASHBERY, BARBARA GUEST, JAMES SCHUYLER, and CLARK COOLIDGE, as well as his interest in the BEATS and the Providence school of poetry, have been equally important in establishing him as a prominent figure of experimental New York–style poetry today. Infused with movement and rhythm, Gizzi's poems explore the joys and sorrows of day-to-day life through lush vocabulary, syntactical breakdowns, crafted verbal play, and dizzying versifications, often relegating us, as Ashbery has noted, "to a place of poignant irresolution," as stated on the back cover of Gizzi's *No Both* (1998).

Gizzi's first collection of poems, *My Grandfather's Pants* (Bench Press, 1973) was soon followed by *Carmela Bianca* (Bonewhistle Press, 1974) and the Burning Deck Press publications: *Bird As* (1976), *Avis* (1979), and *Species of Intoxication* (1983). No further volumes appeared during the 1980s, but Gizzi contributed in other ways to the literary scene, notably as organizer of readings series at Simon's Rock of Bard College and at Arrowhead, the Herman Melville home near Pittsfield, Massachusetts. In the early 1990s he joined the editorial collaborative Hard Press and worked on its journal, *Lingo*. He resumed publishing volumes of his own with *Just Like a Real Italian Kid* (1990) and *Continental Harmony* (Roof Books, 1991). Most recently Gizzi has published *Interferon* (The Figures, 1995), *No Both,* (Hard Press, 1998) and *My Terza Rima* (The Figures, 2001), which includes the previously published books *Too Much Johnson* (The Figures 1999) and *Cured in the Going Bebop* (Paradigm Press, 2000). In 2001 Gizzi began a new publishing venture, Qua Books, in collaboration with Craig Watson, opening with an Ashbery volume, *As Umbrellas Follow Rain.*

Lowell Connector (Hard Press, 1993), a collaborative homage to JACK KEROUAC, with texts by Gizzi, CLARK COOLIDGE, and JOHN YAU, highlights a common orientation shared by Gizzi and Coolidge in particular. A review of *My Terza Rima* in *Publishers Weekly* noted: "In literal dialogue with Clark Coolidge (they did tandem readings last year [2000]), Gizzi has been travelling the 'nameways' of B-movies, cartoons, jazz and its lore with increasing intensity and skill since *Continental Harmony* in 1991." Not to diminish Gizzi's uniqueness, however, the reviewer went on to add: "the knack for surrealistic assemblage, the intricate orchestra-tion of sonic patterns, the unerring ear for all that 'human convoluters' let escape their 'conniption traps,' establish this 'Misteriosi So-and-So' as a soloist of the first order" (78).

Bibliography

DuCharme, Mark. "Michael Gizzi." *Poetry Project Newsletter* 170 (1998): 22–23.

Evans, Steve. "Gizzi's *No Both.*" *Poetics Journal* 10 (1998): 283–286.

Review of *My Terza Rima. Publishers Weekly* 4 June 2001, 78.

Gizzi, Peter (1959–   )

Peter Gizzi is the author of a significant body of verse that is often described as NEW YORK SCHOOL poetry, and rightly so, yet he also draws on other schools of poetics, resulting in work that is complex, vibrant, and nondoctrinaire. Gizzi, who holds a B.A. in classical literature from New York University, also received an M.F.A. from Brown University, and a Ph.D. from the State University of New York at Buffalo, two well-known hotbeds of contemporary experimental poetry of varying stripes.

Gizzi's first book, *Periplum* (Avec, 1992), under-scored its New York School roots with a cover and interior drawings by TREVOR WINKFIELD; the work inside ranged from the classically erudite "Blue Peter" to the more whimsical "A.k.a." ("Maps / don't lead anywhere. / That's it. Geronimo!"). A second volume, *Artificial Heart* (Burning Deck, 1998), displayed a more mature voice with deeper political and philosophical concerns, though a crafted playfulness still animates the surface of the work. Like other New York School poets, Gizzi often "samples" popular culture—in his case rock lyrics, as in *Artificial Heart*'s "New Picnic Time" and "Fear of Music." Sometimes his references to New York School poetry are direct: "A Textbook of Chivalry" was inspired by FRANK O'HARA's "Hotel Transylvanie," while "Rewriting the Other and the Others" is described as "an 'erasure' of the poem 'The Other and the Others' by David Shapiro."

Gizzi's third full-length volume, *Some Values of Landscape and Weather* (Wesleyan University Press, 2003), further extended the poet's impressive range of voice, here using film and history as the primary agents of investigation into modal consciousness. The long poem *Etudes, Evidence, or a Working Definition of the Sun Gear* begins: "In a picture of thought the *f*-stop opens / as when skylarks departing," before going on to offer a litany of sense perception that illustrates "the way / the smallest dot is something's home." *Revival* is a similarly expansive elegy for GREGORY CORSO, though most of the book is organized around compressed lyrics, some in sequences; the sheer density of such poems offers both a diamond-like precision and a refusal to be pinned down, as in the meditative tour de force "Beginning with a Phrase by Simone Weil," which was anthologized in *The Best American Poetry 1995*.

While *The Outernationale* (Wesleyan University Press, 2007) confirmed Gizzi's place at the forefront of young American poets, it is significant that Gizzi's creative life has encompassed more than the writing of books. As the founding editor of the magazine *O-BLEK* (1987–93), easily one of the most influential literary journals of its era, he reenvisioned the parameters of the poetic community along new and invigorating lines, implicitly bridging the gaps between New York School poetry and other experimental poetries. Another editing project, the mammoth anthology *The Exact Change Yearbook* (1995), similarly depicted a poetic landscape that had not yet been imagined, yoking recorded material, work in TRANSLATION, and cutting-edge American poetics together into an unexpected whole; the book included a CD with recordings of JOHN ASHBERY, TED BERRIGAN, and others. And Gizzi's work on collecting Jack Spicer's lectures, in *The House That Jack Built* (Wesleyan University Press, 1998), and poems, in *My Vocabulary Did This to Me* (Wesleyan University Press, 2008), is surely one of the most important archival projects of the last decade.

Critical response to Gizzi's work has been overwhelmingly positive, with most reviews to date centering on *Artificial Heart*: "Many of these poems have the quality of open air studies in which the aim is not to form objects, but rather to suggest a feeling for them," wrote Joshua Green in the *Boston Review* (n.p.), and Ruth Andrews reported in *Rain Taxi*, "Gizzi's gorgeous musicality marries his abstractly conjured imagery in a wedding of nonlinear bliss" (n.p.). Introducing a group of "Young

American Poets" in a Belgian magazine, Marjorie Perloff argued that Gizzi "brings together the indeterminacy of Ashberyian narrative ('Something must be moving at incredible speed') with distinct Keatsian echoes . . . and an absence of 'explanation' that makes Gizzi's striving for self-understanding so moving" (n.p.). Gizzi has received several awards and fellowships for his work, including the Lavan Younger Poet award from the Academy of American Poets (1994, selected by Ashbery), and grants from the Howard Foundation (1998, selected by BARBARA GUEST) and the Foundation for Contemporary Performance Arts (1999, selected by JASPER JOHNS).

Bibliography

Andrews, Ruth. Review of *Artificial Heart*. *Rain Taxi* (Spring 1999). Available online. URL: http://www.raintaxi.com/online/1999spring/gizzi.shtml. Accessed December 18, 2008.

Green, Joshua. Review of *Artificial Heart*. *Boston Review* 27, no. 2 (April–May 2002). Available online. URL: http://www.bostonreview.net/BR27.2/microspoetry.html. Accessed December 18, 2008.

Perloff, Marjorie. Introduction to Portfolio of "Young American Poets." *Yang* (Antwerp, Belgium) 182 (Summer 1998). Available online. URL: http://wings.buffalo.edu/epc/authors/perloff/yang.html. Accessed December 18, 2008.

Godfrey, John (1945–   )

Among the poets of the second-generation NEW YORK SCHOOL, John Godfrey has slipped under the critical radar, but he remains highly influential to younger poets. Godfrey was born in Massena, New York, and graduated from Princeton University in 1967. He began publishing poems in mimeo magazines while an undergraduate and in 1969 moved to the Lower East Side of NEW YORK CITY where he lives to this day.

His first full-length collection, *Dabble: Poems, 1966–1980*, was published in 1982 by Full Court Press. Other books include *Where the Weather Suits My Clothes* (Z Press, 1984), *Midnight on Your Left* (The Figures, 1988), *Push the Mule* (The Figures, 2001), and *Private Lemonade* (Adventures in Poetry, 2003). Formally, his works range from short lyrics to dense prose, but they are always characterized by an urban dynamism that verges, at times, on surrealism. For example, a text simply titled "Poem" begins: "Why even the sun was a vassal on that set / what with them young chicks losing they's / pantyhose in five-second spots, and young / guys in puffy blouses stepping forward / extending microphones to the colossal concrete" (*Dabble* 36).

Godfrey's stance is a tough one, in a world where "The Blessed Virgin Is a '10'," according to the title of one poem. But behind this facade looms a deeper, darker sense of pathos and implicit failure. In the end, Godfrey must admit, "[A]t least I know Mary feels for a pore drunkie like me, and the same to you sister" (*Where the Weather* 24). With the publication of *Push the Mule* and *Private Lemonade*, Godfrey's work has moved toward increasingly complex syntactical patterns. Sentences such as "Young woman in ticket line puts her cheek against the back of her partner's shoulder is a symptom" surprise the reader at nearly every turn ("Pouring Gulf," *Push the Mule* 13).

Later in life, Godfrey returned to school, receiving a degree in nursing from Columbia University. He currently works as a pediatric nurse with homebound AIDS children in Brooklyn, New York.

Bibliography

Godfrey, John. *Dabble: Poems, 1966–1980.* New York: Full Court Press, 1982.
———. *Push the Mule.* Great Barrington, Mass.: The Figures, 2001.
———. *Where the Weather Suits My Clothes.* Calais, Vt.: Z Press, 1984.

Gold, Arthur (1917–1990), and Robert Fizdale (1920–1995) *pianists*

The piano duo of Arthur Gold and Robert Fizdale formed while the two men were students at the Juilliard School and made a vital contribution to New York's MUSIC scene through polished performances both of classical works and of new work they had specially commissioned. In their lifestyle, inspired by legends of prewar Paris, Gold and Fizdale sought "both to interrelate the various arts and to hobnob with artists themselves," according to composer NED ROREM (130). A significant chapter in their relation to poets is their dual love affairs (they did everything as a team) pairing Gold with JAMES SCHUYLER and Fizdale with FRANK O'HARA in 1953.

The biographical significance of these affairs lies in the realignment of relationships. Schuyler's taking up with Gold led to "a serious rift" between Schuyler and EDWIN DENBY, who had had hopes of nurturing his own affair with Schuyler before he made the mistake of introducing him to Gold (Kernan 283–284). More happily, the brief affair with Fizdale helped O'Hara get over the pain of rejection by LARRY RIVERS (Gooch 241). The artistic significance has proved to be longer lasting. Gold and Fizdale commissioned Paul Bowles to compose *A Picnic Cantata* (1954), based on Schuyler's libretto, and Ned Rorem to compose FOUR DIALOGUES FOR TWO VOICES AND TWO PIANOS (1954), based on O'Hara's libretto. In addition to formal commissions, each poet wrote a number of works inspired by his affair with one of the pianists.

In Schuyler's case such works are more difficult to identify, as he was more reticent than O'Hara, especially at this time, and the chronology of his work has been confused by delayed publication. Drawing on Schuyler's recollection that Gold "encouraged me to write in the formal styles" (interview 12), Paul Bauschatz sees this influence reflected in early collections (286 note 6), for instance, in the "Sestina" (a TRANSLATION from Dante) in *Freely Espousing* (1969) or the villanelle ("Poem [I do not always understand]") and "Sonnet" in *The Home Book* (1977). Explicitly, the notion that "Art is formality" is connected to Gold and Fizdale in "Grand Duo," an "improvisation" dedicated to the pianists and referring to their performance of the *Grand Duo* by Franz Schubert.

Both musical references and formal structures distinguish the poems that O'Hara wrote during his affair with Fizdale. Now available in *The Collected Poems* (160–167) and *Poems Retrieved* (118–132), they include titles such as "Appoggiaturas," "Romanze, or, The Music Students," "Tschaikovskiana," and FORMS such as the sestina ("Southern Villages," "Green Words") and "Sonnet." "Sneden's Landing Variations," dedicated to Fizdale, is a formal tour de force in its deployment of rhyme schemes and the repetition of end words. The title refers to the musical form of "theme and variations" and to the small community of Snedens Landing on the Hudson River Palisades, just a few miles north and across the river from NEW YORK CITY, where Gold and Fizdale had rented a house during the summer of 1953. But O'Hara's elegiac mood as well as his experience of love is reflected in the poem's last line: "you were always kissing summer goodbye." In the fall, Gold and Fizdale left for a concert tour of Europe, from which Fizdale wrote a letter ending the affair. "To the Meadow" records O'Hara's response: "my broken heart is in your debt" (*Poems Retrieved* 137).

Schuyler's affair with Gold lasted into 1956 and included a memorable six months (1954–55) when Schuyler traveled with the pianists through Europe, "a lovely ritual / captured in artistic patterns" ("A New Yorker," *Collected Poems* 7). In the artists' world they shared with Schuyler and O'Hara, Gold and Fizdale continued to thrive; in the party-going world of the HAMPTONS, they became famous for offering gourmet meals, a talent that led to their writing a food column for *Vogue* magazine. By the time they retired from public performance in 1982, they had also begun writing biography, focusing on two Parisian legends, the salon hostess Misia Sert and the actress Sarah Bernhardt.

Bibliography

Bauschatz, Paul. "James Schuyler's 'A Picnic Cantata': The Art of the Ordinary." In *The Scene of My Selves: New Work on New York School Poets,* edited by Terence Diggory and Stephen Paul Miller, 267–286. Orono, Me.: National Poetry Foundation, 2001.

Bowles, Paul. *A Picnic Cantata.* Arthur Gold and Robert Fizdale, piano. Sound recording, ML 5068. New York: Columbia, 1955.

Gold, Arthur, and Robert Fizdale. *The Divine Sarah: A Life of Sarah Bernhardt.* New York: Knopf, 1991.

———. *The Gold and Fizdale Cookbook.* New York: Random House, 1984.

———. *Misia: The Life of Misia Sert.* New York: Knopf, 1980.

Gooch, Brad. *City Poet: The Life and Times of Frank O'Hara.* New York: Knopf, 1993.

Kernan, Nathan. "James Schuyler: A Chronology." In *The Diary,* by James Schuyler, 278–298. Santa Rosa, Calif.: Black Sparrow, 1997.

O'Hara, Frank. *The Collected Poems.* Rev. ed. Edited by Donald Allen. Berkeley: University of California Press, 1995.

———. *Poems Retrieved.* Rev. ed. Edited by Donald Allen. San Francisco: Grey Fox, 1996.

Rorem, Ned. *Setting the Tone: Essays and a Diary.* New York: Coward-McCann, 1983.

Schubert, Franz. *Grand Duo for Piano.* Arthur Gold and Robert Fizdale, piano. Sound recording, ML 5068. New York: Columbia Masterworks, 1955.

Schuyler, James. *Collected Poems.* New York: Noonday/Farrar, Straus & Giroux, 1993.

———. Interview by Mark Hillringhouse. *American Poetry Review* 14, no. 2 (March–April 1985): 5–12.

Golden Book of Words, The
Bernadette Mayer (1978)

The Golden Book of Words is unlike most of BERNADETTE MAYER's previous books. As Mayer says, "This is really the only real book of poetry I've published" (excerpt from a lecture 100), although that definition might apply also to *Poetry* (Kulchur, 1976). Mayer's other books revolve around one central thematic concept or experiment. In *The Golden Book of Words,* however, experimentation is confined within the individual poems. For example, in "Very Strong February," Mayer gives herself the restrictive task of placing at least one color in each line. Although Mayer's workshops at the POETRY PROJECT AT ST. MARK'S CHURCH IN-THE-BOWERY fostered future generations of LANGUAGE writers, many of these same poets attacked *The Golden Book of Words* for being less experimental than her earlier work. Even Mayer questions the departure when she writes in the title poem, "Why is my verse so barren of new Pride, / So far from variation or quick change?"

Although *The Golden Book of Words* is singular among Mayer's works, it is also her most characteristically NEW YORK SCHOOL book. A talky voice, full of daily occasions, leads the collection. But in the male-dominated New York School, Mayer's work stands out for expanding the repertoire to feeding babies, fantasies about Carlton Fisk, making ends meet, and marital life. In short, Mayer opens the New York School to women and, more specifically, mothers.

The *Golden Book of Words* was written soon after Mayer moved from NEW YORK CITY to the BERKSHIRES of western Massachusetts. Tension between city life and provincial life is apparent in the isolation and lack of anonymity portrayed in the book. The dislike of western Massachusetts is apparent in "Looking Like Areas of Kansas," which begins, "New England is awful / The winter's five months long." Although Mayer was isolated in Lenox, she still had connections to New York through visits and correspondence from friends. She specifies: "The most interesting thing about [*The Golden Book of Words*] to me was having Joe Brainard do the cover for which Joe asked me what I'd want it to be. Joe wasn't doing many covers at the time either and I loved getting his wonderful printed correspondences so I'd write him as often as possible; in fact, I always did" ("Writing" 591).

There are a variety of references to literary figures, but only a few true influences are apparent in Mayer's work. For example, the influence of surrealism can be seen in her juxtaposition of imagery and tendency toward automatism, such as in the prose portion of "The Marble Faun": "a big guy like a hairsplitter or grasshopper has come now into my room, he's feeling his way upward with five legs and two antennae, a long tail like a fat neck in back, the tree's still moving, this moment still tentative, capitalism and materialism still here, a book about an old man, a young man still at the south pole." But Mayer gives equal presence to literary icons and everyday people; whether it be the local butcher or Nathaniel Hawthorne, each is important in relationship to her.

The Golden Book of Words is a chronologically organized selection of Mayer's writing during the two-year period beginning shortly before the birth of her second daughter. In a letter to her partner at the time, LEWIS WARSH, Mayer writes, "I'm awful tired today but I think my new schedule has to rule out 'working' at night. If I'm gonna work I'll have to do it in daylight. But when? That's why poems are good cause you can dash em off & then you've got this object to return to, even polish it up. What's becoming of my experimental writing?" ("Selected Letters" n.p.). It is no surprise, then, that the book consists of individual poems as opposed to one large, unified project. Though criticized for being

unlike her other books, *The Golden Book of Words* is clearly Mayer in every aspect: motherly, experimental, political, profane, feminist, and otherwise unique among the New York School. As in "Serial Biography," she writes: "Oh I guess poetry can be about all of this."

Bibliography

Mayer, Bernadette. Excerpt from a lecture at the Naropa Institute, 1989. In *Disembodied Poetics: Annals of the Jack Kerouac School,* edited by Anne Waldman and Andrew Schelling, 95–102. Albuquerque: University of New Mexico Press, 1994.

———. *The Golden Book of Words.* Lenox, Mass.: Angel Hair, 1978.

———. "Selected Letters to Lewis Warsh, 1975–76." *Chain* 6 (Summer 1999). Available online. URL: http://people.mills.edu/jspahr/chain/6_mayer.htm.

———. "The Writing of *Moving, Eruditio Ex Memoria* and *The Golden Book of Words.*" In *The Angel Hair Anthology,* edited by Anne Waldman and Lewis Warsh, 590–591. New York: Granary Books, 2001.

Goodman, Paul (1911–1972)

Long before he became a guru to the countercultural youth movement of the 1960s, Paul Goodman exercised a magnetic influence in New York's Downtown bohemia, helping to draw together art and POLITICS in a distinctive blend that reflected his own experience of growing up in New York with the city as his school. "A man's eros turns to the institutions and the customs of the city, that educate character and nurture physical beauty," wrote Goodman, echoing Socrates (*Making Do* 274). This combination of urban experience and erotic impulse, which for Goodman was primarily homosexual, creates the mood of "urban pastoral" that informs Goodwin's many works of FICTION, such as *Empire City* (1964). In his critical writing it is the basis for the vision of "intimate community" that he set forth in a 1951 essay, "Advance-Guard Writing, 1900–1950"—an essay that made a significant impact on the communities of poets that were just then taking shape as the NEW YORK SCHOOL, BLACK MOUNTAIN POETS, and the SAN FRANCISCO RENAISSANCE (Shaw 82–84). In fact, Goodman taught briefly at the University of California, Berkeley (1949–50), and BLACK MOUNTAIN COLLEGE (1951), but he preferred to gather disciples around him in DOWNTOWN MANHATTAN bars such as the SAN REMO, where FRANK O'HARA met him in 1951. Before moving to NEW YORK CITY, O'Hara had written to his friend JANE FREILICHER of his enthusiasm for Goodman: "Just knowing that he is in the same city may give me the power to hurt myself into poetry" (Gooch 187).

The uneasy relationship that developed between O'Hara and Goodman after they met has been narrated in detail by Joe LeSueur, who became O'Hara's roommate through Goodman's introduction. Characteristically, O'Hara described their difference in personal terms, citing "Paul Goodman's estimation of me as shallow and superficial" (Gooch 372). For instance, Goodman did not approve of O'Hara's admiration for the movie star James Dean (Gooch 268) or, for that matter, even the composer Sergei Prokofiev (LeSueur 118). It was equally characteristic of Goodman, however, to couch his difference from O'Hara in more philosophical terms. Whereas O'Hara, following Walt Whitman and Vladimir Mayakovsky, sought "to identify with the world and its faults," Goodman maintained a separation intended "to keep both contestants in the field, I and the world"—a contest, presumably, that held open the possibility of reforming the world's faults (*Five Years* 25). Despite these differences, readers who knew both men have pointed to similarities in their poetry. Richard Howard argues that Goodman was Whitman's "true heir," but when he notes that Goodman was more frequently inclined to "reflexive and restorative irony," he recalls "the manner of the School of New York" detectable in poems by Goodman such as one beginning, "Because I love you, walking with you / Seventh Avenue is blurry" (Howard 192–193; Goodman *Collected Poems* 270). NED ROREM observes that Goodman "composed on the run, for immediate occasions, in the manner Frank O'Hara would make popular" (360). Indeed, in "Advance-Guard Writing in America: 1900–1950," Goodman, citing the authority of Johann Wolfgang von Goethe, declared occasional poetry to be "the highest kind" for its role in shaping "intimate community" (211–212).

There can be no question that Goodman felt more at home in the "intimate community" of artists and writers than in the society of New York intellectuals with which he is sometimes identified. During the 1940s the pacifist anarchism that set Goodman at odds with the editors of *Partisan Review* provided common ground with the founders of the LIVING THEATRE, Julian Beck and Judith Malina, who also joined Goodman in practicing alternatives to orthodox Freudian psychotherapy, such as Wilhelm Reich's "orgone" treatments and Gestalt analysis. During the 1950s the Living Theatre produced more plays by Goodman than any other writer. They were "didactic, singularly undramatic plays," in LeSueur's judgment (18), but they appealed to "direct action" on the part of the audience (Tytell 83), most explicitly at the end of *Faustina* (1952), when the title character berates the audience for not having leapt onto the stage to prevent a murder they have just witnessed. Not surprisingly, Goodman welcomed the "direct action" emphasized in ACTION PAINTING ("What Is a Picture?" 186–187), a theory he had anticipated in his earlier art criticism, according to JOHN BERNARD MYERS (58).

By the time Goodman came to national attention for his analysis of alienated youth, *Growing Up Absurd* (1960), he was well prepared to introduce into social theory what he had learned from the arts. "The young people have latched on to the movement in art that is strongest in our generation, the so-called Action Painting or New York School," he wrote (*Growing Up* 239). He cited the BEATS as representative writers, but the sort of action they represented would apply equally well to the events staged later in the decade by the second-generation New York School poets at the POETRY PROJECT AT ST. MARK'S CHURCH IN-THE-BOWERY: "their persistent effort at the effective community reading, appearing as themselves in their own clothes, and willing to offend or evoke some other live response; and also their creative playing" (*Growing Up* 189). What even Goodman could not have anticipated were the violent confrontations between youth and authority that erupted on college campuses, at political conventions, and in the streets of urban ghettos by the end of the 1960s. Although Goodman criss-crossed the country to encourage meaningful protest where he could, the meanings espoused by New Left leaders too often seemed totalitarian rather than communitarian. Even the Living Theatre, he found, had turned the word *revolution* into a fetish "which connotes a total systematic change—and who needs it?" (Tytell 311). A few days after writing these words to Malina in 1972, Goodman died of a heart attack at his rural retreat in New Hampshire, where since 1961 he had enjoyed pastoral experience in a purer FORM than New York City could provide.

Bibliography

Diggory, Terence. "Community 'Intimate' or 'Inoperative': New York School Poets and Politics from Paul Goodman to Jean-Luc Nancy." In *The Scene of My Selves: New Work on New York School Poets*, edited by Terence Diggory and Stephen Paul Miller, 13–32. Orono, Me.: National Poetry Foundation, 2001.

Gooch, Brad. *City Poet: The Life and Times of Frank O'Hara.* New York: Knopf, 1993.

Goodman, Paul. "Advance-Guard Writing in America: 1900–1950." In *Utopian Essays and Practical Proposals.* New York: Vintage–Random House, 1962, 191–216.

———. *Collected Poems.* Edited by Taylor Stoehr. New York: Random House, 1973.

———. *Empire City.* New York: Macmillan, 1964.

———. *Five Years.* New York: Brussel & Brussel, 1966.

———. *Growing Up Absurd: Problems of Youth in the Organized System.* New York: Random House, 1960.

———. *Making Do.* New York: Macmillan, 1963.

———. "What Is a Picture?" In *Utopian Essays and Practical Proposals.* New York: Vintage–Random House, 1962, 182–189.

Howard, Richard. "Paul Goodman." In *Alone with America: Essays on the Art of Poetry in the United States Since 1950.* Enlarged ed. New York: Atheneum, 1980, 184–194.

King, Richard. "Paul Goodman." In *The Party of Eros: Radical Social Thought and the Realm of Freedom.* Chapel Hill: University of North Carolina Press, 1972, 78–115.

LeSueur, Joe. *Digressions on Some Poems by Frank O'Hara: A Memoir.* New York: Farrar, Straus & Giroux, 2003, 5–19, 117–121.

Myers, John Bernard. *Tracking the Marvelous: A Life in the New York Art World.* New York: Random House, 1983.

Rorem, Ned. "Remembering a Poet" (1972). In *Setting the Tone: Essays and a Diary.* New York: Coward-McCann, 1983, 358–360.

Shaw, Lytle. *Frank O'Hara: The Poetics of Coterie.* Iowa City: University of Iowa Press, 2006.

Tytell, John. *The Living Theatre: Art, Exile, and Outrage.* New York: Grove, 1995.

Great Balls of Fire Ron Padgett (1969)

Appearing at the end of the 1960s, RON PADGETT's *Great Balls of Fire* (Holt, Rinehart and Winston, 1969; reprint Coffee House Press, 1990) provides an impressive overview of the range of experiment with which the NEW YORK SCHOOL poets became identified as the second generation emerged during the preceding decade. In this regard, *Great Balls of Fire*, Padgett's first major solo collection, is comparable to BEAN SPASMS (1967), in which he collaborated with TED BERRIGAN. However, while *Bean Spasms* is a crazy grab bag in which it is hard to imagine anything not fitting, *Great Balls of Fire*, which reprints some material from *Bean Spasms*, acquires a tight coherence in the hands of a single author who has learned the potential of placement as a key—sometimes the only—creative act. It is the lesson of Marcel Duchamp, whose presence is acknowledged in the title of Padgett's poem "After the Broken Arm," reprinted from his earlier collection *In Advance of the Broken Arm* (1964). Duchamp had assigned the latter title to one of his "ready-mades" (1915), a snow shovel that became a work of art simply by being placed on exhibit. In Padgett's poem the consequence of saying "the right word in New York City" is displaced into "the fabulous dry horror of the West," from which Padgett had removed himself when he brought his words to NEW YORK CITY in 1960.

The displacement of words across languages is both a frequent technique and a major theme in *Great Balls of Fire*. The French poets whom Padgett had translated show up repeatedly: Guillaume Apollinaire ("Strawberries in Mexico"), Blaise Cendrars ("You Again," "The Statue of a Libertine"), Max Jacob ("Homage to Max Jacob"), and Pierre Reverdy ("After Reverdy," "Reading Reverdy"). "Some Bombs" experiments with translating Reverdy's *Quelques poèmes* (Some poems,

1916) for the sound of the original words rather than their sense, or sometimes a playful mixture of the two. For instance, *"Le montagne avale tout"* (The mountain swallows all) becomes "The montage swallows a toot" in Padgett's poem. A series of odes ("to the Astronauts," "to the Futurist Painters and Poets," etc.) appear to be TRANSLATIONs, with Italian versions printed at the bottom of the page, but these are by GEORGE SCHNEEMAN, written after Padgett's English poems, whose foreign air derives from manipulation of diction and point of view rather than translation from an "original" source. In "Le mouvement de César Franck" ("Movement by César Franck," the French composer), Padgett goes directly to the source, copying French phrases from various "found" materials and presenting them as a collage, disconnected and untranslated. "Falling in Love in Spain or Mexico" presents phrases from the sort of English phrase book a foreigner might use but transfers them to the speech of a dramatic character who appears to be hurled toward "falling in love" by the momentum of the phrases alone. The absurd comedy that results is reminiscent of Eugène Ionesco's use of similar material in his play *The Bald Soprano* (1949).

The secret of such comedy lies in the inevitable distance between an original and its copy. The distance can be wide, as in "Birches," Padgett's reduction of Robert Frost's famous poem of that title (1916), or very narrow, as in "A Man Saw a Ball of Gold," which is an exact copy of a poem by Stephen Crane (1895) except for one word (Padgett substitutes *gold* for *clay* in the fourth line). The same line ("A man saw a ball of gold") repeated in a different poem ("Tone Arm") is not the same. Within the same poem a repeated phrase is not the same, whether it appears in different line arrangements ("Joe Brainard's Painting *Bingo*") or identically in a string of 14 lines (making "Nothing in That Drawer" a minimalist sonnet). Finally, and initially, the same poem ("Detach, Invading") printed at both the beginning and end of Padgett's volume is not the same poem. Placement makes a difference.

Reviewers of *Great Balls of Fire* enjoyed the fun of Padgett's word play, somewhat to the surprise of "an old sense-monger," as Reed Whittemore described himself (23). Generally, they preferred poems less *abstract*, Padgett's own term ("Reading" n.p.), than "Detach, Invading," poems such as "16 November 1964" (Lehman 226–227) or "Poem for Joan Inglis on Her Birthday" (Martz 555–556). These are "occasional poems," the New York School's most accessible mode, but they contribute to the exploration of repetition and difference throughout Padgett's volume. Although the poet of "16 November" copies down words as he encounters them during the day, when he reads his notebook at night the words themselves appear to be transformed, composing a poem that bears no resemblance to the day's experience. In "Poem for Joan Inglis," resemblance is made literal by the presence of a mirror, which reveals in a familiar scene a deeper world than the speaker had experienced before.

Bibliography

Lehman, David. "The Whole School." *Poetry* 119, no. 4 (January 1972): 224–233.

Martz, Louis. "Recent Poetry: Established Idiom." *Yale Review.* 59, no. 4 (Summer 1970): 551–569.

Padgett, Ron. "Reading of 'Detach, Invading.'" Sound recording. *Susan Howe with Poetry* radio show, WBAI, New York City, 17 June 1975. Companion CD to *All Poets Welcome: The Lower East Side Poetry Scene in the 1960s,* by Daniel Kame. Berkeley: University of California Press, 2003.

Whittemore, Reed. "On the New York Poets." *New Republic*, 13 December 1969, 23–24.

Green, Henry (Henry Vincent York)
(1905–1974) *British poet*

The work of British author Henry Green influenced several first-generation NEW YORK SCHOOL poets. Born Henry Vincent York, Green chose his unremarkable pseudonym because of its very ordinariness. It is not surprising, therefore, that a reverence for the ordinary and mundane should pervade Green's novels.

In each of his nine books the author devotes a surprising amount of attention to minute details, which are usually irrelevant to the narrative. He is interested in evoking a highly specific atmosphere rather than in enticing his readers with the plot. In fact, Green often pushes the plot into the distant background, allowing the nuances and idiosyncrasies of each particular scene to draw the reader's focus.

Green's ambivalence to the plot is accentuated by his oblique wit and impersonal tone. He rarely makes explicit statements about his characters and their relation. Instead, he exposes them to us—along with the details of their milieu—with neither judgment nor affectation. For this reason he has been described by some as an "invisible author."

It is likely that Green's willingness to revel, nonjudgmentally, in the world's tedium, helped endear him to young New York School poets such as JAMES SCHUYLER and JOHN ASHBERY. In his master's thesis on Green, Ashbery argues that the novelist's brilliance lies partly in his "objectiveness." He defines this term as "this light acceptance of the world, this enjoyment of life without feeling called upon to apologize for its boredom or its ugly stretches" (4). In speaking of Green here, Ashbery also suggests what he attempts to bring to his own writing. And the same might be said of his fellow New York School poets, all of whom have been associated with the "art of the everyday."

Another defining feature of Green's work is the author's highly poetic style. Indeed, his prose experiments resemble poetic techniques. For example, he will often omit the definite articles from a phrase in order to manipulate the pace at which a reader encounters his meaning. Green relies most heavily on this sort of conceit in his second novel, *Living,* from which the following passage is taken.

> Mr Craigan smoked pipe, already room was blurred by smoke from it and by steam from hot water in the sink. She swilled water over the plates and electric light caught in shining waves of water which rushed off plates as she held them, and then light caught on wet plates in moons (18).

This selection demonstrates the conversational effect of Green's truncated syntax and staggered rhythm. That poetic expressiveness—coupled with Green's emphasis on everyday details—explains why the author held so much interest among the New York School poets. Just like Green, many of

those poets were searching for a detached but conversational way to capture the aesthetic of ordinary, everyday experience.

Although Green's books never won a broad audience or critical acclaim, he has always commanded a small, passionate group of very prominent readers. In addition to the New York School poets, this group has included W. H. AUDEN, Elizabeth Bowen, Evelyn Waugh, Terry Southern, Eudora Welty, and John Updike.

Green continues to be a fairly obscure figure within British modernism. Even the slight surge in attention that he received in the 1970s has all but disappeared. While some of his collections were reprinted by Penguin in the early 1990s, his work rarely sees print today.

Bibliography

Allen, Brooke. "Reading Henry Green." *New Criterion* (March 1993): 26–27.

Ashbery, John Lawrence. "Three Novels of Henry Green." M.A. thesis. New York: Columbia University, 1950.

Bassoff, Bruce. *Toward Loving: The Poetics of the Novel and the Practice of Henry Green.* Columbia: University of South Carolina Press, 1975.

Green, Henry. *Concluding.* London: Hogarth Press, 1948.

———. *Loving.* London: Hogarth Press, 1945.

———. *Pack My Bag: A Self-Portrait.* London: Hogarth Press, 1940.

———. *Party Going.* London: Hogarth Press, 1939.

Holmesland, Oddvar. *A Critical Introduction to Henry Green's Novels: The Living Vision.* London: Macmillan, 1986.

Mengham, Rod. *The Idiom of the Time: The Writings of Henry Green.* Cambridge: Cambridge University Press, 1982.

Greenberg, Clement (1909–1994) *art critic*

With the publication of two essays, "Avant-Garde and Kitsch" (1939) and "Towards a Newer Laocoon" (1940), critic Clement Greenberg instantly became a major player on the New York art scene. By the time the NEW YORK SCHOOL poets arrived on that scene, Greenberg was on his way to becoming, as W. H. AUDEN said of Freud, "no more a person now/But a whole climate of opinion" (93). For Greenberg, the modern artist's essential task was "to eliminate from the specific effects of each art any and every effect that might be conceivably borrowed from any other art. Thus would each art be rendered 'pure'" (vol. 4 86). Painting had thus to be "purified" of any trace of what Greenberg called "literature"; in practice this meant it would become increasingly abstract. Greenberg boosted the careers of certain artists who seemed to him to meet this stringent standard, most notably JACKSON POLLOCK, and marginalized those who violated it, especially the surrealists, who promoted "a confusion of literature with painting as extreme as any of the past" (vol. 1 36).

When he was editor of the journal *Art & Literature,* JOHN ASHBERY requested permission to reprint Greenberg's critical summa, "Modernist Painting"(1960), calling it "a tremendously important article" that "should be seen by as many readers as possible" (Greenberg, vol. 3 xv). However, Ashbery and company also admired the surrealists precisely for breaking down those distinctions Greenberg sought to maintain, whether between figuration and abstraction or painting and literature. "I grew up under the shadow of Surrealism," BARBARA GUEST recalls, where "there was no recognized separation between the arts" (16). And in an essay on one of Greenberg's bêtes noires, Yves Tanguy, Ashbery notes approvingly that "the arbitrary distinction between abstract and figurative painting did not exist for Tanguy" (27). Nonetheless, although the poets implicitly rebelled against Greenbergian norms, Greenberg's name itself seldom appears in any of their art writings, an omission in keeping with their preference, as critics, for appreciation over polemics.

Their friend, figurative painter FAIRFIELD PORTER, did frequently debate Greenberg both in person and in print; Ashbery alludes to these disagreements in an essay on Porter (310). Early on, Greenberg supported some of the painters most closely allied with the poets, giving LARRY RIVERS's first show a rave review (vol. 2, 301), and recommending Rivers and GRACE HARTIGAN, among others, to Dwight Ripley and JOHN BERNARD MYERS when the two consulted Greenberg before opening the TIBOR DE NAGY GALLERY (Wilkins 22, 26). However, the critic soon withdrew his support of second-generation New York School artists in favor of those exemplars of "pure" abstraction, the color field painters.

Bibliography

Ashbery, John. *Reported Sightings: Art Chronicles, 1957– 1987.* Edited by David Bergman. Cambridge, Mass.: Harvard University Press, 1991.

Auden, W. H. "In Memory of Sigmund Freud." *Selected Poems.* New ed. Edited by Edward Mendelson. New York: Random House–Vintage, 1979, 91–95.

Greenberg, Clement. *The Collected Essays and Criticism.* 4 vols. Edited by John O'Brian. Chicago: University of Chicago Press, 1986.

Guest, Barbara. *Dürer in the Window: Reflexions on Art.* New York: Roof Books, 2003.

Porter, Fairfield. *Fairfield Porter: Art in Its Own Terms: Selected Criticism, 1935–1975.* Edited by Rackstraw Downes. New York: Taplinger, 1979.

Wilkins, Karen. "Tibor de Nagy: The First Fifty Years." In *Tibor de Nagy Gallery: The First Fifty Years, 1950– 2000.* New York: Tibor de Nagy, 2000, 17–40.

Greenwald, Ted (1942–)

A second-generation NEW YORK SCHOOL poet, Ted Greenwald was born in Brooklyn in 1942 and raised in Queens and has lived his entire life in NEW YORK CITY. Known for his playful cadences, linguistic permutations, and reconstruction of the poetic line as a means of conveyance, Greenwald has written a number of books and participated in COLLABORATIONs with other writers and visual artists, including *Poker Blues,* a video made with Les Levine, in which he appears as the sole performer. Along with Charles Bernstein, Greenwald started the reading series at the EAR INN, a bar on Spring Street, inaugurating the series with a performance by JOHN ASHBERY and MICHAEL LALLY in fall 1978. Greenwald himself has read his work at many venues, including the Ear Inn, the POETRY PROJECT AT ST. MARK'S CHURCH IN-THE-BOWERY, and the BOWERY POETRY CLUB.

Because his work often involves syntactic and formal experimentation, Greenwald has been associated with LANGUAGE POETRY since its inception as a movement. Nonetheless, his work shows a more immediate and less theoretical understanding of the rhythms and inflections inherent in the American vernacular. His style is often minimal and comparable to someone like ROBERT CREELEY, though it is more percussive in parts. His collection, *Jumping the Line* (Roof Books, 1999), for example, consists of more than 1,000 tercets organized around a principle of recurrence and repetition, as embodied here:

> You're doing
> No thing
> Makes sense
>
> Makes sense
> No thing
> The object of
>
> Your every word.

According to Charles Bernstein in a blurb on the cover of Greenwald's book, *Jumping the Line*, the poet "has created an ingeniously alluring structure.... The gentle but persistent permutation and context-shifting of this 'ghostly sewing' create 'machine songs' that are semantically open, experimentally spacious and thematically self-reflective." Greenwald's other books include a collection of unpunctuated prose poems, *The Up and Up* (Atelos, 2004); *Something, She's Dead* (1999); *Word of Mouth* (Sun & Moon, 1986); a verbal-visual collaboration with artist Richard Bosman, *Exit the Face* (MOMA, 1982); *Licorice Chronicles* (KULCHUR, 1979); *Common Sense* (L Publications, 1978); and *You Bet* (This Press, 1977). His work has also been anthologized, including an appearance in *The Best American Poetry 2004*, edited by Lyn Hejinian (Scribner).

Greenwald still lives and writes in New York City with partner Joan McClusky and their daughter, Abby.

Groundwater Press (1974–   )

Founded in 1974 in NEW YORK CITY by poets EUGENE RICHIE and ROSANNE WASSERMAN, this independent nonprofit press is a center of recent NEW YORK SCHOOL innovation and collaboration. In 1987, when Richie was JOHN ASHBERY's literary secretary, the press expanded operations to Hudson, New York. Groundwater continues the New York School's traditional poet-painter COLLABORATIONS, working with TIBOR DE NAGY GALLERY and Flow Chart Foundation; British poets and painters JOHN ASH, MARK FORD, and TREVOR WINKFIELD; and Parisians Olivier Brossard and Pierre Martory. The press cosponsors events and publications linking writers and artists surrounding Ashbery, JAMES SCHUYLER, KENNETH KOCH, and BARBARA GUEST. In 1975, working on *City Magazine*, Richie met F. B. Claire, a Bronx-born FICTION writer. With Wasserman, they earned grants for magazine and press projects from the New York State Council on the Arts, National Endowment for the Arts, Coordinating Council of Literary Magazines, and New York City Department of Cultural Affairs. In 1980 Groundwater published *Writers Introduce Writers*, a book of short stories by Diana Maychick, Lee Vassel, Donald Wallace, Mindy Pennybacker, Arkady Rovner, and others, introduced by teacher-mentors including Sarah Wright, Manuel Puig, Marianne Hauser, Arturo Vivante, Al Young, Vance Bourjaily, Judith Guest, and John Barth. It received a *Library Journal* citation.

The Intuflo Editions chapbook series, in conjunction with Marc Cohen and Susan Baran's Intuflo Reading Series, was inspired in 1989, when Wasserman heard GERRIT HENRY's voice in a dream saying, "A person could die without ever getting a book published!" Introduced by established poets such as Koch and Ashbery, these limited editions feature new writers and covers by New York School artists, including the first book by Anne Porter, widow of painter FAIRFIELD PORTER, and Pierre Martory's *Every Question but One*, translated by Ashbery, with a JANE FREILICHER cover. Other writers included Susan Baran, Marc Cohen, Henry, Maggie Paley, Jaime Manrique, Robert Thompson, and Edward Barrett.

In the 1990s Groundwater published *The History of Rain* by Tomoyuki Iino, Tokyo critic and translator of Ashbery; books by Michael Malinowitz and Mary du Passage with grants from Rensselaer County Council for the Arts; volumes by Beth Enson and STAR BLACK; and second volumes by Cohen, Baran, Manrique, Barrett, and Michael Malinowitz. *Short History of the Saxophone* by TOM WEATHERLY appeared in 2006 and along with *The Autobiography of Bill Sullivan* by Manrique, supported by a Furthermore Foundation grant and in conjunction with Sullivan's major retrospective at the Albany Institute of History and Art.

Bibliography

Berger, Joseph. "Thirst for Verse: Poetry Readings Multiply," *New York Times*, 24 October 1987, pp. 33–34.

Groundwater Press Web site. Available online. URL: http://webpage.pace.edu/erichie/groundwater.

Mitgang, Herbert. "New York Issues Guide to Writers' Services," *New York Times*, 30 December 1981, p. C10.

Guest, Barbara (Barbara Ann Pinson)
(1920–2006)

Barbara Guest is the most purely surreal of the first generation of NEW YORK SCHOOL poets, as well as the only woman. Both of these facts presented obstacles during the course of her career, but she resolutely pursued her own path and rose from relative isolation to become an important role model for younger writers, particularly among Language poets (see LANGUAGE POETRY) and women engaged in a wide range of textual experimentation. While the connection of text to painting—the hallmark of the New York School aesthetic—was a constant stimulus for Guest's experimentation, MUSIC set an equally vital example as a means of liberation from what Guest, following William Carlos Williams, called "the tyranny of the image" (*Forces* 64).

Guest was exposed to the modern image in its most tyrannical form as a young woman coming of age in Los Angeles, the capital of the motion picture industry and home to Barbara Ann Pinson, as Guest had been named at her birth in North Carolina. The impression that Hollywood left on Guest, however, was not that of a machine for producing mass entertainment but rather of a private dream space, the realm of the creative imagination. Like the New York she was about to encounter, Hollywood in the 1940s had attracted leading European figures in all of the arts seeking a refuge from the war in Europe. In *Confetti Trees* (Sun & Moon, 1999), a collection of prose poems set in wartime Hollywood, Guest imagines the émigré composer Arnold Schönberg (1874–1951) receiving an invitation to have his opera *Die Glückliche Hand* (The lucky hand) produced as a film. The prospect sends Schönberg into a reverie about the "utmost unreality" that he had hoped his opera would embody. "Utmost unreality" is another name for the surrealism (DADA AND SURREALISM) that Guest went to seek in NEW YORK CITY after graduating from the University of California, Berkeley, in 1943. Schönberg, as Guest portrays him, could only dream of reuniting with the painter Wassily Kandinsky (1866–1944), who would understand what he sought. But in New York Guest would reunite with the painter, sculptor, and architect Tony Smith (1912–80), whom she had met in Los Angeles and who became her guide to the emerging art of the New York School.

By the early 1950s, Guest was a full participant in the New York arts scene. She wrote reviews for *Art News*, read her poems at the artists' CLUB, and published them prominently in the *Partisan Review*, for which she served briefly as poetry editor in the later 1950s. Out of the nucleus of New York School poetry forming at the TIBOR DE NAGY GALLERY came a production of Guest's play *The Ladies Choice* (1953, with designs by JANE FREILICHER); periodical publication in the house organ *Semicolon* (1955); and eventually Guest's first collection of poems, *The Location of Things* (1960), published by Tibor de Nagy Editions, the same series that had previously launched FRANK O'HARA, JOHN ASHBERY, and KENNETH KOCH. Although Guest partied with these writers at favorite hangouts such as the CEDAR STREET TAVERN and grew especially close to the fourth member of the group, JAMES SCHUYLER, there is a certain distance between her and them that can be traced both in her life and in her work. She had ties to a different world through marriage, her second to the English editor and translator Stephen Guest (1948–54), and then to the military historian Trumbull Higgins (1954–90). She had a daughter by her second marriage and a son by her third.

By marriage Guest belonged to a social elite, a world that can be found reflected in such poems as "Belgravia" and "On the Way to Dumbarton Oaks," which appeared in *The Location of Things* and again as the first two poems in Guest's *Selected Poems* (Sun & Moon, 1995). However, the elitism of which some readers accuse Guest is more a matter of aesthetic choice than of social circumstance. Her commitment to "utmost unreality" is not moderated by the pop imagery or colloquial speech of the other New York School poets, which seems to keep them in touch with the ordinary world. Nor is Guest's abstraction modified by expressionism. Although connections can be drawn between her life and her poems, the story they tell is primarily the life of the impersonal imagination, the deity presiding over modernist poetry from Stéphane Mallarmé to Wallace Stevens. Guest confirms the surrealist link in that chain by concluding her essay "Poetry the True Fiction" (1992) with a quotation from André Breton: "to imagine is to see" (*Forces* 32).

Elevation rather than elitism properly designates the tone that characterizes Guest's work. It is addressed, democratically, to any reader, but its goal is "to lift us upward" into a world that is wholly imagined (*Forces* 28). As the paradigm for this movement, "Parachutes, My Love, Would Carry Us Higher" has become one of Guest's best-known poems. The third entry in *Selected Poems*, it first gained wide circulation in DONALD M. ALLEN's anthology *The NEW AMERICAN POETRY, 1945–1960* (1960). The reversal in the title image—we expect parachutes to carry us down, not up—is a typical surrealist technique for breaking the grip of mundane reality. A more typical image for Guest, aimed at the same result, is that of a stairway, as in the title poem of *The Blue Stairs* (Corinth, 1968) or in "The Farewell Stairway," from *Fair Realism* (Sun & Moon, 1989). Like many of Guest's poems, "The Farewell Stairway" is about a work of art, in this case a painting by Giacomo Balla (1909) sometimes known by the same title as Guest's poem. For Guest, the presence of a work of art exerts an upward "pull," much like a stairway, although in the case of "The Farewell Stairway" it is notable that the women are depicted as descending. This may be because, as women, their position in the ordinary world is so paradoxical that for them the way down is the way up. Sarah Lundquist and Rachel Blau DuPlessis have offered powerful feminist readings of "The Farewell Stairway" along these lines, tracing its complex reversals of the simplistic placement of women in surrealist art and specifically in Balla's futurism.

Fair Realism, the volume in which "The Farewell Stairway" appears, marks a significant turning point in Guest's career. It follows a period of more than a decade in which her writing took new forms—the

novel *SEEKING AIR* (Black Sparrow, 1978) and the pioneering biography *HERSELF DEFINED: THE POET H.D. AND HER WORLD* (Doubleday, 1985)—but her production of poetry slowed, as if the new FORMS evolving in that mode needed time to germinate. Their emergence is signaled by the publication of *Fair Realism* by the California-based Sun & Moon Press, associated with Language poetry. However, aesthetic rather than ideological preoccupations account for the new emphasis on music that characterizes Guest's work from this time onward. Her study of H.D. had provided insight into the limitations as well as the possibilities of concentrating poetic energy "in an instant of time," as Ezra Pound had prescribed for imagism (Pound 4). By unfolding in time, music holds out the promise of the "more 'open' poetry" that Guest believed H.D. eventually sought (*Forces* 65) and that Guest now sought for herself. "Musicality," published separately as a chapbook in 1988 and collected in *Fair Realism*, names the sought-after quality "evanescence." Thematically, that quality is evoked by the "farewells" of "The Farewell Staircase" and repeated as the gesture of "waving farewell" in "Nostalgia," the lead poem in Guest's volume *The Red Gaze* (Wesleyan University Press, 2005). Based on a painting by Giorgio de Chirico, *The Nostalgia of the Infinite* (1913), the poem "Nostalgia" testifies that in turning to "Minimal Sound," the title of another poem from *The Red Gaze*, Guest had left neither surrealism nor the art of painting behind.

Bibliography

Chicago Review: Barbara Guest triple issue 53, no. 4, 54, no. 1, 54, no. 2 (Spring 2008).

DuPlessis, Rachel Blau. "The Gendered Marvelous: Barbara Guest, Surrealism and Feminist Reception." In *The Scene of My Selves: New Work on New York School Poets*, edited by Terence Diggory and Stephen Paul Miller, 189–213. Orono, Me.: National Poetry Foundation, 2001.

Guest, Barbara. *The Collected Poems*. Edited by Hadley Haden Guest. Middletown, Conn.: Wesleyan University Press, 2008.

———. *Forces of Imagination: Writing on Writing*. Berkeley, Calif.: Kelsey St. Press, 2003.

Kasper, Catherine, ed. *Women's Studies*: Barbara Guest issue 30, no. 1 (2001).

Lundquist, Sarah. "Reverence and Resistance: Barbara Guest, Ekphrasis, and the Female Gaze." *Contemporary Literature* 38, no. 2 (1997): 260–285.

Nelson, Maggie. *Women, the New York School, and Other True Abstractions.* Iowa City: University of Iowa Press, 2007, 31–45.

Pound, Ezra. *Literary Essays.* Edited by T. S. Eliot. 1954. Reprint, New York: New Directions, 1968.

Guston, Philip (Philip Goldstein)
(1913–1980) *painter*

Among the first generation of NEW YORK SCHOOL painters, Philip Guston is unusual for the increased intensity in his relation to poetry after the poets of the second generation emerged in the 1960s. He had known JACKSON POLLOCK since high school in Los Angeles, honed his craft (and changed his name from the original Goldstein) in the Works Progress Adminstration mural projects during the 1930s, and "joined up" (as CLEMENT GREENBERG expressed it) in the abstract expressionist breakthrough in New York in 1948 (213). Guston's mode of abstraction was less aggressive in gesture than that of Pollock or WILLEM DE KOONING. By the late 1950s, when the mode caught on with some influential critics, Guston's sensitivity of touch and the shimmering FORMS that emerged were commonly identified as *lyrical,* a term that implies an orientation toward poetry. But the poet FRANK O'HARA, a devoted admirer, emphasized "a subtle drama" in Guston's work, "the sense of an unseen presence . . . , perhaps of an actor who has just left the stage or a voice that has just died out" ("Growth" 137–138). O'Hara's poem "It Seems Far Away and Gentle Now" (1956), a response to Guston's *Painting* (1954), translates the theatrical metaphor as a play of surface and depth: "a surface agitation of the waters / means a rampart on the ocean floor is falling" (*Collected Poems* 261).

Guston was deeply moved by O'Hara's death in 1966—"he was our Apollinaire," he told Joe LeSueur at the funeral (Gooch 11)—and it may not be mere coincidence that the following year brought a marked shift in Guston's style from abstraction to representation. It was as if he had plunged beneath the level of "surface agitation" to bring the viewer into direct contact with the fallen ramparts of American culture, shaken by the Vietnam War and racial conflict. Detached heads and hooded figures recalling the Ku Klux Klan populated numerous drawings and, eventually, paintings in a grotesque cartoon style that Guston's former friends in the art world interpreted as a defection to POP ART. Younger poets, however, found affinity with the "underground" comics of R. Crumb and an aesthetic of bedrock grittiness that they cultivated in their own work (Berkson, "New Gustons" 85). The principal intermediary was BILL BERKSON, who had met Guston through O'Hara and wrote a series of consistently favorable reviews of Guston's work, starting with his first "Art Chronicle" in KULCHUR (number 7, August 1962).

Berkson helped arrange for Guston to supply a cover for CLARK COOLIDGE's *ING* (1968) and in 1969 brought the publishers ANNE WALDMAN and LEWIS WARSH to visit Guston in his rural retreat in Woodstock, north of NEW YORK CITY. Coolidge became a frequent visitor after he moved to the nearby region of Massachusetts's BERKSHIRES in 1970. Guston's visits to BOSTON, MASSACHUSETTS, where he taught at Boston University from 1973 to 1978, put him in touch with WILLIAM CORBETT. Guston provided covers for various Angel Hair volumes (ALICE NOTLEY, *Incidentals in the Day World,* 1973; Corbett, *Columbus Square Journal,* 1976) and for magazines edited by Waldman (*The WORLD*), Berkson (*Big Sky*), and Corbett (*Fire Exit*). However, his closest COLLABORATION with poets took the form of drawings paired with, and often incorporating the text of, poems. Berkson's *ENIGMA VARIATIONS* (BIG SKY, 1975) exhibits the former relationship; Coolidge's *Baffling Means* (O-blek, 1991) surveys the most extensive case of the latter. In such cases, Guston reciprocated by reading the poems with the fully human attention that he appreciated in the poets' response to his art. "I like that kind of reaction, compared with reactions like the green works, the blue doesn't work," Guston explained (Balken 33). A specific reaction from Coolidge uncannily recalls O'Hara's response to the abstract work a decade earlier. According to Guston, Coolidge said that a particular work "looked as if an invisible presence had been there, but had left these objects and gone somewhere else" (Balken 33).

Bibliography

Balken, Debra Bricker. *Philip Guston's Poem-Pictures.* Andover, Mass.: Addison Gallery of American Art, Phillips Academy; Seattle: University of Washington Press, 1994.

Berkson, Bill. "The Dark Pictures" (1990). In *The Sweet Singer of Modernism and Other Art Writings, 1985–2003.* Jamestown, R.I.: Qua Books, 2003, 107–110.

———. "The New Gustons." *Art News* 69, no. 6 (October 1970): 44–47, 85.

———. "Pyramid and Shoe: Philip Guston and the Funnies." In *Philip Guston Retrospective,* by Michael Auping, 65–73. Exhibit catalog. Fort Worth, Tex.: Modern Art Museum of Fort Worth; New York: Thames & Hudson, 2003.

Corbett, William. *Philip Guston's Late Works: A Memoir.* Cambridge, Mass.: Zoland, 1994.

Gooch, Brad. *City Poet: The Life and Times of Frank O'Hara.* New York: Knopf, 1993.

Greenberg, Clement. "America Takes the Lead, 1945–1965" (1965). In *The Collected Essays and Criticism.* Vol. 4, *Modernism with a Vengeance, 1957–1969.* Edited by John O'Brian. Chicago: University of Chicago Press, 1995, 212–217.

Guston, Philip. "Dialogue with Philip Guston 11/1/64." Interview by Bill Berkson. *Art and Literature* 7 (Winter 1965): 56–69.

———. "Portrait & Letter." In *Homage to Frank O'Hara,* edited by Bill Berkson and Joe LeSueur, 100–101. Bolinas, Calif.: Big Sky, 1988.

O'Hara, Frank. "Growth and Guston" (1962). In *Art Chronicles 1954–1966.* Rev. ed. New York: Braziller, 1990, 134–141.

———. "It Seems Far Away and Gentle Now" (1956). In *The Collected Poems.* Rev. ed. Edited by Donald Allen. Berkeley: University of California Press, 1995, 261.

Schjeldahl, Peter. "Philip Guston." In *The Hydrogen Jukebox: Selected Writings, 1978–1990.* Berkeley: University of California Press, 1991, 227–231.

Storr, Robert. *Philip Guston.* New York: Abbeville, 1986.

Welish, Marjorie. "The Art of Philip Guston" (1988). In *Signifying Art: Essays on Art after 1960.* Cambridge: Cambridge University Press, 1999, 146–158.

H

Hamptons, the

The area along the southern shore of eastern Long Island is referred to as "the Hamptons" because of the string of towns bearing the name, from Westhampton Beach to East Hampton, celebrated by KENNETH KOCH as "East Hampton glaringest of Hamptons Hampton of sea shine of de Kooning and of leaves" in his poem "A Time Zone." If the presence of "sea shine" attracted such artists as WILLEM DE KOONING, who associated the area with the landscape he had known in Holland, the presence of artists in turn attracted the NEW YORK SCHOOL poets. FAIRFIELD PORTER was particularly hospitable at the home he maintained in Southampton from 1949 until his death in 1975. The "enormous party mesmerizing comers in the disgathering light," on which FRANK O'HARA reports in "Joe's Jacket," was held at the Porters' in August 1959. JAMES SCHUYLER lived with the Porters from 1961 to 1973, and at various times BARBARA GUEST and RON PADGETT spent summers at the Porter home. During TED BERRIGAN's brief residence in Southampton in fall 1970, he and Porter collaborated on the broadside *Scorpion, Eagle and Dove,* with text by Berrigan and a drawing by Porter depicting Southampton's Main Street.

While the Porter household was an extension of the bohemian life that the poets and artists enjoyed together in DOWNTOWN MANHATTAN, the glamor of Uptown wealth came into even closer proximity with bohemian nonchalance in the Hamptons, which have a long-standing tradition as a high-society resort. In this regard the repre-sentative household was that of Leo Castelli in the East Hampton neighborhood of Georgica Pond. Although Castelli had not yet opened his own New York gallery when he began gathering artists and wealthy patrons in the Hamptons, his money and influence were already capable of producing a most powerful mixture. And, in the early 1950s, it was still possible for "a band of vagabonds," as LARRY RIVERS describes the cohort that included fellow artists Nell Blaine and JANE FREILICHER and poets JOHN ASHBERY and Koch, to rent a small bungalow just down the road from the Castellis. Rivers recalls "their huge house with the circular pebble driveway, the money, the important visitors, the da Vinci expert, the long-haired dachshunds" (268). During summer 1952, Willem and Elaine de Kooning had each been provided a separate studio at the Castellis', and JOHN BERNARD MYERS, who was also staying nearby, took the occasion to introduce the de Koonings to his gallery poets, Ashbery, Koch, and O'Hara. In "Day and Night in 1952" O'Hara recorded both the exhilaration and the strangeness that he and his fellow "vagabonds" experienced on such occasions, "grinning and carrying on as if it were a picnic given by somebody else's church."

Although he lived nearby in Springs, JACKSON POLLOCK appeared less frequently on the Castellis' guest list as he proved himself unable to handle the heavy drinking that was part of the social ritual. His death from a drunk-driving accident on the road to Springs in 1956 indelibly stamped the landscape with the Pollock legend. The local cemetery where he is buried has become a monument to the New York School with the addition of graves of many other prominent figures, including O'Hara.

Bibliography

Gruen, John. *The Party's Over Now.* Wainscott, N.Y.: Pushcart Press, 1989.

Harrison, Helen A., and Constance Ayers Denne. *Hamptons Bohemia: Two Centuries of Artists and Writers on the Beach.* San Francisco: Chronicle Books, 2002.

Koch, Kenneth. "A Time Zone." *One Train.* New York: Knopf, 1994, 22–30.

Long, Robert, ed. *Long Island Poets.* New York: Permanent Press, 1986.

Myers, John Bernard. *Tracking the Marvelous: A Life in the New York Art World.* New York: Random House, 1983.

O'Hara, Frank. *The Collected Poems.* Rev. ed. Edited by Donald Allen. Barkeley: University of California Press, 1995.

Rivers, Larry, with Arnold Weinstein. *What Did I Do?* New York: HarperCollins, 1992.

Hanging Loose (1966–)

Hanging Loose magazine began in 1966, the same year as the POETRY PROJECT AT ST. MARK'S CHURCH IN-THE-BOWERY. Though the latter is central and the former only peripheral to the NEW YORK SCHOOL, it is instructive to trace the parallel tracks that each institution has pursued into the present day. A communal, democratic ethic has contributed to the survival of both projects. Unknown writers are encouraged to participate and to keep coming back. Because a sense of the group continues, transitions in leadership are manageable, although in the case of *Hanging Loose,* one editor, Bob Hershon, has remained on the scene almost from the beginning. In 1967 he joined founding editors Ron Schreiber, Emmett Jarrett, and Dick Lourie, each of whom later left NEW YORK CITY. Hershon, Schreiber, and Lourie continue as editors, joined by Mark Pawlak. The policy of collective editing was extended to the reader by the original format of *Hanging Loose,* offering loose mimeographed pages in an envelope, rather than bound, hence the title. A reader could choose which poems to save—the contents were predominantly poems, especially in early issues—and which to throw away. A more conventional bound format was adopted starting with issue 25 (summer 1975).

It is possible to generalize about the poetry published in *Hanging Loose* to distinguish it from the New York School aesthetic, starting with the idea of the "aesthetic" itself. As Burton Hatlen has observed, "the emphasis in *Hanging Loose* has consistently been on 'content'—on what gets 'said,' not on what gets made" (139). However, the increasing representation of New York School writers in *Hanging Loose* in recent years suggests that more contingent factors have influenced the relationship. *Hanging Loose* is based in Brooklyn rather than Manhattan. In the spirit of open democracy, the editors established a policy of not soliciting material but letting submissions find their way to them. Hershon has relaxed that policy and, while keeping the magazine open to new writers, has encouraged submissions by writers he admires, particularly those who have not attracted the attention of commercial publishers. From the mid-1980s onward there has been a significant increase in the number of New York School writers published in *Hanging Loose* and in the book series under that imprint. Among these writers are JACK COLLOM (who appeared in the first issue of the magazine), TIM DLUGOS, MARY FERRARI, EDWARD FIELD, ED FRIEDMAN, MICHAEL FRIEDMAN, CLIFF FYMAN, JOHN GODFREY, YUKI HARTMAN, DAVID LEHMAN, GARY LENHART, JOEL LEWIS, EILEEN MYLES, CHARLES NORTH, MAUREEN OWEN, RON PADGETT, SIMON PETTET, JEROME SALA, Elio Schneeman, TONY TOWLE and PAUL VIOLI. Hanging Loose Press published the second installment of *BROADWAY: A POETS AND PAINTERS ANTHOLOGY,* edited by JAMES SCHUYLER and North (1989), and took over from BILL ZAVATSKY's SUN Press the task of keeping in print Schuyler's *Freely Espousing* (originally published by Doubleday in 1969).

Bibliography

Anderson. Elliott, and Mary Kinzie, eds. *The Little Magazine in America: A Modern Documentary History.* Yonkers, N.Y.: Pushcart Press, 1978, 701–702.

Hatlen, Burton. "*Hanging Loose:* A Profile." *Sagetrieb* 3, no. 1 (March 1984): 131–141.

happenings

A mode of PERFORMANCE ART especially involving visual artists during the period roughly from 1958 to 1964, happenings rejected the plot structure of traditional drama. They just happened. The interest in chance occurrence reflects the teaching of JOHN CAGE, who laid the groundwork for happenings in an event at BLACK MOUNTAIN COLLEGE in 1952 (Duberman 370–379). He invited various members of the college community to perform any action they wished within blocks of time arbitrarily assigned by Cage. Participants included the dancer Merce Cunningham, the painter ROBERT RAUSCHENBERG, and the poet CHARLES OLSON.

Poets were not usually assigned to perform in the later happenings that took place in galleries and lofts in NEW YORK CITY, but poets, especially those with close ties to painters, were often among the audience, and audience participation was encouraged. "I took part in them in the sense that I got that tone of it," recalled FRANK O'HARA. "If Red Grooms decides that he's going to paint his face white, get into some-old fashioned underwear, have a drain dragged across the stage, if a tree is going to fall over in a Jim Dine, and if something in an [Claes] Oldenburg is going to collapse—that is for your *fun*. It's supposed to remind you that art is fun and that we're all children and that it's marvelous" (17). O'Hara echoes Allan Kaprow's remark on the "amazingly childlike" quality of JACKSON POLLOCK (7), whose ACTION PAINTING was an immediate precursor to happenings.

Kaprow (1927–2006) began his career as an abstract expressionist painter, studied with Cage at the New School from 1957 to 1959, and mounted the first happening in New York at the Reuben Gallery in June 1959. In Kaprow's article on "The Legacy of Jackson Pollock," one statement in particular points to both happenings and the poetry of the NEW YORK SCHOOL as legitimate heirs: "Pollock, as I see him, left us at the point where we must become preoccupied with and even dazzled by the space and objects of our everyday life, either our bodies, clothes, rooms, or, if need be, the vastness of Forty-Second Street" (7). Like the poetry of the New York School, the space of happenings was often crammed with "objects of our everyday life," one reason that the artists of happenings, such as those mentioned by O'Hara above, are often associated with POP ART. But in the analogy implied between the scale of a Pollock painting and "the vastness of Forty-Second Street," Kaprow suggests that the new action art must literally "take to the streets," that the city itself is the ultimate happening. O'Hara had already placed his poem "Second Avenue" (1953) in the tradition of "works as big as cities" (40), and his many walk poems construct urban experience on the arbitrary pattern of happenings: "I do this, I do that." It is not surprising that O'Hara claimed KENNETH KOCH's *The Construction of Boston* (1962) "really was a happening" (19). Since none of the collaborators, including Rauschenberg, Nikki de Saint Phalle, and Jean Tinguely, as well as Koch, controlled the action, the city took on a life of its own.

Bibliography

Drucker, Johanna. "Collaboration without Object(s) in the Early Happenings." *Art Journal* 52, no. 4 (Winter 1993): 51–58.

Duberman, Martin. *Black Mountain: An Exploration in Community.* 1972. Reprint, New York: Norton, 1993.

Johnston, Jill. "On the Happenings—New York Scene" (1962). In *Marmalade Me.* New York: Dutton, 1971, 44–51.

Kaprow, Allan. "The Legacy of Jackson Pollock" (1958). In *Essays on the Blurring of Art and Life.* Edited by Jeff Kelley. Berkeley: University of California Press, 1993, 1–9.

O'Hara, Frank. *Standing Still and Walking in New York.* Edited by Donald Allen. San Francisco: Grey Fox, 1983.

Sontag, Susan. "Happenings: An Art of Radical Juxtaposition" (1962). In *Against Interpretation and Other Essays.* New York: Dell/Delta, 1966, 263–274.

Hartigan, Grace (1922–2008) *painter*

Among the leading painters of the second generation of the NEW YORK SCHOOL, Grace Hartigan was perhaps foremost in her interaction with poets and poetry, in her personal relations, in her COLLABORATIONs, and in the role assigned to imagery in her painting. Hartigan met the New York School poets through their association with the TIBOR DE NAGY GALLERY, where she had her first solo exhibit in 1951. She and FRANK O'HARA immediately formed a close bond that developed into a love affair, as Hartigan described it. Although O'Hara's HOMOSEXUALITY prevented them from becoming sexual partners, it deepened their mutual understanding through the role-playing demanded of women and gay men in the macho culture of the time. In the "camp" spirit of the gay poets who referred to one another by women's names, Hartigan first exhibited at the de Nagy Gallery under the name "George." Her practice is honored in the title of O'Hara's early "eclogue," "Grace and George" (1952).

Masking and multiple identities are recurring themes in Hartigan's *Oranges* (1953), a series of paintings based on prose poems by O'Hara, as well as in individual paintings such as *The Masker* and *Masquerade* (both 1954), for which O'Hara posed as a model. Among the many poems that O'Hara composed with Hartigan in mind (including "Poem for a Painter," "Portrait of Grace," "Christmas Card for Grace Hartigan," "For Grace after a Party"), the theme of masquerade finds its culmination in "IN MEMORY OF MY FEELINGS" (1956), where Hartigan's name appears in the dedication and echoes in the line, "Grace to be born and live as variously as possible." In light of the fact that this line is inscribed on O'Hara's gravestone, it assumes retrospectively the mood of elegy, another theme that O'Hara and Hartigan shared. For the memorial volume issued by the Museum of Modern Art, entitled *In Memory of My Feelings* (1967), Hartigan chose to set the text of O'Hara's poem "The DAY LADY DIED" within a design suggestive of gravestones. She also composed a memorial painting, *Frank O'Hara, 1926–1966* (1966), an abstract composition in somber shades of green and gray punctuated by life-affirming reds. In further affirmation of O'Hara, she later depicted him receiving the tribute of a female figure, doubtless symbolizing Hartigan herself, in a painting entitled *Crowning of the Poet* (1985).

The two memorial paintings for O'Hara, one abstract, the other figurative, represent a formal tension in Hartigan's work that O'Hara helped her work through, in defiance of the reigning critical dogma that only "pure" abstraction could be con-

sidered "advanced" painting. The importance of imagery in the poems on which the *Oranges* are based no doubt encouraged Hartigan in the direction of figurative painting, although some of her later work based directly on poems is more abstract, such as the series of prints entitled *Salute* (based on JAMES SCHUYLER), "The Hero Leaves His Ship" (based on BARBARA GUEST), and "*Archaics*" (also based on Guest). O'Hara offered a theoretical argument for the combination of abstract and figurative elements in an essay entitled "Nature and New Painting" (1954). In a section on Hartigan, O'Hara pays particular attention to her painting *Grand Street Brides* (1954), based on displays in the windows of bridal shops in the Lower East Side neighborhood where Hartigan lived. "Permission" to draw on imagery from popular culture is a specific debt for which Hartigan credits O'Hara. It led her in a direction that later historians have associated with POP ART, although Hartigan insists her work is very different in spirit.

When O'Hara saw her painting *Marilyn* in 1962, he misread what is essentially an elegy as a pop parody, in the spirit of ANDY WARHOL's treatments of the recently deceased movie star, Marilyn Monroe. By this time, however, the close friendship between Hartigan and O'Hara had ended. In 1960 Hartigan had married her fourth husband, Dr. Winston Price, and moved to Baltimore, Maryland, where he was engaged in medical research. On the advice of her psychoanalyst she broke off relations with O'Hara in order to strengthen her marriage, but her enduring attachment is evident in her later elegies to him.

Bibliography

O'Hara, Frank. *The Collected Poems*. Rev. ed. Edited by Donald Allen. Berkeley: University of California Press, 1995.

———. "Grace and George: An Eclogue." *Amorous Nightmares of Delay: Selected Plays*. Baltimore: Johns Hopkins University Press, 87–90.

———. "Nature and New Painting." *Standing Still and Walking in New York*. San Francisco: Grey Fox, 1983, 41–51.

Mattison, Robert Saltonstall. *Grace Hartigan: A Painter's World*. New York: Hudson Hills, 1990.

Hartman, Yuki (1939–)

Born and educated in Japan, Yuki Hartman moved with his family to the United States in 1959 and settled in Manhattan in 1965. Married to the painter Susan Greene, he associated with the POETRY PROJECT AT ST. MARK'S CHURCH IN-THE-BOWERY from the mid-1960s onward and also with the Asian American Writer's Workshop beginning in the early 1980s. His first book of poetry is titled *One of My* (Genesis Grasp Press, 1970), which foreshadows, in some sense, Hartman's one-of-a-kind presence on the poetry scene, yet also his modesty. Hartman came to poetry, in part, through studies in literature and exposure to the NEW YORK SCHOOL via workshops at the Poetry Project and as a committed attendee of the poetry reading scene flourishing in DOWNTOWN MANHATTAN in the 1970s and 1980s. His work quickly evinced a confident and unique elongated line and a consistent set of concerns, including dream studies, magic, and Asian poetic and aesthetic traditions, that never seem to waver in the vagaries of poetic fashion. In the tradition of the symbolist poets (a reading of Hartman's work suggested by reviewer Michael Slater), an object of solitary reverie or assemblage of elements that excites the poet's senses is contemplated. In almost painterly, thoughtful application of line, wonderfully concretized by an array of beloved and interesting things and landscapes, a proclivity that Hartman shares with masters such as Li Po and Mei Yaochen, the sense of object and subject devolve. In a layering of perceptions the certainty of categories, the givens of the poem, become reversed, transmuted, shape-shifted, even negated.

A Hartman poem is undeniably only his, despite how the cadence and conversational quality of his work is deeply a part of the New York School flowering of the late '70s. His poems take from the instantaneous urban perceptions of ALLEN GINSBERG. Much of Hartman's work shares affinities with the work of poets CHARLES NORTH, Robert Hershon, MAUREEN OWEN, BERNADETTE MAYER, ED FRIEDMAN, BOB ROSENTHAL, LEWIS WARSH, STEVE LEVINE, Vyt Bakaitis, and the late JIM BRODEY. In his poems one may catch subtle echoes of JOHN GODFREY's inversions and sudden moves, and EILEEN MYLES's humor and making magic out of a minute's apprehension.

Hartman has published seven books and been included in many anthologies, and his work has been reviewed nationally. One discerns from his work that his literary friendships, his private research, and a commitment to the aesthetics of a meaningful everyday life in the flux of NEW YORK CITY, which he shares with painter Susan Greene, more than a larger arena of teaching or widespread literary activities, anchor his sensibility.

He is the author of *Hot Footsteps* (Telephone Books, 1976), *Red Rice* (SWOLLEN MAGPIE PRESS, 1980), *Ping* (Kulchur Foundation, 1984), *New Poems* (Empyreal Press, 1991), *A Coloring Book* (HANGING LOOSE PRESS, 1996), and *Triangle* (Situation Press, 1997). Among the anthologies his work can be found in are *The NuyorAsian Anthology* (Asian American Writers Workshop, 1999), *Out of This World* (Crown, 1992), and BROADWAY: *A POETS AND PAINTERS ANTHOLOGY 1* (Swollen Magpie Press, 1979).

Harwood, Lee (1939–) *British poet*

Lee Harwood was among the first British poets to appreciate tendencies that distinguished NEW YORK SCHOOL poetry within the broader range of New American Poetry. Harwood himself came to represent similar tendencies in new British contexts, from his early volumes with Fulcrum Press (*The White Room*, 1968; *Landscapes*, 1969; *The Sinking Colony*, 1970) to the anthology *Children of Albion: Poetry of the 'Underground' in Britain* (edited with Michael Horovitz, Penguin, 1969) and the Penguin Modern Poets series, in which Harwood shared a volume (number 19, 1971) with JOHN ASHBERY and fellow Briton Tom Raworth (1938–).

For young poets in Britain who were at all disposed to consider the New American Poetry, the BEATS were the obviously new thing and in their raw energy seemed also the most American. ALLEN GINSBERG's *Howl* (1956) echoes in Harwood's early prose-and-poetry assemblage "Cable Street," from his first pamphlet, *title illegible* (Writer's Forum, 1965). However, the rhetoric of Beat poetry troubled Harwood, who disliked "telling people how to live"

(Sheppard, *Poetry of Saying* 42). Meeting Ashbery in London in 1965 opened Harwood's eyes to a different approach: "Poems that created a world and invited the reader to enter, to wander round, to put in their own two cents, to use" (Harwood, "Contributor's Note" 588). While the intimacy of this world fore-stalled rhetoric, its fictionality, as something "created," avoided the bland sincerity of the so-called Movement that then dominated BRITISH POETRY. Of the fictional space he hoped to create, Harwood explained that "the personal was interwoven in this world, but there was much more involved than the personal" ("Contributor's Note" 588).

Although married since 1961, Harwood became romantically involved with Ashbery and followed him to NEW YORK CITY in 1966. Their affair is reflected in Harwood's pamphlet of the same year, *The Man with Blue Eyes,* published as the first in the Angel Hair series of books, with cover design by JOE BRAINARD and introduction by PETER SCHJELDAHL. The anonymously funded Poets Foundation con-ferred on Harwood's book a prize in memory of FRANK O'HARA, whom Harwood had met shortly before O'Hara's death. Although Harwood spent only about two months in the United States in 1966, he began friendships with many New York School poets that would be renewed and extended on later visits. For instance, during a period of residence in BOSTON, MASSACHUSETTS (1972–73), with Judith Walker, a photographer who became Harwood's sec-ond wife, Harwood collaborated with LEWIS WARSH and WILLIAM CORBETT on a mimeograph magazine, *The Boston Eagle* (1973–74). Harwood's volume *Boston-Brighton* (Oasis, 1977) contains poems from the Boston period and from the beginning of his residence in the English seaside city of Brighton, where he and Walker raised their two children and where Harwood maintains his home today. A later prose sequence, *Dream Quilt* (Slow Dancer, 1985), grew out of a year-long residence in BOLINAS, CALIFORNIA (1983–84), following the breakup of Harwood's marriage with Walker. In Bolinas he lived with Bobbie Louise Hawkins (1930–   ), for-mer wife of ROBERT CREELEY. Harwood's relation-ship with Hawkins had begun in the late 1960s and inspired the centerpiece of Harwood's early work, "a notebook" of prose and poetry entitled *The Long Black Veil* and dated 1970–72.

While such biographical connections help to account for the personal element in Harwood's work, the work itself derives as much life from the process of fiction-making as from biographical fact. For instance, during the 1980s Harwood wrote love poems for SANDY BERRIGAN, former wife of TED BERRIGAN, that imagine fictional encounters between Sandy and various artists, including the contemporary Hungarian composers György Kurtág (Harwood, *Collected Poems* 370–72); Istvan Martha (*Collected Poems* 486–88); and the fifth-century Chinese poet Tao-yun (*Collected Poems* 434). If much of Harwood's late work, including the Sandy Berrigan poems, has the air of pastoral, that quality depends on the consciousness of artifice that tradi-tionally distances the pastoral poet from nature: "I look down on this from a high window" ("Gilded White / for Sandy Berrigan," *Collected Poems* 414). Meanwhile, Harwood has continued to explore the modernist tradition of constructing fictional worlds through the technique of collage. According to English poet and critic Robert Sheppard, the collage method employed by Harwood in "Animal Days," from the volume *The Sinking Colony* (Fulcrum, 1979), derives generally from the example of Tristan Tzara, whom Harwood translated (*Selected Poems,* 1975), and specifically from John Ashbery's poem "Europe" (1962) (Sheppard, "It's a Long Road" n.p.). Sheppard sees the continuing influ-ence of "Europe" in Harwood's late work "Days and Nights," from the volume *Morning Light* (Slow Dance, 1998) ("It's a Long Road," part 2 n.p.). The dedication of "Days and Nights" to American artist and sculptor JOSEPH CORNELL (1903–72) serves as a reminder that Ashbery had opened to Harwood the possibility of "creating a Joseph Cornell box with words" (Harwood, "Contributor's Note" 588).

Bibliography

Ashbery, John. "Comment on Lee Harwood's *The White Room*" (1968). In *Selected Prose.* Edited by Eugene Richie. Ann Arbor: University of Michigan Press, 2004, 116.

Ford, Mark. "Emerging Glorious from the Clouds." *The Guardian,* 18 September 2004. Available online. URL: http://books.guardian.co.uk/reviews/poetry/0,6121,1307051,00.html. Accessed December 18, 2008.

Harwood, Lee. Autobiographical essay. In *Contemporary Authors, Autobiography Series* 19, edited by Joyce Nakamura, 135–153. Detroit, Mich.: Gale, 1994.

———. *Collected Poems, 1964–2004*. Exeter, U.K.: Shearsman, 2004.

———. "Contributor's Note." In *The Angel Hair Anthology*, edited by Anne Waldman and Lewis Warsh, 588–589. New York: Granary Books, 2001.

———. "A Faded Memory of Joe Brainard." *Pressed Wafer* 2 (March 2001): 205–208.

Lopez, Tony. "*The White Room* in the New York Schoolroom." In *Something We Have That They Don't: British and American Poetic Relations Since 1925*, edited by Steve Clark and Mark Ford, 137–150. Iowa City: University of Iowa Press, 2004.

Selby, Nick. "'A Generous Time': Lee Harwood in New York." In *Don't Ever Get Famous: Essays on New York Writing after the New York School*, edited by Daniel Kane, 215–241. Champaign, Ill.: Dalkey Archive, 2006.

Sheppard, Robert. "It's a Long Road: A Journey through Lee Harwood's *Collected Poems*." Part 1. Pages. 19 December 2005. Available online. URL: http://robert sheppard.blogspot.com/2005/12/robert-sheppard-review-of-harwoods.html. Accessed December 18, 2008.

———. "It's a Long Road: A Journey through Lee Harwood's *Collected Poems*." Part 2. Pages. 24 January 2006. Available online. URL: http://robertsheppard. blogspot.com/2006/01/robert-sheppard-review-of-harwoods.html. Accessed December 18, 2008.

———. *The Poetry of Saying: British Poetry and Its Discontents, 1950–2000*. Liverpool, U.K.: Liverpool University Press, 2005.

Stannard, Martin. "Lucent Surface, Nourishing Depth." *Staple* 59 (Spring 2004). Available online. URL: http://www.poetrymagazines.org.uk/magazine/record. asp?id=13691. Accessed December 18, 2008.

Weatherhead, A. Kingsley. "Lee Harwood." In *The British Dissonance: Essays on Ten Contemporary Poets*. Columbia: University of Missouri Press, 1983, 173–191.

Hearing Ned Rorem and Kennety Koch (1966)

A cycle of six songs for medium-low voice and piano, *Hearing* was composed in 1966 by NED ROREM to poems written by KENNETH KOCH in 1962. An alternative 1976 version is orchestrated by the composer for soprano, mezzo-soprano, tenor, and baritone voices accompanied by a snare drum, bass drum, triangle, cymbals, xylophone, glockenspiel, gong, and mandolin (or guitar or ukulele).

Rorem, one of the leading American art-song composers of his generation, writes in a neoromantic idiom grounded in traditional tonal practice. The original version of the cycle, published in 1969 by Boosey & Hawkes, opens with "In Love with You," whose MUSIC has three contiguous sections corresponding to its tripartite text. After its opening rhythmically irregular vocal lines ("O what a physical effect it has on me . . .") mingled with scattered keyboard gestures, the song's central section ("We walk through the park . . .") features a perambulating duple-meter ostinato accompaniment, and its concluding passage renders the words "Inside the symposium of your sweetest look's sunflower awning . . ." in a stately fashion, supported by chiming, tertian harmonies. The second song, "Down at the Docks," is a lilting major-key ballad that Rorem indicates as "like a Barcarolle," and the third embodies the despondent tone of Koch's "Poem," with a deliberate, syllabic recitative-like melody over low, sustained piano sonorities whose tempo and harmonic density gradually intensify over the course of the song. Next comes a cheerful presentation of Koch's "Spring" ("Let's take a walk / In the city / Till our shoes get wet . . ."), superimposed over simple, folklike piano themes that contrast dramatically with the dissonant, heavy harmonies of "Initiation," the fifth poem, giving an ominous quality to the text's carefree, spirited mood ("Mediterranean Suns! Shine on in and around"). "Madly Exuberant!" is Rorem's performance direction for the final and longest song, "Hearing," which has no regular meter, the voice's rapid melodic figures rollicking freely over an energetic piano accompaniment that careens between thudding staccato bass tones, chains of massive chords, and light, shimmering textures. Throughout the entire 26-minute cycle, Rorem never deviates from a faithful, linear expression of Koch's words.

Bibliography

Rorem, Ned. *Hearing*. New York: Boosey & Hawkes, 1969.

———. *Rosalind Rees Sings Ned Rorem with the Composer at the Piano.* Sound recording, GSS 104. Saranac Lake, N.Y.: GSS, 1984.

Hell, Richard (Richard Meyers) (1949–)

Famous for performing PUNK ROCK (for which he adopted his stage name), Richard Hell has written song lyrics, prose FICTION, poems, and numerous essays and reviews. The NEW YORK SCHOOL has helped shape not only his poetry but also his openness to diverse means of expression, including performance, and his "do it yourself" attitude, often identified with punk (Taylor 14, 62) but also connected, in Hell's mind, with the POETRY PROJECT AT ST. MARK'S CHURCH IN-THE-BOWERY (statement in *Out of This World* 646–647). Hell has been active at the Poetry Project both as a featured reader and an organizer of a reading series; as a contributor to *The* WORLD; and as the editor of *Cuz,* which briefly replaced *The World* during the 1980s.

Raised in a suburb of Lexington, Kentucky, Richard Meyers was sent, at age 15, to a private school in Delaware (he has called it "a glorified reform school" [Heylin 93]). He soon dropped out in 1966 and made his way to NEW YORK CITY, where he started a magazine, *Genesis: Grasp* (1968–71), to publish his own work and that of other young writers he got to know, including ANDREI CODRESCU, CLARK COOLIDGE, YUKI HARTMAN, and SIMON SCHUCHAT. After his former Delaware schoolmate Tom Miller (1949–) joined him in New York, Meyers conceived a publishing venture, Dot Books, which issued two poetry pamphlets: *Yellow Flowers,* by Andrew Wylie of TELEGRAPH BOOKS, and *Wanna Go Out?* conceived by Miller and Meyers in the guise of a fictional persona, "Theresa Stern."

PATTI SMITH, whom Wylie had introduced to Meyers (Heylin 96), was to have published a third Dot Books volume, but that plan was derailed as Smith, Meyers, and Miller became caught up in rock MUSIC—and in love, in the case of Smith and Miller. Meyers and Miller formed the band The Neon Boys in 1972, re-formed in 1974 as Television, for which Meyers took the name "Richard Hell" and Miller "Tom Verlaine." Hell later performed with The Heartbreakers (1975) and The Voidoids (1976–82), the latter named after an early (1973)

work of experimental prose in which the character Theresa Stern resurfaces, in addition to characters based on Myers, Miller, and Wylie. Rather than participate in the decline of punk into new wave during the 1980s, Hell distanced himself from the music business but found an ironic position for critique by taking on the role of a cynical insider in the movie *Smithereens* (1982).

As a songwriter, Hell is best known for "Blank Generation," the title track of the Voidoids's 1977 album and clearly a synonym for the band's name. The phrase has been interpreted as a gesture of nihilism (McNeil and McCain 281–283), but in the context of New York School poetry, the blank appears as a literary device for generating new meanings. As he prints the lyrics on his [Web site], Hell leaves a blank (___) before the word *generation,* inviting the reader (or listener) to fill in his or her own meaning. The "death of the Author," as Roland Barthes predicted, is simultaneously "the birth of the reader" (1,470). Toward this end, Hell employed the "blank" device in the poem "It" (*Genesis: Grasp,* no. 3, 1970) and it shows up in the following year in TED BERRIGAN's "Train Ride." A character based on Berrigan appears in Hell's second novel, *Godlike* (Little House on the Bowery–Akashic, 2005), as an "amphetamine-addicted, hovering Buddha," in the words of one reviewer (Smith n.p.). While Hell's first novel, *Go Now* (Scribner, 1996), is BEAT influenced in theme (drug addiction) and structure (road trip), *Godlike* transfers the story of Arthur Rimbaud and Paul Verlaine (the source for Hell's and Tom Verlaine's stage names) to the New York School poetry scene of the 1970s. Hell not only bases characters on real poets but also quotes their poems, some authentic, some made up by Hell. Again, similarities with the "Theresa Stern" COLLABORATION with Verlaine suggest that collaboration, another device for undermining authorship, may be Hell's most significant link to the New York School. In the same year as *Godlike,* Hell published *Rabbit Duck* (Repair Books, 2005), a series of poems written in collaboration with DAVID SHAPIRO. Hell's book *Hot and Cold* (PowerHouse, 2001) includes collaborations with Patti Smith, Tom Verlaine (not in the persona of Teresa Stern), Cookie Mueller, and others. Collaborations with the painter Christopher Wool appear in *Psychopts* (JMC & GHB Editions, 2008).

Bibliography

Barthes, Roland. "The Death of the Author" (1968). Translated by Stephen Heath. In *The Norton Anthology of Theory and Criticism*, edited by Vincent B. Leach, 1,466–1,470. New York: Norton, 2001.

Berrigan, Ted. "Train Ride." In *The Collected Poems of Ted Berrigan*. Edited by Alice Notley, Anselm Berrigan, and Edumund Berrigan. Berkeley: University of California Press, 2005. 241–285.

Hell, Richard. "Blank Generation" (1974). Richard Hell: Official site. Available online. URL: http://www.richardhell.com/lyrics2.html. Accessed December 18, 2008.

———. *Hot and Cold: Essays, Poems, Lyrics, Notebooks, Pictures, Fiction*. New York: Powerhouse, 2001.

———. *Spurts: The Richard Hell Story*. Sound recording, R2 74723. Burbank, Calif.: Rhino Records, 2005.

———. Statement in *Out of This World: An Anthology of the St. Mark's Poetry Project, 1966–1991*, edited by Anne Waldman, 646–647. New York: Crown, 1991.

Heylin, Clinton. *From the Velvets to the Voidoids: The Birth of American Punk Rock*. Updated ed. Chicago: A Cappella/Chicago Review Press, 2005.

McNeil, Legs, and Gillian McCain. *Please Kill Me: The Uncensored Oral History of Punk*. New York: Grove, 1996.

Smith, Rod. Review of *Godlike* (excerpt). Richard Hell: Official site. Available online. URL: http://www.richardhell.com/godlike.html#excerpt. Accessed December 18, 2008.

Taylor, Steven. *False Prophet: Field Notes from the Punk Underground*. Middletown, Conn.: Wesleyan University Press, 2003.

Henderson, David (1942–   )

One of the youngest members of the UMBRA poets workshop, David Henderson maintained the longest association with Umbra and with the Lower East Side community where it was based, including the POETRY PROJECT AT ST. MARK'S CHURCH IN-THE-BOWERY. Although he moved to California in 1970, he continued to publish issues of *Umbra* magazine until 1974. His poems appeared frequently in *The WORLD*, the magazine of the Poetry Project, and they are included in all three of the anthologies based on that magazine. Gravitating back to NEW YORK CITY, his hometown, during the

1980s, Henderson has since conducted workshops at the Poetry Project and in BOB HOLMAN's Study Abroad in-the-Bowery program.

Henderson's first collection, *Felix of the Silent Forest*, was published in 1967 by DIANE DI PRIMA's Poets Press, with an introduction by LeRoi Jones (AMIRI BARAKA). The title refers to the cartoon character Felix the Cat, a cat doubly denatured because he is not "real" and because he inhabits the noisy city although he is "of the silent forest." The mood of Henderson's poems swings between a sense of alienation or displacement, grounded in his experience as an African American, and a vision of human unity, of divisions overcome. At the latter pole the tension of city versus forest finds a resolution that resembles the urban pastoral GENRE favored by NEW YORK SCHOOL poets. For instance, in "Poem for Painters," included in TOM WEATHERLY's anthology *Natural Process* (1970), urban chaos and social conflict whirl around a central point of stillness, a single tree growing on the sidewalk outside the Downtown loft of Joe Overstreet (1933–   ), a painter associated with Umbra. The poem's address to a painter is another point in common with the New York School.

However, MUSIC is the other art with which Henderson increasingly aligned his poetry. In his second collection, *De Mayor of Harlem* (Dutton, 1970), "talk of bopping" is a way of talking that captures the life of the street and enlivens poetry with improvised rhythms (as in "Jocko for Music and Dance"). During this period, Henderson performed poems with JAZZ musicians Ornette Coleman (1930–   ) and Sun Ra (1914–93). In 1978 he published the work for which he is still best known, a biography of rock guitarist Jimi Hendrix (1942–70), originally entitled *Jimi Hendrix: Voodoo Child of the Aquarian Age* and retitled in later editions as *'Scuse Me While I Kiss the Sky* (Bantam, 1981; Atria, 2006).

Music remains an important point of reference in Henderson's later collections of poems, which continue to explore tensions in mood through symbolic geography. The title of *The Low East* (North Atlantic Books, 1980) refers to New York's Lower East Side, always a site of ambivalence for Henderson. An early poem, "Downtown-Boy Uptown" (1964), posed the dilemma: "I stand in my low east window looking down. / Am I in the wrong slum?" (Nielsen and Ramey 91). But the east is also the place of the rising sun, a counterthrust to feeling "low." Thus, *The Low East* offers "Hanging Out in Music" as a means of finding "company" even "when you alone" (65). Similarly, the later poem "Third Eye World" seeks to overcome human divisions through music: "Everyone can sing" (*Neo-California* 70). On the other hand, in "Percy Sledge in South Africa," hearing the recorded voice of the American rhythm and blues singer Percy Sledge (1941–   ) in a South African bar prompts reflections on racial apartheid in South Africa, by way of ironic allusion to "When a Man Loves a Woman" (1966), Sledge's theme song:

> *Percy Sledge*
> *will give up all his comforts*
> *and sleep out*
> *in the rain*
> (*Neo-California* 63).

Both "Third Eye World" and "Percy Sledge" appear in Henderson's most recent collection, *Neo-California* (North Atlantic Books, 1998). This title combines not only past and present but also New York and California, the two locations where Henderson has alternately made his home.

Bibliography

Coleman, Ornette. *Science Fiction*. Title track (1971) with poem by David Henderson. Audio recording, KC 31061. New York: Columbia Records, 1972.

Henderson, David. *De Mayor of Harlem*. New York: Dutton, 1970.

———. *The Low East*. Richmond, Calif.: North Atlantic Books, 1980.

———. *Neo-California*. Berkeley, Calif.: North Atlantic Books, 1998.

———. "Poem for Painters." In *Natural Process: An Anthology of New Black Poetry*, edited by Ted Wilentz and Tom Weatherly, 54–63. New York: Hill & Wang, 1970.

Nielsen, Aldon Lynn, and Lauri Ramey, eds. *Every Goodbye Ain't Gone: An Anthology of Innovative Poetry by African Americans*. Tuscaloosa: University of Alabama Press, 2006.

Sun Ra. "Love in Outer Space" (ca. 1977). In *The Singles*. Audio recording, ECD 22164–2. Conshohocken, Pa.: Evidence Music, 1996.

Thomas, Lorenzo. *Extraordinary Measures: Afrocentric Modernism and Twentieth-Century American Poetry*. Tuscaloosa: University of Alabama Press, 2000, 122–127.

Henry, Gerrit (1950–2003)

Gerrit Henry's brilliant poetry is "by turns, sometimes even simultaneously, bitter and very funny, wry and ecstatic, harrowing and soothing" (Ashbery xiii). A comic, lyric genius, Henry wanted "poetry to be as lively and as buoyant as a lyric penned by Jerome Kern for delivery by Billie Holiday" and "to find a poetic language capable of communicating the glamour and the romance of Fred Astaire singing 'Night and Day' in *The Gay Divorcée*" (Lehman, iv). His rhyming couplets and quatrains celebrate Judy Garland or Cole Porter with the wit of KENNETH KOCH, JOHN ASHBERY, FRANK O'HARA, W. H. AUDEN, or the Renaissance troubadours.

Born in New York, Henry grew up on Long Island and earned a B.A. in English from Columbia University (1972), where he studied with Koch. A cabaret singer and songwriter in the 1970s, he also worked at the Museum of Modern Art. Ashbery invited him to write for *ARTnews*, and he became contributing editor. His reviews appeared in publications such as *Art in America*, the *Village Voice*, *People*, *Art International*, and the *New York Times*. He was a guest curator and wrote catalog essays for exhibitions and also the monograph *Janet Fish* (1987). These pieces "shimmer with verbal felicities enough to make them worth reading for their own literary sake" (Ratcliff 142). He received poetry awards from the Cornell Woolrich Fellowship, Ann and Erlo Von Waveren Foundation, Poetry Foundation, New York Foundation for the Arts, and National Endowment for the Arts, and taught poetry at C. W. Post and the School of Visual Arts. He died in Manhattan of a heart attack at 52.

Henry's troubled life sensitized him: "Still, it's the wounded who strive to heal, / And saints who do not know to feel" ("Blue Prelude," published in

Couplets and Ballades, 1998). In "The Confessions of Gerrit" (*The Mirrored Clubs of Hell,* 1991), he playfully begins, "I drink a lot of skimmed milk / . . . I stare long and hard at handsome faces," but also speaks frankly: "I've gotten fat to discourage AIDS / . . . My parlor palm is dying, frond by yellowing frond." As Ashbery suggests, Henry is "a Dante adrift without a Virgil" (xiii) in a Manhattan "Satyricon" populated by devils and angels, friends and loved ones: "The soul realizing / The heart's only end / Say Goodnight / You've found a friend" (*Lullabye* 12).

Bibliography

Ashbery, John. Introduction to *The Mirrored Clubs of Hell,* by Gerrit Henry. New York: Little, Brown, 1991, xiii–xiv.

Henry, Gerrit, With Hilary Lorenz. *Lullabye.* Kasterlec, Belgium: Frans Masereel Center, 2002.

———. *Couplets and Ballades.* Baltimore, Md.: Dolphin, 1998.

Lehman, David. Introduction to *The Lecturer's Aria,* by Gerrit Henry. New York: Groundwater Press/Intuflo Editions, 1989, iv.

Ratcliff, Carter. "Gerrit Henry." *Art in America* (September 2003): 142.

Hernton, Calvin (1932–2001)

Born in Chattanooga, Tennessee, Calvin Hernton became a prominent member of the UMBRA poetry workshop on NEW YORK CITY's Lower East Side in the early 1960s. He is best known for a series of studies linking racism and sexuality, drawing on his training as a sociologist and his work with radical psychiatrist R. D. Laing (1927–89) at the Institute for Phenomenological Studies in London.

Hernton began traveling to New York City while an undergraduate at Talladega College in Alabama (B.A., 1954). After receiving his master's degree in sociology from Fisk University in Nashville, Tennessee (1956), and teaching social science at various institutions, he returned to New York in 1961 and moved to East 6th Street, between First and Second Avenues, at the heart of a vibrant and temporarily interracial bohemia. He began to participate at poetry readings at LES DEUX MÉGOTS on East 7th Street and there met DAVID HENDERSON, who also later joined Umbra.

Raymond Patterson (1929–2001) introduced Hernton to Umbra organizer TOM DENT, and his work began appearing in the journal *Umbra* and other Lower East Side magazines. For instance, "Jitterbugging in the Streets," a poem about the violent protests that were beginning to challenge American indifference to racial injustice, circulated in a magazine called *Streets.* Hernton's engagement in the urban scene is the principal trait he shares with the NEW YORK SCHOOL poets, though Hernton's message is more explicitly political. "The Gift Outraged," about the social victims and outcasts the speaker encounters in Tompkins Square Park, parodies the title of "The Gift Outright," the poem Robert Frost read at the inauguration of President John F. Kennedy in 1961. In his first separate volume, *The Coming of Chronos to the House of Nightsong: An Epical Narrative of the South* (Interim, 1964), Hernton returned to a southern setting and adopted a mythical method derived partly from black folklore and partly from modernist poetry extending from T. S. Eliot to CHARLES OLSON. In this respect his work differs markedly from contemporary New York School poetry.

In 1965 Hernton published his first nonfiction book, *Sex and Racism in America* (Doubleday), on the connections between racial and sexual anxiety in U.S. culture. In the same year he left for London to study with Laing. He returned to the United States in 1969 and in 1970 began teaching at Oberlin College, in Ohio, where he remained until his retirement in 1999. Hernton pursued his analysis of racism, now reinforced by Laing's psychological theories, in *Coming Together: Black Power, White Hatred, and Sexual Hang-Ups* (Random House, 1972) and *The Sexual Mountain and Black Women Writers: Adventures in Sex, Literature, and Real Life* (Doubleday, 1987). A novel, *Scarecrow* (Doubleday, 1974), arrives at a pessimistic conclusion that seems to question the efficacy of Laingian therapy. Hernton's colleague from Umbra days, ISHMAEL REED, published Hernton's two collections of poems: *Medicine Man: Collected Poems* (Reed, Cannon and Johnson, 1976) and *The Red Crab Gang and Black River Poems* (Ishmael Reed Publications, 1999).

Bibliography

Hernton, Calvin. "Umbra: A Personal Recounting." *African American Review* 27, no. 4 (Winter 1993): 579–584.

Oren, Michael. "The Enigmatic Career of Hernton's Scarecrow." *Callaloo* 29, no. 2 (Spring 2006): 608–618.

Thomas, Lorenzo. *Extraordinary Measures: Afrocentric Modernism and Twentieth-Century American Poetry.* Tuscaloosa: University of Alabama Press, 2000. 133–136.

Heroes, The John Ashbery (1950)

JOHN ASHBERY's one-act play *The Heroes* is his most frequently performed work for the THEATER. It has a place in theatrical history as an early production of the LIVING THEATRE (1952), whose director, Judith Malina, described Ashbery's play as "a poetic discussion of the foibles of the figures of the Greek myths, like an 18th century play written by a young 20th century poet whose pen has been dipped in surrealism" (232). Rather than looking back to surrealist antecedents, the poet Richard Howard has used *The Heroes* as a lens for viewing the later development of Ashbery's poetry (though the play itself is written in prose). Theseus's description of the labyrinth, the site of his heroic slaying of the minotaur, becomes, for Howard, an emblem of the Ashbery poem: "the poem as a means of escape from identity, leading into a world of contemplation, indifference, bliss" (29). Theseus explains that the weapon he used to slay the minotaur was "the indifference of the true aesthete" (*Heroes* 7), but he also explains that the minotaur was only a FICTION all along, "a stupid, unambitious piece of stage machinery" (4). This revelation, for DAVID LEHMAN, locates the play in the world of postmodernism, where "artifice doesn't bother to disguise itself" (n.p.).

The literal setting of the play is "a country house near the sea"; much of the dialogue has a contemporary air suggestive of a house party in the HAMPTONS. The characters, however, all derive from Greek myth. The house belongs to Achilles, who shares it with Patroclus, the young friend whose death is central to the action of Homer's *Iliad*. Though it is never stated explicitly, there is a strong suggestion that all or most of the characters, including house guests Ulysses and Circe from Homer's *Odyssey*, are dead, and that the setting is the underworld. "You know how funny people get after they've been down here awhile," Achilles reminds Patroclus (*Heroes* 16). Theseus's ability to leave at the end of the play may be based on the legend about his successful journey into Hades and back to the land of the living. However, a more likely explanation is that Theseus symbolizes the life-giving power of artifice, in contrast to the death-threatening aspect of the minotaur. In André Gide's novella *Thésée* (*Theseus*, 1946), which Ashbery has acknowledged as a model (Ashbery, *Mark Ford* 36), the grand artificer Daedalus, architect of the labyrinth, explains to Theseus: "What happens, in the case of a hero, is this: his mark endures. Poetry and the arts reanimate it and it becomes an enduring symbol" (Gide 1,232–1,233). For Ashbery, however, heroic endurance flattens out into mundane duration. The director Herbert Machiz, who mounted the second production of *The Heroes* for the ARTIST'S THEATRE in 1953, understood Ashbery's characters as antiheroes in this sense, specifically opposed to the heroic postures of World War II: "They are neither gods nor heroes; they simply have a talent for survival. They are authentic post-war *enfants terribles*, with a tenderness imbedded in their speech and a cynicism that might really be going too far were it not for the leaven of a playful wit as innocent as a child's" (Machiz 10).

Bibliography

Ashbery, John. *The Heroes.* In *Three Plays.* Calais, Vt.: Z Press, 1978, 1–29.

———. *John Ashbery in Conversation with Mark Ford.* London: Between the Lines, 2003.

———. "Poet in the Theater." *Performing Arts Journal* 3, no. 3 (Winter 1979): 15–27.

Auslander, Philip. *The New York School Poets as Playwrights: O'Hara, Ashbery, Koch, Schuyler and the Visual Arts.* New York: Peter Lang, 1989, 79–85.

Gide, André. *Theseus.* Translated by John Russell. *Partisan Review* 15, no. 11 (November 1948): 1,159–1,174, 1,227–1,248.

Howard, Richard. "John Ashbery." In *Alone with America: Essays on the Art of Poetry in the United States Since*

1950. Enlarged ed. New York: Atheneum, 1980, 25–56.

Lehman, David. "The Questions of Postmodernism." *Jacket* 4 (July 1988). Available online. URL: http://jacketmagazine.com/04/lehman-postmod.html. Accessed December 18, 2008.

Machiz, Herbert. Introduction to *Artists' Theatre: Four Plays.* New York: Grove, 1960, 7–13.

Malina, Judith. *The Diaries, 1947–1957.* New York: Grove, 1984.

Herself Defined: The Poet H.D. and Her World Barbara Guest (1984)

In the biography *Herself Defined*, BARBARA GUEST produced the most extensive work of nonfiction prose by any NEW YORK SCHOOL poet. That its subject is a poet, Hilda Doolittle, who published under her initials H.D., is, of course, no accident; however, it is the poet's life more than her poems that receives Guest's attention, and it was the circumstances of Guest's life that led her to focus on H.D. Guest's second husband, Stephen Guest, who had been an intimate of H.D., and he revealed to her "an intimate detail" of H.D.'s life, identifying the composer Cecil Gray as the father of H.D.'s child, Perdita. By this time Perdita herself had moved to NEW YORK CITY, where she and Guest became friends, even to the point of sharing an apartment for a while. When Guest embarked on her biography in the late 1970s, Perdita encouraged and assisted her by providing information. Perdita's son, Timothy Schaffner, reissued the biography under the imprint of his Schaffner Press in 2003.

Guest's biography appeared in the midst of a revival of critical interest in H.D., spurred largely by the feminist movement. Feminist critic and H.D. scholar Susan Stanford Friedman preferred Guest's biography to its recent predecessor, Janice S. Robinson's *H.D.: The Life and Work of an American Poet* (1982). However, Friedman was troubled that Guest kept her distance from contemporary scholarship and even from her subject, H.D., toward whom Guest maintains "a critical, ironic stance," Friedman observes (109). These are the traits of Guest's work that most clearly reflect the sensibility of the New York School, and it is no wonder that they were approved by the "New York intellectual"

Alfred Kazin in his review of the biography. Guest refuses to subordinate the individuality of H.D. to the purposes of a movement, whether feminism or imagism. And the central irony of Guest's project is that H.D.'s individuality cannot be defined, neither by herself nor by her biographer.

Herself Defined helps reveal Guest's individuality as a writer when read in the context of her creative work of the period: the prose-poem sequence *The COUNTESS FROM MINNEAPOLIS* (1976); the novel *SEEKING AIR* (1978); "The Türler Losses" (1979), a sequence of poems based in part on research trips to Switzerland; and the sequence of poems *BIOGRAPHY* (1980), which reflects Guest's experience of becoming a biographer. The first two works, in particular, explore the necessary accommodations to ordinary reality of a life devoted almost wholly to the imagination, a life very much like that of H.D. Moreover, each of these works represents, in a different way, an opening out to narrative beyond a concentration on image, which had been the starting point for both H.D. and Guest.

Bibliography

Friedman, Susan Stanford. "H.D." *Contemporary Literature* 26, no. 1 (Spring 1985): 107–113.

Guest, Barbara. "H.D. and the Conflict of Imagism." In *Forces of Imagination.* Berkeley, Calif.: Kelsey St. Press, 2003, 61–73.

———. "The Intimacy of Biography." *Iowa Review* 16, no. 3 (Fall 1986): 58–71.

Kazin, Alfred. "A Nymph of the New." *New York Review of Books* 31, no. 5 (March 29, 1984), 15.

Hess, Thomas B. (1920–1978) *art critic*

As an editor at *Art News* magazine, Tom Hess involved the NEW YORK SCHOOL poets in writing art criticism and provided the major forum for promoting ABSTRACT EXPRESSIONISM, the movement in painting with which the poets of the first generation were most closely allied. According to BARBARA GUEST, the first poet he recruited to *Art News* in 1951, Hess "believed in the instinct of poets to define a painting, no matter how untrained in the formal aesthetics of art" (Wilkin 31). Hess himself had been well trained in formal aesthetics, at private schools, partly in Europe, and at

Yale University (B.A., 1942), but his own instinct seemed to suggest that the new painting emerging in NEW YORK CITY demanded an accounting in terms of process more than FORM. He inaugurated the series of *Art News* articles describing how an individual artist "paints a picture" and wrote one of the most influential installments, "De Kooning Paints a Picture," tracing the development of *Woman* I. Hess and HAROLD ROSENBERG are the two critics most responsible for establishing WILLEM DE KOONING as the leader of the New York art world during the 1950s. ACTION PAINTING, the mode that came to be identified with de Kooning, took its name from an article Rosenberg published in *Art News*.

When Hess joined the staff of *Art News* in 1946, after serving in the air force during World War II, the magazine was a fairly conservative publication with a long history, dating back to 1902. The editor, Alfred M. Frankfurter (1906–65), had held his position since 1936 and would retain it until his death in 1965, when Hess succeeded him; however, in the position of executive editor from 1948 to 1965, Hess played a major role in determining policy, including the hiring of poets to write the monthly "reviews and previews" that aimed to cover every art show in New York. JOHN ASHBERY gave a cynical explanation for these assignments: "[I]t was sort of slave wages, because poets are generally poor, and people who were trained as art historians are not going to write short reviews, for which we got paid something like five dollars" (296). Nevertheless, most of the first generation of poets (Ashbery, EDWIN DENBY, Guest, KENNETH KOCH, FRANK O'HARA, JAMES SCHUYLER) and many of the second generation (BILL BERKSON, TED BERRIGAN, GERRIT HENRY, RON PADGETT, JOHN PERREAULT, CARTER RATCLIFF, PETER SCHJELDAHL) wrote for *Art News* under Hess's editorship. Eventually, Ashbery became the most heavily involved, serving as executive editor from 1966 until sale of the magazine in 1972 led to both Ashbery's and Hess's departure. During the period of their COLLABORATION they coedited the series of *Art News* annuals on specific themes, in addition to preparing monthly issues of the magazine.

Hess's involvement in the art world reached beyond *Art News* into areas where the artists themselves were the primary audience. His influential book, *Abstract Painting* (1951), provided the focus of a series of panels at the artists' CLUB, debating the convergence of abstraction and expressionism that Hess perceived in recent American art. One of the panels (March 7, 1952) became the occasion for introducing the young artists of the TIBOR DE NAGY GALLERY along with their poet ally, O'Hara. Hess would later appear with O'Hara in the pages of the Club's magazine, *It Is. Location,* a magazine that Hess and Rosenberg ran briefly during the 1960s, debuted with LARRY RIVERS's important memoir of his collaboration with O'Hara, "Life among Stones." With his wife, Audrey (1924–74), an heir to the Sears Roebuck fortune, Hess administered the Longview Foundation, which supported artists and writers with individual grants, such as the award to Schuyler announced in the second issue of *LOCUS SOLUS* (1961). Hess also curated retrospective exhibitions at the Museum of Modern Art of two of the artists he most admired, de Kooning (1969) and Barnett Newman (1971). He had just assumed the position of consultative chairman of the department of 20th-century painting at the Metropolitan Museum of Art when he died of a heart attack in 1978, two days after the death of Rosenberg.

Bibliography

Ashbery, John. "An Interview in Warsaw" (1980). In *Code of Signals: Recent Writings in Poetics,* edited by Michael Palmer, 294–314. Berkeley, Calif.: North Atlantic Books, 1983.

Baker, Elizabeth C., et al. Memorial statements on Thomas B. Hess. *Art in America* 66, no. 6 (November–December 1978): 8–13.

Craven, David. "The 'Critique-Poésie' of Thomas Hess." *Art Criticism* 1, no. 1 (Spring 1979): 83–100.

Hamill, Pete. "The First 100 Years of *Art News.*" *Art News* 101 (November 2002): 196–203.

Hess, Thomas. *Abstract Painting: Background and American Phase.* New York: Viking, 1951.

———. "De Kooning Paints a Picture." *Art News* 52 (March 1953): 30–33ff.

O'Hara, Frank, Thomas B. Hess, et al. "Non-American Painting: Six Opinions of Abstract Art in Other Countries." *It Is* 3 (Winter–Spring 1959): 76–78.

Rivers, Larry. "Life Among the Stones." *Location* 1, no. 1 (Spring 1963): 90–98.

Rosenberg, Harold. "The American Action Painters." *Art News* 51 (December 1952): 22–23ff.

Wilkin, Karen. "The First Fifty Years." In *Tibor de Nagy Gallery: The First Fifty Years, 1950–2000.* New York: Tibor de Nagy Gallery, 2000, 17–40.

Highfill, Mitch (1958–   )

In the poetry of Mitch Highfill, FRANK O'HARA's NEW YORK CITY translates to a magical plane:

> Strolling down Second Avenue at midnight
> wing rubbings of insects in my throat.
> I ask my double for a glass of water ("Gemini,"
> Liquid Affairs 1).

Highfill's concept of the poem derives less from the NEW YORK SCHOOL than from the poets of DEEP IMAGE and the SAN FRANCISCO RENAISSANCE (Jack Spicer has been a major influence). However, his interest in language involved him in "procedural" FORMS that led him from the chance operations of JACKSON MAC LOW, reflected in Highfill's first collection, *No Precautions* (Next Century, 1984), to traditional forms favored by the New York School. For instance, Highfill employs sestina and pantoum in *The Blue Dahlia,* written in 1984–85 though not published until 1999 (Detour Press). Like *Turn* (Situations, 1997), *Rebis* (DoubleChange e-book, 2002; Open Mouth chapbook, 2007), and *A Dozen Sonnets* (Faux Press e-books, 2004), *The Blue Dahlia* is a SERIAL POEM, reflecting Spicer's influence. WILLIAM S. BURROUGHS's influence is also evident in the "cut-up" operations performed on the detective FICTION of Raymond Chandler, the source for the title of *The Blue Dahlia.* Highfill proceeded to experiment with "found" poetry in work collected in *Liquid Affairs* (United Artists, 1995), such as "Doctrine of Security" and "Yellow Ribbon"—drawn from political discourse—and in his early participation in the "flarf" list, a group of poets involved in skimming the froth churned up while surfing the Web. Although Highfill's tone in these experiments is closer to the sobriety of LANGUAGE POETRY than the frivolity often expected of the New York School, a related tone, that of "declarative statement," links Highfill, by his own acknowledgement, to his friend and publisher, LEWIS WARSH (Highfill interview n.p.).

Shortly after arriving in New York from Nashville, Tennessee, in 1980, Highfill "inherited" from Warsh the mimeograph equipment on which *United Artists* magazine had been printed. Highfill used the equipment to launch Prospect Books (1983–86) with his wife, KIMBERLEY LYONS, whose *Strategies* was the first title in the series. Later, Highfill, Lyons, DAVID ABEL, and Jim Hydock formed a team to edit *Red Weather* magazine (1988–90). Its three issues reflect a mood of crisis both locally (riots at Tompkins Square on the Lower East Side) and internationally (war in the Persian Gulf). The violent clashes between police and squatters at Tompkins Square in 1988, which Highfill witnessed firsthand, left an impression on his work. For instance, "Seven Thunders" ironically adopts the persona of a religious fundamentalist to compare Tompkins Square with Waco, Texas, where federal agents attacked the Branch Davidian compound in 1993 (*Liquid Affairs* 38–39). After the disruption of their Lower East Side neighborhood, Highfill and Lyons moved to Brooklyn, New York. They maintained ties with the POETRY PROJECT AT ST. MARK'S CHURCH IN-THE-BOWERY, in DOWNTOWN MANHATTAN, where Highfill ran the Wednesday night reading series in 2000.

Bibliography

Highfill, Mitch. Interview by Gary Sullivan. *Readme* 3 (Summer 2000). Available online. URL: http://home.jps.net/~nada/highfill.htm. Accessed December 19, 2008.

———. *Liquid Affairs.* New York: United Artists, 1995.

Snyder, Rick. "The New Pandemonium: A Brief Overview of Flarf." *Jacket* 31 (October 2006). Available online. URL: http://jacketmagazine.com/31/snyder-flarf.html. Accessed December 19, 2008.

Hollo, Anselm (1934–   )

Anselm Hollo was born in Helsinki, Finland, in 1934, and educated there and in the United States. He left Finland in his 20s to work as a writer and translator, first in Germany and Austria, and then in London, where he worked for the BBC. He was responsible for translating ALLEN GINSBERG's *Howl,* as well as many other poems, into Finnish. He has been associated with a number of poetic movements, including the BEATS, the BLACK MOUNTAIN POETS, the Language poets, and both the first and second generations of the NEW YORK SCHOOL. Hollo, a contemporary and personal friend of TED BERRIGAN, JOANNE KYGER, JOHN WIENERS, AMIRI BARAKA, and ANNE WALDMAN, has taught at the State University of New York at Buffalo and the University of Iowa and currently teaches at NAROPA INSTITUTE in Boulder, Colorado.

Hollo's work is marked by a disjunctive and allusive playfulness that moves from witty self-reflexivity to distilled lyricism, as embodied in the following lines from his SERIAL POEM *Where If Not Here:*

> In the jingle-jangle mornings I went following you
> & you & you & you (a love letter to the word
>   "and")
> "You see here before you," Guillaume said, "me"
> Laments, Consolations   And what is not a quo-
>   tation?
> "Words, m'dear, words, not pretty pictures"
> The leaves are detaching themselves.

Hollo is founding member of a few minor poetics movements, including actualism, which originated in Iowa City and emphasizes the importance of quotidian objects (such as toothpaste, which became the name of a journal Hollo contributed to) as subjects of poetry. As Ron Silliman writes, "Actualism was an *-ism* that never sought to be any sort of movement—the anarcho/anti-organizational impulse was very strong. If anything, the Actualist Conventions were themselves a spoof of the least attractive aspect of their surrealist predecessors" (n.p.).

Hollo has published more than 35 books and chapbooks of his poetry, including *Rue Wilson Monday* (La Alameda Press, 2000), *Notes on the Possibilities and Attractions of Existence: Selected Poems, 1965–2000* (Coffee House Press, 2001), and *Braided River: New and Selected Poems, 1965–2005* (Salt, 2005); has translated many contemporary Finnish poets, including Paavo Haavikko and Pentti Saarikoski; and won many prizes, including a National Endowment for the Arts Poet's Fellowship (1979), Gertrude Stein Award in Innovative Poetry (1996), the Finnish Government Prize for

Translation of Finnish Literature (1996), and the San Francisco Poetry Center's Award for Best Book of Poems published in 2001 (2002). He currently makes his home with his wife, the visual artist Jane Dalrymple-Hollo, in Boulder, Colorado.

Bibliography

Hollo, Anselm. "4 from *Where If Not Here*." Poetry Project. Available online. URL: http://www.poetryproject.com/poets&poems/hollo.html. Accessed December 18, 2008.

Notley, Alice. "Hollo's *Corvus*" (1997). In *Coming After: Essays on Poetry*. Ann Arbor: University of Michigan Press, 2005, 41–51.

Silliman, Ron. "Friday, September 27, 2002." Silliman's Blog. Available online. URL: http://ronsilliman.blogspot.com/2002_09_01_archive.html. Accessed October 19, 2008.

Weatherhead, A. Kingsley. *The British Dissonance: Essays on Ten Contemporary Poets*. Columbia: University of Missouri Press, 1983.

Holman, Bob (1948–   )

During the 1990s Bob Holman became one of the most visible advocates for poetry in the United States as producer of the cable channel MTV's "spoken word" videos and the Public Broadcasting Service television series *The United States of Poetry* (1996) and as Web master of several Internet sites. Though he comes from America's heartland, born in Tennessee and raised in rural Ohio, Holman's life in the arts has made him a New Yorker. He has promoted a fusion of SLAM POETRY and hip-hop MUSIC based on his experience as cohost of the NUYORICAN POETS CAFÉ from 1989 to 1996. His orientation toward performance derives from his experience among the NEW YORK SCHOOL poets at the POETRY PROJECT AT ST. MARK'S CHURCH IN-THE-BOWERY during the late 1970s, when Holman produced a number of POETS' THEATER events based on work by Alfred Jarry, Vladimir Mayakovsky, and Tristan Tzara as well as his own COLLABORATIONS with BOB ROSENTHAL (Holman, interview n.p.). During the same period he took workshops at the Poetry Project with TED BERRIGAN, ALICE NOTLEY, and BERNADETTE MAYER. His formal education had ended in 1970 with a B.A. from Columbia

University, where he studied with KENNETH KOCH. FRANK O'HARA's "PERSONISM" provided a model for what Holman wanted to achieve in performance, though Holman has employed new technology to make it "faster" (Holman, "Congratulations" 2).

Holman's first collection of poems, *Tear to Open*, was published in 1979 by Power Mad Press. The editors were BARBARA BARG and Joel Chassler (1944–2002), acquaintances from Holman's sojourn in CHICAGO, ILLINOIS (1972–74), who, like Holman, had relocated to NEW YORK CITY. In LITA HORNICK's reading series at the Museum of Modern Art in 1979, Holman opened his segment by tearing open a paper bag placed over his head, thus performing the title of his book (Holman, interview n.p.). A similar image appears in "Rap It Up" (1980), a poem that reveals Holman's early identification of "rap" music with freedom of expression opposed to any FORM of restraint ("wrap"). However, expressionism for Holman retains a connection with artifice as it does for the New York School in general. For instance, in the "character" of "PanicDJ," Holman performed a text entitled "Hey What Did I Say" (1987), in which the words were arranged in a circular pattern that the performer tore up as he read them, clearing a space for purely oral utterance that appeared to arise spontaneously for the remainder of the performance. In fact, the performer was now reciting a memorized script, "reading" from memory as much as he had previously been reading from the page. What the audience witnessed was not so much the disappearance of the text as its transposition into another mode (Holman, interview n.p.).

The transposition between poetry and VISUAL ART that characterizes so much of New York School poetry has been facilitated, in Holman's case, by involvement in the painter's world through Elizabeth Murray (1940–2007), whom Holman married in 1982. For the Eye and Ear Theater, a project designed to combine the work of poets and painters, under the supervision of ALEX KATZ's wife, Ada, Holman directed three productions: EDWIN DENBY's *Four Plays* (1981), designed by Murray; ED FRIEDMAN's *The White Snake* (1982), designed by Robert Kushner (1949–); and W. H. AUDEN's *Paid on Both Sides* (1983), designed by David Hockney (1937–). In 1988 Holman

and Murray published an artist's book combining poems and drawings, *Cupid's Cashbox* (Jordan Davies). Portraits of both Holman and Murray feature in *A Couple of Ways of Doing Something* (Art of This Century/Pace Editions, 2003), a series of 22 daguerreotypes by Chuck Close, each with an accompanying "praise poem" by Holman about the person portrayed. Fittingly, Murray curated the artwork that adorned the BOWERY POETRY CLUB when it opened under Holman's direction in 2002. Hosting a performance art space is clearly the form of collaboration that Holman most enjoys.

Bibliography

Bob Holman Web site. Available online. URL: http://bobholman.com.

Gates, Henry Louis, Jr. "Sudden Def." *New Yorker*, 19 June 1995, 34–42.

Holman, Bob. *The Collect Call of the Wild*. New York: Holt, 1995.

———. "Congratulations, You Have Found the Hidden Book." In *ALOUD! Voices from the Nuyorican Poets Café*, edited by Miguel Algarín and Bob Holman, 1–2. New York: Holt, 1994.

———. Interview by Monica de la Torre. *Brooklyn Rail* (May 2006). Available online. URL: http://brooklynrail.org/2006/05/poetry/bob-holman-with-monica-de-la-torre. Accessed December 18, 2008.

———. *In with the Out Crowd*. Audio recording. Silverlake, Calif.: Mercury/Mouth Almighty, 1998.

———. *PANIC*DJ: Performance Text*. 2d ed. New York: University Arts Resources, 1990.

———. "Rap It Up." In *Sugar, Alcohol, and Meat*. Audio recording. New York: Giorno Poetry Systems, 1980. Available online. URL: http://www.ubu.com/sound/sam.html. Accessed December 18, 2008.

Holman, Bob, et al., eds. *The United States of Poetry*. New York: Abrams, 1996.

———. *The United States of Poetry*. Videorecording. Miami Lake, Fla.: KQED Video, 1996.

Miller, Stephen Paul. "Ted Berrigan's Legacy: Sparrow, Eileen Myles, and Bob Holman." In *The World in Time and Space: Towards a History of Innovative American Poetry in Our Time*, edited by Edward Foster and Joseph Donahue, 217–223. Jersey City, N.J.: Talisman House, 2002.

People's Poetry Gathering Web site. Available online. URL: http://peoplespoetry.org.

Richardson, Lynda. "A Poet (and Proprietor) Is a Beacon on the Bowery," *New York Times*, 12 November 2002, p. B2.

homosexuality

NEW YORK SCHOOL poetry has been profoundly shaped by, and has in turn helped shape, major transformations in the role of homosexuality in U.S. culture since World War II. Even the language used to describe homosexual experience has been so transformed that terms such as *gay, queer,* or *coming out* no longer mean what they meant at the start of this period. Historian George Chauncey has argued that before the birth of "gay liberation" and the Stonewall protests of 1969, gay men did not locate themselves in or outside of a "closet," but instead viewed themselves as living a double life, symbolized as masking (6). Such an understanding lends historical specificity to the opening of FRANK O'HARA's poem "Homosexuality" (1954)—"So we are taking off our masks, are we" (*Collected Poems* 181)—but it also lends a gay connotation to GRACE HARTIGAN's portrayal of O'Hara in her 1954 painting *The Masker* (Ferguson 92). Gay poets such as O'Hara, JOHN ASHBERY, and JAMES SCHUYLER offered to the painters of the second-generation New York School a means of defining their identity as distinct from the heavily macho posturing and existential agonizing of many first-generation painters. Artists both straight and gay also benefited from the social networks that gay men created as alternatives to the channels of power in mainstream society. A central node in one such network, the TIBOR DE NAGY GALLERY, played an especially important role in connecting the New York School poets with visual artists.

Membership in such a network had less to do with being homosexual than with sharing in the code known as "camp," based in gay subculture. Hartigan recalls that she began exhibiting at de Nagy under the name "George" as a playful reflection of the "camp" female names that many of the men connected with the gallery had privately assumed (Diggory 49). The practice left its imprint on Schuyler's "Dorabella" poems (*Home Book* 84–85), featuring the persona from Wolfgang Amadeus Mozart's opera *Così fan tutte*

that Schuyler assumed in tandem with W. H. AUDEN's lover Chester Kallman, who camped as "Fiordiligi" (Schuyler, *Collected Poems* 368). More pervasive in the texture of New York School poems is the "campy, dry, superior wit" that Joe LeSueur remembers as "the dominant 'in' way of talking at just about every party," where O'Hara, Ashbery, Schuyler, and the painter JANE FREILICHER seemed the in-most of the "in." Significantly, LeSueur, who was gay, felt he could not pick up the style, whereas the "straight" poet KENNETH KOCH picked it up so well that he "could easily have passed for gay" (LeSueur 126–127). Compared to the work of his first-generation colleagues, Koch's poetry most fully embodies qualities that Susan Sontag has identified in an influential essay as salient features of camp: "The Camp insistence on not being 'serious,' on playing, also connects with the homosexual's desire to remain youthful" (290–291).

Poems written by the gay men in Koch's circle—O'Hara, Schuyler, and Ashbery—suggest that the homosexual's chief desire, not unlike that of the heterosexual, is to be desired. "I want to be wanted more than anything else in the world," O'Hara concludes in "Homosexuality" (*Collected Poems* 182). O'Hara and Schuyler expressed that desire in love poems addressed to particular individuals—O'Hara to Vincent Warren (*Collected Poems* 329–406), for instance, or Schuyler to Bob Jordan (*Collected Poems* 120–136)—although in these poems, typically, the beloved is not named, and the fact that he is male is only hinted at. In O'Hara's "Poem 'À *la recherche d'Gertrude Stein*,'" which Stuart Byron has called "the best love poem ever written about one man's love for another" (68), the only clue to the beloved's gender is "the faint line of hair dividing your torso" (*Collected Poems* 349). Ashbery is even more circumspect, leaving critics either to speculate about the absence of homosexuality as a theme in his poems (Vincent; Imbriglio) or to invent ingenious strategies for reading them as "homotextual" code (Shoptaw). In its very elusiveness Ashbery's work conveys the air of menace surrounding homosexual love in a society where it was both tacitly and explicitly outlawed. "Is it asking too much," Ashbery asks in *FLOW CHART* (1991), "to want to be loved, just a little, and then to be satisfied with that? Of course not, / but the police are everywhere" (174).

The policing of homosexuality darkened the atmosphere of surveillance that hung over cold war America and became sufficiently oppressive to induce Ashbery to live outside the country from 1955 to 1964. By the time he returned, a movement of resistance was gathering, and poetry was making its contribution under the banner of free speech. Although the Beat writers were more closely identified with this cause than the New York School, that identification has as much to do with the BEATS' enthusiasm for movements as it does with the content of the poetry. ED SANDERS had no trouble recognizing the spirit of his magazine *FUCK YOU* in O'Hara's account of oral sex in "In the Movies" (*Collected Poems* 206–209). Sanders published O'Hara's poem in 1964, 10 years after it was written but only five years before gay liberation found its collective voice as crowds confronted police at the Stonewall Inn in Greenwich Village in DOWNTOWN MANHATTAN. That event inevitably changed the context for reading work such as JOHN GIORNO's "Pornographic Poem," a fantasy of homosexual gang rape that appeared in RON PADGETT and DAVID SHAPIRO's *ANTHOLOGY OF NEW YORK POETS* in 1970. And when O'Hara's *Collected Poems* appeared the following year, the inclusion of openly gay poems had the significance of establishing O'Hara as "only the third American poet of major stature to be overtly gay—Paul Goodman and Allen Ginsberg were the others" (Byron 65).

O'Hara, PAUL GOODMAN, and ALLEN GINSBERG each represent a component of the new "gay bohemia" that developed in New York and San Francisco during the decade after Stonewall, "compounded," according to Edmund White, "out of the Beat and hippie movements, out of cool, jazz-loving, heroin-shooting New Yorkishness, out of the new gay liberation movement and the New Left in general" (n.p.). This period saw an acceleration of the breakdown between "high art" and popular culture, encouraged by camp taste and the success of POP ART in the mode of the gay ANDY WARHOL. KENWARD ELMSLIE and JOE BRAINARD, lovers and collaborators, kept the New York School up to speed in this regard, while also supplying continuity with the past through their association with O'Hara, who had died in 1966. While Ashbery acquired mainstream recognition for his work dur-

ing the 1970s, he supplied what White describes as "the link between younger gay poets of the ever-growing New York School (Brad Gooch, Tim Dlugos, JOHN ASH) and the older founding generation" (n.p.). TIM DLUGOS, in turn, extended the geographical range of the New York School through his connections with "gay bohemia" in Washington, D.C., and Los Angeles, where DENNIS COOPER and DAVID TRINIDAD were important contacts.

The spread of AIDS in the 1980s brought an end to "gay bohemia," according to White. According to poet EILEEN MYLES, it also caused her to feel an increased sense of isolation as a lesbian in the literary community. Men mourning men grew "ever more protective of their lineage" ("Lesbian Poet" 126) and wrote women out of the history of friendships, such as Myles's with Dlugos (Myles, interview n.p.). Despite the common acknowledgment of Gertrude Stein as an important predecessor, the history of the New York School has so far featured lesbian women less prominently than gay men. However, Myles herself has helped construct a more inclusive lineage in work such as her short story "Chelsea Girls" (Lamm), based on her experience as Schuyler's assistant and echoing the title of a Warhol movie. The title of *The New Fuck You: Adventures in Lesbian Reading,* an anthology edited by Myles and Liz Kotz (Semiotext(e), 1995), deliberately recalls Sanders's magazine. Meanwhile, the PUNK ROCK aesthetic that evolved symbiotically with the New York School in the East Village during the 1970s has influenced "a teeming society of women who identify the postpunk third wave of feminism as the beat we're listening to," Myles explains, "because unlike the taboo-laden feminism of my youth, the new lesbian mise-en-scène is a fierce, wildly infectious, and inclusive cultural force" ("My Intergeneration" n.p.). Perhaps that force will determine the next phase in the relationship between homosexuality and the New York School.

Bibliography

Ashbery, John. *Flow Chart.* New York: Knopf, 1992.
Byron, Stuart. "Frank O'Hara: Poetic 'Queertalk'" (1974).
    In *Frank O'Hara: To Be True to a City,* edited by Jim Elledge, 64–69. Ann Arbor: University of Michigan Press, 1990.

Chauncey, George. *Gay New York: Gender, Urban Culture, and the Making of the Gay Male World, 1890–1940.* New York: BasicBooks, 1994.

Diggory, Terence. "Questions of Identity in *Oranges* by Frank O'Hara and Grace Hartigan." *Art Journal* 52, no. 4 (Winter 1993): 41–50.

Ferguson, Russell. *In Memory of My Feelings: Frank O'Hara and American Art.* Exhibit catalog. Los Angeles: Museum of Contemporary Art; Berkeley: University of California Press, 1999.

Giorno, John. "Pornographic Poem." In *An Anthology of New York Poets,* edited by Ron Padgett and David Shapiro, 254–256. New York: Vintage/Random House, 1970.

Imbriglio, Catherine. "'Our Days Put on Such Reticence': The Rhetoric of the Closet in John Ashbery's *Some Trees.*" *Contemporary Literature* 36, no. 2 (Summer 1995): 249–288.

Kikel, Rudy. "The Gay Frank O'Hara" (1978). In *Frank O'Hara: To Be True to a City,* edited by Jim Elledge, 334–349. Ann Arbor: University of Michigan Press, 1990.

Lamm, Kimberly. "'One Lighting the Other, Seductively': James Schuyler, Eileen Myles, and the Sexuality of Literary Influence." *How2* 1. no. 8 (Fall 2002). Available online. URL: http://www.asu.edu/piper-cwcenter/how2journal/archive/online_archive/v1_8_2002/current/workbook/lamm-essays.htm. Accessed December 18, 2008.

LeSueur, Joe. *Digressions on Some Poems by Frank O'Hara: A Memoir.* New York: Farrar, Straus & Giroux, 2003.

Myles, Eileen. *Chelsea Girls.* Santa Rosa, Calif.: Black Sparrow, 1994.

———. Interview by Kimberly Lamm (2001). *How2* 1, no. 8 (Fall 2002). Available online. URL: http://www.asu.edu/pipercwcenter/how2journal/archive/online_archive/v1_8_2002/current/workbook/lamm-interview.htm. Accessed December 18, 2008.

———. "The Lesbian Poet" (1994). In *School of Fish.* Santa Rosa, Calif.: Black Sparrow, 1997, 123–131.

———. "My Intergeneration." *Village Voice,* 20 June 2000. Available online. URL: http://www.villagevoice.com/2000=06=20/news/my=intergeneration/1.

Nelson, Maggie. "Getting Particular: Gender at Play in the Work of John Ashbery, Frank O'Hara and James Schuyler." In *Women, the New York School, and Other True Abstractions.* Iowa City: University of Iowa Press, 2007, 49–95.

O'Hara, Frank. *The Collected Poems.* Rev. ed. Edited by Donald Allen. Berkeley: University of California Press, 1995.

Ross, Andrew. "The Death of Lady Day" (1989). In *Frank O'Hara: To Be True to a City,* edited by Jim Elledge, 380–391. Ann Arbor: University of Michigan Press, 1990.

Schuyler, James. *Collected Poems.* New York: Noonday/Farrar, Straus & Giroux, 1995.

———. *The Home Book.* Calais, Vt.: Z Press, 1977.

Shoptaw, John. *On the Outside Looking Out: John Ashbery's Poetry.* Cambridge, Mass.: Harvard University Press, 1994.

Sontag, Susan. "Notes on 'Camp'" (1964). In *Against Interpretation and Other Essays.* New York: Delta/Dell, 1966, 275–292.

Vincent, John. "Reports of Looting and Insane Buggery behind Altars: John Ashbery's Queer Poetics." *Twentieth Century Literature* 44, no. 2 (Summer 1998): 155–175.

White, Edmund. "The American Sublime: Living and Dying as an Artist." In *Loss Within Loss: Artists in the Age of AIDS.* Madison: University of Wisconsin Press, 2001. Available online. URL: http://www.artistswithaids.org/artery/centerpieces/centerpieces_white.html. Accessed December 18, 2008.

Hoover, Paul (1946–)

Well known as both a poet and coeditor of NEW AMERICAN WRITING (1986–), Paul Hoover cemented his reputation as consolidator of the considerable energies of the NEW YORK SCHOOL of poetry along with other contemporary avant-garde poetic movements while serving as an anthologist. Hoover edited *The Norton Anthology of Postmodern American Poetry* (1994), still considered a staple in the field. As a reviewer in *Publisher's Weekly* put it, "for anyone carping at the idea of the postmodern or the avant-garde as wanly intellectual, fiercely separatist, beside the point, or even nonexistent, Hoover's large-scale collection of recent experimental American poetry (and a concluding selection of essays about it) should persuade that it's not" (McQuade 88).

Hoover was born in Harrisonburg, Virginia, in 1946, studied English at Manchester College in Indiana, wrote his first poems at the age of 24 while working as a conscientious objector at a CHICAGO, ILLINOIS, hospital, and received his M.A. in creative writing from the University of Illinois in Chicago. It is therefore in Chicago, along with ELAINE EQUI, JEROME SALA, and MAXINE CHERNOFF, whom he married, that Hoover developed as a poet of the New York School. In 1971 he founded the DADA-influenced poetry magazine *OINK!* which achieved cult celebrity and published numerous poets of the New York School until ceasing publication in 1985. In 1986 Chernoff and Hoover founded the widely distributed and influential *New American Writing.* Dedicated to experimental writing, the annual journal includes cover art by leading artists, including ALEX KATZ, Robert Mapplethorpe, and FAIRFIELD PORTER, and poems and essays by JOHN ASHBERY, ROBERT CREELEY, BARBARA GUEST, Lyn Hejinian, Charles Bernstein, among others.

As a poet, Hoover is the author of 11 poetry collections, most recently *Edge and Fold* (Apogee Press, 2006) and *Poems in Spanish* (Omnidawn Publishing, 2005). TALISMAN House issued *Totem and Shadow: New & Selected Poems* in 1999. The book-length work, *The Novel: A Poem* was published by New Directions in 1990. Hoover has appeared in numerous journals and anthologies, including five volumes of *The Best American Poetry* (Scribners). The University of Michigan Press published a book of his critical prose, *Fables of Representation,* in 2004; the lengthy title essay is a study of New York School poetry. Currently, Hoover is visiting professor at San Francisco State University. From 1974 until 2003 he was poet-in-residence at Columbia College Chicago.

About his work poet Mary Jo Bang has written, "there is a cool precision in his poems, a striking aptness in the marrying of word to word. And in many of them, there is an unexpected tenderness only half-masked by Hoover's allegiance to exploring and mapping language's inherent imperfection . . . central to all of them (regardless of language's irrefutable limitations) is his keen intelligence and laconic wit" (n.p.). The poet Gillian Conoley has referred to Hoover's "appetitive inclusionary impulse" (95), and indeed his work ranges from the quietly ruminative to the incandescent, as seen in his poem "But Kenneth," which concludes with an image of Kenneth Koch at work:

> But Kenneth in a portrait
> Reading a book for Fairfield Porter, his type-
>
> Writer gleaming, smudges of light around
> His eyes and the back of his hand a fiery white
> Like the page his mouth is reading.

Bibliography

Bang, Mary Jo. Review of Hoover, *Viridian. Boston Review.* October/November 1997: 55. Available online. URL: http://bostonreview.net/BR22.5/micros.html.

Conoley, Gillian. Review of Hoover, *The Novel: A Poem. Denver Quarterly* 26, no. 2 (Fall 1991): 95.

Hoover, Paul. "But Kenneth." In *Poems in Spanish.* Richmond, Calif.: Omnidawn Publishing, 2005, 59–60.

McQuade, Molly. Review of Paul Hoover, ed., *Postmodern American Poetry. Publishers Weekly* 241, no. 13 (March 28, 1994): 88.

Hornick, Lita (Lita Romola Rothbard)
(1927–2000) *publisher*

As a major patron of NEW YORK SCHOOL poets, Lita Hornick gave generously of both her money and her attention. She helped the poets reach a wider audience through the magazine KULCHUR (1960–65), which she funded and, toward the end, edited. Under the imprint of Kulchur Press (1966–70) and the Kulchur Foundation (1970–1989), she published the first collections of many second-generation poets. A series of poetry readings that Hornick inaugurated at the Museum of Modern Art in 1973 connected downtown bohemia to high society, under the auspices of the Museum's Junior Council. The mixing turned wilder at the annual parties that Hornick and her husband, Morton, a curtain manufacturer, conducted at their Park Avenue apartment from 1961 to 1981. The entertainment followed trends in the arts, from JAZZ combos arranged through LeRoi Jones (AMIRI BARAKA), Hornick's partner in *Kulchur;* to the VELVET UNDERGROUND, arranged through ANDY WARHOL in 1967, the year after he painted Hornick as "Lita Curtain Star"; and on through the "art" music of Philip Glass, Steve Reich, LaMonte Young, and Meredith Monk. Such company made it difficult for poets to compete for attention, but JOHN GIORNO was up to the challenge, showing up at one party, as JAMES SCHUYLER reported, "in Wellington boots and red sash, looking remarkably like a high school crush of mine as he appeared one starry night in the *Pirates of Penzance*" (Schuyler 231).

Growing up in New Jersey as the only child of a well-to-do family, Lita Romola Rothbard discovered poetry as a solution to loneliness (*Green Fuse* 9). After graduating from Barnard College in 1948, she married Morton Hornick and began to raise a family (sons born in 1950 and 1955), but in defiance of 1950s norms for wives and mothers, she pursued further studies in literature at Columbia University, earning her Ph.D. in 1958 with one of the first dissertations on the poetry of Dylan Thomas. Under the title *The Intricate Image,* it was eventually published by JOHN BERNARD MYERS (Gallery Editions, 1972). Reading THE NEW AMERICAN POETRY in 1960 "turned me on with a great flash of renewed insight," Hornick recalled (*Green Fuse* 23). Early issues of *Kulchur* magazine proved the excitement was ongoing, and she wrote to founding editor Marc Schleifer with an eye on poetry, though he turned his eye to her money. Accounts of *Kulchur*'s editorial board meetings suggest that the poets Hornick worked with did not take her seriously (Gooch 387–388; Hettie Jones 198–199), and her tendency to paranoia magnified their attitude into belief in a "plot" against her—one of the factors that led her to terminate the magazine (*Green Fuse* 38–39, 41).

Relations with poets in Hornick's later projects were less tense. Hornick entered into the New York School spirit of COLLABORATION represented in several Kulchur books, notably *Screen Tests* (GERARD MALANGA and Warhol, 1967), *Bean Spasms* (TED BERRIGAN and RON PADGETT, 1967), *Interlocking Lives* (KENNETH KOCH and Alex Katz, 1970), and *Sung Sex* (KENWARD ELMSLIE and JOE BRAINARD, 1989). Hornick's work on the MOMA reading series with PAUL VIOLI, another Kulchur author (*In Baltic Circles*, 1973), can also be counted as a successful collaboration. Hornick and Giorno became especially close, and they collaborated in publishing each others' books. Kulchur Foundation issued Giorno's *Balling Buddha* (1970) and *Grasping at Emptiness* (illustrated by Richard Bosman, 1985), and Giorno Poetry Systems issued three volumes

of Hornick's prose (*Kulchur Queen,* 1977; *Nine Martinis,* 1987; *The Green Fuse,* 1989) and one volume of poetry (*To Elizabeth and Eleanor, Great Queens Who Loved Poetry,* 1993), written by Hornick in collaboration with "poet friends" (including Giorno, ALICE NOTLEY, Padgett, BOB ROSENTHAL, Violi, and ANNE WALDMAN). In the poems one reviewer noted a "consistency of tone," suggesting that Hornick's was "the dominant voice in these exchanges" (Bennett). Reviewing another collection of criticism, *Night Flight* (Kulchur Foundation, 1982), JIM BRODEY was impressed that Hornick "would take the time to go through the entire Dial-A-Poet series [by Giorno] and talk a little about each piece on every record." This documentary approach characterizes Hornick's criticism in general. Focusing on the poets and artists she knew personally, she offers minimal interpretation but records that the work was done and that someone paid attention.

During the 1980s Hornick faced a series of traumatic events, starting in 1982 with a fractured shin and then severe burns when an alcohol rub she applied for therapy ignited from a cigarette. In 1988 her husband died of a heart attack and Hornick decided to end her publishing career and to devote herself "to reading and collecting art" (*Green Fuse* 152).

Bibliography

Bennett, John M. Review of Hornick et al., *To Elizabeth and Eleanor. TapRoot Reviews* 5 (1994). Available online. URL: http://wings.buffalo.edu/epc/ezines/treehome/tree05/horn_gre.html. Accessed December 18, 2008.

Brodey, Jim. Review of Hornick, *Night Flight. Poetry Project Newsletter* 90 (April 1982): n.p.

Gooch, Brad. *City Poet: The Life and Times of Frank O'Hara.* New York: Knopf, 1993.

Hornick, Lita. *The Green Fuse: A Memoir.* New York: Giorno Poetry Systems, 1989.

Jones, Hettie, *How I Became Hettie Jones.* New York: Dutton, 1990.

Schuyler, James. *Just the Thing: Selected Letters of James Schuyler 1951–1991.* Edited by William Corbett. New York: Turtle Point Press, 2004.

Warhol, Andy. *Lita Curtain Star (Lita Hornick).* 1968. Synthetic polymer paint and silkscreen ink on eight canvases. Overall 55 1/2" × 9' 3" (141 × 282 cm). Coll. Museum of Modern Art, New York. Color image available online. URL: http://www.moma.org/collection/.

Hotel Chelsea   *See* CHELSEA HOTEL.

Hotel Lambosa and Other Stories, The
Kenneth Koch (1993)

The relatively slim volume entitled *Hotel Lambosa* contains 88 tightly woven stories by KENNETH KOCH, ranging in length between one and four pages. Most of the stories take place within the emerging bohemian culture of the 1960s, as seen through the eyes of a narrator-protagonist who closely resembles Koch himself. We follow the author as he makes his way from Italy to North Africa to Mexico and elsewhere. Immersed in these foreign settings, Koch depicts an odd combination of actual experiences and impossible scenarios told as though they really occurred. The resulting collection is a kind of half-waking travelogue that critic Bernard F. Dick describes as "an interfacing mirror of the ordinary and the bizarre, characters clearly real and others (perhaps) imagined" (142).

The short tales in *Hotel Lambosa* are filled with highly condensed but often vivid observations of hotels, museums, and beaches, as well as dramatic encounters with local shamans, poets, painters, and musicians (including several NEW YORK SCHOOL associates). As with much of Koch's previous writing, humor is one of the collection's dominant registers, as we see in "The Allegory of Spring," which features talking trees: "One tree said to another: I am prettier than you. And the other said: It is impossible for you to see yourself" (47). The abrupt, rapid-fire length of these stories is particularly well suited to Koch's idiosyncratic sensibility, with its high-velocity plot twists and perpetual shifts in tone and GENRE, from comic-strip slapstick to sober philosophizing and social satire.

But while the book's content retains Koch's characteristic playfulness, its expository style is, in the poet's own words, "more or less realistic" (interview n.p.). Indeed, *Hotel Lambosa* relies far less upon "poetic" language and more upon straight-forward prose, compared, for instance, with the author's earlier work *The RED ROBINS* (1975).

In speaking about his inspiration for writing a book of so-called short-shorts, Koch cites the Japanese author, Yasunari Kawabata (1899–1972), whose own short story collection, *Palm-of-the-Hand Stories,* bears striking resemblances to *Hotel Lambosa* (Koch, interview n.p.). The prose of Victor Shklovsky (1893–1984), the Russian formalist critic who also wrote fiction and memoir, provided Koch with another model for "always surprising" sentences (Koch, interview n.p.).

Published in 1993 by Coffee House Press, *Hotel Lambosa* was one of the first books in the series Coffee to Go: Short-Short Stories for People on the Run! Critical response to the book was generally favorable, though certain reviewers were frustrated by the scarcity of detail provided in certain stories, perhaps due to length restrictions.

Bibliography

Dick, Bernard F. Review of *Hotel Lambosa. World Literature Today* 68, no. 1 (Winter 1994): 142.

Johnson, Peter. Review of *Hotel Lambosa. American Book Review* (February 1994): 12.

Koch, Kenneth. *The Hotel Lambosa and Other Stories.* Minneapolis, Minn.: Coffee House Press, 1993.

———. Interview by David Kennedy. 5 August 1993. University of Pennsylvania Web site. Available online. URL: http://writing.upenn.edu/~afilreis/88/koch.html. Accessed December 18, 2008.

Mort, John. Review of *Hotel Lambosa. Booklist* 89, no. 18 (May 15, 1993): 1,674.

Sowd, David. Review of *Hotel Lambosa. Library Journal* 118, no. 10 (June 1, 1993): 196.

Hymn to Life   **James Schuyler** (1974)

Random House published *Hymn to Life,* the fourth of JAMES SCHUYLER's full-length poetry collections, in 1974, featuring on its dust jacket artwork by FAIRFIELD PORTER. *Hymn to Life* consists of six parts: four series ("Waterbury," "Elsewhere," "Loving You," and "Evenings in Vermont") and two long poems ("The Fauré Ballade" and "Hymn to Life"). Schuyler wrote the majority during a rather turbulent period in his life, beginning April 1971; the collection tracks the course of a rocky two-year affair he had with a married Brooks Brothers salesman. In alternatively euphoric and distressed tones, the poems in "Loving You" all address an absent lover, revealing the bipolar mood swings the relationship exacerbated for the poet. One moment, the lovers are quarreling; the next, they are "reconciled / As though this / light June wind had blown / it all away" ("Was It," *Collected Poems* 182). Feelings of satisfaction—"How good of you / to phone. It set me / up. I'm full of / beans" ("Up," *Collected Poems* 187)—are immediately followed by those of dejection—"This week we / didn't meet I / hate that" ("August Night," *Collected Poems* 189).

In August 1971, while visiting Kenward Elmslie and Joe Brainard in Calais, Vermont, Schuyler was committed to the Vermont State Hospital at Waterbury following his second nervous breakdown of the summer. During his three-and-a-half-week stay at the hospital, he wrote the thin-lined, elegiac poems included in the first section of *Hymn to Life*. Voices uncharacteristic of Schuyler populate the polyphonic verse of "Waterbury": from the rich blues slang of "Beautiful Funerals" to the Lord's Prayer woven through "Our Father." A year later, in fall 1972, Schuyler again visited Elmslie in Vermont, at which point he began writing the pieces included in the volume's fourth section, "Evenings in Vermont." His relative calm comes through in the painterly, observational style of these romantic poems, in stark contrast to those in "Loving You" and "Waterbury." While the boundaries between self and other are still permeable, the consequences of the poet's identity issues are less severe, as nature, here a surrogate for the beloved, becomes a vehicle for introspection and the acceptance of change. It is with a sedate acquiescence, watching autumnal flies buzz about a window pane, that the speaker in "'From the next . . .'" remarks, "It is their dying / season" (*Collected Poems* 196).

The poems in "Elsewhere," the longest of the volume's six sections, do not convey a particular genius loci. Many of them are apostrophes to time (days of the week, months, seasons) or absent friends. From a biographical standpoint, the most notable of these is "To Frank O'Hara," an upbeat, celebratory sequel to his first elegy for Frank O'Hara, "Buried at Springs" (*Collected Poems* 42). Schuyler's esteem for O'Hara is equally apparent in

"The Fauré Ballade," a long piece immediately following "Elsewhere" composed exclusively of quotes, some serious, others frivolous, a dozen of which the poet attributes to O'Hara. Critics have also taken notice of "May, 1972," the only poem Schuyler explicitly wrote about the Vietnam War other than "Scarlet Tanager" in *The Crystal Lithium* (*Collected Poems* 88).

The centerpiece of the volume is its title poem, "Hymn to Life," one of several long-lined observational epics Schuyler wrote over the course of his career, inspired in part by Walt Whitman's "Leaves of Grass." "Hymn to Life," which Tom Clark has described as a "four-hundred-line anthem to nature's plenitude" (13), establishes Schuyler as a legitimate heir not only to Whitman and his expansive catalogs of natural observations, but to the English romantics, particularly John Keats and William Wordsworth. As Wordsworth did before him, Schuyler attempts to capture the disjunctive progression of time, using a rhetoric of accumulation suggestive of time-lapse photography. Unlike the poems in *Loving You*, *Hymn to Life* evokes a poet embracing and at peace with the world.

Initially the publication of *Hymn to Life* did little more for Schuyler than enhance his reputation among the already-loyal followers of New York School poets. Outside that circle the book's critical reception was not as friendly. Vernon Young, reviewing *Hymn to Life* for *Parnassus*, remarked that "there is scant intelligence audible in these bouquet poems" (88), taking issue in particular with the poet's penchant for pathetic fallacy and the passivity of his politics in "May, 1972." The popular endorsement in the poetry world Schuyler sought for his work would not materialize until the publication of *The Morning of the Poem* in 1980.

Bibliography

Clark, Tom. "Schuyler's Idylls: Notes and Reflections on the *Collected Poems*." *American Poetry Review* 23, no. 3 (May 1994): 7–13.

Koestenbaum, Wayne. "Epitaph on 23rd Street: The Poetics of James Schuyler." *Parnassus: Poetry in Review* 21, nos. 1–2 (1996): 33–57.

Lehman, David. *The Last Avant-Garde: The Making of the New York School of Poets*. New York: Doubleday, 1998.

Schuyler, James. *Collected Poems.* New York: Farrar, Straus & Giroux, 1993.

———. *The Diary of James Schuyler.* Edited by Nathan Kernan. Santa Rosa, Calif.: Black Sparrow Press, 1996.

———. *Hymn to Life.* New York: Random House, 1974.

Thompson, Robert. "James Schuyler's 'Spots of Time.'" In *The Scene of My Selves: New Work on New York School Poets,* edited by Terence Diggory and Stephen Paul Miller, 287–308. Orono, Me.: National Poetry Foundation, 2001.

Vendler, Helen. "New York Pastoral." *New York Review of Books* 35, no. 14 (September 29, 1988), 11–12.

Ward, Geoff. *Statutes of Liberty.* New York: Palgrave, 2001.

Wasserman, Rosanne. "James Schuyler: *Selected Poems.*" *American Poetry Review* 18, no. 6 (November 1989): 5–8.

Watkin, William. "'Let's make a list': James Schuyler's Taxonomic Autobiography." *Journal of American Studies* 36 (April 2002): 43–68.

Whedon, Tony. "Occasions for Morning." *American Poetry Review* 18, no. 6 (November 1989): 9–15.

Young, Vernon. "Raptures of Distress." *Parnassus: Poetry in Review* 3, no. 2 (1975): 75–89.

Hymn to the Rebel Café   **Ed Sanders** (1993)

ED SANDERS's *Hymn to the Rebel Café* (Black Sparrow Press) represents three strains of his poetic impulses. He offers tender odes and meditations, poems echoing the tenets of his INVESTIGATIVE POETRY, and satirical comic verse that echoes TALES OF BEATNIK GLORY. As in his other work, *Hymn to the Rebel Café* welds together Sanders's profound attention to social justice and with a concern for artistic FORM. The characteristic rhythms of Sanders's poetic voice and his command of simple, musical speech clearly root *Rebel Café* in the NEW YORK SCHOOL tradition, though the settings are largely drawn from outside NEW YORK CITY.

In the style of earlier poems such as "My Boat Was Overturned," and continued in Sanders's later volume *Cracks of Grace* (Membrane, 1994), many poems in *Rebel Café* speak with a quiet rapture about personal moments of reflection and experiences of beauty. "The Ocean Etude" recounts Sanders's visit to Père Lachaise cemetery in Paris. Contemplating the graffiti scrawled over poet and rock musician Jim Morrison's grave, Sanders notes Morrison's crumbling bust and finds "something / eerily beautiful / about his face / in this / loony Egyptian garden." In this poem, as in "At Century's End," "Images of Miriam," "Cemetery Hill," and "Elegy for Ted Berrigan," Sanders's blend of direct speech, personal revelation, and emotionally charged breath stanzas achieves new poetic power.

Many of the book's poems reflect the rural landscape of upstate New York where Sanders lives. He honors the variety of wildlife in poems such as "In Honor of Catalpa," which seems descended from Ralph Waldo Emerson's "The Rhodora." In "Some Poems from Mead's Mountain Road," Sanders's catalog of animals echoes Walt Whitman's lists in *Leaves of Grass*. Yet together with his glyphs and drawings, the voice that can observe "The shiny white-gray blobs / on the pants leg / from the candles / we held / at the Nagasaki vigil / on the Woodstock Green" evokes how the pastoral landscape has endured through the 20th century in spite of—perhaps because of—America's turbulent recent history. Other of Sanders's nature odes include "The Wetlands at Wilson State Park" and "The Long Sleep of Catullus."

Rebel Café includes two of Sanders's paeans to progressive POLITICS. The title poem, "Hymn to the Rebel Café," lists people and places involved in the tradition of revolution, social progress, and cultural change, such as gatherings in Philadelphia taverns during the American Revolution, socialist meetings at the Café Royale in New York, the artistic tables of Austin's Fox Bar in Paris, and the poetry readings at the Total Assault Cantina of Sanders's own TALES OF BEATNIK GLORY. In another poem, "By Pont Neuf," Sanders chronicles how too many Americans "share a doom / instead of a dream" in a country steeped in western traditions of violence.

Rebel Café also contains two early examples of Sanders's practice of investigative poetry. "Melville's Father" traces a period of hardship in the Melville family's history; "Cassandra" retells the Greek myth in investigative poetic verse form. In both, Sanders ends with morals applicable to America's history of violence and poverty. Sanders's didacticism and direct appeals to moral truths succeed because of the sincerity of his voice.

The final poem in *Rebel Café* is "An East Village Hippie in King Arthur's Court," authored, Sanders claims, by Suncatch, an East Village regular at the PEACE EYE BOOKSTORE. Set on the Lower East Side of *Tales of Beatnik Glory*, the poem relates how Suncatch's "turret tab" of acid transports him to the age of King Arthur. Suncatch meets Merlin and Arthur, and he brings 1960s Lower East Side culture to the Middle Ages, introducing the Round Table to the Beatles and The FUGS. He revises history by building hydraulic generators and guitars, conducts romances, and negotiates settlements of ancient strife before waking back on East 5th Street. The poem is typical of Sanders's impulse to remake the world through the romance of literature and to contest authority with humor.

Bibliography

Ratner, Rochelle. Review of *Hymn to the Rebel Café*. *Library Journal* 118, no. 10 (June 1, 1993): 130.
Sanders, Ed. "My Boat Was Overturned." In *Thirsting for Peace in a Raging Century: Selected Poems, 1961–1985*. Minneapolis, Minn.: Coffee House Press, 1987, 162.

Identikit Jim Brodey (1967)

In prefatory "Notes" JIM BRODEY explains that *Identikit* was "constructed from daily workbooks kept over a period of ten months beginning in September 1965." This origin aligns Brodey's book with various diary projects of roughly the same period, such as LEWIS WARSH's "New York Diary" (begun in 1966) or BERNADETTE MAYER's MEMORY (begun in 1971), but Brodey offers much less daily detail. He focuses intently on the self as "constructed" artifact, as implied by his title. In police investigations an Identi-kit is a file of predefined facial features from which a composite portrait of a crime suspect is drawn, according to the match between certain features and witnesses' accounts. In contrast to the resulting mugshot, the photograph of Brodey that appears on the cover of *Identikit* has the naturalness of a snapshot. According to his friend TOM CLARK, Brodey intended his title to draw an analogy between the police procedure and "the reconstruction of the authorial self in lyric poetry," but Clark goes on to observe: "The usual suspects, however, once released into the dispersive field of the lyric, seem to flee too quickly even for that kind of quasi-random identification" (25). The FORM of *Identikit*, 21 pages that may be read either "as one long work divided into sections or as a book of separate poems," as (Brodey explains in his "Notes"), constitutes just such a "dispersive field," mirrored in the imagery:

first   range   through
New York factory constellations of evening planet

tug & haze-turn   blossoms & aerial arrangements
   (21).

Reviewing *Identikit* for *Poetry* magazine, GILBERT SORRENTINO reported: "Brodey is into a kind of automatic surrealistic writing here, which makes no pattern that I can see" (60). Brodey's surrealism is up to date with the latest NEW YORK SCHOOL models, particularly that of JOE CERAVOLO, whose *Fits of Dawn* (1965) is cited explicitly in *Identikit* (6). To call Brodey's surrealism "automatic," however, is to miss one of the principal patterns informing the book: the opposition between natural impulse and mechanism that descends from the earlier tradition of English romanticism. "No, not ever by machine," Brodey insists (21). His naturalism is based in the body, like the contemporary breath-based poetics of CHARLES OLSON, but for Brodey the measure of impulse is not merely organic but orgasmic, "not in breath-units" but in "sperm bombs" (18). Sexuality proves to be the most elusive aspect of identity explored in *Identikit*. At least one sexual act is described in explicitly heterosexual terms (20), yet HOMOSEXUAL-ITY is implied in much of the imagery as well as the relationships claimed, for instance to EDWIN DENBY, to whom one of the poems is dedicated (6–7), and to FRANK O'HARA and Joe LeSueur, who are invoked cryptically in what may be the remains of one of the "codas" Brodey initially intended for each section:

poem, of Frank
of the silently beguiling, and of
Joe, of the silent deep-six mumble (4).

In 1964 Brodey was a frequent visitor at the apartment O'Hara and LeSueur shared, and on occasion he shared O'Hara's bed, raising in LeSueur's mind the obvious question: "was he straight or gay? Frank didn't seem to care, and neither did Jim" (LeSueur 293). The categories "straight" and "gay" are like the predefined facial features in the police Identi-kit; a portrait constructed on the basis of such definitions is inevitably artificial.

Brodey's acceptance of artifice distances his work from romanticism and points toward a postmodernism that was just beginning to find expression during the mid-1960s. *Identikit* concludes in a gesture of transcendence stimulated by the breakthrough exhibit of MINIMALIST art, *Primary Structures*, at New York's Jewish Museum (1966), and particularly the work of Ronald Bladen (1918–88), the most romantic minimalist. Earlier in the book, balancing the poem dedicated to Denby, Brodey includes a poem "for" Denis Roche (1937–), one of the new French poets associated with the journal *Tel Quel* and introduced by JOHN ASHBERY in *ART AND LITERATURE*. Coincidentally but significantly, Roche's work was of particular interest to the theorist of "poetic artifice," English poet-critic VERONICA FORREST-THOMSON, who published her first collection of poems, also entitled *Identi-kit*, in the same year as Brodey's book. The interrogation of identity was an international trend.

Bibliography

Brodey, Jim. Excerpts from *Identikit*. In *The Angel Hair Anthology*, edited by Anne Waldman and Lewis Warsh, 191–195. New York: Granary Books, 2001.

———. Excerpts from *Identikit*. In *An Anthology of New York Poets*, edited by Ron Padgett and David Shapiro, 299–303. New York: Vintage/Random House, 1970.

———. *Identikit*. New York: Angel Hair, 1967.

Clark, Tom. "Confessions." In *Contemporary Authors, Autobiography Series* 22, edited by Joyce Nakamura, 1–26. Detroit, Mich.: Gale, 1996.

LeSueur, Joe. *Digressions on Some Poems by Frank O'Hara: A Memoir*. New York: Farrar, Straus & Giroux, 2003.

Sorrentino, Gilbert. "Ten Pamphlets." *Poetry* 112, no. 1 (April 1968): 56–61.

"I do this, I do that poem"   *See* GENRE.

Iijima, Brenda (Brenda Uchman) (1967–   )
Brenda Iijima (pronounced ee-JEE-mah) exemplifies a growing dissatisfaction among younger poets with the aesthetic categories of preceding decades. "I never feel I am writing out of or in opposition to the New York School, Language Poetry—however these modes of writing are parsed and termed," she has stated (interview n.p.). Distrusting the "disregard for tangibility" in all such classifications (interview n.p.), Iijima has worked to integrate aesthetic process in broader life processes, expanding poetics to ecopoetics ("Eco-Panel"). Aspects of NEW YORK SCHOOL writing have provided valuable precedents, particularly the tangibility achieved in relation to visual art, which Iijima practices as a painter and photographer, as well as a writer. A pivotal document in Iijima's development is her pamphlet *Color and Its Antecedents* (Yen Agat, 2004), where "color is the élan of the actual," an opening in writing onto the greater tangibility that Iijima desires. Her first example is FRANK O'HARA's poem "Radio," in which the color orange in a WILLEM DE KOONING painting defies containment, "more than the ear can hold" (O'Hara 234). Later examples include JAMES SCHUYLER and JOE CERAVOLO, Jack Spicer and Lyn Hejinian, cited by Iijima without regard to the different "schools" these writers would conventionally be taken to represent (New York School, SAN FRANCISCO RENAISSANCE, LANGUAGE POETRY).

Born Brenda Uchman, she "grew up on the foot of the highest mountain in Massachusetts [Mount Greylock] located in the former mill town of North Adams" (*In a Glass Box*, PRESSED WAFER, 2002). At Skidmore College, where she earned a B.S. in studio art in 1990, she met her future husband, Toshi Iijima, with whom she traveled abroad for several years before the couple settled in NEW YORK CITY in 1997. There, Iijima launched Portable Press, which published the first extensive collection of her poems, *Person(a)*, in 1998, and has since issued volumes by such writers as JACK KIMBALL, Jonas Mekas, Akilah Oliver, Diane Ward, Africa Wayne, and Peter Lamborn Wilson. One of the poems in *Person(a)*, entitled "Believe," introduces the theme of "dark oceanic doubt" that becomes crucial, both formally and thematically, in Iijima's later work. For the most part, however, the sense of FORM in *Person(a)* is more fixed than fluid; several of the poems play variations on the sonnet. In *Around Sea* (O Books, 2004), formal units flow and expand, in keeping with the title theme and with an "oceanic" spirit manifested in contemporary works: for instance, *Emptied of All Ships* (Litmus Press, 2005) by STACY SZYMASZEK, with whom Iijima has collaborated, and *Saline* (Instance Press, 2005) by KIMBERLEY LYONS, whose book bears a cover designed by Iijima. Iijima further develops this "ecopoetics" in *Animate, Inanimate Aims* (Litmus Press, 2007) and in a work-in-progress under the title *Eco Quarry Bellwether* (Segue Reading).

Bibliography

Iijima, Brenda. Interview by C. A. Conrad. *PhillySound Feature* 4 (August 31, 2005). Available online. URL: http://phillysound.blogspot.com/2005_08_01_archive.html. Accessed December 18, 2008.

————. Segue Reading at Bowery Poetry Club. 19 March 2005. Audio file. PennSound, University of Pennsylvania. Available online. URL: http://writing.upenn.edu/pennsound/x/Segue-BPC.html. Accessed December 18, 2008.

Iijima, Brenda, and Stacy Szymaszek. Excerpt from "Sailor Porn." *EOAGH: A Journal of the Arts* 3 (2006). Available online. URL: http://chax.org/eoagh/issue3/issuethree/bracyiimaszek.html. Accessed December 18, 2008.

Iijima, Brenda, et al. "Eco-Panel." Segue Series at Bowery Poetry Club. 21 January 2006. Audio file. PennSound, University of Pennsylvania. Available online. URL: http://writing.upenn.edu/pennsound/x/Segue-BPC.html. Accessed December 18, 2008.

Mlinko, Ange. "Nothing Matters but the Quality of the Inspiration." *Readme* 4 (Spring–Summer 2001). Available online. URL: http://home.jps.net/~nada/angereview.htm. Accessed December 18, 2008.

O'Hara, Frank. "Radio" (1955). In *The Collected Poems*. Rev. ed. Edited by Donald Allen. Berkeley: University of California Press, 1995, 234.

Quartermain, Meredith. "Round about Seeing." *Jacket* 25 (February 2004). Available online. URL: http://jacketmagazine.com/25/quar-iijima.html. Accessed December 18, 2008.

"In Memory of My Feelings"   Frank O'Hara (1956)

FRANK O'HARA's "In Memory of My Feelings" rewrites for the 20th century the *Song of Myself* (1855) that Walt Whitman composed almost exactly 100 years before. The boldness with which O'Hara assimilates French influence, particularly that of Arthur Rimbaud (Perloff 142), is typical not only of NEW YORK SCHOOL cosmopolitanism but also of American self-confidence in the period following World War II. But the multiplication of selves that drives O'Hara's poem prevents the reader from being drawn into confidence, in contrast to the "confessional" mode of poetry that ROBERT LOWELL was about to inaugurate. "Instead," writes critic James Breslin, "the reader is asked to 'open' himself and let the poem invade him in the way the world constantly violates O'Hara's transparent self" (244–245). According to one of the poem's first readers, the painter GRACE HARTIGAN, to whom it is dedicated, "In Memory of My Feelings" is about "how to be *open* but not violated, how *not to panic*" (Perloff 141). Hartigan recalls one of the several passages where O'Hara depicts the self, or selves, in the guise of a serpent:

> My transparent selves
> flail about like vipers in a pail, writhing and hissing
> without panic, with a certain justice of response.

O'Hara expects his reader to render him that justice.

For O'Hara's 30th birthday in 1956, Hartigan threw a party, and "In Memory of My Feelings" is in a way his gift to her in return, as well as a meditation on reaching a milestone age. Previous birthdays recede from him into the abstraction of mere numbers—"My 10   my 19, / my 9,   and the several years"—even as the end of his years seems to be prefigured in the deaths of relatives: "My father, my uncle, / my grand-uncle and the several aunts." Autobiographical details surface in this manner throughout the poem, but they do not supply a unifying ground, because O'Hara lives his life always on at least two planes, that of time and that of timeless art:

> And the mountainous-minded Greeks could
> speak of time as a river and step across it into Persia,
> leaving the pain
> at home to be converted into statuary. I adore the
> Roman copies.

Hartigan's art enters the poem through references to two paintings, *Ocean Bathers* (1953) and *Frank*

O'Hara and the Demons (1952), in which she portrayed O'Hara in multiple guises: "One of me is standing in the waves, an ocean bather, / or I am naked with a plate of devils at my hip" (Perloff 210 note 7). Seeing himself extend into endless possibilities in art, O'Hara was inspired to live his life with as much variety. Punning on his friend's first name, he prays for "Grace / to be born and live as variously as possible." These words were inscribed on his gravestone.

While "the scene of my selves," as O'Hara calls it, is constantly changing, "In Memory of My Feelings" operates within a framework that is perceptible if the reader steps back far enough from the individual lines. There are nearly 200 lines, a fact which in itself makes it difficult to view the poem as a whole, but they are divided into five numbered sections. The first section introduces major themes and images that recur throughout the poem. The next two sections contrast water imagery, especially the sea (section 2), with desert imagery (section 3). A somewhat more abstract contrast of history (section 4) and art (section 5) generates tension between the final sections. The opposition of sea and desert in particular recalls W. H. AUDEN's analysis of the structure of romantic imagery in *The Enchafèd Flood* (1950), a book that O'Hara surely knew. Whether O'Hara consciously had Auden in mind when he was writing "In Memory of My Feelings," the extent to which Auden's analysis applies to O'Hara's poem reveals the depth of its roots in romanticism. For example, what Auden calls "the double-natured hero" (5) is played out in two figures who continually revolve around each other in O'Hara's poem: the "war hero" and the outcast "naked host."

"In Memory of My Feelings" was first published in the *Evergreen Review* (Autumn 1958) and reprinted in *The* NEW AMERICAN POETRY, *1945–1960* (1960). The title has been applied to several other works associated with O'Hara, starting with JASPER JOHNS's painting *In Memory of My Feelings—Frank O'Hara* (1961). Following O'Hara's death in 1966, BILL BERKSON edited a memorial volume published by the Museum of Modern Art, pairing O'Hara's poems with prints by 30 artists. In the prints for the poem "In Memory of My Feelings," Johns once again employed the enigmatic imagery

of fork and spoon that appeared in his earlier painting. In 1999 Russell Ferguson organized for the Museum of Contemporary Art, Los Angeles, the exhibition *In Memory of My Feelings: Frank O'Hara and American Art.*

Bibliography

Auden, W. H. *The Enchafèd Flood; or The Romantic Iconography of the Sea.* 1950. Reprint, New York: Vintage/Random House, 1967.

Breslin, James E. B. *From Modern to Contemporary: American Poetry, 1945–1965.* Chicago: University of Chicago Press, 1985.

Ferguson, Russell. *In Memory of My Feelings: Frank O'Hara and American Art.* Exhibit catalog. Los Angeles: Museum of Contemporary Art; Berkeley: University of California Press, 1999.

O'Hara, Frank. "In Memory of My Feelings." In *The Collected Poems.* Rev. ed. Edited by Donald Allen. Berkeley: University of California Press, 1995, 252–257.

———. *In Memory of My Feelings: A Selection of Poems.* Edited by Bill Berkson. New York: Museum of Modern Art, 1967.

Perloff, Marjorie. *Frank O'Hara: Poet Among Painters.* 1977. Reprint, Chicago: University of Chicago Press, 1998.

Ward, Geoff. "In Memory of My Feelings." In *Statutes of Liberty: The New York School of Poets.* Basingstoke, U.K.: Macmillan, 1993, 70–82.

In Public, In Private Edwin Denby and Rudolph Burckhardt (1948)

EDWIN DENBY's first volume of poems, *In Public, In Private,* is also the first book of poetry published by a NEW YORK SCHOOL poet. Denby raised money from friends and family to pay for its printing at the Press of James A. Decker, in Prairie City, Illinois (Ballowe), a firm that had gained a national reputation for publishing contemporary poets ranging from Edgar Lee Masters (1869–1950) to Louis Zukofsky (1904–78). Denby's poems are accompanied by photographs by RUDOLPH BURCKHARDT.

At a time when the New York School had yet to be conceived, Denby's opening tribute to "the climate of New York" (*Complete Poems* 3) would have been read in relation to the past, extending back to Walt Whitman (1819–92) and Hart Crane (1899–1932). Coincidentally, Denby's first poems appeared in *Poetry* magazine the same year, 1926, that Crane's work first appeared there. And, as Lincoln Kirstein (1907–96) described Denby's poetry, "He shares Crane's quirkiness in implosive short circuits of dense, awkwardly precise rhetoric, odd broken rhymes, reckless rhythm, sharpness of physical imagery and incandescent metaphor" (184). *In Public, In Private* also owes a debt to Gertrude Stein (1874–1946), whose *Four Saints in Three Acts* Denby had championed in Europe during the 1930s. In the prose piece, "Aaron," for example, Denby describes his friend Aaron Copland (1900–90) in phrases that both echo Stein and foreshadow later poets of the New York School: "He once remarked to somebody, 'Tunes are like birds.' He wanted to say it again, but he couldn't remember, so the conversation became general, and he didn't mind" (*Complete Poems* 39). At the book's center a brief selection of song lyrics from librettos for operas written in COLLABORATION with Copland are noteworthy for their interest in the rhythms of American speech; meant to be sung, these simple lyrics also suggest the quality of internalized song distinct to Denby's poems.

Many of the book's poems employ the sonnet FORM, concluding with a rhymed couplet that at first feels like a quip but upon analysis reveals itself as a deflationary gesture. In subject matter most register the experience of an urban inhabitant and pedestrian. Denby's early work has something of the conversational, slangy insouciance of FRANK O'HARA—"Abroad they've still got the pyramid of Whoosis, / Would it last in New York? The answer is, who cares" ("Mid-day Crowd")—but it is contained within a traditionally rigorous albeit idiosyncratic prosody. O'Hara himself viewed *In Public, In Private* as "an increasingly important book for the risks it takes in successfully establishing a specifically American spoken diction which has a classical firmness and clarity under his hand" (179). The meager contemporary critical response that *In Public, In Private* received, however, was not all so sympathetic. In *Partisan Review*, Dudley Fitts (1903–68) wrote that the book contained "mishandled metres, a yammering diction, and a brash inconsequence of intent" (Padgett xx). The book's

"acute and painful sensibility," as it was described by O'Hara (179), nevertheless produced elegant lines such as, "The lunch-hour crowd between glittering glass and signs / Calmly displays the fact of passing time" ("Elegy—The Streets").

Both the poems and Burckhardt's accompanying black-and-white photographs capture such evocative late 1930s and early 1940s tableaux. While some of the poems are specifically identified as "commentary text" for Burckhardt's photographs (*In Public* 73), they by no means function as illustrations; in fact, the interaction of word and image is such that it is impossible to determine whether Burckhardt's pictures instigated texts or Denby's way of seeing inspired the photography. (Such a relation can also be found in the 1948 Burckhardt film *The Climate of New York*, with cinematic "movements" separated by titles and lines from Denby poems.) Even poems that share a title with a particular photograph are not necessarily descriptive of the visual image but are often a kind of free-associating commentary. From "Luncheonette Counter Display," for example, Denby spins out; "What is advertising and what isn't? / . . . Do you want to be refreshed or not be refreshed /. . . Pictures count ten, a word alone a million, / And plenty more where they come from, brother." He uses the language of Madison Avenue in much the way Burckhardt incorporates billboards into his compositions. What Denby, like Burckhardt, chooses to make note of in any particular poem creates its own haphazard arrangement; items from a Queens "desert-landscape" are presented as revelatory "found art": "In this backyard of exploitation and refuse / Chance vistas, weights in the air part and compose . . . / So New York photographed without distortions / Shows we walk among noble proportions" ("Long Island City," published as "Five Reflections" in *Complete Poems*).

Denby and Burckhardt shared an aesthetic of observation without prejudgment; the faces and postures of people riding on the subway could be recorded equally on film and in words. Not the result of a concept or proposal but rather the natural outgrowth of decades spent together, *In Public, In Private* was only one of a series of synergetic books and films the pair made together; it also set a precedent for later New York School poets and visual artists. The abstract frontispiece to *In Public, In Private,* it is worth noting, was provided by Denby and Burckhardt's friend, WILLEM DE KOONING, whose influence is expressly acknowledged in "The Silence at Night."

The social interactions that went along with such COLLABORATIONs are themselves a subject of Denby's poetry. In "A Postcard" he inaugurates the New York School device of cataloging the names of friends in a letter-poem: "Elaine, Nini, Sylvia, Marjorie, Theda, / Each sends you happy wishes for your birthday . . . / Dear Rudy, they all say . . . And Frank, David, John, Aaron, Paul, Harry and / Virgil. . . ." But while friendship is indeed a recurring theme, so too is the relationship of human figure to its meteorological context, to the buildings and streets of the city, and to a community that is at once natural and manmade: "The sky is in the street with the trucks and us, / Stands awhile, then lifts across land and ocean. / We can take it for granted that here we're home / In our record climate I look pleased or glum" ("The Climate").

Bibliography

Ballowe, James. "Little Press on the Pairie." 3 July 2003. IT [*Illinois Times*] Online. Available online. URL: http://www.illinoistimes.com/gyrobase/Content?oid=oid%3A2337.

Burckhardt, Rudy, dir. *The Climate of New York* (1948). With poems by Edwin Denby. In *Films by Rudy Burckhardt.* Videorecording. New York: Poetry Project, 2003.

Denby, Edwin. *The Complete Poems.* Edited by Ron Padgett. New York: Random House, 1986.

———. *In Public, In Private.* Photographs by Rudolph Burckhardt. With frontispiece by Willem de Kooning. Prairie City, Ill.: Press of James A. Decker, 1948.

Kirstein, Lincoln. "Edwin Denby" (1983). In *The Complete Poems,* by Edwin Denby, 183–186. New York: Random House, 1986.

O'Hara, Frank. "The Poetry of Edwin Denby" (1957). In *The Complete Poems,* by Edwin Denby, 179–181. New York: Random House, 1986.

Padgett, Ron. Introduction to *The Complete Poems,* by Edwin Denby, xi–xxvi. New York: Random House, 1986.

Intransit: The Andy Warhol–Gerard Malanga Monster Issue (1968)

In the 220-page issue that GERARD MALANGA guest-edited for the West Coast magazine *Intransit,* the NEW YORK SCHOOL poets play a large role in conferring the status of writing on the work of ANDY WARHOL's pop avant-garde. Compared to the small proportion of BEAT writers—represented only by ALLEN GINSBERG, PHILIP WHALEN, DIANE DI PRIMA, JOHN WIENERS, and British fellow traveler Harry Fainlight—the New York School is abundantly represented: JOHN ASHBERY, EDWIN DENBY, BARBARA GUEST, FRANK O'HARA, TED BERRIGAN, JOE BRAINARD, JIM BRODEY, JOSEPH CERAVOLO, DICK GALLUP, RUTH KRAUSS, LEWIS MACADAMS, BERNADETTE MAYER, RON PADGETT, JOHN PERREAULT, SOTÈRE TORREGIAN, ANNE WALDMAN, and LEWIS WARSH. There was no need to attract any further notoriety to the Warhol circle than they already had; instead, Malanga presents a case for their sophistication. He goes as far as to include more "mainstream" writers such as Richard Eberhart, Jean Garrigue, JAMES MERRILL, and Howard Moss. However, he stops short of including ROBERT LOWELL, who receives the now standard avant-garde lashing in a poem by Lou Reed, the leader of Warhol's house band, The VELVET UNDERGROUND.

Other Warhol associates included in the issue are John Cale, another Velvet Underground musician; Nico, film actress and sometime singer with the Velvets; TAYLOR MEAD and Ingrid Superstar, both "stars" of Warhol films. Each of them is represented as a writer. In fact, given Warhol's base in the visual arts, it is noteworthy that the only visual feature in the entire issue is a brief series of photos presenting clothing designed by Susan Hodes and modeled by Hodes, International Velvet (Susan Bottomly), and Ingrid Superstar. Warhol himself is represented by an excerpt from his experimental prose work *a: a novel* (printed in the *Intransit* issue under its original title *Cock*), a transcription of taped conversations with Ondine (Bob Olivo). This experiment in the production of writing without an author converges with New York School experimentation such as Berrigan's "cut-up" novel CLEAR THE RANGE, also excerpted in *Intransit.*

Intransit magazine was published from 1965 to 1969 in Eugene, Oregon, by Bill Thomas (1934–), who covered a range of avant-garde poetry by recruiting a variety of guest editors, including James Koller (1966), associated with the SAN FRANCISCO RENAISSANCE; and Beat writers Whalen (1967) and Gary Snyder (1969). In a related chapbook series under the imprint of Toad Press, Thomas published two pamphlets by Krauss (*If Only*, 1969; *Under Twenty*, 1970) and the first solo title by Warsh (*The Suicide Rates*, 1967). Warsh attributes the publishing connection to Malanga, who had heard Warsh's poem read by KENNETH KOCH in his New School workshop in 1963 (151).

Bibliography

Warsh, Lewis. Interview by Edward Foster. In *Poetry and Poetics in a New Millennium: Interviews*, edited by Edward Foster, 147–159. Jersey City, N.J.: Talisman House, 2000.

Investigative Poetry Ed Sanders (1976)

Conceived during research for *The Family* (Dutton, 1971), ED SANDERS's book on the Charles Manson murders, *Investigative Poetry* was first presented as a lecture at the NAROPA INSTITUTE in summer 1975 and later published by City Lights Books in 1976. In this manifesto Sanders argues that "poetry should again assume responsibility for the description of history" (3). Like CHARLES OLSON, theorist of "PROJECTIVE VERSE," Sanders believed poetry needed a new imperative in order to stay relevant to the broader culture.

Investigative Poetry is divided into four sections, systematically detailing how poetry must take responsibility for "historical reality" (7). In section 1, Sanders describes his inspirations and precedents, including Hart Crane's *The Bridge* (1930), Ezra Pound's *The Cantos* (1930–69), William Carlos Williams's *Paterson* (1946–58), Allen Ginsberg's *Howl* (1956), and Olson's *The Maximus Poems* (1960–75).

For Sanders, poetry is free from the corrupting influences of ideology and power, whether of government, church, or capitalism. Sanders believes poetry can reveal, expose, and recall in verse what

collective memory inevitably has scattered; moreover, poetry must replace the sanitized language of textbooks with voices of compassion, transgression, and provocation. Sanders clearly intends investigative poetry to supplement the dominant historical narratives told by the authorities of nation-states who may have slim interest in explaining their motives about policies and censorship. Furthermore, Sanders assumes investigative poets will certainly face the censure of those authorities, and he finishes section 1 by listing poets he believed faced such censure, such as William Blake.

Section 2 of *Investigative Poetry* concerns poetic technique. Sanders offers a multidimensional set of guidelines, combining the poetic impetus of "Projective Verse" with the poet's prerogative to open "case files" (22). In his discussion of case files, Sanders emphasizes the importance of detailed research on historical subjects and explains how best to organize notes and files. He addresses the delicate balance poets must strike between poetic language and the relation of facts. Finally, he discusses interviews as an additional method of collecting information.

In section 3 Sanders speculates on the future of investigative poetry while simultaneously listing various ways to present poetry visually on the page. In the final section Sanders emphasizes the importance of public performance. He considers a variety of musical accompaniment, including innovative instruments, chants, choruses, opera, and technological effects. He also includes a "Clue List" that acts as a general bibliography for the authors and works cited throughout *Investigative Poetry*.

In 1981 Station Hill Press published Sanders's follow-up book on investigative poetry, *The Z-D Generation*, Z-D standing for "[Émile] Zola-[Denis] Diderot," two authors who confronted corruption in their own cultures by exposing it in writing. Sanders explicates many of his original ideas while developing additional thoughts on censorship, zealous political conservatives, the search for information, and his vision of a "Z-D Generation."

Sanders has published several books of poetry using the techniques and ideas he advocates. These include *Chekhov* (Black Sparrow, 1995), *1968: A History in Verse* (Black Sparrow, 1997), *The Poetry* and *Life of Allen Ginsberg* (Overlook, 2000), and *America: A History in Verse* (Black Sparrow, 2000; Godine, 2004).

Iovis Anne Waldman (1993–)

ANNE WALDMAN describes her long poem, *Iovis* (pronounced YOH-vis), as a "tantric female epic" (Preface iii). It is epic in its length and the scope of its subject matter, indicated in the title reference to the Roman father-god Jove, who is everywhere, according to Waldman's source in Virgil (Eclogue III): "*Iovis omnia plena,*" "all is full of Jove." Unlike Virgil's *Aeneid* and other classical epics, however, *Iovis* does not tell a continuous narrative; in this regard it resembles modernist models like Ezra Pound's *Cantos*, William Carlos Williams's *Paterson*, and CHARLES OLSON's *Maximus Poems*. But *Iovis* is "female" because, unlike its modernist models, its author is female and because Waldman consciously writes against the gender implications of both modernist FORM and classical epic matter, namely, war. In both of these respects her closest modernist predecessor is H.D. (Hilda Doolittle), author of *Trilogy* and *Helen in Egypt*. The "tantric" aspect of *Iovis* derives from Waldman's study of tantric Buddhism, which ascribes magical power to language, specifically, the power to reenact or perform as ritual "very powerful states of mind" (Waldman, *Vow* 143). In looking to Eastern sources for this attitude toward language, Waldman resembles her colleagues among the BEAT writers. However, for the notion of the long poem as performance, she also acknowledges the influence of Olson in both theory and practice (*Vow* 204–209) and the encouragement of KENNETH KOCH. In typical NEW YORK SCHOOL fashion Koch dispensed with theory in his memorable advice: "just do it, write long and big" (*Vow* 36).

From the time she conceived of the project in the mid-1980s, Waldman seems to have planned *Iovis* as a trilogy (*Vow* 272), another tie to H.D. Books I (1993) and II (1997) have been published; sections of Book III appear in *In the Room of Never Grieve* (2003). Book I addresses many male writers—for instance, "Messieurs Kerouac O'Hara Olson Denby Berrigan" (223)—and engages the subject of war indirectly, through recollections of World War II by Waldman's father. Book II highlights female writers, beginning with Sappho and ending with the countess of Dia, *troubairitz* (female troubadour). War continues as a theme, for instance, in a conversation between Waldman and her son, Ambrose, about the Vietnam War (section XIX), but the overall mood of the book is "elegiac," Waldman notes, adding that "grieving, keening, seems a feminine proclivity" (*Vow* 289). The subtitle of Book III, *The Eternal War*, implies continued need for grieving, as war comes closer than ever to Waldman in the terrorist attack on DOWNTOWN MANHATTAN's World Trade Center, near her "ancestral dwelling" (443). Rather than tracing a dialectical progress toward some triumphant synthesis, the poem's three parts, as published thus far, seem to perform a cycle, in keeping with Waldman's claim, "its weave is narrative yet circular" (Preface iii). What strikes some readers as a lack of narrative is really the lack of climax. In contrast to traditional epic there is no final victory. Instead, there is continuing survival. "I am writing this poem as survival mechanism," Waldman comments, "I see it as a life's work, for it continues on and survives itself" (*Vow* 273).

The work's performance of "itself" may be the aspect of *Iovis* that reveals most clearly Waldman's continuation of the New York School aesthetic. In a much discussed passage of *Iovis* II (Notley 84; DuPlessis), Waldman records ROBERT CREELEY's judgment that her work is too personal to qualify as epic (36–37). This judgment implies both gender bias (personal references do not disqualify Olson from Creeley's definition of epic) and GENRE confusion, reading an instance of "PERSONISM" as if it were confessional. On the contrary, Waldman signals her commitment to "Personism" in her references to FRANK O'HARA's "IN MEMORY OF MY FEELINGS" (1956), from which she takes an epigraph for *Iovis* II and a key representation of the poet's persona in *Iovis* III, "I; myself." "In Memory of My Feelings" concludes with the image of

> the scene of my selves, the occasion of these ruses
> which I myself and singly must now kill
>   and save the serpent in their midst
> (O'Hara 257).

In response, Waldman vows

> *to keep the I; myself*
> (*the occasion* of these ruses)
> *intact for a ceremonial day* (404).

In each case the poet's ability to take on and cast off multiple selves, like the serpent's ability to shed its skin, is a matter of survival, epic matter (Thomas 211).

Bibliography

DuPlessis, Rachel Blau. "Anne Waldman: Standing Corporeally in One's Time." *Jacket* 27 (April 2005). Available online. URL: http://jacketmagazine.com/27/w-dupl.html. Accessed December 18, 2008.

Notley, Alice. "*Iovis Omnia Plena.*" In *Coming After: Essays on Poetry.* Ann Arbor: University of Michigan Press, 2005, 83–94.

O'Hara, Frank. "In Memory of My Feelings." In *The Collected Poems.* Rev. ed. Edited by Donald Allen. Berkeley: University of California Press, 1995, 252–257.

Thomas, Heather. "'Eyes in All Heads': Anne Waldman's Performance of Bigendered Imagination in *Iovis* I." In *We Who Love to Be Astonished: Experimental Women's Writing and Performance Poetics,* edited by Laura Hinton and Cynthia Hogue, 203–212. Tuscaloosa: University of Alabama Press, 2002.

Waldman, Anne. *Iovis: All Is Full of Jove,* Book I. Minneapolis, Minn.: Coffee House Press, 1993.

———. *Iovis: All Is Full of Jove,* Book II. Minneapolis, Minn.: Coffee House Press, 1997.

———. *Iovis: The Eternal War,* Book III. Excerpts in *In the Room of Never Grieve: New and Selected Poems, 1985–2003.* Minneapolis, Minn.: Coffee House Press, 2003, 391–479.

———. Preface to *In the Room of Never Grieve: New and Selected Poems, 1985–2003.* Minneapolis, Minn.: Coffee House Press, 2003, i–iv.

———. *Vow to Poetry: Essays, Interviews, and Manifestos.* Minneapolis, Minn.: Coffee House Press, 2001.

Iowa Writers' Workshop (1936)

During the 1950s the Program in Creative Writing at the University of Iowa, generally known as the Iowa Writers' Workshop, was identified with precisely the poets that the "New American Poetry" set out to oppose. Iowa was where ROBERT LOWELL taught W. D. Snodgrass (1926–   ). When FRANK O'HARA applied to come to Iowa for a semester in 1955, he received a letter of rejection from Lowell (Gooch 236). The New School in NEW YORK CITY, where O'Hara and KENNETH KOCH both taught in the early 1960s, had a tradition of writing workshops dating back to 1931, when Gorham Munson (1896–1969) started a workshop there, whereas the workshops at Iowa were not formally organized into a program until 1936, under Wilbur Schramm (1907–87). More important, the New School had the constant stimulation of the artistic culture of New York City to keep it up to date, whereas Iowa had to import its stimulation. It did just that under the leadership of Paul Engle (1908–91), who directed the program at Iowa from 1941 to 1966. Expanding enrollment by 10 times the size it was when he took over, Engle actively recruited talented students from all over the country and ultimately, with the founding of the International Writing Program in 1967, all over the world.

A brief period of interaction between the NEW YORK SCHOOL poets and the Iowa Writers' Workshop begins with Engle's successor, George Starbuck (1931–96), director from 1966 to 1969. Seeking to expose the already diverse student body at Iowa to a more diverse faculty, in terms of the range of poetic practice, Starbuck hired TED BERRIGAN; Kathleen Fraser (1937–   ); Fraser's husband at the time, Jack Marshall (1936–   ); ANSELM HOLLO; Steve Katz (1935–   ); Seymour Krim (1922–89); and David Ray (1932–   )—"all, at that time," according to Hollo, "regarded as pretty 'cutting edge' makaris, somewhat threatening, even, to the post–Paul Engle neo-Frostian/pseudo-WCWilliamsian 'Iowa' establishment" (Hollo n.p.). The establishment tolerated Berrigan for only one academic year (1968–69) before he was let go, but it was a crucial year for him in many respects. He separated from his wife, SANDY BERRIGAN; formed long-lasting friendships with colleagues such as Hollo and students such as Merrill Gilfillan (1945–   ), MICHAEL LALLY, and ALICE NOTLEY, whom he married in 1972; and launched a career as an itinerant teacher that he pursued for the next decade. Before his year of teaching in England (1973–74), Berrigan's year at Iowa, with its new International Writing Program, helped him spread the word(s) of the New York School among foreign writers such as the British Gordon Brotherston (1939–   ), the Irish Sydney Smith (1936–   ) and the Slovenian Tomaš Šalamun (1941–   ). Smith's "Form of Application to Ted Berrigan for Country or Associate Membership of the New York Poets" has been preserved in his collected poems.

Like New York's Lower East Side during the 1960s, Iowa City during the 1970s became a spawning ground for little magazines and small presses conceived in opposition to the established journals where students at the Iowa Writers' Workshop were expected to publish. Two of the first magazines in the Language movement began in Iowa City: *This* (1971–82), initially edited by Barrett Watten (1948–   ) and Robert Grenier (1941–   ), and *Hills* (1973–83), initially edited by Bob Perelman (1947–   ) and Michael Waltuch. Another movement, the actualists, had their own set of publications, including *Toothpaste* (edited by Allan Kornblum, 1970–72), *Gum* (edited by Dave Morice, 1970–73), *Search for Tomorrow* (edited by George Mattingly, 1970–72), and *The Spirit That Moves Us* (edited by Morty Sklar, 1975–91). In practice, no rigid lines of division were drawn and poets associated with different groups contributed to one another's magazines. Although less well known today than LANGUAGE POETRY, actualism was closer to the dadaist spirit of the New York School and has in fact been dubbed by Language poet Ron Silliman as "the New York School's western cousin" (n.p.). Its principal spokesperson was Darrell Gray (1945–86), author of "The Actualist Manifesto" (*Gum* 9, January 1973). Today, its best-known author may be Dave Morice (1946–   ), creator of *Poetry Comics*—originally an Iowa City magazine (1979–82)—and more recently the subject of several volumes published by the TEACHERS & WRITERS COLLABORATIVE.

By far the most influential publisher among the actualists is Allan Kornblum (1949–   ), who enrolled in the Iowa Writers' Workshop after participating in workshops at the POETRY PROJECT AT ST. MARK'S CHURCH IN-THE-BOWERY in DOWNTOWN MANHATTAN. He got the idea for *Toothpaste* from the mimeograph magazines revolving around the Poetry Project, and while he was producing *Toothpaste* he continued to send contributions to New York magazines such as PAUL VIOLI's *New York Times* (1970–73). Violi's *Waterworks* was one of the first volumes issued by the Toothpaste Press from Kornblum's new home in West Branch, Iowa, where he acquired a letterpress that enabled printing of much higher quality than his initial mimeograph publications. Toothpaste Press went on to publish work by both Kornblum and his wife Cinda and many of the Iowa actualists, including not only Morice but his pseudonymous alter ego, "Joyce Holland." Toothpaste also published Black Mountain (CHARLES OLSON, ROBERT CREELEY, Cid Corman) and Beat authors (ALLEN GINSBERG, DIANE DI PRIMA, GREGORY CORSO, Gary Snyder), but of the writers not based in Iowa, most were of the New York School: JIM CARROLL, JOSEPH CERAVOLO, TOM CLARK, DICK GALLUP, JOHN GIORNO, ROSE LESNIAK, STEVE LEVINE, Notley, RON PADGETT, ED SANDERS, Violi, and ANNE WALDMAN. The last Toothpaste Press volume, Waldman's *Makeup on Empty Space*, was published in 1984, at which time the Kornblums moved to Minneapolis, Minnesota, and established Coffee House Press, named in honor of the typical venue for performance of avant-garde poetry. Coffee House has become one of the leading national publishers for such poetry. New York School authors remain prominent in the list, but Kornblum has maintained an openness to a wide range of styles that recalls his experience at the Iowa Writers' Workshop as a site of avant-garde performance.

Bibliography

Clay, Steven, and Rodney Phillips. "Iowa." In *A Secret Location on the Lower East Side: Adventures in Writing, 1960–1980*. New York: New York Public Library/Granary Books, 1998, 48–50.

Dana, Robert, ed. *A Community of Writers: Paul Engle and the Iowa Writers' Workshop*, Iowa City: University of Iowa Press, 1999.

Gooch, Brad. *City Poet: The Life and Times of Frank O'Hara*. New York: Knopf, 1993.

Hollo, Anselm. "Memorial Note on George Starbuck" (1996). Electronic Poetry Center, University of Buffalo. Available online. URL: http://wings.buffalo.edu/epc/documents/obits/starbuck.html. Accessed December 18, 2008.

Kornblum, Allan. Interview by Jessica Powers (2006). *NewPages.* Available online. URL: http://www.newpages.com/interviews/kornblum_coffee_house_press.htm. Accessed December 18, 2008.

Lenhart, Gary. "The Toothpaste Press." *Sagetrieb* 3, no. 3 (Winter 1984): 135–148.

Morice, Dave. *How to Make Poetry Comics.* New York: Teachers & Writers, 1983.

———. *Poetry Comics: An Animated Anthology.* New York: Teachers & Writers, 2002.

———. *Poetry Comics: A Literary Postcard Book.* New York: Teachers & Writers, 2002.

Silliman, Ron. "Wednesday, October 9, 2002." Silliman's Blog. Available online. URL: http://ronsilliman.blogspot.com/2002_10_01_archive.html. Accessed December 18, 2008.

Sklar, Morty, and Darrell Gray, eds. *The Actualist Anthology.* Iowa City: Spirit That Moves Us Press, 1977.

Smith, Sydney Bernard. "Form of Application to Ted Berrigan for Country or Associate Membership of the New York Poets." In *Poems, 1957–2006* [Ireland]: Little Red Hen, 2006, 123–124.

I Remember Joe Brainard (1970–1975)

In a letter to ANNE WALDMAN, JOE BRAINARD wrote:

> I am way way up these days over a piece I am still writing called "I Remember." I feel I am very much like God writing the bible. I mean, I feel like I am not really writing it but that it is because of me that it is being written. I also feel that it is about everybody else as much as it is about me. And that pleases me. I mean, I feel like I *am* everybody. And it's a nice feeling (Waldman and Warsh 576).

I Remember is an important text of NEW YORK SCHOOL history as well as a poignant account of American life in the 1950s. It was originally published in three installments by Angel Hair Press (*I Remember,* 1970; *I Remember More,* 1972; and *More I Remember More,* 1973) and another installment by the Museum of Modern Art (*I Remember Christmas,* 1973). RON PADGETT edited a collected edition for Full Court Press (1975), later updated by Penguin Books (1995) and Granary Books (2001). Each printing has been enormously successful.

I Remember possesses a simplicity that lends itself well to classroom exercise and, at the same time, is a highly complex and carefully crafted collection of memories and impressions that shift in age and content. Each unit begins with the words "I remember" and extends to varying lengths, from a simple sentence to a complex paragraph.

> I remember the first time I really got drunk. I painted my hands and face green with Easter egg dye and spent the night in Pat Padgett's bath tub. She was Pat Mitchell then (10).

> I remember the day Frank O'Hara died. I tried to do a painting somehow especially for him. (Especially good.) And it turned out awful (13).

> I remember wondering how one would go about putting on a rubber gracefully, in the given situation (117).

In "Self-Portrait: 1971," Brainard recognized: "Writing, for me, is a way of 'talking' the way I wish I could talk" (*New Work* 10). This may refer to his stutter, which was only cured on the page, or it may simply reflect his simple and communicative writing style.

As a writer, Brainard is present and self-critical. The concern with which he crafts each image is evident in a 1972 diary entry from *N.Y.C. Journals:*

> Spent most of today correcting *More I Remember* proofs. And writing a new center section. And a new ending. Still not too happy with it tho. More "forced" than the first volume. More boring details. And not as much personal stuff. I hope people aren't going to be disappointed (*New Work* 52).

This also points to Brainard's modesty and eagerness to please, traits that undoubtedly shape the friendly nature of his work. He leaves empty space wherein readers can make the piece their own. Whether one experienced the 1950s and 1960s or recognizes all of the dated cultural icons, one relates on a simple level of human experience that is both engrossing and comforting. Reading *I Remember* is like listening to your childhood friend recount events of your own life and your friend's. LEWIS WARSH says that Brainard "gave the reader the illusion he was telling everything, without getting heavy or going too deep" (109).

Brainard's impulse to write, as for many of his friends in the second-generation NEW YORK SCHOOL, stemmed from Frank O'Hara's famous directive in "PERSONISM" (1959): to put the poem "between two persons instead of two pages" (O'Hara 499). In another letter to Waldman, Brainard wrote: "You know, I write for people. I really do. When I write I feel like I am talking to people. And telling them (you) things that I want to tell. If there were no magazines and no readings I wouldn't write" (Waldman and Warsh 576).

In an interview with Waldman, Brainard explained that his mind worked more visually than verbally:

JB: When I'm reading my focus is there, but my general focus isn't at all with words. My brain doesn't have compartments to make order of words or something.

AW: But it does with images?

JB: Yes, I'm sure it does with images because I can see things and it all makes sense in my brain and I can recall things in an order that I could never do with words. It's all scrambled with words (Brainard, interview 101).

Perhaps this is why Brainard was so apt to write short passages containing tidy and complete mini-moments and images. In these moments, much like a Brainard drawing or collage, a whole world is revealed; not everything is stated explicitly, yet nothing is missing. When collected, these moments compose a memoir like no other.

Bibliography

Brainard, Joe. Interview by Anne Waldman (1978). In *Joe Brainard: A Retrospective*, by Constance M. Lewallen, 101–105. Exhibit catalog. Berkeley: Art Museum, University of California, Berkeley; New York: Granary Books, 2001.

———. *I Remember*. New York: Granary Books, 2001.

———. *New Work*. Los Angeles: Black Sparrow, 1973.

O'Hara, Frank. "Personism" (1959). In *The Collected Poems*. Rev. ed. Edited by Donald Allen. Berkeley: University of California Press, 1995, 498–499.

Waldman, Anne, and Lewis Warsh, eds. *The Angel Hair Anthology*. New York: Granary Books, 2001.

Warsh, Lewis. "Joe Brainard." *Pressed Wafer* 2 (March 2001): 109–112.

Irish poetry

For the NEW YORK SCHOOL poets, as for their Irish contemporaries, Irish poetry prior to World War II was dominated by "[William Butler] Yeats of the baleful influence" (Koch, *Collected Poems* 123), as KENNETH KOCH referred to the Irish master in "FRESH AIR" (1955). Yeats's bardic utterance was a long way from the colloquial speech that the New York School poets favored, but their resistance to Yeats had less to do with his work than with the academic conventions that had been formulated from his example. Defending Koch against a hostile reviewer in 1954, FRANK O'HARA wrote: "[Koch's] technique is opposed to that Academic and often turgid development by which many young poets gain praise for their 'achievement,' an achievement limited usually to the mastery of one phase of Yeats (and usually the last)" ("Another Word" 59). Both O'Hara and Koch found Yeats's adaptations of the Japanese Noh play useful for their own experiments in the THEATER, where Yeats's example represented an alternative option rather than an imperative paradigm (Koch, interview 202–203; O'Hara, TRY! TRY!).

AMERICAN POETRY offered to many Irish poets an alternative to Yeats. This possibility opened up as part of the rise in America's cultural influence during World War II and the following decades, so it affected the older Irish poets late in their careers. In *Mnemosyne Lay in Dust* (Dolmen, 1966), Austin Clarke (1896–1974) approached the confessional poetry of ROBERT LOWELL (Rosenthal 268–270). In contrast, judging Lowell to be "very dead," Patrick Kavanagh (1904–67) preferred the BEATS (Grennan 388) and read with them at the

International Poetry Incarnation in London's Royal Albert Hall in 1965. The poet of this generation who comes closest to the New York School is Denis Devlin (1908–59). From a highly dense style based on French models, he turned to a more relaxed, more colloquial poetry during the 1940s, when he spent time in America as a diplomat. The critic Eamon Grennan associates Devlin's "Annapolis," written during this period, with O'Hara (Grennan 386), but this is an assertion of affinity rather than influence in either direction. The affinity is confirmed in JOHN ASHBERY's linking of Devlin with the British poet F. T. Prince as exceptional artists who achieved genuinely modern results using traditional FORMS (Ashbery 73, 76).

As in the case of Devlin, travel to the United States has contributed significantly to Irish poets' exposure to international perspectives, as John Montague (1929–), a major advocate of such exposure, has pointed out ("Impact"). News of the SAN FRANCISCO RENAISSANCE and Beat poets made San Francisco a destination during the 1960s for Montague himself and for James Liddy (1934–), an openly gay poet who has been publicly recognized by Ashbery as "one of the most original among living Irish poets," as stated on the jacket of Liddy's *White Thought in a White Shade* (Kerr's Pinks, 1988). Seamus Heaney (1939–), successor to Yeats as recipient of the Nobel Prize (1995), made his way to "Beatsville" in 1970–71 as guest lecturer at the University of California, Berkeley (Heaney 16). His attempt to open himself to "open form" convinced him that "the Whitmanian inheritance" was not for him, a judgment that he later repeated in tracing a line of inheritance from Wallace Stevens to Ashbery (Heaney 16–17). Heaney read Ashbery in the light of his renewed exposure to America during the 1980s through a series of appointments at Harvard University. In 1988 he told an interviewer that Ashbery's "bemused, disappointed but untragic response to the evacuation of meaning in most people's lives" helped to explain Ashbery's popularity, though Heaney himself clearly retained his own reservations (Heaney 16). Paul Muldoon (1951–), a student of Heaney's, has expressed his reservations even more explicitly (Muldoon, interview 24); nevertheless, Muldoon, who has taught at

Princeton University since 1990, is the Irish poet whose name has been linked most frequently with Ashbery's (Grennan 380; Logan 35).

Among other New York School poets, O'Hara shows up in the work of Muldoon (*The Prince of the Quotidian* 11, 161–162) and his fellow Northerner Derek Mahon (1941–) in association with NEW YORK CITY (Mahon 211). However, W. H. AUDEN's association with New York seems to be even more significant for these writers (Muldoon, "7, Middagh Street"; Mahon 203), suggesting that what they share with the New York School may derive from Auden as much as from any direct exchange. Nothing could be more direct than the "Form of Application to Ted Berrigan for Country or Associate Membership of the New York Poets," submitted by Sydney Bernard Smith (1936–) in response to TED BERRIGAN's invitation at a reading in Iowa City in 1969. In general, however, there is little evidence that New York School poets of the second generation have come to the attention of Irish poets. For several poets of that generation (Berrigan, MICHAEL LALLY, EILEEN MYLES), "Irishness" has been an issue, but as a class marker rather than a literary category. Being educated at Harvard seems to have freed O'Hara from any burden that may have been entailed in his Irish-American background. Like contemporary Irish writers, he approached the great modernists James Joyce and Samuel Beckett as members of an international avant-garde rather than Irish exiles (Perloff 31–33).

Bibliography

Ashbery, John. "Tradition and Talent: Philip Booth, Stanley Moss, and Adrienne Rich" (1966). In *Selected Prose*. Edited by Eugene Richie. Ann Arbor: University of Michigan Press, 2004, 73–78.

Devlin, Denis. "Annapolis" (1946). In *Collected Poems*. Edited by J. C. C. Mays. Winston-Salem, N.C.: Wake Forest University Press, 1989, 31–32.

Grennan, Eamon. "The American Connection: An Influence on Modern and Contemporary Irish Poetry" (1990). In *Facing the Music: Irish Poetry in the Twentieth Century*. Omaha, Neb.: Creighton University Press, 1999, 379–400.

Heaney, Seamus. Interview by Randy Brandes (1988). *Salmagundi* 80 (Fall 1988): 4–21.

Joyce, Trevor. "Irish Terrain: Alternative Points of Cleavage." In *Assembling Alternatives: Reading Postmodern Poetries Transnationally,* edited by Romana Huk, 156–168. Middletown, Conn.: Wesleyan University Press, 2003.

Koch, Kenneth. *The Collected Poems.* New York: Knopf, 2005.

———. Interview by Jordan Davis (1995). *The Art of Poetry: Poems, Parodies, Interviews, Essays, and Other Work.* Ann Arbor: University of Michigan Press, 1996, 187–214.

Logan, William. "Abroad and at Home: Ted Hughes, Eavan Boland, John Ashbery, Paul Muldoon" (1991). In *Desperate Measures.* Gainesville: University Press of Florida, 2002, 26–36.

Mahon, Derek. "Hudson Letter" (1996). In *Collected Poems.* Oldcastle, Ireland: Gallery Books, 1999.

Montague, John. "The Impact of International Modern Poetry on Irish Writing" (1973). In *The Figure in the Cave and Other Essays.* Edited by Antoinette Quinn. Syracuse, N.Y.: Syracuse University Press, 1989, 208–220.

Muldoon, Paul. Interviewed by Lynn Keller. *Contemporary Literature.* 35.1 (Spring 1994): 1–29.

———. *The Prince of the Quotidian.* Winston-Salem, N.C.: Wake Forest University Press, 1994.

———. "7, Middagh Street" (1987). In *Poems, 1968–1998.* New York: Farrar, Straus & Giroux, 2001, 175–193.

O'Hara, Frank. "Another Word on Kenneth Koch" (1955). In *Standing Still and Walking in New York.* Edited by Donald Allen. San Francisco: Grey Fox, 1983, 59–61.

———. *Try! Try! A Noh Play* (1951). In *Amorous Nightmares of Delay: Selected Plays.* Baltimore, Md.: Johns Hopkins University Press, 1997, 17–30.

Perloff, Marjorie. *Frank O'Hara: Poet Among Painters.* 1977. Reprint, Chicago: University of Chicago Press, 1998.

Rosenthal, M. L. *The New Poets: American and British Poetry since World War II.* New York: Oxford University Press, 1967.

Smith, Sydney Bernard. "Form of Application to Ted Berrigan for Country or Associate Membership of the New York Poets." In *Poems, 1957–2006* [Ireland]: Little Red Hen, 2006, 123–124.

Wills, Clair. *Reading Paul Muldoon.* Newcastle upon Tyne, U.K.: Bloodaxe, 1998.

J

Jarnot, Lisa (1967–)

Poet, biographer, and memoirist Lisa Jarnot was born in Buffalo, New York, worked with ROBERT CREELEY at the State University of New York at Buffalo (1985–89), and received her M.F.A. in poetry from Brown University (1992–94) in PROVIDENCE, RHODE ISLAND. She then moved to NEW YORK CITY where she became actively involved with the community of the POETRY PROJECT AT ST. MARK'S CHURCH IN-THE-BOWERY. She has edited two small magazines, *No Trees* (1987–90) and *Troubled Surfer* (1991–92), as well as the *Poetry Project Newsletter* and *An Anthology of New American Poetry* (Talisman House Publishers, 1997), which included such poets as PETER GIZZI, CHRIS STROFFOLINO, Thomas Sayers Ellis, and Juliana Spahr.

Jarnot is the author of four full-length collections of poetry: *Some Other Kind of Mission* (Burning Deck Press, 1996), *Ring of Fire* (Zoland Books, 2001), *Black Dog Songs* (Flood Editions, 2003); and *Night Scenes* (Flood Editions, 2008); and numerous chapbooks. Her biography of the San Francisco poet Robert Duncan is forthcoming from University of California Press. She currently teaches at NAROPA University's Jack Kerouac School of Disembodied Poetics, at Bard College, and at Brooklyn College.

Jarnot's poems are cited for their playful disjunctive meandering. They are full of allusive echoes ranging from CHARLES OLSON and FRANK O'HARA to Gertrude Stein and Marlon Brando, and swerve from inside out to the material world, then back in, undulating, "rising on wave after wave of near endless iteration, like a linguistic Mandelbrot set," as Patrick Pritchett has written in *Jacket* (n.p.). Jarnot herself has written: "What I learned to do early in life, as a survival mechanism of sorts, was to invent a self, or a composite of selves, as if my own life was formed out of a distant memory of who all the other versions of me had been throughout the history of my kind. . . . What I had intuited even at that point was that one's identity existed as one's invention, and that as a creative person, one's identification and explanation of the self might always be in flux, like the whole of the universe is in flux, existing as a place of multiple possibilities, formed around one's attentions to the message arriving from the outside."

Bibliography

Jarnot, Lisa. "Biography and Autobiography." *Chain* no. 7 (August 2000): Available online. URL: http://www.temple.edu/chain/MemoirAnti-memoir/content.html. Accessed December 18, 2008.

Pritchett, Patrick. "Patrick Pritchett Reviews *Ring of Fire* by Lisa Jarnot." *Jacket* 15 (December 2001). Available online. URL: http://jacketmagazine.com/15/pritchett-revs-jarnot.html. Accessed December 21, 2008.

jazz

Writers of the post–World War II avant-garde engaged with jazz at significantly different moments. When JACK KEROUAC heard saxophonist Charlie Parker (1920–55), trumpeter Dizzy Gillespie (1917–93), and pianist Thelonious

Monk (1917–82) jam at Minton's Playhouse in Harlem in 1941, he experienced a revolution, a new freedom of expression unlike anything in previous MUSIC, or for that matter, in any of the arts. At first it was simply called "modern" (Scott and Rutkoff 271), but the label that stuck was *bebop*, a term that sounded like the music but deliberately unlike the language of the white audience who had become the primary consumers of earlier big band "swing." Bebop was born Uptown in NEW YORK CITY's Harlem, among black musicians playing for themselves.

When FRANK O'HARA heard Monk and recent arrival John Coltrane (1926–67) play at the FIVE SPOT in Greenwich Village in 1957 (Magee 704), he experienced the Downtown revival of a movement that had nearly died out. A six-year ban on Monk's performance had just been lifted; death had imposed a permanent ban on Parker, who "no longer wails at the Open Door," O'Hara lamented (316); and Gillespie had formed a big band to tour overseas under U.S. State Department sponsorship. While O'Hara became involved in similar official promotion of painting through his job at the Museum of Modern Art, his involvement with jazz reflected its assimilation into a Downtown bohemia that, for the time being, ignored racial differences among artists who shared a common sense of living on the margins of U.S. society. In "The DAY LADY DIED" (1959), O'Hara celebrated Billie Holiday (1915–59) not as a black woman but as a persecuted artist, whom O'Hara heard sing at the Five Spot in 1958, while she was under a performance ban as a result of her conviction on narcotics charges. O'Hara's poem is only the most famous example of a subgenre of NEW YORK SCHOOL elegy focusing on jazz musicians, with notable attention to Monk (Berrigan 589; Brodey, *Heart* 100–101; Corbett, "Thelonius Sphere Monk" 178).

The most important figure in the connection between jazz and the New York School poets was the African-American writer LeRoi Jones. Though later, as AMIRI BARAKA, Jones reasserted the significance of Harlem in maintaining a separate black identity, during the time of his closest friendship with O'Hara (1958–64), Jones identified with "any would-be Bohemian," black or white, in opposition to the denial of freedom and the absence of creativity in mainstream culture (Jones, "Correspondence," 473). Jones and his white wife, Hettie, gathered the forces of opposition in their journal YŪGEN and in their apartment in Chelsea, where parties lasting through the weekend included writers of the Beat, Black Mountain, and New York "schools" along with up-and-coming jazz musicians like Ornette Coleman (1930–), Cecil Taylor (1929–), Archie Shepp (1937–), and Don Cherry (1936–95). These men were leaders of the "new thing" that promised to expand the innovations of bebop into a wide-open field—in musical terms, atonal, like the work of the New York School composers JOHN CAGE and MORTON FELDMAN. A connection to the "all-over" composition and free improvisation of New York School painting was explicitly acknowledged on the cover of Coleman's album *Free Jazz* (1961), which reproduced a work by JACKSON POLLOCK.

While Jones was forward-looking in his advocacy of free jazz, he was equally influential for the sense of jazz history that informed his reviews in trade journals such as *Down Beat* as well as literary periodicals such as the *FLOATING BEAR* and *KULCHUR*. His book *Blues People* (1963) offered the long view, tracing jazz from its roots in blues and its essential connection to the conditions of oppression experienced by black people in America. In this view Jones's report of the clubbing of Miles Davis (1926–91) by policemen, recorded in O'Hara's "Personal Poem" (1959), served as a tragic validation of Davis, whose mellowing of bop into the smooth flow of "cool" jazz made Jones suspicious of a desire to accommodate white taste. White poets could find in Jones validation for their interest in the blues and jazz history. KENNETH KOCH's poem "The History of Jazz" (1962) focuses on a fictitious saxophone player, incongruously named Madeleine Reierbacher, whose "brain floats up into the lyric atmosphere of the sky" when she plays the "Lead Flint Blues" (103). *The SONNETS* (1964, 2000) by TED BERRIGAN are threaded by references to real blues musicians (36, 62, 71–72): Blind Blake (1895–1937), Big Bill Broonzy (1893–1958), Leadbelly (1888–1949), Lonnie Johnson (1899–1970). ANNE WALDMAN joined ALLEN GINSBERG and Bob Dylan in the initial recording sessions (1971) for Ginsberg's *First Blues* (1983), an occasion symbolizing the common ground that blues provided for jazz, folk, and rock music as well as for the BEATS and New York School poets.

"The art of the jazz sentence" (Brodey, *Heart* 241) as practiced by a number of New York School poets inevitably invites comparison with free jazz, insofar as both the poetry and the music abandon the rules of syntax that previously governed each art. In some cases the poets explicitly draw attention to the connection, for example, in CLARK COOLIDGE's "improvisations" on Cecil Taylor or on the Rova Saxophone Quartet; in LORENZO THOMAS's "Spirits You All," dedicated to the Charles Gayle Trio; and in JIM BRODEY's frequent naming of free jazz performers (Coleman, Cherry, Eric Dolphy [1928–64]) among his poems ranging over the entire history of jazz (*Heart* 135, 140, 241–243; "Little Light"). A map of the actual paths of influence, however, would need to include points of multiple convergence as well as areas where jazz and poetry run parallel rather than intersecting. For instance, Coolidge's involvement in jazz extends to his performance as a drummer, but the spirit of jazz in his writing may have as much to do with his reading of Kerouac, whose response to jazz Coolidge has extensively analyzed. In the work of Thomas and Brodey it can seem as if the spirit of jazz arises from "the streets themselves," as Brodey puts it in "Lennie Tristano, No Wind" (*Heart* 32). This sense of "the disorder of tenement streets" (Thomas, "Great Love Duets" 105) composing a kind of jazz order has literary precedent in O'Hara's "Second Avenue" (1953, 1960).

Bibliography
Berrigan, Ted. *The Collected Poems of Ted Berrigan.* Edited by Alice Notley, Anselm Berrigan, and Edmund Berrigan. Berkeley: University of California Press, 2005.

Brodey, Jim. *Heart of the Breath: Poems, 1979–92.* Edited by Clark Coolidge. West Stockbridge, Mass.: Hard Press, 1996.

———. "Little Light/ for Eric Dolphy." In *Broadway: A Poets and Painters Anthology,* edited by James Schuyler and Charles North. New York: Swollen Magpie, 1979, 13.

Coleman, Ornette. *Free Jazz.* Sound recording, R2 75208. San Francisco: Rhino, 1998.

Coolidge, Clark. "From Comes through in the Call Hold (Improvisations on Cecil Taylor)." *Village Voice,* "Jazz Special" supplement, 28 June 1989, pp. 9–10.

———. *Now It's Jazz: Writings on Kerouac and the Sounds.* Albuquerque, N.Mex.: Living Batch Press, 1999.

———. *The Rova Improvisations.* Los Angeles: Sun & Moon, 1994.

Corbett, William. "Ornette Coleman: A Boxed Set" and "Monk: *Live at the It Club.*" In *All Prose: Selected Essays and Reviews.* Cambridge, Mass.: Zoland, 2001, 314–320.

———. "Thelonious Sphere Monk" (1989). In *New and Selected Poems.* Cambridge, Mass.: Zoland, 1995, 178.

Ginsberg, Allen. *First Blues.* Sound recording, Water 166. San Francisco: Water, 2006.

Jones, LeRoi (Amiri Baraka). *Blues People: Negro Music in White America.* 1963. Reprint, New York: Perennial–HarperCollins, 2002.

———. "Correspondence: The Beat Generation." *Partisan Review* 25, no. 3 (Summer 1958): 472–473.

Kerouac, Jack. "The Beginning of Bop" (1959). In *The Portable Jack Kerouac.* Edited by Ann Charters. New York: Penguin, 1996, 555–559.

Koch, Kenneth. "The History of Jazz" (1962). In *The Collected Poems.* New York: Knopf, 2005, 102–104.

Magee, Michael. "Tribes of New York: Frank O'Hara, Amiri Baraka, and the Poetics of the Five Spot." *Contemporary Literature* 42, no. 4 (Winter 2001): 694–726.

O'Hara, Frank. *The Collected Poems.* Rev. ed. Edited by Donald Allen. Berkeley: University of California Press, 1995.

Scott, William B., and Peter M. Rutkoff. "New York Blues: The Bebop Revolution." In *New York Modern: The Arts and the City.* Baltimore, Md.: Johns Hopkins University Press, 1999, 260–288.

Thomas, Lorenzo. "The Blues and the King's English" (1989). In *Disembodied Poetics: Annals of the Jack Kerouac School,* edited by Anne Waldman and Andrew Schelling, 432–447. Albuquerque: University of New Mexico Press, 1994.

———. "Great Love Duets" (1968). In *The Angel Hair Anthology,* edited by Anne Waldman and Lewis Warsh, 105–108. New York: Granary Books, 2001.

———. "Spirits You All." In *Dancing on Main Street.* Minneapolis, Minn.: Coffee House Press, 2004, 52–57.

Jim Carroll Band, The (1980–1983)

After witnessing the success of his friend and fellow poet-musician PATTI SMITH, JIM CARROLL put his poetic talents to the task of writing songs in the mid-1970s. While living in BOLINAS, CALIFORNIA, he joined the band Amsterdam, which then became The Jim Carroll Band. Carroll played a demo tape for Earl McGrath of Rolling Stones Records, a friend from the New York art world who "understood things in literary terms," according to Carroll (Creswell 229). Thanks to McGrath's advocacy, the band released their first album, *Catholic Boy,* with Atco-Atlantic Records in 1980.

Critics reviewed *Catholic Boy* widely, generally finding it modestly successful as a whole, but singling out "People Who Died" for special praise. Part Bob Dylan, part Lou Reed, part Johnny Rotten, Carroll easily applied a poet's "intuitive sense of phrasing" (*Forced Entries* 164) to the electric riffs behind him, alternately singing, chanting, and reciting distinctively when necessary. Arriving before the distinctive synthesizer sound of much early-1980s rock, other *Catholic Boy* songs, such as "I Want the Angel" or "It's Too Late," sound like bridges between the classic grooves of rock anthems such as The Who's "Baba O'Riley" and the Seattle sound of the early 1990s. Critics felt Carroll's presence on other songs, such as "City Drops into Night," as too much poet, not enough songwriter. The band's core personnel play most tracks: Brian Linsley and Terrell Winn on guitar, Steven Linsley on bass, and Wayne Woods on drums. Lenny Kaye of the Patti Smith Band plays guitar on "People Who Died."

"People Who Died" is modeled on a poem of the same title by TED BERRIGAN (1970). In the song, Carroll catalogs various names and types of deaths, with NEW YORK CITY as a frequent backdrop. Carroll's energy, enhanced by the frenetic, punkish guitar chords lashing behind him, gives the song a sticky gravity. He finishes the verses and chorus with announcements of fraternity and eulogy: "They were all my friends, and they just died." Like many of his poems, the song works both as a personal lament and as a communal outcry, but also a dark celebration of the song's characters, who live on the edges of risk, addiction, illness, and war.

The Jim Carroll Band's second album, *Dry Dreams* (Atco-Atlantic, 1982), brought praise for such songs as "Jealous Twin" and "Lorriane" but proved a commercial and critical disappointment. The limitations of Carroll's vocal style, along with lyrics that reviewers found equally limited in expression, caused several to dismiss the record. Yet on songs like "Dry Dreams," Carroll's vocal offers a spirited complement to the straightforward chord progressions. This time, joining Carroll on vocals, Linsley on bass, and Woods on drums, were Paul Sanchez on guitar, Jon Tiven on guitar and organ, Tom Canning on piano, Walter Steding on violin, Sammy Figueroa on percussion, Alan Lanier on synthesizer, and Randy Brecker on trumpet.

The band's final release, *I Write Your Name* (Atlantic, 1983) divided the critics. Though many felt it returned to the promise of *Catholic Boy,* others believed Carroll's performance suffered by comparison with that of other poet-singers such as Smith or Reed. The material, however, stands on its own and converses well with Carroll's spoken word poetry. In particular, "Love Crimes" showcases The Jim Carroll Band at its best: energetic, urgent, and simple. The songs are most successful when neither Carroll nor the music overwhelms the other. In addition to Carroll, Linsley, Woods, and Sanchez, the band included Kaye and Brian Marnell on guitars, Kinny Landrum on keyboards, Will Lee on additional bass, and Michael Caravello on congas and percussion.

Carroll gave up the band when the demands of touring got to be too exhausting and he "wanted to get back to writing" (Carroll, "Unspoken Genius"). "I like performing a lot," he explained, "but I didn't like being on the road and all the psychological paraphernalia." He expresses his attitude through detailed imagery in his poem "On Tour."

Bibliography

Berrigan, Ted. "People Who Died" (1970). In *The Collected Poems of Ted Berrigan.* Edited by Alice Notley, Anselm Berrigan, and Edmund Berrigan.

Berkeley: University of California Press, 2005, 236–237.

Carroll, Jim. *Forced Entries: The Downtown Diaries, 1971–1973.* New York: Penguin, 1987.

———. "On Tour." In *Fear of Dreaming: Selected Poems.* New York: Penguin, 1993, 217.

———. "Unspoken Genius," Interview by Suzan Alteri. *Real Detroit Weekly,* 13–19 January 2000. Available online. URL: http://www.enotes.com/contemporary-literary-criticism/carroll-jim/jim-carroll-with-suzan-alteri- interview-date-13-19. Accessed December 5, 2008.

Carter, Cassie. "Conclusion: Writing as Redemption." In *Shit into Gold: Jim Carroll's* The Basketball Diaries *and* Forced Entries. Catholicboy.com. Available online. URL: http://www.catholicboy.com/chapter4.php. Accessed December 21, 2008.

Creswell, Toby. "People Who Died." In *1001 Songs: The Great Songs of All Time and the Artists, Stories and Secrets behind Them.* New York: Thunder's Mouth, 2006, 299.

Jim Carroll Band, The. *The Best of the Jim Carroll Band: A World without Gravity.* Audio recording, R2 71290. Los Angeles: Rhino, 1993.

Joans, Ted (1928–2003)

Of the African-American poets associated with DOWNTOWN MANHATTAN's bohemia during the 1950s, Ted Joans was the first on the scene. A Midwesterner by birth, he moved to NEW YORK CITY soon after receiving a bachelor's degree in fine arts from Indiana University in 1951. He thought of himself as a painter, found a special excitement in surrealism (see DADA AND SURREALISM), and drew inspiration from contemporary action painters such as WILLEM DE KOONING and Franz Kline (1910–62). To this extent, Joans shared the aesthetic orientation of the NEW YORK SCHOOL poets; however, he was encouraged to practice poetry by ALLEN GINSBERG, who wanted Joans to "jazz up"—literally—the poetry readings that were becoming popular in Greenwich Village coffeehouses in the late 1950s. Joans approached poetry as JAZZ performance, and he has since been identified with the BEAT aesthetic on that basis. Appropriately, his first two volumes are *Beat Poems* (Deretchin, 1957) and *Jazz Poems* (Rhino Review, 1959).

Joans pushed the meaning of performance beyond Beat expression to circle back to the self-reflexive irony that is more typical of the New York School. Being Beat became a concept to play with. In the Corinth Books anthology *The Beat Scene* (1960), which combines Beat (Ginsberg, JACK KEROUAC, GREGORY CORSO) and New York School writers (FRANK O'HARA, KENNETH KOCH, KENWARD ELMSLIE) indiscriminately, Joans's "Playmates" offers the following scenario among others: "Let's play bohemian, and wear odd clothes, and grow a beard or a ponytail, live in the Village for 200.00 a month for one small pad and stroll through Washington Square Park with a guitar and a chick looking sad" (Wilentz 104). Accompanying photos by Fred McDarrah (1926–2007) show Joans in the beard and beret that he helped to establish as the Beat "uniform," though he seems to have regarded it more as a form of packaging, with a cynical eye turned to the American propensity to market the latest lifestyle. He hired himself out through the "Rent-a-Beatnik" program advertised by McDarrah through the *Village Voice,* turning commerce into a GENRE of PERFORMANCE ART that ANDY WARHOL was soon to perfect. As LORENZO THOMAS later observed, "It is not negative criticism to say that Ted Joans's masterpiece was the creation of Ted Joans" (197).

As if to escape the marketing system closing in on the 1960s art world, Joans left the United States in 1961 for extensive travels in Africa and Europe. In the year of his departure he published *All of Ted Joans and No More* (Excelsior) and *The Hipsters* (Corinth). A tone of parody persists in the titles of two volumes published at the end of the decade: *Black Pow-Wow* (Hill and Wang, 1969), published at the height of the Black Power movement in the United States; and *Afrodisia* (Hill and Wang, 1970), reflecting his experience of Africa. His next major volume published in the United States was *Teducation: Selected Poems, 1949–1999* (Coffee House Press, 1999). Joans died in 2003 in Vancouver, British Columbia, Canada.

Bibliography
Fabre, Michel. "Ted Joans: 'The Surrealist Griot.'" In *From Harlem to Paris: Black American Writers in France, 1840–1980.* Urbana: University of Illinois Press, 1991, 308–323.

Fox, Robert Elliot. "Ted Joans and the (b)reach of the African American Literary Canon." *Melus* 29, nos. 3–4 (Fall–Winter 2004): 41–58.

Joans, Ted. "Bird and the Beats" (1981). *Chicken Bones: A Journal.* Available online. URL: http://www.nathanielturner.com/charlieparker.htm. Accessed December 5, 2008.

———. "The Teducated Mouth: An Interview with Ted Joans." Empty Mirror Books Web site. Available online. URL: http://www.emptymirrorbooks.com/teducatedmouth.html. Accessed December 5, 2008.

Thomas, Lorenzo. *Extraordinary Measures: Afrocentric Modernism and Twentieth-Century American Poetry.* Tuscaloosa: University of Alabama Press, 2000.

Wilentz, Elias, ed. *The Beat Scene.* New York: Corinth, 1960.

John Giorno Band (1982–1990)

Despite its name, the John Giorno Band is best understood not as a group of musicians but as a mode of performance that evolved, along with the name, as JOHN GIORNO explored the possibilities of integrating his poetry with rock MUSIC. The style of the music reflects the time and circumstances in which the experiment took place. Living on NEW YORK CITY's Lower East Side and already involved in PERFORMANCE ART, Giorno found the currents of no wave and new wave music swirling around him after the storm of 1970s PUNK ROCK. His first group, not yet called the John Giorno Band, consisted of keyboardist-guitarist Pat Irwin of the Raybeats, bass player Philippe Hagen of the Del-Byzanteens, and experimental percussionist David van Tieghem, who had recorded with Steve Reich, Laurie Anderson, and David Byrne. For the Giorno Poetry Systems label, this group recorded two tracks on the album *Who You Looking At* (1982) and (without Hagen) one track on *Life Is a Killer* (1982). Next, Giorno teamed up with Lenny Kaye, lead guitarist of the recently disbanded PATTI SMITH Group. Giorno produced the only album recorded by the Lenny Kaye Connection, *I've Got a Right* (Giorno Poetry Systems, 1984), and performed with them for one track on the album *You're a Hook* (Giorno Poetry Systems, 1984). Keyboardist C. P. (Charlie) Roth of the Lenny Kaye Connection performed "all instruments" (on synthesizers) behind Giorno for

one track on a third album of 1984, *Better an Old Demon Than a New God,* also released by Giorno Poetry Systems.

The group to which the name John Giorno Band first attached, starting in 1985, formed around Roth. He was joined by his brother Adam on guitar, David Conrad (the son of poet Adrienne Rich) on bass, and Mike Osborn on drums—"a polished white funk quartet," according to Stephen Holden, the *New York Times* critic who reviewed their show at the Bottom Line in Greenwich Village in April 1985. Giorno continued to perform live with this group for the next five years, though he disliked the hassle of managing "all this equipment" on road trips (Giorno, "Subduing" n.p.), a major factor in his eventual decision to dissolve the band. Meanwhile, in the Giorno Poetry Systems studio, they recorded "Scum and Slime" (*A Diamond Hidden in the Mouth of a Corpse,* 1985); "Sucking Mud" (*Smack My Crack,* 1987); and "It's a Mistake to Think You're Special," (*Like a Girl, I Want You to Keep Coming,* 1989). The John Giorno Band never released a single disc or a solo album, a reflection of Giorno's indifference to commercial success and of the excitement he derived from bringing many different sounds together. *A Diamond Hidden in the Mouth of a Corpse* is an especially notable collection in this regard, with tracks by such cutting-edge groups as Hüsker Dü, Sonic Youth, and Cabaret Voltaire, as well as readings by WILLIAM S. BURROUGHS.

When performing with musicians, Giorno chants rather than sings his poems. Music, whether vocal or instrumental, is not an additional layer on top of the words but rather a complement to "the musical qualities inherent in the phrases" (Giorno, interview 162). An essentially musical quality, in Giorno's view, seems to be the ability of certain phrases to lift out of context, lodging in the memory as what might be called "sound bites," though Giorno does not disparage the "short attention span" usually associated with that term (Giorno, interview 163). Rather, he reinforces the separateness of his sound bites by using breathing and repetition as framing devices. The visual connotations of framing become literalized in videos and "poem-prints," two media in which Giorno has extended his performance work. For instance, from the poem "Scum and Slime," the phrase "I want to be filthy and anonymous"—highlighting two terms often applied disparagingly to gay sex—is framed as a kind of badge of honor in both a poem-print and a music video.

Bibliography

Giorno, John. Interview by Nicholas Zurbrugg. In *Art, Performance, Media: 31 Interviews,* by Nicholas Zurbrugg. Minneapolis: University of Minnesota Press, 2004, 156–171.

———. "Subduing the Demons in America." *The Archive* (Leslie-Lohman Gay Art Foundation) 11 (2003). Available online. URL: http://www.leslielohman. org/newsletter/No11/giornopart6.htm. Accessed December 5, 2008.

Holden, Stephen. "Music: Giorno's Poetic Pop," *New York Times,* 4 April 1985, p. C14.

John Giorno Band. "Scum and Slime." In *It's Clean, It Just Looks Dirty.* Videorecording, Giorno Video Pak 3, GPS 037. New York: Giorno Poetry Systems, 1986.

Palmer, Robert. "The Pop Life: David Murray Comes into His Own." *New York Times,* 27 October 1982, p. C20.

Johns, Jasper (1930–) *artist, painter*

Since his paintings of flags and targets stunned the New York art world in his first solo exhibition in 1958, Jasper Johns has been identified with a cooling down of the emotional tone of ABSTRACT EXPRESSIONISM and an ironic appropriation of popular imagery that received the label of POP ART during the 1960s. Johns's connection to NEW YORK SCHOOL poetry, however, depends on the poets' recognition of emotional expression in his work and his difference from pop artists like ANDY WARHOL. While Johns's images are "greeted with delight" because they are "recognizable," in fact, "they are filled with pain," FRANK O'HARA insisted ("Art Chronicle I" 132).

Shortly before Johns's 1958 debut at the Castelli Gallery, O'Hara had met Johns through the latter's lover, ROBERT RAUSCHENBERG. As "Jap," his nickname, Johns appears in O'Hara's poem "Joe's Jacket" (1959), which marks the beginning of O'Hara's love affair with Vincent Warren. O'Hara features more prominently in Johns's memorial to the end of his affair with Rauschenberg, the painting *In Memory of My Feelings—Frank O'Hara* (1961), in which an image of the American flag—a part of Johns's artistic identity—has been nearly obliterated in a layer of gray paint. His association with this painting no doubt gave O'Hara insight into Johns's indirect methods for expressing the pain of loss. Numbers, another favorite emblem of Johns's, perform this function for O'Hara both in the poem "IN MEMORY OF MY FEELINGS" (1956) and in "The Clouds Go Soft" (1963), a poem Johns incorporated in a lithograph, *Skin with O'Hara Poem* (1963–65). A simple fork and spoon appear both in Johns's painting *In Memory of My Feelings* and in his design accompanying the title poem in the memorial volume for O'Hara, also called *In Memory of My Feelings.* Presumably, the meaning attached to these ordinary objects is something like that expressed in O'Hara's poem "Dear Jap" (1963): "that small insufferable things become culinary" (*Collected Poems* 471). In the same poem O'Hara writes: "when I think of you in South Carolina"— John's native state, where he had withdrawn after breaking up with Rauschenberg—"I think of my foot in the sand" (471). O'Hara is referring to Johns's *Memory Piece—Frank O'Hara* (1961–70), a boxlike sculpture in which a mold taken from O'Hara's foot leaves an impression in sand when the lid of the box is closed. In one construction this device "means" transience and simultaneously conceals its meaning.

The critic Marjorie Perloff has argued that O'Hara's connection to Johns may prove to be "more significant" than O'Hara's connection to abstract expressionist painters once seemed to be ("Introduction" xxi), although Perloff emphasizes that Johns's "'cool' Conceptualism" diverges from O'Hara's "PERSONISM" ("Watchman" 218). To Perloff the divergence points in the direction of LANGUAGE POETRY ("Introduction" xxiv–xxv), but within the New York School tradition it is possible to trace a continuing interest in the conceptual dimension of Johns's work that does not repudiate subjectivity, as Language poets claim to do. This branch of the tradition stems from JOHN ASHBERY, who was less close to Johns personally than O'Hara was but took great interest in Johns's art (Ashbery, interview 34). Reviewing a 1966 show at the Castelli Gallery, Ashbery described

Johns's painting *According to What* (1964) as "a sort of equation with insufficient conditions for determining the unknown" ("Brooms and Prisms" 69). The comparison with a mathematical equation highlights the systematic nature of Johns's concerns, articulated in a series of "Sketchbook Notes" that he published in Ashbery's journal ART AND LITERATURE (number 4, spring 1965), in TREVOR WINKFIELD's *JUILLARD* (number 3, winter 1968–69), and in BERNADETTE MAYER's *0 TO 9* (number 6, July 1969), named after Johns's work with numerals. In the same issue of *Art and Literature* that carried his own work, Johns would have read some of TED BERRIGAN's SONNETS, works he admired for their sometimes random, sometimes obsessively systematic rearrangement of "found" materials; Johns used the title page of the Grove Press edition of *The Sonnets* (1967) as found material in *Screen Print 3* (1968; Bernstein 131–133).

Younger poets in the line of Ashbery have shown a marked tendency to recuperate Johns's CONCEPTUALISM as a mode of surrealism (see DADA AND SURREALISM). DAVID SHAPIRO compares Ashbery and Johns as "American Surrealists holding the everyday as the marvelous" (Shapiro 58). JOHN YAU's *Corpse and Mirror*, selected by Ashbery for the National Poetry series, takes it title from one of Johns's abstract paintings of the 1970s, when he covered the entire surface of a canvas with patterns of "cross-hatch" marks traditional in printmaking. The painting *Corpse and Mirror* (1974) suggests, both in its title and its bifurcated design, the surrealist device for collaborative composition known as the "exquisite corpse" (Bernstein 137–138). Yau takes the suggestion further by applying the title to a sequence of neosurrealist prose poems. Later, in a book-length essay on Johns, Yau makes a case for viewing even so mundane an image as Johns's *Flag* (1955) as an effort to combine dream and reality, in the spirit of the Belgian surrealist René Magritte (Yau, *United States* 20–23). The difference, according to MARJORIE WELISH, is that Johns evokes the surreal from materials as much as from images: "It is as if Johns had taken Symbolist concrete thought to an extreme in order, as the Surrealist André Breton might have said, to follow through on the impulse to make the imaginary real" (80).

Bibliography

Ashbery, John. "Brooms and Prisms: Jasper Johns" (1966). In *Selected Prose.* Edited by Eugene Richie. Ann Arbor: University of Michigan Press, 2004, 68–73.

———. Interview by Kenneth Deifik and Stephen Paul Miller. *Unmuzzled Ox* nos. 4 and 5 (1979): 31–35.

Bernstein, Roberta. *Jasper Johns' Paintings and Sculptures, 1954–1974: "The Changing Focus of the Eye."* Ann Arbor, Mich.: UMI Research Press, 1985.

Ferguson, Russell. *In Memory of My Feelings: Frank O'Hara and American Art.* Exhibit catalog. Los Angeles: Museum of Contemporary Art; Berkeley: University of California Press, 1999, 127–136.

O'Hara, Frank. "Art Chronicle I" (1962). In *Standing Still and Walking in New York.* Edited by Donald Allen. San Francisco: Grey Fox, 1983, 126–132.

———. *The Collected Poems.* Rev. ed. Edited by Donald Allen. Berkeley: University of California Press, 1995.

Perloff, Marjorie. "Introduction, 1997." In *Frank O'Hara: Poet Among Painters,* by Marjorie Perloff. New ed. Chicago: University of Chicago Press, 1998, xi–xxx.

———. "Watchman, Spy, and Dead Man: Jasper Johns, Frank O'Hara, John Cage and the 'Aesthetic of Indifference.'" *Modernism/Modernity* 8, no. 2 (April 2001): 197–223.

Shapiro, David. *Jasper Johns Drawings, 1954–1984.* New York: Abrams, 1985.

Welish, Marjorie. "When Is a Door Not a Door? Jasper Johns" (1991). In *Signifying Art: Essays on Art after 1960.* Cambridge: Cambridge University Press, 1999, 76–83.

Yau, John. *Corpse and Mirror.* New York: Holt, Rinehart & Winston, 1983.

———. *The United States of Jasper Johns.* Cambridge, Mass.: Zoland, 1996.

Jones, LeRoi   *See* BARAKA, AMIRI.

Jones, Patricia Spears (1951–   )

The poetry of Patricia Spears Jones, while nourished by her contact with the NEW YORK SCHOOL poetic, just as much exemplifies her involvement with the tradition of the UMBRA workshop and the Nuyorican poetry scene (see NUYORICAN POETS CAFÉ) and her deep readings of international modernism and poetries of the Négritude movement. Born in Forest City, Arkansas, she received a B.A. in communication arts from Rhodes College in Memphis, Tennessee (1973). From there she headed for NEW YORK CITY, where she engaged in a writing workshop led by ALICE NOTLEY at the POETRY PROJECT AT ST. MARK'S CHURCH IN-THE-BOWERY in the late 1970s, along with BOB HOLMAN, EILEEN MYLES, BOB ROSENTHAL, GREG MASTERS, among others. Also in this period she was introduced by TED GREENWALD to a mentor, LORENZO THOMAS, through whom she connected with various developing coteries of New York African-American writers. MAUREEN OWEN, also a mentor and friend, published her book *Mythologizing Always* (Telephone Books, 1981). Jones served as program coordinator of the Poetry Project in the early '80s and taught writing workshops there in 2005, but she has been too intellectually searching to situate herself completely in any one community of writers. However, through her writing, lectures, teaching, and essays, she has represented, with honesty and a crisp forbearance, the importance to her work of the sometimes contentious poetic constellations in which she participates.

In her love of the American songbook, classic B movies, and kitsch, Jones shares ground with writers such as Thomas, KENWARD ELMSLIE, Notley, Charlotte Carter, ED FRIEDMAN, and BILL KUSHNER, coming right down from FRANK O'HARA: "Here in North America where / Carmen Miranda and her mulatto progeny sashayed they stuff / Across Hollywood camera eye / like comets christening the tropics" ("Spanish Lesson" 230). Jones has been deeply committed to the feminist movement and feminist modes of understanding, especially the activist, challenging strand that upset the apple cart of the New York arts scene in the '70s. She was an editor of *Ordinary Women: An Anthology of New York City Women Poets* (Ordinary Women Books, 1978). Her meditation on the great, late African-American actress Diana Sands was published in *Home Girls: A Black Feminist Anthology* (Kitchen Table–Women of Color Press, 1983).

In addition to *Mythologizing Always*, mentioned above, Jones's volumes of poetry include *Knock Knock* (Bench Press, 1981), *Bessie Smith for Beginners* (Writers & Readers, 1987), *The Weather That Kills* (Coffee House Press, 1995), and *Femme du Monde* (Tia Chucha Press, 2006). She has written and collaborated on several theater pieces that incorporate poetry, including *Mother*, commissioned by Mabou Mines (1994), and *Estáis muertos*, based on Cesar Vallejo's poem, produced in COLLABORATION with Cuban composer Mónica Santos Loriga at the Virginia Center for Creative Arts (2002).

Jones is a critic of increasing scope, frequently writing for scholarly and popular journals on the work of African-American writers such as June Jordan, Cornelius Eady, Yusef Komunyakaa, and Lucille Clifton, and musicians such as Duke Ellington and Richie Havens. She is the author of a seminal essay on independent black filmmakers (*Village Voice*, 27 August–2 September 1980). In 2006, at Poets House in New York, Jones delivered a scholarly and loving memorial assessment of the work and influence of Thomas ("Thinking in Words"). In addition to the Poetry Project Jones has taught at Sarah Lawrence College, the NAROPA INSTITUTE, and Parsons School of Design.

Bibliography

Jones, Patricia Spears. "Spanish Lesson." In *Aloud: Voices from the Nuyorican Poets Café*, edited by Miguel Algarín and Bob Holman, 229–230. New York: Holt, 1994.

———. "Thinking in Words: A Talk about Lorenzo Thomas." A Gathering of the Tribes. Available online. URL: http://www.tribes.org/pjones/essays/thomas. Accessed December 18, 2008.

Journalist, The Harry Mathews (1994)

HARRY MATHEWS's *The Journalist* is a fictional collection of journal entries by a nameless, middle-aged man recovering from a nervous breakdown. At first he is encouraged to keep the journal as a way of staying grounded in real life, but the activity ends up doing far more harm than good. The "journalist" becomes obsessed with recording every detail of reality, and he invests so much time and energy into this task that he becomes alienated from, and fiercely suspicious of, those around him. What is more, the journalist finds himself beholden to an increasingly byzantine notation system of his own invention, meant to help catalog the diverse constituents of his experiences (for example, the subjective aspects versus the verifiable aspects, sounds versus sights, etc.). Eventually, the narrator's monumental project consumes him to the point where his life is merely fodder for his journal.

While *The Journalist* is arguably Mathews's most realistic novel, it is, nevertheless, full of the narrative interruptions and formal oddities that pervade his earlier fiction. For example, when the journalist meets a Hungarian waiter at a restaurant, he solicits (and attempts to transcribe) the man's entire life story in painstaking detail, a sequence that snowballs across several pages.

In Mathews's other novels digressions of this sort are justified by the absurdist tenor of the work as a whole; here they are conceived as a product of the narrator's mental instability. The author effectively interiorizes the surreal landscape of *The* CONVERSIONS and *TLOOTH*, making that landscape a feature of his subject's psychology instead of the external world. As a result of the psychological depth suggested in the text, Mathews's characteristic irony toward his protagonist's behavior is necessarily less pronounced than in the author's previous novels. And while there are certainly comic moments, the overall tone of the story is rather serious.

The book's heightened gravity might, in part, derive from the weighty philosophical issues that it engages; most notably, the tension between "real" experience and written record, and the differences between writing for oneself (such as a diary entry) and writing for an audience (such as a novel). Mathews, himself, foregrounds these concerns in numerous essays and interviews.

Initial critical reception to *The Journalist* was generally favorable, though some accused its conclusion of being heavy-handed and insufficiently ambiguous compared with the rest of the text.

Bibliography

Mathews, Harry. *The Journalist.* New York: Godine, 1994.

Moore, Steven. Review of *The Journalist. Review of Contemporary Fiction* (Fall 1994): 205.

Polk, James. Review of *The Journalist. New York Times Book Review*, 26 Mar 1995, 718.

Review of *The Journalist. Kirkus Reviews*, 1 July 1994, 108.

Review of *The Journalist. The Atlantic Monthly*, October 1994, 132.

Shaw, Lytle. "An Interview with Harry Mathews." *Chicago Review* (Spring 1997): 36–52.

Judson Memorial Church

Judson Memorial Church, at 55 Washington Square South, opened its facilities to experimental artists working in DANCE, THEATER, poetry, and the visual arts as part of its mission of community service. In 1890 the distinguished Baptist preacher Edward Judson commissioned architect Stanford White to construct a building that would unite people of disparate classes and provide services to Lower Manhattan's growing immigrant community. This sense of social responsibility persisted within the church through the late 1950s when Reverend Howard Moody began coordinating events around the arts as well as social issues such as civil rights, free expression, abortion rights, and the decriminalization of prostitution.

As early as 1959 POP ART exponents such as Claes Oldenberg, JIM DINE, ROBERT RAUSCHENBERG, and Red Grooms were displaying work in what came to be called the Judson Gallery (a forum to which the public was invited to hang art and poetry representing their concerns). Around that same time Judson began hosting the first "HAPPENINGS"—uncategorizable gatherings that blurred the line separating life and art—led by Carolee Schneemann, Allan Kaprow, and others. In 1961 the Judson Poets' Theatre was founded under the auspices of assistant minister Al Carmines, a composer and, like Moody, a champion of free expression. The first production of the Poets' Theatre was *The Great American Desert* by JOEL OPPENHEIMER (Banes 45–46).

Perhaps the most famous offshoot of the Judson arts program is the Judson Dance Theatre, a troupe that evolved out of an experimental choreography class taught by Robert Dunn at the Merce Cunningham Studio. Members included Yvonne

Rainer, Steve Paxton, Trisha Brown, Deborah Hay, Fred Herko, Lucinda Childs, and others. Like the NEW YORK SCHOOL painters and poets, the troupe celebrated spontaneity and freedom from artistic conventions. Largely through the involvement of composer Philip Corner, the Dance Theatre became connected with such experimental musicians as JOHN CAGE and MORTON FELDMAN and eventually worked with many of the pop artists as well. Today the church continues to host free weekly dance performances.

Though much of the art presented at Judson was controversial (including, in some cases, nudity and mutilation), the church never tried to impose restrictions on its artists, who were in their own way "reaching out for the transcendent," in the words of Oldenburg, or seeking the "beatific," as JACK KEROUAC claimed for the BEATS. Likewise, the church seemed to echo the New York School poets in its desire to unite the world of art with ordinary experience.

Bibliography

Banes, Sally. *Greenwich Village 1963: Avant-Garde Performance and the Effervescent Body.* Durham, N.C.: Duke University Press, 1993.

Judson Memorial Church Web site. Available online. URL: http://www.judson.org/index.html.

Juillard (1968–1972)

The magazine *Juillard* (pronounced ZHWEE-yar), edited by TREVOR WINKFIELD, represents a "second generation" of the project begun by *LOCUS SOLUS* and *ART AND LITERATURE*. Compared to those journals, *Juillard* was a much less lavish production. Financed by Winkfield himself, only two of the nine issues were printed by offset (number 1, spring 1968, and number 3, winter 1968–69); the rest were mimeographed. But Winkfield was directly inspired by the dynamic transaction between French and American literature that he witnessed in the earlier journals, which appeared to him much more exciting than anything going on in England, where Winkfield launched *Juillard* from his hometown of Leeds. While still in college, he had been one of three editors of a magazine called *Icteric* (1967–68).

When it showed signs of failing after two issues, Winkfield used the material that had been gathered for a third issue to start *Juillard*.

Winkfield's enthusiasm for the work of RAYMOND ROUSSEL was the force that first attracted him to JOHN ASHBERY, KENNETH KOCH, and HARRY MATHEWS, each of whom published TRANSLATIONS of Roussel during the 1960s (eventually republished by Winkfield in his Roussel collection, *How I Wrote Certain of My Books* [1995]). Like *Locus Solus*, *Juillard* takes its title from Roussel, in this case from the name of a character in *Impressions of Africa* (1910). Winkfield's translation of Roussel's "The Stopping-Place" appeared in *Juillard* number 7 (fall 1970); the next issue (number 8, winter 1970–71) presented three works by Roussel, including "Among the Blacks," in a collaborative translation by Winkfield and RON PADGETT. *Juillard* consistently accorded a prominent place to translation, particularly of work associated with DADA AND SURREALISM. Issue number 7 is dedicated to Isidore Ducasse (Lautréamont), recognized by the surrealists as a crucial forerunner. Issue number 8 includes work by George Trakl, Pierre Reverdy, and André du Bouchet, in addition to Roussel.

While documenting a tradition, Winkfield was simultaneously discovering new work, much of it by poets of the NEW YORK SCHOOL. *Juillard* published work by Ashbery, BILL BERKSON, JOE BRAINARD, MICHAEL BROWNSTEIN, KENWARD ELMSLIE, LARRY FAGIN, Mathews, CHARLES NORTH, Padgett, JAMES SCHUYLER, TONY TOWLE, ANNE WALDMAN, and BILL ZAVATSKY. The one book issued under a projected series of Juillard Editions was Mathews's first collection of poems, *The Ring* (1970). By the time it appeared, Winkfield had moved to New York; however, the transatlantic perspective that had originally inspired *Juillard* persisted through the final issue in 1972.

Winkfield's involvement in the visual arts as well as literature is reflected in *Juillard*, though mimeograph production imposed limits on visual presentation. Covers were designed by JASPER JOHNS (number 1, spring 1968), JOSEPH CORNELL (number 3, winter 1968–69); Brainard (number 6, summer 1970); Glen Baxter, who went to school with Winkfield (number 8, winter 1970–71); and

Winkfield himself (number 7, fall 1970; number 9, spring 1972). Text written by Johns, an installment of his "Sketchbook Notes" (number 3, winter 1968–69), is the publication that Winkfield recalls with greatest pride. Recently, with generous financial backing, Winkfield has embarked on a new periodical project, *The Sienese Shredder* (number 1, winter 2006–07), coedited by Brice Brown.

The greater emphasis on visual art in this project reflects not only the availability of funds but also Winkfield's sense that contemporary artists are producing more of interest than writers are.

Bibliography

Winkfield, Trevor. Telephone conversation with Terence Diggory, 10 June 2007.

K

Kaplan, Allan (1932–)

Allan Kaplan belongs to New York by birth and to the NEW YORK SCHOOL through his participation in workshops conducted by KENNETH KOCH and FRANK O'HARA at the New School in the early 1960s. His poems appeared in the leading New York School magazines of this period, *LOCUS SOLUS* and *ART AND LITERATURE*, and his reviews appeared in *KULCHUR*. In the early 1970s he was among the small number of second-generation poets who broke into mainstream publishing under the editorship of Fran McCullough at Harper & Row, which published Kaplan's first collection of poems, *Paper Airplane* (1971). Although he has continued to live in Greenwich Village since that time, his poems have appeared somewhat less frequently in magazines less closely tied to the New York School. He has supported himself through teaching, principally in the NEW YORK CITY school system. His second collection, *Like One of Us* (Untitled Press), appeared in 2007.

Kaplan's poetry resembles that of O'Hara and Koch in their most breezy, exuberant moods. Even when Kaplan is in a somber mood, there seems to be something in the act of writing that lifts his spirits, preventing him from taking himself too seriously. Taking on a life of its own, the poem mocks death, as in Kaplan's memorial to O'Hara: "Frank O'Hara's collapsed from too much living. / O darling boy, get up, we love you!" (*Paper Airplane* 27). Kaplan's allusion to O'Hara's "Poem ('Lana Turner has collapsed')" (1962) points to an important area of shared reference—movies and Hollywood stars (Towle 53)—that underwrites both writers' sense of poetry as performance. In his frequent literary allusions Kaplan sometimes performs like the graduate student he was during the 1960s (he received an M.A. from New York University). The act of the imagination that inspires performance may be felt more strongly when the performance itself is imaginary, as in repeated images of the circus, a source of reference that Kaplan shares with Koch. In "Various Performers," "the Earth is galloping like a circus horse" on which the poet and his lover ride "like bareback acrobats" (*Paper Airplane* 9–10). Reflecting perhaps a more mature experience of love in the recent poem "For the Sake of Appearances," the poet admits, "I'll not arrive strolling across a high wire / balance pole spreading out from my shoulders / like wings," but he nevertheless hopes that in his lover's eyes, "I may still appear / more than I am" (43).

Bibliography

Kaplan, Allan. "For the Sake of Appearances." *Hubbub* 21 (2005): 43.

———. *Paper Airplane.* New York: Harper & Row, 1971.

Towle, Tony. *Memoir, 1960–1963.* Cambridge, Mass.: Faux Press, 2001.

Katz, Alex (1927–) *painter*

In the relation between visual art and NEW YORK SCHOOL poetry, the painter Alex Katz holds a unique position of equal importance to poets of the first and second generations. He matches the former in stylistic flair and the latter in toughness of character. EDWIN DENBY celebrated the light in Katz's paintings; RON PADGETT imagined Katz himself stepping out of a detective novel. FRANK O'HARA, who reviewed Katz's first solo show in 1954, declared: "Katz is one of the most interesting painters in America" (*Art Chronicles* 142).

A New Yorker by birth, Katz discovered "the numinous instant" that he wanted to capture in painting in the rural environment of the Skowhegan art school in Maine (Ratcliff 120). Since 1954 he has maintained a home in Maine as well as NEW YORK CITY, and his work draws on both settings to create an "urban pastoral" mode similar to that of Denby and RUDOLPH BURCKHARDT, who followed Katz to Maine in the mid-1960s. In painting, Katz's portrayal of nature aligns him with FAIRFIELD PORTER and JANE FREILICHER, but their painterly style contrasts sharply with the "hard-edged" quality that gives Katz's images the look of commercial art or POP ART, the avant-garde movement with which Katz was sometimes associated in the 1960s.

Unlike the pop artists, who drew imagery as well as style from commercial art, Katz painted the life that he saw around him. The people around him supplied his most important subject—more important than landscape—because Katz is above all a painter of "ordinary social space," as BILL BERKSON has noted (27). Katz's wife, Ada, whom he married in 1958, is his most famous subject, but his poet friends also appear throughout his work, as if to acknowledge that they, too, like the painter, were "dealing with their life as they were living it" (Katz, interview by Storr 34). When JAMES SCHUYLER and Burckhardt showed up at Katz's studio on assignment for *Art News,* they, along with Ada, became the subjects of the picture described in "Alex Katz Paints a Picture." Later, after assigning a portrait of ANNE WALDMAN the generic title *Face of a Poet* (1972), Katz extended the GENRE to a book entitled *Face of the Poet* (Brooke Alexander/Marlborough Graphics, 1978), consisting of 14 portraits, each paired with a text by the poet represented (TED BERRIGAN, KENWARD ELMSLIE, JOHN GODFREY, TED GREENWALD, MICHAEL LALLY, ANN LAUTERBACH, GERARD MALANGA, ALICE NOTLEY, JOHN PERREAULT,

CARTER RATCLIFF, René Ricard, PETER SCHJELDAHL, TONY TOWLE, and BILL ZAVATSKY).

A long series of COLLABORATIONs with poets began in 1962 with the "cut-out" figures of British and American soldiers and props such as Washington's boat that Katz created for a production of KENNETH KOCH's play *GEORGE WASHINGTON CROSSING THE DELAWARE.* The visual paradox of flat painted figures standing alone in three-dimensional space—a strategy that Katz had applied to portraits of O'Hara and other friends since 1959—nicely complemented the ambiguity of "surface" and "depth" in Koch's text, though Katz was disappointed that the play was produced on a conventional deep stage (Katz, interview by Katz 12). On the whole, Katz's images interact with poetry more effectively in the space of a book, particularly in cases where narrative is transposed to the abstract plane of "sequencing" (Katz, interview Katz 12), as in Katz's later collaboration with Koch (*Interlocking Lives,* Kulcher Foundation, 1970), with JOHN ASHBERY (*Fragment,* Black Sparrow, 1969) and with HARRY MATHEWS (*Selected Declarations of Dependence,* Z PRESS, 1977). Throughout the 1970s he produced covers for books (Elmslie, *Motor Disturbance,* 1971; Notley, *Phoebe Light,* 1973) and magazines (*Big Sky* 2 [1972], *The WORLD* 28 [1973], *ZZZZZ* [1977]), forming ties with poets that gathered together in *Face of the Poet,* then spun out a variety of full-scale collaboration in the 1980s: with Ratcliff (*Give Me Tomorrow,* Vehicle Editions, 1985), with his son VINCENT KATZ (*A Tremor in the Morning,* Peter Blum, 1986), and with Padgett (*Light As Air,* Pace Editions, 1989). Also during the 1980s Katz resumed work for the stage in collaboration with Ada, who produced several plays by poets for the Eye and Ear Theater.

A major retrospective exhibition at the Whitney Museum of American Art in 1986 confirmed Katz's position as a master of postwar realist painting. On that occasion Berkson commented on the blend of realism and artifice that ensured Katz's lasting significance to the poets. "Katz's paintings of people," Berkson wrote, "catch perceptible dance-like postures in everyday life, postures that are part of the theatrical forward thrust of character associated with contemporary New York" (30–31).

Bibliography

Berkson, Bill. "First Painter of Character" (1986). In *The Sweet Singer of Modernism and Other Art Writings, 1985–2003*. Jamestown, R.I.: Qua Books, 2003, 27–37.

Denby, Edwin. "Alex Katz Paints His North Window" (ca. 1960). In *Alex Katz*, by Carter Ratcliff et al., 152. London: Phaidon, 2005.

Freilicher, Jane, and Alex Katz. "A Dialogue." *Art and Literature* 1 (March 1964): 205–216.

Katz, Alex. Interview by Robert Storr. In *Alex Katz*, by Carter Ratcliff et al., 7–49. London: Phaidon, 2005.

———. Interview by Vincent Katz. *Poetry Project Newsletter* 184 (April–May 2001): 11–15ff.

———. "Memoir" (1967). In *Homage to Frank O'Hara*, edited by Bill Berkson and Joe LeSueur, 99. Bolinas, Calif.: Big Sky, 1988.

O'Hara, Frank. "Alex Katz" (1954). In *What's with Modern Art?* Edited by Bill Berkson. Austin, Tex.: Mike & Dale's Press, 1999, 19.

———. "Alex Katz" (1966). In *Art Chronicles, 1954–1966*. Rev. ed. New York: Braziller, 1990, 142–148.

Padgett, Ron. "Portrait of Alex for Alex" (ca. 1970). In *Alex Katz*, by Carter Ratcliff et al., 146. London: Phaidon, 2005.

Porter, Fairfield. "A Realist" (1960). In *Art in Its Own Terms: Selected Criticism, 1935–1975*. Edited by Rackstraw Downes. Cambridge, Mass.: Zoland, 1979, 90–91.

Ratcliff, Carter. "Survey." In *Alex Katz*. London: Phaidon, 2005, 51–135.

Schuyler, James. "Alex Katz Paints a Picture" (1962). In *Selected Art Writings*. Edited by Simon Pettet. Santa Rosa, Calif.: Black Sparrow, 1998, 36–44

Katz, Vincent (1960–)

Born in Manhattan, Vincent Katz was befriended as a child by JOE BRAINARD, KENWARD ELMSLIE, KENNETH KOCH, FRANK O'HARA, and JAMES SCHUYLER, all friends of his father, the painter ALEX KATZ. He has written that from this extended family circle he was "able to observe the ease with which these, and other [New York School] writers, integrated their art and daily life" (questionnaire response n.p.). At age six he wrote a poem on the death of O'Hara; his first publication, in 1970, appeared in ADVENTURES IN POETRY. As a teenager (at which time he was already editing and publishing his own work), he attended events at the POETRY PROJECT AT ST. MARK'S CHURCH IN-THE-BOWERY. Katz recalls a nervous reading he gave there of a poem about EDWIN DENBY "with tons of sentiment and emotion in it," after which TED BERRIGAN was heard to say, "Right on, Vinny" (Contributor's note 650). Early poems show (and self-consciously mock) his poetic legacy: "I'm writing a / poem to say / it's good to be writing / a poem" ("Island Music," *Cabal* 69).

Among Katz's most notable collections of poetry are *Rooms* (Open Window, 1978), *Cabal of Zealots* (Hanuman, 1988), *Understanding Objects* (Hard Press, 2000), and *Rapid Departures*, with drawings by Mario Cafiero (Ateliê Editorial, 2005). Katz has also done a series of TRANSLATIONs from Greek and Latin, most significantly, *The Complete Elegies of Sextus Propertius* (Princeton University Press, 2004). Although his Propertius was criticized as "too hip" (Butrica, n.p.), Katz's translations (completed during a Rome Prize Fellowship) nevertheless received an award from the American Literary Translators Association. His wide-ranging professional career as an art critic (Cy Twombly, JIM DINE, Kiki Smith), curator (the exhibition and book, *Black Mountain College: Experiment in Art* [MIT Press, 2002]), and editor (currently the journal *Vanitas* and Libellum books) is consistent with NEW YORK SCHOOL practice. He has also carried on its tradition of collaborative enterprises, working with RUDOLPH BURCKHARDT (*BOULEVARD TRANSPORTATION*), Red Grooms, and Francesco Clemente, as well as with his wife, the photographer Vivien Bittencourt, among many others.

Bibliography

Butrica, J. L. Review of *The Complete Elegies of Sextus Propertius*. *Bryn Mawr Classical Review* (28 November 2004). Available online. URL: http://ccat.sas.upenn.edu/bmcr/2004/2004-11-28.html. Accessed December 5, 2008.

Katz, Vincent. Contributor's note. In *Out of This World: An Anthology of the St. Mark's Poetry Project*, edited by Anne Waldman, 650. New York: Crown, 1991.

———. *Cabal of Zealots*. Madras and New York: Hanuman, 1988.

———. Questionnaire response for *Encyclopedia of the New York School Poets*. 6 December 2005.

Kerouac, Jack (1922–1969)

In a series of novels beginning with *On the Road* (1957), Jack Kerouac earned a place in literary history as a leading representative and popular chronicler of the *beat generation,* a term he claimed to have invented. His fierce ambition, combined with a distrust of "intellectuals" inherited from his working-class background in Lowell, Massachusetts, made him both jealous and suspicious of the artists and writers of the New York avant-garde with whom he began to mingle during the later 1950s. In a notorious exchange during a reading by GREGORY CORSO and FRANK O'HARA in 1959, a drunken Kerouac taunted from the audience, "You're ruining American poetry, O'Hara," to which O'Hara shot back, "That's more than you ever did for it" (Gooch 322). KENNETH KOCH parodied *On the Road* in "On the Go," published in the first issue of *LOCUS SOLUS* (1961). Nevertheless, in the style more than in the content of his writing, Kerouac showed a commitment to experimentation that aligns him with the NEW YORK SCHOOL poets and directly influenced poets of the second generation and later.

Kerouac wrote poetry as well as prose. He is represented in DONALD M. ALLEN's anthology *The NEW AMERICAN POETRY, 1945–1960* (1960) with selections from *Mexico City Blues* (1959), the only collection of Kerouac's verse published during his lifetime. Far more influential, however, is Kerouac's approach to prose as "an endless one-line poem," as he described it in a statement for the Allen anthology (414). Whereas poetry seemed to demand limits—whether they be the implied 12 bars of the blues chorus or the three lines of the haiku, another FORM Kerouac favored—prose invited limitless expansion analogous to the free improvisation practiced in contemporary JAZZ. The resulting "spontaneous prose," as Kerouac called it, is musical in its rhythms and particularly in its pauses, which Kerouac connected with the writer's pattern of breathing in the way that a musician's breath determined the length of time he could "blow." What kept the prose tied to poetry was the notion of an "image" as the subject on which the writer improvised, like the theme at the core of jazz improvisation. This image-based prose tends to drift away from the storytelling function of traditional prose narrative, which still dominates in *On the Road.* Kerouac's more experimental work heads in the direction of visual narrative, as in the "book-movie" inserted at the center of *Dr. Sax* (1959), or the passages from *Old Angel Midnight* incorporated into the largely improvised narration that Kerouac recorded for the film *Pull My Daisy* (1959). Significantly, O'Hara reported to JASPER JOHNS that he thought *Dr. Sax* and *Old Angel Midnight* were Kerouac's best works (Perloff 203 note 42).

Bibliography

Kerouac, Jack. *Dr. Sax.* New York: Grove, 1987.
———. Interview by Ted Berrigan and Aram Saroyan. In *Writers at Work: The Paris Review Interviews,* 4th series, edited by George Plimpton, 359–395. New York: Viking, 1976.
———. *On the Road.* New York: Penguin, 1991.
———. *The Portable Jack Kerouac.* Edited by Ann Charters. New York: Penguin, 1995.
———. Statement. *The New American Poetry 1945–1960.* New ed. Edited by Donald Allen. Berkeley: University of California Press, 1999, 414.
Nicosia, Gerald. *Memory Babe: A Critical Biography of Jack Kerouac.* New York: Grove, 1983.

Kimball, Jack (1954–   )

Jack Kimball lived in NEW YORK CITY for only a brief period during the 1970s, but his travels around the world and on the World Wide Web demonstrate the transportability of the NEW YORK SCHOOL aesthetic. The journey began in Kimball's native BOSTON, MASSACHUSETTS, where Joe Dunn (1935–97) and JOHN WIENERS held weekly meetings that continued the spirit of the poets' gatherings they had known during the heyday of the SAN FRANCISCO RENAISSANCE. The 20-year-old Kimball used these meetings to test responses to writers he was discovering, including JOHN ASHBERY and FRANK O'HARA; he recalls that Dunn's group was "more receptive to O'Hara" (Kimball, e-mail n.p.), who had been a friend of Wieners's. No one could compete with the "sexual as well as poetic glamour" conveyed by the personal presence of Wieners (Kimball, "John" n.p.), but a reading by KENWARD ELMSLIE that Kimball attended at Harvard University came close. Kimball recalls: "It was my introduction to bravura performance and daring lyric, snarly and leaping beyond the confines of the page" (e-mail n.p.). Work by both Wieners and Elmslie appeared in the first issue of *Shell*, a magazine that Kimball founded in 1976. Before the magazine completed its run in 1979, Kimball added a book series, especially notable for issuing ANNE WALDMAN's *Shaman* (1977) and STEVE MALMUDE's *From Roses to Coal* (1980). Meanwhile, Kimball himself was drawn more fully into the New York School orbit, first commuting from Boston to Ashbery's seminar at Brooklyn College and eventually taking up residence in a "poets' building" on the Lower East Side, where other residents included ALLEN GINSBERG, Peter Orlovsky, JIM BRODEY, LARRY FAGIN, JOHN GODFREY, and RICHARD HELL.

While continuing to write poetry, during the 1980s Kimball turned from publishing to teaching back in the Boston area. He worked his way to a doctorate in sociolinguistics at Harvard, then left for nearly a decade of teaching in Japan (1992–2000). Taking advantage of that period's revolution in Web publishing, he started an online magazine called *The East Village* (1998–2002), with one eye fixed on the New York poets and the other eye winking at the fact that while he had moved to the Far East, new media had transformed the world into the "global village" that Marshall McLuhan had predicted (McLuhan 31). Not only did Kimball include Japanese writers among the poets he published, but he also highlighted geographic convergence in special theme issues: "Poetries of Canada" (number 4), "Video Tokyo" (number 6), "Boston 1999" (number 7), "LA/NY" (number 9). A nongeographic theme issue, "Funny Business" (number 11), addressed a particular interest of the New York School, the reintroduction of humor in poetry. It included contributions by RON PADGETT, LISA JARNOT, LEE ANN BROWN, TONY TOWLE, JACK COLLOM, EILEEN MYLES, MICHAEL FRIEDMAN, TOM CLARK, and MICHAEL GIZZI, among others. Towle's association with Kimball has turned out to be especially fruitful. When Kimball, back in the United States to teach at MIT (Massachusetts Institute

of Technology), started a new publishing venture, Faux Press, he issued online versions of two previously unpublished COLLABORATIONs between Towle and O'Hara (2000); the following year, Towle's *Memoir* was the first traditional (paper) book issued by Faux Press, followed by Myles's *On My Way* (2001), JORDAN DAVIS's *Million Poems Journal* (2003), and a reissue of ALICE NOTLEY's *Waltzing Matilda* (2003).

Books of Kimball's own poetry have so far been published mainly by Peter Ganick (1946–   ) at Potes and Poets Press (*Witness Protection*, in collaboration with Ganick, 1997; *Quite Vacation*, 1998; *Frosted*, 2001). The identification of that press with LANGUAGE POETRY has established a context for the reception of Kimball's work. For instance, in a blurb for *Frosted*, Towle noted "mysterious ironies and enjambments, lines that are stunningly odd, and various kinds of oblique narrative that may owe something to 'language' influences, but are often also resonant of Jimmy Schuyler." Though still at an oblique angle, Kimball turned to, or from, Ashbery in the composition of *Post Twyla* (Blue Lion Books, 2006). The original goal, later modified, was "to spoof a diary via devious inspiration, compressing reactions to every page of John Ashbery's FLOW CHART within three-line verses" (Kimball, interview n.p.). Perhaps the most faithful expression of the original stimulus that Kimball found in the New York School occurs in his ELECTRONIC POETRY ("Webpraxis"), where the activity of the text approaches the dynamism that Kimball admired in Elmslie's performance at Harvard. Elsmlie's own Web site confirms the connection.

Bibliography

East Village, The. Available online. URL: http://www.theeastvillage.com/.

Fauxpress.com/e. Available online. URL: http://www.fauxpress.com/e/.

KenwardElmslie.com. Available online. URL: http://www.kenwardelmslie.com/.

Kimball, Jack. E-mail to Terence Diggory, 1 February 2006.

———. Interview by Tom Beckett (2006). E-X-C-H-A-N-G-E-V-A-L-U-E-S. Available online. URL: http://willtoexchange.blogspot.com/2006/09/interview-with-jack-kimball.html. Accessed December 17, 2008.

———. "John and the Four Dunn(e)s." *Jacket* 21 (February 2003). Available online. URL: http://jacketmagazine.com/21/kimb-rev1.html. Accessed December 17, 2008.

———. "Webpraxis." Jack Kimball Web site. Available online. URL: http://www.jackkimball.com/. Accessed December 17, 2008.

McLuhan, Marshall. *The Gutenberg Galaxy.* Toronto, Canada: University of Toronto Press, 1962.

Koch, Kenneth (1925–2002)

In the work of Kenneth Koch (pronounced COKE), the NEW YORK SCHOOL of poets went public, both in a general sense, in the way that "Koch's poems assume an audience" (North 63), and in the sense of a very specific occasion, embodied in Koch's verse-manifesto "FRESH AIR" (1955). Upon its reprinting in *The NEW AMERICAN POETRY, 1945–1960* (1960), that poem announced, in effect, the arrival of the New York School, in the words of the fictional speaker who rises to address "the Poem Society" at the opening: "You make me sick with all your talk about restraint and mature talent! / Haven't you ever looked out the window at a painting by Matisse?" (*Collected Poems* 122). The defiance of maturity in the first line has created more of a problem for Koch than for his fellow poets, because Koch has developed not merely comic moments in his work but a comic mode, inspired by popular cartoons, which some critics have dismissed as childish (for example, Harry Roskolenko). On the other hand, the invitation to see "a painting by Matisse" outside the window suggests that for Koch, as for the rest of the New York School, some of the "fresh air" he hoped to let into poetry was blowing from the avant-garde visual arts. If Koch's work is comic, it is also frequently abstract.

Growing up in Cincinnati, Ohio, Koch developed an early interest in poetry as another, "bigger" world (*Art of Poetry* 157), *A Possible World,* as his 2002 collection was titled (Knopf, 2002). It could not be pinned down to the exotic Pacific islands where he was stationed as an army draftee during World War II or to the intellectual tradition of Harvard University where he took his B.A. degree in 1948. Koch's teachers included DELMORE SCHWARTZ, but the chief lesson of Harvard may

have come from Koch's fellow student, JOHN ASHBERY, who told Koch, after reading the French protodadaist Alfred Jarry, "I think we should be a little crazier" (Koch, *Art of Poetry* 159). Fulbright grants awarded to Koch and, after his marriage in 1954, to his wife, Janice, supported sojourns in France (1950–51) and Italy (1954–55), where their daughter Katherine was born in 1955. As Koch treats it in his poetry, Europe feels like the country of the imagination, but that quality is enhanced by the distance Koch obtains when he writes from NEW YORK CITY, where he eventually made his home. Like Koch, New York is always turning toward a world elsewhere, the situation Koch depicts in his poem "Fate" (1979), where he recalls his friends Ashbery, FRANK O'HARA, and the painter JANE FREILICHER, none of whom had (as of 1951) been to Europe, listening to Koch's account of his first visit. "I / was so happy," Koch explains,

> to be there with them, and my
> Europe, too, which I had, Greece, Italy, France,
> Scandinavia, and England—imagine
> Having all that the first time (*Collected Poems* 307).

The multiplicity of worlds in this passage is characteristic of Koch throughout his career, but the quiet simplicity of the language distinguishes his later, post-1970 work from earlier experiments where a high degree of opacity appears to be an inevitable by-product of the high level of energy. In a note to *Sun Out,* a retrospective collection of poems written between 1952 and 1954, Koch explains that he had been trying "to re-create in English" the "happy confusion" he had experienced while living in France, when "words would have several meanings for me at once" (ix). Responding to Roskolenko's criticism of Koch's first volume, *Poems* (illustrated by Nell Blaine, Tibor de Nagy Editions, 1953), O'Hara defended Koch for trying "to make vivid our sense of the meaning of words. He tends to enlarge where others narrow down" (60). Potentially endless enlargement was the challenge O'Hara and Koch posed to each other in writing their long poems *Second Avenue* (O'Hara) and *When the Sun Tries to Go On* (Koch) in 1953 (*Art of Poetry* 21–22). For both poets, such enlargement had a parallel in abstract expressionist painting, which was notable not only for expanding the size of the typical canvas but also for crowding the composition with a confusion of FORMs that erased the traditional distinction between figure and ground. Koch uses painters' language when he describes the importance of "surface" to him and his fellow poets (*Art of Poetry* 214), but the underlying similarity between painting and poetry lies not in a "look" but a process, argues William Watkin. "Whatever our poems had to say," Koch goes on to explain, "the words got there first" (*Art of Poetry* 214), and they arranged themselves in surprising combinations: "When / The bugle shimmies, how glove towns!" (*Sun Out* 72).

Before *When the Sun Tries to Go On* was published in Alfred Leslie's "one-shot" compilation *The Hasty Papers* (1960), Koch made his debut in a more conventional form of the long poem, the mock epic *Ko, or a Season on Earth* (Grove, 1959). The observance of conventions, whether of narrative or of stanza structure, freed Koch to play in "the gap between the poem's decorous surface and its riotous substance," as Richard Howard observed (333). A conventional component is essential to Koch's success as a "public" poet, according to CHARLES NORTH, who includes among the conventional themes transformed by Koch "the hackneyed subject of young love" (North 58). As if to balance epic with lyric, love poems constitute the core of two collections that Koch published immediately after *Ko: Permanently* (illustrated by Alfred Leslie, TIBER PRESS, 1960) and *Thank You and Other Poems* (Grove, 1962). The theme reaches an astonishing climax in the list poem "Sleeping with Women," collected in the volume *The Pleasures of Peace* (Grove, 1969). Subsequently, Koch's view of "young love" becomes retrospective, his mood frequently elegiac, as in "The Circus" (*The Art of Love*, Random House, 1975) and "To Marina" (*The Burning Mystery of Anna in 1951*, Random House, 1979). This new tone resonates with Koch's sense of his own aging and the gradual breakup of his marriage to Janice, whose death in 1981 is obliquely commemorated in "With Janice" (*Days and Nights*, Random House, 1982).

Autobiographical recollection is a continuous strand running throughout the volumes Koch published during the remainder of his life: *On the Edge* (Viking, 1986), SEASONS ON EARTH (reprinting of *Ko* with two sequels, Knopf 1987), *One Train* (Penguin 1994), *Straits* (1998), and *New Addresses* (Knopf 2000). Overall, however, it is as impossible to define Koch's work by any single strand as it would be to reduce JACKSON POLLOCK to a single line. As O'Hara asked to live variously (Koch, *Art of Poetry* 211), Koch extended his life in writing that seems unbounded in its variety, radiating out from his multifaceted poetry to include plays, FICTION, and COLLABORATIONs with writers (Ashbery, O'Hara), artists (LARRY RIVERS, ALEX KATZ), and musicians (NED ROREM). Unlike other New York School poets of Koch's generation, he wrote little criticism, but he applied his critical intelligence to teaching legendary classes at the New School (1958–66) and Columbia University (1959–2001), where many younger poets received their initiation into the art of the New York School. Koch's success in teaching poetry in grade schools and nursing homes won him much acclaim, as well as a second marriage (1994), to Karen Culler, an educational consultant. The didactic poems in *The Art of Love* derive what Koch calls "the instructional tone" from his teaching experience (*Art of Poetry* 206). The poem "The Art of Poetry" offers characteristic encouragement: "your feelings are changing every instant / And the language has millions of words, and the number of combinations is infinite" (*Collected Poems* 256).

Bibliography

Diggory, Terence, and Stephen Paul Miller, eds. *The Scene of My Selves: New Work on New York School Poets.* Orono, Me.: National Poetry Foundation, 2001. [Includes essays on Koch by David Chinitz, Theodore Pelton, and David Spurr.]

Howard, Richard. "Kenneth Koch." In *Alone with America: Essays on the Art of Poetry in the United States Since 1950.* Enlarged ed. New York: Atheneum, 1980, 331–341.

Koch, Kenneth. *The Art of Poetry: Poems, Parodies, Interviews, Essays, and Other Work.* Ann Arbor: University of Michigan Press, 1996.

———. *The Collected Fiction.* Edited by Jordan Davis, Karen Koch, and Ron Padgett. Minneapolis, Minn.: Coffee House Press, 2005.

———. *The Collected Poems.* New York: Knopf, 2005.

————. *The Gold Standard: A Book of Plays.* New York: Knopf, 1998.

————. *I Never Told Anybody: Teaching Poetry Writing in a Nursing Home.* Rev. ed. New York: Teachers & Writers Collaborative, 1997.

————. "Inspiration and Work: How Poetry Gets to Be Written." *Comparative Literature Studies* 17, no. 2 (June 1980): 206–219.

————. *On the Great Atlantic Rainway: Selected Poems, 1950–1988.* New York: Knopf, 1994.

————. *Rose, Where Did You Get That Red? Teaching Great Poetry to Children.* New York: Random House, 1973.

————. *Sun Out: Selected Poems, 1952–1954.* New York: Knopf, 2002.

————. *Wishes, Lies, and Dreams: Teaching Children to Write Poetry.* New York: Chelsea House, 1970.

Koch, Kenneth, ed. "Special Collaboration Issue." *Locus Solus* 2 (1961). [Includes Koch and Jane Freilicher, "The Car"; Koch and John Ashbery, "Six Collaborations"; Koch, "A Note on This Issue."]

Koch, Kenneth, and Alex Katz. *Interlocking Lives.* New York: Kulchur Foundation, 1970.

Koch, Kenneth, and John Ashbery. "A Conversation" (1965). In *Selected Prose,* by John Ashbery. Edited by Eugene Richie. Ann Arbor: University of Michigan Press, 2004, 55–68.

Kostelanetz, Richard, ed. *The New American Arts.* 1965. Reprint, New York: Collier, 1967. [Includes discussion of Koch in chapters on Poetry, Theatre, and Fiction.]

Lehman, David. "Kenneth Koch: The Pleasures of Peace." In *The Last Avant-Garde: The Making of the New York School of Poets.* New York: Doubleday, 1998, 203–242.

North, Charles. "Kenneth Koch in Public" (1982). In *No Other Way: Selected Prose.* Brooklyn, N.Y.: Hanging Loose, 1998, 50–71.

O'Hara, Frank. "Another Word on Kenneth Koch" (1955). In *Standing Still and Walking in New York.* Edited by Donald Allen. San Francisco: Grey Fox, 1983, 59–61.

Roskolenko, Harry. "On Kenneth Koch Again: A Rebuttal." *Poetry* 86, no. 3 (June 1955): 177–178.

————. "Satire, Nonsense, and Worship" *Poetry* 84, no. 4 (July 1954): 232–234.

Tranter, John, ed. "A Tribute to Kenneth Koch." *Jacket* 15 (December 2001). Available online. URL: http://jacketmagazine.com/15/index.shtml. Accessed December 17, 2008.

Watkin, William. "Surfacing Between Art and Life." In *In the Process of Poetry: The New York School and the Avant-Garde.* Lewisburg, Pa.: Bucknell University Press, 2001, 35–64.

Koethe, John (1945–)

Like much of the poetry of the NEW YORK SCHOOL, the work of John Koethe (pronounced KAY-tee) is often abstract and cerebral, its focus directed inward on the process of its own creation. Koethe counts among his chief influences Wallace Stevens and JOHN ASHBERY, poets who write of the mind's encounter with a world of language and ideas. But amid this philosophically minded tradition, Koethe holds the rare distinction of professional credentials as a distinguished professor of philosophy at the University of Wisconsin–Milwaukee. His work captures the lyricism of abstract thought with a precision not seen perhaps since the *Four Quartets* of that other philosopher-poet, T. S. Eliot. Indeed, Andrew Yaphe suggests that "Koethe is writing the kinds of poems that Eliot would have written, had he been forced to struggle with the influence of Ashbery" (108). Koethe's own explanation of the relationship between philosophy and poetry, outlined in *Poetry at One Remove* (University of Michigan, 2000), hinges on the fact that both are exercises in speculation (2). But in the poem "Moore's Paradox," Koethe signals an important difference between his two professions; poets tend to revel in this uncertainty rather than seek to clarify it, being "worse, or alternately, better / At inhabiting the obviously untrue and / Hoisting flags of speculation in defiance of the real" (*North Point North* 42).

Koethe's earliest work was inspired by Eliot, Ezra Pound, and William Carlos Williams, and to this canon he soon added the BLACK MOUNTAIN POETS, particularly Robert Duncan. But it was his discovery of Ashbery's *The Tennis Court Oath* (1962) in 1965 that became the most important revelation: "It changed my conception of what poetry could be and in a real sense changed my life" (*Poetry at One Remove* 54). Shortly after this conversion Koethe met Ashbery, KENNETH KOCH, and FRANK O'HARA a few months before his death. He was also introduced to younger poets such as TED BERRIGAN and PETER SCHJELDAHL. Like others in this circle, he drew inspiration from the visual arts and worked as a correspondent for *Art News*. These influences are apparent in Koethe's first collection, *Blue Vents* (Audit/Poetry 1968), which offers a perfect example of New York School poetics. His mastery of this aesthetic was recognized when his second book, *Domes* (Columbia University Press, 1973), won the Frank O'Hara Award.

Already in this second book a shift from some of the hallmarks of the New York School is visible. By the end of the 1960s Koethe had begun to move away from collage and disjunction and to experiment with an extended, meditative style exemplified in poems such as "Domes" and "A Long Lesson." His third collection, *The Late Wisconsin Spring* (Princeton, 1984), continues this exploration. At once elegiac and philosophical, poems such as "The Narrow Way" and "In the Park" are meditations of "a mind infatuated with the rhetoric of farewell" (*North Point North* 131), a fitting description for his work ever since. Over the next decade Koethe assembled the poems published in *Falling Water* (HarperPerrenial, 1997), which won the Kingsley Tufts Award, and *The Constructor* (HarperFlamingo, 1999). The title poems of both collections represent Koethe's most impressive work and testify to his mastery of the long poem. "Falling Water," which Peter Campion has called "one of the four or five most impressive poems" of the 1990s (95), offers both a reflection on the architecture of Frank Lloyd Wright and a candid description of the end of the poet's marriage, achieving "an admixture of expansion and restraint" (*North Point North* 238) that exemplifies what Ashbery has called the "one-size-fits-all" autobiographical poem.

Koethe's continued development is evident in the new work among the selected poems of *North Point North* (HarperCollins, 2002) and in *Sally's Hair* (HarperCollins, 2006). Poems such as "Proust" and "Hamlet" in the latter collection engage more directly than previous work with narrative and autobiography. Other poems such as "Poetry and War" are more directly political, interweaving considerations about the beginning of the war in Iraq in 2003 with observations about more personal losses. Achieving a rare synthesis of intelligence and feel-

ing, Koethe's newest work continues to offer proof of his belief that poetry has the resources to represent consciousness in all its dimensions (*Poetry at One Remove* 82). It also demonstrates the degree to which Koethe has made the meditative, discursive mode of Ashbery into something distinctly his own. As James Longenbach suggests, Koethe is thus "perhaps the only poet heavily influenced by Ashbery and utterly distinguishable from him" (29).

Bibliography

Campion, Peter. Review of *North Point North*. *Poetry* 182 (2003): 94–96.

Hahn, Robert. "'Drawing by Michelangelo, Color by Titian': Of Originality, Influence, and the Poetry of John Koethe." *Kenyon Review* (2004): 128–45.

Kane, Paul. "Philosopher-Poets: John Koethe and Kevin Hart." *Raritan* 21 (2001): 94–113.

Koethe, John. *The Continuity of Wittgenstein's Thought*. Ithaca, N.Y.: Cornell University, 1996.

———. *North Point North: New and Selected Poems*. New York: HarperCollins, 2002.

———. *Poetry at One Remove: Essays*. Ann Arbor: University of Michigan, 2000.

———. *Skepticism, Knowledge, and Forms of Reasoning*. Ithaca, N.Y.: Cornell University, 2005.

Longenbach, James. "Disjunction in Poetry." *Raritan* 20 (2001): 20–36.

Spiegelman, Willard. "Wallace Stevens's 'Second Selves' and the Nostalgia of Discursiveness." *Wallace Stevens Journal* 24 (2000): 176–186.

"Strategies for Writing Long Poems." *Writer* 115 (2002): 22–25.

Yaphe, Andrew. "The Romantic Futility of John Koethe." *Chicago Review* 47 (2001): 102–109.

Krauss, Ruth (1901–1993)

Although older than any of the first-generation poets, Ruth Krauss became associated with the NEW YORK SCHOOL during the emergence of the second generation in the 1960s. Her temperament and her prior experience as an author of children's literature made her something of a motherly figure for the younger poets. TONY TOWLE, who met Krauss in KENNETH KOCH's and FRANK O'HARA's workshops at the New School in spring 1963, recalls: "[H]er own poetry was perhaps overly 'childlike,' but she was so wonderfully upbeat that you felt better about yourself after a conversation" (Towle 53).

Krauss was born in Baltimore, Maryland, and entered the New York art world by way of the Parsons School of Fine and Applied Art, where she earned a bachelor's degree. Her first children's book, *A Good Man and His Good Wife* (Harper, 1944), was illustrated by New York School painter Ad Reinhardt (1913–67). Later collaborators included Krauss's husband, Crockett Johnson (David Johnson Leisk [1906–75]) and Maurice Sendak (1928–), who regarded Krauss as his mentor ("Book Life" n.p.). Krauss had won two Caldecott Medals—for *The Happy Day* (Harper, 1949), illustrated by Marc Simont, and *A Very Special House* (Harper, 1953), illustrated by Sendak—by the time her experimental writing began to appear in publications associated with the New York School. Her collage of "found" text from Shakespeare's sonnets and Soviet cosmonaut Yuri Gagarin's radio transmissions appeared in the "COLLABORATION" issue of LOCUS SOLUS (number 2, 1961), edited by Koch. Over the next decade Krauss's work appeared in the WAGNER LITERARY MAGAZINE, "C" magazine, KULCHUR, INTRANSIT, and *The WORLD*. Her principal collections are *There's a Little Ambiguity Over There Among the Bluebells* (Something Else Press, 1968), *This Breast Gothic* (Bookstore Press, 1973), and *Under 13* (Bookstore Press, 1976).

The techniques that Krauss developed as a children's writer carry over into her avant-garde experiments and reflect the interest in the CHILD as a muse of spontaneity within the New York School. Koch, for whom that interest was particularly strong, may well have found inspiration for his ONE THOUSAND AVANT-GARDE PLAYS (1988) in the very short "poem plays" that Krauss produced in the mid-1960s at such Off-Off Broadway venues as the Café Cino and the Judson Poets Theatre (Poland and Mailman). In TAMBOURINE LIFE (1966), TED BERRIGAN praised Krauss's "Hope You Happy Monkey" as "one song I have always liked" (*Collected Poems* 133), and he recommended that LEWIS and Phoebe MACADAMS read it to their baby Ocean Lee (MacAdams 216). A poem found among O'Hara's manuscripts, built on the insistent repetition of the word *lost*, was assumed to be O'Hara's reworking of a poem by Krauss

because the manuscript bore Krauss's name; in fact, it is Krauss's poem, published under her name in *Intransit,* and the refrain is one of the devices she typically used to conjure the child's sense of the magic of words.

Bibliography

Bermel, Albert. "Closet Openings," *The Nation,* 25 August 1969, 156–157.

Berrigan, Ted. "Tambourine Life." In *The Collected Poems of Ted Berrigan.* Edited by Alice Notley, Anselm Berrigan, and Edmund Berrigan. Berkeley: University of California Press, 2005, 121–150.

"Book Life Picks 2005: Picture Books—*Bears,* by Ruth Krauss; illus. Maurice Sendak." *PW Book Life.* Available online. URL: http://www.pwbooklife. com/2005picturebooks.html. Accessed December 17, 2008.

Krauss, Ruth. "Lost." *Intransit: The Andy Warhol—Gerard Malanga Monster Issue* (1968): 162.

———. "Notes on Frank's Workshop at the New School." In *Homage to Frank O'Hara,* edited by Bill Berkson and Joe LeSueur, 128. Bolinas, Calif.: Big Sky, 1988.

MacAdams, Lewis. "Big Ted." In *Nice to See You: Homage to Ted Berrigan,* edited by Anne Waldman, 210–217. Minneapolis, Minn.: Coffee House Press, 1991.

O'Hara, Frank. "Poem (after a poem by Ruth Krauss)." In *Poems Retrieved.* Edited by Donald Allen. San Francisco: Grey Fox, 1996, 230–231. [Originally published in *The World* (no. 7, Oct. 1967) under the mistaken assumption that O'Hara had reworked Krauss's original poem.]

Poland, Albert, and Bruce Mailman, eds. *The Off Off Broadway Book: The Plays, People, Theatre.* Indianapolis, Ind.: Bobbs-Merrill, 1972. [Includes Krauss, *A Beautiful Day,* 25–26.]

Schjeldahl, Peter. "Around the Corner." *Poetry* 117, no. 4 (January 1971): 261–275.

Towle, Tony. *Memoir, 1960–1963.* Cambridge, Mass.: Faux Press, 2001.

Kraut, Rochelle (1952–)

Born in Germany in a camp for those who had been displaced by the destruction of World War II, Rochelle (Shelley) Kraut has made her home in the American avant-garde. "I lay born on the old / and stand living on the new," she writes in her poem "Intensely Song" (1984). In CHICAGO, ILLINOIS, where Kraut majored in art at the University of Illinois branch campus, she and her boyfriend BOB ROSENTHAL were at the center of a group that started the mimeo magazine *Milk Quarterly* and ran a reading series at the Body Politic Theater, a project of Second City cofounder Paul Sills (Holman n.p.). TED BERRIGAN and ALICE NOTLEY, during their sojourn in Chicago in 1972–73, told stories of an even livelier scene in NEW YORK CITY, so Kraut and Rosenthal headed there in 1973, the same year they were married. Although they were eventually drawn into the BEAT circle, with Rosenthal assuming the role of secretary to ALLEN GINSBERG, Kraut lists the NEW YORK SCHOOL poets Berrigan and JAMES SCHUYLER as her chief contemporary influences (Biographical note 235). Berrigan celebrates her as muse in his poems "Shelley" and "After Peire Vidal, & Myself" from his 1982 collection *The Morning Line* (*Collected Poems* 534, 540–541).

The interdisciplinary spirit of the New York arts community has encouraged Kraut to seek many outlets for her creativity. She has produced numerous cover designs for small press books and magazines and frequently performed in "poets theater" and film, including several works by RUDY BURCKHARDT (*Good Evening Everybody*, 1977; *Mobile Homes*, 1979; *The Casserole Dish*, 1979). From 1975 to 1979 Kraut and Rosenthal published Frontward Books, including titles by Berrigan (*A Feeling for Leaving*, 1975) and Notley (*A Diamond Necklace*, 1977)—both with covers by Kraut—as well as Kraut's own principal collection, *Circus Babys* (1975). Most of her poems are scattered throughout the pages of magazines associated with the so-called third-generation New York School, such as *Caveman*, which printed "Conversation with Jackie Curtis," Kraut's evocation of the former ANDY WARHOL star and drag queen who remained active in Lower East Side THEATER until his death in 1985. Following the appearance of the one-shot review *The Ladies Museum* (1977), coedited by Kraut, EILEEN MYLES, and SUSIE TIMMONS, these three women joined a larger group, including BARBARA BARG, ELINOR NAUEN, and Notley, in editing later issues of *Caveman* (Russo 260).

After years of underground circulation, Kraut's work suddenly entered the spotlight when one of her poems from the 1980s, "My Makeup," was featured by Camille Paglia in her discussion of "forty-three of the world's best poems," *Break, Blow, Burn* (2005). The performance of "sexual personae" in Kraut's poem attracted Paglia (212–213), though her commentary gentrifies that performance by linking it to Edna St. Vincent Millay rather than the gender-bending theater of the Lower East Side in which Kraut participated.

Bibliography

Berrigan, Ted. *The Collected Poems of Ted Berrigan*. Edited by Alice Notley, Anselm Berrigan, and Edmund Berrigan. Berkeley: University of California Press, 2005.

Holman, Bob. "Three Generations in the 70s: Memoirs of a Chicago Po-Renaissance." About.com: Poetry. Available online. URL: http://poetry.about.com/od/poetryhistory/a/chicago70s.htm. Accessed December 17, 2008.

Kraut, Rochelle. Biographical note. In *Break Blow Burn*, by Camille Paglia, 235. New York: Pantheon, 2005.

———. "Conversation with Jackie Curtis." *Caveman* (January 30, 1979): n.p.

———. "Intensely Song." In *Out of This World: An Anthology of the St. Mark's Poetry Project, 1966–1991*, edited by Anne Waldman, 504–505. New York: Crown, 1991.

———. "My Makeup." In *Break Blow Burn*, by Camille Paglia, 210. New York: Pantheon, 2005.

———. "Newborn Sleep." Audio Recording. *Sugar, Alcohol, & Meat*. New York: Giorno Poetry Systems, 1980. Ubuweb. Available online. URL: http://www.ubu.com/sound/sam.html. Accessed December 17, 2008.

Paglia, Camille. *Break, Blow, Burn*. New York: Pantheon, 2005.

Russo, Linda. "'F' Word in the Age of Mechanical Reproduction: An Account of Women-Edited Small Presses and Journals." In *The World in Time and Space: Towards a History of Innovative American Poetry in Our Time*, edited by Edward Foster and Joseph Donahue, 243–284. Jersey City, N.J.: Talisman House, 2002.

Kulchur (1960–1965)

Among the many magazines in which NEW YORK SCHOOL poets were involved during the early years of the New American Poetry, *Kulchur* was unique for its concentration on publishing reviews and criticism. The magazine emerged from the circle of writers, artists, and musicians whose unofficial headquarters was the Chelsea apartment of LeRoi Jones (AMIRI BARAKA) and his wife, Hettie, editors of *YŪGEN*. The founding editor was the young poet Marc D. Schleifer (1935–). He soon became caught up in the excitement of the Communist revolution in Cuba, which he left to witness first-hand after assembling the third issue of *Kulchur*, the first under publisher LITA HORNICK (1927–2000), who provided the magazine with financial stability. The next two issues appeared under guest editors, GILBERT SORRENTINO (number 4, 1961) and JOEL OPPENHEIMER (number 5, spring 1962). New York School poets FRANK O'HARA and KENNETH KOCH first appeared in Oppenheimer's issue, though there is some dispute about who solicited their contributions (Sorrentino 313; Hornick 284). It is a matter of record that, starting with issue number 7 (autumn 1962), an editorial board had formed under Hornick as managing editor, with other editors assigned to cover particular arts: LeRoi Jones (MUSIC), Sorrentino (books), O'Hara (art), Joe LeSueur (THEATER), and BILL BERKSON (film).

Kulchur was named after Ezra Pound's *Guide to Kulchur* (1938). The Pound tradition was represented in the magazine's pages by contributions from the Black Mountain group (CHARLES OLSON was listed as "contributing editor" from the first through the 13th issues) and the OBJECTIVISTS (Louis Zukofsky's "Five Statements for Poetry" appeared serially in *Kulchur*). In this context the work of the New York School poets strikes a very different, less "serious," even openly defiant note. Koch's contribution to issue number 5 was a parody of Pound's *Cantos*. O'Hara's contribution, the first of his three "Art Chronicles," treats ABSTRACT EXPRESSIONISM as "the art of serious men" but peppers that treatment with flippant asides, such as a quotation from the popular entertainer Sophie Tucker (1884–1966) about her gold tea set, which O'Hara applies to the new Guggenheim Museum: "It's way out on the nut for service, but it was my dream!" As the second-generation poets got into the act, they turned the act of criticism into an occasion for questioning critical authority. "It would be much easier for me to get something said about this book if I could briefly turn into Charles Olson or John Lennon or Martin Luther King," wrote TED BERRIGAN in a review of O'Hara's *Lunch Poems* (number 17, spring 1965). RON PADGETT aimed his satire especially at the critical pronouncement waiting to become a publicist's "blurb": "When I first read these poems, I had a birthday, got married, and told a joke" (on Berrigan's *The SONNETS*, number 17); "When I read *Literary Days* at night I wake up in the morning" (on TOM VEITCH's *Literary Days*, number 17). Padgett's essay "Sound and Poetry" (number 17) was a "hilarious takeoff of some solemn discussions of poetic form," according to Hornick, who found it "new and refreshing" (Hornick 295).

Hornick seems to have welcomed New York School irreverence because, as she explained, "I was interested in making *Kulchur* an arena for a diversity of opinion and anxious to prevent it from becoming a coterie magazine" (Hornick 295). During this period the New York School itself was expanding beyond its original coterie, as was demonstrated by disagreements between first- and second-generation writers in the pages of *Kulchur*. Berrigan opened a review of HAROLD ROSENBERG, the prophet of "ACTION PAINTING," with the blunt declaration: "Harold Rosenberg, folks, is a dunce" (number 19, autumn 1965). While O'Hara put down POP ART in the third (and last) of his "Art Chronicles" (number 9, spring 1963), Berrigan praised the new style in a later "Art Chronicle" (number 19, summer 1965), building on ground already prepared by GERARD MALANGA's interview with ANDY WARHOL (number 16, winter 1964–65). O'Hara's final appearance in *Kulchur* was in number 12 (winter 1963), which contained his review of John Rechy's *City of Night* and a gathering of essays on civil rights, which O'Hara had helped Jones solicit (Magee 700). After that issue Hornick dissolved the editorial board—or it dissolved under her, depending on whose account is credited (Hornick 291; Gooch 416)—but second-generation New York School writers continued to have ready access to publication in *Kulchur*. Over the course of *Kulchur*'s 20 issues, first-generation writers (EDWIN DENBY, KENWARD ELMSLIE, BARBARA GUEST, Koch, LeSueur, O'Hara) were outnumbered by second-generation writers (Berkson, Berrigan, JOE BRAINARD, JIM BRODEY, TOM CLARK, DICK GALLUP, ALLAN KAPLAN, RUTH KRAUSS, Padgett, ARAM SAROYAN, Veitch).

Like many other magazines of the period, *Kulchur* extended into a project for publishing books. However, in the case of *Kulchur*, book publication began after the magazine ended, a result of Hornick's decision to focus her energies on fewer authors and to concentrate on publishing poetry rather than criticism (Hornick 297).

Note: References to *Kulchur* above cite issue number, not volume. Volume groupings began with volume 2, number 5 (spring 1962), but the entire sequence of issues was numbered consecutively (1–20). Only two issues appeared in each of the first two years (1960, 1961), which were counted as one volume; thereafter, issues appeared four times a year, one volume per year, concluding with volume 5, number 20 (winter 1965–66).

Bibliography

Gooch, Brad. *City Poet: The Life and Times of Frank O'Hara*. New York: Knopf, 1993.

Hornick, Lita. "*Kulchur*: A Memoir" (1975). In *The Little Magazine in America: A Modern Documentary History*, edited by Elliott Anderson and Mary Kinzie, 280–297. Yonkers, N.Y.: Pushcart Press, 1978.

Koch, Kenneth. "Canto CXXIII." In *The Art of Poetry: Poems, Parodies, Interviews, Essays, and Other Work*. Ann Arbor: University of Michigan Press, 1996, 98–99. [Reprint of Pound parody originally published in *Kulchur*.]

Magee, Michael. "Tribes of New York: Frank O'Hara, Amiri Baraka, and the Poetics of the Five Spot." *Contemporary Literature* 42, no. 4 (2001): 694–726.

O'Hara, Frank. *Standing Still and Walking in New York*. San Francisco: Grey Fox, 1983. [Reprints all of O'Hara's contributions to *Kulchur*.]

Sorrentino, Gilbert. "Neon, Kulchur, etc." In *The Little Magazine in America: A Modern Documentary History*, edited by Elliott Anderson and Mary Kinzie, 298–316. Yonkers, N.Y.: Pushcart Press, 1978.

Kushner, Bill (1931–   )

Born in the Bronx to impoverished Russian immigrants, Bill Kushner was first exposed to poetry while attending P.S. 52, an all-boys public school in the Bronx. The work of Walt Whitman particularly spoke to him, and Whitman has remained a lodestone in his work. Kushner used poetry to help him cope with his conflicted anxieties about his sexuality and identity, and though he worked a variety of jobs to support himself, including as an office worker, a hatcheck clerk, and a mail messenger, he wrote persistently throughout this time. The creation of art was also tantamount to the creation of community, and Kushner found a hospitable audience in the NEW YORK SCHOOL.

Influenced by FRANK O'HARA and JOHN ASHBERY, Kushner's work has some of the breezy conversational tone of the former and the paratactic conflation of disparate materials of the latter. His work is also JAZZ inflected, like the opening of the poem "Shaker":

> It happened again. On the way out, oh
> just one simple walk before bed time, a
> check of the moon to make sure it was
> still up there, yeah, doing its ha-ha job.

Kushner also borrows from a more formalist strain: Many of his poems are loosely based on the sonnet FORM. There is also an intimacy of revelation inherent to his work, and he deals with subjects that range from evanescent sex and gay identity to the ambivalence of aging and the discordances of family. His hallmark style is clipped, accelerated lines that flit from image to image with the rapid lyric transience of a hummingbird sipping nectar. As BOB HOLMAN has written about his book *He Dreams of Water*: "Bill Kushner! Master tailor, stitching Comedy and Tragedy together with Art, his is not one-size-fits-all: his is gay and camp, sad and sheer, mad and simply mad about poetry" (n.p.).

Kushner has performed his work for years in such venues as the POETRY PROJECT AT ST. MARK'S CHURCH-IN-THE BOWERY, KGB Bar, Zinc Bar, and Cornelia Street Café. He is a two-time recipient of the New York Arts Fellowship. His books include *In the Hairy Arms of Whitman* (Melville House Publications, 2003), *He Dreams of Water* (Rattapallax Press, 2000), *That April* (United Artists Books, 2000), *Love Uncut* (United Artists Books, 1990), *Head* (United Artists Books, 1986), and *Night Fishing* (Midnight Sun Press, 1980). His work has been anthologized in *Best American Poetry 2002* (Scribner, 2003), *Out of This World* (Crown, 1990), *In Our Time: The Gay and Lesbian Anthology* (St. Martin's Press, 1989), and *Up Late* (4 Walls, 8 Windows, 1987).

Bibliography

Bazzett, Denise. Review of *He Dreams of Waters. New Pages Book Reviews.* Available online. URL: http://newpages.com/bookreviews/archive/reviews/HeDreamsOfWater.htm. Accessed December 18, 2008.

Holman, Bob. Comment about *He Dreams of Waters.* Rattapallax Web site. Available online. URL: http://www.rattapallax.com/kushner_about_book.htm. Accessed December 18, 2008.

Kushner, Bill. "Shaker." *MiPOesias* 16 (spring 2004). Available online. URL: http://www.mipoesias.com/April2004/kushner.htm. Accessed December 18, 2008.

Kyger, Joanne (1934–   )

Usually labeled a BEAT writer, Joanne Kyger employs a "conversational" tone (Friedman 75) and a "gestural" line (Davidson 188) that link her to the NEW YORK SCHOOL, as does her central position in the community of writers in BOLINAS, CALIFORNIA. She was born in Vallejo, California, and, after much relocating while her father pursued a career in the U.S. Navy, attended college in Santa Barbara. There she took classes from Hugh Kenner (1923–2003), the renowned scholar of modernist poetry, but she did not complete her degree, deciding instead to devote herself to writing poetry in San Francisco, where she moved in 1957. She joined the circle of poets gathered around Robert Duncan (1919–88) and Jack Spicer (1925–1965), but a visit from Gary Snyder (1930–   ) led Kyger beyond the confines of a single coterie. From 1960 to 1964, as Snyder's wife, Kyger lived in Japan, engaged in intensive study of Zen Buddhism, and

traveled extensively in India with Snyder, ALLEN GINSBERG, and Peter Orlovsky. Back in the United States, divorced from Snyder, she continued to broaden her circle of acquaintances, including several writers who would soon become identified with the "second generation" of the New York School. She met LARRY FAGIN in San Francisco in 1964; heard TED BERRIGAN read from *The SONNETS* at the BERKELEY POETRY CONFERENCE in 1965; visited TOM CLARK in Paris in 1966 during a trip with her second husband, the painter Jack Boyce; and in 1967 attended the wedding of ANNE WALDMAN and LEWIS WARSH in NEW YORK CITY, where Kyger and Boyce resided briefly. The removal of Tom and Angelica Clark to Bolinas, after their wedding in New York in 1968, foretold "the beginnings of literary adventures" in a setting more agreeable to Kyger's temperament (*Contemporary Authors* 200). She moved to Bolinas with Boyce in 1969, and though their relationship soon ended, Bolinas has remained Kyger's home since.

Although DONALD M. ALLEN did not select Kyger's work for *The NEW AMERICAN POETRY, 1945–1960* (1960), he did publish her first book, *The Tapestry and the Web* (1965), under the imprint of his Four Seasons Foundation. The mythic underpinning of these poems, many of which reenvision the *Odyssey* from Penelope's perspective, reflects Kyger's apprenticeship with Duncan and Spicer, but the voice is already inflected by "a vernacular chattiness that echoes, yet feminizes, what has variously been called the personism, or situational focus, of the New York School poets," as the critic Amy Friedman has characterized it (73). Appropriately, New York School poets provided publishing outlets as Kyger went on to develop this voice in *Joanne* (ANGEL HAIR, 1970), *All This Every Day* (BIG SKY, 1975), and *The Wonderful Focus of You* (Z PRESS, 1980). The repeated naming of friends, a practice characteristic of the New York School, further testifies to Kyger's close connection to these poets, both in her poems and in theirs. A Kyger poem typically enacts abrupt shifts of attention such as the streets of New York stimulated in FRANK O'HARA or Berrigan, though in Kyger the more likely stimulus is the practice of Zen meditation. Both Buddhist and poetic practice have informed Kyger's occasional teaching at the NAROPA INSTITUTE in Boulder, Colorado.

Bibliography

Berkson, Bill. "Joanne Kyger." In *Dictionary of Literary Biography*. Vol. 16: *The Beats: Literary Bohemians in Postwar America*, edited by Ann Charters, 324–328. Detroit, Mich.: Gale, 1983.

Davidson, Michael. *The San Francisco Renaissance: Poetics and Community at Mid-Century.* Cambridge: Cambridge University Press, 1989.

Friedman, Amy L. "Joanne Kyger, Beat Generation Poet: 'a porcupine traveling at the speed of light.'" In *Reconstructing the Beats,* edited by Jennie Skerl, 73–88. New York: Palgrave Macmillan, 2004.

Kyger, Joanne. *About Now: Collected Poems.* Orono, Me.: National Poetry Foundation, 2007.

———. Autobiographical essay. In *Contemporary Authors, Autobiography Series* 16, edited by Joyce Nakamura, 187–203. Detroit, Mich.: Gale, 1992.

———. *The Japan and India Journals, 1960–64.* Bolinas, Calif.: Tombouctou, 1981. Reprint, *Strange Big Moon.* Berkeley, Calif.: North Atlantic, 2000.

Notley, Alice. "Joanne Kyger's Poetry." In *Coming After: Essays on Poetry.* Ann Arbor: University of Michigan Press, 2005, 15–26.

Russo, Linda. "To Deal with Parts and Particulars: Joanne Kyger's Early Epic Poetics." In *Girls Who Wore Black: Women Writing in the Beat Tradition,* edited by Ronna C. Johnson and Nancy M. Grace, 178–204. New Brunswick, N.J.: Rutgers University Press, 2002.

Russo, Linda, ed. "Joanne Kyger Feature." *Jacket* 11 (April 2000). Available online. URL: http://www.jacket magazine.com/11/index.html. Accessed December 18, 2008.

L

Lally, Michael (1942–)

Michael Lally is an autobiographical poet, much affected by FRANK O'HARA's "PERSONISM" but influential himself in broadening the range of possibilities recognized in that concept. TED BERRIGAN's "New Personal Poem" (1977) is addressed to Lally. Lally's long poem *My Life* (1974), which led JOHN ASHBERY to dub him "the François Villon of the seventies" (Lally, questionnaire response n.p.), shares its title with Lyn Hejinian's experimental prose work *My Life* (1980)—no doubt a coincidence, but it signals the common ground on which Lally and the Language poets (see LANGUAGE POETRY) frequently met. In *L=A=N=G=U=A=G=E* magazine (January 1980) Lally emphasized the formal artifice of *My Life* as "the ultimate life-as-list jacket blurb litany etc." ("My Work" 55), perhaps with intentional reference to Ashbery's recent "Litany" (1979).

Lally was born in South Orange, New Jersey, into a working-class Irish-American family, a circumstance that created an immediate bond with Berrigan when Lally enrolled in his workshop at the University of Iowa in 1968. On the other hand, what appeared to be elitism in O'Hara presented a barrier to reading him until Lally had an illumination while teaching O'Hara's work at Trinity College in Washington, D.C., where he was hired after graduating with an M.F.A. from Iowa in 1969. As Lally later explained in his long poem *In the Mood* (Titanic, 1978), he came to realize that what appeared to be elitism in O'Hara was really a form of inclusiveness that respected the reader's individuality while it asserted O'Hara's:

he's our most democratic poet since Whitman,
bringing that "tradition" full circle by
reversing Whitman's posing as the common-man-
brother-to-all which reduced everyone to
the level of anonymity (It's Not Nostalgia 89).

In contrast to the contemporary vogue for displaying "open sores and wounds," as Lally characterized confessional poetry, O'Hara taught the important lessons of writing for the joy of it and living in the same spirit. When Lally, following O'Hara's "beacon," moved to NEW YORK CITY in 1975, he entered a period of "experimentation with male lovers," again with O'Hara's example in mind (Lally, questionnaire response n.p.). Both his lifestyle and the sexual openness of his poetry led to his inclusion in several gay publications during this period, but he has continued relations with women, including three marriages. He separated from his first wife, the poet Lee Lally, just before his move to New York.

Wherever he has lived, Lally has actively promoted the poets' community through various means, not least through the personal network he developed as he moved from place to place. From Iowa he distributed Poetry of the People "underground" newspapers across the country, offering them the latest poems in the way that wire services offered stories to mainstream newspapers. In Washington, D.C., he started the Mass Transit reading series (1971–74), an important incubator for LANGUAGE POETRY, and Some of Us Press, which published books by SIMON SCHUCHAT and

TIM DLUGOS as well as Lally's *The South Orange Sonnets* (1972). In New York, while Lally lived there, NEW YORK SCHOOL and Language poets were dividing into hostile camps, but Lally "tried to create an inclusive community" (Vickery 31), perhaps most successfully between the covers of his anthology *None of the Above* (The Crossing Press, 1976), which included, for instance, New York School poet ALICE NOTLEY and Language poet Ray Di Palma, both of whom had been classmates of Lally's at Iowa.

Lally left New York for Los Angeles in 1982 in order to pursue opportunities in movies and television, both as an actor and a writer. Lally's West Coast connections of consequence to the New York School included DENNIS COOPER, ARAM SAROYAN, DAVID TRINIDAD, JEROME SALA, and ELAINE EQUI. Under the imprint of Little Caesar Press, Cooper published Lally's collection *Hollywood Magic* (1982); he also encouraged Lally's participation in the BEYOND BAROQUE reading series. With Eve Brandstein, Lally started a new series called Poetry in Motion (1988–96), which attracted a good deal of media attention as a scene for Hollywood celebrities. In 1997 Lally married Jaina Flynn, a fellow Jerseyite, and the couple moved back to their home state in 1999. Their story is told in "It Happens," one of the new poems in *It's Not Nostalgia* (Black Sparrow, 1999), a retrospective collection for which Lally received the American Book Award.

Bibliography

Berrigan, Ted. "New Personal Poem." In *The Collected Poems of Ted Berrigan*. Edited by Alice Notley, Anselm Berrigan, and Edmund Berrigan. Berkeley: University of California Press, 2005, 508–509.

Lally, Michael. *It's Not Nostalgia: Poetry and Prose*. Santa Monica, Calif.: Black Sparrow, 1999.

———. Lally's Alley blog. Available online. URL: http://lallysalley.blogspot.com/.

———. "My Work." L=A=N=G=U=A=G=E 3, no. 11 (January 1980): 54–55.

———. Questionnaire response for *Encyclopedia of the New York School Poets*. 13 January 2006.

———. Statement for History Project. DCpoetry. Available online. URL: http://www.dcpoetry.com/history/lally. Accessed December 18, 2008.

Smith, Alexandra. "A Place for Poetry in Land of Pictures," *New York Times*, 12 July 1989, pp. C1, C8.

Vickery, Ann. *Leaving Lines of Gender: A Feminist Genealogy of Language Writing*. Hanover, N.H.: Wesleyan University Press/University Press of New England, 2000.

Lang, Violet R. (Bunny) (1924–1956)

The many poems in which FRANK O'HARA portrays his friend Bunny Lang convey an extravagant impression: "you float regally by on your / incessant escalator, calm, a jungle queen" ("V. R. Lang" [1950]; O'Hara, *Collected Poems* 18). Evidently Lang was just as extravagant in real life. Joe LeSueur reports first meeting her in the apartment he shared with O'Hara where Lang was taking a bath, which she treated as the occasion for an audience, commanding him to sit on the toilet seat while the two of them sipped drinks and got acquainted (LeSueur 36). What seems to have won over O'Hara and LeSueur and other admirers of Lang was her gift for heightening the intensity of ordinary experience. When Lang appeared, along with JOHN ASHBERY, in the first production of O'Hara's play TRY! TRY! by the POETS' THEATRE in Cambridge, Massachusetts (1951), O'Hara wrote to her: "I want / your voice in my ear so the sun / will be hotter" (*Try! Try!* 30)

Lang came to the Poets' Theatre not as a Harvard student, like O'Hara and Ashbery, but as a BOSTON, MASSACHUSETTS, debutante seeking a society on her own terms rather than those dictated by convention. She had left undergraduate study at the University of Chicago to join the Canadian Women's Army Corps during World War II. By the time she returned to Boston she had acquired literary credentials as an editor of the *Chicago Review* and as a writer published in *Poetry* magazine. But the THEATER promised a presence that words alone could not capture. "It never was enough. Words are not *there*," Lang wrote in her poem "Argument" (82). Her taste in theater inclined toward nonliterary modes such as cabaret and burlesque. She enjoyed a stint as a burlesque dancer in Boston in 1951, and her first full-length play, *Fire Exit* (1952), retells the myth of Orpheus and Eurydice as the story of a classical musician who fails to retrieve his wife from a burlesque troupe. Lang succeeded in another attempt at retrieval when she picked up GREGORY CORSO on the streets of New York and installed him in the rooms of her Harvard friends, "probably a deliberate act of sedition," in the judgment of Nora Sayre (102). Lang counted on the Harvard establishment being scandalized by Corso's beatness, an attitude and an idiom that she had already incorporated in her second play, *I Too Have Lived in Arcadia* (1954). Perhaps the key to Lang's theatrical personality is her attachment to the role of jester or Lord of Misrule, as O'Hara recognized in his image of Lang, Corso, and O'Hara himself, acting in Ashbery's *The Compromise* (1956), "bowing to each other and the audience, like jinxes" ("To Hell with It" [1957]; O'Hara, *Collected Poems* 275).

Underlying the comedy in Lang's performance was an acceptance of tragedy that connects her work with the elegiac vein in NEW YORK SCHOOL poetry. *I Too Have Lived in Arcadia* places its "tarnished lovers," as O'Hara called them, in a pastoral setting that enhances the elegiac mood: "There on their island the City presses down upon them, initiating the failure of love, which is death" (O'Hara, "V. R. Lang" 86). The play had its origins in the failure of a love affair between Lang and the painter Mike Goldberg (1924–) and figures the City in the person of a rival for the man's affection—whom Lang understood to be Joan Mitchell (1926–92), in Goldberg's case. But by the time O'Hara wrote his commentary on the play, Lang had died of Hodgkin's disease, and O'Hara had begun mourning her in a series of poems that would extend from "A Step Away from Them" (1956) to "Variations on Pasternak's 'Mein Liebchen, was willst du noch mehr'" (1959). When O'Hara's own untimely death followed 10 years after Lang's, a poem of hers found among his papers was mistaken for his and published in the first edition of his *Collected Poems* as "Words to Frank O'Hara's Angel." In Lang's *Poems and Plays*, under the title "To Frank's Guardian Angel," the poem performs Lang's recognition that words are never enough in the face of tragic knowledge: "You pray for him, you weep instead" (Lang 118).

Bibliography

Gooch, Brad. *City Poet: The Life and Times of Frank O'Hara.* New York: Knopf, 1993.

Lang, V. R. *Poems and Plays.* With a memoir by Alison Lurie. New York: Random House, 1975.

LeSueur, Joe. *Digressions on Some Poems by Frank O'Hara.* New York: Farrar, Straus & Giroux, 2003.

Nelson, Maggie. *Women, the New York School, and Other True Abstractions.* Iowa City: University of Iowa Press, 2007.

O'Hara, Frank. *The Collected Poems.* Rev. ed. Edited by Donald Allen. Berkeley: University of California Press, 1995.

———. *Try! Try!* With "An Epilogue to the Players." In *Amorous Nightmares of Delay: Selected Plays.* Baltimore, Md.: Johns Hopkins University Press, 1997, 17–30.

———. "V. R. Lang: A Memoir" (1957). In *Standing Still and Walking in New York.* Edited by Donald Allen. San Francisco: Grey Fox, 1983, 86–87.

Sayre, Nora. "The Poets' Theatre: A Memoir of the Fifties." *Grand Street* 3, no. 3 (1 March 1984): 92–105.

Language poetry

Language poetry, or Language writing, as many of its practitioners prefer to call it, is a poetic movement and literary sensibility that emerged in the mid-1970s as a development of NEW YORK SCHOOL and Black Mountain poetics (see BLACK MOUNTAIN POETS), as well as a reaction to the political and cultural milieu of the Vietnam War and Richard Nixon's presidency. From the modernist tradition, one of the most significant influences on Language poetry was Gertrude Stein, whose radical experiments with prose served as a model for the assembling and reassembling of language in ways that are always surprising and inherently subversive to traditional concepts regarding language and literature. The movement is also linked to OBJECTIVISTS through a shared focus on the presentation of the concrete objects of reality in the poem—an object in itself—rather than through the poem by means of symbol, metaphor, or their recent variant, "DEEP IMAGE." In Language poetry this translates into a focus on the materiality of language and a rejection of poetry as a means of self-expression or as a statement of individual identity. The most significant figures in Language poetry brought recognition to the movement through the publication of small journals like *Tottel's* (1970–81, edited by Ron Silliman), *This* (1971–82, edited by Barrett Watten and Robert Grenier), *Hills* (1973–83, edited by Bob Perelman), and the Tuumba chapbook series (1976–84, edited by Lyn Hejinian), all based in the San Francisco Bay area. The relatively late emergence in NEW YORK CITY of *Roof* (1976–79, edited by James Sherry) and *L=A=N=G=U=A=G=E* (1978–81, edited by Charles Bernstein and Bruce Andrews) reflects the special conditions that Language poets faced on the home turf of the New York School.

The orientation toward abstraction in the New York School, derived in part from its association with the visual arts, helped lay the groundwork for Language writing in the early 1960s. Important examples included FRANK O'HARA's *Second Avenue* (Totem Press/ Corinth Books, 1960) and *Biotherm* (*Poetry/Audit*, 1964), KENNETH KOCH's *When the Sun Tries to Go On* (*The Hasty Papers*, 1960), JOHN ASHBERY's *The Tennis Court Oath* (Wesleyan University Press, 1962), and TED BERRIGAN's *The SONNETS* ("C" Press, 1964). The development of a network of like-minded writers can be traced through ARAM SAROYAN's *LINES* (1964–65), which published Grenier and CLARK COOLIDGE; Coolidge's *Joglars* (1964–66), coedited with Michael Palmer; and BERNADETTE MAYER's *0 to 9* (1967–69), which published Coolidge, Saroyan, and Hannah Weiner. During the 1970s Weiner participated in Mayer's workshops at the POETRY PROJECT AT ST. MARK'S CHURCH IN-THE-BOWERY, along with other writers who became associated with the Language movement, such as Nick Piombino and Bernstein.

With the New York School firmly established and even institutionalized in the Poetry Project, there was less immediate need for the kind of organizing on behalf of avant-garde poetry that the Bay Area Language poets took part in during the early 1970s. However, by 1974, when Bernstein returned to New York after several years' residence on the West Coast, he saw reason to doubt the direction in which the Poetry Project was heading. As Bernstein recalls, a joint reading by ROBERT LOWELL and ALLEN GINSBERG at the Poetry Project in 1977 "seemed symptomatic of a certain refusal to stand by one's stands, as if fame superseded ideological or aesthetic oppositions, or as if oppositions had no place in poetry" (Waldman 621). In contrast to the anarchic spirit of inclusiveness at the Poetry Project, Language poetry began to separate itself from the New York School as an assertion of "ideological and aesthetic oppositions" (Waldman 621). And the opposition was not merely set against "mainstream" poetics such as Lowell represented but also against a regressive tendency within the avant-garde itself, represented by Ginsberg and the BEATS. As far as the Language poets were concerned, Beat emphasis on self-expression was a throwback to romanticism, and the Poetry Project seemed to have gone Beat. "Perhaps it could have been otherwise," Barrett Watten wrote from his West Coast perspective; "rather than a romance of beginnings that turned into a looking backward to sources in the Beats—as, say, Ted Berrigan's interpretation of his work veered from the terrorist implications of cut-up to the recuperative ones of autobiography—there might have been more of an opening, for instance, to issues in other arts and modes of thought, to a wider intellectual life" (Waldman 684).

While it is hard to imagine any group of poets more open to "issues in other arts" than the New York School, the "wider intellectual life" to which Watten refers definitely met with resistance insofar as it meant "theory," which is what it tended to mean for Watten and his colleagues. New York School writers have always preferred to practice poetry rather than explain it, or worse, prescribe it according to predefined goals. At the Poetry Project, Mayer's workshops were unusual, and particularly important to Language poets, because she assigned reading by the French structuralist critic Roland Barthes or the philosopher of language Ludwig Wittgenstein, but even Mayer resisted the Language poets' use of Marxist theory to attach a political agenda to the practice of poetry (Kane 188, 269 note 12). When theory of all sorts became the fashionable new wave in university English departments during the 1980s, many Language poets rode the wave into the academy, a cause for further alienation from the anti-academic New York School. On the West Coast, especially, alienation occasionally flared up in outright hostility, as it did on the occasion of TOM CLARK's critique of Language poetry, "Stalin as Linguist," published in the Bay Area newsletter *Poetry Flash* (number 148, 1985). Back in New York, Language poetry found room under the big tent of the Poetry Project, where Bernstein was appointed in 1984 to coordinate a series called St. Mark's Talks, modeled on the series of "Talks" that Perelman had promoted in the Bay Area. The St. Mark's series included West Coast Language writers, just as the Bay Area series had included New York School writers such as BILL BERKSON, Berrigan, ALICE NOTLEY, and LORENZO THOMAS.

During the 1990s an especially productive exchange between New York School poets and Language writers revolved around the GENRE of lyric poetry and the voice of the lyric "I," resisted in early Language theory as a symptom of romantic expressionism. Reflecting on Perelman's retrospective account of Language writing, *The Marginalization of Poetry* (1996), ANN LAUTERBACH wondered, in a review in verse form, if:

The resistance isn't so much to
the unified subject, the lyric, or to narrativity per se

but to a certain display *of subjectivity* (n.p.).

The self-consciousness of that display in O'Hara made him a suitable counterpart to Roland Barthes, theorist of "the death of the author," in an imaginary dialogue between O'Hara and Barthes that forms the conclusion to Perelman's book. It was previously published in *Raddle Moon* (number 14, 1995), a Canadian journal oriented toward Language poetry but equally open to an essay by Notley on the subject of "Voice" (number 18, 2000). After confirming the presence of voice, although in different ways, in the work of RON PADGETT and Barrett Watten, Notley goes on to assert, "in poetry women's voices don't sound the same as men's" (152).

Writing by women, across the divisions of "schools," has been a significant site "Where Lyric Tradition Meets Language Poetry," as the title of a 1999 conference at Barnard College put it. According to Bernstein, BARBARA GUEST was "an incandescent center" at this conference (Bernstein, "Introducing" n.p.), a consequence of her development from New York School origins to later experimentation embraced by the Language poets, especially after her move to California in 1994. Bernstein insists on Guest's "aversion to the lyric" as one of the terms of that embrace (Bernstein, "Introducing" n.p.), while

for MARJORIE WELISH, in a paper presented at the Barnard conference, "Guest's lyrical pulse brings early modern materiality of language into vital relation with the free-ranging experiment that is lyric" (n.p.). The interaction between New York School poetry and Language writing provides a measure of that freedom and that range.

Bibliography

Barthes, Roland. "The Death of the Author" (1968). Translated by Stephen Heath. In *The Norton Anthology of Theory and Criticism,* edited by Vincent B. Leach, 1,466–1,470. New York: Norton, 2001.

Bernstein, Charles. *Content's Dream: Essays, 1975–1984.* Los Angeles: Sun & Moon, 1986.

———. "Introducing Barbara Guest." *Jacket* 10 (October 1999). Available online. URL: http://jacketmagazine.com/10/bern-on-gues.html. Accessed December 18, 2008.

Bernstein, Charles, and Bruce Andrews, eds. *The L=A=N=G=U=A=G=E Book.* Carbondale: Southern Illinois University Press, 1984.

Clark, Tom. "Stalin as Linguist" I (1985) and II (1987). In *The Poetry Beat: Reviewing the Eighties.* Ann Arbor: University of Michigan Press, 1990, 65–83.

Dworkin, Craig, ed. Eclipse Website. Available online. URL: http://english.utah.edu/eclipse/projects/. [Includes facsimile issues of *L=A=N=G=U=A=G=E* and *Tottel's* and an index of *This.*]

Foster, Edward, and Joseph Donahue, eds. *The World in Time and Space: Towards History of Innovative American Poetry in Our Time.* Jersey City, N.J.: Talisman House, 2002.

Kane, Daniel. "Bernadette Mayer and 'Language' in the Poetry Project." In *All Poets Welcome: The Lower East Side Poetry Scene in the 1960s.* Berkeley: University of California Press, 2003, 187–201.

Koch, Kenneth. *When the Sun Tries to Go On.* In *Sun Out: Selected Poems, 1952–54.* New York: Knopf, 2002, 71–140.

Lauterbach, Ann. "Lines Written to Bob Perelman in the Margins of *The Marginalization of Poetry.*" *Jacket* 2 (January 1998). Available online. URL: http://jacketmagazine.com/02/laut.html. Accessed December 18, 2008.

Notley, Alice. "Voice." In *Coming After: Essays on Poetry.* Ann Arbor: University of Michigan Press, 2005, 147–157.

O'Hara, Frank. *The Collected Poems*. Rev. ed. Edited by Donald Allen. Berkeley: University of California Press, 1995.

Perelman, Bob. *The Marginalization of Poetry: Language Writing and Literary History*. Princteon, N.J.: Princeton University Press, 1996.

Perelman, Bob, ed. *Writing/Talks*. Carbondale: Southern Illinois University Press, 1985.

Perloff, Marjorie. "Language Poetry and the Lyric Subject: Ron Silliman's Albany, Susan Howe's Buffalo." *Critical Inquiry* 25, no. 3 (Spring 1999): 405–434.

———. "The Word as Such: L=A=N=G=U=A=G=E Poetry in the Eighties" (1984). In *The Dance of the Intellect: Studies in the Poetry of the Pound Tradition*. Cambridge: Cambridge University Press, 1985, 215–238.

Pritikin, Renny. Excerpt from "Program Report from 80 Langton Street, San Francisco/Writer in Residence: Ted Berrigan: June 24–27, 1981." In *Nice to See You: Homage to Ted Berrigan*, edited by Anne Waldman, 19–25. Minneapolis, Minn.: Coffee House Press, 1991.

Rankine, Claudia, and Juliana Spahr, eds. *American Women Poets in the 21st Century: Where Lyric Meets Language*. Middletown, Conn.: Wesleyan University Press, 2002.

Silliman, Ron, ed. *In the American Tree*. Orono, Me.: National Poetry Foundation/University of Maine at Orono, 1986.

Vickery, Ann. *Leaving Lines of Gender: A Feminist Genealogy of Language Writing*. Hanover, N.H.: University Press of New England/Wesleyan University Press, 2000.

Waldman, Anne, ed. *Out of This World: An Anthology of the St. Mark's Poetry Project, 1966–1991*. New York: Crown, 1991.

Ward, Geoff. *Statues of Liberty: The New York School of Poets*. New York: St. Martin's Press, 1993.

Welish, Marjorie. "The Lyric Lately (a Work in Progress)." *Jacket* 10 (October 1999). Available online. URL: http://jacketmagazine.com/10/welish-on-guest.html. Accessed December 18, 2008.

Last Clean Shirt, The Alfred Leslie and Frank O'Hara (1964)

American painter and filmmaker Alfred Leslie (1927–) composed the movie *The Last Clean Shirt* (black and white, 39 minutes) with subtitles by FRANK O'HARA. The film premiered in fall 1964 at NEW YORK CITY's Lincoln Center. Destroyed in a fire in 1966, it was out of circulation until 1989 when Leslie completed the restoration of the negative once thought to be lost.

The film shows two characters, a black man (the driver, Richard White) and a white woman (Ruth Cazalet), driving around Manhattan in a convertible car. The camera is set in the back seat; from Astor Place, the car goes up Third Avenue and finally reaches 34th Street and Park Avenue. The film repeats this scene three times. Leslie commissioned lines from O'Hara and rearranged them as subtitles. In the first part of the triptych, the woman talks to the silent driver in Finnish gibberish. Subtitles are only added in the second part. In the third part the subtitles express the driver's thoughts.

The Last Clean Shirt presents itself as a parody of a foreign educational movie. At the beginning a black screen appears with the white label *EDU* to the sound of James R. Lowell's poem "Once to Every Man and Nation." With its uneventful unfolding the film tests the spectator's attention: Screenings sometimes elicited angry reactions from the audience. Many of the commissioned subtitles come from poems by O'Hara and provide a tense commentary to the images. References from Havana to China and Africa are critical of the United States's foreign policy during the cold war. "I am ashamed of my century / for being so entertaining," excerpted from the poem "Naphtha," provides an ironical counterpoint to the lack of action. The film's entertainment is to be found in the criticism of the emerging consumer society and its commodified boredom.

At the end of each section one hears a funerary hymn. Death pervades the film, whose title refers to the shirt a deceased person is buried in. The song "The Last Clean Shirt" (Jerry Leiber/Mike Stoller/Johnny Otis) brings about the conclusion of each section. Although parodic, the film has a spiritual strain as it urges one to reflect on mortality. The subtitles to the film would later be used by Alfred Leslie in studies for *The Killing Cycle* (1967–1978), a series of paintings about the death of Frank O'Hara.

Bibliography

Brossard, Olivier. "*The Last Clean Shirt*: A Film by Alfred Leslie and Frank O'Hara." *Jacket* 23 (August 2003).

Available online. URL: http://jacketmagazine.com/23/bross-ohara.html. Accessed December 18, 2008.

Ferguson, Russell. *In Memory of My Feelings: Frank O'Hara and American Art.* Los Angeles: Museum of Contemporary Art; Berkeley: University of California Press, 1999.

French, Philip. "Pop Cinema?" *Encounter Magazine* (1964): 55.

Leslie, Alfred, and Frank O'Hara. *The Last Clean Shirt.* In *Films of Alfred Leslie.* Videorecording, no. 1886. West Long Branch, N.J.: Kultur, 1997.

Yohn, Tim. *"The Last Clean Shirt." Art in America* 79 (June 1991): 151–152.

LaTouche, John (1917–1956) *songwriter*

Premature death from heart failure at the age of 38 inscribed the name of John LaTouche along with those of VIOLET R. (BUNNY) LANG and JACKSON POLLOCK in FRANK O'HARA's poem "A Step Away from Them" (1956). By profession, LaTouche was a songwriter, famous in his time for the words of "Ballad for Americans" (1939) and "Taking a Chance on Love" (with Theodore Fetter, 1940), but today most frequently heard (though not recognized) in the lyrics he wrote for Leonard Bernstein's *Candide* (1956). For the NEW YORK SCHOOL poets, LaTouche was a scene maker.

In the early 1950s LaTouche presided over a glittering salon in his penthouse apartment on East 67th Street, where actors, musicians, artists, and writers mingled with high-society figures. Especially notable among the latter was Alice Bouverie, the Astor heiress who became attached to LaTouche because "his wit delighted her almost as much as their shared passion for the night," according to Gore Vidal (246). NED ROREM recalls meeting O'Hara at LaTouche's apartment on the occasion of a party in honor of Sonia Orwell, the widow of novelist George Orwell (39). On another evening O'Hara and his fellow poets JOHN ASHBERY and BARBARA GUEST provided the occasion (Gooch, *City Poet* 226–227), reading from work that, at least in O'Hara's case, managed to shock the most advanced of audiences. According to JAMES SCHUYLER, gallery owner Betty Parsons was "very offended and outraged" by O'Hara's poem "Easter" (159). Even the young KENWARD ELMSLIE, then a

"recent addition" to LaTouche's "complex love life" (Elmslie, "Fifties Probe" 6), was scared by "the violence of the language" in O'Hara's poem (Elmslie, excerpt 171).

Elmslie remained the poet who was closest to LaTouche both in his personal life and in his style of writing. The two men set up a house together in Calais, Vermont, where Elmslie, after LaTouche's death, continued to entertain in a sort of country version of the city salon, and where JOE BRAINARD and RON PADGETT also took up residence. While his poetry eventually embraced the free expression he had once found so frightening in O'Hara, Elmslie has also practiced the discipline of writing for musical THEATER that had first attracted him to LaTouche. Theater, literal scene making, connected LaTouche with other poets as well. He directed a short film, *Presenting Jane,* based on Schuyler's scenario, and featuring JANE FREILICHER (in the title role), Ashbery, O'Hara, JOHN BERNARD MYERS, and Schuyler. From the surviving accounts (Ashbery and Schuyler; Myers 136, 166; Gooch, *City Poet,* 223), it is not clear which was more theatrical: the making of the film on Georgica Pond in East Hampton during the summer of 1952 or the screening of the film as part of a production of Schuyler's play for the ARTISTS' THEATRE the following February. LaTouche's prior involvement in film reveals the range of his connections. He wrote a song to accompany a sequence by the painter Fernand Léger in Hans Richter's film *Dreams That Money Can Buy* (1947). Along with EDWIN DENBY, Aaron Copland, Paul Bowles, and Virgil Thomson, LaTouche acted in RUDOLPH BURKHARDT's first film, *145 W. 21* (1936).

Bibliography

Ashbery, John, and James Schuyler. "Out at Lenore Petit's." In *The World Anthology,* edited by Anne Waldman, 101–102. Indianapolis, Ind.: Bobbs-Merrill, 1969.

Elmslie, Kenward. Excerpt from *Gay Sunshine* interview (1976). In *Homage to Frank O'Hara,* edited by Bill Berkson and Joe LeSueur, 170. Bolinas, Calif.: Big Sky, 1988.

———. "Fifties Probe." In *Blast from the Past.* Austin, Tex.: Skanky Possum, 2000, 5–13.

———. "Touche's Salon." In *Blast from the Past.* Austin, Tex.: Skanky Possum, 2000, 1–4.

Gates, Anita. "Theater Review: Recalling a Sondheim Precursor," *New York Times*, 3 March 2000, p. E3.

Gooch, Brad. *City Poet: The Life and Times of Frank O'Hara*. New York: Knopf, 1993.

———. "Poet's Corner." *House & Garden* 158 (November 1986): 176–181.

Myers, John Bernard. *Tracking the Marvelous: A Life in the New York Art World*. New York: Random House, 1983.

O'Hara, Frank. *The Collected Poems*. Rev. ed. Edited by Donald Allen. Berkeley: University of California Press, 1995.

Rorem, Ned. Excerpt from *The Final Diary* (1974). In *Homage to Frank O'Hara*, edited by Bill Berkson and Joe LeSueur, 39–40. Bolinas, Calif.: Big Sky, 1988.

Schuyler, James. Interview by Carl Little. *Agni* 37 (January 1993): 152–182.

Vidal, Gore. *Palimpsest: A Memoir*. New York: Random House, 1995.

Lauterbach, Ann (1942–)

As a native New Yorker, Ann Lauterbach traces her connection to the NEW YORK SCHOOL through the experience of the city rather than an aesthetic program. "There's a slightly disembodied, mental aspect," she told an interviewer, "which allows for irony or analytical detachment (what is usually called 'abstraction') which probably has to do with the charged quality of urban life in general and the peculiar dissonance of 'inner' and 'outer' life in New York, where what one thinks, says, and does may be out of alignment" (interview by Bendall 23). A common aesthetic orientation is also a relevant connection, however. Lauterbach attended New York's High School of Music and Art while ABSTRACT EXPRESSIONISM was still the supreme standard of advanced painting, and she recalls, "I was enamored of the Abstract Expressionists for the combination of sensuousness and mystery" (interview by Bendall 20).

Lauterbach went on to the University of Wisconsin in 1960 with the intention of studying painting, though she began to redirect her creative energies toward writing. After graduation from Wisconsin in 1964 and a year of graduate study on a Woodrow Wilson Fellowship at Columbia University, she settled in London (1967–74), where she worked in publishing and at the Institute of Contemporary Arts (ICA). She published her first poems in England and Ireland. Returning to New York in 1974, Lauterbach held a series of jobs with art galleries. She has maintained close ties to the visual arts by writing catalog essays and collaborating with artists such as Lucio Pozzi (1935–), Ellen Phelan (1943–), and Ann Hamilton (1956–), but since an initial appointment in the Brooklyn College M.F.A. program in 1985, Lauterbach has been employed mainly in teaching. Since 1991 she has been cochair of writing in the Milton Avery Graduate School of the Arts at Bard College, where she was appointed to the Ruth and David Schwab II chair in language and literature in 1997.

During her residence in London Lauterbach arranged readings at the ICA by a number of poets, including ROBERT CREELEY, TED BERRIGAN, and RON PADGETT. A visit by JOHN ASHBERY in 1971, for a festival Lauterbach had arranged, proved to be transformative for her art. Ashbery's reading from *Three Poems* (Viking, 1972), which he had just completed, presented the possibility "that a poem could be at least as capacious as prose, that it need not be a tidy little bouquet of words tied in a ribbon," she explains (interview by Bendall 19). Although the term *capacious* suggests an interest in how much poetry can include, Ashbery's alternative of "leaving out" (*Three Poems* 3) resonates in explicit references throughout Lauterbach's work (*If* 100; "Misquotations" 147). The concept offers a key to understanding Lauterbach's approach to abstraction and her affinity with Ashbery, the New York School poet with whom she is most often compared (McCorkle). For Lauterbach, Ashbery's most profound lesson is not how to write but how "to listen for the multiplicity, the plurality, of experience" (Lauterbach, "What We Know" n.p.). It is a mode of attention that she connects with the title of Ashbery's book *As We Know* (Viking, 1979), whose major poem, "Litany," enacts "multiplicity" and "plurality" through two voices read or performed simultaneously, as Ashbery and Lauterbach have done together. Lauterbach also "perform[s] a way of knowing through the experience of knowing" in *The Night Sky* (Lauterbach, interview by Bernstein n.p.), a 2005 collection of essays (Viking, 2005) that recall Ashbery's *Three Poems* in their use of prose for poetic purpose.

Besides Ashbery, other New York School writers who have been particularly important to Lauterbach include BARBARA GUEST and JAMES SCHUYLER for their ability to evoke time in the spatial dimension that Lauterbach calls "air" and KENWARD ELMSLIE and JOE BRAINARD for their bond of friendship. Lauterbach has composed an elegiac sequence in memory of Brainard, "Songs for Joe" (*If* 131–136; "Five More"), and expressed a sense of "fury" at Brainard's death in "Missing Ages" (*If* 137–139), dedicated to Elmslie (Lauterbach, interview by Bernstein n.p.). These are specific affinities, not dictated by a sense of belonging to any "school." Lauterbach has pointed to writers outside the New York School who have been important to her in different ways, such as Michael Palmer (1943–   ) and Norma Cole (1945–   ). With the Language poets Lauterbach shares a strong interest in critical theory and philosophy, particularly the American pragmatist tradition extending back to Ralph Waldo Emerson. The influence of LANGUAGE POETRY partly accounts for a significant shift in Lauterbach's poetic practice away from the visual image to becoming "increasingly aware of and attentive to aural values" in her work after 1990 (Lauterbach, interview by Bendall 20). MUSIC, on the other hand, has always been an inspiration to Lauterbach, as it has been to the New York School generally.

If in Time (Penguin, 2001) includes work from Lauterbach's five previous volumes: *Many Times, but Then* (University of Texas Press, 1979), *Before Recollection* (Princeton University Press, 1987), *Clamor* (Viking, 1991), *And for Example* (Penguin, 1994), and *On a Stair* (Penguin, 1997). The title poem of *Hum* (Penguin, 2005) registers Lauterbach's response to the terrorist attack on New York's World Trade Center on SEPTEMBER 11, 2001. A new collection, *Or to Begin Again* (Penguin), is scheduled to appear in 2009.

Lauterbach's many honors include a Guggenheim Foundation fellowship in 1986, an Ingram Merrill Foundation grant in 1988, and a MacArthur Foundation fellowship in 1993.

Bibliography

Ashbery, John. *Three Poems*. New York: Viking, 1972.

Ashbery, John, and Ann Lauterbach. Performance of "Litany" (1980). Audio recording. PennSound. Available online. URL: http://writing.upenn.edu/pennsound/x/Ashbery.html.

Borkhuis, Charles. "Im.age . . . Dis.solve: The Linguistic Image in the Critical Lyric of Norma Cole and Ann Lauterbach." In *We Who Love to Be Astonished: Experimental Women's Writing and Performative Poetics*, edited by Laura Hinton and Cynthia Hogue, 127–139. Tuscaloosa: University of Alabama Press, 2002.

Hume, Christine. "'Enlarging the Last Lexicon of Perception' in Ann Lauterbach's Framed Fragments." In *American Women Poets in the 21st Century: Where Lyric Meets Language*, edited by Claudia Rankine and Juliana Spahr, 367–399. Middletown, Conn.: Wesleyan University Press, 2002.

Lauterbach, Ann. "All View (13 Windows)." In *Ann Hamilton: whitecloth*. Exhibit catalog. Ridgefield, Conn.: Aldrich Museum of Contemporary Art, 1999, 9–35.

———. "Barbara Guest: Architect of Air." In *The Night Sky: Writings on the Poetics of Experience*. New York: Viking, 2005, 189–196.

———. "Fifth Season" [on James Schuyler]. *Denver Quarterly* 24, no. 4 (Spring 1990): 69–76.

———. "Five More Songs for Joe." *Pressed Wafer* 2 (March 2001): 113–115.

———. *If in Time: Selected Poems, 1975–2000*. New York: Penguin, 2001.

———. Interview by Charles Bernstein (2006). Close Listening series. Audio recording. PennSound. Available online. URL: http://writing.upenn.edu/pennsound/x/Lauterbach.html. Accessed December 18, 2008.

———. Interview by Molly Bendall. *American Poetry Review* 21, no. 3 (May–June 1992): 19–15.

———. "Misquotations from Reality." *Diacritics* 26, nos. 3–4 (Fall/Winter 1996): 143–157.

———. "What We Know as We Know It: Reading 'Litany' with JA: *As We Know* (1979)." *Conjunctions* 49 (2007): 341–350. Available online. URL: http://www.conjunctions.com/archives/c49-al.htm. Accessed December 18, 2008.

Lauterbach, Ann, with Ellen Phelan. *A Clown, Some Colors, A Doll, Her Stories, A Song, A Moonlit Cove*. New York: Whitney Museum of American Art, 1996.

Lauterbach, Ann, with Lucio Pozzi. *How Things Bear Their Telling*. Colombes, France: Collectif Génération, 1990.

McCorkle, James. "Nimbus of Sensations: Eros and Reverie in the Poetry of John Ashbery and Ann Lauterbach." In *The Tribe of John: Ashbery and Contemporary Poetry*, edited by Susan M. Schultz, 101–125. Tuscaloosa: University of Alabama Press, 1995.

Lehman, David (1948–) *literary critic*

Born in NEW YORK CITY in 1948, David Lehman is among the principal chroniclers and advocates of the NEW YORK SCHOOL poets, particularly JOHN ASHBERY, a former colleague of his at Brooklyn College, and KENNETH KOCH, under whom he studied as an undergraduate at Columbia University.

Lehman earned his Ph.D. in English from Columbia in 1978, completing a dissertation on prose poetry entitled "The Marriage of Poetry and Prose," followed by a one-year postdoctoral fellowship at Cornell University in 1980. It was his time at Cornell, then a hotbed of critical theory, that prompted him to leave academe and pursue a career in freelance journalism in the early '80s. Lehman spent the next seven years working as a reviewer for *Newsweek*, devoting his spare time to scholarly essays and book projects, among them *Beyond Amazement: New Essays on John Ashbery* (Cornell University Press, 1980), *James Merrill: Essays in Criticism* (with James Berger; Cornell University Press, 1983), and *The Perfect Murder* (Free Press, 1989), a study of detective novels.

As a literary critic, Lehman is best known for his book-length condemnation of deconstruction, *Signs of the Times: Deconstruction and the Fall of Paul de Man* (Poseidon, 1991), and his history of the New York School, *The Last Avant-Garde: The Making of the New York School of Poets* (Doubleday, 1998). The former, prompted by his distaste for critical theory and revelations that Paul de Man had written for a collaborationist newspaper in Belgium during World War II, draws a genealogical relationship between the interpretive practice and the moral failings underlying the critic's wartime journalism. Though not the only critique of the method, the book was perhaps the most readable and won him recognition as one of deconstruction's most outspoken adversaries. *The Last Avant-Garde,* which identified Ashbery, Koch, FRANK O'HARA, and JAMES SCHUYLER as the New York School's

core group, met with mixed reviews. Matt Badura described it as "an enthusiastic and eminently readable portrait of the poets" (195). As Vernon Shetley pointed out, Lehman was "close to many of the subjects that survive" and "profited by access to reminiscences, letters, and other unpublished materials" (132). Still, other critics argued that the book raises additional issues that it fails to resolve, such as Lehman's ambiguous usage of the terms *avant-garde* and *establishment* and his omission of poet BARBARA GUEST.

As a poet, Lehman has published seven volumes to date: *An Alternative to Speech* (Princeton University Press, 1986), *Operation Memory* (Princeton University Press, 1990), *Valentine Place* (Scribner, 1996), *The Daily Mirror: A Journal in Poetry* (Scribner, 2000), *The Evening Sun* (Scribner, 2002), *When a Woman Loves a Man* (Scribner, 2005), and *Jim and Dave Defeat the Masked Man* (Soft Skull, 2006), a series of sestinas written in COLLABORATION with James Cummins. From the start, Lehman's work displays his penchant for word play, polemic, and paradox, often within the framework of traditional forms, as in his often-cited title sestina "Operation Memory." The poems of *Valentine Place*, though equally ironic, take a decidedly autobiographical turn. Named after the street on which Lehman once lived in Ithaca, New York, the collection is a loose autobiography of the author's love life, from boyhood crushes to marriage and divorce. According to Lehman, it was Robert Bly who in 1996 challenged him to write a poem a day for the rest of his life. This "journal in poetry" project, which has apparently dominated most of his creative output since, is clearly reflected in the titles of *The Daily Mirror* and *The Evening Sun*. Critics have responded to this project with measured enthusiasm, noting its striking similarity to the "I do this, I do that" poems of O'Hara.

Lehman's influence in the world of poetry extends well beyond his literary and critical writing, however. Most know Lehman for his editorial accomplishments, recently highlighted by the publication of his canonical ANTHOLOGY, the *Oxford Book of American Poetry* (Oxford University Press, 2006). In editing *Great American Prose Poems: From Poe to Present* (Scribner, 2003), Lehman returned to the FORM studied in his dissertation. He serves as series editor of the annual *Best American Poetry* anthology, which he launched in 1988, and as general editor of the University of Michigan Press's Poets on Poetry Series, which has published two collections of his essays, *The Line Forms Here* (1992) and *The Big Question* (1995). Throughout his career Lehman has actively solicited discussion on the craft of writing from poets. An early anthology, *Ecstatic Occasions, Expedient Forms* (Macmillan, 1987, 1996), features poems self-selected and commented upon by those it includes, while those writers chosen for inclusion in *The Best American Poetry* are asked to provide a note describing the process of the awarded poem's composition.

In 1997 Lehman and STAR BLACK founded a reading series at the KGB Bar in DOWNTOWN MANHATTAN's East Village, subsequently represented in an anthology coedited by Lehman and Black, *The KGB Bar Book of Poems* (Perennial, 2000). Returning to teaching in recent years, Lehman currently serves on the faculty of the New School in New York and the low-residency M.F.A. program at Bennington College in Vermont.

Bibliography

Badura, Matt. Review of *The Last Avant-Garde*. *Review of Contemporary Fiction* 20, no. 1 (Spring 2000): 194–195.

Bayles, Martha. "Cedar Tavern Days." *Wilson Quarterly* 23, no. 1 (Winter 1999): 94–97.

Benfey, Christopher. "The Limits of Fun." *New Republic* 220, nos. 1–2 (January 1999): 37–41.

Diggory, Terence. Review of *The Last Avant-Garde*. *College Literature* 26, no. 2 (Spring 1999): 211–214.

Garner, Dwight. Review of *The Daily Mirror*. *New York Times Book Review*, 9 January 2000, 20.

Hainey, Michael. Review of *The Evening Sun*. *New York Times Book Review*, 14 April 2002, 20.

Lehman, David. Interview by Tom Disch. *The Cortland Review*, September 1999. Available online. URL: www.cortlandreview.com/features/99/09/index. html. Accessed October 22, 2008.

Murphy, Bruce F. Review of *The Evening Sun*. *Poetry* 181, no. 5 (March 2003): 353–355.

Shetley, Vernon. "The New York School of Poetry." *Raritan* 18, no. 4 (Spring 1999): 130–144.

Shoaf, Diann Blakely. Review of *Valentine Place*. *Antioch Review* 54, no. 4 (Fall 1996): 498.

Simon, John. "Partying on Parnassus: The New York School Poets." Review of *The Last Avant-Garde*. *New Criterion* 17, no. 2 (October 1998): 31–38.

Thompson, W. B. "Enlarging the Sphere." *Michigan Quarterly Review* 39, no. 1 (Winter 2000): 173–179.

Lenhart, Gary (1947–   )

NEW YORK SCHOOL poetics turned out to be life transforming for Gary Lenhart, who was first able to imagine himself as a poet after discovering books by TED BERRIGAN and RON PADGETT in the library at the University of Wisconsin–Madison, where Lenhart attended graduate school (M.A., 1973). Berrigan and Padgett "were the first poets who seemed to be writing in my language," recalls Lenhart (102), who had taken a leap from his working-class background in Albany, New York, to study the foreign language known as "literature." After moving to NEW YORK CITY in 1974, Lenhart soon abandoned formal studies to devote himself to poetry in the underclass conditions of the Lower East Side, "in a building where we had no heat or hot water during the first two winters I lived there" (100). But Lenhart and the other poets who occupied the building, including ALLEN GINSBERG, had the "incredible zest and resourceful imagination" that Lenhart witnessed in Berrigan and Padgett, "making poems out of materials that lay to hand" (*Lenhart* 102).

The poems in Lenhart's first collection, *One at a Time* (United Artists, 1983), abound in such materials, like the "beer can or empty / Orange Fanta" that neighbors drop onto the garbage heap outside "the tenement next door" ("Satellites"). His second collection, *Light Heart* (Hanging Loose, 1991), treats the conditions of poverty less lightly, after a sobering decade under "Reagan and his profiteers" ("Ode to Utopia"). *Father and Son Night* (Hanging Loose, 1999) focuses on the basic social unit, the family. Many of the poems in this collection are autobiographical, though Lenhart refuses to separate his personal life from the life of poetry, "Signs of a bliss we are invited to share" ("Cinderella"). The poem that extends this invitation is an instance of sharing typical of the New York School. It is one of a set of 15 poems, each by a different author, issued as a series of broadsides (*Bringing Up Baby*, Coffee House

Press, 1997), with illustrations by Lenhart's wife, the painter Louise Hamlin (1949–   ).

During his years in New York Lenhart edited two magazines, *Mag City* (1977–85, with coeditors GREG MASTERS and MICHAEL SCHOLNICK) and *Transfer* (1986–91). He ran the EAR INN reading series for a period (1978–80), worked as administrative assistant at the POETRY PROJECT AT ST. MARK'S CHURCH IN-THE-BOWERY (1979–81), and helped develop many publications as associate director of the TEACHERS & WRITERS COLLABORATIVE (1984–94). In 1992 he moved with his wife and daughter to Norwich, Vermont, within commuting distance of Dartmouth College, where he and his wife both teach. In 2006 he published *The Stamp of Class: Reflections on Poetry and Social Class*, covering a wide range of poets, including Berrigan, Padgett and EILEEN MYLES.

Bibliography

Lenhart, Gary. *The Stamp of Class: Reflections on Poetry and Social Class.* Ann Arbor: University of Michigan Press, 2006.

Lenhart, Gary, ed. *The Teachers & Writers Guide to William Carlos Williams.* New York: Teachers & Writers Collaborative, 1998.

Les Deux Mégots

The early 1960s witnessed a groundswell of enthusiasm for poetry gatherings staged at coffeehouses around DOWNTOWN MANHATTAN. This development prompted Mickey Ruskin, owner of the crowded Tenth Street Coffee House, to find a larger space for his café's popular poetry readings. He found that space in the basement of an old brick townhouse at 64 East 7th Street, where, in 1962, he and co-owner Bill Mackey opened Les Deux Mégots, or "The Two Cigar Butts"—a play on the name of the well-known Parisian café Les Deux Magots. Shortly thereafter, Ruskin sold his half of the establishment to Mackey, who became the Mégots' sole proprietor and a garrulous fixture behind the café's pastry counter. (Ruskin would later gain recognition as the restaurateur behind The Ninth Circle and Max's Kansas City.)

Located between Second and Third Avenues, Les Deux Mégots was one of the first artistic sanctuaries on the Lower East Side, which, at that time, was primarily a working-class Jewish and Italian neighborhood. The coffeehouse was open from 4 P.M. until midnight and held readings on Monday and Wednesday nights under the auspices of PAUL BLACKBURN, a poet often identified with the Black Mountain school. Some of the figures who read at Les Deux Mégots were Robert Bly, ALLEN GINSBERG, John Harriman, Leroi Jones (AMIRI BARAKA), Robert Kelly, DENISE LEVERTOV, Robert Lima, JACKSON MAC LOW, and Diane Wakoski. The café eventually spawned the literary magazine *Poets at Les Deux Mégots*, which featured a wide range of work from the BEATS and BLACK MOUNTAIN POETS, DEEP IMAGE poets, and younger NEW YORK SCHOOL poets.

In February 1963—after less than one year of operation—the coffeehouse closed down, reopening as a restaurant the following year. Many of the poets from Les Deux Mégots would go on to read at CAFÉ LE METRO and, later, at the POETRY PROJECT AT ST. MARK'S CHURCH IN-THE-BOWERY.

Lesniak, Rose (1955–   ) *artist, filmmaker*

Rose Lesniak, born in CHICAGO, ILLINOIS, on February 26, 1955, is best known for her COLLABORATIONS between poets and filmmakers, spearheading the first mixed-media video-recorded performances in the United States. As the founder of the Manhattan Poetry Video Project, Lesniak helped memorialize the readings of such poets as ALLEN GINSBERG, ANNE WALDMAN, and BOB HOLMAN.

Lesniak studied at Northwestern Illinois University with TED BERRIGAN. With BARBARA BARG and Joel Chassler, she founded *Out There Magazine*, whose mission was to assist nonestablished and experimental writers with publication. Lesniak and Barg edited and published 15 issues of *Out There Magazine*. In 1977 Lesniak moved to NEW YORK CITY, where she helped start "Words to Go," a poetry-on-wheels project that traveled around New York City, dispensing poetry to those people who might not readily encounter it. As Lesniak has said, "I was seeking a return to the tradition of the troubador poets" (Mossin). This work in performance poetry led to Lesniak's interest in poetry videos. Along with Andrea Kirsh, Lesniak founded the nonprofit organization Out There Productions, Inc. The company produced a half-hour documentary video, *Poets in Performance*, that featured poets Berrigan, MAUREEN OWEN, Waldman, Barg, and JOHN GIORNO performing their works in historical areas of the city. Along with Holman, Pedro Pietre, and others, Lesniak also worked in the CETA Artists Project, the largest federally funded artists' project since the Works Progress Administration. It was initiated by President Jimmy Carter under the Comprehensive Employment Training Act.

Lesniak then founded the Manhattan Poetry Video Project, a project that showed readings by contemporary poets and that premiered at Joseph Papp's Public Theater to sold-out audiences. Lesniak won the American Film Festival Blue Ribbon Award for her innovation. Spurred by the urge to disseminate the spoken word widely, Lesniak was instrumental in having these poetry videos covered on National Public Radio, in *Billboard* magazine, and in the *New York Times*. As Lesniak stated at the time, "We have to think of new ways to get poetry out into the world. . . . It's very important for poetry to be different in its approach now, not just stay in the cafes and small reading halls. . . . With video, we have the chance to create a global cafe of sorts" (Mossin).

As a poet, Lesniak has published a number of small-press collections, including *Young Anger* (Toothpaste Press, 1979), *Remember?* (Toothpaste Press, 1980), *Untitled* (Power Mad Press, 1980), and *Throwing Spitballs at the Nuns,* with drawings by Ann Mikolowski (Toothpaste Press, 1982). Her CD-ROM and song "She's So" was produced by Sphiny Productions and appeared on the compilation *Life Is a Killer,* put out by Giorno Poetry Systems.

In 1988 Lesniak moved to Miami Beach and, to this date, works as a child abuse investigator for the Miami Beach Police Special Victims Squad. She continues to write poetry but refuses to publish it at this time, focusing her energies instead on her activism and on studying animal behavior.

Bibliography

Mossin, Andrew. "Poetry Videos: A Global Café of Sorts." *Coda Magazine* (June–July 1985). Available online. URL: http://archive.pw.org/mag/articles/a8506-1.htm. Accessed December 5, 2008.

Levertov, Denise (1923–1997)

NEW YORK CITY was Denise Levertov's home throughout most of the 1950s and 1960s, though in the realm of aesthetics she was closer to the Black Mountain group than to the NEW YORK SCHOOL. The cliquishness of the New York School writers put her off. In her correspondence with William Carlos Williams, which had begun in 1951, she gave a proposed anthology project only a half-hearted endorsement because "the poets, or at least those who are editing it, aren't much good I think; a little clique—John Ashbery, Kenneth Koch, [Frank] O'Hara—rather slick" (Levertov and Williams 51). In the same letter, however, she admits to "very varying feelings about [Charles] Olson," the oracle of BLACK MOUNTAIN POETS. Ultimately, Levertov was unwilling to sacrifice independent judgment to affiliation with any group.

Levertov was always a lyric poet, but she left behind the subjective neoromanticism of her first book, *The Double Image* (1946), published in her native England, when she immigrated to the United States in 1948 with her American husband, the writer Mitchell Goodman. Immersion in American language and culture helped her to "get" Williams's objectivism, and acquaintance with ROBERT CREELEY, a classmate of Goodman's at Harvard, brought her up to date with the latest developments of the OBJECTIVISTS in the pages of *Origin* and *The BLACK MOUNTAIN REVIEW*, where she published her work throughout the 1950s. Her friendship with Robert Duncan, who was more in tune with Levertov's spiritual sensibility than was Creeley, began in 1953 when Duncan responded to some of Levertov's work in *Origin*. Her collection *With Eyes at the Back of Our Heads* (1959) confirmed her full command of her new style and began her lifelong association with the major avant-garde publisher New Directions. The following year she appeared along with Creeley and Duncan in the "Black Mountain" section of DONALD M. ALLEN's *The NEW AMERICAN POETRY, 1945–1960*. Her reputation reached its peak during the 1960s, although her later accomplishments both as a writer and a teacher, primarily at Stanford University (1981–94), added to her distinction.

Against the common background that Levertov shared with the New York School poets, their divergence stands out all the more sharply. In 1955 Levertov reported to Duncan, "Mitch [Goodman] had a violent argument in the Cedar bar with and about Franz Kline and in defense of Lee Bell and Louisa Matthiasdottir" (Levertov and Duncan 23). Bell and his wife, Matthiasdottir, were figurative painters devoted to the School of Paris, closer in aesthetic predilection to Levertov and her husband, who were also their neighbors in Greenwich Village. A similar divergence shows up in the pages of KULCHUR, where in the same issue (number 6, summer 1962), FRANK O'HARA promotes abstract expressionist artists while Levertov reviews contemporary British poets. During this period both O'Hara and Levertov began to encounter a second generation of young poets through teaching workshops, O'Hara at the New School (1963) and Levertov at the 92nd Street Y (1964). Two students in Levertov's workshop, Emmett Jarrett and Dick Lourie, went on to found HANGING LOOSE magazine in 1966. In the same year another young poet, Joel Sloman, whose first book Levertov had recommended to the Norton publishing company, became the first assistant director of the newly formed POETRY PROJECT AT ST. MARK'S CHURCH IN-THE-BOWERY. Levertov read at the Poetry Project, as she had done in the various coffeehouses that preceded it, and she contributed to related publications, including the inaugural issue of ANGEL HAIR (spring 1966). Her passionate engagement in protests against the Vietnam War, for which her husband was imprisoned, involved her in political activity at St. Mark's more deeply than the first-generation New York School poets cared to go. However, she felt even more distant from the work of the second generation, which she dismissed as "a kind of diluted Dada" (interview 57).

Of all the New York School poets, Levertov seems to have been closest in spirit to BARBARA GUEST. She liked Guest in person (Levertov and Duncan 375), and she found Guest's poetry "much less chic & flip, much more felt through" than first impression and, no doubt, prior association had suggested (Levertov and Duncan 459). For Levertov, as for Guest, an essential quality of poetry was "mystery." Writing of H.D. (Hida Doolittle, 1886–1961), for whose work she shared an enthusiasm with Duncan as well as with Guest, Levertov

explained: "She showed a way to penetrate mystery, which means, not to flood darkness with light so that darkness is destroyed, but to *enter into* darkness, mystery, so that it is experienced" ("H.D." 246). Not surprisingly, a poem by Guest that Levertov singled out for praise was "The Brown Studio" (Levertov and Duncan 290), where the speaker senses "an emptiness, beginning to darken" (Guest 77).

Bibliography

Guest, Barbara. *Poems: The Location of Things—Archaics—The Open Sky*. Garden City, N.Y.: Doubleday, 1962.

Levertov, Denise. "H.D.: An Appreciation" (1962). In *The Poet in the World*. New York: New Directions, 1973, 244–248.

———. Interview by Michael Andre (1972). In *Conversations with Denise Levertov*, edited by Jewel Spears Brooker, 52–67. Jackson: University Press of Mississippi, 1998.

———. *Selected Poems*. Edited by Paul A. Lacey. New York: New Directions, 2002.

Levertov, Denise, and Robert Duncan. *The Letters of Robert Duncan and Denise Levertov*. Edited by Robert J. Bertholf and Albert Gelpi. Stanford, Calif.: Stanford University Press, 2004.

Levertov, Denise, and William Carlos Williams. *The Letters of Denise Levertov and William Carlos Williams*. Edited by Christopher MacGowan. New York: New Directions, 1998.

Shapiro, David. "Denise Levertov: Among the Keys." *Twentieth Century Literature* 38, no. 3 (Fall 1992): 299–304.

Levine, Steve (1953–)

Born on Yom Kippur, September 18, 1953, in Brooklyn, New York, Steve Levine attended the University of Chicago but has noted his education is "ongoing" (Levine to Lyons). Levine joined his friend, poet, and translator SIMON SCHUCHAT, in a move to NEW YORK CITY from CHICAGO, ILLINOIS. A cluster of Chicago poets, including BOB ROSENTHAL, ROCHELLE KRAUT, BOB HOLMAN, and BARBARA BARG, most of whom had become affiliated through studies and friendship with TED BERRIGAN and ALICE NOTLEY (who had worked in Chicago for a time), also moved to New York in the mid-1970s, infusing the East Village scene with a new stream of poetic energy constellating around the POETRY PROJECT AT ST. MARK'S CHURCH IN-THE-BOWERY, the NUYORICAN POETS CAFÉ, and other venues. Levine found connections with GARY LENHART and Schuchat to be particularly sustaining. By 1976 Levine was among the participants, including EILEEN MYLES, SUSIE TIMMONS, Jeff Wright, and MICHAEL SCHOLNICK, in Notley's writing workshop at the Poetry Project. Along with GREG MASTERS, SIMON PETTET, ELINOR NAUEN, MAGGIE DUBRIS, and others, this loosely defined third-generation of NEW YORK SCHOOL poets formed the core of a "new pluralism," which DAVID SHAPIRO points to as generated in part by Berrigan as the antiwar activities of St. Mark's wound down (227).

Levine immediately started to publish seriously with the release of *A Blue Tongue* (Toothpaste Press, 1976). Energized by the do-it-yourself permissiveness of the East Village scene, Levine supported the work of his peers Masters, Wright, Scholnick, and Lenhart with his Remember I Did This for You/Power Mad Press, notable for its handsomely bold graphic look (examples of which are in the New York Public Library collection). Levine's own PHILIP GUSTON–like cartoon drawing graced the cover of Myles's *The Irony of the Leash* (Jim Brodey Books, 1978). Levine went on to collect his poems in *Pure Notation* (Coffee House Press, 1992); write a play, *The Cycles of Heaven* (Coffee House Press, 1988); co-author, with Jim Hanson, *Three Numbers* (Toothpaste Press, 1976); and publish *There Is No Leg Room in the Hall of Arms* (Happy Abattoir Publications, 2003).

Levine's laconic, often puncturing wit has been evident in his writings in the privately circulated *Caveman* magazine (1977–1988). Yet, his poems evince a tender, at times delirious sensibility caught in the contradictions of a New York minute less hallowed than the surrealists' fortuitous encounter, and more likely to startle. "Reckless ecstasy on this glorious / Day" ("Poem" 522) results from a "glimpse / Of our planet's random grace" ("Tiny Catullus" 253). Irony and disappointment mediate the data of the senses and the pure language play called *zaum* by the Russian futurists. Levine's poems never gush and rarely extend past the limits of where the poet's full realization has brought him. Levine prefers control and a reining in, a dropping back at unex-

pected junctures so that relationship, situation, and tense shift position. A sense of dread, an evocation of the uncomfortable private moment—"life's wet bar of soap / out from under / Some furniture, to find it covered / with horrific hair" ("Miserable Life" 170)—shares ground with modernists such as Franz Kafka, Robert Musil, and Blaise Cendrars in the rueful disclosure, a trembling unwrapping of armor in the humming traffic of poetic consciousness. In this regard Levine's friendships with the now deceased German poet Daniel Krakauer and American-Lithuanian poet and translator Vyt Bakaitis have been just as important to him as the turmoil and camaderie—"Love and be loved hate and be hated" ("Poem" 522)—found amid the third-generation New York School poets.

Bibliography

Levine, Steve. "Miserable Life." *Nice To See You: Homage to Ted Berrigan*. Edited by Anne Waldman. Minneapolis: Coffee House Press, 1991, 170–171.

———. Personal communication to Kimberly Lyons. February 2006.

———. "Poem." *Out of This World: An Anthology. 1966–1991*. Edited by Anne Waldman. New York: Crown, 1991, 522.

———. "Tiny Catullus." *Up Late: American Poetry Since 1970*. Edited by Andrei Codrescu. New York: 4 Walls 8 Windows, 1987, 252–253.

Shapiro, David. "On a Poet." *Nice To See You: Homage to Ted Berrigan*. Edited by Anne Waldman. Minneapolis: Cofee House Press, 1991, 223–227.

———. *Out of This World: An Anthology, 1966–1991*. New York: Crown, 1991.

Lewis, Joel (1955–)

Born in Brooklyn, New York, Joel Lewis was raised in Hoboken, New Jersey, in a Polish-Jewish politically activist milieu. His father was a survivor of Auschwitz. In 1977 he received a B.A. in political science from William Paterson University, in Wayne, New Jersey. He received master's degrees in social science (William Paterson, 1980), creative writing (City College of New York, 1988), and social work (Yeshiva University, New York, 1993).

In a review of *The Collected Poems of Ted Berrigan*, Lewis wrote, "[I]n the end, it is poets reading other poets and then participating in the underground economy of talking and writing that established a poet's position within the active literary culture" (24). That "underground economy" has been Lewis's cherished habitat for almost 30 years, an environment that he has nourished as poet, critic, editor, teacher, and advocate. His books of poetry are *Vertical's Currency* (Talisman House, 1999) and *House Rent Boogie* (Yellow Press, 1992). *The Tasks of the Youth Leagues* (Oasis Press, 2005) is the most recent of a number of smaller chapbook editions. He has edited *On the Level Everyday: Selected Talks of Ted Berrigan* (Talisman House, 1977), *Reality Prime: Selected Poems of Walter Lowenfels* (Talisman House, 1998), and *Bluestones + Salt Hay: An Anthology of New Jersey Poets* (Rutgers University Press, 1990). To track Lewis's peripatetic, caffeinated travels—via the conveyance of his poems and conversation and projects—through the Northeast Corridor, across the Atlantic, backward in time to his unsentimental vision of modernism and forward to Lewis's wry hopefulness for a retrievable future in his unstinting support of younger poets gives an indication of his "caring enough about the work" (Lewis review, 24). "Who is left among the walking wounded to stake that line & what's with this time?" he queries in his long poem *The Tasks of the Youth Leagues.* In answer, Lewis's poems evoke myriad voices in splinters of repartee (what other poet so firmly ensconced in an urban milieu has such an ear for the idiom of North Atlantic towns?). Introspections, gleaming of self-awareness, give his poem sudden lyrical shots, passages of infused aloneness, and refracted longing.

Lewis became part of the NEW YORK SCHOOL scene by inviting its players over to his house as an organizer (1978–80) of the legendary Lady Jane series in North Bergen and at the Beaten Path in Hoboken, New Jersey. Thereafter, via New Jersey Transit and ferry, Lewis attended readings at the POETRY PROJECT AT ST. MARK'S CHURCH IN-THE-BOWERY, the EAR INN, and other DOWNTOWN MANHATTAN venues; climbed the long stairs to 101 St. Mark's Place, befriending TED BERRIGAN and ALICE NOTLEY; and also became close to MAUREEN OWEN, LEWIS WARSH, JOHN GODFREY, CLARK COOLIDGE, TONY TOWLE, and GARY LENHART. Perhaps Lewis's stubbornly eclectic literary interests

and unabashed identification with New Jersey and political activities precluded closeness with the coteries of the so-called third generation. JORDAN DAVIS has wryly noted that the fourth generation is "one, more or less: Joel Lewis and he chose to stay in New Jersey" (8). Lewis has remarked: "I always recognized the New York School as a STANCE toward writing" (e-mail n.p.). It might be speculated that the stance of the OBJECTIVISTS and modernists such as William Carlos Williams has excited his ongoing projects as well. Rather than advocating a New Jersey regional style, Lewis brings his wide-ranging readings of the poetries of the 20th century to the region where he "hangs his baseball hat" (e-mail n.p.) as a writer, editor, and consultant for Talisman House, a publishing house based in New Jersey; the New Jersey Performing Arts Center; and the Hoboken Historical Museum. Lewis's exemplary use of poetry's means of noticing everything everyday is brought to a larger world in his writings on JAZZ, Yiddish modernism, a White Castle restaurant, and a horseradish bottler, among the many topics covered in articles published in *Poets & Writers*, *Sulfur*, *Time Out*, and the *Utne Reader*.

Bibliography

Davis, Jordan. "Peeling Oranges on Top of the Skyscrapers: Towards a Name-Blind History of Poetry since 1960." *Vanitas* 1 (2005): 5–13.

Lewis, Joel. E-mail to Terence Diggory, 9 May 2006.

———. Review of *The Collected Poems of Ted Berrigan*. *Poetry Project Newsletter* 206 (February–March 2006): 24–25.

Lima, Frank (1939–   )

Frank Lima was one of the first Puerto Rican street poets to emerge in the second generation of the NEW YORK SCHOOL, and he was called by some the "Rimbaud of Spanish Harlem." Of mixed Puerto Rican and Mexican heritage, born in NEW YORK CITY, he wrote poems reflecting his rough-hewn upbringing, which included juvenile delinquency and abuse at the hands of his parents, priests, and other authority figures. In his mid-20s Lima succumbed to substance abuse and spent time in jail and in rehab but reemerged to become a world-class chef and to publish *Inventory: New and*

Selected Poems (1997), his first book in 20 years. The autobiographical poem "Scattered Vignettes" opens that volume and delineates some of what Lima went through as a child: "My first arrest took place in junior high school: / a gun . . . My life was rehabs, / Arrests and jails / Crabs / Syphilis / Hepatitis / And finally / The mad houses."

When asked about his influences, Lima names ROBERT LOWELL, ALLEN GINSBERG, KENNETH KOCH, and perhaps most profoundly, FRANK O'HARA, with whom Lima took a class at the New School. "Frank was the mentor that taught me to take chances in poetry," Lima recalled, "and to be free and enjoy writing it . . . that art was the ultimate experience, and that it should be luxurious and fun" (n.p.). Some of the fun they had together is on record in "Love on the Hoof," a script they wrote collaboratively around 1963 for a film project by ANDY WARHOL that never materialized (LeSueur xxiv). In spring 1963 O'Hara invited Lima and TONY TOWLE to share his apartment on East 9th Street after O'Hara and Joe LeSueur had decided to move to Broadway. In *Memoir* Towle describes the nervousness that he and Lima shared at their first public reading in April 1963 at the Smolin Gallery on 57th Street, in the company of fellow students JIM BRODEY and ALLAN KAPLAN and their mentors, O'Hara and Koch (Towle 59–61).

Though he was acquainted with many of its artists and writers, Lima prefers not to be thought of as a New York School poet, saying, "I do not align my lifestyle or work with the second generation New York School. However, I feel privileged to know them as part of that time. I have, over the years, stayed in contact with many of them and their outstanding and innovative work that continues to be contributory to modern American poetry" (n.p.).

Lima has published five books of poetry, including *Inventory* (TIBOR DE NAGY GALLERY, 1964); *Underground with the Oriole* (Dutton, 1971); *Angel: New Poems* (Norton, 1976); *Inventory: New and Selected Poems*, edited and introduced by DAVID SHAPIRO (Hard Press, 1997); and *The Beatitudes* (Hard Press, 2001). He conducts writing workshops at the POETRY PROJECT AT ST. MARK'S CHURCH IN-THE-BOWERY and is a chef instructor at the New York Restaurant School.

Bibliography

LeSueur, Joe. Introduction (1978). In *Amorous Nightmares of Delay: Selected Plays,* by Frank O'Hara, xv–xxv. Baltimore, Md.: Johns Hopkins University Press, 1997.

Lima, Frank. Interview by Guillermo Parra (2001). Venepoetics Blogspot. Available online. URL: http://interviewfranklima.blogspot.com/. Accessed December 18, 2008.

O'Hara, Frank, and Frank Lima. "Love on the Hoof." In *Amorous Nightmares of Delay: Selected Plays,* by Frank O'Hara 173–176. Baltimore, Md.: Johns Hopkins University Press, 1997.

Towle, Tony. *Memoir, 1960–1963.* Cambridge, Mass.: Faux Press, 2001.

Lines (1964–1965)

For the second generation of the NEW YORK SCHOOL, the six issues of ARAM SAROYAN's mimeograph magazine *Lines* carry a weight of influence far greater than their number. While it was valuable for Saroyan to connect through the magazine with the nucleus of the second generation already forming around TED BERRIGAN, that group, recently arrived from Tulsa, Oklahoma, must also have found validation through association with Saroyan, a native New Yorker whose father, William Saroyan, was a famous writer and who had already published in *Poetry* magazine. In addition to publishing Berrigan, RON PADGETT, DICK GALLUP, TOM VEITCH, and JOSEPH CERAVOLO, *Lines* remained open to a wider literary world by publishing such writers as CHARLES OLSON, Lorine Niedecker, and WILLIAM S. BURROUGHS. At the same time, early work by CLARK COOLIDGE and Robert Grenier, along with Saroyan's own "minimalist" experiments, seemed to point in a new direction that eventually emerged as LANGUAGE POETRY.

Coolidge's association with *Lines* is of particular significance. Saroyan and Coolidge met as magazine editors at a conference on little magazines sponsored by the Library of Congress in Washington, D.C., in April 1965 (Coolidge was editing *Joglars* out of PROVIDENCE, RHODE ISLAND). The subsequent appearance of Coolidge's work in the final issue of *Lines* (November 1965) attracted the attention of readers such as LEWIS WARSH, who "felt an immediate rush of recognition" (xxvi). That rush became part of the impetus for ANGEL HAIR magazine, which Warsh and ANNE WALDMAN launched in 1966, picking up, in a sense, where *Lines* left off. Meanwhile, from 1965 to 1967 Saroyan published a series of pamphlets under the Lines imprint, including Coolidge's first collection, *Flag Flutter and U.S. Electric* (1966), and a second pamphlet entitled simply *Clark Coolidge* (1967). Saroyan's *Works* (1966), also issued in the Lines series, became the occasion for "the first unequivocally positive response I'd gotten in the media," the author recalled (*Street* 104). The review appeared in the *Boston Globe Sunday Magazine* shortly after Saroyan had taken up residence in Cambridge, Massachusetts, in a house he shared with Coolidge.

Bibliography

Clay, Steven, and Rodney Phillips. *A Secret Location on the Lower East Side: Adventures in Writing, 1960–1980*. New York: New York Public Library/Granary Books, 1998.

Dworkin, Craig, ed. Eclipse Web site. Available online. URL: http://english.utah.edu/eclipse/projects/. [Includes facsimile edition of *Lines* magazine.] Accessed December 18, 2008.

Saroyan, Aram. *Friends in the World: The Education of a Writer*. Minneapolis, Minn.: Coffee House Press, 1992.

———. *The Street: An Autobiographical Novel*. Lenox, Mass.: Bookstore Press, 1974.

Warsh, Lewis. Introduction to *The Angel Hair Anthology*. New York: Granary Books, 2001, xix–xxvii.

list poem   *See* GENRE.

Little Caesar (1977–1984)

DENNIS COOPER began *Little Caesar* in Los Angeles in 1977 as a saddle-stitched "punk poetry zine," but by its sixth issue, in which a brief note about its first impetus appeared, the magazine had become the meeting place for young poets on the East Coast as well as the West Coast who savored the milieu of an editor who was unashamedly enamored of pop culture. Blending Cooper's enthusiasm for maverick PUNK ROCK musicians and new-wave bands,

Little Caesar magazine was soon accompanied by a similarly named imprint that issued a flurry of titles. Little Caesar Press solidified Cooper's alliance with young writers in NEW YORK CITY, CHICAGO, and Los Angeles whose artistic genealogies included affiliations with diverse increments of the NEW YORK SCHOOL of poets. In launching and sustaining the magazine and press in a region of the country not best known for its poets, Cooper found inspiration in a renaissance of poetry in Los Angeles that included notable magazines such as *Invisible City, Bachy, Beyond Baroque New,* and *Momentum*. With a self-assurance that belied his youth, Cooper began churning out substantial issues of cultural commentary and poetry and prose by JAMES SCHUYLER, TIM DLUGOS, Steve Hall, Brad Gooch, and TED GREENWALD. Typical covers of *Little Caesar* issues featured Iggy Pop or gay film star Eric Emerson.

Independent literary presses tend to favor whichever coast they happen to be located on, but Cooper's affection for the New York School enabled Little Caesar Press to develop a book list that perhaps indirectly provides an estimate of how thoroughly the New York School by the late 1970s had managed to influence young poets on a national level. Not only did Cooper publish books by poets from Los Angeles such as AMY GERSTLER and DAVID TRINIDAD, who would go on to appear in anthologies edited by ANNE WALDMAN (*Out of This World*), but Cooper also published substantial collections by poets such as LEWIS MACADAMS, TOM CLARK, and PETER SCHJELDAHL as well as MICHAEL LALLY, ELAINE EQUI, Dlugos, and EILEEN MYLES.

The peak years of production for Little Caesar Press were 1979 through 1982, during which Cooper published 18 titles, including one major anthology, *Coming Attractions* (1980). In his brief introduction to *Coming Attractions*, Cooper notes that the book developed out of the insistence by Dlugos that "the younger poets of his hometown New York City had now attained an identity separate from the generation of poets before, that known both affectionately and disparagingly as 'the (third generation) New York School.'" In 1984 Cooper left Los Angeles for New York, and although he issued a large, attractively designed catalog that encapsulated in a pictorial fashion Little Caesar's backlist of books and magazines that seemed to promise continued production, Little Caesar ceased operations, and Cooper concentrated on his own writing.

Bibliography

Cooper, Dennis, ed. *Introduction. Coming Attraction: An Anthology of American Poets in their Twenties.* Los Angeles, Calif.: Little Caesar, 1980.

Living at the Movies Jim Carroll (1973)

The title of JIM CARROLL's collection *Living at the Movies* blurs the boundary between life and art, a characteristic of postmodern art in general and of NEW YORK SCHOOL poetry in particular. Carroll's choice of movies as the representative art is characteristic of the second-generation poets in contrast to the first generation, whose paradigm was painting. A related distinction is the new importance that drugs assumed for the second-generation poets as a means of altering perception; in fact, the poems collected in Carroll's book refer to drugs much more explicitly than to movies, which function rather as an implied metaphor of drug-induced experience (Carter).

As if to acknowledge his roots in the New York School tradition, Carroll opens the volume with "Blue Poles," the title of a painting by JACKSON POLLOCK. The significance of the poem's setting, on a beach in winter, is illuminated in a separately published journal entry, in which Carroll describes his admiration for "the blue clarity of winter" as represented by the horizon line viewed from a beach. Each perception in this context is distinct in itself, "as if the cold froze each frame of moving film." Carroll says he could stare at the horizon line all day just as "I can stare at Pollock or read Frank [O'Hara]'s poems all day" (*Forced Entries* 31).

In contrast to this desire for the frozen frame, Carroll is equally attracted to moving images: "they'll be gone eventually / and new forms will take shape" ("Styro," *Fear* 9). His guide in this direction is TED BERRIGAN, to whom the title poem of *Living at the Movies* is dedicated. Carroll's poem is constructed on the model of Berrigan's SONNETS, intersplicing lines as an editor works with film clips and producing a dizzying effect of repetition within movement, "reaching for a particular moment / to reoccur,"

as Carroll describes the effect in another poem, "Heroin" (*Fear* 22). Berrigan also wrote a "Heroin" poem, which was published along with Carroll's in the same issue of the *PARIS REVIEW* (number 48, fall 1969). Read together, the two poems represent the ambivalence of drug experience in relation to the aesthetic possibilities that Carroll and Berrigan were exploring. Carroll's experience resembles the fixity of the beach in "Blue Poles"—"Sat for three days in a white room" (*Fear* 21)—whereas Berrigan's moves impatiently beyond the horizon:

> I'm going
> way over
> the white
> skyline (223).

In a review of *Living at the Movies* in *Poetry* magazine, GERARD MALANGA expressed a preference for "the fast kind of poetry," such as Carroll's haiku-like "A Fragment." In Malanga's judgment, "Carroll's poems are not so perfect as O'Hara's nor is his vision so intense," but "his range is wider" (165)—an assertion perhaps of those traits that Carroll shares with other second-generation poets. Their presence in Carroll's work creates the impression of a coterie that distinguishes New York School poetry in general. Or, as Malanga states, using an odd choice of metaphor, "[H]is poems are irrigated by friends, by his own kind and consanguinity" (164). A couple of the poems in *Living at the Movies* are in fact COLLABORATIONs, for instance, "Growing Up" (with Berrigan and BILL BERKSON).

Living at the Movies was published in 1973 by Grossman, a trade house with a distinguished list in experimental poetry. A painting by LARRY RIVERS was reproduced on the cover. The volume was dedicated to Devereaux Carson, a girlfriend of Carroll's who is addressed by name in the poem "Gliding." Five poems in *Living at the Movies* had appeared in Carroll's previous pamphlet, *4 Ups & 1 Down* (ANGEL HAIR, 1970), and a number of others had appeared in New York School magazines such as *ADVENTURES IN POETRY,* "*C*," *TELEPHONE,* and *The WORLD.* Penguin published a second edition of *Living at the Movies* in 1981, with Rivers's painting replaced on the cover by a large photo of Carroll, now a rock MUSIC celebrity.

Bibliography

Berrigan, Ted. "Heroin" (1969). In *The Collected Poems of Ted Berrigan*. Edited by Alice Notley, Anselm Berrigan, and Edmund Berrigan. Berkeley: University of California Press, 2005, 222–223.

Carroll, Jim. *Fear of Dreaming: Selected Poems*. New York: Penguin, 1993.

———. *Forced Entries: The Downtown Diaries, 1971–1973*. New York: Penguin, 1987.

Carter, Cassie. "The Sickness That Takes Years to Perfect: Jim Carroll's Alchemical Vision." *Dionysos: The Literature and Addiction. TriQuarterly* 6, no. 1 (winter 1996): 6–19.

Malanga, Gerard. "Traveling & Living." *Poetry* 125, no. 3 (1974): 162–165.

Living Theatre (1948–)

Founded by Julian Beck (1925–85) and Judith Malina (1926–) in 1948, the year they were married, the Living Theatre led the way in the development of avant-garde THEATER in postwar NEW YORK CITY. The NEW YORK SCHOOL poets were present from the beginning, encouraged by their acquaintance with PAUL GOODMAN, whose plays were among the works most frequently performed by the Living Theatre in its early years. The first production by the Living Theatre in a standard theater space, Gertrude Stein's *Doctor Faustus Lights the Lights* at the Cherry Lane Theatre in Greenwich Village in 1951, made an impression on JOHN ASHBERY as "one of the most beautiful things I've ever seen on the stage" ("Poet in the Theater" 18). During the following year Ashbery and FRANK O'HARA performed as two dogs in Pable Picasso's *Desire Trapped by the Tail*, and Ashbery's play *The HEROES* received its premier production, with Beck and Malina performing in principal roles (photo in Tytell). *The Heroes*, full of homosexual innuendo and even presenting a brief DANCE scene between men, was on a double bill with Alfred Jarry's *Ubu Roi*, whose language was apparently still as scandalous to some as it had been when first performed in 1896. Citing fire-code violations, authorities closed the theater building, the first of several instances of government harassment that the Living Theatre has faced throughout its history.

After some years uptown in a converted loft near Columbia University, the Living Theatre moved to a building on the fringes of Greenwich Village, at the intersection of Sixth Avenue and 14th Street, where William Carlos Williams's *Many Loves* opened in January 1959. Jack Gelber's *The Connection*, which opened in July of that year, finally made the breakthrough that Beck and Malina had been working toward by removing all barriers between the reality lived by the audience and the reality performed by the actors. Many left the theater wondering whether they had been watching actors or "real" drug addicts. Following this direction would eventually take the Living Theatre not only off the stage but literally into the streets. For the time being, however, the Living Theatre continued to provide a home for "poetic" plays. As part of a special series of Monday night productions, separate from the main repertory, O'Hara's *Loves Labor* and KENNETH KOCH's *Bertha* premiered together in December 1959. Beck and Malina also encouraged the use of their building for a variety of other events that helped connect members of the avant-garde in all the arts. A famous scene of JACK KEROUAC heckling O'Hara occurred at a reading O'Hara gave with GREGORY CORSO at the Living Theatre in March 1959 (Gooch 322–323). O'Hara returned to participate in benefit readings for *A New Folder* in June and for *YŪGEN* in November (photos in Berkson and LeSueur 71).

Koch's *The Election*, both a political satire and a parody of *The Connection*, was produced at the Living Theatre just before the presidential election of November 1960, in which John F. Kennedy defeated Richard M. Nixon (played, respectively, by poet BILL BERKSON and playwright Arnold Weinstein in Koch's work). However, the New York School poets diverged from the Living Theatre as the latter engaged in more aggressive political activism, including a series of general strikes against cold war militarism (1962–63) and a brutal depiction of a marine corps detention center in Kenneth Brown's play, *The Brig* (1963). A reading that Ashbery conducted from the set of *The Brig* in September 1963 (Howard 39–41; Wolf 86) marked an important homecoming for the New York School poets (Ashbery was still based in Paris) but simultaneously a leave-taking for the theater, which was closed by IRS agents the following month, ostensibly for tax violations. From 1964 to 1984 the Living Theatre operated mainly outside the United States. Beck died in 1985, the year after the Living Theatre returned to New York. In 1988 Malina married Hanon Reznikoff (1949–2008), a member of the company. She continues to run the Living Theatre.

Bibliography

Ashbery, John. *The Heroes.* In *Three Plays.* Calais, Vt.: Z Press, 1978, 1–29.

———. "Poet in the Theater." *Performing Arts Journal 3,* no. 3 (Winter 1979): 15–37.

Berkson, Bill, and Joe LeSueur, eds. *Homage to Frank O'Hara.* Bolinas, Calif.: Big Sky, 1988.

Gooch, Brad. *City Poet: The Life and Times of Frank O'Hara.* New York: Knopf, 1993.

Howard, Richard. "John Ashbery." In *Alone with America: Essays on the Art of Poetry in the United States Since 1950.* Enlarged ed. New York: Atheneum, 1980, 25–56.

Koch, Kenneth. *The Election.* In *A Change of Hearts: Plays, Films, and Other Dramatic Works.* New York: Random House, 1973, 114–129.

LeSueur, Joe. "Our First Theatre of Cruelty." *Kulchur 3,* no. 11 (Autumn 1963): 17–19.

O'Hara, Frank. *Loves Labor, an Eclogue.* In *Amorous Nightmares of Delay: Selected Plays.* Baltimore, Md.: Johns Hopkins University Press, 1997. 155–161.

Tytell, John. *The Living Theatre: Art, Exile, and Outrage.* New York: Grove, 1995.

Wolf, Reva. *Andy Warhol, Poetry, and Gossip in the 1960s.* Chicago: University of Chicago Press, 1997.

Locus Solus (1961–1962)

The first generation of NEW YORK SCHOOL poets took their first shot at editing their own magazine in *Locus Solus,* a title that marks a private space both in its meaning (solitary place) and its derivation. It alludes to a 1914 novel of the same title by RAYMOND ROUSSEL, the obscure French author whose work provided a secret meeting ground for the New York School poets. The idea for the magazine originated with HARRY MATHEWS and JOHN ASHBERY, both living in France at the time. Mathews was able to provide funding through a recent inheritance, but otherwise his interest in the magazine was principally devoted to seeing installments of his novel *The CONVERSIONS* published in the first three issues, though the final issue (number 5, 1962) also contains his poem "The Ring" and his TRANSLATION of a portion of Roussel's *Locus Solus.* Ashbery provided editorial leadership by assembling a "Double Issue of New Poetry" (numbers 3–4, winter 1962) and recruiting JAMES SCHUYLER and KENNETH KOCH to edit other issues. Koch's "Special Collaborations Issue" (number 2, summer 1961) remains a significant reference point for the practice that has become a defining feature of New York School poetry. Schuyler's issues, the first and last (number 1, winter 1961; number 5, 1962), are miscellaneous but nevertheless formed by a deliberate intention to represent a group identity as Schuyler conceived it. In soliciting a contribution from his longtime friend Chester Kallman (1921–75), whose work appeared in the final issue, Schuyler explained that "part of the unstated objective" of *Locus Solus* was to offer "a riposte at *The New American Poetry* [1960], which has so thoroughly misrepresented so many of us" (it did not represent Kallman at all) (*Just the Thing* 129).

As a correction or supplement to *The NEW AMERICAN POETRY, 1945–1960,* the most important contributions of *Locus Solus* are the re-introduction of EDWIN DENBY (represented in the first issue by nine sonnets from MEDITERRANEAN CITIES [1956]) and the forecasting of Ashbery's "experimental" turn in poems later collected in *The Tennis Court Oath* (1962; "The New Realism," *Locus Solus* 3–4) and *Rivers and Mountains* (1966; "Into the Dusk-Charged Air," *Locus Solus* 5). The poets' work in prose is also represented in Schuyler's "Current Events" (*Locus Solus* 1); an early installment of the collaborative novel by Schuyler and Ashbery, *A NEST OF NINNIES* (*Locus Solus* 2); and Denby's memoir "The Thirties" (*Locus Solus* 5). The representation of the first-generation New York School poets in *Locus Solus* is completed with work by KENWARD ELMSLIE, BARBARA GUEST, Koch, and FRANK O'HARA. The second generation begins to emerge with names that were to become prominent (BILL BERKSON, TED BERRIGAN, JOSEPH CERAVOLO, JOHN PERREAULT) and some others who had connected with Koch and O'Hara through their workshops at the New School (Jean Boudin, ALLAN KAPLAN, RUTH KRAUSS). Another workshop student, Michael Benedikt (1935–), though not usually associated with the New York School, made his closest connection in the context of *Locus Solus,* assuming the title of managing editor for the final issue.

Although handsomely printed on fine paper (5 × 7 inch format), *Locus Solus* was not illustrated. It included writing by various authors with ties to the visual arts that were so important to New York School poetry. FAIRFIELD PORTER (and his wife, Anne), Robert Dash (a painter friend of the Porters), Musa McKim (the wife of PHILIP GUSTON), LARRY RIVERS, and HAROLD ROSENBERG all contributed poems. RUDOLPH BURCKHARDT published *Love in Three Acts: A Swiss Play* (*Locus Solus* 1). Using the FORM of a play, JANE FREILICHER and Koch assigned lines to various parts of "The Car" (*Locus Solus* 2) in a demonstration of collaboration on several levels. In the final issue, poems by GERARD MALANGA and Piero Heliczer (1937–93) signal the ANDY WARHOL circle that would expand throughout the coming decade to take in many New York School poets.

Bibliography

Burckhardt, Rudy. *Love in Three Acts: A Swiss Play.* In *Mobile Homes.* Edited by Kenward Elmslie. Calais, Vt.: Z Press, 1979, 109–116.

Clay, Steven, and Rodney Phillips. "*Locus Solus.*" In *A Secret Location on the Lower East Side: Adventures in Writing, 1960–1980.* New York: New York Public Library/Granary Books, 1998, 169.

Denby, Edwin. "The Thirties." In *Dance Writings and Poetry.* Edited by Robert Cornfield. New Haven, Conn.: Yale University Press, 1998, 1–5.

Freilicher, Jane, and Kenneth Koch. "The Car." In *Saints of Hysteria: A Half-Century of Collaborative American Poetry,* edited by Denise Duhamel, Maureen Seaton, and David Trinidad, 12. Brooklyn, N.Y.: Soft Skull Press, 2007.

Roussel, Raymond. "*Locus Solus,* Chapter 1." Translated by Harry Mathews. In *How I Wrote Certain of My Books and Other Writings.* Edited by Trevor Winkfield. Boston: Exact Change, 1995, 57–78.

Sawyer-Lauçanno, Christopher. "*Locus Solus et Socii:* Harry Mathews and John Ashbery." In *The Continual Pilgrimage: American Writers in Paris, 1944–1960.* San Francisco: City Lights, 1992, 233–259.

Schuyler, James. "Current Events." In *The Home Book: Prose and Poems, 1951–1970.* Edited by Trevor Winkfield. Calais, Vt.: Z Press, 1977, 75–82.

———. *Just the Thing: Selected Letters of James Schuyler, 1951–1991.* Edited by William Corbett. New York: Turtle Point Press, 2004.

love poem   *See* GENRE.

Lowell, Robert (1917–1977)

The name of Robert Lowell symbolized the literary establishment that NEW YORK SCHOOL poets sought either to oppose or to ignore. Through his distinguished BOSTON family he was related to the 19th-century poet James Russell Lowell and the modernist Amy Lowell. After transferring from Harvard— an early sign of rebellion against his heritage—he literally went to school with the New Critics, with John Crowe Ransom at Kenyon College (1937–40) and with Cleanth Brooks and Robert Penn Warren at Louisiana State University (1940–41). His work quickly won critical acclaim and honors such as the Pulitzer Prize, awarded to his second collection, *Lord Weary's Castle* (Harcourt, Brace, 1946). By the time of the ANTHOLOGY *The New Poets of England and America* (Meridian, 1957), a selection from Lowell was an inevitable and principal exhibit. It may have prompted FRANK O'HARA's parody "A Web of Saints Near the Sea" (1957).

At the same time Lowell undertook a radical change in style to advance an autobiographical project that was eventually published as *Life Studies* (Farrar, Straus and Cudahy, 1959), a volume that proved to be crucial not only in Lowell's career but also in literary history. It became the touchstone for identifying the work of other poets—notably, John Berryman (1914–72), W. D. Snodgrass (1926–2009), Sylvia Plath (1932–63), and Anne Sexton (1928–74)—as *confessional poetry,* a term introduced by the critic M. L. Rosenthal (1917–96) in a review of *Life Studies.* The willingness to reveal ugly truths about the poet's life and mind may have been encouraged by Beat expressionism; Lowell admitted that a reading tour of the West Coast in 1957 encouraged him to loosen up his style to meet the expectations of audiences attuned to Beat performance (Axelrod 99–100). However, in contrast to the BEATS, Lowell and the other confessional poets typically employ a tight formal structure to maintain dramatic tension between the life revealed and the means of revelation.

In Lowell's work FORM functions less organically than it was supposed to do in the NEW AMERICAN POETRY, whether Beat, Black Mountain (see BLACK MOUNTAIN POETS), or New York School. That is the first difference between Lowell's confessionalism and O'Hara's "PERSONISM," defined in the same year as *Life Studies*. A second difference is that Personism, as O'Hara describes it, is a by-product of sexual energy and the experience of being in love, whereas sterility and the failure of love are as fundamental to Lowell's confessionalism as they are to T. S. Eliot's *The Waste Land* (1922). Referring to "Skunk Hour," the concluding poem in *Life Studies*, O'Hara objected, "I don't think that anyone has to get themselves to go and watch lovers in a parking lot necking in order to write a poem, and I don't see why it's admirable if they feel guilty about it. They should feel guilty. Why are they snooping?" (O'Hara, interview 13).

An encounter now enshrined in New York School legend (Gooch, photo following page 270) took place between Lowell and O'Hara in February 1962 at a joint reading at Wagner College, site of the NEW YORK CITY WRITERS CONFERENCE, in which Lowell had participated the previous summer. O'Hara's reading included "Poem (Lana Turner has collapsed)," which he had written on the way to Wagner College that day in response to a newspaper headline. Lowell began his portion of the reading by remarking wryly that he did not compose so spontaneously. Joe LeSueur, one of the sources of this anecdote (xvi), has tried to correct the idea that O'Hara intended "to tweak Lowell's nose in public" (Lehman 349; LeSueur 265), but each poet's stance was so different that it is difficult simply to describe either one without seeming to imply criticism of the other. Thus, when JOHN ASHBERY stated, in his memorial tribute to O'Hara, that his poetry "does not speak out against the war in Vietnam" (81), Louis Simpson (1923–   ) read the observation as "sneering at the conscience of others," among whom Lowell had made himself prominent when he refused an invitation to the White House in 1965 (Lehman 308–309). In fact, during the 1960s, when NEW YORK CITY was Lowell's principal place of residence, he and his wife, Elizabeth Hardwick (1916–2007), helped to redefine the image of the New York intellectual as members of the group of writers who gathered around the *New York Review of Books,* founded in 1963. The tone of the public intellectual resonates in the titles of Lowell's collections *For the Union Dead* (Farrar, Straus and Giroux, 1964) and *History* (Farrar, Straus and Giroux, 1973).

In the work of second- and third-generation New York School poets, the titles of Lowell's books and even his name float on the surface, as if to deny the possibility of any further similarity. TED BERRIGAN's "Near the Ocean" (1967), echoing the title of Lowell's 1967 volume (Farrar, Straus and Giroux), mocks Lowell's characteristic mode of complaint as crabbiness, playing on the image of a creature that dwells in the ocean. PETER SCHJELDAHL's "Life Studies" (1968) admits that life is always "being / Bungled by someone," but concludes "on the whole / It is quite intricate and entertaining" (395). In the poem "On His Name" (1973), TONY TOWLE presumes a possible kinship with Lowell on the grounds that their last names sound alike, but the Lowell he imagines meeting simply manifests impatience to get out of Towle's poem. Writing "On the Death of Robert Lowell" (1977), EILEEN MYLES offers a punk response—"I don't give a shit" (28)—which seems to concur with the judgment that Schjeldahl had pronounced more formally while Lowell was still alive: "Robert Lowell is the least distinguished poet alive" ("To the National Arts Council" 390). Less harsh judgments were to follow, however. DAVID SHAPIRO attempted a balanced comparison of Lowell and O'Hara: "Lowell's diction determines an approach to things which is serious and heavy and committed. O'Hara's diction determines a corresponding freedom" (n.p.). Similarly, DAVID LEHMAN tips the balance in favor of O'Hara in the third edition of *The Oxford Book of American Poetry* (Oxford University Press, 2006), which represents Lowell with only nine poems and O'Hara with 15, concluding with "Poem (Lana Turner has collapsed)."

Bibliography

Ashbery, John. "Writers and Issues: Frank O'Hara's Question" (1966). In *Selected Prose*. Edited by Eugene Richie. Ann Arbor: University of Michigan Press, 2004, 80–83.

Axelrod, Steven Gould. *Robert Lowell: Life and Art*. Princeton, N.J.: Princeton University Press, 1978.

Berrigan, Ted. "Near the Ocean" (1967). In *The Collected Poems of Ted Berrigan*. Edited by Alice Notley, Anselm Berrigan, and Edmund Berrigan. Berkeley: University of California Press, 2005, 328.

Gooch, Brad. *City Poet: The Life and Times of Frank O'Hara*. New York: Knopf, 1993.

Lehman, David. *The Last Avant-Garde: The Making of the New York School of Poets*. New York: Doubleday, 1998.

LeSueur, Joe. *Digressions on Some Poems by Frank O'Hara: A Memoir*. New York: Farrar, Straus & Giroux, 2003.

Lowell, Robert. *Collected Poems*. Edited by Frank Bidart and David Gewanter. New York: Farrar, Straus & Giroux, 2003.

Myles, Eileen. "On the Death of Robert Lowell." In *A Fresh Young Voice from the Plains*. New York: Power Mad Press, 1981, 28.

O'Hara, Frank. Interview by Edward Lucie-Smith (1965). In *Standing Still and Walking in New York*. Edited by Donald Allen. San Francisco: Grey Fox, 1983, 3–26.

———. "Poem (Lana Turner has collapsed)" (1962). In *The Collected Poems*. Rev. ed. Edited by Donald Allen. Berkeley: University of California Press, 1995, 449.

———. "A Web of Saints Near the Sea (Lowell)" (1957). In *Poems Retrieved*. Rev. ed. Edited by Donald Allen. San Francisco: Grey Fox, 1996, 180–181.

Perloff, Marjorie. *The Poetic Art of Robert Lowell*. Ithaca, N.Y.: Cornell University Press, 1973.

Rosenthal, M. L. *The New Poets: American and British Poets Since World War II*. New York: Oxford University Press, 1967.

———. "Poetry as Confession." *The Nation* 189, no. 8 (19 September 1959): 154–155.

Schjeldahl, Peter. "Life Studies" (1968). In *An Anthology of New York Poets*, edited by Ron Padgett and David Shapiro, 394–395. New York: Vintage/Random House, 1970.

———. "To the National Arts Council" (1968). In *An Anthology of New York Poets*, edited by Ron Padgett and David Shapiro, 390, 393. New York: Vintage/Random House, 1970.

Shapiro, David. Interview by John Tranter (1984). *Jacket* 23 (August 2003). Available online. URL: http://jacket magazine.com/23/shap-iv.html. Accessed December 18, 2008.

Towle, Tony. "On His Name" (1973). In *The History of the Invitation: New and Selected Poems, 1963–2000*. Brooklyn, N.Y.: Hanging Loose Press, 2001, 109.

Lower East Side   *See* DOWNTOWN MANHATTAN.

Luis Armed Story, The   Tom Veitch (1978)

"This will be a strange novel" (25), warns one of the characters in *The Luis Armed Story*, and the author, TOM VEITCH, identifies the strangeness by placing his own name in a list of American writers who are presented as reincarnations of "certain prematurely deceased Dadaists" (60). In particular, Veitch follows WILLIAM BURROUGHS in employing the dadaist technique of assembling new texts out of "cut-up" bits of old texts. Besides employing this procedure literally, Veitch creates a pastiche of several popular GENRES, from crime FICTION to the comic book—the latter a genre that Veitch had turned to professionally by the time *The Luis Armed Story* was published by Full Court Press in 1978.

Rather than following a continuous narrative line, *The Luis Armed Story* revolves in "cyclic" fashion around three central characters: Luis, his brother Robert(o), and their sister and/or Luis's wife, Rosa (the suggestion of incest is one of the book's several assaults on sexual taboos). Their Hispanic background (located variously in Mexico or Puerto Rico) and possible Indian ancestry confer on the Armed family the aura of the *fellaheen*, or native underclass, whom Burroughs and JACK KEROUAC idealized. Of the stories that get told and retold about them throughout the book, some have historical relevance. For instance, the Armed brothers are arrested at the inauguration of President Lyndon Johnson in 1965. Others, such as a long episode set in a monastery, can be traced to the life of the author, who was a Benedictine monk from 1965 to 1968. All of the stories, to judge from the introduction ascribed fictitiously to C. G. Jung, are assumed to have some fundamental meaning relevant to Jung's theories of unconscious archetypes. However, rather than moving in the direction of psychic integration, the main thrust of the novel is toward the disintegration of normal consciousness, fueled by the constant explosion of apocalyptic religious imagery.

If Veitch's religious sensibility aligns him with a Beat writer like Kerouac, his comic sensibility is in the spirit of a NEW YORK SCHOOL writer such as KENNETH KOCH. As in Koch, popular culture and the absurd mingle when Veitch literalizes the biblical image of the stones crying out while Luis Armed delivers an apocalyptic sermon. A stone rolls into the room and takes its place at the head of the table, demanding something to eat. Most unprophetically, it explains, "Cornflakes will do" (143). In a later scene Luis encounters Bugs Bunny and Daffy Duck playing tennis in a parking lot. Daffy delivers what amounts to Veitch's invitation to the reader of his novel: "I had this big dream for you—you can be in it if you want to!" (190).

Bibliography

Veitch, Tom. *The Luis Armed Story*. New York: Full Court Press, 1978.

Lyons, Kimberly (1958–   )

Kimberly Lyons is one of the first NEW YORK SCHOOL poets to manifest in her close-grained and linguistically charged work the multiplicity of the school as it merged with other experimental movements in the 1980s. As a result, she has been an essential part of reworking and expanding the definition of a "New York School" poet, work that continues today through her participation in the ongoing Situations chapbook series.

Born in Tucson, Arizona, and raised in CHICAGO, ILLINOIS, where she studied with PAUL HOOVER, Lyons came to NEW YORK CITY at a time when groups such as the Language school, performance poets, and the NUYORICAN POETS CAFÉ were coalescing, which she witnessed firsthand through her role as program coordinator at the POETRY PROJECT AT ST. MARK'S CHURCH IN-THE-BOWERY from 1987 to 1991 and as the coeditor of *Red Weather* magazine and Prospect Books with her husband, the poet MITCH HIGHFILL.

Lyons counts among her influences (and in many cases as friends) BERNADETTE MAYER, LEWIS WARSH, JOHN ASHBERY, ANNE WALDMAN, ALICE NOTLEY, FRANK O'HARA, MAUREEN OWEN, JOHN YAU, and other New York School poets from all generations. In her essay "The Itineraries of Anticipation," she helped name the succeeding generations of women poets of the New York School. However, her work also remains strongly marked by her long friendship with her teacher Robert Kelly (1935–   ) at Bard College and her interest in the poets Robert Duncan (1919–88) and Gerrit Lansing (1928–   ). Their influences can be seen in Lyons's linguistic apprehensions of worlds within the quotidian world: Ordinary objects and ordinary words are animated by her intense sensibility of their visible and invisible potentialities. Of her book *Abracadabra* (Granary, 2000), Mark Wallace in *Rain Taxi* writes: "[A]ny notion of ourselves as subjective immediately must reckon with the way our consciousness is also created by the things we live among" (n.p.). Lyons's books include *6 Poems* (Lines, 1982), *Strategies* (Prospect Books, 1983), *Oxygen* (Northern Lights/Brooklyn Series, 1991), *In Padua* (St. Lazaire Press, 1991), *Mettle* (with images by Ed Epping, Granary, 1996), *Hemisphere's Planetarium Petals and Three Algonquins* (Situations, 1999), *A Poem for Posada* (Situations, 2001), and *Saline* (Instance, 2005).

Bibliography

Borkhuis, Charles. Review of *Hemisphere's Planetarium Petals. Poetry Project Newsletter* 179 (April–May 2000): 22.

Lyons, Kimberly. "The Itineraries of Anticipation (Women and the Poetry Project)." *Readme* 1 (Fall 1999). Available online. URL: http://home.jps.net/~nada/lyons.htm. Accessed December 19, 2008.

Wallace, Mark. Review of *Abracadbra. Rain Taxi* (Spring 2000). Available online. URL: http://www.rain taxi.com/online/2000spring/lyons.shtml. Accessed December 19, 2008.

Warsh, Lewis. Review of *Abracadabra. Poetry Project Newsletter* 179 (April–May 2000): 21–22.

lyric   *See* GENRE.

M

Maas, Willard (1911–1971)

A poet, filmmaker, and bohemian, Willard Maas was most conspicuous within NEW YORK SCHOOL circles during the period 1958 to 1963, when he taught English at Wagner College on Staten Island, New York; served as faculty adviser to the WAGNER LITERARY MAGAZINE; and hosted the NEW YORK CITY WRITERS CONFERENCE on the Wagner campus. However, for a much longer period, more than two decades, Maas and his wife, Marie Menken (1909–70), made their rooftop apartment in Brooklyn Heights into a social center for New York artists and intellectuals. One party in 1962 represents an iconic moment, when Charles Henri Ford, editor of the surrealist magazine *View* of the 1940s, introduced ANDY WARHOL, about to become the superstar pop artist of the 1960s (Warhol and Hackett 25–26). The continuity was provided by gay subculture, in which Maas, with Menken's full permission, engaged flamboyantly. Conducted by Maas, the opening for a show of Menken's paintings at the TIBOR DE NAGY GALLERY in 1951 entered into gay mythology as a gang bang (Myers 117–118).

Maas was born in Lindsay, California, but during the 1930s he settled in NEW YORK CITY, where he married Menken in 1936 and resumed college coursework, eventually earning a B.A. from Long Island University in 1938. That same year he received *Poetry* magazine's Guarantors Prize (awarded the previous year to W. H. AUDEN) and published his second collection of poetry, *Concerning the Young* (Farrar & Rinehart). His first collection, *Fire Testament* (1935), had been issued by Ronald Lane Latimer's Alcestis Press, publisher of Wallace Stevens and William Carlos Williams. Despite these auspicious beginnings Maas's production of poems dwindled after 1940, but he began a series of experimental "film poems" that earned him a reputation as "one of the most important pioneers of the avant-garde film" (Mekas 287). The first of these, *Geography of the Body* (1943), includes ironic commentary composed and read by the British poet George Barker (1913–91), whose "neoromantic" style represents the category to which Maas's verse is usually assigned (Myers 117). The last collection published during his lifetime, a special section of the final issue of the *Wagner Literary Magazine* (number 4, 1963–64), confirms the aptness of this designation: "And all the troubled history of love speaks the poem" ("The Arrow's Mark"). Though his style looked to the past, Maas's passion for experiment and for youth made him receptive to the new work of the New York School.

Bibliography

Brakhage, Stan. "Marie Menken." In *Film at Wit's End: Eight Avant-Garde Film Filmmakers.* Kingston, N.Y.: McPherson, 2001, 32–47.

Crase, Douglas. *Both: A Portrait in Two Parts.* New York: Pantheon, 2004.

Film-Makers' Cooperative Catalogue 7. New York: Film-Makers' Cooperative, 1989.

Mekas, Jonas. *Movie Journal: The Rise of the New American Cinema, 1959–1971.* New York: Macmillan, 1972.

Myers, John Bernard. *Tracking the Marvelous: A Life in the New York Art World*. New York: Random House, 1983.

Warhol, Andy, and Pat Hackett. *POPism: The Warhol '60s*. New York: Harcourt Brace, 1980.

MacAdams, Lewis (1944–)

Poet, activist, filmmaker, performance artist, cultural historian, and journalist Lewis MacAdams was born in 1944 in West Texas and educated at Princeton University. He has twice held the title of "World Heavyweight Poetry Champion" at the Taos (New Mexico) Poetry Circus and is the author of a dozen books and tapes of poetry. In the late 1960s MacAdams, then at Princeton, became good friends with GREGORY CORSO and soon became a fixture in the poetry scene around DOWNTOWN MANHATTAN's Greenwich Village and the Lower East Side. Steeped in JAZZ bebop, ABSTRACT EXPRESSIONISM, and the innovative poetics being practiced by JOE BRAINARD, KENWARD ELMSLIE, TED BERRIGAN, and others, MacAdams internalized the poetics of space and disjunction while developing a keen ecological sensibility.

As a journalist in the early '80s, he was the American correspondent for the French magazine *Actuel*. From 1980 to 1982 he was the editor of *WET*, "the Magazine of Gourmet Bathing and Beyond," a Los Angeles–based, internationally circulated bimonthly of the avant-garde. Since the mid-1980s he has been a contributing editor of the *L.A. Weekly*. He writes regularly on culture and ecology for *Rolling Stone*, the *Los Angeles Times*, and *Los Angeles Magazine*, among other publications.

In 1985 he founded Friends of the Los Angeles River (FoLAR), a "40-year art work" to bring the Los Angeles River back to life. In the years since, FoLAR has become the river's most important and influential advocate. Two of its current major goals are to create a Los Angeles River Conservancy to oversee restoration of the river, and a "River Watch" program to improve the river's water quality and target polluters. In 1991 MacAdams received the San Fernando Valley Audubon Society's annual Conservation Award.

MacAdams's latest collection of poems, *The River: Books One, Two & Three*, published by Blue Press in 2005, took the Los Angeles River as its generative metaphor. His book *Birth of the Cool: Beat, Bebop and the American Avant Garde* was published in 2001 by Simon & Schuster. He is currently writing a biography of *Rolling Stone* founder Jann Wenner. His other books include *The Poetry Room* (Harper & Row, 1970), *News from Niman Farm* (Tombouctou Books, 1976), and *Live at the Church* (KULCHUR, 1977). Throughout his multiple investigations MacAdams has stayed committed to an ethical engagement with his environment and has been a strident dissident against political corruption, industrial pollution, and corporate greed. As poet and editor Dale Smith has written in a review of *The River: Books One and Two*, "MacAdams' nerve to address powerful interests presents a classic example of American dissent" (n.p.).

Bibliography

Smith, Dale. "Dale Smith Reviews Lewis MacAdams." *Jacket Magazine* 7 (1999). Available online. URL: http://jacketmagazine.com/07/smit-r-mac.html. Accessed December 18, 2008.

Mac Low, Jackson (1922–2004)

An anarchist, Jackson Mac Low was born in CHICAGO, ILLINOIS, in 1922. As ROBERT CREELEY noted in the citation for the Wallace Stevens Award that Mac Low won in 1999, Mac Low's "poetry has long been recognized as the most defining of American experimentalism, both with respect to text and to PERFORMANCE. It is the genius of his art to make poetry again enactment, to make its materials—words and syntax, and all the human echoes each must carry—a resonating, perceptive pattern reaching far beyond the enclosure of imagined subjects or intent" (n.p.). Although Mac Low is not generally regarded as a NEW YORK SCHOOL poet, his use of "chance operations" as a composition technique dovetails well with what DAVID LEHMAN in *The Last Avant-Garde* characterizes as the New York School's adherence to Ezra Pound's dictum: "Make it new" (7).

Of the more than 30 volumes of poetry that Mac Low wrote, some of the most significant include *Stanzas for Iris Lezak* (Something Else Press, 1972), *Bloomsday* (Station Hill Press, 1984), *Representative*

Works: 1938–1985 (Roof Books, 1986), and *Pieces o' Six: Thirty-three Poems in Prose* (Sun and Moon Press, 1992). In addition, Mac Low was a visual and performance artist, as well as a composer. His visual works have been displayed in the United States and abroad. His compositions, which were heavily influenced by JOHN CAGE, have been collected in *Jackson Mac Low: Doings; Performance Works 1955–2002.* Perhaps Mac Low's most famous work, "Verdrous Vangunaria," was performed in the loft of Yoko Ono (the wife of Beatle John Lennon) in 1967.

Although Mac Low's work has not been the subject of a great deal of recent scholarship or criticism, Ellen Zweig, in "Jackson Mac Low: The Limits of Formalism," has noted that Mac Low's "[e]mphasis on chance instead of choice was made in order to attempt to get rid of the ego. Chance operations, he believed, would help him to get rid of the habitual associations which arise from personal history." (82). Poet Ron Silliman gives chance operations less importance in Mac Low's work than does Zweig, but he concurs with Creeley that Mac Low is a pioneer in American experimentalism ("Jackson Mac Low Papers" n.p.).

Bibliography

Creeley, Robert. "Robert Creeley on Jackson Mac Low." American Academy of Poets. Available online. URL: http://www.poets.org/viewmedia.php/prmMID/15898. Accessed October 23, 2008.

"Jackson Mac Low Papers: Background." Recollection Books. Available online. URL: http://recollection books.com/bleed/Encyclopedia/MacLow/mss0180d. html. Accessed October 23, 2008.

"Jackson Mac Low: Short Biography." Available online. URL: http://www.writing.upenn.edu/~afilreis/88/ bio.html. Accessed October 23, 2008.

Lehman, David. *The Last Avant-Garde: The Making of the New York School of Poets.* New York: Doubleday, 1998.

Mac Low, Jackson. *Doings: Performance Works, 1955–2002.* New York: Granary Books, 2002.

———. *Thing of Beauty: New and Selected Works.* Edited by Anne Tardos. Berkeley: University of California Press, 2008.

Zweig, Ellen. "Jackson Mac Low: The Limits of Formalism." *Poetics Today* 3 (1982): 79–86.

Malanga, Gerard (1943–)

During the 1960s Gerard Malanga played a key role in the interaction between the NEW YORK SCHOOL poets and the "superstars" who orbited around ANDY WARHOL. A native New Yorker, Malanga was trained in both poetry and visual art at NEW YORK CITY's High School of Art and Design, where one of his teachers was DAISY ALDAN. A series of college courses never led to a degree but exposed him to a wide range of poet mentors: Richard Eberhart at the University of Cincinnati (1960–61); WILLARD MAAS and, briefly, ROBERT LOWELL at Wagner College on Staten Island (1961–63); and KENNETH KOCH at the New School (1961–63). Warhol met Malanga in 1963 at a reading he gave at the New School with TONY TOWLE, one of his classmates from Koch's workshop. An offer of a summer job as Warhol's studio assistant led to an extended period of COLLABORATION, lasting until 1970.

Malanga shared Warhol's fascination with repetition, the glamour of surfaces, and the creative potential of manipulating preexisting materials rather than producing something wholly new. All of these features are exhibited in Malanga's early poem "Now in Another Way" (*No Respect* 27), dedicated to Warhol, appropriating language from JOHN ASHBERY (Wolf 82–83), and published in "C" magazine (number 3, July–August 1963) by TED BERRIGAN, who was conducting his own experiments in appropriation in *The SONNETS* at this time. The next issue of "C" (number 4, September 1963) exhibited another feature of Malanga that attracted Warhol: his physical beauty and his ambiguous sexuality. The cover of this issue reproduces two photographs taken by Warhol showing EDWIN DENBY, whose writing is the focus of the issue, with Malanga, who is kissing Denby in the photograph on the back cover (Wolf 19–33). It is a provocative performance of the sort that Malanga would repeat for Warhol in a series of films, starting in 1963 with *The Kiss,* and in the 1966 "HAPPENING" known as the Exploding Plastic Inevitable, in which Malanga dances to the MUSIC of The VELVET UNDERGROUND.

Malanga came to prefer a position off-stage, as the voice of a poem or behind the camera, as the observing eye rather than its object. *SCREEN TESTS* (Kulchur Press, 1967), his first major book publication, pairs his poems with Warhol's photographic portraits of their acquaintances, including Ashbery, Denby, Berrigan, and in a kind of mirror reflection, Malanga himself. His own portrait photography, a practice that later became a significant component of his career, began with an iconic portrayal of CHARLES OLSON, taken in 1969 when Malanga interviewed the elder poet for The PARIS REVIEW (Saroyan 49–50). Recognizing the interview as both portraiture and gossip, that mixture of high and low culture that virtually defines the art of the 1960s, Malanga and Warhol founded *Interview* magazine in fall 1969. It was their last collaboration, although *Chic Death* (Pym-Randall Press, 1971) constituted a kind of collaboration in retrospect, presenting reproductions of Warhol's Death and Disaster paintings next to Malanga's poems from the mid-1960s, including "Now in Another Way."

While his work in photography has paid his way, Malanga has continued to write and publish poems. His list of significant influences still includes Ashbery, but he has added Charles Simic and, retrospectively, PAUL BLACKBURN. The title of his recent selected edition, *No Respect*, reflects Malanga's sense that "the poetry mafia in New York" have rejected him out of jealousy over the fame he achieved through his association with Warhol ("Secret Language" n.p.). Although the BERKSHIRES of Massachusetts have served as a retreat, New York has remained Malanga's base of operations.

Bibliography

Bockris, Victor, and Gerard Malanga. *Up-Tight: The Velvet Underground Story.* New York: Quill, 1983.

Malanga, Gerard. *Archiving Warhol: Writings and Photographs.* New York: Creation Books, 2002.

———. Essay in *Contemporary Authors, Autobiography Series* 17, edited by Joyce Nakamura, 95–120. Detroit, Mich.: Gale, 1993.

———. Excerpts from "The Secret Diaries" (1966). In *Out of This World: An Anthology of the St. Mark Poetry Project, 1966–1991,* edited by Anne Waldman, 278–288. New York: Crown, 1991.

———. "In Memory of the Poet Frank O'Hara 1926–1966." In *The World Anthology,* edited by Anne Waldman, 134–136. New York: Bobbs-Merrill, 1969.

———. *No Respect: New and Selected Poems, 1964–2000.* Santa Rosa, Calif.: Black Sparrow, 2001.

———. "The Permanence of Frank O'Hara" (1977). In *Frank O'Hara: To Be True to a City,* edited by Jim Elledge, 392–399. Ann Arbor: University of Michigan Press, 1990.

———. "Remembering Frank" (1969). In *Homage to Frank O'Hara,* edited by Bill Berkson and Joe LeSueur, 79. Bolinas, Calif.: Big Sky, 1988.

———. *Screen Tests, Portraits, Nudes.* Göttingen, Germany: Steidl; London: Thames & Hudson, 2000.

———. "The Secret Language of Poetry." *3AM Magazine* (June 2002). Available online. URL: http://www.3am magazine.com/litarchives/2002_jun/interview_ gerard_malanga.html. Accessed December 18, 2008.

Saroyan, Aram. "In Private, in Public: Notes on the Sixties, Andy Warhol, and the Photography of Gerard Malanga." In *Starting Out in the Sixties: Selected Essays.* Jersey City, N.J.: Talisman House, 2001, 47–63.

Wolf, Reva. *Andy Warhol, Poetry, and Gossip in the 1960s.* Chicago: University of Chicago Press, 1997.

Malmude, Steve (1940–)

Steve Malmude was born into a family of "left wing intellectual bohemians" steeped in the Jewish tradition of DOWNTOWN MANHATTAN's Lower East Side (questionnaire response n.p.). His father, Seymour, was an actor in the Yiddish THEATER on Second Avenue, and Malmude counts among his influences the Yiddish poet Mani Leib Brahinsky (1884–1950), whom he honored in the 1981 poem "Mani Leib" (*The Bundle* 32). At Queens College, Malmude majored in English literature and classics. He recalls: "[M]y best company were Catullus, Propertius, Tibullus, Ovid and Horace, very dead poets, till I met the very live ones at the Poetry Project" (questionnaire response n.p.).

What was especially alive about the NEW YORK SCHOOL poets was their openness to the full range of experience as permissible material for a poem and their delight in juxtaposing their materials in ways that kept the poem energized. "At night I see the gas / station settling a lily," begins "To Portland" (*Bundle* 19), a poem from Malmude's first collection, *Catting* (Adventures in Poetry, 1973). Malmude associates this poem with his "rhapsodic" mood at the time of the birth of his first daughter,

Anna, in 1969. The movement of the poem reflects the influence of KENNETH KOCH, whose "Sleeping with Women" (1969) got Malmude interested in reading Walt Whitman. However, Malmude's poems typically do not rush forward or outward in the way that Koch's or Whitman's do. Instead, they tend to open inward in a series of discrete gestures marked off by stanzas, usually of four lines. They are not long poems, but they "cancel sequentiality and therefore shortness," an effect Malmude associates with the improbable model of A. E. Housman (questionnaire response n.p.).

The other quality that Malmude shares with fellow New York School poets is an acute sensitivity to language itself as the poem's material, a "phrase-yard" ("Danang" [1973], *Bundle* 7) something like a lumberyard. The sounds of words can generate a poem, which in Malmude's case usually rhyme. In his sensitivity to language, though not in the regularity of his arrangements, Malmude resembles CLARK COOLIDGE or LARRY FAGIN, Malmude's first publisher and principal promoter. Of Coolidge, Malmude says, "Language was an in-joke between us, beyond comment" (questionnaire response n.p.). But absence of comment does not imply absence of meaning. As Miles Champion has noted in a review of Malmude's selected edition, *The Bundle* (Subpress/Goodbye, 2002), "Malmude's poems bear comparison to those of Coolidge and [Joe] Ceravolo in that words are used as objects and message carriers equally" (24).

Between *Catting* and *The Bundle*, Malmude published just two volumes, separated by a gap of 16 years: *From Roses to Coal* (Shell, 1982) and *I Got to Know* (Goodbye, 1997). Malmude has shown little interest in making a "career" as a poet. For most of his life he has supported himself as a carpenter, a trade not unrelated to the careful craftsmanship of his poems. He has grown into a family of poets, including his former wife, Carol Szamatowicz, and his former son-in-law, JORDAN DAVIS (his publisher at Goodbye Books). But Malmude's poems give the impression that he relishes "craftbound / solitude," as he states in "A Woodshop," one of the most recent poems in *The Bundle* (78). He now lives in Limerick, Maine, far from the Lower East Side but not too distant to be read with much appreciation in the New York School community.

Bibliography
Champion, Miles. Review of *The Bundle. Poetry Project Newsletter* 196 (October–November 2003): 23–24.
Koch, Kenneth. "Sleeping with Women" (1969). In *The Collected Poems*. New York: Knopf, 2005, 165–169.
Malmude, Steve. *The Bundle: Selected Poems*. Honolulu and New York: Subpress/Goodbye, 2002.
———. Questionnaire response for *Encyclopedia of the New York School Poets*, January 2006.

Masters, Greg (1952–) *writer, publisher*
In 1975 Greg Masters gravitated toward the community of poets at St. Mark's Church as a natural consequence of his decision to move from his native New Jersey to New York's East Village. Generalizing from his own experience, he explains, "It was a decision to abandon the elite, middle class or working class path we'd grown up in in order to pursue a path that freed one from a career objective or the restrictions of starting a family" ("The East Village"). Rather than orienting themselves toward the future, Masters and other poets of his generation rooted themselves in the "now," developing an aesthetic of immediacy that accepted, indeed demanded, a limited audience: "This focus on the common moment confines its appeal to a smaller audience, but an audience that's passionate in its appreciation for small miracles" ("The East Village").

Mimeograph publishing was the perfect medium for this aesthetic, because it involved the audience in the production of the work as well as its consumption. In his journal, Masters recorded an evening of collating ALICE NOTLEY's *A Diamond Necklace* for BOB ROSENTHAL's Frontward Books: "Bob lays out the stacks of pages and around and around we all go making a new Alice Notley book. Reading phrases as I go past the different piles, repeating some of them out loud. Everyone else doing the same thing plus chatter and the usual information exchange" ("I was a Teenage Bohemian"). A similar process produced Masters's two books, *In the Air* (1978), published by STEVE LEVINE as a Power Mad book, and *My Women and Men, Part 2* (1980), under Master's own imprint, Crony Books. In both instances, Masters's "cronies" were GARY LENHART and

MICHAEL SCHOLNICK, who shared the same Lower East Side tenement with Masters as well as the same publishing series (their three Power Mad volumes had similar cover designs to reinforce the series association). These three friends also coedited *Mag City* (1977–83), a mimeograph magazine whose contents Masters has described in terms that apply to his own poetry: "The work is decidedly unacademic, meaning the poems' emphasis is content, not form, leaving rough edges, all the more for impact" (Statement 233).

By the mid-1980s, what Masters has dubbed "The Age of Mimeo," had come to an end, partly as a result of new printing technology, which came to the *Poetry Project Newsletter* while Masters was editor (1981–83), and partly as a result of the disruption of the East Village community amid real estate speculation. Masters has held on as an East Village resident and has been instrumental in asserting the district's continued vitality through the annual Howl festival. In an essay written for the inaugural festival in 2003, Masters acknowledged the challenge facing a community dedicated to the art of "now": "We don't want revivals here. It's not a museum. It's a pulsating life form" ("The East Village").

Bibliography

Masters, Greg. "The East Village: An Introduction." *For the Artists: Music and Literature Reviews.* Greg Masters Homepage. Available online. URL: http://homepage.mac.com/gm437/fortheartists.htm/east village.htm. Accessed December 18, 2008.

———. "I Was a Teenage Bohemian: A Two Month Journal" (December 1977–January 1978). Greg Masters Homepage. Available online. URL: http://home page.mac.com/gm437/bohemian.htm/bohemian3.htm. Accessed December 18, 2008.

———. "Introduction to *The Age of Mimeo*" (1996). *For the Artists: Music and Literature Reviews.* Greg Masters Homepage. Available online. URL: http://homep-age.mac.com/gm437/fortheartists.htm/mimeo.htm. Accessed December 18, 2008.

———. Statement in *A Secret Location on the Lower East Side: Adventures in Writing, 1960–1980,* edited by Steven Clay and Rodney Phillips, 233. New York: New York Public Library/Granary Books, 1998.

Mathews, Harry (1930–) *novelist*

Through JOHN ASHBERY, whom he met in France in 1956, Harry Mathews was linked to other NEW YORK SCHOOL poets and, crucially, to the work of RAYMOND ROUSSEL. According to Mathews, reading Roussel enabled him "to write prose as if it were poetry" (interview by Rubinstein 143). Indeed, following his encounter with Roussel, Mathews has written mainly works of FICTION. And while he has published numerous poems, TRANSLATIONs, and essays, he is known primarily as a novelist.

In 1961 Mathews joined Ashbery, KENNETH KOCH, and JAMES SCHUYLER to cofound *LOCUS SOLUS,* a literary magazine named for one of Roussel's books. Mathews cites the *Locus Solus* group as his "first and most important literary environment." Despite that sense of connectedness, however, he was never a core member of the New York School but rather an "honorary member," as he describes himself (interview by Laurence).

Mathews's first novel, *The CONVERSIONS,* came out in 1962 (Random House). Several aspects of this and later works are distinctly Rousselian. Like Roussel, Mathews relies on his own imagination, rather than firsthand observation, for creative material. Also like Roussel, Mathews uses a bland, indifferent tone to describe wildly absurd situations. The author even adopts Roussel's method of imposing arbitrary (even illogical) rules on his writing.

The latter trait also aligns Mathews with the French novelist George Perec (1936–82), whom he met in 1970. Perec, the author of *La Vie mode d'emploi* (1978; "Life: a user's manual"), introduced Mathews to the OULIPO, a French group that invents and implements formal constraints within the creative process. Mathews became the first American member of that group in 1973. He and Perec remained best friends until the latter's death in 1982. They translated each other's work and engaged in several COLLABORATIONs.

The Oulipo presented Mathews with a new kind of group dynamic. In contrast to the New York School's informal fraternizing, the Oulipo held scheduled meetings once a month. Moreover, Oulipo members rarely discussed the nontheoretical aspects of their work. That emphasis on theory and rules would be anathema to many of the New York School poets. Still, the New York School and the Oulipo share a common interest in creative processes.

Even before he joined the Oulipo Mathews had a propensity for complex riddles, a staple of both the FORM and subject matter of his work. For example, in *The Conversions,* he introduces a character who writes and speaks backward. The reader is forced to decipher two variations of English—one when the man's spoken sounds are reversed, the other when his written letters are reversed. The playfulness of these devices is reminiscent of some New York School poetry. In particular, it resembles the tongue-in-cheek inventiveness of Koch. An excerpt from Mathews's best-known poem, "Histoire" (1984), in the form of a sestina, confirms this similarity:

> Biting his lips, he plunged his militarism into the
>   popular context of her Marxism-Leninism,
> Easing one thumb into her fascism, with his free
>   hand coddling the tip of her Maoism
>   (Armenian Papers 80).

Early poems by Mathews echo the allusiveness of FRANK O'HARA and Ashbery's openness to ambient stimuli. "The Joint Account," from *The Ring* (JUILLARD, 1970), is a case in point:

> White smiles of condescending complicity between
>   your not-silent bites
> Reading poems by Elizabeth Browning or listening
>   to Gianni Schicchi is also agreeable à deux
>   (Armenian Papers 13).

This poem's digressiveness and abrupt shifts of focus are features found in nearly all of Mathews's work. Those traits are especially visible in the narrative tangents that pervade his five novels.

Mathews's 1977 collection, *Trial Impressions* (Burning Deck), conjures forth 30 variations on (or extrapolations of) two stanzas from John Dowland's *Booke of Ayres.* This glib formal exercise includes everything from near-verbatim derivatives to elaborate "choose-your-own-path" versions of Dowland's

poem. The following line is from one of the more jocular versions of the Renaissance original, entitled "Male Chauvinist": "You're a pain, and as long as you hang around, I'll keep playing the field" (Mathews, *Armenian Papers* 89). While the strategy that underlies *Trial Impressions* is clearly Oulipian, its whimsical tone is exceedingly "Kochian." Even so, the book stays within the bounds of witty experimentalism, never veering, as Koch does, into madcap absurdity.

The same is not true of *Selected Declarations of Dependence* (Z Press, 1977), which Mathews dedicated to Ashbery. In that work Mathews does indulge an absurdist sensibility. *Declarations* uses the words from 46 proverbs as its sole vocabulary, with the body of the text structured as a first-person address to an anonymous partner: "You have called me a king, but you look on me as the bones of today that will soon be dead, you put the day away with me, the king, (72). As in Koch's *The RED ROBINS* (1975), there is a sense of heartfelt emotion cloaked within the nonsense of what is said. As a result, the text seems to possess a kind of otherworldly wisdom. That impression is only strengthened by the poems interspersed throughout the book, which catalog every conceivable mixture of the 46 proverbs:

> Every dog leads to Rome.
> Look before you do as the Romans do:
> Rome wasn't built with a silver lining.
> When in Rome, take the hindmost.
> Sticks and stones lead to Rome (Selected
>   Declarations 38).

Mathews's more recent work, *Singular Pleasures* (Dalkey Archive Press, 1993), also shows hints of Koch's aesthetic. The book is a series of prose poems, each relating an act of masturbation. As with Koch's own treatment of sexual material, the stories range in tone from the ridiculous to the erotic to the obscene.

Mathews was married to the artist Niki de Saint-Phalle (1930–2002) from 1949 to 1960. In 1992 he married the French novelist Marie Chaix (1942–   ). He currently divides his time between France and the United States.

Bibliography

Beer, John. "Reading Harry Mathews." July 2001. Center for Book Culture. Available online. URL: http://www.centerforbookculture.org/context/no8/beer.html. Accessed December 19, 2008.

Laurence, Alexander. "The Novels of Harry Mathews." University of Alberta Web site. Available online. URL: http://www.ualberta.ca/~stefan/Oulipo/Laurence/hm-novel.html. Accessed December 19, 2008.

Mathews, Harry. *Armenian Papers: Poems, 1954–1984.* Princeton, N.J.: Princeton University Press, 1987.

———. *The Case of the Persevering Maltese: Collected Essays.* Normal, Ill.: Dalkey Archive Press, 2003.

———. Interview by Alexander Laurence. University of Alberta Web site. Available online. URL: http://www.ualberta.ca/~stefan/Oulipo/Laurence/hm-interv1.html. Accessed December 19, 2008.

———. Interview by Lytle Shaw (1994). *Chicago Review* 43, no. 2 (Spring 1997): 36–52.

———. Interview by Meyer Raphael Rubinstein. *Silo* (1978): 140–145.

———. *Mid-Season Sky: Poems, 1954–1991.* Manchester, U.K.: Carcanet, 1992.

———. *Selected Declarations of Dependence.* Calais, Vt.: Z Press, 1977.

———. *The Way Home: Collected Longer Prose.* London: Atlas Press, 1999.

Review of Contemporary Fiction, Harry Mathews issue, 7, no. 3 (Fall 1987). [Includes contributions by John Ash, John Ashbery, Barbara Guest, and Kenneth Koch.]

Ryan, Michael. "Introducing Harry Mathews" (2004). University of Pennsylvania Web site. Available online. URL: http://nickm.com/misc/mathews_intro.html. Accessed December 19, 2008.

Mayer, Bernadette (1945–)

A pivotal figure in NEW YORK SCHOOL poetry during the 1960s and 1970s, Bernadette Mayer (pronounced as in the "mayor" of a city) has remained influential into the present. A native New Yorker, she earned a B.A. from the New School in 1967. Her early OULIPO-esque writing experiments and the workshops she conducted at the POETRY PROJECT AT ST. MARK'S CHURCH IN-THE-BOWERY starting in 1971 were very influential for younger poets, some of whom formed the core of the East Coast Language school. After receiving an inheritance, she relocated in 1975 to western Massachusetts, where she and LEWIS WARSH launched the magazine UNITED ARTISTS (1977–83). She soon returned to NEW YORK CITY and the Poetry Project, which she directed from 1980 to 1984. She has also worked for the TEACHERS & WRITERS COLLABORATIVE and the New School.

By the 1970s the second-generation New York School had carved its own niche in AMERICAN POETRY and its membership seemed firmly established, but Mayer opened the doors to future generations of experimental writers. As Juliana Spahr says, Mayer's "New York is very similar to the New York chronicled by the New York School, but hers is a less elitist and more inclusive New York" (Spahr 102). Mayer's attention to the plasticity of language suggests the influence of Gertrude Stein, derived by a circuitous route, as Mayer recalls: "[O]ne of my teachers, the poet Bill Berkson, told me I wrote too much like Gertrude Stein. I said, 'Hmm, that's interesting, I've never read Gertrude Stein,' and then I read all of Stein. That was illuminating" (Kane 85). But the full range of her influences can be seen in the reading lists she made for her Poetry Project workshops, which included Stein, poststructuralist criticism, philosophy, children's books, and 19th-century American writers such as Nathaniel Hawthorne and Herman Melville.

0 TO 9 (1967–69), the groundbreaking magazine Mayer edited with Vito Acconci (1940–), had a different aesthetic than other second-generation New York School magazines. TED BERRIGAN and RON PADGETT submitted collaborative works that Mayer and Acconci rejected. "I guess it was because of their style or something," Mayer says (Rifkin n.p.). Her connection to Acconci implies a parallel to CONCEPTUAL ART, which can be seen in MEMORY (exhibit, 1972; book, North Atlantic Books, 1975). Described by Mayer as an "emotional science project" (*Studying Hunger* 9), *Memory* was a multimedia installation piece that documented the month of July 1971 using 1,200 photographs, seven hours of audio recording, and text.

Mayer's magazine *Unnatural Acts* (1972–73) was made up of collaborative poems written in her workshop at the Poetry Project. The writers are not credited for their individual contributions, thus challenging ideas about authorship. "None of the women had problems with the anonymity of it," Mayer recalls, "yet quite a few men came up to me and asked, 'Well, who's going to know what I wrote?' A lot of men want you to know that a specific line is their territory" (Kane 86).

The book *Moving* (Angel Hair, 1971), as Mayer describes it, arose from "the task of not writing as much as possible. Only writing when I absolutely felt compelled" ("A Lecture" 96). The book is organized in the format of the children's book *The How & Why Wonder Book of Our Earth* (1960) and also includes works solicited from other writers. Of *Studying Hunger* (Adventures in Poetry / Big Sky, 1975), Mayer writes, "I wanted to try to record, like a diary, in writing, states of consciousness, my states of consciousness, as fully as I could, every day, for one month" (*Studying Hunger* 7). Mayer tore pages at random from her old journals and used them to write *Eruditio ex Memoria* ("Learning from memory," Angel Hair, 1977). These process-oriented experiments expanded poetic possibility outside the parameters established by the first-generation New York School. As LISA JARNOT has remarked, Mayer believes "that patterns and forms should always be shifting" (Kane 85).

In "The Obfuscated Poem" (1983), Mayer writes: "The best obfuscation bewilders old meanings while reflecting or imitating or creating a structure of a beauty that we know" (659). This bewilderment is present in *Incident Reports Sonnets* (Archipelago, 1984), which "surrealistically describe[s] surrealistic events and everyday things," according to Mayer ("A Lecture" 102). The content of *Sonnets* (Tender Buttons, 1989), a series of semi-traditional sonnets, ranges from incident reports to GI Joe. *The Formal Field of Kissing* (Catchword, 1990) consists of loose translations of and poems inspired by the classical Roman poets Catullus and Horace.

Mayer's work is full of sex, references to popular culture, weather, life in New England, literary figures, and such daily acts as cleaning and nursing. However, the key to her work is in her study of perception and states of consciousness. In order to write the first part of *Midwinter Day* (Turtle Island, 1992; New Directions, 1999), a book-length poem written in a single day, Mayer spent about two weeks training to remember her dreams. *The Desires of Mothers to Please Others in Letters* (Hard Press,

1994) is a series of letters written during the course of pregnancy with her third child; thus, the book is a record of her consciousness during this period. These experiments bear a strong relationship to surrealism, an influence that is perhaps her strongest connection to other New York School poets. Works such as *The 3:15 Experiment* (Owl Press, 2001), for which Mayer and three other poets (Jen Hofer, Danika Dinsmore, and LEE ANN BROWN) woke daily at 3:15 A.M. in order to write, are similar to the earlier surrealist experiments of André Breton, Philippe Soupault, and Robert Desnos.

Although most of Mayer's books represent a single theme or writing experiment, she has published three more conventional collections of poems at various stages of her career: *Poetry* (Kulchur Foundation, 1976), *The GOLDEN BOOK OF WORDS* (Angel Hair, 1978), and *Scarlet Tanager* (New Directions, 2005). *A Bernadette Mayer Reader* (New Directions, 1992) presents a retrospective selection from earlier volumes along with new poems.

Bibliography

Berkson, Bill, and Bernadette Mayer. *What's Your Idea of a Good Time? Letter and Interviews, 1977–1985.* Berkeley, Calif.: Tuumba Press, 2006.

Dinsmore, Danika, et al. "The 3:15 Experiment." Available online. URL: http://www.315experiment.com/.

Dworkin, Craig, ed. Eclipse Web site. Available online. URL: http://english.utah.edu/eclipse/projects/. [Includes facsimile editions of Mayer's *Ceremony Latin* (1964), *Story* (1968), *Moving* (1971), *Memory* (1975), *Studying Hunger* (1975), *Poetry* (1976), *Eruditio ex Memoria* (1977).]

Gordon, Nada. *Form's Life: An Exploration of the Works of Bernadette Mayer* (1986). Available online. URL: http://home.jps.net/~nada/mayer2.htm. Accessed December 19, 2008.

Kane, Daniel. "The Live Poet's Society: Where Feminism and Poetry Intersect." *Ms.* 11, no. 4 (June–July 2001): 84–87.

Mayer, Bernadette. *A Bernadette Mayer Reader.* New York: New Directions, 1992.

———. Excerpt from "A Lecture at the Naropa Institute, 1989." In *Disembodied Poetics: Annals of the Jack Kerouac School,* edited by Anne Waldman and Andrew Schelling, 95–102. Albuquerque: University of New Mexico Press, 1994.

———. "The Obfuscated Poem" (1983). In *Postmodern American Poetry,* edited by Paul Hoover, 658–659. New York: Norton, 1994.

———. *Studying Hunger.* New York: Adventures in Poetry; Bolinas, Calif.: Big Sky, 1975.

Nelson, Maggie. "What Life Isn't Daily? The Gratuitous Art of Bernadette Mayer." In *Women, the New York School, and Other True Abstractions.* Iowa City: University of Iowa Press, 2007, 99–129.

Rifkin, Libbie. "'My Little World Goes on St. Mark's Place': Anne Waldman, Bernadette Mayer and the Gender of an Avant-Garde Institution." *Jacket* 7 (April 1999). Available online. URL: http://www.jacketmagazine.com/07/rifkin07.html. Accessed December 19, 2008.

Russo, Linda. "Poetics of Adjacency: 0–9 and the Conceptual Writing of Bernadette Mayer & Hannah Weiner." In *Don't Ever Get Famous: Essays on New York Writing after the New York School,* edited by Daniel Kane, 122–150. Champaign, Ill.: Dalkey Archive Press, 2006.

Shaw, Lytle. "Faulting Description: Clark Coolidge, Bernadette Mayer and the Site of Scientific Authority." In *Don't Ever Get Famous: Essays on New York Writing after the New York School,* edited by Daniel Kane, 151–172. Champaign, Ill.: Dalkey Archive Press, 2006.

Spahr, Juliana. "'Love Scattered, Not Concentrated Love': Bernadette Mayer's Sonnets." *Differences* 12, no. 2 (Summer 2001): 98–120.

Vickery, Ann. "Desire not a Saint: The Pathography of Bernadette Mayer." In *Leaving Lines of Gender: A Feminist Genealogy of Language Writing.* Hanover, N.H.: University Press of New England/Wesleyan University Press, 2000, 150–166.

McCain, Gillian (1966–)

The DOWNTOWN MANHATTAN sensibility that evolved as PUNK ROCK in tandem with NEW YORK SCHOOL poetry during the 1970s achieves ironic historical distance in the work of Gillian McCain. She is herself a historian of punk, coauthor with Legs McNeil of *Please Kill Me: The Uncensored Oral History of Punk* (Grove, 1996). As a poet, she writes prose that manages to be both playful and deadly serious in its criticism of its own FORM, the forms of contemporary society, and the forms of opposition to society that readers of New York School poetry

may take for granted a little too readily. "It was necessary for me to detach in order to become reattached," writes McCain in her first collection, *Tilt* (1996); then she turns on her reader: "And what makes you think you're any different?" (21).

Born in New Brunswick, Canada, McCain completed a B.A. at Dalhousie University in Halifax, Nova Scotia, in 1987, then moved to NEW YORK CITY. She studied in the NAROPA INSTITUTE's summer program in 1988 and completed an M.A. at New York University in 1990. Private study with LARRY FAGIN, however, has informed her work most profoundly, by introducing her to the prose poem form that has become a Fagin specialty. Comparing three writers of what he calls "Faginescas," JORDAN DAVIS calls Carol Szamatowicz the "Anthony Trollope of the form," after the 19th-century novelist; Michael Friedman the "Fred Astaire," after the movie actor; and McCain the "Susan Sontag," after the hip culture critic and theorist of "camp." Reviewing McCain's second volume, *Religion* (The Figures, 1999), Mark Wallace draws a direct comparison to the New York School: "Her work features 'I did this then I did that' New York school immediacy, but undermines it with ironic distance that collapses any naïve faith in the immediate as a clear source of value" (26).

McCain has played a formal role in the central institution of the New York School, the POETRY PROJECT AT ST. MARK'S CHURCH IN-THE-BOWERY, since 1991, when she became program coordinator. She edited a magazine, *Milk,* in connection with the Friday night reading series there. In 1994 she moved to a new position as editor of the *Poetry Project Newsletter,* which she held through 1995. As of 2008, she is a member of the Poetry Project's board of directors. McCain met Jim Marshall, a writer, at the Poetry Project, and married him in 2002.

Bibliography

Davis, Jordan. "Poets in Review" (1 November 1996). Electronic Poetry Center. Available online. URL: http://epc.buffalo.edu/documents/poetsinreview/carll_szam.html. Accessed December 19, 2008.

McCain, Gillian. *Tilt.* West Stockbridge, Mass.: The Figures/Hard Press, 1996.

Wallace, Mark. Review of *Religion. Poetry Project Newsletter* 176 (October–November 1999): 26.

———. Review of *Tilt. Poetry Previews.* Available online. URL: http://www.poetrypreviews.com/poets/poet-mccain.html. Accessed December 19, 2008.

Mead, Taylor (1924–)

A legendary actor in underground film and THE-ATER, Taylor Mead is also a poet whose work reflects both BEAT and NEW YORK SCHOOL influences. Certain features of his writing style are common to both "schools"—the diary mode, the sense of writing as talk—but in his persona as poet, which he also adopts as an actor, he is more "queer" New York School than "hip" Beat. His inclination is to cruise rather than to drive. Much has been made of a cross-country road trip that Mead took in 1963 with ANDY WARHOL as a deliberate reenactment of JACK KEROUAC's *On the Road* (Wolf 130–134), but it was Warhol who pinpointed urban drifting, the basis of FRANK O'HARA's walk poems, as characteristic of Mead: "That's what Taylor used to love to do all day—drift all over town in that way he had that people called pixieish or elfin or wistful" (Warhol and Hackett 35).

"Pixieish" might describe the performance that established Mead's underground reputation, as the title character in *The Flower Thief* (1960), a film by Ron Rice, who referred to Mead's character simply as "the poet" (Sitney 301). In a similar vein were Mead's role as Peter Pan in Charles Ludlam's Off-Off Broadway play *The Conquest of the Universe* (1967) and the coy feminine persona sometimes adopted in his poems. "Could this be me, poor little rich girl from Grosse Pointe?" he asks in "I Was in a Drugstore" (1972).

Mead's upbringing in a wealthy and politically powerful family in Grosse Pointe, Michigan, produced in him a hostility to power that helps explain the paradoxical aura of powerlessness he generates in performance. It also helps explain his uncanny success in portraying figures of power, figures whose authority is comically subverted when the "pixieish" Mead inhabits them. Examples include his roles as the President of the United States in Robert Downey's film *Babo 73* (1964), the General in O'Hara's play *The GENERAL RETURNS FROM ONE PLACE TO ANOTHER* (1964), and Tarzan in two films, Warhol's *Tarzan and Jane Regained . . . Sort Of* (1963),

which Mead edited, and RUDOLPH BURKCHARDT's *Tarzam* (1969), which Mead wrote. In Warhol's film a scene in which skinny Mead and muscular Dennis Hopper flex biceps together epitomizes the absurdity of having Mead "embody" Tarzan in the first place. In Burckhardt's film the body humor includes a scene in which "Tarzam" (Mead) gets sick from eating berries and is cured when a missionary doctor, played by EDWIN DENBY, administers an enema.

Mead's performances in later work by New York School poets have tested his versatility. He played five roles in the stage version of KENNETH KOCH's *The RED ROBINS* (1978) and two roles in DAVID SHAPIRO and STEPHEN PAUL MILLER's *Harrisburg Mon Amour,* performed at The Kitchen in COLLAB-ORATION with Laurie Anderson (1980). His poetry readings have extended his range of performance, from early scenes such as CAFÉ LE METRO to the POETRY PROJECT AT ST. MARK's CHURCH IN-THE-BOWERY, the Museum of Modern Art, and, most recently, the BOWERY POETRY CLUB, where he currently appears in weekly shows. Some of the work from those shows is included in *A Simple Country Girl* (YBK, 2005), the only book of Mead's poems that has achieved noticeable circulation.

Bibliography
Mead, Taylor. "I Was in a Drugstore." In *Totally Corrupt.* Sound recording, GPS 008-009. New York: Giorno Poetry Systems, 1976.

Sitney, P. Adams. *Visionary Film: The American Avant-Garde, 1943–2000.* 3rd ed. New York: Oxford University Press, 2002.

Warhol, Andy, and Pat Hackett. *POPism: The Warhol Sixties.* 1980. Reprint, San Diego, Calif.: Harcourt-Harvest, 1990.

Wolf, Reva. *Andy Warhol, Poetry, and Gossip in the 1960s.* Chicago: University of Chicago Press, 1997.

Wright, Jeffrey Cyphers. "Throwaway Genius." *Tool a Magazine* (2005). Available online. URL: http://www.toolamagazine.com/MeadSimple.html. Accessed December 19, 2008.

Mediterranean Cities Edwin Denby and Rudolph Burckhardt (1956)

The second of the EDWIN DENBY–RUDOLPH BURCKHARDT book COLLABORATIONS, *Mediterranean*

Cities (Wittenborn) is the result of travels in Greece and Italy while Denby had the support of an extended Guggenheim Fellowship (1948–52). Once again the poet and photographer's distinct perspectives are purposefully overlaid to give their shared work extraordinary three-dimensionality. But while the subject of their earlier book, IN PUBLIC, IN PRIVATE, was NEW YORK CITY as observed by the Swiss-born photographer and the American Denby, in *Mediterranean Cities* roles are reversed; it is the "Yank" poet now "to whom darling Europe is foreign" (Denby 87, 92).

Most of Burckhardt's photographs exhibit the same unromantic eye that regarded the shapes and faces of Manhattan, now responding to "streets glummer than New York's but possessing / Capacious idols dead magicians begot" (Denby 90). Midtown's "built canals of air," as Denby had described them in *In Public, In Private* (Denby 13), now modulate into the actual canals and streets of Venice, the architectural composition of grilled window and gondola dock supplanting the arc of a gaspipe or American neoclassical stonework. A Neapolitan girl's lusciousness, captured by Burckhardt's tender objectivity, differs from that of a New Yorker only in her evident eagerness to be photographed.

On the other hand, Denby, approaching 50, described on the book jacket as an "awkwardly intense middle-aged traveler," projects himself onto everything he sees. Denby's Europe is a place of dreamy decadence, mirrored in an unnamed photograph of the overgrown steps of a Mediterranean garden, perhaps "the decayed park of a long dead pope" (Denby 87), urns marking the path up to a shadowy assignation. Denby is in love with an animate Europe, enamored of the "soft voices" of boys "easy in grace" (Denby 102). The poems' subject is less Europe than the sexuality of an aging man. "Villa Adriana" (the summer house of Emperor Hadrian and his young lover, Antinous) is described by the self-reflective Denby as "Peculiar like a middle-aged man undressed" (95). Animated by memories of Denby's youth, these poems perform the traditional role of elegy in the fact of loss: "lost is the Greece when I was ten that / Seduced me, god-like it shone" (106). They are also poems of "cultural maturity" as FRANK O'HARA described them (179): "So slowly desire

turns her grace / Across the years, and eases the grief we bear / And its madness to merely a powerful song" (Denby 103).

Not only are these sonnets among Denby's best, but *Mediterranean Cities* is widely praised as "one of the finest examples of poet/artist collaborative books" (Katz n.p.). Comparing it to the 1961 series published by TIBER PRESS, FAIRFIELD PORTER determined: "One wonders about the whole series, is this done for the artists' or the poets' sake? Do the prints enhance the poems, or the poems glamorize the prints? For me, Denby and Burckhardt's *Mediterranean Cities* remains a more organic collaboration" (225). Perhaps the book's achievement stems from a particularly acute awareness of the processes of time that photography and poetry share; certainly Denby's measured sonnets are a meditation on the fleeting experience of individual mortality, as well as on the endeavor of art. As O'Hara writes of Denby's lines, "the ambiguous nature of temporality [is] made clear by the timeless exertion of the consciousness" (181).

Mediterranean Cities concludes with an image of Burckhardt's own son seated in the Roman Forum; the photograph faces the collection's final poem, "Ciampino": "But Jacob, a two year old American / Is running in the garden in August delight; / 'Forum not a park, Forum a woods,' he opines." Time and locale suddenly jump forward a year (such startling shifts will become more evident in Denby's later sonnets), and the poet records: "Now in New York Jacob wants to have my cat / He goes to school, he behaves aggressively / He is three and a half, age makes us do that." Finally, Denby anticipates his farewell to life itself: "And fifty years hence will he love Rome in place of me? / For with regret I leave the lovely world men made / Despite their bad character, their art is mild" (Denby 115).

Bibliography

Denby, Edwin. *The Complete Poems.* Edited by Ron Padgett. New York: Random House, 1986.

Katz, Vincent. Headnote to "Maine Sonnets by Edwin Denby." *Rudy Burckhardt's Maine* (2003). New York Studio School Web site. Available online. URL: http://www.nyss.org/rudy/MaineSonnets.html. Accessed December 19, 2008.

O'Hara, Frank. "The Poetry of Edwin Denby" (1957). In *The Complete Poems,* by Edwin Denby, 179–181. New York: Random House, 1986.

Porter, Fairfield. "Poets and Painters in Collaboration" (1961). In *Art in Its Own Terms: Selected Criticism, 1935–1975.* Edited by Rackstraw Downes. Cambridge, Mass.: Zoland, 1979, 220–225.

Memorial Day Ted Berrigan and Anne Waldman (1971)

In clear, gentle tones and at a meditative pace, TED BERRIGAN and ANNE WALDMAN read their collaborative poem *Memorial Day* to an audience at the POETRY PROJECT AT ST. MARK'S CHURCH IN-THE-BOWERY on Wednesday, May 5, 1971. They had originally thought their joint reading had been scheduled on Memorial Day (May 30), so that title naturally suggested itself for their COLLABORATION. Additionally, both poets were in the mood to commemorate recent deaths, including that of FRANK O'HARA, whose gravesite features in the poem, and JACK KEROUAC, whose death had affected Berrigan "like I got hit in the head with a hammer," he told TOM CLARK (51). Through Clark's position as poetry editor of the *PARIS REVIEW,* O'Hara's "Memorial Day 1950" had been published posthumously just the previous summer, no doubt reinforcing the uncanny sensation that the dead "speak to us with sealed lips," as Berrigan and Waldman put it.

The pervasive theme of death confers on *Memorial Day* both a unity and a somberness that are unusual in NEW YORK SCHOOL collaborations. Nevertheless, typical devices of collaboration produce a countervailing mood of playfulness. Mirroring structures give the effect of statement and counterstatement, most notably in the variations on the word *open* at the beginning and *closed* at the end. Lists encourage collaboration by holding open the possibility of endless extension, ranging in structure from simple ("Deaths, causes": tuberculosis, syphilis, dysentery, etc.) to complex ("50 States": state of grace, Oregon, statement, etc.). Single lines of text ("Girl for someone else in white walk by"; "Guillaume Apollinaire is dead") reappear in later contexts; indeed, the original context of the line about Guillaume Apollinaire is Berrigan's Sonnet XXXVII, here reproduced in its entirety. Collaborating with voices from the past, even one's own, becomes a way of communicating with the dead, with a ghost writer, so to speak. Another of the lists in the poem "riffs" on the word *ghost* ("ghost the little children," "ghost radio," "ghost toast," etc.).

In performing the poem, Berrigan and Waldman alternated their reading of sections by a design that was "orchestrated," Waldman explained (Fischer 42), that is, the goal was to produce a musical effect, not to identify a particular poet as the author of a particular section. An amusing passage about the communication of dolphins figures the inextricable blending of voices in collaboration: "within the clicks of one / you can hear the squeaks of the other." References to other participants in the scene at St. Mark's extend the sense of a collaboration to an entire community. In retrospect, however, individual identities reappear; for instance, we can identify Berrigan as the "I" who reports an exchange with RON PADGETT about composing an epitaph. Padgett proposes "OUT TO LUNCH," while Berrigan opts for "NICE TO SEE YOU." At the suggestion of MICHAEL BROWNSTEIN, Waldman chose *Nice to See You* as the title for the memorial volume for Berrigan that she assembled after his death in 1983.

Bibliography

"Anne Waldman." PennSound, University of Pennsylvania. Available online. URL: http://www.writing.upenn.edu/pennsound/x/Waldman.html. Accessed December 19, 2008.

Berrigan, Ted, and Anne Waldman. *Memorial Day.* New York: Poetry Project, St. Mark's Church In-the-Bowery, 1971. Unpaginated bound mimeograph sheets with cover design by Donna Dennis.

———. *Memorial Day.* London: Aloes Books, 1974.

———. *Memorial Day.* In *So Going Around Cities: New and Selected Poems, 1958–1979,* by Ted Berrigan. Berkeley, Calif.: Blue Wind, 1980.

———. *Memorial Day.* In *The Collected Poems of Ted Berrigan.* Edited by Alice Notley, Anselm Berrigan, and Edmund Berrigan. Berkeley: University of California Press, 2005.

———. *Memorial Day.* Sound recording, May 5, 1971 (five-minute excerpt). In *All Poets Welcome: The Lower East Side Poetry Scene in the 1960s,* by Daniel

Kane. CD accompanying text. Berkeley: University of California Press, 2003.

Clark, Tom. *Late Returns: A Memoir of Ted Berrigan.* Bolinas, Calif.: Tombouctou Books, 1985.

Fischer, Aaron. *Ted Berrigan: An Annotated Checklist.* New York: Granary Books, 1998.

Waldman, Anne. *Alchemical Elegy.* CD. Boulder, Colo.: Naropa University/Fast Speaking Music, 2001.

Memory Bernadette Mayer (1972, 1975)

As both a gallery exhibition and a book, BERNADETTE MAYER's *Memory* demonstrates the continuing interaction between NEW YORK SCHOOL writing and visual art as "CONCEPTUAL ART" began to challenge the primacy of the visual in the early 1970s. The subject of *Memory* is mental process in general and specifically the processes of memory, dream, and vision as ordinary sense perception. To explore this subject Mayer made herself the subject of an "emotional science project" or "experiment" (excerpt from *Studying Hunger* 413, 410), committing to taking a full roll (35 exposures) of color slide film every day during the month of July 1971, and simultaneously writing and drawing in a journal. In taking the photographs she tried to avoid formal composition, "but just to take them to reflect what actual vision is, and not romanticize it" (excerpt from "A Lecture" 101). The journal recorded daily events but also subjective states such as dreams. Memory came into play during the process of bringing together the objective, photographic record with the subjective, written record. In the first presentation of *Memory* (1972), at Holly Solomon's gallery at 98 Greene Street in SoHo, DOWNTOWN MANHATTAN, 3 × 5-inch color prints from all of the slides were displayed on a 40-foot wall, and the text was played from a tape recording that lasted eight hours from start to finish. In book form (1975), published by North Atlantic Books, *Memory* presented 195 pages of text, composed "around the pictures" and the original journal entries (excerpt from "A Lecture" 98), concluding with a kind of postscript entitled "Dreaming." Only a few of the photographs are reproduced, in black and white on the book's cover (Vickery 153).

In the art gallery context, *Memory* fits a contemporary trend known as "story art," or "narrative art," identified with artists such as John Baldessari (1931–), William Wegman (1943–), and Roger Welch (1946–), who frequently combined photographs with text. In the context of New York School writing, *Memory* extends long-standing interests in the theme of dailiness, the form of the diary, and an emphasis on the surface qualities of language, which Mayer maintains despite the potential psychological depth of her subject. Gertrude Stein, an important precursor for the New York School, appears to have been Mayer's principal model (excerpt from "A Lecture" 98–99). As with Stein, Mayer writes prose that flows freely, without conventional paragraph divisions, for instance. It is a mistake to identify this freedom with formlessness, however. Complex patterns of repetition, again as in Stein, infuse Mayer's prose with a poetic quality. Mayer's quest is to "find structures" in what might at first appear an undifferentiated "accumulation of data," a phrase that *Village Voice* photography critic A. D. Coleman applied to the gallery show and that Mayer objected to (excerpt from *Studying Hunger* 410, 413). Mayer continued this quest for structure in subsequent work such as *Studying Hunger* (ADVENTURES IN POETRY/BIG SKY, 1975) and *Midwinter Day* (Turtle Island Foundation, 1982), but *Memory* was the project that placed Mayer at the forefront of radical experimentation in the New York School.

Bibliography

Baker, Peter. "Language, Poetry and Marginality: Coolidge, Palmer and Mayer." In *Obdurate Brilliance: Exteriority and the Modern Long Poem.* Gainesville: University of Florida Press, 1991, 150–161.

Gordon, Nada. "Memory." In *Form's Life: An Exploration of the Work of Bernadette Mayer.* 1986. Available online. URL: http://home.jps.net/~nada/mayer5.htm. Accessed December 19, 2008.

Mayer, Bernadette. Excerpt from "A Lecture at the Naropa Institute, 1989." In *Disembodied Poetics: Annals of the Jack Kerouac School,* edited by Anne Waldman and Andrew Schelling, 95–102. Albuquerque: University of New Mexico Press, 1994.

———. Excerpt from *Studying Hunger.* In *In the American Tree,* edited by Ron Silliman, 410–424. Orono: National Poetry Foundation/University of Maine at Orono, 1986.

———. *Memory* (1975). Facsimile ed. Edited by Craig Dworkin. Eclipse Web site. Available online. URL: http://english.utah.edu/eclipse/projects/MEMORY/html/contents.html. Accessed December 19, 2008.

Vickery, Ann. "Desire not a Saint: The Pathography of Bernadette Mayer." In *Leaving Lines of Gender: A Feminist Genealogy of Language Writing.* Hanover, N.H.: University Press of New England/Wesleyan University Press, 2000, 150–166.

Merrill, James (James Ingram Merrill) (1926–1995)

Born in NEW YORK CITY, James Merrill was a contemporary of JOHN ASHBERY and the first NEW YORK SCHOOL poets. After graduating in 1947 from Amherst College, he and his partner, David Jackson, settled in Connecticut, and the two traveled between Stonington and Athens, Greece, for years afterward. In New York, Merrill was connected with the gay arts network that included JOHN BERNARD MYERS of the TIBOR DE NAGY GALLERY. He participated in the ARTISTS' THEATRE and published in both of Myers's periodicals, *Semi-Colon* (1953–56) and *Parenthèse* (1975–79). As the son of Charles Merrill of the Merrill, Lynch brokerage firm, he was in a position to direct financial assistance to many writers through a family foundation.

Merrill modeled himself upon the same artistic masters as Ashbery and thus shares a literary lineage with the New York School, but the divergent yet equally influential style of his later work demonstrates how widely differing poetic "schools" may develop from a single tradition. Like Ashbery's early verse, Merrill's work from *The Black Swan* (privately printed, 1946) to *The Country of a Thousand Years of Peace* (Knopf, 1959) is influenced by W. H. AUDEN's formal precision and Wallace Stevens's embodiments of abstract ideas. His mind moves with agility from contemplating minute details like "Robins' eggs hollowed by a pin and puff" to flights of spectacular vision, like his pursuit of memory's phoenix: "And when the wild wings rose, on foot I followed" (*Collected Poems* 33). In 1962, when Ashbery began to experiment with disjunction and fragmentation in *The Tennis Court Oath* (Wesleyan University Press, 1962), Merrill took a contrary route, softening his conventional metric FORMs with a more straightforward, personal tone in *Water Street* (Atheneum, 1962). Merrill preserves the characteristic New York School proclivity for wit and word games, but his later work became increasingly opposed to Ashbery's style following SELF-PORTRAIT IN A CONVEX MIRROR (Viking, 1975), aiming rather at clarity and precision rather than difficulty and disjuncture. His later poems favor regular meter and the mannered, conversational mode of Auden, abandoning the dense style he learned from Stevens. While Ashbery's later verse (and that of his literary "descendants," such as Charles Bernstein and ANN LAUTERBACH) has become increasingly opaque and disjointed, Merrill's most acclaimed work, *The Changing Light at Sandover* (Atheneum, 1982), deliberately supplants "fancy narrative concoctions" with a straightforward, "unseasoned" style (*Changing Light* 3). *The Changing Light at Sandover* aims to be an all-encompassing, epic cosmogony: "ABSOLUTES ARE NOW NEEDED," Merrill's spirit-muse declares (*Changing Light* 113). Merrill's later work addresses human emotions and existence on a broader scale, and its admirers range from New Formalists such as J. D. McClatchy and Mary Jo Salter to Richard Wilbur and W. S. Merwin. If formal experiment is the touchstone of New York School poetry, Merrill carries the classicist torch, more characteristic of poetry in postwar Britain than in the United States. He innovates within the constraints of convention, invoking the shades and forms of tradition as guides to distinguish the passing from the permanent, or "to tell part the earth's pull / From heaven's gravities" (*Collected Poems* 472).

Bibliography

Merrill, James. *The Changing Light at Sandover: A Poem.* New York: Knopf, 2001.

———. *Collected Poems.* Edited by J. D. McClatchy and Stephen Yenser. New York: Knopf, 2001.

———. *A Different Person: A Memoir.* New York: Knopf, 1993.

Shoptaw, John. "James Merrill and John Asbery." In *The Columbia History of American Poetry,* edited by Jay Parini and Brett C. Miller, 750–806. New York: Columbia University Press, 1993.

Mesmer, Sharon (1960–)

Sharon Mesmer was born and raised in CHICAGO, ILLINOIS, where she earned her B.A. from Columbia College and cofounded the energetic literary newspaper *Letter eX*. In 1988 she moved to NEW YORK CITY, ostensibly to study poetry with ALLEN GINSBERG. She earned an M.F.A. at Brooklyn College in 1990 and was awarded that college's MacArthur Fellowship Prize. Meanwhile, she became engaged in multiple poetry and performance activities, including at the alternative and edgy venues of the Lower East Side, such as ABC No Rio and the NUYORICAN POETS CAFÉ. She performed as lead singer for The Mellow Fuckin Woodies, a short-lived, iconoclastic MUSIC poetry ensemble. Throughout the 1990s she participated in the "Unbearables," a literary collective that conducted hilarious outdoor literary escapades. More recently, she has been an active member of the Flarf Collective. Her COLLABORATIONs include an artist's book with David Humphrey and a poetry comic with David Borchart.

Mesmer's studies with poet PAUL HOOVER in Chicago and Ginsberg in New York were complemented by workshop studies with ALICE NOTLEY at the POETRY PROJECT AT ST. MARK'S CHURCH IN-THE-BOWERY and elsewhere. Early influences were Chicago's affinity for world surrealism (see DADA AND SURREALISM), PATTI SMITH, BEAT poetry, 1970s rock and roll, Peter Lamborn Wilson, and ANDREI CODRESCU. Early poems evoked a NEW YORK SCHOOL style filtered through Chicago's literary vernacular and shaped by slams and punk performance. Her first published poem was in MAUREEN OWEN's magazine TELEPHONE in 1980. Mesmer's poem "Passive Womanhood Planet" is like a little sister to ANNE WALDMAN's "Fast Speaking Woman." Along with her peers, such as Todd Colby, EDWIN TORRES, CONNIE DEANOVICH, Deborah Pinotelli, Tracey McTague, Jim Behrle, Nada Gordon, Brendan Lorber, DAVID TRINIDAD, Tracey Morris, and Cynthia Nelson, Mesmer helped to open the New York School to the wide range of poetic sources and modes fermenting in the '90s.

Mesmer's vivid short stories are marked by a shift of vernacular from high church to barroom confession. Her readings are memorable for her energizing, focused delivery. Mesmer's poetry has always had an outrageous, daring flare—a scoping of the self and other selves in the service of a tenuous survivalist, surreal beauty, scraping away any pretension, even at the expense of normative self-esteem. Mesmer's poems ask powerful, increasingly universal questions and reverberate with an Augustinian vision and abjection, desire, and repugnance. She is the author of *Vertigo Seeks Affinities* (a poetry chapbook, Belladonna Books, 2006); *In Ordinary Time* (stories, HANGING LOOSE PRESS, 2005); *Ma Vie à Yonago* (stories in French TRANSLATION, Hachette Litterateurs, France 2005); *Lonely Tylenol* (limited edition, with David Humphrey, Flying Horse Editions, 2003); and *Half Angel, Half Lunch* (Hard Press, 1998). Her work appears in numerous anthologies, including *An Exquisite Corpse Reader* (Black Sparrow); the *Outlaw Bible of American Poetry* (Thunder's Mouth Press) and *Heights of the Marvelous* (St. Martin's Press). She has written articles and reviews for journals internationally and is on the teaching staff of the New School.

Metro Café   *See* CAFÉ LE METRO.

Miller, Stephen Paul (1951–)

Born on Staten Island, New York, Stephen Paul Miller participated in the NEW YORK SCHOOL–influenced Lower East Side poetry scene of DOWNTOWN MANHATTAN in the 1970s and 1980s while coediting the little magazines *National Poetry Magazine of the Lower East Side* and *Poetry Mailing List*, which featured numerous New York School poets. He also collaborated with JOHN CAGE and exhibited his collaborative multimedia work at P.S. 1 in Queens.

In the 1980s Miller published several chapbooks of poetry and drama, but his first full collection is a long poem, *Art Is Boring for the Same Reason We Stayed in Vietnam* (1992). This stanzaless poem of extremely short lines is influenced in its relaxed, conversational tone by the work of FRANK O'HARA, and in its associative leaps and philosophical musings by JOHN ASHBERY and DAVID SHAPIRO's poetry. Critiquing the George H. W. Bush administration's war rhetoric and attempt to control mass-media coverage of the Persian Gulf conflict, congressional censorship of artists, and other questionable social practices, all the while speculating on deconstructive notions of context and limitation, Miller vigorously advocates an expansion of possibilities for dialogue and democratic structures in *Art Is Boring*.

In *The Bee Flies in May* (2002) Miller's penchant for casual, conversational, exploratory poetry and scrutiny of political conditions is most evident in the long poem *Row*, which draws on many sources to propose challenging connections among the Holocaust, IBM's systems of classification, the American suburb's emergence, Bob Dylan's song "Desolation Row," and Alan Turing's work on artificial intelligence in relation to his HOMOSEXUALITY. The poem promotes wariness of the dangers of data centralization and mass-produced lifestyles, but New York School skepticism tempers the aura of a dark conspiracy theory. Poems like "Dr. Shy" exhibit the New York School tendency to allow conflicting aims—here, "official" elegy for the poet's father, ironic psychological investigation, and tender narratives leading to ontological bafflement—to coexist. "Ralph Kramden Emerson Tonight" typifies Miller's proclivity in plays to "merge" disparate historical and fictional figures. "I Was on a Golf Course the Day John Cage Died of a Stroke," which appeared in the 1993 *Best American Poetry* anthology and takes off on O'Hara's "The DAY LADY DIED," meditates on chance, programmatic aesthetics, and openness to materials as it braids together several previously unrelated stories.

The poems "I'm Trying to Get My Phony Baloney Ideas about Metamodernism into a Poem," "Pleasure," and "'The Hustle' and Its Liquid Totems of Holocaust, Suburb, and Computer" in Miller's most recent collection, *Skinny Eighth Avenue* (2005), continue the poet's trend since *Art Is Boring* to write complex, politically inflected long poems that behave like "cultural studies" texts in bringing various historical strands into relation while maintaining a casual, conversational, yet also lyrically charged surface characteristic of New York School poetry. The book features numerous drawings by Miller's young son, Noah Mavael Miller, whose questions and assertions are sometimes quoted in the poems.

An accomplished cultural critic, Miller has authored *The Seventies Now: Culture as Surveillance* (1999), which includes a reading of Ashbery's "SELF-PORTRAIT IN A CONVEX MIRROR" against a JASPER JOHNS painting series and the Watergate affair. In addition, he coedited *The Scene of My Selves: New Work on New York School Poets* (2000).

Bibliography

Diggory, Terence, and Stephen Paul Miller. *The Scene of My Selves: New Work on New York School Poets.* Orono, Me.: National Poetry Foundation, 2000.

Fink, Thomas. "Probings of Coalition and Broad Community: Melvin Dixon, Joseph Lease, Stephen Paul Miller, and Gloria Anzaldua." In *"A Different Sense of Power": Problems of Community in Late-Twentieth-Century U.S. Poetry*. Madison, N.J.: Fairleigh Dickinson University Press, 2001, 174–196.

Miller, Stephen Paul. *Art Is Boring for the Same Reason We Stayed in Vietnam.* New York: Unmuzzled Ox Press, 1992.

———. *The Bee Flies in May.* New York: Marsh Hawk Press, 2002.

———. *The Seventies Now: Culture as Surveillance.* Durham, N.C.: Duke University Press, 1999.

———. *Skinny Eighth Avenue.* New York: Marsh Hawk Press, 2005.

minimalism

As a movement in visual art, minimalism posed one of the two great challenges to ABSTRACT EXPRESSIONISM during the 1960s, the other being POP ART. While pop had content, minimalism remained rigorously abstract, opposing expressionism by limiting FORM to regular geometrical shapes. This reductive tendency had precedent in some earlier painting, such as that of Barnett Newman, but the objectifying of shape in minimalism naturally led to the production of objects. The most representative works of the movement can be categorized as sculpture, although that term had outdated aesthetic connotations for the most representative artist, Donald Judd (1928–94).

In NEW YORK SCHOOL poetry a renewed interest in the tradition of objectivism during the 1960s helped prepare for engagement with minimalist art. Personal connections also helped. One of the first group exhibitions of minimalists, "Shape and Structure," was hosted by JOHN BERNARD MYERS at the TIBOR DE NAGY GALLERY in January 1965. The following year the Jewish Museum presented the more widely noticed "Primary Structures" show, curated by Kynaston McShine, sometime lover of FRANK O'HARA. Two of the artists included in that show, Tony Smith (1912–80) and Ronald Bladen (1918–88), had long-standing connections with the poets' community dating back to the 1950s. Their work retained "poetic" qualities that kept it on the margins of minimalism but made it more amenable to treatment in poetry. JIM BRODEY's IDENTIKIT (Angel Hair, 1967) concludes with a reference to Bladen—specifically to the Jewish Museum show—and BARBARA GUEST's The COUNTESS FROM MINNEAPOLIS (Burning Deck, 1976) concludes with a reference to Smith.

The hard-line minimalism of Judd has most in common with the poetry that ARAM SAROYAN and CLARK COOLIDGE were writing during the second half of the 1960s. "I remember Aram and I used to talk about people like Don Judd a lot," recalls Coolidge (n.p.), who includes among "people like" Judd the artist Dan Flavin (1933–96), sculptor of fluorescent lights. Saroyan reduced a poem to a single word (Aram Saroyan, Random House, 1968), while Coolidge broke words down to syllables (ING, Angel Hair, 1968). The magazine 0 TO 9, where minimalist tendencies in art and poetry most frequently met, featured "pages" from Coolidge's Suite V, where one word appears at the top, another at the bottom of each page (for example, "taps / buns"; number 6 [July 1969]). In the same issue LARRY FAGIN offers a variant on this form—four words per page, each in one of the four corners—titled "For Don Judd." RON PADGETT's "Nothing in That Drawer" (1969) appears to translate into verbal form the rows of identical boxes Judd would attach to a wall; Padgett's poem simply repeats the title for 14 lines (the number of lines in a sonnet). In this case it is unclear whether the poem is moving toward reduction (the nothing in the title) or away from it—toward the implied narrative of a desperate person searching for lost valuables. Such ambivalence is typical of New York School poets' response to minimalism. Reviewing a show of Judd's work at the Whitney Museum in 1968,

JOHN ASHBERY confessed that the work in a previous show at the Castelli Gallery had seemed to him "malevolent"; now he was willing at least to apply Judd's own preferred term, "interesting" (Reported Sightings, 254–255).

During the 1970s the influence of minimalism as a movement dispersed in a variety of directions, including CONCEPTUAL ART, installation art, and PERFORMANCE ART. The work of individual artists connected with the original breakthrough of minimalism received periodic reassessment by New York School poets. Ashbery's further appreciation of Judd is evident in the form he adopted for the poems in Shadow Train (Viking, 1981), each consisting of four quatrains, which Ashbery compared to Judd's boxes ("Imminence" 75–76). The repetition of quatrains makes them, in Judd's terms, "unrelational" (Judd and Stella 151); each one stands as an independent whole, rather than growing together in some organic sequence. MARJORIE WELISH examined this logic further, again with specific reference to Judd, both in critical essays (Signifying Art) and in the most recent poems collected in the title section of The Annotated 'Here'" (Coffee House Press, 2000). Meanwhile, a renewed concern for aesthetic quality in the "post-minimalism" of Richard Tuttle (1941–) has made his work an object of special attention among the poets (CARTER RATCLIFF, CHARLES NORTH). Tuttle has collaborated with Fagin (Poems, 1977) and BARBARA GUEST (The ALTOS, Limestone Press, 1991), and he designed Guest's collection of art criticism, Dürer in the Window (Roof Books, 2003). Personal connections, once again, are a factor in this relationship, Guest having become a friend of Tuttle's wife, the poet Mei-Mei Berssenbrugge (1947–). However, it is at least equally important that Guest's late work constitutes the most intensive application of a post-minimalist aesthetic in New York School poetry.

Bibliography
Ashbery, John. "The Imminence of a Revelation" (1981). In Acts of Mind: Conversation with Contemporary Poets, edited by Richard Jackson, 69–76. Tuscaloosa: University of Alabama Press, 1983.
———. Reported Sightings: Art Chronicles 1957–1987. Edited by David Bergman. Cambridge, Mass.: Harvard University Press, 1992.

Berkson, Bill. "Bladen's Mounds" (1991/1992). In *The Sweet Singer of Modernism & Other Art Writings, 1985–2003*. Jamestown, R.I.: Qua Books, 2003, 111–118.

———. "Ronald Bladen: Sculpture and Where We Stand." *Art and Literature* 12 (Spring 1967): 139–150.

Coolidge, Clark. Interview by Tom Orange. *Jacket* 13 (April 2001). Available online. URL: http://jacketmagazine.com/13/coolidge-iv.html. Accessed December 19, 2008.

Judd, Donald, and Frank Stella. "Questions to Stella and Judd" (1964/1966). In *Minimal Art: A Critical Anthology*, edited by Gregory Battcock, 148–164. New York: Dutton, 1968.

North, Charles. "Richard Tuttle: Small Pleasures" (1975). In *No Other Way: Selected Prose*. Brooklyn, N.Y.: Hanging Loose, 1998, 20–24.

Padgett, Ron. "Nothing in That Drawer." In *Great Balls of Fire*. 1969. Reprint, Minneapolis, Minn.: Coffee House Press, 1990, 5.

Perreault, John. "Minimal Abstracts" (1967). In *Minimal Art: A Critical Anthology*, edited by Gregory Battcock, 256–262. New York: Dutton, 1968.

Ratcliff, Carter. "Exhibition at Betty Parsons Gallery." *Art International* 14 (May 1970): 76.

Schjeldahl, Peter. "Minimalism." In *The Hydrogen Jukebox: Selected Writings, 1978–1990*. Berkeley: University of California Press, 1991, 204–226.

Welish, Marjorie. *Signifying Art: Essays on Art After 1960*. Cambridge: Cambridge University Press, 1999.

Mlinko, Ange (1969–)

Born in Philadelphia, Ange Mlinko (pronounced AN-gie MLINK-o) has a decisively sophisticated urban vision, at once spontaneous and complex: "I'm so happy! Stop grading papers and make love to me!" ("Happiness in Harness," *Matinees* 25). Her "intoxicating, cerebral poems display a unique sense of humor and mystery," noted the *New Yorker* in 2005 (n.p.).

In BOSTON, poet WILLIAM CORBETT, first introduced her to NEW YORK SCHOOL poets, among whom she counts FRANK O'HARA, KENNETH KOCH, JOHN ASHBERY, KENWARD ELMSLIE, BERNADETTE MAYER, and CHARLES NORTH as influences. BOB HOLMAN, when he chose her second book, *Starred Wire* (2005), for the National Poetry Series, extended her range of sources: "O'Hara conversation, Ashbery sophistication, Schuyler shapeliness, [Barbara] Guest adventures, [Alice] Notley grain, Mayer utopia, [Ron] Padgett whimsy, Oulipo oofs." One hears her interweavings of such overtones in lines such as "So maybe Lisbon's like Philadelphia, losing all its stars / to New York, in its case Paris?" ("Là," *Starred Wire* 1).

Mlinko adds a cybernetic presence to the New York School with her monthly blog, Bachelardette, named in homage to French philosopher Charles Bachelard, begun May 2005. She posts comments and reviews topics, from Oprah's book choices to MARCELLA DURAND, claiming, "I loathe the outright campaign to shame poets into being 'readable,' advanced by the likes of everyone from Ted Kooser to Camille Paglia."

With a B.A. in philosophy and mathematics from St. John's College, Annapolis (1991), she values such intellectual lyric poets as JOHN KOETHE, Anne Carson, and Susan Stewart; other favorites are Marianne Moore, Hart Crane, and Wallace Stevens. While pursuing an M.F.A. in poetry from Brown University (1998), she studied with August Kleinzahler, C. D. Wright, and Keith and Rosmarie Waldrop. She worked one year at al-Akhawayn University, in Ifrane, Morocco, coordinating the writing center there. Her first collection, *Matinees* (1990), featured a cover by JOE BRAINARD. In it, the prose poem "Editorial for Compound Eye #2" celebrates a visit to Boston photographer Ben Watkins: "I died tissue-thin deaths just then completely sentimentalizing my city: I know those trees and that bridge . . . Look, I live here. Aren't I moving to New York, San Francisco, Seattle, every day?" (51). In New York she edited the *Poetry Project Newsletter* (2000–02), for which she interviewed North and Fred Moten and reviewed works by Koethe and others; in summer 2001 she was a visiting writer at NAROPA INSTITUTE. Currently she resides in Brooklyn with her husband and son.

Bibliography

"Briefly Noted: Poets and Poetry." *New Yorker*, 29 August 2005, n.p. Formerly available online. URL: http://www.newyorker.com/critics/content/articles/050829crbn_brieflynoted.

"Daniel Kane Interviews the Poet Ange Mlinko, July 2000." Poets on Poetry: Poets Chat. Teachers & Writers. Formerly available online. URL: http://www. twc.org/forums/poetschat/poetschat_amlinko.html.

———. Matinees. Cambridge, Mass.: Zoland Books, 1999.

———. Starred Wire. Minneapolis, Minn.: Coffee House Press, 2005.

modernist poetry in English

In responding to modernism as an international movement, the NEW YORK SCHOOL poets did not stop at language barriers, relying on TRANSLATION where necessary, even in the case of poetry, which is so often said to be untranslatable. French and Russian literature especially attracted attention within the New York School, but writers in other languages are frequently evident, for example, Federico García Lorca (FRANK O'HARA), Rainer Maria Rilke (KENNETH KOCH), Giorgos Seferis (BARBARA GUEST), and Giuseppe Ungaretti (TED BERRIGAN). Nevertheless, poetry written in English, and especially by American poets, carried the greatest weight in the modernist inheritance transmitted to the New York School—"weight" in the sense both of value and of burden. Indeed, one of the chief motives that led New York School poets to foreign models was the desire to get out from under the burden of modernist giants such as W. B. Yeats (1865–1939) and T. S. Eliot (1888–1965). It was also a desire to avoid the staleness of their numerous imitators (O'Hara, "Another Word" 59; Ashbery, "Reverdy" 110–111).

At an early stage of his career Eliot had drawn heavily on French models, but, like Yeats, he became identified with the symbolist mode, a poetry of indirection in which "hidden" meanings lay behind the images. The French poets who were especially important to the New York School had moved beyond symbolism to a "transparent" poetry, as JOHN ASHBERY described the work of Pierre Reverdy (1889–1960) in contrast to Eliot's ("Reverdy" 110). Reverdy's images, in other words, directly described a world, though it might be a dream world, or an activity, though it might be purely the act of the mind. "The poem of the act of the mind" was Wallace Stevens's definition of the modern poem ("Of Modern Poetry," 1940; Stevens,

Collected Poems 240), and Ashbery and O'Hara had determined to "abandon Eliot for Stevens" while they were still undergraduates at Harvard, according to Harold Brodkey (Gooch 138).

No other modernist poet has an importance to the first-generation New York School poets equal to that of Wallace Stevens (1879–1955). In "The Duplications" (1977), Koch describes a factory "Kept busier than the mind of Wallace Stevens" (Seasons 254), as if nothing busier in the act of invention could be imagined. Guest draws on Stevens's "Notes Toward a Supreme Fiction" (1948) to describe the modern conception of reality as a process of endless invention, "variable, . . . open-ended in form and matter" ("Poetry" 27). To JAMES SCHUYLER, Stevens's conception of reality justifies consideration of a realist painter like FAIRFIELD PORTER as also a modernist (8–9). Stevens shared with the New York School poets a strong interest in "The Relations Between Poetry and Painting," the title of a lecture he delivered at the Museum of Modern Art in New York in 1951 (Stevens, Necessary Angel 157–176). When HAROLD ROSENBERG formulated his definition of "ACTION PAINTING" in 1952, he drew on another lecture by Stevens ("The Figure of the Youth as Virile Poet," 1943) to explain the new painting by analogy to what Stevens called "the process of the personality of the poet" (Rosenberg 29; Stevens, Necessary Angel 45). In other words, action painting was the painting of the act of the mind.

Although he mentioned Stevens, DONALD M. ALLEN gave much more prominence to Ezra Pound (1885–1972) and William Carlos Williams (1883–1963) in explaining the modernist background of the New American Poetry (xi). This emphasis reflects the extent to which Allen's view of the new poetry was shaped by the BLACK MOUNTAIN POETS and the BEATS, for whom Pound and Williams were foundational. To O'Hara, "the Pound heritage" took itself too seriously so that poets like CHARLES OLSON became preoccupied with "saying the important utterance" (Standing Still 13). Second-generation writers, more open to Olson and the Beats, tended also to be more open to Pound. With The Cantos (1917–69) in mind, Berrigan claimed that "most of us" got "the idea of a poem as being made up of a lot of fragments" from Pound (interview 93), an indication that the possibility of being influenced by Eliot had been ruled out by this time. Berrigan referred to himself as "the self-appointed chief Pound(er) of my generation" (PADGETT, *Ted* 67), referring to his opinionated stance and his presumption that his opinions represented a movement, but he did not take himself entirely seriously in this role. He employed self-parody as a defense against "the important utterance," just as his friend RON PADGETT employed parody ("The Unwobbling Jello") to defend against Pound ("the unwobbling pivot" was Pound's translation of a central concept of Confucius [Kenner 452–458]).

Williams offered a welcome antidote to the depressing mood that accompanied the high seriousness of poetry in the Eliot-Pound tradition. "I was very grateful to William Carlos Williams," explained Koch, "because he seemed happy so much of the time" (interview 160). Against divorce, "the sign of knowledge in our time" (Williams, *Paterson* 17), Williams wrote a poetry of marriage, as O'Hara recognized in celebrating the marriage of JANE FREILICHER and Joe Hazan as both "William-Carlos Williamsian" and "most modern," in the sense of "vanguard" opposition to the social condition of modernity ("Poem Read at Joan Mitchell's," 1957; O'Hara, *Collected Poems* 265). In the same spirit LEWIS WARSH celebrated the marriage of Angelica and TOM CLARK in "Dreaming as One," which takes its title from Williams's *Paterson* (133). At a dark time in her marriage to Berrigan, "immobile pregnant and isolate and unhappy" (Notley, *Doctor Williams* n.p.), ALICE NOTLEY wrote her way through Williams's "Asphodel, That Greeny Flower" (1955), literally typing it out, to emerge with her own *Songs for the Unborn Second Baby* (United Artists, 1979). That experience became the basis for Notley's imaginary lineage for women of the second-generation New York School, descended from two "male-females," O'Hara and PHILIP WHALEN, who were themselves the offspring of a "marriage" between William Carlos Williams and Gertrude Stein (Notley, *Doctor Williams* n.p.).

Gertrude Stein (1874–1946), Marianne Moore (1887–1972), and H.D. (Hilda Doolittle, 1886–1961) are the three women poets of the modernist period who have meant most to the New York School. Whether it mattered that they were women is a question that gives rise to some ambivalence. For EILEEN MYLES, commenting on Stein, "[T]he fact that our century's greatest poet is a lesbian is nothing to sneeze at," yet what mattered most is "that a woman, unwriting herself, flooding the world with her details, standing in such an endangered place could be free" (131)—presumably, free also from the condition of being a woman under patriarchy. What Myles refers to as Stein's "unwriting" has concerned poets who are more interested in exploring the conditions of language than the conditions of gender. In his statement for PAUL CARROLL's *The Young American Poets*, CLARK COOLIDGE subscribed to the position that "Stein has most clearly & accurately indicated, Words have a universe of qualities other than those of descriptive relation: Hardness, Density, Sound-Shape, Vector-Force, & Degrees of Transparency/Opacity" (149). On this basis, poets such as Coolidge and BERNADETTE MAYER have been placed in the line of LANGUAGE POETRY, for which Stein is a significant precursor. Yet for Mayer especially, Stein's experiments in language are also experiments in psychology; she is as much concerned with "the act of the mind" as is Stevens, as evidenced in MEMORY. And, "Mind Gertrude Stein" was the title of a course that ANNE WALDMAN taught at the NAROPA INSTITUTE in summer 1978 (Waldman, "Loom"; Hornick 96–98, 111–112).

From a similar perspective, Ashbery has praised both Stein and Moore as poets of a "way of happening" (*Selected Prose* 12–13, 87–88), by which he means the continuous flow of experience that modern novelists have sought to capture in the technique known as "stream of consciousness." Even when the contents of the stream are sharply delineated, as they are so often in Moore, the sensation of flow is abstract, above or below such conventional demarcations as gender. In making his case for Moore as "our greatest modern poet" (*Selected Prose* 108), Ashbery argued against a gendered reading of her work: "these are not the manners of a governess" (*Selected Prose* 111). Different readers have presented a different case for Moore's friend H.D. Although she remained critically detached from her subject, Guest wrote her biography, *HERSELF DEFINED: THE POET H.D. AND HER WORLD* (Doubleday, 1984), in full awareness of the issues raised by contemporary feminism.

In subsequent criticism Guest explicitly tied H.D.'s development as a writer away from imagism to her struggle as a woman against domination by Pound, who had declared her the representative "Imagiste" (Guest, *Forces* 61–73). The breakthrough was not H.D.'s wartime *Trilogy* (1944–46), still essentially composed in fragments after the manner of Pound and Eliot, but rather *Helen in Egypt* (1961), a new attempt at epic narrative. Pursuing the "'feminine' epic" after H.D.'s example (Notley, "'Feminine' Epic" 174), Notley, with *The DESCENT OF ALETTE* (1992), and Waldman, with *IOVIS* (1993–   ), have brought New York School writing closer to the mythic consciousness that had been a basic "way of happening" in modern poetry since Eliot's *The Waste Land* (1922).

Bibliography

Allen, Donald. Preface to *The New American Poetry, 1945–1960*. 1960. Reprint, Berkeley: University of California Press, 1999, xi–xiv.

Altieri, Charles. "Ann Lauterbach's 'Still' and Why Stevens Still Matters." In *Postmodernisms Now: Essays on Contemporaneity in the Arts*. University Park: Pennsylvania State University Press, 1998, 136–151.

Ashbery, John. "Reverdy en Amérique." *Mercure de France* 1,181 (January 1962): 109–112.

———. *Selected Prose*. Edited by Eugene Richie. Ann Arbor: University of Michigan Press, 2004.

Berrigan, Ted. Interview by *CITY* magazine (1977). In *Talking in Tranquility: Interviews with Ted Berrigan*, edited by Stephen Ratcliffe and Leslie Scalapino, 90–105. Bolinas, Calif.: Avenue B; Oakland, Calif.: O Books, 1991.

———. "Life of a Man" (1967). In *The Collected Poems of Ted Berrigan*. Edited by Alice Notley, Anselm Berrigan, and Edmund Berrigan. Berkeley: University of California Press, 2005, 187–191. [Title from Ungaretti.]

Coolidge, Clark. Contributor's statement. In *The Young American Poets*, edited by Paul Carroll, 149. Chicago: Follett, 1968.

Gooch, Brad. *City Poet: The Life and Times of Frank O'Hara*. New York: Knopf, 1993.

Guest, Barbara. *Forces of the Imagination: Writing on Writing*. Berkeley, Calif.: Kelsey St. Press, 2003.

———. "Poetry the True Fiction" (1992). In *Forces of Imagination: Writing on Writing*. Berkeley, Calif.: Kelsey St. Press, 2003, 26–32.

———. "'Who Will Accept Our Offering at This End of Autumn?'" In *Poems: The Location of Things/Archaics/ The Open Skies*. Garden City, N.Y.: Doubleday, 64. [Title from Seferis.]

Hornick, Lita. *The Green Fuse: A Memoir*. New York: Giorno Poetry Systems, 1989.

Kenner, Hugh. *The Pound Era*. Berkeley: University of California Press, 1973.

Koch, Kenneth. "Aus Einer Kindheit" (1962). In *Collected Poems*. New York: Knopf, 2005, 81–82. [Title from Rilke.]

———. Interview by Jordan Davis (1995). In *The Art of Poetry: Poems, Parodies, Interviews, Essays, and Other Work*. Ann Arbor: University of Michigan Press, 1996, 187–214.

———. *Seasons on Earth*. New York: Penguin, 1987.

Myles, Eileen. "The Lesbian Poet" (1994). In *School of Fish*. Santa Rosa, Calif.: Black Sparrow, 1997, 123–131.

Notley, Alice. *Doctor Williams' Heiresses*. Berkeley, Calif.: Tuumba Press, 1980.

———. "The 'Feminine' Epic" (1995). In *Coming After: Essays on Poetry*. Ann Arbor: University of Michigan Press, 2005, 171–180.

———. *Songs for the Unborn Second Baby*. Lenox, Mass.: United Artists, 1979.

O'Hara, Frank. "Another Word on Kenneth Koch" (1955). In *Standing Still and Walking in New York*. Edited by Donald Allen. San Francisco: Grey Fox, 1983, 59–61.

———. *Collected Poems*. Rev. ed. Edited by Donald Allen. Berkeley: University of California Press, 1995.

———. *Standing Still and Walking in New York*. Edited by Donald Allen. San Francisco: Grey Fox, 1983.

———. "Young Girl in Pursuit of Lorca" (1960). In *Poems Retrieved*. Rev. ed. Edited by Donald Allen. San Francisco: Grey Fox, 1996, 203–204.

Padgett, Ron. *Ted: A Personal Memoir of Ted Berrigan*. Great Barrington, Mass.: The Figures, 1993.

———. "The Unwobbling Jello." In *Tulsa Kid*. Calais, Vt.: Z Press, 1979, 72–73.

Rosenberg, Harold. "The American Action Painters" (1952). In *The Tradition of the New*. 1960. Reprint, New York: Da Capo, 1994, 23–39.

Schuyler, James. "An Aspect of Fairfield Porter's Paintings" (1967). In *Selected Art Writings*. Edited by Simon Pettet. Santa Rosa, Calif.: Black Sparrow, 1998, 8–17.

Stevens, Wallace. *Collected Poems*. New York: Vintage/
Random House, 1990.

———. *The Necessary Angel: Essays on Reality and the
Imagination*. New York: Vintage/Random House,
1951.

Waldman, Anne. "Loom Down the Thorough Narrow"
(1978). In *Vow to Poetry: Essays, Interviews, and
Manifestos*. Minneapolis, Minn.: Coffee House Press,
2001, 89–99.

Warsh, Lewis. "Dreaming as One." In *Part of My History*.
Toronto, Canada: Coach House Press, 1972, n.p.

Williams, William Carlos. "Asphodel, That Greeny
Flower." In *Collected Poems*. Vol. 2: *1939–1962*.
Edited by Christopher MacGowan. New York: New
Directions, 1988, 310–337.

———. *Paterson*. Rev. ed. Edited by Christopher
MacGowan. New York: New Directions, 1992.

Mother (1964–1969)

Even before NEW YORK CITY became the official publishing address for *Mother*, the magazine
became an important outlet for the work of NEW
YORK SCHOOL poets. It was founded at Carleton
College, Minnesota, by PETER SCHJELDAHL and a
classmate, Jeff Giles. Schjeldahl had his eye on
New York, where he eventually settled in 1965, and
he opened the pages of the magazine to the Tulsa
group centered on TED BERRIGAN, a recent arrival
in New York himself. While Schjeldahl spent time
in Europe (1964–65), he was replaced as coeditor
by another Carleton student, David Moberg, for
issues 3–5, but the New York School connection
was already well established, with JOE BRAINARD
supplying covers for issues 3 and 5, and Berrigan,
RON PADGETT, DICK GALLUP, KENWARD ELMSLIE,
JOSEPH CERAVOLO, JOHN PERREAULT, DAVID
SHAPIRO, LORENZO THOMAS, TONY TOWLE, and
TOM VEITCH—as well as Schjeldahl—all contributing writing. First-generation writers responded
to the invitation of the second generation. HARRY
MATHEWS and BARBARA GUEST were introduced in
the fifth issue (summer 1965).

Issues 6 (Thanksgiving 1965) and 7 (Mother's
Day 1966) were published from New York with
Schjeldahl and LEWIS MACADAMS as coeditors. One
new contributor to number 6 was JOHN GIORNO,
whose book *Poems* (1967) was to be one of only

two titles issued independently by Mother Press
(the other was Gallup's *The Bingo* [1966]). Among
first-generation writers, JAMES SCHUYLER contributed "Four Poems/to Frank O'Hara" to number 5,
and JOHN ASHBERY contributed a play, *The Coconut
Milk*, to number 6 (reprinted from *Semi-Colon* 2
[1955]). An unusual contribution by KENNETH
KOCH extends over both of these issues. Parodying
the current TRANSLATIONs of South American poets
by Robert Bly and others, Koch made up his own
Argentine movement, *hasosismo* (meaning "the art
of the fallen limb," according to Koch), and presented supposed translations from representative
(fictitious) poets. The most notorious publication
in *Mother* (number 6) was another hoax. Berrigan
lifted excerpts from various interviews published
elsewhere (with such subjects as CHARLES OLSON,
Bob Dylan, and playwright Fernando Arrabal) and
presented the combined results as his interview
with JOHN CAGE, who was never consulted in the
project. When this interview was selected for a cash
prize and publication in *The AMERICAN LITERARY
ANTHOLOGY* (Farrar, Straus and Giroux, 1968),
Berrigan had to reveal his fabrication to editor
George Plimpton, who decided that publication
could proceed with the addition of an explanatory
note (Berrigan, interview 99–101).

As Schjeldahl became increasingly involved
in writing art criticism, he again withdrew from
editing *Mother*. MacAdams was joined by another
poet, Duncan McNaugton (1942–), in editing
the final issues. Issue number 8, the last to appear in
print format, was published from Buffalo, New York,
where McNaughton was pursuing graduate studies.
The most notable New York School publications
in this issue were Schuyler's "A Picnic Cantata"
and Berrigan's "TAMBOURINE LIFE." The remaining
issues (numbers 9 and 10) appeared as long-playing
records, with contributors (including McNaughton
and MacAdams, Ceravolo, TOM CLARK, and Elmslie)
reading from their work. McNaughton soon founded
a new magazine titled *Fathar* (1970–75), as the successor to *Mother*, which he continued to edit from
the poets' community in BOLINAS, CALIFORNIA.

Bibliography

Berrigan, Ted. Interview by CITY magazine (1977). In
Talking in Tranquility: Interviews. Edited by Stephen

Ratcliffe and Leslie Scalapino. Bolinas, Calif.: Avenue B; Oakland, Calif.: O Books, 1991, 90–105.

———. "Tambourine Life." In *The Collected Poems of Ted Berrigan.* Edited by Alice Notley, Anselm Berrigan, and Edmund Berrigan. Berkeley: University of California Press, 2005, 121–150.

Koch, Kenneth. "Some South American Poets." In *The Art of Poetry: Poems, Parodies, Interviews, Essays, and Other Work.* Ann Arbor: University of Michigan Press, 1996, 61–71.

Schuyler, James. "A Picnic Cantata" and "Four Poems/for Frank O'Hara." In *The Home Book.* Edited by Trevor Winkfield. Calais, Vt.: Z Press, 1977, 16–25, 66–72.

Mounting Tension (1950)

Mounting Tension is the first of many "home movies" in which filmmaker RUDOLPH BURCKHARDT collaborated with NEW YORK SCHOOL poets other than his friend of long standing, EDWIN DENBY. Leading actors in *Mounting Tension* include JOHN ASHBERY, JANE FREILICHER, and LARRY RIVERS, the nucleus of the group of artists and writers who would soon become associated with the TIBOR DE NAGY GALLERY. The film makes NEW YORK CITY's Museum of Modern Art an object of fun "in much the way that the police or the bigwigs in city hall had functioned in the silent movies," Jed Perl notes (399). Indeed, *Mounting Tension* follows the format of silent movies, with a soundtrack of MUSIC (Duke Ellington and Thelonious Monk), but with subtitles for dialogue, since Burckhardt could not afford synchronous sound. The film stock is 16mm, black and white.

The film's simple story, covered in 20 minutes, is easily summarized (using the actors' first names only, to distinguish fictional characters from real persons). We first meet Larry, an artist, painting imaginary nudes and sublimating his desire for real nudes by playing on his saxophone. Anne (Aikman, a friend of Burckhardt's) wanders into Larry's apartment by mistake. She shows an interest in art, while Larry shows considerable interest in her, so much so that she has to run out of the apartment to escape his clutches. She runs through a park where she meets John, an all-American boy who, after a game of catch, offers to take her to a baseball game, but she persuades him to visit the Museum of Modern

Art instead. (The museum's willingness to permit filming on location is an indication of how good its relations with the young upstart artists had already become.) In a hilarious scene John is evicted from the museum for wielding his baseball bat, and Anne unhappily follows him onto the streets, where they argue. Meanwhile, Larry has been stumbling through the streets like a dopefiend (the character he originally proposed to Burckhardt), though the "fix" he needs is obviously sexual. A sign leads him to the office of Jane, "a combination of palm-reader and psychoanalyst" (Burckhardt, catalogue description n.p.). She probes into Larry's earliest memories—playfully rendered by Burckhardt in a montage sequence—then gets him to dance with her. At this point John and Anne enter the office, seeking help for their lovers' quarrel. Larry grabs for Anne, and he and John fight while a picture of Sigmund Freud shakes on the wall. In the next scene, "two weeks later," all have been happily reconciled. On a lake in the park, Larry rows by with Anne, while Jane, on the shore, models for a painting by John—though his painting is abstract. In the excitement of greeting his friends Larry falls from the rowboat into the water, and the movie ends.

Burckhardt explained that *Mounting Tension* "made fun of modern art and psychoanalysis, two pretty sacred subjects at that time" (Burckhardt and Pettet 142), but the fun conveyed by the film has less of the spirit of satire than of improvisation and COLLABORATION. "We sort of made it up as we went along," Burckhardt recalled (catalog). It is clear that the actors are having fun, and it is not surprising that they would appear in later films by Burckhardt: Rivers in *A Day in the Life of a Cleaning Woman* (1953), Freilicher in *The Automotive Story* (1954), and Ashbery in *Money* (1968). Rivers had a role along with ALLEN GINSBERG and GREGORY (NUNZIO) CORSO in *Pull My Daisy* (1959), the film by Alfred Leslie and Robert Frank that is often heralded as the birth of the New American Cinema. The date of *Mounting Tension* proves that the movement had already been stirring for quite some time.

Bibliography

Burckhardt, Rudy. Catalog description for *Mounting Tension.* Film-Makers' Cooperative Catalog. Available

online. URL: http://www.film-makerscoop.com/
catalog/b.html. Accessed December 19, 2008.
———. *Mounting Tension.* 1950. 16mm film. New York:
   Film-Makers' Cooperative.
Burckhardt, Rudy, and Simon Pettet. *Talking Pictures: The
   Photography of Rudy Burckhardt.* Cambridge, Mass.:
   Zoland Books, 1994.
Perl, Jed. *New Art City: Manhattan at Mid-Century.* New
   York: Knopf, 2005.

Moxley, Jennifer (1964–   )

Born in San Diego, California, Jennifer Moxley's
connections to the NEW YORK SCHOOL are mani-
fold, though they have not been a major factor in
the reception of her work. For example, Moxley
and many of the original New York School poets
share FRENCH POETRY—Charles Baudelaire, Arthur
Rimbaud, and Guillaume Apollinaire—as an influence. The poems in *Imagination Verses* (Tender
Buttons, 1996), her acclaimed debut volume, owe
also a debt to FRANK O'HARA, BERNADETTE MAYER,
and Stephen Rodefer (poets of what might be called
the first, second, and third generations of the New
York School, respectively): They are topical, insistently lyrical, and fuse erotic and political content
within the textures of a teeming subjectivity equally
at home in pop culture and high literary artifice.
In *The Sense Record* (Edge, 2002), Moxley's poems
modulate toward more sustained and intricately
articulated structures. The long title poem cites
and was influenced in part by a rereading of JOHN
ASHBERY's SELF-PORTRAIT IN A CONVEX MIRROR
(1974), and the nine-page "Impervious to Starlight"
exhibits an elasticity and porousness of structure,
along with a sharp eye for the telling of quotidian detail, that call to mind, without having been
consciously influenced by, JAMES SCHUYLER's longer
poems ("Crystal Lithium," *The Morning of the Poem,*
etc.). A more explicit investigation of Schuyler's
handling of the long poem is evident in two poems
by Moxley published in the debut issue of *The Poker*
(Winter 2003), "Taking My Own Advice (After
Schuyler)" and "And A Second (After Schuyler)."
A third poem, *Clampdown,* exceeds its origins in the
homage-to-Schuyler sequence and stands as one of
Moxley's most distinctive and accomplished long
poems to date. It was completed in 2002 and pub-

lished in *Explosive* magazine in 2003 but remains
uncollected at this time.

Often Capital (2005, Flood) gathers two early
works by Moxley: "The First Division of Labour"
(originally published as a chapbook in 1995) and
"Enlightenment Evidence" (originally published
in the United Kingdom by Rem press in 1996).
Concerned with the interpenetration of psychological and political violence, these early texts
foreground devices and themes not much explored
within the New York School poetic: Susan Howe's
work, the poetry and life of George Oppen and
other OBJECTIVISTS, and feminist historiography
are the more pertinent points of comparison here.
Moxley's fourth volume, *The Line,* was published by
Post-Apollo Press in 2007. A sequence of 43 prose
poems patterned structurally—though not thematically—on Rimbaud's *Illuminations,* this volume
delivers affectively charged and often oneiric utter-
ances in a straightforward syntax that contrasts
sharply with the elaborate rhetorical periods of *The
Sense Record.*

In addition to collections of poems published
between 1996 and 2006, Moxley has published
a lengthy memoir, *The Middle Room* (Subpress,
2007), detailing her emergence as a poet in San
Diego in the mid- to late 1980s alongside writers
such as Helena Bennett, Bill Luoma, Scott Bentley,
Douglas Rothschild, and others. A retrospective of
JOE BRAINARD's work at the University of California,
San Diego, art gallery in 1986 that included ANNE
WALDMAN, KENWARD ELMSLIE, BILL BERKSON, and
Brainard himself reading from their works was just
one of the many New York School–related events
to occur in San Diego during this period. From
San Diego Moxley moved to PROVIDENCE, RHODE
ISLAND, in 1989. In part through PETER GIZZI (then
editing *O-BLEK* magazine) and LEE ANN BROWN
(publisher of Tender Buttons), Moxley became
acquainted with many of the poets working in the
New York School tradition, the most important
being Mayer, whose life in poetry stood as an early
model for Moxley's own. For 16 months starting in
1998, Moxley lived in Paris, where she formed a
close friendship with ALICE NOTLEY and her husband, the British poet DOUGLAS OLIVER. Moxley's
reflections on Notley's *The DESCENT OF ALETTE*
(Penguin, 1996) appeared in the pages of *The Poker*

(number 2, spring 2003). Since 1999 Moxley has lived in Orono, Maine, with her partner, the poetry critic Steve Evans. She is an assistant professor of English at the University of Maine, poetry editor to *The Baffler* magazine, and contributing editor to *The Poker*. Each of Moxley's first two volumes received starred reviews in *Publishers Weekly*, and her widely anthologized and translated work has commanded serious attention both in the field of avant-garde and experimental poetries and in broader venues such as the *Boston Review, Village Voice, Chicago Review, San Francisco Chronicle*, and *The Best American Poetry*.

music

Not music, but sound is what confers coherence on the bewildering array of musical styles and GENRES to which NEW YORK SCHOOL poets have responded. MORTON FELDMAN, the composer who was closest to the painters, explains: "The new painting made me desirous of a sound world more direct, more immediate, more physical than anything that had existed heretofore" (5). To establish the claim that painting was about paint, painters had to renounce representation, to make painting abstract—a task challenging enough. But music, already abstract, had an internal barrier to immediacy: the system of controlled relationships that traditionally conferred on the materials of music the status of notes rather than sounds. To free sounds from the restriction of system, the New York School composers explored various modes of indeterminacy, for instance, randomizing the process of decision making in composition, as in the case of JOHN CAGE, or, in the case of Feldman, approaching the score itself less as a space for notation and more as an "arena in which to act," as HAROLD ROSENBERG defined the field of "ACTION PAINTING."

The first generation of New York School poets, who faithfully attended recitals by Cage, Feldman, and their associates, celebrate music in their poems because it provides access to the "sound world" that Feldman desired: "an entity of sound / into which being enters," as JOHN ASHBERY describes it in "THE SKATERS" (1964; *Rivers and Mountains* 34). This entrance is simultaneously an opening—"sound opens sound," BARBARA GUEST

writes (169)—so that the "sound world" expands to include sounds in the world as well as in the recital hall. To FRANK O'HARA's ear, "the wind sounded exactly like / Stravinsky" (292). The same principle of expansiveness may account for the wide range of O'Hara's tastes in music. If he could hear Igor Stravinsky, he was also capable of hearing Arnold Schoenberg, "father of sound" (69), though O'Hara's romantic temperament inclined him to favor the Franco-Russian tradition (Stravinsky) in 20th-century music over the Austro-German (Schoenberg). O'Hara wrote as many as seven poems "On Rachmaninoff's Birthday" and inspired JAMES SCHUYLER to write in celebration of "Rachmaninoff's Third [Symphony]." O'Hara's enthusiasm for Rachmaninoff may have come not only from his love for the Russian tradition but also from his respect for Rachmaninoff as a concert pianist. Before he devoted himself to poetry, O'Hara had aspired to become a pianist and had begun training at the New England Conservatory in BOSTON, MASSACHUSETTS. He thus stands at the head of a distinguished list of classically trained instrumentalists among the poets, including DAVID SHAPIRO (violin) and CHARLES NORTH (clarinet).

Language was the instrument upon which the poets, as poets, performed with expertise, and composers have been eager to join them in COLLABORATION. KENNETH KOCH's work "wanted music," in the judgment of Virgil Thomson (Tommasini 454), famous for two operas based on the work of Gertrude Stein. Thomson composed a song cycle, "Mostly About Love" (1959), based on four unpublished poems by Koch, and together they planned an opera, *Angelica*, that was never completed. NED ROREM set Koch's *Bertha* as a chamber opera (1968) after composing numerous songs on texts by Koch, Ashbery, and O'Hara. A step beyond the song cycle in the direction of opera, the genre of cantata loosely embraces Rorem's FOUR DIALOGUES (1954), with text by O'Hara; Paul Bowles's *Picnic Cantata* (1954), with text by Schuyler; and Elliott Carter's *Syringa* (1978), with text by Ashbery. The New York School poet with most extensive involvement in opera is KENWARD ELMSLIE, who has supplied librettos for Rorem (*Miss Julie*, 1965), Jack Beeson (*The Sweet Bye and Bye*, 1957; *Lizzie Borden*, 1965), and Thomas Pasatieri (*The Seagull*, 1972; *Three Sisters*,

1986; *Washington Square,* 1976). Among classical operas that supply reference points for the poets, Giacomo Puccini's are especially prominent, with *Turandot* (1926) furnishing the title of Ashbery's first collection (1953) and a line from *Tosca* (1900) featured as the title of Ashbery's later volume *And the Stars Were Shining* (1994). Koch refers to the same line, from the aria "E lucevan le stelle," in his poem "At the Opera" (1994).

The attraction of vocal music carries over to JAZZ, where the New York School poets attend especially to the singers (O'Hara, "The DAY LADY [Billie Holiday] DIED" [1959]; Schuyler, "Let's All Hear It for Mildred Bailey!" [1987]), as opposed to the instrumentalists whom the BEATS idolized. Although Koch tried reading to the accompaniment of LARRY RIVERS's saxophone (Lehman 198), this mode of performance, too, remained largely the preserve of the Beats. Popularizing poetry was not a concern for the first-generation New York School nor was most popular music. The poetry they wrote during the 1950s barely registered the revival of folk music and the rise of rock and roll. Classical or "art" music remained a touchstone to some later poets (for example, TONY TOWLE, "Some Musical Episodes" [1992]), but during the 1960s, as rock came to dominate the soundscape through a proliferation of hybrid modes such as folk rock, New York School poets added distinctive ingredients to the mix. For instance, TED BERRIGAN's "TAMBOURINE LIFE" (1966) refers to many of the hit songs from the period when it was written, including Bob Dylan's "Mr. Tambourine Man," a 1965 hit in a version by The Byrds. But Berrigan also claims to be writing the poem "using the John-Cage-Animal-Cracker / Method of Composition" (125). When TOM CLARK composed *Neil Young* (1970), he de-composed the lyrics of his favorite singer by cutting them up and rearranging the fragments, a collage technique common to Cage, Ashbery, and WILLIAM S. BURROUGHS.

As rock lyrics and poetry converged, it seemed only natural for poets to perform in rock bands, as a long list of performers testifies: ED SANDERS, JOHN GIORNO, JIM CARROLL, CLARK COOLIDGE, MAGGIE DUBRIS, SUSIE TIMMONS, BARBARA BARG, EDMUND BERRIGAN, CHRIS STROFFOLINO. As a style of performance, PUNK ROCK emerged from the same Lower East Side scene as the POETRY PROJECT AT ST. MARK'S CHURCH IN-THE-BOWERY and bears distinctive marks of the New York School tradition, both in the surrealist imagery of its lyrics and in the raw physicality of its sound. Indeed, punk moves a step further toward the fulfillment of Feldman's prophecy that when music truly finds its freedom it will occur not in a "sound world" but a world of noise: "Sound is all our dreams of music. Noise is music's dream of us" (Feldman 2).

Bibliography

Ashbery, John. "The Skaters." In *Rivers and Mountains.* 1966. Reprint, New York: Ecco, 1977, 34–63.

Bauschatz, Paul. "James Schuyler's 'A Picnic Cantata': The Art of the Ordinary." In *The Scene of My Selves: New Work on New York School Poets,* edited by Terence Diggory and Stephen Paul Miller, 267–286. Orono, Me.: National Poetry Foundation, 2001.

Berrigan, Ted. *The Collected Poems of Ted Berrigan.* Edited by Alice Notley, Anselm Berrigan, and Edmund Berrigan. Berkeley: University of California Press, 2005.

Clark, Tom. Excerpts from *Neil Young* and author's note. In *The Angel Hair Anthology,* edited by Anne Waldman and Lewis Warsh, 287–292, 579–580. New York: Granary Books, 2001.

Feldman, Morton. *Give My Regards to Eighth Street: Collected Writings.* Edited by B. H. Friedman. Cambridge, Mass.: Exact Change, 2000.

Guest, Barbara. "Dissonance Royal Traveller" (1992). In *Selected Poems.* Los Angeles: Sun & Moon, 1995, 169–173.

Johnson, Steven, ed. *The New York Schools of Music and Visual Arts.* New York: Routledge, 2002.

Koch, Kenneth. *The Collected Poems.* New York: Knopf, 2005.

Kramer, Lawrence. "'Syringa': John Ashbery and Elliott Carter." In *Beyond Amazement: New Essays on John Ashbery,* edited by David Lehman, 255–271. Ithaca, N.Y.: Cornell University Press, 1980.

Lehman, David. *The Last Avant-Garde: The Making of the New York School of Poets.* New York: Doubleday, 1998.

O'Hara, Frank. *The Collected Poems.* Rev. ed. Edited by Donald Allen. Berkeley: University of California Press, 1995.

Schuyler, James. *Collected Poems.* New York: Noonday/Farrar, Straus & Giroux, 1995.

Tommasini, Anthony. *Virgil Thomson: Composer on the Aisle.* New York: Norton, 1997.

Towle, Tony. *Some Musical Episodes: Poetry and Prose.* Brooklyn, N.Y.: Hanging Loose Press, 1992.

Myers, John Bernard (1920–1987) *gallery director*

John Bernard Myers was the man who first applied the label "NEW YORK SCHOOL" to a group of poets. His art was to gather together artists in a group and ride the wave of energy that resulted. His first artistic outlet was the THEATER—puppet theater—and he approached the community of the arts in theatrical terms, including the role he chose to play in a "camp" style that advertised his HOMOSEXUALITY. FRANK O'HARA and LARRY RIVERS captured Myers's style and his interests in their play, *Kenneth Koch: A Tragedy* (1954): "Why, my dears, haven't you heard? I have a gallery of the liveliest, more original, and above all youngest painters in America, and for every painter there's a poet. You know we've discovered something called 'the Figure' that's exciting us enormously this season" (O'Hara and Rivers 128).

The TIBOR DE NAGY GALLERY, which Myers directed from its inception in 1950 until 1970, became identified with painters of the second-generation New York School, including LARRY RIVERS, GRACE HARTIGAN, Alfred Leslie, and JANE FREILICHER—many of whom explored figurative or representative painting as an alternative to pure abstraction during the 1950s. But Myers was concerned less with a particular look than with the imaginative act that produced *the marvelous,* a term he adopted from the surrealist poet André Breton (1896–1966). Surrealism and a parallel movement in painting, neoromanticism (associated with artists Pavel Tchelitchew [1898–1957] and Eugene Berman [1899–1972]) had inspired Myers while he was growing up in Buffalo, New York, and provided the opportunity for his escape to the cultural capital of NEW YORK CITY, where he was invited to work on the magazine *View.* A showcase for many European artists and writers in temporary exile in the United States, *View* ceased publication in 1947, but Myers hoped to perpetuate its spirit in the Tibor de Nagy Gallery. "For me," he recalled, "it was like being back at *View* magazine, when poets and painters were invariably making collaborations" (Myers, *Tracking* 147).

Myers promoted COLLABORATION by functioning simultaneously as gallery director, publisher, and theater producer. In 1951 Tibor de Nagy Editions began with the publication of O'Hara's first collection, *A City Winter,* accompanied by drawings by Rivers. Volumes by KENNETH KOCH (*Poems,* with prints by Nell Blaine) and JOHN ASHBERY (*Turandot,* with drawings by Freilicher) followed in 1953, and many more volumes in later years. Also in 1953 Myers launched the ARTISTS' THEATRE with his lover, Herbert Machiz, and a periodical broadside, *Semi-Colon* (1953–56), where the work of "house poets" such as Ashbery, O'Hara, Koch, and JAMES SCHUYLER appeared amid an eclectic mix of authors, including Wallace Stevens (1879–1955), W. H. AUDEN, JAMES INGRAM MERRILL, and Saul Bellow (1915–2005). By 1962 Tibor de Nagy Editions had taken on a sufficiently distinct identity for Myers to advertise his list as "the New York School of Poets" (*WAGNER LITERARY MAGAZINE,* number 3), a term he explained in introducing a sampling of the poets for the journal *Nomad.* A more substantial representation appeared at the end of the decade in Myers's anthology, *The POETS OF THE NEW YORK SCHOOL* (1969).

Throughout the 1960s Myers suffered defections from his gallery as opportunities in the art world expanded and prices escalated. When Myers himself left Tibor de Nagy in 1970 to set up a gallery under his own name, a few artists left with him, notably Red Grooms (1937–   ) and Neil Welliver (1929–2005). But Myers had lost his place at the center of an art world that no longer seemed to have any center, and his growing disgust with that world led him to close his gallery in 1975. As he faced further discouragement in his personal life, including the death of Machiz in August 1976 and news of the cancer to which Myers eventually succumbed, his involvement with poets continued to sustain him. In a new magazine, *Parenthèse* (1975–79), Myers published old friends such as Ashbery and BARBARA GUEST along with new discoveries such as DOUGLAS CRASE and complemented the poetry with distinguished FICTION by such writers as Guy Davenport (1927–2005) and Walter Abish

(1931–   ). Reproductions of work by a wide range of visual artists were equally important to the project. As Myers explained, "the founding principle was my belief in 'interaction'" (*Tracking* 271).

Bibliography

Myers, John. "Frank O'Hara: A Memoir." In *Homage to Frank O'Hara,* edited by Bill Berkson and Joe LeSueur, 34–38. Bolinas, Calif.: Big Sky, 1988.

———. *Tracking the Marvelous: A Life in the New York Art World.* New York: Random House, 1983.

O'Hara, Frank, and Larry Rivers. *Kenneth Koch: A Tragedy.* In *Amorous Nightmares of Delay: Selected Plays,* by Frank O'Hara, 121–132. Baltimore, Md.: Johns Hopkins University Press/PAJ Books, 1997.

Rivers, Larry, with Arnold Weinstein. *What Did I Do? The Unauthorized Autobiography.* New York: HarperCollins/Aaron Asher Books, 1992.

Sokolowski, Thomas, et al. *A Memorial Service for John Bernard Myers.* New York: Sea Cliff Press, 1988.

Myles, Eileen (1949–   )

Born in Cambridge, Massachusetts, in 1949, Myles offers personal narratives in prose and poetry, with an unpolished physical immediacy that recalls JACKSON POLLOCK's ACTION PAINTINGS. Interfacing NEW YORK SCHOOL and BEAT styles, she both worked with JAMES SCHUYLER and befriended ALLEN GINSBERG. Her work includes plays and opera librettos, Dial-a-Poem contributions, and international spoken-word tours. Her working-class background, both Polish and Irish, energizes an anarchic, inventive personality; she has been not only a lesbian spokeswoman but a write-in candidate for U.S. president in 1992.

After Catholic school, where she seems to have terrorized the nuns at least as much as they terrorized her, she graduated in 1971 from the University of Massachusetts, BOSTON, and moved to NEW YORK CITY in 1974: "I wanted a home and / New York is the biggest home / you could possibly have" ("New York" in *Maxfield Parrish*). Her first reading was at CBGB's, the famous DOWNTOWN MANHATTAN venue for underground rock; she came out in 1977 as both poet and lesbian, when reading with JOSEPH CERAVOLO. PAUL VIOLI, ALICE NOTLEY, and TED BERRIGAN were among her teach-

ers at the POETRY PROJECT AT ST. MARK'S CHURCH IN-THE-BOWERY, which she later directed from 1984 to 1986. From 1977 to 1979 she edited the magazine *dodgems* and assisted Schuyler, based at the CHELSEA HOTEL, as the title story of Myles's collection CHELSEA GIRLS (Black Sparrow, 1992) records. *Maxfield Parrish: Early & New Poems* (Black Sparrow, 2006) offers material from her earlier books *Sappho's Boat* (Little Caesar Press, 1982), *A Fresh New Voice from the Plains* (Power Mad Books, 1981), and *The Irony of the Leash* (JIM BRODEY Books, 1978). Her work in publishing and THEATER is also notable: *The New Fuck You: Adventures in Lesbian Reading* (Semiotext(e), 1995), coedited with Liz Kotz, was nominated for a Lamda Award, and she won the Lamda for *School of Fish* (Black Sparrow, 1997), *Not Me* (Semiotext(e), 1999), *On My Way* (Faux Press, 2001), and *Skies* (2001). Two plays, *Feeling Blue, Parts 1, 2, and 3* and *Modern Art,* were both performed at P.S. 122, and her opera, *Hell,* has toured with St. Mark's. Her articles have appeared in many magazines and journals, including *The Nation, Art in America,* the *Village Voice,* and *Paper.* Although she has taught at the Schoolhouse Center in Provincetown, Rhode Island, NAROPA INSTITUTE in Boulder, Colorado, and University of California, San Diego, in addition to New York's Bard College and Pratt Institute, her home is still the East Village.

Along with Schuyler, her influences include FRANK O'HARA, JOHN WEINERS, and ROBERT CREELEY. Although the irony of such heavily masculine influence is not lost on her, as a poet she is more interested in "a private person's public nature," and she claims that she cannot locate "a culture of feminism" (interview by Lamm). Nevertheless, feminists and lesbians both respect her stance and appreciate her writing, and a younger generation of both genders that has felt her influence admires her outspoken and theatrical pronouncements. Heroic, extroverted, and deeply committed to the joy of New York City, Myles's life and work have the kind of mythic quality associated with JACK KEROUAC and O'Hara. She sees life itself as a rehearsal for the performance of poetry, despite language's inadequacies to fully capture it.

One of the strongest New York School influences on her style is in the mixture of genders and classes that poetry can catalyze in order to create the intuition of a superior world in which the poet is naturally ennobled. "School of Fish" reveals the effects of these mixes, as Myles sees blue—her socks, her dog's leash, a bicycle—then leaps to the story of a friend who "for a week or two . . . lived in the streets & / it was such an illumination. What's this human / addiction to light." Such revelations are rooted in the moment: "A poem is a series of conditions, and you're trying to strike some charm that will bring it all together," she says in an interview. "Don't impose a pre-ordained agenda. It's something that doesn't begin to be separate from you until you finish it" (Kane n.p.). As she observes in an untitled poem in *Skies* (Black Sparrow, 2001). "Language / takes / the size / of your / life." For Myles, poetry is "a performance of being," (interview by Kane), unwriting, "not really thinking about a void you write into . . . allowing the poem to happen" (interview by Lamm).

Bibliography

Eileen Myles Web site. Available online. URL: http://www.eileenmyles.net/.

Kane, Daniel. "Interview with Eileen Myles." Teachers & Writers. Formerly available online. URL: http://www.twc.org/forums/poetschat/poetschat_em0199.html.

Lamm, Kimberly. "Interview with Eileen Myles." *How2*. Formerly available online. URL: http://www.scc.rutgers.edu/however/v1_8_2002/current/workbook/lamm-interview.shtm.

Myles, Eileen. *Sorry, Tree*. Seattle, Wash.: Wave, 2007.

Nelson, Maggie. "When We're Alone in Public: The Metabolic Work of Eileen Myles." In *Women, the New York School, and Other True Abstractions*. Iowa City: University of Iowa Press, 2007, 169–208.

N

Naropa Institute/Jack Kerouac School
(1974–)

Located in Boulder, Colorado, Naropa Institute was founded by the Tibetan Buddhist teacher Chögyam Trungpa (1940–87) as a center for Buddhist education. In the tradition from which Trungpa descended, poetry had an important place, embodied, for instance, in the 11th-century poet-saint Milarepa, himself an inheritor of the teachings of the monk Naropa at Nalanda University in India. In the United States poets had more recently been involved in educational experiments that shared similarities with Nalanda. With BLACK MOUNTAIN COLLEGE in mind (and JOHN CAGE on hand to explain that "it all came together at lunch" [Waldman, essay 283]), Trungpa invited ALLEN GINSBERG and ANNE WALDMAN to design a poetry program at Naropa, which began in summer 1975. It was named the Jack Kerouac School of Disembodied Poetics to honor JACK KEROUAC's assimilation of Buddhist principles in his writing and to invoke the presence not only of Kerouac but of an entire tradition of writers who, though dead, would participate in the discussions at Naropa in "disembodied" form. "Sappho, [William] Blake, [Walt] Whitman, H.D. [Hilda Doolittle], [Gertrude] Stein, [Ezra] Pound, W. C. Williams, Lorine Niedecker, Frank O'Hara" are the names that Waldman specifically connects with the curriculum of the Kerouac School (essay 283).

Although named for a Beat writer (see BEATS), the Kerouac School has become an important gathering place for writers in every branch of contemporary experimentation, or the "outrider tradition," as it has come to be known at Naropa. As indicated by the presence of FRANK O'HARA's name in Waldman's list quoted above, NEW YORK SCHOOL poets have had a significant presence at Naropa, not least in the person of Waldman herself, who had been eager to find "some way to live off the Lower East Side a spell" (Waldman, essay 283). JOHN ASHBERY taught in the first summer program and contributed poems to two of the first magazines that Naropa would spawn over the years: *Bombay Gin,* edited by Bonnie Shulman, Cindy Shelton, and Bill St. Clair; and *Roof,* edited by James Sherry and TOM SAVAGE (soon to become a major outlet for the Language poets). TED BERRIGAN taught at Naropa repeatedly from 1975 until his death in 1983; transcripts of several of his classes have been collected in *On the Level Everyday.* LARRY FAGIN directed the poetics program from 1982 to 1984, during a period when Waldman was on leave. By this time Naropa had become the starting point for New York School connections for such writers as REED BYE, who married Waldman in 1980, and JACK COLLOM, who helped organize the Naropa outreach event in Boulder where Bye and Waldman met. Bye continues on the core faculty of the Department of Writing and Poetics at Naropa, along with ANSELM HOLLO and Bobbie Louise Hawkins, former wife of ROBERT CREELEY. Collom is a member of the adjunct faculty, along with MAUREEN OWEN and LISA JARNOT.

As Waldman has acknowledged ("Take Me" 87–88), the coexistence of an institute devoted to Buddhist practice and a school devoted to poetic practice led to some tension from the start of the Naropa experiment. An explosion occurred as early as 1975, when Trungpa forcibly staged the public humiliation of the poets W. S. Merwin and Dana Naone at the Vajradhatu Seminary in Snowmass, Colorado. Although the seminary was not part of Naropa, the principals in the drama were involved in both institutions, and subsequent efforts by the leaders of the Jack Kerouac School to defend Trungpa divided the community of poets nationwide. A seminar in "Investigative Poetry [see INVESTIGATIVE POETRY]," taught by ED SANDERS at Naropa in 1977, documented the incident (*The Party*). TOM CLARK assembled another set of documents (*The Great Naropa Poetry Wars*) and composed a fictionalized version (*The Master*). Whatever poets thought of Trungpa, their respect for Ginsberg and Waldman remained such that the Jack Kerouac School continued to thrive. Different challenges have arisen as Naropa has grown into a university—its title since 1999—enrolling undergraduate as well as graduate students (about 400 of each) and submitting to rules of accreditation that are potentially even more at odds with Trungpa's "crazy wisdom" than the ancient license accorded poets.

Bibliography

Berrigan, Ted. *On the Level Everyday: Selected Talks on Poetry and the Art of Living.* Edited by Joel Lewis. Jersey City, N.J.: Talisman House, 1997.

Clark, Tom. *The Great Naropa Poetry Wars.* Santa Barbara, Calif.: Cadmus, 1980.

———. *The Master.* Milwaukee, Wisc.: Pentagram Press, 1979.

Naropa University Web site. Available online. URL: http://www.naropa.edu/index.html.

Sanders, Ed, and Investigative Poetry Group. *The Party: A Chronological Perspective on a Confrontation at a Buddhist Seminary.* Woodstock, N.Y.: Poetry, Crime & Culture Press, 1977.

Trungpa, Chögyam. *Crazy Wisdom.* Boston: Shambhala, 1991.

Waldman, Anne. Essay in *Contemporary Authors, Autobiography Series* 17, edited by Joyce Nakamura, 267–294. Detroit, Mich.: Gale, 1993.

———. "'Take Me to Your Poets!'" In *Vow to Poetry: Essays, Interview, and Manifestos.* Minneapolis, Minn.: Coffee House Press, 2001, 81–88.

Waldman, Anne, and Andrew Schelling, eds. *Disembodied Poetics: Annals of the Jack Kerouac School.* Albuquerque: University of New Mexico Press, 1994.

Waldman, Anne, and Marilyn Webb, eds. *Talking Poetics from Naropa Institute: Annals of the Jack Kerouac School of Disembodied Poetics.* 2 vols. Boulder, Colo.: Shambhala, 1978–79.

Nauen, Elinor (1952–   )

Born in Sioux Falls, South Dakota, Elinor Nauen came to NEW YORK CITY in 1976 and "immediately went to my first poetry reading ever, the Frank O'Hara memorial in November (at the Poetry Project . . .). I was stunned. Glamour, beauty, wit. That great big party that made poetry the most exciting thing you could possibly do" (605). Nauen then enrolled in JIM BRODEY's workshop at the POETRY PROJECT AT ST. MARK'S CHURCH IN-THE-BOWERY, where she met STEVE LEVINE, EILEEN MYLES, SUSIE TIMMONS, GREG MASTERS, MICHAEL SCHOLNICK, and BARBARA BARG, a constellation of writers sometimes termed the third generation of NEW YORK SCHOOL poets. Nauen became one of a circle of friends around ALICE NOTLEY and TED BERRIGAN who helped to nourish their projects. The larger community of writers important to Nauen has included MAUREEN OWEN, BOB ROSENTHAL, ROCHELLE KRAUT, BOB HOLMAN, ED FRIEDMAN, RICHARD HELL, YUKI HARTMAN, GARY LENHART, and Murat Nemat-Nejat.

Nauen's high spirits helped create an atmosphere of spontaneity, optimism, and verve on the DOWNTOWN MANHATTAN poetry scene. In the mid-1980s, along with MAGGIE DUBRIS and Rachell Walling, Nauen edited *Koff* Magazine Press while also contributing to the publishing enterprises of Levine, Masters, and others. Issues 1 and 2 of *Koff* featured nude centerfolds of poets PAUL VIOLI and of LEWIS WARSH. Issue 3 featured photos of 12 nude poets. The disruption of conventional expectations of gender roles evident in *Koff* has extended to Nauen's interventions into the traditionally male domains of baseball and cars, with her groundbreaking anthologies: *Line Drive: 100*

Baseball Poems (Southern Illinois University Press, 2002); *Diamonds Are a Girl's Best Friend* (Faber, 1994); and *Ladies Start Your Engines* (Faber, 1996).

Although Nauen's poetry is identified with the NEW YORK SCHOOL, the narrative duration and almost raconteur quality of her poems is very much her own. The combination of personal and local history and the casual allusions to admired literary and cultural figures is most akin to the work of Owen and KENNETH KOCH. The prose of EDWARD SANDERS and JACK KEROUAC comes to mind also. Nauen's sustained narrative line and her wry sense of incident and relaying of random encounters seem as much reflections of early years in the Midwest and decades of travel and hitchhiking as lessons learned from the New York School. Her poems often evoke flatness, plains, ground, and sky. In the accomplished long rhyming poem, "Pink Highways" the sustained increment of line as in "Standing alone on a road by a field / At daybreak, with the fresh grassy air / Rising in whips, sky lavender and teal / Cattle regarding you with solemn stare / The top of your head about to yield / To its most feathery impulse . . ." characteristically holds the instance of realization several beats longer than the enjambed, instantaneous, urban sequences in the work of her generation. Nauen confidently takes the measure that it takes to tell the story that is there. "Pink Highways" is part of an unpublished book-length poem, *So Late into the Night,* composed in OTTAVA RIMA.

Nauen's first book, *Cars and Other Poems* (Misty Terrace Press, 1980), is a classic of the mimeo GENRE and was featured in the New York Public Library's defining 1998 exhibition *A Secret Location on the Lower East Side: Adventures in Writing. American Guys* was published in 1996 by HANGING LOOSE PRESS. Anthology appearances include *Up Late: The American Poetry Scene Since 1970* (Four Walls, Eight Windows, 1987), *Out of This World* (Crown, 1991), *Cult Baseball Players* (Simon & Schuster, 1991), and the *Portable Boog Lit Reader* (Boog Lit, 2000). Nauen has written for *Family Circle, Inside M.S., Fitness, Self, Health, Organic Style,* and other periodicals and is an editor for *Newsweek International* and MediaChannel.org. She has edited books of writings of Paul Krassner and Senator George Mitchell. She lives in New York City with novelist Johnny Stanton.

Bibliography

Elinor Nauen. Web site. Available online. URL: http://www. elinornauen.com/index.htm. Accessed December 19, 2008.

Nauen, Elinor. Contributor's Statement. *Out of This World: An Anthology of the St. Mark's Poetry Project 1966–1991.* Edited by Anne Waldman. New York: Crown, 1991, 664–665.

Nest of Ninnies, A John Ashbery and James Schuyler (1969)

This satirical novel is the product of a long-term COLLABORATION between NEW YORK SCHOOL poets JOHN ASHBERY and JAMES SCHUYLER. While the details of their partnership are somewhat vague, we know that it extended over the course of some 16 years. Ashbery and Schuyler met in 1951 through their mutual friend, art critic JOHN BERNARD MYERS, and they conceived *A Nest of Ninnies* during a car trip the following year. The two men worked on the project sporadically over the next decade and a half, often meeting at the home of painter FAIRFIELD PORTER and, for a brief period, at their shared apartment on East 49th Street (previously occupied by FRANK O'HARA and Joe LeSueur). *A Nest of Ninnies* was finally published by Dutton in 1969, the same year as Schuyler's first major poetry collection, *Freely Espousing.* JOE BRAINARD, a close associate of the New York School poets, provided the cover art for the first edition.

The novel is an arch look at the attitudes and mores of upper-middle-class suburbanites. It follows a handful of roughly interchangeable characters—ranging in age from late teens to early 50s—who repeatedly cross paths while visiting popular tourist destinations in Florida, France, Italy, and Manhattan. Along the way they host dinner parties, attempt to play and appreciate classical MUSIC, and share recipes for gourmet cuisine. For the most part the book's satirical tenor remains understated and unassisted by authorial commentary; instead, the authors use the characters' own dialogue as an object of implicit ridicule (a technique employed by Schuyler in his earlier novel, *ALFRED AND GUINEVERE*). The plot is deliberately uneventful, and its sparse narration lends a sense of monotony to what little action there is. The following passage, which takes place at a party hosted by Mrs. Kelso and her son, Irving, is representative:

> "How do you do," Mrs. Kelso said. "This is Fluffy. He's a little out of sorts today, so don't pay too much attention to him."
>
> No one made any motion toward the white cat which lay, outstretched and watchful, at Mrs. Kelso's feet. Fluffy got up and left the room. "Oh dear," Mrs. Kelso said, "it must be one of you doesn't like cats.". . .
>
> "What a lovely painting, Mrs. Kelso," Fabia said. "Did some member of your family do it?"
>
> "Yes, they did," Mrs. Kelso said, "and no one so very far away."
>
> "Could that be the famous haunted castle?" Fabia asked.
>
> "It has certain features of that castle," Irving said with a blush, "but the basic idea came from my own head."
>
> "I heard a most interesting broadcast today," Mrs. Kelso said firmly.
>
> Fluffy entered the room carrying a dead mouse.
>
> "Funny, I never noticed that place on the ceiling before," Irving said.
>
> "If you're looking at the place I am," Fabia said, "I think it's the shadow of the knob on that lamp" (34–35).

The novel's formal blandness and its eye for quotidian detail reinforce the tastelessly insipid qualities of the bourgeoisie.

The principal characters are natives of a fictional town, Kelton, in upstate New York, a social milieu with which the authors—Ashbery, from Rochester, and Schuyler, who spent his teens near Buffalo—were intimately familiar. While writing the book, the two poets took turns lampooning Kelton's residents. "We started out alternating almost sentence by sentence," Schuyler once told an interviewer. "John and I were always trying to cap each other as it went on" (183–184). Indeed, the text frequently hints at a substratum of authorial dialogue beneath the hackneyed sentiments and provincial gossip of its characters.

A Nest of Ninnies met with mixed reviews upon its release. Some admired its subtle wit and social commentary; W. H. AUDEN, whom Schuyler had befriended after World War II, declared that it was "destined to become a minor classic" (20). Other critics, however, accused it of being overly cynical; Sara Blackburn wrote:

> Like satires about the emptiness of advertising . . . it is the kind of novel whose existence depends on readers who find their own lives absurd but see no possibility for making them otherwise (475).

The original documents from the poets' writing process are among the James Schuyler Papers in the Mandeville Special Collections of Geisel Library at the University of California, San Diego.

Bibliography

Ashbery, John, and Schuyler, James. *A Nest of Ninnies.* 1969. Reprint, Calais, Vermont: Z Press, 1983.

Auden, W. H. Review of *A Nest of Ninnies. New York Times Book Review,* 4 May 1969, pp. 5, 20.

Blackburn, Sara. Review of *A Nest of Ninnies. Nation,* 14 April 1969, 475.

Downes, Rackstraw, et al. *Fairfield Porter: A Catalogue Raisonné.* New York: Hudson Hills Press, 2001.

Schuyler, James. Interview by Carl Little. *Agni* 37 (June 1993): 152–182.

Stitt, Peter. "The Art of Poetry XXXIII: An Interview with John Ashbery." *Paris Review* 90 (Winter 1983): 30–59.

New American Poetry, 1945–1960, The
(1960)

The enormously influential anthology *The New American Poetry,* edited by DONALD M. ALLEN and published by Grove Press, established the canon of the first generation of NEW YORK SCHOOL poets and set them in context of a broader avant-garde movement (44 poets in all) that had emerged since 1950. Despite the earlier date announced in the title, 1950 is the effective starting date that CHARLES OLSON, one of Allen's principal advisers, cited to justify exclusion of earlier writers in the tradition (Golding 187–188). The key criterion was the date of emergence as a writer rather than date of birth, as Allen explains in his preface to justify, explicitly, the exclusion of writers such as ROBERT LOWELL and ELIZABETH BISHOP and, implicitly, the inclusion of their senior, Olson. The effect of such juggling was to draw an absolute division between *cooked* and *raw* poets, to use the terms Lowell employed in his acceptance speech for the National Book Award in 1960 (Rasula 233–234). The latter were gathered in *The New American Poetry*, the former in *New Poets of England and America* (Meridian, 1957), edited by Donald Hall, Robert Pack, and Louis Simpson, who had included Lowell (Shapiro 6). The contrast has entered literary history as "the war of the anthologies" (Carroll 226–228; Rasula 223–247).

A concern for literary history motivated Allen to adopt what he admits to be "the unusual device of dividing the poets into five large groups" in the preface (xii): BLACK MOUNTAIN, SAN FRANCISCO RENAISSANCE, BEAT Generation, New York Poets, and a fifth miscellaneous group. In order of birth, which determines the sequence within each group, the New York Poets are BARBARA GUEST, JAMES SCHUYLER, EDWARD FIELD (whose inclusion seemed an anomaly even at the time), KENNETH KOCH, FRANK O'HARA, and JOHN ASHBERY. Allen does not call them "the New York School," a designation that JOHN BERNARD MYERS first used in print slightly later to connect the poets with the New York School of painters. In fact, Allen's brief description of these poets in his preface sets them in the context of THEATER rather than painting: the POETS' THEATRE at Harvard, the LIVING THEATRE and the ARTISTS' THEATRE in New York. However, in a section of "Statements on Poetics" at the back of the anthology, Schuyler's "Poet and Painter Overture" emphasizes the relation to painting as the key to understanding New York poetry. It also provides the key to understanding the claims Allen is making for the New American Poetry: namely, that such poetry is poised to extend the cultural influence of America internationally, as only JAZZ MUSIC and abstract expressionist painting had done previously. The title of Allen's anthology echoes the title of an exhibition, *The New American Painting* (1958–59), that had recently toured eight European countries under the auspices of New York's Museum of Modern Art (Gooch 354; Golding 186 note).

Apart from Schuyler, the only other New York poet represented by a statement on poetics is O'Hara, in an uncharacteristically perfunctory performance that pales by comparison to his manifesto for "PERSONISM," which Allen had turned down. *The New American Poetry* demonstrates that the poetics of the New York School must be sought primarily in the poetry itself, in contrast, for instance, to the case of Olson, whose essay on "PROJECTIVE VERSE," reprinted by Allen, has exercised perhaps more influence than his poetry. Among the poems by O'Hara that Allen presents, "WHY I AM NOT A PAINTER" obviously enacts the situation described in Schuyler's "Poet and Painter Overture," while offering countless younger poets an example of "how I could write too," as TED BERRIGAN expressed it (47). No theoretical statement could possibly embody Allen's "rejection of all those qualities typical of academic verse" (preface xi) as compellingly as Koch's poem "FRESH AIR," which, for that reason, became the central exhibit in Harvey Shapiro's review of *The New American Poetry* in the *New York Times Book Review*. In a front-page review in the *New York Herald Tribune Book Review*, Marianne Moore found "treasure" in Schuyler's "Salute" and "pleasure" in Ashbery's "The Instruction Manual." Guest's "Parachutes, My Love, Could Carry Us Higher" seemed "as far afield as one could imagine from the battering 'confessional' model" associated with Lowell, according to the young Kathleen Fraser, who heard Guest read the poem at the TIBOR DE NAGY GALLERY in 1964 (Fraser 127). *The New American Poetry* established not only the canon of New York School poets but also the poems with which each was identified for many years thereafter.

Bibliography

Allen, Donald. *The New American Poetry, 1945–1960*. New ed., Berkeley: University of California Press, 1999.

Berrigan, Ted. Interview by Barry Alpert (1972). In *Talking in Tranquility*. Edited by Stephen Ratcliffe and Leslie Scalapino. Bolinas, Calif.: Avenue B; Oakland, Calif.: O Books, 1991, 31–54.

Carroll, Paul. *The Poem in Its Skin*. Chicago: Follett, 1968.

Fraser, Kathleen. "Barbara Guest: The Location of Her (A Memoir)" (1994). In *Translating the Unspeakable: Poetry and the Innovative Necessity.* Tuscaloosa: University of Alabama Press, 2000, 124–130.

Golding, Alan. "*The New American Poetry* Revisited, Again." *Contemporary Literature* 39, no. 2 (1998): 180–211.

Gooch, Brad. *City Poet: The Life and Times of Frank O'Hara.* New York: Knopf, 1993.

Moore, Marianne. "The Ways Our Poets Have Taken in Fifteen Years Since the War" (1960). In *The Complete Prose.* Edited by Patricia C. Willis. New York: Viking, 1987, 535–539.

Perloff, Marjorie. "Whose New American Poetry? Anthologizing in the Nineties." *Diacritics* 2, nos. 3–4 (Fall–Winter 1996): 104–123.

Rasula, Jed. *The American Poetry Wax Museum: Reality Effects, 1940–1990.* Urbana, Ill.: National Council of Teachers of English, 1996.

Shapiro, Harvey. "Rebellious Mythmakers." *New York Times Book Review,* 28 August 1960, p. 6.

New American Writing/OINK! (1971–)

Founded by poets PAUL HOOVER and MAXINE CHERNOFF in CHICAGO, ILLINOIS, and edited since 1994 from their home in Mill Valley, California, this annual literary magazine quickly established itself as one of the leading innovative literary journals of the post-1975 period. Nationally distributed by Ingram Periodicals, *New American Writing* holds a rank and editorial focus comparable to Clayton Eshleman's *Sulfur,* which ran 46 issues from 1981 to 2000, and Bradford Morrow's ongoing and influential *Conjunctions.* Of the three, *New American Writing* has been most dedicated to the poetry of the NEW YORK SCHOOL and, increasingly since the early 1990s, work influenced by LANGUAGE and "post-Language" poetics. Work from the magazine has frequently been selected for the annual anthologies *The Best American Poetry* and *The Pushcart Anthology.* In l988 the magazine was named one of the nation's 10 outstanding literary magazines by the Coordinating Council of Literary Magazines. The magazine is also distinguished by its inclusiveness. Numerous younger poets who have gone on to significant careers made their first appearance in its pages.

In 2001, the magazine was honored at the National Arts Club in NEW YORK CITY, for 30 years of consecutive publication including its earlier embodiment as *OINK!,* which published 19 issues from 1971 to 1985. *OINK!* began as a small, saddle-stitched quarterly edited by Dean Faulwell, James Leonard, and Hoover, graduate students in the Program for Writers at the University of Illinois, Chicago. Its editorial disposition was whimsical and surrealist. The first issue featured the editors' own poetry, with a cover portraying a doleful, large-eyed hound saying "OINK!," and opened with a series of manifestos, one of which proclaimed: "We like the paintings of Willem de Kooning. They're so messy and delicate, and I don't know, brilliantly stupid. Our motto is simply 'oink.' Our goal is to uncover the true dirt of the unconscious ('in all of its purity')." Contributors in early issues were largely of the New York School: RON PADGETT, PETER SCHJELDAHL, TED BERRIGAN, ALICE NOTLEY, and ANNE WALDMAN. After the fourth issue of *OINK!* Faulwell moved to California, where he published one issue of *BOINK!* Leonard moved to Wisconsin after the sixth issue, and Chernoff joined Hoover as coeditor. The prose poet Russell Edson became a regular contributor, and issue 13 (1977) consisted entirely of his chapbook, *Edson's Mentality.* By *OINK!*'s last issue, number 19 (1985), which had cover art by JOE BRAINARD, it had developed into a professionally typeset, perfect-bound volume of 132 pages. The opening work was "You Can Go Home Again: A Letter from Paris" by NED ROREM. The previous issue, number 18 (1984), had cover art by ALEX KATZ; contributors included Notley, ANDREI CODRESCU, Lyn Hejinian, Barrett Watten, Lydia Davis, AMY GERSTLER, ELAINE EQUI, and EILEEN MYLES, figures typical of the *NEW AMERICAN WRITING* issues to come.

As *OINK!* gave way to *New American Writing* in 1986, circulation immediately tripled and grew thereafter to more than 6,000. By number 10 (1992) it appeared in bookstores and newsstands nationally, and contributors included BARBARA GUEST, Hilda Morley, KENNETH KOCH, Lydia Davis, Carl Rakosi, DENISE LEVERTOV, Susan Wheeler, Charles Bernstein, PETER GIZZI, Karen Garthe, Joan Retallack, and Gillian Conoley, a cross-section of experimental activity. The magazine's use of cover art by noted artists (Jennifer Bartlett, LARRY RIVERS, Elizabeth Murray) was made more effective by the use of the four-color printing process. Nevertheless, from its inauguration to the present day the magazine has been a cottage industry, edited out of a wicker laundry basket.

In the late 1980s the magazine began to include special features: contemporary AUSTRALIAN POETRY, edited by John Tranter (number 4, 1988); censorship and the arts (number 5, 1989), occasioned by the National Endowment of the Arts censorship scandal over a Robert Mapplethorpe cover; New British Poetry, edited by Ric Caddel (numbers 9–10, 1991); Lies About the Truth: 14 Brazilian Poets, edited by Régis Bonvicino (number 18, 2000), somewhat controversial in Brazil for its implicit attack on concretism; Russian absurdist poetry of the 1930s, edited by Eugene Ostashevsky (number 20, 2002), with Kazimir Malevich cover art; and Richter 858 Poets, edited by David Breskin (number 21, 2003), based on a show of Gerhard Richter's abstract "scrape" paintings (cover by the artist) at the Museum of Modern Art in San Francisco. Issue 23 (2005) contained four special features: new poems by Mahmoud Darwish; César Vallejo's *Black Heralds*, translated by Clayton Eshleman; a 100-page supplement of New Canadian Poetry edited by Todd Swift; and Nine Contemporary Vietnamese Poets, edited and translated by Nguyen Do and Hoover.

With continued interest in new poetics and its recently added focus on TRANSLATION and an international scope, *New American Writing* continues into its fourth decade. Only one small press dedicated to the innovative, Keith and Rosmarie Waldrop's Burning Deck Press, has had a longer continuous history of publication.

Bibliography

Eshelman, Clayton, Paul Hoover, and Maxine Chernoff. "*Sulfur* and *New American Writing*: A Dialogue." *Jacket* 36 (2008). Available online. URL: http://jacket magazine.com/36/iv-eshleman-chernoff-hoover. shtml. Accessed December 19, 2008.

New American Writing Web site. Available online. URL: http://www.newamericanwriting.com.

New York City

In his introduction to FRANK O'HARA's *Collected Poems* (1971), JOHN ASHBERY allows that the space experienced in O'Hara's work is "not only the space of NEW YORK SCHOOL painting but also the space of New York itself, that kaleidoscopic lumber-room where laws of time and space are altered" (Ashbery, Introduction x). Ashbery intends to distinguish O'Hara's work from that of other poets, including himself, for whom New York was "merely a convenient place to live and meet people." Ashbery's tendency to swerve from the real to an imaginary city, as in "The Instruction Manual" (1956), has helped to make the New York School mode available to poets who do not live in New York. Still, the history of the New York School has ensured that New York City continues to leave its stamp even on works of imagination created elsewhere.

The vast size of New York City has been an inspiration and a challenge to the poets as it is to anyone who lives or works there or merely makes the effort to pass through. In 1950 the greater New York area was the largest urban concentration in the world, with roughly 12.5 million people (Rosenberg, "Top Ten" n.p.). By 2005 it had been surpassed by Tokyo, but New York's population remains huge, with an estimated 17.8 million in the greater area (Rosenberg, "Largest Cities" n.p.), about 8.1 million in the city proper (Department of City Planning n.p.). The expansion of the city into the surrounding area was promoted by construction of a network of highways that had begun before World War II. After the war the white middle class (as many as 800,000 during the 1950s) followed these highways to settle in homes in the suburbs (Wallock 31), commuting to jobs in office towers that sprang up in Midtown Manhattan. To the poet walking the streets these buildings were the most visible evidence of expanding scale. O'Hara was particularly taken by the Seagram Building (1958), designed in the modernist International Style by Mies van der Rohe and Philip Johnson. The building shows up repeatedly in O'Hara's poems: "The Lay of the Romance of the Associations" (1959), "Personal Poem" (1959), "Steps" (1960), "Walking" (1964). O'Hara did not live to see the ultimate giant, the World Trade Center, designed by the relatively unknown architect Minoru Yamasaki and featuring the tallest building in the world (110 stories, 1,368 feet [417 meters]) at the time of completion (1972). Construction began in 1968, and later poets took notice. BERNADETTE MAYER's snapshot of the twin towers appeared on the spine of her book MEMORY (1975), and, of course, the towers' destruction was the occasion of many elegies after SEPTEMBER 11, 2001.

The New York School artists drew the poets to New York in the first place, and the artists, with their "works as big as cities" (O'Hara, *Standing Still* 40), provided the key to the poets' response to the city's scale. Viewing WILLEM DE KOONING's *Suburb in Havana* (1958), O'Hara asked, "Why should it have this overpowering effect when we have the House of Seagram in front of us?" (O'Hara, *Standing Still* 95). The implied answer is that the painting, while abstract, still expresses personality, whereas impersonality seems to shape the building as much as it did the poetic theory of T. S. Eliot. O'Hara's sense of personality, which he passed on to later New York School poets in his essay on "PERSONISM," is distinctively urban. It can be anonymous, an advantage to a gay man cruising the streets, and it can be collective so that the "them" with whom O'Hara engages in "A Step Away from Them" (1956) includes not only intimate acquaintances, like VIOLET R. (BUNNY) LANG, but also "laborers" on their lunch break, "a Negro [who] stands in a doorway," "a blonde chorus girl" whose high heels click on the sidewalk, "a lady in foxes" and "several Puerto Ricans" (*Collected Poems* 257–258).

EDWIN DENBY, whom O'Hara invokes in "A Step Away from Them," led the way in expressing this sense of collective personality ("Mid-Day Crowd" [1948]) in New York School poetry. He also captured something even more ineffable, which Denby called "the climate of New York" ("The Climate" [1948]; Denby 9). It is as if the weather, or the ability to feel it, humanizes the relations that the city otherwise reduces to mere commerce: "The sky is in the streets with the trucks and us," writes Denby (9). "The scruffy skies of New York" that Ashbery observes in FLOW CHART (174) make the city, despite his denial, more than "a convenient place to live and meet people." For younger poets,

such as JORDAN DAVIS in "A Little Gold Book," the sky returns to the city streets to be redeemed by their immediacy: "Fragile sky in the ugly city you see on tv / Turns to gold on the terrible street" (30). However "terrible" the city may appear, the New York School poets have found a way of inhabiting it so that, in Denby's words, "We can take it for granted that here we're home" (9).

Bibliography

Ashbery, John. *Flow Chart.* New York: Knopf, 1992.

———. "The Instruction Manual." In *Some Trees.* 1956. Reprint, New York: Ecco, 1978, 14–18.

———. Introduction to *The Collected Poems,* by Frank O'Hara. Rev. ed. Edited by Donald Allen. Berkeley: University of California Press, 1995, vii–xi.

Davis, Jordan. "A Little Gold Book." In *An Anthology of New (American) Poets,* edited by Lisa Jarnot, Leonard Schwartz, and Chris Stroffolino, 30–33. Jersey City, N.J.: Talisman House, 1998.

Denby, Edwin. *Dance Writings and Poetry.* Edited by Robert Cornfield. New Haven, Conn.: Yale University Press, 1998.

Department of City Planning, New York City. "New York: A City of Neighborhoods." New York City Web site. Available online. URL: http://www.nyc.gov/html/dcp/pdf/neighbor/neighbor.pdf. Downloaded December 19, 2008.

Diggory, Terence. "Picturesque Urban Pastoral in Post-War New York City." In *The Built Surface.* Vol. 2: *Architecture and the Pictorial Arts from Romanticism to the Twenty-First Century,* edited by Karen Koehler, 283–303. Aldershot, U.K.: Ashgate, 2002.

Mayer, Bernadette. *Memory.* Plainfield, Vt.: North Atlantic Books, 1975.

O'Hara, Frank. *The Collected Poems.* Rev. ed. Edited by Donald Allen. Berkeley: University of California Press, 1995.

———. "Larry Rivers: *The Next to Last Confederate Soldier*" (1959). In *Standing Still and Walking in New York.* Edited by Donald Allen. San Francisco: Grey Fox, 1983. 95–96.

Rosenberg, Matt. "Largest Cities in the World." About.com. Available online. URL: http://geography.about.com/od/urbaneconomicgeography/a/agglomerations.htm. Accessed December 14, 2008.

———. "Top Ten Cities of the Year 1950." About.com. Available online. URL: http://geography.about.com/

library/weekly/aa011201g.htm. Accessed December 19, 2008.

Wallock, Leonard. "New York City: Capital of the Twentieth Century." In *New York: Culture Capital of the World, 1940–1965.* New York: Rizzoli, 1988, 17–51.

New York City Ballet (1948–)

Founded in 1948 by impresario Lincoln Kirstein (1907–96) and choreographer George Balanchine (1904–83), the New York City Ballet (NYCB) represented the distillation of several decades of experiments in DANCE that rejuvenated that moribund court entertainment, the ballet. Balanchine's movement vocabulary remained strictly classical, but he gave his traditional means a modernist twist, attracting in the process a nontraditional audience. "A faithful band of intellectuals, delighting in Balanchine's latest masterpieces," is how FRANK O'HARA's lover Vincent Warren (1938–) describes the artists, writers, and academics who frequented the NYCB (Berkson and LeSueur, *Homage* 75), especially in its early years, before it acquired a permanent home and an establishment aura at Lincoln Center (1964–).

Virtually all of the poets and many of the artists associated with the NEW YORK SCHOOL burned incense at Balanchine's altar; among the most devoted were O'Hara, poet and critic EDWIN DENBY, and O'Hara's Harvard roommate Edward Gorey (1925–2000), who never missed a performance. Like O'Hara's poems, Balanchine's ballet has a French basis, a Russian inflection, and American aims. Whereas traditional ballet staging reflects the sense of hierarchy of its erstwhile aristocratic audience, "Balanchine proposes a different magic," Denby writes, one which derives from his rigorous "attention to the craft of dancing"; this focus on dancing for dancing's sake "makes one moral law for all" (Denby 231). In a 1955 review O'Hara also emphasizes Balanchine's democratizing impulse: In his work, "the differentiation between the two main dancers and the corps is kept to a minimum . . . they are part of society, they exist in and because of the corps as lovers did in the 19th century and don't anymore. They may exit solo, but they enter with

their peers and are beheld in their midst, bowing" (*Standing Still* 72).

The NYCB figures in another of O'Hara's erotically charged visions of a tight-knit society of peers, his epithalamium for JANE FREILICHER, "Poem Read at Joan Mitchell's" (1957). "[D]ear New York City Ballet Company, you are quite a bit like a wedding yourself!" he exclaims, and imagines that his friend's marriage won't stand in the way of "more discussions in lobbies of the respective greatnesses of [NYCB stars] Diana Adams and Allegra Kent" (*Collected Poems* 266). The scene in the NYCB lobby could be as lively as the one on stage. There, JOHN ASHBERY was introduced to Marianne Moore (Ashbery n.p.) and JOHN BERNARD MYERS to Tibor de Nagy (Myers 97); and Myers once shouted at O'Hara and LARRY RIVERS (quoting Mrs. Paul Verlaine), "There they are, all covered with blood and semen," an incident memorialized in a plate in the O'Hara-Rivers COLLABORATION *Stones* (Perloff 103).

Other O'Hara poems containing NYCB references are "Aix-en-Provence" (1955), "John Button Birthday" (1957), "Variations on Pasternak's 'Mein Liebchen, Was Willst du Noch Mehr'"(1959), "Glazunoviana, or Memorial Day" (1960), "Ode to Tanaquil LeClerq" (1960), "Variations on Saturday" (1960), and "BIOTHERM" (1962).

Bibliography

Ashbery, John. Unpublished letter to John Warner Moore, 14 February 1967. Rosenbach Museum and Library, Philadelphia, Pa.

Bender, Thomas. "The New York City Ballet and the Worlds of New York Intellect." In *Dance for a City: Fifty Years of the New York City Ballet,* edited by Lynn Garafola, with Eric Foner, 53–72. New York: Columbia University Press, 1999.

Berkson, Bill, and Joe LeSueur, eds. *Homage to Frank O'Hara.* Bolinas, Calif.: Big Sky, 1978.

Denby, Edwin. *Dance Writings and Poetry.* Edited by Robert Cornfield. New Haven, Conn.: Yale University Press, 1998.

Garis, Robert. *Following Balanchine.* New Haven, Conn.: Yale University Press, 1995.

Myers, John Bernard. *Tracking the Marvelous: A Life in the New York Art World.* New York: Random House, 1981.

O'Hara, Frank. *The Collected Poems of Frank O'Hara*. Rev. ed. Edited by Donald Allen. Berkeley: University of California Press, 1995.

———. *Standing Still and Walking in New York*. Edited by Donald Allen. San Francisco: Grey Fox, 1983.

O'Hara, Frank, and Bill Berkson. "Notes from Row L" (1961). In *Hymns of St. Bridget and Other Writings*. Woodacre, Calif.: Owl Press, 2001, 39–40.

Perloff, Marjorie. *Frank O'Hara: A Poet Among Painters*. 1977. Reprint, Chicago: University of Chicago Press, 1998.

New York City Writers Conference
(1956–1965)

Based at Wagner College on Staten Island, New York, the New York City Writers Conference provided an important staging ground for NEW YORK SCHOOL poets in the early years of the emergence of the second generation. To some extent the Wagner College conference provided an experience for the New York School similar to that provided for the BEAT, BLACK MOUNTAIN, and SAN FRANCISCO RENAISSANCE poets by the conference held at the University of British Columbia in Vancouver, Canada, during the summer of 1963. Representatives of all of these groups then converged at the BERKELEY POETRY CONFERENCE in 1965.

The New York City Writers Conference was founded in 1956 as a 10-day summer school program under the direction of Gorham Munson (1896–1969), who had for many years taught a popular writing workshop at the New School. The conference personnel shifted noticeably toward the avant-garde when WILLARD MAAS took over as director for a brief period in the early 1960s. KENNETH KOCH taught poetry, Edward Albee playwriting, and the FICTION workshop alternated between PAUL GOODMAN and Kay Boyle, who succeeded Maas as conference director in 1964. A group of younger poets followed Koch to study with him, including, in 1962, FRANK LIMA and DAVID SHAPIRO, and, in 1963, JIM BRODEY, Kathleen Fraser, and TONY TOWLE. GERARD MALANGA, a Wagner College student and protégé of Maas, was present both years and provided his own connections to the avant-garde. In his *Memoir* Towle recounts an expedition that Malanga led to ANDY WARHOL's Factory, where Malanga had just begun to work (79–80). The Gotham Book Mart provided a link to the old avant-garde by sponsoring a writing award, in which Lima, Shapiro, and Towle each had a share.

In addition to workshops the conference sponsored readings and "round-table, coffee-hour discussions" with visiting writers and artists. Under Maas the guests included poets FRANK O'HARA, BILL BERKSON, KENWARD ELMSLIE, LeRoi Jones (AMIRI BARAKA), and GREGORY CORSO, as well as representatives of other arts, for instance, the composer Ben Weber, Julian Beck and Judith Malina of the LIVING THEATRE, and Amos Vogel of Cinema 16. A wintertime counterpart to these events, a "Fine Arts Festival" held on the Wagner campus every February, became the occasion for the notorious joint appearance of O'Hara and ROBERT LOWELL in 1962, when O'Hara read "Poem (Lana Turner has collapsed)," just composed on the ferry ride over to Staten Island, and Lowell responded dryly that the poems he would read had taken more time to write (Gooch 386–387). In February 1964 Malanga organized a panel billed as "The New Decadents," consisting of himself, JOE BRAINARD, TED BERRIGAN, DICK GALLUP, LORENZO THOMAS, Peter Orlovsky, and RON PADGETT (Padgett 66–68).

Bibliography

Gooch, Brad. *City Poet: The Life and Times of Frank O'Hara*. New York: Knopf, 1993.

Padgett, Ron. *Joe: A Memoir of Joe Brainard*. Minneapolis, Minn.: Coffee House Press, 2004.

Towle, Tony. *Memoir, 1960–1963*. Cambridge, Mass.: Faux Press, 2001.

New York Poets Theatre (1961–1965)

Despite the similarity in name, the New York Poets Theatre (sometimes known as the American Poets Theatre) was not simply a theatrical outlet for NEW YORK SCHOOL poetry. It produced a number of plays by New York School poets, but the productions sought theatrical effect primarily through means other than text and treated text as one more theatrical effect. DIANE DI PRIMA, one of the theater's founders, describes her plays as "'word scores' for a director to do with as s/he wills" (di Prima, *Recollections* 376). The directors involved in the project, James Waring, John Herbert MacDowell, and Alan Marlowe, had roots in DANCE and MUSIC rather than "literary" theater. The fifth member of the founding board, LeRoi Jones (AMIRI BARAKA), was just beginning to write for THEATER and saw his first play produced, along with di Prima's *The Discontent of the Russian Prince* and Michael McClure's *The Pillow,* in the first program of the New York Poets Theatre, at the Off-Bowery Theater on East 10th Street in October 1961. A "New York School" response was registered by Joe LeSueur, who regretted that "supple and evocative language" of Jones's play, from *The System of Dante's Hell,* was overwhelmed by the "no holds barred" staging of a homosexual rape in an army camp.

The New York Poets Theatre offered a second series of one-act plays in 1961, featuring work by James Waring, JOHN WIENERS, and Robert Duncan, but did not manage another season until the spring of 1964, when it opened at the New Bowery Theater (also known as the Bridge Theater) on St. Mark's Place, with a triple bill consisting of FRANK O'HARA's *Loves Labor, An Eclogue,* Wallace Stevens's *Three Travelers Watch a Sunrise,* and di Prima's *Murder Cake.* O'Hara's play stole the show with a huge cast highlighted by drag queen Frankie Francine in the role of Venus. According to di Prima, O'Hara did not mind the fact that Venus could not remember her lines and had to read them from her fan, although James Waring, who had directed the original production of the play for the LIVING THEATRE in 1959, objected to the amateurish effect (Gooch 417; di Prima, *Recollections* 376). Later in the season, after the police had expelled the company from the New Bowery Theater for showing "obscene" films, KENNETH KOCH's *Guinevere, or The Death of the Kangaroo* opened in a converted loft on Bleecker Street, with sets and costumes by Red Grooms, followed in June by McClure's *The Blossom, or Billy the Kid,* with the entire theater turned into an installation by West Coast artist George Herms. The stark contrast between these plays, which di Prima regarded as paradigmatic of a contrast in East and West Coast sensibilities (*Recollections* 389), extends to their handling of text, with

Koch's words flying free of sense and McClure's reabsorbed in the physical senses.

Having decided that she preferred McClure, di Prima was inevitably disappointed in the final season of the New York Poets Theatre in 1965, consisting entirely of New York School work: BARBARA GUEST's *Port,* JAMES SCHUYLER's *Shopping and Waiting,* and Schuyler's COLLABORATION with KENWARD ELMSLIE, *Unpacking the Black Trunk* (di Prima, *Recollections* 407). In *Shopping and Waiting,* "a picture book that makes sounds like the pictures when you turn the pages" (Schuyler 86) offers an ironic commentary on the visceral language that the New York Poets Theatre sought to develop.

Bibliography

di Prima, Diane. *Recollections of My Life as a Woman: The New York Years.* New York: Viking, 2001.

———. *ZipCode: The Collected Plays.* Minneapolis, Minn.: Coffee House Press, 1992.

Gooch, Brad. *City Poet: The Life and Times of Frank O'Hara.* New York: Knopf, 1993.

Jones, LeRoi. "The Eighth Ditch (Is Drama)." In *The System of Dante's Hell.* New York: Grove, 1965, 79–91.

Koch, Kenneth. *Guinevere, or The Death of the Kangaroo.* In *Bertha and Other Plays.* New York: Grove, 1966, 24–33.

McClure, Michael. *The Mammals.* San Francisco: Cranium Press, 1972.

O'Hara, Frank. *Loves Labor, An Eclogue.* In *Amorous Nightmares of Delay: Selected Plays.* Baltimore, Md.: Johns Hopkins University Press, 1997, 155–161.

Schuyler, James. *Shopping and Waiting.* In *The Home Book.* Calais, Vt.: Z Press, 1977, 86–88.

Stevens, Wallace. *Three Travelers Watch a Sunrise.* In *Opus Posthumous.* Rev. ed. Edited by Milton J. Bates. New York: Vintage–Random House, 1990, 149–162.

New York School

The term *New York School* was first applied by Robert Motherwell to a group of painters he was associated with in New York, alternatively labeled "abstract expressionists" or "action painters." Motherwell sought to distinguish this group from the School of Paris, the dominant movement in modern art up to that time, derived from the innovations of Paul Cézanne, Pablo Picasso, and Henri Matisse. In the first published reference to the New York School (1951), Motherwell emphasized spontaneity at both the beginning and the end of the painting process; the painter begins "without preconceived ideas" and the completed painting may seem "'unfinished,' in comparison with our young contemporaries of Paris" (Motherwell 83). The absence of preconceived ideas includes the idea of the New York School itself, which makes it very difficult to assign any fixed meaning to the term. Nevertheless, the continuation of this difficulty from New York School painting to poetry is one of the surest signs that they share something in common. In 1968, just as the term was becoming accepted in reference to poetry, JOHN ASHBERY reluctantly attempted an explanation: "[T]his is very hard because our program is the absence of any program. I guess it amounts to not planning the poem in advance but letting it take its own way" ("New York School" 115).

In addition to the conceptual difficulty and the resistance any artist might feel to being pinned down with a label, another reason for Ashbery's reluctance to define a *New York School of poets* is that the term was not invented by one of the poets, as Motherwell was one of the painters, but rather by JOHN BERNARD MYERS, director of the TIBOR DE NAGY GALLERY (Ashbery, "Robert Frost Medal" 249). Hoping to capitalize on the success of the New York School painters, Myers wanted to highlight the poets' association with the painters as a way of promoting them and his gallery. The fact that his gallery had published the poets is one of the common characteristics that Myers assigns in his first published reference to the "New York School of Poetry" in the magazine *Nomad* (Myers, "In Regards" 30). He claims to have been using the phrase informally "for the past four or five years"; ads for Tibor de Nagy Editions tout the "New York School of Poetry" (*WAGNER LITERARY MAGAZINE* 3 [1962]) at the same time as Myers's essay in *Nomad*. Other common traits Myers claims for the poets in that essay are that "they have all lived in New York simultaneously at one time or another" (30)—a geographical definition that both Motherwell (83) and Ashbery ("Introduction" 133) would object to—and that "they share a sharp distaste for literary pretentiousness" (30)—an echo of the lack of "finish" that Motherwell observed in the paintings.

No sooner had the existence of the New York School of poets attained mainstream recognition, in an article by Stephen Koch in the *New York Times Book Review* (1968), than qualifications and dissensions arose, starting with the inventor of the term. In response to Koch's article, Myers wrote a letter to the *Times* stating (erroneously) that he had been careful not to refer to a "New York School of poets" but rather to "poets of the New York School," the title of an anthology that Myers was currently preparing (and promoting by writing this letter). The intention, further elaborated in the preface to Myers's anthology (1969), was to restrict the term *New York School* to the painters and to assert merely that the poets had a connection to the painters, not that the poets constituted a school of their own, though Myers allowed that they might constitute a "coterie" ("Poets of the New York School" 7–8). When RON PADGETT and DAVID SHAPIRO published *AN ANTHOLOGY OF NEW YORK POETS* the following year, they recoiled from "the gruesome possibility of 'the New York School of Poets' label," which they blamed (again erroneously) on "reviewers, critics and writers either sustained by provincial jealousy or the bent to translate everything into manageable textbookese" (Padgett and Shapiro, Preface xxx). Padgett and Shapiro excluded the word *school* from the title of their book. Instead, they presented *an*, not *the* anthology, of *some*, not *the* New York poets (Padgett, interview 111).

The term *school* appears in Padgett and Shapiro's preface only in the context of Ashbery's joke about the "*soi-disant* [self-proclaimed] Tulsa School" (Padgett and Shapiro, Preface xxx), which would include Padgett, if it existed (see TULSA SCHOOL). Such playfulness has continued to provide poets (CHARLES NORTH, JORDAN DAVIS) with a means of accepting the term *New York School* without violating the New York School spirit, which Stephen Koch characterized in the title of his article as "the serious at play."

Bibliography

Ashbery, John. "Introduction to *The Collected Poems of Frank O'Hara*" (1971). In *Selected Prose*. Edited by Eugene Richie. Ann Arbor: University of Michigan Press, 2004, 128–134.

———. "The New York School of Poets" (1968). In *Selected Prose*. Edited by Eugene Richie. Ann Arbor: University of Michigan Press, 2004, 113–116.

———. "Robert Frost Medal Address" (1995). In *Selected Prose*. Edited by Eugene Richie. Ann Arbor: University of Michigan Press, 2004, 243–252.

Davis, Jordan. "Peeling Oranges on Top of the Skyscrapers: Towards a Name-Blind History of Poetry since 1960." *Vanitas* 1 (2005): 5–13.

Koch, Stephen. "The New York School of Poets: The Serious at Play." *New York Times Book Review*, 11 February 1968, 4–5.

Motherwell, Robert. "Preface ['The School of New York'] to *Seventeen Modern American Painters*" (1951). In *Collected Writings*. Edited by Stephanie Terenzio. New York: Oxford University Press, 1992, 82–84.

Myers, John Bernard. "In Regards to This Selection of Verse, or Every Painter Should Have His Poet." *Nomad New York* nos. 10–11 (Autumn 1962): 30.

———. Letter to the editor. *New York Times Book Review*, 31 March 1968, 22.

———. "The Poets of the New York School." In *The Poets of the New York School*, edited by John Bernard Myers, 7–29. Philadelphia: Department of Fine Arts, University of Pennsylvania, 1969.

North, Charles. "New York Schools" (1988). In *No Other Way: Selected Prose*. Brooklyn, N.Y.: Hanging Loose Press, 1998, 103–109.

———. "The N.Y. Poetry Scene/Short Form" (1983). In *No Other Way: Selected Prose*. Brooklyn, N.Y.: Hanging Loose Press, 1998, 74–81.

Padgett, Ron. Interview by Edward Foster (1991). In *Poetry and Poetics in a New Millennium*, edited by Edward Foster, 100–114. Jersey City, N.J.: Talisman House, 2000.

Padgett, Ron, and David Shapiro. Preface to *An Anthology of New York Poets*. New York: Vintage–Random House, 1970, xxix–xxxvii.

New Zealand poetry   *See* AUSTRALIAN AND NEW ZEALAND POETRY.

Nomad New York (1962)

The phrase *New York School of Poetry* (as distinguished from simply *New York Poets*) first appeared in print in JOHN BERNARD MYERS's brief introduction to a selection of poems in the special New York double issue (number 10–11, autumn 1962) of the magazine *Nomad*, based in Los Angeles. Myers introduces the phrase apologetically, insisting that there is little in common besides "a sharp distaste for literary pretentiousness" in the work of these poets: KENNETH KOCH, BILL BERKSON, FRANK O'HARA, BARBARA GUEST, KENWARD ELMSLIE, JAMES SCHUYLER, JOHN ASHBERY. But the poets' relation to NEW YORK CITY and to the art of the New York School justifies appropriation of that term, Myers implies (30).

The *Nomad New York* issue, which turned out to be the final issue of a venture begun in 1959, illustrates the complex interaction between the visual and literary avant-gardes at this time, as well as the variety of connections that existed among literary "schools," both aesthetically and geographically. One of *Nomad*'s coeditors, Donald Factor (1934–   ), was closely involved in the nascent gallery scene in Los Angeles, both as a patron of artists associated with the Ferus Gallery and as an early contributor to *Artforum*, founded in 1962. In *Nomad New York* Factor published a pioneering essay on four emerging pop artists (though he avoids giving them that name): Roy Lichtenstein, James Rosenquist, JIM DINE, and Claes Oldenburg. During a visit to New York, Factor's interests as a collector had taken him to the TIBOR DE NAGY GALLERY, where he met Myers. Factor had met his coeditor, Anthony Linick (1938–   ), while they were college students, Factor at the University of Southern California and Linick at the University of California, Los Angeles. Linick's interest in the contemporary avant-garde was both literary and historical, the latter reflected eventually in his doctoral dissertation on "A History of the American Literary Avant-Garde Since World War II" (1965) and in his grouping of poets in the introduction to the *Nomad New York* issue. Linick acknowledges a debt to DONALD M. ALLEN's *The NEW AMERICAN POETRY, 1945–1960* for three of the groups represented in *Nomad*: BLACK MOUNTAIN, New York School, and BEAT. *Nomad* adds the "DEEP IMAGE" group, a special section devoted solely to JACKSON MAC LOW and a group of "eight independent voices," including Michael Benedikt, whom Linick had come to know well during summers spent in New York.

Two other writers connected with *Nomad* later developed close ties with the New York School. ANSELM HOLLO, who was responsible for an interview with GREGORY CORSO excerpted in *Nomad New York,* had been recruited as European correspondent through the magazine's London-based publisher, Villiers. JOHN PERREAULT, whose work was first published in *Nomad* 8 (autumn 1960), appears as one of the "independent voices" in *Nomad New York,* with a poem entitled "Politics."

Bibliography

International Guide to Literary and Art Periodicals. Vols. 1 and 2. London: Villiers, 1960–61.

Lehman, David. *The Last Avant-Garde: The Making of the New York School of Poets.* New York: Doubleday, 1998, 27.

Linick, Anthony. "Anthony Linick on *Nomad.*" 25 May 2007. Reality Studio Web site. Available online. URL: http://realitystudio.org/bibliographic-bunker/bunker-interviews/anthony-linick-on-nomad/. Accessed December 19, 2008.

Myers, John Bernard. "In Regards to This Selection of Verse, or Every Painter Should Have His Poet." *Nomad* 10/11 (autumn 1962): 30.

North, Charles (1941–)

Born in NEW YORK CITY, Charles North has long made his home on Manhattan's Upper West Side, preserving his independence from the Downtown poetry scene while absorbing the principles of his art from leading practitioners of the NEW YORK SCHOOL. After completing his formal education (B.A. in English and philosophy, Tufts University, 1962; M.A. in English and comparative literature, Columbia University, 1964), North enrolled in KENNETH KOCH's last workshop at the New School in 1966–67. He published his first poems in *The WORLD* in 1968 and gave his first poetry reading at the POETRY PROJECT AT ST. MARK'S CHURCH IN-THE-BOWERY in 1970, the same year he joined a Poetry Project workshop led by TONY TOWLE, where he also met PAUL VIOLI. The three became close friends and poetic allies and in the late 1970s began meeting once a week at a Downtown café. (Bob Hershon of Hanging Loose Press joined the group in the 1990s.) Through

Towle, North was introduced to JAMES SCHUYLER, who had been an admirer of North's poetry from afar (Schuyler's "Light from Canada" [1971] is dedicated to North). In the late 1970s North and his wife, Paula, a painter, frequently entertained Schuyler at their home, and North and Schuyler collaborated in producing two installments of *BROADWAY: A POETS AND PAINTERS ANTHOLOGY* (1979, 1989). Meanwhile, North had embarked on a teaching career at Pace University, where he is currently full-time poet-in-residence.

While exploring an astonishing variety of FORMs, North has maintained a consistent "double / vision of the city" ("Two Architectural Poems" [1989], *New and Selected* 105). One of the entries in the diary-poem "Aug.–Dec. for Jimmy Schuyler," from the "new" section in *New and Selected Poems* (1999), presents the vision succinctly: "The important buildings elevated just enough for light to pass underneath forming a human chain, air to people to air" (184). While the "important buildings" mark this vision as urban, it is rendered "idyllic," fulfilling Schuyler's characterization of North's work, not only by the elevation of the buildings but also by the flow of light (and "human" traffic) that passes between and even underneath them, North would have us believe. That this "urban idyll" is achieved through movement rather than the suspension of movement in calm, as in traditional pastoral, is typical of North's paradoxical yet passionate involvement in tradition. Throughout his work movement is as important an effect as image, and MUSIC as important an influence as painting, the former tending toward abstraction by opening up the structures (buildings) suggested by the latter. *Elizabethan and Nova Scotian Music,* North's first collection (ADVENTURES IN POETRY, 1974), includes "Some Versions of Reeds," based on North's experience as a clarinetist. The poem begins, "If the box is tightly sealed, break it open" (24).

In pursuit of open FORM, North has broken into (and out of) many traditional forms: sonnet, sestina, villanelle, pantoum. He has also invented his own forms, including "lineups," a variant of the list poem that assigns a baseball batting order and field positions to any imaginable set of people, places, or things; and "sixteens," a 16-line stanza that indents the central section of eight lines. North's lines typically move in syntactical leaps—(*Leap Year* [Kulchur Foundation, 1978]) is the title of his "first big book" (North, interview by Mlinko 13)—but the effect is different from the parataxis that North has identified as the "prevailing style" of the contemporary avant-garde (*No Other Way* 121). While the units of parataxis separate from each other, the units of North's poetry join together more closely than in ordinary syntax. The corresponding device in traditional rhetoric is zeugma, the hinging of disparate phrases on a single word. "Zeugma" stars as the pitcher in North's "lineup" of rhetorical figures, and the long poem "Shooting for Line," is built entirely on the figure: "To break the silence or your newly acquired Ming vase." The title of North's recent volume, *The Nearness of the Way You Look Tonight* (Adventures in Poetry, 2001), brings together two popular song titles, "The Nearness of You" and "The Way You Look Tonight," hinged on the single word *you*. Much of North's rhetoric seems to be aimed at provoking in the reader the question put by Sarah Fox in an interview: "[W]ho is 'you'?" (167). In some exquisite love poems North addresses "you" as the Beloved, but just as frequently, "you" seems to be any link in the chain of urban experience, "air to people to air," as in the "cloud-famished city" of "Song," where "I am pressed up against you / Like air pressed up against the sky" (*New and Selected Poems* 177).

Bibliography

Ash, John. Review of *The Year of the Olive Oil. Washington Post Book World*, 31 December 1989, p. 6.

Jacob, John. Review of *New and Selected Poems. American Book Review* (May–June 2000): 26–27.

North, Charles. *Cadenza*. Brooklyn, N.Y.: Hanging Loose Press, 2007.

———. *Complete Lineups*. Brooklyn, N.Y.: Hanging Loose Press, 2009.

———. Interview by Ange Mlinko. *Poetry Project Newsletter* 183 (February–March 2001): 10–14, 27.

———. Interview by Sarah Fox. *Verse* 20, nos. 2–3 (2004): 158–168.

———. *New and Selected Poems*. Los Angeles: Sun & Moon Press, 1999.

———. *No Other Way: Selected Prose*. Brooklyn, N.Y.: Hanging Loose Press, 1998.

———. *The Year of the Olive Oil*. Brooklyn, N.Y.: Hanging Loose Press, 1989.

Schuyler, James. "Light from Canada" (1971). In *Collected Poems*. New York: Farrar, Straus & Giroux/Noonday, 1995, 100–101.

Notley, Alice (1945–)

In relation to NEW YORK SCHOOL poetry Alice Notley occupies a complicated position both inside and out. Coming to NEW YORK CITY to study at Barnard College (B.A., 1967) was Notley's means of escaping the isolation of her hometown, Needles, California, in the Mojave Desert, yet the desert landscape returns repeatedly as a setting for her poetry, and Notley has said, "I resist thinking of myself as a New York poet" (interview by Foster 64). While pursuing graduate study at the University of Iowa, Notley met TED BERRIGAN. In 1972 she married him and automatically became a New York School "insider." After a period of shifting residences in New York; BOLINAS, CALIFORNIA; CHICAGO, ILLINOIS; and England, the couple settled in 1976 in New York with their children, the future poets ANSELM and EDMUND BERRIGAN. Their apartment at 101 St. Mark's Place served as a social center for the DOWNTOWN MANHATTAN poets, and their workshops at the POETRY PROJECT AT ST. MARK'S CHURCH IN-THE-BOWERY helped to form a third generation of the New York School.

Berrigan's death in 1983 was the first of a series of losses that profoundly affected Notley over the course of a decade: EDWIN DENBY (1983); Kate Berrigan (1987), Ted's daughter from his first marriage, who had grown close to Notley; Notley's brother, Albert (1988); and poet Steve Carey (1989), a close friend. Eventually a new relationship with DOUGLAS OLIVER, whom Notley had met during her earlier residence in England, helped her through this difficult time. She married Oliver in 1988 and in 1992 moved with him to Paris, where she still resides. Her distance from New York geographically provides a symbolic measure of the distance achieved stylistically in her work since the 1980s.

Notley's first collection of poems, *165 Meeting House Lane* (1971), was published by Berrigan's "C" Press. The title refers to the address where Notley and Berrigan lived in Southampton on the eastern end of Long Island during the winter of 1970–71. Like Berrigan's SONNETS and Denby's "Later Sonnets"—a fresh discovery for her—Notley's collection employs the sonnet FORM both for its artifice and for its immediacy, "a kind of progression of action—recalled later but written as if in the present, as in an O'Hara poem," Notley explains ("Intersections" n.p.). Notley's sequence of 24 sonnets reads like a diary, and a sense of "dailiness" is the outstanding quality that reflects her New York School context throughout the decade of the 1970s. *Incidentals in the Day World* (ANGEL HAIR, 1973) explores the specific challenges to "the form of the day" faced by a mother caring for a young child ("Three Strolls" 417), a source of anxiety in *Songs for the Unborn Second Baby* (UNITED ARTISTS, 1979), written while Notley was living in England (1973–74). The collection *For Frank O'Hara's Birthday*, published in Britain (Street Editions, 1976), includes "Your Dailiness" (1973), which Notley describes as "possibly the most 'inspired' poem I've ever written, in that it came to me whole." Its "proselike line dominated by the sentence" (essay 225), compared with the terse lines and fragmentary phrases of the sonnets, shows Notley to be experimenting with a wide variety of forms at this time (essay 225).

Reviewing *How Spring Comes* (Toothpaste Press, 1981) and *Waltzing Matilda* (KULCHUR, 1981) in the early 1980s, PETER SCHJELDAHL caught a hint of "bottomless subjective depths" beneath the "playful manipulation of a verbal surface," particularly in "The Prophet" (1979), a tour de force from *How Spring Comes* that Notley describes as "serio-comic" (essay 230). "You can't be in the New York School without being humorous," she has observed (interview by Dick n.p.), yet this is precisely the quality in her work that was temporarily eclipsed during the dark period following Berrigan's death (essay 232). Her mood found elegiac expression in the title poem of *At Night the States* (Yellow Press, 1985) and in a play, *Anne's White Glove*, produced by the Eye and Ear Theater at the La Mama Annex in 1985. She developed a new style in the course of writing "Beginning with a Stain" (1987), simultaneously an elegy for Kate Berrigan and a love poem for Oliver; "White Phosphorous" (1988), an elegy for

her brother; and the epic *The DESCENT OF ALETTE* (1990). All three works were collected in *The SCARLET CABINET*, coedited by Notley and Oliver (Scarlet Editions, 1992). When Penguin reissued *The Descent of Alette* in 1996, Notley broke into "mainstream" publishing.

The Descent of Alette inaugurates Notley's new mode of long poems with a strong narrative line, explicitly feminist POLITICS, and an otherworldly metaphysics representing the "bottomless subjective depths" that Schjeldahl sensed in the volumes of 1981. Dialogues with the dead are central to *Close to Me & Closer . . . (The Language of Heaven)* (1991) and *Désamère* (1992), published together in one volume in 1995 (♀ Books), and to *Alma, or The Dead Women* (Granary Books, 2006). The New York School legacy is more clearly in evidence in two dialogues with the self, *Mysteries of Small Houses* (Penguin, 1998) and *Disobedience* (Penguin, 2001). *Mysteries* is an autobiographical sequence that re-creates Notley's earlier lyrical forms as a vehicle for memories, many of which describe her life with Berrigan. *Disobedience* is a combination of diary and dream journal covering a year from August 1995 through August 1996. Both in its attention to the facts of daily life and in its humor, this work owes some of its creative freedom to the New York School, but the title signals Notley's refusal to be owned by any school or ideology (Notley, "Poetics" n.p.).

Notley has received a number of citations and honors for her work, including the Academy of American Poets Lenore Marshall Prize (2007), Griffin Poetry Prize (2002), American Academy of Arts and Letters Literature Award (2001), Poetry Society of America's Shelley Memorial Award (2001), *Los Angeles Times* Book Award for Poetry (1998), and San Francisco Poetry Center Book Award (1982). In addition to writing poetry she has edited three magazines, *Chicago* (1972–75), *Scarlet* (1990–92), and *Gare du Nord* (1998–99), and collections of work by both of her husbands: Berrigan's *A Certain Slant of Sunlight* (1988) and *The Collected Poems of Ted Berrigan* (University of California Press, 2005) and Oliver's *Arrondissements* (Salt, 2003). An important collection of her critical prose is entitled *Coming After* (University of Michigan Press, 2005), reflecting the sense of "being *after* the

Truly Greats" that Notley shared with her fellow poets of the second-generation New York School during the 1970s (Notley, essay 229).

Bibliography

Alice Notley issue. *Talisman* 1 (Fall 1988).

Davidson, Ian. "Creative Disobedience." *Jacket* 32 (April 2007). Available online. URL: http://jacketmagazine.com/32/davidson-ian-notley.shtml. Accessed December 19, 2008.

Holden, Stephen. "Stage: 'White Glove,'" *New York Times,* 19 April 1985, p. C26.

Nelson, Maggie. "Dear Dark Continent: Alice Notley's Disobediences." In *Women, the New York School, and Other True Abstractions.* Iowa City: University of Iowa Press, 2007, 131–167.

Notley, Alice. *Doctor Williams' Heiresses.* Berkeley, Calif.: Tuumba Press, 1980.

———. Essay in *Contemporary Authors Autobiography Series* 27. Edited by Joyce Nakamura. Detroit, Mich.: Gale, 1997, 221–240.

———. *Grave of Light: New and Selected Poems, 1970–2005.* Middletown, Conn.: Wesleyan University Press, 2006.

———. "Intersections with Edwin's Lines." *Jacket* 21 (February 2003). Available online. URL: http://jacketmagazine.com/21/denb-notl.html. Accessed December 19, 2008.

———. Interview by Edward Foster (1988). In *Poetry and Poetics in a New Millennium,* edited by Edward Foster, 64–87. Jersey City, N.J.: Talisman House, 2000.

———. Interview by Jennifer Dick. *Double Change* 3 (2002). Available online. URL: http://www.doublechange.com/issue3/notleyint-eng.htm. Accessed December 19, 2008.

———. *In the Pines.* New York: Penguin, 2007.

———. "The Poetics of Disobedience" (1998). Electronic Poetry Center, University of Buffalo. Available online. URL: http://wings.buffalo.edu/epc/authors/notley/disob.html. Accessed December 19, 2008.

———. "Three Strolls." In *The Angel Hair Anthology,* edited by Anne Waldman and Lewis Warsh, 415–418. New York: Granary Books, 2001.

Perelman, Bob. "'fucking / me across the decades like we / poets like': Embodied Poetic Transmission." In *Don't Ever Get Famous: Essays on New York Writing after the New York School,* edited by Daniel Kane, 195–214. Champaign, Ill.: Dalkey Archive Press, 2006.

Schjeldahl, Peter. "Lines from L.A. and N.Y." *New York Times Book Review,* 17 January 1982, p. 13.

Nuyorican Poets Café (1974–)

This celebrated poetry venue, located at 236 East 3rd Street, between Avenues B and C, was founded in 1974 by poet Miguel Algarín (1941–) to accommodate the raucous literary gatherings formerly held in his apartment on East 6th Street. Algarín, a second-generation Puerto Rican immigrant, wanted to create a public forum that would bring poetry into the lives of working-class people. To that end he rented a pub (The Sunshine Café) across the street from his apartment and called it the Nuyorican Poets Café, an homage to the Spanglish term (an amalgam of *New York* and *Puerto Rican*) for those of Puerto Rican heritage born in New York. As well as a deeply Puerto Rican flavor, the original Nuyorican Poets Café was marked by its dive-bar ambiance, which firmly aligned it with the populist values of its founder.

In addition to its Puerto Rican habitués (including Miguel Piñero [1946–88], author of the play *Short Eyes* [1974]), the bar quickly attracted like-minded poets from other ethnic groups, such as WILLIAM S. BURROUGHS and ALLEN GINSBERG, who read to increasingly large crowds. By 1980 the Nuyorican's audience had expanded so much that it moved to a larger space on East 3rd Street. Just two years later, though, the café closed its doors.

When it reopened in 1989, it became home to some of the very first poetry slams, rowdy competitions in which poets are rated on a scale of 1 to 10 by judges selected at random from the audience. Ever since that time the Nuyorican Poets Café has been a SLAM POETRY mecca and even gained a foothold in mainstream culture with appearances on MTV and Hollywood patronage in the 1990s. This explosion of media attention was thanks, in large part, to the publicizing efforts of BOB HOLMAN, a veteran of the East Village arts scene. Holman helped reopen the café and ran the Nuyorican Poetry Slams from 1992 until 1996 when he and Algarín had a falling out.

Like many of his contemporaries, Holman was inspired by the BEATS and the founding NEW YORK SCHOOL poets, particularly KENNETH KOCH, who was Holman's first poetry professor at Columbia University. Among other things Koch instilled in Holman the importance of creating community through art. In this sense Holman was a point of intersection between these otherwise discrete groups of poets from the New York School and the Nuyorican Poets Café. Indeed, the Nuyorican has come to embody many of the same principles that united the New York School: disdain for the "high seriousness" of academia, emphasis on personal expression and the everyday realities of urban life, and a desire to play freely and spontaneously with language. To this day the Nuyorican Poets Café attracts dozens of poetry aficionados and neophytes to its crowded, nightclub-style atmosphere (complete with bouncer) for slam competitions, script readings, stand-up comedy, plays, MUSIC, and DANCE performances.

Bibliography

Algarín, Miguel, and Bob Holman, eds. *Aloud: Voices from the Nuyorican Poets Café*. New York: Holt, 1994.

Bastidas, Grace. "Bard Wired." *Village Voice* 45, no. 17 (2000), 53.

Holman, Bob. "A Community of Poets: Fact and Myth" (1998). About.com: Poetry. Available online. URL: http://www.about.com/arts/poetry/library/weekly/aa072898.htm. Accessed December 19, 2008.

———. "What Is American about American Poetry?" (1999). Poetry Society of America Web site. Available online. URL: http://www.poetrysociety.org/holman.html. Accessed December 19, 2008.

Morales, Ed. "Grand Slam." *Village Voice* 42, no. 41 (1997), 62–63.

Nuyorican Poets Café Web site. Available online. URL: http://www.nuyorican.org/.

objectivists

The objectivist poets reemerged from silence and obscurity during the 1960s in time for rediscovery amid the ferment of poetic experimentation that had been stimulated by *The NEW AMERICAN POETRY, 1945–1960* (1960). DONALD M. ALLEN had not included the objectivists in that anthology because they seemed to represent a past moment in literary history (Golding 186). They had appeared as a group as early as 1931, in a special issue of *Poetry* magazine (February) edited by Louis Zukofsky (1904–78). Although Zukofsky included a number of very different poets, the three others who became most closely identified with the objectivist label were George Oppen (1908–84), Carl Rakosi (1903–2004), and Charles Reznikoff (1894–1976). Ezra Pound had promoted the group to *Poetry*, but these poets had more in common with William Carlos Williams, whose *Autobiography* (1951) provides a more lucid account of objectivist theory than the disparate assemblage of commentary that Zukofsky offers in *Poetry*.

According to Williams (264–265), objectivism is an advance beyond imagism. Pound's insistence on "direct treatment of the thing" as an imagist principle agrees with the meaning of the word *objective* as it is usually understood. But the call for an objectivist poetry, Williams explains, was intended to focus attention on the poem as object, as a thing made, and thus to revive a concern for measure that could not be satisfied by image alone or by image set adrift on so-called free verse. In a parallel way the revival of objectivism during the

1960s offered what Ron Silliman has described as a corrective to the extremes of "open-form" poetry—the sort of poetry that had grown out of CHARLES OLSON's theory of "PROJECTIVE VERSE," ironically embraced by Williams in his *Autobiography* as the next step forward.

If the BEATS represent the extreme version of open FORM as expressionist voice and LANGUAGE POETRY represents the "correction" that was to come, there was room between these extremes where the NEW YORK SCHOOL could find common ground with the objectivists. In a joint interview with TED BERRIGAN and Oppen conducted in 1973, Berrigan shrewdly located his divergence from "the voice poets": "the place where I deviate from them is that most of the structure of my work is based upon, really, what you do on the page that corresponds to what you do when you make music" (Berrigan and Oppen 71). Here is the same insistence on form as measure—musical structure—that was one of the founding principles of objectivism. Yet Oppen distinguishes himself from Berrigan on the basis of another founding principle, the concept of image as "a thing which hasn't been said," that "doesn't yet have words" (Berrigan and Oppen 69). Berrigan agrees that his poetry, by contrast, is "mostly talk" (Berrigan and Oppen 70), but he quickly adds that talk does not imply rhetoric, the disease that imagism was invented to cure. Instead, Berrigan characteristically identifies talk with "a walk to the store to buy the paper and back," both talk and walk being experienced as conversation, urban and urbane. In cultivating these modes Berrigan is closer to the native New Yorker Charles Reznikoff, "a lovely old man," as Berrigan called him ("Things to Do in New York City"), whose walk poems have been compared to those of EDWIN DENBY and FRANK O'HARA (Lopate). Talk also mobilizes the work of Carl Rakosi, whom BILL BERKSON recommended to Berrigan as "a really terrific man" (Berrigan and Oppen 70).

Years of neglect had made Zukofsky a difficult man, deliberately keeping his distance from the poetry community in Manhattan though welcoming younger poets who made the pilgrimage to his apartment in Brooklyn Heights (Terrell 72–73). A sense of taking himself too seriously could come across on the page, putting off Berrigan, for instance, from Zukofsky's homophonic TRANSLATIONs of Catullus, which Berrigan might have been expected to appreciate. Not put off were TOM CLARK and ARAM SAROYAN, who each reviewed Zukofsky for *Poetry* magazine, Saroyan offering his review of *A 13–21* as a collage of quotation, another experimental technique that Zukofsky's own practice helped validate. Along with CLARK COOLIDGE, Saroyan represents a minimalist pole of the New York School aligned with Zukofsky in tension with the maximalist pole aligned with Olson, but the tension also exists within each of the predecessors. In Zukofsky's case the paradoxical example is the long poem *A*, assembled from minimal units in 24 sections over a period of 50 years.

ANNE WALDMAN embraces the paradox by ironically including Zukofsky along with Williams, Pound, and Olson in the list of "epic masters" whose challenge she takes on in her feminist epic *IOVIS*. The impulse to cut words, editorially, may be linked, Waldman implies, to the male propensity for cutting up bodies, traditionally glorified by the epic celebration of war. In a passage centered on Zukofsky's Catullus translations (*Iovis* 235), Waldman accepts cuts recommended by a male companion, but she prints the original along with the reduced version, refusing to choose between the projectivist and objectivist modes ("Vow" 128–129), while simultaneously critiquing both.

Bibliography

Berrigan, Ted. "Things to Do in New York City" (1969). In *The Collected Poems of Ted Berrigan*. Edited by Alice Notley, Anselm Berrigan, and Edmund Berrigan. Berkeley: University of California Press, 2005, 162.

Berrigan, Ted, and George Oppen. Interview by Ruth Gruber (1973). In *Talking in Tranquility: Interviews with Ted Berrigan*. Edited by Stephen Ratcliffe and Leslie Scalapino. Bolinas, Calif.: Avenue B; Oakland, Calif.: O Books, 1991, 55–72.

Clark, Thomas. Review of *All: The Collected Short Poems, 1923–1958*. *Poetry* 107 (October 1965): 55–59.

DuPlessis, Rachel Blau, and Peter Quartermain, eds. *The Objectivist Nexus: Essays in Cultural Poetics.* Tuscaloosa: University of Alabama Press, 1999.

Golding, Alan. "*The New American Poetry* Revisited, Again." *Contemporary Literature* 39, no. 2 (1998): 180–211.

Grenier, Robert. "Notes on Coolidge, Objectives, Zukofsky, Romanticism, And &." In *In the American Tree*, edited by Ron Silliman, 530–543. Orono: National Poetry Foundation/University of Maine at Orono, 1986.

Lopate, Phillip. "The Pen on Foot: The Literature of Walking Around." *Parnassus: Poetry in Review* 18, no. 2/19, no. 1 (1993): 176–212.

Messerli, Douglas, ed. *From the Other Side of the Century: A New American Poetry, 1960–1990*. Los Angeles: Sun & Moon, 1994.

Saroyan, Aram. Review of *A 13–21*. *Poetry* 117 (November 1970): 118–122.

Silliman, Ron. "Third Phase Objectivism." *Paideuma* 10, no. 1 (Spring 1981): 85–89.

Terrell, Carroll F. "Louis Zukofsky: An Eccentric Profile." In *Louis Zukofsky: Man and Poet*. Orono: National Poetry Foundation/University of Maine at Orono, 1979, 31–74.

Waldman, Anne. *Iovis*. Minneapolis, Minn.: Coffee House Press, 1993.

———. "Vow to Poetry: A Conversation with Randy Roark" (1991). In *Vow to Poetry: Essays, Interviews, and Manifestos*. Minneapolis, Minn.: Coffee House Press, 2001, 107–136.

Williams, William Carlos. *The Autobiography*. New York: New Directions, 1951.

Zukofsky, Louis, with Celia Zukofsky, trans. *Catullus*. London: Cape Goliard; New York: Grossman, 1969.

O-blek (1987–1993)

Edited by poets PETER GIZZI and Connell McGrath (1961–   ) and published by the Garlic Press in

Stockbridge, Massachusetts, *O-blek* was one of the premier literary magazines of its day. Subtitled *A Journal of Language Arts*, the magazine ran no mission statement or editor's notes, instead presenting different dictionary entries for the word *oblique* at the start of each issue; the editors further eschewed standard practice by running no biographical notes on its contributors. Thus, *O-blek* elevated the obliquity of poetry as a value.

Often mistaken as a LANGUAGE POETRY vehicle, *O-blek* more accurately presented a dynamic cross-section of the adventurous end of contemporary AMERICAN POETRY—narrowly focused, perhaps, but without adherence to any one school. Poets broadly associated with Language writing, including CLARK COOLIDGE, Lyn Hejinian, and Michael Palmer, did frequently appear in the journal's pages, but so did unaffiliated writers such as Fanny Howe, Robert Kelly, Rosmarie Waldrop, and JOHN WIENERS, as well as significant younger voices such as Jena Osman, Elizabeth Robinson, Roberto Tejada, and Elizabeth Willis. As part of this mix, and in keeping with its attention to poetries skewed away from the mainstream, *O-blek* often showcased the work of poets associated with latter-day NEW YORK SCHOOL practice, including TED BERRIGAN, KENWARD ELMSLIE, BERNADETTE MAYER, CHARLES NORTH, ALICE NOTLEY, RON PADGETT, DAVID SHAPIRO, MARJORIE WELISH, JOHN YAU, and others. Although the magazine did not have theme issues, its fifth number was "dedicated to the editors of the journal *LOCUS SOLUS*" and contained an evident New York School focus, including work by JOSEPH CERAVALO, JOHN ASHBERY, BARBARA GUEST, JAMES SCHUYLER, KENNETH KOCH, BILL BERKSON, and FRANK O'HARA, as well as a cover by TREVOR WINKFIELD.

While the first 11 issues of *O-blek* were published in a short, nearly square format, its 12th and final issue was a massive, two-volume compendium entitled *Writing from the New Coast*, which focused exclusively on the work of new and emerging writers. Divided into "Presentation" and "Technique," the latter volume was edited by Gizzi and poet Juliana Spahr and largely derived from a conference held at the State University of New York at Buffalo; its short papers offer a useful look at the poetics of a generation coming of age in the wake of post-structuralism. The former volume presented the work of more than 100 young poets, though in an uncharacteristic editor's foreword, Gizzi was quick to call the book "not an anthology but the result of six months' work," thereby highlighting its provisional status in the shifting landscape of poetry. "The new coast," Gizzi wrote, "is the curve of an earth as witnessed from elsewhere."

In addition to its 12 issues, *O-blek* published a handful of books under the rubric O-blek Editions, including a lengthy sequence by Emmanuel Hocquard translated by Palmer, a COLLABORATION between Coolidge and artist PHILIP GUSTON, and chapbooks by Pam Rehm, Elizabeth Willis, and others. As intriguing as these books are, it is for the editorial vision and widespread influence of its journal that the name *O-blek* holds a paradoxically central place in literary history.

occasional poem   *See* GENRE.

ode   *See* GENRE.

O'Hara, Frank (1926–1966)

The NEW YORK SCHOOL of poets can be said to begin with the arrival of Frank O'Hara in NEW YORK CITY in August 1951. His magnetic personality drew other writers as well as artists in every medium into interaction with O'Hara and one another. His poetry seemed an extension of his personality and his personal life, where his many friends could read about themselves and their world yet experience the magical transformation that was the purpose of art as O'Hara understood it. The tragic circumstances of O'Hara's death at the age of 40, when he was fatally struck by a beach taxi on Fire Island, New York, transformed his life into myth and, for many who knew him, marked the end of an era.

Born in Baltimore, Maryland, and raised in Grafton, Massachusetts, O'Hara sought wider horizons immediately after graduating from high school in 1944, first in the navy, then at Harvard

University. Rather than providing a gateway to the establishment, Harvard gave O'Hara his first access to a community based on experimentation in both art and lifestyle. His friend JOHN ASHBERY, who graduated from Harvard a year ahead of O'Hara, introduced him to the arts community in NEW YORK CITY, which he made his home after a year of graduate study at the University of Michigan.

In New York the world of the painters, who led the avant-garde, provided the foundation for O'Hara's life. He earned his income by writing reviews for *Art News* and working at the Museum of Modern Art, first as a clerk at the front desk, later in a series of progressively more responsible curatorial positions. In 1952 the TIBOR DE NAGY GALLERY, the principal showcase for the younger painters of the New York School, published O'Hara's first collection of poems, *A City Winter*, with two drawings by LARRY RIVERS. In 1953 the same gallery published *Oranges* in connection with an exhibition of paintings by GRACE HARTIGAN based on O'Hara's text. O'Hara continued to produce COLLABORATIONs with visual artists throughout his career.

Though his voice is already distinctive, O'Hara's early poetry explores a wide variety of influences, FORMs, and themes. Sonnets of the English Renaissance are the model for the title sequence of *A City Winter*. In addition to the pervasive influence of surrealism (see DADA AND SURREALISM), modern FRENCH POETRY contributes specific models, from Arthur Rimbaud's prose poems (the principal source of *Oranges*) to Stéphane Mallarmé's inscriptions for fans (the source of "Yet Another Fan" in *A City Winter*). The VISUAL ARTS make their appearance in references both to paintings ("Early Mondrian") and to painters. "Jane Awake" addresses O'Hara's close friend, the painter JANE FREILICHER. Although they can seem distracting in individual poems, O'Hara's references by name to personal acquaintances help compose the theme of friendship that supplies an important thread of continuity throughout his work. Another major theme emerging at this stage, signaled in the title *A City Winter*, is the experience of city life, often mediated by the idealization of nature in the pastoral tradition, signaled in the subtitle of *Oranges: 12 Pastorals*. The major city poem of this period is the long work *Second Avenue*, written in

1953 but not published in its entirety until 1960 (Totem/Corinth).

Meditations in an Emergency (1957), the first collection of O'Hara's poems to be issued by a commercial publisher, Grove Press, provided the occasion for the first critical notices of O'Hara's work. They were generally "friendly but puzzled," as O'Hara's biographer Brad Gooch aptly characterizes them (300). Reviewers recognized that O'Hara was not producing ordinary poetry, but to explain what he was producing they floundered about amid references to ABSTRACT EXPRESSIONISM, surrealism, and JAZZ. In a review in the *New York Times*, Kenneth Rexroth provided perhaps the most insightful commentary by distinguishing O'Hara's work from ABSTRACT EXPRESSIONISM, however much the poet might admire the painters, and emphasizing instead its quality of realism, a "flat, dead-pan colloquialism" (300).

The new realism in O'Hara's work developed into a new GENRE that he dubbed his "I do this I do that" poems, because they follow the poet on a seemingly random itinerary through the urban scene. Poems in this genre make up O'Hara's best-known work from the later 1950s, including "A Step Away from Them," "The DAY LADY DIED," and "Personal Poem," all eventually collected in the volume *Lunch Poems* that O'Hara published in 1964 with the West Coast firm City Lights. "Personal Poem" also belongs to a series arising out of O'Hara's love affair with the dancer Vincent Warren from 1959 to 1961. A selection was published by the Tibor de Nagy Gallery in 1965 under the title *Love Poems (Tentative Title)*. *Tentative* aptly expresses O'Hara's attitude toward love but also his hesitation about whether it is the love or the poetry that comes first in a love poem. From the experience of writing "Personal Poem," he abstracted the concept of "PERSONISM," "sustaining the poet's feelings towards the poem while preventing love from distracting him into feeling about the person" (*Collected Poems* 499).

A tendency that runs counter to intimacy, barely hinted at in O'Hara's description of Personism, is more pronounced in a series begun around the same time as the "I do this I do that poems" and collected in 1960 under the title *Odes* (Tiber Press) Traditionally the public speech of the ode contrasts with the private speech of the love poem. In the American tradition it is the mode of Walt Whitman's oratorical style. It also provides a kind of justification for the extremes of imagery that had attracted O'Hara to French surrealism. Frequently O'Hara directs the violence inherent in such imagery against the self or images of the self, as in the conclusion of "IN MEMORY OF MY FEELINGS" (1956), which belongs to this series although it is not formally designated an ode. Here, the poet revisits "the scene of my selves," which he declares he "must now kill." O'Hara continued to explore the consequences of this act in later poems such as "BIOTHERM (for BILL BERKSON)" (1961), which presents, in both form and imagery, an amorphous body washed up on the shore of "the ego-ridden sea." If Warren is the muse of the love poems, Bill BERKSON is the ultimate destination of the odes, serving literally as the addressee of a series of curiously fragmented and impersonal poems titled with some form of the corporate abbreviation F.Y.I (for your information).

After a substantial selection of O'Hara's work appeared in the anthology *The NEW AMERICAN POETRY, 1945–1960* (1960), he rapidly acquired a following among younger poets such as Berkson. TED BERRIGAN, RON PADGETT, DICK GALLUP, and JOE BRAINARD traveled all the way from Tulsa, Oklahoma, to meet O'Hara and to experience firsthand the bohemian life his poems enacted. FRANK LIMA, TONY TOWLE, GERARD MALANGA, JOSEPH CERAVOLO, and JIM BRODEY enrolled in a poetry workshop that O'Hara taught at the New School during the academic year 1962–63. Imitations of the "I do this I do that" poem mark the early spread of O'Hara's influence. The odes and their offshoots, such as the Berkson poems, have resonated in later developments, such as the Language writing that emerged in the 1970s, after the full scope of O'Hara's work became available in *The Collected Poems* (Knopf 1971). A volume of *Selected Poems*, edited by Mark Ford, was published by Knopf in 2008.

Bibliography

Elledge, Jim, ed. *Frank O'Hara: To Be True to a City.* Ann Arbor: University of Michigan Press, 1990.

Ferguson, Russell. *In Memory of My Feelings: Frank O'Hara and American Art.* Los Angeles: Museum of Contemporary Art; Berkeley: University of California Press, 1999.

Gooch, Brad. *City Poet: The Life and Times of Frank O'Hara.* New York: Knopf, 1993.

O'Hara, Frank. *Art Chronicles 1954–1966.* Rev. ed. New York: Braziller, 1990.

———. *The Collected Poems of Frank O'Hara.* New ed. Edited by Donald Allen. Berkeley: University of California Press, 1995.

———. *Early Writing.* Edited by Donld Allen. Bolinas, Calif.: Grey Fox, 1977.

———. *Poems Retrieved.* Rev. ed. Edited by Donald Allen. San Francisco: Grey Fox, 1996.

———. *Standing Still and Walking in New York.* Edited by Donald Allen. Bolinas, Calif.: Grey Fox, 1983.

Perloff, Marjorie. *Frank O'Hara: Poet Among Painters.* 1977. Rev. ed. Chicago: University of Chicago Press, 1998.

O'Hara Songs, The Morton Feldman and Frank O'Hara (1962)

MORTON FELDMAN's *O'Hara Songs* consists of three separate musical settings of FRANK O'HARA's poem "Wind," for bass-baritone, chimes, piano, violin, viola, and violoncello. Feldman wrote that O'Hara, whom he met during the early 1950s, "admired my music because its methodology was hidden" (*Give My Regards* 104), and the poet himself explained that Feldman resisted "the clichés of the International School of present-day avant-garde"—the highly systematic "serial" technique employed by postwar composers like Pierre Boulez and Karlheinz Stockhausen—and undertook "a personal search for expression which could not be limited by any system" (*Give My Regards* 212).

Feldman's atonal score is notated on conventional five-line staff paper, with unstemmed noteheads indicating exact pitches. All of the pitches belong to the traditional 12-note chromatic tempered scale. The score designates only the order of pitch events in each vocal or instrumental part, and the rhythmic organization is otherwise indeterminate; there are no barlines to establish metrical groupings, and there is no regular pulse.

In his performance directions prefacing the score, Feldman writes that "the first and last song begin with voice and given instruments sounding simultaneously. The duration of each sound thereafter is chosen by the singer and instrumentalists." He prescribes that the MUSIC unfold at a measured pace of between 66 and 84 pitch-events per minute, and "all sounds should be played with a minimum of attack. Dynamics are very low." Simultaneities are not predetermined because the individual performers may pace their parts independently. The vocal line's melodic countours are highly disjunct, and the text setting is exclusively syllabic, with no explicit wordpainting.

Supported by an extremely discontinuous accompanimental texture, the effect is one of static detemporalization in keeping with the poem's expression of a mode of subjectivity rather than a progressive narrative. In the first song, which is approximately five minutes in duration, the male voice sings O'Hara's entire text straight through with no omissions or repetitions, and the accompaniment is played by a muted violin and a cello, both of which employ a variety of timbral effects—artificial harmonics, sounds played by bowing on the instrument's bridge, and pizzicato. The second song, about two minutes long, sets only the poem's broken first line, "Who'd have thought that snow falls," which repeats the same descending series of pitches five times, accompanied by piano and chimes. And the third, about four minutes' duration, returns to a linear rendering of the complete poem with solo viola accompaniment.

Bibliography

Feldman, Morton. *Chamber Music.* Sound recording, WER 6273-2. Mainz, Germany: Wergo, 1996.
———. Composer's note to *The O'Hara Songs.* New York: C. F. Peters, 1963.
———. *Give My Regards to Eighth Street: Collected Writings.* Edited by B. H. Friedman. Cambridge, Mass.: Exact Change, 2000, 104, 212.
LeSueur, Joe. *Digressions on Some Poems by Frank O'Hara: A Memoir.* New York: Farrar, Straus & Giroux, 2003.
O'Hara, Frank. "Wind" (1957). In *The Collected Poems.* Rev. ed. Edited by Donald Allen. Berkeley: University of California Press, 1995, 269.

OINK!   *See* NEW AMERICAN WRITING/OINK!

Old Place, The

There are few records of the 1950s gay bar The Old Place (139 West 10th Street) other than FRANK O'HARA's poem "At the Old Place" (1955). Joe LeSueur, O'Hara's former roommate, describes the bar as a "seedy, out-of-the-way basement bar" (54). In contrast to the orgiastic gay clubs that began to spring up in the 1970s, The Old Place was fairly tame—in LeSueur's words, "about as wild as a high school prom of years past" (55). O'Hara patronized the bar primarily because he loved to dance.

Opened in 1941 by David Bright and Matilda Tarigo, The Old Place was one of several Greenwich Village bars that catered primarily to gay men during the 1940s and 1950s. These establishments were frequent targets of police raids and harassment by city officials. When a crime wave hit the city in summer 1959, authorities used it as an excuse to shut down scores of gay bars by revoking their liquor licenses. This is probably one reason why The Old Place closed its doors around that time. This antihomosexual atmosphere laid the ground for the riots that took place in 1969 at the Stonewall Inn, a gay-friendly bar located not far from The Old Place. In the spirit of "gay liberation" that followed that event, O'Hara's "At the Old Place" was published for the first time in the journal *New York Poetry* (November 1969).

On the summer evening of 1955 recorded in O'Hara's poem, the cast of characters includes O'Hara; his roommate Joe (LeSueur); the painter (John) Button; Howard (Griffin), a poet and sometime secretary to W. H. AUDEN; "Ashes" (JOHN ASHBERY); the composer Dick (Stryker); Alvin (Novak), Button's lover; the poet Jack (Spicer); Earl (McGrath), secretary to Gian Carlo Menotti and later producer of Rolling Stones records; and a mysterious "Someone." Spicer, a central figure in the SAN FRANCISCO RENAISSANCE, had recently "come to New York to escape the claustrophobia of being a big fish in a small pond," according to his biographers (Ellingham and Killian 63), but O'Hara registers his discomfort in moving from a bar like the SAN REMO, where the poem starts out, to the unabashedly camp atmosphere of "a *gay* dance bar" like The Old Place (LeSueur 54). By the end of 1955 Spicer had fled NEW YORK CITY for BOSTON, where O'Hara reencountered him in the company of JOHN WIENERS (Ellingham and Killian 70), but by the end of 1956 Spicer had returned to San Francisco. The camp style that repelled him became absorbed into NEW YORK SCHOOL poetry regardless of the poet's sexual orientation. Button's coded appeal, "L G T TH O P," for "let's go to The Old Place," is remembered in TED BERRIGAN's poem "L. G. T. T. H.," for "let's go to the Hop," from the 1950s pop MUSIC hit.

Bibliography

Berrigan, Ted. "L. G. T. T. H." (ca. 1973). In *The Collected Poems of Ted Berrigan*. Edited by Alice Notley, Anselm Berrigan, and Edmund Berrigan. Berkeley: University of California Press, 2005, 398–399.

Ellingham, Lewis, and Kevin Killian. *Poet Be Like God: Jack Spicer and the San Francisco Renaissance*. Hanover, N.H.: University Press of New England/Wesleyan University Press, 1998.

LeSueur, Joe. "At the Old Place." *Digressions on Some Poems by Frank O'Hara*. New York: Farrar, Straus & Giroux, 2003, 53–58.

O'Hara, Frank. "At the Old Place" (1955). In *The Collected Poems*. Rev. ed. Edited by Donald Allen. Berkeley: University of California Press, 1995, 223–224.

Olin, Jeni (1974–)

Jeni Olin was born in Houston, Texas, and studied in North Carolina and at the NAROPA INSTITUTE. She is the author of a two-part debut collection of poetry, *Blue Collar Holiday and a Valentine for Frank O'Hara* (Hanging Loose, 2005), which includes original color prints, drawings, and reproductions of paintings by NEW YORK SCHOOL artist LARRY RIVERS, with whom she lived and collaborated for the last five years of his life. Olin's poetry is liquid in its forward momentum and shifts register from irony to unabashed joy with quicksilver speed, registering the effects of DOWNTOWN MANHATTAN and pop culture on a speaker who partakes of Blakean innocence and experience. As poet and

critic John Latta writes, "Olin's willing to admit sleaze, and trash, and several degrees and varieties of 'hard core' into her poems—with disarming innocence. Rather like the innocence and pathos that soak through Nan Goldin's photographs. And humor, no holds barred and ferocious" (n.p.).

The opening of the title poem of Olin's collection, "Blue Collar Holiday," which appeared anthologized in the *Best American Poetry 2004,* edited by Lyn Hejinian and DAVID LEHMAN (Scribner, 2004), demonstrates this swerving diction and accumulation of allusion, both literary and pop cultural:

> *And if I feel like a woman looming over Lautrec*
> *with water weight & panties and murderous*
>   *fuchsia underfoot*
> *those dying balloons on Job's Lane sag around*
>   *like saline breast implants*
> *and pineal sunbeams sneak through my hair*
> *dirty but focused as screwy detectives or Plexiglas.*

Olin has published her work in such journals as *The Hat, Exquisite Corpse, Blue Book, Jacket, RealPoetik, PuppyFlowers,* and *The East Village* and read her work at such venues as the POETRY PROJECT AT ST. MARK'S CHURCH IN-THE-BOWERY, the Frequency Series at the Four-Faced Liar, the Zinc Bar, and Pete's Candy Store in Brooklyn, New York. Her poems have appeared on *Radio Poetique,* a show dedicated to Brooklyn poets and housed at the Penn Sound archives. Olin's poem "New York Red-Eye to Love" is featured in the Artists for Peace, Liberties & Civil Justice fine art gallery and anthology online. Olin's work also appeared in *Free Radicals: American Poets Before Their First Books,* edited by Sarah Manguso and Jordan Davis (Subpress, 2004).

Bibliography

Olin, Jeni. "Blue Collar Holiday." *Jacket* 16 (March 2002). Available online. URL: http://jacketmagazine. com/16/olin-poems.html. Accessed August 15, 2008.

Latta, John. "Attention Span 2006, a Production of Third Factory." Available online. URL: http://www.third factory.net/attentionspan2006p3.html. Accessed August 15, 2008.

Oliver, Douglas (1937–2000)
British poet, writer

Douglas Oliver was born in 1937 in Southampton and grew up in nearby Bournemouth on the south coast of England. Although he dropped out of school at 16, he wrote and taught poetry, journalism, and FICTION in England, Paris, and eventually NEW YORK CITY. As evidenced by the tribute volume *A Meeting for Douglas Oliver* (2002), he was a poet's poet, concerned with poetry's ability to provoke personal integrity and political justice. It was only in the final years of his life that he began to attract the positive critical attention he deserved. He had three related connections to NEW YORK SCHOOL poetry: He nurtured it as a reader and an editor; he was involved with poetry in New York and wrote poetry himself during his time there during the late 1980s and early 1990s; and he even married into it—through the person of poet ALICE NOTLEY in February 1988.

After two decades of writing for the *Cambridge Evening News*, translating for the Agence France-Press, and publishing pieces of prose and FICTION through Peter Riley's *The English Intelligencer*, Tim Longville's Grosseteste Press, and Andrew Crozier's Ferry Press, Oliver was brought to prominence in Britain by his inclusion in Longville and Crozier's 1987 collection, *A Various Art*. He was affiliated to the so-called Cambridge School of poets, and his poetry, despite its proud anachronistic formalism, bore the marks of AMERICAN POETRY and especially that of the BEATS.

During the later periods of his life in New York and Paris, Oliver collaborated with his wife, Notley. He had previously been friendly with both her and her husband TED BERRIGAN, also a poet, who died in 1983. In 1987 Notley and Oliver met again, and in February 1988 they married and moved to New York. Although he developed his friendship with KENNETH KOCH and continued to read and publish American poetry after they moved to Paris in 1992, most notably in the fascicle *Gare du Nord*, it was in New York where he formed his closest ties to New York poets, including, among many others, ANNE WALDMAN and ANSELM HOLLO.

While living there, Oliver wrote PENNILESS POLITICS (Hoarse Commerce, 1991), his most important contribution to New York School poetry.

It was a bitter polemic against the divisive, deadly POLITICS of the Reagan-Bush era and provided an insight into Notley and Oliver's departure from the United States in 1992. Although largely ignored outside the poetry community in the United States, it won a powerful review from Howard Brenton in the *Guardian* who compared it favorably to T. S. Eliot's *The Waste Land*.

Along with Notley he continued to edit the innovative poetic periodical *Scarlet*, which ended with the publication of an anthology of their own related work called *The* SCARLET CABINET (1992). Apart from marital ties to Notley, Oliver also developed friendships with the poets EDMUND and ANSELM BERRIGAN, her sons, as well as with a number of New York poets who submitted their work to *Scarlet*. Oliver died of cancer on April 21, 2000, in Paris.

Bibliography

Brenton, Howard. "Poetic Passport to a New Era," *Guardian*, 7 April 1992, p. 3.

Crozier, Andrew, and Greg Chamberlain. "Obituary: Douglas Oliver, a Poet Articulating Ethical Values in a World of Injustice and Joy," *Guardian*, 6 May 2000, p. 28.

Notley, Alice, and Douglas Oliver. *The Scarlet Cabinet: A Compendium of Books*. New York: Scarlet Editions, 1992.

Oliver, Douglas. Essay in *Contemporary Authors Autobiography Series* 27. Edited by Joyce Nakamura. Detroit, Mich.: Gale, 1997, 241–261.

———. *Kind*. London: Allardyce, Barnett, 1987.

———. *A Meeting for Douglas Oliver and 27 Uncollected Poems*. Cambridge: Infernal Methods, 2002.

Olson, Charles (1910–1970)

It is impossible to separate poet, teacher, and revolutionary in an assessment of Charles Olson's influence on postwar AMERICAN POETRY. The concept of "composition by field" in Olson's essay on "PROJECTIVE VERSE" (1950) defined, in more ways than one, the field of experimental poetry for this period. Of greater significance for the NEW YORK SCHOOL poets, who tended not to subscribe to theoretical programs, was Olson's insistence on writing as experimental action. "Take chances, jump in there, and see what happens" (Duberman 406) is the lesson recalled repeatedly by Olson's students at BLACK MOUNTAIN COLLEGE, where he taught from 1951 to 1956. "The Kingfishers," the poem by Olson that leads off the anthology *The NEW AMERICAN POETRY, 1945–1960* (1960), points to "the risk of beauty" and links it to cultural revolution through reference to Mao Zedong, whose Communist revolution had taken over China just months before Olson wrote the poem in 1949. Earlier, in 1945, Olson had decided to devote the remainder of his life to literature, turning his back on prospects that might have opened up through his work for Franklin D. Roosevelt's final presidential campaign.

Olson was born in Worcester, Massachusetts, where Frank O'Hara later attended high school, but the coastal town of Gloucester became identified with Olson as the site of his serial epic *The Maximus Poems* (published in 1960, 1968, and 1975). This project is modeled on William Carlos Williams's *Paterson* and Ezra Pound's *Cantos*—rather too closely, in FRANK O'HARA's opinion (O'Hara 13; Perloff 15), though for younger poets Olson's association with Williams and Pound, with whom he had personal as well as literary contact, contributed to Olson's aura. Another factor was the force of his physical presence, enhanced by his size—6 feet 7 inches and some 260 pounds—his penchant for oracular utterance, and a tremendous need for response from his listeners. The emphasis in Olson's poetics on both oral performance and open FORM arose from this need. An especially famous demonstration occurred at the BERKELEY POETRY CONFERENCE in 1965, which ANNE WALDMAN vividly recalls: "It was incredible to watch a poet seemingly enact his whole life—from infancy to old age—up there in front of you: very scary, but also moving, profound, and vulnerable. Up there without props, without a script, every idea of text or presentation tossed to the wind. Probably inebriated, not giving you any sort of line, not dishing out some message or propaganda, but just opening up his head in public" (27).

Olson's interaction with the New York School consisted largely of personal encounters of this kind during the last decade of this life. During the summer of 1962 he made a brief appearance on the New York scene as the guest of LeRoi Jones (AMIRI BARAKA), who helped publish Olson's work in *YŪGEN, The FLOATING BEAR,* and *KULCHUR* (Clark 298–299; Olson, "Reading at Berkeley" 133). In summer 1963, at a poetry conference in Vancouver, British Columbia, Olson urged CLARK COOLIDGE and Michael Palmer to start a magazine, which eventually became *Joglars* (Coolidge 237). In fall 1964 O'Hara gave a reading at the State University of New York at Buffalo, where Olson taught from 1963 to 1965. *"BIOTHERM,"* a poem in "projective" style, particularly impressed Olson at O'Hara's reading and upon rereading it in the Buffalo student magazine *Audit* (Olson, "Interview and Note"). The following year O'Hara helped arrange for Olson to read at the Festival of Two Worlds, in Spoleto, Italy, where he was introduced by JOHN ASHBERY, and then went on to the poetry conference at Berkeley. Olson held his own "Gloucester Poetry Conference," as he called it (Clark 331), during the summer of 1966, with JOHN WIENERS and ED SANDERS, two of his favorite companions among the younger poets, helping lift his spirits as much through chemical as through poetic stimulation. The next summer in London, following the International Poetry Festival, LARRY FAGIN was on hand to witness Olson, again in a party mood, lift Mick Jagger off his feet in a big bear hug (Fagin 586). The cost of living life at this pitch of intensity is evident in the responses, some of them nearly incoherent, that Olson provided when GERARD MALANGA interviewed him for the *PARIS REVIEW* in spring 1969.

Within 10 months Olson was dead of cancer of the liver. His former student at Black Mountain, JOEL OPPENHEIMER, paid him tribute in the *Village Voice*: "Maybe it was Charles writing furiously to Creeley and Duncan and all of us that made it impossible to ignore a whole new school of poetry that insisted that poetry was life *and* art, and that in the end could not be denied" (9).

Bibliography

Clark, Tom. *Charles Olson: The Allegory of a Poet's Life.* New York: Norton, 1991.

Coolidge, Clark. Statement in Steven Clay and Rodney Phillips. *A Secret Location on the Lower East Side: Adventures in Writing, 1960–1980.* New York: New York Public Library/Granary Books, 1998.

Duberman, Martin. *Black Mountain: An Exploration in Community.* New York: Norton, 1993.

Fagin, Larry. "True Passion: My Life with Angel Hair." In *The Angel Hair Anthology,* edited by Anne Waldman and Lewis Warsh, 585–587. New York: Granary Books, 2001.

Kelleher, Michael, and Ammiel Alcalay. Olson Now blog. Available online. URL: http://www.olsonnow. blogspot.com/.

O'Hara, Frank. Interview by Edward Lucie-Smith (1965). In *Standing Still and Walking in New York.* Edited by Donald Allen. San Francisco: Grey Fox, 1983, 3–26.

Olson, Charles. *The Collected Poems.* Edited by George F. Butterick. Berkeley: University of California Press, 1987.

———. *Collected Prose.* Edited by Donald Allen and Benjamin Friedlander. Berkeley: University of California Press, 1997.

———. "Interview and Note." In *Homage to Frank O'Hara,* edited by Bill Berkson and Joe LeSueur, 177–178. Bolinas, Calif.: Big Sky, 1988.

———. *The Maximus Poems.* Edited by George F. Butterick. Berkeley: University of California Press, 1983.

———. "*Paris Review* Interview" (1969). In *Muthologos: The Collected Lectures and Interviews.* Vol. 2. Edited by George F. Butterick. Bolinas, Calif.: Four Seasons, 1979, 105–153.

———. "Reading at Berkeley" (1965) In *Muthologos: The Collected Lectures and Interviews.* Vol. 1. Edited by George F. Butterick. Bolinas, Calif.: Four Seasons, 1978, 97–156.

Oppenheimer, Joel. "Charles Olson 1910–1970." *Village Voice,* 15 January 1970, p. 9.

Perloff, Marjorie. *Frank O'Hara: Poet Among Painters.* Chicago: University of Chicago Press, 1998.

Saroyan, Aram. "The Poet's Father (Charles Olson)." In *Starting Out in the Sixties: Selected Essays.* Jersey City, N.J.: Talisman House, 2001, 64–69.

Waldman, Anne. "My Life a List" (1976). In *Vow to Poetry: Essays, Interviews, and Manifestos.* Minneapolis, Minn.: Coffee House Press, 2001, 25–50.

One Thousand Avant-Garde Plays
Kenneth Koch (1988)

KENNETH KOCH's *One Thousand Avant-Garde Plays* (1988) is actually a collection of 112 short pieces, imaginative and improvisatory in their consistent portrayals of the comic drama of life. These poetic flashes achieve their comic repercussions primarily through the juxtapositions of incongruous situations and by means of rapid (many are less than half a page in length), often unpredictable changes in language, character, and scene, from, for example, Mary Magdalene to little Red Riding Hood.

The plays echo and imitate older dramatic FORMs such as the Elizabethan chronicle ("The Mediterranean" and "The Black Spanish Costume"), frequently appropriating the earlier dramatic conventions, such as court masques ("Watteau's Reputation" and "The Boat from Mandaki"), as well as Noh and Kabuki plays ("The Choice in Shanghai") and PERFORMANCE ART ("A Song to the Avant-Garde").

In assembling the collection, Koch told an interviewer: "I wanted to bring together in writing them moments of excitement in the present and things that happened in the past which were—in one way and another 'momentous'—either for the world now, or the momentous at the time for the people that lived them" (Tranter n.p.). At his best Koch is a good, amusing playwright and a fine parodist. And, although he is a playwright of limited tonal range yet a wide and resourceful vision, his deployment of structures—whether metered, vers libre, or the flat line—gives his plays freedom and surprise that occasionally astonish. Just as often, however, as in "Hippopotamus Migration in Africa," a piece in which hippos appear on a stage and speak a simple aside of their existence, or "Olive Oyl Commandeers Popeye's Gunboat and Sails Off to Attack Russia," the works seem simple and formless with varying slack results.

In appraising Koch's poetic output, Geoff Ward wrote, in what could accurately be said of his plays: "They are upbeat, comic and almost cartoon-like in their vibrancy. The most frantically and farcically humorous of all poets, Koch often draws his best jokes from a self-reflexive attention to the world" (7–8).

Koch's achievement, finally, consists of small surprises, enchantments of image and allusion, phrase and idea. His plays rarely move or instruct, but they do entertain.

Bibliography

Koch, Kenneth. *One Thousand Avant-Garde Plays.* New York: Knopf, 1988.

Tranter, John, "Very Rapid Acceleration: An interview with Kenneth Koch" (1989). *Jacket* no. 5 (October 1998). Available online. URL: http://jacketmagazine.com/05/koch89.html. Accessed October 26, 2008.

Ward, Geoff. *Statues of Liberty: The New York School of Poets.* New York: St. Martin's Press, 1993. (pp. 7–8)

Oppenheimer, Joel (1930–1988)

Joel Oppenheimer was born in Yonkers, New York, in 1930 and died from cancer in 1988. While not allied with the poets of the NEW YORK SCHOOL, Oppenheimer was a thorough New Yorker. He was part of the group of poets and painters who drank and talked at the Cedars Tavern; he was an avid sports fan and wrote a book on the Mets called *The Wrong Season* (Bobbs-Merrill, 1973); he was a longtime resident of the West Village in DOWNTOWN MANHATTAN and a connoisseur of its restaurants and its political and social events; and between 1969 and 1984 he wrote a regular column for the *Village Voice* on baseball, public issues, and political themes, and the news of the city. But most of all he was the founding director of the POETRY PROJECT AT ST. MARK'S CHURCH IN-THE-BOWERY, and from 1966 to 1968 he initiated the "Poets in the Schools" program, which KENNETH KOCH and other poets made famous.

Oppenheimer grew up in a middle-class Jewish family and attended public schools, then Cornell University and the University of Chicago briefly before finding his place at BLACK MOUNTAIN COLLEGE in North Carolina. He studied with M. C. Richards, but it was CHARLES OLSON who challenged him into his life as a writer. His early books, *The Dancer* (1951) and *The Dutiful Son* (1956) were published by Jonathan Williams at his Jargon Society, but it was with *The Love Bit and Other Poems* (Totem Press, 1962) that he found a discursive poetic FORM, based on short lines, intricate rhythmic structures, the exclusive use of lowercase letters, and the admittance of all kinds of information into the poem. He lived in NEW YORK CITY and worked in print shops in the period leading up to his first major book, *In Time: Poems, 1962–1968* (Bobbs-Merrill, 1969). *On Occasion: Some Births, Deaths, Weddings, Birthday, Holidays, and Other Events* (Bobbs-Merrill, 1973) followed. The occasional poem, which became his signature poem, functions as a part of life, and is an actual benefit to society, he thought.

In the *Village Voice* articles he wrote about political movements, mainly the Vietnam War protests, public issues of life in New York, and family affairs. He reserved poetry, therefore, for meditations on other subjects, as evidenced in *The Woman Poems* (Bobbs-Merrill, 1975). He took a lead from Robert Bly's book *Sleepers Joining Hands* (1973) about the eternal female goddess, but he added his own obsessions about sex and women and intense personal relationships. He wrote a SERIAL POEM in which each poem explores one aspect of the central theme but together form a sustained, meditative narrative. This major effort was followed by *Names, Dates & Places* (Saint Andrews, 1978) and *At Fifty: A Poem* (Saint Andrews, 1982). By the next collection, *New Spaces: Poems, 1975–1983* (Black Sparrow, 1985), he was moving on to other concerns without forgetting the great value of ordinary events. His later books, which include *Why Not* (Press of the Good Mountain, 1985), *The Uses of Adversity* (Zelot, 1987), and *New Hampshire Journal* (Perishable Press, 1994), are collected in *Collected Later Poems* (University of Buffalo, 1997).

Oppenheimer was a master of the occasional poem whose discursive style reached great refinement. He celebrated living and the rituals of living and insisted that life, love, and erotic desires should be celebrated along with marriages, the new season, births, and deaths. In his late poems he achieved a reductivist poetics in which complex ideas and perceptions appear in carefully measured lines, and in this accomplishment showed that he shared with JOHN ASHBERY and FRANK O'HARA a direct line from the later writing of Wallace Stevens and William Carlos Williams.

Bibliography

Bertholf, Robert. "Joel Oppenheimer." In *Dictionary of Literary Biography*. Vol. 193, edited by Joseph Conte, 252–265. Detroit, Mich.: Gale Research, 1998.

Gilmore, Lyman. *Don't Touch the Poet: The Life and Times of Joel Oppenheimer.* Jersey City, N.J.: Talisman House, 1998.

ottava rima

The stanza FORM known by its Italian designation ottava rima (octave rhyme) has descended in the English tradition as eight lines in iambic pentameter, rhyming *abababcc*. Since Ludovico Ariosto employed the form in *Orlando Furioso* (1516), it has been associated with epic narrative and with a mixture of serious and comic tones, associations reinforced by the most famous example in English, Lord Byron's *Don Juan* (1819–24). In modern poetry W. B. Yeats adopted ottava rima for serious lyric in "Among School Children" (1927) and "Sailing to Byzantium" (1927), but the Byronic spirit revived only with W. H. AUDEN, and even he substituted a seven-line stanza in "Letter to Lord Byron" (1937) for fear that he might "come a cropper" (take a heavy fall) in ottava rima (42). When KENNETH KOCH faced the challenge fully in his narrative poems *Ko, or a Season on Earth* (1959) and *The Duplications* (1977), collected in SEASONS ON EARTH (1987), ottava rima became one of the levers by which the NEW YORK SCHOOL pried opened the windows of poetry to let in fresh air.

The length of the ottava rima stanza encourages poets to pack a lot in, and the pattern of alternating sounds invites variety. As Koch writes in the middle of one of his stanzas in *The Duplications*:

> *This stanza is a help, a splendid churn to*
> *Make oppositions one, to bring Khartoum,*
> *Venice, and Oz into the self-same urn; to*
> *Put silverfoil and rags on the same loom*
> (*Seasons* 211)

Once the machinery of the form is set in motion, it can threaten to overwhelm the poet, forcing him or her to perform comic acrobatics (churn to / urn to) to keep up the pace. Koch, however, finds creative stimulus in the sense that the poem may actually get ahead of him. "The whole plot comes from the rhyme, from the need for rhymes," he has explained (interview n.p.). For instance, in the last line of the first canto of *Ko*, "Let's pause a moment, like a

dairy truck," the dairy truck seems to be introduced solely to rhyme with "unstuck" at the end of the preceding line. But now that it has appeared, the truck becomes the focus of action in the beginning of the next canto, which describes in detail various pictures that the milkman has painted on the bottles the truck is transporting. Even the movement of the truck can be said to be driven by the poem's form, since the repetition of sound in ottava rima accumulates a powerful forward momentum that suits both the purposes of narrative and, when it seems to escape control, of comedy.

Later approaches to ottava rima in the New York School tradition appear in DOUGLAS OLIVER's PENNILESS POLITICS (Hoarse Commerce, 1991; Bloodaxe, 1994) and ELINOR NAUEN's *So Late into the Night* (in progress). Nauen concedes, "Although Byron's my model more than Koch / I honor Kenneth and his fine rima" (n.p.).

Bibliography

Auden, W. H. *Collected Longer Poems.* London: Faber, 1974.

Koch, Kenneth. Interview by Anne Waldman. *Jacket* 15 (December 2001). Available online. URL: http://www.jacketmagazine.com/15/koch-waldman.html. Accessed December 19, 2008.

———. Commentary on Byron, *Don Juan*, excerpts. In *Making Your Own Days: The Pleasures of Reading and Writing Poetry.* New York: Scribner, 1998.

———. *Seasons on Earth.* New York: Penguin, 1987.

Nauen, Elinor. Excerpt from *So Late into the Night.* Real Poetik (2003). Available online. URL: http://www.scn.org/realpoetik/elinor-nauen03.htm. Accessed December 19, 2008.

Oliver, Douglas. Essay in *Contemporary Authors Autobiography Series* 27. Edited by Joyce Nakamura. Detroit, Mich.: Gale, 1997, 241–261.

Padgett, Ron. "Ottava Rima." In *The Teachers & Writers Handbook of Poetic Forms.* 2d ed. New York: Teachers & Writers Collaborative, 2000, 124–125.

Oulipo (1960–)

The French literary association Oulipo was conceived by the writer Raymond Queneau (1903–76) and the mathematician François Le Lionnais (1901–84) as a means of developing a literature that would have the formal elegance and productive potential of mathematics. The name *Oulipo* (pronounced oo-lee-POH) derives from the first two letters of each of the key words in its official title: Ouvroir de littérature potentielle (workshop of potential literature). Oulipo is important to NEW YORK SCHOOL poets for its ongoing attention to the procedures of RAYMOND ROUSSEL, whom the poets had discovered before Oulipo was founded in 1960. As a proven *roussellâtre* (disciple of Roussel), HARRY MATHEWS was admitted to membership in Oulipo in 1973, providing New York School poetry with a formal link to the French avant-garde going back to Alfred Jarry (1873–1907). Oulipo began as a branch of the College of Pataphysics, founded in 1948 and named after the proto-dadaist "science" that Jarry announced, in opposition to metaphysics, in 1893. Dadaist artist Marcel Duchamp (1887–1968) joined Oulipo in 1962. The official Oulipo Web site lists a total of "34 members, of whom 13 are excused due to death."

Oulipo is better known for FICTION than for poetry, through the work of members Georges Perec (1936–82) and Italo Calvino (1923–85), as well as Queneau (*Zazi dans le Métro*, 1959) and Mathews. However, the "constraints," or rules, that Oulipians apply to their work has led to "fiction that was organized the way poetry is," as Mathews has explained (interview 14). It is typical of Oulipian poetry to adopt a traditional FORM, such as the sonnet, and apply new constraints, as Queneau did for his *100,000,000,000,000 Poems,* the title indicating the potential number of poems that might be produced by rearranging the lines in 10 sonnets provided by Queneau. The work was published (1961) in the form of a children's "flip" book, with the lines cut into strips so the reader could rearrange them. Mathews has favored the sestina, again with new constraints added (as in "Histoire" and "Presto"). The collaborative sestina by KENNETH KOCH and JOHN ASHBERY, "Crone Rhapsody," is Oulipian in this sense. Not only does it repeat end words according to the requirements of a sestina, but it satisfies the additional requirements that "all the end-words are pieces of office furniture," and further, "that every line contain the name of a flower, a tree, a fruit, a game, and a famous old lady" (Koch 196).

The issue of *LOCUS SOLUS* (number 2, 1961) in which "Crone Rhapsody" was published may be considered the most comprehensive collection of New York School work in the Oulipian mode. It includes an installment of Mathews's novel *The CONVERSIONS,* built on a complex tale-within-tale structure after the manner of Roussel; FRANK O'HARA's "Choses Passagères" (Passing things), mined from a French dictionary (Epstein), a favorite Oulipian tool; and Ashbery's "To a Waterfowl," an example of the ancient form of the cento in which all the lines come from previously published poems by various authors. Mathews included another cento by Ashbery, "The Dong with the Luminous Nose," in the *Oulipo Compendium,* the best survey of the movement available in English. Continuing interest in Oulipo as a stimulus to experimental writing was demonstrated by the Noulipo Conference held at the California Institute of Arts in 2005, in which both Mathews and BERNADETTE MAYER participated.

Bibliography

Ashbery, John. "The Dong with the Luminous Nose." In *Wakefulness.* New York: Farrar, Straus & Giroux, 1999, 75–76.

———. "To a Waterfowl." *Locus Solus* 2 (1961): 7–9.

Ashbery, John, and Kenneth Koch. "Crone Rhapsody." *Locus Solus* 2 (1961): 157–162.

Epstein, Andrew. "Frank O'Hara's Translation Game." *Raritan* 19, no. 3 (2000): 144–161.

Koch, Kenneth. "A Note on This Issue." *Locus Solus* 2 (1961): 193–197.

Mathews, Harry. "Histoire" (1982). In *Postmodern American Poetry,* edited by Paul Hoover, 206–208. New York: Norton, 1994.

———. Interview by Marcella Durand. *Poetry Project Newsletter* 199 (April–May 2004): 13–15, 18.

———. "Presto" (1984). In *An Exaltation of Forms: Contemporary Poets Celebrate the Diversity of Their Art,* edited by Anne Finch and Kathrine Varnes, 389. Ann Arbor: University of Michigan Press, 2002.

Mathews, Harry, and Alastair Brotchie, eds. *Oulipo Compendium.* Rev. ed. London: Atlas Press; Los Angeles: Make Now Press, 2005.

Motte, Warren F., Jr., ed. *Oulipo: A Primer of Potential Literature.* Lincoln: University of Nebraska Press, 1986.

Nielsen, Aldon Lynn. "Oulipian Poetry." In *An Exaltation of Forms: Contemporary Poets Celebrate the Diversity of Their Art*, edited by Anne Finch and Kathrine Varnes, 385–390. Ann Arbor: University of Michigan Press, 2002.

Noulipo Conference Program. California Institute of the Arts Web site. Formerly available online. URL: http://www.calarts.edu/redcat/season/0506/cnv/noulipo.php.

O'Hara, Frank. "Choses Passagères." *Locus Solus* 2 (1961): 128–129.

Oulipo Web site. Available online. URL: http://www.oulipo.net/.

Owen, Maureen (1943–)

Born to an Irish-American family in Graceville, Minnesota, Maureen Owen trained horses and traveled the racing circuit before moving to NEW YORK CITY, where she established herself as a poet, editor, teacher, and publisher. She served as program coordinator of the POETRY PROJECT AT ST. MARK'S CHURCH IN-THE-BOWERY from 1976 to 1980 and founded TELEPHONE magazine and books, a seminal press that published the work of three generations of NEW YORK SCHOOL poets. As a poet, Owen has transfigured the quotidian into the outlandish, swerving through unexpected syntax, caesuras, and fields of white space peppered with minimal punctuation to arrive at revelations bracketed by quietude on both sides. As an editor and teacher, Owen has been at the center of the New York School of poets and has marshaled her considerable energies to help both emerging and established poets and artists.

Upon arrival in New York in the summer of 1968, Owen immediately sensed the communal environment for creating artistic work that existed at that time. As she has written, "When I moved to New York . . . I was a friend of Ron [Padgett's] from Tulsa days, [so I] gravitated over to the [Poetry] Project. I had two little children in tow and was living on the Lower East Side. I was meeting a lot of terrific writers, a lot of them women who were around, who were writing, who were writing seriously, and weren't really getting published anywhere, despite the Project's magazine *The World*—there was never enough room in it for everyone anyway. People who didn't feel part of the group weren't getting in, were intimidated by the scene even though the Project was quite open" ("Notes" n.p.). Owen set about to change this by founding *Telephone* magazine, and she thanks ANNE WALDMAN and LARRY FAGIN for helping her get started, teaching her about the mimeograph format, how to use stencils, and ultimately how to put together a poetry journal.

Owen published a number of emerging women poets in *Telephone*, including Rebecca Wright, Janine Pommy Vega, and Rebecca Brown, and the magazine quickly became one of the signature small-press imprints of the time. Owen would go on to publish complete poetry collections. As Owen has said, "I just love to publish. If you teach writing, it's like you're only teaching half of it. You have to show people how to get their work out. . . . I enjoy making books and magazines. I try to be playful about it, do a few wild political things or use some of the media around. There's so much you can pull into a publication. I love to do end papers by cutting up magazine ads (or the *New York Times* magazine section!), a cheap way to use colors—use cut up ads. There's so much junk around you can use. You can make your magazine or book much more beautiful and it's free" ("Notes" n.p.).

During Owen's term as program coordinator, the St. Mark's Poetry Project began including more women poets and consciously addressing the skewed gender balance that had existed for some time in the New York School. Owen also institutionalized a sense of archiving, of writing bylaws, of fixing formal procedures that allowed the Poetry Project to go from being a kind of loose collective to a more cohesive arts organization. During this time Owen deepened her friendships with many New York School poets, including RON PADGETT and BERNADETTE MAYER, and other experimentalists, such as Susan and Fanny Howe.

Since *Country Rush* (ADVENTURES IN POETRY, 1973), Owen has published more than 10 volumes of poetry. Seven of them are excerpted in *American Rush: Selected Poems* (Talisman House, 1998), a finalist for the *Los Angeles Times* Book Prize. *AMELIA EARHART* (Vortex Editions, 1984) received the American Book Award. The title of *Erosion's Pull* (Coffee House, 2006), referring to the geology of mountain ranges, reflects her current residence in the mountains of Colorado, where she teaches at NAROPA University.

Bibliography

Foster, Edward, ed. Maureen Owen issue. *Talisman* nos. 21–22 (Winter–Spring 2001).

Owen, Maureen. "Notes on Publishing: From a Telephone Interview with Marcella Durand, February 1999." *Jacket* 11 (April 2000). Available online. URL: http://jacketmagazine.com/11/owen-durand.html.

———. "When as a Girl on the Plains of Minnesota." In *The Grand Permission: New Writings on Poetics and Motherhood,* edited by Patricia Dienstfrey et al., 11–16. Middletown, Conn.: Wesleyan University Press, 2003.

P

Padgett, Ron (1942–   )
While the zany laughter of Woody Woodpecker resonates throughout Ron Padgett's poetry (Notley 35–36), his pragmatism and historical perspective have lent stability to the NEW YORK SCHOOL, though he regards the notion of such a "school" with skepticism (Padgett, interview 111). As early as his high school years in Tulsa, Oklahoma, when Padgett encountered the range of New American Poetry featured in the *Evergreen Review,* he not only confirmed his own identity as an "outsider" poet (Padgett, interview 101) but also started a magazine, the *WHITE DOVE REVIEW,* enlisting his friends DICK GALLUP and JOE BRAINARD as coeditors and attracting TED BERRIGAN as a contributor. Padgett was the first of the Tulsa group to arrive in NEW YORK CITY, in the fall of 1960. He had decided to study at Columbia University because it was in New York and because "[Jack] Kerouac and [Allen] Ginsberg had gone there" (Padgett, interview 103). From several courses with KENNETH KOCH, starting with freshman humanities, Padgett learned the joys of comic literature and the creative possibilities of TRANSLATION, which he practiced on the early modernist French poets Guillaume Apollinaire, Blaise Cendrars, Max Jacob, and Pierre Reverdy. Meanwhile, Padgett's efforts to publish Berrigan and another Tulsa acquaintance, David Bearden, in the *Columbia Review* aroused objections from university authorities on grounds of obscenity and prompted Berrigan to launch "C" magazine (1963), in which Padgett eventually collaborated as a guest editor.

Padgett's enthusiasm for COLLABORATION shows up especially in early publications such as *BEAN SPASMS,* with Berrigan (Kulchur, 1967); *The ADVENTURES OF MR. AND MRS. JIM AND RON,* with artist JIM DINE (Grossman, 1970); and *ANTLERS IN THE TREETOPS,* with TOM VEITCH (Coach House Press, 1973). Throughout Padgett's career the spirit of collaboration has informed his many other contributions to the community of writers. As coeditor, with DAVID SHAPIRO, of *AN ANTHOLOGY OF NEW YORK POETS* (Random House, 1970), he helped compile a record of "the crisscrossing of friendships" that the editors found "surprising and inspiring" (Padgett and Shapiro xxx). In 1973 he established new channels within that network as founding editor of the *Poetry Project Newsletter* and as a cofounder, with ANNE WALDMAN and Joan Simon, of Full Court Press. Later, as director of the POETRY PROJECT AT ST. MARK'S CHURCH IN-THE-BOWERY (1978–80), he encouraged collaborative performance, such as the memorable 1979 event, "Popeye and William Blake Fight to the Death" by Koch and ALLEN GINSBERG ("Talk of the Town" 29–31). Above all, as fellow-collaborator BILL ZAVATSKY reported, "in his extensive work with children as a teacher of poetry writing, the collaboration was central to Ron's approach. It loosens up writers of any age, gets them laughing, it makes poetry joy" (Eshelman 14). Padgett has taught students of all ages in various Poets-in-the-Schools programs, ranging as far afield as South Carolina (1976–78), and at Brooklyn and Columbia Colleges. Starting in 1969 he served the TEACHERS & WRITERS

COLLABORATIVE in several roles, culminating in the position of director of publications, which he held for 20 years (1980–99).

Closely related to Padgett's interest in collaboration is his attitude toward authorship, which has left him relatively free of "the anxiety of influence" analyzed by Harold Bloom. With regard to the influence of the first-generation New York School poets, Joe LeSueur suggests a certain amount of anxiety in recalling that both Padgett and Berrigan maintained a formal distance between themselves and FRANK O'HARA, a stance that LeSueur interprets as a sign of "awe" (LeSueur 196). On the other hand, in "Strawberries in Mexico" (1969), a poem that takes its title from Apollinaire, Padgett presumes such familiarity with O'Hara that he freely appropriates his work (specifically, the poem "Rhapsody"), "as anyone familiar with his poetry will tell" (*New and Selected* 106). Such open acknowledgment is in the spirit of "The New Plagiarism," a movement that Padgett announced in 1964 in a mock-manifesto that echoes both O'Hara's "PERSONISM" and the "New Realism" that became established in the New York art world under the alternative title, POP ART. In its appropriation of popular imagery—including one of Padgett's favorite sources, cartoons—and in its embrace of mechanical processes such as silkscreening, pop art brought a kind of honesty to the act of copying that felt refreshing after the long tradition of "dressing up" influences, which Padgett opposed in "The New Plagiarism." Yet Padgett did not intend an outright rejection of the "Personism" associated with O'Hara and abstract expressionist art. Rather, by directly appropriating "found" texts, translating texts from one language to another, and producing new texts through collaboration, Padgett cultivated a kind of multiple personality. The mystery of the mental processes that permit such a state is opened to the reader's interpretation in "Poem (Funny, I hear)" (1976), where Padgett's ability to hear O'Hara's voice in his head is starkly juxtaposed with a memory of JAMES SCHUYLER hallucinating O'Hara's presence as if he were still alive (*New and Selected* 17).

The proliferation of voices in Padgett's work frees it from the confines of conventional criticism that seeks to identify a single voice as distinctive of the author or to mark a particular book as a distinct "stage" in a continuous process of development. Clayton Eshelman locates an extreme of "opaqueness" in Padgett's first major solo collection, GREAT BALLS OF FIRE (Holt, Rinehart and Winston, 1969), and a move toward greater transparency in volumes of the 1970s, when "Padgett became Padgett," according to Eshelman (8, 11). Whatever this claim might mean, its validity is limited by the persistence of moments when the later poems resist meaning as language turns back on itself. For instance, "Louisiana Perch," from *Toujours l'Amour* (SUN, 1976), highlights "the great words . . . without meaning," *from, a, their, or,* and so on (*New and Selected* 7). In the long poem *Cufflinks,* from *Triangles in the Afternoon* (SUN, 1979), the word *cufflink* redundantly inscribed on a pair of cufflinks renders meaningless the "final devastating chord" about to be played on a grand piano by the hands that wear the cufflinks (*New and Selected* 90). In an interview with Padgett, Ed Foster attempted to distinguish *Great Balls of Fire* from *The Big Something* (The Figures, 1989) on the basis of the dramatic role assigned to death in the later volume. For instance, "Who and Each," a response in part to the death of Waldman's mother, Frances, abruptly introduces the death of friends at the end of a detailed description of a dictionary search (*New and Selected* 14); "Dog" laments that "The New York streets look nude and stupid / With Ted [Berrigan] and Edwin [DENBY] no longer here" (*New and Selected* 86). Again, Padgett calls for modification of the straight "developmental" view, in this case by directing Foster's attention to "a certain preoccupation with death" as early as *Great Balls of Fire* (Padgett, interview 112). In another interview, with EDMUND BERRIGAN, Padgett has described how "something made me avoid Comedy Court" while writing "Morning," from *You Never Know* (Coffee House Press, 2002). That "something" is an urge "to avoid writing a 'Ron Padgett' poem," to remain "mercurial," "multifaceted" (Padgett, "Ron Padgett Lifts Off" 14). Padgett's goal, always, is to make something new, a challenge he met in his *New and Selected Poems* (Godine, 1995) by treating old poems as "found" material to be interspersed with the newer work, with no indication of dates. Reviewing this volume, Karen Volkman successfully captured a sense of the authentic unity that emerges from all of Padgett's variousness: "This *New & Selected* is a fine sampling of a restless, hilarious, and haunting lyric intelligence, a 'phony' whose variable voices form a rare and raucous orchestration: the real thing" (V21).

Bibliography

Apollinaire, Guillaume. *The Poet Assassinated.* Translated by Ron Padgett. Illustrated by Jim Dine. New York: Holt, Rinehart & Winston, 1968.

Bloom, Harold. *The Anxiety of Influence: A Theory of Poetry.* New York: Oxford University Press, 1973.

Cendrars, Blaise. *Complete Poems.* Translated by Ron Padgett. Berkeley: University of California Press, 1992.

Eshelman, Clayton. "Padgett the Collaborator." *Chicago Review* 43, no. 2 (Spring 1997): 8–29.

LeSueur, Joe. "Duologue for Ted." In *Nice to See You: Homage to Ted Berrigan,* edited by Anne Waldman, 191–197. Minneapolis, Minn.: Coffee House Press, 1991.

Notley, Alice. "Ron Padgett's Visual Imagination" (1998). In *Coming After: Essays on Poetry.* Ann Arbor: University of Michigan Press, 2005, 27–40.

O'Hara, Frank. "Rhapsody." In *Collected Poems.* Rev. ed. Edited by Donald Allen. Berkeley: University of California Press, 1995, 325–326.

Padgett, Ron. *How to Be Perfect.* Minneapolis, Minn.: Coffee House Press, 2007.

———. Interview by Edward Foster (1991). In *Poetry and Poetics in a New Millennium,* edited by Edward Foster, 100–114. Jersey City, N.J.: Talisman House, 2000.

———. *Joe: A Memoir of Joe Brainard.* Minneapolis, Minn.: Coffee House Press, 2004.

———. *New and Selected Poems.* Boston: Godine, 1995.

———. "The New Plagiarism." *Adventures in Poetry* 2 (July 1968): n.p.

———. *Oklahoma Tough: My Father, King of the Tulsa Bootleggers.* Norman: University of Oklahoma Press, 2003.

———. "Poets and Painters in Paris, 1919–39." *Art News Annual* 34 (1968): 88–95.

———. "Ron Padgett Lifts Off." *Poetry Project Newsletter* 203 (April–May 2005): 11–15.

———. *The Straight Line: Writings on Poetry and Poets.* Ann Arbor: University of Michigan Press, 2000.

———. *Ted: A Personal Memoir of Ted Berrigan.* Great Barrington, Mass.: The Figures, 1993.

———. *Tulsa Kid.* Calais, Vt.: Z Press, 1979.

Padgett, Ron, and David Shapiro. Preface to *An Anthology of New York Poets.* New York: Vintage–Random House, 1970, xxix–xxxvii.

Schneeman, George. "Collaborating with Poets: A Conversation with George Schneeman." In *Painter Among Poets: The Collaborative Art of George Schneeman,* edited by Ron Padgett, 34–62. New York: Granary Books, 2004.

"Talk of the Town: Poems." *New Yorker,* 28 May 1979, 29–31.

Volkman, Karen. "The Tulsa Kid." *Village Voice,* 3 September 1996, p. V21.

"Painter, The" John Ashbery (1948)

"The Painter" is the earliest of a series of "artist poems" (including FRANK O'HARA's "WHY I AM NOT A PAINTER" and KENNETH KOCH's "The ARTIST") that reflect the NEW YORK SCHOOL poets' engagement with the visual arts. In fact, "The Painter" predicts such engagement, since it was written while JOHN ASHBERY was still a student at Harvard University and largely unaware of developments in the visual arts after SURREALISM. He was aware of the existence of avant-garde experimentation in the arts in general and recognized the relative lack of experimental poetry. "The Painter" may be read both as a parable of the avant-garde artist and as a way of asking, "Is it now possible to write poetry?" That was the question W. H. AUDEN heard when "The Painter" was published in *Some Trees* (1956), selected by Auden for the Yale Younger Poets series.

The shoreline setting of "The Painter" represents a liminal space between nature and art, "between the sea and the buildings." The people in the buildings accept their removal from nature and expect the same of art, that is, that it be "a means to an end," a medium of representation. But the Painter wants his art to be nature without mediation; he seeks a nonrepresentational, or abstract, art. At first, he merely offers a blank canvas, onto which he expects the sea to "Plaster its own portrait." When nothing happens, he makes a concession to the people in the buildings and portrays his wife, "making her vast, like ruined buildings," symbolizing art's undoing. The results encourage the Painter to return to the sea as his subject, aiming now not merely at symbolic ruin but at the actual wreck of his canvas. His attack on art, now more dadaist than abstract, arouses the people to throw the Painter "from the tallest of the buildings."

Paradoxically, the final defeat of the Painter may be the key to the success of his art. If his "perfectly white" final canvas anticipates the white paintings of ROBERT RAUSCHENBERG (1952), the death of the Painter embraces the self-extinguishing silence explored by Rauschenberg's advocate, JOHN CAGE. Like Cage, who employed chance techniques in MUSIC to remove the composer's control, Ashbery let the FORM of the sestina compose "The Painter." Two days later he explained in a letter to Koch that he liked sestinas because "they practically write themselves" (Lehman 132). They are the poetic equivalent of allowing the subject of a painting to "Plaster its own portrait on the canvas."

Bibliography

Ashbery, John. *Some Trees.* With foreword by W. H. Auden. New Haven, Conn.: Yale University Press, 1956.

Lehman, David. *The Last Avant-Garde; The Making of the New York School of Poets.* New York: Doubleday, 1998, 132–135.

painting *See* ART, VISUAL.

Paris Review (1953–)

As its name implies, the *Paris Review* was founded on an assumption opposite to the implications of the term NEW YORK SCHOOL. The magazine's founder, Peter Matthiessen (1927–), and his friend George Plimpton (1927–2003), who served as editor-in-chief for the rest of his life, assumed that Paris following World War II was still the capital of the avant-garde and could again offer young American writers the creative stimulus and bohemian lifestyle that the post–World War I "lost generation" had made legendary. That legend, along with the Ivy League connections of the founders, helped the *Paris Review* acquire prestige

very quickly. It distinguished itself from other leading "reviews" of the 1950s (*Hudson, Kenyon, Partisan, Sewanee*) by focusing on "primary" work and avoiding criticism or theory, except insofar as writers themselves chose to engage in such discussion in the famous series of interviews for which the *Paris Review* is best known.

Ironically, while FRENCH POETRY played a formative role in the development of the New York School, the poetry found in the pages of the *Paris Review* under its first two poetry editors, Donald Hall (until 1961) and X. J. Kennedy (1961–64), reflected a conservative Anglo-American tradition. This orientation changed radically when TOM CLARK was appointed to succeed Kennedy as poetry editor, on the recommendation of Hall, Clark's former professor at the University of Michigan. Suddenly, in the words of Plimpton, "the magazine made up for modernist lost time" (Plimpton et al., "Paris Review Sketchbook" 385), and Clark filled a good part of the gap with New York School poets.

At the time of his appointment Clark was in England, studying with poet and Pound scholar Donald Davie at Cambridge University. Following up, in a sense, on Hall's interview with Ezra Pound in the *Paris Review,* number 28 (summer–fall 1962), the first selections of poetry that Clark edited, starting with number 32 (summer–fall 1964), traced Pound's legacy as represented by the OBJECTIVISTS and the BLACK MOUNTAIN group. Meanwhile, Clark searched for new developments in his own generation, and he found them in the mimeograph magazines that were pouring out from NEW YORK CITY's Lower East Side and somehow ending up in bookstores in London and Paris, next to more stylishly dressed European relations such as ART AND LITERATURE. Clark wrote to the poets whose work appealed to him in these magazines and invited them to contribute to the *Paris Review,* which was rather like asking a sandlot baseball player if he wanted to pitch in a major league game (a dream realized by editor Plimpton [*Out of My League*]). The response to Clark's invitation was so enthusiastic that he was able to produce his own series of mimeograph magazines (*Once, Twice, Thrice,* and so on) from the "generous overflow" of manuscripts (Clark 17), beyond what he could use for the *Paris Review.* New

York School writing came to dominate the pages of the *Paris Review* to the extent that poets who were not of a "neosurrealist" disposition may simply have stopped submitting, as critic Charles Molesworth speculates (185). The trend reached a climax in number 41 (summer–fall 1967), in which the entire roster of poets consists of JOHN ASHBERY, Michael Benedikt, BILL BERKSON, PAUL CARROLL, Clark, CLARK COOLIDGE, DICK GALLUP, BARBARA GUEST, KENNETH KOCH, FRANK LIMA, HARRY MATHEWS, RON PADGETT, JAMES SCHUYLER, TONY TOWLE, and PHILIP WHALEN. Clark continued to serve as poetry editor through number 56 (spring 1973), after which the magazine underwent several changes, including the relocation of its headquarters to New York and the appointment of Benedikt (1935–) to succeed Clark.

Prior to Clark's tenure at the *Paris Review*, poets of the first-generation New York School intersected with the magazine's social circle through mutual involvement in the artists' colony that formed in the HAMPTONS on Long Island during the 1950s. Patsy Southgate (1928–98), the wife of Matthiessen at the time of the magazine's founding and later the wife of painter Mike Goldberg, reported on "The Eastern Long Island Painters" in a special feature of *Paris Review*, number 21 (spring–summer 1959). Southgate, FRANK O'HARA, and the novelist Terry Southern, who had debuted in the first issue of the *Paris Review*, circulated among the magazine's "Quality Lit" crowd, as Southern dubbed them (114–115), with a hipness that set them apart. Also on the scene at this time was Maxine Groffsky (ca. 1937–), rebounding from an affair with Philip Roth, another *Paris Review* discovery. When a new affair with LARRY RIVERS broke up (Gruen 137–140), Groffsky left for Europe and took on the job of Paris editor of the *Paris Review* (1966–70). Groffsky also played a role in Paris Review Editions, a short-lived publishing venture in association with the firm of Doubleday. Titles in the series included Mathews's *TLOOTH* (1966), Schuyler's *Freely Espousing* (1969), and KENWARD ELMSLIE's *The Orchid Stories* (1973). Starting in 1980, Groffsky served as Schuyler's literary agent and no doubt shares responsibility with the poetry editor at the time, Jonathan Galassi, for the publication of the "Payne Whitney Poems" (number 79, spring 1981) and "A Few Days" (number 96, summer 1985), among the most significant works of New York School poetry to appear in the *Paris Review*. *The Paris Review Anthology*, edited by Plimpton (Norton, 1990), gathers work by Ashbery, AMIRI BARAKA, TED BERRIGAN, Clark, Coolidge, Koch, JOHN KOETHE, O'Hara, Padgett, ED SANDERS, ARAM SAROYAN, Schuyler, and ANNE WALDMAN.

Bibliography

Clark, Tom. *Late Returns: A Memoir of Ted Berrigan.* Bolinas, Calif.: Tombouctou, 1985.

Gruen, John. *The Party's Over Now: Reminiscences of the Fifties—New York's Artists, Writers, Musicians, and Their Friends.* Wainscott, N.Y.: Pushcart Press, 1989.

Molesworth, Charles. *The Fierce Embrace: A Study of Contemporary American Poetry.* Columbia: University of Missouri Press, 1979.

Plimpton, George. *Out of My League.* New York: Harper, 1961.

Plimpton, George, et al. "The Paris Review Sketchbook." *Paris Review* 79 (Spring 1981): 308–420.

Sawyer-Laução, Christopher. "The Paris Review." In *The Continual Pilgrimage: American Writers in Paris, 1944–1960.* San Francisco: City Lights, 1992, 143–159.

Southern, Terry. "Frank's Humor." In *Homage to Frank O'Hara*, edited by Bill Berkson and Joe LeSueur, 112–116. Bolinas, Calif.: Big Sky, 1988.

Southgate, Patsy. "My Night with Frank O'Hara." In *Homage to Frank O'Hara*, edited by Bill Berkson and Joe LeSueur, 119–121. Bolinas, Calif.: Big Sky, 1988.

Talese, Gay. "Looking for Hemingway." *Esquire* 60 (July 1963): 44–47ff.

Part of My History Lewis Warsh (1972)

Marking a turning point in the life of the author, LEWIS WARSH, *Part of My History* intersects with the history of the NEW YORK SCHOOL and of the United States in significant ways. During 1969, the year when Warsh wrote most of the work collected in the book, his marriage to ANNE WALDMAN was breaking up, and he was growing "old," as the arrival of his 25th birthday seemed to threaten. Like a number of other New York School writers, Warsh left NEW YORK CITY for the

West Coast and the rural environment around BOLINAS, CALIFORNIA. Meanwhile, the country was in political turmoil following the 1968 presidential election and major losses in the war in Vietnam. While traveling across country, Warsh attended the opening of the "Conspiracy Trial" of seven war protesters in CHICAGO, ILLINOIS—an aftershock of the Democratic Party convention held in that city the previous summer. In Iowa City Warsh participated in one of many "Moratorium Day" rallies held across the country on October 15, 1969, in opposition to the war.

At the Iowa City rally Warsh read three poems: FRANK O'HARA's "My Heart," TED BERRIGAN's "Peace," and Warsh's own "Rolling Through Air," which he had written the night before in ALICE NOTLEY's apartment. All three are printed in *Part of My History*. This selection is typical of the tendency of New York School writers to engage in POLITICS only indirectly, imagining a personal alternative to public crisis. At the same time what passes for "personal" in a New York School context is made problematic by various strategies of appropriation, in this case, Warsh's decision to publish other people's poems in "his" book, along with other texts written in COLLABORATION with Waldman, Berrigan, and TOM CLARK. Clark has described the circumstances of his collaboration with Warsh, a sequence of poems entitled "Chicago." Although the title alludes to the Conspiracy Trial, the mood of the poems overall is "pastoral," grounded in the natural and domestic tranquillity of Clark's home in Bolinas, where the collaboration took place. In another poem, "Dreaming as One" (the title quotes William Carlos Williams's *Paterson*), Clark and his wife, Angelica, seem to figure an ideal marriage in contrast to the failed marriage of Warsh and Waldman. Warsh's own emotional investment in the Bolinas community is deliberately concealed within an aesthetic problem he has learned from the action painters: Trying to discover the truth of emotions "is like trying to discover the artist / and the action of painting."

Among several prose works included in *Part of My History*, "New York Diary" and "California Diary" display the style of deadpan reporting of daily trivia for which Warsh became well known. In the context of this book, the restlessness and

purposelessness of the "New York Diary" suggest reasons for Warsh's departure from New York, but "California Diary" is not markedly different. Warsh even notes the similarity at one point: "I don't feel on top or on bottom I just feel distracted and then what's the point? remembering the almost similar scenes at Bill [Berkson]'s before leaving New York." The emotional range of this book is best gauged not between the two coasts but between the two GENREs of prose and poetry. In this respect an especially interesting prose work is "With Bill at Belle Terre," a diary entry that describes the composition, in successive drafts, of a poem of the same title, reprinted in a separate section of the book. The act of writing the poem seems to put Warsh in touch, in his prose, with the coast of Long Island, viewed from BILL BERKSON's house at Belle Terre. Anticipating the role of natural scenery in the Bolinas poems, a felt relationship to nature, rather than details of the scenery itself, hints at the possibility of a healing of Warsh's relationship with Waldman: "as if nature were trying to send me a message—from Anne, I'd like to think, and I hope she's OK."

Part of My History was published in an edition of 1,000 copies by Coach House Press in Toronto, one of the leading outlets for experimental writing in Canada. The format is six inches square, with text (unpaginated) in dark blue ink on light blue paper. Photographs of Warsh's friends and, in one case, a drawing (of Berkson) punctuate the text. The cover design, showing stylized phases of the moon in a repeating pattern, is by JOE BRAINARD. "Landscapes," the last poem in the volume, was written in response to Brainard's request for a text to accompany a series of drawings of Vermont landscapes.

Bibliography

Warsh, Lewis. "Halloween 1967" (part of "New York Diary") and "Chicago" (with Tom Clark). In *The Angel Hair Anthology*, edited by Lewis Warsh and Anne Waldman, 210–211, 275–279. New York: Granary Books, 2001.
———. "New York Diary 1967." In *Nice to See You: Homage to Ted Berrigan*, edited by Anne Waldman, 63–67. Minneapolis, Minn.: Coffee House Press, 1991.

pastoral   *See* GENRE.

Peace Eye Ed Sanders (1965)

ED SANDERS's collection of poems *Peace Eye* (Frontier Press) wittily captures his characteristically playful perspective from within DOWNTOWN MANHATTAN's burgeoning alternative culture. Influenced by ancient Egypt, William Blake, Walt Whitman, CHARLES OLSON, and ALLEN GINSBERG, *Peace Eye* also evokes the humor of NEW YORK SCHOOL poets such as KENNETH KOCH to offer a broad range of sometimes satirical, sometimes critical narrative poetry, replete with Sanders's idiosyncratic blend of mythology, allegory, symbolism, and incantation.

Many of the poems in *Peace Eye* appeared in mimeographs and other little magazines on the Lower East Side during the 1960s. The collection is divided into four sections: "Soft-man Poems," "The Toe Queen Poems," "The Gobble Gang Poems," and "Cemetery Hill." The first section collects seven poems that originally appeared in early issues of *FUCK YOU: A MAGAZINE OF THE ARTS*. In these Sanders develops allegorical references to NEW YORK CITY and examines the confrontation between the dominant American culture and the new, radically different community of artists, activists, and authors.

"Soft-man is denizen / of Rot City," Sanders begins the first poem, which presents "Soft-man" as a kind of everyman citizen "goosed in the dread Hustle," lost in the antihumanism of New York's working world and consumer culture. Sanders depicts Soft-man as losing his spirit inside the "crotch-lake," which is the "Rot City" of New York and, by extension, American life. The following poem, "Soft-man 2," delivers an incantation in praise of purer values: "may the paste of ourselves be cast aside . . . & may we descend in the petals to th' Peace Eye."

For Sanders, the "Peace Eye" represents the presiding spiritual authority, "dimensionless in the time drama" of human violence, war, repression, and censorship. Throughout the "Soft-man Poems" the Peace Eye stands as an idealized symbol of the values Sanders promoted in *Fuck You* and in earlier works like *Poem from Jail* (City Lights, 1963). In the "Soft-man Poems" Sanders depicts the struggle of the "real bomb children" against the "Control Team" masterminding "Blob Culture," with its "Hustlers" and "Blood Munchers," who will ultimately face defeat by the forces of "Goof City," presented as both an ideal place and the actual community of the Lower East Side, where Sanders opened his PEACE EYE BOOKSTORE.

The satiric "Toe Queen Poems" present Tillie the "Toe Queen," a kind of prostitute for toe fetishists, such as the "export banker" who "liked hang-nail toe dirt / in his mouth." Tillie hustles a series of perverse customers while trying to evade arrest. In the section's foreword, purportedly by one "Consuela," Sanders echoes the theme of *Fuck You* by urging "dope freaks, poets, space cadets, submarine boarders, Toe Queens, cock scarfs, & lower east side peace creeps" to "Keep Freaking! Munch away! Total Assault on the Culture!"

Later in the book, Sanders relates similar adventures in "The Gobble Gang Poems," which recount the exploits of a "young Consuela," a "chief turkey / in a Gobble Gang / in the arcade / at times square." In this series of poems Conseula encounters investment bankers and other high-powered notables while police raids interrupt business. Sanders includes a section of mock rabble-rousing exclamations: "PLEASURE-GIVERS / OF THE WORLD / AID SOFT MAN! ARTISTS, BULL DIKES, CONSUELA! GOBBLE GOBBLE IS CALL TO RESISTANCE!" Shortly afterward the tone turns darker, when a client drugs Consuela with cocaine and causes her death. A concluding prayer calls for nonviolence and for "love . . . / in the domain / of the creepers."

In both "The Toe Queen Poems" and "The Gobble Gang Poems" Sanders revels in the innocence of sex and in the corruption of the sex industry. He describes both Tillie and Consuela as tough women struggling in a society dominated by men obsessed with power. By linking them both to artists and "Soft-man," as in "The Gobble Gang Poems," Sanders unites the Lower East Side community of artists and writers with other disenfranchised members of the New York underground—in this case, hustlers who expose and exploit the weaknesses of powerful Wall Street types.

In addition to poems linked by a narrative thread, the first two sections of *Peace Eye* include individual poems designed to amuse and outrage, such as "The Fugs," "Hymn to the Vagina of Mercy," "For Marilyn Monroe," "Sheep-Fuck Poem," and "Blow Job Poem." In "The Fugs," named after his own band, Sanders declares, "The Rolling Stones are as / important as the Magna Carta," a leveling of low and high culture that critics have come to regard as typical of postmodernism. More specifically, Sanders's affiliation with the New York School is evident in his mixing of levels and abrupt shifts of tone.

In the final section, "Cemetery Hill," Sanders enters fully into the spirit of the "Peace Eye." The section consists of three poems from 1964— "Cemetery Hill," "Arise Garland Flame," and "The Pilgrimage"—each in its own way a peaceful elegy that reflects on Sanders's visits to his mother's grave.

Bibliography

Sanders, Ed. *Peace Eye.* Buffalo, N.Y.: Frontier Press, 1965.

Younkins, Jerry. Review of *Peace Eye. Work* [Artists Workshop, Detroit, MI] 2 (Fall 1965): 98–101.

Peace Eye Bookstore (1965–1969)

In late 1964 ED SANDERS rented a former butcher shop on East 10th Street and transformed it into the Peace Eye Bookstore, an important community center for poets, writers, artists, and alternative press on the Lower East Side in DOWNTOWN MANHATTAN. To acknowledge the neighborhood's roots, Sanders left the "Strictly Kosher" sign on the front window, while adding his own "Peace Eye" symbol, representing the Egyptian gods Horus and Ra.

Next door to Peace Eye lived Tuli Kupferberg (1923–), whom Sanders published in FUCK YOU: A MAGAZINE OF THE ARTS and who became Sanders's principal collaborator in the folk-rock group The FUGS. At the grand opening of Peace Eye in February 1965, The Fugs played their first concert, attended by WILLIAM S. BURROUGHS and featuring cloth wall banners by ANDY WARHOL (Wolf 55–57). Neighborhood kids hassled those attending the opening by throwing firecrackers, until ALLEN GINSBERG went outside and pacified the kids with his chanting (Morgan 132).

In addition to distributing a variety of alternative press publications through the bookstore,

Sanders turned it into his publishing headquarters for pamphlets issued under the Fuck You imprint. The most famous of these were unauthorized editions of W. H. AUDEN's obscene poem *The Platonic Blow* (1965) and Ezra Pound's *Cantos CX–CXVI* (1967). Not all of the literary merchandise offered through the store was textual. For instance, Sanders marketed a collection of pubic hairs contributed by famous writers, including Ginsberg, FRANK O'HARA, and Italian poet Giuseppe Ungaretti (1888–1970), whose donation Sanders solicited at a party given by O'Hara in Ungaretti's honor (Gooch 419–420).

In January 1966 the New York police raided the bookstore and arrested Sanders on obscenity charges, of which he was finally acquitted in summer 1967. Meanwhile, he was spending less time at the store, which was taken over as a crashpad by some of the young hippies who were flocking to the East Village during this period (Sukenick 182–183). In early 1968 Sanders reopened Peace Eye on Avenue A, in the former offices of the *East Village Other* newspaper. This new site frequently hosted art shows, including "one of the first ever underground comix exhibitions" (Sanders n.p.) in November 1968, featuring Art Spiegelman (1948–), R. Crumb (1943–), and Spain Rodriguez (1940–), the *Trashman* artist who designed the new store sign ("Peace Eye Books"). Sanders soon gave up the bookstore as he became absorbed in researching the Charles Manson murders for the *Los Angeles Free Press.*

Bibliography

"Frank O'Hara and Ed Sanders." *USA: Poetry.* WNET/ Channel Thirteen TV, 1966. [The Sanders segment is filmed at the Peace Eye bookstore.]

Gooch, Brad. *City Poet: The Life and Times of Frank O'Hara.* New York: Knopf, 1993.

Morgan, Bill. *The Beat Generation in New York: A Walking Tour of Jack Kerouac's City.* San Francisco: City Lights, 1997.

"Peace Eye Books." The Fugs Web site. Available online. URL: http://www.thefugs.com/fugspeace_eye.html. Accessed December 19, 2008.

Sanders, Ed. "Free Thoughts on Angels, Yowells & Electric Stencil Cutting: A Short Conversation with Ed Sanders 9/07/2004." Detroit Artists Workshop Web site. Available online. URL:

http://www.detroitartistsworkshop.org/Literature/
EdSandersInterview/EdSandersInterview.htm
#PeaceEye. Accessed December 19, 2008.

Sukenick, Ronald. *Down and In: Life in the Underground.*
New York: Beech Tree/Morrow, 1987.

Wolf, Reva. *Andy Warhol, Poetry, and Gossip in the 1960s.*
Chicago: University of Chicago Press, 1997.

Penniless Politics Douglas Oliver (1991)

Written following the Tompkins Square Park
riots in 1988 and originally published in London
by Hoarse Commerce books in 1991, *Penniless
Politics* was reproduced in *The* SCARLET CABINET
(1992) before being reprinted and distributed by
Bloodaxe Books in 1994. *Penniless Politics*, subtitled
A Satirical Poem, presented an indictment of the
supply-side economics and impoverished national
POLITICS at the end of the Ronald Reagan–George
H. W. Bush era.

In *The Infant and the Pearl* (Silver Hounds,
1985) DOUGLAS OLIVER had already written an
extended political polemic in poetic FORM. An
indictment of (Margaret) Thatcherite politics in
Great Britain using the form of the 14th century alliterative poem *Pearl*, it was well received,
although it still only reached a small audience.
Now living near Tompkins Square Park on NEW
YORK CITY's Lower East Side and seeing the disparity in worldview between the tent dwellers of the
park and the gentrifying renters in the apartments
surrounding it, Oliver was again roused by the
apparent injustice.

It is a lively, uncynical political poem whose
formal conception is reminiscent of his earlier *The
Infant and the Pearl* but far less bitter. Its opening line—"All politics the same crux: to define
humankind richly"—starts the hope that politics,
as poetry, can move toward embracing diversity.
It follows the trials of a new political party called
Spirit that comes to power in a strange and powerful vision, which then dissipates, having changed
some things.

The poem centers on and is often narrated by
the eponym Will Penniless. He is quite like Oliver
himself, an expatriate Anglo-Saxon in the midst
of a multitude of varied colors and creeds in the
melting pot of America. Oliver felt worried that

his tone would likewise be seen as patronizing, but
when he performed sections at poetry slams at the
NUYORICAN POETS CAFÉ the reception was largely
favorable, even winning one night's competition.
The poem is conducted in OTTAVA RIMA but with
the lines "klutzed" to get a "squawking New York
effect" as Oliver explained it (essay 258).

Penniless Politics was likened by Howard Brenton
in the *Guardian* to T. S. Eliot's *The Waste Land* for
its indictment of the zeitgeist and its formal innovation.

Bibliography

Brenton, Howard. "Poetic Passport to a New Era."
Guardian, 7 April 1992, 3.

Notley, Alice. "Douglas Oliver's New York Poem" (1999).
In *Coming After: Essays on Poetry*. Ann Arbor:
University of Michigan Press, 2005, 108–116.

Oliver, Douglas. Essay in *Contemporary Authors
Autobiography Series* 27. Edited by Joyce Nakamura.
Detroit: Gale, 1997, 241–261.

———. *The Infant and the Pearl*. London: Silver Hounds,
1985.

See, Carolyn. "Attempting to Cope with the Impossible."
Los Angeles Times, 23 September 1991, E2.

performance art

The various forms of action art that became
identified as "performance art" during the 1970s
grew out of the "HAPPENINGS" of the early 1960s.
However, while visual artists created the first happenings, musicians provided another important
stimulus to performance art at both the "high"
and "low" ends of aesthetic frequency. "High" art
influences, especially that of JOHN CAGE, informed
the "events" conceived by members of the Fluxus
group, including Nam June Paik (1932–2006), Yoko
Ono (1933–), and LaMonte Young (1935–).
Meanwhile, the first stirrings of PUNK ROCK MUSIC
drew on rock and roll performance. The involvement of poets in both movements (for instance,
JACKSON MAC LOW in Fluxus and ED SANDERS in
protopunk) led to the development of a subgenre of
performance art known as performance poetry, or
"perf-po," as Sanders calls it (Waldman 138).

In the context of performance art, the notorious "dead pan" reading style of first-generation

NEW YORK SCHOOL poets can be recognized as the performance that it is. Parallel to the development of MINIMALISM at the same time, many of the first performance art events had a minimalist or reductive quality. For instance, Vito Acconci (1940–) simply stared at each member of the audience for 15 seconds in *Performance Test* (1969), and in *Breathing Space* (1970) Acconci and a partner merely breathed into microphones (Kostelanetz 145–146). Acconci has New York School roots as a poet and as coeditor, with BERNADATTE MAYER, of the magazine 0 TO 9, but his handling of text as well as performance looks ahead to the divergence from the New York School by LANGUAGE poets. Charles Bernstein (1950–), for instance, has emphasized both "anti-expressivist" and antitheatrical qualities in poetry readings (Bernstein 10–11), whereas ANNE WALDMAN, through her long association with the POETRY PROJECT AT ST. MARK'S CHURCH IN-THE-BOWERY, has helped identify that New York School headquarters with a highly theatrical performance style.

Waldman's *Fast Speaking Woman* (City Lights, 1975, 1996) provides an index of the multiple intersections between New York School poetry and performance art, past, present, and future. Essays added to the later edition trace influences ranging from ethnographic recordings of chants by Maria Sabina (1896–1985), a shaman of the Mazatec people in Mexico (37); through the live performance by CHARLES OLSON that Waldman witnessed at the BERKELEY POETRY CONFERENCE in 1965 (145); to personal contact with BEAT writers (especially WILLIAM S. BURROUGHS [152]). The cover of *Fast Speaking Woman* shows Waldman made up for performance in *The Palm Casino Revue* (1974), a cabaret event in which poet KENWARD ELMSLIE also participated. Staged at the Bowery Lane Theater across the street from CBGB's, the review carried on the camp excess of ANDY WARHOL's Factory (with "superstars" Jackie Curtis [1947–85] and Candy Darling [ca. 1946–74]), launched various punk performers (including Tomata du Plenty [1948–2000], soon to be at the center of Los Angeles punk with The Screamers), and anticipated the ascendancy of cabaret as a principal mode for performance art in the East Village during the 1980s.

The pages of *Fast Speaking Woman* can do no more than provide the script for a performance in which the poet's voice is fully embodied and poet and audience are incorporated together as a collective entity. As Waldman explains, "I am interested in extending the written word off the page into a ritual vocalization and event, so that 'I' is no longer a personal 'I'" (128). The intended effect is represented more completely in recordings of Waldman performing texts from *Fast Speaking Woman,* assembled by JOHN GIORNO, along with recordings of his own work, in one of the series of albums he issued though Giorno Poetry Systems (1977). An outgrowth of Giorno's Dial-a-Poet project, this series not only brings poetry off the page but places poets among performance artists such as Robert Wilson (1941–), Meredith Monk (1942–), Laurie Anderson (1947–), and Karen Finley (1956–). Waldman has acknowledged Finley's "body art" as an extreme instance of the embodiment Waldman seeks in her own performance (142), yet, like Anderson, the body Waldman performs is more the result of poetic projection than of physical subjection. Technological projection—voice synthesizers, computerized imagery, etc., for which Anderson is well known—has not played an especially important role in New York School performance. However, Anderson collaborated with poets DAVID SHAPIRO and STEPHEN PAUL MILLER in a cybernetically enhanced production of their antinuclear play *Harrisburg Mon Amour,* performed by TAYLOR MEAD at The Kitchen, one of the leading performance spaces in NEW YORK CITY at the time (1980). At around the same time the Poetry Project planted the seeds for a low-tech performance format that later blossomed as the poetry slam.

Bibliography

Battcock, Gregory, and Robert Nickas, eds. *The Art of Performance: A Critical Anthology.* New York: Dutton, 1984.

Bernstein, Charles. Introduction to *Close Listening: Poetry and the Performed Word.* New York: Oxford University Press, 1998, 3–26.

Giorno, John, and Anne Waldman. *A Kulchur Selection.* Sound recording, GPS 010–011. New York: Giorno Poetry Systems/Kulchur Foundation, 1977. Available online. URL: http://www.ubu.com/sound/giorno_waldman.html. Accessed December 18, 2008.

Kirby, Michael, ed. "East Village Performance" special issue. *The Drama Review* 29, no. 1 (Spring 1985).

Kostelanetz, Richard. "The New Poetries" (1973). In *The Old Poetries and the New*. Ann Arbor: University of Michigan Press, 1981, 121–149.

Rothenberg, Jerome. "How We Came into Performance: A Personal Accounting." (2005). UbuWeb Papers. Available online. URL: http://www.ubu.com/papers/rothenberg_performance.pdf. Downloaded December 18, 2008.

Schimmel, Paul. *Out of Actions: Between Performance and the Object, 1949–1979*. Exhibit catalog. Los Angeles: Museum of Contemporary Art; New York: Thames & Hudson, 1998.

Waldman, Anne. *Fast Speaking Woman*. New expanded ed. San Francisco: City Lights, 1996.

Perreault, John (1937–   )

Born in NEW YORK CITY, John Perreault (pronounced purr-O) is an emblematic figure when it comes to the sensibilities of the NEW YORK SCHOOL; he is, as Richard Kostelanetz would call it, a "polyartist," someone more interested in making art than in classifying his work into any particular GENRE. Perreault is an art critic, curator, poet, FICTION writer, and visual artist, and his fusion of different media is indicative of the way the arts often commingled in the New York School.

From 1966 to 1974 Perreault was the art critic for the *Village Voice*, and then from 1975 to 1983 he was the senior art critic and art editor for the *Soho News*. His writings on art have appeared in many of the leading art journals and anthologies, including *Art in America* and *Artforum*. From 1978 to 1981 he was the president of the American section of the International Association of Art Critics, and he won the Penny McCall Foundation Award for Art Criticism in 2002. He currently is on the editorial advisory board of *Sculpture* magazine and is a trustee of the Tiffany Foundation and a regular contributor to *N.Y. Arts Magazine* and *American Ceramics*. Perreault published two books of poetry in the 1960s, *Camouflage* (Lines Press, 1966) and *Luck* (Kulchur Press, 1969). He has also published a number of monographs on contemporary artists, including *On the Work of Sylvia Sleigh* (A.I.R. Gallery, 1978), *Philip Pearlstein: Drawings and Watercolors* (Hacker Art Books, 1988), and *Diane Burko, 1985–1987* (Locks Gallery, 1990).

Perreault considers KENNETH KOCH, JOHN ASHBERY, and JOSEPH CERAVOLO influential in his development: Koch because Perreault attended his New School writing workshop, Ashbery because of his poems and because he published Perreault in ART AND LITERATURE and LOCUS SOLUS, and Ceravolo because he was a good friend. His interest in and prolific writing on art makes him most comparable to FRANK O'HARA in the New York School, but his artistic production as a painter and installation artist separates him from O'Hara. As critic Robert Morgan has written, "John Perreault has always struggled to separate the things he likes to do from the things he does best. In this way, he maintains a discrete repertory of objects, words, and events." In his typical digressive and unpredictable way Perreault himself fabricated an interview in 1996 with Marcel Duchamp (1887–1968) for *Review* magazine. From Duchamp he elicits a definition of art that can stand as Perreault's:

> You once said that art had a smell that only lasted thirty years. And in the interview I published in the *East Village Other* in 1965, I quoted you as saying that art left a scent behind, even when it was removed to another room, another state, another country.

Bibliography

Morgan, Robert. "John Perreault: Pataphysician." *NY Arts Magazine* 8, no. 5 (May 2003): Available online. URL: http://www.nyartsmagazine.com/index.php?option=com_content&task=view&_id=1299&Itemid=687. Accessed December 19, 2008.

Perreault, John. "Dada Perfume: A Duchamp Interview." *Review* (December 1996). Available online. URL: http://plexus.org/review/perreault/dada.html. Accessed August 15, 2008.

"Personism" Frank O'Hara (1959)

To the extent that the NEW YORK SCHOOL of poets has a manifesto, it is FRANK O'HARA's essay "Personism," subtitled "A Manifesto," but often referred to as a "mock-manifesto" (Gooch 338) because it makes fun of "lofty ideas" and insists that "everything is in the poems." The chief virtue of the poems, as reflected in the essay, is spontaneity. Like the action painter, the poet should have no preconceived plan for a particular poem or general theory of poetry, such as manifestos traditionally proclaim, before engaging in the act of writing. "You just go on your nerve," O'Hara declares. Extending the theatrical metaphor employed in HAROLD ROSENBERG's essay on "ACTION PAINTING," O'Hara makes it clear that action poetry is a performance intended for an audience. He grounds rhetorical effect in sexual desire: "As for measure and other technical apparatus, that's just common sense: if you're going to buy a pair of pants you want them to be tight enough so everyone will want to go to bed with you."

Like many of O'Hara's poems, "Personism" arises from a particular occasion. DONALD M. ALLEN had requested a statement for The NEW AMERICAN POETRY, 1945–1960 anthology, and O'Hara's procrastination forced him into the position of sitting down to write something at the last minute on a September evening in 1959, while Allen was on his way to pick up the promised piece. In the course of writing, a recent poem came to mind: "Personal Poem," about having lunch with LeRoi Jones (AMIRI BARAKA) while such an ordinary occasion seemed charged with the energy of O'Hara's love for the dancer Vincent Warren (Lehman 184–193). The trick of Personism, as O'Hara explains it, is to generalize from such a specific emotional charge, to move from wanting to go to bed with someone to writing a poem that makes everyone want to go to bed with you. O'Hara describes this process of generalization as a FORM of abstraction, with a nod to ALLEN GINSBERG's recent essay on "Abstraction in Poetry" in the painters' journal It Is.

Allen rejected "Personism" for The New American Poetry because he did not think it adequately accounted for O'Hara's odes (Gooch 339), which featured prominently in the selection Allen had chosen for his anthology. O'Hara wrote another, rather perfunctory statement for Allen and gave "Personism" to Jones for publication in YŪGEN (number 7, 1961). It was subsequently reprinted in the O'Hara issue of Audit/Poetry (volume 4, number

1, 1964) but did not become widely available until it was quoted in full in the preface to RON PADGETT and DAVID SHAPIRO's An ANTHOLOGY OF NEW YORK POETS (1970) and reprinted in The Collected Poems of Frank O'Hara (1970) and The Poetics of the New American Poetry (1973). An annotated version, identifying O'Hara's many allusions, is available in Jahan Ramazani's updated edition of The Norton Anthology of Modern and Contemporary Poetry (2003), volume 2.

Bibliography

Encke, Jeff. "Why I Am Not a Manifestor: Postwar Avant-Gardism and the Manifestos of Frank O'Hara" (2003). Octopus Magazine 3. Available online. URL: http://www.octopusmagazine.com/issue03/encke_ohara.html. Accessed December 19, 2008.

Gooch, Brad. City Poet: The Life and Times of Frank O'Hara. New York: Knopf, 1993.

Lehman, David. The Last Avant-Garde: The Making of the New York School of Poets. New York: Doubleday, 1998.

O'Hara, Frank. "Personism: A Manifesto." In The Collected Poems of Frank O'Hara. Edited by Donald Allen. Berkeley: University of California Press, 498–499.

Silverberg, Mark. "Ashbery, O'Hara, and the Neo-Avant-Garde Manifesto." Arizona Quarterly 59, no. 1 (Spring 2003): 137–165.

Pettet, Simon (1953–)

Born in Kent, England, Simon Pettet moved to NEW YORK CITY's Lower East Side in 1978, where he continues to live and write. In an interview Pettet described poetry as a "form of magic" because the poetic reaches across time and space to connect one human to another in a vibrant, cosmic instant. His poems are often understated and unassuming in their efforts to distill the complexity of an encounter into a compact, lyric instant. In this way Pettet embraces significant and recurring motifs of NEW YORK SCHOOL poetry: His poems are personal, direct, composed with an air of inspired spontaneity, and built of familiar diction, with an often lyric "I" addressing a recognizable "you." The poem "Sonne" is illustrative: "You just need to be alone but you don't / Say so everybody thinks you're sick / In need of something strong well / These things get around." These four lines, excerpted from the middle of a 10-line poem, develop a tension between leaving and staying. The line breaks divide familiar phrases, "You don't / say" and "Well / these things get around," which syncopate the poem's rhythm. Understated poems are not often well served by grandiose interpretations, but it seems appropriate here to observe that life itself is a sequence of moments before parting.

Pettet cites influences that range from the Greek lyric poet Sappho to the American PAUL BLACKBURN, both as a poet himself and as a translator of the French troubadours. Even this range fails to capture the scope of Pettet's reading, as bookshelves swell the walls of his apartment, with volumes flowing casually onto the floors and tabletops.

In addition to *An Enigma and Other Lyrics* and *21 Love*, small pamphlets published in London, Pettet has published *Lyrical Poetry* (Archipelago Press, 1992), *Selected Poems* (Talisman House, 1995), and, most recently, *Some Winnowed Fragments* (Talisman House, 2005). Pettet's contributions to New York School scholarship include *The Selected Art Writings of James Schuyler* (Black Sparrow Press, 1998), which provides a much-needed overview of JAMES SCHUYLER's art criticism during and after the zenith of ABSTRACT EXPRESSIONISM; and two COLLABORATIONs with photographer and filmmaker RUDOLPH BURCKHARDT: *Conversations with Rudy Burckhardt About Everything* (Vehicle Editions, 1987) and *Talking Pictures* (Zoland Books, 1994). Recently he has worked with the artist Duncan Hannah, who individually colored the drawings in each copy of *Abundant Treasures* (Granary Books, 2001). In this artists' book Pettet's poems and Hannah's watercolors carry forward the New York School tradition of collapsing the boundary between visual and literary art. His presence on the Internet is also evolving. The February 2004 issue of the zine *Jacket* features his poetry, an appreciation by ROBERT CREELEY, and an interview with ANSELM BERRIGAN.

Bibliography

Pettet, Simon. Personal interview for *Encyclopedia of the New York School Poets*, 28 February 2004.

————. "Summer." *Selected Poems*. Jersey City, N.J.: Talisman House, 1995, 12.

Simon Pettet feature. *Jacket* 25 (February 2004). Available online. URL: http://jacketmagazine.com/25/index.shtml. Accessed December 19, 2008.

photography　*See* ART, VISUAL.

***Plain Grief*　Maxine Chernoff** (1991)

Plain Grief, by MAXINE CHERNOFF, is the story of Sarah Holm, a wife and mother whose dutifully maintained household teeters on the verge of collapse. The book opens on Thanksgiving Day at Sarah's house in CHICAGO, ILLINOIS, where the reader learns that both she and her husband are having extramarital affairs. Prompted by the impending divorce of her parents, 12-year-old Carrie has run away with her visiting cousin, Deenie, an anorexic and sexually precocious 14-year-old. As Sarah and her Native American lover, Jeremy Bone Shoulder, search for the girls, the text alternates between the runaway adolescents and their adult pursuers. Into this mixture Chernoff adds brief interludes that center on Sarah's husband, Larry, her sister, Mae, and her mother, Ivy.

The six chapters depict consecutive days following Carrie and Deenie's escape. Instead of provoking dramatic suspense, however (there is never serious reason to doubt the children's safety), the story thrives on a kind of voyeuristic curiosity about how the characters will settle their grievances once they are (inevitably) reunited.

The author makes frequent use of flashback in order to suggest how her characters' pasts have shaped their present dilemmas. These sequences deal with everything from Sarah's relationship with her deceased father to her introduction to Jeremy. The latter meeting occurs during one of several scenes set in a group therapy workshop for victims of grief. These sessions strike interesting parallels with the psychiatric ward in JAMES SCHUYLER's *WHAT'S FOR DINNER?* Both books emphasize the disparity between the topics deemed suitable during therapy versus those discussed at home.

Also like Schuyler's novel, *Plain Grief* retains a sense of whimsy in the face of its somber subjects. (At one point Sarah admits that radishes are one of the objects she associates with the grief in her life.) Moreover, Chernoff seems to share Schuyler's fascination with everyday reality, and, notwithstanding her ironic gestures at romantic intrigue, her book consists of rather commonplace feelings and events (hence the title).

Released in 1991 from Summit Books, *Plain Grief* garnered praise for the independence of its heroine (Sarah) and for its vibrant depiction of the two young cousins. Still, more than one reviewer saw the abundant flashback sequences as a drag on the action.

Bibliography

Chernoff, Maxine. *Plain Grief.* New York: Summit Books, 1991.

Eckoff, Sally S. Review of *Plain Grief. Village Voice Literary Supplement*, November 1991, 6.

Fialkoff, Francine. Review of *Plain Grief. Library Journal* (July 1991): 131.

Hoffman, Roy. "Coming Apart." *New York Times Book Review*, 22 September 1991, 19.

Joyce, Alice. Review of *Plain Grief. Booklist* (August 1991): 2,097.

See, Carolyn. "Attempting to Cope with the Impossible," *Los Angeles Times*, 23 September 1991, p. E2.

Steinberg, Sybil. Review of *Plain Grief. Publishers Weekly* (5 July 1991): 56.

Wolitzer, Hilma. "When Mourning Comes." *Chicago Tribune*, 29 September 1991, p. 146.

"Poem (Khrushchev Is Coming on the Right Day!)" Frank O'Hara (1960)

FRANK O'HARA's 1959 "Poem (Khrushchev Is Coming on the Right Day!)" first appeared in 1960 in DONALD M. ALLEN's compilation of contemporary poetry, *The NEW AMERICAN POETRY, 1945–1960*. The poem would also be featured in various collections, including the Lawrence Ferlinghetti and Nancy Peters pocket edition of *Lunch Poems* (1964) and a hardbound, illustrated selection of O'Hara poetry, *In Memory of My Feelings* (1967), compiled as a posthumous tribute by associates and admirers at the Museum of Modern Art.

One reason for the enduring popularity of this particular poem is that it is representative of O'Hara's thematic and stylistic devices at their most effortless and topical. It is a lunch-hour poem, recording the names and faces that drift through the poet's thoughts as he makes his daily rounds. It is also a thoroughly NEW YORK CITY piece, featuring landmarks such as Pennsylvania Station, daily events, and the very newspaper headlines that occasion his own ruminations: Soviet premier Khrushchev's arrival in the United States at the height of cold war tensions. Another feature notable in O'Hara's lyric poetry and clearly present in this poem is his penchant for cataloging ready material, for instance, things he has done during the day, sometimes labeled as "I do this, I do that" verse. In this poem he lists the full names of "unknown figures" that float through his mind in bed, names removed from actions, undesignated in the texture of his own experience.

In the foreground, the poet blithely references his coterie of friends, among them the dancer Vincent Warren, whom O'Hara had met earlier that same year. "Blonde haired" Piedie Gimbel is remembered, as is the ABSTRACT EXPRESSIONIST painter Hans Hofmann. O'Hara goes on to casually celebrate GRACE HARTIGAN, who painted his portrait and collaborated with him in *Oranges*, his first text and painting series in 1953, though in this poem he plugs her new work, *Sweden*.

The comings and goings of his own busy circle are at once presented alongside the names of international poets, playwrights, and personages. Warren is quoted as saying that Eugene Ionesco is greater than Samuel Beckett, "that's what I think," his assessment easily holding the floor on the topic. The poem goes on to contrast the dark life of François Villon, whom O'Hara reads over coffee, with the seemingly eternal, blinding light of New York City. Nikita Khrushchev, too, is a figure among others in the "tossing, hurrying on up" city. He is mentioned three times throughout the poem, once in the beginning, middle, and end. But consistently his political carriage and encumbrances are scattered by the autumn wind and the directness of September light. Khrushchev, we discover, has chosen the right day to come merely because the day in itself is an accommodation.

Bibliography

O'Hara, Frank. *In Memory of My Feelings: A Selection of Poems by Frank O'Hara.* Edited by Bill Berkson. New York: Museum of Modern Art, 1967.

———. *Lunch Poems.* Edited by Lawrence Ferlinghetti and Nancy J. Peters. San Francisco: City Lights, 1964.

Perloff, Marjorie. *Frank O'Hara: Poet Among Painters.* Austin: University of Texas, 1979.

Smith, Alexander, Jr. *Frank O'Hara: A Comprehensive Bibliography.* New York: Garland, 1979.

Vendler, Helen. "Frank O'Hara, the Virtue of the Alterable." In *Part of Nature, Part of Us: Modern American Poets.* Cambridge, Mass.: Harvard University Press, 1980, 179–194.

poem-painting

The distinguishing characteristic of the poem-painting as a work of art is that text and image are placed within a single visual field rather than side by side, as in an illustrated book, or above and below, as in the relation of picture and caption. The poem-painting provides ideal expression for the close relationship to visual art that inspired NEW YORK SCHOOL poetry at its origin. However, the poets drew additional inspiration from the specific practice of poem-painting in other times and places. For instance, when LARRY RIVERS referred to *Stones* (Universal Limited Art Editions, 1957–60), a series of lithographs produced in COLLABORATION with FRANK O'HARA, as a "Trans-Siberian, Paris, New York project" (Rivers 92), he had in mind the rich culture of collaboration between poets and painters that Paris fostered in the early 20th century and specifically *La Prose du Transsibérien* ("Prose of the Trans-Siberian [Railway]," 1913), by the poet Blaise Cendrars and the painter Sonia Delaunay. When BILL BERKSON claimed "the spirits of Lady Murasaki's imperious dilettantes" to be present in the *Poem-Paintings* by Norman Bluhm (1920–1999) and O'Hara (1960), he invoked the fusion of literature, painting, and calligraphy in the East Asian tradition that also gave birth to Lady Murasaki's novel *The Tale of Genji* (ca. 1020).

In several respects the poem-paintings of the New York School poets reflect the contemporary aesthetic of abstract expressionist painting (which extends to printmaking, as did the practice of poem-painting). Emphasis on the flat canvas or paper rather than the illusion of three-dimensional space encouraged analogy between the surface of painting and the surface of writing. The nonobjective images that appeared especially in early ABSTRACT EXPRESSIONISM were often read as FORMS of writing, pictographs or hieroglyphs (O'Hara, "Jackson Pollock" 24–25), and as these images grew increasingly abstract, they drew attention to the painter's gesture as an act of writing (O'Hara, "Jackson Pollock" 31). The visual trace of that action was so important aesthetically that GRACE HARTIGAN did not trust O'Hara to write the texts of his own poems into the series of paintings entitled *Oranges* (1952), the earliest poem-paintings in the New York School (Hartigan 160). Later Rivers realized that the writing O'Hara produced on the prints for *Stones* made him "almost as important as myself in the overall *visual* force of the print" (Rivers 94). As Rivers explained, "the size of his letters, the density of the color brought on by how hard or softly he pressed on the crayon, where it went on the stone (which many times was left up to him) were not things that remained separated from my scratches and smudges" (96). The fact that even the matter of placement could be decided by either the poet or the painter, without prior agreement, was owing to their mutual acceptance of abstract expressionist composition, in which pictorial incidents occurred "all-over," randomly and spontaneously, rather than gathering around a dominant center.

The more the creation of text became part of the process of creating a poem-painting, the less likely it became that the text could stand alone. O'Hara's *Collected Poems* includes all of the "Orange" poems (5–9) written before Hartigan had conceived her paintings, but only four of the 12 texts for *Stones* (290, 312, 315) and none of the texts from the *Poem-Paintings* with Bluhm. Although new separate poems rarely arose from the production of poem-paintings, the experience of producing them undoubtedly reinforced qualities that distinguish New York School poetry overall. The gossipy quality of the "occasional poem" is taken to an extreme in the poem-painting, conceived as "a conversation between friends," as Bluhm described his collaboration with O'Hara (Bluhm 11). Rivers described *New York, 1950–1960*, a poem-painting he produced with KENNETH KOCH (1960), as "devoted to mutually experienced parties, neighborhoods, resorts, houses, studios, people and restaurants" (98).

But the words in a poem-painting are not merely "about" such experiences; in association with painting, the words also take on a material quality, the sort of quality that critics of New York School poetry sometimes misleadingly label "abstract." "Rather than writing a long poem 'about' the vase" that Mary Abbott (1921–) drew for the poem-painting *Honey or Wine?* (1971), BARBARA GUEST wrote lines of a poem on strips of paper that were then physically attached to the drawing, simultaneously absorbing the drawing into the poem's syntax (Guest 9). A similar physical-syntactical relation exists between the place-name *Peoria*, as RON PADGETT wrote it in "bold, stuffed-sausage script" (Padgett 72), and JIM DINE's drawing of a pig that appears below it, in one of the plates of their collaboration *Oo La La* (Petersburg Press, 1970). Meaningless out of context, "Peoria" in the context of the print packs a wallop similar to the "little-smear-whack in the rear" that Dine applied to his pig.

Padgett and Dine, Berkson and JOE BRAINARD, TED BERRIGAN and GEORGE SCHNEEMAN are just a few of the teams that continued the tradition of the poem-painting beyond the "first generation." Awareness of the tradition has specially inflected the work of JOHN YAU, who sought out O'Hara's collaborator Bluhm to produce a series of "poem prints" (1987) and whose ongoing series of collaborations with Archie Rand (1950–) since 1987 were, in Rand's words, "loosely modeled on the O'Hara/whomever precedent" (Rand 73).

Bibliography

Berkson, Bill. "'It's raining / and I'm thinking . . .'" In *Poem-Paintings,* Frank O'Hara and Norman Bluhm. Exhibit catalog. New York: New York University Art Collection, 1967, n.p.

———. "Working with Joe [Brainard]." *Modern Painters* 14, no. 3 (Autumn 2001): 62–65.

Bluhm, Norman. "26 Things at Once." *Lingo* 7 (1997): 10–18.

Diggory, Terence. *Grace Hartigan and the Poets: Paintings and Prints.* Exhibit catalog. Saratoga Springs, N.Y.: Schick Art Gallery, Skidmore College, 1993.

Ferguson, Russell. *In Memory of My Feelings: Frank O'Hara and American Art.* Exhibit catalog. Los Angeles: Museum of Contemporary Art; Berkeley: University of California Press, 1999. [Includes color reproductions of the complete set of the O'Hara-Rivers *Stones* and of 11 of the O'Hara-Bluhm *Poem-Paintings*.]

Fischer, Aaron. *Ted Berrigan: An Annotated Checklist.* New York: Granary Books, 1998. [Includes reproductions of Berrigan-Schneeman collaborations.]

Guest, Barbara. "Mary Abbott." In *Dürer in the Window: Reflexions on Art.* New York: Roof Books, 2003, 8–9.

Hartigan, Grace. Interview by Cindy Nemser. In *Art Talk: Conversations with 12 Women Artists*, by Cindy Nemser, 148–172. New York: Scribner's, 1975.

Koch, Kenneth. *Collaborations with Artists.* Exhibit catalog. New York: Tibor de Nagy Gallery, 1994.

O'Hara, Frank. *The Collected Poems.* Rev. ed. Edited by Donald Allen. Berkeley: University of California Press, 1995.

———. "Jackson Pollock" (1959). In *Art Chronicles, 1954–1966.* Rev. ed. New York: Braziller, 1990, 12–39.

Padgett, Ron. Statement in Debra Bricker Balken, ed. "Interactions between Artists and Writers." *Art Journal* 52, no. 4 (Winter 1993): 72.

Perloff, Marjorie. "Poem-Paintings." *Frank O'Hara: Poet Among Painters.* 1977. Reprint, Chicago: University of Chicago Press, 1998, 96–112.

Rand, Archie. Statement in Debra Bricker Balken, ed. "Interactions between Artists and Writers." *Art Journal* 52, no. 4 (Winter 1993): 73–74.

Rivers, Larry. "Life Among the Stones." *Location* 1, no. 1 (Spring 1963): 90–98.

Yau, John, and Archie Rand. *100 More Jokes from the Book of the Dead.* St. Helena, Calif.: Meritage Press, 2001.

Yau, John, and Norman Bluhm. *Poem Prints.* Exhibit catalog. New York: Cone Editions, 1987.

Poetry in Motion **Ron Mann** (1982)

Ron Mann's documentary film *Poetry in Motion* is an invaluable record of performance styles after more than a decade of experimentation in NEW YORK CITY and elsewhere, but before the emergence of "spoken word" and "slam" performance as popular FORMs. In Toronto, Canada, where Mann (1958–) lives, he saw JOHN GIORNO and WILLIAM S. BURROUGHS perform at a rock club called the The Edge and learned about the Dial-a-Poem recordings from Giorno during a break. Mann conceived the idea of preparing an anthology of "post-Beat" poets, on the model of DONALD M. ALLEN's *The NEW AMERICAN POETRY, 1945–1960*, except on film rather than in print (Mann, e-mail n.p.). Through contacts made in part through Giorno, Mann proceeded to film more than 75 performances by nearly 40 poets. The advice of New York filmmaker Emile de Antonio (1919–89) proved crucial in the process of paring down this material to a manageable 90 minutes and providing continuity by interspersing performance segments with excerpts from an interview with Charles Bukowski (1920–94), as representative "outsider." Despite the role assigned to Bukowski, based in Los Angeles, and the inclusion of a good number of Canadian poets, representing Mann's home, New York is the film's principal source of the energy.

For sheer expenditure of energy nothing beats ALLEN GINSBERG singing "Capitol Air," backed up by a full rock band. KENWARD ELMSLIE ("Who'll Prop Me Up in the Rain") foregrounds verbal MUSIC by playing recorded instrumental accompaniment from a boombox that he holds in his lap as he sings. The chanting of ANNE WALDMAN ("Makeup on Empty Space") and Giorno ("We Got Here Yesterday/We're Here Today/And I Can't Wait To Leave Tomorrow") relies on the performer's voice as the only instrument, though a few brief clips are shown from another performance by Giorno that incorporates echo reverberation produced by the microphone and amplifier. The film also offers a quick glimpse of ED SANDERS's "Talking Tie," and in his main performance ("The Cutting Prow/For Henri Matisse") he plays his Pulse Lyre, a synthesizer activated by contact points that he wears on his fingers. The minimal gestures required to play this device complement the intimacy of the studio setting where Sanders performs, in contrast to Ginsberg's, Elmslie's, Waldman's, and Giorno's performances before a live audience. But an intimacy similar to Sanders's is achieved by JIM CARROLL ("Just Visiting") and TED BERRIGAN ("Whitman in Black"), each of whom gently leads the listener-viewer into the interior space of reading. The fact that Berrigan was to die only a year after this film was released makes his reading especially a moment to be treasured.

Mann went on to make a number of other documentaries after *Poetry in Motion*, which was only his second full-length film. In 1995 he issued *Poetry in Motion II* on CD-ROM, including much of the material edited out of the original version, hence the list of poets expands beyond the 24 originally featured. NEW YORK SCHOOL poets in the expanded version include TOM CLARK, BOB HOLMAN, ROSE LESNIAK, EILEEN MYLES, and ALICE NOTLEY.

Bibliography

Mann, Ron. E-mail to Terence Diggory, 3 August 2006.
——. *Poetry in Motion.* VHS. Sphinx Productions (Toronto) and Giorno Poetry Systems (New York). New York: Voyager, 1982.
——. *Poetry in Motion II.* CD-ROM. Santa Monica, Calif.: Voyager, 1995.

Poetry Project at St. Mark's Church in-the-Bowery (1966–)

The Poetry Project at St. Mark's Church in-the-Bowery is the institutional headquarters of NEW YORK SCHOOL poetry. A kind of anti-academy, the Poetry Project has been open to the full range of contemporary nonacademic poetry. ALLEN GINSBERG claimed, "St. Mark's has become my church, my religion place" (xxvi). But New York School lineage has provided the thread of continuity that has held the Project together over the years. At the outset the influence of the BLACK MOUNTAIN POETS was dominant. PAUL BLACKBURN moved poetry readings to St. Mark's Church early in 1966 after CAFÉ LE METRO proved inhospitable. JOEL OPPENHEIMER was appointed the first director of the Poetry Project that summer; his first assistants were Joel Sloman (1931–), a student of DENISE LEVERTOV's, and Sam Abrams (1935–), a friend of GILBERT SORRENTINO's. This administrative team quickly dissolved, however, and ANNE WALDMAN rose from her initial position as secretary, through a brief term as assistant director, and ultimately to the position of director, which she held for 10 years (1968–78). She was succeeded by RON PADGETT (1978–80), BERNADETTE MAYER (1980–84), EILEEN MYLES (1984–86), ED FRIEDMAN (1986–2003), ANSELM BERRIGAN (2003–07), and STACY SZYMASZEK (2007–).

With roots going back to Dutch settlement in Manhattan—the Bouwerie was the farming estate of Peter Stuyvesant, who is buried on the church grounds—St. Mark's (consecrated as an Episcopal church in 1799) has a progressive record of involvement in social and cultural affairs. The rector during the 1960s, Reverend Michael Allen (1927–), viewed the arts as allies in his mission to challenge an unjust establishment. In 1964 he hired Ralph Cook (1928–) to oversee ministry in the arts, and Cook promptly founded the experimental playwrights' workshop, Theater Genesis, based at the church. John Brockman (1941–) ran a film series there before he became manager of the Filmmakers' Cinematheque. Thus, it was natural for Blackburn to seek a home for poetry readings at St. Mark's. What formalized these activities as "projects" was Allen's agreement to participate in a grant from the federal Department of Health, Education and Welfare, administered through the New School and designed to control juvenile delinquency by channeling the wayward energies of Lower East Side youth into creative forms of expression. Luckily for the projects, whose artists regarded government officials as Vietnam War criminals, the federal grant lasted only two years. By the end of that period other sources of funding had come through, though the film project had already broken away to pursue an independent existence as the Millennium Film Workshop. In 1974 DANCE joined the St. Mark's consortium in a project called Danspace, cofounded by poet LARRY FAGIN and dancer Barbara Dilley (1938–). Theatre Genesis ceased operation in 1978, the year a major fire disrupted all activity at the church. An outpouring of support for the Poetry Project at that time generated new momentum that has helped carry it into the present day.

Programs sponsored by the Poetry Project include workshops, publications, weekly readings, special events, such as an annual New Year's Day marathon reading, and occasional symposia. TED BERRIGAN, Sloman, and Abrams led the poetry workshops in the first year of operation. Since that time the workshops have spun out a complex web of affiliations, for instance, the close association of TONY TOWLE, CHARLES NORTH, and PAUL VIOLI that began in Towle's workshop in 1970. A few years later Mayer's workshops attracted Charles Bernstein, Nick Piombino, Hannah Weiner, and others who formed the nucleus of the New York branch of LANGUAGE POETRY. An important document for that movement, a list of writing "Experiments," grew out of Mayer's workshop, as did the magazine *Unnatural Acts* (1972–73), edited by Mayer and workshop member Friedman—one of several workshop-based publications that have appeared over the years. The official magazine of the Poetry Project, *The WORLD*, began in 1967 under Sloman's editorship, soon taken over by Waldman. The *Poetry Project Newsletter* was launched by Padgett in 1973. The series of readings has produced many memorable moments, many of which are preserved in a large archive of recordings maintained at St. Mark's. The CD accompanying Daniel Kane's *All Poets Welcome* includes the interruption of KENNETH KOCH's reading of "To My Audience" by a mock shooting (1968), Waldman and Berrigan's joint performance of their collaborative poem MEMORIAL DAY (1971), and other readings by Levertov, Armand Schwerner, Clayton Eshelman, BILL BERKSON, DICK GALLUP, and LORENZO THOMAS.

Bibliography

Friedman, Ed. Statements on the Poetry Project and the *Poetry Project Newsletter*. In *A Secret Location on the Lower East Side: Adventures in Writing, 1960–1980*, edited by Steven Clay and Rodney Phillips, 184–185, 189. New York: New York Public Library/ Granary Books, 1998.

Ginsberg, Allen. Foreword to *Out of This World: An Anthology of the St. Mark's Poetry Project, 1966–1991*, edited by Anne Waldman, xxiv–xxx. New York: Crown, 1991.

Kane, Daniel. *All Poets Welcome: The Lower East Side Poetry Scene in the 1960s*. Berkeley: University of California Press, 2003.

Lyons, Kimberly. "The Itineraries of Anticipation (Women and the Poetry Project)." *Read Me* 1 (Fall 1999). Available online. URL: http://home.jps.net/~nada/lyons.htm. Accessed December 19, 2008.

Mayer, Bernadette. "Experiments." Poetry Project Web site. Available online. URL: http://www.poetryproject.com/features/mayer.html. Accessed December 19, 2008.

North, Charles. "New York Schools" (1988) and "Leaping and Creeping: Several Lectures" (1991). In *No Other Way: Selected Prose*. Brooklyn, N.Y.: Hanging Loose Press, 1998, 103–109, 120–132.

Poetry Project Web site. Available online. URL: http://www.poetryproject.com/.

Rifkin, Libbie. "My Little World Goes on St. Mark's Place: Anne Waldman, Bernadette Mayer and the Gender of an Avant-Garde Institution." *Jacket* 7 (April 1999). Available online. URL: http://jacketmagazine.com/07/rifkin07.html. Accessed December 19, 2008.

Waldman, Anne. Introduction to *Out of This World: An Anthology of the St. Mark's Poetry Project, 1966–1991*. New York: Crown, 1991, 1–6.

———. Statement on *The World*. In *A Secret Location on the Lower East Side: Adventures in Writing, 1960–1980*, edited by Steven Clay and Rodney Phillips, 186–188. New York: New York Public Library / Granary Books, 1998.

poetry slam   *See* SLAM POETRY.

Poets of the New York School, The (1969)

The first anthology devoted exclusively to "the Poets of the New York School" was issued under that title by JOHN BERNARD MYERS, the man who invented the label. Through his Tibor de Nagy Editions, Myers had previously published a book by each of the nine poets represented in the anthology. As director of the TIBOR DE NAGY GALLERY, he had actively promoted the poets' involvement in the visual arts, which is reflected in every aspect of the anthology, from the introduction to the design, including photographs of the poets by the fashion photographer Francesco Scuvullo and reproductions of work by artists associated with the poets (in the case of JAMES SCHUYLER, a portrait painted by FAIRFIELD PORTER takes the place of a photograph). The anthology was published by the Graduate School of Fine Arts at the University of Pennsylvania, founded in 1966 by Neil Welliver, another Tibor de Nagy artist whose work appears in the book.

Myers's intimate acquaintance with the poets allowed him to construct particularly meaningful pairings with painters: JOHN ASHBERY with Porter, JOSEPH CERAVOLO with Red Grooms, KENWARD ELMSLIE with JOE BRAINARD, BARBARA GUEST with Robert Goodnough, KENNETH KOCH with ALEX KATZ, FRANK LIMA with Neil Welliver, FRANK O'HARA with Norman Bluhm, Schuyler with JANE FREILICHER, and TONY TOWLE with Alan D'Arcangelo. In some cases the basis for the pairing is obvious. For instance, one of Elmslie's poems is entitled "For Joe Brainard." In other cases the association seems more playful. In pairing Lima with Welliver, known for his landscape painting, Myers may have been thinking along the lines of Helen Vendler in a review of the anthology: "The flora and fauna of 100th Street become, in the poetry of Frank Lima, another, competitive, nature" (16).

In Myers's introduction, the spirit of play becomes the characteristic that distinguishes the work of these poets from that of their predecessors, the surrealists, whose personal importance to Myers he discusses at some length. As a disciple of André Breton, Myers presents himself as a target of O'Hara's irreverence: "When I was sometimes pompous or overly serious about a particularly far-out painting or object he [O'Hara] had a wonderful way of pricking the balloon and letting out the gas" (20). But according to Myers, "O'Hara's passion for wanting others, everyone he knew, to share his capacity to 'see'" is the inheritance from the surrealists, and from visual art, that he transmitted "to the poets in this book, especially those now writing in the Sixties" (20). In presenting Ceravolo, Elmslie, Lima, and Towle, Myers made a gesture toward that emerging "second generation," though not as broadly as RON PADGETT and DAVID SHAPIRO did in *An* ANTHOLOGY OF NEW YORK POETS, which appeared the following year. Myers might have been expected to extend his list at least to BILL BERKSON, whom Myers had sponsored in earlier publications. However, a misunderstanding based on a rumor had led Myers to drop Berkson from the anthology, and though Myers later reversed his decision, Berkson by that point was not disposed to cooperate, though he squelched a boycott that other poets had been prepared to mount on his behalf (Schuyler 182).

Bibliography

Lask, Thomas. "Lines from Gotham," *New York Times*, 6 June 1970, p. 29.

Myers, John Bernard, ed. *The Poets of the New York School.* Philadelphia: Graduate School of Fine Arts, University of Pennsylvania, 1969.

Reeve, F. D. "Fresh Airs." *Poetry* 119, no. 1 (October 1971): 39–44.

Schuyler, James. *Just the Thing: Selected Letters, 1951–1991.* Edited by William Corbett. New York: Turtle Point Press, 2004.

Vendler, Helen. "27 poets, 363 poems—9 poets, 95 poems." *New York Times Book Review*, 15 November 1970, 16.

Poets' Theatre (1950–1968, 1986–)

FRANK O'HARA and JOHN ASHBERY were both directly involved in the Poets' Theatre in Cambridge, Massachusetts, from its inaugural production in February 1951. During their recent years at Harvard they had become friends with two of the prime movers in the venture, Lyon Phelps (1923–), a fellow student, and VIOLET R. (BUNNY) LANG, a BOSTON native. The initial program, staged in the basement of Christ Church Parish House, featured Richard Eberhart's *The Apparition;* Phelps's *3 Words in No Time;* Ashbery's *Everyman: A Masque,* with MUSIC composed by O'Hara; and O'Hara's TRY! TRY! A *Noh Play,* directed by Lang, designed by O'Hara's former roommate Edward Gorey (1925–2000), and with Lang and Ashbery playing two of the three characters. The play by Eberhart (1904–2005) was directed by Molly Howe (Mary Manning, 1905–99), the wife of a Harvard law professor and the mother of two daughters who were to become leading experimental poets: Susan (1937–) and Fanny Howe (1940–). As a former actress at Ireland's Abbey Theatre under W. B. Yeats, Molly Howe connected the Poets' Theatre to its principal model in the modernist tradition.

For O'Hara, Ashbery, and Lang, however, the cabaret style of W. H. AUDEN and Christopher Isherwood was as much a model as the ritualism of Yeats. The contrast between these modes caused something of a problem for the selection of plays as well as some conflict between the intention of the young performers and the expectations of the old guard. On opening night Thornton Wilder (1897–1975) scolded audience members who had laughed at O'Hara's *Try! Try!;* they would laugh again at O'Hara's *Change Your Bedding!* presented later the same year. In 1952 Cid Corman (1924–2004), who had become a local authority on the avant-garde through *Origin* magazine and a weekly radio show, stormed out of a production of his own play, *The Circle,* a tragedy staged by Lang as a farce. That same year she presented her own *Fire Exit,* subtitled *Vaudeville for Eurydice.* In 1953 Lang regretted the decision to produce *This Music Crept by Me upon the Waters* by Archibald MacLeish (1892–1982) because, she predicted, a flood of professors' plays would follow, from which "we will all die of boredom" (Lurie 15). Dylan Thomas helped alleviate boredom with the first public reading of *Under Milk Wood* at the Poets' Theatre in April 1953, though it took some time for the audience to catch on; "perhaps no one was expecting to be made to laugh," Thomas's biographer speculates (Ferris 289). Further challenge to those expectations came with productions of JAMES SCHUYLER's *Shopping and Waiting* (1953), Lang's *I Too Have Lived in Arcadia* ("a pastoral, in the present time," 1954), GREGORY CORSO's *In This Hung-Up Age* (1955), and Ashbery's *The Compromise* (1956).

Ashbery's play, spoofing a silent-era movie about the Canadian Mounties, included performances by Lang, Corso, and O'Hara, who was back in Cambridge for a residency at the Poets' Theatre sponsored by the Rockefeller Foundation. O'Hara's poem "To Hell with It" (1957) records his "memories of Bunny and Gregory and me in costume / bowing to each other and the audience, like jinxes" (275). By the time O'Hara wrote this poem, Lang had died from Hodgkin's disease. The Poets' Theatre continued until 1968, when the small THEATER on Palmer Street that had been its home for over a decade burned down. In 1986, under the leadership of Andreas Teuber of Brandeis University, the Poets' Theatre revived along with its ties to the NEW YORK SCHOOL; for instance, an adaptation of KENWARD ELMSLIE's *26 Bars* was performed at Boston's Institute of Contemporary Art in 1989.

Bibliography

Ashbery, John. *The Compromise.* In *Three Plays.* Calais, Vt.: Z Press, 1978, 31–119.

———. "Poet in the Theater." Interview by Roger Oliver. *Performing Arts Journal* 3, no. 3 (Winter 1979): 15–37.

Corso, Gregory. "In This Hung-Up Age: A One Act Farce Written 1954." *Encounter* 18, no. 1 (January 1962): 83–90.

Eberhart, Richard. *Collected Verse Plays.* Chapel Hill: University of North Carolina Press, 1962.

Ferris, Paul. *Dylan Thomas: A Biography.* New York: Dial Press, 1977.

Gooch, Brad. *City Poet: The Life and Times of Frank O'Hara.* New York: Knopf, 1993.

Lang, V. R. *Fire Exit* and *I Too Have Lived in Arcadia.* In *Poems and Plays.* New York: Random House, 1975, 149–297.

Lurie, Alison. "V. R. Lang: A Memoir." In *Poems and Plays,* by V. R. Lang, 1–71. New York: Random House, 1975.

MacLeish, Archibald. *This Music Crept by Me upon the Waters.* Cambridge, Mass.: Harvard University Press, 1953.

O'Hara, Frank. "The Hell with It." In *The Collected Poems.* Rev. ed. Edited by Donald Allen. Berkeley: University of California Press, 1995, 275.

———. *Try! Try!, Change Your Bedding!* and appendix. In *Amorous Nightmares of Delay: Selected Plays.* Baltimore, Md.: Johns Hopkins University Press, 1997, 17–30, 51–61, 218–225.

Sayre, Nora. "The Poets' Theatre: A Memoir of the Fifties." *Grand Street* 3, no. 3 (Spring 1984): 92–105.

Schuyler, James. *Shopping and Waiting.* In *The Home Book.* Calais, Vt.: Z Press, 1977, 86–88.

Teuber, Andreas. "The Poets' Theatre." Available online. URL: http://people.brandeis.edu/~teuber/pt.html. Accessed December 19, 2008.

Thomas, Dylan. *Under Milk Wood: A Play for Voices.* New York: New Directions, 1954.

politics

NEW YORK SCHOOL poets do not theorize about politics, but they enact the principle of "intimate community" set forth in PAUL GOODMAN's essay "Advance-Guard Writing, 1900–1950" (376), which "is really lucid about what's bothering us both besides sex," FRANK O'HARA reported enthusiastically to JANE FREILICHER (Gooch 187). For Goodman, "intimate community" is the equivalent of the Greek *polis,* the foundation of politics, and the antidote to the modern condition of estrangement that David Riesman, in 1950, tagged with the title *The Lonely Crowd: A Study of the Changing American Character* (see O'Hara, *Collected Poems* 267). The "advance-guard" writer, in Goodman's view, engages in politics by bringing estranged individuals into community, "putting his arms around them and drawing them together" (375). One paradigm for such writing is O'Hara's "Personal Poem" (1959), in which news of wide-ranging social import—the clubbing of black JAZZ musician Miles Davis by white policemen—reaches O'Hara in an intimate context, during lunch with LeRoi Jones (AMIRI BARAKA). It is easy to read the poem as dismissing the significance of the Davis incident, but a more accurate reading recognizes the poem's construction of a relationship between the clubbing and the lunch. The outline of such a relationship may be clearer in JOHN ASHBERY because he typically handles these matters more abstractly. For instance, in "Pyrography," commissioned by the U.S. government to commemorate the country's bicentennial in 1976, Ashbery envisions a structure in which,

> *not just the major events but the whole incredible*
> *Mass of everything happening simultaneously and*
>   *pairing off,*
> *Channeling itself into history, will unroll*
> *As carefully and as casually as a conversation in*
>   *the next room (Houseboat* 10).

The major events of history have loomed over the casual conversations of New York School poetry since it emerged in the aftermath of World War II (1939–45). O'Hara, KENNETH KOCH, and JAMES SCHUYLER saw military service during the war (Ashbery reached draft age just as the war ended). O'Hara's roommate Joe LeSueur reports: "Frank never in the nine and a half years I lived with him talked about what he did during the war" (xvi). O'Hara's play TRY! TRY! (1951), as LeSueur points out, stands as an exceptional instance of a depiction of the war in O'Hara's work. The politics of the play is posed in intimate terms, not as a question of the war itself but rather of reintegrating into community after the war (updated to the Korean War [1950–53], in the revised version presented in New York in 1953). As in O'Hara's later play The GENERAL RETURNS FROM ONE PLACE TO ANOTHER (1964), based loosely on General Douglas MacArthur's role in World War II and Korea, the problem of returning is reduced to an absurdity that is comic but not hopeful. Koch and Schuyler, meanwhile, waited until the end of their careers to express the extremity of World War II. The FORM of New Addresses (2000), poems addressed to personified abstractions in the antiquated manner of the 18th century, supplies the premise for Koch's "To World War II" and just enough absurdity to contain the horror of the final line: "You died of a bomb blast in Nagasaki, and there were parades" (Collected Poems 602). In "Let's All Hear It for Mildred Bailey" (1987), Schuyler relies on a parenthesis to contain "the silence" of boxcars bearing "Jews, gypsies, nameless / forever others" toward "The Final Solution," while Mildred Bailey sings in a nightclub "in war-haunted, death-smeared / NY" (398). Earlier, Schuyler had employed a similar "here-there" contrast to write about the Vietnam War in "May, 1972," which appeared in a special issue of Poetry magazine "Against the War" (September 1972).

During the 1960s the equation of politics and protest—"Against the War"—generated a view of New York School poetry as standing apart from politics. This view ignores the oppositional role that poetry plays by virtue of what it is rather than what it is about. BARBARA GUEST, in her cryptic "anti-war poem," "The Handbook of Surfing" (1967), celebrated "the artful dare" (50), creative imagination, in contrast to mere "protest" (49). Leaving "the Horrors of War" to his contemporaries, who seemed preoccupied with the subject, Koch enumerated "The Pleasures of Peace" (1968), just as O'Hara had converted the threats of the

cold war into the pleasure of feeling cold air on his face, in "POEM (KHRUSHCHEV IS COMING ON THE RIGHT DAY!)" (1959). The idea "that art is human willpower deploying every means at its disposal to break through to a truer state than the present one" is the political idea at the heart of Ashbery's memorial essay, "Frank O'Hara's Question" (83), which has ironically become exhibit A in the case for viewing New York School poetry as apolitical. Ashbery concedes that O'Hara's poetry "does not speak out against the war in Vietnam or in favor of civil rights" (81), but in saying that, Ashbery is claiming that O'Hara's poetry lacks a political "message" (81), not that it lacks politics. The lesson was not lost on TED BERRIGAN, who adapted a section of Ashbery's essay as a "found" poem of the same title, substituting the word message, which Ashbery applied to so-called committed poetry, for the word measure in a line that Ashbery quoted from O'Hara's "BIOTHERM" (1962). In its reworked version the line affirms the New York School poet's commitment to the poem as "a truer state than the present one," to be defended at all costs: "I am guarding it from mess and message" (Berrigan, Collected Poems 160).

While Ashbery was attacked by Louis Simpson for separating poetry and protest (Herd 93–95), second-generation poets like Berrigan faced pressure toward protest from the example of the BEATS and the poets of Black Power. Berrigan responded with an "Anti-War Poem" (1970; Collected Poems 223–224) modeled on O'Hara's list of likes and dislikes in "Personal Poem" (Berrigan does not like Engelbert Humperdinck but he "loves" the Incredible String Band). Under the title "Black Power" (1970; Collected Poems 210–211), Berrigan celebrated the pleasures of drinking coffee (presumably black). Other poets who were temperamentally more inclined toward Beat activism included ED SANDERS, who joined ALLEN GINSBERG in the demonstrations at the Democratic National Convention in CHICAGO, ILLINOIS, in 1968, and ANNE WALDMAN, whose work with Ginsberg at the NAROPA INSTITUTE naturally led to collaborative protest at the Rocky Flats nuclear weapons plant outside Denver, Colorado (Ginsberg, "Plutonian Ode" [1978]; Waldman, "Warring God Charnel Ground" [1994]). As an African

American, LORENZO THOMAS acknowledged the mythic appeal of Black Power—"They once built pyramids / With they power" ("Better Physics")—but as a navy veteran returning from the Vietnam War, he confronted the powerlessness of the black man in his own country with an irony that echoes O'Hara on the theme of return: "Why all de slaves am not singing / For the return of the Kid" (*Fit Music* 388). Poetry's complicity in suspect political power becomes the target of Thomas's irony in "Inauguration" (1979), a parody of the poem, "The Gift Outright," that Robert Frost read at the inauguration of President John F. Kennedy in 1961 (Nielsen 148–50). New York School satire of liberal as well as conservative politics dates back to Koch's play *The Election* (1960), in which BILL BERKSON played the role of Kennedy. Thomas's parody of an inaugural poem looks ahead to *On the Pumice of Morons,* a rewriting by LARRY FAGIN and CLARK COOLIDGE of the poem read by Maya Angelou, "On the Pulse of Morning," at the inauguration of President Bill Clinton in 1993. To produce their "Unaugural Poem," Coolidge and Fagin employed an OULIPO technique, replacing every noun in Angelou's poem with a noun that appeared seven words later in a dictionary. With an attitude typical of the New York School, Coolidge disavowed any "revolutionary" intent but noted that some readers took the experiment "way too seriously" (Coolidge n.p.; Perelman 103–104).

The readers whom Coolidge thus characterized were Language poets, the next movement to challenge the New York School's resistance to "committed" or "serious" poetry—a movement, in fact, that emerged during the 1970s out of the protest movement against the Vietnam War. EILEEN MYLES reports an exchange with Charles Bernstein, a leader of the Language group, that not only reveals differences with New York School poetry at the time (late 1970s) but also differences between Myles's generation and the first-generation New York School. On learning that Myles had attended the University of Massachusetts (UMass) BOSTON, Bernstein recalled that the radical students at his university, Harvard, had hoped to mobilize "the children of the working class" at UMass (Myles 53). It had not occurred to the Harvard students, Myles realized, that the UMass students had no time to

join demonstrations because they were working at part-time jobs to put themselves through school. This is a very different limitation on protest than the defense of art mounted by Ashbery and his fellow Harvard alumni in the first-generation New York School, and it points to the emergence of a new political issue, that of social class, which poets such as Berrigan and RON PADGETT brought to the second generation, not as an "issue" but as an integral part of their identity (Lenhart 98–111). By the time Myles came on the scene a whole set of identities—based on class, race, gender, sexual orientation—were becoming abstracted as issues in what eventually would be called "identity politics." New York School poets explored these identities in their work but kept their distance from the politics insofar as that term implied subscribing to a collective "movement." Noting the prominent role played by women in the magazine *Caveman* when MAUREEN OWEN was in charge (ca. 1979), ALICE NOTLEY adds, "it was too anarchic to be called feminist" (Russo 260). During her write-in campaign for president in 1992, Myles spoke as a woman, but her "issue" was free speech for all.

The anarchism of the New York School, for which Goodman supplied a philosophical framework, was tested under laboratory conditions in the isolated community of BOLINAS, CALIFORNIA, to which several of the poets migrated for some period of time during the 1970s. To the city poets the natural beauty of the California coast seemed exotic; it reminded Berrigan of Korea (Kyger 207), where he had been stationed during postwar military service (1954–55). For a while it seemed that a human community might flourish there as naturally as the biological community, but an oil spill off the coast in 1971 stirred up the residents to organize around the Public Utilities board, the only government entity with local roots (Opstedal). Environmental activism left its mark in poetry, notably that of LEWIS MACADAMS (*The River,* Blue Press, 2005). Similar connections have been forged in Colorado at Naropa (COLLOM). Back in NEW YORK CITY, what might be called urban environmentalism informed DOUGLAS OLIVER's *PENNILESS POLITICS* and Notley's *The DESCENT OF ALETTE,* published together in *The SCARLET CABINET* (1992). In *Désamère* (O Books, 1992),

Notley weaves into one the degradation of the natural environment, the destruction of human lives in war, and the poet's perpetual task to return from the isolation of art with a message of hope for the community. Through the figure of French poet Robert Desnos, Notley writes:

> I'm condemned to return in future deserts
> Dreaming the truth for others, until
> A more human future is won for us (Grave 226).

Bibliography

Angelou, "On the Pulse of Morning" (1993). In *The Complete Collected Poems*. New York: Random House, 1994, 269–273.

Ashbery, John. *Houseboat Days*. New York: Penguin, 1977.

———. "Writers and Issues: Frank O'Hara's Question" (1966). In *Selected Prose*. Edited by Eugene Richie. Ann Arbor: University of Michigan Press, 2004, 80–83.

Berrigan, Ted. *The Collected Poems of Ted Berrigan*. Edited by Alice Notley, Anselm Berrigan, and Edmund Berrigan. Berkeley: University of California Press, 2005.

Collom, Jack. "On, at, around Active Eco-Lit." In *Disembodied Poetics: Annals of the Jack Kerouac School*, edited by Anne Waldman and Andrew Schelling, 110–130. Albuquerque: University of New Mexico Press, 1994.

Coolidge, Clark. Interview by Tyler Doherty. *Jacket* 22 (May 2003). Available online. URL: http://jacketmagazine.com/22/doher-cooli.html. Accessed December 19, 2008.

Diggory, Terence. "Community 'Intimate' or 'Inoperative': New York School Poets and Politics from Paul Goodman to Jean-Luc Nancy." In *The Scene of My Selves: New Work on New York School Poets*, edited by Terence Diggory and Stephen Paul Miller, 13–32. Orono, Me.: National Poetry Foundation, 2001.

Fagin, Larry, and Clark Coolidge. *On the Pumice of Morons*. Great Barrington, Mass.: The Figures, 1993.

Frost, Robert. "The Gift Outright" (1942). In *The Poetry*. Edited by Edward Connery Lathem. New York: Holt, 1979, 348.

Ginsberg, Allen. "Plutonian Ode" (1978). In *Collected Poems, 1947–1980*. New York: Harper & Row, 1984, 702–705.

Gooch, Brad. *City Poet: The Life and Times of Frank O'Hara*. New York: Knopf, 1993.

Goodman, Paul. "Advance-Guard Writing in America, 1900–1950." *Kenyon Review* 13, no. 3 (Summer 1951): 357–380.

Guest, Barbara. "A Handbook of Surfing" (1967). In *Selected Poems*. Los Angeles: Sun & Moon, 1995, 42–50.

Herd, David. *John Ashbery and American Poetry*. New York: Palgrave, 2000.

Koch, Kenneth. *The Collected Poems*. New York: Knopf, 2005.

———. *The Election*. In *A Change of Hearts: Plays, Films, and Other Dramatic Works*. New York: Random House, 1973, 114–129.

Kyger, Joanne. "Day after Ted Berrigan's Memorial Reading" (1983). In *Nice to See You: Homage to Ted Berrigan*, edited by Anne Waldman, 207. Minneapolis, Minn.: Coffee House Press, 1991.

Lenhart, Gary. *The Stamp of Class: Reflections on Poetry and Social Class*. Ann Arbor: University of Michigan Press, 2006.

LeSueur, Joe. Introduction to *Amorous Nightmares of Delay*, by Frank O'Hara, xv–xxv. Baltimore, Md.: Johns Hopkins University Press, 1997.

Myles, Eileen. Interview by Edward Foster (1997). In *Poetry and Poetics in a New Millennium*, edited by Edward Foster, 50–63. Jersey City, N.J.: Talisman House, 2000.

Nielsen, Aldon Lynn. *Black Chant: Languages of African-American Postmodernism*. Cambridge: Cambridge University Press, 1997.

Notley, Alice. *Grave of Light: New and Selected Poems, 1970–2005*. Middletown, Conn.: Wesleyan University Press, 2006.

O'Hara, Frank. *Amorous Nightmares of Delay: Selected Plays*. Baltimore, Md.: Johns Hopkins University Press, 1997.

———. *The Collected Poems*. Rev. ed. Edited by Donald Allen. Berkeley: University of California Press, 1995.

Opstedal, Kevin. "A Literary History of the San Andreas Fault: Bolinas Section." *Jack Magazine* 1, no. 3 (2001). Available online. URL: http://www.jackmagazine.com/issue3/renhist.html. Accessed December 19, 2008.

Perelman, Bob. *The Marginalization of Poetry: Language Writing and Literary History*. Princeton, N.J.: Princeton University Press, 1996.

Riesman, David. *The Lonely Crowd: A Study of the Changing American Character*. New Haven, Conn.: Yale University Press, 1950.

Russo, Linda. "The 'F' Word in the Age of Mechanical Reproduction: An Account of Women-Edited Small Presses and Journals." In *The World in Time and Space: Towards a History of Innovative American Poetry in Our Time,* edited by Edward Foster and Joseph Donahue, 243–284. Jersey City, N.J.: Talisman House, 2002.

Schuyler, James. *Collected Poems.* New York: Noonday/Farrar, Straus & Giroux, 1995.

Thomas, Lorenzo. "Better Physics." *Chicago* 5, no. 1 (November 1, 1972): n.p.

———. *Fit Music: California Songs 1970* (1972). In *The Angel Hair Anthology,* edited by Anne Waldman and Lewis Warsh, 382–389. New York: Granary Books, 2001.

———. "Inauguration" (1979). In *Every Goodbye Ain't Gone: An Anthology of Innovative Poetry by African Americans,* edited by Aldon Lynn Nielsen and Lauri Ramey, 253. Tuscaloosa: University of Alabama Press, 2006.

Waldman, Anne. "Warring God Charnel Ground (Rocky Flats Chronicles)" (1994). In *Vow to Poetry: Essays, Interviews, and Manifestos.* Minneapolis, Minn.: Coffee House Press, 2001, 229–237.

Pollock, Jackson (1912–1956) *artist*

There is a mythic dimension in both the life and work of Jackson Pollock that is crucial to understanding the response of the NEW YORK SCHOOL poets, both positive and negative. His birth in the West (in Cody, Wyoming, though he spent most of his boyhood in California), along with his macho behavior, encouraged an association with cowboy legends. "They'll / never fence the silver range," writes FRANK O'HARA in his "Digression" (1956) on Pollock's painting *No. 1, 1948* (*Collected Poems* 260). However, JOHN ASHBERY notes something tiring in "the swashbuckling energy, wide-open spaces and 'O Pioneers' stance of much American abstract expressionism," and Ashbery's terms make it clear that he has the Pollock myth in mind (136). Of more interest to the poets was the myth of the avant-garde, which Pollock seemed to exemplify by producing work "of the kind that cannot be destroyed by acceptance, because it is basically unacceptable," Ashbery explained (392). As JAMES SCHUYLER put it, Pollock was "the painter who invented a new mode of freedom" (126).

The invention that made Pollock's reputation, both in the art world and in the popular press, was the technique of dripping, rather than brushing, paint as he walked around canvases laid flat on the floor, rather than propped on an easel. The resulting weblike patterns of lines were first exhibited at the Betty Parsons Gallery in NEW YORK CITY in 1948, and by 1949 *Life* magazine was asking whether Pollock was "the Greatest Living Painter in the United States." The question was an incredulous response to claims made by CLEMENT GREENBERG, who felt that Pollock had broken through to a mode of abstraction more pure than cubism and at the same time broken away from the surrealist (see DADA AND SURREALISM) imagery that had characterized Pollock's work of the early 1940s. When imagery began to reappear in Pollock's work in 1950, Greenberg felt he was backsliding (228).

In contrast to Greenberg's emphasis on abstraction, the poets responded to the expressive possibilities of Pollock's drip technique. Expressionism led directly from surrealism to Pollock. According to Ashbery, Pollock realized in painting the surrealist ideal of automatic writing (26), a device for liberating the unconscious. (see ABSTRACT EXPRESSIONISM and DADA AND SURREALISM.) According to O'Hara, when images appear to resurface in Pollock's work of the early 1950s, "they are not images at all, but ideographs" (O'Hara, "Jackson Pollock 1912–1956" 25), that is, writing—just like the hieroglyphs that O'Hara found at the center of Pollock's work of 1943, *Guardians of the Secret* (O'Hara, *Jackson Pollock* 24–25). Viewing Pollock's painting as a FORM of writing thus provides an argument for the unity of his career and an inspiration for the writing of poetry. Poetry that somehow "dissolved its signs," as O'Hara felt Pollock had done in his "classic" work of 1947–50, would produce, like Pollock, "a lyricism of immediate impact and spiritual clarity" (O'Hara, *Jackson Pollock* 25). This is the immediacy that O'Hara requests of Pollock as muse in "Ode on Causality" (1958): "a sexual bliss inscribe upon the page of whatever energy I burn for art" (*Collected Poems* 302). In contrast to the melodramatic "swashbuckling energy" that Ashbery found to be tiresome in the cowboy myth, the myth of burning energy carries the tragic overtones of "burning out." Pollock's self-destructive behavior, fueled by alcohol, may have led to a decline in his art during the 1950s, in the view of some critics, but it enhanced the mythic aura that surrounded him. That aura became permanently attached to his name after Pollock and one of his passengers died when he lost control of his car near his home in the Springs, Long Island, in 1956.

The timing of Pollock's death relative to the development of New York School poetry meant that much of what the poets wrote about Pollock was filtered through the lens of elegy. O'Hara's "Ode on Causality," which was formally titled an "elegy" in one manuscript (*Collected Poems* 542), centers on Pollock's grave at the Springs. Later, in an extended essay, the first study of Pollock to be published as a separate book (1959), O'Hara broadened the focus by connecting the personal doom that hung over Pollock with the fear of "universal destruction" that cold war tensions and nuclear weapons had instilled in American society at large (*Jackson Pollock* 26). For the New York arts community, the sense of tragic pattern was reinforced 10 years after Pollock's death when O'Hara was killed by a beach vehicle and buried in the same cemetery as Pollock. "Frank's head is at Jackson's feet," remarked Pollock's widow, the painter Lee Krasner (Gooch 4). KENNETH KOCH's suite of poems "Homage to Frank O'Hara" interweaves references to Pollock throughout. One of the poems is entitled "To My Pollock," with the clear implication that Koch is not merely addressing a drawing by Pollock that he owns but also his friend O'Hara, *his* Pollock, elevated to tragic status by "vanishing" (68).

For the generation of poets who emerged after Pollock's death, the legend of his life faded and the influence of his art dispersed in a variety of directions that led away from formal innovation, although the latter received renewed attention in art criticism as Greenberg's authority increased. In contrast to Greenberg's formalism, Allan Kaprow, an early instigator of "HAPPENINGS," proposed that "The Legacy of Jackson Pollock" was to be sought, quite literally, in the streets, a suggestion that echoes in a repeated line of TED BERRIGAN's SONNETS (1964): "Harumscarum haze on the Pollock streets" (*Collected Poems* 39, 54). In retrospect, tracing Pollock's influence

through the work of ALEX KATZ, BILL BERKSON emphasized the haze of sensation, "essentially nondimensional, a rush, weightless and mobile, a drift of unruly impulse felt before you have a name to fix it with" (Berkson 231). For Berkson, as for O'Hara, Pollock's "mythopoeic sign language" transforms into immediate feeling when inscribed on the "skin" of the canvas: "his image-making became an immediate fact" (237).

Bibliography

Ashbery, John. *Reported Sightings: Art Chronicles, 1957–1987.* Edited by David Bergman. Cambridge, Mass.: Harvard University Press, 1991.

Berkson, Bill. "The Sensational Pollock" (2000). In *The Sweet Singer of Modernism and Other Art Writings, 1985–2003.* Jamestown, R.I.: Qua Books, 2003, 228–238.

Berrigan, Ted. *The Collected Poems.* Edited by Alice Notley, Anselm Berrigan, and Edmund Berrigan. Berkeley: University of California Press, 2005.

Frank, Elizabeth. *Jackson Pollock.* New York: Abbeville, 1983.

Gooch, Brad. *City Poet: The Life and Times of Frank O'Hara.* New York: Knopf, 1993.

Greenberg, Clement. "'American-Type' Painting" (1955, 1958). In *Art and Culture: Critical Essays.* 1961. Reprint, Boston: Beacon, 1965, 208–229.

"Jackson Pollock: Is He the Greatest Living Painter in the United States?" *Life* 27, 8 August 1949, 42–44.

Kaprow, Allan. "The Legacy of Jackson Pollock." *Art News* 57, no. 6 (October 1958): 24–26ff.

Koch, Kenneth. "Homage to Frank O'Hara." In *Broadway 2: A Poets and Painters Anthology,* edited by James Schuyler and Charles North, 65–68. Brooklyn, N.Y.: Hanging Loose Press, 1989.

O'Hara, Frank. *The Collected Poems.* Rev. ed. Edited by Donald Allen. Berkeley: University of California Press, 1995.

———. *Jackson Pollock* (1959). In *Art Chronicles, 1954–1966.* New York: Braziller, 1990, 12–39.

———. "Jackson Pollock, 1912–1956" (1959). In *What's with Modern Art?* Edited by Bill Berkson. Austin, Tex.: Mike & Dale's Press, 1999, 25–26.

Schuyler, James. "Jackson Pollock II" (1957). In *Selected Art Writings.* Edited by Simon Pettet. Santa Rosa, Calif.: Black Sparrow, 1998, 126.

pop art

When pop art arrived on the New York art scene in the early 1960s, in the work of such artists as ANDY WARHOL, Roy Lichtenstein (1923–97), James Rosenquist (1933–), and Tom Wesselmann (1931–2004), it was received enthusiastically by a broad segment of the popular press and the general public, who were tired of the anguish, alienation, and abstraction they had endured under the long reign of NEW YORK SCHOOL painting, or ABSTRACT EXPRESSIONISM. The New York School poets were more ambivalent about pop, not only because of their allegiance to New York School painting. Second-generation painters such as GRACE HARTIGAN and LARRY RIVERS, with whom the poets were most closely allied, had, in fact, already moved away from abstraction and, partly following the poets' lead (Hartigan n.p.), experimented with the incorporation of popular imagery from advertising, merchandising, entertainment, and POLITICS. More recently, ROBERT RAUSCHENBERG and JASPER JOHNS had approached such material from a more detached, ironic perspective, but one that remained intensely subjective, and thus still expressionist, in a sense. What was most disturbing about pop art, therefore, was that some of it seemed to be not only about objects but by objects. The artist had become a machine, as Warhol said "everybody" should (118).

For first-generation poets trained in abstract expressionism, the adjustment required to "see" pop art was aided by their familiarity with a parallel movement in France, dubbed "New Realism" (*nouveau réalisme*) by art critic Pierre Restany. This was the title of an exhibition at the Sidney Janis Gallery in NEW YORK CITY in 1962 that provided an important breakthrough for American pop artists whose work was shown along with that of European peers. JOHN ASHBERY wrote an essay for the exhibition catalog as well as a poem entitled "The New Realism," collected in *The Tennis Court Oath* (1962). Reviewing the exhibition in one of his "Art Chronicles" for *KULCHUR* magazine, FRANK O'HARA placed the European artists ahead of the Americans in "the struggle into existentiality" (148). That phrase echoes the common application of French existentialist philosophy to abstract expressionism while also resonating with Ashbery's

claim that the New Realists struggled "to come to grips with the emptiness of industrialized modern life" (81). Also in 1962, KENNETH KOCH collaborated with Rauschenberg and two European New Realists, Nikki de Saint Phalle (1930–2002) and Jean Tinguely (1925–91), in a HAPPENING called *The CONSTRUCTION OF BOSTON*. Happenings had provided a kind of incubator for the development of American pop (O'Hara 148), for instance, in the work of JIM DINE, who later collaborated with Koch as well as several second-generation poets.

Second-generation poets sometimes approached Warhol's machine ideal in their repetition and appropriation of imagery—strategies Warhol employed in his multiple images of Campbell's soup cans. An obvious example is KENWARD ELMSLIE's "GIRL MACHINE" (1971), which resulted from a commission by poet GERARD MALANGA for Warhol's *Interview* magazine (volume 1, number 2 [1969]). When performed by Elmslie, this piece reveals a playful exuberance that is not immediately evident in the text alone, though various editions have evoked performance by including still photographs from the Busby Berkeley films that inspired the text. The comic strip, a GENRE much favored by the poets, goes further in this direction, taking full advantage of the page itself as the space of performance. In this genre the poets, from O'Hara to Elmslie, had their "own" pop artist to work with, JOE BRAINARD, who drew most of the strips for two issues of "C" Comics (1964), a spin-off of TED BERRIGAN's "C" magazine. The more canonical pop artist Lichtenstein set the precedent for the appropriation of comics in painting, just as the precedent in poetry was set by Koch, one of the contributors to "C" Comics and eventually a collaborator with Lichtenstein, whose stylized cutout airplane was a central prop in a production of Koch's play *The RED ROBINS* (1978). What Koch has said about his relation to Lichtenstein may apply more broadly to the whole question of precedence in this case: "[T]here was a common feeling, as much as there was influence" (interview 8). As for the nature of the feeling, Koch emphasized that the laughter he expected his work to generate was not grounded in contempt for popular culture: "It appeals to you, it arouses you, it moves you. At the same time, you can feel that sometimes it's stupid and empty and dopey. But I think these things can be expressed simultaneously" (interview 9). Once again, for the poet, the expression of feeling is pop's saving grace.

Bibliography

Ashbery, John. "The New Realists." In *Reported Sightings: Art Chronicles, 1957–1987*. Edited by David Bergman. Cambridge, Mass.: Harvard University Press, 1991, 81–83.

De Salvo, Donna, and Paul Schimmel. *Hand-Painted Pop: American Art in Transition, 1955–62*. Exhibit catalog. Los Angeles: Museum of Contemporary Art; New York: Rizzoli, 1992.

Elmslie, Kenward. "Girl Machine" and Author's Note. In *The Angel Hair Anthology*, edited by Anne Waldman and Lewis Warsh, 353–358, 584–585. New York: Granary Books, 2001.

Elmslie, Kenward, with Steven Taylor and Joe Brainard. "Girl Machine." In "Nite Palais." Kenward Elmslie Web site. Available online. URL: http://www.kenwardelmslie.com/interactive/index02.html. Accessed December 19, 2008.

Hartigan, Grace. Interview by Irving Sandler (11 November 1994). In "Artists Talk on Art" (unpub.). New York: Fulcrum Gallery.

Koch, Kenneth. *The Gold Standard: A Book of Plays*. New York: Knopf, 1998. [Book cover shows color photograph of Lichtenstein's "airplane" for *The Red Robins*.]

———. Interview by David Spurr (1979). *Contemporary Poetry* 3, no. 4 (1980): 1–12.

Lewallen, Constance. *Joe Brainard: A Retrospective*. Berkeley: Art Museum, University of California at Berkeley; New York: Granary Books, 2001. [Reproduces examples of "*C*" *Comics* on pp. 34–35.]

O'Hara, Frank. "Art Chronicle III" (1963). In *Standing Still and Walking in New York*. Edited by Donald Allen. San Francisco: Grey Fox, 1983, 140–151.

Warhol, Andy, et al. "What Is Pop Art?" (1963). In *Pop Art: The Critical Dialogue*, edited by Carol Ann Mahsun, 111–137. Ann Arbor: University of Michigan Research Press, 1989.

Wolf, Reva. *Andy Warhol, Poetry, and Gossip in the 1960s*. Chicago: University of Chicago Press, 1997. [Reproduces page layout from *Interview* magazine showing Elmslie's "Time Step Ode," the original version of "Girl Machine," on p. 52.]

Porter, Fairfield (1907–1975) *artist*

Although he was a realist painter, Fairfield Porter's place in the New York art world and in NEW YORK SCHOOL poetry is based on the friendship and mutual admiration between Porter and WILLEM DE KOONING. They met around 1940, after Porter had moved to the New York area from his native CHICAGO, ILLINOIS. In 1951 de Kooning's recommendation was decisive in persuading JOHN BERNARD MYERS to represent Porter in the newly formed TIBOR DE NAGY GALLERY, and Elaine de Kooning recommended Porter to replace her as a writer for *Art News*. These were the two main contexts through which Porter came to interact with the New York School poets. Like the poets, whose medium required a certain degree of reference to reality, Porter found in de Kooning a sense of abstraction that applied equally well to his own practice of realist painting. In each case the intention was not to "translate" the visible world but to communicate the artist's "kinetic and visual sense of the world" as an "immediate reality," present in the painting or poem (F. Porter, "Abstract Expressionism" 111). "Many of Porter's paintings," wrote FRANK O'HARA, "have a look of spontaneity and effortless felicity, an anonymous and silent placidity of the paint itself" (54). "The paint is itself a palpable fact," JAMES SCHUYLER seconded, "that holds an imprint of life and infuses life into the image" ("An Aspect" 15). Yet words could be similarly infused with "kinetic and visual sense." "Jimmy, you're *much* more visual than I am," Porter remarked after reading the title poem of Schuyler's *The Crystal Lithium* (Random House, 1972), for which Porter provided a cover image. Porter's remark was "the greatest compliment any poem of mine ever had," Schuyler recalled (Schuyler, interview 182).

The scenes in Porter's paintings depict "everyday life" (Schuyler, "An Aspect" 16), another interest the painter shared with the poets. However, compared with the NEW YORK CITY lofts and tenements that were typical surroundings for the poets, the environment that Porter's inherited wealth provided was both more comfortable and more expansive in its openness to the natural world. At his home in Southampton, on Long Island, Porter hosted many gatherings of New York School poets from both the first and second generations. This "enchanting place" (Ashbery 11), purchased by Porter in 1949, became an early outpost for the new wave of artists and writers who soon colonized the HAMPTONS area, yet the impression of the scene produced by Porter's paintings is not glamorous but "intimist," in keeping with one of his principal influences, the French painter Édouard Vuillard (1868–1940). Among interior scenes that include Porter's wife, Anne (1911–)—a poet—or some of their six children, Schuyler frequently appears (for example, *The Screen Porch*, 1964), since the Porters took Schuyler into their family after a bout of mental illness in 1961 and he lived with them until 1973. Porter's first portrait of Schuyler dates back to 1955, when the poet visited the Porter family property on Great Spruce Head Island off the coast of Maine, a scene memorably recorded in photographs by Eliot Porter (1901–90), Fairfield's brother. In Schuyler's poetry the impressions of Maine are idyllic (as evidenced in the section of *The Crystal Lithium* entitled "The Island"), whereas those of Southampton are more simply domestic. Porter recognized himself "putting out the garbage on a snowy morning" in "The Crystal Lithium" (F. Porter, letter 289). The two moods combine in an untitled collaborative poem that Porter and KENNETH KOCH wrote from Great Spruce Head to Schuyler and O'Hara, recalling their earlier visits to the island (F. Porter, *Collected Poems* 64–65).

As his occasional poems and, even more, his extensive critical writing demonstrate, Porter was an immensely literate man, able to draw fully on his education (at Harvard, 1924–28) and his wide reading. Although the poets understandably felt at home with this quality in Porter, what they seem to have admired most in his painting was distinctly nonverbal and subtly disturbing. "The coziness," JOHN ASHBERY explained, "is deceiving. It reverberates in time the way the fumbled parlor-piano tunes in the 'Alcotts' section of Ives' *Concord* Sonata do. The local color is transparent and porous, letting the dark light of space show through" (Ashbery 13). BARBARA GUEST marked the death of "the great painter" in her novel *SEEKING AIR* (1978), where she identifies him as "the painter of interiors and lawns. Of incorrigible silences" (90).

Bibliography

Ashbery, John. "Respect for Things as They Are." In *Reported Sightings: Art Chronicles, 1957–1987*. Edited by David Bergman. Cambridge, Mass.: Harvard University Press, 1991, 313–317.

Guest, Barbara. *Seeking Air*. 1978. Reprint, Los Angeles: Sun & Moon, 1997.

O'Hara, Frank. "Porter Paints a Picture" (1955). In *Standing Still and Walking in New York*. Edited by Donald Allen. San Francisco: Grey Fox, 1983, 52–58.

Porter, Anne. *Living Things: Collected Poems*. Hanover, N.H.: Zoland, 2006.

Porter, Eliot. *Summer Island: Penobscot County*. San Francisco: Sierra Club, 1966.

Porter, Fairfield. "Abstract Expressionism and Landscape" (ca. 1962). In *Art in Its Own Terms: Selected Criticism, 1935–1975*. Edited by Rackstraw Downes. Cambridge, Mass.: Zoland, 1979, 107–111.

———. *The Collected Poems with Selected Drawings*. Edited by John Yau, with David Kermani. New York: Tibor de Nagy Editions/Promise of Learnings, 1985.

———. Letter to James Schuyler, 19 August 1971. In *Material Witness: The Selected Letters*. Edited by Ted Leigh. Ann Arbor: University of Michigan Press, 2005, 288–290.

Schjeldahl, Peter. "Stern Beauty." *New Yorker*, 17 April 2000, 122–123.

Schuyler, James. "An Aspect of Fairfield Porter's Paintings" (1967). In *Selected Art Writings*. Edited by Simon Pettet. Santa Rosa, Calif.: Black Sparrow, 1998, 8–17.

———. Interview by Carl Little. *Agni* 37 (January 1993): 152–182.

Spring, Justin. *Fairfield Porter: A Life in Art*. New Haven, Conn.: Yale University Press, 2000.

Pressed Wafer (1999–)

A BOSTON press, Pressed Wafer was founded by WILLIAM CORBETT and Joseph Torra (1955–). Others have worked on production and/or as contributing editors, including Jim Behrle, Dan Bouchard, and Chris Mattison. The press takes its name from a book by JOHN WIENERS (1967). Since its conception in 1999, Pressed Wafer has published journals, chapbooks, full-length books, postcards, and foldouts.

The first issue of the journal of the same name, published in 2000, included Rodrigo Moynihan, Ann Kim, JAMES SCHUYLER, Wieners, Paul Metcalf, Michael Palmer, Monica Peck, Paul Petricone, and others. Issue number two, published in 2001, featured a tribute to JOE BRAINARD. The issue also included Stephen Jonas, August Kleinzhaler, Sam Cornish, ANGE MLINKO, JENNIFER MOXLEY, MARCELLA DURAND, Torra, and others.

Pressed Wafer has printed a substantial number of chapbooks. A partial list includes titles by BRENDA IIJIMA, Beth Anderson, Fred Moten, Mike County, Jim Behrle, Del Ray Cross, Karen Weiser, Corbett, Jim Dunn, Seido Ronci, Sean Cole, Wieners, and Patricia Pruitt. The press's perfect-bound book titles include *Rub Out* by Ed Barrett (2003), *After the Chinese* by Torra (2004), *October Snow* by Sam Reifler (2004), *February Sheaf* by Gerrit Lansing (2003), and *Ten in the Morning* (2004), with images by Gerald Coble and text by Corbett.

In 2000 Pressed Wafer, along with Granary Books, published a tribute to Wieners, *The Blind See Only This World: Poems for John Wieners*. Edited by Corbett, MICHAEL GIZZI, and Torra, this anthology contained work by JOHN ASHBERY, Lansing, Mlinko, ALLEN GINSBERG, Paul Auster, Fanny Howe, Jim Harrison, ANNE WALDMAN, LEWIS WARSH, BARBARA GUEST, BERNADETTE MAYER, RON PADGETT, Robert Duncan, Susan Howe, Ken Irby, ROBERT CREELEY, KENWARD ELMSLIE, and others.

Pressed Wafer has also produced postcards by artists Gerald Coble, Robert Nunnelly, Elsa Dorfman, Paula and CHARLES NORTH, Nancy Pike, Behrle, Dan Bouhcard and Neal Fernley, and Roy Arenella. In addition, a number of foldouts have brought poetry to the fingertips of Pressed Wafer's readers. Authors include Maureen McLane, James Cook, Dasha Lymar, Ed Barrett, Fanny Howe, Gizzi, and others.

Pressed Wafer is an independent press and receives no public or institutional funding. Corbett, Torra, and Mattison remain dedicated to publishing work of younger as well as established writers, maintaining the tradition of the small press in America.

printmaking   *See* ART, VISUAL.

"Projective Verse" Charles Olson (1950)
CHARLES OLSON's essay "Projective Verse," first published in the magazine *Poetry New York* in 1950, offers a theoretical formulation of free verse practiced by Olson's primary models, Ezra Pound and William Carlos Williams. Olson claims

for poetry the process-oriented aesthetic that HAROLD ROSENBERG's essay on "The American Action Painters" would claim for painting two years later. When Rosenberg describes the painter approaching the canvas "as an arena in which to act" (25), he is essentially describing what Olson calls "composition by field" in "Projective Verse" (387). It is an open field, because its shape is not predetermined by a FORM the artist is attempting to fill in or a subject the artist is attempting to depict. Rather than seeking to re-present a past event, whether physical or imagined, the artist seeks to present the work of art itself as an event. It takes place in the present moment, yet it is oriented—projected—toward an undetermined future. It may be called "abstract" (Olson "Letter" 398) in this special sense of being open ended and nonrepresentational.

In *The NEW AMERICAN POETRY, 1945–1960,* which reprints "Projective Verse," editor DONALD M. ALLEN credits Olson with defining "the dominant new double concept: 'composition by field' and the poet's 'stance toward reality'" shared by the various movements included in the anthology (xiv). However, on the issue of the poet's stance, the NEW YORK SCHOOL differed from Olson in a way that can be illuminated by Olson's difference from Rosenberg. Rosenberg emphasized the artificiality of creative acts; he called them "dramas of 'as if'" (27). Drama is also important to Olson ("Projective Verse" 386, 396), who taught a course on THEATER as "projective art" at BLACK MOUNTAIN COLLEGE (Olson, *Collected Prose* 424). In "Projective Verse," however, the poet's "stance toward reality" is primarily a matter of "how he conceives his relation to nature" (395; for Olson, the poet is always male). Criticizing subjective self-consciousness, Olson wants to return "man" to nature, as one other object in the field. Since the field of nature, as Olson conceives it, is essentially a force field, charged with energy ("Projective Verse" 387), the poet restored to that field becomes in turn a force of nature. JACKSON POLLOCK may have boasted "I am nature," but by 1952, when "The American Action Painters" appeared, Rosenberg was warning against the mysticism of "the cosmic 'I'" (34), and the New York School poets shared his skepticism. They rejected that aspect of projective verse that projected the human to superhuman scale, the scale implied by the name "Maximus" that Olson adopted for the persona of his major epic sequence (published in 1960, 1968, 1975).

Among other aspects of projective verse, perhaps the most congenial to the New York School poets was the emphasis on forward propulsion driving a poem through a constantly changing series of impressions. "Keep it moving as fast as you can, citizen," Olson wrote (149). Whether it derived directly from Olson, this principle generated the long poems of FRANK O'HARA (*Second Avenue,* 1960), KENNETH KOCH (*When the Sun Tries to Go On,* 1960), JAMES SCHUYLER (*The Morning of the Poem,* 1980), and JOHN ASHBERY (FLOW CHART, 1991). A second principle that can be traced directly to Olson is "the use of the typewriter as an instrument, not just a recorder of thought," as O'Hara puts it, citing "Projective Verse" in notes for a talk at the artists' CLUB in 1952 (34). The date demonstrates how early the concepts of "Projective Verse" entered into New York School conversation, and the specific reference testifies to O'Hara's acquaintance with the original 1950 publication of Olson's essay, since the passage about the typewriter ("Projective Verse" 393) does not appear in the extensive excerpt that William Carlos Williams reprinted in his *Autobiography* in 1951 (329–332). At the same time O'Hara's divergence from Olson in the context of painting is already evident. In conceiving of the typewriter "as an instrument," O'Hara is seeking the equivalent of the painter's brush, or the other implements that Pollock used in place of the brush in an effort to transfer the painter's action as directly as possible onto the canvas. The typewritten page becomes the equivalent of the canvas for O'Hara and other New York School writers, as their attention to the visual appearance of the text implies. For Olson, by contrast, the page is the equivalent of the musical score, a set of instructions, made all the more precise thanks to the mechanism of the typewriter but ultimately intended for realization by the natural organism that projects breath as human voice. This aspect of projective verse was taken up by the second generation of the New York School as they explored live performance as a medium for poetry.

Bibliography

Allen, Donald, ed. *The New American Poetry, 1945–1960.* 1960. Reprint, Berkeley: University of California Press, 1999.

Creeley, Robert. "On the Road: Notes on Artists and Poets, 1950–1965" (1974). In *Collected Essays.* Berkeley: University of California Press, 1989, 367–376.

O'Hara, Frank. "Design etc." (1952). In *Standing Still and Walking in New York.* Edited by Donald Allen. San Francisco: Grey Fox, 1983, 33–36.

Olson, Charles. *Collected Prose.* Edited by Donald Allen and Benjamin Friedlander. Berkeley: University of California Press, 1997.

———. "Letter to Elaine Feinstein" (1959). In *The New American Poetry, 1945–1960,* edited by Donald Allen, 397–400. Berkeley: University of California Press, 1999.

———. "Projective Verse" (1950). In *The New American Poetry, 1945–1960,* edited by Donald Allen, 386–397. Berkeley: University of California Press, 1999.

Perloff, Marjorie. "Charles Olson and the Inferior Predecessors: 'Projective Verse' Revisited." *ELH* 40, no. 2 (Summer 1973): 285–306.

Rosenberg, Harold. "The American Action Painters" (1952). In *The Tradition of the New.* 1960. Reprint, New York: da Capo, 1994, 23–39.

Stein, Charles. "Projection." In *Code of Signals: Recent Writings in Poetics,* edited by Michael Palmer, 67–78. Berkeley, Calif.: North Atlantic Books, 1983.

Williams, William Carlos. *The Autobiography.* New York: New Directions, 1951.

prose poem   *See* FORM.

Providence, Rhode Island

The most obvious connections between Providence and NEW YORK SCHOOL poets involve the second generation. TED BERRIGAN, CLARK COOLIDGE, and Hannah Weiner (1928–97) were born here. Coolidge and BILL BERKSON attended Brown University, and across town Berrigan spent time at Providence College. From 1964 to 1966, while living in Providence, Coolidge edited the magazine *Joglars* with Michael Palmer. Coolidge's activity in the city is probably the most sustained of any major figure connected with the New York School. The poetry scene then was, otherwise, largely academic.

Literary activity in Providence, however, flourished by the early 1970s, stimulated by the creative writing program at Brown University, which began in the mid-1960s. In 1968 Keith Waldrop (1932–   ) joined the Brown faculty and brought along Burning Deck Press, coedited by his wife, Rosmarie Waldrop (1935–   ). The Waldrops' predilection for experimental literature created a solid niche for the avant-garde in Providence as Burning Deck published Rochelle Owens, HARRY MATHEWS, BARBARA GUEST, KENWARD ELMSLIE, JACKSON MAC LOW, and others.

Following Burning Deck's lead, Tom Ahern, a student of Keith Waldrop's, ran Diana's Monthly Press from 1972 to 1986, first as a magazine and later as a series of chapbooks and almanacs. Included in Diana's catalog were selections from Hannah Weiner's *Code Poems* and *Clairvoyant Journals* and Kathy Acker's *Florida*.

Throughout the '70s and '80s several reading series took place at Brown and community venues. Craig Watson held readings at Roger Williams Park Museum of Natural History. The Anyart Gallery, an independent space on Steeple Street, also served as a popular reading forum. Among the poets appearing were JOHN ASHBERY, TOM CLARK, Elmslie (including performances of *26 Bars* and *Postcards on Parade*), Mac Low, Mathews, BERNADETTE MAYER, and Weiner.

Subsequent activity has maintained associations with the New York School. LEE ANN BROWN began Tender Buttons Press while living in Providence with the 1989 publication of Mayer's *Sonnets*. Rosmarie Waldrop put together a two-year program of readings at the Providence Athenaeum that brought Guest and others to the city. In 2001 MICHAEL GIZZI and Craig Watson initiated Qua Books with *As Umbrellas Follow Rain*, poems by Ashbery, and in 2003 published *The Sweet Singer of Modernism*, art writings by Berkson. Another reading series—at Tazza, a downtown bar—was begun by Gizzi and Michael Magee in 2004 and has featured Berkson, Coolidge, Mayer, and JOHN YAU. Other notable publishing ventures include Gale Nelson's Paradigm Press, Magee's *Combo*, Jen

Tynes's Horse Less Press, and JENNIFER MOXLEY's *Impercipient*, which ran from 1992 to 1995.

Bibliography

Januzzi, Marisa. "Kerouac, Berrigan, and the Poetics of Providence." *Titanic Operas* (2003). Dickinson Electronic Archives. Available online. URL: http://www.emilydickinson.org/titanic/material/januzzi.html. Accessed December 19, 2008.

punk rock

The one FORM of MUSIC that can be said to have originated at the POETRY PROJECT AT ST. MARK'S CHURCH IN-THE-BOWERY is punk rock. For her first poetry reading, on a double-bill with GERARD MALANGA at the Poetry Project on February 10, 1971, PATTI SMITH invited guitarist Lenny Kaye to accompany her on a few pieces. The pairing of Smith and Kaye became the nucleus of the Patti Smith Group that released the album *Horses* in 1976, the beginning of punk's emergence into mainstream recognition. The pairing of Smith and Malanga is equally significant, however. Both Smith and Malanga thought of themselves primarily as poets, and Malanga was to be instrumental in arranging the publication of Smith's first collection of poems, *Seventh Heaven*, with TELEGRAPH BOOKS in 1972. However, like Malanga, who had performed as a dancer with the protopunk band The VELVET UNDERGROUND during the 1960s, Smith had reconceived the role of the poet as a matter of performance as much as language (McNeil and McCain 160–161).

Music, too, like language, was a means to an end. While it is possible to characterize punk in purely musical terms—minimal chord structure, pounding rhythm, deliberately amateurish technique—such a characterization misses the essential nature of punk as total PERFORMANCE ART. This distinction became a source of friction between another formative pair in the development of punk, RICHARD HELL and Tom Verlaine (Thomas Miller; 1949–   ) of the band Television (1974–75). While Verlaine concentrated on music, Hell, in his own words, "wanted us to stand for something in everything we did. And that included clothes and the look of our graphics and all that imagery kind of thing" (Heylin 122). An understanding of imagery was the primary contribution to punk by poets like Hell, who also started out at the Poetry Project. Compared to poetry, music's advantage was its ability to attract a bigger audience. Punk's poet-musicians sought to eliminate the distance between audience and performer that large concert venues had created in mainstream rock and that the silent page created for printed poetry. The preferred venue for punk performance was the small, intimate club, such as CBGB on the Bowery, where the Patti Smith Group and Television played a now legendary double-bill in spring 1975. It was "the official beginning of the scene" (McNeil and McCain 172), and it was the same scene that has sustained the Downtown poetry community, with the Poetry Project located just a few blocks north and, eventually, the BOWERY POETRY CLUB located right across the street from CBGB, which closed in 2005.

Punk's move to overcome the distance between performer and audience was staged as part of a broader assault on a corrupt social system that reserved all the benefits to an elite group of "stars" while relegating the masses to the status of non-entities or "punks." As an institution, the Poetry Project was regarded with some suspicion by Smith and Hell as part of a "star system" (McNeil and McCain 109–110; Heylin 98), like the record companies. However, as a tradition, poetry supplied models of the outcast rebel. There was the *poète maudit* (accursed poet) Arthur Rimbaud, who was a major hero for Smith (as evidenced in her poems "rimbaud dead" and "dream of rimbaud," in *Babel*) and whose legend inspired the stage names taken by Hell (recalling Rimbaud's *Season in Hell*) and Verlaine (after Rimbaud's lover and fellow poet, Paul Verlaine). Among contemporary writers there were the BEATS (Bockris), whose name carries many of the same meanings as the word *punk,* though punks repudiated both the passivity and the pastoralism that were the grounds on which the Beats met the more recent "hippies" (McNeil and McCain 203, 282).

NEW YORK SCHOOL poets could be suspect on similar grounds. Nevertheless, as in the Beats, there is in the New York School an attitude to performance that feeds directly into the attitude of punk rock. FRANK O'HARA's standard for form—"if you're going to buy a pair of pants you want them to be tight enough so everyone will want to go to bed with you" ("Personism" 498)—echoes in Smith's declaration: "[Y]ou only perform because you want people to fall in love with you" (McNeil and McCain 161). An awareness that one is performing, that the self on display belongs to "imagery" rather than nature, involves punk more integrally in the New York School tradition than in that of the Beats, at least in this one respect. The three strands have continued to intertwine as the tradition has extended in GENRE from bands (BARBARA BARG, SUSIE TIMMONS, MAGGIE DUBRIS) to SLAM POETRY (JEROME SALA, ELAINE EQUI, BOB HOLMAN) and in territory from East Coast to West (DENNIS COOPER in Los Angeles, JIM CARROLL in San Francisco). From 1978 on, the geography of punk was further complicated by the reimportation from Britain of models that had originated in New York in a very different, more poetically oriented context (McNeil and McCain 198–199; Taylor 64–65).

Bibliography

Blank Generation—The New York Scene. Sound recording, R2 71175. Santa Monica, Calif.: Rhino Records, 1993.

Bockris, Victor. *Beat Punks: New York's Underground Culture from the Beat Generation to the Punk Explosion.* New York: Da Capo, 1998.

Heylin, Clinton. *From the Velvets to the Voidoids: The Birth of American Punk Rock.* Updated ed. Chicago: A Cappella/Chicago Review Press, 2005.

Kral, Ivan, and Amos Poe. *Blank Generation—Dancing Barefoot.* Videorecording, DR-4323. Oaks, Pa.: MVD, 2000.

McNeil, Legs, and Gillian McCain. *Please Kill Me: The Uncensored Oral History of Punk.* New York: Grove, 1996.

O'Hara, Frank. "Personism" (1959). In *The Collected Poems.* Rev. ed. Edited by Donald Allen. Berkeley: University of California Press, 1995, 498–499.

Smith, Patti. *Babel.* New York: G. P. Putnam's Sons, 1978.

Taylor, Steven. *False Prophet: Field Notes from the Punk Underground.* Middletown, Conn.: Wesleyan University Press, 2003.

Q

Quill, Solitary Apparition Barbara Guest (1996)

The qualities of "space, sparseness and openness" (Guest, interview 24) that BARBARA GUEST sought to develop in her work following the publication of *Fair Realism* (1989) reach a culmination in *Quill, Solitary Apparition* (1996), a sequence of seven poems. Taking the modernist technique of fragmentation to an extreme, Guest scatters only a few words across each page so that they seem suspended in or about to disappear into blank space. Some of the blankness has been produced by erasure, a practice that Guest began to employ in composing her poem "Chalk" (1989), collected in *Defensive Rapture* (1993). Thematically the effect is one of *evanescence*, a key term whose repetition links "Finally, to the Italian Girl," the opening poem in *Quill*, to "Musicality" (1988), collected in *Fair Realism*.

In musical rather than visual terms the blank spaces of *Quill* function either as silence or as dissonance. The composer Arnold Schoenberg provides the model here as elsewhere in Guest's work of this period. While dissonance interrupts lyrical (or melodic) flow, represented by the image of water in the poem "Pallor," it simultaneously redirects the flow from its "natural" horizontal or descending course into a vertical construction that Guest figures alternatively as a fountain or a musical chord—"the fourth chord" employed distinctively by Schoenberg and his followers. On the last page of "Pallor," the institution of the fourth chord is associated with the emergence in the poem of the

"persona," whose ghostlike pallor identifies her with the blankness of the white page, now animated by the author's inscription.

Guest discusses the full set of associations in her essay "Shifting Persona" (1990), pointing toward the imagery of the concluding poem from which *Quill, Solitary Apparition* takes its title. The reader, Guest explains, "is lifted by the author's inked quill, a euphemism for time, to project beyond singularity." Opened to multiple possibility, we "watch for the apparitions of ourselves moving alongside the characters" ("Shifting Persona" 38)—characters in the sense both of fictional personae and of letters of the alphabet, moving across the page. Guest's identification of the quill as "a euphemism for time" tells us how much she is conscious of time as the medium of poetry, as of MUSIC. But she is equally concerned with time as the medium of culture or history. Quotations from past texts and echoes of the styles of earlier periods make the music of *Quill, Solitary Apparition* polyphonic. One series of allusions to modern authors, from Charles Baudelaire to James Joyce to Guest's younger contemporary, MARJORIE WELISH, leads up to the assertion in the title of the next-to-last poem that we are "Leaving Modernity," another topic on which Guest has commented outside her poetry (Guest, interview 24–26). This poem, however, observes a "disorder" that "interrupts Modernity" rather than displacing it entirely, just as dissonance interrupts the flow of the melodic line without eliminating the music. The complexity of Guest's sense of music, poetry, and time allows for the possibility that "Leaving Modernity" may mean "leaving (without ending)."

Bibliography

Guest, Barbara. *Defensive Rapture.* Los Angeles: Sun & Moon, 1993.

———. *Fair Realism.* Los Angeles: Sun & Moon, 1989.

———. Interview by Mark Hillringhouse. *American Poetry Review* (July–August 1992): 23–30.

———. "Shifting Persona." In *Forces of Imagination: Writing on Writing.* Berkeley, Calif.: Kelsey St. Press, 2003, 36–42.

———. *Quill, Solitary Apparition.* Sausalito, Calif.: Post-Apollo Press, 1996.

Kaufman, Robert. "A Future for Modernism: Barbara Guest's Recent Poetry." *American Poetry Review* (July–August 2000): 11–16.

Mueller, Robert. "'Understanding What It Means to Understand Music': Barbara Guest and Wittgenstein." Electronic Poetry Center, University at Buffalo. Available online. URL: http://epc. buffalo.edu/authors/guest/mueller.html. Accessed December 19, 2008.

R

Ratcliff, Carter (1941–)

Carter Ratcliff is one of a number of NEW YORK SCHOOL poets (including GERRITT HENRY, JOHN PERREAULT, and PETER SCHJELDAHL) who have extended the affinity between poetry and painting into a career in art criticism. In his criticism the language is animated by the act of poetic imagination, an act as essential to engagement with a work of art as with the ordinary world. In turn, the worlds he has encountered in art inform his poetry. "For instance," he explains, "writing about Jackson Pollock, Barnett Newman, and other painters of their generation led me to consider certain peculiarly American ideas about space (infinite), order (contingent), and individuality (untrammeled)—in short, the American sublime, which had always tinged my poetry but, at some point late in the 1980s, began to supply it with explicit topics" (questionnaire response n.p.).

Ratcliff was raised in the Midwest and attended the University of Chicago (B.A., 1963). After serving in the army, he moved to NEW YORK CITY in 1967 in order to connect with the poets who most interested him, the New York School poets who were just then establishing a center of operations at the POETRY PROJECT AT ST. MARK'S CHURCH IN-THE-BOWERY. For several years Ratcliff participated in TED BERRIGAN's workshop, for which he composed a "things to do" poem. In 1968 he began issuing a magazine under a different title for each issue: *Reindeer* (1968), *Seaplane* (1969), *Cicada* (1970). He began writing criticism for *Art News* in 1968, the year he met Phyllis Derfner, also an art critic, whom Ratcliff married in 1974.

Poems by Ratcliff have appeared in some of the most important magazines associated with the New York School, from classic second-generation showcases such as *The WORLD*, *ADVENTURES IN POETRY*, and *Sun* to recent initiatives such as TREVOR WINKFIELD's *The Sienese Shredder* and VINCENT KATZ's *Vanitas*. Ratcliff has published only two collections: *Fever Coast* (Kulchur Foundation, 1973) and *Give Me Tomorrow* (Vehicle Editions, 1983), the latter a COLLABORATION with the painter ALEX KATZ. Both its publisher, LITA HORNICK, and a reviewer, Nick Piombino, connected *Fever Coast* with the work of JOHN ASHBERY, Hornick citing in particular the air of mystery and "those long sentences, which manage to maintain a logical syntax, though nearly swamped by the accumulating images" (Hornick 62–63). Attracted to the "gangster-type poems" in *Give Me Tomorrow*, Katz created fictional portraits of "people who looked like they could come out of a movie, glamourous people," in the style of Humphrey Bogart (Katz 13). Ratcliff's association with Katz has been fruitful for both his poetry and his criticism. He is one of the 14 poets featured in Katz's album *Face of a Poet* (Brooke Alexander/Marlborough Graphics, 1978), and his catalog essay for a 1979 exhibition of Katz's *Cutouts* (Robert Miller Gallery) was praised by Ashbery as "the best piece of criticism I have ever seen on this hard to elucidate artist" (232).

Bibliography

Ashbery, John. "Neil Welliver and Alex Katz" (1979). In *Reported Sightings: Art Chronicles, 1957–1987.* Edited by David Bergman. Cambridge, Mass.: Harvard University Press, 1991, 231–232.

Hornick, Lita. *The Green Fuse: A Memoir.* New York: Giorno Poetry Systems, 1989.

Katz, Alex. Interview by Vincent Katz. *Poetry Project Newsletter* 184 (April–May 2001): 11–15ff.

Piombino, Nicholas. Review of *Fever Coast. The World* 29 (April 1974): 88.

Ratcliff, Carter. *The Fate of a Gesture: Jackson Pollock and Postwar American Art.* New York: Farrar, Straus & Giroux, 1996.

———. "Joe Brainard's Quiet Dazzle." In *Joe Brainard: A Retrospective,* by Constance M. Lewallen, et al., 49–68. Exhibit catalog. Berkeley: University of California Berkeley Art Museum; New York: Granary Books, 2001.

———. Questionnaire response for *Encyclopedia of the New York School Poets,* 23 February 2006.

———. "Schneeman and Company: How to Do Things with Words and Pictures." In *Painter Among Poets: The Collaborative Art of George Schneeman,* edited by Ron Padgett, 11–34. New York: Granary Books, 2004.

———. "The Sublime Was Then: The Art of Barnett Newman." In *Sticky Sublime,* edited by Bill Beckley, 211–239. New York: School of Visual Arts/Allworth Press, 2001.

———. "Things to Do in Ted Berrigan's Workshop." In *The World Anthology: Poems from the St. Mark's Poetry Project,* edited by Anne Waldman, 127–128. Indianapolis, Ind.: Bobbs-Merrill, 1969.

Ratcliff, Carter, et al. *Alex Katz.* London: Phaidon, 2005.

Rauschenberg, Robert (1925–2008) *artist*

More than one critic, including FRANK O'HARA, has described Robert Rauschenberg as the "*enfant terrible* of the New York School" (O'Hara, "Bob Rauschenberg" 20), a role he acted out most famously in 1953 when he requested a drawing from WILLEM DE KOONING in order to erase it. With a debut exhibition at Betty Parsons's gallery in 1951, Rauschenberg was present from the beginning of the NEW YORK SCHOOL, irreverently foreboding its overthrow in developments of the 1960s such as POP ART, MINIMALISM, CONCEPTUAL ART, and PERFORMANCE ART. He was an early associate of JOHN CAGE, who purchased a painting from the 1951 exhibition and later invited Rauschenberg's participation in his pioneering HAPPENING at BLACK MOUNTAIN COLLEGE in 1952. A series of all-white paintings that Rauschenberg was working on at the same time anticipated Cage's silent composition *4'33"* (1952) as devices for capturing "whatever fell on them" (Cage 98), tuning the attention of viewers or listeners to their immediate environment.

The New York School poets were attracted to the immediacy of Rauschenberg's work, but they tended to find in it less "poetry" than in the work of JASPER JOHNS, Rauschenberg's closest associate in visual art and his lover from 1953 to 1961. O'Hara reviewed an important show by Rauschenberg at the Charles Egan Gallery in 1954, in which Rauschenberg showed early versions of his "combines," assembled from found objects. "For all the baroque exuberance of the show, quieter pictures evidence a serious lyrical talent," reported O'Hara ("Bob Rauschenberg" 20), suggesting both a less than serious motive and a less than poetic effect in the "baroque exuberance." Looking back on the same show a decade later, JOHN ASHBERY found an affinity with JOSEPH CORNELL in Rauschenberg's presentation of "the object and its nimbus of associations," but in tracing the next step toward "the radical simplicity" of minimalism, Ashbery raises doubts about the loss of the poetical "nimbus" (17). Such a loss clearly concerns O'Hara in his poem "For Bob Rauschenberg" (1959), which responds to the artist's counsel to "put everything / aside but what is there" (*Collected Poems* 322). Where does that leave "the heavenly aspirations of / Spenser and Keats and Ginsberg," O'Hara wonders.

More prominent than the "lyrical talent" in Rauschenberg was a theatrical talent that defined his reception by the poets throughout the 1960s, though it is evident earlier. O'Hara compared the more "extrovert" work in Rauschenberg's 1954 exhibition with his designs for *Minutiae* (1954), his first COLLABORATION with choreographer Merce Cunningham. In a 1959 exhibition his "combine" *Monogram,* the now-famous assemblage of stuffed goat and automobile tire, evoked JAZZ performance in BILL BERKSON's recollection. "It struck a chord," Berkson later wrote, "compounded of one part

Ornette Coleman [Rauschenberg's fellow Texan who meanwhile had arrived from L.A. and checked into the Five Spot], one part Jack Kerouac braying [on another record recently acquired] 'Laugh to hear the crazy music!'" (259). In 1962 Rauschenberg himself performed, nominally under Cunningham's direction, in KENNETH KOCH's play *The CONSTRUCTION OF BOSTON*. In 1967 Rauschenberg was one of 12 performers in JOHN GIORNO's first recording, a reading of Giorno's "Pornographic Poem" (Giorno 166). However, according to Giorno, it was not in the realm of performance that Rauschenberg "strongly influenced" him, but rather in the transformation of "found" materials (160). While Rauschenberg himself grew more distant from the circle of New York School poets—particularly after he moved his studio to Florida in 1970—his approach to "collaborating with materials" (Tomkins 204, 232) remained influential. TONY TOWLE dedicated his poem "Random (Re-arrangeable) Study for *Views*" (1976) to Rauschenberg, and MARJORIE WELISH chose the phrase "Collaborating with Materials" to designate a section of her collection *The Annotated "Here"* (2000).

Bibliography

Ashbery, John. "Joseph Cornell" (1967). In *Reported Sightings: Art Chronicles, 1957–1987*. Edited by David Bergman. Cambridge, Mass.: Harvard University Press, 1991, 13–18.

Berkson, Bill. "A New York Beginner" (1998). In *The Sweet Singer of Modernism and Other Art Writings, 1985–2003*. Jamestown, R.I.: Qua Books, 2003, 255–264.

Cage, John. "On Robert Rauschenberg, Artist, and His Work" (1961). In *Silence: Lectures and Writings* (1961). Reprint, Middletown, Conn.: Wesleyan University Press, 1973, 98–108.

Giorno, John. Interview by Nicholas Zurbrugg. In *Art, Performance, Media: 31 Interviews*. Minneapolis: University of Minnesota Press, 2004, 156–171.

Koch, Kenneth. *The Construction of Boston* (1962). In *The Gold Standard: A Book of Plays*. New York: Knopf, 1998, 47–64.

O'Hara, Frank. "Bob Rauschenberg" (1955). In *What's with Modern Art?* Edited by Bill Berkson. Austin, Tex.: Mike & Dale's Press, 1999, 20.

———. *The Collected Poems*. Rev. ed. Edited by Donald Allen. Berkeley: University of California Press, 1995.

Tomkins, Calvin. "Robert Rauschenberg." In *The Bride and the Bachelors; Five Masters of the Avant-Garde*. New York: Penguin, 1976, 189–237.

Towle, Tony. "Random (Re-arrangeable) Study for *Views*" (1976). In *The History of the Invitation: New & Selected Poems, 1963–2000*. Brooklyn, N.Y.: Hanging Loose Press, 2001, 160–161.

Welish, Marjorie. "Collaborating with Materials." In *The Annotated "Here" and Selected Poems*. Minneapolis, Minn.: Coffee House Press, 2000, 33–42.

Red Robins, The Kenneth Koch (1975)

First published in 1975, KENNETH KOCH'S extravagant novel *The Red Robins* epitomizes the NEW YORK SCHOOL poet's idiosyncratic sense of humor. The book's eponymous heroes are a group of young airplane pilots searching for the mythical Asian city of Tin Fan, with the assistance of the President and Santa Claus. The latter is on a mission to defeat his archrival, the Easter Bunny, who is aligned with villainous forces (including Dr. Pep and Dracula) intent on diverting the Red Robins from their goal. Koch introduces an array of offbeat characters, such as Mike the Tiger and Jim the Plant, to give the story a kind of ironic naïveté.

Although the novel is written primarily in prose, it incorporates an eclectic mix of other literary FORMS, such as the sonnet, haiku, and popular song. Likewise, the tone of the book is quite fluid, routinely switching from weepy, overwrought melodrama to aphoristic New Age pseudo-wisdom (led by the "celebrated Asian philosopher," Ni Shu) to comic strip action-adventure. This last GENRE probably receives the greatest stress in the novel, and it is the one most likely to upset the academic poets satirized in Koch's most famous poem, "FRESH AIR" (1956). Whimsical and freewheeling in its use (and abuse) of popular culture, *The Red Robins* shows the influence of rock singers such as The Beatles and Cat Stevens and writers like Kurt Vonnegut, Jr., J. R. R. Tolkien, and Ken Kesey.

Muted political overtones surface throughout this Vietnam-era novel, with jabs at American arrogance and misguided paternalism, but these are never more than passing concerns for Koch, who consciously avoids the use of symbolism and "deeper meaning." In this respect his approach resembles the playful experiments of the dadaists (see DADA AND SURREALISM).

In 1977 Koch adapted his novel into a stage play, which was first produced at Guild Hall in East Hampton and then in NEW YORK CITY's Theater at St. Clement's. Both productions were directed by Don Sanders and the second featured a set designed by artists Rory McEwen, JANE FREILICHER, Red Grooms, ALEX KATZ, and Roy Lichtenstein. The poet was present for all of the rehearsals and perpetually revised the script in conjunction with the director. The play is very similar to its source in terms of plot, but it is much shorter and written almost exclusively in verse.

Bibliography

Dickison, Steve. "Kenneth Koch: A Partial Bibliography." *Jacket* 15 (December 2001). Available online. URL: http://www.jacketmagazine.com/15/index.html. Accessed December 19, 2008.

Koch, Kenneth. *The Red Robins*. New York: Random House Trade Paperbacks, 1975.

———. *The Red Robins: A Play*. New York: Theatre Arts Journal Publications, 1979.

Review of *The Red Robins*. *Choice* (Fall 1976): 1,572.

Weatherford, John. Review of *The Red Robins*. *Library Journal* (May 15, 1980): 1,182.

Reed, Ishmael (1938–)

Born in Tennessee and raised in Buffalo, New York, Ishmael Reed participated in the UMBRA workshop in NEW YORK CITY and later in the POETRY PROJECT AT ST. MARK'S CHURCH IN-THE-BOWERY. Best known for his GENRE-bending novels, Reed has published a prolific body of work over more than four decades. In addition to the novel *Mumbo Jumbo* (Doubleday, 1972), a canonical work of African-American literature, Reed has published volumes of poetry, plays, and essays and edited several anthologies. Although his relationship with the NEW YORK SCHOOL and New York City may be described as ambivalent, Reed, like many members of the Umbra workshop, developed as a writer there, refining the style and ambition he later carried west.

Reed became an active member in Umbra soon after arriving in New York City in 1962. His relationships with authors like CALVIN HERNTON, DAVID HENDERSON, Joe Johnson, Steve Cannon, and TOM DENT proved valuable and productive. As the Umbra workshop evolved into the BLACK ARTS MOVEMENT and as the philosophy of Black Power grew in influence, Reed developed independently of many of his colleagues, remaining occasionally isolated during a decade of profound division over definitions of the "black aesthetic." While many black authors and artists left the Lower East Side as a gesture of black separatism in the mid-1960s, Reed remained active Downtown, while simultaneously editing a black weekly newspaper, the *Advance*, in Newark, New Jersey.

In 1965 Reed appeared with Carla Blank in the play *Black* at the Bridge Theater on St. Mark's Place. In the same year he helped found and also name the *East Village Other* (Reed, interview 276)—though the naming honor has also been claimed for TED BERRIGAN (Padgett 85). The first issue of the paper (October 1965) carried Reed's account of the fight at CAFÉ LE METRO involving some of the Umbra poets that prompted a search for a new venue for poetry readings and ultimately led to the founding of the Poetry Project (Kane 55). In 1966 Reed ran the first FICTION workshop at the Poetry Project, but "there's no record of that," he has observed critically, because "black people have been completely excised out of the 1960s history" of avant-garde and counterculture (Reed, interview 276–277).

Reed's history as a fiction writer remains more visible, since it is connected from the beginning with mainstream publishers. On the recommendation of Langston Hughes (1902–67), the firm of Doubleday took an interest in Reed's work and published his first novel, *The Free-Lance Pallbearers* in 1967. However, reviewers "missed the allusions," according to LORENZO THOMAS, preferring to place a book by a black man in the context not of literary tradition but of black experience—"dada in the housing projects," as Thomas characterized the reaction (Kane 86). Both Reed and Thomas left New York around the same time, Reed in 1967 for California, Thomas in 1968 for service in the navy and eventually residence in Texas, but their continued interaction testifies to the importance of early Umbra contacts for both men. Reed's second novel, *Yellow Back Radio Broke Down* (Doubleday, 1969), takes its title from Thomas's poem "Modern Plumbing Illustrated" (Zamir 1,234 note 113). Thomas reviewed Reed's third novel, *Mumbo Jumbo*, in the *Village Voice* (15 March 1973). Reed published Thomas's collection *The Bathers* in 1981 as part of his series of "I. Reed" books.

Reed's first collection of poetry was a small-press production, *catechism of d neoamerican hoodoo church* (1970), published in London in Paul Breman's Heritage series of black poetry but distributed in the United States through the Broadside Press in Detroit, Michigan, a leading outlet for the Black Arts Movement. The University of Massachusetts Press published *Conjure: Selected Poems, 1963–1970* (1972), and a trade publication soon followed, *Chattanooga* (Random House, 1973). Ten years elapsed between *Secretary to the Spirits* (NOK, 1978) and *New and Collected Poems* (Atheneum, 1988), which has been updated in several editions. Elliptical and elusive, Reed's poetry resembles his fiction in its consistent use of historical and literary references, its comic timing, and its conscious allusions to African-American traditions and forms. Despite these similarities, however, his poetry is distinctive for its autobiographical use of the first person and its reliance on condensed, musical messages in place of longer narratives. Both of these qualities call to mind the voices of first- and second-generation New York School poets such as KENNETH KOCH and ED SANDERS.

Bibliography

Kane, Daniel. *All Poets Welcome: The Lower East Side Poetry Scene in the 1960s.* Berkeley: University of California Press, 2003.

Padgett, Ron. *Joe: A Memoir.* Minneapolis, Minn.: Coffee House Press, 2004.

Reed, Ishmael. Interview by Shamoon Zamir (1988). In *Conversations with Ishmael Reed*, edited by Bruce Dick and Amritjit Singh, 271–302. Jackson: University Press of Mississippi, 1995.

———. *New and Collected Poems, 1964–2007.* New York: Thunder's Mouth, 2007.

———. *The Reed Reader.* New York: Basic Books, 2000.

———. *Shrovetide in Old New Orleans.* Garden City, N.Y.: Doubleday, 1978.

Zamir, Shamoon. "The Artist as Prophet, Priest and Gunslinger: Ishmael Reed's Cowboy in the Boat of Ra." *Callaloo* 17, no. 4 (Autumn 1994): 1,205–1,235.

Richie, Eugene (1951–   )

Eugene Richie writes intimate collagist poetry that celebrates the humor, surprise, grit, and beauty so essential to the NEW YORK SCHOOL sensibility. He details earthly life, layering familiar and miraculous sights and language like sea glass into poems, recalling JOSEPH CORNELL's shadowboxes: "Are these the turns and twists of fate, / or the way back to the garden of Eden, / that shopping mall on the side of the expressway?" ("Lights on the Sound," *Island Light* 95).

Born in Winona, Minnesota, Richie earned a B.A. in English at Stanford University (1974), where he studied with Al Young, David MacDonald, Rod Taylor, and Donald Davie; befriended Belle Randall; and published *Disciplines* (1974) with Jack Kenealy. For his poetry M.F.A. at Columbia University (1974–76) he worked with David Ignatow, Richard Eberhardt, Mark Strand, Galway Kinnell, and Manuel Puig. He also studied with Mark Mirsky and JOEL OPPENHEIMER at City College, in New York, and edited *City Magazine* and *Gnosis Anthology*. He has translated, with Raimundo Mora, works by Jaime Manrique, Isaac Goldemberg, and Matilde Daviu. He and ROSANNE WASSERMAN founded GROUNDWATER PRESS in 1974, married in 1977, and had a son, Joseph, in 1990. Richie participated in JOHN ASH's "Ash Wednesday" workshops and developed funding for Marc Cohen and Susan Baran's Intuflo Reading Series, held in a Columbus Avenue hardware store. He also published, through Groundwater, chapbooks of Intuflo readers, with covers by New York artists.

After earning a comparative literature doctorate (New York University, 1987), he published *Moiré* (1989), *Island Light* (1998), and *Place du Carousel* (2001). He was JOHN ASHBERY's literary secretary from 1984 to 2004 and has edited Ashbery's *Selected Prose*. A trustee of Ashbery's Flow Chart Foundation, Richie currently leads poetry seminars and is the director of writing at Pace University, where he is a colleague of CHARLES NORTH and Thomas Breidenbach.

Richie's work, which Ashbery calls "truly romantic poetry," depicts "the landscape of love we all carry around with us, that we use to accost, identify and finally to understand the 'real' one yapping at our ankles" (*Moiré* iv). Influences include John Keats, Friedrich Hölderlin, Novalis, Rainer Maria Rilke, Wallace Stevens, Marianne Moore, ELIZABETH BISHOP, JAMES SCHUYLER, ANN LAUTERBACH, and James Tate. In "No Rhyme nor Reason," he asks, "Have you already talked to the one you love / Or will the afternoon slip away again?" (*Moiré* 1). As in "No Reservations," exceptional generosity of spirit prevails: "This is for you. / It's the best I have in the world" (*Island Light* 47).

Bibliography

Richie, Eugene. *Island Light.* New York: Painted Leaf Press, 1998.

———. *Moiré.* Introduction by John Ashbery. New York: Groundwater Press/Intuflo Editions, 1989.

Richie, Eugene, et al., eds. *Gnosis Anthology of Contemporary American and Russian Literature and Art.* 2 vols. New York: Gnosis Press, 1982; Moscow: Medusa Press, 1994.

Richie, Eugene, with Jack Kenealy. *Disciplines.* Introduction by Al Young. San Jose: Calif.: Globe Press, 1974.

Richie, Eugene, with Rosanne Wasserman. *Place du Carousel.* Art by Antanas Andziulis. Vilna, Lithuania: Zilvinas & Daiva Publications, 2001.

Rivers, Larry (Irving Grossberg) (1923–2002) *artist*

More than any other painter of the second-generation NEW YORK SCHOOL, Larry Rivers approached the canvas as "an arena in which to act," the scene that HAROLD ROSENBERG assigned to "ACTION PAINTING" (25). Never content with any one scene, however, Rivers played a dynamic role in the interaction between painting and New York School poetry.

"Larry Rivers" was the stage name he took as a JAZZ saxophonist during the 1940s; he had been born in the Bronx, New York, to an immigrant Jewish family named Grossberg, who named their son Yitzroch Loiza, later changed to Irving. Fellow musician Jack Freilicher and his wife, JANE FREILICHER, introduced him to painting, more of a "class" act than jazz, Rivers quickly intuited. Class also attached to Rivers's first impressions of FRANK O'HARA, both for his HOMOSEXUAL style and his Harvard background. However, by the time they met in 1950, Rivers had already acquired the credentials he needed for success in the art world, having studied with Hans Hofmann, toured the museums in Paris, and attracted favorable notice from CLEMENT GREENBERG. Greenberg recommended that JOHN BERNARD MYERS recruit Rivers for the new TIBOR DE NAGY GALLERY. His first show there was in 1951, the same year Tibor de Nagy Editions published O'Hara's first book, *City Winter,* with drawings by Rivers.

Over the years Rivers's artwork appeared with other texts by O'Hara: as the set for the ARTISTS' THEATRE production of *TRY! TRY!* (1953), which O'Hara rewrote out of gratitude for Rivers's efforts; as drawing fully integrated with writing in *Stones* (1957), the only instance of true COLLABORATION that O'Hara felt he had undertaken (O'Hara, *Standing Still* 4); and as the cover for *Second Avenue* (1960), a poem in which O'Hara provides a glimpse of Rivers at work as a sculptor. As a writer, Rivers collaborated with O'Hara on an unproduced play, *Kenneth Koch: A Tragedy* (ca. 1954), and on the art-world spoof, "How to Proceed in the Arts" (1961). According to O'Hara, Rivers also wrote "good poems of a diaristic (boosted by surrealism) nature" (*Standing Still* 172). If this description also fits O'Hara's poetry, it is because a shared view of art as "a diary of . . . experience" (O'Hara, *Standing Still* 171) connects Rivers and O'Hara, as it connects their art and lives. For instance, Rivers's painting *The Studio* (1956) documents his "Bohemian household," as O'Hara called it, in all its "staggering complexity" (*Standing Still* 173), with images of Rivers himself; his two sons, Joseph and Steven; his mother-in-law, Berdie; his ex-wife, Augusta; and O'Hara. O'Hara's volume *Meditations in an Emergency* (1957) charts a brief love affair between O'Hara and the bisexual Rivers in 1954, from declaration ("To the Harbormaster") to dissolution, the "emergency" referred to in the title poem. In life, Rivers appears to have been more committed to the "I do this, I do that" principle articulated by O'Hara (*Collected Poems* 341) than O'Hara himself wanted to be. Responding to critics who have read the unevenness of his art as a sign of lack of commitment, Rivers explained, "I go from this to that, and why be ashamed of it? It seems to me this is the human experience" (Kimmelman B11).

A more public dimension of the human experience connects Rivers and KENNETH KOCH, the New York School poet to whom Rivers was closest, after O'Hara. Rivers achieved notoriety in the New York art world with his painting *Washington Crossing the Delaware* (1953), purchased by the Museum of Modern Art but vilified by old guard abstract expressionists as a regression to representational painting in its stalest "academic" mode, history painting. While O'Hara responded to the "intimate" emotion Rivers had uncovered beneath the historic icon (*Collected Poems* 234), Koch reproduced the icon in deliberately flat prose in his play GEORGE WASHINGTON CROSSING THE DELAWARE (1962), dedicated to Rivers. In treating this theme both Koch and Rivers intended parody, in part, but both also found serious inspiration in the grand scale that history painting provided Rivers, whose further exploration of the GENRE ranged from a *History of the Russian Revolution* (1965) to a *History of Matzo: The Story of the Jews* (1984–85). Starting with *New York, 1950–1960,* Rivers and Koch collaborated on a series of POEM-PAINTINGs that enlarge personal history to epic scale. Koch drew on the epic tradition in literature in his novel *The* RED ROBINS (1975) and in his epic compilation SEASONS ON EARTH (1987), both published with covers designed by Rivers. With regard to parody both Koch and Rivers have been identified with the spirit of POP ART on the basis of their appropriation of imagery from mass culture. "Portions of Camel Cigarette packs, the front grill of a 1960 Buick, French Money, Rembrandt's Syndics of the Drapery Guild from Dutchmasters Cigars, Vocabulary Lessons, A Menu, Playing Cards, etc." appear in Rivers's own inventory of such images in his work. However, he makes it clear that he wants his treatment of these images to turn the viewer toward his real subject: "I hope you feel a thrill and think about something different and then maybe think about Art and Me" ("Statement" 103).

Bibliography

Ashbery, John. "Larry Rivers" (1979). In *Reported Sightings: Art Chronicles, 1957–1987.* Edited by David Bergman. Cambridge, Mass.: Harvard University Press, 1991, 217–220.

———. "Larry Rivers Was Dying. He Asked to See Friends" (2002). In *Selected Prose.* Edited by Eugene Richie. Ann Arbor: University of Michigan Press, 2004, 286–290.

Gruen, John. *The Party's Over Now: Reminiscences of the Fifties.* Wainscott, N.Y.: Pushcart Press, 1989.

Kimmelman, Michael. "Larry Rivers, Artist with an Edge, Dies at 78," *New York Times,* 16 August 2002, pp. B1, B11.

Koch, Kenneth. "Collaborating with Painters" (1993). In *The Art of Poetry: Poems, Parodies, Interviews, Essays, and Other Work.* Ann Arbor: University of Michigan Press, 1996, 168–175.

———. *George Washington Crossing the Delaware* (1962). In *Bertha and Other Plays.* New York: Grove, 1966, 43–66.

Myers, John Bernard. *Tracking the Marvelous: A Life in the New York Art World.* New York: Random House, 1983.

O'Hara, Frank. *The Collected Poems.* Rev. ed. Edited by Donald Allen. Berkeley: University of California Press, 1995.

———. *Standing Still and Walking in New York.* Edited by Donald Allen. San Francisco: Grey Fox, 1983.

O'Hara, Frank, and Larry Rivers. "How to Proceed in the Arts" (1961). In *Art Chronicles, 1954–1966,* by Frank O'Hara, 92–98. Rev. ed. New York: Braziller, 1990.

———. "Kenneth Koch: A Tragedy." In *Amorous Nightmares of Delay: Selected Plays,* by Frank O'Hara, 121–132. Baltimore, Md.: Johns Hopkins University Press, 1997.

Rivers, Larry. "Larry Rivers: 'Why I Paint As I Do'" (1959). In *Art Chronicles, 1954–1966,* by Frank O'Hara, 106–120. Rev. ed. New York: Braziller, 1990.

———. "Life Among the Stones." *Location* (Spring 1963): 90–98.

———. "Six Poems." *Locus Solus,* nos. 3–4 (Winter 1962): 38–48.

———. "Speech Read at Frank O'Hara's Funeral, Springs, Long Island, July 27, 1966." In *Homage to Frank O'Hara,* edited by Bill Berkson and Joe LeSueur, 138. Bolinas, Calif.: Big Sky, 1988.

———. "Statement" (1963). In *Pop Art Redefined*, edited by John Russell and Suzi Gablik, 103–104. New York: Praeger, 1969.

Rivers, Larry, and David Hockney. "Beautiful and Interesting." *Art and Literature* 5 (Summer 1965): 94–117.

Rivers, Larry, with Carol Brightman. *Drawings and Digressions*. New York: Clarkson N. Potter, 1979.

Rivers, Larry, with Arnold Weinstein. *What Did I Do? The Unauthorized Biography*. New York: HarperCollins, 1992.

Rose, Barbara, et al. *Larry Rivers: Art and the Artist*. Exhibit catalog. Boston: Little, Brown; Washington, D.C.: Corcoran Gallery of Art, 2002.

Rosenberg, Harold. "The American Action Painters" (1952). In *The Tradition of the New*. 1960. Reprint, New York: Da Capo, 1994, 23–39.

Schjeldahl, Peter. "At the Mad Fringes of Art." *New York Times Book Review*, 18 November 1979, 7, 38.

———. "Larry Rivers: 'Achingly Erratic,'" *New York Times*, 27 December 1970, p. 85.

Schuyler, James. "Larry Rivers" (1962). In *Selected Art Writings*. Edited by Simon Pettet. Santa Rosa, Calif.: Black Sparrow, 1998, 188–190.

Rocks on a Platter Barbara Guest (1999)

The title of BARBARA GUEST's *Rocks on a Platter* recalls Wallace Stevens's "The Planet on the Table" (1950). In each case the poet offers an image of the poem itself as a combination of nature and artifice, and the specific items combined are chosen for their incongruity, lending an air of surrealism. Going beyond the presentation of an image of the poem, the text of *Rocks on a Platter* embodies in poetic FORM an entire theory of poetry. In this respect it is comparable to Stevens's "Notes Toward a Supreme Fiction" (1942), a text on which Guest comments explicitly in her essay "Poetry the True Fiction."

The immediate precursors of *Rocks on a Platter* are two poems by Guest: "Others" (1994), the first poem Guest wrote after relocating from the East to the West Coast, and "Startling Maneuvers" (1997), written as a contribution to a birthday celebration for the French poet Anne-Marie Albiach. As the title suggests, "Others" is about the poet's ability to identify with other selves, and to produce other, fictive selves in the course of writing a poem. Guest

had in mind John Keats's assertion that the poet "has no Identity—he is continually in for—and filling some other Body" (338). The phrase "fills some other Body," in fact, concludes section 3 of *Rocks on a Platter* (34), a section that consists entirely of the text of "Others" as it was published in *Avec* in 1995. Earlier sections of *Rocks on a Platter* identify the theme of self in poetry more directly: "the moss of subjectivity" (section 1, 11), "remnant of self" (section 2, 16). At the end of section 3 Keats's image of filling another body marks a stage in the progressive absorption of such ideas into the form, the body, of the poem itself, a process that culminates in section 4 in repeated references to the body of the dolphin, for whom "what occurs [is] absorbed in the skin" (41). In "Poetry the True Fiction" Guest writes of measuring the life of a poem by "the vibrancy of its skin" (30). In *Rocks on a Platter* we can measure the vibrancy that Guest achieves through the image of the dolphin by comparing the function of absorption as embodied in the dolphin's skin and as abstracted in the epigraph to section 4, quoted from T. W. Adorno's *Aesthetic Theory*: "The Moment a limit is posited it is overstepped, and that against which the limit was established is absorbed" (35; Adorno 6).

Evidence provided by Robert Kaufman from earlier versions of the poem suggests that another quotation from Adorno has been absorbed in the final version into the single word *mimesis*, appearing just above the quotation from Keats at the end of section 3. The concept of *mimesis*, central to the Western tradition of aesthetic theory, is often reduced to the simple notion of imitation as the function of art, the grounds for realism. However, following Adorno, in the passage Guest originally quoted (Adorno, 54), Guest connects mimesis with magic, which operates in the belief that imitation of an object in nature is equivalent to becoming that object: "hawk chin / you are also a hawk," to cite one instance of this equation in *Rocks on a Platter* (24). The poet's ability to identify with other beings is an extension of this principle, and it imbues poetry with an irremediable magical quality. At the same time, and still in agreement with Adorno, Guest recognizes that magic belongs to the past; she spells the word in archaic form, *magick*, and sets it in opposition to "the empirical sun" (18).

Caught in the tension between magic and empiricism, "art threatens to be pulled apart," according to Adorno (54). Guest registers that threat in the degree to which her poem appears to have been pulled apart already, to exist as merely a jumble of fragments. Nevertheless, her gamble is that the reader will experience the pull in another direction, into the poem, the direction taken initially by the author in the act of composition. "A Reverie on the Making of a Poem" opens with a description of this pull, as a sensation both on the physical and the metaphysical, or magical, plane: "*pull in the composition* physical—remember, a contradictory tug, phantom-like." Under the guise of "solid objects," on the one hand, and "invisibility," on the other hand, the same forces are at work in a passage from "A Reverie" that found its way into *Rocks on a Platter* (16). Here the forces seem to combine to encourage a "spectacular jump" (16) or "leap" (7), on which Guest has commented: "That's taking chances, and writing that doesn't take a chance isn't worth the old-fashioned—I remember my father's saying 'It's not worth a tinker's damn'— and he said that in North Carolina" ("A Talk" 10).

Bibliography

Adorno, Theodor W. *Aesthetic Theory*. Edited by Gretel Adorno and Rolf Tiedemann. Translated by Robert Hullot-Kentor. Minneapolis: University of Minnesota Press, 1997.

Guest, Barbara. "Others." *Avec* 9 (1995): 21–32.

———. "Poetry the True Fiction." In *Forces of Imagination: Writing on Writing*. Berkeley, Calif.: Kelsey Street Press, 2003, 26–32.

———. "A Reverie on the Making of a Poem." *American Letters and Commentary* 10 (1998): 79–83.

———. *Rocks on a Platter*. Hanover, N.H.: University Press of New England/Wesleyan University Press, 1999.

———. "Summon Song (from *Others*)." *American Letters and Commentary* 7 (1995): 21.

———. "A Talk on 'Startling Maneuvers.'" *Poetry Project Newsletter* 172 (December 1998–January 1999): 8, 10.

Kaufman, Robert. "A Future for Modernism: Barbara Guest's Recent Poetry." *American Poetry Review* (July–August 2000): 11–16.

Keats, John. Letter to Richard Woodhouse. October 27, 1818. *The Selected Poetry of John Keats*. Edited by Paul de Man. New York: Signet—New American Library, 1966, 337–338.

Lundquist, Sara. "Dolphin Sightings: Adventures in Reading Barbara Guest." *How2* 1, no. 3 (2000). Formerly available online. URL: http://www.scc.rutgers.edu/however/v1_3_2000/current/readings/lundquist.html.

Qureshi, Ramez. Review of *Rocks on a Platter*. *Jacket* 10 (October 1999). Available online. URL: http://jacketmagazine.com/10/gues-r-by-q.html. Accessed December 19, 2008.

Waldrop, Rosmarie. "Guest's *Rocks on a Platter* and *Miniatures*." In *Dissonance (If You Are Interested)*. Tuscaloosa: University of Alabama Press, 2005, 121–122.

Rorem, Ned (1923–) *musician*

The leading composer of American "art song," Ned Rorem has frequently set texts by NEW YORK SCHOOL poets whom he has known personally. Nevertheless, he stands in ambivalent relation to their aesthetic and to the avant-garde with which they are identified. When JOHN BERNARD MYERS introduced FRANK O'HARA to Rorem at one of JOHN LATOUCHE's parties in 1952, O'Hara made the mistake of saying, "You're from Paris and I think [Pierre] Boulez is gorgeous" (Rorem, excerpt 39), referring to the French composer who had made serial or atonal MUSIC a touchstone of the contemporary avant-garde. Although Rorem had taken up temporary residence in Paris, it was not to ally himself with Boulez, whom he later characterized as "having radically constipated music for three decades" (*Setting the Tone* 166). Throughout this period Rorem remained committed to traditional tonal composition. That commitment cost him a place in the musical vanguard but did not lower his standing in the eyes of the poets, who after all were quite ready to embrace traditional figurative painters like FAIRFIELD PORTER and JANE FREILICHER when avant-garde painting was still defined by abstraction (Ross 205). From Rorem's perspective, the avant-garde poets were the ideal collaborators. "The best collaboration," he declared, "is between conservative and avant-garde, but when two artists of the same persuasion work together the result is redundant" (*Setting the Tone* 228).

Talented, beautiful, and *queer*—the term he prefers to "gay" (*Setting the Tone* 105)—Rorem had attracted the attention of PAUL GOODMAN as early as 1938, when Goodman was studying at the University of Chicago, in the city where Rorem was raised. When Rorem arrived in NEW YORK CITY in 1944 to continue musical studies, Goodman helped to provide entry into gay, artistic, and intellectual circles, which frequently intersected. For Myers, who sought to inject a bohemian tone into the Greenwich Village gay bar Mary's, Goodman and Rorem collaborated on raunchy blues songs (*Setting the Tone* 360). Goodman's more elevated poem, "The Lordly Hudson," served as the text for an art song by Rorem that was recognized by the Music Library Association as the best published song of 1948. Though traditional in FORM, the song is in the New York School spirit of boasting that New York can match the best that Paris has to offer, as Rorem suggested in the liner notes to *Rosalind Rees Sings Ned Rorem*. Rorem's residence in Paris from 1949 to 1958 appears less of a contradiction in the light of similar sojourns by the New York School poets, especially JOHN ASHBERY, as well as the poets' assimilation of French models into a distinctly American idiom. As the novelist Edmund White has remarked of Rorem, "He was able to import French culture while remaining a thoroughly American figure" (Keller 34).

Rorem began setting texts by New York School poets while living in Paris, when FOUR DIALOGUES FOR TWO VOICES AND TWO PIANOS (1954), based on texts by O'Hara, was commissioned for performance by the duo piano team of ARTHUR GOLD and ROBERT FIZDALE in dialogue with male and female vocalists (Gooch 244). This was the first of several quasi-operatic works that make up one GENRE of Rorem's New York School COLLABORATION, including *Miss Julie* (based on the August Strindberg play, with libretto by KENWARD ELMSLIE, 1965, 1979), *Hearing* (based on texts by KENNETH KOCH, 1966, 1976), and *Bertha* (based on a play by Koch, 1968, 1973). The other genre consists of individual songs or song cycles, including "For Poulenc" (on a poem by O'Hara, 1968), *SOME TREES* (on three poems by Ashbery, 1968), *Nantucket Songs* (including Ashbery and others, 1981), *The Schuyler Songs* (setting for orchestra based on eight poems by JAMES SCHUYLER, 1987), and *Another Sleep* (including Ashbery and others, 2002).

Although Rorem's success as a vocal composer has eclipsed his instrumental works, which are numerous, he received the Pulitzer Prize in 1976 for an orchestral suite, *Air Music*. Publication of his diaries, starting with *The Paris Diary* (1966), and essays, starting with *Music from Inside Out* (1967), has earned him a considerable reputation as a writer.

Bibliography

Gooch, Brad. *City Poet: The Life and Times of Frank O'Hara.* New York: Knopf, 1993.

Keller, Joanna. "His Masterpiece May Be Himself, Remade as Fiction," *New York Times,* 26 October 2003, section 2, p. 23ff.

Rorem, Ned. Excerpt from *The Final Diary* (1974). In *Homage to Frank O'Hara,* edited by Bill Berkson and Joe LeSueur, 39–40. Bolinas, Calif.: Big Sky, 1988.

———. *The Paris Diary and the New York Diary, 1951 to 1961.* New York: Da Capo, 1998.

———. *Rosalind Rees Sings Ned Rorem with the Composer at the Piano.* Sound recording, GSS 104. Saranac Lake, N.Y.: GSS, 1984.

———. *Setting the Tone: Essays and a Diary.* New York: Coward-McCann, 1983.

———. *War Scenes, Five Songs, Four Dialogues.* Donald Gramm, bass-baritone; Eugene Istomin, piano. Sound recording, PHCD 116. Cliffdale Park, N.J.: Phoenix USA, 1991.

———. *Women's Voices, Some Trees, The Nantucket Songs and Other Songs.* Various artists. Sound recording, CRI CD 657. New York: CRI, 1993.

Ross, Alex. "Musical Events: The Gentleman Composer: Eighty Years of Ned Rorem." *New Yorker,* 20 October 2003, 203–205.

Rosenberg, Harold (1906–1978) *art critic*

The critic Harold Rosenberg established the terms on which the NEW YORK SCHOOL poets engaged with contemporary painting and, more broadly, with postwar American society. Unlike rival critic CLEMENT GREENBERG, who emphasized formal features specific to the medium of painting, Rosenberg employed "the terminology of feeling" to evoke what painting shared with other aspects of modern culture—"with poetry, with history, and with politics" (Rosenberg quoted in Gruen 174). A poet himself, Rosenberg viewed painting as metaphorical action, the basis of what he famously dubbed "ACTION PAINTING." Although he shared Greenberg's background in the Marxism of the American avant-garde during the 1930s, Rosenberg began writing art criticism after World War II by rejecting the historical determinism to which Greenberg continued to cling. For Rosenberg, reflecting the philosophy of the French existentialists, the creative act was supremely an individual act. However, to perform such an act in an age threatened by conformity from both the Right and the Left was necessarily a form of political protest. With his words, "The existence of the highbrow has become a political issue in the United States," written in 1953, Rosenberg supplied a political framework for the New York School poetry featured in *Semi-Colon*, the broadside of the TIBOR DE NAGY GALLERY that JOHN BERNARD MYERS invited Rosenberg to introduce (Myers 147–148).

In the great breakthrough year for New York School painting, 1948, Rosenberg's presence was especially notable in connection with the painter Robert Motherwell (1915–91). They coedited a journal, *Possibilities*, so-named as an assertion of the artist's freedom "as the political trap seems to close around him" (Motherwell and Rosenberg 490). For a second issue of the journal, which was never published, Motherwell responded to a Rosenberg poem with a drawing in which he discovered the abstract motif that generated his *Elegy to the Spanish Republic* series, spanning Motherwell's career (Carmean). WILLEM DE KOONING, however, became the painter most closely identified with Rosenberg, both through the concept of action painting, for which de Kooning was the paradigm (Rosenberg, "De Kooning" 117), and through the DOWNTOWN MANHATTAN arts scene, in which Rosenberg and de Kooning, unlike Greenberg or Motherwell, were fully involved. This was the context in which the poets engaged with Rosenberg. For instance, at the artists' CLUB on Eighth Street in 1957, FRANK O'HARA participated in a panel, moderated by Rosenberg, on the topic "The Painter As His Own Poet" (Sandler 78–79). Rosenberg and O'Hara also shared the pages of the journal *It Is*, an outgrowth

of the Club. To the poets' journal LOCUS SOLUS (number 5, 1962), Rosenberg contributed, tellingly, a political essay, "Liberalism, Conservatism—and Literature." JAMES SCHUYLER reported that Rosenberg pressed him about this essay at a party in the HAMPTONS (Schuyler 139), another scene in which Rosenberg and his wife, May, played a prominent role as pioneer "colonizers."

To the younger poets who were drawn to the New York School during the 1960s, Rosenberg remained a presence, though at some distance. His tall form (over six feet) was easy to pick out on the street as he walked to and from his apartment on Tenth Street, just a few doors away from St. Mark's Church (Malanga n.p.). On the other hand, as "the guardian and protector of abstract expressionism," Rosenberg seemed determined to stand in the way of "newer trends in art," such as POP ART—a position for which TED BERRIGAN denounced him in a 1965 review in *Kulchur* (Berrigan 84). Feeling increasingly alienated from the artists' community, Rosenberg sought new audiences as a professor at the University of Chicago (starting in 1966) and as art critic for the *New Yorker* (starting in 1967). From the distance of time the poet and artist MARJORIE WELISH has passed favorable judgment on Rosenberg's legacy "as a model of the independent, imaginative, and intellectual critic at a time when not only our politics and our art but also our art criticism has become conservative and self-serving" (Welish 144).

Bibliography

Berrigan, Ted. Review of *The Anxious Object. Kulchur* 18 (Summer 1965): 84–85.

Carmean, E. A., Jr. "Robert Motherwell: The Elegies to the Spanish Republic." In *American Art at Mid-Century: The Subjects of the Artist,* by E. A. Carmean, Jr., and Eliza E. Rathbone, with Thomas B. Hess, Washington, D.C.: National Gallery of Art, 1978.

Gruen, John. *The Party's Over Now: Reminiscences of the Fifties.* Wainscott, N.Y.: Pushcart Press, 1989.

Malanga, Gerard. "The Poetry in Something." *Rain Taxi* (Summer 2004). Available online. URL: http://www.raintaxi.com/online/2004summer/malanga.shtml. Accessed December 19, 2008.

Motherwell, Robert, and Harold Rosenberg. "The Question of What Will Emerge Is Left Open." In

Theories of Modern Art: A Source Book by Artists and Critics, edited by Herschel B. Chipp, 489–490. Berkeley: University of California Press, 1971.

Myers, John Bernard. *Tracking the Marvelous: A Life in the New York Art World.* New York: Random House, 1983.

Rosenberg, Harold. "The American Action Painters" (1952). In *The Tradition of the New.* 1960. Reprint, New York: Da Capo, 1994, 23–39.

——. "De Kooning 1: 'Painting Is a Way'" (1963). In *The Anxious Object.* 1966. Reprint, Chicago: University of Chicago Press, 1982, 108–120.

Sandler, Irving. "Sweeping Up after Frank." In *Homage to Frank O'Hara,* edited by Bill Berkson and Joe LeSueur, 78–80. Bolinas, Calif.: Big Sky, 1988.

Schuyler, James. Letter to John Ashbery, December 1961. In *Just the Thing: Selected Letters of James Schuyler, 1951–1991.* Edited by William Corbett. New York: Turtle Point, 2004, 138–140.

Welish, Marjorie. "Harold Rosenberg: Transforming the Earth" (1985). In *Signifying Art: Essays on Art after 1960.* Cambridge: Cambridge University Press, 1999, 127–145.

Rosenthal, Bob (1950–)

Bob Rosenthal was recruited to the NEW YORK SCHOOL from his native CHICAGO, ILLINOIS, when TED BERRIGAN and ALICE NOTLEY arrived there in 1972. Though he was formally enrolled at the University of Illinois–Chicago, Rosenthal sat in on some of Berrigan's classes at Northeastern Illinois University. He remembers Berrigan teaching him to use a mimeograph machine, a skill Rosenthal soon applied in publishing *Milk Quarterly* out of Chicago and, later (1976–79), Frontward Books out of New York (Rosenthal, "Mimeography" 219). Berrigan recalls thinking "there's obviously a lot more to Bob Rosenthal / than meets the eye" after being introduced to Rosenthal's girlfriend, ROCHELLE KRAUT (Berrigan 534).

With Berrigan's encouragement, Rosenthal and Kraut moved to NEW YORK CITY in 1973, the year they were married. They settled on St. Mark's Place and were quickly caught up in the activities surrounding the POETRY PROJECT AT ST. MARK'S CHURCH IN-THE-BOWERY, at the time a scene of exciting convergence of BEAT and New York School

influence. Rosenthal became secretary to ALLEN GINSBERG in 1977 and continues to this day as trustee of the Allen Ginsberg Trust. While still in Chicago, Rosenthal had published two collections, *Morning Poems* (1972) and *Sweet Substitute* (1973), with the Yellow Press in Chicago, a spinoff of *Milk Quarterly.* In New York his first book publications were *Bicentennial Suicide* (Frontward Books, 1975), a "performance novel" written in COLLABORATION with BOB HOLMAN, whom he had met in Chicago; *Lies About the Flesh* (Frontward Books, 1977), a collection of poems; and *Cleaning Up New York* (Angel Hair, 1977), a prose narrative about his experiences in a part-time job, written in response to writing classes with both Francine du Plessix Gray, at City College, in New York, and BERNADETTE MAYER, at the Poetry Project. Later collections have appeared less frequently: *Rude Awakenings* (Yellow Press, 1982) and *Viburnum* (White Fields Press, 1994).

Rosenthal's poetry reflects the changing times during which it was written. Early work is personal in the New York School manner, peppered with references to fellow poet-friends and evoking "New York's mind" ("On Sarah Bernhardt's Birthday," 1974). "FMLN" (1986), registers political concerns with an explicitness typical of the 1980s, though still personally inflected. Rosenthal picks up on the language of his young son to conclude: "I sit in the land of the bad people & pay my dues." "Eleven Psalms" (2000) lifts the dilemma of being "happy in a world of pain" to a spiritual plane, reflecting the influence of Buddhist studies with Ginsberg. As Rosenthal summarizes the lesson: "Allen taught us to breathe in the poison and breathe it out again as nectar" (Allen Ginsberg Trust).

Bibliography

Allen Ginsberg Trust Web page. Available online. URL: http://www.inflightstudio.com/sites/ginsberg/index.php?page/about.

Berrigan, Ted. "Shelley" (1982). In *The Collected Poems of Ted Berrigan.* Edited by Alice Notley, Anselm Berrigan, and Edmund Berrigan. Berkeley: University of California Press, 2005, 534.

Rosenthal, Bob. Excerpt from *Cleaning Up New York.* In *The Angel Hair Anthology,* edited by Anne Waldman and Lewis Warsh, 495–501. New York: Granary Books, 2001.

———. Excerpt from "Eleven Psalms." In *Healing Poems* (2000). Available online. URL: http://sstoth0.tripod. com/healingpoems/id15.html. Accessed December 19, 2008.

———. Excerpt from "Mimeography: Friends Forever." In *A Secret Location on the Lower East Side: Adventures in Writing, 1969–1980*, edited by Steven Clay and Rodney Phillips, 219. New York: New York Public Library/Granary Books, 1998.

———. "FMLN." In *Out of This World: An Anthology of the St. Mark's Poetry Project, 1966–1991*, edited by Anne Waldman, 558. New York: Crown, 1991.

———. "On Sarah Bernhardt's Birthday." *Out There* 6 (1974): 63.

———. "True Reality Fiction" (1980). Audio recording. Internet Archive. Available online. URL: http://www.archive.org/details/Bob_Rosenthal_class_True_reality_fiction_August_1980_80 P134. Accessed December 19, 2008.

———. "Walking with Ted" and "Ted Dancing" (1984). In *Nice to See You: Homage to Ted Berrigan*, edited by Anne Waldman, 165–166. Minneapolis, Minn.: Coffee House Press, 1991.

Roussel, Raymond (1877–1933)
French poet, writer

Raymond Roussel was born into a wealthy family in Paris in 1877, and died in Palermo, Sicily, in 1933. His very peculiar poetry, novels, and plays influenced the work of various NEW YORK SCHOOL writers: KENNETH KOCH, JOHN ASHBERY, HARRY MATHEWS, TREVOR WINKFIELD, and RON PADGETT have all acknowledged the impact of Roussel's writings on their development, and all have published TRANSLATIONs of his texts. Most of these have been collected in *How I Wrote Certain of My Books*, edited by Winkfield (1995). Roussel's work falls into four distinct phases. At the age of 17 he experienced what he called *"la gloire,"* a conviction that he was destined to literary fame equal to that of Dante or Shakespeare. He set about writing an enormously long novel in verse called *La Doublure* (1897), most of which is devoted to describing in minute detail the costumes worn by revelers at a carnival in Nice. Its successor, *La Vue* (1904), presents just as meticulously a beach scene set in the lens of a penholder. While both anticipate the

methods of *nouveaux romanciers* such as of Alain Robbe-Grillet, they received little attention from Roussel's contemporaries.

Disappointed, Roussel turned to prose FICTION: His two novels, *Impressions d'Afrique* (1910) and *Locus Solus* (1914) were composed using a method based on puns that he kept secret until his death, only revealing it in the posthumously published *Comment j'ai écrit certains de mes livres* (1935; *How I Wrote Certain of My Books*). This method generated a series of narratives and inventions that are highly ingenious; the most celebrated, or notorious, is the statue of a Spartan helot fashioned from whalebones placed on a whalebone trolley that runs on tracks made of calves' lungs. Roussel, desperate for fame, had both novels dramatized and performed on the Parisian stage, where they were jeered at by audiences and derided by critics but championed by Roussel's only fans, the SURREALISTS. His two plays, *L'Étoile au front* (1925) and *La Poussière de soleils* (1927), fared no better, despite the enormous sums he lavished on sets, costumes, and actors. His final poem, *Nouvelles Impressions d'Afrique* (1932), took him 15 years to write and is perhaps the most singular of all his texts. It consists of four cantos in alexandrines, each made up of a single sentence interrupted by a bewildering number of parentheses and footnotes and illustrated by 59 woodcut prints of staggering banality.

Bibliography
Ford, Mark. *Raymond Roussel and the Republic of Dreams.* Ithaca, N.Y.: Cornell University Press, 2001.

Roussel, Raymond. *How I Wrote Certain of My Books.* Edited by Trevor Winkfield. Berkeley, Calif.: Exact Change, 1995.

Russian poetry

The NEW YORK SCHOOL poets' engagement with Russian literature is intense but narrowly focused on two modern poets, Boris Pasternak (1890–1960) and Vladimir Mayakovsky (1893–1930). The great 19th-century novelists are acknowledged in passing references, for instance, to Leo Tolstoy in KENNETH KOCH's "Aus Einer Kindheit" ("The maid read *Anna Karenina* and told us secrets"; 1962; *Collected Poems* 81) and to Fyodor Dostoyevsky in FRANK

O'HARA's "Lines Written in *A Raw Youth*" (1954; *Collected Poems* 177). However, Pasternak and Mayakovsky are the two Russian writers judged to be "still of our time" in Koch's "FRESH AIR" (1955; *Collected Poems* 123). The definition of "our time" is complicated by the fact that Walt Whitman was an important source for the "new FORMS" that Mayakovsky especially worked to import into Russian poetry ("Order No. 2 to the Army of the Arts," 1921), so to move into the future with Mayakovsky involved American poets in a reencounter with their own past. An additional complication, extended through O'Hara's passion for Russian MUSIC, was the romantic identification of Russia with a past that never was,

> last mystic land
> of the great split soul
>
> and the rite of spring ("A Poem About Russia," 1951; O'Hara, *Collected Poems* 51).

The Russian connection thus brings into focus a paradoxical combination of modernist zeal and romantic nostalgia that distinguishes New York School poetry at its origin.

The revolution of modernity was formally enacted in the Russian Revolution of 1917, which both Mayakovsky and Pasternak supported, the latter with more ambivalence than the former. The wholesale discarding of the old order raised a question about the continued relevance of poetry. Futurism, the movement with which Mayakovsky became identified, celebrated modern industry and portrayed the poet as the engineer of a new humanity: "Hearts are motors too. / The soul is a fine machine" ("The Worker Poet" 201). Pasternak resisted this assimilation, for which he won O'Hara's approval: "you sound above the factory's ambitious gargle. / Poetry is as useful as a machine!" ("Memorial Day 1950"; *Collected Poems* 18). While Pasternak inspires imagery of nature in O'Hara's work (for example, "Snapshot for Boris Pasternak," 1952), Mayakovsky provides means for treating the modern city. O'Hara connected "Second Avenue" (1953) with Mayakovsky, to whom the poem is dedicated, and WILLEM DE KOONING, because "they both have done works as big as cities where the life

in the work is autonomous (not about actual city life) and yet similar" (O'Hara, *Collected Poems* 497). For Mayakovsky, scale was as much a matter of the poet's persona as his subject; following Whitman, he developed a voice that preserved the tone of one-on-one conversation at that same time that it seemed to address multitudes, the "intimate yell" that JAMES SCHUYLER described as Mayakovsky's gift to O'Hara (O'Hara, *Collected Poems* vii). Similarly, O'Hara praised the balance of "intimacy" and "epic structure" in Pasternak's novel *Doctor Zhivago* (1957), which achieved a "perfect scale" that O'Hara associated with two 19th-century novels, one Russian (Mikhail Lermontov's *A Hero of Our Times*) and one French (Gustave Flaubert's *A Sentimental Education*) (O'Hara, *Collected Poems* 506).

Of the several poems by O'Hara that refer to Mayakovsky or Pasternak, the two that distill the essence of the relationship are "A True Account of Talking to the Sun at Fire Island" (1958; *Collected Poems* 306–307) and "Variations on Pasternak's 'Mein Liebchen, was willst du noch mehr?'" (1959; *Collected Poems* 339). "A True Account" is based on "An Extraordinary Adventure Which Happened to Me, Vladimir Mayakovsky, in a Summer Cottage" (1920), in which Mayakovsky addresses the Sun as a rival, in the manner of Whitman at the conclusion of section 24 of *Song of Myself*. Mayakovsky establishes terms of equality with the Sun by inviting "him" to tea, and they part with the assurance that their combined sources of energy, "an explosion of poetry and light," will endure "to the end of time—/and to hell with everything else!" (Mayakovsky, translated by Fagin 40). In his dialogue with the Sun, O'Hara achieves a comparable balance of the sublime and the colloquial but darkens the mood considerably by introducing at the end a mysterious "they" who call the Sun away and who, the Sun explains, are calling O'Hara, too. As in "A Step Away from Them" (1956), "they" are clearly the dead, whose presence orients O'Hara's poem toward a past that has already ended rather than toward Mayakovsky's open-ended future. These two moments combine in O'Hara's "variation" on Pasternak: "time moves, but is not moving" (*Collected Poems* 339). O'Hara feels he has moved on from mourning the death of VIOLET R. (BUNNY) LANG and entered a timeless moment in his love for Vincent Warren. The details of this poem seem further removed from the source in Pasternak than in the case of Mayakovsky, but in fact the combination of hopeful love and elegiac despair remains faithful not only to Pasternak but to Henrich Heine, the source of Pasternak's German title, which translates, "My love, what more do you desire?"

Mayakovsky died by his own hand in 1930, just before the official imposition of "socialist realism" under Joseph Stalin froze the possibility of creative expression in literature. Pasternak survived the period, which lasted through Stalin's death in 1953, by occupying himself mainly with TRANSLATION. His final years were embroiled in controversy centering on *Doctor Zhivago*, suppressed in Russia but translated in Europe (1957) and the United States (1958), and the award of the 1958 Nobel Prize in literature, which Pasternak declined in response to Soviet criticism. O'Hara and Koch sent off a telegram of congratulations for the Nobel Prize, without much hope that it would ever reach Pasternak (Koch, "Frank O'Hara" 209–210). In an essay on "Zhivago and His Poems," first published in the *Evergreen Review* in 1959, O'Hara defended Pasternak against charges from leftist critics that his novel betrayed the spirit of the Russian Revolution and specifically the embodiment of that spirit in Mayakovsky. Turning the tables on the critics, O'Hara argued that Mayakovsky, whom he identified with the character of Strelnikov in the novel, was reactionary in his romantic conception of life as "a landscape before which the poet postures," while Pasternak was more progressive in his identification of the conditions of life as "the very condition of his inspiration in a deeply personal way" (*Collected Poems* 503). This is the identification that made the work of JACKSON POLLOCK "an occasion for American culture," as O'Hara argued in his 1959 monograph on Pollock, which takes its epigraph from Pasternak's description of the composer Antonin Scriabin as an occasion for Russian culture (O'Hara, "Jackson Pollock" 12).

While O'Hara was engaged in his defense of Pasternak, Russian culture was experiencing a youth rebellion parallel to the movement in the United States that was popularly identified with Beat writers. Young Russian poets, most notably Yevgeny Yevtushenko (1933–), self-consciously drew inspiration from the BEATS, and the Beats in turn helped to introduce British and American readers to the "Red Cats," Russian poets, the title suggested by ALLEN GINSBERG for an anthology published by City Lights Books (1962) containing ANSELM HOLLO's translations of Yevtushenko, Andrei Voznesenski (1933–), and Mayakovsky's friend Semyon Kirsanov (1906–72). O'Hara dismissed these writers for producing "tiresome imitations of Mayakovsky" and issued an "Answer to Voznesensky & Evtushenko" (1963) that seemed also to announce an end to his love affair with Russian literature: "I do not love you any more since Mayakovsky died and Pasternak / theirs was the death of my nostalgia for your tired ignorant race" (*Collected Poems* 468). Nevertheless, enthusiasm for Mayakovsky in particular, inspired partly by O'Hara and partly by the "tiresome imitations" of the younger Russians, has persisted in the New York School (TED BERRIGAN, SOTÈRE TORREGIAN, BARBARA GUEST, RON PADGETT, LEE ANN BROWN). Poetry performance has been stimulated by Mayakovsky's declamatory style and by the works he composed for THEATER, such as *Mayakovsky: A Tragedy*, which BOB HOLMAN staged at St. Mark's Church in the late 1970s. ANNE WALDMAN, who recalls Berrigan pushing her to "be Mayakovsky" in her performance of poetry (Waldman 221), presented Mayakovsky's "Extraordinary Adventure" and O'Hara's "True Account" to a class at the NAROPA INSTITUTE in 1976. While she praised Russian poets in general, including Yevtushenko and Voznesenski, for being "tremendous orators" (Waldman 40), she specially commended O'Hara's poem for "its intimacy" (44).

Bibliography

Berrigan, Ted. "Homage to Mayakofsky" (1963). In *The Collected Poems of Ted Berrigan*. Edited by Alice Notley, Anselm Berrigan, and Edmund Berrigan. Berkeley: University of California Press, 2005, 659–660.

Brown, Lee Ann. "Mayakovsky." In *Polyverse*. Los Angeles: Sun & Moon, 1999, 35.

Cavanagh, Clare. "Whitman, Mayakovsky, and the Body Politic." In *Rereading Russian Poetry*, edited by Stephanie Sandler, 202–222. New Haven, Conn.: Yale University Press, 1999.

Guest, Barbara. "Eating Chocolate Ice Cream: Reading Mayakovsky" (1968). In *The Angel Hair Anthology*, edited by Anne Waldman and Lewis Warsh, 104–105. New York: Granary Books, 2001.

Heine, Heinrich. *Buch der Lieder: Die Heimkehr* 61: "Du hast Diamenten und Perlen." In *Sämtliche Werke*, vol. 1. Edited by Oskar Walzel. Leipzig, Germany: Insel, 1911, 139.

Koch, Kenneth. *Collected Poems*. New York: Knopf, 2005.

———. "Frank O'Hara and His Poetry." In *American Writing Today*, edited by Richard Kostelanetz, 201–211. Troy, N.Y.: Whitston, 1991.

Mayakovsky, Vladimir. "An Extraordinary Adventure." Read in Russian by Mayakovsky. Audio file. PennSound. Available online. URL: http://writing.upenn.edu/pennsound/x/Mayakovsky.html. Accessed December 19, 2008.

———. "An Extraordinary Adventure" (1920). Translated by Larry Fagin. In *Vow to Poetry: Essays, Interviews, and Manifestos*, edited by Anne Waldman, 37–40. Minneapolis, Minn.: Coffee House Press, 2001.

———. "Order No. 2 to the Army of the Arts" (1921). Translated by George Reavey. In *The Bedbug and Selected Poetry*. Edited by Patricia Blake. New York: Meridian, 1960, 144–149.

———. "The Worker Poet" (1918). Translated by Babette Deutsch. In *A Treasury of Russian Verse*, edited by Avrahm Yarmolinsky, 200–201. New York: Macmillan, 1949.

O'Hara, Frank. *Collected Poems*. Rev. ed. Edited by Donald Allen. Berkeley: University of California Press, 1995.

———. "Jackson Pollock" (1959). In *Art Chronicles, 1954–1966*. Rev. ed. New York: Braziller, 1990, 12–39.

Padgett, Ron. "Talking to Vladimir Mayakovsky." In *New and Selected Poems*. Boston: Godine, 1995, 4.

Pasternak, Boris. "Mein Liebchen, was willst du noch mehr?" (1923). In *Selected Poems*. Translated by J. M. Cohen. London: Ernest Benn, 1958, 11–12.

Schmidt, Paul. "Frank's Russia." In *Homage to Frank O'Hara*, edited by Bill Berkson and Joe LeSueur, 194–195. Bolinas, Calif.: Big Sky, 1988.

Shaw, Lytle. "Combative Names: Mayakovsky and Pasternak in the American 1950s." In *Frank O'Hara: The Poetics of Coterie*. Iowa City: University of Iowa Press, 2006, 115–150.

Torregian, Sotère. "After Mayakovsky" (1967). In *The Angel Hair Anthology*, edited by Anne Waldman and Lewis Warsh, 68–69. New York: Granary Books, 2001.

Waldman, Anne. *Vow to Poetry: Essays, Interviews, and Manifestos*. Minneapolis, Minn.: Coffee House Press, 2001.

Whitman, Walt. *Song of Myself*: Section 24. In *Leaves of Grass: Comprehensive Reader's Edition*. Edited by Harold W. Blodgett and Sculley Bradley. New York: Norton, 1965, 52–54.

S

Sala, Jerome (1951–)

Born and raised in CHICAGO, ILLINOIS, Jerome Sala was a pioneer of the performance poetry phenomenon in that city that was later to be known as the poetry slam. As early as 1980, according to a history of SLAM POETRY, "Sala constructed his own poetry competition based on a boxing match" (Heintz n.p.). An admirer of the public declamatory style of the Russian poet Vladimir Mayakovsky, Sala is connected to NEW YORK SCHOOL poetics through his wry wit and bold approach to the uses of popular culture. With ELAINE EQUI, he was also associated with the establishment of the 1980s punk poetry scene in Chicago, and with the poets DENNIS COOPER and MICHAEL LALLY, in Los Angeles.

According to NEW YORK CITY performance poet BOB HOLMAN, in 1979 TED BERRIGAN and ANNE WALDMAN donned boxing gloves in a poetry competition based on "rounds" (Heintz n.p.). Sala's first match was in 1980 with a local Chicago musician, Jimmy Desmond, who became rowdy when he lost the bout. Two days later the poet Al Simmons, who was later to found the Taos Poetry Circus, approached him to engage in a rematch with Desmond, which Sala also won. A series of matches organized by Simmons ensued, later to become the model for Marc Smith in developing the now-famous poetry slams in 1985, first at Chicago's Get Me High Lounge and later at the Green Mill Tavern (one of Al Capone's main hangouts in the 1920s) on Lawrence Avenue.

According to Sala, he did not participate in much poetry performance during the years 1981–84. Nevertheless, he continued to publish his work, and he grew in fame as an instigator of the punk poetry scene. In 1988 he moved with Equi to New York City to take a position in advertising, which he still holds. He also began the pursuit of a Ph.D. in critical theory at New York University.

Sala's first collection, *Spaz Attack* (Stare Press, 1980), contains the poem "I Beat Up Willem de Kooning," which opens with the surrealistic line: "no longer am I mystified as a cannibal who finds a toaster in the jungle." PETER SCHJELDAHL wrote of *Spaz Attack:* "May I call Sala an honorable hysteric? Whatever he is, he writes poetry of a wide-open, funny/horrifying, sneaky-serious sort that I haven't seen the like of in many years" (298).

Sala's other books are *I Am Not a Juvenile Delinquent* (Stare Press, 1985), *The Trip* (Highlander Press, 1987), *Raw Deal: New and Selected Poems* (Another Chicago Press, 1994), and *Look Slimmer Instantly* (Soft Skull Press, 2005). His work appears in numerous anthologies, including *Coming Attractions: An Anthology of American Poets in Their Twenties*, edited by Cooper (Little Caesar Press, 1980); *Up Late: American Poetry Since 1970*, edited by ANDREI CODRESCU (Four Walls, Eight Windows, 1987); and the *Oulipo Compendium* (Atlas Press, 1998), edited by HARRY MATHEWS.

Bibliography

Heintz, Kurt. "An Incomplete History of Slam." e-poets. network. Available online. URL: http://www.e-poets. net/library/slam/. Accessed December 19, 2008.

Schjeldahl, Peter. "Cabin Fever." *Parnassus* 9 (Spring–Summer 1981): 284–300.

Sanders, Ed (Edward Sanders) (1939–   )

Poet, novelist, activist, musician, and scholar, Ed Sanders is a second-generation NEW YORK SCHOOL author with close ties to the BEAT Generation and the countercultural movements of the 1960s. His genius for inventive bold satire and poetic craftsmanship and his ceaseless desire to integrate literature, performance, and history ensure his unique place among American authors of the past 40 years.

Born in Kansas City, Missouri, Sanders was president of his high school class and played football and basketball. His mother died when he was 17; he discovered ALLEN GINSBERG's *Howl* and JACK KEROUAC's *On the Road* shortly afterward and hitchhiked to NEW YORK CITY in spring 1958. Enrolling at New York University and majoring in Greek, he supported himself working nights at a Times Square cigar store. In 1961 he married the artist and writer Miriam Kittell.

In the same year Sanders was arrested, along with seven other antiwar protesters, for attempting to board a nuclear submarine in Groton, Connecticut. After refusing to pay a fine, he served time in jail, the inspiration for his *Poem from Jail* (City Lights, 1963). In 1962 Sanders began publishing *FUCK YOU: A MAGAZINE OF THE ARTS* in the basement office of Dorothy Day's *Catholic Worker.* The motto of *Fuck You* was "Total Assault on the Culture," and Sanders demonstrated his self-proclaimed slogan that he would "print anything." As Sanders distributed the magazine for free, *Fuck You* grew into one of the leading mimeographs then proliferating on the Lower East Side, eventually featuring some of the New York School's leading poets: FRANK O'HARA and JOHN ASHBERY, as well as Ginsberg and many others. Sanders published 13 issues of *Fuck You* until, in January 1965, police arrested him for obscenity charges related to the magazine and his experimental films *Amphetamine Head* and *Mongolian Cluster Fuck.* Sanders also started Fuck You Press, for which he edited the anthologies *Poems for Marilyn* (1962), *Despair: Poems to Come Down By* (1964), and *Bugger: An Anthology of Buttockry* (1964).

In 1964 Sanders opened the PEACE EYE BOOKSTORE in a former kosher butcher shop on East 10th Street and moved *Fuck You*'s printing operations there. Peace Eye became a meeting place for two generations of the New York School and, as Sanders described it, a "scrounge lounge" for the Lower East Side's alternative magazines. Peace Eye's catalogs have themselves become collector's items for such unusual features as the sale of the poet Ginsberg (not his books), at $1.5 million.

Sanders began his "folk-rock poetry satire group," The FUGS, in 1965, along with core members Tuli Kupferberg and Ken Weaver. A musical parallel to *Fuck You,* The Fugs released seven albums and toured extensively during 1965–70. In the bold satire of songs like "Kill for Peace" and the playful invention of "Slum Goddess," The Fugs experimented with MUSIC unplayable on radio. They performed on bills with Ginsberg, Country Joe and the Fish, the Mothers of Invention, Jimi Hendrix, Janis Joplin, The Doors, and Frank Zappa, among others. The Fugs' mixture of THEATER, protest, and shocking subject matter attracted a cult following to their festive, comic concerts, and they became the house band of the Players Theater on MacDougal Street. The Fugs occasionally reunite and tour. In 2003 Sanders produced their recording *The Final Fugs Album, Part One.*

Meanwhile, Sanders continued his career as a writer. His 1963 *Poem from Jail,* written on cigarette packs in an ancient Greek meter, introduces the technical proficiency, inventive wordplay, and politically charged subject matter that would become the hallmark of Sanders's poems. In 1965 he published PEACE EYE (Frontier Press), a collection of poems in which he refined his satirical impulses. The influences in these poems include CHARLES OLSON's "PROJECTIVE VERSE," KENNETH KOCH's wit, and Ginsberg's dramatic images. In 1967 Sanders and The Fugs brought protest poetry off the page, chanting, "Out, demons, Out!" during an anti–Vietnam War exorcism of the Pentagon. *Life* magazine featured Sanders on its cover, and Johnny Carson asked him onto his *Tonight Show,* an invitation rescinded when Sanders insisted The Fugs play "Kill for Peace." Sanders's participation in the peace demonstrations at the 1968 Democratic convention in CHICAGO, ILLINOIS, with its violent police attacks upon the protesters, led to his first novel *SHARDS OF GOD* (Grove, 1970), a satirical fantasy about the activities of the Youth International Movement, or Yippies, during the protests.

The Charles Manson cult's 1969 murders of Sharon Tate and others inspired Sanders to investigate Manson's appropriation of countercultural ideas, dress, language, and values for his own mad, violent purposes. Sanders penetrated Manson's interconnected communities, at times using disguises and assumed identities. His surprising discoveries of southern California's gothic underground societies produced the definitive book on the Manson killings, *The Family: The Story of Charles Manson's Dune Buggy Attack Battalion* (Dutton, 1971), which detailed how Manson ruled his group through terror, drugs, and intimidation.

In the early 1970s Sanders moved to Woodstock, New York. In 1972 he cowrote *Vote!* with fellow Yippies and former Chicago protesters Jerry Rubin and Abbie Hoffman. His literary reputation growing, in 1975 Sanders delivered a series of lectures called "Investigative Poetry" at the NAROPA INSTITUTE. The lectures, with the thesis that "poetry should again assume responsibility for the description of history" (*Investigative Poetry* 3), became a published manifesto. INVESTIGATIVE POETRY (City Lights, 1976) is an essential key to Sanders's work; it inspired several of his most ambitious and successful projects, including his series AMERICA: A HISTORY IN VERSE (Black Sparrow, 2000; Godine, 2004).

20,000 AD (North Atlantic Books, 1976) drew on Sanders's knowledge of Egyptian hieroglyphs and contained stirring elegies to the poets Olson and PAUL BLACKBURN. He then embarked on his four-volume autobiographical series TALES OF BEATNIK GLORY (Stonehill, 1975; Citadel Underground, 1990; Thunder's Mouth, 2004), about the Lower East Side during 1959–70. FAME AND LOVE IN NEW YORK (Turtle Island, 1980), a novel satirizing the New York art world, was followed by *The Z-D Generation* (Station Hill, 1981), a sequel to *Investigative Poetry*. Sanders's selected poems, *Thirsting for Peace in a Raging Century,* came out in 1988 (Coffee House Press). In 1993 he published HYMN TO THE REBEL CAFÉ (Black Sparrow), a collection of poetic reflections, personal meditations, and long poems that anticipate later investigative poetry books such as *Chekhov* (Black Sparrow, 1995), and *1968: A History in Verse* (Black Sparrow, 1997). In the new century, Sanders's literary production has accelerated impressively. The year 2000

alone saw his biography *The Poetry and Life of Allen Ginsberg* (Overlook), as well as volumes one and two of *America: A History in Verse* (Black Sparrow).

Over the past 40 years, Sanders has received numerous awards, honors, and distinctions, including the Frank O'Hara Prize (Modern Poetry Association, 1967), a Guggenheim Foundation Fellowship for poetry (1983–84), two National Endowment for the Arts fellowships (1966, 1987–88), and the American Book Award (1988) for *Thirsting for Peace in a Raging Century.* He is a member of the PEN board of governors.

While Sanders's reputation has never eclipsed those of more widely celebrated New York School or Beat authors, accomplishments like the dynamic *America: A History in Verse* confirm his importance to American literature. With an individual language attuned to the struggles of ordinary people and an extraordinary sense of the interrelationships among poetry, music, and social justice, Sanders creates in the bardic tradition of Walt Whitman a poet singing the narratives of a nation, with prophecy, melody, and urgency.

Bibliography

Horvath, Brooke, ed. Ed Sanders issue. *Review of Contemporary Fiction* 19, no. 1 (Spring 1999).

Sanders, Ed. *Investigative Poetry.* San Francisco: City Lights, 1976.

———. *Thirsting for Peace in a Raging Century: Selected Poems, 1961–1985.* Minneapolis, Minn.: Coffee House Press, 1987.

San Francisco Renaissance

Throughout the 1950s New York and San Francisco stood at opposite poles in the circuit of energy moving through contemporary poetry, with the Beat writers closing the circuit, so to speak, by their shuttling back and forth across the country. The "renaissance" in San Francisco is sometimes identified as a Beat phenomenon, but its separate treatment in DONALD M. ALLEN's *The NEW AMERICAN POETRY, 1945–1960* reflects important differences. As the term *renaissance* implies, the older bohemian tradition in San Francisco preserved a courtly atmosphere in which the BEATS, when they invaded, were barely tolerated. Starting in the 1940s the leaders of the San Francisco Renaissance exerted influence by holding court in the form of literary gatherings—Kenneth Rexroth (1905–82), the established elder, at his apartment in the city; Robert Duncan (1919–88) and Jack Spicer (1925–65) at a house in Berkeley that they shared with other aspiring writers—in the spirit of knights gathered at the round table. Poetry was the Holy Grail, always sought for but never finally achievable as an ideal FORM.

This air of medievalism was a major source of tension between the San Francisco poets and the resolutely modern poets of the NEW YORK SCHOOL, as ALLEN GINSBERG attempted to explain to Duncan in connection with a rebuff Duncan had received from FRANK O'HARA: O'Hara "felt any gesture he made was poetry, and poetry in that sense was totally democratic. So that there were no kings and queens of poetry. So when you wrote him, he saw you as the Queen of Poetry, giving him the scepter, and he said 'Well, I don't want a scepter from that old queen!'" (149). As Ginsberg implies, homosexual POLITICS was also a source of tension. Although Duncan and Spicer were gay, they did not import camp style into their poetry in the manner of the New York School. Privately, Spicer mocked JOHN ASHBERY's volume *Some Trees* (1956) as *Thumb Twees* (Ellingham 75). On the other hand, the elegiac poetry of their mutual acquaintance JOHN WIENERS moved both Spicer and O'Hara to tears on one occasion when the three men were together in BOSTON, MASSACHUSETTS (Wieners 64).

The famous evening in 1956 at the 6 Gallery, where Rexroth presided and Ginsberg gave his first public reading of "Howl," marks the arrival of the Beats on the San Francisco scene, but it also symbolizes aspects of the San Francisco Renaissance that connect it with the New York School. The fact that the event took place at an art gallery testifies to interaction between poetry and the visual arts that may appear in retrospect less significant in San Francisco than in New York, if only because New York painters have supplied the more recognizable points of reference. For instance, the reputation of Jess Collins, a painter who was Duncan's partner, has grown only gradually beyond the San Francisco Bay area. In the overview Rexroth contributed to the "San Francisco Scene" issue of *Evergreen Review*

(1957), Dylan Thomas, JACKSON POLLOCK, and Charlie Parker provide the coordinates for locating the scene on the map of contemporary aesthetics. The JAZZ musician Parker is relevant to the 6 Gallery reading as an instance of performance, "like a jam session," as JACK KEROUAC memorialized the occasion in *The Dharma Bums* (14). In this case the influence moved from San Francisco to New York, where coffeehouses like LES DEUX MÉGOTS and CAFÉ LE METRO offered opportunities for poets to perform on the model of North Beach venues like The Cellar, where Rexroth read to jazz accompaniment, or The Place, where Spicer promoted weekly Blabbermouth nights. Such performance caught on particularly with the second generation of the New York School, many of whom were exposed to the San Francisco scene firsthand at the BERKELEY POETRY CONFERENCE in 1965 or, in the case of LARRY FAGIN, HARRIS SCHIFF, and LEWIS WARSH, in the bars that served as Spicer's headquarters. A few years later poets migrating from both San Francisco and New York converged on the seaside community of BOLINAS, CALIFORNIA, where many took up extended residence.

With regard to poetic structure, the influence of the San Francisco Renaissance helped make "open form" the common currency of the New American Poetry. Duncan in particular promoted the views of CHARLES OLSON, whom Duncan had joined as a colleague at BLACK MOUNTAIN COLLEGE in 1955 and 1956. Spicer and his close friend Robin Blaser (1925–) applied the principle of "open form" to units larger than the individual poem in their concept of the "SERIAL POEM," which influenced efforts by many New York School writers to write in longer forms, as ANNE WALDMAN, for one, has acknowledged (xxiv). The related concept of "dictation," as Spicer applied it to the creative process, works like the New York School practices of COLLABORATION and appropriation to undermine traditional views of authorship.

Bibliography

Allen, Donald, and Warren Tallman, eds. *The Poetics of the New American Poetry.* New York: Gove, 1973.

Davidson, Michael. *The San Francisco Renaissance: Poetics and Community at Mid-Century.* Cambridge: Cambridge University Press, 1991.

Ellingham, Lewis, and Kevin Killian. *Poet Be Like God: Jack Spicer and the San Francisco Renaissance.* Hanover, N.H.: University Press of New England/Wesleyan University Press, 1998.

Ferlinghetti, Lawrence, and Nancy J. Peters. *Literary San Francisco.* San Francisco: City Lights/Harper & Row, 1980.

Ginsberg, Allen. *Allen Verbatim: Lectures on Poetry, Politics, Consciousness.* Edited by Gordon Ball. New York: McGraw-Hill, 1974.

Kerouac, Jack. *The Dharma Bums.* 1958. Reprint, New York: Penguin, 1986.

Rexroth, Kenneth. "San Francisco Letter." *Evergreen Review* 1, no. 2 (1957): 5–14.

Waldman, Anne. Introduction to *The Angel Hair Anthology.* New York: Granary Books, 2001, xix–xxvii.

Wieners, John. "Chop-House Memories." In *Homage to Frank O'Hara,* edited by Bill Berkson and Joe LeSueur, 64–66. Bolinas, Calif.: Big Sky, 1988.

San Remo

The San Remo, at 93 MacDougal Street, was an early haven for the bohemian subculture that flourished in Greenwich Village after World War II. Under proprietor Joe Santini, it was very much like other bars in (what was then) Little Italy, complete with pressed-tin ceiling, black-and-white tile floors, and wooden booths. Nevertheless, the bar's relatively tolerant acceptance of gays and interracial couples (not to mention women wearing jeans), made it attractive to avant-garde writers and artists. The San Remo was the inspiration for the "Black Mask" bar featured in JACK KEROUAC's interracial love story *The Subterraneans.* At one point in the book Kerouac zooms in on the ultimate hipster (based on his friend Bill Keck): "suddenly you'd see him in the Black Mask sitting there with head thrown back thin dark eyes watching everybody as if in sudden slow astonishment and 'Here we are little ones and now what my dears,' but also a great dope man, anything in the form of kicks" (4). Ron Sukenick summed up the San Remo as "an actual Village-Bohemian-literary-artistic-underground-mafioso-pinko-revolutionary-subversive-intellectual-existentialist-anti-bourgeois café" (19).

Although JACKSON POLLOCK could be seen there occasionally, the San Remo was "the literary bar" complementing "the artists' bar," the CEDAR STREET TAVERN, according to FRANK O'HARA ("Larry Rivers" 169). O'Hara met one of his literary heroes, PAUL GOODMAN, at the San Remo, though he was disappointed in Goodman's manner of maintaining himself at the center of an elite inner circle (Gooch 201). The poem "On the Way to the San Remo" (1954) typifies O'Hara's contrasting approach, weaving the destination seamlessly into the fabric of city life.

The San Remo is now called Carpo's Café, a coffeehouse that features live JAZZ.

Bibliography

Gooch, Brad. *City Poet: The Life and Times of Frank O'Hara.* New York: Knopf, 1993.

Kerouac, Jack. *The Subterraneans.* New York: Grove, 1958.

O'Hara, Frank. "Larry Rivers: A Memoir" (1965). In *Standing Still and Walking in New York.* Edited by Donald Allen. San Francisco: Grey Fox, 1983, 169–173.

———. "On the Way to the San Remo" (1954). In *The Collected Poems.* Rev. ed. Edited by Donald Allen. Berkeley: University of California Press, 1995, 205–206.

Sukenick, Ronald. *Down and In: Life in the Underground.* New York: William Morrow, 1987.

Saroyan, Aram (1943–)

From the dislocations of "Upper Bohemia," as it has been called, Aram Saroyan came to the NEW YORK SCHOOL in search of family as much as art. His father was the celebrated novelist William Saroyan, an early influence on JACK KEROUAC, but a disturbingly elusive father to Aram. His mother, Carol Marcus, was a New York debutante and actress who married the actor Walter Matthau after divorcing (for the second time) Aram's father. Aram Saroyan formed an early determination to become a writer, choosing ROBERT CREELEY as his principal model, partly in opposition to William Saroyan's style. Early success in placing his poems in *The Nation* (1963) and *Poetry* (1964) encouraged the young Saroyan to abandon his formal education, which he had pursued half-heartedly over a sequence of semesters at the University of Chicago, New York University, and Columbia

University. He began the magazine LINES (1964–65) as a means of connecting with other young writers. The project put him in touch with RON PADGETT, CLARK COOLIDGE, and TED BERRIGAN, among others. Berrigan especially provided a crucial demonstration of the possibility of combining "fine attention to sound," which Saroyan had learned from Creeley, with the romantic spontaneity that FRANK O'HARA had encouraged in Berrigan (Friends 37–38). Equally important, Berrigan's way of being fully present to younger colleagues, like Saroyan, to some extent filled the gap in Saroyan's life left by his distant father.

The style that Saroyan explored during the 1960s could not have been less like the "chatty" style sometimes associated with New York School writers. Taking Creeley's sparseness several steps further, Saroyan wrote *concrete* or *minimalist* poems. These terms suggest affinity with the visual arts, but the significance to Saroyan of "fine attention to sound" makes it seem equally relevant to include his project in the "aesthetics of silence" that the critic Susan Sontag described at the time (1967). The placement of very few words, sometimes only one, on a page draws attention to the blank space. Indeed, while publishing two volumes of such work with a commercial publisher, Random House (*Aram Saroyan*, 1968; *Pages*, 1969), Saroyan took the decidedly uncommercial step of issuing a "book" in the form of a wrapped and commercially labeled ream of otherwise blank typing paper; the only assertion of authorship was the stamped notice "© Aram Saroyan 1968 Kulchur Press." From this point it would seem logical to stop writing altogether, as Saroyan did for a period lasting to 1972.

Major changes in his life led Saroyan to resume writing in a very different style. He had married Gailyn McClanahan, a painter (1968), fathered a daughter (1970, the first of three children), and moved to BOLINAS, CALIFORNIA (1972), where he reconnected with Creeley and many poets he had known previously in NEW YORK CITY. The experience of raising a family converged with a sense of being welcomed into a larger family where art and life merged rather than conflicted. Life now rushed in to fill the previously empty spaces of Saroyan's poems. The new poems, collected in *Day and Night: Bolinas Poems* (Black Sparrow, 1998), combine the diary structure cultivated by the New York School with the "transparent" personality that Saroyan admired in the BEATS. The more Saroyan has turned his attention to narrative and character study, however, the more he has turned to prose, including biographies of his parents (*Last Rites*, Morrow, 1982; *William Saroyan*, Harcourt Brace Jovanovich, 1983; *Trio*, Simon and Schuster, 1985) and personal memoir, as both FICTION (*The Street*, Bookstore Press, 1974) and nonfiction (*Friends in the World*, Coffee House Press, 1992). He left Bolinas in 1984 and currently resides in Los Angeles.

Bibliography

Aram Saroyan. Web site. Available online. URL: http://www.aramsaroyan.com/.

Dworkin, Craig, ed. Eclipse Web site. Available online. URL: http://english.utah.edu/eclipse/projects/.

Padgett, Ron, and David Shapiro, eds. *An Anthology of New York Poets.* New York: Random House, 1970.

Saroyan, Aram. *Complete Minimal Poems.* New York: Ugly Duckling, 2008.

———. *Friends in the World: The Education of a Writer.* Minneapolis, Minn.: Coffee House Press, 1992.

———. "A Personal Memoir." In *Nice to See You: Homage to Ted Berrigan,* edited by Anne Waldman, 135–138. Minneapolis, Minn.: Coffee House Press, 1991.

———. "Saroyan, Aram." In *Contemporary Authors Autobiography Series* 5. Detroit, Mich.: Gale, 1987, 211–223.

———. *Starting Out in the Sixties: Selected Essays.* Jersey City, N.J.: Talisman House, 2001.

Sontag, Susan. "The Aesthetics of Silence." In *Styles of Radical Will.* New York: Doubleday-Anchor, 1991, 3–34.

Savage, Tom (1948–   )

Tom Savage was born in NEW YORK CITY and has been active in NEW YORK SCHOOL poetry both as a writer and a publisher. As a participant in the summer session of the Jack Kerouac School at NAROPA INSTITUTE in 1976, he coedited the first issue of *Roof* magazine with James Sherry. In New York from 1984 to 1987 he published *Gandhabba* magazine, the title of which reflects Savage's interest in Eastern philosophy and religion and Buddhism in particular. However, the magazine grappled directly with issues close at hand. For instance, issue number 4 (1986) is devoted to political poetry and opens with Savage's editorial challenge: "The term 'political poetry' has a bad ring to it for some members of our community." From 1992 to 2001 Savage edited a third magazine, *Tamarind*.

Savage's poems abide in the social inequities of urban life and swerve toward and away from an idea of a communicable divine presence, particularly in his later books, which he wrote and published after recovering from serious brain surgery to cure his epileptic fits. As he writes in "Surviving Grace":

> I have survived your grace,
> Possibly existent God.
> I have survived brain surgery,
> Falling off a Himalayan cliff,
> Nearly being shot in Turkey,
> And many, many epileptic seizures.

That poem appeared in *Brain Surgery Poems* (Linear Arts Books, 1999). His most recent collection is *Brainfits* (Straw Gate, 2008). Previously he published six other books of poems, starting with *Personalities* (Jim Brodey Books, 1978). *Slow Waltz on a Glass Harmonica* and *Filling Spaces* both appeared in 1980 under Savage's own imprint, Nalanda University Press. More recent titles include *Housing, Preservation and Development* (Cheap Review, 1988), *Processed Words* (Coffee House, 1990), and *Political Conditions Physical States* (United Artists, 1993). Savage's individual poems have been published in many periodicals including Hanging Loose, Talisman, and *The World*.

Savage has taught workshops at the Poetry Project at St. Mark's Church in-the-Bowery, the Juilliard School, and Encore Community Center, a senior citizens center that is part of St. Malachy's Church, the "actor's chapel." He also continues to keep abreast of the various generations of New York School poets, writing reviews for *A Gathering of Tribes*, including a recent piece on *Great American Prose Poems: From Poe to the Present* (Scribner, 2003), edited by David Lehman. In that review, which reflects his own attitudes toward poetics, Savage writes that poetry "only bites the mind when the brain needs to be jarred out of its pop culture morass of 'short attention span music'

(my term for the 3 to 5 minute limited expanse of most popular music) and the mass hypnosis presented by TV, computers, the daily drudgery of most people's work, etc." (n.p.). Savage's peculiar brain surgery aims to cure such mass hypnosis.

Bibliography

Savage, Tom. "Prose Poetry or Poetic Prose: Which Would Baudelaire Choose to Write in America?" (2003). *A Gathering of the Tribes*. Available online. URL: http://www.tribes.org/cgi-bin/form.pl?karticle=343. Accessed December 19, 2008.

Scarlet Cabinet, The   Alice Notley and Douglas Oliver (1992)

The Scarlet Cabinet: A Compendium of Books is the culminating collection from the married couple Alice Notley and Douglas Oliver, editors of the poetry magazine *Scarlet*, which appeared briefly at the beginning of the 1990s. Notley and Oliver published the compendium, which also functioned as the sixth and final issue of the magazine, themselves in New York City in 1992 just before they moved to Paris. Unlike previous issues of *Scarlet* in which they published the work of other New York poets, such as Jerome Rothenberg, Clark Coolidge, and Anne Waldman, *The Scarlet Cabinet* includes only completed works by Notley and Oliver—showing not only their poetic involvement with each other but also their shared belief that poets can self-publish successfully. *The Scarlet Cabinet* consists of seven books of poetry and prose and stretches to more than 400 pages. Although largely overlooked by a mainstream press that had generally begun to take note of their writing, *The Scarlet Cabinet* was recognized as providing the definitive collection of Oliver and Notley's work together in New York.

Four of the books are by Notley and three are by Oliver, but this double authorship is only the start of the variety of form and subjects engaged by the book. After two short introductions—one by each author—the collection begins with Penniless Politics, a political satire by Oliver that follows the adventures of a truly alternative political party in the Ronald Reagan–George H. W. Bush era. *The Descent of Alette*, by Notley, which follows it, is the longest and arguably most ambitious book in the collection. The working unit of this four-book poem is a four-line stanza with no discernible rhyme scheme but with a complicated rhythm indicated by the numerous quotation marks interspersing the narrator's sentences.

Following *Descent*, Oliver's *Sophia Scarlett* is the only prose in the volume. A 100-page prose novella in 21 chapters—a tongue-in-cheek "Historical Romance"—it makes up the bulk of the rest of the volume. Ostensibly written in the style of Robert Louis Stevenson by a recently deceased academic, *Sophia* traces the adventures of the eponymous heroine. After this interlude the next three books are collections of Notley's poetry: first, *Beginning with a Stain,* which is dedicated to Oliver; then *Twelve Poems without Mask*; and, finally, *Homer's Art,* including *White Phosphorus*. These continue, with their individual variations, the project that *Descent* began, with the sections *Twelve Poems* and *White Phosphorus* even echoing it formally.

To close the volume, Oliver's *Nava Sûtra: or The Sutra of Marudevi Chopra, a Fiction,* is modeled on the Jaina bible, the Tattvartha Sutra, and arranged in six headed sections as a series of wisdom statements. Although Oliver was a profound respecter of Jain beliefs he notes that "no jain would accept the above doctrines."

Bibliography

Notley, Alice, and Douglas Oliver. *The Scarlet Cabinet: A Compendium of Books.* New York: Scarlet Editions, 1992.

Schiff, Harris (1944–   )

A "post-capitalist utopian poet," as he describes himself in the magazine *Big Bridge* (n.p.), Harris Schiff was the publisher of the mimeographed poetry magazine the *Harris Review* (two issues, 1971) and founder in 1996 of the e-zine *$lavery—Cyberzine of the Arts.* Schiff is a resident of NEW YORK CITY's East Village and has a long-running association with the POETRY PROJECT AT ST. MARK'S CHURCH IN-THE-BOWERY. Throughout the 1970s and 1980s he served there in various administrative and creative capacities, running the weekly open readings and serving as a board member, a co-coordinator, a workshop instructor, and editor of *The WORLD.*

Schiff's own first publication was in the magazine *Open Space* in San Francisco (1963), where he participated in the Jack Spicer circle along with LEWIS WARSH, a friend from high school (Ellingham and Killian 265–268, 373–375). In the later 1960s he spent time living as a resident of the Morningstar Commune in Arroyo Hondo, New Mexico, details of which are captured in the prose poem "I Should Run for Cover but I'm Right Here."

Schiff's aesthetic sensibility is perhaps best characterized by his ability to assimilate tangential information into the body of a poem. A poem like "Grieving Aloud" (*Big Bridge* 9, 2003), for example, includes a tag from an email, "12/3/2003 10:32:53 AM," snippets of unattributed dialogue, and portions of a flattened, plain-spoken internal monologue: "I have a great deal of paper work and computer work to do." Other poems delve into sexuality, urban life, and psychic disassociation with a comic ease of delivery traceable to FRANK O'HARA and TED BERRIGAN.

Schiff is the author of a number of books, including *Secret Clouds* (ANGEL HAIR, 1970), *I Should Run for Cover but I'm Right Here* (Angel Hair, 1978), and *In the Heart of the Empire* (UNITED ARTISTS, 1979). *Yo-Yo's with Money* (United Artists, 1979) is a COLLABORATION with Berrigan consisting of a play-by-play account of a Yankees–Red Sox game which the poets had attended, transcribed from tape and mimeographed for distribution. Schiff's work has been widely anthologized, and he has received grants from the Coordinating Council of Literary Magazines, the National Endowment of the Arts, and the New York Foundation for the Arts. Schiff's poem "Here Comes the Descent," a commentary on SEPTEMBER 11, 2001, was published in *The Arts Paper* of Boulder, Colorado (December 2001–January 2002), and his work has appeared in many other journals, including the PARIS REVIEW, *Ploughshares,* and *Big Bridge.*

Bibliography

Ellingham, Lewis, and Kevin Killian. *Poet Be Like God: Jack Spicer and the San Francisco Renaissance.* Hanover, N.H.: University Press of New England/Wesleyan University Press, 1998.

Schiff, Harris. "Grieving Aloud" and "Contributor's Note." *Big Bridge* 9 (2003). Available online. URL:

http://www.bigbridge.org/issue9/ochstitlepage.htm. Accessed December 19, 2008.

Schiff, Harris, ed. *$lavery—Cyberzine of the Arts.* Available online. URL: http://www.cyberpoems.com.

Waldman, Anne, and Lewis Warsh, eds. *The Angel Hair Anthology.* New York: Granary Books, 2001.

Schjeldahl, Peter (1942–)

As art critic for the *New Yorker* since 1998, Peter Schjeldahl (pronounced SHELL-doll) has attained a level of professional prominence that may seem to be far above the "underground" world of NEW YORK SCHOOL poetry where he started out. However, when in 1977 he was at the point of abandoning poetry in order to devote all of his writing energy to criticism, he made it clear in "Dear Profession of Art Writing" that he looked up to the poets, particularly "my heroes," as he called them: "[Allen] Ginsberg, [Kenneth] Koch, [John] Ashbery, [James] Schuyler, [Ron] Padgett. Up there, hello!" (*Since 1964* 18). Moreover, he committed himself to "the poet-critic tradition," including Charles Baudelaire, Guillaume Apollinaire, and FRANK O'HARA (*Since 1964,* 16). Above all, this means writing as a "fan" of the artists whom Schjeldahl reviews (Storr), something he achieves by projecting onto them the position he still identifies as "me-as-a-poet" (Schjeldahl, Introduction 9).

Born in Fargo, North Dakota, Schjeldahl attended Carleton College in Northfield, Minnesota, where he cofounded MOTHER magazine and got to know a group of aspiring avant-gardists who moved to NEW YORK CITY at about the same time, including artists Donna Dennis and Martha Diamond and musician Lee Crabtree, later a member of The FUGS. In 1964 Schjeldahl dropped out of Carleton, married classmate Linda O'Brien, and passed through New York only briefly on his way to Europe. There, two transformative experiences opened his eyes to visual art, which he never studied formally: With GEORGE SCHNEEMAN he visited Piero della Francesca's *Pregnant Madonna* (*Madonna del Parto,* ca. 1467) in a small chapel in Monterchi, Italy ("George Inside" 63); and in Paris he stumbled upon ANDY WARHOL's show of flower paintings. "'Oops,' I thought. 'Wrong city! Go home!'" Schjeldahl recalls of that moment ("Andy Warhol" 101). New York was where "it" was happening; "exactly what was 'it'? I forgot," Schjeldahl comments sardonically ("Andy Warhol" 102). He returned to New York in 1965, found an apartment on the Lower East Side, resumed his editorial role in *Mother,* and "did art criticism for money and bonus prestige" ("Introduction" 9). As a poet, he threw himself into the whirlwind pursuit of the new (in both art and lifestyle) for which Warhol provided a paradoxically calm center. Schjeldahl explained: "The sixties went too fast for absolutely anybody, except somebody [like Warhol] who would live only on the surface" (Sukenick 222). When Warhol was shot in 1968, "it" was over, as Schjeldahl records in his poem "Shot" (*Since 1964* 87).

Some of Schjeldahl's poetry registers the fluctuations of changing experience using devices that have come to be associated with the New York School. For instance, "The Paris Sonnets" (*Since 1964* 71–80), which appeared in Schjeldahl's first collection, *White Country* (Corinth Books, 1968), recycle lines through a sequence of poems, producing an effect similar to looking into a kaleidoscope, after the manner of TED BERRIGAN's SONNETS (1964). *Dreams* (Angel Hair, 1973), a set of prose poems, employs a diary format to filter ordinary experience through the skewed perspective of the subconscious. As dream images of TOM DISCH, ANNE WALDMAN, JOHN ASHBERY, and others surround Schjeldahl, naked in bed, he learns that the St. Mark's Christmas Reading is about to be held in his tiny apartment ("The Reading"; *Since 1964* 59). Symbolically, this situation may foreshadow Schjeldahl's eventual choice in favor of writing criticism, "doing something both more noticed and less naked than poetry" (Schjeldahl, Introduction 9). But other poems point in the same direction less symbolically, through stylistic traits that are not typical of the New York School.

Schjeldahl likes to indulge in "big ideas," to take positions and to hold on to them, rather than to move through them as O'Hara and Ashbery do. Framing the shooting of Warhol in the context of other recent violence, including the assassinations of Martin Luther King Jr. and Robert Kennedy, Schjeldahl takes his poem "Shot" to the point of generalization—"This year has its own logic"—but he knows he cannot go farther because "logic"—or for that matter generalization—can tear the fabric of feeling in a poem (Schjeldahl, Introduction 10). He is able to go farther in his review of the Warhol retrospective at the Museum of Modern Art in 1989: "The '60s were about erasing boundaries. Warhol did it best because the boundaries—between high and low, art and commerce, etc.—scarcely existed for him in the first place" ("Andy Warhol" 102). For Schjeldahl, choosing to write criticism rather than poetry became vital as a means of maintaining boundaries.

Bibliography

Atlas, James. "A Chronicle of Younger Poets." *Poetry* 113, no. 6 (March 1969): 428–433.

Pritchard, William H. "Criticisms of Life: Sound and Half-Sound." *Hudson Review* 32, no. 2 (Summer 1979): 252–268.

Schjeldahl, Peter. "Andy Warhol: Museum of Modern Art" (1989). In *The 7 Days Art Columns, 1989–1990.* Great Barrington, Mass.: The Figures, 1990, 101–104.

———. "George Inside." In *Painter Among Poets: The Collaborative Art of George Schneeman,* edited by Ron Padgett, 63–66. New York: Granary Books, 2004.

———. *The Hydrogen Jukebox: Selected Writings, 1978–1990.* Berkeley: University of California Press, 1991.

———. Introduction to *Columns and Catalogues.* Great Barrington, Mass.: The Figures, 1994, 9–12.

———. *Since 1964: New and Selected Poems.* New York: SUN, 1978.

Seidman, Hugh. "Images, Artifacts, Entertainments." *New York Times Book Review,* 8 July 1979, 4.

Storr, Robert. Introduction to *The Hydrogen Jukebox,* by Peter Schjeldahl. Berkeley: University of California Press, 1991, xv–xxii.

Sukenick, Ronald. *Down and In: Life in the Underground.* New York: Beech Tree Books/William Morrow, 1987.

Schneeman, George (1934–2009) *artist*

The art of George Schneeman conveys a utopian spirit that harmonized perfectly with the spirit of the poets' community that gathered around the POETRY PROJECT AT ST. MARK'S CHURCH IN-THE-BOWERY in its early days. In 1966 Schneeman, his wife, Katie, and their three young sons arrived in NEW YORK CITY's Lower East Side from Italy, where they had already met the poets PETER SCHJELDAHL, RON PADGETT, and BILL BERKSON. Accounts of gatherings at the Schneemans' apartment infuse bohemian New York with the culture and courtesy of an Italian Renaissance court but none of the regal air. The Schneeman ambience was "familiar" (BROWNSTEIN 83) in the sense of "family"—"the first real family of artists I'd ever known," recalls LEWIS MACADAMS (67). Two of Schneeman's sons, Paul (1960–) and Elio (1961–97), grew up writing poetry as a natural extension of their family life. Although Schneeman exhibited at the Fischbach and Holly Solomon Galleries during the 1970s, his reputation has remained largely confined to the New York poets' community. As a reviewer of a recent show at the First Floor Gallery observed, "Schneeman made art not to be received by an international corporate art world, but a small group of brilliant friends" (Holzman n.p.).

The art and landscape that Schneeman experienced in Italy, where he was sent as a U.S. Army draftee in 1958, inspired him to seriously devote himself to painting, in which he was self-taught. Previously, in his native Minnesota, he had pursued literary studies as far as the graduate level. Thus he was fully prepared to respond to the poets he joined in New York and to collaborate with them in numerous visual works where their freshness as amateurs enlivened the art. Expert technique was not the goal, according to Schneeman, but rather to "invent a sort of utopia in the form of a visual field filled with pleasure, quickness, and wit" ("Collaborating" 56). In *Yodeling into a Kotex* (1969), a COLLABORATION between Schneeman and Padgett, the technique of chiaroscuro, or tonal contrast, identified with the realism of the Italian Renaissance, is deliberately misidentified as the name of "a painter of the realistic school" about whom "little is known." The scholarly tone of that statement, in staid typewritten lettering, is countered by wildly collaged text that reads, "No he's her," from which an arrow points to an image of a bunny rabbit that might have been lifted from a children's book.

In his collaborations and equally numerous cover designs for books and magazines, Schneeman performs so variously that it is impossible to identify his hand with any one style. The character of the work, rather, more usually reflects the personality of the poet involved. For instance, TED BERRIGAN "bullied his way into art," according to Schneeman ("Collaborating" 51). In their collaboration *In the Nam What Can Happen?* (1967–68), texts and images messily contend for the same space, suggesting a more personal struggle than that of the Vietnam War to which the title refers. In contrast, *Landscape* (1972), a collaboration with LARRY FAGIN, separates text and image. In the spirit of Fagin's MINIMALISM, Schneeman's drawings are neatly done and vary from each other only minimally as the sequence progresses, each frame adding a new element of (disconnected) narrative into the same landscape.

Paradoxically, Schneeman's portraits of his poet friends and family members convey his own identity more clearly than the collaborations. Their broad, flat areas of color and simplified backgrounds have been compared with the style of ALEX KATZ (Padgett 32). However, Schneeman refuses to associate this effect with the tendency toward abstraction in NEW YORK SCHOOL painting. "They're not in a void," he says of his "idealized" figures, "they're in some perfect world, you know, they're in some Platonic world" (interview 128).

Bibliography

Berrigan, Ted, and George Schneeman. *In the Nam What Can Happen?* New York: Granary Books, 1997.

Brownstein, Michael. "For George." In *Painter Among Poets: The Collaborative Art of George Schneeman*, edited by Ron Padgett, 83. New York: Granary Books, 2004.

Fagin, Larry, and George Schneeman. *Landscape.* In *The Angel Hair Anthology*, edited by Anne Waldman and Lewis Warsh, 395–403. New York: Granary Books, 2001.

Holzman, Eric. "George Schneeman." *Brooklyn Rail* (November 2006). Available online. URL: http://brooklynrail.org/2006/11/artseen/george-schneeman. Accessed December 19, 2008.

MacAdams, Lewis. In *Painter Among Poets: The Collaborative Art of George Schneeman*, edited by Ron Padgett, 67. New York: Granary Books, 2004.

Padgett, Ron. "Finishing Touches: On the Painting of George Schneeman." In *Poets and Painters*, edited by Dianne Perry Vanderlip, 32. Exhibit catalog. Denver, Colo.: Denver Art Museum, 1979.

Padgett, Ron, and George Schneeman. *Yodeling into a Kotex.* New York: Granary Books, 2003.

Schneeman, George. "Collaborating with Poets." *Painter Among Poets: The Collaborative Art of George Schneeman*, edited by Ron Padgett, 35–57. New York: Granary Books, 2004.

———. Interview by Alice Notley (1977). In *Waltzing Matilda*, by Alice Notley, 101–132. 1981. Reprint, Cambridge, Mass.: Faux Press, 2003.

Waldman, Anne. "'Surprise Each Other': The Art of Collaboration" (1998–99). In *Vow to Poetry: Essays, Interviews, and Manifestos*, Minneapolis, Minn.: Coffee House Press, 2001, 319–327.

Scholnick, Michael (1953–1990)

As editor and publisher, Michael Scholnick embraced writing that emanated from the NEW YORK SCHOOL, Beat, and Nuyorican milieux. His own poems were inimitable and beyond category; KENNETH KOCH called them "the real thing, part of the small amount of it there ever is." From 1977 to 1986 he coedited the lively magazine *Mag City* and published chapbooks under his own imprint, Misty Terrace.

After growing up in the Bronx, New York, and Wilkes-Barre, Pennsylvania, Scholnick attended Wilkes College and Rutgers University, where he received a B.A. in 1975. While at Rutgers he studied with Miguel Algarín, founder of the NUYORICAN POETS CAFÉ, at which Scholnick became a regular after moving to NEW YORK CITY's Lower East Side. In 1976 he spent the summer at NAROPA INSTITUTE, where he was a teaching assistant to ALLEN GINSBERG. In 1977 he persuaded GREGORY MASTERS and GARY LENHART to join with him to publish *Mag City*, a mostly mimeographed literary magazine that continued publication for almost 10 years.

In 1978 Scholnick was one of 10 young poets to appear in a selection edited by Ginsberg—who praised Scholnick's "beat optimist élan"—for *New Directions*, number 37. In that same year his first chapbook of poems, *Perfume*, was published under STEVE LEVINE's Remember I Did This for You imprint, and his first play, *Providence*, was produced as part of BOB HOLMAN's POETS' THEATRE workshop. In 1980 Scholnick received a Fellowship in Poetry from the National Endowment for the Arts, and his second chapbook, *Beyond Venus*, was published by Crony Books. In 1982 he was an organizer of the Ear of the Dog Poets' Theatre Festival, where his second play, *Pay Day,* was performed.

In that same year Scholnick married Nellie Villegas and began to teach in New York City high schools. During the remaining eight years of his life, he put together two unpublished manuscripts of poems, "Heart Melodies" and "Glancing at My Life," wrote a four-act play (*You Got to Understand Something*), and wrote the catalog essay for ALEX KATZ's 1987 exhibition of paintings at the Robert Miller Gallery. While pursuing an M.A. in English and American literature at New York University, he studied with Harold Bloom and wrote the critical appreciation "Shaking Hands with James Schuyler." A heart attack abruptly ended his life in 1990. *Clinch: Selected Poems of Michael Scholnick,* was published posthumously by Coffee House Press in 1998.

Bibliography

Koch, Kenneth. Publisher's blurb for *Clinch* by Michael Scholnick. Coffee House Press, Web site. Available online. URL: http://www.coffeehousepress.org/clinch reviews.asp. Accessed December 19, 2008.

Schuchat, Simon (1954–)

Simon Schuchat (pronounced SHOO-chat) lived in NEW YORK CITY for a brief but crucial period (1975–78), when a third generation of NEW YORK SCHOOL poets was beginning to emerge. The geographical extent of New York School connections is amply demonstrated in Schuchat's career in Washington, D.C., and CHICAGO, ILLINOIS, prior to his New York sojourn, and afterward, when he took up assignments in Russia, Japan, and China as a U.S. Foreign Service officer.

Growing up outside Washington, D.C., where he was born, Schuchat reached out to the avant-garde poets who excited him early on. He arranged for ALLEN GINSBERG to give a reading at his high school. In the year he graduated, 1971, he launched a magazine, *Buffalo Stamps* (1971–73), which included TED BERRIGAN, LEWIS MACADAMS, and RICHARD HELL among its contributors. Schuchat's first book, *Svelte* (Genesis: Grasp, 1971), with an introduction by MacAdams, was published by Richard Hell in New York, but his second book, *Blue Skies* (Some of Us

Press, 1972), was published in D.C. at the instigation of MICHAEL LALLY, who had encouraged Schuchat to read Berrigan's work and even to make a special trip to New York to meet him. Berrigan became the center of the poets' circle that Schuchat entered while studying at the University of Chicago (1971–75) and that regathered around Berrigan and ALICE NOTLEY when they returned to New York in 1977. Schuchat's third book, *Light and Shadow* (Vehicle Editions, 1977), was reviewed by Berrigan in the *Poetry Project Newsletter.* Schuchat edited two New York–based magazines, *432 Review* (1976–78) and *Caveman* (1977–81), maintaining a connection with the latter even after moving to Shanghai, China, to teach English at Fudan University (1978–81). Schuchat returned to the United States to pursue East Asian studies at Yale and Harvard and joined the Foreign Service in 1985. His most recent position (2007–) is that of deputy consul general in Shanghai. Under the pressures of diplomatic affairs, he has not published a collection of verse since *At Baoshan* (Coffee House Press, 1984).

Among the range of options provided by the New York School aesthetic, Schuchat turns away from self-conscious reflection on art and toward urban encounter. "Stately and Toward" (*Out There* 6, 1974), written in Chicago, concludes with a prose statement: "I wouldn't mind writing something that was correlative to [the painter J. M. W.] Turner, but it's obvious that it's more necessary to write something exactly correlative to the two black girls, about fifteen, that I just saw, walking south." A similar encounter with a "young girl grinning / at me" is recorded in "Heavenly Ford Road Anecdote," from *At Baoshan.* Here, however, the otherness of the girl, encountered on a street in Shanghai, is marked by cultural rather than racial difference: "is this what / They mean . . . by / Losing face?" the poet muses. Most of Schuchat's recent writing poses that question—"Is this what they mean?"—through the act of TRANSLATION, for instance, of the classical Chinese poet Lu You or the Russian conceptualist poet D. A. Prigov.

Schuyler, James (1923–1991)

James Schuyler (pronounced SKY-ler) has been called an "urban pastoral" poet (Clark, Vendler,

Gray): Some of his best and best-known poetry is written in response to nature, but his response encompasses urban experience, human emotions, and the passage of time, in addition to landscapes, skies, forms of plants, and effects of light. Often compared to visual art—in particular to the paintings of his friend FAIRFIELD PORTER—Schuyler's poems are less a description than the record of a process of discovery. The result is what JOHN ASHBERY has called "inspired utterance couched in everyday terms" (Ashbery 209).

Schuyler was born in CHICAGO, ILLINOIS, and spent his early childhood in Washington, D.C., and later in a suburb of Buffalo, New York. Tensions with his stepfather at home and with the "jock" culture at school made for an unhappy adolescence, but he discovered the poetry of William Carlos Williams, Marianne Moore, and Wallace Stevens and decided to become a writer. After two years at the small, religious Bethany College in West Virginia and about a year in the navy, Schuyler moved to NEW YORK CITY in 1944. Meeting W. H. AUDEN there brought him further into the writer's world. With his lover Bill Aalto, Schuyler spent time with Auden and Chester Kallman on the Italian island of Ischia during 1948–49. While typing Auden's manuscripts, Schuyler's first impression was, "if this is poetry, I'm certainly never going to write any myself" (interview by Little 161).

Initially Schuyler planned to write FICTION. His first published works, three very short stories, appeared in the literary journal *Accent* in summer 1951. A poem in the same issue, FRANK O'HARA's "The Three-Penny Opera," made a strong impression on Schuyler and led to his meeting O'Hara through JOHN BERNARD MYERS, whom Schuyler had known from Buffalo (interview by Little). Soon, O'Hara's "jazzy" rhythms and line breaks inspired Schuyler to write his first poems in fall 1951. One of these, "Salute," was his first published poem (in *New World Writing I* [1952]) and has been much anthologized. Schuyler wrote "Salute" while in a hospital recuperating from a nervous breakdown, the first of several such episodes that mark turning points in his life. After his release in January 1952, his acquaintance with O'Hara and Ashbery deepened into friendship and provided welcome confirmation of Schuyler's talent, perhaps

"*the* most important moment in my life," Schuyler later recalled (interview by Schjeldahl n.p.). That summer Schuyler and Ashbery began writing the novel A NEST OF NINNIES together. In the fall, Schuyler and O'Hara began to share an apartment at 326 East 49th Street.

The 1950s was the period of Schuyler's most intense social involvement with the other poets and the painters of the NEW YORK SCHOOL, an involvement reflected in the range of his writing. He published poems in periodicals ranging from the *New Yorker* to DAISY ALDAN's *FOLDER*, but he also wrote plays, fiction, and art exhibition reviews. His play *Presenting Jane* (now lost) was produced by the ARTISTS' THEATER in 1953 as part of a triple bill with O'Hara's *TRY, TRY* and KENNETH KOCH's *Red Riding Hood*. Another short play, *Shopping and Waiting,* was produced at the POETS' THEATRE in Cambridge, Massachusetts, the same year. In 1953 Schuyler was commissioned by ARTHUR GOLD, his lover at the time, to write A *Picnic Cantata*, the libretto for a composition for voice, two pianos, and percussion with a score by Paul Bowles. In 1958 Schuyler's first solo novel, ALFRED AND GUINEVERE, was published by Harcourt, Brace & Company.

The '60s opened with the publication of Schuyler's first book of poems, *Salute* (Tiber Press), a limited edition folio with scrigraphs by GRACE HARTIGAN. Also in 1960 DONALD M. ALLEN's influential anthology, THE NEW AMERICAN POETRY, *1945–1960,* presented four poems by Schuyler, along with his essay "Poet and Painter Overture." In June 1961, following another breakdown and hospitalization, Schuyler moved in with the painter FAIRFIELD PORTER and his family in Southampton, Long Island. Though Schuyler referred to Porter simply as his "best friend," their relationship was also ambiguously romantic. Porter's style of painterly realism had a profound effect on Schuyler's poetry. Both based their work on depicting "things as they are" (Schuyler, *Collected Poems* 234). Porter also provided a sense of security and shared family life amid surroundings of inspiring natural beauty—both in Southhampton and on Great Spruce Head Island in Maine's Penobscot Bay, where the Porters spent most summers.

Schuyler's next book, *May 24th or So* (Tibor de Nagy Editions, 1966), was for the most part incorporated in *Freely Espousing* (Doubleday, 1969), his first full-length, commercially published book of poems. *Freely Espousing* contains many of Schuyler's best short poems, including "Freely Espousing," "February," "December," "A Man in Blue," "An Almanac," and "May 24th or So." Its range encompasses urban poems from the early '50s, when (inspired by DADA artists) he was experimenting with FORMS of literary collage, to poems written in response to landscape and the rhythms of nature in Southampton and in Maine. The book was praised by JOHN KOETHE in *Poetry* as embodying "the sort of vision that periodically reawakens us to the infinite range of possibilities open to the poet" (Lehman 255).

Schuyler's next two books, *The Crystal Lithium* (Random House, 1972) and HYMN TO LIFE (Random House, 1974), each bore a cover image by Porter. Both books include sections of nature poems, love poems, and long title poems, the longest Schuyler had written so far. The unusually long line of "The Crystal Lithium," which Schuyler would later adopt for "HYMN TO LIFE," "The Morning of the Poem," and "A Few Days," was determined by setting the margins of the typewriter to the edges of the paper, "so long as the breath didn't give out" (interview by Little 171). *The Crystal Lithium* also introduced Schuyler's trademark "skinny" poems—poems with very short (two- or three-word) lines such as "Letter to a Friend: Who Is Nancy Daum," "Blue," and "Janis Joplin's Dead: Long Live Pearl."

In summer 1971 Schuyler suffered two serious nervous breakdowns, requiring further hospitalization. Having been asked to leave the Porters, he moved back to New York City by 1973. This decade was a difficult one for Schuyler: He suffered a devastating breakup with a lover, the sudden death of Porter, and further breakdowns and hospital stays, including one for serious injuries sustained when he accidentally set fire to his room by smoking in bed. In 1979 Schuyler moved from a seedy single-room-occupancy hotel to the CHELSEA HOTEL. There, with a succession of young assistants to help him, Schuyler's life and mental condition improved steadily through the 1980s, though physical ailments, eventually traced to diabetes, continued to plague him.

The Morning of the Poem (Farrar, Straus & Giroux, 1980) showed Schuyler working at the height of his creative powers despite his personal difficulties. The volume, awarded the Pulitzer Prize in 1981, contains a range of emotional contrast, from the bleak, withdrawn "Payne Whitney Poems," named for one of the hospitals where Schuyler spent time, to the expansive and engaging *The Morning of the Poem,* which is continued, in a sense, by the title poem of *A Few Days* (Random House, 1985). In 1988 Schuyler published *Selected Poems* (Farrar, Straus & Giroux) and on November 15 gave his first-ever public reading, at the Dia Foundation in New York. Shyness had kept him from reading before, but the enthusiastic response to the Dia event encouraged Schuyler to give several more readings before his death on April 12, 1991, following a stroke.

Bibliography

Ashbery, John. "Introduction to a Reading by James Schuyler" (1988). In *Selected Prose.* Edited by Eugene Richie. Ann Arbor: University of Michigan Press, 2004, 208–210.

Ashbery, John, and James Schuyler. *A Nest of Ninnies.* New York: Dutton, 1969.

Clark, Tom. "Schuyler's Idylls: Notes and Reflections on the *Collected Poems.*" *American Poetry Review* (May–June 1994): 7–13.

Gray, Timothy. "New Windows on New York: The Urban Pastoral Vision of James Schuyler and Jane Freilicher." *Genre* 33 (Summer 2000): 171–198.

Lehman, David. *The Last Avant-Garde.* New York: Doubleday, 1998.

Revell, Donald, ed. "James Schuyler: A Celebration" special issue. *Denver Quarterly* 24, no. 4 (Spring 1990).

Schuyler, James. *Alfred and Guinevere.* With introduction by John Ashbery. New York: New York Review Books, 2001.

———. *Collected Poems.* New York: Farrar, Straus & Giroux, 1993.

———. *The Diary of James Schuyler.* Edited by Nathan Kernan. Santa Rosa, Calif.: Black Sparrow Press, 1997.

———. Interview by Carl Little. *Agni* 37 (January 1993): 152–182.

———. Interview by Peter Schjeldahl. Tape recording. January 1977. Unpub.

―――. *Just the Thing: Selected Letters of James Schuyler, 1951–1991*. Edited by William Corbett. New York: Turtle Point Press, 2004.

―――. *Selected Art Writings*. Edited by Simon Pettet. Santa Rosa, Calif.: Black Sparrow Press, 1998.

―――. *What's for Dinner?* With afterword by James McCourt. New York: New York Review Books, 2006.

Vendler, Helen. "New York Pastoral: James Schuyler." In *Soul Says: On Recent Poetry*. Cambridge, Mass.: Harvard University Press, 1995, 62–70.

Schwartz, Delmore (1913–1966)

After winning much acclaim for his debut volume, *In Dreams Begin Responsibilities* (1938), a collection of poems and short FICTION, Delmore Schwartz lived under the curse of high expectations that he could not fulfill, in his own judgment as well as others'. By 1952, in a panel on "New Poets" at the artists' CLUB, FRANK O'HARA characterized Schwartz as "the brave young poet who is willing to take up any challenge, but one defeats him if encountered" (Gooch 217). Choosing T. S. Eliot as his model, Schwartz took on a challenge in which the NEW YORK SCHOOL poets chose not to compete. He wrote poetry of philosophical and cultural alienation in the dark mood assumed by later "confessional" poets such as ROBERT LOWELL. The passing of that baton was symbolically achieved in 1959, when Schwartz received the Bollingen Prize for *Summer Knowledge* and Lowell published *Life Studies*, with a poem entitled "To Delmore Schwartz."

Schwartz loomed over the New York School poets as a figure of authority in person as well as in his writing. He taught at Harvard University while JOHN ASHBERY, KENNETH KOCH, and O'Hara were students there—his classes seem to have left the deepest impression on Koch—and during their first years in NEW YORK CITY he was poetry editor of the *Partisan Review,* the main outlet for the so-called New York Intellectuals. To Schwartz's credit and to the young poets' delight, he published their work, including Ashbery's "The Picture of Little J. A. in a Prospect of Flowers" (volume 18, number 4 [1951]), BARBARA GUEST's "People in Wartime" and "This Way to Pity" (volume 18, number 5 [1951]), and O'Hara's "On Looking at *La Grande Jatte,* the Czar Wept Anew*" (volume 19, number 2 [1952]). O'Hara's poem offers an especially pointed comparison with Schwartz's poem alluding to the same painting by Georges Seurat, "Seurat's Sunday Afternoon Along the Seine," first published in *Summer Knowledge*. Where Schwartz meditates on the irresolvable tension between changeless art and changing reality, O'Hara celebrates "a change in the season" as an ideal to which art should aspire (O'Hara, *Collected Poems* 63), perhaps looking to Wallace Stevens rather than Schwartz as his model.

During the 1960s Schwartz's art declined as he suffered bouts of heavy drinking and paranoia. Eventually he broke ties with all of his friends and died alone and destitute in a Manhattan hotel on July 11, 1966, just two weeks before O'Hara was fatally struck by a beach taxi on Fire Island. In the course of time, the surviving New York School poets have looked back on Schwartz with admiration. His *Last and Lost Poems* (1979) appeared with a jacket blurb from Ashbery: "This posthumous collection will perhaps help to re-establish Delmore Schwartz as one of the major twentieth-century American poets." Koch's posthumous volume, *A Possible World* (2002), includes "A Momentary Longing to Hear Sad Advice from One Long Dead," the "one" in question being Schwartz. Facing the end of his own life, Koch hears in Schwartz's characteristic mood a wisdom that modifies Koch's own obsession with happiness: "People say yes everyone is dying / But here read this happy book on the subject. Not Delmore. Not that rueful man" (Koch, *Collected Poems* 664).

Bibliography

Atlas, James. *Delmore Schwartz: The Life of an American Poet.* New York: Farrar, Straus & Giroux, 1977.

Gooch, Brad. *City Poet: The Life and Times of Frank O'Hara.* New York: Knopf, 1993.

Koch, Kenneth. *The Collected Poems.* New York: Knopf, 2005.

O'Hara, Frank. *The Collected Poems.* Rev. ed. Edited by Donald Allen. Berkeley: University of California Press, 1995.

Schwartz, Delmore. *Screeno: Stories and Poems.* New York: New Directions, 2004.

―――. *Selected Essays.* Edited by Donald A. Dike and David H. Zucker. Chicago: University of Chicago Press, 1970.

Screen Tests/A Diary Andy Warhol and Gerard Malanga (1967)

JOHN ASHBERY, TED BERRIGAN, EDWIN DENBY, and RON PADGETT are among the 54 figures subjected to scrutiny by ANDY WARHOL and GERARD MALANGA in their *Screen Tests/A Diary*, one of the first books published by LITA HORNICK's KULCHUR Press. Warhol's close-up photographs of faces—still images taken from film segments lasting three minutes each—"subject" the sitter in the sense of forcing submission (Koestenbaum 99), treating the person as an object. Malanga's poems corresponding to each photograph seem to offer a counterbalancing subjectivity, though whose subjectivity is represented remains very much in question. The suggestion that the poems are diary entries makes it possible to read the entire book as a portrait of Malanga, whose face appears in one of the "screen tests" and on both the front and back cover of the book. However, the format of the book as a kind of portrait gallery, along with Malanga's constant obsession with "the friends" in the texts of the poems, disperses identity into multiple facets. The multiplicity of identity is further suggested by the fact that at least two frames of each screen test are reproduced in the photographic portraits, recalling the multiple images of celebrities—Marilyn Monroe, Liz Taylor, Jackie Kennedy—for which Warhol was already famous. Indeed, *Screen Tests/A Diary* appears to be another of Warhol's experiments in the production of celebrity by means of the reproduction of images, an experiment in which poets are included in the mix of "socialites and thieves, models, consumers of amphetamines, painters, filmmakers, musicians" that Warhol's Factory constantly recycled (Wolf, "Collaboration" 59).

Although celebrity remained confined to a coterie among the NEW YORK SCHOOL poets, they were as fascinated as Warhol was by the theme of multiple identity, by the interplay of objective and subjective states, and by the compulsion to repeat that drives various techniques of reproduction. Malanga recognizes this fascination in his poems written to accompany the poets' screen tests. His poem for Ashbery opens with the line, "What had you been thinking about," reproduced without acknowledgment from Ashbery's poem "The Tennis Court Oath" but thereby acknowledg-ing a debt to the technique of appropriation that Ashbery employed to construct his poem (Wolf, *Andy Warhol* 104–105). Similarly, by addressing the poem for Berrigan like a letter, "Dear Ted," Malanga is simultaneously translating Berrigan, who began a number of his own poems with this form of address. Malanga acknowledges Padgett's fascination with translating French poets by referring to "the Pierre Reverdy birthday / cake" in his poem for Padgett. The poem for Denby, however, probes more deeply than any of the others into the essential problem of translating subjective desire into objective image:

> *He is not*
> *the young boy disturbing your mind*
> *with his "good looks."*

He is not because, presumably, he exists objectively, in a different state from the subjective ideal in "your mind." Malanga's complicated involvement with Denby, for instance, in their double portrait by Warhol on the cover of Berrigan's "C" magazine (number 4, September 1963), makes him one candidate for "the young boy" this poem refers to, in which case the pronoun *he* is a screen for *I*.

Bibliography

Angell, Callie. *Andy Warhol Screen Tests: The Films of Andy Warhol, Catalogue Raisonné.* New York: Abrams/Whitney Museum of American Art, 2006.

Koestenbaum, Wayne. *Andy Warhol.* New York: Viking Penguin, 2001.

Wolf, Reva. *Andy Warhol, Poetry, and Gossip in the 1960s.* Chicago: University of Chicago Press, 1997.

———. "Collaboration as Social Exchange: *Screen Tests/A Diary* by Gerard Malanga and Andy Warhol." *Art Journal* 52, no. 4 (Winter 1993): 59–66.

sculpture *See* ART, VISUAL

Seasons on Earth Kenneth Koch (1987)

In the book entitled *Seasons on Earth*, KENNETH KOCH brought together three poems written at different stages of his career, also collected post-humously in *On the Edge: Collected Longer Poems*

(Knopf, 2007). His work in the GENRE of the comic epic is represented by two long narrative poems, *Ko, or a Season on Earth* (Grove, 1959) and *The Duplications* (Random House, 1977), previously published separately. Serving as a preface, "Seasons on Earth" (1987) precedes the narratives, reflecting on their relation to his life. The two narratives share certain characters. All three poems are linked formally by Koch's use of the eight-line stanza FORM, OTTAVA RIMA, derived from the Italian Renaissance poets Ariosto and from Lord Byron's *Don Juan*. The multiple implications of the title, *Seasons on Earth,* also circulate through all three poems. In the singular, as the subtitle to *Ko,* it refers literally to the baseball season and metaphorically to the human tendency to organize time in some artificial structure, the rules of a game. The allusion to Arthur Rimbaud's title *A Season in Hell* both acknowledges another literary debt and, by contrast, underscores Koch's commitment to the here and now, to life on earth rather than either heaven or hell. Yet the book, as a retrospective exhibit of Koch's career, necessarily concerns itself with more than one moment in time, so the expansion of "seasons" to the plural form evokes the traditional representation of the stages of a person's life as the passage of the seasons from spring to winter.

Ko, the first volume Koch issued through a commercial publisher, consists of 438 stanzas divided into five cantos. Koch (whose name is playfully echoed in the title) wrote the poem in a burst of inspiration during the spring of 1957, while living in Florence, Italy, with his wife, Janice, who had received a Fulbright fellowship, and their baby daughter. Happiness became the poem's subject and spring was its season, so one of the first events in the poem is the arrival of the Japanese baseball player, Ko, at the spring training camp of the Brooklyn Dodgers in Florida, where his powerful fast ball—capable of drilling a hole in the backstop—persuades the Dodgers to take him on immediately. But the first word of the poem is *Meanwhile,* so we do not linger long with Ko or with any of several other characters whose simultaneous stories occasionally intersect: a disfigured proletarian named Huddle who crosses a millionaire gangster nicknamed Dog Boss; secret agent Andrews and his flame, Doris; and another couple, Pemmistrek

("a quite distant cousin of Dog Boss" [72]) and Alouette. Koch shows little interest in the lives of these characters except for what they can do for the poem, which is primarily to keep it moving, one pole in the "tension between the moment of ecstasy and the movement elsewhere" that structures the poem, according to Richard Howard (333). Like the work of Doris's father, Joseph Dah (Koch's wink at DADA), *Ko* is "an Action Poem" (39). The happiness Koch was experiencing may have freed him for the action of writing, but within that arena, the feeling of happiness is conveyed to the reader primarily through the continuously surprising conjunctions of "rhyme and chance," as Koch explains in "Seasons on Earth" (9).

Comic rhyme (Disney / miss me / frisbee [262]) continues to supply the energy as well as to suggest the title of *The Duplications,* but in this poem there is a tighter correspondence—duplication—between form and content. Within the story the central duplication is the production of copies of cities. Commander Papend re-creates Venice in Peru to provide an appropriate setting for his lovemaking with "thousands of young girls fresh as clover" (138). In the case of another group, the Early Girls, lovemaking produces copies of cities, the first example being Philadelphia (164), as if the name of the "city of brotherly love" were taken literally. Mickey and Minnie Mouse and their friends move back and forth between literal and figurative realms throughout the poem. Pemmistrek, Alouette, and Huddel reappear from *Ko.* Ironically, the one personage who seems to lack this power of resurrection is the author himself, who struggles to resume the poem after its single canto break and finds his "mind less leaping / Than when I saw you last" (211). From this point a remarkable glimpse into the mind of the author, his intentions for his poem (to be "endless), and its relation to this life (sadly not endless) extends for several stanzas—the most "interesting" section of the poem, according to Helen Vendler. Ultimately, the narrative resumes and ultimately exceeds (by 14 stanzas) the length of *Ko.*

Autobiographical reflection comes into focus once again in the most recent poem in the volume, "Seasons on Earth." Looking back, addressing his wife, Janice, Koch recalls that the conditions of his life when he was writing *The Duplications,* from 1968 to 1977, were very different from the ecstatic three months when he wrote *Ko:*

> There was no Florence anymore, however,
> And no sweet feeling of a Quattrocento
> Harmonious mix of you, me, and the weather—
> (12).

In fact, his marriage broke up before he finished *The Duplications,* and shortly afterward, in 1981, Janice died. Despite these losses, "Seasons on Earth" declares Koch's persistent faith not in the words of the poems he is reprinting but in something that the words could never quite capture and that there-fore still retains an imaginative freshness:

> O possibility, sweet chance that there is
> A wholeness only hinted by the stanzas (19).

Bibliography

Howard, Richard. "Kenneth Koch." In *Alone with America: Essays on the Art of Poetry in the United States Since 1950.* Enlarged ed. New York: Atheneum, 1980, 331–341.

Koch, Kenneth. *Seasons on Earth.* New York: Penguin, 1987.

Lang, Nancy. "Comic Fantasy in Two Postmodern Verse Novels: Slinger and Ko." In *The Poetic Fantastic: Studies in an Evolving Genre,* edited by Patrick D. Murphy and Vernon Ross Hyles, 113–121. Westport, Conn.: Greenwood, 1989.

McHale, Brian. "Telling Stories Again: On the Replenishment of Narrative in the Postmodernist Long Poem." *Yearbook of English Studies* 30 (2000): 250–262.

Tassoni, John Paul. "Play and Co-Option in Kenneth Koch's Ko, or a Season on Earth: 'Freedom and the Realizable World!'" *Sagetrieb* 10, nos. 1–2 (Spring–Fall 1991): 123–132.

Vendler, Helen. "The Wonder Man." *New York Review of Books,* 24 November 1977, p. 10ff.

Seeking Air Barbara Guest (1978)

BARBARA GUEST's novel *Seeking Air* (Santa Barbara, Calif.: Black Sparrow, 1978; Los Angeles: Sun and Moon, 1997) has been described by the author as "essentially a prose-poem" (Hillringhouse 29). Not surprisingly, the little attention it has received in print has come mostly from poets, notably MICHAEL LALLY and Kathleen Fraser, although the FICTION editor of London's *Sunday Times,* Peter Ackroyd, praised it as "a delight to read" (Manousos 296).

The book's lyric qualities serve the larger purpose of charting the development of a fictional character, one of the traditional functions of the novel. The protagonist is Morgan Flew, a writer, perhaps an academic (to judge from occasional references to his "colleagues"). The book's very brief numbered chapters record Morgan's thoughts, fantasies, and reflections on incidents in his daily life. The chapters may be thought of as entries in Morgan's diary, and one of the models that Guest has acknowledged is Jonathan Swift's letters to Vanessa, an epistolary diary, which supplies the epigraph to *Seeking Air.* However, many of the chapters convey such a sense of immediacy that the reader experiences the illusion of having gained direct access to Morgan's consciousness rather than something he has written. The relevant model in this case is modernist experimentation in "interior monologue" or "stream of consciousness." Guest acknowledges a pioneer in this mode, the novelist Dorothy Richardson, by naming Morgan's lover, Miriam, the name of the protagonist in Richardson's multivolume *Pilgrimage* (1915–1938).

Morgan and Miriam inhabit the world that Guest and her husband, the historian Trumbull Higgins, experienced during the time that Guest was writing *Seeking Air.* Morgan's Manhattan apart-ment, with its view of the East River, is modeled on a studio on East 94th Street that a friend provided for Guest to use as a retreat for writing. The HAMPTONS on the eastern end of Long Island provide another pole of the fictional couple's existence, as they did for Guest and her husband. In the novel, association with the Hamptons especially establishes Morgan's and Miriam's place in the art world. Throughout the book Morgan makes references that imply his friend-ship with writers and artists who were in fact Guest's friends: the painter FAIRFIELD PORTER (referred to as "the great painter"), the sculptor Tony Smith, and the writer HARRY MATHEWS (the last two referred to by name). Even more significant as keys to Morgan's character are his constant references to works of art and literature. It is clear that these works not only exist in his world but are his world. His problem is to maintain a foothold in the real world, to avoid being swallowed up entirely into the world of Dark, his romantic designation for the great writing project at which he works obsessively yet inconclusively.

Morgan's problem is one that much preoccupied Guest throughout the decade of the 1970s. The metaphor of the title *Seeking Air* has its roots in the verse collection *Moscow Mansions* (1973), particularly in the poem "Roses," which takes its epigraph from a remark by Gertrude Stein: "painting has no air." "Rosy Ensconcements," from the same collection, describes the apartment assigned to Morgan in the novel, with "its air enriched by plants," a natural presence "transcending purely artistic considerations." The accommodation of art, or the life of the imagination, to nature, or the life of ordinary material existence, generates a narrative line in *The* COUNTESS FROM MINNEAPOLIS (1976), as it does in *Seeking Air*. However, art triumphs at the end of *The Countess* in the form of Tony Smith's sculpture *Amaryllis*, the shape of a plant abstracted and cast in metal, whereas nature triumphs, or at least asserts equal rights, at the end of *Seeking Air*. In Miriam, a real woman, Morgan finally recognizes the White he needs to counterbalance Dark.

In the spirit of broader cultural movements during the decade, it is possible to read the conclusion of *Seeking Air* from a feminist perspective and to understand Morgan's acknowledgment of Miriam's independent existence as a rejection of his earlier desire for total possession, which he himself calls "chauvinism" (72). According to Fraser, the possibility of performing such a critique arises from Guest's decision to write from the male point of view, inverting the procedure of Richardson. However, Morgan's residence in the apartment that Guest used for writing suggests that it may be as much Guest's consciousness as Morgan's to which the reader gains access in *Seeking Air*. Gender may be one of the "partitions, screens" that Morgan recalls from the houses in Japanese films (108) and that Guest employs to construct her House of Art.

Bibliography

Fraser, Kathleen. "'One Hundred and Three Chapters of Little Times': Collapsed and Transfigured Moments in the Cubist Fiction of Barbara Guest." In *Translating the Unspeakable: Poetry and the Innovative Necessity.* Tuscaloosa: University of Alabama Press, 2000, 161–173.

Guest, Barbara. Interview by Mark Hillringhouse. *American Poetry Review* (July–August 1992): 23–30.

———. *Seeking Air*. Los Angeles: Sun & Moon, 1995.

Johnson, Honor. "Barbara Guest and Lyric Atmospheres." *HOW(ever)* 1, no. 3 (February 1984). Available online. URL: http://www.scc.rutgers.edu/however/print_archive/alerts0284.html#guest. Accessed December 19, 2008.

Lally, Michael. Rev. *Seeking Air. American Book Review* 1, no. 3 (Summer 1978): 14.

Manousos, Anthony. "Barbara Guest. *Dictionary of Literary Biography* 5, Part 1. Edited by Donald J. Greiner. Detroit, Gale, 1980, 295–300.

"Self-Portrait in a Convex Mirror"
John Ashbery (1974)

JOHN ASHBERY's most famous poem, "Self-Portrait in a Convex Mirror," is not often discussed in the context of the NEW YORK SCHOOL because it marks the moment of his full acceptance into the mainstream of contemporary AMERICAN POETRY. "Self-Portrait" first appeared in the venerable magazine *Poetry* (August 1974) and then as the title poem of a volume (Viking, 1975) that was awarded the Pulitzer Prize, the National Book Award, and the National Book Critics Circle Award. In contrast to the disorientation that many readers experienced in Ashbery's earlier work, "Self-Portrait" seemed to offer the reader a stable position: standing in front of the 1524 painting by the Italian mannerist painter Parmigianino from which Ashbery's long poem takes its title. Certain passages of the poem provide detailed description of the painting or quote from art historical sources (Parmigianino's contemporary Giorgio Vasari and the modern art historian Sydney Freedberg), so that the reader seems to be provided not only with a definite object to "look at" but also with authoritative commentary on its meaning. But this "essayistic thrust," as Ashbery himself calls it, is suspended in a poetic process, as Ashbery explains: "It's really not about the Parmigianino portrait, which is a pretext for a lot of reflections and asides that are as tenuously connected to the core as they are in many of my poems" (Kostelanetz 108). The movement that Ashbery's poems have in common is also common to the New York School.

Like "the scene of my selves" in FRANK O'HARA's "IN MEMORY OF MY FEELINGS" (1956), the self-portrait in Ashbery's poem functions as "the occasion of these ruses" (O'Hara 256). Both poets operate on the assumptions that define New York School painting, or more specifically, the "ACTION PAINTING" defined by HAROLD ROSENBERG: "With traditional aesthetic references discarded as irrelevant, what gives the canvas its meaning is not psychological data but *rôle*, the way the artist organizes his emotional and intellectual energy as if he were in a living situation" (Rosenberg 29). "Self-Portrait in a Convex Mirror" opens by imagining just such a situation: "As Parmigianino did it" (68). The poem's conclusion repeats the full trajectory that Rosenberg outlines, starting with the discarding of "traditional aesthetic references," or what Ashbery calls "frozen gestures," "conventions." "The sooner they are burnt up / The better for the roles we have to play," he writes (82). Readers who find security in Ashbery's choice of a traditional painting as his starting point may miss the radical implications of this conclusion. However, as Ashbery's earlier art criticism makes clear, he viewed Parmigianino as a precursor of modernist painters, a distorter of FORM like Pablo Picasso and a conjuror of dream like Giorgio de Chirico (Ashbery, "Parmigianino"). The paradox of the particular portrait in question is that the techniques of "straight" realism produce the effect of illusion because the medium of vision itself, the mirror, is convex (a shape reproduced by the wooden surface on which Parmigianino painted). In a parallel process Ashbery turns the "essayistic" language of Sydney Freedberg toward the effect of poetry: "The forms retain a strong measure of ideal beauty [Freedberg] / As they forage in secret on our idea of distortion [Ashbery]" ("Self-Portrait" 73).

Although Parmigianino's self-portrait shows almost nothing beyond the face of the painter, the device of the convex mirror carries the potential for reflecting more of the external world than would have appeared, say, in an ordinary flat mirror. According to Vasari, in language that Ashbery adopts, this potential for inclusiveness was the original stimulus for the painting: "With great

art to copy all that you saw in the glass" ("Self-Portrait" 72). Critics of Ashbery's poem have debated whether he might be taking the painting as an occasion for turning outward toward a larger social reality than the private dreamscape evoked in his earlier volume *The Double Dream of Spring* (Dutton, 1970), a title taken from de Chirico. Among New York School poets, STEPHEN PAUL MILLER has gone to the extreme of placing "Self-Portrait in a Convex Mirror" in the contemporary political context of the Watergate scandal and President Richard Nixon's self-destructive obsession with surveillance, while DAVID LEHMAN, dismissing Miller's thesis as "delightfully flaky," presents the poem as "a soulful meditation" on art, "without topical reference or political intent" (313). Within the poem a passage on "the shadow of the city" seems to proceed through these extremes in a dialectical manner ("Self-Portrait" 75). The first city invoked is Rome, where Parmigianino was living during the sack of the city by the troops of Charles I, a decidedly political event. The next city invoked is Vienna, where Ashbery encountered Parmigianino's self-portrait at firsthand "with Pierre in 1959," an occasion both of art and private experience, "Pierre" being Ashbery's lover at the time. Finally, Ashbery takes us to "New York / where I am now, which is a logarithm / Of other cities." In its logarithmic function NEW YORK CITY serves as a lens, like a convex mirror, for expanding or multiplying experiences, personal and political, temporal and spatial. As a poem of the New York School, "Self-Portrait in a Convex Mirror" reflects "the space of New York" as Ashbery saw it reflected in the work of O'Hara: a "kaleidoscopic lumber-room where laws of time and space are altered" (Ashbery, Introduction x).

Bibliography

Ashbery, John. Introduction to *The Collected Poems*, by Frank O'Hara, Rev. ed. Edited by Donald Allen. Berkeley: University of California Press, 1995, vii–xi.

———. "Parmigianino" (1964). In *Reported Sightings: Art Chronicles, 1957–1987*. Edited by David Bergman. Cambridge, Mass.: Harvard University Press, 1991, 31–33.

———. "Self-Portrait in a Convex Mirror." In *Self-Portrait in a Convex Mirror*. 1975. Reprint, New York: Penguin, 1976, 68–83.

———. "Self-Portrait in a Convex Mirror." Audio recording. *Voice of the Poet: John Ashbery,* edited by J. D. McClatchy. New York: Random House Audio Books, 2001.

———. *Self-Portrait in a Convex Mirror: The Poem with Original Prints.* [By Richard Avedon, Elaine de Kooning, Willem de Kooning, Jane Freilicher, Jim Dine, Alex Katz, R.B. Kitaj, and Larry Rivers.] Limited ed. San Francisco: Arion Press, 1984.

Bloom, Harold. "The Breaking of Form." In *John Ashbery: Modern Critical Views.* New York: Chelsea House, 1985, 115–126.

Davidson, Michael. "Ekphrasis and the Postmodern Painter Poem." *Journal of Aesthetics and Art Criticism* 42 (1983): 69–79.

Freedberg, Sydney J. *Parmigianino: His Works in Painting.* Cambridge, Mass.: Harvard University Press, 1950.

Kostelanetz, Richard. "John Ashbery." In *The Old Poetries and the New.* Ann Arbor: University of Michigan Press, 1981, 87–110.

Lehman, David. *The Last Avant-Garde: The Making of the New York School of Poets* New York: Doubleday, 1998.

Miller, Stephen Paul. *The Seventies Now: Culture as Surveillance.* Durham, N.C.: Duke University Press, 1999, 108–115.

O'Hara, Frank. *The Collected Poems.* Rev. ed. Edited by Donald Allen. Berkeley: University of California Press, 1995.

Rosenberg, Harold. "The American Action Painters" (1952). In *The Tradition of the New.* 1960. Reprint, New York: Da Capo, 1994, 23–39.

Shoptaw, John. *On the Outside Looking Out: John Ashbery's Poetry.* Cambridge, Mass.: Harvard University Press, 1994.

Sokolsky, Anita. "A Commission That Never Materialized." In *John Ashbery: Modern Critical Views,* edited by Harold Bloom, 233–250. New York: Chelsea House, 1985.

Vasari, Giorgio. *Lives of the Most Eminent Painters, Sculptors, and Architects.* Vol. 3. Translated by Mrs. Jonathan Foster. London: Bohn, 1851.

Vendler, Helen. "John Ashbery and the Artist of the Past." In *Invisible Listeners: Lyric Intimacy in Herbert, Whitman, and Ashbery.* Princeton, N.J.: Princeton University Press, 2005, 57–80.

Ward, Geoff. *Statutes of Liberty: The New York School of Poets.* Basingstoke, U.K.: Macmillan, 1993.

Watkin, William. *In the Process of Poetry: The New York School and the Avant-Garde.* Lewisburg, Pa.: Bucknell University Press, 2001.

September 11, 2001

The destruction of the twin towers of the World Trade Center in DOWNTOWN MANHATTAN by terrorists commanding two passenger jets inscribed the date of September 11, 2001, in the historical record of mass catastrophe. Whether it is possible to inscribe the event in poetry has been a challenge to all poets, not just those of the NEW YORK SCHOOL. However, the challenge to the New York School is particularly acute because, on the one hand, the lives of the many poets who lived Downtown were directly affected by the disaster and, on the other hand, the New York School aesthetic is keyed to the individual rather than the mass, to dailiness rather than singular acts that change history.

"What Is a Day?" is the question ANN LAUTERBACH used to frame her initial meditation on "9/11" (225), echoing an assertion in the title poem of *Hum* (2005), "I know what days are," despite the unknowable nature of *that* day. "To narrate oneself into a catastrophe with unknowable global consequences seems trivial, or vain, or both," she admits in her prose meditation (225). In *In the Dust Zone,* MAGGIE DUBRIS narrates events she experienced directly as a paramedic at the World Trade Center site, but the narration keeps swerving in search of "facts" to undergird the unreality of the experience: "Pliny the Elder recorded more than 20,000 facts that survive to this day. Here are some of them: The earth is divided into three continents; Africa, Asia, and Urupaa. Al [a fellow paramedic] has just almost gotten killed." In an e-mail posting to the University of Buffalo Poetics List on September 11, Charles Bernstein concluded with a bald fact, "It's 8:23 in New York," deliberately echoing the opening of FRANK O'HARA's "THE DAY LADY DIED": "It's 12:20 in New York." It is clear that O'Hara's intimate relation to the death of "Lady Day" cannot be replicated in relation to the deaths of more than 2,700 people in the twin towers.

As if in reaction against the monumentality of the towers themselves, the elegiac strain in the New York School goes minimalist in the wake of the towers' destruction. Simply, "We / miss you," concludes EILEEN MYLES in "Flowers," her contribution to an anthology of *Poetry After 9/11* (Johnson and Merians 63). In general, the consequences after 9/11, rather than what happened then, provide a more manageable means for poetry to approach the subject. There are the immediate consequences of having to show identification in order to reach your Downtown home, the problem posed at the opening to a section of ANNE WALDMAN's *Iovis* III: "Identity posits control. Who is enemy? Who are fleeced?" (443). Complementary to the threat of state control is the threat of militarism, satirized in PAUL VIOLI's "House of Xerxes" in the language of a fashion publicist (Johnson and Merians 71–76). Above all, the consequences for language itself after September 11 become an explicit focus of concern in New York School poetry. These consequences can be seen as aesthetic, since "wit, laughter / and ambiguity" are now burdened by "gloom, / lamentation and humorlessness," according to TONY TOWLE (Johnson and Merians 47). They also can be seen as political, since "our language . . . is our nation," as CARTER RATCLIFF puts it (Johnson and Merians 21). Ultimately, they appear to be universal. In "The Pilots," a poem about the terrorists who piloted the planes on September 11, TOM CLARK asks:

> How to build sentences of such transparency
> The strange accidence of those pictures of the dead
> Peels away to reveal a grammar of humanness
>   (310).

The ethics of COLLABORATION that has evolved such a rich tradition in the New York School are fully tested in the poetic response to September 11. BOB HOLMAN organized the building of Twin Towers of Words at the People's Poetry Gathering Web site. One hundred and ten lines, one for each floor in the original building, were assembled for each "tower" out of text submitted to the Web site either spontaneously or by invitation. The names of contributors to the second, invited "tower" include such poets with national reputations as ROBERT CREELEY, Galway Kinnell, and Adrienne Rich, along with a large number of poets recognizable within the New York School, including BILL BERKSON,

ANSELM BERRIGAN, BRENDA COULTAS, ELAINE EQUI, ED FRIEDMAN, MICHAEL GIZZI, Holman, VINCENT KATZ, DAVID LEHMAN, GARY LENHART, Myles, MAUREEN OWEN, ED SANDERS, DAVID TRINIDAD, Waldman, MARJORIE WELISH, and JOHN YAU.

Bibliography

Bernstein, Charles. Posting on "Poetics" listserv (11 September 2001) Buffalo, N.Y.: University at Buffalo.

Clark, Tom. "The Pilots." In *Light & Shade: New and Selected Poems.* Minneapolis, Minn.: Coffee House Press, 2006, 310.

Dubris, Maggie. Excerpt from *In the Dust Zone.* Maggie Dubris Web site. Available online. URL: http://www.maggiedubris.com/events.htm. Accessed December 19, 2008.

Johnson, Dennis Loy, and Valerie Merians, eds. *Poetry After 9/11: An Anthology of New York Poets.* Hoboken, N.J.: Melville House, 2002.

Lauterbach, Ann. *Hum.* New York: Penguin, 2005.

———. "9/11." In *The Night Sky: Writings on the Poetry of Experience.* New York: Viking Penguin, 2005, 225–234.

O'Hara, Frank. "The Day Lady Died" (1959). In *The Collected Poems.* Rev. ed. Edited by Donald Allen. Berkeley: University of California Press, 1995, 325.

People's Poetry Gathering Web site. Available online. URL: http://www.peoplespoetry.org.

Waldman, Anne. Selections from *Iovis, Book III: The Eternal War.* In *In the Room of Never Grieve: New and Selected Poems, 1985–2003.* Minneapolis, Minn.: Coffee House Press, 2003, 391–479.

serial poem

The serial poem is a distinctly postmodernist version of the long poem. Unlike the epic, it does not narrate a story; unlike the lyric sequence, it does not trace the continuous development of a mood. It thrives, rather, on discontinuity and presents its parts as fragments, often by keeping the parts short and marking them off from one another by a system of numbering or graphic punctuation (for example, a series of asterisks or a line drawn across the page). However, as discrete units, the parts are expected to collide, generating a field of energy that remains, at least in theory, open to further additions or intrusions. In this respect the serial poem can be regarded as a type of "PROJECTIVE VERSE," as proposed by CHARLES OLSON. The term *serial poem* comes from the San Francisco poet Jack Spicer, who explained, "It simply means that you go from one point to another to another to another, not really knowing where you are from point A to point B" (73).

The development of the serial poem during the 1960s demonstrates the complex interaction between the NEW YORK SCHOOL and other trends in experimental poetry and even calls into question the conventional lines of division. The style of Spicer and his companion Robin Blaser—sonorous, sensual, symbol laden—is evident in early work by a number of poets who were soon to become identified with the second generation of the New York School: "The Suicide Rates" by LEWIS WARSH (1963); "Procris and Cephalus" by LARRY FAGIN (1964; Ellingham and Killian 314); "The DeCarlo Lots" by ANNE WALDMAN (1966). Fagin and Warsh both spent time in the Spicer circle in San Francisco during the early 1960s; Waldman had read Spicer and Blaser (both are represented in *The NEW AMERICAN POETRY, 1945–1960*) while still in high school. During the later 1960s in NEW YORK CITY, Warsh, Fagin, and Waldman came into contact with TED BERRIGAN, whose turn to the serial FORM in "TAMBOURINE LIFE" (1966)—which jokingly refers to "cereal poems" (*Collected Poems* 125)—marks a significant shift from the sequence form of *The SONNETS* (1964). The arbitrary succession of events in daily experience, from which Berrigan's sonnets draw much of their content, permeates the form as well in "Tambourine Life." The shift from myth to diary as the underpinning of the serial poem may be the New York School's most significant contribution to the form. It is evident in the later serial works of Waldman ("Giant Night," 1970) and Warsh (*PART OF MY HISTORY*, 1972). Meanwhile, in *Twelve Poems* (1972), Fagin had tapped into another source of the serial poem in the OBJECTIVIST tradition, extending from ROBERT CREELEY's *Pieces* (1968) back to George Oppen's *Discrete Series* (1934).

As Berrigan acknowledged in "Tambourine Life," again half-jokingly, other arts besides literature affected the handling of the serial poem within the New York School. "The John-Cage-Animal-Cracker / Method of Composition" that Berrigan claims to employ (*Collected Poems* 125) alludes to Cage's interest in creating MUSIC that accorded equal value to each sound, rather than assigning roles such as "dominant" and "subdominant" within a tonal hierarchy. The composer of "serial music," as the modernist tradition from which Cage derives is sometimes called, faces a challenge similar to that posed to the writer of serial poems: how to honor the equivalence of the parts while at the same time assembling them into a larger whole. Applying the analogy of *12-tone composition*, another term for "serial music," to "all-over" or abstract expressionist painting, CLEMENT GREENBERG thought the challenge could be met: "Like the 'twelve-tone composer,' the 'all-over' painter weaves his work of art into a tight mesh whose scheme of unity is recapitulated at every meshing point" (156–157).

Bibliography

Bernstein, Charles. "Reznikoff's Nearness." In *The Objectivist Nexus: Essays in Cultural Poetics*, edited by Rachel Blau DuPlessis and Peter Quartermain, 210–239. Tuscaloosa: University of Alabama Press, 1999.

Berrigan, Ted. *The Collected Poems of Ted Berrigan*. Edited by Alice Notley, Anselm Berrigan, and Edmund Berrigan. Berkeley: University of California Press, 2005.

Conte, Joseph M. "Seriality and the Contemporary Long Poem." *Sagetrieb* 11 (Spring–Fall 1992): 35–45.

———. *Unending Design: The Forms of Postmodern Poetry.* Ithaca, N.Y.: Cornell University Press, 1991.

Ellingham, Lewis, and Kevin Killian. *Poet Be Like God: Jack Spicer and the San Francisco Renaissance*. Hanover, N.H.: University Press of New England/Wesleyan University Press, 1998.

Golding, Alan. "George Oppen's Serial Poems." In *The Objectivist Nexus: Essays in Cultural Poetics*, edited by Rachel Blau DuPlessis and Peter Quartermain, 84–103. Tuscaloosa: University of Alabama Press, 1999.

Greenberg, Clement. "The Crisis of the Easel Picture" (1948). In *Art and Culture: Critical Essays*. Boston: Beacon, 1965, 154–157.

Spicer, Jack. "Vancouver Lecture 2: The Serial Poem and *The Holy Grail*." In *The House That Jack Built: The Collected Lectures*. Edited by Peter Gizzi. Hanover, N.H.: University Press of New England/Wesleyan University Press, 1998, 49–96.

Waldman, Anne, and Lewis Warsh, eds. *The Angel Hair Anthology.* New York: Granary Books, 2001.

Shapiro, David (1947–)

Born in Newark, New Jersey, David Shapiro was a violin prodigy who played with several orchestras. In pursuit of a parallel interest in poetry he attended the NEW YORK CITY WRITERS CONFERENCE at the ages of 14 and 15, entering the circle of the NEW YORK SCHOOL poets. When, at 18, Shapiro published his first book of poems, *January* (Holt, Rinehart and Winston, 1965), he decided that the pursuit of poetry would take precedence over MUSIC for him.

As STEPHEN PAUL MILLER noted in his master's thesis, Shapiro's early work features an "expressive surrealism" (24). Soon, inspired by Gertrude Stein's investigations of grammar and syntax, JOHN ASHBERY's *The Tennis Court Oath* (Wesleyan University Press, 1962), and JOSEPH CERAVOLO's work, Shapiro pursued collage experiments in poems such as "The Heavenly Humor" and "Poems from Deal"—both collected in his 1969 volume, *Poems from Deal* (Dutton)—to see how far he could depart from conventional meanings. In other poems he frequently tailored the parodic, chatty, casually allusive, associative modes of KENNETH KOCH, JAMES SCHUYLER, and FRANK O'HARA to his own intense preoccupation with political anger and family romance—largely absent from the elder poets' work—as well as erotic love.

In spring 1968 political anger against the Vietnam War and establishment complacency erupted on many college campuses, including Columbia University, where Shapiro was a student ("Cynical Idealists"). He was one of the protesters who temporarily occupied the office of university president Grayson Kirk, and a photo of Shapiro sitting in Kirk's chair and smoking a cigar appeared in newspapers around the country ("Where Are They Now"). After graduation Shapiro taught for a while at Columbia, where his students included future poet MARJORIE WELISH and future filmmaker Jim Jarmusch (1953–), but his past involvement in protests prevented him from receiving tenure, he feels. He went on to a tenured position in art history at William Patterson University in New Jersey

and an adjunct position at Cooper Union in NEW YORK CITY.

A Man Holding an Acoustic Panel (Dutton, 1971), Shapiro's third book, was nominated for a National Book Award. Its title poem constitutes his first major long poetic sequence and features a multiplicity of topics, tones, and images—framed only by a sense of movement among various geographical scenes—that anticipates the increasing complexity of his later sequences and long poems. One section is an elegy to the Czech martyr Jan Palach, which inspired architect John Hejduk's monument to Palach in Prague. Hejduk (1929–2000) was a close friend and colleague of Shapiro's at Cooper Union. The title sequence of *Burning Interior* (Overlook, 2002) is an elegy to Hejduk.

Shapiro's New York School association was cemented by his coediting *An* ANTHOLOGY OF NEW YORK POETS (Random House, 1970) with RON PADGETT. He wrote the first dissertation (1974), which became the first book (Columbia University Press, 1979), on Ashbery, and he joined several New York School elders in writing art criticism, including monographs on Piet Mondrian, JASPER JOHNS, and JIM DINE. Like other New York School poets, Shapiro has engaged in poetic COLLABORATION, including with his sister Debra (in *January*) and his son Daniel (in *A Burning Interior*). Other collaborative projects have incorporated Shapiro's poems, for instance, RUDOLPH BURCKHART's film *Mobile Homes* (1979). He has done cartoon poems with Alfred Leslie (1927–) and GEORGE SCHNEEMAN.

Shapiro's volumes *The Page-Turner* (Lateness, 1972) and *Lateness* (Overlook, 1977) parallel developments in the emerging movement of LANGUAGE POETRY. From his sixth collection, *To an Idea* (Overlook, 1983), until the present, Shapiro has written many poems that explore the conditions, limitations, and opportunities of language as a medium of representation and as a "solid" material entity. While precursors like Wallace Stevens and Ashbery exhibit this concern, Shapiro tends to make his investigations of representation more persistent and explicit than those of these predecessors. In poems such as "To an Idea" (1983), "Commentary Text Commentary Text Commentary Text" (1983), and "The Lost Golf Ball" (in *House [Blown Apart]*, Overlook, 1988), and in the sequences "House

(Blown Apart)" (1988), "After a Lost Original" (in the volume of the same title, Overlook, 1994), "The Seasons" (1994), and "A Burning Interior" (2002), Shapiro continually doubts yet entertains possibilities of recuperating origins amid endless "TRANSLATION," of arriving at a "pure" center while haunting the margins, of untangling "inside" from "outside," and of converting stark absence into palpable presence through the pursuit of traces.

Denying that Shapiro's poetry concerns "revelation or the production of meaning," Carl Whithaus argues that "it is about loss and memory, those fleeting traces of the past inscribed imperfectly in words." However, Miller, Thomas Fink, Jorie Graham, and other critics have found Shapiro's preoccupation with meaning and its failures to be bound up with his emphasis on elegy. Further, as CHRIS STROFFOLINO has noted about *After a Lost Original*, Shapiro's complex handling of the old "theme of father and son as a grid" (74), tied to the questioning of origins and after-effects, enables "a range of non-patriarchal possibilities" (74) to enrich the development of this theme (74). Shapiro's love poems, such as "An Exercise in Futility" and "A Song" (both 1983), spotlight the uncertainties of erotic attachments and power relations in such a way that they parody concepts of male dominance and drain them of authority.

If Shapiro is often dubbed "a poet's poet," it is partly because he foregrounds poetic language's complex conditions. But it is also because he achieves an elegant modulation of (free-verse) line length in carefully sculpted stanzas; exhibits a gift for assonance and the uncanny rhyme or slant-rhyme; deploys surprising, seamless shifts in tone, parodies with panache; and productively exploits ambiguities.

Bibliography

Beckley, Bill, and David Shapiro, eds. *Uncontrollable Beauty: Toward a New Aesthetics*. New York: Allworth Press/School of Visual Arts, 1998.

"The Cynical Idealists of '68." *Time*, 7 June 1968, 78–83.

Fink, Thomas. "David Shapiro's 'Possibilist Poetry.'" *Jacket* 24 (November 2003). Available online. URL: http://jacketmagazine.com/23/shap-fink.html. Accessed December 19, 2008.

———. *The Poetry of David Shapiro*. Rutherford, N.J.: Fairleigh Dickinson University Press, 1993.

———. "Tracing David Shapiro's 'The Seasons.'" *Contemporary Literature* 37, no. 3 (fall 1996): 416–438.

Fink, Thomas, and Joseph Lease, eds. *"Burning Interiors": David Shapiro's Poetry and Poetics*. Madison, N.J.: Fairleigh Dickinson University Press, 2007.

Gordon, Noah Eli. "Written and Rewritten to Order: The Gift of Generative Possibility in the Work of David Shapiro." *Octopus Magazine* 9. Available online. URL: http://www.octopusmagazine.com/issue09/gordon.htm. Accessed December 19, 2008.

Graham, Jorie. "Poets Wondering Who They Are." *New York Times Book Review*, 4 March 1984, p. 14.

Miller, Stephen Paul. "Jasper Johns and David Shapiro: An Analogy." Master's thesis, City College of New York, 1983.

———. "Periodizing Ashbery and His Influence." In *The Tribe of John: Ashbery and Contemporary Poetry*, edited by Susan M. Schultz, 146–167. Tuscaloosa: University of Alabama Press, 1995.

Shapiro, David. *New and Selected Poems (1965–2006)*. Woodstock, N.Y.: Overlook Press, 2007.

———. "Pluralist Music." *Rain Taxi* (Fall 2002). Available online. URL: http://www.raintaxi.com/online/2002fall/shapiro.shtml. Accessed December 19, 2008.

Stroffolino, Chris. Review of *After a Lost Original*. *Lingo* 4 (1995): 72–80.

Tranter, John, ed. David Shapiro feature. *Jacket* 23 (August 2003). Available online. URL: http://jacketmagazine.com/23/index.shtml. Accessed December 19, 2008.

"Where Are They Now." *Newsweek*, 13 October 1969, 24.

Whithaus, Carl. "Immediate Memories: (Nostalgic) Time and (Immediate) Loss in the Poetry of David Shapiro." *Rocky Mountain Modern Language Association* (1997). Available online. URL: http://rmmla.wsu.edu/ereview/53.1/articles/whithaus.asp. Accessed December 19, 2008.

Shards of God Ed Sanders (1970)

ED SANDERS's first novel, *Shards of God*, is subtitled *A Novel of the Yippies*. Sanders blends his own participation in the Left-wing movement of artists, writers, and dissidents—members of the Youth International Party, who became known as the "Yippies"—with colorfully exaggerated accounts of the hippie movement that satirize the media's portrayal of the counterculture. With its mosaic of characters, nearly all based on actual people, the work pays rapt homage to the counterculture and its heroes during the 1968 Democratic National Convention in CHICAGO, ILLINOIS. *Shards of God* engages the maelstrom of American life during that time of upheaval through a voice that alternately praises and scorns.

The narrative focuses on a series of absurd, imaginative conflicts between the Yippies and the institutions of American power. Abbie Hoffman and Jerry Rubin, real-life dissident leaders and organizers, initiate acts of civil disobedience and lead merry crowds against the Pentagon, the FBI, the CIA, the federal government, and the Chicago police led by Mayor Richard Daley. Hoffman and Rubin aim to replace the "total vomit" that "rules the nations of the west" with a "new magical Aeon of community" that would "create an era of justice and sharing" (15–17).

The story begins in summer 1967 during "The Great Pentagon Hunching Contest," where Sanders describes Hoffman as a god with powerful global connections to an impending revolution. The "Hunching Contest" pits Hoffman against a Pentagon-designed android in a sexual endurance contest. When the android loses, the Pentagon reneges on its agreement to share intelligence on the "Council of Eye Forms," a cosmic leadership instructing the Yippies. The council's members include Buddha, Ra, Jesus, Che Guevera, Karl Marx, and Malcolm X.

The narrative soon moves to Rubin's apartment for a Yippie initiation, which allows Sanders to relate Yippie goals, such as "a constitution to service a workable government of freedom and sharing"; to reveal its director, Jesus Christ; and to name such sympathizers and members as ALLEN GINSBERG, Ho Chi Minh, Raquel Welch, Bob Dylan, and a fleet of flying saucers (37).

After their space adventures Rubin and Hoffman lead the planning for the Chicago convention. Their tactics include computerized tapping of "electric information . . . from the CIA, from the FBI, from banks" (56). They also plan to sabotage the "Hate Computer" located at the University of Chicago that ultimately protects the "oil people" (59).

Sanders interrupts this narrative of Yippie planning with three chapters describing a government concentration camp for countercultural dissidents. Guevera instructs Rubin in the proper methods of resistance for the Chicago demonstrations, with which Sanders deals directly in five chapters, most memorably "The Festival of Life," "Terry Southern," and "The Battle of the Hilton." In his final chapter, "Orgy of Triumph with the Sauceroids," Sanders celebrates the implicit victory of the Yippies during the convention.

Sanders himself describes the book as a "failure," explaining that "it didn't live up to what I intended" ("Ed Sanders" 29). Nevertheless, *Shards of God* is an engaging document of the late 1960s and partially fulfills in novel form the poetic theory Sanders later championed, INVESTIGATIVE POETRY.

Bibliography

Boddy, Kasia. "*Shards of God:* An Epicurian to the Heroes of the Peace-Swarm." *Review of Contemporary Fiction* 9, no. 1 (Spring 1999): 61–80.

Sanders, Ed. "Ed Sanders on His Fiction." *Review of Contemporary Fiction* 9, no. 1 (Spring 1999): 24–30.

———. *Shards of God.* New York: Grove, 1970.

Shaw, Lytle (1967–)

FRANK O'HARA revolutionized AMERICAN POETRY by intimately involving in his work the current world about him—including at-the-time shocking subjects such as movie stars and the goings-on of his lovers and friends. Poet and art writer Lytle Shaw, who wrote his dissertation on O'Hara, "Frank O'Hara: The Poetics of Coterie" (University of Iowa, 2006), updates O'Hara's ambulatory and quotidian impulse; however, Shaw, is also highly influenced by the art and literary movements of the last quarter of the 20th century, such as CONCEPTUAL and environmental art. Shaw's *Cable Factory 20* (Atelos, 1999), inspired by Robert Smithson's descriptions of the landscape surrounding the Spiral Jetty in Utah's Great Salt Lake, juxtaposes 20 site-specific poems with associated visual images. More recent work includes an ongoing identity-twisting COLLABORATION with artist Jimbo Blachly, in which they investigate the city- and artscapes about them through the eyes of two dandies named the Chadwicks.

Their projects (which also reveal the torquing influence of HARRY MATHEWS, on whom Shaw wrote his undergraduate thesis) include "Errant Walker: Lodging the Chadwicks," in which they avariciously comment on the hypercharged real estate arena of NEW YORK CITY, and "Wandering Plots: A Grand Tour of Matta-Clark's Queens," a "tour" of artist Gordon Matta-Clark's land acquisitions throughout the borough. With O'Hara-like irreverence, Shaw's sharp sense of the banal strips the lyric of any lingering sentimentality and, like CLARK COOLIDGE with geological terms, introduces into it a vocabulary drawn from architecture and art theory, which he initially studied at Cornell University in his home town of Ithaca, New York. In fact, the title alone of his chapbook *Low Level Bureaucratic Structures: A Novel* (Shark, 1998) may have helped usher in a new era of poetry focused on the extreme ridiculousness of late-stage capitalism.

Shaw, along with his wife and frequent collaborator, visual artist Emilie Clark, is the editor of *Shark*, a journal of poetics and art writing, and the curator of the Line Reading Series at the Drawing Center, which has featured JOHN ASHBERY, BERNADETTE MAYER, Lyn Hejinian, and JACKSON MAC LOW. Other books by Shaw, who currently teaches American literature at New York University, include *Ten Masters and the Method* (Shark, 2005); *The Lobe* (Roof, 2002); *A Side of Closure* (a+bend, 2000); *The Rough Voice*, with Clark (Idiom, 1998); *Principles of the Emeryville Shellmound* (Shark, 1998); and *Flexagon*, with Clark (ghos-ti-, 1998).

Sikelianos, Eleni (1965–   )

In the latest generation of NEW YORK SCHOOL poets, there are few who have the range and mastery that poet and memoirist Eleni Sikelianos does. Drawing from "lines of . . . ancestors laid out in filaments" (*Book of Jon* ix), she explores in often-epic prose and verse her family's past as redemptive prologue. The great-granddaughter of Greek poet Angelos Sikelianos (who was nominated for the Nobel Prize) and granddaughter of Eva Palmer Sikelianos (after whom Sikelianos's own daughter is named), a THEATER director and lover of Nathalie Barney and burlesque dancer Melena the Cat Lady,

Sikelianos, born in Santa Barbara, California, in 1965, is also the niece of ANNE WALDMAN. In *The Book of Jon* (City Lights, 2004) she explores in visceral and poetic prose (demonstrating her formidable ability to mix GENREs) the life of her father, Jon Sikelianos, a musician and heroin addict. But in addition to chronicling her family, she explores the geography of her early childhood, lately culminated in her epic remaking of the pastoral, *The California Poem* (Coffee House Press, 2004).

The NEW YORK SCHOOL influence, particularly that of FRANK O'HARA and JAMES SCHUYLER, can be found in her close and exacting eye for FORM and detail, as well as her deeply felt linguistic depictions of love, as evident in collections such as *Earliest Worlds* (Coffee House Press, 1994)). The presence of ALICE NOTLEY and BERNADETTE MAYER, both of whom were Sikelianos's teachers, are found in the development of her strong and unique line, which utilizes the full space of the page in various medium-crossing forms, including poetic "essays." She also takes from Waldman her sense of the poet as a public presence, using a range of voices to convey linguistic and political dissent. Like most subsequent generations of the New York School poets, Sikelianos looks to other literary traditions, such as the OBJECTIVISTS, especially Lorine Niedecker, and poets such as H.D. (Hilda Doolittle) and Fanny Howe, as well as prose writers Marcel Proust and Herman Melville. Other books include *The Monster Lives of Boys & Girls* (Green Integer, National Poetry Series, 2003), *The Book of Tendons* (Post-Apollo, 1997), and *To Speak While Dreaming* (Selva Editions, 1993). Married to the FICTION writer Laird Hunt, Sikelianos lives in Boulder, Colorado.

Bibliography

Sikelianos, Eleni. *The Book of Jon*. San Francisco: City Lights, 2004.

Sinking of the Odradek Stadium, The
Harry Mathews (1975)

This fanciful yet dense novel by HARRY MATHEWS consists of letters sent between an oddly matched pair of newlyweds: Zachary, a librarian at the University of Miami, and Twang, an expatriate of the fictional Southeast Asian country, Pan-Nam, now residing in Italy. Separated by a vast geographical expanse, the lovers conspire to locate a cache of gold that dates back to Renaissance Italy. As fragments of the gold's tortuous history emerge, however, Twang seems increasingly distant, and Zachary begins to lose his grip on reality.

The world of *The Sinking of the Odradek Stadium* is a contorted reflection of our own, in which junkies get high sniffing sulfur, Native Americans host semi-clothed nudist colonies for the sexually timid, and infants learn to chew with "Manducation" apples, specially bred for softness. On top of these idiosyncrasies, the novel is complicated by Twang's pidgin English, which is riddled with a bizarre combination of Pannamese-influenced grammar and spelling mistakes, often resulting in hilarious, Joycean puns. For example, she relates how an impotent lover "falls prostate," instead of "prostrate," at her feet (58).

Twang's command of the language gradually improves, but it remains difficult to decipher for most of the book. For Zachary, this challenge is exacerbated by the failed delivery (indicated via footnote) of a crucial letter, in which Twang tells him that, for security, the couple must no longer be candid with each another in writing. The resultant rift that forms between the lovers underlines the theme of language as a fallible system of shared discursive rules; having never received his wife's letter (and, thus, her new rules), Zachary misconstrues all of her subsequent correspondence as emotional neglect.

In terms of its quirky, tongue-in-cheek exuberance and eclectic mix of styles, Mathews's novel resembles the work of fellow NEW YORK SCHOOL alumnus KENNETH KOCH. Mathews, however, stops short of Koch's madcap frivolity, and his two main characters are never so absurd as to exclude them from the reader's sympathy.

The Sinking of the Odradek Stadium first saw print in the *PARIS REVIEW*, in 1971–72, but it was then rejected more than 25 times before Harper & Row released it in a volume with Mathews's earlier novels, *The CONVERSIONS* and *TLOOTH*, in 1975. When it finally came out, the book was very well received, and it has been reprinted several times, wryly appended by an index that offers clues to various allusions made in the text and also to the novel's enigmatic title.

Bibliography
Ash, John. "A Conversation with Harry Mathews." *Review of Contemporary Fiction* (Fall 1987): 21–32.
Mathews, Harry. *The Sinking of the Odradek Stadium and Other Novels.* New York: Harper & Row, 1975.
———. *The Way Home.* London: Atlas Press, 1999.
McPheron, William. "Harry Mathews: A Checklist." *Review of Contemporary Fiction* (Fall 1987): 197–226.
Shaw, Lytle. "An Interview with Harry Mathews" (1994). *Chicago Review* (Spring 1997): 36–52.

"Skaters, The" John Ashbery (1964)

In critical discussion of JOHN ASHBERY, his long poem "The Skaters" has come to mark a turning point in his development, though what he was turning from or to is characterized differently, depending on the critic. For DAVID LEHMAN, "The Skaters" marks the beginning of Ashbery's "maturity" (161). For Harold Bloom, the poem and the volume in which it appeared, *Rivers and Mountains* (Holt, Rinehart and Winston, 1966), restored Ashbery to the tradition of American Romanticism, from which, according to Bloom, he had regrettably strayed in the radically experimental work of his preceding volume, *The Tennis Court Oath* (Wesleyan University Press, 1962; Bloom 116). John Shoptaw goes so far as to claim that "The Skaters" is "a kind of farewell to the poetics of the New York school" (89). That claim overlooks the poem's impact on the rising second generation, at least one of whom, GERARD MALANGA, makes a cameo appearance in "The Skaters," in a reference to "Gerard's letters" ("The Skaters" 36; Wolf 89–90). Reading the poem in manuscript as a freshman at Columbia University was for DAVID SHAPIRO "one of the ten greatest aesthetic experiences of my life" (Lehman 237). Not long afterward, thanks to the teaching of KENNETH KOCH, Columbia students were comparing "The Skaters" to T. S. Eliot's *The Waste Land*, a comparison that "did not seem exaggerated to me," Lehman recalls (114).

The relation of "The Skaters" to the NEW YORK SCHOOL and the nature of the "turn" that this poem marks in Ashbery's career can be illuminated by the concept of ABSTRACT EXPRESSIONISM derived from the painting that defined the avant-garde in which New York School poetry developed. If *The*

Tennis Court Oath takes abstraction to an extreme limit, *Rivers and Mountains* restores a balance with expressionism, but it does not leave abstraction behind altogether. The pattern of development is explicitly outlined in the poem: "the rhythm of the series of repeated jumps, from abstract into positive and back to a slightly less diluted abstract" ("The Skaters" 39). The more diluted abstraction is "This leaving-out business" to which Ashbery refers in a passage immediately preceding the one just quoted, a passage to which critics have returned repeatedly in an attempt to define Ashbery's poetics (McHale 583). Leaving out achieves abstraction by reduction, shutting out the recognizable world to which both poetry and painting have traditionally referred and even eliminating the structures of relationship that imitate relations in the world. "What is the matter with plain old-fashioned cause-and-effect?" Ashbery asks in "The Skaters" (39). In contrast to the highly fragmented style of a poem such as "Europe," from *The Tennis Court Oath*, "The Skaters" restores relations of continuity at the levels both of grammar and of reference. But it circles back toward a less diluted abstraction by "wanting to put too much in" ("The Skaters" 38). Putting in and taking out had been defined as alternative modes of abstraction by the abstract expressionist painter WILLEM DE KOONING (de Kooning 557). In *Three Poems* (Viking, 1972) Ashbery was still weighing the alternatives: "I had thought that if I could put it all down, that would be one way. And next the thought came to me that to leave all out would be another, and truer, way" (*Three Poems* 3).

The expressionism of "The Skaters" has autobiographical roots. Ashbery has described the poem as "a meditation on my childhood which was rather solitary" (interview 119). No doubt, as many critics have suggested, the theme of solitude was reinforced by Ashbery's experience of "being an exile" ("Skaters 57) in Europe during the time he wrote the poem. However, the poem treats the clichéd image of the isolated artist largely as a subject for parody (Shapiro 112–114). The specific problem that Ashbery associates with his solitary childhood is not romantic agony—or *schmerzen*, as the poem calls it with an ironic eye on German romanticism ("The Skaters" 39)—but simply "boredom"

(interview 119). Several passages in *The Skaters* are lifted from an activity book entitled *Three Hundred Things a Bright Boy Can Do*, with suggestions ranging from perspective drawing ("The Skaters" 47–48) to "fire designs" (50) to skating. When skating is first introduced at the opening of Ashbery's poem, it is presented as an escape from boredom into the delight of "novelty":

> it is novelty
> That guides these swift blades o'er the ice
> Projects into a finer expression (but at the expense
> Of energy) the profile I cannot remember
> ("The Skaters" 34).

To the extent that the New York School had a theory of the avant-garde, this is it. "The history of art and the history of each artist's development are the response to the discomforts of *boredom*," LARRY RIVERS told FRANK O'HARA (Rivers 113). The "finer expression" that results from the quest for novelty is not the expression of "the old, imprecise feelings" ("The Skaters" 40) but rather the satisfaction of formal precision, like the skater's figure 8 that Ashbery later describes (47). If Ashbery parodies the *schmerzen* of German romanticism, he is still fascinated by its FORMs, such as the four-part sonata structure that underlies the four sections of "The Skaters" (Shapiro 109; Herd 109). Similarly, while the details of Ashbery's personal history remain "the profile I cannot remember," "The Skaters" "projects into a finer expression" what Ashbery has called "forms of autobiography" (interview 123).

Bibliography

Ashbery, John. Interview by Janet Bloom and Robert Losada. In *The Craft of Poetry: Interviews from* The New York Quarterly, edited by William Packard, 111–132. Garden City, N.Y.: Doubleday, 1974.

———. "The Skaters." In *Rivers and Mountains*. 1966. Reprint, New York: Ecco Press, 1977, 34–63.

———. *Three Poems*. 1972. Reprint, New York: Penguin, 1977.

Bloom, Harold. "John Ashbery: The Charity of the Hard Moments" (1973). In *Contemporary Poetry in America: Essays and Interviews*, edited by Robert Boyers, 110–138. New York: Schocken, 1974.

de Kooning, Willem. "What Abstract Art Means to Me" (1951). In *Theories of Modern Art: A Source Book by Artists and Critics,* edited by Herschel B. Chipp, 556–561. Berkeley: University of California Press, 1971.

Herd, David. *John Ashbery and American Poetry.* New York: Palgrave, 2000.

Lehman, David. *The Last Avant-Garde: The Making of the New York School of Poets.* New York: Doubleday, 1998.

McHale, Brian. "How (Not) to Read Postmodernist Long Poems: The Case of Ashbery's 'The Skaters.'" *Poetics Today* 21, no. 3 (Fall 2000): 561–590.

Rivers, Larry. "Larry Rivers: 'Why I Paint as I Do'" (1959). In *Art Chronicles, 1954–1966,* by Frank O'Hara, 106–120. Rev. ed. New York: Braziller, 1990.

Shapiro, David. "'The Skaters': An Analysis." In *John Ashbery: An Introduction to the Poetry.* New York: Columbia University Press, 1979, 93–131.

Shoptaw, John. "Taurus, Leo, Gemini: *Rivers and Mountains.*" In *On the Outside Looking Out: John Ashbery's Poetry.* Cambridge, Mass.: Harvard University Press, 1994, 74–99.

Wolf, Reva. *Andy Warhol, Poetry, and Gossip in the 1960s.* Chicago: University of Chicago Press, 1997.

slam poetry

As early as 1979 the POETRY PROJECT AT ST. MARK'S CHURCH IN-THE-BOWERY hosted experiments in adversarial COLLABORATION that later developed into the type of PERFORMANCE ART known as the poetry slam. ANNE WALDMAN and TED BERRIGAN confronted each other with boxing gloves at a joint reading, and KENNETH KOCH and ALLEN GINSBERG improvised alternating lines representing the antagonists in "Popeye and William Blake Fight to the Death." Al Simmons brought the idea from NEW YORK CITY to CHICAGO, ILLINOIS, where it took root in a punk poetry scene that included JEROME SALA and ELAINE EQUI, who would later move to New York. The slam as an outright contest, with the audience boisterously taking sides, took shape under the leadership of Marc Smith at two Chicago bars, Get Me High and the Green Mill. Inspired by a visit to Chicago, BOB HOLMAN introduced the slam model in New York at the NUYORICAN POETS CAFÉ in 1992 and promoted cross-fertilization between slam poetry and rap (Gates).

The spread of poetry slams nationwide has inevitably led to variations in practice. Typically, however, the format consists of each competitor performing for a limited time (usually three minutes); receiving scores from a panel of judges, as in Olympic competition; and, depending on the score received, either dropping out or advancing to further rounds, until a final winner is determined. Under these conditions, and in response to the need to connect immediately with a rowdy audience, slam poetry has evolved as a distinctive style, employing insistent patterns of rhythm and other sound effects, often including rhyme, and delivering provocative content as bluntly as possible while constantly entertaining. As a participant in the World Heavyweight Championship Poetry Bout in Taos, New Mexico, part of the annual Poetry Circus established by Simmons, Waldman has described the creative exhilaration: "As contestants, both Victor Hernandez Cruz and I pulled out all the stops, egged on by the fury of the mob and by our own sense of drama, display, and incantation" (143).

The Taos festival, held annually between 1982 and 2003, retained an association with the Poetry Project through its invited participants and, through the practice of invitation, became identified with one pole in a continuing tension among advocates of slam poetry. As a competition, the slam format inevitably produces stars, and it seems only natural that "championship" events invite stars to participate, rather than preserving the "open mike" policy through which both competitors and judges have been recruited at the Green Mill and the Nuyorican Poets Café. On the other hand, the punk ethos in which slam poetry originated demands that the star performer stand for the audience, sending the message, "You could be doing this as easily as I can."

Bibliography

Gates, Henry Louis, Jr. "Downtown Chronicles: Sudden Def." *New Yorker,* 19 June 1995, 34–42.

Heintz, Kurt. "An Incomplete History of Slam." E-poets. network. Available online. URL: http://www.e-poets. net/library/slam/. Accessed December 19, 2008.

Kane, Daniel. "Epilogue: Bob Holman, the Poetry Project, and the Nuyorican Poets Café." In *All Poets Welcome: The Lower East Side Poetry Scene in the 1960s*. Berkeley: University of California Press, 2003, 203–208.

Koch, Kenneth, and Allen Ginsberg. "Popeye and William Blake Fight to the Death." Audio file. *Jacket* 15 (December 2001). Available online. URL: http://www.jacketmagazine.com/15/koch-popeye. html. Accessed December 19, 2008.

Waldman, Anne. *Fast Speaking Woman*. New expanded ed. San Francisco: City Lights, 1996.

Waldman, Anne, and Victor Hernandez Cruz. *The Battle of the Bards*. Videorecording. Los Angeles: Lannan Literary Foundation, 1990.

Smith, Patti (1946–) *musician*

To see through the legendary rock star to the formative Patti Smith, you must imagine a young woman living the poetic paradox: She quietly digests the French symbolist Arthur Rimbaud while listening to The Rolling Stones, her own rock gods (Smith, "Rise of the Sacred Monsters"). Her musical mode is inflected by the cerebral twisting of Bob Dylan as much as the sexual stomp of James Brown. Her NEW YORK SCHOOL affiliation owes as much to the painters as to the poets. She tried painting, but "frustrated with the image I'd draw words instead—rhythms that ran off the page onto the plaster. Writing lyrics evolved from the physical act of drawing words" (*Patti Smith Complete* 21). Perhaps the ultimate paradox in her makeup is captured in an early poem, "Neo Boy," where she creates a persona as "altar kneeler / action painter," reflecting her religious upbringing as well as her artistic inclination (*Babel* 36).

Born in CHICAGO, ILLINOIS, Smith moved with her family to Philadelphia when she was three, and eventually settled in Woodbury, New Jersey, when she was nine. She enrolled in Glassboro State Teachers College but dropped out at age 20. The following year, 1967, she moved to NEW YORK CITY and connected with a number of emerging artists, including playwright Sam Shepard (1943–), with whom she collaborated in *Cowboy Mouth* (1971), and photographer Robert Mapplethorpe (1946–89). In the early 1970s Smith embarked on a double career as both poet and rock singer. In 1971 she read at the POETRY PROJECT AT ST. MARK'S CHURCH IN-THE-BOWERY with backup by guitarist Lenny Kaye. In 1972 her first poetry collection, *Seventh Heaven,* was published by TELEGRAPH BOOKS. By 1974, for her first recording session, Smith had assembled some of PUNK ROCK's finest, from keyboardist Richard Sohl (1954–90) to Television guitarist Tom Verlaine (1949–).

Smith discovered that her poems "were great performed," but "they weren't such hot shit written down" (McNeil and McCain 161). While the MUSIC sometimes displays the rampant improvisation of free JAZZ, most of her lyrics have the ethereal control of free verse or of the prose poetry favored by the French symbolists. JIM CARROLL, fellow poet and sometime boyfriend, recalls, "She could just let it all loose, but formwise she wasn't that disciplined." In performance, however, "she could just go nuts and counterpoint it with this sweet self and let go with this weird-angry-magic self, too" (McNeil and McCain 111).

Smith's image was uncompromising. Rejecting the constraints of gendered performance, she cultivated an androgynous look, a clear departure from glamorous doo-wop groups that dominated 1960s popular music. She was aggressive, penning radio-hostile tunes that countered snappy, overplayed disco. Free to be (or to remake) herself, she developed a wide range of expression in recordings. "Gloria," the lead track on her debut album, *Horses* (1975), is frontal nudity in church, complete with choir refrain, Smith's lonely sacrament for the blues bum to take on his lonely way. Tinkling, sober piano keys inform the depressive pleading in "Pissing in a River" (*Radio Ethiopia*, 1976), while "Babelogue" (*Easter*, 1978) is a coarse, weighty "spoken word" piece read at rapid speed.

Throughout her career Smith has stayed in touch with the action painter who brought about the union of the poet and the performer. In "Rock n Roll Nigger" (*Easter*), she revalued the term of racial hatred by connecting it with the rebel artist: "Jackson Pollock was a nigger." In 1980 Smith brought the first phase of her career to a close at a benefit concert in Detroit, Michigan, where she and Fred "Sonic" Smith (1948–94), whom she married that year, improvised an accompaniment to a film of Jackson Pollock painting (Heylin 280–281). During a period of retirement from concert touring, Smith gave birth to two children, the first a son named Jackson. Upon her return to active recording, a track on *Peace and Noise* (1997), named after Pollock's painting *Blue Poles*, recalls the connection between drawing and writing that launched Smith's career: "Blue poles infinitely winding, as I write, as I write."

Bibliography

Heylin, Clinton. *From the Velvets to the Voidoids: The Birth of American Punk Rock.* Updated ed. Chicago: A Cappella/Chicago Review Press, 2005.

McNeil, Legs, and Gillian McCain. *Please Kill Me: The Uncensored Oral History of Punk.* New York: Grove, 1996.

Noland, Carrie Jaurès. "Rimbaud and Patti Smith: Style as Social Deviance." *Critical Inquiry* 21, no. 3 (Spring 1995): 581–610.

Smith, Greg. "'And All the Sinners, Saints': Patti Smith, Pioneer Musician and Poet." *Midwest Quarterly* 41, no. 2 (Winter 2000): 173–190.

Smith, Patti. *Auguries of Innocence.* New York: Ecco, 2005.

———. *Babel.* New York: G. P. Putnam's Sons, 1978.

———. *Early Work: 1970–1979.* New York: W. W. Norton, 1994.

———. *Land 1975–2002.* Sound recording, 22-14708-2. New York: Arista Records, 2002.

———. *Patti Smith Complete, 1975–2006: Lyrics, Reflections and Notes for the Future.* New York: Harper Perennial, 2006.

———. "Rise of the Sacred Monsters." In *Rock and Roll Is Here to Stay,* edited by William McKeen, 372–383. New York: W. W. Norton, 2000.

———. *Strange Messenger.* Exhibit catalog. Pittsburgh, Pa.: Andy Warhol Museum, 2002.

———. *Woolgathering.* New York: Hanuman Books, 1992.

Something Wonderful May Happen (2001)

The only documentary film focusing on New York School poetry, *Something Wonderful May Happen: New York School of Poets and Beyond* was produced by a team of Danish filmmakers—Lars Movin (1959–), Niels Plenge (1959–), and Thomas Thura (1963–)—as part of a film series for a poetry program called "In the Making." John Ashbery, Kenneth Koch, and Frank O'Hara represent the first-generation New York School, the first two in fresh footage of readings and interviews, O'Hara in clips from a *USA: Poetry* segment produced by Richard Moore for National Educational Television in 1966. The view "beyond" the New York School, promised in the film's subtitle, is provided by David Lehman and Charles Bernstein (1950–), who read their poems and offer commentary throughout, and Jordan Davis, who comments briefly on youthful exuberance as an enduring legacy of the New York School. Lehman's and Bernstein's comments offer conflicting views, with Lehman emphasizing the poets' use of ordinary speech and their affirmative view of life, while Bernstein stresses the torquing of the ordinary by self-conscious artifice in the service of social critique. The seductively "natural" style of the film glosses over these conflicts in the politics of poetry.

Interviews with Jane Freilicher, Larry Rivers, and Alfred Leslie (1927–) represent the important relationship between New York School painting and poetry. Freilicher alludes to the politics of painting in connection with her own decision to paint figuratively at a time when abstraction was dominant. Unfortunately, the film does not show what the dominant, abstract expressionist mode looked like—in the work of Jackson Pollock and Willem de Kooning, for instance—and only a glimpse of Freilicher's work is shown. More of Rivers's work appears in a segment during which he bluntly describes the tensions of collaborating with poets whose work he did not always like. One of the segments featuring Leslie shows rare footage from his film *The Birth of a Nation* (1965), for which O'Hara wrote captions.

The title of the film, taken from O'Hara's journal (O'Hara 108–109), takes on ironic coloring in the context of the time in which it was made. Koch and Rivers both died during summer 2002. With more wide-ranging impact, the World Trade Center towers, which appear repeatedly in the film's views of the New York skyline, disappeared in the terrorist attack of September 11, 2001. One of the poems Lehman reads in the film is "The World Trade Center," recording his more positive view of the towers after the bombing attempt in 1993. The affirmative view of life that he ascribes to the New

York School was to be tested more severely when the towers fell.

Bibliography

Lehman, David. "The World Trade Center." In *Valentine Place*. New York: Scribner, 1996, 48.

Movin, Lars, et al. *Something Wonderful May Happen.* Videorecording. 57 minutes. New York: Filmmakers Library, 2001.

O'Hara, Frank. "A Journal" (1948–49). In *Early Writing*. Edited by Donald Allen. Bolinas, Calif.: Grey Fox, 1977, 97–110.

Some Trees: Three Poems for Three Voices
Ned Rorem and John Ashbery (1968)

Some Trees: Three Poems for Three Voices consists of songs for soprano, mezzo-soprano, and bass-baritone soloists with piano accompaniment, composed in 1968 by NED ROREM to texts by JOHN ASHBERY from the mid-1950s. It was published by Boosey & Hawkes. Rorem, who is renowned both as a song composer and a prolific diarist, eschews the austere atonality of mid-20th-century musical avant-gardists, preferring a tonally grounded neoromantic style. *Some Trees*, his first work for an ensemble of soloists rather than a single singer, was written as a finale for a Town Hall recital of his MUSIC. Rorem considers the works of Ashbery and other NEW YORK SCHOOL poets to be "ideal for madrigal combinations meant for the joy of collective unity in the modern home and hall," as he wrote in liner notes. The opening song, "Some Trees," is set to music that contravenes the text's stanzaic organization and rhyming couplets. The trio of singers declaim the initial line, "These are amazing," in unison, and the vocal writing remains primarily homophonic, although Rorem initiates several phrases with staggered, imitative entries so that a line or word of text is reiterated across the ensemble (for example, "A silence already filled . . ."). Its energetic tempo is sustained with a dense, active keyboard accompaniment. A more somber tone is presented by the second song, "The Grapevine," which opens with an explicit harmonic reference to the prelude to Richard Wagner's opera *Tristan und Isolde*. The voices render the text one after another, a line or two at a time, only singing together at the line "But things get darker," midway through Ashbery's final stanza. The last and longest poem, "Our Youth," receives the most complex musical setting, its comparatively dissonant harmonic language occasionally veering toward atonality. Commencing with the male voice deliberately intoning the first stanza a cappella, Rorem's score closely follows and dramatizes the text's narrative. Its pace gradually accelerates, the texture growing increasingly dense, toward the penultimate stanza, "Blue hampers . . . Explosions, Ice . . . ," in which the piano accompaniment abruptly ceases, exposing the vocal trio exchanging overlapping fragments of text. Following a brief solo keyboard interlude, the poem's final lines—"It's true we have not avoided our destiny . . . ,"—are set in the manner of a church chorale, slow and solemn.

Bibliography

Rorem, Ned. Liner notes to *Women's Voices, Some Trees, The Nantucket Songs, and Other Songs.* Various artists. Sound recording, CRI CD 657. New York: CRI, 1993.

Sonnets, The Ted Berrigan (1964)

TED BERRIGAN wrote *The Sonnets* in the spring of 1963, little more than two years after he moved from Tulsa, Oklahoma, to NEW YORK CITY. After its publication Berrigan liked to cultivate the myth that the book was a sort of dynamo waiting to be put into operation: "I came to New York to become this wonderful poet . . . and I was to be very serious. Not to become but to be. To find out how to work at it. That only took about a year and a half, then I wrote this major work and there I was" (Pritikin 20). In reality, the book is the culmination of an intense poetic education and apprenticeship. *The Sonnets* is largely influenced by the DADA techniques of cut-up and collage, Hans Hoffman's notion of "push and pull," and Berrigan's close reading of JOHN CAGE's *Silence* (1961), Alfred North Whitehead's *Process and Reality* (1929), and first-generation NEW YORK SCHOOL poets FRANK O'HARA and JOHN ASHBERY. Despite the book's myriad influences and appropriations, it was, as RON PADGETT said, "not a question of plagiarization . . . it was a matter of using 'found' lines to create an entirely different work" ("On *The Sonnets*" 9). In one short passage from Sonnet II, for example, one can see an imitation of O'Hara's "The DAY LADY DIED" (1959) and a reference to Ashbery's "How Much Longer Will I Be Able to Inhabit the Divine Sepulcher . . ." (1962) collaged with a more openly lyric voice:

> It's 8:30 p.m. in New York and I've been running
>   around all day
> old come-all-ye's streel into the streets. Yes, it
>   is now,
> How Much Longer Will I Be Able to Inhabit
>   The Divine
> and the day is bright gray turning green (2).

None of the poems strictly fits the traditional definition of a sonnet, but most conform thematically to the Petrarchan model or to a 4-4-4-2 arrangement, and, as Padgett noted, "the feel of the well-crafted 'little song' hovers behind them all" ("On *The Sonnets*" 10). Like William Shakespeare's *Sonnets*, the book has a narrative arc that involves friendships and love triangles. From Shakespeare, Berrigan also

> discovered that the basic unit of the sonnet was the line. . . . I wanted every line, you see, to be able to be read as a separate unit by itself. I didn't necessarily want it to have meaning by itself, but it had to be there, it had to exist the way that the squares in a Josef Albers work or the way the stripes do in a Jasper Johns flag (Berrigan, "Sonnet Workshop" 92–93).

Many of the poems, especially those in the latter third of the book, are composed entirely from lines rearranged from earlier poems, sometimes according to a discernable pattern, sometimes by ear. Each time a line appears, it is transformed by its placement according to the material surrounding it.

Although *The Sonnets* was extremely influential in avant-garde circles, it has received surprisingly little critical attention. The longest and most notable essays on *The Sonnets* are JOEL LEWIS's "'Everything Turns into Writing': The Sonnets of

Ted Berrigan" and the chapter on Berrigan in Libbie Rifkin's *Career Moves*. While Lewis's essay primarily summarizes information that can be gleaned from the many interviews and lectures Berrigan gave on *The Sonnets*, Rifkin tries at great length to explain *The Sonnets* as part of Berrigan's careerist strategy aimed at self-canonization. As Daniel Kane aptly points out, however,

> Rifkin is certainly correct in pointing out that Berrigan was hyper-aware of audience and reception, [but] his poetry and his work as an editor might be read more fruitfully as works of microcommunity building that both echoed and complicated the utopian aspects of 1960s counterculture. . . . The idea of secure canonicity would probably have seemed ludicrous to Berrigan, since the writers he most respected were entirely dismissed by the academic establishment throughout the 1960s and early 1970s (107).

Ironically, as Kane suggests elsewhere, the reprinting of *The Sonnets* by Grove Press in 1967 was a symbolic event that marked the beginning of the dissemination of the second-generation New York School, as many left for teaching positions and their work was picked up by larger publishing houses.

Despite the fact that *The Sonnets* is still Berrigan's best-known work, he always maintained that the book was the end of one way of writing, not the beginning. If one considers that after *The Sonnets* Berrigan's work turned toward a more openly diaristic style, this appears to be true. As ALICE NOTLEY suggests, however, Berrigan's perpetual tinkering with the book and occasional revisiting of *The Sonnets*'s compositional method shows his "continuing interest in the poems as movable parts of space-time and in the ongoing applicability of their method" (Berrigan, *Sonnets* 84).

The Sonnets has been published in four separate editions—in 1964 ("C" Press), 1967 (Grove), 1982 (United Artists), and 2000 (Penguin)—and is included in *The Collected Poems of Ted Berrigan* (University of California Press, 2005). A recording of Berrigan reading the complete *Sonnets* in 1981 is available at PennSound.

Bibliography

Ashbery, John. "How Much Longer Will I Be Able to Inhabit the Divine Sepulcher . . ." In *The Tennis Court Oath*. Middletown, Conn.: Wesleyan University Press, 1962, 25–27.

———. "Review of Ted Berrigan's *The Sonnets*" (1968). In *Selected Prose*. Edited by Eugene Richie. Ann Arbor: University of Michigan Press, 2004, 117–119.

Berrigan, Ted. *The Sonnets*. New York: Penguin, 2000.

———. "Sonnet Workshop." In *On the Level Everyday: Selected Talks on Poetry and the Art of Living*. Edited by Joel Lewis. Jersey City, N.J.: Talisman House, 1997, 82–96.

———. "Ted Berrigan" audio recording archive. PennSound. Available online. URL: http://writing. upenn.edu/pennsound/x/Berrigan.html. Accessed December 18, 2008.

Hofmann, Hans. "The Search for the *Real* in the Visual Arts" (1948). In *Search for the Real and Other Essays*. Rev. ed. Edited by Sara T. Weeks and Bartlett H. Hayes, Jr. Cambridge, Mass.: MIT Press, 1967, 40–48.

Kane, Daniel. *All Poets Welcome: The Lower East Side Poetry Scene in the 1960s*. Berkeley: University of California Press, 2003.

Lewis, Joel. "'Everything Turns into Writing': The Sonnets of Ted Berrigan." *Transfer* 2, no. 1 (1988): 129–155.

Lopez, Tony. "'Powder on a Little Table': Ted Berrigan's Sonnets and 1960s Poems." *Journal of American Studies* 36, no. 2 (2002): 281–292.

O'Hara, Frank. "The Day Lady Died." In *The Collected Poems*. Rev. ed. Edited by Donald Allen. Berkeley: University of California Press, 1995, 325.

Padgett, Ron. "On *The Sonnets*" (1978). In *Nice to See You: Homage to Ted Berrigan*, edited by Anne Waldman, 9–11. Minneapolis, Minn.: Coffee House Press, 1991.

———. Review of *The Sonnets*. *Kulchur* 17 (Spring 1965): 94–95.

Pritikin, Renny. Excerpt from "Program Report from 80 Langton Street, San Francisco/Writer in Residence :: Ted Berrigan :: June 24–27, 1981." In *Nice to See You: Homage to Ted Berrigan*, edited by Anne Waldman, 19–25. Minneapolis, Minn.: Coffee House Press, 1991.

Rifkin, Libby. "'Worrying About Making It': Ted Berrigan's Social Poetics." In *Career Moves: Olson, Creeley, Zukofsky, Berrigan, and the American Avant-Garde*. Madison: University of Wisconsin Press, 2000, 108–135.

Sorrentino, Gilbert (1929–2006)
fiction writer, editor

As a participant in NEW YORK CITY's literary avant-garde during the 1950s and 1960s, Gilbert Sorrentino is most closely identified with the BLACK MOUNTAIN writers. A native New Yorker, he attended Brooklyn College, where in 1956 he started a magazine, *Neon*, to which writers such as JOEL OPPENHEIMER and Fielding Dawson turned in the hope of continuing the tradition of the *BLACK MOUNTAIN REVIEW*. Sorrentino had already tapped the sources of the tradition by entering into correspondence with Ezra Pound and William Carlos Williams. A lengthy passage from a prose sketch by Sorrentino appears in book 5 of Williams's *Paterson* (1958), just a few pages after an excerpt from ALLEN GINSBERG.

To Sorrentino's tastes the BEATS were too romantic and the NEW YORK SCHOOL writers too campy, but he held common cause with them as part of the broader movement represented by DONALD M. ALLEN's *NEW AMERICAN POETRY, 1945–1960*, (1960), in which Sorrentino appears in the final group of unclassified, independent voices. Looking back on "New Yorkisme," as he called it, Sorrentino explained, "Although its rationale would seem to be 'fun,' it will be remembered that this fun was in direct response to the numbing drivel that crowded the pages of literary quarterlies from 1945 to 1960" ("New York School" 249). In other words, the playfulness of the New York School was justified by its critical edge, according to Sorrentino. His interest in sharpening that critical edge brought Sorrentino into the company of New York School writers in the pages of *YŪGEN*, the *FLOATING BEAR*, and *KULCHUR*. Sorrentino, for example, always respected the work of FRANK O'HARA, his colleague on the editorial board of *Kulchur*, though he did not compromise critical judgment for the sake of collegiality. His review of *Lunch Poems* (1964) in *Bookweek* offers a finely balanced assessment of O'Hara: "his camping is saved by his intelligence" (Sorrentino, "New Note" 6).

O'Hara's image in fictional guise survives reasonably well in *Imaginative Qualities of Actual Things* (1971), Sorrentino's satirical novel about the New York art world (which led JOEL OPPENHEIMER to stop speaking to Sorrentino). Although he continued to write poetry, Sorrentino became better known for his FICTION, in which he allowed himself the sort of playfulness that made him suspicious of New York School poetry. His fiction has been compared to the work of HARRY MATHEWS and one novel in particular, *Under the Shadow* (1991), is directly inspired by RAYMOND ROUSSEL.

From 1965 to 1970 Sorrentino worked as an editor for Grove Press. During the 1970s his income derived from freelance editing, book reviewing, and occasional teaching at the New School. In 1982 he left New York to teach creative writing at Stanford University, from which he retired in 1999.

Bibliography

Andrews, David. "Of Love, Scorn and Contradiction: An Interpretative Overview of Gilbert Sorrentino's *Imaginative Qualities of Actual Things*." *Review of Contemporary Fiction* 23, no. 1 (Spring 2003): 9–44.

Sorrentino, Gilbert. Interview by Alexander Laurence (1994). The Write Stuff. Available online. URL: http://www.altx.com/int2/gilber.sorrentino.html.

———. Interview by David Ossman. In *The Sullen Art: Interviews.* New York: Corinth Books, 1963, 46–55.

———. "*Neon, Kulchur,* etc." In *The Little Magazine in America: A Modern Documentary History,* edited by Elliott Anderson and Mary Kinzie, 298–316. Yonkers, N.Y.: Pushcart Press, 1978.

———. *New and Selected Poems: 1958–1998.* Los Angeles: Green Integer, 2004.

———. "The New Note" (1966). In *Frank O'Hara: To Be True to a City,* edited by Jim Elledge, 15–16. Ann Arbor: University of Michigan Press, 1990.

———. "The New York School, continued," *New York Times,* 19 September 1976, p. 249.

Space Clark Coolidge (1970)

The poems in CLARK COOLIDGE's *Space* defy conventional understanding. They do not tell or imply a story, they do not express the feelings of a speaker, and they do not even arrange words according to the rules of grammar. Frequently they present merely word particles rather than whole words. "Say there are no rules, let's see what can be written"—this is Coolidge's summary of his attitude at the time (interview 2). Yet his confidence that something can be written—and read—starting from this premise reveals his faith in a rule-making energy inherent in words; his project is to free that energy from preexisting structures and to observe what new structures emerge when words that appear to be unrelated come into relation. "Space" is one name for that act of relating.

Coolidge's "space" is clearly one version of the open field that CHARLES OLSON advocated for the practice of "PROJECTIVE VERSE." While the field metaphor easily slides toward the misleading impression of a static arrangement, however, Coolidge did not miss Olson's insistence on the importance of movement within the field, "the changes from one word to the very next word," as Coolidge describes it (Reading). Movement provides the basis for Coolidge's distinction between two other predecessors, Gertrude Stein and JACK KEROUAC, who are often invoked by critics attempting to explain Coolidge's work. "Turning the objects on a table," which is Stein's form of movement, according to Coolidge, "is different from going along at speed seeing things out of the car window" (interview 19). Coolidge clearly identifies more closely with the latter "sort of momentum" that he feels in Kerouac and in the JAZZ improvisation that provided the score, so to speak, for Kerouac's vision. Coolidge's own experience as a jazz drummer makes the identification more than metaphorical. At the same time he recognized a similar vision in the NEW YORK SCHOOL poets and the painters who inspired them. Recalling the value WILLEM DE KOONING placed in peripheral vision, Coolidge points out qualities in the work of FRANK O'HARA that are also outstanding features of Coolidge's *Space*: "The way things go by him in his lines, to the side & away, just catching the edges of. An inclusion of vectors inexplicable to syntax" ("FO'H Notes" 184).

The dynamism of "vectors," in contrast to the structuralism of "syntax," ties the work of *Space* more closely to the action aesthetic of the New York School than Coolidge's later work, which has been championed by the Language poets. An untitled poem that also appears in RON PADGETT and DAVID SHAPIRO's ANTHOLOGY OF NEW YORK POETS (Random House, 1970) has received the most extensive explication from Coolidge himself ("Arrangement" n.p.), in connection with his reading of JOHN ASHBERY's *The Tennis Court Oath* (1962). Usually designated by its first three words, "ounce code orange" (*Space* 68), Coolidge's five-line poem locates its center by way of "vectors," as Coolidge calls them, linking *a* in the second line and *the* in the third line to both the top and the bottom lines: "the ounce" or "a code"; "a trilobite" or "the trilobite" (the bottom line reads: "trilobite trilobites"). Energy thus flows around the poem as through an electrical circuit, an analogy confirmed by the word *ohm* that stands alone in the fourth line. But the circuit is kept open by the crucial addition of the letter *s* on the repeated *trilobite*, which makes the word, as Coolidge reads it, into a verb as well as a plural noun. "I feel, as [Ernest] Fenollosa pointed out, that every noun is a verb," Coolidge explains, underscoring once again the principle of dynamism ("Arrangement").

The publishing history of *Space* encompasses some of the most important outlets available to the New York School at the time. As Tom Orange has analyzed, section 1 consists of poems that had appeared previously in *Flag Flutter & U.S. Electric* (LINES 1966) or were soon to appear in *The So* (ADVENTURES IN POETRY, 1971). Section 2 consists of poems not previously collected by Coolidge, although "Styro" had appeared in PAUL CARROLL's *The Young American Poets* (Follett, 1968), as well as in the Padgett and Shapiro anthology. Section 3 represents poems from *Clark Coolidge* (Lines, 1967), and section 4, from *ING* (Angel Hair, 1968). *Space* itself represents a brief moment when the work of New York School writers (including TOM CLARK, DICK GALLUP, and LEWIS MACADAMS, as well as Coolidge) found favor with the mainstream publisher Harper & Row, through the good offices of editor Fran McCullough. The cover of *Space*, designed by JASPER JOHNS, shows a ruler bearing Coolidge's name, as if to suggest that Coolidge, like the trilobite, is irreducible to any measure but his own.

Bibliography

Bernstein, Charles. "Maintaining Space: Clark Coolidge's Early Work." In *Content's Dream: Essays, 1975–1984.* 2d ed. Evanston, Ill.: Northwestern University Press, 2001. Available online. URL: http://epc.buffalo.edu/authors/coolidge/bernstein.html. Accessed December 18, 2008.

Coolidge, Clark. "Arrangement." In *Talking Poetics from the Naropa Institute: Annals of the Jack Kerouac School of Disembodied Poetics* 1. Edited by Ann Waldman and Marilyn Webb. Boulder, Colo.: Shambala, 1978. Available online. URL: http://epc.buffalo.edu/authors/coolidge/naropa.html. Accessed December 18, 2008.

———. "FO'H Notes." In *Homage to Frank O'Hara,* edited by Bill Berkson and Joe LeSueur, 183–185. Bolinas, Calif.: Big Sky, 1988.

———. Interview by Ed Foster. In *Poetry and Poetics in a New Millennium,* by Ed Foster, 1–20. Jersey City, N.J.: Talisman House, 2000.

———. "Reading at Franconia College, Franconia, N.H., ca. 1971." Sound recording (2-minute excerpt). CD accompanying *All Poets Welcome: The Lower East Side Poetry Scene in the 1960s,* by Daniel Kane. Berkeley: University of California Press, 2003.

———. *Space.* New York: Harper & Row, 1970. Available online. URL: http://www.princeton.edu/~eclipse/. Accessed December 19, 2008.

Golston, Michael. "At Clark Coolidge: Allegory and the Early Works." *American Literary History* 13, no. 2 (2001): 295–316.

Kostelanetz. Richard. "The New Poetries." In *The Old Poetries and the New.* Ann Arbor: University of Michigan Press, 1981, 121–149.

McGann, Jerome [under pseudonym Anne Mack and Jay Rome]. "Truth in the Body of Falsehood." *Parnassus: Poetry in Review* 15, no. 1 (1989): 257–280.

Orange, Tom. "Arrangement and Density: A Context for Early Clark Coolidge" *Jacket* 13 (April 2001). Available online. URL: http://jacketmagazine.com/13/coolidge-o-a.html. Accessed December 19, 2008.

Watten, Barrett. "Total Syntax: The Work in the World." In *Artifice and Indeterminacy: An Anthology of New Poetics,* edited by Christopher Beach, Tuscaloosa: University of Alabama Press, 1998. Available online. URL: http://epc.buffalo.edu/authors/coolidge/watten.html. Accessed December 19, 2008.

Spellman, A. B. (Alfred Bennett Spellman, Jr.) (1935–)

A leading practioner of avant-garde poetics in New York in the early 1960s, A. B. Spellman was born in

North Carolina and attended Howard University, where he was a classmate of LeRoi Jones (AMIRI BARAKA). Spellman joined Jones in NEW YORK CITY in 1958 and quickly became acquainted with the writers and artists associated with YŪGEN magazine, including the NEW YORK SCHOOL poets. With DIANE DI PRIMA, Spellman planned a magazine that never materialized, though it left a trace in FRANK O'HARA's whimsical poem "What Happened to 'The Elephant at the Door'" (1961). A more substantial result, drawing on material submitted for the aborted magazine, was the FLOATING BEAR, edited by di Prima and Jones, in which a number of the poems from Spellman's series The Beautiful Days appeared (number 13, September 1961). A volume entitled The Beautiful Days was published in 1965 by di Prima's Poets Press, with a preface by O'Hara.

In his preface O'Hara praised Spellman's "lean, strong, sexy poems" and seems to have been especially attracted to an elegiac note in Spellman's treatment of the themes of love and death. Rather than being distracted by experimental FORM, O'Hara felt he heard Spellman's "real voice sounding above the inspired or the willed (in the moral sense) technical choices" (181). In retrospect Spellman himself has judged that his real voice did not emerge until the BLACK ARTS MOVEMENT challenged him with the example of "insistently oral" poetry. "Before," he explains, "I was much more into a [Robert] Creeley-ish concern with enjambments, with ways of making the eye dance with line breaks" (n.p.). Another encouragement to "become more comfortable in the vernacular" was the sound of JAZZ, to which Spellman attuned his ear as a discerning critic. His jazz reviews appeared in KULCHUR as well as trade journals such as Metronome and Downbeat. In 1966 he published Four Lives in the Bebop Business (Pantheon), an account of Cecil Taylor (1929–), Ornette Coleman (1930–), Herbie Nichols (1919–63), and Jackie McLean (1932–2006), which has since gone through many editions, most recently as Four Jazz Lives (University of Michigan Press, 2004).

Spellman's work at the height of the Black Arts Movement appears in magazines such as the Journal of Black Poetry and Cricket, the journal of "Black Music in Evolution" that he coedited with Jones and Larry Neal (1937–81) from 1968 to 1969.

However, a series of teaching appointments, starting with Morehouse College in Atlanta, Georgia, in 1969, took Spellman away from New York and distracted him from assembling another collection of poems. Then, in 1975, he began a 30-year career as an administrator with the National Endowment for the Arts in Washington, D.C. He did not return to writing poetry until he was in his 60s. Things I Must Have Known (Coffee House Press, 2008) includes poems from the Black Arts period, such as "When Black People Are" (1968), as well as new poems of autobiographical reminiscence, such as "The First Seventy," in which the elegiac mood that attracted O'Hara resurfaces from even greater depths of experience.

Bibliography

Funkhouser, Christopher. "LeRoi Jones, Larry Neal, and 'The Cricket': Jazz and Poets' Black Fire." African American Review 37, nos. 2–3 (Summer–Autumn 2003): 237–244.

Nielsen, Aldon Lynn. Black Chant: Languages of African-American Postmodernism. Cambridge: Cambridge University Press, 1997.

O'Hara, Frank. "Preface to A. B. Spellman's The Beautiful Days." In Standing Still and Walking in New York. Edited by Donald Allen. San Francisco: Grey Fox, 1983, 181.

———. "What Happened to 'The Elephant at the Door.'" In Poems Retrieved. Rev. ed. Edited by Donald Allen. San Francisco: Grey Fox, 1996, 207.

Spellman, A. B. "On Things I Must Have Known: A. B. Spellman in Conversation with Pearl Cleage." Coffee House Press Web site. Available online. URL: http://www.coffeehousepress.org/thingsimusthaveknown interview.asp. Accessed December 19, 2008.

Spoleto Festival of Two Worlds (1965)

The eighth annual Festival of Two Worlds, held in Spoleto, Italy, from June 24 to July 18, 1965, provided an international showcase for the New American Poetry in general and for the NEW YORK SCHOOL in particular. The composer Gian Carlo Menotti, the festival's founder and director, decided to introduce a "Poetry Week" into the program that year, and he consulted FRANK O'HARA for recommendations of American writers. Although O'Hara's duties at the Museum of Modern Art prevented him from attending, poets who did participate on O'Hara's recommendation included JOHN ASHBERY, BILL BERKSON, Lawrence Ferlinghetti, BARBARA GUEST, CHARLES OLSON, and JOHN WIENERS. Olson and Wieners would conclude their tour of readings at the BERKELEY POETRY CONFERENCE later in July. Also attending at Spoleto, and in some cases participating in unofficial events surrounding the festival, were JOE BRAINARD, KENWARD ELMSLIE, LEWIS MACADAMS, PETER SCHJELDAHL, and GEORGE SCHNEEMAN.

According to Berkson, O'Hara had also recommended ALLEN GINSBERG and GREGORY CORSO, but Menotti decided against inviting them, fearful that they might violate decorum. The rock concert air in which Ginsberg performed at the International Poetry at London's Albert Hall the previous month would have borne out Menotti's fears. As it turned out, cold war POLITICS proved to be a more serious threat to the Spoleto festival, since Menotti had given top billing to an appearance by Ezra Pound, whose 1922 ballet *Le Testament,* based on the poem by François Villon, would receive its first full production at Spoleto. In protest against Pound's affiliation with Italian fascism during World War II, Soviet authorities prevented the appearance of Russian poet Yevgeny Yevtushenko until, at the last minute, he was "delivered" by a high official of the Italian Communist Party, according to the *New York Times* (Neville 7). In the small THEATER used for these occasions (seating 350), Yevtushenko read with the Italian poet Lino Curci and the American Allen Tate—not one of O'Hara's choices. Pound read on a later day in a program that led off with Ashbery, Wieners, and Swedish poet Johannes Edfelt. Pound read only TRANSLATIONs, including work by Marianne Moore and ROBERT LOWELL as well as his own. His performance was largely inaudible, due to frail health, but he was warmly applauded as an icon of modern literature. After being introduced to Pound at an outdoor café, Brainard wrote to RON PADGETT, "He does not look real. He looks like he belongs on a coin" (Padgett 88).

In introducing Guest as a member of "the New York School of poets," English poet Stephen Spender noted that "they all write about painting"

(Berkson n.p.). The full range of the arts that provided a context for the New York School was well represented at Spoleto. An exhibition of *Recent Landscapes by Nine Americans,* organized by O'Hara for the Museum of Modern Art, was on display, and there were performances of LeRoi Jones's (AMIRI BARAKA) play *Dutchman,* MORTON FELDMAN's percussion piece *The King of Denmark,* and several ballets by George Balanchine, presented by the NEW YORK CITY BALLET.

Bibliography

Berkson, Bill. "Fresh Air." Int. Robert Gluck. *Jacket* 29 (April 2006). Available online. URL: http://www.jacketmagazine.com/29/berk-gluc-iv.html. Accessed December 19, 2008.

Clark, Tom. *Charles Olson: The Allegory of a Poet's Life.* New York: Norton, 1991.

"Ezra Pound Hailed at Spoleto Reading, Despite Weak Voice," *New York Times,* 2 July 1965, p. 16.

Neville, Robert. "A Podium of Poets." *New York Times Book Review,* 25 July 1965, 7.

Padgett, Ron. *Joe: A Memoir of Joe Brainard.* Minneapolis, Minn.: Coffee House Press, 2004.

Wieners, John. "Ezra Pound at the Spoleto Festival 1965." In *Cultural Affairs in Boston: Poetry and Prose, 1956–1985,* edited by Raymond Foye, 63–64. Santa Rosa, Calif.: Black Sparrow, 1988.

Stroffolino, Chris (1963–)

Chris Stroffolino was born in Reading, Pennsylvania. He received his B.A. in English/philosophy from Albright College, his M.A. in English from Temple University in 1988, and a Ph.D. from the State University of New York–Albany in 1998, with a dissertation on William Shakespeare's middle comedies. Since then, Stroffolino has taught at a number of universities, including New York University, Rutgers, Long Island University, Drexel University, University of Massachusetts, and St. Mary's College. He is also a keyboardist and lead vocalist for the indie rock band Continuous Peasant, which has released two albums, *Exile in Babyville* (2003) and *Intentional Grounding* (2005).

As the author of an essay entitled "Against Lineage" that questions the very value of literary heritages and the political agenda behind them that often goes unarticulated, it may seem inappropriate to speak of Stroffolino's work as NEW YORK SCHOOL. Stroffolino nonetheless confesses indebtedness, or at least abiding interest, in the work of FRANK O'HARA and JOHN ASHBERY, and he has pointed out affinities with such figures as JOHN YAU, KENNETH KOCH, BERNADETTE MAYER, DOUGLAS CRASE, ALICE NOTLEY, DAVID SHAPIRO, and JIM BRODEY. He also speaks of Bob Dylan as a contemporary poet and, in his practice, blurs the often-arbitrary distinction between GENRES. As he has written, "In my poetry as in my literary criticism, I have attempted to show that many of the dichotomies by which poetry is traditionally understood ('text-based' vs. 'oral' traditions; 'serious' vs. 'comic;' 'avant-garde' vs. 'mainstream;' 'political' vs. 'personal;' etc.) place reductive limitations on an artform whose primary function is, or should be, to go beyond specialization and factionalism to appeal to a sense of common humanity" (n.p.). Though he claims the term never adequately represented the range of his poetry, Stroffolino was also associated with post–LANGUAGE POETRY, which as defined by Mark Wallace had two primary characteristics: "hybridity . . . mixing traditions, crossing boundaries, and critiquing notions of form as pure or singular . . . [and] resistance to definition" ("Definitions" n.p.).

Stroffolino coedited *An Anthology of New (American) Poetry* (Talisman, 1998) with LISA JARNOT and Leonard Schwartz. He has published a collection of essays, *Spin Cycle* (Spuyten Duyvil, 2001), and three full-length books of poetry, *Speculative Primitive* (Tougher Disguises, 2004), *Stealer's Wheel* (Hard Press, 1999), and *Oops* (Pavement Saw, 1994). *Stealer's Wheel* gestures toward a New York School lineage on its cover, which reproduces a COLLABORATION by GRACE HARTIGAN and her colleague Rex Stevens. Reviewing *Stealer's Wheel* for the *Poetry Society Newsletter*, Wallace identified Stroffolino's intentional use of mixed metaphor as "perhaps his signature linguistic twist . . . one comparison undermined by another and then another until comparisons are shown to be no more than temporary and partial" (review 24).

Bibliography

Stroffolino, Chris. "Bipolar Worlds." *Rain Taxi* (Fall 2005). Available online. URL: http://www.raintaxi. com/online/2005fall/stroffolino.shtml.   Accessed December 19, 2008.

Wallace, Mark. "Definitions in Process, Definitions as Process/Uneasy Collaborations: Language and Postlanguage Poetries." Available online. URL: http://www.flashpointmag.com/postlang.htm. Accessed December 19, 2008.

———. Review of *Stealer's Wheel. Poetry Project Newsletter* 177 (December 1999–January 2000): 23–24.

SUN (1971–1985)

Midway through the course of its existence, in 1978, the SUN publishing venture was hailed by MICHAEL LALLY in the pages of the *Washington Post* as "one of the most important of the country's small presses." The four books of 1977 that Lally chose to review reflected the eclectic tastes of the publisher, BILL ZAVATSKY. Two were important works of NEW YORK SCHOOL poetry: PAUL VIOLI's *Harmatan* and TONY TOWLE's *Autobiography and Other Poems*, the latter published in association with Coach House South, an extension of Coach House Press brought from Toronto, Canada, to NEW YORK CITY by the poet David Rosenberg. The other two SUN titles reviewed by Lally were by DEEP IMAGE poet George Economou (*Ameriki*) and CHICAGO surrealist Bill Knott (*Selected and Collected Poems*). Knott's book won the 1977 Elliston Book Award, administered by the University of Cincinnati, for the best volume of poetry published by an independent literary press.

Although Zavatsky eventually found publishing books "more gratifying" ("On Publishing" n.p.), *SUN* began as a magazine that evolved out of *Sundial*, a publication run by Columbia University students but funded by the Episcopal Office there. The magazine subscribed to no doctrine, however, and it lost its funding in 1968 because the priest responsible for the project participated in the student uprising at Columbia in ways that diocesan officials deemed inappropriate (Zavatsky, "Brodey Questionnaire" n.p.). By the time Zavatsky became editor in 1970, the magazine was at the point of extinction, so he used his own funds to finance the first issue of *SUN* in 1971. Four more issues followed, erratically numbered and at irregular intervals up to 1983. As a spin-off of *SUN*, Zavatsky published two issues of a journal entitled *Roy Rogers*, the first (1970) concentrating on the cowboy hero as subject, the second (1974) devoted to the FORM of the "one line poem."

The first SUN books presented poets of New York, though not of the New York School: Philip Lopate (*The Eyes Don't Always Want to Stay Open*, 1972; redesigned and reissued, 1976), a friend of Zavatsky through Columbia connections; and Harvey Shapiro (*Lauds*, 1975), Zavatsky's first poetry workshop instructor. Zavatsky's own volume, *Theories of Rain and Other Poems* (1975), belongs in this company as much as in that of the many New York School poets he went on to publish (including, besides Towle and Violi, MAUREEN OWEN, RON PADGETT, PETER SCHJELDAHL, JAMES SCHUYLER, and MARJORIE WELISH). The complete list of 36 titles published by SUN is distinguished not only by collections of new poems but also by TRANSLATION projects. Especially notable for New York School involvement are RAYMOND ROUSSEL's *How I Wrote Certain of My Books* (translated by TREVOR WINKFIELD, 1975; reissued in 1977 in an expanded edition including two essays on Roussel by JOHN ASHBERY and a translation of Canto III of Roussel's poem *New Impressions of Africa* by KENNETH KOCH); and Max Jacob's *The Dice Cup: Selected Prose Poems* (edited by MICHAEL BROWNSTEIN, 1979; with translations by Ashbery, David Ball, Brownstein, Padgett, Zack Rogow, and Zavatsky).

Bibliography

Lally, Michael. "Economou and Company," *Washington Post Book World*, 1 January 1978, p. E7.

Zavatsky, Bill. "The Brodey Questionnaire." Unpublished manuscript (ca. 1978) for a project by Jim Brodey about New York School poets.

———. "On Publishing My First Book of Poems in Thirty Years." In "Dispatches: Journals." Poetry Foundation Web site. Available online. URL: http://www.poetry foundation.org/dispatches/journals/2006.08.14. html. Accessed December 19, 2008.

surrealism   *See* DADA AND SURREALISM.

Swollen Magpie Press (1970–1982)

As Ezra Pound had employed the emblem of "a swollen magpie" in the "Pull down thy vanity"

passage of Canto LXXXI (from The Pisan Cantos, 1948), it seemed to PAUL VIOLI to be an appropriate emblem for the "vanity press" he launched in 1970 by publishing two of his own pamphlets, *She'll Be Riding Six White Horses* and *Automatic Transmissions*. One more book, Phillip Lopate's novella, *In Coyoacan*, was added to the list in 1971. Meanwhile, Swollen Magpie had hatched a magazine, *New York Times* (not associated with the newspaper), coedited by Violi and Allen Appel (1945–   ). Operating out of Appel's apartment on East 10th Street in DOWNTOWN MANHATTAN, from 1970 to the winter of 1972–73 they produced four issues of the magazine with work by many second-generation NEW YORK SCHOOL writers, including JIM BRODEY, DICK GALLUP, CHARLES NORTH, RON PADGETT, CARTER RATCLIFF, PETER SCHJELDAHL, TONY TOWLE, and BILL ZAVATSKY. From Iowa City, Allan Kornblum and ANSELM HOLLO sent their own work as well as that of other poets whom they discovered there. From England, F. T. Prince unwittingly contributed a poem, a consequence of editorial casualness that dovetailed with a tenet circulating at the POETRY PROJECT AT ST. MARK'S CHURCH IN-THE-BOWERY among some who regarded poetry as communal property. Violi recalls that Prince seemed "pleased and amused" after hearing of the publication when they later met (e-mail).

Appel eventually left Swollen Magpie to pursue other interests, which eventually led to a successful career as a novelist. After a brief hiatus Violi resumed book publishing, this time in partnership with North, whose wife, Paula, designed the project's logo. Between 1976 and 1982 they published volumes of poetry by Towle, JOSEPH CERAVOLO, MARY FERRARI, YUKI HARTMAN, and Martha LaBare, as well as by Violi and North. North brought two COLLABORATIONs to the list: *Gemini* (1981), a book of collaborative poems written by North and Towle, and *BROADWAY: A POETS AND PAINTERS ANTHOLOGY* (1979), edited by North and JAMES SCHUYLER. (The same editors published a second *Broadway* anthology with Hanging Loose Press in 1989). One book of criticism appeared under the Swollen Magpie imprint: *David Antin: Debunker of the Real* by LITA HORNICK, who was working with Violi on a series of readings at the Museum of Modern Art.

The press was helped by grants from the National Endowment for the Arts and the Coordinating Council of Literary Magazines. Like most projects of this sort, however, Swollen Magpie was a low-budget, hands-on affair. North retains a vivid physical memory of using the back of a teaspoon to flatten the spine of every book before stapling.

Bibliography

North, Charter. Letter to Terence Diggory, August 24, 2005.

Violi, Paul. E-mail to Terence Diggory, September 1, 2005.

Szymaszek, Stacy (1969–)

In July 2007 Stacy Szymaszek (pronounced sih-MAH-zik) became the eighth director of the POETRY PROJECT AT ST. MARK'S CHURCH IN-THE-BOWERY. She had only recently moved to NEW YORK CITY from her native Milwaukee, Wisconsin, where she worked as literary program manager at Woodland Pattern Book Center (1999–2005) and edited *Gam: A Journal of Great Lakes Writing* (2003–05). Experienced in the social forms of the poetry community—the public reading, the little magazine, and the independent press (she is a coeditor of Instance Press)—Szymaszek brings to her own poetry a mode of sociality different from what she has called "the revelry in friendship and conversation associated with the New York School" (Szymaszek, review 25). In her work-in-progress under the title *hyper glossia*, "every organ babbles" (Segue reading n.p.). The reader or listener experiences the body of the text physically: "It wasn't a word but a plosive cluster burst from my lips" (Segue reading n.p.). Any conversation resulting from these bursts appears to take place internally, among different components of the same psyche, or differently gendered experiences of the same body. Szymaszek describes the dramatis personae of *hyper glossia* as a female narrator, no longer living; her male double, who is living; and "a villainous colonizer presence" (Segue reading n.p.).

"Archetype, ethnicity, and myth are categories for understanding her approach to meaning," writes Kenneth Warren (27) in a review of *Emptied of All Ships* (Litmus Press, 2005), Szymaszek's major publication to date. Appropriately, Warren ties these categories to "the lineage of Herman Melville and Charles Olson," modified by the feminist narrative of Susan Howe (Warren 28). Names more closely identified with the NEW YORK SCHOOL might be added to this list if Szymaszek's personae are considered as functions of voice rather than narrative. Like FRANK O'HARA, Szymaszek presents "the scene of my selves" (O'Hara 257), in which the multiplication of personae reflects queer identity in the mirror of straight society. Szymaszek, an "out" lesbian, adopted a male persona in *Pasolini Poems* (Cy Press, 2005), "filtered" through the voice of Pier Paolo Pasolini (1922–75), an Italian poet and film director (Szymaszek, interview n.p.). Out of Melville's *Moby-Dick,* crossed with Virginia Woolf's *To the Lighthouse,* emerged a character Szymaszek calls James, who appears in *Some Mariners* (Etherdome, 2004), later incorporated in *Emptied of All Ships.* As Szymaszek describes the latter work, "A lot of the initial building of the poem was around the prefix 'trans'—across, beyond, into another state or place. Transatlantic, transonic, transcribe, the whole thing with James trans-lating Chinese poetry is supposed to be humorous underneath all that angst. So, yes, (James as) trans-sexual but really in a fantastical sense of pan-gendered, a body beyond (trans) anything we currently know" (Szymaszek, interview n.p.).

Bibliography

O'Hara, Frank. "In Memory of My Feelings" (1956). In *The Collected Poems.* Rev. ed. Edited by Donald Allen. Berkeley: University of California Press, 1995, 252–257.

Szymaszek, Stacy. Interview by Kate Greenstreet (2006). Every Other Day: First Book Interviews. Available online. URL: http://www.kickingwind.com/5406.html. Accessed December 19, 2008.

———. Review of *Some Clear Souvenir. Poetry Project Newsletter* 209 (December 2006–January 2007): 25–26.

———. Segue reading at Bowery Poetry Club, 14 January 2006. Audio file. PennSound. Available online. URL: http://writing.upenn.edu/pennsound/x/Segue-BPC.html. Accessed December 19, 2008.

Warren, Kenneth. Review of *Emptied of All Ships. Poetry Project Newsletter* 207 (April–May 2006): 27–28.

T

Tales of Beatnik Glory Ed Sanders
(1975–2004)

Composed of four volumes written by ED SANDERS over three decades, *Tales of Beatnik Glory* is a set of serial short stories that trace a community of characters living on Manhattan's Lower East Side during the 1960s. The volumes cover the period chronologically: 1957–62 (volume 1), 1963–65 (volume 2), 1966–67 (volume 3), 1967–69 (volume 4). The series has been published cumulatively, starting with volume 1 (Stonehill, 1975), then volumes 1 and 2 together (Citadel Underground, 1990), and then a comprehensive edition of four volumes (Thunder's Mouth, 2004).

Sanders blends the inner lives of his characters into a collage of cold war POLITICS, news headlines, peace protests, gallery openings, the mimeograph revolution, academic conferences, and jazz concerts, creating a kaleidoscopic vision of the era of affordable housing, burgeoning radicalism, and idealistic social discovery. Stylistically witty and irreverent, the *Tales* are fictional exaggerations that render the bold and unpredictable developments Sanders witnessed and at times led during those years. He chronicles the spirit of the neighborhood from the perspective of both observer and participant, gently mocking its excesses while celebrating its unique virtues.

Volume 1, written during 1973–74, depicts the Lower East Side with an optimistic tone emphasizing the young innocence of the early 1960s, even when confronted with a disapproving, conservative mainstream culture. The story "The Poetry Reading," for instance, describes an evening inside the Gaslight Café, which Sanders presents as it probably often appeared, with readers like ALLEN GINSBERG and JACK KEROUAC, and the first strains of "Beat-fever" spreading through the media and youth culture. In "A Book of Verse" Sanders recounts the impact of Ginsberg's *Howl.* "Raked Sand," in which the Cuban missile crisis inspires his characters' contemplation of mortality, best illustrates Sanders's ambition to integrate history into FICTION. Other stories, such as "The Total Assault Cantina" and "An Editorial Conference," showcase Sanders's skill at presenting archetypal counterculture moments in comic vignettes.

With volume 2, written during 1984–89, Sanders registers changes taking place within the counterculture, introducing a new tone that characterizes the remainder of the series. In stories such as "It's Like Living with a Mongol" he also addresses some aspects of BEAT generation bohemia that look less attractive in retrospect, such as gender inequalities. The story that opens volume 2, "I Have a Dream," displays Sanders's range, as his characters behold Martin Luther King, Jr.'s speech at the March on Washington, discuss Ezra Pound's anti-Semitic radio broadcasts, and feel the Vietnam War stirring up civil strife: "Sam saw a time of crazed peril for America. There was a crackle of insane electricity in the brains of madmen, and planes swooping low over villages with fire that would not stop" (*Tales* 1–2: 299).

Through it all, the Lower East Side remains the ever-present theater. Sanders's own mimeograph publication, *FUCK YOU: A MAGAZINE OF THE*

459

ARTS, plays a role in volume 1, and his PEACE EYE BOOKSTORE appears briefly in "The Van Job" in volume 2. Likewise, in "Wild Women of East Tenth," from the same volume, The FUGS's rehearsals at Peace Eye introduce a story that catalogs real and imaginary places, people preparing for an ANDY WARHOL party, and, in an engaging comic episode, a police raid on the filming of an avant-garde movie called *Meat Fit.*

Yet despite the exuberance of the Lower East Side stories, Sanders also reflects on the disheartening cultural wars raging nationally. The final story of volume 2, "Freedom Summer," changes the setting to Mississippi during the struggle for civil rights. Sanders's description of a church bombing reinforces how the values and optimism of the Lower East Side in volume 1 could only persist by carrying those ideas elsewhere in America. Sanders's preoccupation with social justice here, as in his work generally, defines the emotion behind his characters' enthusiasms and relationships.

Bibliography

Dewey, Joseph. "Helter Shelter: Strategic Interment in *Tales of Beatnik Glory.*" *Review of Contemporary Fiction* 9, no. 1 (Spring 1999): 101–111.

Herd, David. "'After All, What Else Is There to Say?' Ed Sanders and the Beat Aesthetic." *Review of Contemporary Fiction* 9, no. 1 (Spring 1999): 122–137.

Sanders, Ed. "Edward Sanders on His Fiction." *Review of Contemporary Fiction* 9, no. 1 (Spring 1999): 24–30.

———. *Tales of Beatnik Glory vols. 1 and 2.* New York: Citadel Press, 1995.

———. *Tales of Beatnik Glory vols. 1–4.* New York: Thunder's Mouth, 2004.

Yohalem, John. "Fun and Games in East Village." *New York Times Book Review* 9 November 1975, 22.

Talisman (1988–)

Talisman magazine and its publishing arm Talisman House have become a major outlet for work by and about NEW YORK SCHOOL poets of the second and later generations. The project's founder, Edward Foster (1942–), was an undergraduate at Columbia University (B.A., 1965) at the same time as RON PADGETT, DAVID SHAPIRO, and BOB HOLMAN. After earning a Ph.D. from Columbia in 1970, he began to construct a conventional academic career as a professor of English and American literature at Stevens Institute of Technology, across the Hudson River from NEW YORK CITY in Hoboken, New Jersey. In 1980, at the urging of ALLEN GINSBERG, Foster helped TED BERRIGAN get an appointment as a distinguished visiting professor at Stevens. Discovering Foster's love for poetry, which he had not written since college, Berrigan prodded him "to construct a life that . . . admitted only poetry" (Foster, essay 127). He did not find a way of doing this until after Berrigan died in 1983 and Foster spent 1985–86 on a second Fulbright Fellowship in Turkey, where the call for prayer from a mosque brought a moment of realization that "I was free to do as I wished" (Foster, essay 124). Back in the United States, he began to make plans for *Talisman* magazine with his friends Joseph Donahue (1954–) and Zoe English (1952–)—magazine editing being one of the activities that Berrigan thought might properly occupy a poet when he was not writing poems. The first issue of *Talisman,* in 1988, featured an interview with Berrigan's widow, ALICE NOTLEY. In 1993 Foster extended the *Talisman* enterprise to publish two books that he was especially interested in, one being Notley's *Selected Poems,* the other being William Bronk's *The Mild Day.*

Apart from his allegiance to Bronk (1918–99), a singular figure who spent his life outside poetry circles, Foster has ranged widely in his attention to the New American Poetry, both in his work on *Talisman* and in his own critical writing. He has written a study of Jack Spicer of the SAN FRANCISCO RENAISSANCE (Western Writers Series, Boise State University, 1991), complementary volumes on *Understanding the Beats* (University of South Carolina Press, 1992) and *Understanding the Black Mountain Poets* (University of South Carolina Press, 1994), and a memoir of Berrigan, *Code of the West* (Rodent Press, 1994). He has resisted LANGUAGE POETRY both for its emphasis on critical theory and for its attack on an inner rather than a socially constructed self, undermining the traditional basis of lyric poetry. Interviews—one of the distinctive features of *Talisman,* which have been collected in two books (*Postmodern Poetry* [1994] and *Poetry and Poetics in a New Millennium*

[2000])—arose as "an opportunity for poets to talk about themselves and their work in ways other than as emanations of some political or historical process," Foster has explained (Foster, interview n.p.). In the same interview he expresses his admiration for both Berrigan and Notley as lyric poets in particular. In his own poems, however, Foster avoids the autobiographical detail associated with New York School "PERSONISM." The desire that drives the poems can sometimes be identified as homosexual desire, but it is abstracted, as in Spicer or Bronk, rather than explicitly described, as in FRANK O'HARA or Ginsberg.

The list of individual volumes of poetry published by Talisman House includes, besides Notley's Selected Poems, work by JOHN ASH, PAUL HOOVER, JOEL LEWIS, STEPHEN PAUL MILLER, DOUGLAS OLIVER, and SIMON PETTET. However, the more distinctive contribution that Talisman has made to contemporary poetry has taken the FORM of comparative and critical contexts. Lewis's collection of Berrigan's talks, On the Level Everyday (1997), is one example of such work by a single author, and ARAM SAROYAN's Starting Out in the Sixties (2001) is another. Talisman has also issued notable anthologies such as Primary Trouble: An Anthology of Contemporary American Poetry (edited by Leonard Schwartz, Joseph Donahue, and Foster, 1996), Moving Borders: Three Decades of Innovative Writing by Women (edited by Mary Margaret Sloan, 1998), An Anthology of New (American) Poets (edited by LISA JARNOT, Leonard Schwartz, and CHRIS STROFFOLINO, 1998), and Word of Mouth: An Anthology of Gay American Poetry (edited by Timothy Liu, 2000). A massive anthology of essays "towards a history of innovative American poetry in our time" was issued in 2002 as Talisman numbers 23–26. Its title, The World in Time and Space, quotes William Bronk, but its essays survey the full field, extending even to Language poetry. John Olson, Peter Bushyeager, Miller, and Thomas Fink contribute essays focused on the New York School, and Foster includes his second interview with Notley.

Bibliography

Foster, Edward. Answerable to None: Berrigan, Bronk and the American Real, Essays and Reviews. New York: Spuyten Duyvil, 1999.

——. Essay in Contemporary Authors Autobiography Series 26, edited by Shelly Andrews, 109–130. Detroit, Mich.: Gale, 1997.

——. Interview by Olivier Brossard (2002). Double Change 3. Available online. URL: http://www.double change.com/issue3/foster.htm. Accessed December 18, 2008.

——. What He Ought to Know: New and Selected Poems. East Rockaway, N.Y.: Marsh Hawk Press, 2006.

"Tambourine Life"   Ted Berrigan   (1967)

After the high-wire act of The SONNETS, TED BERRIGAN came down to earth in his long poem "Tambourine Life." In doing so, he produced "one of the milestones of the generation," as PAUL CARROLL predicted when he included "Tambourine Life" in his anthology The Young American Poets, which exposed the poem to a wide audience (119). Within that audience were many poets who read the poem as a model they could use, whereas the complex system of verbal permutations in The Sonnets defied imitation. There seemed to be no system to "Tambourine Life" other than the ordinary life everybody shares. Anything that happened, any words or thoughts that came to mind during the act of writing could enter into the poem. For instance, the title alludes to Bob Dylan's song "Mr. Tambourine Man," which was playing on the radio repeatedly, in a hit version by The Byrds, while Berrigan was writing. In turn, the act of writing extended into life simply because Berrigan determined to write something every day over a period of many days; "Tambourine Life" is dated "Oct. 1965–Jan. 1966." In the spirit of ACTION PAINTING, he also determined that his writing should be "spontaneous" (Berrigan, Talking 95). His goal was to produce a long poem, but not in the manner of John Milton's Paradise Lost, with a plot, or of William Wordsworth's The Prelude, with a pattern of psychological development. Composed, or "NOT composed" (Berrigan, Collected Poems 125), as a field of colliding particles with the potential to expand infinitely, "Tambourine Life" is an outstanding example of the postmodern SERIAL POEM, or "cereal poem," as Berrigan playfully calls it (Berrigan, Collected Poems 125).

The challenge to the writer of such a poem is "guarding it from mess and measure" (O'Hara,

444), as FRANK O'HARA advised in "BIOTHERM" (1962), a likely inspiration for Berrigan, according to ALICE NOTLEY (Berrigan, *Collected Poems* 677). To be more than a "mess" the poem required some FORM, but traditional closed form, or "measure," risked closing the poem off from life. The alternative "open form" (Berrigan, *Talking* 37) of "Tambourine Life" developed in two stages. First, Berrigan kept writing until life itself prompted closure, on the tragic occasion of the death of Anne Kepler, a friend of Berrigan's going back to his days in Tulsa, Oklahoma. On December 20, 1965, she died in a fire at the Jewish Community Center in Yonkers, New York (not "the Yonkers Children's Hospital," as Berrigan mistakenly reports in "People Who Died" [1970; Berrigan, *Collected Poems* 237]). Section 66 of "Tambourine Life," very close to the end of the poem's 70 numbered sections, begins:

> *Now*
> *in the middle of this*
> *someone I love is dead*
> (Berrigan, *Collected Poems* 149).

In a later interview Berrigan recalled, "I was slapped in the face with this real-life happening, which made it so I couldn't do anything. I mean, my whole life as it was just stopped, kind of. And I had this poem" (Berrigan, *Talking* 178).

The poem that Berrigan had at this point was not yet the one first published in MOTHER magazine (number 8, May Day 1967). He resumed making daily entries for a few days in January 1966 and then let the manuscript lie in a desk drawer for several months, until LEWIS MACADAMS asked Berrigan if he had something "substantial" to contribute to *Mother* (Berrigan, *Talking* 178). The idea of publishing "Tambourine Life" as a whole, rather than in separate units, as *The Sonnets* had first appeared in various magazines, stimulated Berrigan to reconceive the basic unit of composition. Initially he had written in lines arranged in a column flush left to the margin, in the style of RON PADGETT's long poem "Tone Arm" (1966), another of Berrigan's models, according to Notley (Berrigan, *Collected Poems* 676). Now, following the "open form" layout used by O'Hara and PAUL BLACKBURN (Berrigan, *Talking* 38), Berrigan spaced his words over the entire page, filling the "white expansiveness" (Berrigan, *Collected Poems* 121) as Kepler had "filled my life when I felt empty" (Berrigan, *Collected Poems* 149). However, an uncanny result of Berrigan's shift from the line to the page as his unit of composition is that the blank spaces on the page fill the poem as much as the words do, just as Kepler's entrance at the end of the poem is simultaneously a departure, filling Berrigan's life with her absence. An image of this effect appears in "American Express," a poem that seems to be an early arrangement of lines from "Tambourine Life," though it was published later, in the collection *In the Early Morning Rain* (1970). At the conclusion of "American Express," clouds "filled / with holes" appear to the poet "alight with borrowed warmth, / just like me" (*Collected Poems* 109).

"Tambourine Life" has provided a point of departure both for NEW YORK SCHOOL poets who want a poem to sound "just like me," with a strong personal voice, and for Language poets who emphasize "writing's lethal and consuming importance," as Charles Bernstein does in an essay that concludes with a quotation from "Tambourine Life" (Bernstein 155). Commenting on the poem in her introduction to *The Collected Poems of Ted Berrigan*, Notley attempts to balance these views: "it sounds like him talking, though it also sounds 'constructed,' in unexpected and witty ways" (6).

Bibliography

Bernstein, Charles. "Writing Against the Body" (1983). In *Nice to See You: Homage to Ted Berrigan*, edited by Anne Waldman, 154–157. Minneapolis, Minn.: Coffee House Press, 1991.

Berrigan, Ted. *The Collected Poems of Ted Berrigan*. Edited by Alice Notley, Anselm Berrigan, and Edmund Berrigan. Berkeley: University of California Press, 2005.

———. *Talking in Tranquility: Interviews with Ted Berrigan*. Edited by Stephen Ratcliffe and Leslie Scalapino. Bolinas, Calif.: Avenue B; Oakland, Calif.: O Books, 1991.

Carroll, Paul. Editor's note on Ted Berrigan, "Tambourine Life." In *The Young American Poets*. Chicago: Follett/Big Table, 1968, 119.

O'Hara, Frank. *The Collected Poems*. Rev. ed. Edited by Donald Allen. Berkeley: University of California Press, 1995.

Padgett, Ron. "Tone Arm." In *Great Balls of Fire*. Rev. ed. Minneapolis, Minn.: Coffee House Press, 1990, 63–78.

Teachers & Writers Collaborative

NEW YORK CITY's Teachers & Writers Collaborative (T&W) was founded in 1967 by like-thinking writers and professors who met through a series of government-funded education conferences. These scholars were united by their dissatisfaction with the teaching of English and, specifically, with instruction methods that severed literature from the real life of students. Among the many originators of the nonprofit collaborative were poets Betty Kray, DENISE LEVERTOV, Grace Paley, Muriel Rukeyser, and Anne Sexton, along with Robert Silvers from the *New York Review of Books* and Herbert Kohl, a former inner-city schoolteacher who served as the collaborative's first director. According to its mission statement, the group set out to provide "a link between New York City's rich literary community and the public schools." To meet that goal T&W recruited professional writers (and, later on, artists) to work with students in grades K–12.

Given their emphasis on bringing the academic art of writing into contact with everyday experience, it is not surprising that T&W drew sympathetic attention from the NEW YORK SCHOOL poet KENNETH KOCH. During his brief tenure with the collaborative, Koch wrote two groundbreaking books about how to teach poetry to children: *Wishes, Lies, and Dreams* (Chelsea House, 1970) and *Rose, Where Did You Get That Red?* (Vintage, 1973).

Additionally, Koch enlisted second-generation New York Schoolers such as RON PADGETT (who now serves on the board of directors), LARRY FAGIN, DAVID SHAPIRO, and DICK GALLUP to the organization; BILL BERKSON had come to T&W shortly ahead of Koch. Like Koch, these young poets were interested in linguistic experimentation and tended to privilege aesthetic issues over the social and political concerns of other collaborative members. Regardless of their particular interests, a kind of communal learning took place as all the writers who joined T&W were required to keep diaries and to share their teaching experiences with one another.

In 1992 the group opened the Center for Imaginative Writing at the Union Square headquarters, which serves as a forum for writers and educators to engage in workshops, readings, and seminars. Additionally, T&W sponsors free after-school programs, a literacy initiative for teen mothers, and an educational radio show. The Teachers & Writers Collaborative also publishes a quarterly newsletter and curriculum guides for creative writing instructors.

Bibliography

Teachers & Writers Collaborative Web site. Available online. URL: http://twc.org. Accessed December 19, 2008.

Telegraph Books (1971–1972)

Telegraph Books publishing venture was a COLLABORATION between ARAM SAROYAN, Andrew Wylie (1950–), and Victor Bockris (1949–). Unlike many other series that published books by NEW YORK SCHOOL writers (for instance, Saroyan's earlier Lines), Telegraph Books was not associated with a magazine. It was modeled on the City Lights Pocket Poet series and, like City Lights, took its name from a bookstore, in this case run by Wylie in Greenwich Village. While still based in NEW YORK CITY, the project reflects the dispersal or expansion, depending on how it is viewed, of New York School activity. In 1971–72, Saroyan was living in Cambridge, Massachusetts, where he had earlier met Wylie while the latter was still an undergraduate at Harvard University. Wylie introduced Saroyan to Bockris, a recent graduate of the University of Pennsylvania whose Philadelphia connections provided for the physical production of Telegraph Books as well as another node in an avant-garde network developing along the East Coast.

As if to confirm that the New York School had now gone on the road, the Telegraph Books publication that most fully reflects the New York School of the previous decade takes the FORM of a trip diary, *Back in Boston Again* (1972), a collaboration by TED BERRIGAN, TOM CLARK, and RON PADGETT based on a visit with Saroyan. Saroyan's own contributions, *The Rest* (1971) and *Poems* (1972), are in his minimalist mode, evidently an influence on the volumes by Bockris (*In America* [1972]) and Wylie (*Tenderloin* [1971] and *Gold* [1972]). Another Telegraph author, TOM WEATHERLY (*Thumbprint* [1971]), shares with Saroyan roots in Black Mountain poetry (see BLACK MOUNTAIN POETS) that Weatherly adapts to a self-consciously black aesthetic.

Bockris and Wylie were fascinated by the instant celebrity produced in New York by ANDY WARHOL's Factory and worldwide by the publicity agents of pop MUSIC. Like rock stars on album covers, Telegraph Book authors are glamorized in large photos that appear on each book cover. GERARD MALANGA, a close associate of Warhol, is one of the authors (*Poetry on Film* [1972]), and he is responsible for bringing two others into the series. Brigid Polk, as Brigid Berlin was known in the Warhol circle, published *Scars* (1972), which reproduces imprints of people's scars (taking Weatherly's *Thumbprint* to a literal level) along with comments by each contributor. PATTI SMITH, on the verge of stardom in the emerging PUNK ROCK scene, published *Seventh Heaven* (1972), her first collection of poems, in which she glances back at the shooting star of French modernist poet Arthur Rimbaud.

Telegraph Books came to an end when Saroyan left for BOLINAS, CALIFORNIA, seeking a very different culture from the personality cult that flourished at Max's Kansas City in Manhattan. Bockris and Wylie went on to conduct celebrity interviews published under the brand name "Bockris-Wylie." By 1980 they were working independently, Bockris as a biographer of such figures as WILLIAM S. BURROUGHS, Warhol, and Smith and Wylie as an influential literary agent.

Bibliography

Clay, Steven, and Rodney Phillips. *A Secret Location on the Lower East Side: Adventures in Writing, 1960–1980.* New York: New York Public Library/Granary Books, 1998.

Saroyan, Aram. *Friends in the World: The Education of a Writer.* Minneapolis, Minn.: Coffee House Press, 1992.

Telephone (1969–1984, 1999–   )

Edited by MAUREEN OWEN, *Telephone* magazine applied the principle of FRANK O'HARA's "PERSONISM" that writing could be as personal as talking on the telephone (O'Hara 499). Production of the magazine itself, using the mimeograph equipment at the POETRY PROJECT AT ST. MARK'S CHURCH IN-THE-BOWERY, was a community event, and publication was a continuation of the writing process. Owen believes, "The purpose of a good little magazine is not the printed completion of a work. It's a kind of ongoing thing. Here's what people are doing. What do you think?" (Owen n.p.). In the spirit of inclusiveness the magazine grew to outsize proportions, gathering as many as 144 pages and 74 authors in a single issue (number 17, August 1981)—"as big as a telephone book," conceptually (Owen n.p.). Eventually the series of books that Owen began issuing in 1972 under the Telephone imprint included a work entitled *The Telephone Book* (1979), transcripts of several weeks of telephone conversations conducted by ED FRIEDMAN.

In both concept and format *Telephone* resembled *The WORLD*, in which Owen had a hand through her association with the Poetry Project. However, in her own publication Owen could offer personal encouragement to women writers who "just weren't knocking on the door" at St. Mark's (Owen n.p.). Both the magazine and the series of Telephone books are notable for the appearance of SANDY BERRIGAN, Rebecca Brown (1948–   ), Susan Cataldo (1952–2001), Janet Hamill (1945–   ), Fanny Howe (1949–   ), Susan Howe (1937–   ), Janine Pommy Vega (1942–   ), and Rebecca Wright (1942–   ). The presence of the Howe sisters places *Telephone* in the "feminist genealogy of Language writing" traced by Ann Vickery. Since reviving the Telephone books imprint in 1999, Owen has published new volumes by both Hamill and (posthumously) Cataldo.

Telephone magazine ended in 1982, a few years after Owen had left NEW YORK CITY for Guilford, Connecticut. Like *United Artists,* which ended in the same year, *Telephone* served as "a bridge between the generations" (Clay and Phillips 41) in the NEW YORK SCHOOL. An unusual representation of the first generation is the reproduction of a 1957 letter from O'Hara to the painter Mike Goldberg (*Telephone,* number 6, Spring 1972), in which O'Hara quotes the full text of JOHN ASHBERY's "They Dream Only of America," sent to O'Hara by Ashbery from Paris.

Several of the leading men of the second generation appear in the second issue of *Telephone* (1970), characteristically in collaborative teams: BILL BERKSON, TED BERRIGAN, and JIM CARROLL; LEWIS MACADAMS, TOM VEITCH, and CLARK COOLIDGE; RON PADGETT and DICK GALLUP. LITA HORNICK's "Ted Berrigan/Romantic Formalist," a rare instance of critical prose in *Telephone*, appears in issue number 14 (July 1978) along with early appearances of a new generation of writers, such as BARBARA BARG, EILEEN MYLES, TOM SAVAGE, and SIMON SCHUCHAT. An unusual twist on the theme of generations in *Telephone* was the inclusion of poets' children, some grown up, like Hadley Haden-Guest, daughter of BARBARA GUEST; some less than 10 years old, like Kate Berrigan, daughter of Ted and Sandy; and Wayne Padgett, son of Ron and Pat Padgett. Owen was raising two sons at the time (both appear in *Telephone*) and she regarded them as members of the community that her magazine represented. "I used to bring the kids to readings a lot," she recalled. "They would come to the collating too—they were very helpful" (Owen n.p.). Publication of their writing reflected the confidence in the creative spontaneity of the CHILD that the New York School inherited from romanticism.

Bibliography

Clay, Steven, and Rodney Phillips. *A Secret Location on the Lower East Side: Adventures in Writing, 1960–1980.* New York: New York Public Library/Granary Books, 1998.

O'Hara, Frank. "Personism" (1959). In *The Collected Poems.* Rev. ed. Edited by Donald Allen. Berkeley: University of California Press, 1995, 498–499.

Owen, Maureen. "Notes on Publishing" (1999). *Jacket* 11 (April 2000). Available online. URL: http://jacketmagazine.com/11/owen-durand.html. Accessed December 19, 2008.

Vickery, Ann. *Leaving Lines of Gender: A Feminist Genealogy of Language Writing.* Hanover, N.H.: University Press of New England/Wesleyan University Press, 2000.

theater

Poetry entered the theater of postwar NEW YORK CITY from various directions. There was an interest in reviving verse as a medium for dramatic language, on the model of the Elizabethan stage. T. S. Eliot's *The Cocktail Party,* a leading example of this movement, had a successful Broadway run in 1950. Of more interest to the NEW YORK SCHOOL poets was the work of Tennessee Williams (1911–83) and his successor, Edward Albee (1928–), often called "poetic" for its mood and symbolism. Williams and Albee were known personally to the poets who circulated in New York's gay subculture. However, the connection with theater that was most specific to the New York School was the opposition of "poetry" to "realism," particularly conventions such as the drawing-room set that Eliot and even Williams and Albee still employed. In this respect poetry was allied with "abstraction," as Julian Beck made clear in a 1959 manifesto for his LIVING THEATRE (Beck X3). As a painter who had exhibited with JACKSON POLLOCK, Beck derived his understanding of abstraction from the sources of the New York School. Like many other avant-garde theater directors, he turned to the New York School poets for language, often not written as verse, that can "take us beyond this ignorant present" into the unconscious realms of "self-understanding" and "an understanding of the nature of all things" (Beck X3).

As in the case of painting, the closer ties to Europe that had developed through World War II proved to be stimulating for the New York theater. The rise of Off-Broadway theaters was fed largely by a European repertoire, from classics by Henrik Ibsen and Anton Chekhov to the latest "theater of the absurd" by Eugène Ionesco and Samuel Beckett (a favorite of FRANK O'HARA's [LeSueur, Introduction xxi]). Among the wartime émigrés who took refuge in New York, a central figure in the theater was the one-time colleague of Bertolt Brecht, Erwin Piscator (1893–1966). In 1940 Piscator founded the Dramatic Workshop at the New School, which produced many influential alumni, including Judith Malina, Beck's wife and cofounder with him of the Living Theatre in 1948. Also in 1948, Piscator's wife, Maria Ley Piscator (1898–1999), launched the POETS' THEATRE at the 92nd Street Y with a program consisting of two "Noh" plays by PAUL GOODMAN (*Dark* and *Stoplight*) and Jean Genet's *The Maids* (Malina 37). The program was organized by JOHN BERNARD MYERS, later director of the TIBOR DE NAGY GALLERY and producer of many plays by New York School poets under the aegis of the ARTISTS' THEATRE.

The Living Theatre, the Poets' Theatre, and the Artists' Theatre were forerunners of the movement that became known by 1960 as Off-Off Broadway, noncommercial performances supported by the same network of Downtown coffeehouses and lofts that sponsored poetry readings. The Caffe Cino, usually cited as the pioneer in this movement, produced work by many poet-playwrights, including BARBARA GUEST (*The Office*, 1963) and RUTH KRAUSS (*38 Haikus*, 1964; *Newsletters*, 1966). "Poets' theaters" proliferated, from the Judson Poets' Theatre, based at JUDSON MEMORIAL CHURCH, to the Hardware Poets' Playhouse, located above a hardware store on 54th Street. The NEW YORK POETS THEATRE, under the leadership of DIANE DI PRIMA, produced the most work by New York School poets. At St. Mark's Church, Theatre Genesis was founded by Ralph Cook (1928–   ) in 1964. It preceded the founding (1966) of the POETRY PROJECT AT ST. MARK'S CHURCH IN-THE-BOWERY, but unlike the Poetry Project, it did not survive the fire at the church in 1978. Known primarily as the incubator for the work of Sam Shepard (1943–   ), Theatre Genesis developed a list of playwrights that did not overlap with the list of poets involved in the Poetry Project. However, the two ventures shared "a feeling about the spoken word as an almost shamanistic act, incantatory, ritualistic, as opposed to the theatrical [dialogue] tradition," according to Murray Mednick (1939–   ) of Theatre Genesis (Bottoms 116).

Much of the original energy of Off-Off Broadway had dissipated by 1970 owing largely to economic pressures, and much of the energy that survived was channeled into the "theatre of images" associated with Richard Foreman (1937–   ) and Robert Wilson (1941–   ), in which language is "flattened out" (Marranca 3) rather than animated in the way Mednick describes. There were parallel developments in New York School poetry, but with rare exceptions (for instance, CLARK COOLIDGE and TOM VEITCH) they did not look to the theater to be realized. However, the theater of Wilson, in work such as *Einstein on the Beach* (1976), moved KENNETH KOCH not toward reduction of language but expansion of scale (Koch, interview 203).

Koch's first full-length play, *The RED ROBINS*, was produced in New York in 1978 with lavish décor (by JANE FREILICHER, Red Grooms, ALEX KATZ, and Roy Lichtenstein, among others) that threatened to overwhelm the words. The preferred balance was reflected in the title of the Eye and Ear Theater, under the direction of Katz's wife, Ada, which produced KENWARD ELMSLIE's *City Junket*, designed by Grooms (1980); a stage version of JOHN ASHBERY's *Litany*, designed by Alex Katz (1980); and a revival of Pablo Picasso's *Desire Caught by the Tail*, designed by Lynda Benglis (1984).

Since the mid-1990s, Foreman's Ontological-Hysteric Theater (founded in 1968) has occupied the space once used by Theatre Genesis at St. Mark's Church. A COLLABORATION with the Poetry Project—"finally," according to the press release—took the FORM of "A Poets-Theater Festival," cocurated by LEE ANN BROWN, Corina Copp, and Tony Torn in May 2006. While not literary in any conventional sense, Foreman's use of language in the theater bears an affinity to the use of the theater as a metaphor for the human condition in New York School poetry. For instance, in "Pyrography" (1976) Ashbery asks:

> How are we to inhabit
> This space from which the fourth wall is invariably missing,
> As in a stage-set or dollhouse, except by staying as we are . . . ? (9).

Bibliography

Aronson, Arnold. *American Avant-garde Theatre: A History*. London: Routledge, 2000.

Ashbery, John. "Pyrography." In *Houseboat Days*. New York: Penguin, 1977, 8–10.

Auslander, Philip. *The New York School Poets as Playwrights: O'Hara, Ashbery, Koch, Schuyler and the Visual Arts*. New York: Peter Lang, 1989.

Beck, Julian. "Why Vanguard?" *New York Times*, 22 March 1959, pp. X1ff.

Bottoms, Stephen J. *Playing Underground: A Critical History of the 1960s Off-Off-Broadway Movement*. Ann Arbor: University of Michigan Press, 2004.

Coolidge, Clark, and Tom Veitch. *To Obtain the Value of the Cake Measure from Zero: A Play in One Act*. San Francisco: B. Presson, 1970.

Koch, Kenneth. Interview by Jordan Davis (1995). In *The Art of Poetry: Poems, Parodies, Interviews, Essays, and Other Work.* Ann Arbor: University of Michigan Press, 1996, 187–214.

———. *The Red Robins.* In *The Gold Standard: A Book of Plays.* New York: Knopf, 1998, 65–140.

LeSueur, Joe. Introduction to *Amorous Nightmares of Delay: Selected Plays,* by Frank O'Hara. Baltimore, Md.: Johns Hopkins University Press, 1997, xv–xxv.

———. "Theatre Chronicle." *Kulchur* 3, no. 10 (Summer 1963): 37–43.

Malina, Judith. *The Diaries, 1947–1957.* New York: Grove, 1984.

Marranca, Bonnie, ed. *The Theatre of Images.* New ed. Baltimore, Md.: Johns Hopkins University Press, 1996.

"Plays on Words: A Poets-Theater Festival." Press release (May 2006). Poetry Project at St. Mark's Church-in-the-Bowery, New York.

Poland, Albert, and Bruce Mailman, eds. *The Off Off Broadway Book: The Plays, People, Theatre.* Indianapolis, Ind.: Bobbs-Merrill, 1972.

Thomas, Lorenzo (1944–2005)

Born in Panama, Lorenzo Thomas immigrated with his parents to the United States in 1948. He became an important member of the Umbra poetry workshop in the early 1960s and continued publishing poetry and essays while teaching at the University of Houston until his death in 2005. His sensitive poems reveal a broad range of intellectual influences and an astute assimilation of American popular culture and political history. A perceptive essay by Alice Notley highlights key traits that link Thomas with the concerns of the New York School: "Thomas has invented a form that allows for an innovative coincidence of the public and the private" (96), Notley writes, and "Thomas's poems are self-consciously musical and are also about music" (102).

Thomas learned English growing up in the Bronx and Queens. While attending Queens College, he joined the Umbra poets workshop, where he met other practicing poets and young authors, including Ishmael Reed, Calvin Hernton, David Henderson, and Tom Dent. He contributed to the Umbra magazines distributed by the group. Like Reed and Henderson, in Umbra Thomas learned to combine original imagery in his poems with references to American popular culture, African-American folklore, headline news, and location and landscape. Many of his early poems are first-person meditations on race, desire, America, the economy, and POLITICS, their tones ranging from comic to angry. He has been compared with Aimé Césaire (Dent 318), the Afro-Caribbean poet who injected surrealism (see DADA AND SURREALISM) into poems questioning the structures of identity.

Thomas graduated from Queens in 1967, the same year he published his first book of poems, *A Visible Island,* with Adlib Press in Brooklyn. His poetry written in NEW YORK CITY during the 1960s focused on the social and political tensions and victories of the Civil Rights movement and the political struggle between African Americans and others in the African diaspora. Although the Umbra workshop dissolved after 1964, many of its leading authors appeared together in numerous anthologies of the late 1960s and 1970s as part of the BLACK ARTS MOVEMENT, a national and international renaissance of African diaspora thought. Thomas contributed to *Black Fire: An Anthology of Black American Writing* (Morrow, 1968), *New Black Voices* (New American Library, 1972), and *The Poetry of Black America* (Harper & Row, 1973).

Thomas left New York in 1968 for the U.S. Navy, serving as a communications adviser in Vietnam. He credits ANNE WALDMAN and Elleased Southerland (Ebele Oseye) with "holding on to my lifeline" during this period (Thomas, Memoir 604). He returned to New York in 1972, working briefly as a librarian at Pace University before leaving New York for good, the next year to become writer in residence at Texas Southern University in Houston. He remained in Houston to conduct workshops for the new Black Arts Center from 1974 to 1976 and decided to settle in the South. However, his next publications, *Fit Music: California Songs, 1970* (1972) and *Dracula* (1973), were both issued by Angel Hair, reflecting Thomas's continued connection with the New York School. Based on the popularity of vampire films, *Dracula* meditates on the American desire for conquest and bloodlust, but also on the victims of that desire, such as African Americans, "charged . . . with the presence of the unwanted / The necessary black negro" (Thomas, *Dracula* 408).

Thomas included *Dracula* in his 1981 collection called *The Bathers*, issued under Reed's publishing imprint. The collection as a whole reflects Thomas's capacity to bring together emotional explorations of subjects as disparate as film and his identity within the African diaspora. The title poem, originally published in 1970, juxtaposes the mythology of ancient African cultures, like Egypt, with the African-American civil rights struggle. Although "Bathers" are a traditional subject in painting, Thomas refers to the famous photographs of black demonstrators being fire-hosed by police in Birmingham, Alabama, in 1963.

Thomas's work continued to expand in range of FORM and reference during his time in Houston. He learned even more about African-American folk traditions, which he began to discuss in essays and poems alike. In addition to his poems Thomas pursued a distinguished academic career as a professor at the University of Houston starting in 1976. After focusing on journal articles for *African American Review* and *Callaloo*, among others, Thomas completed work on his important collection of essays *Extraordinary Measures: Afrocentric Modernism and Twentieth Century American Poetry* (University of Alabama Press, 2000). This versatile book showcases Thomas's penetrating historiography on figures such as Fenton Johnson, William Stanley Braithwaite, Melvin B. Tolson, and AMIRI BARAKA. Several chapters deal directly with subjects like Umbra, the Black Arts Movement, poetry readings, and regional poetry groups. In 2004, Thomas published *Dancing on Main Street* (Coffee House Press), his final book of poems.

When Thomas died in 2005, some surviving members of Umbra, including Henderson and Lloyd Addison, held a memorial poetry reading at the BOWERY POETRY CLUB in New York City. Thomas's legacy as an artist became integrated with his leadership and activism in an artistic community far from his beginnings in New York. However, reflecting on the group of writers who eventually dispersed across the country—Dent to New Orleans, A. B. SPELLMAN to Atlanta, Reed to Oakland—Thomas maintained that their "cultural and political activism was the fruit of their New York experience"

(*Extraordinary Measures* 121), and the same could certainly be said of Thomas himself.

Bibliography

Dent, Tom. "Lorenzo Thomas." In *Dictionary of Literary Biography*, Vol. 41: *Afro-American Poets Since 1955*, edited by Trudier Harris and Thadious M. Davis, 315–326. Detroit, Mich.: Gale, 1985.

Jones, Patricia Spears. "Thinking in Words: A Talk About Lorenzo Thomas." A Gathering of the Tribes. Available online. URL: http://www.tribes.org/pjones/essays/thomas. Accessed December 19, 2008.

Nielsen, Aldon Lynn. *Black Chant: Languages of African-American Postmodernism*. Cambridge: Cambridge University Press, 1997.

Notley, Alice. "Lorenzo Thomas: A Private Public Space" (1997). In *Coming After: Essays on Poetry*. Ann Arbor: University of Michigan Press, 2005, 95–107.

Thomas, Lorenzo. "Between the Comedy of Matters and the Ritual Workings of Man: An Interview with Lorenzo Thomas." *Callaloo* 4 (February–October 1981): 19–35.

———. *Dracula* (1973). In *The Angel Hair Anthology*, edited by Anne Waldman and Lewis Warsh, 404–410. New York: Granary Books, 2001.

———. *Extraordinary Measures: Afrocentric Modernism and Twentieth-Century American Poetry*. Tuscaloosa: University of Alabama Press, 2000.

———. Interview by Hermione Pinson. *Callaloo: A Journal of African-American and African Arts and Letters* 22, no. 2 (Spring 1999): 287–303.

———. Memoir in *The Angel Hair Anthology*, edited by Anne Waldman and Lewis Warsh, 603–604. New York: Granary Books, 2001.

Tiber Press (1953–1977)

While promoting COLLABORATION between poets and artists of the NEW YORK SCHOOL during the 1950s, the Tiber Press was itself the product of an intimate collaboration. It was founded in 1953 by Floriano Vecchi (1920–2005) and Richard Miller (1920–71), who were lovers, and DAISY ALDAN (1923–2001), who was Miller's wife (Field 77). They had ties with an international avant-garde through personal contacts, such as the translator William Weaver, who sponsored Vecchi's immigration to the United States from his native Italy; and institutions, such as the artists' CLUB, which Aldan attended with Frederick Kiesler, and the Downtown Gallery, a headquarters of American modernism, where Miller worked for a time. Employing Vecchi's experience in printmaking, Tiber Press produced prints by a number of Downtown Gallery artists (Stuart Davis, Georgia O'Keefe, Ben Shahn, Charles Sheeler), but for the most part these were reproductions based on existing work. The production of original prints began with younger artists (GRACE HARTIGAN, Alfred Leslie, Gandy Brodie, Felix Pasilis), who contributed their work to the Tiber Press journal, FOLDER. In this way Vecchi introduced a number of second-generation New York School painters to the medium of silkscreen printing, as he was to do slightly later with ANDY WARHOL, who made the medium his trademark (Castleman 144).

Apart from *Folder*, the principal project through which Tiber Press provided a showcase for New York School poets, was a series of four artist's books, officially published in 1960, pairing the work of a poet with prints by an artist of the same "school": JOHN ASHBERY with Joan Mitchell in *The Poems*; KENNETH KOCH with Alfred Leslie in *Permanently*; FRANK O'HARA with Mike Goldberg in *Odes*; and JAMES SCHUYLER with Hartigan in *Salute*. In the case of Mitchell and Goldberg this was their first exercise in printmaking. In Schuyler's case this was his first collection of poems. Except in the case of Ashbery, most of the texts were reprinted in later, more widely distributed collections by each poet. In the Tiber Press volumes, each limited to an edition of 225 copies, the generous size of the pages (17-by-14½ inches), the fine quality of the handmade paper, and the richness of color in the prints enhance the visual presentation. On a more abstract level of vision there are correspondences between the poems and prints. Reviewing the series for the *Evergreen Review*, FAIRFIELD PORTER noted the "luminosity" in both Schuyler and Hartigan, and the impression that, next to an Ashbery poem, a Mitchell print "looks like writing" (225). Text and image are kept to separate pages, however, except on the covers, title pages, and one instance of thoroughly integrated collaboration, O'Hara's "Ode on Necrophilia" (*Collected Poems* 280). Here the text, in O'Hara's handwriting, merges with

Goldberg's drips, the signature of ACTION PAINTING (Ferguson 70). The practical difficulty of pinning down Goldberg during the production of the book is humorously recorded in O'Hara's poem "To Richard Miller" (1958; *Collected Poems* 301).

After the completion of this ambitious series, Aldan, whose marriage to Miller had been annulled, left Tiber Press and went on to publish Folder Editions, featuring some of her own text and image collaborations. Out of financial necessity Miller and Vecchi increasingly focused on producing upmarket greeting cards. In 1977, six years after Miller died in an automobile accident, Vecchi sold Tiber Press and subsequently concentrated on his own artwork.

Bibliography

Aldan, Daisy. "An Interview on *Folder*." In *The Little Magazine in America: A Modern Documentary History*, edited by Elliott Anderson and Mary Kinzie, 263–279. Yonkers, N.Y.: Pushcart Press, 1978.

Castleman, Riva. "Floriano Vecchi and the Tiber Press." *Print Quarterly* 21 (2004): 127–145.

Diggory, Terence. *Grace Hartigan and the Poets: Paintings and Prints*. Saratoga Springs, N.Y.: Schick Art Gallery, Skidmore College, 1993.

Ferguson, Russell. *In Memory of My Feelings: Frank O'Hara and American Art*. Los Angeles: Museum of Contemporary Art; Berkeley: University of California Press, 1999.

Field, Edward. *The Man Who Would Marry Susan Sontag and Other Intimate Portraits of the Bohemian Era*. Madison: University of Wisconsin Press, 2005.

O'Hara, Frank. *The Collected Poems*. Rev. ed. Edited by Donald Allen. Berkeley: University of California Press, 1995.

Porter, Fairfield. "Poets and Painters in Collaboration" (1961). *Art in Its Own Terms: Selected Criticism, 1955–1975*. Edited by Rackstraw Downes. 1979. Reprint, Cambridge, Mass.: Zoland, 1993, 220–225.

Tibor de Nagy Gallery (1950–)

As headquarters for the "second generation" of NEW YORK SCHOOL painters, the Tibor de Nagy Gallery (pronounced TEE-bore-de-NAJSH) provided the launch site for the New York School of poets, for whom the painters provided vital creative stimulus. The gallery's founding director, JOHN BERNARD MYERS, actively promoted interaction between artists and writers and stirred the mixture with a considerable amount of sexual energy transmitted through his connections in New York's gay subculture. Myers's business partner, Tibor de Nagy (1908–93), helped balance Myers's flamboyance with sober pragmatism, grounded in banking experience in his native Hungary. After fleeing Soviet occupation in 1948, Nagy (who later added the "de" to his name to lend a touch of class to the gallery) arrived in New York with very little money. Financial support for the gallery initially came from Dwight Ripley (1908–73), a member of the international set associated with Peggy Guggenheim (1898–1979). Hoping to fill a void left by Guggenheim's departure from New York and the closing of her gallery in 1947, Ripley brought together Myers's ambitions as an arts impresario and CLEMENT GREENBERG's astuteness as an art critic. Most of the artists whom Greenberg recommended to Myers to start his gallery, including Robert Goodnough (1917–   ), GRACE HARTIGAN, Alfred Leslie (1927–   ), and LARRY RIVERS, had been selected by Greenberg and Meyer Schapiro (1904–96) for the landmark *New Talent* show they mounted at the Kootz Gallery in 1950.

Since its opening at 206 East 53rd Street in December 1950, the Tibor de Nagy Gallery has been located at various addresses, all in Midtown Manhattan (currently 724 Fifth Avenue, just off 57th Street). Unlike the Downtown cooperative galleries that made 10th Street virtually synonymous with the "look" of ABSTRACT EXPRESSIONISM during the 1950s, Tibor de Nagy was always a commercial gallery (though it made little profit in its first years), and it was free to reflect the personal and very eclectic tastes of its director. With no interest in perpetuating the "macho" image of the New York painter, Myers was unusually receptive to women painters. Hartigan, JANE FREILICHER, Helen Frankenthaler (1928–   ), and Nell Blaine (1922–96) were repeatedly featured in early shows. The division between abstract and representational work, drawn as a battle line in some parts of the contemporary art world, was easily bridged at Tibor de Nagy. The figurative painter FAIRFIELD PORTER joined the gallery on the strong recommenda-tion of abstract expressionist pioneer WILLEM DE KOONING. Goodnough, an abstract painter, was Myers's personal favorite among the artists at Tibor de Nagy—at least so he declared in retrospect, after stars like Rivers had defected to other galleries (Myers 157). Myers did not brood on the past, however. In 1965 the Tibor de Nagy Gallery was one of the first to feature "minimalist" work, in a group exhibition entitled *Shape and Structure*. Myers was cool toward POP ART, but he embraced Red Grooms as a "fantasist" (Myers 206).

The association of the Tibor de Nagy Gallery with poetry evolved along with the art. Ironically, by inventing the label "the New York School of Poets," Myers meant to celebrate the boldness of individual imagination that he admired in his artists rather than conformity to any group style. The series of Tibor de Nagy Editions that first published FRANK O'HARA, JOHN ASHBERY, KENNETH KOCH, BARBARA GUEST, and KENWARD ELMSLIE extended during the 1960s to second-generation writers such as BILL BERKSON, FRANK LIMA, JOSEPH CERAVOLO, and TONY TOWLE. After Myers left the gallery in 1970, its ties to poetry slackened somewhat. However, such ties remained important to individual artists such as Archie Rand (1950–   ), who had been recruited to the gallery by Nagy himself in 1966. When Ashbery's partner, David Kermani, became gallery director in 1977, the interaction of "poets, writers and artists" resumed on a regular basis, as Rand recalls (Wilkin 37). Kermani was instrumental in reviving the Tibor de Nagy Editions imprint for the publication of Porter's *Collected Poems* in 1985. The series has continued under Andrew Arnot and Eric Brown, former assistants to Nagy who took over the gallery after his death in 1993. Under their leadership the Tibor de Nagy Gallery has mounted exhibitions of work by JOE BRAINARD, RUDOLPH BURCKHARDT, GEORGE SCHNEEMAN, and TREVOR WINKFIELD, artists with a long history of association with New York School poets.

Bibliography

Crase, Douglas. *Both: A Portrait in Two Parts.* New York: Pantheon, 2004. [Double biography of Dwight Ripley and Rupert Barnaby.]

Myers, John. *Tracking the Marvelous: A Life in the New York Art World.* New York: Random House, 1983.

Wilkin, Karen. "The First Fifty Years." In *Tibor de Nagy Gallery: The First Fifty Years, 1950–2000.* Exhibit catalog. New York: Tibor de Nagy Gallery, 2000, 17–40.

Timmons, Susie (1955–)

Born in CHICAGO, ILLINOIS, and raised in New Jersey, Susie Timmons came to NEW YORK CITY in 1974 after some time on the West Coast, including study at the University of Oregon. In New York Timmons was introduced to the Downtown poetry scene by Billy McKay, then editor of the *Poetry Project Newsletter.* She started writing poetry in workshops led by BILL ZAVATSKY and JIM BRODEY. She became active in the arts COLLABORATIONs and peripatetic escapades of the third-generation NEW YORK SCHOOL poets that included BOB HOLMAN, STEVE LEVINE, ROSE LESNIAK, ROCHELLE KRAUT (who published Timmons in the magazine she edited with SIMON SCHUCHAT, *432 Review*), BOB ROSENTHAL (whose Frontward Books published her first book), BARBARA BARG (Timmons performed instrumentals and vocals in Barg's band, the G-Spots, in the 1980s), GREG MASTERS, MICHAEL SCHOLNICK, ELINOR NAUEN, MAGGIE DUBRIS (Timmons was a comrade in Nauen and Dubris's Consumptive Poets League), and Susan Cataldo. The work of RON PADGETT and David Rattray, her friendship with TED BERRIGAN, and a workshop in 1978 with ALICE NOTLEY were formative to Timmons's poetics. In Notley, Timmons found an especially encouraging and challenging mentor.

Timmons lived in New York's East Village, and her jobs included baby-sitting for the children of Phillip Glass and bookkeeping for ALLEN GINSBERG. Diving into the various worlds and GENREs of the Downtown scene, she was invited to collaborate in events and performances of multiple media. Timmons brought to these appearances the same qualities found in her poems: a witty delivery and timing and capacity to mix seemingly quotidian, almost embarrassingly naked disclosure with sudden and compact lyric interjections and edgy, unpredictable shifts in diction and use of space and caesura. Disparate, odd observations ranging from the minuscule detail to large socioeconomic realities are drawn together in an inescapable and personal logic. The work of Notley, MAUREEN OWEN,

JOE BRAINARD, and EILEEN MYLES comes to mind in association with Timmons's phrasing and use of subjectivity. Timmons appeared as Sylvia Plath in Myles's play *Patriarchy,* coming on stage with a cardboard stove over her head. Timmons performed with musician-composers John Zorn and Charles K. Noyse and with bands led by Carol Parkinson, Ikue Mori, and Cinnie Cole. She appeared in Christian Marclay's 1985 opera *Dead Story* and the film *Money* by filmmaker Henry Hills.

Timmons's poetry has been published in the magazines *Dodgems* (edited by Myles), *Bom, Mag City* (edited by Scholnick and Masters), *Gandhabba, Shiny, Cuz* (edited by RICHARD HELL), and *Ecstatic Piece* (edited by Thurston Moore). Timmons herself edited issue number 39 of the Poetry Project's *The WORLD* and a short-lived but cogent magazine, *Bingo,* which appeared on newsprint. She is the author of *Hogwild* (Frontward Books, 1979) and *Locked from the Outside* (1990), winner of the first Ted Berrigan Prize. In her preface to the latter volume, Alice Notley wrote: "Timmons' poetry voice has wit, has personality, never tells us what's really going on (is not confessional or even explicit, though there's a lot of apartment & city décor) & yet manages to effect in the reader a sense that the experience of given poems is complete" (n.p.).

Timmons left New York in the early 1990s, disheartened by the loss of several close friends to AIDS. She received a degree from Smith College in 1995 and pursued graduate studies in invertebrate paleontology, all the while continuing to write profusely. She now lives in Brooklyn.

Tlooth   Harry Mathews (1966)

The 1966 novel *Tlooth,* by HARRY MATHEWS, chronicles the picaresque adventures of an androgynous prison escapee, determined to exact revenge on his/her romantic rival. Like the author's previous novel, *The CONVERSIONS, Tlooth* is narrated by its protagonist and incorporates a series of strange and comical "nested" stories, recounted by eccentric supporting characters. For example, shortly after the narrator breaks out of prison, fellow escapee Robin Marr describes his/her struggle to make sense of a notebook sheet found inside a library copy of Robert Frost's *Lives of Eminent Christians.* (Mis)construing the paper's contents as a craftily coded message, Marr invents a dozen ingenious ciphers for the unintelligible scribbles. The alleged brainteaser even ignites a debate among scholars about its proper interpretation. But no sooner are we enmeshed in this puzzle than the page is revealed as meaningless and the matter is abandoned.

In interviews Mathews has expressed interest in the way these narrative diversions affect the primacy and relevance of the main storyline, yet *Tlooth* is actually less digressive and more overtly episodic than *The Conversions,* which relies on similar tale-within-a-tale plot devices. In *Tlooth* the protagonists' journey can be traced, with only minor interruptions, from a religiously segregated prison camp in Russia, to the mustard-rich plains outside Afghanistan, to a jail in Kabul, and onward to India and Europe. In his depiction of these places Mathews consistently blurs the line between reality and fantasy—a fact that has led more than one reviewer to link his novel with the work of Italian filmmaker Frederico Fellini. (This comparison is further suggested by a series of chapters in part 3 where the central text is actually displaced by a film script).

As in his other fiction, Mathews depicts fantastical events in a deceptively nonchalant voice; the most astonishing incidents are, in the words of Roderick Cook, "blandly handed to you" (142). In an interview with JOHN ASH the author attributes his disarming rhetorical simplicity to the influence of RAYMOND ROUSSEL.

Bibliography

Ash, John. "A Conversation with Harry Mathews." *Review of Contemporary Fiction* (Fall 1987): 21–32.

Cook, Roderick. Review of *Tlooth. Harper's Magazine,* November 1966, 142.

Gettes, Anthony. "Pursuit and Escape." *New York Times Book Review,* 30 October 1966, 72.

Mathews, Harry. "Fearful Symmetries." *Literary Review: An International Journal of Contemporary Writing* (Spring 2002): 444–452.

———. *Tlooth.* Garden City, N.Y.: Doubleday, 1966.

Torregian, Sotère (1941–   )

More than most NEW YORK SCHOOL poets, Sotère Torregian subscribed to "orthodox surrealism" (bio-graphical note 438; see DADA AND SURREALISM), but in his work, "marvelous" imagery in the mode of André Breton jostles with the accidents of everyday life in the casual manner of FRANK O'HARA. "See me drop my last piece of tuna / to the ants," writes Torregian in "After Mayakovsky" (1967), just before ascending to the surreal sublime: "I stuff my magic letters down the / throat of the cyclone" (66). The poem's title points to the legacy of RUSSIAN POETRY that was just as important to the New York School as French surrealism.

Born in Newark, New Jersey, Torregian attended the New College of Rutgers University and quickly entered into both the political and the literary scene across the Hudson River, in NEW YORK CITY. At the Free University of New York (FUNY), an outgrowth of the New Left antiwar movement, Torregian offered a two-year course on "Poetry and Revolution." He also introduced JOHN ASHBERY at his reading at FUNY in celebration of the publication of *Rivers and Mountains* (Holt, Rinehart and Winston) in March 1966. The full range of New York School magazines, from ART AND LITERATURE to *The* WORLD, published Torregian's work. Angel Hair published one of his first chapbooks, *The Golden Palomino Bites the Clock* (1967), with a cover by GEORGE SCHNEEMAN. Along with many other poets of the second-generation New York School, Torregian enjoyed his first broad public exposure in PAUL CARROLL's anthology *The Young American Poets* (Follett, 1968), where Torregian's selection included two poems in honor of O'Hara.

When Torregian left New York for California in 1967, his affiliations outside the New York School became more visible in his publications and other activities. Oyez Press in Berkeley published *The Wounded Mattress* with an introduction by Philip Lamantia (1927–   ), the leading American surrealist. At Stanford University, where Torregian taught from 1969 to 1973, he became involved in the founding of the Black Studies program under St. Clair Drake (1911–90). Although Torregian introduced himself in Carroll's anthology as of "all-around Mediterranean descent" (biographical note 438), his ties to North Africa were especially meaningful at a time when African Americans were taking the lead in the revolutionary cause that Torregian espoused. His work is included in *New*

Black Voices: An Anthology of Contemporary African-American Literature (New American Library, 1972), edited by Abraham Chapman. However, the first extensive collection of Torregian's work, *The Age of Gold* (KULCHUR Foundation, 1976), drew on his New York School connections. To return to New York for the publication party at the Gotham Book Mart, Torregian took a cross-country train trip, which became the occasion for a journal in prose and poetry. MAUREEN OWEN, who had suggested the journal, published it as *Amtrak Trek* (1978), in her series of TELEPHONE books. The final section, composed in New York, is in part a COLLABORATION with TED JOANS.

Torregian continues to reside in California, where he has become less visible over the years, confining his appearances to occasional poetry readings, university lectures, and small-press publications. The full range of his work has become available only recently in a collected edition, *"I Must Go" (She Said) "Because My Pizza's Cold": Selected Works, 1957–1999* (Skanky Possum, 2002). As the title indicates, Torregian continues to ground his surrealism in the accidents of everyday life, in the spirit of the New York School.

Bibliography

Sotère Torregian Web site. Available online. URL: http://www.soteretorregian.com/. Includes facsimile and plain text of *Amtrak Trek* journal.

Torregian, Sotère. "After Mayakovsky." In *The Angel Hair Anthology*, edited by Anne Waldman and Lewis Warsh, 66–69. New York: Granary Books, 2001.

———. Biographical note in *The Young American Poets*, edited by Paul Carroll, 438–439. Chicago: Follett/Big Table, 1968.

Torres, Edwin (1958–)

Poet and performer Edwin Torres has injected a much-needed shot of bilingual performative experimentalism into the NEW YORK SCHOOL. One of the original SLAM POETRY performers at the NUYORICAN POETS CAFÉ, Torres's interests range from the work of the Russian futurists (including Velemir Khlebnikov), Kurt Schwitters, the Fluxus artists JOHN CAGE, Gertrude Stein, and JACKSON MAC LOW to the ABSTRACT EXPRESSIONIST artists JACKSON POLLOCK and WILLEM DE KOONING. In the 1990s he moved to other media that allowed him to more fully explore the experimental possibilities of poetry both on and off the page. Torres's poetic performances—incorporating typography, visual art, DANCE, MUSIC, THEATER, and multiple languages—have taken place at Dixon Place, The Kitchen, the Museum of Modern Art, the Guggenheim Museum, and the Whitney Museum of American Art, among other venues. As a board member of the POETRY PROJECT AT ST. MARK'S CHURCH IN-THE-BOWERY, he continues to push the boundaries of what (and who) constitutes the New York School and to remind it of its innovative roots.

BRENDA COULTAS writes, "The nomad is a constant in Torres's work, an alter ego for this poet who is claimed by a diverse group of avant-garde factions that include: The Nuyorican Poets Cafe, Poetry Project, and the L=A=N=G=U=A=G=E school. Thus he finds himself a nomad, a traveler among poets. There is a reason why Torres is claimed by all poetic camps, and that is because he is an extraordinary poet" (Coultas 19). His books include *The Popedology of an Ambient Language* (Atelos, 2007), *The All-Union Day of the Shock Worker* (Roof, 2001), *Fractured Humorous* (Subpress, 1999), and *SandHomméNomadNo* (self-published, 1997). His CDs of word and sound include *Novo* (OozeBap, 2003), *Please* (Faux Press, 2002), and *Holy Kid* (Kill Rock Stars, 1998).

Born in the Bronx, Torres received his B.A. at the Pratt Institute. He is married to the visual artist Elizabeth Castagna.

Bibliography

Coultas, Brenda. Review of *Fractured Humorous*. *Poetry Project Newsletter* 179 (April–May 2000): 19–20. Available online. URL: http://epc.buffalo.edu/authors/torrese/fractured.html. Accessed December 19, 2008.

Torres, Edwin. "Holy Kid" (1999). About.com:Poetry. Available online. URL: http://poetry.about.com/library/weekly/aa042799.htm. Accessed December 19, 2008.

———. "The Limit Is Limitless: On Performance Poetry in the Digital Age." About.com:Poetry. Available online. URL: http://poetry.about.com/cs/reviewsessays/a/perfpoetorres.htm. Accessed December 19, 2008.

Towle, Tony (1939–)

For Tony Towle (rhymes with "soul"), the NEW YORK SCHOOL has been more of a school in the formal sense than it has for most poets. Having been attracted to the New York poets initially as the most intriguing in DONALD M. ALLEN's *The NEW AMERICAN POETRY, 1945–1960* and then having heard KENNETH KOCH and FRANK O'HARA read at the New School in late spring 1962, Towle enrolled in their New School workshops in the spring semester of 1963. That summer he took another workshop with Koch at the NEW YORK CITY WRITERS CONFERENCE at Wagner College and emerged with a share of the Gotham Book Mart Avant-Garde Poetry Prize. In his poem "Addenda" (1971), Towle enumerates what he learned from O'Hara and Koch, as well as JOHN ASHBERY and JAMES SCHUYLER, but he also makes it clear that poetry for him is much more than knowledge of a craft. "From January 1963," he writes, "I knew it would have to be poetry or nothing" (*History* 93). "Nothing" is frequently glimpsed just over the edge of a poem by Towle, where "dark ironies," as the poet himself describes them (interview n.p.), seem designed to nudge the reader just up to the edge. Against the threat of falling, poetry flies "Up, gracing the void with intellect" ("The Morgan Library" [1970], *History* 89).

In his early work Towle frequently collages "found" texts, a technique encouraged by Ashbery's recent work in *The Tennis Court Oath* (1962) and inspired by comic books and romance magazines that JOE BRAINARD scavenged on the streets along with objects for his own art. Brainard and Towle briefly shared an apartment that Towle had taken over from O'Hara. For Towle, his collage work culminates in "Lines for the New Year" (1964–65), which has been a favorite with other second-generation poets such as LARRY FAGIN, who published it in 1975 as the title poem of an Adventures in Poetry pamphlet, and RON PADGETT, who introduces the section of early poems in Towle's collection *The History of the Invitation* (2001). Towle eventually grew dissatisfied with "pop collage," as he calls it, sensing that he was "sidestepping myself, avoiding the deeper water" (interview n.p.). O'Hara's death in 1966 plunged Towle into that deeper water, leading to "Sunrise: Ode to Frank O'Hara," which Towle describes as "a formal but personal elegy, more personal than I was used to being, and it seemed to usher in an easier, more fluent tone in the poems that came after it" (interview n.p.). This new tone characterizes the volumes *After Dinner We Take a Drive into the Night* (Tibor de Nagy Editions, 1968) and *North* (Columbia University Press, 1970), which was published as that year's recipient of the Frank O'Hara Award. At the same time Towle's place in the history of the movement was further secured by his inclusion in both JOHN BERNARD MYERS's *The POETS OF THE NEW YORK SCHOOL* (1969) and Padgett and DAVID SHAPIRO's *ANTHOLOGY OF NEW YORK POETS* (1970).

In Towle's later work the elegiac mood persists, held in check by a satirical wit that he frequently aims at himself. If collage is less deliberately part of the procedure for producing poems, it remains a quality of their texture. "Their cohesive look," CHARLES NORTH has observed, "masks a pervasive and frequently enigmatic disjunction featuring surreal and cinematic jumps, dramatic shifts in voice, narrative that doesn't add up, strings of participial phrases that don't clearly refer, false parallels, and the like" (Towle, *History* 49). Nevertheless, cohesion is achieved through "the power of the narrative flow," as noted by MICHAEL LALLY in a review of *AUTOBIOGRAPHY* (SUN/Coach House South, 1977) and brilliantly exemplified in that volume's long title poem. Longer works again supply title and anchor for subsequent collections: *Works on Paper* (SWOLLEN MAGPIE, 1978), *Some Musical Episodes* (Hanging Loose, 1992), and *Winter Journey* (Hanging Loose, 2008), although in the last case the title poem is not the longest in the book.

MUSIC, primarily modernist classical, has provided crucial inspiration to Towle as well as his particular entrée into the New York School sensibility. The more expected influence of the visual arts is also abundantly evident, however. References to artists in Towle's poems range from Rembrandt to ROBERT RAUSCHENBERG, and the roster of artists who have provided covers for Towle's volumes is impressive: JASPER JOHNS, Allan D'Arcangelo, Robert Motherwell, LARRY RIVERS, Jean Holabird, and James Rosenquist. From 1964 to 1981 Towle worked as secretary to Tatyana Grosman at Universal Limited Art Editions (ULAE) on Long Island, which engaged many of the leading artists of the time in printmaking projects. Towle's COL-LABORATION with Lee Bontecou, *Fifth Stone, Sixth Stone,* was published by ULAE in 1968.

Bibliography

Ashbery, John. "Introduction to a Reading by Tony Towle" (2001). In *Selected Prose.* Edited by Eugene Richie. Ann Arbor: University of Michigan Press, 2004, 285–286.

Bolton, Ken. Review of *The History of the Invitation. Jacket* 16 (March 2002). Available online. URL: http://www.jacketmagazine.com/16/ov-bolt-r-towl. html. Accessed December 19, 2008.

Lally, Michael. "Economou and Company." *Washington Post Book World,* 1 January 1978, p. E7.

Lehman, David. "The Whole School." *Poetry* 119, no. 4 (January 1972): 224–233.

Tony Towle Web site. Available online. URL: http://www.tonytowle.com/index.html.

Towle, Tony. *The History of the Invitation: New & Selected Poems, 1963–2000.* Brooklyn, N.Y.: Hanging Loose Press, 2001.

———. Interview. *Pataphysics* 9 (2003). Formerly available online. URL: http://www.pataphysicsmagazine.com/towle_interview.html.

———. *Memoir, 1960–1963.* Cambridge, Mass.: Faux Press, 2001.

———. "Two Conversations with Lee Bontecou." *Print Collector's Newsletter* 2, no. 2 (May–June 1971): 25–27.

translation

A voracious appetite for adventurous foreign poetry, a passion for all things French, and a corollary fascination with the art of translation played a major role in the development of NEW YORK SCHOOL poetry. Although countless 20th-century poets have tried their hand at translating and have drunk deep from the well of European poetry, few movements have found as much inspiration in reading and in undertaking poetic translations as the New York School. Like many writers of the post–World War II period, the young New York School poets turned to the literatures of other languages in their search for an alternative to the conservative, decorous, highly formal model of writing poems that had come to dominate AMERICAN POETRY at mid-century, thanks to the long shadow of T. S. Eliot and the New Criticism. Poets such as KENNETH KOCH, FRANK O'HARA, and JOHN ASHBERY discovered an exhilarating source of inspiration in the writings of the European avant-garde—particularly in modern FRENCH POETRY and in the RUSSIAN POETRY of Boris Pasternak and Vladimir Mayakovsky. From the first, the poets found the example of French avant-garde writing, in particular, tremendously liberating and even set out to learn French in order to be able to read it in the original. Koch and Ashbery both lived in France (the latter for nearly a decade) and studied French literature, and all were deeply influenced by their absorption of the French tradition, from Arthur Rimbaud to Marcel Proust, from RAYMOND ROUSSEL to Guillaume Apollinaire and the surrealists. Their desire to find fuel for their own work and to spread the word about their exciting discovery of these non-English writers often led the poets to translate the foreign writers most important to them.

The two most significant aspects of the New York School's interest in translation are the poets' influential notion of translation as a kind of invigorating language game—a mischievous approach to translating that highlights its slippery, creative aspects and revels in cross-language play—and the often remarkable and important translations the poets produced and what they tell us about New York School aesthetics and influences.

If, as Robert Frost famously observed, "poetry is what gets lost in translation" (Untermeyer 18), the New York School poets find the mystery and beauty of that very loss endlessly inspiring. For them, the slippages of meaning between one language and the other, the tantalizing gap between a phrase and its corresponding version in another tongue, are more fascinating and funny than frustrating. This is why the poets are drawn to such unusual practices as intentional mistranslation, "homophonic" versions of foreign works (based on conveying the sound of the original, rather than sense), exercises in self-translation, and so on. One finds examples of such experiments in every corner of the New York School. For example, there is O'Hara's strange "found language" poem entitled "Choses Passagères," which he wrote in French by lifting a series of nearly untranslatable idiomatic phrases from a French-English dictionary and stitching them together (Epstein). Or, there is O'Hara's "Aus Einem April," a very "loose" version of a Rainer Maria Rilke poem: It actually renders the sounds of the German poem homophonically so that Rilke's "Wieder duftet der Wald," which means "Again the forest is fragrant," becomes "We dust the walls" in O'Hara's poem (Lehman, "Questions" n.p.; O'Hara, *Collected Poems* 186). Or, there is Ashbery's "French Poems," an experiment with self-translation where he decided to compose a series of poems in French and then translate them himself into English "with the idea of avoiding the customary word-patterns and associations" of his native tongue (Ashbery 95). Or, there is Ashbery's habit of asking his creative writing students to "translate a poem from an unfamiliar language to stimulate the students to do something different from what they have written before" (Kostelanetz 89). As DAVID LEHMAN has noted, for these poets "the deliberate mis-translation became a self-assigned exercise" and, more broadly, "poetry was, or could be, a species of mis-translation" (*Last Avant-Garde* 221–222).

Not only did New York School poets find creative *frisson* in the game of translation for their own poetry, but they also became accomplished translators themselves. For example, Ashbery is considered one of the best translators of Pierre Reverdy and Max Jacob and has published versions of works by Charles Baudelaire, Roussel, Giorgio de Chirico, Arthur Cravan, Pierre Martory, and others. Koch published translations of Dante, Rimbaud, Apollinaire, Ovid, and so on. O'Hara's translations of Friedrich Hölderlin, Stéphane Mallarmé, Rimbaud, René Char, and Rilke appeared in a special translation issue of *The WORLD* (number 27, 1973), edited by RON PADGETT, the first of several such issues that have appeared throughout that magazine's run. ANNE WALDMAN's anthology *Out of This World* (Crown, 1991) represents the continuing tradition in three sections of "Translation."

Later generations of New York School poets have been equally, if not more, devoted to the art of translation, whether in TED BERRIGAN's appropriations of Rimbaud and Henri Michaux in *The SONNETS* or in Padgett's highly regarded, career-long efforts at translating French poets. With his much-lauded edition of Blaise Cendrars's *Complete Poems* (University of California Press, 1992), Padgett became known as one of the premier American translators of French poetry. In 1964 both Padgett and Berrigan also produced homophonic translations of Reverdy, the former in "Some Bombs," collected in *Great Balls of Fire* (1969); the latter in "The Secret Life of Ford Madox Ford," finally collected in *The Collected Poems of Ted Berrigan* (University of California Press, 2005). DAVID SHAPIRO has practiced homophonic translation and related modes of transforming texts with less explicit acknowledgment of the original source, in the light of a theoretical understanding that questions the originality—or the secondariness—of any text. The title poem of Shapiro's volume *After a Lost Original* (Overlook, 1994) considers what happens "When the translation and the original meet," and suggests "The original feels lost like a triple pun / And the translation cries, without me you are lost" (Shapiro, *New and Selected* 186). In *Cadenza* (Hanging Loose, 2007), CHARLES NORTH offers a series of "Translations" of his own previously published poems, a process of transformation more attentive to language itself than the standard, content-focused process of "revision."

If nothing else, the long list of writers whom New York School poets have chosen to translate offers an illuminating map of the guiding influences that helped shape their aesthetics. At the same time the practice of translation serves as an important arena for the poets' profound self-consciousness about the nature of language itself. As such, translation should be considered a crucial feature of the distinctive, influential poetics developed by the poets of the New York School.

Bibliography

Ashbery, John. *The Double Dream of Spring.* New York: Dutton, 1970.

Epstein, Andrew. "Frank O'Hara's Translation Game." *Raritan* 19, no. 3 (2000): 144–161.

Kostelanetz, Richard. "John Ashbery" (1976). In *The Old Poetries and the New.* Ann Arbor: University of Michigan Press, 1981, 87–110.

Lehman, David. *The Last Avant-Garde: The Making of the New York School of Poets.* New York: Doubleday, 1998.

———. "The Questions of Postmodernism." *Jacket* 4 (1998). Available online. URL: http://www.jacket-magazine.com/04/lehman-postmod.html. Accessed December 18, 2008.

Lundquist, Sara. "Légèreté et Richesse: John Ashbery's English 'French Poems.'" *Contemporary Literature* 32, no. 3 (Fall 1991): 403–421.

O'Hara, Frank. *The Collected Poems of Frank O'Hara.* Rev. ed. Edited by Donald Allen. Berkeley: University of California Press, 1995.

Padgett, Ron. "Foreign Language." In *The Straight Line: Writings on Poetry and Poets.* Ann Arbor: University of Michigan Press, 2000, 25–32.

Shapiro, David. *New and Selected Poems (1965–2006).* Woodstock, N.Y.: Overlook Press, 2007.

Untermeyer, Louis. *Robert Frost: A Backward Look.* Washington, D.C.: Library of Congress, 1964.

Trinidad, David (1953–)

Born in Los Angeles to a Portuguese father and German–French Canadian mother, David Trinidad became an active California poet, studying with Ann Stanford and participating at the BEYOND BAROQUE Literary/Arts Center in Venice. Not until 1988 did Trinidad move to NEW YORK CITY to study for his M.F.A. in creative writing at Brooklyn College. There he worked with ALLEN GINSBERG and befriended NEW YORK SCHOOL poets JOE BRAINARD, ALICE NOTLEY, EILEEN MYLES, and JAMES SCHUYLER. Trinidad's work is equal parts autobiographical confession and camp postmodern narration, and his poems are known for their laconic exploration of love and human frailty as well as their digestion and reconstitution of many strains of American pop culture. The Supremes, *The Patty Duke Show, The Munsters,* Elvis Presley, *Gilligan's Island,* Barbie, and many other films, television shows, radio hits, and personalities make their appearance in his work. Trinidad came of age during the height of the gay liberation movement and the fact that so many New York School poets were gay and wrote openly about their sexuality was deeply inspirational to him.

Trinidad is the author of more than 10 books of poetry, ranging from *Pavane* (Sherwood, 1981) to *The Late Show* (Turtle Point, 2007). *Plasticville* (Turtle Point, 2000) shows Trinidad at the height of his powers, experimenting in many FORMS, including villanelles, prose poems, sonnets, couplets, and terza rima, while delving into varied themes, some deadly serious like the onset of the AIDS epidemic and the death of friends and others comic and deadpan, skimming the collective unconsciousness of consumer culture and discussing a childhood doll collection. Trinidad manages to conflate high and low culture so thoroughly that Lord Byron and Matthew Arnold find themselves sharing space with Marilyn Monroe and Nick at Nite, and many of the poems in the collection are assemblages that utilize found materials that surprisingly cohere into poems of emotional depth and intellectual complexity. In a blurb on the back cover of *Plasticville,* Notley wrote of Trinidad's work that it is "intensely pleasurable, it appeals to one's ever-present childhood, though its mysterious emotional content is not just childlike and not just happy. . . . there is an unwavering light in all of Trinidad's work that turns individual words into objects, new facts."

Collaboration holds a special interest for Trinidad. A *Taste of Honey* (Cold Calm Press, 1990), written with Bob Flanagan (1952–1996), was followed by two volumes composed in collaboration with Jeffery Conway (1964–) and Lynn Crosbie (1963–): *Phoebe 2002: An Essay in Verse* (Turtle Point, 2003) and *Chain Chain Chain* (Ignition, 2000). A similar interest has inspired Trinidad's work as an editor, which includes *Saints of Hysteria: A Half-Century of Collaborative American Poetry* (with Denise Duhamel and Maureen Seaton, Soft Skull Press, 2007), *Holding Our Own: The Selected Poems of Ann Stanford* (with Maxine Scates, Copper Canyon Press, 2001), *Hello Joe: A Tribute to Joe Brainard* (with WILLIAM CORBETT and ELAINE EQUI, PRESSED WAFER, 2001), and *Powerless: Selected Poems, 1973–1990* by TIM DLUGOS (High Risk Books/Serpent's Tail, 1996).

In an interview in 1999 Trinidad was asked about his proclivity, like FRANK O'HARA, whom he lists as an early influence, to use his friends' names in his poems. Trinidad responded: "[A]t a certain point I decided I wanted to include people's names in my poems—rather than a bunch of mysterious 'you's.' It makes the whole endeavor more personal, I think. I like that intimacy, and the sound of the names affects the music in the poem" (Marranca and Koros 329). Elsewhere in the same interview, when asked about his use of popular culture in his poems, Trinidad said: "I grew up in a suburb of Los Angeles and was exposed, during the sixties, to a tremendous amount of popular culture. A bombardment, really. Comic books, games, songs, television shows, movies. I was deeply affected by these things. . . . It makes sense that I'd try to capture, in my work, how important that stuff was (and still is) to me. It all has a permanent place in my imagination and memory" (Marranca and Koros 326).

Bibliography

Marranca, Richard, and Vasiliki Koros. "Pop Culture and Poetry: An Interview with David Trinidad." *Literary Review: An International Journal of Contemporary Writing* (Winter 1999): 323–332.

True Bride, The Amy Gerstler (1986)

During the eight years between her graduation from college and the publication of her first major collection, *The True Bride* (Lapis Press, 1986), AMY GERSTLER eagerly read "'New York School' writers, and St. Mark's *Newsletter,* and numerous East Coast small-press magazines and anthologies," to which DENNIS COOPER had introduced her (Gerstler, "Contributor's Note" 642). *The True Bride* reflects that influence in the polish of its shimmering surfaces and in its focus on "the chaotic inner-contemporary life" (Gerstler, interview n.p.). Pursuing the "direction" of the New York School while making her own discoveries (Gerstler, "Contributor's Note" 642), Gerstler produces poems that are pleasurable, witty, racy, parodic, and flippant, in conversation with popular culture as well as high art traditions, and capable of generating profound social and psychological insights within their hip style.

In his introduction to *The True Bride,* poet TOM CLARK explained that Gerstler's "most salient gift is her awesome capacity for surrendering authorial identification with the voicing of the work" (n.p.). Sven Birkerts similarly identified the poet's strength as being "the creation of a persona," combined with her humor and "sudden switches of idiom" (177–178). Amy Robbins, meanwhile, emphasized the volume's darker themes: a "preoccupation with death and the afterlife" and "women's sexual and life experience" (140). Rise and Steven Axelrod contrasted the poems' "lively, witty" style with an often "morose" subject matter, arguing that the poems "interfere with an Enlightenment logic of linear narrativity, opening new spaces of collaborativity, bafflement, and ironized knowledge" (88–89).

The volume's title prose-poem manifests many of these characteristics. The sinister, probably mad male speaker, who believes that women should be "pruned in early girlhood," sings the praises of disabled, anorexic Elaine, thus calling into question women's bodies in patriarchy. At the same time, the poem considers the possible autonomy of representation, since the bride's "dear flat realities" are all verbal or pictographic, and since she may not exist at all apart from the speaker's discourse. "The True Bride" ends with a voyeuristic fantasy of disabled brides hobbling across the map of a desert—the speaker's "ideal pornography," implying his (and our) investment in unreal, humiliated fetish objects.

Other poems mourn the predicament of women: "To remain in place is a woman's ailment" (13); "why kiss such a clod?" (56). Others meditate pop transcendence: "Television commercials for Jello, the jewel-colored / food of childhood" (31). Yet others tell disturbingly inchoate stories: "He knew nothing of her checkered past . . . was unaware that, like Poland, she'd been 'taken over' many times. You can assemble a narrative out of the stains on the ceiling" (58).

Just as the NEW YORK SCHOOL reflects the vigor and insouciance of mid-century Manhattan, so *The True Bride* evokes the weirdness and smarts of the Western metropolis toward century's end.

Bibliography

Axelrod, Rise B., and Steven Gould Axelrod. "Amy Gerstler's Rhetoric of Marriage." *Twentieth Century Literature* 50, no. 1 (Spring 2004): 88–105.
Birkerts, Sven. "Prose." *Parnassus* 15 (1989): 163–184.

Clark, Tom. Introduction to *The True Bride,* by Amy Gerstler, n.p. Santa Monica, Calif.: Lapis Press,1986.

Gerstler, Amy. "Contributor's Note." In *Out of this World: An Anthology of the St. Mark's Poetry Project, 1966–1991,* edited by Anne Waldman, 642. New York: Crown, 1991.

———. Interview. *Ignition* 1. Available online. URL: www.ignitionmag.net/issue1/agi.html. Accessed March 9, 2003.

———. *The True Bride.* Santa Monica, Calif.: Lapis Press, 1986.

———. "What Is American about American Poetry?" Poetry Society of America Web site. Available online. URL: http://www.poetrysociety.org/gerstler.html. Accessed March 11, 2003.

Robbins, Amy Moorman. "Amy Gerstler." In *Contemporary American Women Poets: An A-to-Z Guide,* edited by Catherine Cucinella, 138–141. Westport, Conn.: Greenwood Press, 2002.

Try! Try! Frank O'Hara (1951, 1953)

In two distinct versions FRANK O'HARA's one-act verse play *Try! Try!* featured in inaugural productions: at the POETS' THEATRE in Cambridge, Massachusetts (1951), and the ARTISTS' THEATRE IN NEW YORK CITY (1953). The original version is modeled on Japanese Noh THEATER, a highly stylized mode that W. B. Yeats adapted for Western verse drama at the start of the 20th century. However, in deriving his plot and characters from the contemporary situation rather than some mythical heroic age, O'Hara follows T. S. Eliot's example in such plays as *The Cocktail Party* (1950).

The plot of *Try! Try!* involves a husband returning to his wife "after any war," according to the original stage directions (O'Hara 18)—after the Korean War, according to Herbert Machiz, the director of the New York production (Machiz 9). In the original production the wife was played by VIOLET R. ("BUNNY") LANG, who also directed, and the husband by her friend Jack Rogers. The names of the characters, Violet and Jack, derive from these actors, as is also the case with the one additional character, John, originally played by JOHN ASHBERY. This third role underwent the most change between the two versions of the play. In the original version John stands apart from the action

and serves the function of a chorus, or of the musicians in Noh theater. In addition to his speeches he supplies musical commentary by playing records on "an old-fashioned gramophone" throughout the course of the action (O'Hara 17). In the later version he enters the action as the third party in a love triangle, having moved in with Violet while her husband was away. Accordingly, O'Hara completely rewrote John's speeches for the later version, while he retained speeches for both Violet and Jack that mark them as romantic idealists. John's realism, only hinted at in the poetic structure of the original version, becomes part of the dramatic structure in the later version:

> *I suppose I'm the snake-in-the grass but*
> *I can't say I'm sorry. Someone has to smile*
> *at her as she comes back from the bathroom*
>   (O'Hara 48).

Although both versions cite war as the immediate cause of Violet and Jack's separation, all three of the characters express a sense of alienation that seems more existential than historical. In theatrical terms they have been cast in roles with which they do not identify. Violet, in the first version, does not identify with her own name, and her distance from Jack suggests a distance from the role that a wife was expected to play. On the set of the first version, designed by O'Hara's former Harvard roommate Edward Gorey (1925–2000), the principal prop is an ironing board, and the version concludes with John's warning that "the kitchen's full of knives" (O'Hara 28 and "Appendix"). John also states that "your heroes are all dead" (O'Hara 28), an allusion to Jack's alienation from his role as a war hero. John's ability to find "lyricism" in this situation (O'Hara 22) points to the poetic core of O'Hara's play and predicts the direction that Ashbery's own poetry was to take. In fact, some lines spoken by John in the first version, about the suspension of time "when the subway stops / just before reaching a station" (O'Hara 22), echo a paradigmatic speech in Ashbery's play *The* HEROES (1950), in which Theseus describes watching a couple in the next train when "my train had stopped in the station directly opposite another" (Ashbery 10). Theseus's sense that he can understand what the couple are saying even though he cannot hear them is very much like the relation of John, and the audience, to Violet and Jack in O'Hara's play. In LARRY RIVERS's set for the New York production, a painted backdrop mirrored the alienation of the audience in the guise of "large-eyed figures placed in a city scape that suggested Istanbul," as JOHN BERNARD MYERS described it (Myers 35; O'Hara "Appendix").

Since the first performance of *Try! Try!*, when Thornton Wilder scolded the audience for laughing (Gooch 181), critics have erred either in taking the play too seriously or dismissing it as "merely silly" (Perloff 169). In the most balanced assessment, Charles Altieri suggests that the play "provides the most ready access to many characteristics of [O'Hara's] fictive world," starting with the premise that "man needs the artifice of witty and elaborate speech because without it he would have only the pressure of an absurd and oppressive reality" (189–190). Actors and poets have valued *Try! Try!* as an occasion for performance rather than philosophy. In a second New York production in 1968, director Ann MacIntosh exploited "the play's soap opera–like situation and made the proceedings almost light-hearted," Joe LeSueur recalled (xviii). In 1979 poets associated with the new Language movement (Bob Perelman, Steve Benson, Carla Harryman, and Nick Robinson) presented *Try! Try!* at the Grand Piano coffeehouse in San Francisco. Appropriately, in view of the play's origins, that performance led to the establishment of a new poets theater (Vickery 7, 119).

Bibliography

Altieri, Charles. "From 'Varieties of Immanentist Expression'" (1979). In *Frank O'Hara: To Be True to a City*, edited by Jim Elledge, 189–208. Ann Arbor: University of Michigan Press, 1990.

Ashbery, John. *The Heroes*. In *Three Plays*. Calais, Vt.: Z Press, 1978, 1–29.

Gooch, Brad. *City Poet: The Life and Times of Frank O'Hara*. New York: Knopf, 1993.

LeSueur, Joe. Introduction to *Amorous Nightmares of Delay: Selected Plays*, by Frank O'Hara. Baltimore, Md.: Johns Hopkins University Press, 1997, xv–xxv.

Machiz, Herbert. Introduction to *Artists' Theatre: Four Plays*. New York: Grove, 1960, 7–13.

Myers, John Bernard. "Frank O'Hara: A Memoir" (1977). In *Homage to Frank O'Hara*, edited by Bill Berkson and Joe LeSueur, 34–38. Bolinas, Calif.: Big Sky, 1988.

O'Hara, Frank. *Try! Try!* [2 versions] and "Appendix: Documents." In *Amorous Nightmares of Delay: Selected Plays*. Baltimore, Md.: Johns Hopkins University Press, 1997, 17–49, 218–225.

Perloff, Marjorie. *Frank O'Hara: Poet Among Painters*. 1977. Reprint, Chicago: University of Chicago Press, 1998.

Vickery, Ann. *Leaving Lines of Gender: A Feminist Genealogy of Language Writing*. Hanover, N.H.: Wesleyan University Press/University Press of New England, 2000.

Tulsa School

The notion of a "Tulsa School" of poets within or in tandem with the NEW YORK SCHOOL has been one of the in-jokes that defines the group (or groups). TED BERRIGAN, RON PADGETT, JOE BRAINARD, and DICK GALLUP all moved to NEW YORK CITY from Tulsa, Oklahoma, in the early 1960s. Berrigan was an easterner by birth, but after military service in Korea he was sent to Tulsa as an adviser for the army reserve and eventually enrolled in the University of Tulsa to study for a master's degree in English literature. He got to know Padgett, Brainard, and Gallup through their magazine, the WHITE DOVE REVIEW. Once in New York they shared living arrangements in various configurations and collaborated in such ventures as "C" magazine, so it was natural that others would identify them as a cohesive group. To call them the "*soi-disant* [self-proclaimed] Tulsa School," as JOHN ASHBERY did (Padgett and Shapiro xxx), was to poke fun at the provinciality of Tulsa, from the perspective of New York, and to turn the tables on Berrigan, who jokingly authorized himself to enroll people in the New York School for a five-dollar fee (Berrigan 91). TOM VEITCH kept the tables spinning by enrolling himself in the Tulsa School. In his contributor's note for Richard Kostelanetz's *New American Writers*, Veitch listed Tulsa as his place of birth, though in fact he was born in Vermont (336).

Since the Tulsa School never actually existed, it has no defining characteristics. Nevertheless,

Padgett cites his western background as a basis for distinguishing his work from that of other New York School poets: "The work of the others was more sophisticated, urbane, and witty. But my work was quick and light, with a lot of the cowboy-hillbilly that was natural to my feeling, that I didn't find in theirs" (Padgett 107). Although Padgett's involvement with FRENCH POETRY might seem, by contrast, ultra-sophisticated, he points out that the poets whose work has engaged him the most—Guillaume Apollinaire, Pierre Reverdy, Blaise Cendrars, and Max Jacob—each approached the Parisian avant-garde from a foreign or provincial background. "Maybe," Padgett speculates, "I felt a little sympathy for them because I was a little displaced" (106).

Bibliography

Berrigan, Ted. "Interview with CITY" (1977). In *Talking in Tranquility: Interviews.* Edited by Stephen Ratcliffe and Leslie Scalapino. Bolinas, Calif.: Avenue B; Oakland, Calif.: O Books, 1991, 90–105.

Padgett, Ron. Interview by Edward Foster (1991). In *Poetry and Poetics in a New Millennium,* edited by Edward Foster, 100–114. Jersey City, N.J.: Talisman House, 2000.

Padgett, Ron, and David Shapiro. Preface to *An Anthology of New York Poets.* New York: Vintage-Random House, 1970, xxix–xxxvii.

Veitch, Tom. Contributor's note in *The New American Writers,* edited by Richard Kostelanetz, 336. New York: Funk & Wagnalls, 1967.

U

Umbra (1962–1964)

Contemporary to the second-generation NEW YORK SCHOOL and precursor to the BLACK ARTS MOVEMENT, Umbra was a workshop consisting mostly of young black men who shared and critiqued one another's poetry, gave readings at Lower East Side venues like LES DEUX MÉGOTS and CAFÉ LE MÉTRO, and published the journal *Umbra*. The title, evoking the many connotations connecting race and color, derives from the poem "Umbra" by Lloyd Addison (1931–). TOM DENT edited the first issue of *Umbra* in 1963, with CALVIN HERNTON and DAVID HENDERSON as associate editors. An editorial statement announced: "*Umbra* has a defined orientation: 1) the experience of being Negro, especially in America; and 2) that quality of human awareness often termed 'social consciousness'" (Clay and Phillips 154). Umbra poets grappled with aesthetics, philosophy, and activism in a climate of increasing social tension and cultural anxiety over race. Although most Umbra poems were political, members disagreed about political direction, a factor in the group's dissolution by 1964. Henderson produced the fifth and final issue of *Umbra* magazine in California in 1974.

Early Umbra members Dent, Henderson, Hernton, Addison, Art Berger (who was white), Joe Johnson, Raymond Patterson, Oliver Pitcher, and Rolland Snellings (Askia Mohammed Touré) met regularly at Dent's apartment on East 2nd Street, and before long two dozen or so poets had joined, including Steve Cannon, Ray Durem, Albert Haynes, Charles and William Patterson, Norman Pritchard, LORENZO THOMAS, James Thompson, Lenox Raphael, and ISHMAEL REED. Though in fewer numbers, there were women members, such as Jane Logan, Mildred Hernton, Maryanne Raphael, Ann Guilfoyle, and Brenda Walcott. JAZZ musicians Archie Shepp and Cecil Taylor and painters Tom Feelings and Joe Overstreet were also associated with the group. Although never formally a member of Umbra, LeRoi Jones (AMIRI BARAKA) became an important bridge figure to both the New York School poets and the BEATS, and, later, to the Black Arts Movement.

Umbra's stylistic and formal concerns resembled those of the New York School poets: a focus on ordinary speech, an assertive MUSIC and layered rhythms, experimental structure and page layout, and lively public readings. Members shared a desire for innovation and experimentation, working in the idiom of "black speech" rooted in African-American identity, and in such musical traditions as jazz, rhythm and blues, and gospel call and response. As in the case of the New York School, Umbra poetry sometimes foregrounds and mythologizes other group members, as well as NEW YORK CITY itself. Many set their work in Harlem, and several, including Baraka, moved there from the Lower East Side around 1965, giving rise to the Black Arts Movement.

Umbra's rich variety of poetic voices marks it as a dynamic but little-known poetic movement of the 1960s. As Reed has commented, the contribution of black artists of the Lower East Side seems "excised," and "the story of black bohemia has not been told" (277).

Bibliography

Addison, Lloyd. "Umbra." In *Every Goodbye Ain't Gone: An Anthology of Innovative Poetry by African Americans,* edited by Aldon Lynn Nielsen and Lauri Ramey, 6–9. Tuscaloosa: University of Alabama Press, 2006.

Clay, Steven, and Rodney Phillips. *A Secret Location on the Lower East Side: Adventures in Writing, 1960–1980.* New York: New York Public Library/Granary Books, 1998.

Dent, Tom. "Umbra Days." *Black American Literature Forum* 14, no. 3 (1980): 105–108.

Kane, Daniel. *All Poets Welcome: The Lower East Side Poetry Scene in the 1960s.* Berkeley: University of California Press, 2003.

Nielsen, Aldon Lynn. "A New York State of Mind." In *Black Chant: Languages of African-American Postmodernism.* Cambridge: Cambridge University Press, 1997, 78–169.

Oren, Michael. "The Umbra Poets Workshop, 1962–1965: Some Socio-Literary Puzzles." In *Belief vs. Theory in Black American Literary Criticism,* edited by Joe Weixlman and Chester J. Fontenot. 177–223. Greenwood, Fla.: Penkevill Publishing, 1986.

Panish, John. "'As Radical as Society Demands the Truth to Be': Umbra's Racial Politics and Poetics." In *Don't Ever Get Famous: Essays on New York Writing after the New York School,* edited by Daniel Kane, 50–73. Champaign, Ill.: Dalkey Archive Press, 2006.

Reed, Ishmael. Interview by Shamoon Zamir (1988). In *Conversations with Ishmael Reed,* edited by Bruce Dick and Amritjit Singh, 271–302. Jackson: University Press of Mississippi, 1995.

Thomas, Lorenzo. "Alea's Children: The Avant-Garde on the Lower East Side, 1960–1970." *African American Review* 27, no. 4 (1993): 573–578.

———. "The Shadow World: New York's Umbra Workshop & Origins of the Black Arts Movement." *Callaloo,* no. 4 (October 1978): 53–72.

United Artists (1977–   )

Born in the relative isolation of Lenox, Massachusetts, where coeditors LEWIS WARSH and BERNADETTE MAYER had taken up residence,

United Artists's magazine and books embody Warsh's recognition "that a community of poets could exist through the actual writing and publishing of the work, and that the social scene . . . was secondary to this other activity" (interview Foster 151). On the other hand, given its relatively late emergence in the development of the NEW YORK SCHOOL, United Artists inevitably registered not only continuity but also fractures within the community. It has been called "a bridge between the generations" (Clay and Phillips 41), helping introduce younger writers such as GARY LENHART, Steve Carey, and TOM SAVAGE to the company of established second-generation writers such as BILL BERKSON and TED BERRIGAN. But a misunderstanding over the publication of a new edition of Berrigan's SONNETS (1982) caused a rift between Berrigan and Warsh that led TOM CLARK, from the distance of California, to lament the displacement of formerly youthful exuberance by "pain and suffering" (Clark 55; Warsh, "Publishing Ted" 17–20).

A more general rift between the New York School and the emerging LANGUAGE poets extended to United Artists because Mayer and CLARK COOLIDGE, a neighbor in the BERKSHIRES, were perceived by some of the Language writers as backsliding during the period of their involvement with the magazine. Although both had pioneered experimental techniques, "in the course of Mayer's later editing of United Artists, the stylistic opening-up returns all these techniques to the self," according to Barrett Watten, who would prefer to see writing move away from the self that dominated traditional lyric poetry (Watten 57). A more generous assessment is offered by Steven Clay and Rodney Phillips, who call United Artists "adventuresome in its combination of the personal and the experimental, pioneering in the publication of journal and diary entries" (41). The elegantly plain design moved Clay and Phillips also to call United Artists "the apotheosis of the mimeograph magazine" (41). Warsh, more humbly, calls it "probably the last of the great mimeo magazines" (statement 199), going on to explain that booksellers' requirements and computerized desktop publishing promoted a glossier look in a new wave of magazines in the mid-1980s. United

Artists ceased publication as a magazine in 1983, after 18 issues. The book series, begun in 1979, has been continued by Warsh to the present day. The 33rd title in the series, *Across the Big Map* by Ruth Altmann (2004), was praised by Language poet Ron Silliman as proof that "the New York School was still evolving" (n.p.), continuing to experiment even with received FORMs.

Bibliography

Clark, Tom. *Late Returns: A Memoir of Ted Berrigan.* Bolinas, Calif.: Tombouctou, 1985.

Clay, Steven, and Rodney Phillips. *A Secret Location on the Lower East Side: Adventures in Writing, 1960–1980.* New York: New York Public Library/Granary Books, 1998.

Silliman, Ron. "Tuesday, November 30, 2004." Silliman's Blog. Available online. URL: http://ronsilliman.blogspot.com/2004_11_01_ronsilliman_archive.html.

Warsh, Lewis. Interviewed by Edward Foster (1991). In *Poetry and Poetics in a New Millennium,* edited by Edward Foster, 147–159. Jersey City, N.J.: Talisman House, 2000.

———. "Publishing Ted." In *Ted Berrigan: An Annotated Checklist,* by Aaron Fischer, 15–20. New York: Granary Books, 1998.

———. Statement in *A Secret Location on the Lower East Side: Adventures in Writing, 1960–1980,* by Steven Clay and Rodney Phillips, 199. New York: New York Public Library/Granary Books, 1998.

Watten, Barrett. *Total Syntax.* Carbondale: Southern Illinois University Press, 1985.

V

Veitch, Tom (1941–)

One of the more eclectic members of the NEW YORK SCHOOL, Tom Veitch has produced works in multiple GENRES, including poetry, essays, tape experiments, graphic novels, and comic books. Veitch was in the class of 1963 at Columbia University, where he met RON PADGETT and, through him, TED BERRIGAN and JOE BRAINARD. During his first semester Veitch was inexplicably overwhelmed with terrifying experiences of the inevitability of death and the realization that college was a waste of time. His initial response to this existential quandary was to get involved with friends who were experimenting with peyote. Veitch took a leave of absence for a year and traveled to San Francisco where he wrote stories (unpublished) and worked as a desk clerk. Finally, after six months, he decided to return to Columbia and finish his education.

Back at Columbia Veitch continued his experiments with mind-altering substances and found one drug experience to be akin to instant psychoanalysis. At the end of the process, he passed into a state of clear self-awareness that lasted for weeks after the drug wore off—what the Hindus call a *samadhi*. At this point he began work on a novel called *The Transfigured,* of which only one chapter is extant today, and also wrote a short novel called *Whats.* Berrigan and Veitch wrote a collaborative novel called *Malgmo's End,* which became the first "C" Press book, under the title *Literary Days* (1964). Around this time Veitch wrote the core section of *The LUIS ARMED STORY* (of which versions appeared in PETER SCHJELDAHL's magazine *MOTHER* and then in JOHN ASHBERY's magazine *ART AND LITERATURE*). The novel was eventually published in full at Full Court Press (1978) by Padgett, Veitch's collaborator in *ANTLERS IN THE TREETOPS* (Coach House Press, 1973).

Veitch then abandoned New York to enter a contemplative Benedictine monastery in Vermont, where he stayed as a monk from 1965 to 1967. He next moved to San Francisco, where he connected with CLARK COOLIDGE and met his future wife. In San Francisco Veitch wrote *Eat This* (Angel Hair, 1974) and a long COLLABORATION with LEWIS MACADAMS that exists in fragments and on an audio tape that bookseller Julia Newman made. He gave readings at Intersection and started a free-form musical event called "The Poets Orchestra," in which the audience was invited to pick up instruments and play along with the performers. Veitch also started *Tom Veitch Magazine* (which ran four issues, 1970–72) and met Greg Irons, a San Francisco poster artist, who did illustrations and one of the covers for *Tom Veitch Magazine.* Through Irons Veitch contributed to the burgeoning "underground comix" scene. He also set up a printing press that printed Barrett Watten's *This* magazine, among other work. His last collection of poems is *Death College and Other Poems (1964–1974)* (Big Sky, 1976), which reprints a number of earlier small-press volumes. The collection concludes with an afterword by ALLEN GINSBERG, whom Veitch met while teaching at the NAROPA INSTITUTE.

After returning to the East coast, Veitch built on his experience in alternative comics. With Scottish artist Cam Kennedy he created a graphic novel called *The Light and Darkness War* (Marvel/Epic, 1988–89), about a fantastic afterlife realm populated by warriors and soldiers from all earth's wars. This led to contracts with DC Comics and Dark Horse, where Kennedy and Veitch wrote a serial for George Lucas—*Star Wars: Dark Empire* (Dark Horse Comics, 1993, 1995). The underlying theme in the comic books was the mutability of reality and the powers of consciousness. In 1995 Veitch retired from comics and has been writing poetry, essays, and fiction, while living in relative seclusion in Vermont.

Velvet Underground, The (1965–1970)

Recognized today as a precursor of PUNK ROCK bands, The Velvet Underground during its brief existence was as much a scene as a sound. The group made the scene in April 1966 when ANDY WARHOL presented them as part of a multimedia HAPPENING, "The Exploding Plastic Inevitable," at the Dom on St. Mark's Place, also a home of The FUGS. Their last gig with lead singer Lou Reed (1942–) was at Max's Kansas City on Union Square, "the exact place," according to Warhol, "where Pop Art and pop life came together in New York in the sixties, teeny boppers and sculptors, rock stars and poets from St. Mark's Place" (Warhol and Hackett 186). Although The Velvet Underground briefly reunited for a European tour in 1993, for the most part band members have pursued separate careers, with Reed maintaining the closest ties to NEW YORK SCHOOL poetry.

New York School MUSIC fed directly into The Velvets' sound through band member John Cale (1942–), who was playing in an experimental music ensemble formed by LaMonte Young (1935–), an associate of JOHN CAGE, when Cale met Reed in 1964. The Velvets' identification with "electricity and machines," as Reed describes it (Bockris and Malanga 61), was due largely to Cale. His electric viola produced "a drone that sounded like a jet engine" (Bockris and Malanga 13). Reed brought a background in poetry, acquired in part through study with DELMORE SCHWARTZ at

Syracuse University. Like many New York School poets, Reed placed himself in opposition to ROBERT LOWELL ("The People" 53), though for an ally he looked past the first-generation New York School, none of whom showed any more interest in rock music than Schwartz did. "[Arthur] Rimbaud's really where it's at!" Reed declared ("The People" 50), not because the turn-of-the-century French poet could have known about rock, but because he represented the youthful rebellion that Reed wanted rock to stand for. As for later punk musicians, Rimbaud for Reed occupied a place that did not belong to FRANK O'HARA but that James Dean occupied in O'Hara's imagination and to some extent in Reed's ("The People" 53). In "Walk on the Wild Side," Reed's most popular song, from the post-Velvets album *Transformer* (1972), one of the characters "just speeding away / thought she was James Dean for a day."

The recognition that "she had to crash" after speeding lends to the work of Reed and The Velvet Underground an elegiac undertone that second-generation New York School poets picked up on. TED BERRIGAN's "Sunday Morning" (1975), dedicated to Reed, takes its title from a track on The Velvets' first album, *The Velvet Underground and Nico* (1967), produced by Warhol. Reed's song is in a "morning-after" mood, but Berrigan, perhaps with an eye on Wallace Stevens's post-Christian "Sunday Morning," playfully expands the vision to the "epoch after": "In former times people who committed adultery got stoned; / Nowadays its just a crashing bringdown" (354). JIM CARROLL takes Berrigan as his model for the list poem but takes The Velvet Underground as if the band were a drug in "10 Things I Do When I Shoot Up" (1970). Two of the "things" are "put on the Velvet Underground / nod out" (n.p.). Maintaining the connection, one of the poems from Carroll's *The Book of Nods* (Viking, 1986), "Dueling the Monkey," is dedicated to Reed and his wife, Sylvia. Performance as well as poetry forged close ties between Carroll and Reed. In 1984 they read together at St. Mark's Church, and Reed joined The JIM CARROLL BAND in a music video of Reed's song "Sweet Jane," which dates to The Velvet Underground's gig at Max's. With ironic nostalgia, the lyrics recall a time "when all the poets studied rules of verse."

Bibliography

Berrigan, Ted. "Sunday Morning." In *The Collected Poems of Ted Berrigan*. Edited by Alice Notley, Anselm Berrigan, and Edmund Berrigan. Berkeley: University of California Press, 2005, 354–355.

Bockris, Victor, and Gerard Malanga. *Up-Tight: The Velvet Underground Story*. New York: Quill, 1983.

Carroll, Jim. "Sweet Jane." Music video. Catholicboy.com. Available online. URL: http://www.catholicboy.com/ catholicboy.com-asp//video.asp. Accessed December 19, 2008.

———. "10 Things I Do When I Shoot Up." Catholicboy. com. Available online. URL: http://www.catholic boy.com/catholicboy.com-asp//tedb.asp. Accessed December 19, 2008.

Carter, Cassie. "Friends and Influences: Lou Reed and the Velvet Underground." Catholicboy.com. Available online. URL: http://www.catholicboy.com/ catholicboy.com-asp//reed.asp. Accessed December 19, 2008.

Reed, Lou. "The People Must Have to Die for the Music." *Intransit: The Andy Warhol–Gerard Malanga Monster Issue* (1968): 50–53.

———. *Transformer*. Sound recording, 07863 65132 2. 30th anniversary ed. New York: RCA/BMG Heritage, 2002.

Velvet Underground, The. *Peel Slowly and See*. Sound recording, 31452 7887-2. Hollywood, Calif.: Polydor, 1995.

Warhol, Andy, and Pat Hackett. *POPism: The Warhol Sixties*. 1980. Reprint, San Diego, Calif.: Harcourt-Harvest, 1990.

Vermont Notebook, The John Ashbery and Joe Brainard (1975)

Written by JOHN ASHBERY with drawings by JOE BRAINARD, *The Vermont Notebook* (Black Sparrow, 1975) exemplifies the possible interplay between verbal and VISUAL ART. Although created after the book was written, Brainard's drawings are not simply illustrations, which confine a text through specificity; they are additions that develop alternate perspectives or directions. Brainard finds perfect complementary images to reveal further delicate facts and observations throughout.

The simple and often silhouetted FORMs of Brainard's ink drawings give the feeling of a sketch-book dashed off quickly, yet with an immaculate quality, with no line out of place or without purpose. Similarly, Ashbery's writing feels dashed off and pared down. Lists and observations fill the book with the sense of jotted notes—"Call Southern New England Telephone Co." (47)—rather than crafted poetry. *The Vermont Notebook* is a diaristic record of "The climate, the cities, the houses, the streets, the stores, the lights, people" (9).

These lists catalog society and record time and distance. The journey is littered with organizations, companies, crimes, and cities. By the last page of lists, the form takes on a more narrative role; "before, sleep, come, mouth, asshole, behaving, foundered, sleep, reef, perfect, almost" (29). After sifting through the capitalist imagery and lists of cultural icons, Ashbery is able to find a semblance of human experience, but one gets the sense that it was a difficult struggle.

The drawings implicate and involve the reader. As the narrator tells of being on a previously traveled highway, Brainard visually tells of any highway; the drawing of an indiscriminate blank sign invites the reader to write in the highway name and relate personally. The indeterminate imagery makes nearly every location in the book relatable. To "our own president plays it right into the lap of big business and uses every opportunity he can to fuck the consumer and the little guy" (59), Brainard implicates the reader by presenting an anonymous washer and drier head on. Though the image comes as a surprise, the viewer never feels assaulted; he references complex subjects, but does so without force. The washer and drier speak directly to the viewer, but without cold provocation.

Ashbery's writing in *The Vermont Notebook* feels distilled compared to his other works; the lists and simple images become complex only in their juxtapositions. *The Vermont Notebook* was published in the same year as SELF-PORTRAIT IN A CONVEX MIRROR (Viking, 1975), which received the Pulitzer Prize for poetry, the National Book Critics Circle Award, and the National Book Award. By producing such an entirely different book, Ashbery refuses to be pinned to the style that brought him so much critical success.

Working collectively and individually, both Ashbery's poetry and Brainard's drawings form *The*

Vermont Notebook, which would simply be incomplete without either of its dynamic elements. The juxtaposition of drawing and writing are crucial to the full experience of the book, creating otherwise impossible, fantastic, and complete images.

Bibliography

Ashbery, John, and Joe Brainard. 1975. Reprint, *The Vermont Notebook.* New York: Granary Books, 2001.

Violi, Paul (1944–)

Raised on Long Island, New York, educated at Boston University (B.A. in English, 1966), Paul Violi settled in NEW YORK CITY in 1968 after extensive travel, including a year in Nigeria that began as a Peace Corps assignment. Walking the streets of New York sent him back to the stimulating contrasts and the energy of abundance that he had experienced in "the vast African markets" (Hillringhouse n.p.) and eventually led to his long poem about Nigeria, *Harmatan* (SUN, 1977). "Abundance," the title of a later poem (in *Likewise Hanging Loose,* [1988]), was also being drawn from the streets of New York in contemporary art that Violi admired, from ROBERT RAUSCHENBERG's "combines" to Claes Oldenburg's installations. The place to engage in comparable experiments in poetry was the POETRY PROJECT AT ST. MARK'S CHURCH IN-THE-BOWERY, where Violi enrolled in a workshop led by TONY TOWLE in spring 1970, the occasion for his meeting CHARLES NORTH. From 1972 to 1974 Violi worked as managing editor for the *Architectural Forum* and was introduced to formative concepts of postmodernism. Later he helped administer the Poetry Project as interim director (1977) and advisory board member (1978–81). With LITA HORNICK, whose KULCHUR Foundation published Violi's collection *In Baltic Circles* (1973), Violi coordinated a series of poetry readings at the Museum of Modern Art (1974–83). He also ran his own press, SWOLLEN MAGPIE, first from New York City (1970–73), then from Putnam Valley in upstate New York, where Violi moved with his wife, Ann, a teacher, and their daughter in 1976. A son was born shortly after the move. Several teaching positions, at New York University, Columbia University, and the New School, have helped Violi maintain his ties with the city.

Of the first-generation NEW YORK SCHOOL poets most frequently cited as a predecessor to Violi is KENNETH KOCH, as a strong comic streak runs through the work of both. Koch's comedy is primarily a matter of verbal surface, however, whereas Violi's opens onto depths both of situation and character. While Koch's flat, cartoonlike characters are typically postmodernist, Violi's personae derive from the modernist tradition, particularly from Ezra Pound, whom Violi has acknowledged as a formative influence (Hillringhouse; Violi, interviewed by Stannard 43). Pound's impersonations of the troubadours echo in Violi's poems such as "To Cisco in the Swamps" (in *Waterworks* [Toothpaste Press, 1972]) and "One for the Monk of Montaudon" (in *Splurge* [SUN, 1982]). "Impersonation," as Violi understands it (interviewed by Stannard 40), extends to his practice of adopting for poetic purposes a utilitarian GENRE—a TV schedule, a chart of berths assigned to boats at a marina, a catalog of fireworks. "Index," the last poem both in *Some Poems* (Swollen Magpie, 1976) and in *Splurge,* has become the best known among these experiments through its appearance in anthologies. Presented as an excerpt from the index to a book of artists' biographies, its inherently fragmentary FORM ironically mirrors the disruptions caused by inexplicable accidents in the life of its fictional subject.

Interruption is fundamental both to Violi's worldview and to his technique. The title poem of *The Curious Builder* (Hanging Loose, 1993), reprinted in the selection of long poems entitled *Breakers* (Coffee House, 2000), is conceived on the paradoxical notion of "continuous interruption," according to Violi (Hillringhouse n.p.). It moves from a mock catalog of dream imagery to an account of a particular dream, swerves abruptly to recollect an auto accident, enters a restaurant of infinitely expanding rooms where the waitress delivers the mail rather than the expected meal, and concludes with an excerpt from the English Renaissance poet Samuel Daniel (the source of the title phrase). Elsewhere Violi exploits interruption to introduce a poetic freedom into conventional narrative, most obviously in the prose collection

Selected Accidents, Pointless Anecdotes (Hanging Loose, 2002). These prose pieces originally appeared in 1995 in the first of a series of COLLABORATIONS between Violi and the British artist Dale Devereux Barker, suggesting that "interference" of visual and verbal modes, as Mary Ann Caws has analyzed it, provides Violi further opportunity for interruption. The text for another collaboration with Barker, collected in Violi's volume *Fracas* (Hanging Loose, 1999), refers to the experience as "Anamorphosis." Its distortions make it impossible for the reader to tell whether a particular image refers to life or to art. Like Rauschenberg, Violi chooses "to act in the gap between the two" (Tomkins 193).

Bibliography

Caws, Mary Ann. *The Art of Interference: Stressed Readings in Visual and Verbal Texts.* Princeton, N.J.: Princeton University Press, 1989.

Diggory, Terence. "A Maze of Openings." *American Book Review* 22 (May–June 2001): 21.

Genega, Paul. "Wild Ellipsis." *American Book Review* 11 (July–August 1989): 14.

Hillringhouse, Mark. Review of *Selected Accidents, Pointless Anecdotes. Literary Review* (Fall 2002). Available online. URL: http://www.findarticles.com/p/articles/mi_m2078/is_1_46/ai_94983807. Accessed December 19, 2008.

Lally, Michael. "Economou and Company." *Washington Post Book World*, 1 January 1978, E7.

Lehman, David. Review of *Splurge. Newsday*, 19 December 1982, 20, 19.

Tomkins, Calvin. *The Bride and the Bachelors: Five Masters of the Avant-Garde.* New York: Penguin, 1976.

Violi, Paul. "Index" and author's commentary. In *Ecstatic Occasions, Expedient Forms,* edited by David Lehman, 216–219. 2d ed. Ann Arbor: University of Michigan Press, 1996.

———. Interview by Mark Hillringhouse. *Joe Soap's Canoe* 16 (1993): n.p.

———. Interview by Martin Stannard. *The North* 35 (2004): 39–44.

———. Interview by Kemel Zaldivar. *MiPoesias* 19, no. 3 (2005). Available online. URL: http://www.mipoesias.com/Volume19Issue3Gudding/violiinterview.html. Accessed December 19, 2008.

———. *Overnight.* Brooklyn: Hanging Loose, 2007.

visual art   *See* ART, VISUAL.

W

Wagner Literary Magazine (1959–1964)

The four issues of the *Wagner Literary Magazine* document the rapid occupation by NEW YORK SCHOOL poets of territory that had been opened by the BEATS. As the newly appointed faculty adviser to the literary magazine at Wagner College on Staten Island, New York, WILLARD MAAS encouraged students to demonstrate a higher level of ambition by launching a new series in spring 1959, newly titled (the magazine was previously entitled *Nimbus*) and substantial, with more than 100 pages in 5½-by-8 inches format. Catching a trend, the first issue opens with a symposium on the Beats. ALLEN GINSBERG, GREGORY CORSO, and Peter Orlovsky responded to comments from major writers and thinkers, including Marianne Moore, Herbert Read, Philip Rahv, Paul Tillich, Lionel Trilling, ROBERT LOWELL, William Carlos Williams, Norman Mailer, e. e. cummings, and Edmund Wilson. The last issue of the series (1963–64), coinciding with Maas's departure from the college, shows more confidence in the right of the new voices to speak for themselves. Only one "name" poet, Richard Eberhart, introduces a group of younger writers, who include JOE BRAINARD, TED BERRIGAN, DICK GALLUP, LORENZO THOMAS, RON PADGETT, JOSEPH CERAVOLO, FRANK LIMA, DAVID SHAPIRO, TONY TOWLE, and JIM BRODEY—writers today identified as "New York School" rather than "Wagner Poets," as the magazine classifies them.

Officially these poets received the "Wagner" designation by participating in some capacity in the NEW YORK CITY WRITERS CONFERENCE or in a corresponding "Fine Arts Festival," both held on the Wagner campus. Unofficially they gained entry through association with GERARD MALANGA, who was a student at Wagner from 1961 to 1964 and editor of the last two issues of the magazine. Earlier, Malanga had studied both with Eberhart and with DAISY ALDAN, who comments on the first presentation of "Wagner Poets" in the magazine's second issue (1960–61). Malanga's training in visual art and his preference for a certain artfulness of style in any medium inclined him more toward the New York School than the Beats, an inclination that would have been reinforced by Maas's predilections.

Other arts besides literature are abundantly represented in the *Wagner Literary Magazine*, but it is the "art music" of Ben Weber and Lucia Dlugoszewski that is represented rather than JAZZ, the "art film" of Marie Menken (Maas's wife) and Stan Brakhage rather than Hollywood. Hollywood is refracted through the lens of ANDY WARHOL, whose "Marilyns" are reproduced to accompany an article on Warhol by Henry Geldzahler (number 4, 1963–64). In an earlier issue (number 2, 1960–61), an article on Alice Neel by a student writer, George Semsel, had been illustrated with Neel's portraits of Ben Weber and FRANK O'HARA, as if they, too, were popular icons in the culture the *Wagner Literary Magazine* sought to foster.

Waldman, Anne (1945–)

The diverse energies that make up the NEW YORK SCHOOL can all be traced in the career of Anne

Waldman, who describes herself as "poet, editor, performer, professor, curator, cultural activist" (faculty listing n.p.). Her poems range from open FORM ("Up Thru the Years") to complex pantoums and sestinas (FIRST BABY POEMS), from one-line MINIMALISM ("Moment") to multivolume epic (IOVIS). She has collaborated in projects involving visual art, DANCE, film, THEATER, and MUSIC. As an editor, she shaped two magazines that defined the second-generation New York School, ANGEL HAIR and The WORLD. As a visionary leader, she has helped ensure the continuing legacy of the New York School within the broader context of the New American Poetry at two institutions, the POETRY PROJECT AT ST. MARK'S CHURCH IN-THE-BOWERY and NAROPA INSTITUTE/University.

Raised in a "bohemian household" in NEW YORK CITY's Greenwich Village (Waldman, Introduction xx), Waldman came naturally to the life of a poet. Her mother, Frances LeFevre Waldman (1909–82), regarded poetry as "the highest art" (Waldman, essay 268–269). Eventually Frances brought to the Poetry Project, at which she served as newsletter editor (1976–78), the spirit of utopian community that she had absorbed during the 1930s as a member of the Sikelianos family in Greece, through her first marriage. Waldman's father, John Waldman (1909–94), became a writer and university professor while Anne was growing up, but she dates her "birth" as a poet to witnessing a performance by CHARLES OLSON, a "poet-father," at the BERKELEY POETRY CONFERENCE in 1965 (Waldman, Fast Speaking 146, 152). Also at Berkeley she met LEWIS WARSH, whom she married in 1967. During the previous year Waldman had graduated from Bennington College, launched Angel Hair magazine with Warsh, and started work at the Poetry Project, where she served as director from 1968 to 1978.

Waldman has aptly characterized the style of her work collected in early volumes such as Giant Night (Corinth, 1970), Baby Breakdown (Bobbs-Merrill, 1970), and No Hassles (Kulchur, 1971): "I was writing to talk to myself, writing notes to myself and to my friends. Telling, spilling out the fast takes in my head. These early poems have energy, naivete, are guileless. Intimate. Dailiness is the measure" (Waldman, essay 279). Over the

course of the next decade her work expanded beyond the surface of dailiness and the immediate circle of friends. She traveled widely, to the West Indies, Central and South America, and eventually to India, where MICHAEL BROWNSTEIN and JOHN GIORNO accompanied her in 1973. After a meeting in Vermont in 1970 with the Tibetan Buddhist teacher Chögyam Trungpa (1940–87), Waldman became increasingly involved in the study of Tantric Buddhism, more action oriented than contemplative modes such as Zen. She discovered a parallel tradition among the indigenous peoples of Central and South America, particularly in the magical chanting of Mexican shaman Maria Sabina (1896–1985). These influences are apparent in the performance-oriented poetry of Fast-Speaking Woman (City Lights, 1975, 1996), first published in the same year that Waldman and ALLEN GINSBERG, at Trungpa's invitation, launched the Jack Kerouac School of Disembodied Poetics at NAROPA.

Waldman's close association with Ginsberg and WILLIAM S. BURROUGHS, her immersion in Buddhism and her use of poetry performance as a vehicle for social protest (Uh-Oh, Plutonium!) have led to her identification with the BEATS in some accounts of literary history (Knight; Puchek). However, the history of Waldman's development is not a matter of moving from New York School origins towards Beat identity but rather a constant effort to pursue "both paths" (Waldman, Vow 129). Immediately after lifting poetry off the page in Fast Speaking Woman, she published Journals and Dreams (Stonehill, 1976), including "pieces . . . strictly for the page, not to be read aloud, too private or something" (Waldman, Vow 47). Personal references abound in a letter addressed to JOE BRAINARD; poems dedicated to JIM CARROLL, LORENZO THOMAS, EDWIN DENBY, and KENWARD ELMSLIE; and COLLABORATIONS with TED BERRIGAN ("MEMORIAL DAY," 1970) and BERNADETTE MAYER ("Rattle Up a Deer," 1974).

The emergence of a "decidedly female landscape," which Waldman regarded as a "breakthrough" in Journals and Dreams (contributor's note 42), owes something to the breakup of her marriage to Warsh, reflected particularly in the poems "29 at Belle Vue" and "Divorce Work." In First Baby Poems (Rocky Ledge Cottage, 1982; Hyacinth Girls,

1983), Waldman's "female landscape" expands to include the experience of motherhood, following her marriage to REED BYE and the birth of their son, Anselm, in 1980 (this marriage broke up in 1991). However, rather than valuing these poems for their personal associations, Waldman describes them as "free of the stain of ego, ownership" (essay 286). Guided by this Buddhist value, she has directed much of her subsequent work to the challenge of writing out of personal experience in a way that has general, even cosmological significance. Not surprisingly this project has taken the form of epic (*Iovis*) or book-length SERIAL POEMS (*Marriage* and *The Structure of the World Compared to a Bubble*), in which Waldman pushes against the conventions both of GENRE and gender. She constructs a voice that is "half male, half female" (*Iovis* I 172), like the married couple, a constant yet changing pattern (in 2003 Waldman married for a third time, to the filmmaker Ed Bowes). She constructs a form that is part linear narrative, part circular monument, like the Buddhist stupa of Borobudur in Java, Indonesia, which supplies the pattern for *The Structure of the World*.

Waldman is the recipient of a National Endowment for the Arts grant (1980) and the Shelley Prize of the Poetry Society of America (1996). She is currenlty Distinguished Professor and Chair of the Summer Writing Program at Naropa University, codirector of the Study Abroad on the Bowery project in New York, and faculty member in the low-residency M.F.A. program at New England College.

Bibliography

Anne Waldman issue. *Talisman* 13 (Fall 1994–Winter 1995).

Gilbert, Alan, and Daron Mueller, eds. "Feature: Anne Waldman." *Jacket* 27 (April 2005). Available online. URL: http://jacketmagazine.com/27/index.shtml. Accessed November 4, 2008.

Knight, Brenda, ed. *Women of the Beat Generation: The Women, Artists and Muses at the Heart of a Revolution.* Berkeley, Calif.: Conari, 1996.

Puchek, Peter. "From Revolution to Creation: Beat Desire and Body Poetics in Anne Waldman's Poetry." In *Girls Who Wore Black: Women Writing the Beat Generation,* edited by Ronna C. Johnson and Nancy M. Grace, 227–250. New Brunswick, N.J.: Rutgers University Press, 2002.

Waldman, Anne. Contributor's note. In *The Postmoderns: The New American Poetry Revised,* edited by Donald Allen and George F. Butterick, 428. New York: Grove, 1982.

———. Essay in *Contemporary Authors Autobiography Series* 17, edited by Joyce Nakamura, 267–294. Detroit, Mich.: Gale, 1993.

———. Faculty listing. M.F.A. Program in Poetry. New England College Web site. Available online. URL: http://www.nec.edu/graduate-and-professional-studies/mfa-in-poetry/mfa-faculty-list. Accessed December 19, 2008.

———. *Fast-Speaking Woman.* 2d ed. San Francisco: City Lights, 1996.

———. *First Baby Poems.* 2d ed. New York: Hyacinth Girls, 1983.

———. *Helping the Dreamer: New and Selected Poems, 1966–1988.* Minneapolis, Minn.: Coffee House Press, 1989.

———. Introduction to *The Angel Hair Anthology.* New York: Granary Books, 2001, xix–xxvii.

———. *Iovis: All Is Full of Jove* [I]. Minneapolis, Minn.: Coffee House Press, 1993.

———. *Iovis: All Is Full of Jove* [II]. Minneapolis, Minn.: Coffee House Press, 1997.

———. *Iovis: The Eternal War* [III, excerpts]. In *In the Room of Never Grieve: New and Selected Poems, 1985–2003.* Minneapolis, Minn.: Coffee House Press, 2003, 391–479.

———. *Marriage: A Sentence.* New York: Penguin, 2000.

———. "Moment." In *Baby Breakdown.* New York: Bobbs-Merrill, 1970, 71.

———. *The Structure of the World Compared to a Bubble.* New York: Penguin, 2004.

———. *Uh-Oh, Plutonium!* Audio recording. New York: Hyacinth Girls Music, 1982. Videorecording. In *Manhattan Poetry Video Project.* New York: Out There Productions, 1984.

———. "Up Thru the Years" (1969). In *The Angel Hair Anthology.* New York: Granary Books, 2001, 347–348.

———. *Vow to Poetry: Essays, Interviews, Manifestos.* Minneapolis, Minn.: Coffee House Press, 2001.

Waldman, Anne, and Lisa Berman, eds. *Civil Disobediences: Poetics and Politics in Action.* Minneapolis, Minn.: Coffee House Press, 2004.

Warhol, Andy (Andrew Warhola)
(1928–1987) *artist, filmmaker*

As the leading man of POP ART, Andy Warhol presided over a major shift in the New York art world during the 1960s, evident in everything from the look of a painting (precise renderings of soup cans replacing abstract brushstrokes) to the atmosphere of the artists' hangout (the disco glitz of Max's Kansas City replacing the bohemian seediness of the CEDAR STREET TAVERN). In contrast to JACKSON POLLOCK's macho style, Warhol's style was unabashedly gay, a fact that made him both enticing and threatening to the gay NEW YORK SCHOOL poets JOHN ASHBERY and FRANK O'HARA. Warhol's lower-class origins—he was born Andrew Warhola to Czechoslovakian immigrants in Pittsburgh—formed a largely unspoken bond with second-generation poets TED BERRIGAN and RON PADGETT.

The deliberate inexpressiveness of Warhol's art, which seemed a direct challenge to the emotional tenor of ABSTRACT EXPRESSIONISM, has reinforced an image of Warhol himself as nonverbal. In fact, he had a profound understanding of the power of the word, though he kept himself at an objective distance from that power, as if to prevent being manipulated by it and to be in a better position to perform his own manipulations. The writer Truman Capote supplied the inspiration for drawings exhibited in Warhol's first solo show in NEW YORK CITY, in 1952 at the Hugo Gallery. His work as a commercial artist throughout the decade focused on the placement of a product's brand name within a visual composition, a key component of the painting *200 Campbell's Soup Cans* that he later exhibited in the breakthrough pop exhibition, *The New Realists*, at the Sidney Janis Gallery in 1962. Although Ashbery's catalog essay for that exhibition does not name Warhol or any other artist, Ashbery's residence in Paris gave him the opportunity to track the subsequent growth of Warhol's international reputation in a series of gallery reviews (Wolf 83–87). Warhol's ability to attract the words of eloquent writers was one form of his manipulation of the power of the word.

O'Hara rebuffed Warhol's approaches in person, though eventually he offered some words of praise in print (Gooch 392–399). The personal tension arose because Warhol seemed to O'Hara both too effeminate and too cold. To produce the latter effect Warhol deliberately played up the mechanical nature of the media he preferred, from silkscreen printing to photography. On one occasion in 1964 that particularly offended O'Hara, Warhol expressed a wish to have been present at the suicide of the dancer Freddie Herko in order to film it (Gooch 397). However, the objectification that Warhol sought through the camera proved attractive to other poets, starting with JOHN GIORNO, who treated Herko's death through the lens of a "found poem" taken from the *Village Voice* (Giorno 148). In 1963 Giorno "starred" in Warhol's first film, *Sleep*, a series of close-ups of Giorno's body, filmed while he was sleeping and edited to last up to eight hours, the scientifically approved norm for sleep in a 24-hour period (Malanga 39). Among a series of responses to *Sleep* published in *Film Culture* (in 1964), TED BERRIGAN contributed "The Upper Arm," JOE BRAINARD "Andy Warhol's Sleep Movie," and RON PADGETT a "Sonnet," consisting of 14 lines filled entirely by the letter z (Wolf 95–97, 108–109).

With the encouragement of Warhol's assistant GERARD MALANGA, a poet himself, Berrigan and Padgett were among several poets, including also Ashbery, EDWIN DENBY, ED SANDERS, and TONY TOWLE, who sat before Warhol's camera for "screen tests." Some of these were reproduced as stills in Warhol's COLLABORATION with Malanga, SCREEN TESTS/A DIARY (1967). Somewhat earlier, a collaborative film project initiated by O'Hara's roommate Joe LeSueur was to have provided Warhol with scripts—unusual in Warhol's practice—written by Denby, FRANK LIMA, O'Hara, Padgett, and other acquaintances. The film was never produced, and only the segment written in collaboration by O'Hara and Lima has been published, under the title "Love on the Hoof." The structure of the script, which plays two simultaneous telephone conversations against each other, anticipates the double-screen format that Warhol employed for one of his most popular films, *The Chelsea Girls* (1966), based on the lives of residents of the CHELSEA HOTEL. A decade later Ashbery recalled this film as one model for the double-column format he used in his poem "Litany" (Wolf 175 note 30).

The "underground" that connected filmmaking and poetry adjoined a darker domain of hustlers, thieves, drug addicts, and psychopaths, from whom Warhol sought to insulate himself after a shooting incident in 1968 that left him critically wounded. The success of his paintings, meanwhile, gave him access to wealthy patrons who were eager to pay for portraits that would enshrine them in the series Warhol had begun with his depictions of Marilyn Monroe, Elvis Presley, and Liz Taylor in the early 1960s. Throughout the '70s, commissioned portraits and other business ventures preoccupied Warhol, while the chorus of charges that he had "sold out" built to a crescendo when the portraits were shown together at the Whitney Museum of American Art in 1979. During the '80s his reputation rebounded somewhat through his association with younger artists (Jean-Michel Basquiat, Francesco Clemente, Keith Haring) and through his inscription into postmodernist theory (Roland Barthes, Arthur Danto, Fredric Jameson). Warhol died in 1987 following gallbladder surgery.

Bibliography

Ashbery, John. "Litany." In *As We Know*. New York: Viking Penguin, 1979, 1–68.

———. "The New Realists." In *Reported Sightings: Art Chronicles, 1957–1987*. Edited by David Bergman. Cambridge, Mass.: Harvard University Press, 1991, 81–83.

Barthes, Roland. "That Old Thing, Art . . ." (1980). In *Pop Art: The Critical Dialogue*, edited by Carol Ann Mahsun, 233–240. Ann Arbor, Mich.: UMI Research Press, 1989.

Danto, Arthur C. *The Transfiguration of the Commonplace: A Philosophy of Art*. Cambridge, Mass.: Harvard University Press, 1981.

Giorno, John. "Andy Warhol's Movie 'Sleep'" (1989). In *You Got to Burn to Shine: New and Selected Writings*. London and New York: High Risk Books/Serpent's Tail, 1994, 123–163.

Gooch, Brad. *City Poet: The Life and Times of Frank O'Hara*. New York: Knopf, 1993.

Jameson, Fredric. "The Cultural Logic of Late Capitalism" (1984). In *Postmodernism, or, The Cultural Logic of Late Capitalism*. Durham, N.C.: Duke University Press, 1991, 1–54.

Koestenbaum, Wayne. *Andy Warhol*. New York: Viking Penguin, 2001.

Malanga, Gerard. *Archiving Warhol: Writings and Photographs*. New York: Creation Books, 2002.

O'Hara, Frank, and Frank Lima. "Love on the Hoof" (ca. 1964). In *Amorous Nightmares of Delay: Selected Plays*, by Frank O'Hara. Baltimore, Md.: Johns Hopkins University Press, 1997, 173–176.

Ratcliff, Carter. *Andy Warhol*. New York: Abbeville, 1983.

Schjeldahl, Peter. "Andy Warhol" (1989). In *The 7 Days Art Columns, 1988–1990*. Great Barrington, Mass.: The Figures, 1990, 101–104.

Warhol, Andy, and Pat Hackett. *POPism: The Warhol Sixties*. 1980. Reprint, San Diego, Calif.: Harcourt-Harvest, 1990.

Wolf, Reva. *Andy Warhol, Poetry, and Gossip in the 1960s*. Chicago: University of Chicago Press, 1997.

Yau, John. *In the Realm of Appearances: The Art of Andy Warhol*. Hopewell, N.J.: Ecco, 1993.

Warsh, Lewis (1944–)

Lewis Warsh has become firmly identified with the NEW YORK SCHOOL as coeditor of ANGEL HAIR (1966–75) and UNITED ARTISTS (1977–), frequent contributing editor of *The* WORLD, and cohost of the Lower East Side version of the literary salon in apartments he shared with ANNE WALDMAN (1966–69) and BERNADETTE MAYER (1980–84). Yet Warsh's writing demonstrates, as he asserts, that "no two people write alike, even if they're associated with a so-called 'school'" (interview by Kane 161). And as a student of "schools" in the poetry world as well as an eclectic reader, Warsh concludes that boundaries matter less than the "enmeshment" of various types of writing and the writers' lives (interview by Foster 151), a theme he has pursued in his work (for example, "Enmeshment," 1984). Certainly Warsh's life dispels the misconception that the New York School is confined to any geographical boundaries. Although born and educated in New York (City College B.A., 1966; M.A., 1975), Warsh met Waldman in California at the BERKELEY POETRY CONFERENCE. After his marriage with Waldman ended in 1969, he spent some time in BOLINAS, CALIFORNIA. In 1975 he moved with Mayer to the BERKSHIRES of Massachusetts for the remainder of the decade. Currently he lives in Lower Manhattan with the playwright-teacher Katt Lissard, whom he married in 2001. He teaches at Long Island University in Brooklyn, where he holds the position of associate professor of English.

When Warsh first read *The NEW AMERICAN POETRY, 1945–1960* in 1960, at age 15, he was least attracted to the New York School (Warsh, introduction xx). Although he studied with KENNETH KOCH at the New School in 1963, the most notable poem Warsh wrote in that workshop, "The Suicide Rates," reflects his interest in Jack Spicer and his circle in the SAN FRANCISCO RENAISSANCE, poets who "internalized experience" (Warsh, introduction xxi). The attention to surface typical of the New York School entered Warsh's work at the prompting of TED BERRIGAN, who met Warsh in 1966 after Warsh and Waldman solicited Berrigan's work for *Angel Hair* (Warsh, "Publishing Ted" 15). Berrigan encouraged Warsh not only to use his knowledge of popular culture in his poems but also to bring himself to the poem's surface, the point at which it engages with daily experience (Warsh, interview by Foster 152–153). The result is evident in Warsh's first collection, *Moving Through Air* (Angel Hair, 1968), which includes "The Suicide Rates" but also "Halloween 1967," an extract from Warsh's "New York Diary," later represented more fully in *PART OF MY HISTORY* (Coach House, 1972). In the diary FORM Warsh developed a distinctive version of the New York School "personal poem," marked by a "deliberately very flat" tone that may derive from Warsh's reading of French "new novelists" such as Alain Robbe-Grillet and Marguerite Duras (Warsh, interview by Foster 152–153). In the New York School context, as Warsh's contemporary David Rosenberg explains, this development took Warsh "beyond either Frank [O'Hara] or Ted [Berrigan] to record the literal goings-to-and-fro of the day, to the exclusion of even a moment's distracting thought about it" (595).

In addition to *Moving Through Air*, Warsh has published other collections of poems, including *Dreaming as One* (Corinth Books, 1971), *Blue Heaven* (Kulchur, 1978), and *Information from the Surface of Venus* (United Artists, 1987). He has also continued the exploration of the formal possibilities of the book as a whole—as something more than a collection—that he began in *Part of My History*. A related interest in arrangement rather than expression is a "conceptual" aspect of Warsh's work that he associates with his partnership with Mayer, balancing the "personal" aspect

that Berrigan encouraged (Warsh, interview by Foster 154). For instance, Warsh has arranged "found" material (*The Maharajah's Son* [Angel Hair, 1977]; *Methods of Birth Control* [Sun & Moon, 1982]), composed extended prose fictions (*AGNES AND SALLY* [Fiction Collective, 1984]; *A FREE MAN* [Sun and Moon, 1991]; *Ted's Favorite Skirt* [Spuyten Duyvil, 2002]), and created collage-like works (*Avenue of Escape* [Long News, 1995]; *The Origin of the World* [Creative Arts, 2001]). Composed of units falling "somewhere between a sentence and a poetic line," according to Daniel Kane (154), the collage texts reflect Warsh's interest in hybrid forms, evident also in *Touch of the Whip* (Singing Horse, 2001), which combines poetry and short prose FICTION, and *Debtor's Prison* (Granary Books, 2001), which juxtaposes stills from the video art of Julie Harrison with brief responses written by Warsh.

Bibliography

Kane, Daniel. Introduction to interview with Lewis Warsh. In *What Is Poetry: Conversations with the American Avant-Garde.* New York: Teachers & Writers, 2003, 154–155.

Lewis Warsh issue. *Talisman* 18 (Fall 1998).

Rosenberg, David. Contributor's note. In *The Angel Hair Anthology*, edited by Anne Waldman and Lewis Warsh, 594–596. New York: Granary Books, 2001.

Schjeldahl, Peter. "Around the Corner." *Poetry* 117, no. 4 (January 1971): 261–275.

Waldman, Anne, and Lewis Warsh, eds. *The Angel Hair Anthology.* New York: Granary Books, 2001.

Warsh, Lewis. "Enmeshment" (1984). In *Out of This World: An Anthology of the St. Mark's Poetry Project, 1966–1991*, edited by Anne Waldman, 388–389. New York: Crown, 1991.

———. Interview by Peter Bushyeager. *Poetry Project Newsletter* 187 (December 2001–January 2002): 12–15.

———. Interview by Edward Foster (1991). In *Poetry and Poetics in a New Millennium*, edited by Edward Foster, 147–159. Jersey City, N.J.: Talisman House, 2000.

———. Interview by Daniel Kane. In *What Is Poetry: Conversations with the American Avant-Garde*, edited by Daniel Kane, 157–162. New York: Teachers & Writers, 2003.

———. Introduction to *The Angel Hair Anthology.* New York: Granary Books, 2001, xix–xxvii.

———. "Publishing Ted." In *Ted Berrigan: An Annotated Checklist,* by Aaron Fischer, 15–20. New York: Granary Books, 1998.

Washington Crossing the Delaware   *See* GEORGE WASHINGTON CROSSING THE DELAWARE.

Wasserman, Jo Ann (1968–)

In her remarkable book *The Escape* (European Books, 2003) Jo Ann Wasserman explores— through a cycle of sometimes excruciating, sometimes hilarious prose-poem/journal entries, sestinas, and short poems—the fraught relationship between a daughter and her mother, as well as between a writer and writing. The bold use of the sestina for such a family project beautifully complicates the distinctions between all kinds of "schools" of writing and embodies questions about the relationships between social and familial structures, individuals, language, and the FORMS that language takes.

Born in New York, Wasserman has worked at a number of key New York literary institutions since the 1990s. Most notable is the POETRY PROJECT AT ST. MARK'S CHURCH IN-THE-BOWERY, where from 1992 to 1997 she was assistant coordinator and coedited *The WORLD.* It might be said that the form of Wasserman's connection to the NEW YORK SCHOOL can be traced to this relationship between New York's "alternative" literary institutions and the labor involved in making them run. Like many poets of her generation, living in and producing poems in NEW YORK CITY might be the main reason to call her a New York School poet, and like the so-called first generation of the so-called New York School, Wasserman resists such classification. Still, there are many ways in which Wasserman's writing builds on the engaged, inventive work of poets such as BERNADETTE MAYER and ALICE NOTLEY. Like earlier generations of the New York School, Wasserman feels a connection between the dailiness of living and the act of writing and, like them, too, has expanded the field of what might be considered the act of the poem. Besides *The Escape,* Wasserman is the author of two chapbooks, *we build mountains* (a + bend press, 1999) and *what counts as proof* (1999).

Wasserman, Rosanne (1952–)

Rosanne Wasserman writes poems with "beautiful surface textures and music" while she "bends language to make unusual illuminations," as Ruth Stone says of "Sweeter Than Wine" in the introduction to Wasserman's *Apple Perfume:* "Imagine us missing the train! But it finally / Amethyst into the station" (2). Her poetry embodies the NEW YORK SCHOOL's fascination with language, FORM, humor, and irreverence. In "Singapore," written for JOHN YAU, lines pun on the title: "Sing a pair in nude gold arms, posed as isles, ringd / With fire. / Sanguine peer, answer namesake's gamesters: under? inside?" (Wasserman, *Other Selves* 65).

Born in Louisville, Kentucky, Wasserman designed her B.A. (1974) in poetry and poetics at Indiana University, studying with Stone and Philip Appleman. She worked with David Ignatow for a poetry M.F.A. from Columbia University (1974–76). She and EUGENE RICHIE founded the GROUNDWATER PRESS (1974), married in 1977, and had a son, Joseph, in 1990. An editor at the Metropolitan Museum of Art (1977–81), Wasserman taught in the Poetry in the Schools program (1986–91), earned her English Ph.D. (1986) at the City University of New York's Graduate Center, graduated cum laude from the Greek Institute there, and began translating Sappho. In JOHN ASH's "Ash Wednesday" workshops she conceived Groundwater's Intuflo chapbook series to complement Marc Cohen and Susan Baran's Intuflo Reading Series, giving many younger New York School poets their first publications. In the 1990s she received a poetry fellowship from the New York Foundation for the Arts, attended Yau's West Side YMCA poetry workshop, and interviewed Pierre Martory and JAMES SCHUYLER for *American Poetry Review.* A trustee of JOHN ASHBERY's Flow Chart Foundation, she currently teaches at the United States Merchant Marine Academy.

Early influences include William Blake, James Joyce, W. B. Yeats, Dylan Thomas, Gertrude Stein, and Marianne Moore, whose connections with New York School poets Wasserman has studied. Later influences are Ashbery, ELIZABETH BISHOP, and OULIPO. Her formal virtuosity in *The Lacemakers* (1992), *No Archive on Earth* (1995), *Other Selves*

(1999), and *Place du Carousel* (2001) includes variants on Moore's stanzas; Ezra Pound's ancient Greek, Chinese, and Provencal forms; centos, sestinas, pantoums, and Oulipo games. In *Lacemakers*, women named for lace implements and mythic figures alternate voices; "Boustrophedon" is inspired by a Greek vase with letters written backward and forward. Simultaneously, however, as Tod Thilleman writes, her meditations take us "into a spell-like, trance-like state of apprehending" (107), as in the first line of "Inuit and Seal," which Ashbery selected for *Best American Poetry* (1988): "Who has been drinking our air from the other side?" (*No Archive on Earth* 3).

Bibliography

Thilleman, Tod. Review of *No Archive on Earth*. *American Letters and Commentary* (1998): 107.

Wasserman, Rosanne. *Apple Perfume*. Introduction by Ruth Stone. New York: Groundwater Press–Intuflo Editions, 1989.

———. "Boustrophedon." *How2* (2002). Available online. URL: http://www.scc.rutgers.edu/however/v1_8_2002/current/new_writing/wasserman.shtm. Accessed December 19, 2008.

———. *The Lacemakers*. New York: Gnosis Press, 1992.

———. "Marianne Moore and the New York School: O'Hara, Ashbery, Koch." *Sagetrieb* 6, no. 3 (1987): 67–77.

———. *No Archive on Earth*. New York: Gnosis Press, 1995.

———. *Other Selves*. New York: Painted Leaf Press, 1999.

———. *Pomes*. Louisville, Ky.: Innominate Press, 1971.

———. *Willing Suspensions*. New York: Groundwater Press, 1974.

Wasserman, Rosanne, with Eugene Richie. *Place du Carousel*. Artwork by Antanas Andziulis. Vilna, Lithuania: Zilvinas & Daiva Publications, 2001.

Weatherly, Tom (1942–)

"I'm the grandson of Wallace Stevens and Hilda Doolittle, Jimmy Rogers and Sippie Wallace, and first cousin to Paul Blackburn," says Weatherly (questionnaire response n.p.), whose work "condenses the wisdom of a life and vast readings into brilliantly compact music," writes ANDREI CODRESCU (*Short History* blurb); the critic Howard Kissel calls him "a mystic with a sense of humor . . . an American Zen master" (*Short History* blurb).

Born in Scottsboro, Alabama, Weatherly is the son of a chemist, mathematician, and school administrator father and a schoolteacher mother. He left George Washington Carver High School in 11th grade for Morehouse College in 1958; transferring to Alabama A&M College, he was expelled for publishing an underground paper, *The Saint*. In NEW YORK CITY by 1968, he attended City College one summer, Hofstra University for three sessions, and later David Ignatow's seminar at Columbia University. Working at the Lion's Head Pub, he befriended many writers, artists, and musicians, notably JOEL OPPENHEIMER and Dave von Ronk. For three decades he worked at the Strand Bookstore, returning to Scottsboro after his mother's death. He has a daughter, Regina, with Mary Virginia Harris and a son, Thomas Elias, with Carolyn Samuels. His other significant partners have been Susan Ellene Christoffersen, Muriel Michal Hollander, Janet Rosen, and Ursula Huebner-Bromberger. Long-distance bicyclist and computer maven, Weatherly maintains a blog, *Eclectic Git*.

Weatherly began the Natural Process Workshop in East Harlem in 1968, which in the early 1970s merged with the POETRY PROJECT AT SAINT MARK'S CHURCH IN-THE-BOWERY. He taught Afro-Hispanic art at Rutgers University–Newark and has conducted poetry workshops at grade schools, universities, prisons, and poetry projects, as well as privately with Madeline Tiger, Julia Kasdorf, and others. New York poets whom he names as influences are Oppenheimer, Sam Abrams, and Ignatow, and he has "learned many esoteric bits from" Jerrold Greenberg, Ronald Edson, Michael Stephens, Codrescu, Esther Levenberg, Marcel Flamm, TED BERRIGAN, ANSELM HOLLO, Giant Night, Sam Allen, and Alma.

Three collections appeared in the early 1970s: *Maumau American Cantos*, *Thumbprint*, and *Climate/Stream*. In the 30 years between then and his next published book, *Short History of the Saxophone* (2006), Weatherly honed his language to an exquisite degree, while his themes remained flesh and spirit, gender and racial conflict, science and POLITICS. His innovative FORM, the glory, resembles Chinese poetry's grids of patterned sound; "musick," below, is a double glory:

bluesy subtle bluest
thence beauty blooms
sunlit bluets center
whence brutal musics
humans vent as blues
    (*Short History* 5).

Bibliography

Weatherly, Tom. Eclectic Git blog. Available online. URL: http://bluestbluetsspace.live.com.

———. *Maumau American Cantos*. New York: Corinth Books, 1970.

———. Questionnaire response for *Encyclopedia of the New York School Poets*, 27 March 2006.

———. *Short History of the Saxophone*. Hudson, N.Y.: Groundwater Press, 2006.

———. *Thumbprint*. New York: Telegraph Books, 1971.

Weatherly, Tom, and Ken Bluford. *Climate/Stream*. Philadelphia: Middle Earth Books, 1972.

Wilentz, Ted, and Tom Weatherly, eds. *Natural Process: An Anthology of New Black Poetry*. New York: Hill & Wang, 1970.

Welish, Marjorie (1944–   )

While Marjorie Welish's work resembles LANGUAGE POETRY in her rigorous attention to the artificiality of any verbal construction, she insists on the continuing relevance of NEW YORK SCHOOL poetry for its concern with musicality. "The problematic of incommensurate orders" is a creative stimulus to Welish, and Language and New York School poetries are only two of the "orders" that her work sets in tension (Welish, "What Is Black" n.p.). Other oppositions reach across media (Welish is both a writer and a painter) or between the "creative" and "critical" modes within the single medium of writing (Welish is both a poet and a critic). Ideally these oppositions exist within a single work. For instance, her villanelle "Street Cries" (1987) constructs "a fusion of cry and song" (Welish, commentary 224), the noise of the street and the MUSIC of the court. In abstract paintings that Welish insists can be "read" like a text, the triad of primary colors (red, yellow, blue) offsets the two-part logic of black versus white (Welish, "What's Black" n.p.). One logic might even be said to "read" the other from a "metapoetic" or

critical position. Such readings occur in passing in the work of FRANK O'HARA, Welish notes ("New York School" n.p.), but they are sustained and more fully developed in the work of JOHN ASHBERY, BARBARA GUEST, and DAVID SHAPIRO, the three New York School writers who are most important to Welish's own development.

A native New Yorker, Welish took a degree in art history at Columbia University (B.A., 1968), where she went on to study poetry with Jill Hoffman and Shapiro (1970–73). Shapiro encouraged her to read New York School poetry, but its potential was fully opened to her through hearing work read at the POETRY PROJECT AT ST. MARK'S CHURCH IN-THE-BOWERY ranging from ISHMAEL REED's expressionism—a mode she chose not to use—to Ashbery's constructivism (Welish, interview by Casper 79). She did not "get" Ashbery until she ceased listening for personal "voice" and instead recognized his work as a construction built of "sociolects and idiolects"—language circulating as common discourse (Welish, interview by Casper 79). Reviewing Welish's first volume, *Handwritten* (SUN, 1979), PETER SCHJELDAHL worried that Ashbery's example might lead Welish to discard "the basic poetic fiction of a peculiar human voice" altogether (Schjeldahl 292), but Ashbery himself responded favorably, choosing for his *Best American Poetry* anthology (1988) the poem "Respected, Feared, and Somehow Loved," later the opening poem of Welish's collection *The Windows Flew Open* (Burning Deck, 1991). Welish's next volume, *Casting Sequences* (University of Georgia Press, 1993) bore blurbs by Ashbery, Shapiro, and Guest, but the ultimate tribute came from Guest when she quoted from *Casting Sequences* in her own poem "Pallor" (in QUILL, SOLITARY APPARITION [Post-Apollo Press, 1996]). Welish returned the compliment, quoting from "Pallor" in "Textile 1," collected in *Word Group* (Coffee House Press, 2004). In her critical writing Welish has cited Guest's work repeatedly as a touchstone for the "non-imitative, verbal music" that is the essence of postmodern lyric, as Welish defines it ("The Lyric Lately" n.p.).

Since 1990 Welish has taught at the Pratt Institute in Brooklyn, and she has held visiting appointments at a number of universities, including Brown, Columbia, NAROPA, and the New School in the United States, and abroad at Cambridge and Goethe University (in Frankfurt). In 2002 her work in both poetry and painting was the subject of a symposium at the University of Pennsylvania under the auspices of the Slought Foundation, which issued a companion volume, *Of the Diagram* (edited by Aaron Levy and Jean-Michel Rabaté). Selected art criticism appears in Welish's *Signifying Art* (Cambridge University Press, 1999). Of her poetry collections, *The Annotated "Here"* (Coffee House Press, 2000) is the most comprehensive, presenting new work as well as selections from each of her previous volumes, while *Isle of the Signatories* (Coffee House Press, 2008) is the most recent.

Bibliography

Levy, Aaron, and Jean-Michel Rabaté, eds. *Of the Diagram: The Work of Marjorie Welish.* Philadelphia: Slought Books, 2003.

McDaniel, Ray. Review of *Word Group. The Constant Critic* (24 June 2004). Available online. URL: http://www.constantcritic.com/archive.cgi?rev=Ray_McDaniel &name=Word%20Group. Accessed December 19, 2008.

Quartermain, Meredith. "Undecorating the Lyric." *Jacket* 25 (February 2004). Available online. URL: http://jacketmagazine.com/25/quar-weli.html. Accessed December 19, 2008.

Schjeldahl, Peter. "Cabin Fever." *Parnassus* 9 (Spring–Summer 1981): 284–300.

Tysh, Chris. Review of *The Annotated "Here."* *Jacket* 15 (December 2001). Available online. URL: http://jacketmagazine.com/15/tysh-r-welish.html. Accessed December 19, 2008.

Welish, Marjorie. Commentary on "Street Cries." In *Ecstatic Occasions, Expedient Forms,* edited by David Lehman, 222–224. 2d ed. Ann Arbor: University of Michigan Press, 1996.

———. "Diagramming Here." *Web Conjunctions* (17 August 2004). Available online. URL: http://www.conjunctions.com/webconj.htm. Accessed December 19, 2008.

———. Interview by Daniel Kane. In *What Is Poetry? Conversations with the American Avant-Garde,* by Danie Kane. 164–74. New York: Teachers & Writers Collaborative, 2003.

———. Interview by Robert N. Casper et al. *Jubilat* 7 (2003): 71–87. Available online. URL: http://www.januaryriver.net/wellish.pdf. Downloaded December 19, 2008.

———. "The Lyric Lately." *Jacket* 10 (October 1999). Available online. URL: http://jacketmagazine.com/10/welish-on-guest.html. Accessed December 19, 2008.

———. "The New York School and the Metapoetic Lyric." Unpub. paper read at the conference "Opening of the Field: The 1960s." National Poetry Foundation, University of Maine at Orono. June 2000.

———. "What Is Black and White and Read All Over?" *How2* 2, no. 1 (Spring 2003). Available online. URL: http://www.asu.edu/pipercwcenter/how2journal//archive/online_archive/v2_1_2003/current/in_conference/resisting-type/welish.htm. Accessed December 19, 2008.

Whalen, Philip (1923–2002)

"A line of poetry drunkenly scrawled on the margin of a quick / splashed picture" is Philip Whalen's image of the inheritance he honors in the Chinese masters ("Hymnus ad Patrem Sinensis," *Overtime* 32), and it could serve equally well as an image of the inheritance that the NEW YORK SCHOOL honors in Whalen. TED BERRIGAN explained his intention in *The SONNETS* (1964) with reference to Whalen's concept of poetry as "a picture or graph of a mind moving," as he described it in his statement for *The NEW AMERICAN POETRY, 1945–1960* (Berrigan 77). In that anthology Whalen is placed at the head of the group of independent writers, though he is now usually categorized as Beat due to his background. As a student at Reed College in Portland, Oregon, he roomed with Gary Snyder and Lew Welch, and in 1955 he participated with Snyder, ALLEN GINSBERG, and others in the famous "Six Gallery" reading in San Francisco, from which the Beat movement is often dated. Interest in Buddhism, common among the BEATS, led in Whalen's case to his ordination as a Zen monk in 1973.

Whalen's distance from the first-generation New York School is carefully measured in an interview with David Meltzer: "Frank O'Hara was always very nice to me, but I never could really get excited about his writing somehow or another. It's very good, I gather. I am totally unable to read John Ashbery. Kenneth Koch is very funny, and he hates to be funny" ("Whatnot" n.p.). To the second-generation poets, on the other hand, Whalen offered welcome encouragement and even helped to forge connections. CLARK COOLIDGE first heard of Berrigan and "C" magazine from Whalen in 1963 during the Vancouver (Canada) Poetry Conference, which featured ROBERT CREELEY, Robert Duncan, Ginsberg, DENISE LEVERTOV, CHARLES OLSON, and Whalen. In this context, Coolidge recalls, Whalen "was the antidote to the whole sort of furrowed brow scene that was going on. I don't know whether it is a Buddhist attitude, I guess it is, but it's just a sort of lighter sense of everything without avoiding the issues" (n.p.). Whalen exhibits this attitude, very congenial to the New York School, in poems addressed to Berrigan, Coolidge, BILL BERKSON, TOM CLARK, and ALICE NOTLEY, many of whom extended their acquaintance with Whalen during his residence in BOLINAS, CALIFORNIA, during the early 1970s. Notley in particular cites Whalen as "one of my biggest influences" (Notley, interview 530). In her 1980 lecture, "Dr. Williams' Heiresses," she pairs Whalen with FRANK O'HARA as "male-females" playing a crucial role in a mythic lineage of modern poetry, opening the line to the many women writers in the next generation.

Bibliography

Berrigan, Ted. Interview by Ralph Hawkins. In *Talking in Tranquility: Interviews with Ted Berrigan.* Edited by Stephen Ratcliffe and Leslie Scalapino. Bolinas, Calif.: Avenue B; Oakland, Calif.: O Books, 1991, 73–89.

Coolidge, Clark. Interview by Tyler Doherty. *Jacket* 22 (May 2003). Available online. URL: http://jacketmagazine.com/22/doher-cooli.html. Accessed December 19, 2008.

Davidson, Michael. *The San Francisco Renaissance: Poetics and Community at Mid-Century.* Cambridge: Cambridge University Press, 1991.

Notley, Alice. *Dr. Williams' Heiresses.* Berkeley, Calif.: Tuumba Press, 1980.

———. Interview by Edward Foster. In *The World in Time and Space: Towards a History of Innovative American Poetry in Our Time,* edited by Edward Foster and Joseph Donahue, 526–535. Jersey City, N.J.: Talisman House, 2002.

Whalen, Philip. "Desperately Awaiting the Arrival of the China Dinner Man" and "Impatient Poetry for Ted and Alice B." In *Nice to See You: Homage to Ted Berrigan,* edited by Anne Waldman, 90–91. Minneapolis, Minn.: Coffee House Press, 1991.

———. "Friendship Greetings" and "Inside Stuff." In *Homage to Frank O'Hara,* edited by Bill Berkson and Joe LeSueur, 67. Bolinas, Calif.: Big Sky, 1988.

———. *Overtime: Selected Poems.* Edited by Michael Rothenberg. New York: Penguin, 1999.

———. Statement in *The New American Poetry, 1945–1960,* edited by Donald Allen, 420. 1960. Reprint, Berkeley: University of California Press, 1999.

———. "Whatnot." *Jacket* 11 (April 2000). Available online. URL: http://www.jacketmagazine.com/11/whalen-iv-by-meltzer.html. Accessed December 19, 2008.

What's for Dinner? James Schuyler (1978)

Like his previous novel, A NEST OF NINNIES (written in conjunction with JOHN ASHBERY), JAMES SCHUYLER's *What's for Dinner?* revolves around two neighboring suburban households: the Taylors and the Delahanteys. The Taylors are a childless couple whose marriage is strained when wife Charlotte ("Lottie") enters a rehabilitation facility to treat her alcohol dependency, leaving her husband, Norris, free to have an affair with a local widow. Meanwhile, the tight-knit Delahantey clan—comprised of aging Grandmother Biddy; her disciplinarian (and possibly alcoholic) son, Bryan; his wife, Maureen; and their twin sons, Patrick and Michael—is quietly coming unstrung. It is briefly hinted that the teenage twins secretly have an incestuous relationship, but the source of greatest concern for their parents is the boys' suspected use of marijuana.

Although there is more narration in *What's for Dinner?* than in Schuyler's previous novels, its tone remains coolly objective, even, to use Stephen Spender's term, "clinical" (47), and the bulk of the story is still conveyed through dialogue. The author does not tell us how to feel about the players but selectively organizes their own clichéd words to determine their effect. In this manner Schuyler constructs an outsider's critique of "straight" bourgeois values, aided also by continual movement among the three major backdrops: the Taylors' house, the Delahanteys' house, and the psychiatric ward, where Lottie is confined. The fluid rotation of these settings implicitly blurs the line between "healthy" domestic behavior and the dysfunctional state of Lottie's fellow patients. The text suggests that normative middle-class ideals are a dangerous, culturally sanctioned form of repression—a repression of drugs, alcohol, artistic self-expression, and, most of all, sex. It is the latter domain that Schuyler foregrounds at the end of the book with three scenes that depict sex, either metaphorically or literally, in connection with sudden violence, held in check.

Schuyler completed the manuscript for *What's for Dinner?* in 1975, but it was rejected by Random House, triggering a severe anxiety attack. In the end Schuyler backed away from Random House and submitted his work to Black Sparrow Press, which released the book in 1978, with cover art by JANE FREILICHER. The poet's decision to use a small company rather than a major publishing house may have been responsible for the relative lack of critical attention that the novel received.

Bibliography

Ottenberg, Eve. Review of *What's for Dinner?* *Village Voice*, 16 July 1979, 68.

Schuyler, James. *What's for Dinner?* New York: Black Sparrow Press, 1978.

Spender, Stephen. "Meat Loaf." *New York Review of Books*, 11 October 1979, 47.

White Dove Review (1959–1960)

Published in Tulsa, Oklahoma, the *White Dove Review* provided a rallying point for the group of writers who soon migrated from Tulsa to NEW YORK CITY and became prominent members of the second generation of NEW YORK SCHOOL poets. The founding editors were RON PADGETT and DICK GALLUP, with art editors JOE BRAINARD and Michael Marsh—all students at Tulsa's Central High School. TED BERRIGAN, then enrolled at the University of Tulsa, submitted his work through the Lewis Meyer Bookstore, where Padgett worked and displayed the magazine. The two met and quickly became friends, reinforcing each other's enthusiasm for new writing as the circle of writers they were acquainted with expanded.

The editors' vision for the *White Dove Review* combined high ambition and modesty. In their "introductory" statement in the first issue, they dedicated themselves to "culture" and "civilization": "We hope the Schliemanns of the year 4000 do not find only beer cans and long cars in their excavations." From the example of *YŪGEN*, to which Padgett subscribed, he learned that "little things stapled together" could be produced easily and cheaply (Padgett, interview by Foster 103), so there was no practical obstacle to prevent high school students from doing that kind of thing. To ensure high quality, Padgett wrote to LeRoi Jones (AMIRI BARAKA) and other writers who appeared in magazines like *YŪGEN* and asked them to contribute. "I (and the rest of the staff) would be deeply honoured and gratified if you could save that poem you are considering tearing up, and send it to us," Padgett wrote to PAUL BLACKBURN (Kane 245 note 162). Blackburn complied, and his poem "Winter Solstice" appeared in the first issue, along with JACK KEROUAC's "Thrashing Doves" blues and Padgett's poem "Bartok in Autumn." Jones appeared in the second issue along with Berrigan. Other writers from the national scene who published in one of the magazine's five issues were ALLEN GINSBERG, ROBERT CREELEY, GILBERT SORRENTINO, and Clarence Major, the African-American writer who had just started his own magazine, *Coercion Review*, in CHICAGO, ILLINOIS.

Poets of the first-generation New York School are conspicuously absent from this list, although Padgett and Berrigan knew FRANK O'HARA's work, at least. His poem "IN MEMORY OF MY FEELINGS" had appeared in the issue of the *Evergreen Review* (autumn 1958) that bore on its cover a picture of a girl holding a white dove—the source of the title for the *White Dove Review*. Berrigan recalled that he "wasn't ready to write in my own voice" at this time—the sort of writing that, paradoxically, O'Hara might have inspired (Berrigan 47). Describing himself as "very serious" at the time, Padgett recalls being simply "baffled" by the humor in KENNETH KOCH's poetry (interview by Foster 104). Both Padgett and Berrigan quickly changed their attitudes after they arrived in New York, but their first round of introductions to New York's literary scene was drawn from the list of contributors to the *White Dove Review* (Padgett, *Joe* 24).

Bibliography

Berrigan, Ted. Interview by Barry Alpert (1972). In *Talking in Tranquility: Interviews*. Edited by Stephen Ratcliffe and Leslie Scalapino. Bolinas, Calif.: Avenue B; Oakland, Calif.: O Books, 1991, 31–54.

Clay, Steven, and Rodney Phillips. *A Secret Location on the Lower East Side: Adventures in Writing, 1960–1980*. New York: New York Public Library/Granary Books, 1998, 158–159.

Ginsberg, Allen. "My Sad Self." In *Collected Poems, 1947–1980*. New York: Harper & Row, 1984, 201–202.

Kane, Daniel. *All Poets Welcome: The Lower East Side Poetry Scene in the 1960s*. Berkeley: University of California Press, 2003.

Kerouac, Jack. "The Thrashing Doves." In *Postmodern American Poetry*, edited by Paul Hoover, 79–80. New York: Norton, 1994.

Padgett, Ron. Interview by Edward Foster (1991). In *Poetry and Poetics in a New Millennium*, edited by Edward Foster, 100–114. Jersey City, N.J.: Talisman House, 2000.

———. Interview by Noel Black (1998). Puppyflowers Web site. Available online. URL: http://www.puppyflowers.com/arch/rp.htm. Accessed December 19, 2008.

———. *Joe: A Memoir of Joe Brainard*. Minneapolis, Minn.: Coffee House Press, 2004.

———. *Ted: A Personal Memoir of Ted Berrigan*. Great Barrington, Mass.: The Figures, 1993.

"Why I Am Not a Painter" Frank O'Hara
(1956)

In breezy, colloquial style and straightforward narrative structure, FRANK O'HARA's poem makes the question posed in the title appear arbitrary. O'Hara says he would rather be a painter, but he just happens to write poems rather than create paintings. He makes the point by comparing the process leading to the creation of *Sardines* (1955), a painting by his friend Mike Goldberg, and his own series of prose poems, *Oranges* (1949). These are actual creations by each artist, but O'Hara's suggestion that they were created at the same time is fictional; for readers aware of this fact, the distinction between moments in time becomes one of several distinctions the poem undermines, including the distinctions between prose and poetry and

between painting and poetry. Goldberg's painting employs the poet's medium—words—presented unpoetically to the painter in his studio; the word *EXIT*, from the sign over the door, clearly appears at the painting's upper right, and the letters of *SARDINES*—perhaps from a can that would provide the painter's lunch—are still visible at the lower edge. Though it has been mostly erased in the painting, the word *Sardines* persists in the painting's title, just as O'Hara's poems draw on the painter's medium—color—in the collective title *Oranges*. The fact that the poems never mention "orange," like the fact that Goldberg obliterated the word *sardines*, involves both poem and painting in a major question about the nature of abstraction in the aesthetic of the NEW YORK SCHOOL: What goes into the work of art and what is taken out?

O'Hara's poem typifies the close interaction between the New York School poets and contemporary painters. Its various appearances during O'Hara's lifetime provide an index of the rapid increase in public exposure to work by the New York School. First published in the *Evergreen Review* (1957), it was reprinted in DONALD M. ALLEN's anthology *The NEW AMERICAN POETRY, 1945–1960* (1960) and then read on the CBS-TV program *Creative America* by the actor Ossie Davis (1963), seated in front of Goldberg's painting. The poem's style, including the "I do this, I do that" pattern, has proved to be enormously influential. Younger poets from TED BERRIGAN to DAVID LEHMAN have testified to the revelatory experience of reading O'Hara's poem in *The New American Poetry* (1960), and it is has appeared in numerous later anthologies.

Bibliography

Berrigan, Ted. Review of *Lunch Poems*. *Kulchur* 5, no. 17 (Spring 1965): 91–94.

Ferguson, Russell. *In Memory of My Feelings: Frank O'Hara and American Art*. Los Angeles: Museum of Contemporary Art; Berkeley: University of California Press, 1999.

Lehman, David. *The Last Avant-Garde; The Making of the New York School of Poets*. New York: Doubleday, 1998.

O'Hara, Frank. *The Collected Poems*. Edited by Donald Allen. Berkeley: University of California Press, 1995.

Wieners, John (1934–2002)

Although he described himself as "a Boston poet" (Wieners, interview 295), John Wieners drew inspiration from NEW YORK SCHOOL, BEAT, BLACK MOUNTAIN, and SAN FRANCISCO RENAISSANCE poetics to create a unique body of work that can finally be located only in the unstable geography of his own mind. He wrote a very personal poetry influenced through personal contacts. After hearing CHARLES OLSON read in BOSTON, MASSACHUSETTS, in 1954, the year Wieners received his B.A. from Boston College, he decided to follow Olson to BLACK MOUNTAIN COLLEGE, where he spent spring 1955 and summer 1956. In spring 1956 Wieners met FRANK O'HARA in Cambridge, Massachusetts, where they were both involved in the POETS THEATRE production of JOHN ASHBERY's *The Compromise*. Wieners published a section of O'Hara's *Second Avenue* in the first issue of his new journal *Measure* (1957–62), but by that time Wieners was in San Francisco attending the workshops where Jack Spicer and Robert Duncan instructed initiates in the "magic vocabulary" of the San Francisco Renaissance (Brady 331). At the same time Wieners threw himself into San Francisco street life with a sense of abandon that jibed perfectly with the emerging Beat sensibility. "After all / what have we got left," he exclaimed in "Poem for Cocksuckers" (*Selected Poems* 36; Kane), one of the *The Hotel Wentley Poems* (Auerhahn, 1958) collection that Wieners named after the San Francisco flophouse where he crashed.

After his return to the East Coast in 1959 and a period of hospitalization for mental illness (1960–61), O'Hara and Olson again became leading contenders for Wieners's attention. Between 1961 and 1964 Wieners spent most of his time in NEW YORK CITY, sometimes staying in O'Hara's apartment (Gooch 370). A group of poems he published in the *FLOATING BEAR* (number 10, 1961) included "For F O'H / After *meditations* [*in an emergency*]," a nod to O'Hara that returned the favor already shown to Wieners in O'Hara's poems "To John Wieners" (1956), "A Young Poet" (1957), and "Les Luths" (1959). In summer 1965, on O'Hara's recommendation, Wieners and Olson participated in the SPOLETO FESTIVAL OF TWO WORLDS. They went on to the BERKELEY POETRY CONFERENCE and eventually to the University of Buffalo, where Olson had offered Wieners a teaching position. Wieners's relations with both Olson and O'Hara were broken in 1966, in the former instance by rivalry over a woman (significant to Wieners despite his HOMOSEXUALITY) and in the latter case by O'Hara's death, remembered by Wieners in his elegy "After Reading *Second Avenue*" (*Selected Poems* 220–221). The complicated legacy each of these mentors left in Wieners's work has been succinctly summarized by Andrea Brady, who remarked on "O'Hara's cosmopolitanism and humor taken to extremes in Wieners's obsession with Hollywood and camp melodramatics, and Olson's emphasis on the present and the personal providing the springboard for Wieners's early Rimbaudian writing" (345). Olson had recommended the French poet Arthur Rimbaud to Wieners while they were at Black Mountain College.

Wieners's legacy, in turn, to later poets of the New York School starts to become evident with the publication of his two Angel Hair books: *Asylum Poems* (1969) and *Hotels* (1974). As Wieners had resettled in Boston in 1970, he provided orientation to the local scene to New York poets who had moved there temporarily, such as ARAM SAROYAN and Angel Hair editor LEWIS WARSH. On the other hand, for a young Boston poet like JACK KIMBALL, Wieners provided a vital link to New York and the broader world of the avant-garde. As a means of establishing avant-garde credentials, Wieners's work has been featured in the inaugural issues of Boston-area publications from *The Boston Eagle* (1973–74), edited by WILLIAM CORBETT, LEE HARWOOD, and Warsh, to *Pressed Wafer* (1999–   ), edited by Corbett and Joseph Torra. *Pressed Wafer*, which takes its title from a volume Wieners had published in Buffalo (Gallery Upstairs, 1967), issued a volume in tribute to Wieners (*The Blind See Only This World*, 2000) with contributions by many writers associated with the New York School, including Ashbery, KENWARD ELMSLIE, BARBARA GUEST, BERNADETTE MAYER, ANGE MLINKO, RON PADGETT, ANNE WALDMAN, and Warsh.

Bibliography

Berkson, Bill, and Joe LeSueur, eds. *Homage to Frank O'Hara*. Bolinas, Calif.: Big Sky, 1988. [Includes

Wieners, "Chop-House Memories" and "After Reading *Second Avenue*."]

Brady, Andrea. "The Other Poet: Wieners, O'Hara, Olson." In *Don't Ever Get Famous: Essays on New York Writing after the New York School*, edited by Daniel Kane, 317–347. Champaign, Ill.: Dalkey Archive Press, 2006.

Clay, Steven, and Rodney Phillips. "Measure." In *A Secret Location on the Lower East Side: Adventures in Writing, 1960–1980*. New York: New York Public Library/Granary Books, 1998, 76.

Corbett, William, Michael Gizzi, and Joseph Torra, eds. *The Blind See Only This World: Poems for John Wieners*. New York: Granary Books; Boston: Pressed Wafer, 2000.

Creeley, Robert. "How Is It Far If You Think It?" *New York Times Book Review*, 23 November 1986, 15–16.

Gooch, Brad. *City Poet: The Life and Times of Frank O'Hara*. New York: Knopf, 1993.

Kane, Daniel. Companion CD to *All Poets Welcome: The Lower East Side Poetry Scene in the 1960s*. Berkeley: University of California Press, 2003. [Includes audio recording of Wieners reading "Poem for Cocksuckers" at Café Le Metro, 1963.]

Kimball, Jack. "John and the Four Dunn(e)s." *Jacket 21* (February 2003). Available online. URL: http://jacketmagazine.com/21/kimb-rev1.html. Accessed December 19, 2008.

Moxley, Jennifer. "Rimbaud's Foolish Virgin, Wieners's 'Feminine Soliloquy,' and the Metaphorical Resistance of the Lyric Body." *Talisman* 34 (Winter–Spring 2007): 71–79.

O'Hara, Frank. *The Collected Poems*. Rev. ed. Edited by Donald Allen. Berkeley: University of California Press, 1995.

Sorrentino, Gilbert. "Emerald on the Beach." *Something Said*. 2d ed. Chicago: Dalkey Archive Press, 2001, 168–172.

Wieners, John. *Cultural Affairs in Boston: Poetry & Prose, 1956–1985*. Santa Rosa, Calif.: Black Sparrow Press, 1988.

———. Interview by Charley Shively (1973/1977). In *Selected Poems, 1958–1984*. Santa Rosa, Calif.: Black Sparrow Press, 1986, 293–308.

———. *Selected Poems, 1958–1984*. Edited by Raymond Foye. Preface by Allen Ginsberg. Santa Rosa, Calif.: Black Sparrow Press, 1986.

———. *707 Scott Street*. Los Angeles: Sun & Moon Press, 1996.

Winkfield, Trevor (1944–   ) *artist*

Painter Trevor Winkfield is, with GEORGE SCHNEEMAN and JOE BRAINARD, the artist most often associated with the second generation of NEW YORK SCHOOL poets. He was born in Leeds, England, in 1944, where his schoolboy passion for Marcel Duchamp led to the writer RAYMOND ROUSSEL (a great influence on Duchamp), which in turn led to an interest in JOHN ASHBERY's TRANSLATIONs of Roussel, and ultimately to Ashbery himself as a poet. He has paradoxically noted, "My two favourite twentieth-century artists are Marcel Duchamp—cerebral—and [Georges] Braque—sensuosity" (Corbett, "Mysterious Clarity" 94), and his own work may be seen as an attempt to reconcile these two forces. Though he attended Leeds College of Art and the Royal College of Art, Winkfield regards himself as a self-taught painter. In 1969 he moved from London to NEW YORK CITY, where he continues to live and exhibit.

In both his life and his work Winkfield provides an object lesson for the culture of the New York School poets. Winkfield has produced artist books in COLLABORATION with many of the principal poets of both the first and second generations of the New York School. Though primarily a painter, early in his career Winkfield devoted time and energy to both editing and translating and more recently has written critical art essays (even writing prose poems of his own prior to his career as a painter). Speaking about painters who have also been poets, Winkfield has remarked, "If it was good enough for Francis Picabia it's good enough for me!" (Winkfield and Devaney). Art critic Jed Perl has noted, "Winkfield would no doubt say that painters can learn from writers (and vice versa)" (Perl, n.p.). Indeed, the cornerstone of Winkfield's give-and-take collaborations is his lifelong friendships with the writers involved.

Appreciating the greater context of Winkfield's milieu and its frequent cross-pollinations requires expanding the notion of collaboration to reflect how the everyday nature of his friendships and work often intersect. To name but one example, in 1988, just after Ashbery's mother had died, Ashbery was suffering from writer's block when, during a car ride, Winkfield suggested that Ashbery write about his late mother, albeit allusively (Winkfield and Devaney). This was the origin of FLOW CHART

(1991), for which Winkfield supplied one of his most striking covers.

A tabulation of Winkfield's most important efforts as a collaborator, editor, and translator would include the following: *Icteric* (coeditor, 1967–68), JUILLARD (1968–72), and *The Lewis Carroll Circular* (1972–73). He also edited JAMES SCHUYLER's *The Home Book* (Z PRESS, 1977). In 1970 he published HARRY MATHEWS's first book of poems, *The Ring* (Juillard Editions). He edited and (along with Ashbery, Mathews, and KENNETH KOCH) contributed translations for Roussel's *How I Wrote Certain of My Books* (Exact Change, 1995), a text from which Winkfield derived many of his early painting methods. Mysterious, matter-of-fact, and marvelous, Winkfield's paintings have been used as book covers by several of his friends. He designed covers for the second editions of Schuyler's *Freely Espousing* (SUN, 1979) and Ashbery's *Rivers and Mountains* (Ecco, 1977) and *Three Poems* (Ecco, 1989). He has worked on several books with KENWARD ELMSLIE, including CYBERSPACE (Granary Books, 2000) and *Snippets* (Tibor de Nagy Editions, 2003). Finely produced limited editions of his collaborations include RON PADGETT's *How to Be a Woodpecker* (Toothpaste, 1983), Ashbery's *Novel* (Grenfell, 1998), LARRY FAGIN's *Dig and Delve* (Granary Books, 1999), BARBARA GUEST's *Outside of This, That Is* (Z Press, 1999), and CHARLES NORTH's *Tulips* (Phylum, 2004). His earlier collaborative book with Mathews, *The Way Home*, was reprinted as part of Mathews's *The Human Country: New and Selected Stories* (Dalkey Archive Press, 2002), which also featured Winkfield's painting *The Poet* on the cover. In 2004 Bamberger Books published *Trevor Winkfield's Drawings*, the most complete collection of the artist's drawings to date, including an extensive checklist.

Bibliography

Ashbery, John. "Trevor Winkfield" (1986). In *Reported Sightings: Art Chronicles, 1957–1987*. Edited by David Bergman. 1989. Reprint, Cambridge, Mass.: Harvard University Press, 1991, 169–173.

Corbett, William. "A Mysterious Clarity." *Modern Painters* 15, no. 2 (Summer 2002): 92–95.

———. "Trevor Winkfield's Altarpieces." In *All Prose: Selected Essays and Reviews*. Cambridge, Mass.: Zoland, 2001, 139–141.

Esplund, Lance. "Winkfield's Vocations." *Art in America* 91, no. 1 (January 2003): 92–95.

North, Charles. "Trevor Winkfield's Radical Daftness" and "Trevor Winkfield's Prose Writings." In *No Other Way: Selected Prose*. Brooklyn, N.Y.: Hanging Loose Press, 1998, 47–49, 162–163.

Perl, Jed. *Trevor Winkfield's Pageant*. Introduction by John Ashbery. West Stockbridge, Mass.: Hard Press, 1997.

Winkfield, Trevor. "How They Wrote Certain of My Drawings." In *Trevor Winkfield's Drawings*. Whitmore Lake, Mich.: Bamberger Books, 2004.

———. *In the Scissors' Courtyard: Selected Writings, 1967–75*. Flint, Mich.: Bamberger Books, 1994.

———. "A Resurrected Childhood." *Arts Magazine* 60, no. 9 (May 1986): 36–40.

Winkfield, Trevor, and Tom Devaney. Conversation and personal correspondence, 2003–2004.

World, The (1967–)

The spirit of community that animated the POETRY PROJECT AT ST. MARK'S CHURCH IN-THE-BOWERY has found its ideal expression in *The World*, the project's official journal. ANNE WALDMAN, the editor who has been involved in the journal most consistently, explains: "the magazine's the real meeting place & it's seeing all these works next to each other that's the big secret of COMMUNITY" (Waldman, "Welcome," *Another World* n.p.). Her phrase "all these works" reflects the expansiveness of the editorial policy that shaped *The World*—or rendered it shapeless, in the view of critics—and helped determine its title. The title is also intended to suggest a newspaper (Waldman, "Outrider" 159). The Poetry Project's founders wanted a publication that would treat poetry as news, presenting some work as soon as it was written. After one issue they abandoned a glossy "art" magazine called *The Genre of Silence* and "copied" the mimeo format of TED BERRIGAN's "C" magazine, according to Joel Sloman, the first editor of *The World* (Kane 155). According to Waldman, who began to assume responsibility with the second issue, "there's that sense of immediacy and lack of pretension, because the mimeo format is a fairly modest one, and it also has that kind of fly-by-night underground quality" ("Outrider" 159). In later years computerized desktop publishing gave *The World* a more polished look without sacrificing spontaneity.

Not surprisingly, early issues of *The World* feature an unusual number of COLLABORATIONs and related works that employ "intertextual collage," as Daniel Kane has noted (157). The first issue (January 1967) opens with a sequence of texts coauthored by Berrigan, LEWIS WARSH, Waldman, and MICHAEL BROWNSTEIN. The atmosphere of close friendship is further intensified by frequent references to the intersections of the authors' personal lives. For instance, "80th Congress," a collaborative poem by Berrigan and DICK GALLUP in the third issue (May 1967), begins: "It's 2 a.m. at Lewis & Anne's, which is where it's at / On Saint Mark's Place." FRANK O'HARA, the poet most responsible for this mode of writing, had died just before *The World* was launched, but his work survives in the pages of the magazine not only in the form of imitation but in his own collaborations. "Poem (after a poem by Ruth Krauss)" (number 7, October 1967) actually *is* a poem by RUTH KRAUSS, mistakenly identified as O'Hara's when it was found among his papers. O'Hara's authentic collaboration with BILL BERKSON, "N.F.T.I.," appeared in a special issue of *The World* devoted to collaboration (number 12, June 1968), along with JOHN ASHBERY's first appearance in the magazine, in collaborations with LEE HARWOOD ("Train Poem") and JAMES SCHUYLER ("Out at Lenore Petit's" and "The Rash"). Both O'Hara and Ashbery are represented in a later special issue devoted to TRANSLATION (number 27, April 1973), guest-edited by RON PADGETT. Ashbery translates six sonnets by the 16th-century French poet Jean-Baptiste Chassignet. O'Hara is represented by a poem he had written in French, "Choses Passagères," translated by John Bátki as "Passing Things." When KENNETH KOCH originally published "Choses Passagères" in the "collaboration" issue of *LOCUS SOLUS* (number 2, summer 1961), he listed O'Hara and "the French language" as coauthors, a view that helps explain the association between translation and collaboration in *The World.*

The World has been published on an irregular schedule. For instance, Padgett's translation issue was succeeded the following month by an issue of autobiographical writing (number 28, May 1973) edited by Warsh, but a year went by before the next issue (number 29, April 1974), the first of two devoted to a variety of critical prose and commentary (the second appeared two years later [number 30, July 1976]). The first seven years saw publication of half of the total number of issues that appeared up to 2002, when publication was suspended after issue number 58. In June 2005 the Poetry Project published a more streamlined magazine, *The Recluse,* in place of *The World,* which was described as "currently on hiatus."

Waldman has edited three anthologies drawn mostly from work published in *The World.* The first and second volumes (1969, 1971) coincided with the appearance of JOHN BERNARD MYERS's *The POETS OF THE NEW YORK SCHOOL* (1969) and Padgett and DAVID SHAPIRO's *ANTHOLOGY OF NEW YORK POETS* (1970). A valuable feature of Waldman's first volume is an appendix reproducing the covers of the first 12 issues of *The World,* including three by GEORGE SCHNEEMAN and one by JOE BRAINARD. Artists who designed covers for later issues include PHILIP GUSTON, LARRY RIVERS, and ALEX KATZ.

Bibliography

Kane, Daniel. *All Poets Welcome: The Lower East Side Poetry Scene in the 1960s.* Berkeley: University of California Press, 2003.

O'Hara, Frank. "Poem (after a poem by Ruth Krauss)." In *Poems Retrieved.* Edited by Donald Allen. San Francisco: Grey Fox, 1996, 230–231.

Reeve, F. D. "Fresh Airs." *Poetry* 119, no. 1 (October 1971): 39–44.

Waldman, Anne. "The Outrider Legacy" (1992). In *Vow to Poetry: Essays, Interview, and Manifestos.* Minneapolis, Minn.: Coffee House Press, 2001, 157–170.

———. Statement in *A Secret Location on the Lower East Side: Adventures in Writing, 1960–1980,* by Steven Clay and Rodney Phillips, 186–188. New York: New York Public Library/Granary Books, 1998.

———. "Welcome." In *Another World: A Second Anthology of Works from the St. Mark's Poetry Project.* Indianapolis, Ind.: Bobbs-Merrill, 1971.

———. *Out of This World: An Anthology of the St. Mark's Poetry Project, 1966–1991.* New York: Crown, 1991.

———. *The World Anthology: Poems from the St. Mark's Poetry Project.* Indianapolis, Ind.: Bobbs-Merrill, 1969.

Yau, John (1950–) *art critic*

John Yau was born in Lynn, Massachusetts, a small mill town north of BOSTON, MASSACHUSETTS, in 1950, shortly after his parents emigrated from China. He grew up mainly in Boston and attended Boston University for two years before transferring to Bard College, where he studied with the poet Robert Kelly (1935–) and received his B.A. in 1972. In 1977 Yau received his M.F.A. from Brooklyn College, where he studied with JOHN ASHBERY. Since then he has gone on to become a well-established art critic, having contributed articles to every major American art periodical as well as dozens of catalogs and written books on JASPER JOHNS and ANDY WARHOL, among others. He has taught at numerous institutions, including Bard College, Brown University, Emerson College, Maryland Institute College of Art, and the University of California at Berkeley. Yau has received numerous fellowships, grants, and awards, including a grant from the National Endowment for the Arts and the Academy of American Poets' Lavan Younger Poets Award. In the late 1990s he established Black Square Editions, a small press that publishes both innovative young writers and books in TRANSLATION. In 2002 he was named a Chevalier des Arts et Lettres by the French government for his service to the arts. He currently lives in Manhattan with his wife, the artist Eve Aschheim, and their daughter.

When asked by Edward Foster whether he thought it was a mistake to associate his work with that of the NEW YORK SCHOOL, Yau replied, "Yes, I think so" (interview 46). At first glance Yau's state-

ment appears to be correct. His work contains none of the quotidian references that are so prominent in the work of FRANK O'HARA, JAMES SCHUYLER, TED BERRIGAN, and many other New York School poets. In fact, Yau's work interrogates the entire notion of poetic subjectivity. He states:

> To write about one's life in terms of a subjective "I" is to accept an academicized, historical legacy—it is to fulfill the terms of the oppressor. I suppose I don't know who this "I" would or could speak for. Myself, what for? Maybe because I don't think what's autobiographical is necessarily interesting because it happens to one but because it might happen to more than one (Yau, interview 49).

Each of Yau's poems seems to originate from a different point of view. At times the perspective even shifts mid-poem, as in "Double Self-Portrait," which cleverly fuses the identities of Warhol and Chairman Mao (*My Heart* 153–158). The "I" in Yau's work literally becomes—to borrow Arthur Rimbaud's phrase—"an other" (Rimbaud 6), a politicized gesture that is often read by critics as commenting on Yau's position as a first-generation Chinese American. Although it may seem different from O'Hara's "PERSONISM," Yau's presentation of multiple subjectivities can be seen as deriving from Ashbery's pronoun slippage.

Like O'Hara and Ashbery, Yau spent many years working as an art critic, and his close relationship to the art world has affected his work in different ways. He has collaborated with several artists; an especially notable instance is BIG CITY PRIMER (Timken Publishers, 1991), with the photographer Bill Barrette. Yau has written works inspired by various artworks, such as the title poem from his book *Corpse and Mirror* (Holt, Rinehart and Winston, 1983), which takes its name from a Johns painting. At times Yau's work even adopts the structure of the work that inspires it. "830 Fireplace Road," for example, is a sonnet composed of variations on the JACKSON POLLOCK statement: "When I am *in* my painting, I'm not aware of what I'm doing." The poem functions gesturally in a manner similar to Pollock's drip paintings, twisting Pollock's original sentence into lines like, "In my am, not am in my, not of when I am, of what" (*Borrowed Love* 12). Yau's work is also often characterized by intense imagery that is reminiscent of the early imagist poets, but with a surrealist twist, for example, "One Hundred Views of the Outskirts of Manhattan," which begins with the couplet: "An immense copper moth / enters the new firehouse" (*Borrowed Love* 87).

The process of composition in Yau's work is often more important than its content. In the late 1970s Yau met HARRY MATHEWS, who introduced him to word substitution games and other OULIPO techniques. Yau has drawn on these techniques—as well as classic literary FORMs such as the pantoum, sestina, and villanelle—throughout his career in order to shift the focus of his work in this process-oriented direction. Yau also takes formal inspiration from film, from "that kind of *speed* of seeing, the seamless jumps, the echoes, and the way something dissolves into something else" (Yau, interview 48). This montage technique can be seen in many of Yau's poems, especially those that are composed of couplets. As Charles Borkhuis points out, the effect of this is to create a sort of "parasurrealism that examines its own lyrical structure as it proceeds, often in the form of serial lists that, like conceptual art, utilize variety within repetition" (Borkhuis 251). The above-mentioned sample of "One Hundred Views of the Outskirts of Manhattan," for example, shifts from the image of the moth entering the firehouse to "The sole refurbisher of car / upholstery clutches his throat" in the very next couplet (*Borrowed Love*

87). The poem accrues meaning through the juxtaposition of disparate images, a process that Yau also relates back to ABSTRACT EXPRESSIONISM: "If you think of an abstract painting by Jackson Pollock, each brushstroke stands on its own. Nevertheless, each brushstroke, each pour of paint adds up to something. I'm interested in the couplet being like a brushstroke that stands on its own, that doesn't describe anything but itself" (Yau, "Poets Chat" n.p.). Yau also takes inspiration from film iconography, for instance, in his series of poems GENGHIS CHAN: PRIVATE EYE (1987–   ).

Most criticism of Yau has dealt primarily with his position as a Chinese-American poet, a fact that makes Yau rather uneasy. "The authority on poetry announced that I discovered I was Chinese when it was to my advantage to do so," he writes in "Ing Grish" (383). In fact, Yau's work has been engaged with the paradox of Chinese-American identity since his first book, *Crossing Canal Street* (Bellevue, 1976). In terms of NEW YORK CITY geography, Canal Street is, of course, the boundary that separates Chinatown from the art world of SoHo. Identity POLITICS is only one of the many rich subtexts that flow beneath Yau's work. Future readings of Yau will benefit from the revisionary strand of surrealism that is currently being theorized by younger poet-critics.

Bibliography

Borkhuis, Charles. "Writing from Inside Language: Late Surrealism and Textual Poetry in France and the United States." In *Telling It Slant: Avant-Garde Poetics of the 1990s,* edited by Mark Wallace and Steven Marks, 237–253. Tuscaloosa: University of Alabama Press, 2002.

Foster, Edward, ed. John Yau issue. *Talisman* 5 (Fall 1990).

O'Hara, Frank. "Personism: A Manifesto" (1959). In *Collected Poems.* Rev. ed. Edited by Donald Allen. Berkeley: University of California Press, 1995, 498–499.

Rimbaud, Arthur. Letter to Georges Izambard, May 1871. In *Collected Poems.* Edited by Oliver Bernard. London: Penguin, 1986, 5–7.

Yau, John. *Borrowed Love Poems.* New York: Penguin, 2002.

———. *Edificio Sayonara.* Santa Rosa, Calif.: Black Sparrow, 1992.

————. *Forbidden Entries*. Santa Rosa, Calif.: Black Sparrow, 1996.

————. "Ing Grish." *Conjunctions* 37 (Fall 2001): 381–384.

————. Interview by Edward Foster. *Talisman* 5 (Fall 1990): 31–50.

————. *In the Realm of Appearances: The Art of Andy Warhol*. Hopewell, N.J.: Ecco, 1993.

————. *My Heart Is That Eternal Rose Tattoo*. Santa Rosa, Calif.: Black Sparrow, 2001.

————. "Poets Chat." February 2000. Teachers & Writers Collaborative. Formerly available online. URL: http://www.writenet.org/poetschat/poetschat_jyau.html.

————. *Radiant Silhouette: New & Selected Work, 1974–1988*. Santa Rosa, Calif.: Black Sparrow, 1989.

————. *The United States of Jasper Johns*. Cambridge, Mass.: Zoland Books, 1996.

Yūgen (1958–1962)

Sensing "a new consciousness in arts and letters," as he announced on the cover of the first issue (Jones, interview 318), LeRoi Jones (later AMIRI BARAKA) began *Yūgen* with Hettie Cohen (1934–   ) in the hope of gathering energies that were in the air rather than arguing a case for a specific "movement." The initial contributors were simply people whom Jones had gotten to know in the New York arts scene. Several, like Jones, were African American (Bobb Hamilton, Allen Polite, Tom Postell, A. B. SPELLMAN), but they disappeared from later issues, a fact that Jones looked back on with regret (*Autobiography* 231). To the extent that *Yūgen*'s identity could be characterized, it was Beat, a consequence of the early involvement of ALLEN GINSBERG as a contributor and promoter. The magazine's Japanese title reflects the BEATS' interest in Eastern religion, particularly Zen Buddhism; however, Jones's immediate source was a classical statement on Noh drama (*Autobiography* 220), and it seems likely that his interest in a standard that prescribed "even the most casual utterance will be graceful" was as much theatrical as religious (Seami 260). From this perspective *Yūgen* is an appropriate channel for the publication of both "Personal Poem" (number 6, 1960) and the related manifesto "PERSONISM" (number 7, 1961) by FRANK O'HARA, who was alerted to *Yūgen* by

Ginsberg and soon became a close friend of Jones's. As for Eastern influences, O'Hara's attitude is implied in a POEM-PAINTING he produced with Norman Bluhm, which was reproduced in *Yūgen* number 7 (64). The style of "ACTION PAINTING" recalls the performance of Japanese calligraphy, a connection Hettie Jones acknowledged (55). But O'Hara's words seem to come from offstage: "No / I don't feel / very haiku / today."

Like DONALD M. ALLEN's *NEW AMERICAN POETRY, 1945–1960* of the same period, *Yūgen* records the confluence of several streams of experimental poetry: Beat (Ray Bremser, WILLIAM S. BURROUGHS, GREGORY CORSO, DIANE DI PRIMA, Ginsberg, JACK KEROUAC, Michael McClure, Gary Snyder, PHILIP WHALEN, JOHN WIENERS), BLACK MOUNTAIN (PAUL BLACKBURN, ROBERT CREELEY, Larry Eigner, Ed Dorn, CHARLES OLSON, JOEL OPPENHEIMER), NEW YORK SCHOOL (JOHN ASHBERY, BARBARA GUEST, KENNETH KOCH, O'Hara), and SAN FRANCISCO RENAISSANCE (Robin Blaser, Ron Loewinsohn, David Meltzer, George Stanley). Jones claimed that another influential editor, PAUL CARROLL, took his bearings in contemporary poetry partly from *Yūgen* (Jones, interview 319). Ashbery's "Leaving the Atocha Station," the subject of a chapter in Carroll's *The Poem in Its Skin* (1968), appeared in *Yūgen* number 7 following the appearance of a poem by Carroll in the preceding issue. In its final issues *Yūgen* itself began to publish critical prose, as exemplified by O'Hara's "Personism" or "Some Notes" by GILBERT SORRENTINO, both in issue number 7. But, as Sorrentino later observed, *Yūgen* "simply did not have the room to print anything more than short critiques," and Jones did not have the money to make more room (Sorrentino 310–311). He let *Yūgen* die as he pursued two alternatives, the *FLOATING BEAR*, a cheap mimeograph newsletter, and *KULCHUR*, a professionally printed journal like *Yūgen* in appearance but unlike *Yūgen* in its having solid financial backing. Both of these publications would continue Jones's involvement with New York School poets that had begun through *Yūgen*.

Bibliography

Jones, Hettie. *How I Became Hettie Jones*. New York: Dutton, 1990.

Jones, LeRoi (Amiri Baraka). *The Autobiography of LeRoi Jones*. Chicago: Lawrence Hill, 1997.

———. "An Interview on *Yūgen*" (1960). In *The Little Magazine in America: A Modern Documentary History*, edited by Elliott Anderson and Mary Kinzie, 317–323. Yonkers, N.Y.: Pushcart Press, 1978.

Seami Motokiyo. "On Attaining the Stage of *Yūgen*." Translated by Ryusaku Tsunoda and Donald Keene. In *Anthology of Japanese Literature*, edited by Donald Keene, 260–262. UNESCO Collection of Representative Works (Japanese Series). New York: Grove, 1955.

Sorrentino, Gilbert. "*Neon, Kulchur,* etc." In *The Little Magazine in America: A Modern Documentary History*, edited by Elliott Anderson and Mary Kinzie, 298–316. Yonkers, N.Y.: Pushcart Press, 1978.

Z

Zavatsky, Bill (1943–)

Growing up in Bridgeport, Connecticut, Bill Zavatsky felt the lure of NEW YORK CITY through JAZZ MUSIC, which he aspired to play professionally, and through the light in his uncle's eyes when he spoke of his days at Columbia University, "where people really cared / about the mind!" ("My Uncle at the Wake" [1977], *Where* X 69). When Zavatsky arrived at Columbia himself in 1965, the *Columbia Review* was about to be taken over by students of KENNETH KOCH, "the young New York School elite," as Zavatsky perceived them ("Brodey Questionnaire" n.p.). He did not join the movement, feeling himself to be an outsider both by circumstance (he was enrolled in General Studies, the university's adult-education division) and by temperament: "my extended life as a Catholic boy had scorched any tendencies to become a disciple" ("Brodey Questionnaire" n.p.). Zavatsky became involved with another student publication, *Sundial,* with a more eclectic editorial policy. Eventually, under Zavatsky's editorship, *Sundial* became the independent magazine *SUN* (1971–83). Under the SUN imprint Zavatsky also published a series of books (1972–85), including his own first collection, *Theories of Rain* (1975) and important volumes by many other NEW YORK SCHOOL poets (MAUREEN OWEN, RON PADGETT, PETER SCHJELDAHL, JAMES SCHUYLER, TONY TOWLE, PAUL VIOLI, MARJORIE WELISH).

Besides editing and publishing, teaching and translating have especially drawn Zavatsky into the New York School orbit. From his present perspec-

tive as a teacher at the Trinity School in New York for more than 20 years, he observes, "My writing is almost unthinkable without the whetstone of teaching" (questionnaire response n.p.). From 1975 to 1977 he taught workshops at the POETRY PROJECT AT ST. MARK'S CHURCH IN-THE-BOWERY, where participants included third-generation New York School poets such as MAGGIE DUBRIS, EILEEN MYLES, and SUSIE TIMMONS. In 1974 Zavatsky began conducting workshops for the TEACHERS & WRITERS COLLABORATIVE, and he has contributed to many of its publications, including *The Whole Word Catalogue 2* (1977), coedited with Padgett. Padgett was also Zavatsky's collaborator in his first major TRANSLATION project, *The Poems of A. O. Barnabooth* by Valéry Larbaud (Grossman, 1975). Other French authors whom Zavatsky later translated include Max Jacob, Robert Desnos, and André Breton.

Of the first-generation New York School poets, Zavatsky shows most affinity with FRANK O'HARA and Schuyler for their realism and range. Though the New York City that O'Hara depicted was essentially "imaginary" ("Brodey Questionnaire" n.p.), in Zavatsky's view, it shared specific place-names with the real city where Zavatsky lived. As for the world of jazz, in which O'Hara evoked names such as Billie Holiday and Miles Davis, Zavatsky was quite willing to follow the lead of the imagination in his own poems, such as "Elegy (For Bill Evans, 1929–1980)" (1980), "For Steve Royal" (1985), and "*Live at the Village Vanguard*" (2005). More than O'Hara, Zavatsky finds, "James Schuyler remains for me the best, the most complete, of the first-generation New York School poets" (questionnaire response n.p.). He is especially proud to have kept in print Schuyler's volume *Freely Espousing* (Doubleday, 1969) through a SUN reissue (1979). As Schuyler grew even more candid in his later work, he "found a way into his loss and its attendant grief that I don't see in his New York School peers," Zavatsky states, "and the gravitas that he found (without letting it sink his work) makes him more three-dimensional than the other poets" (questionnaire response n.p.).

"Loss and its attendant grief" define major themes for Zavatsky, too. His ability to suspend those themes between the poles of wit and sentimentality make for the "dazzling high-wire act" for which the poet Hugh Seidman (1940–) praises Zavatsky's volume *Where X Marks the Spot* (2006), only his second collection in 30 years, in a back-cover blurb. The delay in publication may have something to do with the "demons of anger, self-pity, loneliness, and regret" that Zavatsky's longtime friend Padgett names in his comment on the back cover of the volume. But the work presented, Padgett adds, is "capacious enough for elegy and humor."

Zavatsky was awarded a Guggenheim Fellowship in poetry for 2008–09.

Bibliography

McHenry, Eric. Review of *Where X Marks the Spot. New York Times Book Review*, 10 December 2006, 15.

Saroyan, Aram. "Look We've Come Through!" *Jacket* 30 (July 2006). Available online. URL: http://jacketmagazine.com/30/saroy-zavat.html. Accessed December 18, 2008.

Yau, John. "Still Believe in the Rainbow." *Brooklyn Rail* (June 2006). Available online. URL: http://brooklynrail.org/2006/6/books/still-believe-in-the-rainbow. Accessed December 18, 2008.

Zavatsky, Bill. "The Brodey Questionnaire." Unpublished manuscript prepared ca. 1978 for a project by Jim Brodey about New York School poets.

———. "On Publishing My First Book of Poems in Thirty Years." Poetry Foundation Web site. Available online. URL: http://www.poetryfoundation.org/dispatches/journals/2006.08.14.html. Accessed December 18, 2008.

———. Questionnaire response for *Encyclopedia of the New York School Poets,* 14 December 2005.

———. *Where X Marks the Spot.* Brooklyn, N.Y.: Hanging Loose Press, 2006.

0 to 9 (1967–1969)

In the six issues of *0 to 9* magazine, edited by BERNADETTE MAYER and Vito Acconci (1940–), NEW YORK SCHOOL poets met visual artists at the intersection of MINIMALISM, CONCEPTUAL ART, and PERFORMANCE ART. Although the mimeograph format limited the magazine's ability to reproduce visual art, texts by artists featured prominently, including "Sentences on Conceptual Art" (number 5, January 1969) by Sol LeWitt (1928–) and a set of "Sketchbook Notes" (number 6, July 1969) by JASPER JOHNS that describe his *0 through 9* works, alluded to in the magazine's title. In what was widely perceived as a challenge to ABSTRACT EXPRESSIONISM, Johns's numerals provided the artist with a starting point at a zero-degree of emotion, expressing nothing. "Nothing" is the title of a sequence of 13 poems by CLARK COOLIDGE that leads off issue number 4 of *0 to 9* (June 1968). The first line reads: "the a." In the previous issue (January 1968), Coolidge's rival in minimalism, ARAM SAROYAN, comes even closer to Johns in printing columns of the same number repeated down the middle of the page, "22" on page 22 and "23" on page 23. Pages 32 and 33 are entirely blank except for the page number at bottom right and the name "Aram Saroyan" on page 32 at top left. Of course, it is not strictly accurate to say that the pages are otherwise blank, because they consist of a material substance, paper. The elimination of expressionism in *0 to 9* served to foreground the properties of the medium, a basic principle of modernist abstraction. An important literary precedent in this respect is the treatment of words as things in the work of Gertrude Stein, who is represented in issue number 2 of *0 to 9* (August 1967) by "In" (1913), from *Bee Time Vine and Other Pieces* (1953). Mayer's *Story* (1968), one of several pamphlets published separately under the auspices of *0 to 9*, is strongly influenced by Stein.

Mayer and Acconci were related through Acconci's marriage to the artist Rosemary Mayer

(1943–   ), Bernadette's sister, and through a common dissatisfaction with the "PERSONISM" of New York School poetry. With obvious exceptions, such as Coolidge and Saroyan, the editors seem to have been reluctant to include New York School work in *0 to 9*. The work they did include is not particularly representative of the poets. KENNETH KOCH, the only first-generation poet to make an appearance, offers a brief poem, "The Conquest of PIZARRO" (number 5), that plays with the sound of "Peru" to turn it into "Europe." LARRY FAGIN presents seven words and one fragment on a two-page spread (number 6) as an homage to minimalist artist Donald Judd (1928–94). RON PADGETT and TOM CLARK made it into issue number 2 as "friendly enemies," Acconci recalls (Acconci 9). Mayer recalls that they never accepted any of the COLLABORATIONS submitted by Padgett and TED BERRIGAN (Rifkin n.p.), though, in fact, one was published ("Inner Landscapes," number 3).

Of the works contributed by poets associated with the New York School, those by JOHN PERREAULT and JOHN GIORNO come closest to the path both Acconci and Mayer were to take in the direction of performance and conceptual art. Several of Perreault's texts (numbers 5 and 6) are scripts for or reports on actions to be undertaken in nontheatrical settings, such as the "situation" described by Acconci in *Street Works* (March–May 1969), a compilation by various authors (including ANNE WALDMAN and LEWIS WARSH) published as a supplement to the final issue of *0 to 9*. Acconci reports: "I stood on a corner, noted (mentally) a person walking from that corner to the next, noted the time, ran from that corner to the next," etc. Having stepped off the page into the street, Acconci soon decided to leave words behind altogether. He became an important pioneer in the use of the artist's body as the material for performance. Mayer, who grew closer to the New York School in the following years, remained committed to words. On the pages of *0 to 9* (for example, "Poems," number 3), they perform in ways that sometimes resemble the patterns of repetition that Giorno developed from the experience of performing before an audience (for example, "Groovy and Linda," number 4).

Bibliography

Acconci, Vito. "10 (A Late Introduction to *0 to 9*)." In *0 to 9: The Complete Magazine: 1967–1969*. Reprint, Brooklyn, N.Y.: Ugly Duckling Presse, 2006, 7–11.

Bernstein, Roberta, et al. *Jasper Johns: Numbers*. Exhibit catalog. Cleveland, Ohio: Cleveland Museum of Art, 2003.

Connor, Maureen. "The Pleasure of Necessity: The Work of Rosemary Mayer." *Woman's Art Journal* 6, no. 2 (Autumn 1985–Winter 1986): 35–40.

Kane, Daniel. *All Poets Welcome: The Lower East Side Poetry Scene in the 1960s*. Berkeley: University of California Press, 2003.

Linker, Kate. *Vito Acconci*. New York: Rizzoli, 1994.

Mayer, Bernadette. "Rock, Paper, Scissors." In *0 to 9: The Complete Magazine: 1967–1969*. Reprint, Brooklyn, N.Y.: Ugly Duckling Presse, 2006, 13–14.

Rifkin, Libbie. "'My Little World Goes on St. Mark's Place': Anne Waldman, Bernadette Mayer and the Gender of an Avant-Garde Institution." *Jacket* 7 (April 1999). Available online. URL: http://jacketmagazine.com/07/rifkin07.html. Accessed December 19, 2008.

Russo, Linda. "Poetics of Adjacency: 0–9 and the Conceptual Writing of Bernadette Mayer & Hannah Weiner." In *Don't Ever Get Famous: Essays on New York Writing after the New York School*, edited by Daniel Kane, 122–150. Champaign, Ill.: Dalkey Archive Press, 2006.

"*0 to 9*." In *A Secret Location on the Lower East Side: Adventures in Writing, 1960–1980*, by Steven Clay and Rodney Phillips, 206–207. New York: New York Public Library/Granary Books, 1998.

Z Press (1973–   )

In 1973 poet and librettist KENWARD ELMSLIE was invited to edit an issue of the POETRY PROJECT AT ST. MARK'S CHURCH IN-THE-BOWERY's literary magazine, *The WORLD*. As he gathered the material he wanted to use and considered its quality, he decided he wanted it presented in a less ephemeral FORM. He founded Z Press with the anthology Z, which included the material meant for *The World*. The cover drawing that TREVOR WINKFIELD created for this first anthology became the Z Press logo. Only Z lists NEW YORK CITY as its location.

The publications that followed were all issued from Calais, Vermont.

Other anthologies followed: ZZ, ZZZ, and so on through ZZZZZZ. Between 1973 and 1987 Z Press issued 47 items, including books, two broadsides, several postcard sets—including *12 Postcards* by JOE BRAINARD—an audiocassette, and four LPs of Elmslie's musical works. Many familiar NEW YORK SCHOOL authors appear on the Z Press list, including JOHN ASHBERY, KENNETH KOCH, JAMES SCHUYLER, and HARRY MATHEWS, but Elmslie never limited himself to any particular sensibility. There are a number of surprises as well, including *Heroic Emblems* by Ian Hamilton Finlay and Ron Costley, and in a later series of pamphlets, a poem by ROBERT CREELEY and a linocut by JASPER JOHNS. Other highlights include *The Home Book* (1977), which gathers up stray short pieces by Schuyler; *Three Plays* (1978)

by Ashbery; and *26 Bars* (1987), Elmslie's fantasy drinking-establishment COLLABORATION with artist Donna Dennis.

In 1987, feeling that the press had accomplished what he had hoped it would, Elmslie took a break from issuing new titles for a decade. Then between 1998 and 2000 Z Press issued a half-dozen slim, elegant pamphlets pairing a single poem with an artwork tipped in. Pairings include ANN LAUTERBACH with Brainard, BARBARA GUEST with Winkfield, and Norman Dubie with Vivien Russe.

Bibliography

Bamberger, William C. *Kenward Elmslie, a Bibliographical Profile*. Flint, Mich.: Bamberger Books, 1993.

Clay, Steven, and Rodney Phillips. *A Secret Location on the Lower East Side: Adventures in Writing, 1960–1980*. New York: New York Public Library/Granary Books, 1998, 190–191.

TIME LINE

1944
James Schuyler discharged from navy; settles in New York City

1946
John Ashbery meets Kenneth Koch at Harvard University

Barbara Guest moves to New York City

1948
Edwin Denby publishes *In Public, In Private*, with photos by Rudolph Burckhardt (James A. Decker)

Breakthrough shows by Jackson Pollock (Betty Parsons Gallery) and Willem de Kooning (Egan Gallery)

Charles Olson first lectures at Black Mountain College

1949
John Ashbery meets Frank O'Hara at Harvard University

1950
Charles Olson publishes "Projective Verse"

Tibor de Nagy Gallery founded; John Bernard Myers is director

1951
First published reference to "the School of New York" painters in Robert Motherwell's preface to *Seventeen Modern American Painters*

Frank O'Hara completes master's degree at University of Michigan, Ann Arbor; joins

John Ashbery and Kenneth Koch in New York City; meets James Schuyler and Barbara Guest

O'Hara publishes *A City Winter* (Tibor de Nagy)

1953
Artists' Theatre debut, with works by Kenneth Koch, Frank O'Hara, and James Schuyler

Koch's *Poems* published (Tibor de Nagy)

John Ashbery's *Turandot* published (Tibor de Nagy)

1955
John Ashbery begins decade of residence in France

"6 Poets at the 6 Gallery" in San Francisco includes Allen Ginsberg reading part of "Howl"

1956
Allen Ginsberg publishes *Howl and Other Poems* (City Lights)

John Ashbery publishes *Some Trees* and wins Yale Younger Poets prize (selected by W. H. Auden)

Death of Jackson Pollock

1957
Jack Kerouac publishes *On the Road* (Viking)

Frank O'Hara publishes *Meditations in an Emergency* (Grove)

1958
The New American Painting (Museum of Modern Art) begins European tour

1959
Frank O'Hara writes "Personism: A Manifesto"

1960

The New American Poetry, 1945–1960 (Grove), edited by Donald M. Allen, is published

Barbara Guest's *The Location of Things* published (Tibor de Nagy)

Tiber Press publishes artists' books by John Ashbery (*The Poems,* with Joan Mitchell), Kenneth Koch (*Permanently,* with Alfred Leslie), Frank O'Hara (*Odes,* with Michael Goldberg), and James Schuyler (*Salute,* with Grace Hartigan)

Ron Padgett, Joe Brainard, and Dick Gallup move to New York City from Tulsa, Oklahoma, followed by Ted Berrigan (January 1961)

1961

Kenward Elmslie publishes *Pavilions* (Tibor de Nagy)

Bill Berkson publishes *Saturday Night* (Tibor de Nagy)

1962

First published reference to "New York School of Poetry" by John Bernard Myers in *Nomad*

John Ashbery's *The Tennis Court Oath* published (Wesleyan University Press)

Kenneth Koch's *Thank You and Other Poems* published (Grove)

Harry Mathews's *The Conversions* published (Random House)

The New Realism show (Janis Gallery), pop art breakthrough

1963

Edward Field's *Stand Up, Friend, with Me* published (Grove)

1964

Frank O'Hara's *Lunch Poems* published (City Lights)

Ted Berrigan's *The Sonnets* published ("C" Press)

Frank Lima's *Inventory* published (Tibor de Nagy)

1965

Edward Sanders publishes *Peace Eye* (Frontier)

David Shapiro publishes *January* (Holt, Rinehart & Winston)

John Ashbery resumes residence in New York City

International Poetry Incarnation at Royal Albert Hall, London

New York School poets participate in Spoleto Festival of Two Worlds

Berkeley Poetry Conference

1966

Poetry Project founded at St. Mark's Church in-the-Bowery, with Joel Oppenheimer as director

John Ashbery publishes *Rivers and Mountains* (Holt, Rinehart & Winston)

Death of Frank O'Hara

1967

Joseph Ceravolo's *Wild Flowers Out of Gas* published (Tibor de Nagy)

Poetry Project begins publication of *The World*

Teachers & Writers Collaborative founded

1968

Joe Ceravolo's *Spring in This World of Poor Mutts* wins Frank O'Hara Award

Tony Towle publishes *After Dinner We Take a Drive Into the Night* (Tibor de Nagy)

Anne Waldman appointed director of the Poetry Project

Ted Berrigan teaches at Iowa Writers' Workshop, beginning nearly a decade of various teaching appointments outside New York

1969

The Poets of the New York School (University of Pennsylvania) is published; edited by John Bernard Myers

Kenneth Koch publishes *The Pleasures of Peace* (Grove)

Michael Brownstein's *Highway to the Sky* wins Frank O'Hara Award

Ron Padgett publishes *Great Balls of Fire* (Holt, Rinehart & Winston)

John Ashbery and Allen Ginsberg win American Academy of Arts and Letters Awards

Death of Jack Kerouac

1970

An Anthology of New York Poets published (Random House); edited by Ron Padgett and David Shapiro

John Ashbery's *The Double Dream of Spring* published (Dutton)

Clark Coolidge's *Space* published (Harper & Row)
Tony Towle's *North* wins Frank O'Hara Award
Anne Waldman's *Baby Breakdown* published
(Bobbs-Merrill)
Bill Berkson moves to California
Death of Charles Olson

1971
Frank O'Hara's *Collected Poems* (Knopf) wins
National Book Award
Kenward Elmslie's *Motor Disturbance* wins Frank
O'Hara Award

1972
John Ashbery publishes *Three Poems* (Viking)
Bernadette Mayer exhibits *Memory* (Holly
Solomon Gallery)
Patti Smith publishes *Seventh Heaven* (Telegraph)
Lewis Warsh publishes *Part of My History* (Coach
House)

1973
John Ashbery wins Shelley Memorial Award,
Poetry Society of America
Jim Carroll's *Living at the Movies* published
(Grossman)
John Koethe's *Domes* wins Frank O'Hara Award

1974
James Schuyler publishes *Hymn to Life* (Random
House)

1975
John Ashbery's *Self-Portrait in a Convex Mirror*
(Viking) wins National Book Award, National
Book Critics Circle Award, and Pulitzer Prize
Kenneth Koch publishes *The Art of Love* (Random
House)
Edward Field wins Shelley Memorial Award,
Poetry Society of America
Jack Kerouac School of Disembodied Poetics
founded at Naropa Institute

1976
Barbara Guest's *The Countess from Minneapolis*
published (Burning Deck)
Kenneth Koch wins American Academy of Arts
and Letters Award

Bill Berkson's *Blue Is the Hero* published (L
Publications)
Ted Berrigan returns to New York after nearly a
decade of itinerant teaching

1977
James Schuyler wins American Academy of Arts
and Letters Awards

1978
Bernadette Mayer publishes *The Golden Book of
Words* (Angel Hair)
Ron Padgett appointed director of the Poetry
Project

1979
Kenneth Koch publishes *The Burning Mystery of
Anna in 1951* (Random House)
Tim Dlugos publishes *Je Suis Ein Americano* (Little
Caesar)

1980
James Schuyler's *The Morning of the Poem* (Farrar,
Straus & Giroux) wins Pulitzer Prize
Ted Berrigan's *So Going Around Cities* published
(Blue Wind)
Maureen Owen's *Hearts in Space* published
(Kulchur)
Bernadette Mayer appointed director of the Poetry
Project

1981
Douglas Crase publishes *The Revisionist* (Little,
Brown)
Eileen Myles publishes *A Fresh Young Voice from
the Plains* (Power Mad)
Alice Notley publishes *How Spring Comes*
(Toothpaste)
Lorenzo Thomas publishes *The Bathers* (Reed)

1982
Anne Waldman's *First Baby Poems* published
(Rocky Ledge)
Paul Violi's *Splurge* published (SUN)

1983
Deaths of Ted Berrigan and Edwin Denby

1984

Eileen Myles appointed director of the Poetry Project

1985

John Ashbery receives Bollingen Prize and MacArthur Fellowship

1986

Clark Coolidge publishes *The Crystal Text* (The Figures)
Amy Gerstler publishes *The True Bride* (Lapis)
Ed Friedman appointed director of the Poetry Project

1987

Kenneth Koch's *Seasons on Earth* published (Penguin)
Douglas Crase receives MacArthur Fellowship

1988

Ted Berrigan's *A Certain Slant of Sunlight* published (O Books)
Death of Joe Ceravolo

1989

Barbara Guest publishes *Fair Realism* (Sun & Moon)
Charles North publishes *The Year of the Olive Oil* (Hanging Loose)
John Yau publishes *Radiant Silhouette* (Black Sparrow)

1990

Amy Gerstler's *Bitter Angel* (North Point) wins National Book Critics Circle Award
David Lehman's *Operation Memory* published (Princeton University Press)
David Lehman wins American Academy of Arts and Letters Award

1991

John Ashbery's *Flow Chart* published (Knopf)
Harry Mathews wins American Academy of Arts and Letters Award
Ann Lauterbach's *Clamor* published (Viking)
Gary Lenhart's *Light Heart* published (Hanging Loose)
Death of James Schuyler

1992

The Scarlet Cabinet (containing Alice Notley's *The Descent of Alette* and Douglas Oliver's *Penniless Politics*) published
Alice Notley and Douglas Oliver move to France

1993

James Schuyler's *Collected Poems* published (Farrar, Straus & Giroux)
Anne Waldman publishes *Iovis* I (Coffee House)
Ann Lauterbach receives MacArthur Fellowship

1994

Barbara Guest moves to California
Kenneth Koch wins Shelley Memorial Award, Poetry Society of America
Death of Joe Brainard

1995

John Ashbery awarded Frost Medal, Poetry Society of America
Kenneth Koch wins Bollingen Prize

1996

Anne Waldman wins Shelley Memorial Award, Poetry Society of America

1997

Anne Waldman publishes *Iovis* II (Coffee House)
Vincent Katz publishes *Boulevard Transportation*, with photos by Rudy Burckhardt (Tibor de Nagy)
Frank Lima publishes *Inventory* (Hard Press)
Deaths of Willem de Kooning and Allen Ginsberg

1999

Barbara Guest's *Rocks on a Platter* published (Wesleyan University Press)
Guest awarded Frost Medal, Poetry Society of America
Ron Padgett wins American Academy of Arts and Letters Award
Lee Ann Brown publishes *Polyverse* (Sun & Moon)

2000

Bill Berkson's *Serenade* published (Zoland)
Clark Coolidge's *On the Nameways* published (The Figures)

2001

Alice Notley wins Shelley Memorial Award, Poetry Society of America; American Academy of Arts and Letters Award; and Griffin Poetry Prize (Canada) International Award for *Disobedience* (Penguin)

2002

Death of Kenneth Koch

2003

Anselm Berrigan appointed director of the Poetry Project

2005

Kenneth Koch's *Collected Poems* published (Knopf)
Ted Berrigan's *Collected Poems* published (University of California Press)
Death of Lorenzo Thomas

2006

Death of Barbara Guest
John Koethe publishes *Sally's Hair* (Harper)

2007

John Ashbery wins Griffin Poetry Prize (Canada) International Award for *Notes from the Air: Selected Later Poems* (Ecco)

Edward Field's *After the Fall* published (University of Pittsburgh Press)
Eileen Myles's *Sorry, Tree* published (Wave)
Charles North's *Cadenza* published (Hanging Loose)
Alice Notley's *In the Pines* published (Penguin)
Ron Padgett's *How to Be Perfect* published (Coffee House)
David Shapiro's *New and Selected Poems, 1965–2006* published (Overlook)
Paul Violi's *Overnight* published (Hanging Loose)
Stacy Szymaszek appointed director of the Poetry Project

2008

John Ashbery's *Collected Poems 1956–1987* published (Library of America)
Joe Brainard's *The Nancy Book* published (Siglio)
Marcella Durand's *Area* published (Belladonna)
John Godfrey's *City of Corners* published (Wave)
Barbara Guest's *Collected Poems* published (Wesleyan University Press)
Lisa Jarnot's *Night Scenes* published (Flood Editions)
Tony Towle's *Winter Journey* published (Hanging Loose)
Lewis Warsh's *Inseparable* published (Granary Books)
Marjorie Welish's *Isle of the Signatories* published (Coffee House Press)

SELECTED BIBLIOGRAPHY

For collections of poems by individual authors, see author entries.

BOOKS

Allen, Donald, ed. *The New American Poetry 1945–1960*. 1960. Reprint, Berkeley: University of California Press, 1999.

Allen, Donald, and Warren Tallman, eds. *The Poetics of the New American Poetry*. New York: Grove, 1973.

Anderson, Elliott, and Mary Kinzie, eds. *The Little Magazine in America: A Modern Documentary History*. Yonkers, N.Y.: Pushcart, 1978.

Ashbery, John. *Other Traditions*. Cambridge, Mass.: Harvard University Press, 2000.

———. *Reported Sightings: Art Chronicles, 1957–1987*. Edited by David Bergman. Cambridge, Mass.: Harvard University Press, 1991.

———. *Selected Prose*. Edited by Eugene Richie. Ann Arbor: University of Michigan Press, 2004.

Baraka, Amiri. *The Autobiography of LeRoi Jones*. Chicago: Lawrence Hill Books, 1984.

Berkson, Bill. *Sudden Address: Selected Lectures, 1981–2006*. Berkeley, Calif.: Cuneiform Press, 2007.

———. *The Sweet Singer of Modernism and Other Art Writings, 1985–2003*. Jamestown, R.I.: Qua Books, 2003.

Berkson, Bill, and Bernadette Mayer, *What's Your Idea of a Good Time? Letters and Interviews, 1977–1985*. Berkeley, Calif.: Tuumba Press, 2006.

Berkson, Bill, and Joe LeSueur, eds. *Homage to Frank O'Hara*. Bolinas, Calif.: Big Sky, 1978.

Berrigan, Ted. *On the Level Everyday: Selected Talks on Poetry and the Art of Living*. Edited by Joel Lewis. Jersey City, N.J.: Talisman House, 1997.

———. *Talking in Tranquility: Interviews*. Edited by Stephen Ratcliffe and Leslie Scalapino. Bolinas, Calif.: Avenue B; Oakland, Calif.: O Books, 1991.

Clark, Tom. *Late Returns: A Memoir of Ted Berrigan*. Bolinas, Calif.: Tombouctou, 1985.

———. *The Poetry Beat: Reviewing the Eighties*. Ann Arbor: University of Michigan Press, 1990.

Clay, Steven, and Rodney Phillips, eds. *A Secret Location on the Lower East Side: Adventures in Writing, 1960–1980*. New York: New York Public Library/Granary Books, 1998.

Corbett, William. *All Prose: Selected Essays and Reviews*. Cambridge, Mass.: Zoland, 2001.

———. *Philip Guston's Late Work: A Memoir*. Cambridge, Mass.: Zoland, 1994.

Denby, Edwin. *Dance Writings and Poetry*. Edited by Robert Cornfield. New Haven, Conn.: Yale University Press, 1998.

Diggory, Terence, and Stephen Paul Miller, eds. *The Scene of My Selves: New Work on New York School Poets*. Orono, Me.: National Poetry Foundation, 2001.

Elledge, Jim, ed. *Frank O'Hara: To Be True to a City*. Ann Arbor: University of Michigan Press, 1990.

Epstein, Andrew. *Beautiful Enemies: Friendship and Postwar American Poetry*. New York: Oxford University Press, 2006.

Ferguson, Russell. *In Memory of My Feelings: Frank O'Hara and American Art*. Exhibit catalog. Los Angeles: Museum of Contemporary Art; Berkeley: University of California Press, 1999.

Field, Edward. *The Man Who Would Marry Susan Sontag and Other Intimate Portraits of the Bohemian Era*. Madison: University of Wisconsin Press, 2005.

Foster, Edward. *Code of the West: A Memoir of Ted Berrigan.* Boulder, Colo.: Rodent Press, 1994.

Foster, Edward, ed. *Poetry and Poetics in a New Millennium: Interviews.* Jersey City, N.J.: Talisman House, 2000.

———. *Postmodern Poetry: The Talisman Interviews.* Hoboken, N.J.: Talisman House, 1994.

Foster, Edward, and Joseph Donahue, eds. *The World in Time and Space: Towards a History of Innovative American Poetry in Our Time.* Jersey City, N.J.: Talisman House, 2002.

Gooch, Brad. *City Poet: The Life and Times of Frank O'Hara.* New York: Knopf, 1993.

Goodman, Paul. *Five Years.* New York: Brussel & Brussel, 1966.

Gruen, John. *The New Bohemia.* Chicago: A Cappella Books, 1966.

———. *The Party's Over Now: Reminiscences of the Fifties.* Wainscott, N.Y.: Pushcart, 1989.

Guest, Barbara. *Dürer in the Window: Reflexions on Art.* New York: Roof Books, 2003.

———. *Forces of Imagination: Writing on Writing.* Berkeley, Calif.: Kelsey St. Press, 2003.

Hoover, Paul. *Fables of Representation: Essays.* Ann Arbor: University of Michigan Press, 2004.

Hornick, Lita. *The Green Fuse: A Memoir.* New York: Giorno Poetry Systems, 1989.

———. *Kulchur Queen.* New York: Giorno Poetry Systems, 1977.

———. *Night Flight.* New York: Kulchur Foundation, 1982.

———. *Nine Martinis.* New York: Kulchur Foundation, 1987.

Jones, Hettie. *How I Became Hettie Jones.* New York: Dutton, 1990.

Kane, Daniel. *All Poets Welcome, The Lower East Side Poetry Scene in the 1960s.* Berkeley: University of California Press, 2003.

Kane, Daniel, ed. *Don't Ever Get Famous: Essays on New York Writing after the New York School.* Champaign, Ill.: Dalkey Archive Press, 2006.

———. *What Is Poetry: Conversations with the American Avant-Garde.* New York: Teachers & Writers, 2003.

Katz, Vincent, ed. *Rudy Burckhardt.* Exhibit catalog. Valencia, Spain: IVAM Centre Julio González, 1998.

Koch, Kenneth. *The Art of Poetry: Poems, Parodies, Interviews, Essays, and Other Work.* Ann Arbor: University of Michigan Press, 1996.

Koethe, John. *Poetry at One Remove: Essays.* Ann Arbor: University of Michigan Press, 2000.

Lehman David. *The Big Question.* Ann Arbor: University of Michigan Press, 1995.

———. *The Last Avant-Garde: The Making of the New York School of Poets.* New York: Doubleday, 1998.

———. *The Line Forms Here.* Ann Arbor: University of Michigan Press, 1992.

Lehman, David, ed. *Beyond Amazement: New Essays on John Ashbery.* Ithaca, N.Y.: Cornell University Press, 1980.

Lenhart, Gary. *The Stamp of Class: Reflections on Poetry and Social Class.* Ann Arbor: University of Michigan Press, 2006.

LeSueur, Joe. *Digressions on Some Poems by Frank O'Hara: A Memoir.* New York: Farrar, Straus & Giroux, 2003.

Lewallen, Constance M. *Joe Brainard: A Retrospective.* Exhibit catalog. Berkeley: Art Museum, University of California at Berkeley; New York: Granary Books, 2001.

Myers, John Bernard. *Tracking the Marvelous: A Life in the New York Art World.* New York: Random House, 1983.

Myers, John Bernard, ed. *The Poets of the New York School.* Philadelphia: Graduate School of Fine Arts, University of Pennsylvania, 1969.

Nelson, Maggie. *Women, the New York School, and Other True Abstractions.* Iowa City: University of Iowa Press, 2007.

North, Charles. *No Other Way: Selected Prose.* Brooklyn, N.Y.: Hanging Loose Press, 1998.

Notley, Alice. *Coming After: Essays on Poetry.* Ann Arbor: University of Michigan Press, 2005.

O'Hara, Frank. *Art Chronicles, 1954–1966.* Rev. ed. New York: Braziller, 1990.

———. *Standing Still and Walking in New York.* Edited by Donald Allen. Bolinas, Calif.: Grey Fox, 1973.

Padgett, Ron. *Joe: A Memoir of Joe Brainard.* Minneapolis, Minn.: Coffee House Press, 2004.

———. *Ted: A Personal Memoir of Ted Berrigan.* Great Barrington, Mass.: The Figures, 1993.

Padgett, Ron, ed. *Painter Among Poets: The Collaborative Art of George Schneeman.* New York: Granary Books, 2004.

Padgett, Ron, and David Shapiro, eds. *An Anthology of New York Poets.* New York: Random House, 1970.

Perloff, Marjorie. *Frank O'Hara: Poet Among Painters.* 1969. Reprint, Chicago: University of Chicago Press, 1998.

Ratcliff, Carter. *The Fate of a Gesture: Jackson Pollock and Postwar American Art.* New York: Farrar, Straus & Giroux, 1996.

Rifkin, Libbie. *Career Moves: Olson, Creeley, Zukofsky, Berrigan, and the American Avant-Garde.* Madison: University of Wisconsin Press, 2000.

Rivers, Larry, with Arnold Weinstein. *What Did I Do?* New York: HarperCollins, 1992.

Saroyan, Aram. *Friends in the World: The Education of a Writer.* Minneapolis, Minn.: Coffee House Press, 1992.

———. *Starting Out in the Sixties: Selected Essays.* Jersey City, N.J.: Talisman, 2001.

Schjeldahl, Peter. *The Hydrogen Jukebox: Selected Writings, 1978–1990.* Berkeley: University of California Press, 1991.

Schultz, Susan, ed. *The Tribe of John: Ashbery and Contemporary Poetry.* Tuscaloosa: University of Alabama Press, 1995.

Schuyler, James. *The Diary.* Edited by Nathan Kernan. Santa Rosa, Calif.: Black Sparrow, 1997.

———. *Just the Thing: Selected Letters, 1951–1991.* Edited by William Corbett. New York: Turtle Point Press, 2004.

———. *The Letters of James Schuyler to Frank O'Hara.* Edited by William Corbett. New York: Turtle Point Press, 2006.

———. *Selected Art Writings.* Edited by Simon Pettet. Santa Rosa, Calif.: Black Sparrow, 1998.

Shapiro, David. *Jasper Johns Drawings, 1954–1984.* New York: Abrams, 1985.

———. *Jim Dine: Painting What One Is.* New York: Abrams, 1981.

———. *John Ashbery: An Introduction to the Poetry.* New York: Columbia University Press, 1979.

Shaw, Lytle. *Frank O'Hara: The Poetics of Coterie.* Iowa City: University of Iowa Press, 2006.

Sukenick, Ronald. *Down and In: Life in the Underground.* New York: Beech Tree Books/William Morrow, 1987.

Taylor, Marvin J. *The Downtown Book: The New York Art Scene, 1974–84.* Princeton, N.J.: Princeton University Press, 2006.

Waldman, Anne. *Vow to Poetry: Essays, Interviews, and Manifestos.* Minneapolis, Minn.: Coffee House Press, 2001.

Waldman, Anne, ed. *Nice to See You: Homage to Ted Berrigan.* Minneapolis, Minn.: Coffee House Press, 1991.

———. *Out of This World: The Poetry Project at the St. Mark's Church in-the-Bowery, an Anthology, 1966–1991.* New York: Crown, 1991.

Waldman, Anne, and Andrew Schelling, eds. *Disembodied Poetics: Annals of the Jack Kerouac School.* Albuquerque: University of New Mexico Press, 1994.

Waldman, Anne, and Lewis Warsh, eds. *The Angel Hair Anthology.* New York: Granary Books, 2001.

Waldman, Anne, and Marilyn Webb, eds. *Talking Poetics from Naropa Institute: Annals of the Jack Kerouac School of Disembodied Poetics.* 2 vols. Boulder, Colo.: Shambhala, 1978–79.

Ward, Geoff. *Statutes of Liberty: The New York School of Poets.* 2d ed. New York: Palgrave, 2001.

Watkin, William. *In the Process of Poetry: The New York School and the Avant-Garde.* Lewisburg, Pa.: Bucknell University Press, 2001.

Welish, Marjorie. *Signifying Art: Essays on Art after 1960.* Cambridge: Cambridge University Press, 1999.

Wolf, Reva. *Andy Warhol, Poetry, and Gossip in the 1960s.* Chicago: University of Chicago Press, 1997.

Yau, John. *In the Realm of Appearances: The Art of Andy Warhol.* Hopewell, N.J.: Ecco, 1993.

———. *The United States of Jasper Johns.* Cambridge, Mass.: Zoland Books, 1996.

WEB SITES

Eclipse. Edited by Craig Dworkin. URL: http://english.utah.edu/eclipse/.

Electronic Poetry Center, University at Buffalo. URL: http://wings.buffalo.edu/epc/.

Jacket magazine. URL: http://jacketmagazine.com/00/home.shtml.

PennSound, University of Pennsylvania. URL: http://www.writing.upenn.edu/pennsound/.

Poetry Project. URL: http://www.poetryproject.com/.

Small Press Distribution. URL: http://www.spdbooks.org/root/index.asp.

UbuWeb. URL: http://www.ubu.com/.

LIST OF ENTRIES BY SUBJECT

ANTHOLOGIES

Texts
  American Literary Anthology, The (Plimpton)
  Anthology of New York Poets, An (Padgett and Shapiro)
  New American Poetry, 1945–1960, The (Allen)
  Poets of the New York School, The (Myers)
  Scarlet Cabinet, The (Notley and Oliver)
Topics
  Allen, Donald M.
  anthologies, canonical
  anthologies, polemical
  Carroll, Paul

ART, VISUAL

Names
  Brainard, Joe
  Cornell, Joseph
  de Kooning, Willem
  Dine, Jim
  Freilicher, Jane
  Greenberg, Clement
  Guston, Philip
  Hartigan, Grace
  Hess, Thomas B.
  Johns, Jasper
  Katz, Alex
  Myers, John Bernard
  Pollock, Jackson
  Porter, Fairfield
  Rauschenberg, Robert
  Rivers, Larry
  Rosenberg, Harold
  Schneeman, George
  Warhol, Andy
  Winkfield, Trevor
Topics
  abstract expressionism
  action painting
  art, visual
  conceptual art
  happenings
  minimalism
  performance art
  pop art
  Tibor de Nagy Gallery

COLLABORATION

Adventures of Mr. and Mrs. Jim and Ron, The (Padgett and Dine)
Altos, The (Guest and Tuttle)
Antlers in the Treetops (Padgett and Veitch)
Bean Spasms (Berrigan and Padgett)
Big City Primer (Yau and Barrette)
Boulevard Transportation (Katz and Burckhardt)
collaboration
Cyberspace (Elmslie and Winkfield)
Enigma Variations (Berkson and Guston)
George Washington Crossing the Delaware (Rivers, O'Hara, Koch, Katz)
In Public, In Private (Denby and Burckhardt)
Mediterranean Cities (Denby and Burckhardt)
Memorial Day (Berrigan and Waldman)
Nest of Ninnies, A (Ashbery and Schuyler)
Screen Tests/A Diary (Malanga and Warhol)
Vermont Notebook, The (Ashbery and Brainard)

CRITICISM

Herself Defined: The Poet H. D. and Her World (Guest)
Investigative Poetry (Sanders)

Thomas, Lorenzo
Torregian, Sotère
Towle, Tony
Veitch, Tom
Violi, Paul
Waldman, Anne
Warsh, Lewis
Welish, Marjorie
Zavatsky, Bill

POETS, NEW YORK SCHOOL, LATER GENERATIONS
(PUBLISHED OR CONNECTED AFTER 1975)

Abel, David
Ash, John
Barg, Barbara
Berrigan, Anselm
Berrigan, Edmund
Black, Star
Brown, Lee Ann
Bye, Reed
Carroll, Jim
Chernoff, Maxine
Cooper, Dennis
Coultas, Brenda
Davis, Jordan
Deanovich, Connie
Dlugos, Tim
Dubris, Maggie
Durand, Marcella
Edgar, Christopher
Elliot, Joe
Equi, Elaine
Friedman, Ed
Friedman, Michael
Fyman, Cliff
Gerstler, Amy
Gizzi, Michael
Gizzi, Peter
Henry, Gerrit
Highfill, Mitch
Holman, Bob
Hoover, Paul
Iijima, Brenda
Jarnot, Lisa
Jones, Patricia Spears
Katz, Vincent
Kimball, Jack
Kraut, Rochelle
Lenhart, Gary
Lesniak, Rose

Levine, Steve
Lewis, Joel
Lyons, Kimberly
Masters, Greg
McCain, Gillian
Mesmer, Sharon
Miller, Stephen Paul
Mlinko, Ange
Moxley, Jennifer
Myles, Eileen
Nauen, Elinor
Olin, Jeni
Pettet, Simon
Richie, Eugene
Rosenthal, Bob
Sala, Jerome
Savage, Tom
Scholnick, Michael
Schuchat, Simon
Shaw, Lytle
Sikelianos, Eleni
Stroffolino, Chris
Szymaszek, Stacy
Timmons, Susie
Torres, Edwin
Trinidad, David
Wasserman, JoAnn
Wasserman, Rosanne
Yau, John

POETS, OTHER

Aldan, Daisy
Auden, W[ystan] H[ugh]
Baraka, Amiri (LeRoi Jones)
Bishop, Elizabeth
Blackburn, Paul
Codrescu, Andrei
Corso, Gregory (Nunzio)
Creeley, Robert
Dent, Tom
di Prima, Diane
Ford, Mark
Forrest-Thompson, Veronica
Ginsberg, Allen
Goodman, Paul
Harwood, Lee
Henderson, David
Hernton, Calvin
Hollo, Anselm
Joans, Ted

LIST OF CONTRIBUTORS

Erik Anderson   University of Denver

Rise Axelrod   University of California at Riverside

Steven Axelrod   University of California at Riverside

William Bamberger   Publisher, Bamberger Books

Robert Bertholf   State University of New York at Buffalo

Olivier Brossard   Université Paris Est, Marne-la-Vallée

Paul Cappucci   Georgian Court University

William Corbett   Poet

Anthony Cuda   Emory University

Tom Devaney   Poet

Marcella Durand   Poet

Bernie Earley   State University of New York at Cortland

Jeff Encke   Poet

Andrew Epstein   Florida State University

Carrie Etter   Bath Spa University

Steve Evans   University of Maine, Orono

Nicolas Luis Fernandez-Medina   Stanford University

Thomas Fink   Laguardia Community College, City University of New York

Mark Ford   Poet

Edward Foster   Editor and publisher, *Talisman* magazine and books

Dan Friedman   Yale University

Frank Gaughan   Hofstra University

Benjamin Givan   Skidmore College

Michael Gizzi   Poet

Brian Glavey   University of Virginia

Mitch Highfill   Poet

Paul Hoover   Poet

Daniel Kane   University of Sussex

Jamison Kantor   University of Virginia

Gary Kerley   North Hall High School, Gainesville, Georgia

Nathan Kernan   Poet

Jack Kimball   Poet

Gary Lenhart   Poet

Ellen Levy   Vanderbilt University

Erie Lorberer   Editor, *Rain Taxi*

Kimberly Lyons   Poet

Mary Maxwell   Poet

Bill Mohr   Poet

Nick Moudry   University of Massachusetts, Amherst

Jennifer Moxley   Poet

Judith Mulcahy   City University of New York

Mary Murphy   Alberta College of Art and Design, University of Calgary

William Murray   New School

Anna Priddy   Louisiana State University

Nate Pritts   Louisiana School for Math, Science and the Arts

Chris Pusateri   University of Washington

Raymond Ragosta   Rhode Island College

Eugene Richie   Poet

Justin Rogers-Cooper   City University of New York

Rebecca Rosen   University of Massachusetts, Amherst

Mark Salerno   Poet

Gerald Schwartz   Poet

Ravi Shankar   Editor, *The Drunken Boat*

Eleni Sikelianos   Poet

Douglas Texter   University of Minnesota

Joe Torra   Poet

Mark Tursi   University of Denver

Rosanne Wasserman   Poet

John Woznicki   Georgian Court University

INDEX

Note: **Boldface** numbers indicate major treatment of a topic. Page numbers in *italic* indicate illustrations.